C.S. LEWIS

A Companion & Guide

Books by C.S. Lewis
available from Fount Paperbacks

The Abolition of Man
The Business of Heaven
Christian Reflections
Christian Reunion
Compelling Reason
The Dark Tower
Fern-seed and Elephants
The Four Loves
God in the Dock
The Great Divorce
Letters
Letters to Children
Mere Christianity
Miracles
Narrative Poems
The Pilgrim's Regress
Poems
Prayer: Letters to Malcolm
The Problem of Pain
Readings for Reflection and Meditation
Reflections on the Psalms
The Screwtape Letters
Screwtape Proposes a Toast
Surprised by Joy
Till We Have Faces

Books for children available from Lions

The Chronicles of Narnia:
The Lion, the Witch and the Wardrobe
The Magician's Nephew
The Horse and his Boy
Prince Caspian
The Voyage of the 'Dawn Treader'
The Silver Chair
The Last Battle

C.S. LEWIS

A Companion & Guide

BY WALTER HOOPER

HarperSanFrancisco

A Division of HarperCollins*Publishers*

HarperCollins Web Site:
http://www.harpercollins.com

HarperCollins®, ♣®, and HarperSanFrancisco™ are
trademarks of HarperCollins Publishers Inc.

First published in Great Britain in 1996 by
HarperCollins*Publishers*.

ISBN 0-06-063879-6 (cloth)
ISBN 0-06-063880-X (paper)

98 99 00 01 02 RRDH 10 9 8 7 6 5 4 3 2 1

To my godson

JEREMY DYSON

CONTENTS

PREFACE

'Find out what the author wrote and what the hard words meant and what the allusions were to, and you have done far more for me than a hundred new interpretations or assessments could ever do.' Thus C.S. Lewis characterized 'Dryasdust' critics in *An Experiment in Criticism* (1961). While it seems a strange claim to make, those proud words define pretty closely what I hoped to accomplish in this book. But even if it does not clear up all the 'hard words' and 'allusions', there are a number of other reasons why a Companion and Guide was needed.

Vast changes have occurred between the time of Lewis's birth in 1898 and the present day. Many young readers of the 'Chronicles of Narnia' will find it hard to believe that the author of those stories was tutored by a governess before he went to school, was a grown man by the time his home had electric lights, and died the same day as President John F. Kennedy. Perhaps they will understand just how fast time flies when, one of these days, *their* children say to them, 'You were born before Internet?!' I have tried to bridge the gap between generations with information about Lewis's life, his times, his writings, his ideas and his friends.

It has been over thirty years since Lewis died. Yet, as I write, many of his friends are still about, and they have given me much help. The youngest of those friends is Lewis's stepson, Douglas Gresham. Many of his reminiscences about his years with his mother and Lewis are found in his book *Lenten Lands* (1988), but he gave me much help in addition to what is found there. I have also been fortunate in being able to consult the three remaining members of that group known as The Inklings: Owen Barfield, Colin Hardie and Christopher Tolkien. Lewis had this generation in mind when he gave his inaugural address at Cambridge in 1954. Speaking of the changes separating his hearers from the culture in which he was brought up, he said: 'Use your specimens while you can.

There are not going to be many more dinosaurs.'[1] Mr Barfield, who first met Lewis in 1919 and is his exact contemporary, celebrated his ninety-seventh birthday on 9 November 1995. The help he gave me with the *Companion* was invaluable.

Lewis wrote so well in several subjects – scholarly, fantastic, theological – that it was his misfortune to be mistaken for several authors. One aim of the *Companion* is to make him appear as one. It bothered him that the connection between these various 'authors' was not clear, and in his letter to the Milton Society of America of 2 February 1955 he attempted to put the matter right: 'There is a *guiding thread*,' he said. 'The imaginative man in me is older, more continuously operative, and in that sense more basic than either the religious writer or the critic. It was he who made me first attempt ... to be a poet. It was he who, in response to the poetry of others, made me a critic, and it was he who, after my conversion, led me to embody my religious belief in symbolical or mythopoeic forms, ranging from *Screwtape* to a kind of theologized science fiction. And it was, of course, he who has brought me ... to write the series of Narnian stories for children.'[2] Even if most admirers of Narnia never learn to enjoy Lewis's literary criticism, it is the intention of this book to help them discover what it is about. Others who have read only his theology will be led by that 'guiding thread' to other of his writings. In my effort to be as comprehensive as possible it was impossible to avoid some duplication (W.H. Lewis's birthday is mentioned in the **Chronology**, the **Life** and the **Who's Who**). I am sorry about this. Some will gasp at the size of the *Companion*. But, as they can see from the **Bibliography**, Lewis was a very prolific author. Despite my attempt to bring in all sides of his genius, it was still not possible to discuss all his writings.

Another reason for this *Companion* is Lewis's popularity. In speaking of this, let us begin by noting that nearly all Lewis's readers mention 'prophetic' as a particularly outstanding quality in his writing. And yet if there is one way in which he was *un*prophetic it was about himself. 'I am going to be (if I live long enough),' he wrote to a friend on 20 December 1951, 'one of those men who *was* a famous writer in his forties and dies unknown.'[3] How could he have thought this? The Narnian stories were only just beginning to appear, but some of his theological books were

---

[1] *'De Descriptione Temporum'*, in *Selected Literary Essays*, edited by Walter Hooper (1969), p. 14.

[2] *Letters of C.S. Lewis*, edited by W.H. Lewis (1966); Revised and Enlarged Edition, edited by Walter Hooper (1988), p. 444.

[3] Ibid., p. 415.

then, as now, among the most popular religious apologetics in Britain. I
believe the best explanation for this lacuna in Lewis's makeup was
provided by Owen Barfield who said: 'What I think is true is, that at a
certain stage in his life he deliberately ceased to take any interest in
himself except as a kind of spiritual alumnus taking his moral finals ...
and I suggest that what began as deliberate choice became at length (as he
had no doubt always intended it should) an ingrained and effortless habit
of soul. Self-knowledge, for him, had come to mean recognition of his
own weaknesses and shortcomings and nothing more ... At best, there
was so much else, in letters and in life, that he found much *more*
interesting!'[4]

Lewis's works have found large audiences throughout the world and
are translated into many languages, including such unusual ones as
Welsh and Hawaiian. His popularity continues to grow in his own
country, particularly since Richard Attenborough's film *Shadowlands* was
shown in 1993. But there is no doubt that his greatest fame is in the United
States. From the time his picture appeared on the cover of *Time* on 8
September 1947, the outpouring of warmth and love from that side of the
Atlantic has not ceased. Americans believe admiration demands action –
'Let's *do* something!' One of their many fine achievements has been the
founding of Lewis Societies devoted to the reading and study of his
writings. I regret there was not room enough to include sketches of all of
them in the **What's What** section of this book. Perhaps the most touching
aspect of American admiration has been the stream of letters to Lewis
from young admirers of his Narnian stories, even this long after his death.
(Many of those letters are preserved in the Bodleian Library.) Despite the
fact that most children are told that he is dead, some write to him anyway.
A high compliment was paid to the enduring quality of the Narnian
stories when one little boy from New Jersey, having been told that Lewis
had 'passed away', nevertheless began his letter: 'Dear Mr Lewis, I'm
sorry you died.'

Why is he so popular? In the section entitled **Key Ideas** I mention some
of the qualities which I think explain this. Lewis's vivid and luminous
imagination is certainly one. His was an imagination not only of *invention*
– with the creation of such worlds as Malacandra, Perelandra, Narnia and
Glome. It reveals what in his Preface to *George MacDonald: An Anthology*
(1947) he called the 'divine, magical, terrifying, and ecstatic reality' of the
world we actually live in. Lewis's writings are also graced with a clarity
that almost takes your breath away. This, in combination with his

---

[4] *Owen Barfield on C.S. Lewis*, edited by G.B. Tennyson (1989), pp. 24–5.

powerful reason, makes it possible for his works on Christianity to be understood by nearly everyone, including some who are not easily convinced. We could mention as well Lewis's moral toughness, his charity, his love of God, and a wisdom which made him willing to be happy on God's terms.

Although he did not invent the term, 'Mere Christianity' has become synonymous with Lewis. When theologians began to lose touch with people, Lewis set himself the task of being a *translator*, 'one turning Christian doctrine,' he said, 'into language that unscholarly people would attend to and could understand.'[5] The result has been what he defined in the Preface to *Mere Christianity* as 'the belief that has been common to nearly all Christians at all times', which is not 'put forward as an alternative to the creeds of the existing communions', and 'is what it is and was what it was long before I was born and whether I like it or not.' Again, 'Mere Christianity' is not, he said in 'On the Reading of Old Books', an 'insipid denominational transparency, but something positive, self-consistent, and inexhaustible.' Lewis's theological books appeal to all manner of Christians, and this, in addition to the fact that they are praised by churchmen as varied as Billy Graham and Pope John Paul II, has dealt a mighty blow to the divisions within Christendom.

There is a good deal of cross-referencing in the book, and I do not think the reader will find this difficult to pick up. Four sections of the book are designated by symbols or words: **THE LIFE OF C.S. LEWIS** is represented by **LIFE; KEY IDEAS** by §; **WHO'S WHO** by *; and **WHAT'S WHAT** by ‡. A key to the Symbols and Abbreviations used is found on pages xiv–xvi. I wish my references to Lewis's books could have included chapter and page numbers. However, there are so many editions of many of the books, each with a different pagination, that it seemed best to provide chapter numbers only. A great many of Lewis's essays are quoted in the book, and readers have only to consult the section of the **BIBLIOGRAPHY** on 'Books' to see the particular collection(s) in which they are found. That section also lists the volumes of Lewis's letters which have been published. When letters from these collections are quoted this is indicated by an abbreviation, such as '**L**' for *Letters of C.S. Lewis*. The absence of an abbreviation means that the letter is unpublished, but that the original or a copy may be consulted in the Bodleian Library,‡ Oxford, or the Wade Center,‡ Wheaton College, Wheaton, Illinois. The reciprocal arrangement between those two libraries makes it possible to examine the

---

[5] 'Rejoinder to Dr Pittenger', *God in the Dock: Essays on Theology and Ethics* (1970) and *Timeless at Heart* (Fount, 1987).

unpublished letters in both. The Index would have become too long if I had listed every title in the **Bibliography** and for this reason the Index stops at the end of the Book section on page 816.

In a work of this size the author is almost certain to have depended to a great extent upon the kindness of others. I owe more than I am able to say to Owen Barfield, Douglas Gresham, James Como, Colin Hardie, George Sayer, Christopher Tolkien, Michael Ward and Francis Warner. Others to whom I am indebted include Father Jerome Bertram and Father Seán Finnegan, the Reverend Peter Bide, Sir Richard Dunbar of Hempriggs, Karen Dyson, Monsignor Peter J. Elliott, Elizabeth Gibb, David Gresham, Laurence Harwood, John Havard, Richard Mullen, James Munson, Lois Olivier, Mary Clare Sheahan and J.I. Wilson.

Walter Hooper

OXFORD 25 JANUARY 1996

ABBREVIATIONS & SYMBOLS

LIFE = Life of C.S. Lewis in this volume
MEMOIR = by W.H. Lewis in **L** (see below)
* = WHO'S WHO
‡ = WHAT'S WHAT
§ = KEY IDEAS

ABT   *C.S. Lewis at the Breakfast Table, and other Reminiscences*, ed. James T. Como (1979; 1992)

AGCI   *And God Came In: The Extraordinary Story of Joy Davidman, Her Life and Marriage to C.S. Lewis* by Lyle W. Dorsett (1983). Renamed *Joy and C.S. Lewis* (1994)

AGO   *A Grief Observed*

AMR   *All My Road Before Me*

AOL   *The Allegory of Love*

AOM   *The Abolition of Man*

AT   *Arthurian Torso*

B   *Bodleian Library*‡

BF   *Brothers and Friends: The Diaries of Major Warren Hamilton Lewis*, ed. Clyde S. Kilby and Marjorie Lamp Mead (1982)

BIO   *C.S. Lewis: A Biography*, by Roger Lancelyn Green and Walter Hooper (1974)

BOH   *The Business of Heaven*

BP   *Beyond Personality*

BOX   *Boxen*

BT   *Broadcast Talks* (= *The Case for Christianity*)

CANCSL   *The Canadian C.S. Lewis Journal*

CB   *Christian Behaviour*

CE   *Critical Essays on C.S. Lewis* (Critical Thought Series: I), ed. George Watson (Aldershot: Scolar Press, 1992)

CFC *The Case for Christianity* (= *Broadcast Talks*)

CP *Collected Poems*

CR *Christian Reflections*

CRR *Christian Reunion*

D *Dymer*

DI *The Discarded Image*

DNB *Dictionary of National Biography*, Oxford University Press

DT *The Dark Tower*

ECW *Essays Presented to Charles Williams*, ed. C.S. Lewis (1947)

EIC *An Experiment in Criticism*

EL *English Literature in the Sixteenth Century*

FE *Fern-seed and Elephants*

FL *The Four Loves*

FST *First and Second Things*

GD *The Great Divorce*

GID *God in the Dock* (Eerdmans 1970) (= *Undeceptions*)

gid *God in the Dock* (Fount 1979)

GMD *George MacDonald: An Anthology*

HHB *The Horse and His Boy*

IHW *C.S. Lewis: Images of His World* by Clyde S. Kilby and Douglas Gilbert (1973)

INK *The Inklings* by Humphrey Carpenter (1978)

ISO *In Search of C.S. Lewis*, ed. Stephen Schofield (1983)

Jack *Jack: C.S. Lewis and his Times*, George Sayer (1988)

L *Letters of C.S. Lewis*, ed. with a **Memoir** by W.H. Lewis (1966); Revised and Enlarged Edition also with **Memoir**, ed. W. Hooper (1988), which is quoted throughout this book

LAL *Letters to an American Lady*

LB *The Last Battle*

LCSL *Light on C.S. Lewis* ed. Jocelyn Gibb (1965)

LDGC *Letters: C.S. Lewis – Don Giovanni Calabria*

LJRRT *The Letters of J.R.R. Tolkien*, ed. Humphrey Carpenter (1981)

LL *Lenten Lands: My Childhood with Joy Davidman and C.S. Lewis* by Douglas Gresham (1988)

LTC *Letters to Children*

LTM *Letters to Malcolm*

LP 'Lewis Papers: Memoirs of the Lewis Family, 1850–1930' (unpublished)

LWW *The Lion, the Witch and the Wardrobe*

M *Miracles*

MC *Mere Christianity*

MCA   *Mere Christianity, anniversary edition*

MN   *The Magician's Nephew*

NP   *Narrative Poems*

NYCSL   *CSL: The Bulletin of the New York C.S. Lewis Society*

OBCSL   *Owen Barfield on C.S. Lewis*, ed. G.B. Tennyson (1989)

OOW   *Of Other Worlds*

OS   *On Stories (= Of This and Other Worlds)*

OSP   *Out of the Silent Planet*

OTOW   *Of This and Other Worlds (= On Stories)*

P   *Poems*

PC   *Prince Caspian*

PER   *Perelandra*

PH   *The Personal Heresy*

PP   *The Problem of Pain*

PPL   *A Preface to 'Paradise Lost'*

PR   *The Pilgrim's Regress*

PRCON   *Present Concerns*

PWD   *Past Watchful Dragons* by Walter Hooper (1979)

R   *Rehabilitations*

ROP   *Reflections on the Psalms*

SBJ   *Surprised by Joy*

SC   *The Silver Chair*

SIB   *Spirits in Bondage*

SIW   *Studies in Words*

SL   *The Screwtape Letters*

SL&SPT   *The Screwtape Letters* and *Screwtape Proposes a Toast*

SPT   *Screwtape Proposes a Toast*

SLE   *Selected Literary Essays*

SMRL   *Studies in Medieval and Renaissance Literature*

T   *Transposition (= The Weight of Glory)*

TAFP   *They Asked for a Paper*

TAH   *Timeless at Heart*

TJB   *Through Joy and Beyond* by Walter Hooper (1982)

TST   *They Stand Together*

TWHF   *Till We Have Faces*

U   *Undeceptions (= God in the Dock)*

VDT   *The Voyage of the 'Dawn Treader'*

W   Wade Center‡

WB   Wade Center and Bodleian Library

WG   *The Weight of Glory (= Transpositions)*

WG (Rev)   *The Weight of Glory And Other Addresses*, Revised and Expanded Edition (1980)

WLN   *The World's Last Night*

LIFE OF C.S. LEWIS

I: Childhood in Belfast

Clive Staples Lewis was born on 29 November 1898 in one of a pair of semi-detached houses called Dundela Villas‡ in an inner suburb of Belfast. They were demolished in 1952 and their place is now taken by some modern flats. It is not only the area of Dundela that has undergone changes in Lewis's homeland. The greatest change since Lewis's birth occurred in 1922, when the island was partitioned into Ireland or the Republic of Ireland in the south, and the six counties that make up Northern Ireland – a part of the United Kingdom – in the north. Belfast, in County Down, is the capital of Northern Ireland. That war-torn city had been formed in the seventeenth century by the English crown, and was originally made up mainly of English and Scottish settlers. It was intended to be a Protestant city, but this was a time of economic expansion, and with the growth of its industries and shipping many Catholics had gone there to work.

Clive's father, Albert James Lewis,* was a police court solicitor, whose father, Richard (1832–1908), a master boiler maker, had emigrated from Wales to Cork and eventually to Belfast in 1868. Albert was educated at Lurgan College, in Lurgan, County Armagh. When he was there (1877–79) the headmaster was that remarkable man Mr William T. Kirkpatrick,* who was to play such an important part in the lives of Albert and his sons.

Clive's mother, Florence Augusta 'Flora' Hamilton,* was the daughter of the Rector of St Mark, Dundela, the Rev. Thomas Hamilton (1826–1905). Thomas came from a long line of Church of Ireland (Anglican) ecclesiastics. His father, Hugh, had been Rector of Benmore, Enniskillen, and his grandfather, Hugh Hamilton (1729–1805), had been Bishop of Clonfert and later Bishop of Ossory. Flora was a graduate of

Queen's College in mathematics and logic. Years later, Clive Lewis compared the two families: 'My father's people were true Welshmen, sentimental, passionate, and rhetorical, easily moved to anger and to tenderness; men who laughed and cried a great deal and who had not much of the talent for happiness. The Hamiltons were a cooler race. Their minds were critical and ironic and they had the talent for happiness in a high degree' (**SBJ** I).

Albert and Flora had one other child, Warren Hamilton (or 'Warnie'), who was born in 1895. The combination of good Christian parents and a loving elder brother ensured Clive a very happy childhood. The year 1905 was an eventful year for the family. In April the family moved into a large house, 'Little Lea', on the outskirts of Belfast, which Albert Lewis had specially built for them. Warnie was not destined to enjoy Little Lea for very long. Like so many other Anglo-Irish parents, Mr Lewis wanted his sons to be educated in English public schools, and he wrote to the educational agents, Gabbitas Thring and Co., for advice about where he might send Warnie. They contacted the Rev. Robert Capron* of Wynyard School in Watford, Hertfordshire. With no experience in the matter at all, and in complete innocence, Albert and Flora delivered Warnie, and later Clive, into the hands of a headmaster whose school was near collapse. Wynyard is the school referred to as 'Belsen' in *Surprised by Joy*.

While Warnie was at Wynyard, Clive was being tutored at home by his mother and a governess, Miss Annie Harper. Both parents were fond of reading, and it is perhaps not surprising that Clive should give early evidence of his own remarkable ability with words. Before he was two years old his mother said he was 'talking like anything'. 'Clive' and 'Staples' were family names from the Hamilton side and, disliking both of them, C.S. Lewis announced before he was four years old that he was 'Jacksie' – later amended to Jack – which name he always used after that. It was at Little Lea that Jack created his own imaginary world of 'Boxen' and peopled it with characters, thus training himself to be a novelist.

It was also as a young boy that the future C.S. Lewis, champion of Reason, emerged. Warren Lewis has given us an example of that 'dexterity of riposte' for which his brother later became so famous. It was 1907 and the family were preparing for a holiday in France. Warren said, 'Entering the study, where my father was poring over his account books, Jack flung himself into a chair and observed, "I have a prejudice against the French." My father, interrupted in a long addition sum, said irritably, "Why?" Jack, crossing his legs and putting his finger tips together, replied, "If I knew *why* it would not be a prejudice"' (**TJB** I).

II: 'Joy'

It was about the time of this holiday Warnie and Jack had with their mother in Normandy that Jack had three related experiences which, while unobserved by others, he regarded as initiating 'the central story' of his life (**SBJ** I). He tells in *Surprised by Joy* how one day, as he was standing beside a flowering currant bush, he was visited by the 'memory of a memory' of a day in Dundela Villas when his brother had brought his toy garden into the nursery. 'It is difficult to find words strong enough for the sensation which came over me,' he wrote. 'Milton's "enormous bliss" of Eden ... comes somewhere near it.' It was, he said, a sensation of desire, but before he knew what he desired 'the desire itself was gone, the whole glimpse withdrawn, the world turned commonplace again, or only stirred by a longing for the longing that had just ceased.' A second 'glimpse' came through Beatrix Potter's *Squirrel Nutkin* which, he said, 'troubled me with what I can only describe as the Idea of Autumn.' A third glimpse came through a few lines of Longfellow's translation of Esaias Tegner's *Drapa*:

> I heard a voice that cried,
> 'Balder the beautiful
> Is dead, is dead!'
> And through the misty air
> Passed like the mournful cry
> Of sunward sailing cranes.

'I knew nothing about Balder,' he said, 'but instantly I was uplifted into huge regions of northern sky, I desired with almost sickening intensity something never to be described (except that it is cold, spacious, severe, pale, and remote) and then, as in the other examples, found myself at the very same moment already falling out of that desire and wishing I were back in it.' He described the three experiences as having in common 'an unsatisfied desire which is itself more desirable than any other satisfaction. I call it Joy ... It might almost equally well be called a particular kind of unhappiness or grief. But then it is a kind we want' (**SBJ** I).

A few months later Jack began the first of his diaries. It bears the title *My Life During the Exmas Holadys of 1907* and from it we catch a glimpse of the domestic life of the Lewis family. After describing the servants, he goes on, with his distinctive spelling, to say:

> Papy of course is the master of the house, and a man in whom you
> can see strong Lewis features, bad temper, very sensible, nice wen

not in a temper. Mamy is like most middle-aged ladys, stout, brown hair, spectaciles, kniting her chief industry, etc., etc. I am generaly wearing a jersy ... I have left out an important member of the family namly my grand-father, who lives in a little room of his own upstairs. He is a nice old man in some ways but he pitys himself rather much, how-ever all old people do that ... Hoora!! Warnie comes home this morning. I am lying in bed waiting for him and thinking of him, before I know where I am I hear his boots pounding on the stairs, he comes into the room, we shake hands and begin to talk ... Well I was glad to have him but of course we had our rows afterwards ... (LP III:88–92).

Only a few months after this, in February 1908, Mrs Lewis was found to have cancer. She was operated on at home and for a while it seemed she would be all right. In a few months' time, however, they realized how ill she was. Flora Lewis died at home on 23 August 1908. Writing about her later in his autobiography, Lewis said that 'With my mother's death all settled happiness, all that was tranquil and reliable, disappeared from my life ... It was sea and islands now; the great continent had sunk like Atlantis' (SBJ I). For Albert Lewis the tragedy seemed endless. His father had died a few months before his wife, and his brother Joseph (1856–1908) died a few weeks later.

III: Wynyard, Campbell, Cherbourg and Malvern

Albert Lewis, heart-broken, and intending to do the best he could, sent Jack with Warnie to Wynyard School – 'Belsen' – in September 1908. It was a terrible introduction to England. The Rev. Robert Capron, a native of Devon, had taken a BA degree and a BSc degree from the University of London in 1873 and 1875 respectively, and had been ordained in 1878. He served as a curate in Staffordshire for two years, then went into the schoolmastering business in 1882 when he acquired a pair of semi-detached yellow brick houses in Watford. There was success at first, and in the early days he had as many as thirty pupils. By the time Warnie arrived there in 1905, 'Oldy' – as the boys called him – had had a High Court action taken against him for brutality. His sanity had long been in dispute, and now his erratic behaviour had driven away all but a handful of boys. Besides his bouts of sudden and fierce anger, Warnie lists among the catalogue of horrors he found at Wynyard the dirtiness of the place. 'If a boy was sick,' he said, 'he was accommodated in an attic which served the double purpose of sanatorium and lumber room' (**LP** III:35).

Jack arrived there, with Warnie, on 18 September 1908. The next day he wrote to his father, saying: 'I think I will be able to get on with Mr Capron though to tell the truth he is rather eccentric' (**LP** III:140). Then, on 29 September the full blast of Oldy's temper fell upon Warnie, and that evening he wrote to his father: 'You have never refused me anything Papy and I know you won't refuse me this – that I may leave Wynyard. Jack wants to too' (**LP** III:146). Warnie made his escape in April 1909 and went to Malvern College‡, Malvern, the following month. Jack managed to survive until 1910 when Robert Capron had a High Court action brought against him, and the school collapsed. After one very pleasant term at Campbell College‡ in Belfast, Jack and Warnie returned to England in January 1911; Warnie to Malvern College, and Jack to a small preparatory school overlooking it called Cherbourg House.‡ Here, during the years 1911–13 Jack's education began in earnest under the excellent guidance of the headmaster, Arthur C. Allen.

Jack had been there nearly a year when he was visited by that same 'Joy' which had swept over him two years before. He chanced upon the Christmas number of *The Bookman* for December 1911. In the coloured supplement were some of Arthur Rackham's illustrations to a translation of Richard Wagner's *Siegfried and the Twilight of the Gods*. The combination of the words – 'Siegfried' and 'the Twilight of the Gods' – and Rackham's drawings caused pure 'Northernness' to engulf him: 'a vision of huge, clear spaces hanging above the Atlantic in the endless twilight of Northern summer, remoteness, severity ... and almost at the same moment I knew I had met this before, long, long ago ... in Tegner's *Drapa*, that Siegfried ... belonged to the same world as Balder and the sunward-sailing cranes. And with that plunge back into my own past there arose at once, almost like heartbreak, the memory of Joy itself, the knowledge that I had once had what I had now lacked for years, that I was returning at last from exile and desert lands to my own country ... And at once I knew (with fatal knowledge) that to "have it again" was the supreme and only important object of desire' (**SBJ** V).

It was also at Cherbourg House that he lost the faith. He came under the influence of the School Matron, Miss G.E. Cowie, who was 'floundering in the mazes of Theosophy, Rosicrucianism, Spiritualism, the whole Anglo-American Occultist tradition.' 'Little by little,' Lewis wrote, 'she loosened the whole framework, blunted all the sharp edges, of my belief ... The whole thing became a matter of speculation: I was soon altering "I believe" to "one does feel"' (**SBJ** IV).

By the time Jack Lewis won a scholarship to Malvern College in 1913 he was an apostate. In *Surprised by Joy* the chapter on Malvern is called 'Bloodery'. He defined a 'Blood' as 'a member of the school aristocracy ... The most important qualification is athletic prowess ... good looks and personality will help. So of course will fashion, as fashion is understood at your school. A wise candidate for Bloodery will wear the right clothes, use the right slang, admire the right things, laugh at the right jokes.' Although he was always to love walking and swimming, Lewis never cared for 'games', and because they were enforced, he complained that 'a school day contains hardly any leisure for a boy who does not like games.' He, nevertheless, discovered two 'blessings' at Malvern. One was the Classics master, Harry Wakelyn Smith (1861–1918), or 'Smewgy', who taught him 'the right sensuality of poetry, how it should be savoured and mouthed in solitude.' The other blessing was 'the Gurney', or school library. Nevertheless, even with these compensations, the effect of Malvern was to leave him 'dog-tired, cab-horse tired, tired (almost) like a child in a factory.' While Warnie had never been happier than at Malvern College, and loved it all his life, Mr Lewis saw that it did not suit his other son, and he consented to Jack's leaving after only a year there. It was to be an extraordinarily wise decision.

IV: W.T. Kirkpatrick

Albert Lewis's old headmaster from Lurgan College, Mr William Thompson Kirkpatrick,* was living in semi-retirement in Great Bookham, Surrey, and taking one or two pupils for private tuition. Jack was later to devote a whole chapter of his autobiography to 'The Great Knock', as the family called him. Warnie was with 'The Great Knock' during September-December 1913 preparing for his Army entrance examination. He was placed twenty-first out of 201 candidates and entered the Royal Military Academy at Sandhurst as a prize cadet on 3 February 1914.

Jack arrived at Great Bookham on 19 September 1914. His time there was to be a stunning success intellectually, and a powerful influence upon his abilities as a reasoner. Except that Mr Kirkpatrick probably did not share Jack's imaginative interests, his talk was not only the kind the young man enjoyed, but it was very nearly what Jack's friends remember his own as being. First, Mr Kirkpatrick is described in **SBJ** IX as disliking the practice of 'making conversation' just so that someone is talking. 'If ever a man came near to being a purely logical entity,' Lewis wrote, 'that man was Kirk ... The idea that human beings should exercise their vocal organs for any purpose except that of communicating or discovering truth was to him preposterous.' It was 'red beef and strong beer' to Jack because 'Here was a man who thought not about you but about what you said. No doubt I snorted and bridled a little at some of my tossing; but, taking it all in all, I loved the treatment. After being knocked down sufficiently often I began to know a few guards and blows, and to put on intellectual muscle.'

Mr Kirkpatrick, without intending it, did not help Lewis spiritually. He had studied in a Presbyterian seminary many years before, but was now an atheist of 'the anthropological and pessimistic kind ... great on *The Golden Bough* and Schopenhauer' (ibid.). Now, under Mr Kirkpatrick, Lewis's own atheism began to take shape. It was carefully concealed from his father, but he was open with his friend, Arthur Greeves. Writing to him on 12 October 1916 he said: 'I believe in no religion. There is absolutely no proof for any of them, and from a philosophical standpoint Christianity is not even the best. All religions, that is, all mythologies to give them their proper name, are merely man's own invention' (**TST**).

V: Oxford and Mrs Moore

Lewis arrived in Oxford for the first time on 4 December 1916 and lodged in 'the first house on your right as you turn into Mansfield Road out of Holywell' (**SBJ** XII) while he sat for a scholarship examination. He won a scholarship to University College‡ and arrived in Oxford on 26 April 1917 to read Classics. He joined the Officers' Training Corps as soon as he arrived. Lewis's letters to Arthur Greeves show the next few months to have been idyllic, but there was evidence of the war everywhere. All but a small part of University College was serving as an army hospital (see photos in **TJB** II). There were only 315 students in residence in all the colleges, and of these 50 were Oriental students, 25 were refugees, 30 were medical students, and about 120 were members of the Officers' Training Corps. Lewis was one of only six men in his college. Even so, he extracted what juice there was from his classical studies, the punting on the Cherwell and the library of the Oxford Union.

He was forced to give up all this on 8 June when he joined the Army and was sent across Oxford to be billeted in Keble College. There he shared a room with a young Irishman named Edward Francis Courtney 'Paddy' Moore.* Paddy's mother, Mrs Janie King Moore,* was in Oxford with her twelve-year-old daughter, Maureen,* staying in rooms in Wellington Square, a few minutes' walk from Keble College. Mrs Moore, who was 45 at this time, was born in 1872 in Pomeroy, County Tyrone, the eldest child of the Rev. William James Askins. When her mother died in 1890 she spent much of her time bringing up her brothers and sisters in Dunany, County Louth, where her father was Vicar. In 1897 she married Courtney Edward Moore, a civil engineer in Dublin. In 1908 she separated from her husband, and emigrated to Bristol with Paddy and Maureen.

Lewis took an instant liking to this family, and spent a large part of the short time he still had left with them. On 25 September 1917 he was gazetted into the 3rd Somerset Light Infantry and given a month's leave. He disappointed his father greatly by spending three weeks of this with the Moores at their home in 56 Ravenswood Road, Redlands, Bristol. This marked preference for Mrs Moore – and it was Mrs Moore, not Paddy – worried Albert Lewis. It was on this visit to Bristol that Maureen heard Lewis and Paddy promise that if one or the other should survive the War he would look after Paddy's mother and Lewis's father, a promise about which Mrs Moore was later to write to Albert Lewis (LP VI:44–5).

VI: War

At the beginning of October 1917 Paddy went to France with the Rifle Brigade, and on 19 October Lewis joined his regiment in Crown Hill, near Plymouth. On 15 November the 3rd Somerset Light Infantry was ordered to the front after a forty-eight-hour leave. Lewis could not have gone to Ireland in that time, and he spent it with Mrs Moore in Bristol. He crossed to France on 17 November and arrived in the front line trenches of France on his nineteenth birthday, 29 November 1917, a Second Lieutenant in the Somerset Light Infantry. Warnie had been in France with the British Expeditionary Force during November 1914–February 1915, and he returned to France in September 1915. On the day Jack arrived there Warnie was promoted to Captain. It was impossible for either to tell Mr Lewis exactly where they were. Jack's Commanding Officer, Major V.H.B. Majendie, later wrote *A History of the 1st Battalion The Somerset Light Infantry ... July 1st 1916 to the end of the War* (1921) which traces that part of the war in France which Jack knew first-hand.

He fell ill of 'trench fever' in February 1918 and spent three weeks in the hospital at Le Tréport. Arthur Greeves was worried that he had been replaced in Jack's affections by Mrs Moore, and in Jack's letter to Arthur of 2 February we learn something of what he now felt for the lady. 'As for the older days of real walks far away in the hills,' he assured Arthur, 'perhaps you don't believe that I want all that again, because other things more important have come in: but after all there is room for other things besides love in a man's life' (**TST**).

Lewis rejoined his battalion at Fampoux on 28 February 1918 and was one of those who faced the final German attack on the Western Front. He took part in the Battle of Arras and was wounded on Mount Bernenchon on 15 April 1918. 'I was really hit in the back of the left hand, on the left leg from behind and just above the knee, and in the left side just under the armpit,' Lewis wrote to his father on 4 May from the Liverpool Merchants Mobile Hospital at Etaples (**L**). Before that, Warnie had been so anxious for his brother that on 24 April he borrowed a bicycle and rode the fifty miles from Doullens to Etaples to be with him.

On 25 May 1918 Jack was invalided to the Endsleigh Palace Hospital in London. Despite his urging, Mr Lewis did not get over to see him. Mrs Moore, on the other hand, was a frequent visitor. She and Jack were to see even more of one another after 25 June when he was sent to convalesce at Ashton Court, Long Ashton, Bristol. Her son Paddy had been a Second Lieutenant with the 2nd Battalion of the Rifle Brigade and had been on the receiving end of the great German attack which began on 21 March 1918. He had last been seen on 24 March when he was defending a position against infinitely superior numbers of the enemy, and Mrs Moore was informed that he was missing. In September she learned that he was dead. 'They tell me he was taken a prisoner,' Mrs Moore wrote to Albert Lewis on 1 October 1918, 'overthrew his guards, got back to our lines to be sent over again, was wounded in the leg, and as his man was bandaging him up, was shot through the head and killed instantaneously … I had built such hopes on my only son, and they are buried with so many others in that wretched Somme … Jack has been so good to me. My poor son asked him to look after me if he did not come back' (**LP** VI:44–5).

Besides looking after Mrs Moore, Lewis was very busy with a project he had been engaged on since he arrived in France. During the whole of his life he had the extraordinary ability of being able to write almost anywhere. During his time in France he carried a notebook in his pocket, and he managed to write a number of poems. After he was invalided to the hospital in London in May 1918, and later at several other army hospitals, he continued writing what might be called his 'war poems'. They reflected his increasing despair about God, whom he describes in one as 'a phantom called the Good'. These poems were combined with others he had written during the years with Mr Kirkpatrick and sent to William Heinemann, who accepted them for publication. Jack's first book, *Spirits in Bondage: A Cycle of Lyrics*, was published on 10 March 1919 when he was twenty years old.

VII: Return to Oxford

He returned to University College, Oxford, on 13 January 1919. Now that her own son was dead, Mrs Moore and Maureen moved to 28 Warneford Road, Oxford, to be near Lewis. This was the beginning of a joint household between Lewis and the Moores, which Lewis thereafter was to call 'the family'. He was required to spend one year in college, but after that he also moved into 28 Warneford Road. The family seemed constantly on the move. In his diary of 4 July 1923 (**AMR**) Lewis lists the eight different houses they lived in between 1919 and July 1923. Despite the constant moving, the arrangement Lewis had with Mrs Moore was to last for the rest of her life.

Sadly, the unspoken rift between Lewis and his father, which had lasted for some years, became worse. While it would appear that Mr Lewis never discussed with his son the attachment to Mrs Moore, it worried him greatly. When Warnie learned of it he wrote to his father on 10 May 1919 saying, 'The whole thing irritates me by its freakishness' (**LP** VI:118). Mr Lewis replied on 20 May that 'If Jacks were not an impetuous, kind-hearted creature who could be cajoled by any woman who has been through the mill, I should not be so uneasy. Then there is the husband whom I have always been told is a scoundrel – but the absent are always to blame' (**LP** VI :123). Mr Lewis soon realized, as did Warnie, that Jack now disliked his rare visits to Belfast, and regarded the Moores as his 'real family'. However, despite the distractions and the expense of this arrangement – for Lewis was having to pay most of 'the family's' expenses – he performed brilliantly in all his work.

He took a First Class degree in Classical Honour Moderations‡ in April 1920, a First in *Literae Humaniores*‡ or 'Greats' in August 1922, and a First in English‡ in July 1923. What makes this success all the more remarkable is that Lewis also kept up a very long diary, since published as *All My Road Before Me*, during the years 1922–27. He records there such things as his 'rage against poverty' (20 June 1923) and such a state of exhaustion at the end of English Schools that he was left pondering the 'pleasures of death' (8 September 1923). The diary also records the many fellowships in Oxford that Lewis was passed over for, and the fact that he would have been unable to continue at all had it not been for his father's generosity over the lean years.

Lewis's first job was in his own college. He was asked to deputize for his Philosophy tutor, E.F. Carritt, while the latter was in the United States during the academic year 1924–25. Then in May 1925 he was elected, not to a fellowship in Philosophy, but to one in English at Magdalen College.‡ He was given room 3 on staircase 3 of New Buildings. The strain between him and his father was eased enormously now that he was independent. Mr Lewis asked if he regretted the move to English from Philosophy. 'I am rather glad of the change,' Jack replied. 'I have come to think that if I had the mind, I have not the brain and nerves for a life of pure philosophy ... At any rate I escape with joy from one definite drawback of philosophy – its solitude. I was beginning to feel that your first year carries you out of the reach of all save other professionals. No one sympathizes with your adventures in that subject because no one understands them: and if you struck treasure trove no one would be able to use it' (L 14 August 1925). Actually, there was no sudden move from one subject to another because for a good many years Lewis taught both English and Philosophy in Magdalen.

Lewis did not learn to *like* his father's company, but he was much more attentive from the time his position at Magdalen made him independent. In 1927 Mr Lewis began to suffer cruelly from rheumatism, and Jack was very attentive, trying to get his father to visit him in Oxford. In the summer of 1929 Albert Lewis was found to have cancer, and Jack rushed over to Belfast to be with him. From this point on, and until Albert Lewis's death on 25 September 1929, he was a much better son, spending as much time as he could possibly spare in Belfast with his father. Even so, in the years to come he was appalled by his earlier behaviour. He told one correspondent 'I treated my own father abominably and no sin in my whole life now seems to be so serious.'[1]

VIII: Conversion

It is not unlikely that the knowledge that he would soon lose his father contributed to another great change in Lewis's life. For years he had tried to keep God at bay. Even so his atheism began to crumble at about the time his father became ill. He read G.K. Chesterton's *Everlasting Man* and 'saw the whole Christian outline of history set out in a form that seemed to me to make sense.' At the same time his friends Owen Barfield,* J.R.R. Tolkien,* and Hugo Dyson* were helping him to find the answers to the questions which had bothered him so long: 'Where has religion reached its true maturity? Where, if anywhere, have the hints of all Paganism been fulfilled?'

[1] Letter to Rhona Bodle of 24 March 1954.

In **SBJ** XIV Lewis says 'In the Trinity Term of 1929 I gave in, and admitted that God was God, and knelt and prayed: perhaps, that night, the most dejected and reluctant convert in all England.' This was a conversion to Theism. Lewis did not know how Christ fitted into this until two years later. Dyson was teaching at Reading University when he came over on 19 September 1931 to spend the weekend with Lewis. Tolkien dined with them in Magdalen, and afterwards they began a long and momentous conversation about Myth and its relation to Truth, which lasted half the night. 'What Dyson and Tolkien showed me,' Lewis wrote to Arthur Greeves afterwards, was 'that the idea of a dying and reviving god ... moved me provided I met it anywhere *except* in the gospels ... Now the story of Christ is simply a true myth: a myth working on us in the same way as the others, but with this tremendous difference that *it really happened*' (**TST** 18 October 1931). On 28 September 1931 he went to Whipsnade Zoo in the sidecar of Warnie's motor cycle, and the final piece fell into place. 'When we set out I did not believe that Jesus Christ is the Son of God, and when we reached the zoo I did' (**SBJ** XV). Tolkien's part in the evening's conversation of 19 September 1931 is the subject of his 'Mythopoeia', a poem addressed 'To one who said that myths were lies and therefore worthless, even though "breathed through silver"' (Lewis). It is found in Tolkien's *Tree and Leaf*.

Two other important changes had occurred during the course of Lewis's conversion. Since their arrival in Oxford together in 1919 Lewis and Mrs Moore – or 'Minto' as the Lewis brothers called her – lived in hope that one day they would have a place of their own. In 1930 they found such a place as they had dreamed of. This was The Kilns‡ in Headington Quarry, about four miles from the centre of Oxford. There were nine acres of woodlands and even a large bathing pool. Warnie was stationed at Bulford at this time, but he had, following his father's death, been invited to make his home with Lewis and the Moores. He came over from Bulford and helped them move into The Kilns on 11 October 1930.

The following year, on 13 May 1931, Warnie recorded in his diary: 'I started to say my prayers again after having discontinued doing so for more years than I care to remember.' 'This was no sudden impulse,' he went on, 'but the result of a conviction of the truth of Christianity which has been growing on me for a considerable time: a conviction for which I admit I should be hard put to find a logical proof, but which rests on the inherent improbability of the whole of existence being fortuitous, and the inability of the materialists to provide any convincing explanation of the origin of life' (**BF**).

Following another tour of duty in China, Warnie applied for retirement, and he returned home in December 1932 to find that Lewis and Mrs Moore had added two extra rooms to The Kilns especially for him. Jack also gave him one of his two sitting-rooms in Magdalen. Unlike his brother, who was hopeless with any kind of machinery, Warnie had picked up typing and he now owned a Royal typewriter. Following Albert Lewis's death in 1929 they found that he had preserved a vast quantity of family papers – particularly letters and diaries. These were brought back to the room Jack gave Warnie in Magdalen, added to Jack's and Warnie's diaries and other papers, and the whole arranged in chronological order. During 1933–35 Warnie typed the lot with two fingers. The sheets were then bound into eleven volumes and given the name **Lewis Papers: Memoirs of the Lewis Family 1850–1930.**‡ It is a remarkable piece of editing, with hundreds of explanatory notes written by Warnie. There was always a shortage of space, and in about 1936 Jack burnt nearly all the original documents that went into the **Lewis Papers**.

Despite the fact that Warnie and Mrs Moore were, as he said in his diary of 21 December 1933, 'on very good terms with each other', he complained that 'She is quite incapable of thought … and supplies its place with a bundle of prejudices, whose origin, when it can be traced at all, proves to be a point of personal selfishness' **(BF)**. In that same entry of his diary he touched on what was to Mrs Moore a very sore point and one which became worse as time went on: her unhappiness over Jack's conversion. Although the daughter of an Anglican clergyman, with a brother, William, who was Dean of Kilmore Cathedral from 1931 to 1955, Mrs Moore was an atheist. She blamed God for Paddy's death, and now, says Warnie in that entry of 21 December 1933, 'She nags J about having become a believer, in much the same way that P[apy] used to nag me in his latter years about my boyish fondness for dress, and with apparently just the same inability to grasp the fact that the development of the mind does not necessarily stop with that of the body' **(BF)**. It wasn't just Jack's conversion she resented. She chided both of them for going to those 'blood feasts' in their parish church every Sunday morning. It is hard to resist thinking that Lewis may have had Mrs Moore in mind when, in his **Answers to Questions on Christianity**, he said 'It is extraordinary how inconvenient to your family it becomes for you to get up early to go to church. It doesn't matter so much if you get up early for anything else, but if you get up early to go to church it's very selfish of you and you upset the house.'

IX: The Inklings

'There's no sound I like better than adult male laughter,' said Lewis,[2] and no words can more perfectly describe the delight he found in the 'Inklings'. This was a group of friends, centred on Lewis, who met from about 1930 to 1963 to talk and read aloud their compositions. Some scholars give the probable date of its beginning as 1933; others suggest that it goes much further back. Whatever date we decide to give it, a clue as to why it existed is found in *The Four Loves*. 'In this kind of love,' wrote Lewis of Friendship, *'Do you love me?* means *Do you see the same truth? –* or at least, Do you *care about* the same truth? The man who agrees with us that some question, little regarded by others, is of great importance, can be our friend. He need not agree with us about the answer' (IV).

Apart from the special love he had for Warnie and Arthur Greeves, the friend who most nearly 'saw the same truth' as himself and very often did not agree about the 'answer' was Owen Barfield.* They met in the autumn of 1919 when Lewis was at University College and Barfield was an undergraduate of Wadham College. Thus began for these Inklings a golden age of talk about poetry, language, myth, imagination. 'We got into conversation on fancy and the imagination' is a typical entry from Lewis's diary (28 June 1922). 'Barfield towers above us all,' he said on 10 July 1922. Shortly after this Barfield began his B.Litt. thesis on 'Poetic Diction' – later to be an indispensable book to Lewis and the other Inklings. In 1923 Barfield and Cecil Harwood became Anthroposophists and this, though it did not hurt the friendship, was nevertheless the beginning of the decade-long 'Great War'‡ between Lewis and Barfield.

J.R.R. Tolkien had been an undergraduate at Exeter College 1911–15, and he returned to Oxford in 1925 as the Professor of Anglo-Saxon. He and Lewis had possibly run into one another before, but Lewis records their first conversation in his diary of 11 May 1926 (**AMR**). By 1929 they were meeting on a weekly basis in Lewis's rooms in Magdalen, when Tolkien often brought along some of the manuscripts which were to make up *The Silmarillion*. They usually met on Monday mornings, and in a letter to Warnie of 22 November 1931 Jack described his meetings with Tolkien. 'This is one of the pleasant spots in the week,' he said. 'Sometimes we talk English school politics: sometimes we criticize one another's poems: other days we drift into theology or "the state of the nation": rarely we fly no higher than bawdy and "puns"' (**L**).

[2] From a sketch Lewis wrote for the dust jacket of the American edition of *Perelandra* (1944).

In these early days Lewis and Tolkien were also members of a literary club of dons and undergraduates actually named 'The Inklings'. This group was founded in about 1930 by an undergraduate of University College called Edward Tangye Lean.* In a letter to William Luther White of 11 September 1967 Tolkien said that this society, which had been meeting in Lean's rooms, died in 1933 when Lean left Oxford. 'Its name,' he said, 'was then transferred (by C.S.L.) to the undetermined and unelected circle of friends who gathered about C.S.L., and met in his rooms in Magdalen. Although our habit was to read aloud compositions of various kinds (and lengths!), this association and its habit would in fact have come into being at that time, whether the original short-lived club had ever existed or not. C.S.L. had a passion for hearing things read aloud, a power of memory for things received in that way, and also a facility in extempore criticism, none of which were shared (especially not the last) in anything like the same degree by his friends' (**LJRRT**).

Barfield was living in London, but he joined them whenever he could. Hugo Dyson, who with Tolkien played such an important part in Lewis's conversion, came over several times a year from Reading. Other early Inklings included Warnie Lewis, who came regularly to the meetings when he retired from the Army in 1932, and Colin Hardie* who became Classical Tutor at Magdalen in 1936. Adam Fox* became Dean of Divinity at Magdalen in 1938 and was soon a member of the group. The year 1939 saw the most numerous, and perhaps the most valuable additions to the Inklings. Lewis met his doctor, Robert Havard* (later nicknamed 'Humphrey') in December of 1939, James Dundas-Grant* within a few months of that, and Charles Williams* arrived in Oxford the same month (September) that Warnie was recalled to active service. Other members were J.A.W. Bennett,* Lord David Cecil,* Nevill Coghill,* Father Gervase Mathew,* R.B. McCallum,* C.E. 'Tom' Stevens,* Christopher Tolkien,* John Wain* and Charles Wrenn.*

Lewis and Charles Williams came to one another's attention at the same time. In February 1936 Nevill Coghill lent Lewis a copy of Williams's 'spiritual shocker' *The Place of the Lion*. 'Twenty-four hours later,' he said in the Preface to **ECW**, 'I found myself, for the first time in my life, writing to an author I had never met to congratulate him on his book. By return of post I had an answer from Williams, who had received my letter when he was on the point of writing a similar letter to me about my *Allegory of Love*. After this, as may be supposed, we soon met and our friendship rapidly grew inward to the bone.'

Charles Williams had worked for the Oxford University Press most of his life, and when war broke out he moved to Oxford with the Press and found rooms in 9 South Parks Road, while his family stayed behind in London. By this time the Inklings were meeting twice a week, on Tuesday mornings during Term in the back room of the Eagle and Child ('Bird and Baby')‡ and on Thursday evenings in Lewis's rooms in Magdalen. Williams quickly became one of them. The Tuesday meetings, Warnie noted in his **Memoir**, picked up 'a certain notoriety' because they are mentioned in a detective novel of the period. The novel is Edmund Crispin's *Swan Song*. In chapter 8 Gervase Fen and some others are 'sitting before a blazing fire in the small front parlour of the "Bird and Baby" ... "There goes C.S. Lewis," said Fen suddenly. "It must be Tuesday."' Beginning in 1937 they began listening to Tolkien's magnificent *Lord of the Rings* as it was being written. Charles Williams was persuaded to read aloud what was to be his last novel, *All Hallows' Eve*. During 1944 Warnie read his *The Splendid Century* and over the years the Inklings read and criticized *Out of the Silent Planet, The Problem of Pain, The Screwtape Letters* and many other of Lewis's works.

X: Tutor and Lecturer

The theological books of C.S. Lewis are so well known that it is easy to forget that he earned his living at something else. He was a very busy college tutor, university lecturer, and literary historian. A tutorial is the period of an hour that an undergraduate spends each week with his tutor or tutors, reading an essay or discussing his work. Sometimes a tutor takes two pupils at a time.

One of Lewis's first pupils was the future Poet Laureate, John Betjeman.* It would have been reasonable to suppose that tutor and pupil would have liked one another, but this was not to be. There are numerous references to Betjeman in Lewis's diary, and from them it would seem that, besides his manner, which Lewis disliked, Betjeman simply would not work. On 27 May 1926 Lewis recorded: 'Betjeman appeared in a pair of eccentric bedroom slippers and said he hoped I didn't mind them as he had a blister. He seemed so pleased with himself that I couldn't help replying that I should mind them very much myself but that I had no objection to *his* wearing them – a view which, I believe, surprised him.' On 19 January 1927 he wrote: 'I was rung up on the telephone by Betjeman speaking from Morton in the Marsh, to say that he hasn't been able to read the [Old English], as he was suspected for measles and forbidden to look at a book. Probably a lie, but what can one do?' In the end, Betjeman left Oxford without a degree.

Perhaps if Lewis had been older he and Betjeman could have got on better. But the truth is that Lewis was a very popular tutor, as testified by those many pupils who have said what it was like to be taught by him in those rooms in New Buildings. 'No one knew better how to nourish a pupil with encouragement and how to press just criticism when it was needed, without causing resentment,' wrote Harry Blamires, who began reading English with Jack in 1936, and whose reminiscences are included in Warnie's **Memoir**. 'He did not think of himself as taking pupils through a course; rather he saw his pupils as having two years or so under his guidance, during which they could start on a process which would occupy the responsive ones for the rest of their lives. The literature stood waiting on the shelves; the pupil's appetite was to be whetted and fed ... There was a good deal of fun about tutorials. Lewis sat there on his vast Chesterfield, smoking a pipe and cigarettes alternately, periodically beaming and bouncing with good humour in a hugely expansive way. He looked big, sitting down opposite one, with his great fist bulging round a pipe bowl, eyes wide open and eyebrows raised behind a cloud of smoke.'

'The thick-set body, the red face with its huge domed forehead,' wrote John Wain in *Sprightly Running* III, 'the dense clouds of smoke from a rapidly puffed cigarette or pipe, the brisk argumentative manner, and the love of debate which kept the conversation going at the pace of some breathless game – all these were, and are, familiar to thousands. And for one hour a week, twenty-four weeks in the year, I had them to myself.' One of Lewis's American students, George Bailey, has said: 'Lewis had three standard forms of comment on an essay. If the essay was good: "There is a good deal in what you say." If the essay was middling: "There is something in what you say." If the essay was bad: "There *may* be something in what you say." His other fairly standard comments were: "Too much straw and not enough bricks," and "Not with brogans, please, slippers are in order when you proceed to make a literary point." Lewis was sparing of compliments – the highest I know of was "Much of that was very well said" – but he was quick to notice any excellence of usage. He spent five minutes praising one word I had used to describe Dryden's poetry (the word was "bracing").'[3]

Lewis's first lectures in the University were the ones he gave when he was standing in for his Philosophy tutor, E.F. Carritt, during the academic year 1924–25. His lectures then had been on 'The Good, and its position

[3] George Bailey, 'In the University', *C.S. Lewis: Speaker and Teacher*, ed. Carolyn Keefe (1971), p. 81.

among the values'. As a tutor in English Language and Literature he took pupils who were reading Philosophy as well as those who were reading English. His lectures were, from Michaelmas Term 1925 onwards, on English. The first ones he gave in Oxford's English School were in October 1925 when his subject was 'Some Eighteenth-Century Precursors of the Romantic Movement'. In 1928 he began his twice-weekly lectures on 'The Prolegomena to Medieval and Renaissance Studies', which were to make him one of the most popular lecturers in Oxford. In Hilary Term 1929 he began lecturing on 'Elyot, Ascham, Hooker and Bacon'. In Trinity Term 1930 he gave his first lectures on Milton, and in Michaelmas Term 1930 he had taught 'Textual Criticism' for the first time. It was, however, the Prolegomena lectures which were outstanding.

'As a lecturer,' said Harry Blamires in Warnie's **Memoir**, 'he was the biggest "draw" the English School had in the nineteen-thirties. He could fill the largest lecture rooms. He was popular because his lectures were meaty. He purveyed what was wanted in a palatable form. Proportion and direction were always preserved, but without forcing. Points were clearly enumerated; arguments beautifully articulated; illustrations richly chosen.' These lectures were eventually published as *The Discarded Image: An Introduction to Medieval and Renaissance Literature* (1964).

Since 1928 Lewis had also been writing what was to be his magisterial *The Allegory of Love: A Study in Medieval Tradition*. This was published in 1936, to be followed by other outstanding works of literary history and criticism such as *A Preface to 'Paradise Lost'* and *English Literature in the Sixteenth Century*.

But it was science fiction that Lewis chose as his first vehicle for reaching the mass of his unbelieving fellow countrymen. In 1938 he published *Out of the Silent Planet*, the first of his three interplanetary novels. The Christian purpose of the book was hidden from all but a few, and from this Lewis discovered that 'any amount of theology can be smuggled into people's minds under cover of romance without their knowing it' (L 9 August 1939). This was followed by two sequels, *Perelandra* (1943) and *That Hideous Strength* (1945).

One of Lewis's greatest pleasures was an annual walking tour. Warnie's diary contains an account of the third walking tour he took with his brother from 1–18 January 1934. On this occasion, carrying no more than would go into a haversack, they took a train to Hereford. From there they set out across the Wye into Wales, walking all day and putting up in pubs at night. 'My happiest hours,' Lewis said in the little sketch on the dust jacket of the American edition of *Perelandra*, 'are spent with three or four old friends in old clothes tramping together and putting up in small pubs

– or else sitting up till the small hours in someone's college rooms talking nonsense, poetry, theology, metaphysics over beer, tea and pipes.' In January 1939 Jack and Warnie spent their eighth tour walking in the Welsh marches.

Warnie was fonder of travel by water than by foot, and in 1936 he acquired a small two-berth cabin cruiser. It was moored at Salter's Boatyard on the Thames, beside Folly Bridge. The cruiser was named the *Bosphorus* after the one operated by Captain Macgoullah 'The shrewd, honest master of the schooner Bosphorus' in one of the Boxen stories the brothers were specially fond of – *Boxen or Scenes from Boxonian city life* (I). Warnie was planning to take Jack and Hugo Dyson on a holiday up the river in August 1939 when his army commitments intervened.

XI: World War II and the Emergence of the Apologist

The brief popularity of the Munich Pact which Hitler had signed with Great Britain, France and Italy in 1938 was now over, and war looked certain. The Germans invaded Poland on 1 September 1939, and the next day Lewis and Mrs Moore welcomed the first of the many evacuated schoolgirls who were to live at The Kilns during the next few years. Nineteen schools were evacuated from London to Oxfordshire, many of which were relocated in Oxford itself. On 4 September Warnie was recalled to active service and posted to Catterick in Yorkshire. The next month he was sent to Le Havre in France.

Jack, who would be 40 on 29 November, wrote to him on 18 September about his own position. 'Men between 18 and 41 are liable,' he said, '"if and when called up". No one seems to think it likely that they will want men of 40 this year, so that if it means "under 41 at the time of being called up" it is not likely to concern me ... For the moment dons are a reserved occupation: and as long as they stick to their present plans of not calling up boys between 18 and 20 there will, of course, be a full generation of freshmen each year who must do something between leaving school and joining the army.' As the age of conscription was 18, the University decided that those undergraduates who faced the call-up should be examined on the basis of a shortened curriculum. If they passed their work, they could obtain a special certificate – a 'war degree'. When the war ended they were allowed to return to Oxford and convert it into a full honours degree.

The Government had decided, meanwhile, that they would need Magdalen's New Buildings, and Lewis had to move all his books into the cellars. They were hardly put away when the Government changed its mind and the books had to be brought up again. While waiting to know whether or not he would be called up, Lewis got on with his teaching and looking after the series of evacuated children from London. After the fall of France he joined the Home Guard; writing to his brother on 11 August 1940 he said his duty began 'with the 1.30 a.m. patrol on what they call Saturday morning and mortals call Friday night' (L).

Meanwhile, the Inklings were enjoying the company of their new member, Charles Williams. Jack wrote to Warnie on 5 November 1939 about a meeting at which Tolkien, Charles Williams and Charles Wrenn were present. Wrenn, a University Lecturer in Anglo-Saxon since 1930, was probably meeting Williams for the first time, and he 'almost seriously expressed,' said Jack, 'a strong wish to burn Williams, or at least maintained that conversation with Williams enabled him to understand how inquisitors had felt it right to burn people. Tolkien and I agreed afterwards that we just knew what he meant ... The occasion was a discussion of the most distressing text in the Bible ('narrow is the way and few they be that find it') and whether one really could believe in a universe where the majority were damned and also in the goodness of God. Wrenn, of course, took the view that it mattered precisely nothing whether it conformed to your ideas of goodness or not, and it was at that stage that the combustible possibilities of Williams revealed themselves to him in an attractive light. The general sense of the meeting was in favour of a view on the lines taken in Pastor Pastorum – that Our Lord's replies are never straight answers and never gratify curiosity, and that whatever this one meant its purpose was certainly not statistical' (L).

When he wrote on 11 November 1939 about another meeting he said 'I have never in my life seen Dyson so exuberant – "a roaring cataract of nonsense". The bill of fare afterwards consisted of a section of the new Hobbit book from Tolkien, a nativity play from Williams (unusually intelligible for him, and approved by all) and a chapter out of the book on The Problem of Pain from me ... The subject matter of the three readings formed almost a logical sequence, and produced a really first-rate evening's talk of the usual, wide-ranging kind – "from grave to gay, from lively to severe". I wished very much we could have had you with us' (L). Williams 'is an ugly man,' Lewis told Dom Bede Griffiths on 21 December 1941, 'with rather a cockney voice. But no one thinks of this for five minutes after he has begun speaking. His face becomes almost angelic. Both in public and private he is of nearly all the men I have met the one whose address most overflows with love.'

Shortly after Lewis had written to Warnie about that last Inklings meeting, he managed to smuggle Charles Williams on to the Oxford lecture list, and when we read Lewis's letter to Warnie of 11 February 1940 about Williams's lecture on *Comus* we get the impression it was not only his subject but his love which was communicated to his hearers. The lecture was in the Divinity School on 29 January 1940:

> C.W. lectured nominally on *Comus* but really on Chastity. Simply as criticism it was superb – because here was a man who really started from the same point of view as Milton and really cared with every fibre of his being about 'the sage and serious doctrine of virginity' which it would never occur to the ordinary modern critic to take seriously. But it was more important still as a sermon. It was a beautiful sight to see a whole room full of modern young men and women sitting in that absolute silence which can *not* be faked, very puzzled, but spell-bound: perhaps with something of the same feeling which a lecture on *un*chastity might have evoked in their grandparents – the forbidden subject broached at last. (L)

The Problem of Pain, which Lewis began writing in the summer of 1939 and which he dedicated to the Inklings, was published in 1940. It opened with the arresting words 'Not many years ago when I was an atheist ...' and from that point on the reader is introduced to Lewis's wonderful combination of orthodoxy, scholarship and imaginative creativity. This was his first straight work of theology. Having found what turned out to be his primary 'war work', C.S. Lewis the Christian apologist emerged.

XII: Christianity in Britain

To appreciate his impact upon Great Britain at that time we need to know something of the context in which he wrote. A work which does this well is Adrian Hastings' *A History of English Christianity 1920–1990* (1991). Very briefly, for centuries the heart of traditional Christianity had lain in the historic Incarnation, the belief that God became Man, but by the time Lewis was converted to Christianity in 1931 Agnosticism was everywhere. The reliability of biblical scholarship had been punctured a good many years before by a number of things, amongst which were those 'prophets of enlightenment': Charles Darwin, Karl Marx, Friedrich Nietzsche, Sigmund Freud and Émile Durkheim – all of whose works Lewis could probably have been introduced to by Mr Kirkpatrick. Not

unrelated to this was 'Modernism', a movement within the Roman
Catholic Church which aimed at bringing Catholic belief into closer
relation with the modern outlook in philosophy, history and science.
Although formally condemned in 1907, Modernism reached the heights
of its influence in England in the first years of this century under the
leadership of George Tyrell, whose demythologizing Lewis criticizes
in his essay, 'Fern-seed and Elephants'. The common ground between
Modernism in the Catholic Church and Modernism in the Anglican
Church lay particularly in biblical criticism.

However, one big difference peculiar to Anglicanism was that its
modernism was strongly affected by the philosopher Hegel (1770–1831)
and his system of 'Absolute Idealism'. Hegel and his followers conceived
the whole of reality to be the expression of an Idea, while challenging the
specificity of historical Christianity. Hegel was followed by the British
Idealist School which offered a way of retaining Christian values without
Christianity. Its principal spokesmen were T.H. Green, F.H. Bradley and
Bernard Bosanquet, whose books Lewis came across in the 1920s while
reading Classical Moderations. These philosophers believed that the only
true reality was to be found, not in any historical figure such as Jesus
Christ, but in an all-inclusive experience, the 'Absolute'. They asserted
the primacy of spiritual reality, which was essentially one of divine
immanence rather than transcendence – the spirit within man and all
reality, rather than a personal Father above him. This 'Idealism', which
Lewis had come across in the early 1920s, reached the common man in the
form of a diffused, vague pantheism.

Writing about the 'watered Hegelianism' which affected his last days as
an atheist, he said, 'There were in those days all sorts of blankets,
insulators and insurances which enabled one to get all the conveniences
of Theism, without believing in God. The English Hegelians, writers like
T.H. Green, Bradley and Bosanquet (then mighty names), dealt in
precisely such wares ... We could talk religiously about the Absolute: but
there was no danger of Its doing anything about us. It was "there"; safely
and immovably "there". It would never come "here", never (to be blunt)
make a nuisance of Itself' (SBJ XIII).

Lewis did not read much theology at this time, but he would have
known how greatly the Idealist mood had already affected the
theologians. The Oxford and Cambridge schools of Divinity contained
many 'Modernists' such as William Sanday and B.H. Streeter at Oxford,
and F.C. Burkitt at Cambridge. They had parted from biblical fund-
amentalism and supernaturalism and were trying to establish something
Sanday called 'Reduced Christianity'. Another theological presence was

the Modern Churchmen's Union which was founded in 1898 for the advancement of liberal religious thought in the Church of England. The Union had no time for miracles, and at its conference in 1921 the strategist of Anglican modernism, H.D.A. Major, summed up their position:

> We believe that there is only one substance of the Godhead and the Manhood, and that our conception of the difference between Deity and Humanity is one of degree. The distinction between Creator and creature, upon which ... the older theologians place so much emphasis, seems to us to be a minor distinction (Hastings, *A History of English Christianity*, chapter 12).

While traditional Christianity still had giants such as William Temple, Ronald Knox and G.K. Chesterton, Christian belief was highly discredited amongst the intellectuals of the 1920s. T.S. Eliot was the darling of the Bloomsbury Group until he was baptized and confirmed in the Church of England in 1927. This was shocking behaviour for the author of *The Waste Land* and the editor of *The Criterion*, and Virginia Woolf wrote to a friend on 11 February 1928 saying: 'I have had a most shameful and distressing interview with dear Tom Eliot, who may be called dead to us all from this day forward. He has become an Anglo-Catholic believer in God and immortality, and goes to church. I was shocked. A corpse would seem to me more credible than he is. I mean, there's something obscene in a living person sitting by the fire and believing in God' (Hastings, op. cit. chapter 12).

XIII: Champion of Orthodoxy

Lewis would have understood most of the theological terms of this period. He said in the Preface to the Third Edition of *The Pilgrim's Regress* of 1943: 'On the intellectual side my own progress had been from "popular realism" to Philosophical Idealism; from Idealism to Pantheism; from Pantheism to Theism; and from Theism to Christianity.' Very few people outside Oxford knew who Lewis was between the time of his conversion and the publication of *The Problem of Pain* in 1940. However, as he was changing from a 'hard-boiled atheist' to a champion of orthodoxy, we get a fleeting glimpse of how 'obscene' his Christianity seemed in the place he called 'big brutal Magdalen'.

The American literary critic and philosopher, Paul Elmer More (1864–1937), was in Oxford in the spring of 1933 and dining at Magdalen

College only days before *The Pilgrim's Regress* was published. Writing to Christian Gauss on 11 May 1933, More said:

> I have dined several times at Magdalen, with old J.A. [Smith], and more recently with a Fellow and Tutor of English named Lewis, who interested me more than any other Oxonian I have met for a long time. You will smile when I tell you that this is partly, not wholly, because he has gone through a deep and today unusual religious experience; this he has written out in a book, in more or less disguised form I presume, which is to appear shortly and a copy of which he promises to send me.[4]

More returned to Oxford in July, having read *The Pilgrim's Regress*. This time he was lunching in Magdalen College with the Tutor in Philosophy, John Frederick Wolfenden (1906–85). As it happened, T.S. Eliot had been giving a lecture in Oxford, and he was present. Writing about his conversation with Wolfenden to A.H. Dakin on 7 December 1933, More said:

> I asked him about Lewis, what the story of his experience was and whether he had become a Roman Catholic, and what was meant by 'Mother Kirk' to which his Pilgrim returns. Wolfenden said he didn't know much about it all, but was sure Lewis had not become an R.C. And then he added this tale. He, Wolfenden, and several other Fellows were talking together one day, when a friend came into the room in a state of high excitement. I say, said the newcomer, do you know what's going on with Lewis? So and so tells me he happened to see Lewis in the college chapel the other day, and, being amazed and making enquiries, discovered that he has been going there for weeks without anyone's knowing anything about it.
>
> This brought out one of Eliot's sly little sarcastic digs: It's quite apparent that if anybody in an Oxford college wishes to escape detection, the one place for him to go to is the chapel![5]

What distinguished Lewis from the liberal theologians of that time as well as the present is that, for him, Christianity was, first of all, a matter of

---

[4] Arthur Hazard Dakin, *Paul Elmer More* (Princeton: Princeton University Press, 1960), p. 327.
[5] Op. cit., p. 332.

objective fact; secondly, even though Christianity is sometimes difficult to understand, it is of the utmost importance and for this reason it is worth fighting for. He put it in a nutshell when he said in **The Weight of Glory**:

> If our religion is something objective, then we must never avert our eyes from those elements in it which seem puzzling or repellent; for it will be precisely the puzzling or the repellent which conceals what we do not yet know and need to know.

The same muscular appetite for truth came up a few years later when Lewis was addressing some Welsh clergymen on **Christian Apologetics**. They must remember, he told them, that 'Christianity is a statement which, if false, is of *no* importance, and, if true, of infinite importance. The one thing it cannot be is moderately important.' He went on to say to them that the truth we need most is 'hidden precisely in the doctrines you least like and least understand'. Scientists make progress because scientists 'instead of running away from such troublesome phenomena or hushing them up, are constantly seeking them out':

> In the same way, there will be progress in Christian knowledge only as long as we accept the challenge of the difficult or repellent doctrines. A 'liberal' Christianity which considers itself free to alter the Faith whenever the Faith looks perplexing or repellent *must* be completely stagnant. Progress is made only into a *resisting* material.[6]

Lewis gave a wonderful example of this by attempting to show in his very first work of apologetics – *The Problem of Pain* – why, even in a world of such appalling suffering, we can believe that God is good. Years later, when attacked for the 'vulgarity' of the imagery in his books, he explained in his **Rejoinder to Dr Pittenger** what Modernist Christianity was like when he started writing. 'When I began,' he said, 'Christianity came before the great mass of my unbelieving fellow countrymen either in the highly emotional form offered by revivalists or in the unintelligible language of highly cultured clergymen. Most men were reached by neither. My task was therefore simply that of a *translator* – one turning Christian doctrine, or what he believed to be such, into the vernacular, into language that unscholarly people would attend to and could understand.'

6 See **Repellent Doctrines.**§

It was precisely because he did not shy away from 'repellent doctrines' and was a 'translator' of remarkable ability and clarity of thought that so many turned to Lewis for help. Dr James Welch, the Director of the British Broadcasting Corporation's Religious Broadcasting Department, wrote to him on 7 February 1941 to say how impressed he was by the 'quality of his thinking' and the 'depth of his conviction', and urged him to give a series of talks over the BBC. Lewis agreed, and he was then contacted by the Rev. Eric Fenn, a Presbyterian who had been the Headquarters Secretary of the Student Christian Movement 1926–37, and who was now in the BBC's Religious Broadcasting Department. He explained the wartime restrictions imposed upon all broadcasters during World War II. All scripts had to be passed for security by the official Censor, and then rigidly adhered to. No silence was permitted in the course of a talk lest the gap be filled by the British traitor 'Lord Hawhaw' speaking from Germany. Lewis went up to London every Wednesday in August 1941 and gave four live fifteen-minute talks on 'Right and Wrong: A Clue to the Meaning of the Universe'.

These talks on **Right and Wrong**, heard by more than a million people, were so well received that others in the BBC invited him to broadcast to the Armed Forces and over their Overseas Services. People in Australia and New Zealand were particularly keen on hearing him. Lewis felt he had to turn these invitations down. 'I'm afraid in view of my other commitments,' he wrote on 30 September 1941, 'I should be "over-talked" if I accepted the job you kindly suggest for me. I'm talking already to the RAF, to the general public, to nuns, to undergraduates, to societies. The gramophone will wear out if I don't take care!' (Introduction **MCA**). By the time the war was over his list of engagements would be much longer. Still, we get some idea of what his war work was like by looking at a few. The 'general public' could have been reading *The Screwtape Letters* as they appeared in thirty-one weekly instalments in the church newspaper, *The Guardian*,‡ beginning 2 May 1941. This was a series of delightfully witty letters from Screwtape, who is in the Administration of the Infernal Civil Service, to Wormwood, a junior colleague engaged in trying to secure the damnation of a young man on Earth.

When they were published as a book in 1942 they were found to have a particular appeal for those whose religion was beset by doubts and hesitations. C.E.M. Joad, reviewing the book in the *New Statesman and Nation* (16 May 1942), said 'Mr Lewis possesses the rare gift of making righteousness readable.' As for the 'undergraduates', they could have heard Lewis lecture in the university almost any day of the week and, beginning in January 1942, they could have seen him arguing vigorously for the Christian Faith at the Socratic Club.‡ Or, they could have been sitting in the pews, or standing in the aisles of the University Church of St Mary the Virgin on 8 June 1941 when Lewis preached his famous sermon, **The Weight of Glory**.

The 'nuns' were the Sisters of the Community of St Mary the Virgin in Wantage, one of the first Anglican religious orders founded since the Reformation. Lewis's friend, the scholarly Sister Penelope,* had invited him to stay in their Gate House from 21–22 April 1942 and lecture to the Junior Sisters on 'The Gospel in Our Generation'. 'What odd tasks God sets us,' he replied on 10 April 1941. 'If anyone had told me ten years ago that I should be lecturing in a convent – !' (L). Still he accepted and after spending the night in the convent he went directly to London to give the Annual Shakespeare Lecture on **Hamlet: The Prince or the Poem?**

Lewis's broadcasts on Natural Law§ had proved so provoking that Dr Welch and Eric Fenn were able to persuade Lewis to return to the microphone for three further series. He gave five talks on **What Christians Believe** during January and February 1942; eight talks on **Christian Behaviour** during September to November 1942; and seven talks on **Beyond Personality** during February to April 1944. At this time people did not like programmes to be recorded, and Lewis spent many hours travelling back and forth to London during bombings and air raids, to talk live over the air. During the last series, however, he was allowed to record talks 2, 6 and 7, of which only the last has survived in the archives of the BBC. The broadcasts were later rewritten and published as *Mere Christianity* (1952), which work, more than any other, abounds in examples of Lewis's ability to put complex matters into language anyone can understand. 'Mr Lewis is that rare being – a born broadcaster; born to the manner as well as to the matter' said Robert Speaight in *The Tablet* of 26 June 1943. 'He neither buttonholes you nor bombards you; there is no false intimacy and no false eloquence. He approaches you directly, as a rational person only to be persuaded by reason. He is confident and yet humble in his possession and propagation of truth. He is helped by a speaking voice of great charm and style of manifest sincerity.'

XIV: The Royal Air Force

In the winter of 1941 Lewis had a visit from the Chaplain-in-Chief of the Royal Air Force, Maurice Edwards, and his assistant, the Rev. Charles Gilmore. They asked him to give talks on theology to members of the Royal Air Force, and a lectureship was set up. Lewis certainly took the job seriously. When Dr Emrys Evans asked him to give some lectures at the

University College of North Wales in November 1941, Lewis replied on 14 March 1941: 'I am at present in the state of having promised to undertake some lecturing to the forces which may, or may not, develop into a full-time job.'

It did not, in fact, turn into a full-time job, but it nevertheless absorbed nearly all his weekends. Lewis gave the first of these talks at the RAF base in Abingdon in May 1941. 'As far as I can judge,' he told Sister Penelope in a letter of 15 May 1941, 'they were a complete failure ... One must take comfort in remembering that God used an *ass* to convert the prophet' (L). After this, and throughout the war, he was away for two or three days at a time, and then home for two or three. 'I had never realized,' he told Arthur Greeves on 23 December 1941, 'how tiring perpetual travelling is (specially in crowded trains). One felt all the time as if one had just played a game of football – aching all over. None the less I had some interesting times and saw some beautiful country. Perthshire, and all the country between Aberystwyth and Shrewsbury, and Cumberland, are what chiefly stuck in my mind. It also gave me the chance in many places to see and smell the sea and hear the sound of gulls again, which otherwise I would have been pining for' (TST).

Lewis said later in **Christian Apologetics**, 'Where a speaker has that gift, the direct evangelical appeal of the "Come to Jesus" type can be as overwhelming today as it was a hundred years ago ... I cannot do it: but those who can ought to do it with all their might. I am not sure that the ideal missionary team ought not to consist of one who argues and one who (in the fullest sense of the word) preaches. Put up your arguer first to undermine their intellectual prejudices; then let the evangelist proper launch his appeal.'

We see how Lewis went about the task from his letters to the Rev. Lewis John Collins (1905–82) who, during the war, was a Church of England Chaplain at the RAF base at Yatesbury, Wiltshire. After Collins had told Lewis something of what he could expect there, he replied on 12 July 1942:

> I'm a little surprised (though of course, pleased) at the size of the audience you expect. You mean a *voluntary* one, I trust? I shouldn't like to address an audience that has been (even indirectly and by velvet glove methods!) coerced. This means, of course, that I am prepared to risk getting *no* audience: which, indeed, has often happened to me.
>
> Before deciding which of the suggested subjects I'd talk on, I'd like to know whether the audience is likely to consist of believers or enquirers.

Following an assurance that the audience was voluntary, Lewis replied on
17 July:

> Dear Padre – the conditions are what I regard as ideal. By all means
> put me on to talk to the mixed mass first and then let the serious
> ones come for a follow up in a smaller room afterwards if they like.
> I have known that work well at other stations. I shall talk (roughly)
> on the relation between Christianity and the social order; if you
> don't think it too flippant it might be called 'Christianity isn't a
> patent medicine'.

Two RAF chaplains have left reminiscences about Lewis as a speaker:
Charles Gilmore's 'To the RAF' in *C.S. Lewis at the Breakfast Table*, and
Stuart Barton Babbage's 'To the Royal Air Force' in *C.S. Lewis: Speaker and
Teacher*. It is from Lewis himself that we learn what he found to be the
chief difficulty in presenting the Christian Faith to modern unbelievers
amongst the RAF and his other audiences. In **God in the Dock** he said:

> The ancient man approached God (or even the gods) as the accused
> person approaches his judge. For the modern man the roles are
> reversed. He is the judge: God is in the dock. He is quite a kindly
> judge: if God should have a reasonable defence for being the god
> who permits war, poverty and disease, he is ready to listen to it.
> The trial may even end in God's acquittal. But the important thing
> is that Man is on the Bench and God in the Dock.

It was during Lewis's visit to the RAF base at Abingdon in May 1941 that
his **Screwtape Letters** began appearing in *The Guardian*.‡ Lewis was paid
£2 per letter, and from the first he instructed the editor to pay all £62 into
a fund for 'Clergy Widows'. Much the same happened with the fees from
the BBC. They paid ten guineas, with railway vouchers, for each of his
talks in the first and second series, eight guineas each for the third series,
and ten guineas each for the fourth (a guinea, or £1.05, was worth $5.25 at
the time). After the first series of talks Lewis sent the BBC a list of widows
to whom the fees should be paid. One of those, a 'Mrs Boshell', was a
friend of Mrs Moore and living at The Kilns during this time. When the
BBC saw that her address was the same as that of their broadcaster's they
sent the fee to Lewis to pass on. He returned it at once, making it clear
that it must not be seen coming from *him*!

He had never understood the difference between gross and net profit,
and in the spring of 1942 he discovered to his horror that he owed a hefty

tax bill on all the monies he'd been giving away. Before things got out of hand, Owen Barfield, now a lawyer in the family firm of Barfield and Barfield, intervened and helped Lewis set up a charitable trust – the Agape Fund‡ or the 'Agapargyry' (love + money), as they called it. Thereafter, and until his marriage in 1957, Lewis had two-thirds of all his royalties paid into the 'Agapargyry' for the supplying of anonymous gifts of money to various people in need.

Another side of Lewis's religious life which remained hidden from all but a few was his practice of weekly confession. In his letter to Sister Penelope of 24 October 1940 he said that he was making his first confession the following week. 'The *decision* to do so was one of the hardest I have ever made,' he said, 'but now I am committed (by dint of posting the letter before I had time to change my mind).' He chose as a *directeur*, or spiritual director, Father Walter Adams SSJE, one of the priests of the Anglican Society of Saint John the Evangelist in Cowley, better known as the 'Cowley Fathers'.‡ 'If I have ever met a holy man, he is one,' he wrote to Mary Neylan on 30 April 1941 (*The Chesterton Review*, XVII, August and November 1991, p. 409).

XV: Warnie Returns from the War

But no account of Lewis's 'war work' would be complete without mentioning the one we now see the most of. From the time of his first broadcasts over the BBC Lewis had been inundated with letters. As he gained more and more readers the pile of letters got bigger. In the end the business of answering them would have been impossible without his brother's help. During the time he was in Dunkirk Warnie had been promoted to the rank of Major. Following his evacuation in May 1940 he was sent to Wales, and on 16 August 1940 he arrived home. He had been ill and in hospital most of the time he was in France, and now that he had been transferred to the Reserve of Officers, he decided to serve as a private soldier in the 6th Oxford City Home Guard Battalion. During the summer months he served by going up and down the Thames in the *Bosphorus* as part of the 'floating' Home Guard.

Jack's duties with the Home Guard were less interesting; they involved, as he told Arthur Greeves on 27 December 1940, spending 'one night in nine mooching about the most depressing and malodorous parts of Oxford with a rifle' (**TST**). Maureen Moore had been teaching music in the Oxford High School since 1935, and on 27 August 1940 she married Leonard James Blake, the director of Music at Worksop College in

Nottingham, and of course moved away. Warnie was thus able to move his bedroom upstairs to the room Maureen had occupied, and he turned the larger of the two rooms built on to The Kilns for him into a very snug study.

Warnie's desk was one that had belonged to his father, and one of the things on it now was the portable Royal typewriter. He undertook the job of helping his brother with the daily mail. Those who received letters typed on Warnie's Royal will know what they look like. He practised a military discipline in some areas of his life, and this was one of them. At the top of the right-hand side of the letters he typed the address of The Kilns, and at the top of the left side was a number such as 'REF. 46/19'. This is from a letter to Dorothy L. Sayers* dated 7 January 1946, and the number indicates that it was the nineteenth letter he wrote that year. This was a great help, and Warnie wrote in his diary of 9 September 1967 – when the Royal broke down – that on it he had typed 'at least twelve thousand of J's letters' (**BF**). Even with this help, Jack answered by return of post most of the letters. His practice was to sit down after breakfast with a nib pen and spend at least an hour nearly every morning answering the post. We'll never know how he managed this.

There were sometimes compensations for receiving such a huge amount of mail. Jack often received letters from vastly interesting people that he would have felt it presumptuous to write to himself. One of these was Dorothy L. Sayers. Some time before Lewis heard from her, Miss Sayers had written to a member of the Guild of Catholic Writers saying: 'I am engaged ... in getting together a group of people, mostly writers, to do books, articles, lectures, etc., about national reconstruction and a creative spirit, not precisely under the Christian banner, but certainly on a basis of Christian feeling.'[7] The result was a series of books called *Bridgeheads*, one of which was her own *The Mind of the Maker* (1941).

Dorothy L. Sayers was very impressed by *The Screwtape Letters*, and she had possibly singled out Letter XIX as containing much good sense about Love and Marriage. 'Marriage, though the Enemy's invention,' Screwtape had said, 'has its uses. There must be several young women in your patient's neighbourhood who would render the Christian life intensely difficult to him if only you could persuade him to marry one of them.' About the beginning of April 1942 Dorothy L. Sayers asked Lewis to write on this subject for her *Bridgeheads* series. In his reply, which is undated, he said:

[7] Barbara Reynolds, *Dorothy L. Sayers: Her Life and Soul* (1993), p. 307.

But why not write the book yourself? Either a novel, in which the familiar contrast of love-and-marriage *versus* career is replaced by the new (or so old as to be called new) contrast of love-and-marriage *versus* happiness and marriage *without* 'Love' ... In a novel [one] can *suggest* more than one would feel justified in *stating*.

She would not give up, and asked again for a book. He replied on 6 April 1942: 'Come and lunch on 2 or 3 June – I've booked both. Yes, I understood quite well that you wanted a book for your series: but every word you wrote showed that you had the book in your own head and were just straining at the leash.'

After their first meeting in June 1942 Lewis and Dorothy L. Sayers met from time to time and they corresponded often. Replying to a question about her many years later, Lewis said: 'She was the first person of importance who ever wrote me a fan letter. I liked her, originally, because she liked me; later for the extraordinary zest and edge of her conversation – as I like a high wind.'[8] While Lewis never contributed a book to *Bridgeheads*, much of what Dorothy L. Sayers probably asked him to say went into the character of the unhappily married Jane Studdock in *That Hideous Strength*.

XVI: Domestic Life at The Kilns

These were very busy times for everyone. Mrs Moore had become quite frail, and with Maureen married, more responsibility fell upon Jack. 'Have you room for an extra prayer?' he asked Sister Penelope on 9 November 1941. 'Pray for *Jane* if you have. She is the old lady I call my mother and live with (she is really the mother of a friend) – an unbeliever, ill, old, frightened, full of charity in the sense of alms, but full of uncharity in several other senses. And I can do so little for her' (L). There seems to have been an enormous number of maids employed at The Kilns for brief spells. This was because Mrs Moore seemed always to be quarrelling and making up with them. This type of 'uncharity' became worse as time went on.

The great exception was Fred Paxford*, the gardener and general factotum, who had been there since 1930. He had his own little bungalow in the orchard, and he it was who looked after the chickens and – after the

---

[8] C.S. Lewis, 'Wain's Oxford', *Encounter*, xx, 1 (January 1963), p. 81.

war began – the rabbits. Mrs Moore was devoted to him, and he to her. As far back as 1934 Warnie had discovered that he was being unfair to Paxford for something for which Mrs Moore – 'Minto' – was really to blame. 'I suddenly got very bored with M's conversation tonight,' he wrote on 23 August 1934. 'She has lately developed a tiresome habit of becoming a mere compendium of Paxford's views: every conceivable topic is met with a reply beginning "Paxford says ...". I am resigned to being addressed by my new name of "Pax-Warnie", but if she is to become a mere conduit of the Paxford philosophy, it will be a very great bore. Further, it makes me angry with myself to find that the perfectly natural, and utterly unfair result is that I begin to dislike Paxford, no exercise of will convincing me that it is not the unfortunate P who is boring me with his views on everything under the sun' (BF).

Warnie and Jack were meanwhile very busy. Jack had been invited to give the Ballard Matthews Lectures in University College, North Wales. The three lectures he gave there on Milton in December 1941 were the basis for his book, *A Preface to 'Paradise Lost'* (1942). He came home from North Wales to prepare his talks on **What Christians Believe** which he delivered over the air in January and February 1942. He had also been occupied on behalf of Charles Williams. He felt Williams's talents should be utilized, and now Charles Williams was tutoring and lecturing on a regular basis for the English Faculty. Humphrey Havard had been called up to serve in the Navy, but many of the regular Inklings were in the Sheldonian Theatre on 18 February 1943 when the University conferred on Charles Williams an honorary Master of Arts.

Warnie was finding plenty to do. As a diarist he was far more able than his brother, and he had been keeping a diary off and on since he was a schoolboy. Now because of the war he broke off writing from 1939 until 1944. This was because he was busy during 1942 writing a draft of what became *The Splendid Century: Some Aspects of French Life in the Reign of Louis XIV*. During 22–25 February 1943 Jack and Warnie were able to combine pleasure with business when they had their first jaunt together since before the war. They went by train to Durham where Jack was giving the Riddell Memorial Lectures over a period of three successive evenings in nearby Newcastle-upon-Tyne. These are the lectures later published as *The Abolition of Man*.

By the summer of 1943 domestic life at The Kilns had become very tiring. Sister Penelope invited Lewis to come over for a rest in their Gate House, but he replied on 10 August 1943 'I *should* like a few days at Wantage, but things are so bad at home that I'm cancelling several of my RAF engagements. Pray for me, Sister, and for poor Jane (*very* bad with her varicose ulcer) and for "Muriel" (a kind of lady gardener and "help" who is putting off an operation she ought to have, out of funk, and getting hysterical and going into rages, and losing her faith) and for poor dear Margaret (certified "mental deficient" maid, at times the humblest, most affectionate, quaintest little person you can imagine, but subject to fits of inexplicable anger and misery). There is never any time when *all* three women are in a good temper. When A is in B is out: and when C has just got over her resentment at B's last rage and is ready to forgive, B is just ripe for the next, and so on!' (**L**).

Fortunately, help was at hand. That same summer there arrived at The Kilns the delightful Jill 'June' Flewett, a Catholic girl of sixteen who had to be evacuated from her convent school in London during the Blitz. She stayed nearly two years, winning the hearts of everyone. Two years later Warnie said in his diary of 2 January 1945: 'I have met no one of any age further advanced in the Christian way of life. From seven in the morning till nine at night, shut off from people of her own age, almost grudged the time for her religious duties, she has slaved at The Kilns, for a fractional 2d [1p] an hour; I have never seen her other than gay, eager to anticipate exigent demands, never complaining, always self-accusing in the frequent crises of that dreary house' (**BF**).

Years later, after Jill was married to Sir Clement Freud, and with five children of her own, she wrote down some of her memories of this time for Stephen Schofield to use in his *In Search of C.S. Lewis* (1983). At first she had no idea that the 'Jack' Lewis she knew at The Kilns was the author of the books. 'When I did learn who he was,' she said, 'I was shocked. He had such a great understanding of human nature that I felt he must have known my every thought.' She described Warnie as being 'by nature a gentler, less demanding person, and less stimulating. He was comfy to be with all the time and obviously highly intelligent. But he was not looking for an intellectual response from you in the same way that Jack Lewis did.' There have been so many uncomplimentary things said about Mrs Moore that it might redress the balance somewhat to quote what Jill says about her:

> To Mrs Moore, Lewis showed the greatest loving care. He waited on her, filled her hot water bottle, made her a hot drink, saw that she was tucked in each night. The only time I ever heard Jack Lewis's voice rise in annoyance with her was once when she had said something derogatory about his brother. She was strong-willed, and had a great sense of humour. Mrs Moore and Jack Lewis had happy times together. She adored him absolutely. Her

whole life was centred around him and around him alone. The running of the house, the cooking, the meals – everything she did – was geared for Jack's happiness and comfort ... When she became ill she took all Jack's letters, piles of letters she had received from him over a period of about twenty-five years, and I think also the letters from her own son, Paddy – Lewis's great friend who was killed in the First World War – and threw them all into the old-fashioned boiler in the kitchen. She burned the lot.

It is doubtful if Jack minded at all about the burning of his letters. In any event, he was probably too busy to think much about it. He had always found immense solace in writing and, with June there to help, he was able to finish writing *That Hideous Strength* before Christmas 1943, complete the first six chapters of *Miracles*, and compose his seven talks on **Beyond Personality** for the BBC.

XVII: Charles Williams and the Inklings

Things picked up from this time through to the end of the war. Before delivering his talks on **Beyond Personality** over the BBC during February to April 1944, Lewis encountered one of his major critics at the Socratic Club on 24 January. This was the eminent philosopher, C.E.M. Joad, who gave a paper on 'Being Reviewed by Christians'. Professor Joad had only just returned from agnosticism to Christianity, and Jack was the best arguer the Socratic had. The Socratic was now one of the best-attended and most exciting clubs in Oxford, due primarily to Lewis. His friend Austin Farrer,* then the Chaplain of Trinity College, was a member too and in *The Christian Apologist* he said: 'So far as the argumentative business went, he was a bonny fighter ... I went in fear and trembling, certain to be caught out in debate and to let down the side. But there Lewis would be, snuffing the imminent battle and saying "Aha!!" at the sound of the trumpet. My anxieties rolled away. Whatever ineptitudes I might commit, he would maintain the cause; and nobody could put Lewis down' (**LOL**).

Lewis was in such demand as a preacher in Oxford that 'Peterborough' in *The Daily Telegraph* of 26 February 1944 described him as 'Modern Oxford's Newman': 'Ascetic Mr C.S. Lewis, Magdalen's English Literature tutor and author of *The Screwtape Letters*, is becoming ever more of a power in Oxford. Though a layman he often occupies one or other of the pulpits in the University. An elderly Oxford don remarked to

me the other day that there has been no preacher with Mr Lewis's
influence since Newman. He more than fills the University church of
St Mary's. Preaching on a recent Sunday morning at Mansfield College,
to a congregation in which there were many senior members of
the University, including the Warden of All Souls, he made a deep
impression.'

'"Ascetic Mr Lewis – !!!"' Tolkien wrote to his son Christopher on 1
March 1944. 'I ask you! He put away three pints in a very short session we
had this morning, and said he was "going short for Lent"' (**LJRRT**). The
Inklings were meeting more frequently now than at any time. Tolkien was
devoting as much time as he could spare to *The Lord of the Rings*, and as
each chapter was written it was read to Lewis and some of the others. He
wrote to Christopher on 15 April 1944 about an Inklings meeting he had
just attended at which both Lewis brothers read from their own works,
Warnie from a rewriting of *The Splendid Century* and Jack from *Who Goes
Home?*, later to be called *The Great Divorce*. 'The best entertainment,' he
said, 'proved to be the chapter of Major Lewis's projected book – on a
subject that does not interest me: the court of Louis XIV; but it was most
wittily written (as well as learned). I did not think so well of the
concluding chapter of C.S.L.'s new moral allegory or "vision", based on
the medieval fancy of the Refrigerium, by which the lost souls have an
occasional holiday in Paradise' (**LJRRT**).

He thought even better of Warnie's book as he heard more, and when
he wrote on 31 May 1944 it was to say of a meeting of the Inklings that
'The chief entertainment was provided by a chapter of Warnie Lewis's
book on the times of Louis XIV (very good I thought it); and some
excerpts from C.S.L.'s *Who Goes Home?* – a book on Hell, which I
suggested should have been called rather "Hugo's Home".' Tolkien went
on to say that he was 'occupied by the desperate attempt to bring "The
Ring" to a suitable pause, the capture of Frodo by the Orcs in the passes of
Mordor ... By sitting up all hours, I managed it: and read the last two
chapters ('Shelob's Lair' and 'The Choices of Master Samwise') to C.S.L.
on Monday morning. He approved with unusual fervour, and was
actually affected to tears by the last chapter' (**LJRRT**).

Charles Williams had found time from his work with the Oxford
University Press and his duties in the University to finish his second
Taliessin volume of poetry, *The Region of the Summer Stars*, and write
another novel. The latter was begun in 1943 and read to Lewis and
Tolkien as it was being written during 1943–1944. 'I was in fact a sort of
midwife at the birth of *All Hallow's Eve*,' Tolkien wrote to Anne Barrett on
7 August 1964, 'read aloud to us as it was composed, but the very great

changes made in it were I think mainly due to C.S.L.' (**LJRRT**). Williams clearly felt at home in Oxford, and he had written to his wife on 5 February to say: 'I have found myself thinking how admirable it would be if I could get a Readership here when I retire. I know it may be only a dream; on the other hand, C.S.L. and Tolkien are only human, and are likely to take more trouble over a project which would enable them to see a good deal more of me than over anything which didn't.'[9] Before the end of the year Lewis and Tolkien were proposing a *Festschrift* for Williams in the form of a volume of essays.

For some time now Lewis had been troubled by some shrapnel he had been carrying since the last war, and in August 1944 he had it removed. About the same time Mrs Moore had a stroke which left her without the use of her left arm. Now confined to her bed, she had Paxford bring in the makings of a pudding and stand watching while she mixed the ingredients sitting up in bed. After this had happened a number of times she said, 'Paxford, you've seen me do this often enough. It's time you gave it a try.' In time he became more than a tolerable cook. The family always fasted from meat on Fridays, and Paxford's excellent fish and chips was the usual meal for Friday evenings.

The news from the front was hopeful, and this was reflected in a letter Tolkien wrote to his son Christopher on 23–25 September 1944. 'Lights are steadily increasing in Oxford. More and more windows are being unblacked ... I actually went out to an "Inklings" on Thursday night, and rode in almost peacetime light all the way to Magdalen for the first time in five years. Both Lewises were there, and C. Williams; and beside some pleasant talk, such as I have not enjoyed for moons, we heard the chapter of Warnie's book and an article of C.S.L. ... The Inklings have already agreed that their victory celebration, if they are spared to have one, will be to take a whole inn in the country for a week, and spend it entirely in beer and talk, without reference to any clock!' (**LJRRT**).

It had always displeased Lewis intensely to see *vers libre* replacing traditional forms of poetry, and he placed much of the blame on T.S. Eliot. As far back as 1926, when Eliot was editing the literary journal, *The Criterion*, Lewis came up with the idea of writing 'Eliotic' verses that he could sneak into Eliot's journal under a false name. At the end of a tutorial on 10 June 1926 he mentioned the idea to a pupil. 'I broached to him the idea of my literary dragonnade: a series of mock Eliotic poems to be sent up to the *Dial* and the *Criterion* until, sooner or later, one of these

[9] Alice Mary Hadfield, *Charles Williams: An Exploration of His Life and Work* (1983), chapter 13, p. 226.

filthy editors falls into the trap' (**AMR**). Although many 'Eliotic' poems were sent to Eliot, none was ever published. Later he attacked Eliot's criticism of Milton and the ugly 'stock responses'§ of his poetry in *A Preface to 'Paradise Lost'*.

Now, some time between the autumn of 1944 and the winter of 1945, Charles Williams invited Eliot to Oxford so that he and Lewis could meet. Apparently Williams never imagined that it would be a merry meeting, and that is what it certainly was not. Father Gervase Mathew was present and he recalled how unamused Lewis was by Eliot's opening remark: 'Mr Lewis, you are a much *older* man than you appear in photographs.' As Lewis stood facing him in silence, Eliot tried to be polite in saying, 'I must tell you, Mr Lewis, that I consider your *Preface to 'Paradise Lost'* your best book.'

The year 1945 began with the loss of June Flewett, who left on 3 January to pursue a career on the stage. 'Pray for us always,' Lewis wrote to Sister Penelope that same day, 'we are not a very happy house.' However, Maureen Blake returned for a short while, and on 8 January she gave birth to a son, Richard Francis, in the Radcliffe Infirmary. The war in Europe came to an official end on Wednesday 9 May, and there was rejoicing in the streets of Oxford. Lewis was filled with gratitude when, the following day, he wrote to his former pupil, Dom Bede Griffiths.* 'Every one of us,' he said, 'has escaped by a series of Providences, some not far short of miracles.' He went on to say that the writing of a book on Miracles had caused him to be 'much occupied by the idea of the New Creation ... New heavens and earth – the resurrection of the body – how we have neglected these doctrines and indeed left the Romantics and even the Marxists to step into the gap.'

This faith was very soon tested. That same day – 10 May – Charles Williams was seized with pain. His wife arrived on Friday and Williams was taken to the Radcliffe Infirmary where he was operated on for an internal trouble he had been bothered with years before. The following Tuesday, 15 May, Lewis went to the Infirmary to call on Williams before joining the others in the 'Bird and Baby'. 'I heard of his death at the Infirmary itself,' Lewis wrote, 'having walked up there with a book I wanted to lend him, expecting this news that day as little (almost) as I expected to die that day myself ... I thought he would have given me messages to take on to the others. When I joined them, with my actual message – it was only a few minutes' walk from the Infirmary but, I remember, the very streets looked different – I had some difficulty in making them believe or even understand what had happened. The world seemed to us at that moment primarily a *strange* one' (**ECW**).

The death of Charles Williams was a great loss to all the Inklings, but to none more than Lewis. They had been planning a 'Victory Inklings' when the war ended, but there was little jubilation about it now. The celebration consisted of three days in nearby Fairford. Warnie and Tolkien went over on Tuesday, 11 December, and put up at 'The Bull'. Jack joined them on Wednesday. Barfield was ill, and Humphrey Havard could only come over for lunch one day. Warnie's diary of 15 December includes some of the details of their walks in the vicinity of Fairford: 'Whelford, a mere hamlet, has a simple little church where we all felt that God dwells ... There, to my surprise and pleasure, Tollers said a prayer. Down on the river was a perfect mill house where we amused ourselves by dreaming of it as a home for the Inklings ... Friday morning was again fine ... and we walked to Coln St Aldwyn, a dream village ... here we drank beer at the "Pig and Whistle", which opened at 10 a.m. – the first time in my life I have ever met a pub of that name' (**BF**).

A bright note of this period was, however, the return of Tolkien's son, Christopher, to Oxford. He had been a pilot in the RAF during the war, and he now resumed his studies at Trinity College. Jack and Warnie had always been fond of him, and he was soon made a member of the Inklings. After a time he took over the reading of *The Lord of the Rings* from his father, who was often inaudible, and everyone agreed that this was an improvement.

XVIII: Post-War Oxford

Post-war Oxford was austere, and with rationing there was even more hunger than existed during the war. Because there was hardly any electricity and coal, most photographs of Lewis taken in his college rooms show him wearing a dressing gown on top of his cardigan and jacket. Many of his pupils were ex-servicemen, as he himself had been in 1919. There were men who had fought at El Alamein, many who had been wounded, and others who had been prisoners of war. Most were on government grants. Everywhere you looked there were men in army greatcoats and uniforms with the insignia torn off. A good many of the pupils who were to become Lewis's life-long friends were amongst these servicemen.

There was one of Lewis's pupils who did not fit this description. Kenneth Tynan* – the future theatre critic and producer of the all-nude revue *Oh! Calcutta!* – had come direct from Birmingham, and he appeared for his tutorials in a purple suit in fine doeskin. 'Later,' wrote his biographer, 'there was a cloak with a blood-red lining, and a bottle-green suit, reputedly made of billiard baize and worn with creamy silk shirts. There were broad gold velvet ties, bowties – changed frequently during the course of a day – and soft green suede shoes.'[10] Tynan's love of extravagance far outdid that of John Betjeman, and it might have been expected that Lewis would have been provoked by such a spectacle. But he was older now, he was a Christian, and he seems to have liked the colourful Tynan from the first. And Tynan, unlike Betjeman, liked Lewis.

Kenneth Tynan had a bad stutter at the time, and Lewis volunteered to read his essays aloud for him. An excellent piece of advice which Lewis scribbled on one of his essays was: 'Keep a strict eye on eulogistic and dyslogistic adjectives – they should *diagnose* (not merely blame) and distinguish (not merely praise).' Many of his pupils remembered Lewis's remarkable memory, but Tynan gave an interesting description of it to Stephen Schofield:

> He had the most astonishing memory of any man I have ever known. In conversation I might have said to him, 'I read a marvellous medieval poem this morning, and I particularly liked this line.' I would then quote the line. Lewis would usually be able to go on to quote the rest of the page. It was astonishing.
>
> Once when I was invited to his rooms after dinner for a glass of beer, he played a game. He directed, 'Give me a number from one to forty.'
>
> I said, 'Thirty.'
>
> He acknowledged, 'Right. Go to the thirtieth shelf in my library.' Then he said, 'Give me another number from one to twenty.'
>
> I answered, 'Fourteen.'
>
> He continued, 'Right. Get the fourteenth book off the shelf. Now let's have a number from one to a hundred.'
>
> I said, 'Forty-six.'
>
> 'Now turn to page forty-six! Pick a number from one to twenty-five for the line of the page.'
>
> I said, 'Six.'
>
> 'So,' he would say, 'read me that line.' He would always identify it – not only by identifying the book, but he was also usually able to quote the rest of the page. This is a gift. This is something you can't learn. It was remarkable.
>
> But the great thing about him as a teacher of literature was that he could take you into the medieval mind and the mind of a

[10] Kathleen Tynan, *The Life of Kenneth Tynan* (1987), chapter 5.

classical writer. He could make you understand that classicism and medievalism were really vivid and alive – that it was not the business of literature to be 'relevant' to us, but *our* business to be 'relevant' to it. (*In Search of C.S. Lewis.*)

With so many new students to teach, and with many other commitments as well, Lewis was furiously busy. One of his most impressive religious books, *The Great Divorce*, began appearing in instalments under the title *Who Goes Home?* in *The Guardian‡* in November 1944. In October 1944 his publishers brought out the text of his fourth series of radio broadcasts, *Beyond Personality*. Lewis was in demand as a speaker everywhere, but nowhere was he so admired as in the Socratic Club. The end of the war brought the Club a great many dabblers in theosophy and psychical research, all keen to be heard. Because he could think so well on his feet, Lewis was nearly always called upon to answer these speakers. During this period there were papers on: 'Marxist and Christian Views of the Nature of Man' (26 November 1945); 'The Atomic Bomb – and After' (3 December 1945); 'Can Science Provide a Basis for Ethics?' (11 February 1946); and 'The Significance of Psychical Research' (6 May 1946). Lewis had, of course, to be in Magdalen for tutorials and for other meetings. However, he spent every moment he could at The Kilns looking after Mrs Moore.

Warnie could take little interest in most things connected with the University, and he was restless when Jack was not around. He was delighted when, during June of 1946, he was able to accompany his brother to Scotland where Jack was being made a Doctor of Divinity by the University of St Andrews on 28 June. Warnie had loved trains all his life, and now as the one taking them to St Andrews made its way into Scotland he recorded in his diary of 27 June that after 'miserable, hungry England', here they had 'real porridge, of which I had almost forgotten the taste, plenty of butter, edible sausages, toast, marmalade, coffee!' (**BF**). At the degree ceremony Lewis's promoter, Professor D.M. Baillie, Dean of the Faculty of Divinity, said this about him:

With his pen and with his voice on the radio Mr Lewis has succeeded in capturing the attention of many who will not readily listen to professional theologians, and has taught them many lessons concerning the deep things of God. For such an achievement, which could only be compassed by a rare combination of literary fancy and religious insight, every Faculty of Divinity must be grateful. In recent years Mr Lewis has arranged a new kind of marriage between theological reflection and poetic imagination, and this fruitful union is now producing works which are difficult to classify in any literary genre: it can only be said in respectful admiration that he pursues 'things unattempted yet in prose or rhyme'. It is not very frequently that the University confers its Doctorate of Divinity upon a lay theologian, but it may well be proud to give this acknowledgement to the work of C.S. Lewis (From *St Andrews Citizen* of 29 June 1946).

Back in Oxford, Warnie complained of 'our slatternly straggling Kilns' (25 July 1946, **BF**). The truth is that ever since Warnie had moved into The Kilns he had been complaining about a number of things in his diary, especially Mrs Moore. He resented her interference in his brother's life, and he disliked her dominance of The Kilns. Shortly after he moved in, he wrote (21 December 1933): 'It fills me with both admiration and irritation to see how completely the whole of J's life is subordinated to hers – financially, socially, recreationally: the pity of it is that on his selflessness her selfishness fattens' (**BF**). By 14 October 1946 it was much worse. 'It is an appalling thing to say,' he wrote, 'but she seems to me to be going mad through trying to live on hate instead of love: though goodness knows my own efforts to live on love are feeble enough. Still, I *do* see love as an ideal to work towards, whereas her ideal seems to be hate. I feel that she has been dying for years, and all is white ash now except the flame of greed and hate which is burning even more brightly than it did ten or fifteen years ago' (**BF**).

XIX: Warnie in Ireland

The year 1947 was to be a particularly exhausting one for Lewis. While it was not difficult to find maids to work with Mrs Moore it was extremely difficult to *keep* them. He could not give unlimited attention to matters at The Kilns because many others wanted his help as well. On 7 January Laurence Whistler, the writer and glass engraver, wrote to say that he and Andrew Young were hoping to found a periodical to challenge *Horizon*, and that they already had Ruth Pitter* and Richard Church in favour of the scheme. If he had had the leisure and the freedom to move around Lewis would gladly have taken a lead in this venture. He wrote to Whistler on 9 January saying: 'I am pleased, to the point of being excited, by your suggestion. I have said again and again that what we very badly need is a new, frankly high-brow periodical *not* in the hands of the Left ... I entirely agree that it should not be specifically Christian, much less Anglican: the Tao (in that sense) is to be the ring fence ... I shall be delighted to see you whenever you call. I will also attend the meeting *if I can*: but I am so domestically tied (to the bedside of an elderly invalid) that I can never be sure of being able to leave Oxford.' On 6 March Laurence Whistler called on Lewis at Magdalen, but despite his great interest in the periodical (which was never published), he was unable to meet with the others.

He had at the same time a letter (8 March 1947) from the Marquess of Salisbury (James Edward Hubert Gascoyne-Cecil, 1861–1947), former Conservative MP, who was an authoritative speaker on ecclesiastical matters, inviting him to join a group, which included the Archbishops of Canterbury and York, to discuss the future of the Church of England. 'My mother is old and infirm,' Lewis replied on 9 March, 'we have little and uncertain help, and I never know when I can, even for a day, get away from my duties as a nurse and a domestic servant (there are psychological as well as material difficulties in my house). But I will come if I possibly can.'

Although Lewis did manage to attend a single meeting with the Marquess and the Archbishops at Lambeth Palace on 26 March, he was, as he said in a letter to Sir George Rostrevor Hamilton on 11 March, 'a tethered man'. Mrs Moore had come down with pneumonia in early March and was very ill for some weeks. After her recovery Warnie complained (17 March 1947): 'Here is a woman, who has been, if not at Death's door, at least at his front gate: and the very minute returning strength enables her to do so, she is hard at work building up again the flame of her envy, hatred and malice' (**BF**).

The next month he and Jack had a holiday in Maureen's house in Malvern while she was in Oxford looking after her mother. Warnie loved Malvern, and he dreaded going back to The Kilns. 'Though I can still force myself to see that it is beautiful objectively,' he wrote on 17 April 1947, the day they returned, 'I loathe every stick and stone and sound of it: my Christian dream is to live to see it vanish into a road identical with Netherwoods [Road]' (**BF**). Finally, a note of jubilation appears in his diary. 'The incredible has happened,' he wrote on 11 June 1947, 'I am off on my Irish adventure.' He is, nevertheless, 'feeling very guilty at leaving poor J alone with that horrid old woman in that abominable house, though if I had stopped there I would not have been allowed to do anything to ease his burden.'

The next day he was in Ireland. Warnie had hoped to enjoy a holiday with his friend, Colonel Herbert Denis Parkin, but Colonel Parkin was unable to join him, and he was alone in a small cottage in Dunany, a small coastal town in County Louth. One of those who knew Warnie well, George Sayer,* has described him in *Jack* (chapter 14) as a 'binge drinker'. As to what exactly caused these binges, it is not easy to say. Lewis accepted the belief that his brother might be genetically disposed towards alcoholism, but he nevertheless thought he could help himself if he tried. Certainly a number of things were known to trigger a binge: boredom, depression, excitement, dislike of Mrs Moore, and, of course, simply enjoyment of alcohol. This particular binge began on the way to Ireland and was more serious than any before.

Warnie was extremely frightened when he learned that on 20 June he was taken unconscious to Our Lady of Lourdes Hospital in Drogheda, a town in County Louth, lying 32 miles north of Dublin and 81 miles south of Belfast. The hospital and the Medical Missionaries of Mary who ran it were founded in 1940 by Mother Mary Martin (1892–1975) who became over time a much loved friend to Warnie.

Dr G.P. Costello, who was to be Warnie's doctor for the next twenty-six years, had been appointed to the hospital in 1943.[11] After receiving his wire, Jack rushed over to Ireland, and arrived in Drogheda on 23 June. He stayed in the White Horse Hotel for a week, making twice-daily visits to see his brother, and also had a number of meetings with Mother Mary Martin. As her Order was celebrating their first ten years, she invited him to contribute an essay to their book, *The First Decade: Ten Years' Work of the Medical Missionaries of Mary 1937–1947* [1948]. The essay he wrote in the White Horse was **Some Thoughts**.

While Jack was still in Drogheda, Warnie left the hospital and joined his brother in the 'White Horse'. He refused, however to accompany Jack back to Oxford on 30 June but spent the rest of his holiday at the 'White Horse', remaining there until 27 July. He found St Peter's Anglican Church near the hotel, and began going to services. Drogheda was to be his home-away-from-home for the rest of his life.

Lewis had met Arthur Greeves very briefly when he went to Ireland to see Warnie, and writing to him on 4 July 1947 he said, 'The daily letter writing without W to help me is appalling – an hour and a half or two hours every morning before I can get to my own work' (**TST**).

They were not entirely without help. Mrs Moore's god-daughter, Miss Vera Henry, had a little cottage, 'Golden Arrow', at Annagasan, a few miles from Drogheda in County Louth. Jack and Warnie were very fond of Vera and her brother, Frank Henry, and when they took holidays

[11] See Mary Purcell, *To Africa with Love: The Life of Mother Mary Martin, Foundress of the Medical Missionaries of Mary* (Dublin: Gill and Macmillan, 1987).

together in Ireland they usually stayed in Vera's cottage.[12] Vera helped look after them at The Kilns during the years following the war.

XX: Discovered by America

Lewis had been getting a great many letters from American admirers since *The Screwtape Letters* was published in the United States in 1943. Not long after he returned from Ireland another of his best-known works was published in England and the States. This was *Miracles: A Preliminary Study* (1947), and this meant even more fan letters. It is an indication of how seriously he was taken in the United States that the 8 September 1947 issue of *Time* magazine featured him on its cover. The picture, which shows an angel wing on one side and Screwtape on the other, was painted by Boris Artzybasheff. Underneath, the caption runs: 'Oxford's C.S. Lewis, His heresy: Christianity.' Inside is an article entitled 'Don v. Devil' in which Lewis is included in a growing band of such 'heretics' as T.S. Eliot, W.H. Auden, Dorothy L. Sayers and Graham Greene – intellectuals who believed in God.

A year earlier one of those intellectuals who believed in God published an article entitled 'C.S. Lewis, Apostle to the Skeptics' in *The Atlantic Monthly* of September 1946. This was Chad Walsh,* an associate professor of English at Beloit College in Wisconsin. His wife Eva urged him to expand this into a book, and after arranging an appointment with Lewis, he met him in Oxford during the summer of 1948. During the visit Chad Walsh discovered that Lewis had started writing *Surprised by Joy* as well as 'completing a children's book which he has begun "in the tradition of E. Nesbit"'.

This discovery by American readers had already occasioned much more work for Warnie. He spent a large part of every morning at his little Royal, typing replies to many of his brother's correspondents. No one could have done it better, or so willingly. However, it was not long before he discovered that there was more to acknowledge from America than letters. At this time Britain was experiencing severe rationing, and it was getting worse all the time. In his diary of 10 November 1947 Warnie wrote: 'A staggering blow in the papers this morning: potatoes are put "on rations" on a scale of 3 lbs per week for the bourgeois. And so the last "filler" food disappears from the diet, and

---

[12] There is a photo of Jack and Warnie at Vera Henry's bungalow in *Brothers and Friends* between pp. 212 and 213.

the days of real hunger come upon us' (**BF**). Jack's American admirers had been unable to show any tangible appreciation for his books during the war, but with the blockade removed they showered him with gifts.

There are too many names to recall in this short biography, but several of them must be mentioned not only for their generosity but because they corresponded with Jack and Warnie for the rest of their lives. Vera Gebbert (later Mrs Mathews) of Beverly Hills, California, and Mrs Edward A. Allen and her son Edward Allen, of Westfield, Massachusetts, were as much Warnie's friends as Jack's. Another to whom Jack wrote many excellent letters over the years was Dr Warfield M. Firor. Dr Firor, who was born in Baltimore, Maryland, in 1896, was Professor of Surgery at Johns Hopkins University in Baltimore. Beginning in 1945 he inundated Lewis with whatever seemed to be needed: writing paper, cheese, chickens, sardines, lard, syrup, butter and – more noticeable than anything – *hams*. 'A ham such as you sent lifts me up into our millionaire class,' Lewis wrote on 1 October 1947. 'Such a thing couldn't be got on this side unless one was very deep in the Black Market.' 'The arrival of that magnificent ham leaves me just not knowing what to say,' he wrote on 2 March 1948. 'If it were known that it was in my house, it would draw every housebreaker in the neighbourhood more surely than would a collection of gold plate!'

During all these years the gifts from American admirers were shared with many others beside those who lived at The Kilns. Some were given to the servants of Magdalen College, and many others were divided among the Inklings. Often the Firor hams were eaten by Lewis and his fellow 'hamsters' in his college rooms. Writing about the post-war Inklings meetings in *Sprightly Running*, John Wain has said:

> I can see that room so clearly now, the electric fire pumping heat into the dank air, the faded screen that broke some of the keener draughts, the enamel beer-jug on the table, the well-worn sofa and armchairs, and the men drifting in (those from distant colleges would be later), leaving overcoats and hats in any corner and coming over to warm their hands before finding a chair. There was no fixed etiquette, but the rudimentary honours would be done partly by Lewis and partly by his brother, W.H. Lewis, a man who stays in my memory as the most courteous I have ever met – not with mere politeness, but with a genial, self-forgetful considerateness that was as instinctive to him as breathing. Some-times, when the less vital members of the circle were in a big

majority, the evening would fall flat; but the best of them were as good as anything I shall live to see.

This was the bleak period following a ruinous war, when every comfort (and some necessities) seemed to have vanished for ever; Lewis had American admirers who sent him parcels, and whenever one of these parcels had arrived the evening would begin with a distribution. His method was to scatter the tins and packets on his bed, cover them with the counterpane, and allow each of us to pick one of the unidentifiable humps; it was no use simply choosing the biggest, which might turn out to be prunes or something equally dreary. Another admirer used to send a succulent ham now and then; this, too, would be shared out (chapter V).

XXI: No More Thursday Inklings

It would not have been easy for Lewis to understand why for so many writing is, as the maxim goes, like 'extracting blood from a turnip'. When he was seventeen and at Mr Kirkpatrick's house in Surrey, he learned that Arthur Greeves was ill, and wrote to him on 30 May 1916 saying: 'Cheer up, whenever you are fed up with life, start writing: ink is the great cure of all human ills, as I have found out long ago' (**TST**).

This was certainly to be the case over the next few years. In February 1949 he was about half-way through writing the first of his stories about Narnia, *The Lion, the Witch and the Wardrobe*, when Warnie had another bout with alcohol. If very ill Jack had to get his brother into the Acland Nursing Home and this is what happened in February.

When Warnie arrived back at The Kilns on 4 March 1949 he said in his diary 'I emerged from the Acland yesterday morning, where I had been as a finale to the wearisome cycle of insomnia–drugs–depression–spirits–illness. The saddest feature of the thing is that I can see that J, mine own familiar friend, doesn't believe this to be the cycle, but assumes it to be spirits–insomnia–drugs–depression–spirits–illness. But his kindness remains unabated, and what more can I want? The contrast between the warm cosy Acland and this cold dreary house was disastrous; went in to make my bow to Minto and was given a lecture on the extreme coal shortage, the iniquities of Betty, and an enquiry as to how long I proposed to stay cured this time? Went down to the refrigerated study feeling that I was indeed "home" again. Whether from cold, temper, depression, or all three, I had a shocking night, and when I tried to pray I found the line "dead"' (**BF**).

When Lewis's friend Roger Lancelyn Green* dined with Lewis in Magdalen College on 10 March 1949, Jack read him the first two chapters of *The Lion*, and Green went away with the impression that the book was finished (see **NARNIA** IV). When Green visited him again on 14 June Lewis read aloud from one of his notebooks the two chapters he had written of a new story. This was eventually to become *The Magician's Nephew*, but the story was not going well and was postponed while he turned to write *Prince Caspian*, which he finished by the beginning of December 1949.

For some time now Lewis had been urging Dr Firor – 'Firor-of-the-Hams' as Lewis called him in a letter of 22 January 1949 – to visit him whenever he came to England. In February Dr Firor announced that he would be coming over in the summer, and Lewis wrote on 4 March 1949 saying 'You must manage at least a dinner, night and breakfast here. I've probably told you how I live – tied to an invalid with one night out (i.e. one night in College) a week. That night is normally a Thursday and can never be a Saturday or Sunday. So earmark a weekday as early as possible.' A meeting was planned for July. However, after spending a weekend in Malvern with Mr and Mrs George Sayer,* Warnie arrived home on 13 June to find Jack being taken to the Acland in an ambulance. The following day he recorded in his diary:

> A very anxious day indeed. J was light-headed during the night, and obviously a very sick man when I went in to see him; he is having injections of penicillin every three hours. I could get little out of Humphrey [Havard] except that it is 'a very serious illness for a man of fifty'. Pray God it is going to be all right ... Humphrey explained to me that J's real complaint is exhaustion ... To my joy, he added that when he got him on his legs again, he would insist that he accepted no responsibility for J's health unless he took a good holiday away from The Kilns. I got home sick with fright and savage with anger, and let her ladyship have a blunt statement of the facts: stressing the exhaustion motif and its causes. I ultimately frightened her into agreeing to grant J a month's leave.

He went on to record on 16 June that after breaking the news of a holiday to Jack 'he agreed almost at once, and his delight did me good. Poor man, it will be the first holiday he has had for at least fifteen years' (**BF**). After leaving the nursing home, Jack wrote to Arthur Greeves on 21 June 1949 saying: 'I have been ill and am ordered a real change. I'm coming home (Belfast) for a month ... Can you find me a nice little hotel (or decent rooms) near your cottage? ... I shall be free for once. The sooner you reply the happier I shall be. It seems too good to be true' (TST).

It was, as George Sayer said in *Jack* 18, 'too good to be true. Even as he was writing, Warnie was starting to drink heavily again, this time to assuage his feelings of guilt because he could not bear the thought of staying at The Kilns and of looking after Mrs Moore while Jack was in Ireland.' Warnie was, in fact, in the White Horse Hotel in Drogheda from 14 August to 27 September, and Jack wrote to Arthur Greeves on 2 July 1949 cancelling his holiday:

> This bout started about ten days ago. Last Sunday the Doctor and I begged him to go into a Nursing Home (this has always effectively ended previous bouts) and he refused. Yesterday we succeeded in getting him in: but alas, too late. The Nursing Home has announced this morning that he is out of control and they refuse to keep him. Today a mental specialist is to see him and he will be transferred, I hope for a *short* stay, to what is called a hospital but is really an asylum. Naturally there is no question of a later Irish jaunt for me this year. A few odd days here and there in England is the best I can hope for (TST).

Soon after this Lewis got over to Malvern for a weekend with George Sayer and his wife, Moira. Sayer found him physically out of condition, easily tired when he went out for a walk. 'I'm sure,' Mr Sayer said in *Jack* 18, 'that for months he had not been able to find time for much exercise. A full week in Malvern would have put him right.' He goes on to say:

> From this time on, he spoke freely to me and to other friends about Warren's alcoholism. In the past, he had usually spoken of the causes of Warren's ill-health as 'insomnia or nerves'. But it now seemed certain that Warren's drinking problem would be a permanent part of his life and one that he would be unable to conceal from his friends. Perhaps, too, he wanted our advice. He was devoted to his brother and deeply worried about his future. Yet, except through prayer, he was powerless to help. There seemed to be no clear course of action, no straightforward, expert advice on how best to help Warren. Was it necessary for him to stop drinking altogether, or could he try to limit himself to a single glass? Was it a moral or a medical problem or both? He once asked me if I thought he should 'show his teeth' to his brother. 'There is nothing I should dislike more,' he said. 'But it might work. The

knowledge that he causes vast expense and upsets the entire household influences him not at all.'

Dr Firor called on Lewis when he was in England during July 1949, and the visit was a great success. From this time on Dr Firor made minute enquiries into Lewis's health, and over the later years begged him to join him for a rest in the Rocky Mountains where he had a cabin in Cody, Wyoming. If he had been able to accept this was exactly the kind of holiday Lewis would have liked. Mrs Vera Matthews, of California, also urged him to come to the United States, promising to make him as comfortable as possible. Writing to her on 7 November 1953 he said:

> You think that streamlined planes and trains would attract me to America. What I want to see there is yourself and three or four other good friends, after New England, the Rip Van Winkle Mts, Nantucket, the Huckleberry Finn country, the Rockies, Yellowstone Park, and a sub-arctic winter. And I should never come if I couldn't manage to come by sea instead of air: preferably on a cargo boat that took weeks over the voyage. I'm a rustic animal and a maritime animal: no good at great cities, big hotels, and all that ... I'd love to see a bear, a snow-shoe, and a real forest.

Warnie returned from Drogheda in August 1949 and over the next few months he and his brother were both busy writing. Jack was working on the third Narnian story, *The Voyage of the 'Dawn Treader'*, and although Warnie was yet to publish his first book, *The Splendid Century*, he was now writing a sequel, *The Sunset of the Splendid Century*.

Sadly, they were nearing the end of the Thursday night Inklings meetings. Warnie recorded on Thursday 27 October 1949: 'Dined with J at College ... No one turned up after dinner, which was just as well as J has a bad cold and wanted to go to bed early' (**BF**). On Thursday 10 November 1949 he wrote: 'No Inklings tonight, so dined at home' (**BF**). The Tuesday morning gatherings went on much as before, but the word 'Inklings' no longer appeared in Warnie's diary.

XXII: Cheerful Insecurity

Lewis was not a man who experienced much depression, but by the autumn of 1949 overwork and exhaustion had taken their toll. He believed that he had come to the end of his productive years. Since 1947 he had been corresponding in Latin with Father Giovanni Calabria* of Verona, the founder of an order called the Poor Servants of Divine Providence. This priest had been deeply impressed by *The Screwtape Letters*, and he was encouraging Lewis to do even more to encourage Church unity. On 14 January 1949 Lewis had written to say: 'I would not wish to deceive you with vain hope. I am now in my fiftieth year. I feel my zeal for writing, and whatever talent I originally possessed, to be decreasing; nor (I believe) do I please my readers as I used to. I labour under many difficulties. My house is unquiet and devastated by women's quarrels. I have to *dwell in the tents of Kedar*.[13] My aged mother, worn out by long infirmity, is my daily care. Pray for me, Father, that I ever bear in mind that profoundly true maxim: "If thou wish to bring others to peace, keep thyself in peace" (**LDGC**).'

By the end of the year, when he wrote to Dr Firor on 15 October 1949, he admitted that the subject uppermost in his mind was 'Old Age'. 'These two feelings – the twitch of the tether and the loss of promise I have had for a long time,' he said. 'What has come lately is much harsher – the arctic wind of the future catching one, so to speak, at a corner. The particular corner was the sharp realization that I shall be compulsorily "retired" in 1959, and the infernal *nuisance* (to put it no higher) of patching up some new sort of life somewhere' (**L**). How was he to regard his afflictions? When he wrote to Dr Firor again on 5 December 1949 he saw that such things as 'insecurity, war, poverty, pain, unpopularity, loneliness' can be used by God to help detach us from the world. 'We must be taught that this tent is not home,' he concluded. 'And, by Jove, how terrible it would be if all sufferings, including death itself, were *optional*, so that only a very few voluntary ascetics ever even attempted to achieve the end for which we are created.'

Apart from the Inklings, it is doubtful if others would have known how keenly he was feeling that 'arctic wind'. Since she was converted to Christianity through hearing Lewis's *Mere Christianity* broadcasts, the poet Ruth Pitter* had been corresponding with him regularly. She had several times visited him in Oxford, and on 20 September 1949 Lewis and Barfield had lunched with her at her flat in Chelsea. Now Lewis invited

[13] Psalm 120:4–6:

> Woe is me, that I am constrained to dwell
> with Mesech: and to have my habitation among the tents of Kedar.
> My soul hath long dwelt among them: that are enemies unto peace.
> I labour for peace, but when I speak unto them thereof:
> they make them ready to battle.

her to a luncheon party he gave in the 'Wilde Room' of Magdalen on 31 December 1949. He had finished writing *The Lion, the Witch and the Wardrobe* and the luncheon was given primarily for the purpose of meeting the lady who had been chosen to illustrate his book, Pauline Baynes.* Other guests included Owen Barfield and Marjorie Milne, to whom Lewis dedicated the second impression of *Dymer* in 1950. Pauline Baynes was young and quite overawed by such company, but Lewis did all he could to put her at her ease, and one of her memories of the occasion was seeing Lewis 'picking the chestnuts out of the brussels sprouts with his fingers and saying it was a pity to waste them at the end of the Magdalen lunch' (**PWD** 6).

The new year brought changes. Although Chad Walsh could not see the significance of it at the time, his *C.S. Lewis: Apostle to the Skeptics* had been published in the States in November of 1949, and one of those who had come to know him through his writings on Lewis was Joy Davidman Gresham* of Staatsburg, New York. She owed her conversion to Lewis's books, and on 10 January 1950 Lewis received his first letter from her.

It came at a time when his troubles were mounting swiftly. Mrs Moore had been semi-paralysed for some time now, and because she fell out of bed so often she had to be watched almost constantly. Finally, on 29 April, after falling out of bed three times during the night, Lewis had had to get her into 'Restholme', a nursing home run by Miss Dorothy Watson at 230 Woodstock Road. He had been planning for the summer of 1950 the holiday he did not get in Ireland the previous year. He wrote to Arthur Greeves on 2 May 1950 saying, 'Once again the axe has fallen. Minto was removed to a Nursing Home … and her doctor thinks this arrangement will probably have to be permanent. In one way it will be an enormous liberation for me. The other side of the picture is the crushing expense – ten guineas a week which is well over £500 a year. (What on earth I shall do if poor Minto is still alive nine years hence when I have to retire, I can't imagine.) The order of the day thus becomes for me stringent economy, and such things as a holiday in Ireland are fantastically out of the question. So cancel all. I hardly know how I *feel* – relief, pity, hope, terror, and bewilderment have me in a whirl. I have the jitters!' (**TST**).

He and Warnie had The Kilns to themselves now, and gradually he began to feel less anxious. 'My daily visits to Minto,' he wrote to Arthur Greeves on 15 June 1950, 'are very grievous to me, but I don't think things are too bad for her … Remember that if you can get over to England The Kilns is *now* a house less horrible to stay in than I know it was before, and except for an hour in the afternoon when I go to the Nursing Home we would have all our time to ourselves ... I'm fine, as I now get much more exercise. I have spent a good deal of this last fortnight *in* the river' **(TST)**. And writing to Sister Penelope on 30 December 1950 he said: 'There is no denying – and I don't know why I should deny to you – that our domestic life is both more physically comfortable and more psychologically harmonious for her absence. The expense is of course very severe and I have worries about that. But it would be very dangerous to have no worries – or rather, no *occasions* of worry. I have been feeling very much lately: that *cheerful insecurity* is what Our Lord asks of us' **(L)**.

Although Lewis had been worried earlier about old age, he was now enjoying one of the most fecund periods of his life. *The Lion, the Witch and the Wardrobe* had been published in October 1950, and by March 1951 Lewis had finished writing *Prince Caspian, The Voyage of the 'Dawn Treader'* and *The Silver Chair*. By July of that same year he had finished *The Horse and his Boy* and was at work on *The Magician's Nephew*.

The College gave Lewis a sabbatical year, beginning with the Michaelmas Term of 1951, for the purpose of completing the most ambitious of all his works; this was Volume III of the Oxford History of English Literature, entitled *English Literature in the Sixteenth Century, excluding Drama* (1954). It had reached what he called its 'embryonic stage' as the Clark Lectures which he gave in Cambridge in 1944, but most of it was written during 1951–52. Dame Helen Gardner, who had seen him working on this in the Duke Humphrey Library of the Bodleian, said: 'One sometimes feels that the word "unreadable" had no meaning for him. To sit opposite him in Duke Humphrey when he was moving steadily through some huge double-columned folio in his reading for his Oxford History was to have an object lesson in what concentration meant. He seemed to create a wall of stillness around him.'[14] He was to be almost wholly occupied with this work for two years.

XXIII: Quieter Times

Dr Firor tried to extract a promise from Lewis to have a holiday at his ranch in Wyoming in the summer of 1951, but Lewis replied on 6 December 1950: 'The old lady's retirement to a Nursing Home has made me a good deal freer in a small way. I can plan my days and count on some domestic leisure as I have not been able to do these last fifteen years.

[14] 'Clive Staples Lewis 1898–1963', *The Proceedings of the British Academy*, LI [1965], p. 419.

But it has hardly made me free on such a large scale as you suppose. I visit her pretty nearly every day, and I should certainly like to be at hand when the end comes. Also, I naturally have to be a good deal more frugal than before, since the Nursing Home makes a pretty big hole in my income. The patient is nearly always perfectly placid now and does not seem to suffer at all. Very interested, for the first time in her life, in food. These bedside experiences have much allayed my fear of paralysis: I had not realized that it could be such a quiet return to infancy, or even animality. I suppose one need not be surprised that the evening twilight sometimes is exactly like the morning twilight.'

Mrs Moore died peacefully at 'Restholme' at about 5 o'clock on the evening of Friday, 12 January 1951. On Monday, 15 January she was buried in the churchyard of Holy Trinity Church‡ in Headington Quarry. She shares a grave there with a friend, Alice Hamilton Moore, the widow of Robert Moore. 'And so ends,' Warnie wrote on 17 January, 'the mysterious self-imposed slavery in which J has lived for at least thirty years' (**BF**).

This same year Lewis was proposed for the Professorship of Poetry. This Chair was founded in 1708 and is tenable for five years. Voting is open for all Senior Members of the University, whether they are in residence or not. Lewis was running against the poet and detective novelist Cecil Day-Lewis (1904–72), and he might have stood a good chance of being elected but for the tireless campaigning by the colourful French scholar of Somerville College, Enid Starkie (1897–1970), to elect 'a practising poet'. Warnie recorded in his diary of 8 February 1951: 'While we were waiting at the Royal Oxford – Barfield, Humphrey, David [Cecil], Jaw Bennett [J.A.W. Bennett], J and I – came the bad news that J had been defeated by 194 votes to 173. J took it astonishing well, much better than his backers ... Hugo told me that one elector whom he canvassed announced his intention of voting for CDL *on the ground that* J had written *Screwtape*!' (**BF**).

Lewis had been arranging a holiday with Arthur Greeves in Ireland since Mrs Moore's death, and when the plans were finalized he wrote on 12 March saying, 'Looking forward! – yes, I can't keep the feeling within bounds. I know now how a bottle of champagne feels while the wire is being taken off the cork. Pop!!' (**TST**). Jack and Warnie travelled to Ireland together on 14 August 1951, and Jack spent the next fortnight with Arthur at Crawfordsburn, County Down.

Things were not, however, going as well as Lewis thought. For some time a Mrs Hooker, pretending to be Lewis's wife, had been living on her 'husband's' credit in the Court Stairs Hotel, run by Alan and Nell

Berners-Price in St Lawrence in Thanet, Ramsgate, Kent. As Douglas Gresham has said in _Lenten Lands_ (chapter 9) 'a certain lady had evolved a clever and simple means of living very cheaply; she would move into a hotel somewhere saying that her husband, a rather well-known, though not too well-known, writer, would be arriving to join her, and that he would (of course) meet all her expenses. She would then settle down to a few weeks of leisure and luxury on credit. After a while the proprietors of the hotel would be told that the husband had been delayed by pressure of business or on some other pretext, and then finally the lady would vanish one night, leaving a polite note explaining that she had been urgently called away, and that all her bills should be sent at once to her "husband".'

XXIV: Joy Gresham

Lewis's old _directeur_, Father Walter Adams SSJE, died on 3 March 1952. Writing to Don Giovanni Calabria on 14 April, he said, 'Pray for me, especially at present when I feel very much an orphan because my aged confessor and most loving father in Christ has just died. While he was celebrating at the altar, suddenly, after a most sharp but (thanks be to God) very brief attack of pain, he expired; and his last words were, "I come, Lord Jesus." He was a man of ripe spiritual wisdom – noble minded but of an almost childlike simplicity and innocence' (**LDGC**).

Lewis needed Father Adams at this time because the woman who told Mr and Mrs Berners-Price that she was 'Mrs C.S. Lewis' had been living at the Court Stairs Hotel for over a year. Her husband, she assured them, would pay her bill as soon as he arrived. Finally, in April 1952 Mrs Berners-Price went to Oxford with a mass of unpaid bills and confronted Lewis in Magdalen College. 'I've come to ask about your wife,' she said. 'But I'm not married,' he replied. Mrs Berners-Price was as surprised by this as Lewis had been in learning of his 'wife'.

Following the advice of his solicitor, Owen Barfield, Lewis took out an injunction of 'Jactitation of Marriage' against the woman pretending to be his wife. Mrs Hooker, to give the lady her real name, was arrested. Lewis spent the night of 7 May 1952 with Mr and Mrs Berners-Price, and he served as a witness when Mrs Hooker appeared at the court in Canterbury the following day. It turned out that Mrs Hooker had been in jail a number of times for the same offence. Writing to Mrs Berners-Price on 9 May he said: 'The actual scene in court was horrid. I never saw Justice at work before, and it is not a pretty sight. Any creature, even an animal, at bay, surrounded by its enemies, is a dreadful thing to see: one felt one was committing a sort of indecency by being present.' Lewis was in Canterbury again on 19 May for Mrs Hooker's trial. She was found guilty and sent to Holloway Prison.

While all this was going on Lewis had his first visit from one of his 'pen friends' in America, Mrs Joy Gresham. Mrs Gresham had been born Helen Joy Davidman* in New York City on 18 April 1915, of Jewish parents who had abandoned the Jewish religion some time before she was born. After receiving a BA in English from Hunter College in 1934 and an MA from Columbia University in 1935, she was a school teacher for a few years and then gave it up so that she could write. She summarized these early years in an autobiographical sketch entitled 'The Longest Way Round', saying: 'In 1929 I believed in nothing but American prosperity; in 1930 I believed in nothing. Men, I said, are only apes. Virtue is only custom. Life is only an electrochemical reaction. Mind is only a set of conditioned reflexes, and anyway most people aren't rational like ME. Love, art and altruism are only sex. The universe is only matter. Matter is only energy. I forget what I said energy was only.'[15]

One effect of the Depression of the 1930s was that she became an atheist and a Communist. 'I was getting a little too old for the flitting-butterfly stuff,' she explained in 'The Longest Way Round'. 'For another, though I myself was prosperous and secure, my friends were not. To live entirely for my own pleasures, with hungry men selling apples on every street corner, demanded a callousness of which I seemed incapable ... I wanted to *do* something, so I joined the Communist Party.' The Party soon gave her work as a journalist and critic on their magazine *New Masses*. Joy was still living at home, and while continuing as an active member of the Communist Party she completed her first volume of verse, *Letter to a Comrade* (1938), which won the Yale Series of Younger Poets Award for 1938. After six months in Hollywood as a script writer for MGM, she returned to New York and in 1940 she published her first novel, *Anya*.

Soon afterwards she joined the League of American Writers, and while editing a volume of anti-imperialist war poetry eventually published as *War Poems of the United Nations* in 1943, she met William Lindsay 'Bill' Gresham. He was born in Baltimore, Maryland, on 20 August 1909, but his family had moved to New York in 1917 and he graduated from high school in Brooklyn. He at one time considered being a Unitarian minister.

[15] In *These Found the Way: Thirteen Converts to Protestant Christianity*, ed. David Wesley Soper (Philadelphia: The Westminster Press, 1951), pp. 15–16.

Then in about 1935 he married a New York woman and set out to become a writer. He and his wife soon parted, and after a number of short-lived jobs he headed for Spain as a freedom fighter in the Civil War. When he returned fifteen months later he was mentally ill and, after an aborted attempt at suicide, he found solace in psychoanalysis and the Communist Party. It was through the Party that he met Joy Davidman.

Joy and Bill Gresham were married on 2 August 1942 and, living in an apartment in Sunnyside, Queens, New York, Joy continued to work at *New Masses* while Gresham continued as a free-lance writer. Besides the difficulty of making a living, Bill Gresham already had a serious problem with alcohol. Their son David Lindsay Gresham* was born on 27 March 1944, and their son Douglas Howard Gresham* on 10 November 1945. In 1946 they moved to Ossining, New York. Problems mounted. Bill Gresham was having an extra-marital affair and approaching a mental collapse. Writing about it in 'The Longest Way Round', Joy said: 'All my defences – the walls of arrogance and cocksureness and self-love behind which I had hid from God – went down momentarily. And God came in.' Helped by the writings of C.S. Lewis, Joy and Bill Gresham both became Christians. They joined the local Presbyterian Church and Joy and her sons were baptized in 1948.

Meanwhile, Bill's first novel, *Nightmare Alley*, was published in 1946, and the film rights from the book made it possible to buy a large house in Staatsburg, New York. Bill's second novel, *Limbo Tower*, was published in 1949, and Joy's second novel, *Weeping Bay*, in 1950. At this same time Joy came across Chad Walsh's *C.S. Lewis: Apostle to the Skeptics* (1949) and began corresponding with both him and Lewis. Writing about it in his diary of 5 November 1956, Warnie said: 'Until 10 January 1950 neither of us had ever heard of her; then she appeared in the mail as just another American fan, Mrs W.L. Gresham from the neighbourhood of New York. With, however, the difference that she stood out from the ruck by her amusing and well-written letters, and soon J and she had become "pen-friends"' (**BF**). Unfortunately, only three of Lewis's letters to Joy Davidman have survived (one of 1953 and two from 1959), and only one from Joy to Lewis (8 March 1959). However, we get some notion of what Lewis's response to the letter of 10 January 1950 was from Joy's letter to Chad Walsh of 27 January 1950:

> Just got a letter from Lewis in the mail. I think I told you I'd raised an argument or two on some points? Lord, he knocked my props out from under me unerringly; one shot to a pigeon. I haven't a scrap of my case left. And, what's more, I've seldom enjoyed

anything more. Being disposed of so neatly by a master of debate, all fair and square – it seems to be one of the great pleasures of life, though I'd never have suspected it in my arrogant youth. I suppose it's *unfair* tricks of argument that leave wounds. But after the sort of thing that Lewis does, what I feel is a craftsman's joy at the sight of a superior performance (**AGCI**, chapter 3, p. 70).

The prosperity of the Gresham family was short-lived. Bill's writing was not going well and he was fast becoming unstable. He had become interested in Dianetics, the form of Scientology invented by Ron Hubbard, and in time he became fascinated with Zen Buddhism. In 1952 Joy's first cousin, Mrs Renée Pierce, who also had two small children and was having difficulty with her marriage, brought the children with her on a visit to Staatsburg. For a variety of reasons Joy wanted to be away from her husband. 'I was so much under Bill's influence that I had to run away from him physically,' Joy wrote to Mrs Pierce on 9 July 1953, 'and consult one of the clearest thinkers of our time for help' (**AGCI**, chapter 3, p. 79.)

Joy had started writing *Smoke on the Mountain: An Interpretation of the Ten Commandments* and, being an Anglophile, she took this with her when she sailed for England in August 1952. After arriving she stayed with another 'pen friend', Phyllis Williams, in London. They invited Lewis to have lunch with them in the Eastgate Hotel in Oxford, across the street from Magdalen College, on 24 September. Lewis then returned the favour by inviting the two women to have lunch with him in Magdalen. The fourth member was meant to be Warnie, but when he withdrew George Sayer was asked to take his place. Recalling the luncheon in *Jack* 19, Sayer said:

The party was a decided success. Joy was of medium height, with a good figure, dark hair, and rather sharp features. She was an amusingly abrasive New Yorker, and Jack was delighted by her bluntness and her anti-American views. Everything she saw in England seemed to her far better than what she had left behind. Thus, of the single glass of sherry we had before the meal, she said: 'I call this civilized. In the States, they give you so much hard stuff that you start the meal drunk and end with a hangover.' She was anti-urban and talked vividly about the inhumanity of the skyscraper and of the new technology and of life in New York City … She attacked modern American literature … 'Mind you, I wrote that sort of bunk myself when I was young.' Small farm life was the only good life, she said. Jack spoke up then, saying that, on his father's side, he came from farming stock. 'I felt that,' she said. 'Where else could you get the vitality?'

It was not long after this that Lewis gave Joy another luncheon in Magdalen, this time inviting more of his friends. Warnie was able to be there, and recalling it in his diary of 5 November 1956, he found her 'quite extraordinarily uninhibited. Our first meeting was at a lunch in Magdalen, where she turned to me in the presence of three or four men, and asked in the most natural tone in the world, "Is there anywhere in this monastic establishment where a lady can relieve herself?" But her visit was a great success, and a rapid friendship developed' (**BF**).

That friendship led to Lewis's inviting Joy to The Kilns for Christmas. In his little essay on **What Christmas Means to Me** he said that while he liked 'merry-making and hospitality' at Christmas, he thought the 'commercial racket' with its obligation to exchange cards and gifts caused 'more pain than pleasure'. He must, nevertheless, have felt sorry for Joy being away from home at this time, and he made her a gift of a copy of George MacDonald's *Diary of an Old Soul* with the inscription in the author's hand: 'Charlotte Kölle with kindest regards from George and Louisa MacDonald, April 27, 1885.' Lewis wrote in the flyleaf 'Later: C.S. Lewis to Joy Davidman, Christmas 1952.'

They no doubt talked about the poetry each was writing. Lewis showed her a poem he had written in 1942 – 'The Apologist's Evening Prayer' – but which had not been published. Joy copied it into *The Diary of an Old Soul*, adding 'Written by C.S. Lewis, Copied into this book by Joy Davidman, January 1, 1953.'

Joy had her own copy of *The Great Divorce* with her, and instead of merely signing his name in it, Lewis wrote:

There are three images in my mind which I must continually forsake and replace by better ones: the false image of God, the false image of my neighbours, and the false image of myself.

C.S. Lewis 30 December 1952
(from an unwritten chapter on Iconoclasm)

'Satire is a glass in which the reader commonly sees every face except his own.'

Swift, quoted from memory

When Joy left on 3 January 1953 she had been there for over a fortnight. Writing to Chad Walsh about it on 25 January, Joy said: 'Quite an experience it was, Christmas with the Lewises! (An enormous turkey, and burgundy from the Magdalen cellars to go with it; I stole a wineglassful to put in the gravy, and they thought it was practically *lèse-majesté* – till they tasted the gravy.) Being on vacation, Jack was taking life easy – he was merely writing his book on prayer ... correcting OHEL [Oxford History of English Literature] proofs, setting scholarship and fellowship exam papers, doing a college edition of Spenser for an American publisher, and finishing the *seventh* Narnia book ... also, of course, answering the endless letters ... Also there was a lot of walking and talking ... I've become a complete Anglomaniac anyway, can't wait to transplant' (**AGCI**, chapter 3, pp. 88–9). Her Christian faith had undergone a deep change as well. She had apparently informed Lewis of this, for in a letter to Chad Walsh of 24 January 1953, he said, 'It was pleasant news that she is about to join the church, and will shortly be confirmed.' Joy's confirmation in the Episcopal Church took place in the Cathedral of St John the Divine in New York.

But Joy had another reason for wanting to transplant. While she was spending Christmas with the Lewis brothers, she had a letter from Bill Gresham saying that he knew Joy never could be anything but a writer, whereas 'Renée has a different orientation; her only interest is in taking care of her husband and children and making a home for them.' The 'optimum solution', as he saw it, 'would be for you to be married to some really swell guy, Renée and I to be married, both families to live in easy calling distance so that the Gresham kids could have Mommy and Daddy on hand' (**AGCI**, chapter 3, pp. 90–1).

'Now this occurrence was, or at least seems to have been, so inevitable,' wrote Douglas Gresham many years later, 'that in honesty I must ask myself if in fact Mother saw Renée's arrival in our household as an opportunity not to be missed and left for England, not only aware of the likelihood of their falling in love, but also hoping that they would, thus giving her the chance of escaping from a marriage which was fast disintegrating' (**LL** 2). His elder brother, David, took much the same view. 'As far as I can recollect,' he said, 'the purpose of my mother's trip to England was not to complete that ... book of hers, *Smoke on the Mountain*, but to meet C.S. Lewis, with whom she had been corresponding.'

XXV: The Greshams in London

Since she went to jail, Lewis had been inundated by letters from Mrs Hooker, who really believed that, if she and Lewis were not actually married they were certainly engaged. In January 1953 Mr and Mrs

Berners-Price learned from the Chaplain of Holloway that Mrs Hooker believed that she was dying. She wanted to see Lewis one last time. At Lewis's request Mrs Berner-Price visited her in Holloway on 25 January. She found that, like so much else, Mrs Hooker had lied even about this. 'Poor creature,' Lewis wrote to Mrs Berners-Price on 20 March 1953, 'there's not much of her when one takes away the fantasies.'

That same day Joy, back in Staatsburg, New York, wrote to Chad Walsh saying, 'My cousin has left now – for Florida, to divorce her husband ... whom she left a year or so ago. But for more than a month she and Bill and I were all here together, and she was tortured by guilt and embarrass-ment and worry, and would take to her bed with crying fits – whereupon Bill lectured me for my lack of Christian charity in not enabling her to enjoy her love affair more. I *did* tell her that I felt it would be a blessing for me in the end, was not jealous, and didn't – knowing my Bill – blame her for what had happened between them' (**AGCI** chapter 3, p. 93).

While Joy was busy completing *Smoke on the Mountain*, and raising the funds to return to England, Lewis continued his proof-reading of *English Literature in the Sixteenth Century*. Between batches of proofs he returned to the writing of the last two Narnian books. Five of the Chronicles had been written between the summer of 1948 and March 1950, and these had now been published: *The Lion, the Witch and the Wardrobe* in 1950, *Prince Caspian* in 1951, *The Voyage of the 'Dawn Treader'* in 1952, *The Silver Chair* in 1953. The fifth story, *The Horse and His Boy*, was sent to the publisher, Geoffrey Bles, on 20 March 1953.

Lewis had been having difficulties with *The Magician's Nephew* since he first tried to tell that story in 1949. Putting it aside, he began the last of the series – *The Last Battle*. Roger Lancelyn Green read the first half when he was staying with Lewis in Magdalen on 12–13 February 1953, and on 11 March Lewis wrote to his publisher, Geoffrey Bles, to say 'You will hear with mixed feelings that I have just finished the seventh and really the last of the Narnian stories.' Lewis then returned to *The Magician's Nephew*, and it was ready for Roger Lancelyn Green to read in February 1954, after which it was sent to the publishers.

Lewis was quite ill during the Winter with sinusitis, and Warnie gave him much help with his correspondence. However, after Easter he was well enough to spend a few days with George and Moira Sayer (8–11 April). On 17 April 1953 they learned of the death of their beloved Vera Henry. She had returned to Ireland the year before, and they now had a new housekeeper, Mrs Maude Miller, who lived nearby in Kiln Lane. Despite their problems, this was an important year for the Inklings. The galleys of the first volume of Tolkien's *The Lord of the Rings – The*

Fellowship of the Ring was sent to him in July and he worked on them during the summer.

On 20 August Jack and Warnie set off for Ireland together, and during their jaunt they went to Dundalk ('as near heaven as you can get in Thulcandra,' Lewis told Roger Lancelyn Green on 15 September 1953), Belfast and Rostrevor. The latter is a small seaport in the south of County Down in Carlingford Lough. Walking in the mountains above the Lough, Jack told Warnie that this lovely place was his idea of Narnia. The brothers parted after a week and Jack spent the rest of his holiday with Arthur Greeves, returning to England on 14 September. Warnie's immensely readable *The Splendid Century* was published on 30 October 1953.

The first week in November 1953, Joy sailed for England with her sons, David and Douglas. After reaching London they took rooms in the Avoca House Hotel, 43 Belsize Park, Hampstead. Soon after their arrival she settled the boys in Dane Court School near Woking, in Surrey. Then came their first visit to Oxford for a four-day visit to Jack and Warnie. The Gresham boys met the Lewis brothers for the first time on 17 December. Douglas had read the first four Narnian stories, and expecting an 'heroic figure', he was disappointed to find that C.S. Lewis was a 'slightly stooped, round-shouldered, balding gentleman' (**LL** 7). Nevertheless, he found that he had 'never met a man whose face was more expressive of the vitality of his person.' He remembered Warnie as 'a slightly stouter man, with a full but neat moustache, nicotine-stained' who was 'better dressed than Jack, though in much the same style, softer spoken, though with equal pitch and effect' and who 'possessed as lively a wit and a wider, though less powerful, mind' (Ibid.).

When Joy wrote to Bill Gresham on 22 December, she told him that 'both boys were a big success with the Lewises' and that the visit included 'long walks through the hills, during which Jack reverted completely to schoolboy tactics and went charging ahead with the boys through all the thorniest, muddiest, steepest places.' The Lewis brothers taught David chess, and Joy told his father that 'he astonished them by learning instantly and doing very well', while Douglas pleased them by 'sawing huge armfuls of firewood'.

Lewis was pleased but exhausted by the visit. Writing to Vera Mathews on 23 January 1954, he said: 'The energy of the American boy is astonishing: this pair thought nothing of a four-mile hike across broken country as an incident in a day of ceaseless activity, and when we took them up Magdalen tower, they said as soon as we got back to ground, "Let's do it again".' In a letter to his friend, Ruth Pitter, written the day after Joy and the boys left (21 December 1953), he said: 'We have had an American lady staying in the house with her two sons aged 9½ and 8. I never knew what we celibates are shielded from. I will never laugh at parents again. Not that the boys weren't a delight: but a delight like surf-bathing which leaves one breathless and aching. The energy, the tempo, is what kills.'

Miss Pitter had recently moved to the nearby village of Long Crendon, and she was exactly Lewis's age. A number of Lewis's friends felt that, if he was to marry, she would be the ideal wife. In his biography of Lewis, George Sayer said that after driving Lewis over for a visit to Ruth Pitter in 1955, Lewis 'remarked that, if he were not a confirmed bachelor, Ruth Pitter would be the woman he would like to marry. "One could have with her the kind of relationship described by Patmore in *The Angel in the House*," he said' (*Jack* 19). In the letters Lewis wrote to her at this time he gives the impression that he wanted to see much more of her. In a letter of 4 January 1954 he said: 'You're sure to have to come to Oxford one day, aren't you? Dentist? Bookshop? Bodleian? Let me know and let us lunch together.' '*Bravissima!*' he said in a note of 26 January, after she'd agreed to lunch with him at the Eastgate Hotel on 1 February. Much to Miss Pitter's chagrin, Lewis had invited Joy to have luncheon with him as well. This was the only time the two women met.

XXVI: Cambridge

For many years Tolkien and others had hoped and expected that Lewis would be made a Professor at Oxford. Writing to Christopher Tolkien on 30 January 1945, Tolkien said: 'Five years ago ... my ambition was to get C.S.L. and myself into the two Merton Chairs' (**LJRRT**). Tolkien achieved his ambition of becoming the Merton Professor of English Language and Literature, but his friend had not been elected the Merton Professor of English Literature. That Chair went instead to Lewis's old tutor, F.P. Wilson. Shortly afterwards the Goldsmith's Chair of English Literature at New College became vacant, and this time Lewis was passed over for Lord David Cecil. In her obituary of Lewis for the British Academy, Helen Gardner suggested that 'a suspicion had arisen that Lewis was so committed to what he himself called "hot-gospelling" that he would have had little time for the needs of what had become a very large undergraduate school and for the problems of organization and supervision presented by the rapidly growing numbers of research students in English Literature. In addition, a good many people thought that shoemakers should stick to their lasts and disliked the thought of a professor of English Literature winning fame as an amateur theologian.'

As it turned out, Cambridge University was far less sceptical about Lewis's religious popularity. On 18 January 1954 the Council of the Senate of Cambridge University stated its need for a Professor in Medieval and Renaissance English, because the King Edward VII Chair, held by Basil Willey, was mainly concerned with modern literature and thought. On 31 March the newly-formed Chair of Medieval and Renaissance English was announced as vacant. Then in May the Electors of this newly-established Chair met to elect its first holder. The Electors included Tolkien, F.P. Wilson and Professor Basil Willey, and the meeting was presided over by Sir Henry Willink, who was Master of St Mary Magdalene College‡ and Vice-Chancellor of Cambridge University. On 11 May 1954 the Vice-Chancellor wrote to Lewis to say that the decision to elect him was 'unanimous with a warmth and sincerity which could not have been exceeded.' Lewis replied the following day, saying:

> I feel more pleased and honoured than I can express at your invitation; and the prospect (socially and academically considered) of migrating from Oxford to Cambridge would be more an incentive than a deterrent. The very regretful and very grateful refusal which I have to make is based on different grounds. Domestic necessities govern all our lives at present, and by moving I should lose an invaluable servant. I have, moreover, led another possible candidate to believe that I was not in the field. Thirdly, I come of a stock that grows early old and I already know myself to have lost a good deal of the energy and vigour which the first holder of this important chair most certainly ought to have. It is very difficult to say that the decision I have based on these reasons is now quite fixed without seeming to suppose, like a coxcomb, that you might press me. You will understand that my only motive is a wish to save you from any waste of your time.[16]

The second choice, as Lewis probably knew, was Helen Gardner, at that time Fellow of English at St Hilda's College, Oxford, and later Merton Professor of English Literature. Sir Henry Willink wrote to Lewis again on

[16] The correspondence between Lewis, Sir Henry Willink, and the Electors over Lewis's election are found in the Magdalene College Archives, Group F, Private Papers. From these papers John Constable has written an excellent account of Lewis's move from Oxford to Cambridge entitled 'C.S. Lewis: From Magdalen to Magdalene', *Magdalene College Magazine and Record*, 32, 1988, pp. 42–6. Reprinted in **CE**.

14 May saying that he would not write to their second choice until June, this way hoping to persuade Lewis to accept. But Lewis really did have Warnie and Paxford, his gardener, to think about, and he replied on 15 May:

> I am most moved by your extremely kind letter. But you offer persuasion to one who needs liberation. You knock at my door but I can't unlock it because I haven't the key. The more I look at it the less possible it seems to transport the peculiar domestic set-up of my brother, our man, and myself. There is a whole network of conveniences and life-lines already built up here (my brother, in your ear, is not always in perfect psychological health) which I really dare not abandon. I am assuming, of course, that your Chair involves residence at Cambridge, at any rate in term (as it certainly *ought* to).

There seemed nothing the Electors could do after this, and in his letter to Lewis of 18 May, Sir Henry said: 'It is abundantly clear that you have cogent reasons for not making the move which we had so much hoped would be possible.'

Meanwhile, Tolkien was determined that Lewis should have the Chair, and in a conversation with him on 17 May he convinced Lewis that he would not let down Warnie and Paxford by going to Cambridge. That same day Tolkien wrote to Sir Henry saying: 'Besides being the precise man for the job, Lewis would probably be happy there, and actually be reinvigorated by a change of air. Oxford has not, I think, treated him very well, and though he is incapable of "dudgeon", or of showing resentment, he has been a little dispirited. After our talk he said he would *accept*! It was as I thought: the chief obstacle is domestic. He has a house and some dependants ... But if he could be assured that Cambridge would provide him with the equivalent (more or less) of his rooms in Magdalen ... then I think you can have him.' On 17 May Tolkien also wrote to another of the Electors, Henry Stanley Bennett, a University Reader in English and the Librarian of Emmanuel College, Cambridge, telling him 'I think you will get Lewis. If he can be assured that he need not transfer his whole household to Cambridge ... if Cambridge can provide him something more or less equivalent to his quarters in Magdalen which he will lose – he will come. So he assured me this morning.' Other friends, such as Basil Willey, wrote saying 'Come over into Macedonia and help us!'

Before Tolkien's news could reach Sir Henry Willink, the latter invited Helen Gardner to accept the Chair. Lewis, meanwhile, wrote to him on 19 May reopening the matter:

> It is I who should apologize as the cause of multiplied letter writing, the more so since I am now writing again, and in a strain which may make me rather ridiculous. Since my last letter to you I have had a conversation with Tolkien which has considerably changed my view. He told me, first, that the electors would in no case elect a philologist. This is to me important, for it sets me free (in honour) – I had thought myself bound to refuse it by certain words I had already said to another candidate. If, as now appears, he is not effectively eligible, then I am not bound. He told me, in the second place, that full residence, with an 'establishment' in Cambridge, was not thought necessary: that four days a week in term time (less or more – there would of course be periods of pressure when I might be there for a fortnight or so) would fill the bill. Tolkien's lively mind sometimes leads him (with perfectly innocent intentions) to overstate things. Is his view correct? If so, it would remove my difficulty. As long as my normal housekeeping can be at Oxford, so that the life-lines I told you of are intact, and it is a question of rooms in Cambridge (could any College supply me with them?) I could manage well. I can both work and sleep in trains so that the prospect of spending much of my life on the Bletchley route does not alarm me. I have no right to assume these conditions – they seem too good to be true – but if they are the real conditions I should like nothing better.
>
> I feel a fool in saying all this. But you know how it is when a man has a possible change before him. It is impossible not to toy with the idea of what you *would* do, or *would have done*, if you accepted. I have begun composing imaginary lectures and this has had a good deal to do with it: you know what good lectures those ones always are!
>
> Tolkien also said all the Oxford members of the committee had warned you that I was not a great exponent of 'Research'.
>
> It would not be honest not to add that if *I* were an elector I should prefer a fully resident Professor to a semi-resident one even if he were slightly less desirable in other respects.
>
> Whatever your conclusion, I shall always be grateful for your kindness and rather ashamed of the trouble I have given.

Sir Henry Willink, who must have felt he knew Lewis well by this time, wrote in a friendly manner that 'If Choice No 2 refuses, I hope you will feel that it will be very well worth while for us to have a meeting and a talk.' Lewis, also relaxed, wrote on 26 May:

> Whatever the upshot (and unless No 2 is as trickily placed as myself, I can't quite see him turning down the offer) I shall long remember your inexhaustible kindness, and if I don't reach Cambridge as a Professor I shall come to Magdalene as a week-ender at the first opportunity in the hope of making your acquaintance.

As it turned out, Miss Gardner had been undecided about what to do as she had been offered a University Readership in Renaissance English Literature at Oxford. When the rumour reached her that Lewis had changed his mind, she turned down the offer from Cambridge. Sir Henry Willink wrote to Lewis on 3 June to say: 'No 2 has declined, and I am filled with hope that after all Cambridge will obtain the acceptance of No 1, in spite of the fact that No 1 will appear to No 2 – who will, I hope, be thoroughly discreet – to have been No 2.'

Lewis understood perfectly, and writing to the Vice-Chancellor on 4 June, he said: 'Thank you for your letter of the 3rd. I feel much pleasure and gratitude in accepting the Chair of Medieval and Renaissance English.'

As the Chair was completely new it was not attached to any particular college, and Lewis was delighted when Sir Henry Willink's college offered him a Fellowship with rooms in St Mary Magdalene. Explaining the change to Sister Penelope on 30 July Lewis said: 'Yes, I've been made Professor of "Medieval and Renaissance English" at Cambridge: the scope of the chair (a new one) suits me exactly. But it won't be as big a change as you might think. I shall still live at Oxford in the Vac. and on many weekends in term. My address will be Magdalene, so I remain under the same Patroness. This is nice because it saves "Admin" re-adjustments in Heaven: also I can't help feeling that the dear lady now understands my constitution better than a stranger would' (L).

XXVII: From Magdalen to Magdalene

Jack and Warnie were hoping to celebrate the end of these Cambridge deliberations with a jaunt during August 1954 in County Donegal, Northern Ireland. They were to begin their holiday in Rathmullan on

Lough Swilly, and after three weeks together Jack was to spend a week with Arthur Greeves in Crawfordsburn. On the day they were to leave, however, 6 August, it had to be cancelled. Writing to Arthur, Jack said, 'We ought to have been crossing tonight, but Warnie is in a nursing home (the usual thing). I will get across by hook or crook for my jaunt with you, arriving Crawfordsburn Monday, 30 August' (**TST**), However, after a week in 'Restholme', the same nursing home Mrs Moore had been in, Warnie had recovered and they had a week together in the south of Ireland. Lewis then had his usual holiday with Arthur. Shortly after he got home his massive 'O Hell!' volume, *English Literature in the Sixteenth Century*, Vol. III in the Oxford History of English Literature was published on 16 September.

Sometime before this in the United States Renée Pierce had divorced her husband, and Bill Gresham had filed for a divorce from Joy on the grounds of desertion and incompatibility. In Miami, Florida, on 5 August 1954 Bill Gresham received his divorce from Joy and married Renée (**AGCI** chapter 4).

After his return from Ireland Jack was so busy that he sometimes wondered if he had made the right decision in accepting the Chair at Cambridge. However, as he told Sister Penelope, the 'scope' of the new job suited him exactly. Another attraction was that, as a Professor, he would not be required to give any more tutorials, something which had sapped much of his energy over the years. Warnie noted in his diary of 3 December 1954: 'J finished his last tutorial at ten minutes to one today: after twenty-nine years of it' (**BF**).

Before that last tutorial Lewis joined Dorothy L. Sayers in London for a debate. In 1953 Kathleen Nott had published *The Emperor's Clothes*, described as 'An Attack on the dogmatic orthodoxy of T.S. Eliot, Graham Greene, Dorothy L. Sayers, C.S. Lewis and others.' Miss Sayers felt there should be a debate, and it was scheduled for 27 October 1954 in St Anne's Church, Soho, London. Lewis wrote to her on 12 June to say that he would be present for the 'Nicking of Nott'. At the last minute, however, Kathleen Nott pulled out, and her friend G.S. Frazer faced Lewis and Dorothy L. Sayers before a large and lively audience.[17] Joy's parents were visiting her from New York, and Lewis met them for tea before the debate. Afterwards, Lewis introduced them to Dorothy L. Sayers. Writing about the occasion to William Gresham two days later, Joy described Miss Sayers as an 'enormously witty and very eloquent speaker, a forthright

---

[17] There is an account of it by John Wren-Lewis, 'The Chester-Lewis', in *The Chesterton Review*, XVII, Nos. 3, 4, (August, November 1991), pp. 562–5.

old lady who wears rather mannish clothes and doesn't give a damn about her hairdo' (**AGCI** chapter 4, p. 111). This was probably the only occasion on which Joy and Dorothy L. Sayers met.

Not long after he met Joy's parents, Lewis was in London again to visit Joy at her flat in an annex of the Avoca House Hotel. This was in 14 Belsize Park. Joy and the boys had become friends with an Australian family who were staying there, and Joy wanted them to meet Lewis. The Rev. Leslie Llewelyn Elliott arrived there in November 1954 with his wife and their two sons on an eight-months leave of his Anglican parish in Melbourne to organize an international trade fair. The elder of the Elliott boys, writing forty years later as Monsignor Peter J. Elliott of the Vatican's Pontifical Council for the Family, remembered the occasion well. 'One evening,' he said:

> Joy announced that C.S. Lewis was in London and would like to meet us. Some time later he strode into the hotel dining room where we had just finished supper. I can still see him through the eyes of an eleven-year-old, who had already devoured and savoured three of his Narnian Books.
>
> Here was the 'great man' who could take you into another world, more wonderful and exciting than shabby post-war London or the suburban sprawl of Melbourne. But I had the same disconcerting surprise experienced by many others on first meeting Lewis. Instead of what one expected, that is, an ascetical academic, one was confronted by a country squire. He was plump and tweedy, with a round ruddy face, a pipe, balding dark hair and two bright twinkling mirthful eyes. Those eyes ... they glinted with joy, Christian joy looking out confidently at the created world, knowing that, in spite of old Screwtape and the 'Great Divorce', it is still 'good'...[18]

Even though Lewis did not move to Cambridge until the New Year, his Inaugural lecture, '*De Descriptione Temporum*', as the new Professor of Medieval and Renaissance English was given in Cambridge on 29 November 1954 – his fifty-sixth birthday. His audience was vast, with many old friends going over from Oxford, including Joy Davidman. Writing about it when his own chance came to hold the same Chair, J.A.W. Bennett said that 'a platoon of them who had made the journey

[18] Peter J. Elliott, 'A Child's Memories of C.S. Lewis', *In Review: Living Books Past and Present*, I, 3 (Summer 1994), pp. 33–6.

from Oxford could find no place to sit save on the dais, on which they ranged themselves like a *sceldtruma* or shield-wall resolved to defend their liege lord.'[19] Because she could not be there herself, Dorothy L. Sayers asked her friend Barbara Reynolds to go to the lecture and write to her about it. 'He had a very good house,' she began her letter to Miss Sayers:

> the largest lecture room in Mill Lane was packed and people coming late had to sit on the floor. He was introduced by the Vice-Chancellor (Willink, Master of Magdalene) who said that the unanimous eagerness with which the electors had invited Lewis to come to Cambridge was probably unique among such events ... There is no doubt he was warmly received this evening. He spoke from very few notes, apparently extempore, so I don't see how it can be published as Inaugurals usually are, and that seems a pity in a way. On the other hand, the note he struck was no doubt deliberately informal, and was an expression of his personality as much as of his ideas. His main theme was the problem of periods in literary history, or as he called them in the title of his lecture, 'times' (*aetates*) ...[20]

We discover here something very important about Lewis's lecturing. The lecture was written out in full, and was indeed published immediately after it was given by Cambridge University Press, and yet an experienced lecturer assumed it was given extempore.[21]

A less restrained report of the Inaugural was given by Joy in a letter to Chad Walsh of 23 December 1954. After telling him that she 'shouldn't be surprised to see him strike roots in Cambridge and move there altogether after a couple of years', she described the lecture as

> brilliant, intellectually exciting, unexpected, and funny as hell – as you can imagine. The hall was crowded, and there were so many capped and gowned dons in the front rows that they looked like a

[19] J.A.W. Bennett, *The Humane Medievalist* (1965). Reprinted in **CE**.

[20] Barbara Reynolds, 'Memories of C.S. Lewis in Cambridge', *The Chesterton Review*, XVII, Nos 3, 4 (August, November 1991), p. 378.

[21] The lecture, which was entitled *De Descriptione Temporum*, was published by Cambridge University Press in 1955, and is now reprinted in his *Selected Literary Essays*. Lewis gave the same lecture over the BBC as 'The Great Divide' on 1 April 1955 (see Recordings of C.S. Lewis‡).

rookery. Instead of talking in the usual professorial way about the continuity of culture, the value of traditions, etc., he announced that 'Old Western Culture', as he called it, was practically dead, leaving only a few scattered survivors like himself ... How that man loves being in a minority, even a lost-cause minority! Athanasius *contra mundum*, or Don Quixote against the windmills ... He talked blandly of 'post-Christian Europe', which I thought rather previous of him. I sometimes wonder what he would do if Christianity really did triumph everywhere; I suppose he would have to invent a new heresy.

Lewis took up residence in Cambridge on 1 January 1955. Magdalene College treated him very handsomely by giving him a set of rooms in the First Court above the Parlour and the Old Library. Without Warnie's help he had nearly all his letters to answer. Besides this, there were the lectures to prepare. In his first term there, 'Lent Term', as it is called, he gave a series of twice-weekly lectures entitled 'Prolegomena to the Study of Our Earlier Poetry'. The following term, which in Oxford would have been called 'Trinity Term' but was called 'Easter Term' in Cambridge, he lectured twice a week on Milton. In the years that followed he lectured on 'Some Major Texts: Latin and Continental Vernacular', 'English Literature 1300–1500', 'Spenser's *Faerie Queene*', and 'Some Difficult Words'. This last series of lectures was later published as *Studies in Words*.

After he had been there for a while Lewis was asked to write an essay comparing Oxford and Cambridge. In his **Interim Report**, which appeared in *The Cambridge Review* LXXVII (21 April 1956), he remarked that he soon

discovered that there is something at Cambridge which fills the same place philosophy filled at Oxford: a discipline which overflows the faculty of its birth and percolates through all the others and about which the freshman must pick up something if he means to be anybody. This is Literary Criticism (with the largest possible capitals for both words). You were never safe from the philosopher at Oxford; here, never from the Critic.

At this time everyone at Oxford and Cambridge knew that the one man in Cambridge who embodied all that Lewis meant by 'Critic', and whose attitude towards literature was the antithesis of his own, was F.R. Leavis (1895–1978). This 'stormy spirit', as Lewis called him, had been at Cambridge for many years and was a lecturer in Downing College. One great difference between them was their respective attitudes towards 'Culture'. As Leavis made clear in his *Education and the University* (1943), he wanted to see Culture made the basis of a humane society, but without it being based on any objective standard, and certainly not Christianity. Amongst educated people he believed there to be 'sufficient measure of agreement, overt and implicit, about essential values to make it unnecessary to discuss ultimate sanctions, or to provide a philosophy, before starting to work'. To this end Leavis had founded the periodical *Scrutiny* in 1932.

Lewis believed the opposite. When he saw an article by George Every in *Theology* XXXVIII (March 1939) entitled 'The Necessity of *Scrutiny*', he replied with a very powerful essay on **Christianity and Culture** published in *Theology*, XL (March 1940), and reprinted in *Christian Reflections*. In it he deplored 'the whole tradition of educated infidelity from Arnold to *Scrutiny*' which he said appeared to him 'as but one phase in that general rebellion against God which began in the eighteenth century'. But nowhere was the difference between Lewis's attitude towards literature and culture and that of F.R. Leavis – and, indeed, the modern Deconstructionists – more aptly summed up than in Lewis's *Preface to 'Paradise Lost'*:

> It is not that [Dr Leavis] and I see different things when we look at *Paradise Lost*. He sees and hates the very same that I see and love. Hence the disagreement between us tends to escape from the realm of literary criticism. We differ not about the nature of Milton's poetry, but about the nature of man, or even the nature of joy itself. For this, in the long run, is the real question at issue; whether man should or should not continue to be 'a noble animal, splendid in ashes and pompous in the grave'. I think he should. I wish to see 'ceremonies of bravery' continued even in the present 'infamy of his nature'. The opposite view is held by very different people (XIX).

John Wain had been sorry to see his friend migrate to Cambridge and thought it must be 'like leaving an overblown and neglected rose-garden for a horticultural research station on the plains of Siberia. For Cambridge, in sharp contrast to the cultured *accidie* of Oxford, is dominated (as far as literature is concerned) by an orthodoxy.'[22]

---

[22] John Wain, 'C.S. Lewis Throws Down a Challenge', *The Observer* (22 October 1961), p. 31. A review of *An Experiment in Criticism*.

Despite the Critic and his astringent orthodoxy, Lewis liked the *place* and in his 'Interim Report' he said 'Cambridge is very much more like the Oxford I first knew ... I was bred at a small college in Oxford; I am now, most gratefully and happily, domiciled in a small college at Cambridge.' He was indeed. He enjoyed in Magdalene what John Constable called 'a nearly solidly Anglican Fellowship of some twelve men'. It was so different from what he was used to that he was thereafter to speak of the Cambridge college as the 'penitent Magdalene', as opposed to the '*im*penitent Magdalen' at Oxford.

Of the many friends he made in the penitent Magdalene, one of the closest was Richard Ladborough,* a University lecturer in French. Dr Ladborough later provided an interesting account of Lewis 'In Cambridge' (**ABT**) in which he said Lewis's 'rooms in college, which with their panelling and antique appearance, could have been made attractive with little cost and even with little thought, were, it seemed to me, merely a laboratory for his work and his writings. Here he would sit with pen and ink in a hard chair before an ugly table and write for hours on end ... Until his decline in health, Lewis would go for an afternoon walk. He was good with a map and soon had tracked down most of the footpaths in and around Cambridge. Just occasionally, he would start in the morning with a visit to a pub. He liked the atmosphere of a pub, and he liked beer ... He was essentially a college rather than a university man ... He was ignorant of anything to do with finance, and during debates on figures his eyes closed and he was even known to snore ... It seems needless to say that the chapel was the centre of his life in college. He daily attended weekday Matins at 8.00 o'clock and, when he was well enough, he walked in the Fellows' Garden beforehand ... His normal existence followed an extremely orderly pattern: early rising, chapel, Communion at least once a week, early breakfast, and then attendance to his huge correspondence that came from all over the world. In Cambridge he had no secretary and answered most of his letters in his own hand.' It was in the little Chapel of Magdalene that Lewis was to preach his last sermon – **A Slip of the Tongue** – on 29 January 1956.

Another Fellow, John Walsh, the historian, who later migrated to Oxford, came to Magdalene as a Bye-Fellow in 1952. Lewis, he said,

flowered in Magdalene, which he found a far more congenial – and Christian – home than the more abrasive society of the other Magdalen, which he sharply depicted in *That Hideous Strength*. For a shy junior don, sitting in the candle-lit half-circle of the Combination Room over coffee and port night after night, keeping one's conversational end up with Lewis was part ordeal, part delight, and certainly an education. He did not pick arguments, but if he did, he liked to win them; in a debate with him I always felt at the wrong end of a Socratic dialogue. Lewis seemed not only to have read everything but to have remembered it as well; if one quoted – say – an obscure bit of Calvin, as likely as not he would continue or complete the quotation. He was the best-read man I have ever met, almost too well read. In conversation with tired scientists just in from a hard day at the lab he would throw off lines of Euripides, not at all with the intention of displaying his learning, but in the simple, optimistic belief that everyone had ranged across European literature from Homer to Kipling as he had done. [23]

Other members of Magdalene whom Lewis came to know and like included F.McD.C. Turner, D.W. Babbage, J.F. Burnet, R.W. M. Dias, and J.E. Stevens. There were friends outside Magdalene as well. Lewis had dinner on numerous occasions with those friends he had known since the 1930s – Henry Stanley Bennett and his wife Joan, who was a Fellow of Girton College. Soon there were others whose friendship was a source of great pleasure to Lewis. He enjoyed years of exactly the kind of friendly disputation he relished with the Classicist Nan Dunbar of Girton College. They argued about the Latin poet Statius, and when Miss Dunbar invited him to dine at Girton, Lewis replied (23 April 1956): 'I will certainly come – did you think I was *afraid*?' After years of such sprightly friendship, he spoke of her (18 October 1963) as 'the liveliest and learnedest of my daughters'.

On Saturday, 5 November 1955, Lewis had a visit from Dr Billy Graham who was in Cambridge to lead a Mission sponsored by the Cambridge Inter-Collegiate Christian Union. Graham had many critics, and stringent security precautions had to be taken. Lewis knew about this, and in conversation with Billy Graham he said, 'You know you have many critics, but I have never met one of your critics who knows you personally.'

Most of the time Lewis went home to The Kilns for the weekends and the holidays. The regular Tuesday morning Inklings meetings were changed to Monday to accommodate him. There was a regular train service between Oxford and Cambridge at the time, called the 'Cantab Crawler' because of its slowness. It took three hours to travel the eighty

---

[23] 'Reminiscences' (1) Magdalene, 1948–58, *Magdalene College Magazine and Record*, New Series, No. 34 (1989–90) pp. 45–9.

miles from one university to the other. After the Inklings meetings in the 'Bird and Baby', he would take the 'Cantab Crawler' back to Cambridge. Writing to Mrs Edward A. Allen on 5 December 1955 he said: 'The weekend journeys are no trouble at all. I find myself perfectly content in a slow train that crawls through green fields stopping at every station. Just because the service is so slow and therefore, in most people's eyes *bad*, these trains are almost empty and I have the compartment ... to myself, where I get through a lot of reading and sometimes say my prayers' (L).

At the beginning and end of every term Lewis would ask his driver friend, Clifford Morris, to take him by car. 'If it were in wintertime,' said Morris, 'we generally found a snug little inn, somewhere on the way, and had a meal there; if it were in the summer, we generally took sandwiches and picnicked where we fancied ... Dr Lewis was a great lover of the natural scene, and he was always delighted to be taken through Woburn Park, where the herds of deer and other animals come wandering down to the public highway; and where, in its season, the magnificent rhododendron drive is a sight to behold.'[24]

During the spring holiday of 1955 Joy was visiting Jack and Warnie at The Kilns when Jack complained that he could not find an idea for a book. Writing to Bill Gresham on 23 March, Joy said that she and Lewis 'kicked a few ideas around till one came to life. Then we had another whisky each and bounced it back and forth between us.' 'The next day,' she went on to say, 'without further planning, he wrote the first chapter!' He was soon about half-way through writing what he came to regard as his best book, *Till We Have Faces*. Writing to Katharine Farrer* about the book on 2 April 1955 he said that his version of the Cupid and Psyche myth 'is the story of every nice, affectionate agnostic whose dearest one suddenly "gets religion", or even every luke-warm Christian whose dearest gets a Vocation. Never, I think, treated sympathetically by a Christian writer before.' When Joy wrote to Gresham again on 29 April 1955 she was able to say that Jack was 'about three-quarters of the way through his new book ... and says he finds my advice indispensable.'

XXVIII: Register Office Marriage

During June 1955 Joy had a visit from Chad and Eva Walsh and their daughters Damaris and Madeline. One day they visited Lewis in Oxford, and writing about it later in the Afterword to the Bantam Edition of *A*

[24] Clifford Morris, 'A Christian Gentleman', **ABT**.

Grief Observed, Chad Walsh said that they 'had a chance to observe Joy and Lewis together. She seemed to be at The Kilns a good deal. My wife firmly declared, "I smell marriage in the air." Whether Lewis smelled it is more doubtful.'

In August Joy and the boys moved to a house in 10 Old High Street, Headington, a mile or so from The Kilns, and Jack began visiting there every day. In September he went to Ireland for a holiday with Arthur, and while there he told Arthur that he was thinking of marrying Joy in a private civil ceremony.

For whatever reason, the Home Office refused Joy permission to live and work in England. However, as she wanted to stay and Lewis certainly wanted her to stay, the only solution he could think of was that they go through a civil marriage ceremony. Such a 'marriage' would give Joy and her sons British nationality. In regarding such a legal form as totally different from a true marriage Lewis was following the teaching of the Anglican Church. That church believed, as does the Catholic Church, that in marrying a divorcée one is committing adultery. The ceremony, then, would not and could not make them man and wife. Lewis would remain in his house, and Joy would remain in hers. He did not intend to tell many people about the legal 'marriage', but he nevertheless felt that some old friends, such as Arthur Greeves, should know what his intentions were should they hear about the civil contract. Arthur seems to have questioned his friend's judgement because, when Jack replied on 30 October 1955, he said:

> The other affair remains where it did. I don't feel the point about a 'false position'. Everyone whom it concerned would be told. The 'reality' would be from my point of view adultery, and therefore mustn't happen. (An easy resolution when one doesn't in the least want it!)

By April of 1956 it would seem that Lewis and Joy had not been able to find a way of persuading the Home Office to renew Joy's permission to remain in Britain. Lewis thought it necessary to act. Before that he talked to George Sayer, who was a Roman Catholic. 'I raised objections,' said Sayer:

> A civil marriage with Joy could not possibly be a formality, I said, but would, in fact, make him legally responsible for maintaining the boys if Joy were unable to earn enough to do so. And what if Joy wanted to contract a real marriage with someone else? Jack answered that, in the eyes of the Church, she could not marry

anyone else, since she was already married. I asked if her marriage to Bill had been a Christian marriage. Had she and her husband been baptized? Did they accept the Christian view of marriage? Had Jack told me that Bill had already been married, my case would have been stronger. But he did not agree with my view of marriage, and he contended that the civil marriage would make no difference at all to his relationship with Joy. (*Jack* 19).

Lewis and Joy were 'wed' at the little Register Office in St Giles, Oxford, on Monday 23 April 1956. Dr R.E. Havard and Austin Farrer were there as witnesses. When Lewis was entertaining Roger Lancelyn Green in Cambridge two days later he explained that the 'marriage' was 'a pure matter of friendship and expediency. A register office wedding was simply a legal form and had nothing to do with marriage' (**BIO** XI).

XXIX: The Wedding

Of course Jack had talked with Warnie about his intentions, and Warnie felt some of the same apprehension expressed by George Sayer. In his diary of 5 November 1956, he wrote: 'J assured me that Joy would continue to occupy her own house as "Mrs Gresham", and that the marriage was a pure formality designed to give Joy the right to go on living in England: and I saw the uselessness of disabusing him. Joy, whose intentions were obvious from the outset, soon began to press for her rights, pointing out with perfect truth that her reputation was suffering from J's being in her house every day, often stopping until eleven at night; and all the arrangements had been made for the installation of the family at The Kilns, when disaster overtook us'. (**BF**).

For some time Joy, who had just turned 42, had been complaining of pains in her left leg, back and chest. The doctor diagnosed her problem as rheumatism and fibrositis, an inflammation of the tissues surrounding the muscles which causes pain and stiffness. Lewis was back in Cambridge when, on the evening of 18 October 1956, Katharine Farrer* suddenly knew something was wrong with Joy. 'I *must* ring her!' she said to her husband. She dialled the number. Before it could ring Joy, in her house in Headington, tripped over the telephone wire, bringing the telephone down as she fell to the floor. The fall caused the femur of her leg to snap like a twig. But with the pain was Katharine Farrer's voice, asking if she could help. Joy was admitted to the Wingfield-Morris Orthopaedic Hospital on 19 October. X-rays showed that the left femur, almost eaten through by cancer, broke when Joy fell. Further examination revealed a malignant tumour in her left breast, as well as secondary sites in her right leg and shoulder. 'In the following month,' as George Sayer points out, 'she underwent three operations: the cancerous part of the femur was cut out, and the bone was repaired. The tumour in her breast was cut out, but she was spared a mastectomy. Her ovaries were also removed' (*Jack* 19).

Although there was still no Eros or romantic love on Lewis's part, he felt, as he later told Dom Bede Griffiths, a great pity for Joy. He was asking everyone for their prayers, and as it seemed certain that Joy was dying he wanted to take her to The Kilns where she could die as his wife. He felt this would be wrong without a Christian marriage and this was impossible without ecclesiastic approval. On 17 November Lewis went to see Harry Carpenter, the Bishop of Oxford. By this time Lewis had one particular reason for supposing an ecclesiastic marriage to be allowable. William Gresham had been legally married before he met Joy, and as this first wife was alive at the time of his second legal marriage to Joy, Lewis argued that the second of these marriages was therefore invalid. While that is indeed the position of the Roman Catholic Church, the official position of the Anglican Church is that every legal marriage is valid.

Humphrey Carpenter, the biographer, is the son of Harry Carpenter, and he recalls how his father felt about the matter:

My father was Bishop of Oxford, and Lewis had come to see him to ask if the Church of England would bend the rule it had in those days of not remarrying divorced persons. Lewis wanted the Church's blessing on his union with Joy Gresham, née Davidman, an American divorcée whom he had already married in a registry office. My father said no. When I talked to him about it many years later, he explained that, while he personally felt that it was a harsh rule which could justifiably be relaxed now and then, he did not consider that this would be possible in the case of Lewis, simply because of Lewis's celebrity. If permission were given to such a public figure (argued my father), everyone would demand the right to follow suit. My father told me that Lewis did not see the force of this argument ... and seemed to be hurt and upset. He went on to say that he himself was glad when a clergyman in another diocese, a former pupil of Lewis's, shortly afterwards performed the marriage service at Joy Gresham's bedside ... This mildly illicit

[25] 'Of more than academic interest', the cover story about *Shadowlands* in 'The Culture' section of *The Sunday Times* (27 February 1994), p. 2.

solution seemed to my father a convenient get-out from the church's ruling; he had no animosity against the marriage as such.[25]

However, before this 'mildly illicit solution' could be arrived at there were so many rumours floating about that Lewis felt he had to clear things up. Not only about Joy, but about another lady as well.

For the last fifteen years – since he gave his first series of radio broadcasts – Lewis had been bombarded with letters from an antique dealer in London. It began with requests for advice. Soon, however, the lady began treating Lewis's books as 'love letters' to which she alone had the 'key'. When he saw what was going on, Lewis stopped writing. This did not make the lady any less fervent, and in 1955 she began writing as many as three letters a day, with the occasional telephone call and cable thrown in. Again, Lewis sought help from Owen Barfield, but there was little he could do because there are few ways one can stop a person from writing letters. Lewis coped with it the best way he could, usually by taking the letters directly from the postman's hand and throwing them in the fire.

Then, on Thursday, 25 October 1956, Lewis had a visit in Cambridge from Paul Sargent of London's *Daily Mail*. He had come about the antique dealer who had told them that she and Lewis were being married at a Register Office in London on Saturday morning, 27 October. On 26 October the *Daily Mail* carried an article entitled 'MARRY? I'LL BE MILES AWAY, SAYS THE PROFESSOR,' and which began:

> Professor C.S. (*Screwtape Letters*) Lewis … learned yesterday that a marriage has been arranged … between himself and a woman admirer who fell in love with him through the highbrow pages of his books. The astounded bachelor-professor also learned that he should attend Marylebone Register Office tomorrow to take the hand in marriage of … a 46-year-old London antique dealer … As far as Professor Lewis was concerned he will 'be miles from London on Saturday'.

The paper carried a photograph of Lewis, and one of the lady surrounded by her 'objets d'art, bric-à-brac, china cats, dogs, and smiling cherubs'.

At the same time there were so many rumours about Lewis being married to *someone* that Lewis finally had the following announcement put in *The Times* (24 December 1956): 'A marriage has taken place between Professor C.S. Lewis, of Magdalene College Cambridge, and Mrs Joy Gresham, now a patient in the Churchill Hospital, Oxford. It is requested that no letters be sent.' That same day the *Oxford Mail* carried a story entitled **Wedding of Former Oxford Don** which mentioned both Joy Gresham and the antique dealer.

Lest his friends misunderstand the issue, Lewis wrote to a good many of them explaining to some extent the nature of his 'marriage'. In a letter to Dorothy L. Sayers of 24 December 1956 he said: 'You may see in *The Times* a notice of my marriage to Joy Gresham. She is in hospital (cancer) and not likely to live; but if she gets over this go she must be given a home here. You will not think that anything wrong is going to happen. Certain problems do not arise between a dying woman and an elderly man. What I am mainly acquiring is two (nice) stepsons' (**L**).

The Rev. Peter Bide,* of the Diocese of Chichester, had been Lewis's pupil, and he had performed what Lewis regarded as a miracle. Lewis asked him to come to Oxford for the night of 20 March and lay his hands on Joy. 'Shortly after my arrival at The Kilns,' said Bide, 'he said to me, "Peter, I know this isn't fair, but do you think you could marry us? I asked the Bishop; I've asked my parish priest; I've asked all my friends on the Faculty; and they've said no. Joy is dying and she wants the Sacrament before she dies."' 'I asked Jack to leave me alone for a while and I considered the matter. In the end there seemed only one Court of Appeal. I asked myself what He would have done and that somehow finished the argument.'

The marriage took place in the Wingfield-Morris Hospital on 21 March 1957, and a most touching account of it is found in Warnie's diary of that day:

> One of the most painful days of my life. Sentence of death has been passed on Joy, and the end is only a matter of time. But today she had one little gleam of happiness; it has worried her all along that hers and J's marriage was only a registry office one, because the Bishop of Oxford objected to a religious ceremony. But this J's old friend and pupil Peter Bide consented to perform – a notable act of charity, for he is not of this Diocese, and had no right to do so without the Bishop's authority. However, at 11 a.m. we all gathered in Joy's room at the Wingfield – Bide, J, Sister, and myself, comm-unicated, and the marriage was celebrated. I found it heartrending, and especially Joy's eagerness for the pitiable consolation of dying under the same roof as J: though to feel pity for anyone so magnificently brave as Joy is almost an insult.
>
> She is to be moved here next week, and will sleep in the common-room, with a resident hospital nurse installed in Vera's room. There seems little hope but that there may be no pain at the end. (**BF**)

In April Joy was moved to The Kilns where it was expected she would soon die.

XXX: Recovery and Loss

Jack had always found Joy's accomplishments and nature attractive, and after the move her illness, together with the approach of Thanatos brought him to an open admission of his love for her. In one of the books she liked so much, *The Great Divorce*, Lewis distinguished the *passion* of Pity from the *action* of Pity. He defined the first as 'the ache that draws men to concede what should not be conceded and to flatter when they should speak truth.' The *action* of Pity, on the other hand, is a 'weapon' used by God. 'It leaps quicker than light from the highest place to the lowest to bring healing and joy, whatever the cost to itself. It changes darkness into light and evil into good' (XIII).

Lewis now felt Eros, or romantic love, for the first time. Explaining how this change in his feelings for Joy came about, Lewis said in a letter to Dorothy L. Sayers of 25 June 1957: 'They say a rival often turns a friend into a lover. Thanatos, certainly (they say) approaching but at an uncertain speed, is a most efficient rival for this purpose. We soon learn to love what we know we must lose' (L). Nowhere is this change more clearly put than in a letter to Dom Bede Griffiths of 24 September 1957: 'It is nice to have arrived at all this,' he said, 'by something which began in Agape, proceeded to Philia, then became Pity, and only after that, Eros. As if the highest of these, Agape, had successfully undergone the sweet humiliation of an incarnation' (L).

One friend whom Lewis failed to notify about both these marriages was Tolkien. On the very day that Lewis and Joy were married by Peter Bide, Tolkien said in a letter to Katharine Farrer:

I believe you have been much concerned with the troubles of poor Jack Lewis. Of these I know little beyond the cautious hints of the extremely discreet Havard. When I see Jack he naturally takes refuge in 'literary' talk (for which no domestic griefs and anxieties have yet dimmed his enthusiasm) (LJRRT).

Lewis's failure to mention his marriage to Tolkien was a very serious oversight, and it was one of the main reasons for the cooling between them. 'We were separated first by the sudden apparition of Charles Williams,' Tolkien wrote to his son, Michael, in 1963, 'and then by his marriage. Of which he never even told me; I learned of it long after the event' (LJRRT, p. 341). Of course Lewis knew that news of his marriage would eventually reach Tolkien, but who likes to learn of things this way?

No doubt Lewis knew that to Tolkien marrying a divorced woman was a very serious matter. It had been a point of disagreement between them ever since Lewis devoted a chapter to 'Christian Marriage' in *Christian Behaviour*. He had there said: 'The majority of the British people are not Christians and, therefore, cannot be expected to live Christian lives. There ought to be two distinct kinds of marriage: one governed by the State with rules enforced on all citizens, the other governed by the Church with rules enforced by her on her own members.' Tolkien was appalled by this. 'I should like to know on what grounds you base your "two-marriage" system!' he wrote to Lewis. In a long rebuttal of this 'two-marriage system' he insisted that:

> No item of compulsory Christian morals is valid only for Christians ... Toleration of divorce – if a Christian does tolerate it – is toleration of a human abuse ... And wrong behaviour (if it is really wrong on universal principles) is progressive, always: it never stops at being 'not very good', 'second best' – it either reforms, or goes on to third-rate, abominable (LJRRT, pp. 60–1.)

It is not easy to understand why Lewis did not simply *tell* his friend what had been going on. Although both men took to heart the misfortunes of their friends, Tolkien was – as Lewis himself admitted – the more observant of the two.

Gradually, Joy had begun to improve, and Jack had been willing to leave her in Warnie's hands when he was in Cambridge. As they saw more and more of one another they became very close, and Warnie introduced Joy to his favourite pastime, the Court of Louis XIV. *The Sunset of the Splendid Century* was published on 28 November 1955, and he was now writing a biography of *Louis XIV*. However, when Jack came home in July 1957 he left his writing to go to Ireland.

It was not long before Jack had a telephone call from the landlord of the White Horse Inn in Drogheda to say that Warnie was 'dead drunk' and that they were trying to get him into Our Lady of Lourdes Hospital. Writing about it to Arthur Greeves on 21 August 1957, Jack said that Warnie had written to say 'he has been diagnosed as having a heart complaint which will kill him in a year. It *may* not be true – he says anything in his alcoholic spasms – and I've written to the Rev. Mother asking for the facts' (TST). He was soon able to tell Arthur of Mother

Mary Martin's diagnosis that Warnie's trouble was 'slight and curable ... a by-product of acute alcoholism and pneumonia' (**TST** 5 September 1957).

By the autumn of 1957 Joy's cancer was arrested, and she was improving. For some time now Lewis had been praying that God would allow him to accept her pains into his body. And this is what really seems to have happened. The fullest account of this particular 'Way of Exchange or Substitution' – the bearing of one another's burdens – which Charles Williams spoke about so often, is found in Lewis's letter to Sister Penelope of 6 November 1957:

> When they sent Joy home from hospital last April, they sent her home to die. The experienced nurses expected her life to be a matter of weeks. She could not even be moved in bed without a lifting squad of three of us, and, with all our care, we nearly always hurt her. Then it began to appear that the cancer had been arrested; the diseased spots in the bones were no longer spreading or muitiplying. Then the tide began to turn – they were disappearing. New bone was being made. And so little by little till the woman who could hardly be moved in bed can now walk about the house and into the garden – limping and with a stick, but walking. She even found herself getting up *unconsciously* to answer the telephone the other day. It is the unconsciousness that is the real triumph – the body which would not obey the most planned volition now begins to act on its own. General health and spirits excellent ...
>
> Did I tell you I also have a bone disease? It is neither mortal nor curable: a prematurely senile loss of calcium. I was very crippled and had much pain all summer but am in a good spell now. I was losing calcium just about as fast as Joy was gaining it, and a bargain (if it were one) for which I'm very thankful (**L**).

Lewis mentioned this 'substitution' to many of his friends, and there is an account of it by Nevill Coghill in *Light on C.S. Lewis* in which he says that shortly after his marriage Lewis brought Joy to lunch with him. 'It was then,' said Coghill, 'that he told me of having been allowed to accept her pain. "You mean" (I said) "that her pain left her, and that you felt it for her in your body?" "Yes," he said, "in my legs. It was crippling. But it relieved hers."'

'My own news continues better than we ever dared to hope,' Lewis wrote to Sheldon Vanauken on 27 November 1957, the cancerous bones have rebuilt themselves in a way quite unusual and Joy can now *walk* ... I forget if I had begun my own bone disease ... when you were with us. Anyway, it is much better now and I am no longer in pain ... The intriguing thing is that while I (for no discoverable reason) was losing the chalcium [sic] from my bones, Joy, who needed it much more, was gaining it in hers. One dreams of a Charles Williams substitution! Well, never was a gift more gladly given; but one must not be fanciful (*A Severe Mercy*, X, 1977).[26]

XXXI: 'Startling Frankness'

By Christmas 1957 Joy had improved so much that she could limp around the house and into the garden. She now saw more of her son, David, because he became a student at Magdalen College School in September. Jack's osteoporosis was also much better, though he had to wear a surgical belt for the rest of his life. He had just finished writing *Reflections on the Psalms* and he and Joy were now wondering what reply he should make to the Episcopal Radio-TV Foundation of Atlanta, Georgia.

[26] Perhaps the best description of what is meant by Charles Williams' 'Way of Exchange or Substitution' is that given by Lewis in **AT**, 'Williams and the Arthuriad', III: 'The doctrine, which he called that of Exchange or Substitution, may be summed up in three propositions. (1) The Atonement was a Substitution, just as Anselm said. But that Substitution, far from being a mere legal fiction irrelevant to the normal workings of the universe, was simply the supreme instance of a universal law. "He saved others, himself he cannot save" is a *definition* of the Kingdom. All salvation, everywhere and at all times, in great things or in little, is vicarious. The courtesy of the Emperor has absolutely decreed that no man can paddle his own canoe and every man can paddle his fellow's, so that the shy offering and modest acceptance of indispensable aid shall be the very form of the celestial etiquette. (2) We can and should "bear one another's burdens" in a sense much more nearly literal than is usually dreamed of. Any two souls can ("under the Omnipotence") make an agreement to do so: the one can offer to take another's shame or anxiety or grief and the burden will actually be transferred. This Williams most seriously maintained, and I have reason to believe that he spoke from experimental knowledge. (3) Such "exchanges", however, are not made only by mutual compact. We can be their beneficiaries without our own knowledge or consent, as when our god-parents became our substitutes at the font. Such is the coinherence of all souls that they are not even limited by Time.'

This organization had been founded in the 1940s by the Episcopal laywoman, Mrs Caroline Rakestraw, who believed that radio (and later television) could be used as a means of evangelization. She brought together an impressive board of trustees, which included some of the senior Episcopal clergy of the United States. Backed up by Chad Walsh, one of her trustees, Bishop H.I. Louttit of South Florida asked Lewis if he would make some tape-recordings to be played over the air in the United States.

Replying to the Bishop on 5 January 1958, Lewis agreed to the suggestion. 'The subject I want to say something about in the near future in some form or other,' he said, 'is the four loves – Storge, Philia, Eros and Agape. This seems to bring in nearly the whole of Christian ethics.'

Joy had meanwhile improved a great deal. In the New Year she undertook to clean and paint her new home. When she wrote to Katharine Farrer on 30 January 1958 she said:

> I'd have telephoned you, but the telephone is now lost in clouds of whitewash and plaster – I'm redecorating with a vengeance. My bedroom has come out very well and I'm about to move into it, thus restoring the common-room (as it's known here) for sitting purposes; do come and sit!
>
> One pleasant surprise; underneath a horrid yellow finish like congealed egg-yolk the old bedroom chests and wardrobe turned out to be nice simple oak pieces. That's always like finding buried treasure.
>
> I grow stronger daily – can now drive about freely, and rush about the house like mad, scaring dogs and cats and making fires and opening windows ... but everywhere I go I see more things that need repair! If one moves the books, the walls fall in ...
>
> W's in 'Restholme', I've got no nurse, I'm All Alone most afternoons; come and see!

For some time Jack had been going with various friends for a drink or dinner to Studley Priory at Horton-cum-Studley, a few miles from Oxford. It now became customary for Jack and Joy to have dinner there on Sundays. 'It was on one of these visits to the Priory,' said Douglas Gresham, 'that a meeting took place that was to have a remarkable impact on Mother's life and an even greater one on mine...

> Mother was at the Priory one day when a lady walking carefully and painfully with the aid of a sturdy 'shooting stick' came into the bar.

Mother, of course, also walked with the aid of a stick. Soon, Mother was introduced to Jean Wakeman. Jean was a motoring journalist who had worked her way up to the top of that tough profession by sheer determination, talent, hard work and courage, at the same time battling the pain of her disability. Mother told me that Jean had been lame all her life as a result of injuries she had sustained at the time of her birth ... When Jack, David and I were away at college and school, The Kilns, despite Warnie's kindly presence, must have seemed a lonely place, and the disease of loneliness would have been hard for Mother to bear on top of her other troubles. Jean rescued her, taking her on long trips around the country (LL 10).

By May Joy was well enough to begin planning with Jack a 'belated honeymoon' in Ireland – Joy's first trip there. At the beginning of July they flew to Belfast where they were met by Arthur Greeves. He drove them to the Old Inn near his home at Crawfordsburn, two miles west of Bangor on the Belfast Lough. During the week spent there Jack gave a dinner at the Old Inn so that his Irish relations could meet his bride. Amongst those present were Dr and Mrs Joseph Lewis and their daughter Joan, who remembered Joy being very popular with the Lewises. Joy was also taken to meet Jack's and Warnie's old friend Jane McNeill.* After a week at Crawfordsburn they drove to Rathmullan, on Lough Swilly in County Donegal, where they spent a week at the Royal Fort Hotel.

After they returned to Oxford Joy and Jean Wakeman took David and Douglas for a holiday in Solva, Pembrokeshire, between 30 August and 6 September. Writing to Mrs John Watt on 28 August, Lewis said:

> We had a holiday – you might call it a belated honeymoon – in Ireland and were lucky to get that perfect fortnight at the beginning of July. We visited Louth, Down and Donegal, and returned drunk with blue mountains, yellow beaches, dark fuchsia, breaking waves, braying donkeys, peat-smell, and the heather just beginning to bloom.

The talks for the Episcopal Radio-TV Foundation, which later served as a basis for the book *The Four Loves* (1960), were finished by the summer of 1958. Lewis met Mrs Rakestraw in London where they were recorded 19–20 August. He was paid $300 for them. While it did not affect one word of the talks, Lewis did not get on well with Mrs Rakestraw. To begin with, he kept imagining her name to be 'Cartwheel'. It was, however, her desire to change his scripts which annoyed him greatly. '*Why* did you get my poor Jack mixed up with the insufferable Rakestraw, or whatever her name was?' Joy wrote to Chad Walsh on 29 December 1958:

> She began by criticizing his opening words – 'Today I want to discuss ...' 'Professor Lewis, couldn't you say instead *Let us think together, you and I, about...*' No, he couldn't. 'But we want you to give the feeling of *embracing* them!' Jack said if they wanted an embracer they had the wrong man. 'Well, perhaps I mean a feeling of *involvement*...' Ugh! At the end she made him sit absolutely silent before the microphone for a minute and a half 'so they could feel his living presence'.

There was worse to come. After Mrs Rakestraw returned to Atlanta with the recordings, the Foundation began a huge advertising campaign which made it sound as if Lewis would be in America giving the talks. There was an article entitled 'Announcing Dr Lewis' in the Episcopal Church's magazine, *The Living Church*, vol. 137 (28 September 1958) which said:

> C.S. Lewis, churchman, author, lecturer, philosopher and professor of English at Cambridge University, will speak to American radio audiences in 1959 on the weekly Episcopal Hour program, March 29 to May 31. This will be the first time that the author of *Screwtape Letters*, *Problem of Pain*, and *Case for Christianity* has spoken to Americans, although several of his books were first presented as radio addresses...
>
> The coming program, produced by the Episcopal Radio-TV Foundation, Inc., will be broadcast over more than 325 stations as part of the year-round Protestant Hour program, and is available to cities where it is not already scheduled (p. 26).

But this was before the bishops on the board of the Foundation knew what Lewis had said about Eros. After hearing the tapes they decided they were 'too frank for the American people'. The whole series was then cancelled, and an article, 'Love Talks', appeared in *The Living Church*, vol. 137 (23 November 1958) saying:

> Ten talks on love by C.S. Lewis, originally announced as the spring offering of the Episcopal Radio Hour, led to some lively discussion among those responsible for the program when they listened to tape-recorded previews. The noted English author had pulled no

punches in discussing sex and explaining its place in the Christian view of love.

The combination of a high intellectual level and startling frankness seemed to demand a specific type of audience, rather than a place in the format of this well established segment of the Protestant Hour Network.

A new series will be substituted on the Episcopal Hour ... The C.S. Lewis talks will be channelled into college and urban communities for a more sophisticated audience (p. 26).

On being told about this, Joy wrote to Chad Walsh on 29 December 1958 saying: 'Now we learn, not from the organization, but through a friend – that they decided to suppress the whole series because of Jack's "startling frankness" in sexual matters.'

It fell to Mrs Rakestraw to explain to Lewis that his 'startling frankness' was occasioned by the talks on Eros. 'Professor Lewis,' she said to him, 'I'm afraid you brought sex into your talks on Eros.' 'My dear Mrs Cartwheel,' he replied, 'how can you talk about Eros and *leave it out*?' (**BIO** IX). In the end Mrs Rakestraw was not able to broadcast the talks over the Foundation's radio, but they were offered to individual radio stations across the country. Better still, in 1970 she issued them for sale on cassettes entitled *Four Talks on Love* (see **Recordings‡**).

Lewis's *Reflections on the Psalms* was published in September 1958, and shortly afterwards he had a letter from the Archbishop of Canterbury (Geoffrey Fisher) inviting him to become a member of the 'Commission to Revise the Psalter'. The Terms of Reference of the Commission were: 'To produce for the consideration of the Convocations a revision of the text of the Psalter designed to remove obscurities and serious errors of translation yet such as to retain, as far as possible, the general character in style and rhythm of Coverdale's version and its suitability for congregational use.'[27] As it happened, the Coverdale translation of the Psalms was the one Lewis had used in his *Reflections on the Psalms*. Replying to the Archbishop on 14 November 1958, Lewis said:

I have thought over Your Grace's letter and come to the conclusion that I cannot refuse to serve on this Commission if I am wanted. I wish I were better qualified, but there is no use in multiplying words about that.

[27] G.A. Chase, *A Companion to The Revised Psalter* (1963), pp. 1–2.

That Christmas was a busy one at The Kilns and clouded only by the arrival of what Lewis never liked – Christmas cards. In her letter to Chad Walsh of 29 December 1958 Joy complained that they 'descend by thousands from all sorts of people we don't know'. Besides revising a series of lectures he had given at Cambridge, *Studies in Words*, Lewis returned from church on Christmas Day to answer a pile of letters. One of those he wrote on Christmas Day was to Mary Willis Shelburne of Washington, D.C. who began corresponding with Lewis in 1950. Her own letters were filled with complaints about her family and friends, but Lewis, who thought her 'a very silly, tiresome, and probably disagreeable woman' knew she was also 'old, poor, sick, lonely, and miserable.'[28] For this reason he always took time to answer each of them with letters that are perfect gems in their way. Many of the 138 letters he wrote to her between 1950 and 1963 were published as *Letters to an American Lady* (1967).

XXXII: Revising the Psalms

Lewis returned to Cambridge in early January 1959 for his twice-weekly lectures on the 'Prolegomena to the Study of Our Earlier Poetry'. He had to get an early train to London on 22 January for the first meeting of the Commission to Revise the Psalter. This was held in Lambeth Palace beginning at 11 in the morning and running until 5 that afternoon. The other members of the Commission were the Archbishop of York, the Most Rev. F.D. Coggan; the Rt Rev. G.A. Chase (Bishop of Ripon 1946–59); J. Dykes Bower (Organist of St Paul's); Gerald H. Knight (Director of the Royal School of Church Music); D. Winton Thomas (Regius Professor of Hebrew in the University of Cambridge); and another scholar who, with Jack, was to advise on literary merit – T.S. Eliot.

Eliot was on holiday in the Bahamas at the time, and because of this he and Lewis did not meet until the next meeting of the Commission at Lambeth on 13 April. Much had changed since their last meeting. Besides the fact that both had mellowed, Eliot had married Valerie Fletcher the same year that Lewis had wed Joy, and they had much in common. Lewis said afterwards that, after getting to know Eliot, he found it easy to 'love' him.

One of the friends Lewis saw most often in both Cambridge and Oxford was Roger Lancelyn Green. He and his wife had been especially welcoming to Joy. Writing about his frequent visits to The Kilns, Roger Lancelyn Green said:

[28] Letter to Hugh Kilmer of 17 February 1961.

It was a delight to visit The Kilns in 1958 and 1959 and see the sheer happiness and contentment that Lewis was finding in his brief St Martin's summer: the solicitude for his wife, the simple delight in her company, the argument, badinage and rollicking fun that betokened the perfect relationship. Lewis the Family Man was a role he accepted with kindly amusement – 'see how I have dwindled into a husband' he quoted with delight (**BIO** XI).

Roger Lancelyn Green spent the night of 9 June as Lewis's guest in Magdalene College. Roger and his wife had been on a 'Wings' tour of Greece in April 1959, and as Joy had wanted nearly all her life to visit Greece, the men talked about a similar tour for both couples in April of 1960.

Meanwhile, Lewis and Joy had a fortnight's holiday in Ireland to look forward to. When Easter Term ended at Cambridge, they flew to Ireland on 25 June and were met by Arthur Greeves. During the week spent at the Old Inn at Crawfordsburn Arthur drove them south to that portion of the world Jack thought most resembled Narnia – the Carlingford Mountains in County Louth, which lie just across the Lough from the equally beautiful Mourne Mountains. From there they drove north to Rathmullan, where they spent a few days in the Royal Fort Hotel.

The Lewises arrived back in Oxford on 10 July. They went together to Cambridge on 19 July, the following morning Lewis had a meeting in Magdalene with the young man who turned out to be his last pupil.

This was Francis Warner, the poet and dramatist, then a postgraduate at St Catharine's College. He hoped Lewis would agree to supervise his doctoral thesis on what became 'A Bibliographical Edition of the Latin Text of *De Occulta Philosophia* by H. Cornelius Agrippa, edited together with a revision of the translation of the text published by J.F. in 1651.' Later, as Lord White Fellow in English Literature at St Peter's College, Oxford, Dr Warner recalled his weekly tutorials with Lewis during 1959–61:

> I went regularly, on Wednesday mornings, to Professor Lewis's rooms in Magdalene to show him my week's work on the text of Agrippa. Other research students envied my regular contact with my supervisor – such weekly meetings were, for arts post-graduates, not the Cambridge custom. I replied that they probably enjoyed more sleep than I did, as I lay awake most of Tuesday nights aware of my shortcomings in the three languages necessary for the task (Latin, Greek and Hebrew). My supervisor was

generous with more than his time, though. To spare my blushes, he took the original volume in his hands, and with one finger travelling along the buckled lines, translated 'off the cuff', having told me to stop him when he went wrong. I took this to be his polite way of saying 'Make a note where we differ and correct if you are wrong.' When we reached some Hebrew he asked me to take over. Both he and I were seeing Professor Winton Thomas of my own college, St Catharine's: I for instruction in Hebrew, he as they were both members (with T.S. Eliot) of the Commission to Revise the Psalms. When I asked about Eliot's attitude to the project he said that whenever he himself wanted something changed, Eliot always wanted the Prayer Book version retained.

I would knock on his door at 10.30, and we would sit at an angle together, neither facing nor side by side, until 12.45. My notes show the pace at which we worked. On 25 January 1961, for instance, we stopped at the end of Chapter V. The following week, on 1 February, at the end of Chapter IX. He would make me note down references neither of us knew, and in the intervening week each of us would look them up, and compare our answers the following Wednesday. He was fascinated by this chasing of sources for the innumerable quotations, and was awe-inspiringly well-read. I, for my part, paid particular attention to the bibliographical side, the alternative readings in the folio copies of this work I was laboriously collating letter by letter in the University Library's Anderson Room. He cheered me on: 'Praestat difficilior lectio' he would say again and again.

His notes made during the week showed keen zest. Often he would give the reference he had found, and the Latin or Greek quotation, together with ancillary linguistic material if needed; then a reference to English literature. An example is his comment on the word Echeneis:

Echeneis 1. Adj. ἐχε–νηις, 'ship-detaining.' Hence used of lack of winds, or unfavourable winds (Aeschylus *Agamemnon* 149.) 2. As Noun: a shell-fish credited with the power of holding a ship back = Lat. *echeneis remora*. For which cf. Donne, *Elegy* XVIII, 58; *Letter to Sir H. Wootton*, 8; Grierson's note on the Letter; also Thos. Browne, *Errors* III, cap. 28 last para. but two.

Over and above these marathon sessions (so they seemed to me), he would question me about my poetry, and write at length by letter on my sources, rhythms, etc. 'The general danger at present is that of becoming (like early Keats) "too darn poetical". You know what I mean? ... I like the body of III but not its alexandrine ... Now for details. You mean *Perennia* and *Salacia* as fem. singulars. But remember how *perennis* and *salax* are declined! Your forms could only be neuter plurals. This simply must be altered' (27 October 1961).

'Dear Warner, you bowl me out middle stump about Salacia and Perennis! I just didn't know this' (1 November 1961).

I asked him how he wrote his OHEL volume. He replied that he tried to read every book in that century, much of the reading being done in the Duke Humfrey. Every time he read an author he wrote himself an essay on the subject, dated it, and put it in a drawer for a year and a day. He would then take it out and mark it. Any essay falling below a clear alpha was sent back to be done again. I returned to my college and looking through the book saw that it was, indeed, made up of individual essays clearly written at different stages of his development. I also learned a valuable lesson in consistent self-disciplined planning, sustained through two decades to publication.

There was no small-talk. When I came in he would knock out his pipe, we would each don our gowns, and he would take the leather-bound book from me and begin. Only once did I pluck up the courage to ask him a personal question. 'I hope,' I said quietly, as we gowned, 'the black tie is not what it seems?' 'You are married?' 'Yes,' I replied. 'You are lucky. My wife has just died. Now let's begin.'

Immediately after his first meeting with Francis Warner, Lewis joined T.S. Eliot and the other members of the Commission to Revise the Psalms at Selwyn College for their conference on 20–22 July. After the conference Joy joined Lewis and they had lunch with Eliot and his wife on 23 July. Lewis and Eliot met again at Lambeth Palace on 22 September for further work on the Commission.

On 21 September Lewis sent Roger a note of the days (3–14 April) that would be most suitable for them for a holiday in Athens, Rhodes and Crete, and they planned a meeting at The Kilns on 3 October to discuss the Greek trip.

Lewis had already gone back to Cambridge to begin his lectures on 'English Literature 1300–1500' when he returned to Oxford to take Joy for a routine check at the Churchill Hospital on 13 October. Expecting to find her unchanged, the results left them very depressed. When Lewis wrote to Mary Willis Shelburne on 18 October, he said 'Apparently the wonderful recovery Joy made in 1957 was only a reprieve, not a pardon. The last X-ray check reveals cancerous spots returning in many of her bones. There seems to be some hope of a few years' life still and there are still things the doctors can do. But they are all in the nature of "rear-guard actions". We are in retreat' (**LAL**). He wrote to Chad Walsh on 21 October with the same news, adding 'Dare one hope for a second resurrection?'

Joy at once began to receive X-ray treatment and radiotherapy, and when Jack wrote to George Sayer in November 1959 he was able to tell him that the 'doctors say there is some hope of her being able to live without pain for a year or two. Well, we've enjoyed the fruits of a miracle. I'm not sure it would be right to ask for another. Nor do I think it would be given if I did. They tell me that there is no example on record of anyone who was granted the same miracle twice.'

Lewis could see Joy only on the weekends because during the Lent Term of 1960, which ran from 12 January to 11 March, he had an exceptionally heavy schedule of lectures. After finishing the 'Prolegomena' lectures, he gave eight on one of the writers he most loved – Edmund Spenser's *Faerie Queene*. It was then home to prepare for Greece.

XXXIII: The Glittering Isles of Greece

Despite the fact that she was in pain and probably dying, Joy could not be held back from seeing Greece. Lewis knew it could be extremely problematical, but he agreed to the risk. He told Roger and June Lancelyn Green that he and Joy would meet them at the airport on Sunday, 3 April 1960.

One of Lewis's most endearing Narnian characters, Puddleglum the Marshwiggle, had been modelled on his gardener, Paxford. This was because Paxford's conversation tended to enlarge on the gloomy side of things. Lewis and Joy had just got into the taxi to go to the airport when he appeared to see them off. Leaning through the window of the taxi, Paxford said: 'Well, Mr Jack, there was this bloke just going on over the wireless. Says an airplane just went down. Everybody killed – burnt beyond recognition. Did you hear what I said Mr Jack? – *Burnt beyond recognition!*'

Happily, their plane did not crash, and the trip to Greece was one of the most memorable experiences of all their lives. Roger Lancelyn Green kept a diary while they were there, and much of it was published in chapter XI of the Green-Hooper *Biography* (1974). After leaving London the party were forced to make an extra landing in Naples, and this meant that they did not get to Athens until after midnight. 'With a long walk from the 'plane to the Airport buildings, which was rather painful for Joy,' said Green, 'we immediately learned the Greek for a wheel-chair... We drove straight to the Hotel Cosmopolis, near Omonia Square.'

The next day, 4 April, Joy was not up to going to Marathon, but she and Jack met the Greens for an afternoon tour of Athens. 'Joy was able to get right up to the Acropolis, where she and Jack found a seat on the steps of the Propylaea and sat drinking in the beauty of the Parthenon and Erechtheum – columns of honey gold and old ivory against the perfect blue sky.' They made an early start on Tuesday, 5 April, and went by coach to Mycenae. Lewis was immensely impressed, Green recalled, by the towering walls of Cyclopean masonry and the Lion Gate. 'I shall never forget the way he paused suddenly and exclaimed: "My God! The Curse is still here," in a voice hushed between awe and amazement.'

Wednesday, 6 April, was to prove the most memorable day of the tour and one which 'Jack said afterwards was among the supreme days of his life.' The four of them set out in a car with a driver on a private excursion. Going via Daphni...

> we drove down to the head of the Gulf of Corinth, a superbly lovely drive down and down through vineyards, and richly scented pine woods with many of the trees tapped for resin, and through olive groves shining silver in the sunlight to the tiny village of Aegosthena ... After exploring the ruins we settled down at the one tiny taverna right on the shore, with Cithairon towering up on one side and the mountains behind Megara on the other, for a marvellous meal. To accompany our pre-luncheon ouzo we had pickled octopus, and the meal itself began with fried red mullets which our host brought to us still wet from the sea before cooking; and after these fried squid, the tenderest I have ever found in Greece, followed by ewe's milk cheese and fresh oranges. And with this came measure after measure of retsina freshly drawn from the great cask in the half-cellar of the taverna. We sat there for several hours, the usual vivid conversation lapsing into contented silence broken only by the gentle lapping of the waves, the pervading hum of bees and the call of cicadas: the misty blue of the Gulf and the miraculously clear light of Greece working a charm of absolute contentment.

On Thursday, 7 April, they flew to the Island of Rhodes and settled in the Hotel Thermai, where that evening they sampled several Cretan wines. They had a very pleasant all-day excursion to Lindos on 9 April, and during dinner that evening there was 'Splendid verbal sparring between Jack and Joy, each enjoying it to the full: we could barely keep up with them.' After returning to Rhodes they attended an Easter Service at the Orthodox Cathedral on Sunday, 10 April. That afternoon they flew to Iraklion on the northern coast of Crete. The next morning, 11 April, they visited the Palace of Minos at Knossos.

On Tuesday, 12 April, there was an excursion across the island to Gortyna, Phaistos and Agia Triada. At Phaistos 'Jack was the life and soul of the party, keeping "the table in a roar".' They stopped again at Gortyna on the way back, and Green said 'I had the drinks waiting for Jack and Joy by the time the party had thought of ordering theirs. We'd realized for some time that Joy was often in pain, and alcohol was the best alleviation: so I had become adept at diving into the nearest taverna, ordering "tessera ouzo", and having them ready at a convenient table.'

On Wednesday, 13 April, they flew to Pisa in Italy for a night there, and the next day they flew back to London. 'My last sight of Joy,' said Green, 'was of Jack wheeling her briskly in an invalid chair towards the waiting car.'

In an account of the trip which Lewis wrote for Chad Walsh on 23 May, he said it was as if Joy had been 'divinely supported' during the trip, and she had returned to Oxford 'in a *nunc dimittis* frame of mind, having realized, beyond hope, her greatest, lifelong, this-worldly, desire.'

XXXIV: Farewell to Shadowlands

Mercifully, Lewis was not lecturing during the Easter Term of 1960, but he nevertheless had to spend some time during the next few months at Cambridge. He was at home on the weekends, before taking the 'Cantab Crawler' back to Cambridge. On 25 April he attended a meeting of the Inklings with Roger Lancelyn Green and others.

On Saturday afternoon, 14 May, Professor and Mrs Nicholas Zernov came to tea. Mrs Zernov took some photographs of Joy – the last to be made – and they show her in the common-room of The Kilns looking remarkably well and happy as she sits crocheting an afghan.[29] But Joy's health was deteriorating fast. Since the trip to Greece, Jack told Chad

[29] Mrs Zernov's photographs are published in **TJB**.

Walsh in a letter of 23 May, 'there has been a recrudescence of the original growth in the right breast which started the whole trouble. It had to be removed last Friday – or, as she characteristically put it, she was "made an Amazon". This operation went through, thank God, with greater ease than we had dared to hope. By the evening of the same day she was free from all severe pain and from nausea, and cheerfully talkative. Yesterday she was able to sit up in a chair for fifteen minutes or so ... I had some ado to prevent Joy (and myself) from relapsing into Paganism in Attica! At Daphne it was hard not to pray to Apollo the Healer. But somehow one didn't feel it would have been very wrong – would have only been addressing Christ *sub specie Apollinis*' (L).

For some time now Lewis had been taking Joy to the Acland Nursing Home (now Hospital) for treatment, and it was during this time that Joy ran into Tolkien's wife, Edith. Mrs Tolkien was a patient there at the same time as Joy, and on one warm day the nurses rolled their beds outside so they could enjoy the sun. They met and, as they talked, they discovered each other's identity. Shortly afterwards Tolkien and Lewis bumped into one another when they arrived at the Acland to visit their wives, and Tolkien was introduced to Joy. This appears to be the only occasion on which they met.

Joy loved going for drives, and on Saturday, 11 June Mrs Miller, the housekeeper at The Kilns, and her husband took her out in their car. She came back refreshed. The story is now taken up by Warnie, who, writing in his diary on 21 June said:

On the following Tuesday [14 June] which was a glorious day, I pushed her to the library, and afterwards up as far as the pond, with stops for her to inspect her favourite flower bed; and from there we went to the greenhouse where she got out and looked at her plants. This was to be her last outing. She had been complaining for a day or two of indigestion, and it got worse, accompanied by constant retching and vomiting; diagnosed by her doctor as gastric infection, of which there is a lot in the town. She did not feel up to making the usual end-of-term visit to Cambridge on Saturday last, and that and the taxi for Studley Priory on Sunday were cancelled.

The last time I spoke to Joy (or I suppose ever will), was at about 10.15 on Sunday night, the 19th, when she seemed much better and said she would shout for me if she needed help during the night. When I got downstairs on Monday morning J told me that he had been up with her all night, and, poor thing, she had been vomiting, or at least trying to vomit all the time. About 10 a.m. she said to

Hibbie, 'Nurse, this is the end, I know I'm dying. Telegraph for Doug.' But even then the old courage was still there; almost the last thing she said before falling into a drug-induced coma was, 'I've got enough cancers now to form a Trades Union of the darned things.' And to the doctor she said, 'Finish me off quick, I won't have another operation'...

There is now nothing left to pray for but that she may die without recovering consciousness. Jack of course went in with the ambulance at 4 p.m., and to me fell the task of breaking the news to the boys. I met David at the bottom of the drive and broke the position to him as gently as I could ... Poor Doug arrived in tears, having heard the news from his Headmaster who, with really wonderful kindness, had motored him down all the way from central Wales. (BF)

David had come down from Magdalen College School and Douglas all the way from Lapley Grange School in Machynlleth, Montgomeryshire. 'The first thing she said,' wrote Douglas, 'was, "Doug, congratulations on passing your Common Entrance examinations." I held her in my arms and merely wept. I was now taller than she would have been had she been able to stand, but as usual it was she who comforted me' (LL 13).

But 'Once again,' wrote Warnie on 8 July, 'Joy has made fools of the doctors and nurses' (BF). She returned from the Radcliffe Infirmary on Monday, 27 June feeling quite well. By Sunday, 3 July she was well enough to go to Studley Priory for dinner, and the following day she went for a drive in the Cotswolds. The reprieve was, however, to be very brief. When Warnie went to bed on 12 July, Jack and Joy were playing Scrabble. At 6 a.m. the next day the household was awakened by her screaming, and Jack called the doctor. The ambulance arrived soon afterwards and, once again, Joy was rushed to the Radcliffe Infirmary where Jack persuaded Till,[30] the surgeon, to give her a private room.

Warnie was at home all day waiting for news. Late that night Jack was collected from the Radcliffe by his friend Clifford Morris who drove him home. At 11.40, said Warnie,

I heard J come into the house and went out to meet him. Self: 'What news?' J: 'She died about twenty minutes ago.' She was, he tells me, conscious up to the last, just before Till called J out of the room to say she was dying rapidly. J went back and told Joy, who agreed with him that it was the best news they could now get. During the

---

[30] Dr Anthony Stedman Till.

afternoon and evening she dozed from time to time, but was fully sensible whenever she was awake.

She asked during these final hours that she should be cremated, left her fur coat as a parting gift to K. Farrer, and was able to receive Absolution from Austin [Farrer], whom she asked to read the funeral service over her at the crematorium. Once during the afternoon she said to J, 'Don't get me a posh coffin; posh coffins are all rot.' God rest her soul (**BF**).

Four days later, on Monday, 18 July, Jack, Warnie, David and Douglas went by taxi to the Crematorium. There were others there too including, of course, Jean Wakeman. The service of the dead was read by Austin Farrer. 'At the end,' wrote a grieving Warnie that same day, 'the coffin was withdrawn and curtains, pulled invisibly, hid it from us for ever' (**BF**).

Joy had liked the 'Epitaph' which later appeared in Jack's *Poems* and asked him to rewrite a version of it for her. Of course he did, and the poem was cut into a marble plaque which is near where her ashes were scattered at the Oxford Crematorium:

Remember
Helen Joy
Davidman
D. July 1960
Loved wife of C.S. Lewis

Here the whole world (stars, water, air,
And field, and forest, as they were
Reflected in a single mind)
Like cast-off clothes was left behind
In ashes yet with hope that she,
Re-born from holy poverty,
In lenten lands, hereafter may
Resume them on her Easter Day.

XXXV: A Grief Observed

'Perhaps being maddeningly busy is the best thing for me,' Lewis wrote to Vera Gebbert on 5 August 1960. 'Anyway, I am. This is one of those things which makes the tragedies of real life so *very* unlike those of the stage' (**L**).

When he wrote those words Lewis may have had in mind a man who hoped to adapt one of his books for the stage. For years Donald Swann had been haunted by the beauty of Lewis's imagination, and during a recent American tour with Michael Flanders of their highly successful *At the Drop of a Hat* and other musicals, he wrote a postcard to his fellow composer in England, David Marsh, saying:

What about *Perelandra* as an opera?

David Marsh agreed at once. He would write the libretto and Donald Swann the music. They found Lewis completely in sympathy with their project, and thus began a number of meetings between the three of them. Lewis had apparently not found it possible to cancel all the appointments he had made before Joy died, and Donald Swann said in his autobiography, *Swann's Way*:

There is one episode I shall always remember. This was during one of our occasional meetings when David and I were starting on *Perelandra*. It was a quiet morning and we went to Lewis's home in Oxford for breakfast. We strolled around his lovely garden with him, talking about the opera. After about an hour he said: 'I hope you will excuse me. I must go now because my wife died last night.' He left us. I was very moved. Quite overcome. It is just another story of this very gracious gentleman who always looked after his guests. I mean, at a time like that! What did *we* matter? [31]

In the end, this work was to give Lewis much pleasure. He met Donald Swann and David Marsh again on 8 September, and Marsh was back in Oxford to lunch with Lewis on 20 September. Over the next three years they proceeded to set *Perelandra* to music.

Another who saw a good deal of Lewis at this time was Bill Gresham, Joy's first husband. Gresham had been planning a visit to Oxford before Joy died, and she had last written to him on 2 July about things to bring the boys. Lewis wrote to him on the day of the funeral (15 July) saying, 'Joy died on 13 July. This need make no change in your plans, but I thought you should arrive knowing it.' Bill Gresham arrived on 3 August and put up at the Old Black Horse Inn in St Clement's Street, Oxford. Lewis met him several times during his stay.

[31] Donald Swann, *Swann's Way: A Life in Song*, ed. Lyn Smith (1991), p. 205.

It cannot have been an easy visit for either man. Besides losing Joy, Gresham had lost his sons as well. Remembering this reunion some years later, Douglas said: 'I was an English schoolboy by then ... so I shook his hand and said, "How do you do, sir?" In truth, I confess I felt no emotion for him at all. He was a stranger; we could not bridge the gap of the years of separation. We spent considerable time together and became friends, but really that was all. When he left to go back to America and his new family, I missed him less than I did before he had come' (LL 15). It was much the same for David. After their father returned home on 15 August his fourth book was published – *Houdini: The Man Who Walked Through Walls* (1960). None of his works had enjoyed the success of *Nightmare Alley*, and it wasn't long after this that he was ill himself.

Warnie had gone to Ireland on 25 July and it wasn't long before Jack was informed that Warnie was in Our Lady of Lourdes Hospital in Drogheda. Writing to Arthur Greeves on 30 August about Joy's last days, he said: 'W is away on his Irish holiday and has, as usual, drunk himself into hospital. Douglas – the younger boy – is, as always, an absolute brick, and a very bright spot in my life. I'm quite well myself. In fact, by judicious diet and exercise, I've brought myself down from thirteen stone to just under eleven' (**TST**).

As he could not take a holiday until Warnie returned, Lewis found, as he had so often in the past, that 'ink is the great cure for all human ills' (**TST**, 30 May 1916). In August he wrote *A Grief Observed*, a powerful work of Christian apologetics based on the grief caused by Joy's death. Describing what Warnie called 'this harrowing book' (**Memoir**) to his former pupil, Sister Madeleva C.S.C., in a letter of 3 October 1963, Lewis said:

> It is 'A Grief *Observed*' from day to day in all its rawness and sinful reactions and follies. It ends with faith but raises all the blackest doubts *en route*.

This book was published in September 1961 under a pseudonym Lewis had never used before – 'N.W. Clerk'.

XXXVI: An Entangled Man

After completing *A Grief Observed* Lewis found himself in a whirl of activity. He was also worried about money. He had spent so much over the last few years that he now began keeping a minute account of his expenses.

Austin Farrer had become the Warden of Keble College, and he and his wife 'K' invited Lewis to dine with them there on 15 September. They knew he needed a holiday, but the planned visit to Roger and June Lancelyn Green up in Cheshire now looked less and less probable. David had been a day-boy at Magdalen College School since 1957 and, beginning on 20 September, Douglas would be going there as well. But he could not leave them alone at The Kilns with Warnie still away. On 15 September he wrote to Roger saying:

> Oh Hell! What a trial I am to you both! If Warnie really came home on the 23rd – and if he did not come home so drunk as to have to be put straight into a nursing home – I could and would with delight come to you on the 24th. But neither is really at all probable. And of course I can't leave this house with no grown-up in charge. What it comes to is that you must count me out. I am *very* sorry. *Don't* make any further efforts to accommodate such an entangled man as me.

In the end Warnie returned in time for Lewis to go back to Cambridge on 5 October. He spent the next night at the Athenaeum Club in London in order to attend the Committee on the Revision of the Psalms at Lambeth Palace the following morning. Then, back in Cambridge he began his twice-weekly lectures on English Literature between 1300 and 1500.

Joy had been helpful when Lewis wrote 'Screwtape Proposes a Toast' which had appeared in *The Saturday Evening Post* of 19 December 1959. Even before that Lewis had conceived the idea of what he called *The Whole Screwtape* – a volume to include both the 'Toast' and the original *Screwtape*. His publisher, Jocelyn 'Jock' Gibb* of Geoffrey Bles, visited him in Cambridge on 29 November 1959 to talk about it. Lewis wrote a new Preface to this *Whole Screwtape* which he sent to Gibb a month later, and since that time they had been busy planning the new book.

'Drat that omnibus!' Lewis wrote to Gibb on 9 October 1960, after being reminded yet again that it would have been impossible for the 'Patient' Screwtape wrote about in Letter I to see 'a No 73 bus going past' the British Museum. Numerous readers had pointed out that the thing was impossible, and now a solution must be found. 'It need not be visible *from* the B.M.,' Lewis wrote to Jock Gibb –

> It need be visible only in some neighbouring street which the patient might see on his way to or from lunch. If you can provide the number of any bus that might be seen in some such neighbouring street, and then emend *street* to *streets* in the last line of p. 24, we shall

have saved our bacon. If this is impossible then take your choice of *green coach, jeep, fire engine, Rolls, police car,* or *ambulance.*

Jock Gibb agreed and a problem which had nagged at Lewis for over twenty years was solved by altering the original words 'Once he was in the street the battle was won. I showed him a newsboy shouting the midday paper, and a No 73 bus going past' to read 'Once he was in the streets the battle was won. I showed him ...'

'I believe we've got it right,' Lewis wrote to Gibb on 12 October. They finished the rest of their planning in Magdalene College on 30 November, and the book was published the next year as *The Screwtape Letters and Screwtape Proposes a Toast.*

While Lewis was trying to 'save his bacon' over the No 73 omnibus, he found himself in a violent tussle with the 'Leavisites'. In his 'Interim Report', he had pointed out that Cambridge is dominated by Literary Criticism and that one is never safe from 'the Critic'. It was easy for Lewis to remember that English as an Honour School had only come into existence after the First War, and he did not want to see it degenerate into nothing but feeling. His fears for a fact-less curriculum were expressed in the person of one of the main characters in *That Hideous Strength*, Mark Studdock, whose education was described as being

> merely 'Modern'. The severities both of abstraction and of high human tradition had passed him by ... He was a man of straw, a glib examinee in subjects that require no exact knowledge (chapter 9, part ii).

Lewis was already at work on *An Experiment in Criticism* (1961) while he was writing *A Grief Observed,* and in it he said that, of those who had helped him most in understanding literature, the 'Evaluative Critics' are at the bottom of the list, while the 'Dryasdust' editors, textual critics, commentators and lexicographers are at the top:

> Find out what the author actually wrote and what the hard words meant and what the allusions were to, and you have done far more for me than a hundred new interpretations or assessments could ever do (chapter XI).

Lewis was not deterred by the hostility of the Leavisites, and when the little Cambridge *Broadsheet* asked him in Lent Term of 1960 for a comment about undergraduate criticism, he provided it for them in a nutshell. In the issue of 9 March 1960 he said:

The faults I find in contemporary undergraduate criticism are these: (1) In adverse criticism their tone is that of personal resentment. They are more anxious to wound the author than to inform the reader. Adverse criticism should diagnose and exhibit faults, not abuse them. (2) They are far too ready to advance or accept radical reinterpretations of works which have already been before the world for several generations. The *prima facie* improbability that these have never till now been understood is ignored. (3) Most European literature was composed for adult readers who knew the Bible and the Classics. It is not the modern student's fault that he lacks this background; but he is insufficiently aware of his lack and of the necessity for extreme caution which it imposes on him. He should think twice before discovering 'irony' in passages which everyone has hitherto taken 'straight'. (4) He approaches literature with the wrong kind of seriousness. He uses as a substitute for religion or philosophy or psychotherapy works which were intended as *divertissements*. The nature of the comic is a subject for serious consideration; but one needs to have seen the joke and taken it as a joke first.

Of course none of these critical vices are peculiar to undergraduates. They imitate that which, in their elders, has far less excuse.

After going unremarked for some months, the undergraduate literary magazine, *Delta* (No 22), of October 1960 devoted a twelve-page article to attacking 'Professor C.S. Lewis and the English Faculty'. The editors, Simon Gray of Trinity College and Howard Burns of King's, were incensed that he should think the Bible and the Classics important in understanding most European literature. 'In placing the stress there,' they complained, 'Professor Lewis appears to be indicating both a contempt for the undergraduate's preoccupation with literature, and even more seriously, what amounts to contempt for the highly individual sensibilities and imaginations ... that have created so differently in our literature' (p. 7). After striking bitterly at every point of Lewis's article, they conclude that its tone was

distasteful in its arrogance, distasteful in its authoritarian self-righteousness, distasteful finally in the contempt for the undergraduate that it suggests (p. 9).

This was picked up by the Cambridge University newspaper, *Varsity*, which in an article called 'Detachment' (15 October), said 'Professor C.S. Lewis, when asked to comment on the attacks on him in last week's *Delta* ... informs us that "(a) he can't bear interviews ... (b) he never heard of *Delta* and knows nothing about the articles." See what they mean?' From there news of it spread to *The Listener* (20 October). A leader entitled 'English – Left or Right' stated that 'What we are witnessing is one more skirmish in the battle between "tradition" (the Classics, "Q", the historical approach) and "nonconformity" (Dr Leavis, psychology, sociology and practical criticism) ... There must be an agreed hard core of fact. You cannot start selecting until you have some idea what there is to select *from*. It is all very well to sneer at Aristotle as irrelevant to our time. But who are the editors of *Delta*, who is any man, that they or he should call Aristotle irrelevant?'

This, in its turn, elicited a very long letter from F.R. Leavis himself, who in *The Listener* of 3 November (p. 801) said he could not see anything in *Delta* 'that is not decent and intelligent. Professor Lewis himself, in launching such an attack, will hardly have expected to remain unanswered.' At the end of a very heated debate that was to go on for many months, and in which *The Times Literary Supplement* (25 November) and *The Spectator* (16 December) took part, Lewis finally responded with a Letter to the Editors in *Delta* (No 23, February 1961) in which he said:

> I complained that the tone of undergraduate criticism was too often 'that of passionate resentment'. You illustrate this admirably by accusing me of 'Pecksniffian disingenuousness', 'shabby bluff' and 'self-righteousness'. Do not misunderstand. I am not in the least deprecating your insults; I have enjoyed these twenty years *l'honneur d'être une cible* and am now pachydermatous. I am not even rebuking your bad manners; I am not Mr Turveydrop and 'gentlemanly deportment' is not a subject I am paid to teach. What shocks me is that students, academics, men of letters, should display what I had thought was an essentially uneducated inability to differentiate between a disputation and a quarrel. The real objection to this sort of thing is that it is all a distraction from the issue. You waste on calling me liar and hypocrite time you ought to have spent on refuting my position. Even if your main purpose was to gratify a resentment, you have gone about it the wrong way. Any man would much rather be called names than proved wrong (p. 5).[32]

[32] For more on this see Ian MacKillop, *F.R. Leavis: A Life in Criticism* (1995), pp. 298–9.

Warnie had returned home in October, determined to live the life of a teetotaller. When Jack returned to The Kilns he found him at work on his fifth book about the *ancien régime*. His third book, *Assault on Olympus*, had been published on 7 March 1958, *Louis XIV* on 29 May 1959, and the new book was to be called *The Scandalous Regent: A Life of Philippe, Duc D'Orléans 1674–1723 and of his family*. Warnie had been delighted when Joy became interested in this favourite period of his, and she had read the manuscript of this book. On Saturday, 3 December, Jack went out for lunch with two fellow Inklings. R.E. Havard and James Dundas-Grant,* and over the next few weeks there were dinners with Colin and Christian Hardie, Nevill Coghill, the Farrers and other old friends.

It was back to Cambridge immediately after Christmas for a meeting at St Catharine's College of the Commission to Revise the Psalter, 28–30 December.

XXXVII: Illness

A few days before Jack left for Cambridge, Warnie was still deep in seventeenth-century France. *The Scandalous Regent* was published on 7 April 1961, and now he was re-reading the Memoirs of the diplomat and adventurer, the Chevalier d'Arvieux, towards the idea of writing a book about him. 'I began to re-read *Arvieux* and make notes on what I read, with an eye to manufacturing a book out of him,' he wrote on 13 January 1961. 'I see I last read *Arvieux* in 1930: how little I then imagined that I would ever live to be the author of five books on my pet subject!' (**BF**). He continued with his agreeable hobby and *Levantine Adventurer: The Travels and Missions of the Chevalier d'Arvieux, 1653–1697* was published on 30 November 1961.

In Cambridge Jack faced a heavy schedule of lectures. He followed his twice-weekly lectures on the 'Prolegomena to Renaissance Literature' with eight lectures on Spenser's *Faerie Queene*. Several times during the term he met with D. Winton Thomas, Regius Professor of Hebrew, to work on the Psalms, and on 28 February and 1 March he joined the rest of the Commission at Lambeth Palace. February 23 was the birthday of Samuel Pepys (1633–1703), whose Library and Diary are some of the great treasures of Magdalene College. Lewis was invited to give a talk on Pepys that evening. Writing about the event, Richard Ladborough said:

It is always a matter of astonishment to me that during the whole of his period at Magdalene, Cambridge, he should only once have visited the Pepys Library, and that for only twenty minutes when incited to do so by two eminent Oxford visitors. And yet he read the whole of Pepys's Diary with insight and, of course, with intelligence, and made one of the best speeches on Pepys I have ever heard. This was in hall at the annual dinner held to celebrate Pepys's birthday. Pepys in fact was a late acquaintance of his, and he took it for granted, with his usual modesty, that his hearers knew the text as well as *he* did (**ABT**).

Lewis was also at work on a number of his own things. For several years he had been collecting and revising his poems, and he mentioned the possibility of publishing them when he wrote to Jock Gibb, on 4 December 1960: 'If you and Spencer [Curtis Brown] favour the idea of any poems I'll make a choice.' He continued working on the poems, but it was not a project he would live to finish.

He was also working on a collection of essays published in 1962 as *They Asked for a Paper*. Lewis was always at his best when writing about Heaven, and now he found a way of making his thoughts even clearer. On 12 April 1961 he sent Jock Gibb a new passage he had written for 'Transposition', a sermon he had preached at Mansfield College on 28 May 1944. It is about the 'transposition' of something from a 'higher medium', such as our supernatural life, into those elements which make up our 'natural life'. In the new passage Lewis tackles the problem of why our notion of Heaven involves 'perpetual negations'. We think of Heaven, he said, as a place where there is 'no food, no drink, no sex, no movement, no mirth, no events, no time, no art.' Why?

Lewis constructed a 'fable' in which he imagines a boy who is brought up by his mother in a dungeon. As he has no first-hand experience of the outside world, his mother tries to show him what it is like by drawing pictures. All goes well until, says Lewis,

it dawns on her that he has, all these years, lived under a misconception. 'But,' she gasps, 'you didn't think that the real world was full of lines drawn in lead pencil?' 'What?' says the boy. 'No pencil marks there?' And instantly his whole notion of the outer world becomes a blank ... He has no idea of that which will exclude and dispense with the lines, that of which the lines were merely a transposition – the waving treetops, the light dancing on the weir, the coloured three-dimensional realities which are not enclosed in lines but define their own shapes at every moment with a delicacy and multiplicity which no drawing could ever achieve ...

So with us. 'We know not what we shall be'; but we may be sure we shall be more, not less, than we were on earth. Our natural experiences ... are only like the drawing, like pencilled lines on flat paper. If they vanish in the risen life, they will vanish only as pencil lines vanish from the real landscape, not as a candle flame that is put out but as a candle flame which becomes invisible because someone has pulled up the blind, thrown open the shutters, and let in the blaze of the risen sun.

Halfway through Easter Term 1961 Lewis had a letter from his old friend, Arthur Greeves, who was planning a visit to England and wanted to spend a few days with him. 'Your letter has brightened my whole sky,' Lewis said on 8 May (**TST**). On 22 June Lewis and his driver collected Arthur from London and returned with him to Oxford. Lewis described their two days together in his letter of 30 June 'as one of the happiest times I've had for many a long day' (**TST**). Arthur scribbled a note for himself saying that Jack 'was looking very ill'.

He was ill. Immediately following Arthur's visit Lewis went to the Acland Nursing Home where he was examined by Mr (now Sir) John Badenoch, Director of Clinical Studies in the University of Oxford, and a Consultant Physician with the Oxfordshire Health Authority. 'My trouble,' he told Arthur on 27 June, 'has been diagnosed as one very common at our time of life, namely an enlarged prostate gland. I shall soon be in a nursing home for the necessary operation' (**TST**). The operation was set for Sunday, 2 July, but in the end the surgeon decided it was too dangerous. In September, when Roger Lancelyn Green suggested coming down for a visit, Lewis was still waiting for the doctors to decide whether or not to operate. Writing to Roger on 6 September, he said:

It's a bit tricky. I am awaiting an operation on my prostate: but as this trouble upset my kidneys and my heart, these have to be set right before the surgeon can get to work. Meanwhile, I live on a no-protein diet, wear a catheter, sleep in a chair, and have to stay on the ground floor. I'm quite capable of having a guest, but it depends on how the weekly blood-tests go. This means that, for all I know, it might come just when you want to be here so I think you'd better make alternative arrangements, which could be abandoned in favour of coming to The Kilns if, when the time comes, I should be here and not in the Acland. I'd hate to miss the chance of a visit from you if it turns out to be feasible. Is this all too bothersome?

You needn't pity me too much. I am in no pain and I quite enjoy
the hours of uninterrupted reading which I now get (**L**).

Jack had been planning a trip to Scotland with Jean Wakeman and the boys,
but this now had to be called off. Besides problems with his health, Lewis
was having to consider what was best for his eldest stepson. Unlike
Douglas, who had settled down in the Church of England, David had been
interested in Judaism since he was eleven. Now, increasingly, he was trying
to understand the faith that his maternal grandparents had abandoned. He
was also devoted to *not* being English, and this, as well as a need for an
identity, led him to memorize the conjugations of Hebrew irregular verbs
during the Greek lessons at Magdalen College School. His mother had
encouraged him to have Hebrew lessons, with Jack's complete approval.

Lewis admired his efforts to learn and allowed him to have private
lessons in Hebrew from Ronald May who was working as a proof-reader
for the Oxford University Press, and who later taught at the Oxford
Centre for Post-Graduate Hebrew Studies. At the same time that David
was being taught Hebrew, he started to learn Yiddish by himself. One of
the world's leading Yiddish scholars, Professor Chone Shmeruk of the
Hebrew University of Jerusalem, was in Oxford during the winter of
1961–62 and he gave him lessons in Yiddish. David passed the Hebrew
O-Level examination.

In the meantime Lewis was not well enough to go back to Cambridge
for Michaelmas Term 1961, but stopped at home with his brother and the
boys. Warnie had been a teetotaller since his return from Ireland the
previous September, and we learn from his diary that he started writing
his new book on d'Arvieux on 22 May and finished it on 9 August 1961.
In his diary of 5 September he said:

Completed typing and correcting of d'Arvieux book which will be
sent off to Curtis Brown tomorrow. Whether it is any good or not I
can't say, but I'm rather proud that it should have been done at all.
The bulk of it was written while [in] constant anxiety about J, over-
worked, in pain with a strained Tendon Achilles, and bitterly
disappointed at the loss of my summer holiday, twelve days before
I was due to go (**BF**).

When an operation proved impossible, Lewis, under the care of Mr
Badenoch, began a long series of blood transfusions every few weeks.
They helped enormously, and when Warnie wrote to Mary Willis
Shelburne on 7 October, he said:

The result was that he came home a week ago most definitely improved; with not only the permission but the encouragement of his doctors, he now gets up in the morning and cooks his own breakfast, and every day he goes out for half an hour's walk. Better still, he has been put on a more generous diet and enjoys his meals. But perhaps the best sign is that he tells me he is getting very bored with invalid life and is itching to get back to work. As for the impending operation, the surgeon now talks of it as a thing quite in the future – six, or even twelve months ahead he says. Which naturally is an enormous relief to me, for if they are taking this view there cannot be anything very urgent the matter (**LAL**).

Two days later Lewis wrote to his colleague at Magdalene, Richard Ladborough, saying: 'I grow quite homesick for college and very much hope that though not good for much, I'll be back in January...' This, however, proved impossible, and pretty soon the question was whether he would be well enough to go back in March 1962. Reluctantly, Lewis had to ask that someone else supervise his pupil, Francis Warner. Explaining his problem to Warner in a letter of 6 December 1961, he said:

The position is that they can't operate on my prostate till they've got my heart and kidneys right, and it begins to look as if they can't get my heart and kidneys right till they operate on my prostate. So we're in what an examinee, by a happy slip of the pen, called 'a viscous circle'. Still, it is not *quite* closed. Meanwhile, I have no pain and am neither depressed nor bored.

XXXVIII: Return to Cambridge

Lewis enjoyed the attention of his friends, and over the next months he was surrounded by many of them. On Mondays Humphrey Havard and Jim Dundas-Grant collected him and took him to the Bird and Baby, often going on to The Trout at Godstow afterwards for lunch. Although Lewis was able to get to the church on Sundays, his parish priest, Father Ronald Head,* always celebrated the Eucharist at The Kilns for him on Wednesday mornings. The many who visited him at home included Owen Barfield, Cecil Harwood, Roger Lancelyn Green, John Wain, Kenneth Tynan and Christopher Derrick. Lewis once said to a friend, 'You can't get a cup of tea large enough or a book long enough to suit me,[33] and during this time he re-read many old favourites including *War and Peace* and the *Orlando Furioso*. He also read, and loved, Thomas Merton's *No Man is an Island*.

David was by now eighteen and he was not doing well at Magdalen College School. Encouraged by Rabbi M.Y. Young, a master at Carmel College, a Jewish secondary school in Wallingford, David visited a *yeshivah* – a Jewish traditional academy devoted primarily to the study of rabbinic literature – at Gateshead in the north of England. There he conferred with one of the rabbis who advised him to go to a Jewish school in London to finish his A-level examinations before going to a *yeshiva*. On 15 April he went to London, and after a few months he became a student at the North West London Talmudical College at 961 Finchley Road, where he was to remain for a year.

Lewis was well enough to go back to Cambridge on 24 April, and during Easter Term he resumed his twice-weekly lectures on *The Faerie Queene*. He had several long sessions over the Psalter during the next few months with Bishop Chase and Professor D. Winton Thomas. When he returned home in July, Warnie was already in Drogheda ('I drank from 22 June until 27 August while I was in Ireland', Warnie wrote in his diary for 2 January 1963). Jack wanted to visit Ireland himself, but this was not possible. Writing to Sister Penelope on 23 June 1962, he said:

> It is kind of you to want to know my plight (by the way, apart from everything else, what a *bore* the subject of one's own health is! Like wearisomely enumerating for the police all the contents of a lost handbag). It begins to look as if I shall not be fit for that operation in any reasonable time – doctor's euphemism for NEVER? – but I've apparently developed a 'tolerance' for the state of my blood and kidneys and can carry on, on a low diet and strict economy of exertion. So they let me [go] back to Cambridge last term 'as an experiment'. The experiment, *Laus Deo*, has proved a wholly unexpected success and I am now very definitely better than I've ever been since last June...
>
> You know I'm on the commission for revising the prayer book Psalter? It has been delightful work, with delightful colleagues, and I've learned a lot. We finished our first draft of Psalm 150 a fortnight ago.

Although he was unable to venture far from home, Lewis passed a pleasant summer. For some months he had been writing the book 'behind' his highly-respected lectures on the 'Prolegomena to Medieval and

---

[33] Preface to *Of Other Worlds* (1966).

Renaissance Literature', and he finished it in July. It was given the name *The Discarded Image: An Introduction to Medieval and Renaissance Literature*, and is dedicated to the friend who heard those lectures in Oxford, Roger Lancelyn Green. Besides numerous visitors, Lewis enjoyed a few excursions in and around Oxford. He had seen his old friend, Owen Barfield, a good deal recently, and on 12 July Barfield drove him over to Long Crendon for a visit with Ruth Pitter. This was so successful that on 15 August he invited Ruth to visit him at The Kilns. Times had changed since he gave his wartime broadcasts, and on 11 September the BBC came to The Kilns where they recorded Lewis reading an essay on Bunyan's *Pilgrim's Progress*.

This peaceful autumn was suddenly interrupted. Bill Gresham had been troubled with cataracts on his eyes. He had lost the sight of one eye, and he was threatened with total loss of vision. He had also learned that he had cancer of the tongue and throat. On Thursday, 13 September, he left his home in New Rochelle, New York, and booked into the Dixie Hotel in New York City. He took an overdose of sleeping pills and was found dead on Friday, 14 September. An article entitled **Gresham, A Writer is Found Dead Here** appeared in *The New York Times* of 16 September 1962. It said:

> William Lindsay Gresham, the 53-year-old author of *Nightmare Alley* and other books on carnival life, was found dead Friday afternoon in a room at the Dixie Hotel ...
>
> A hotel spokesman said that Mr Gresham had registered there on Thursday under the name of Asa Kendall, giving his address as 217 Talbott Road, Baltimore. Papers on the body disclosed Mr Gresham's identity, the police said. A family friend said that he lived at 27 Locust Avenue, New Rochelle, N.Y., with his second wife, Renée Rodriguez. He had two sons by a previous marriage. They were said to be living in England.
>
> Mr Gresham was born in Baltimore and grew up in Brooklyn where he was graduated from Erasmus Hall High School. He received his initial taste for carnival life at the side-shows at Coney Island. He also performed as a human target for a circus knife thrower (p. 85).

This dreadful news was followed by a warm tribute by Albert M. Morehead in *The New York Times* of 25 September (p. 34). By a cruel irony, Bill Gresham's last book, published a few months before his death, is entitled *The Book of Strength: Body Building the Safe, Correct Way*. It was dedicated 'To my Boys, Davy and Doug Gresham'.

Lewis had now to tell David and Douglas the news of their father. He then returned to Cambridge on 8 October and resumed his lectures on 'English Literature 1300–1500'. They were to be the last he would give. He heard from Tolkien twice this term. Although Tolkien continued to resent Lewis's marriage, he nevertheless loved his old friend and urged him to attend a dinner to celebrate the publication of *English and Medieval Studies Presented to J.R.R. Tolkien on the Occasion of his Seventieth Birthday* (1962), to which Lewis had contributed an article. Replying on 20 November 1962, he said:

> Dear Tollers – what a nice letter. I also like beer less than I did, though I have retained the taste for general talk. But I shan't be at the *Festschrift* dinner. I wear a catheter, live on a low protein diet, and go early to bed. I am, if not a lean, at least a slippered, pantaloon.

A few days before Christmas, Tolkien wrote to him again. 'Thanks for your most kind letter,' Lewis said on 24 December. 'All my philosophy of history hangs upon a sentence of your own "Deeds were done which were not *wholly* in vain." Is it still possible amid this ghastly racket of "Xmas" to exchange greetings for the Feast of the Nativity? If so, mine, very warm, to both of you.'

XXXIX: Requiescat in Pace

After Christmas Douglas left Magdalen College School and went to a small private school, Applegarth, in Godalming, Surrey. And Jack, following one of his usual visits to the Acland, returned to Cambridge. He had not been back long when on 7 February 1963 he had a visit from the painter, Juliet Pannet. *The Illustrated London Times* had commissioned her to do a likeness of him in pastels, and Lewis agreed to sit for the portrait, which appeared in the magazine on 27 July 1963.

Ever since 1952 Lewis had been trying to write a book on Prayer, and until this term nothing had come of the idea. What had been holding him back was not lack of things to say, but a technique for expressing those thoughts. While Lewis was never afraid of defending the clearly defined dogmas of the Church, he found he could not treat prayer in the same way. Early in 1963 it occurred to him that he might use once again the semi-fictional method which had worked so well for *The Screwtape Letters* and *The Great Divorce*. After this his *Letters to Malcolm: Chiefly on Prayer* (1963) fairly wrote itself. The book was finished in April.

While he was writing *Letters to Malcolm*, the religious world of England was suddenly caught up in what Adrian Hastings, in his *History of English Christianity 1920–1990*, called a mood of 'heady and optimistic novelty' (p. 536). *The Observer* newspaper launched one of the biggest 'media events' of all time. Nearly a million people bought their paper on 17 March so that they could read a special extract from the Bishop of Woolwich's (J.A.T. Robinson) *Honest to God*, in which he stated that if Christianity is to mean anything in the future to more than 'a tiny religious remnant' it would have to learn a new language in which 'the most fundamental categories of our theology – of God, of the super-natural, and of religion itself – must go into the melting.' He suggested that we are even called to a 'Copernican Revolution' in which 'the God of traditional theology' must be given up 'in any form'.

Lewis was one of several *The Observer* asked to comment on the book, and for their issue of 24 March he wrote a piece beginning

> The Bishop of Woolwich will disturb most of us Christian laymen less than he anticipates. We have long abandoned belief in a God who sits on a throne in a localized heaven. We call that belief anthropomorphism, and it was officially condemned before our time. There is something about this in Gibbon.

In his *History*, Adrian Hastings went on to say:

> It is possible that without the almost fortuitous publicity...the book might never have made the national, and indeed inter-national impression that it did. It went through four impres-sions that March and nearly a million copies were sold within three years. Only the Bible could rival it. English religion of the 1960s will always remain more associated with *Honest to God* than with any other book ...
>
> In this, as in several of his other books, John Robinson was with little doubt the most effective writer of popular religious literature since C.S. Lewis, if in many ways Lewis's opposite. Both were highly persuasive. Lewis was a man for the fifties, suspicious of modernity, unwilling to allow the smallest particle of traditional doctrine to be thrown overboard unexamined. Robinson was a man for the sixties, apparently willing to de-mythologize almost anything of which modernity might conceivably be suspicious (p. 537).

Various magazines pleaded with Lewis to give more time to Bishop Robinson's book, but his reason for refusing is found in a letter of 29 April to Edward Dell of *The Episcopalian* in New York. 'A good deal of my utility, ' he said, 'has depended on my having kept out of all dog-fights between professional schools of "Christian" thought. I'd sooner preserve that abstinence to the end.'

Before Lewis went home for the Easter Vacation he planned a trip to his native Ireland. As he explained to Arthur, he could no longer carry his own bag, and he was bringing Douglas with him. Eventually it was decided that he, Warnie and Douglas would go over on 15 July. 'Bravo!' he wrote on 22 March after Arthur had found them rooms. 'We're both too old to let our remaining chances slip!' (**TST**).

Unfortunately, by the time Lewis arrived home from Cambridge on Friday, 7 June, Warnie had anticipated the trip and was already in Ireland. That afternoon he gave tea to a young man from North Carolina, Walter Hooper, who was teaching in the University of Kentucky. They had been corresponding since 1954, and during the weeks that followed Lewis saw a great deal of him at The Kilns, and he took him along to the meetings of the Inklings. Lewis enjoyed a number of treats during the summer, including dining with friends at The Old Swan in Minster Lovell (20 June) and at Studley Priory (26 June). Certainly one of the most memorable was a visit to Cirencester on 29 June to hear Donald Swann's and David Marsh's *Perelandra*. 'He loved it when he heard it,' Donald Swann wrote in *Swann's Way* (chapter 11):

> The first performance took place in a beautiful country house in Cirencester. He came with his friend Dr Havard, the doctor character in the book who packs Ransom into the spacecraft when he sets off for Perelandra. It was sung by myself at the piano together with a team of singers who exemplified parts of it. Later he wrote that it moved him to tears and I know it would have been the most wonderful collaboration if we could have reached the point where he fed his ideas to producers and directors.

The old trouble with his heart flared up in July. On the day he was to have left for his holiday, 15 July, Lewis went to the Acland Nursing Home for an examination. Immediately upon getting there he had a heart attack and went into a coma. The doctors informed the Farrers that Lewis was dying, and they alerted other friends. At two o'clock the next afternoon the Rev. Michael Watts of the Church of St Mary Magdalen gave him

Extreme Unction, the Church's practice of anointing with oil when the patient is *in extremis*.

To everyone's surprise, an hour later Lewis woke from his coma and asked for his tea. He assumed he had been asleep for only a few minutes, and had no notion of what had happened. Over the next two weeks in the Acland he improved, and he saw many visitors including Tolkien and Maureen, who had just become by inheritance Lady Dunbar of Hempriggs, with a castle and estate in Scotland. When George Sayer visited him in the Acland on 18 July, Lewis, he said, 'made a reference to Mrs Moore as if she were still living, and I saw that he was suffering from delusion.' In *Jack* 22, he goes on to say:

> He then asked me if I had met Walter Hooper. 'I've engaged him as my secretary,' he said. 'I want you to like him. I want all my friends to like him. He is a young American. Very devoted and charming. He is almost too anxious to please, but no fool. Certainly not a fool. I must have someone in the house when I go home. Warnie has deserted me and David and Douglas have gone away. There will be hundreds of letters. I must have a secretary.

Attempts were made by George Sayer and the Farrers to contact Warnie, but without success. However, when Lewis went home on 6 August, he had Hooper and a male nurse, Alec Ross, in case he was taken ill during the night. Lewis realized that he would not be able to return to Cambridge and, after resigning his post, he sent Douglas and Walter Hooper to Cambridge on 14 August to clear his college rooms and sort out his books and papers. Not since 1925 had he had all his many books and other belongings in one place, and this meant disposing of many things and rearranging The Kilns. Nevertheless, it was accomplished and Lewis now awaited anxiously for Warnie to return. Writing to Sister Penelope on 17 September, he said:

> I was unexpectedly revived from a long coma – and perhaps the almost continuous prayers of my friends did it – but it would have been a luxuriously easy passage and one almost…regrets having the door shut in one's face. Ought we to honour Lazarus rather than Stephen as the protomartyr? To be brought back and have all one's dying to do *again* was rather hard.
>
> If you die first, and if 'prison visiting' is allowed, come down and look me up in Purgatory.
>
> It *is* all rather fun – solemn fun – isn't it? (L).

Meanwhile, Walter Hooper had to return to the United States to teach one final term before rejoining Lewis in January, and Douglas returned to Applegarth. David was away as well. He had now left the North West London Talmudical College and gone to New York. There he studied at the Yeshiva Rabbi Chaim Berlin, founded in 1939 by the eminent rabbinic scholar, Rabbi Isaac Hutner.

Still, this left Alec Ross, Paxford and, during the day, Mrs Miller. Then, at the end of September Warnie returned and they settled down quite comfortably. His retirement was announced in *The Times* of 14 October:

> Professor C.S. Lewis has resigned because of ill health his appointment as Professor of Medieval and Renaissance English at Cambridge and his fellowship at Magdalene College...
>
> He said he could be driven in a car but he could not walk more than a short distance and was unable to climb stairs. 'It could be very much worse, at least it does not hurt like toothache,' he said ...
> He is now correcting the proofs of the 'Discarded Image' – 'a sort of background to medieval literature,' he said. 'I always have a hundred major projects in mind. It is nice to have leisure and I may be able to get down to all those books I have never written' (p. 12).

During the autumn Father Head came twice a week to give Lewis Communion, and he had visits from many old friends. Roger Lancelyn Green spent the night of 26 September at The Kilns and on leaving the next day he was so certain this was 'goodbye' indeed that he groped his way down Kiln Lane in tears. Another visitor was Tolkien who came with his son John, a Catholic priest. Recalling the event, Father Tolkien said:

> We drove over to The Kilns for what turned out to be a very excellent time together for about an hour. I remember the conversation was very much about the *Morte d'Arthur* and whether trees died (**TJB**, p. 110).

However, the final picture of Lewis must come from his beloved brother, Warnie. In his **Memoir** he wrote:

> Once again – as in the earliest days – we could turn for comfort only to each other. The wheel had come full circle: once again we were together in the little end room at home, shutting out from our talk the ever-present knowledge that the holidays were ending, that a

new term fraught with unknown possibilities awaited us both.

Jack faced the prospect bravely and calmly. 'I have done all I wanted to do, and I'm ready to go,' he said to me one evening. Only once did he show any regret or reluctance: this was when I told him that the morning's mail included an invitation to deliver the Romanes lecture. An expression of sadness passed over his face, and there was a moment's silence: then 'Send them a very polite refusal.'

Friday, 22 November 1963, began much as other days: there was breakfast, then letters and the crossword puzzle. After lunch he fell asleep in his chair: I suggested that he would be more comfortable in bed, and he went there. At four I took in his tea and found him drowsy but comfortable. Our few words then were the last: at five-thirty I heard a crash and ran in, to find him lying unconscious at the foot of his bed. He ceased to breathe some three or four minutes later.

Lewis's funeral was held at the parish church on 26 November. Many of his friends failed to hear of Lewis's death in time to go because President John F. Kennedy also died on 22 November, and the newspapers were mainly given over to him. *The Times* of 27 November (p. 14) published this record of the funeral:

The funeral of Prof. C.S. Lewis took place yesterday at Holy Trinity, Headington Quarry, Oxford. The Rev. R.E. Head officiated, assisted by the Rev. E.J. Payne and the lesson was read by Dr A.M. Farrer, Warden of Keble College. Among those present were:- Mr Douglas Gresham (stepson), Lady Dunbar, Mr Leonard Blake, Miss J. Wakeman, the President and Vice President of Magdalen College, Mr P.C. Bayley (representing the Master and Fellows of University College), Prof. J.R.R. Tolkien, Mr Christopher Tolkien, Prof. John Lawlor, Dr N. Zernov, Commander J.H. Dundas-Grant, Dr R.E. Havard, Mr O. Barfield, Mr G.S. Sayer, Mr A.C. Harwood, Mr F. Paxford, the Rev. G.C. Matthews, the Rev. P.W. Bide, the Rev. K.C. Thompson and the Rev. T.C. Stiff.

On his tombstone Warnie had cut those words which were found on the Shakespearian calendar the day their mother died – 'Men must endure their going hence.'

Since his death thousands of pages have been written about Lewis, his work, and his world. Because it is wise to be guided, at least in part, by those who knew Lewis and lived in that same world, the last words should be reserved for Austin Farrer. The occasion was a Memorial Service for C.S. Lewis held in the Chapel of Magdalen College on 7 December 1963:

> His characteristic attitude to people in general was one of consideration and respect. He did his best for them and he appreciated them. He paid you the compliment of attending to your words. He did not pretend to read your heart. He was endlessly generous. He gave without stint, to all who seemed to care for them, the riches of his mind and the effort of his wit: and where there was need, he gave his money. I will not say what I know about his charities. When he had entered into any relationship his patience and his loyalty were inexhaustible. He really was a Christian – by which I mean, he never thought he had the right to stop.
>
> As he gave, so he took. Everything went into that amazing capacity of mind, his living friends as much as the authors on his shelves. Not to name those who are still with us, his debts in personal wisdom and in literary inspiration to his wife and to Charles Williams were visible to all. He had no affectation of originality. He did not need it.
>
> I must not let myself be led into a panegyric, still less a critique, of his writings. You will estimate them, and are free to estimate them very variously; and what another generation will say, who can guess? Perhaps the force of his style, the concreteness of his invention, and the solidity of his scholarship are unlikely to lack appreciators. But it is not the work of Lewis's pen, it is the work of God's fingers that we are to praise. Truly He has made man in His image, and where the lineaments are visible he will glorify the maker.
>
> The life which Lewis lived with zest he surrendered with composure. He was put almost beside himself by his wife's death; he seemed easy at the approach of his own. He died at the last in a minute. May he everlastingly rejoice in the Mercy he sincerely trusted.[34]

[34] 'In His Image: in commemoration of C.S. Lewis', from Austin Farrer, *The Brink of Mystery,* ed. Charles C. Conti (1976).

CHRONOLOGY OF
C.S. LEWIS'S LIFE

1862 18 May: FLORENCE AUGUSTA ('FLORA') HAMILTON,* mother of C.S. Lewis, born in Queenstown, County Cork, Ireland.

1863 23 August: ALBERT JAMES LEWIS,* father of C.S. Lewis, born in Cork, County Cork, Ireland.

1894 29 August: Marriage of **Albert James Lewis** and **Florence Augusta ('Flora') Hamilton** at St Mark's, Dundela, Belfast.

1895 16 June: WARREN HAMILTON LEWIS,* C.S. Lewis's brother born.

1898 29 November: CLIVE STAPLES LEWIS born.

1899 29 January: **Lewis baptized** in St Mark's,‡ Dundela.

1905 21 April: Lewis family moves into 'Little Lea'.‡

1908 23 August: **Death of Flora Lewis**.

1908 18 September: **Lewis** enrolled at Wynyard School.

1910 September–December: **Lewis** at Campbell College,‡ Belfast.

1911 January: **Lewis** enrolled at Cherbourg House,‡ Malvern. He ceases to be a Christian.

1913 September: **Lewis** enrolled at Malvern College,‡ Malvern.

1914 19 September: **Lewis** meets WILLIAM T. KIRKPATRICK* at Great Bookham, Surrey, and is tutored by him until 20 March 1917.

30 September: **Warren** made Second Lieutenant in Royal Army Service Corps.

4 November: **Warren** sent to France with 4th Company 7th Divisional Train, British Expeditionary Force.

6 December: **Lewis confirmed** at St Mark's, Dundela.

1917 29 April: **Lewis** at University College,‡ Oxford.

8 June: Joins Army and billeted in Keble College with E.F.C. 'PADDY' MOORE*. First meetings with MRS JANIE MOORE*.

25 September: Gazetted into Somerset Light Infantry.

Paddy Moore joins Rifle Brigade and sent to France.

17 November: **Lewis** crosses to France.

     29 November: Arrives in Trenches.

1918 1–28 February: **Lewis** in hospital at Le Tréport.

     24 March: **Paddy Moore** missing in action.

     15 April: **Lewis** wounded in Battle of Arras.

     April: **Paddy Moore** reported dead.

     25 May: **Lewis** arrives Endsleigh Palace Hospital, London.

     25 June–17 November: Convalesces in English hospitals.

     11 November: Armistice signed.

     23 December: Arrives home.

1919 13 January: **Lewis** arrives back in Oxford.

     Mrs Moore and **Maureen*** find rooms in Oxford.

     20 March: *Spirits in Bondage* published.

1920 31 March: **Lewis** takes First in Classical Honour Moderations‡ and begins reading *Literae Humaniores*.‡

1921 24 May: **Lewis** wins Chancellor's Prize for an English Essay.

1922 22 April: **Lewis** begins *Dymer,* poem in rhyme royal.

     1 August: **Lewis** and **Moores** move into 'Hillsboro', 14 Holyoake Road, Headington, where they were to live most of the time until 1930.

     4 August: **Lewis** takes First in *Literae Humaniores*.

     October: **Lewis** begins reading English Language and Literature.‡

1923 16 July: **Lewis** takes First in English Language and Literature.

1924 14 October: **Lewis** gives first lectures in University of Oxford on 'The Good, its position among values'.

1925 20 May: **Lewis** elected Fellow of Magdalen College.‡

1926 23 January: **Lewis** gives first lecture in English School on 'Some Eighteenth-Century Precursors of the Romantic Movement'.

     11 May: First recorded meeting with J.R.R. TOLKIEN.*

     18 September: *Dymer* published.

     21 December–8 January: **Lewis, Warren** and **Albert** together for last time.

1927 11 April: **Warren** sails for China.

1928 2 May: **Albert** retires.

     17 October: **Lewis** begins lectures on 'The Romance of the Rose and its Successors'.

1929 25 July: **Albert** found to have cancer.

     13 August–22 September: **Lewis** nurses father.

     25 September: **Death of Albert Lewis.**

1930 24 February: **Warren** leaves Shanghai for home.

     4 March: While standing before the Dibutsu Buddha at Kamakura in Japan **Warren** becomes convinced of the truth of Christianity.

16 April: **Warren** arrives back in England.

23–24 April: **Lewis** and **Warren** at 'Little Lea' for last time.

11 October: **Lewis** and family move into **The Kilns**.‡

1931 9 May: **Warren** returns to belief in Christianity.

19 September: after talk with **Tolkien** and HUGO DYSON,* **Lewis** *'nearly* certain' Christianity true.

28 September: **Lewis** certain 'that Jesus Christ is the Son of God'.

9 October: **Warren** leaves for second tour of duty in China.

1932 18 January: **Lewis** begins lectures on 'Prolegomena to Medieval Poetry'.

15–29 August: Writes *The Pilgrim's Regress*.

14 December: **Warren** arrives home.

21 December: **Warren** retires from RASC and moves into The Kilns.

1933 25 May: *The Pilgrim's Regress* published.

Since early 1930s **Lewis** and **Tolkien** were members of a club at University College called THE INKLINGS.‡ When it ended in 1933 they transferred the name to circle of friends who gathered about **Lewis** in Magdalen.

1934 31 July–31 August: **Lewis**, **Mrs Moore** and **Maureen** in Ireland.

26 August: **Mrs Moore** meets the Lewis Family.

1936 Spring: **Lewis** meets CHARLES WILLIAMS.*

21 May: Publication of *The Allegory of Love*.

1938 23 September: *Out of the Silent Planet* published.

1939 1 September: Germany invades Poland.

2 September: First evacuated children arrive at The Kilns.

3 September: **War declared**.

4 September: **Warren** recalled to active service.

7 September: **Charles Williams** moves with OUP to Oxford.

October: **Warren** at Le Havre, France.

1940 25 April (Thursday): **First weekly Inklings meeting**.

May: **Warren** evacuated from Dunkirk to Wales.

21 July: **Lewis** conceives the idea for *The Screwtape Letters*.

16 August: **Warren** transferred to Reserve of Officers and returns to Oxford.

18 October: *The Problem of Pain* published.

1941 April: First talk to **Royal Air Force**.

2 May: First *Screwtape Letter* published in *The Guardian*.‡

8 June: 'The Weight of Glory' preached in St Mary's, Oxford.

6–27 August: Four talks on 'Right and Wrong' (Book I of *Mere Christianity*) given over BBC.

1942 11 January–15 February: Talks on 'What Christians Believe' (Book II of *Mere Christianity*) given over BBC.

26 January: First meeting of **Oxford University Socratic Club**.‡

9 February: *The Screwtape Letters* (the book) published.

20 September–8 November: 'Christian Behaviour' (Book III of *Mere Christianity*) talks given over BBC.

13 July: *Broadcast Talks* published.

1943 24–26 February: **Lewis** gives Riddell Memorial Lectures, later published as *The Abolition of Man*.

19 April: *Christian Behaviour* published.

20 April: *Perelandra* published.

1944 22 February–4 April: Seven talks on 'Beyond Personality' (Book IV of *Mere Christianity*) given over BBC.

9 October: *Beyond Personality* published.

10 November: First instalment of *The Great Divorce* appears in *The Guardian*.

1945 9 May: End of World War II.

15 May: Death of **Charles Williams**.

16 August: *That Hideous Strength* published.

1946 14 January: *The Great Divorce* published.

28 June: **Lewis** made honorary Doctor of Divinity by University of St Andrews.

1947 12 May: *Miracles* published.

8 September: **Lewis** on cover of *Time* magazine.

1948 2 February: G.E.M. Anscombe's* 'Reply' to *Miracles* at Socratic Club.

Summer: after a brief start in 1939, **Lewis** begins to write *The Lion, the Witch and the Wardrobe*.

Elected Fellow of Royal Society of Literature.

1949 20 October: Last Thursday evening meeting of **Inklings**.

1950 10 January: **Lewis** receives letter from JOY DAVIDMAN GRESHAM.

29 January: **Mrs Moore** retires to nursing home.

16 October: *The Lion, the Witch and the Wardrobe* published.

1951 12 January: **Mrs Moore dies.**

1952 August: **Joy Gresham** sails from New York to Liverpool.

22 September: **Lewis** made Honorary Doctor.

24 September: **Lewis** meets **Joy Gresham** over lunch in Eastgate Hotel.

November: **Joy** dines with **Lewis** twice in Magdalen College.

December: **Joy** spends two-week Christmas visit at The Kilns with **Lewis** and **Warren**.

1953 3 January: **Joy Gresham** returns to the United States.

30 October: **Warren**'s *The Splendid Century* published.

November: **Joy** returns to England with sons, DAVID* and DOUGLAS* and takes a house in London.

18–21 December: **Joy** and sons with **Lewis** at The Kilns.

1954 4 June: **Lewis** accepts Chair of Medieval and Renaissance English at Cambridge University.

5 August: **Joy** divorced from WILLIAM GRESHAM.

16 September: Publication of *English Literature in the Sixteenth Century*.

29 November: **Lewis** gives Inaugural Lecture at Cambridge.

3 December: **Lewis's** last tutorial in Magdalen College.

1955 7 January: **Lewis** takes up residence in Magdalene College.‡

Lent Term: 'Prolegomena to the Study of Our Earlier Poetry' lectures in Cambridge.

July: elected member of The British Academy.

August: **Joy** and sons move to 10 Old High Street, Headington, Oxford.

19 September: *Surprised by Joy* published.

1956 23 April: **Lewis** and **Joy Gresham** married in Registry Office.

19 October: **Joy** taken to Wingfield-Morris Hospital suffering from cancer.

December: **Joy** transferred to Churchill Hospital.

1957 21 March: **Lewis** and **Joy married** in Wingfield-Morris Hospital by THE REV. PETER BIDE.* **Bide** also performs healing service for **Joy** who is believed to be dying.

April: **Joy** moved to The Kilns.

December: **Joy** is able to walk again.

1958 June: **Joy's** cancer diagnosed as arrested.

July: **Lewis** and **Joy** spend ten days in Ireland.

1959 26 March: **Lewis** elected Honorary Fellow of University College, Oxford.

13 May: **Lewis** made Doctor of Letters by Manchester University.

June: **Lewis** on Commission for Revision of the Psalter.

October: **Joy's** cancer returns.

1960 28 March: *The Four Loves* published.

3–14 April: **Lewis** and **Joy** in **Greece**.

13 July: **Death of Joy Davidman Lewis**.

August: **Lewis** writes *A Grief Observed*.

1961 24 June: **Lewis** diagnosed as having enlarged prostate gland.

2 July: Doctors decide operation too dangerous.

October: **Lewis** too ill to teach.

1962 April: **Lewis** returns to Cambridge.
Summer: writes *The Discarded Image*.
Lewis given Honorary Doctorate by University of Dijon.

1963 January–April: **Lewis** writes *Letters to Malcolm*.
He is given Honorary Doctorate by University of Lyon.
7 June: he returns to Oxford for summer.
15 July: goes to hospital with heart attack.
6 August: returns home from hospital.
22 November: **Death of C.S. Lewis**.

1973 9 April: **Death of Warren Hamilton Lewis**.

WRITINGS

JUVENILIA

⋰⋱

Boxen

BOXEN: THE IMAGINARY WORLD OF THE YOUNG C.S. LEWIS (1985)

Background

I: Animal-Land, India and Boxen

The Lewis family moved to 'Little Lea'‡ on the outskirts of Belfast in April 1905, and it was there that C.S. 'Jack' Lewis wrote his first stories of an imaginary world. We learn from *Surprised by Joy* I that the earliest stories, about a medieval 'Animal-Land', were written in about 1906 when he was seven or so. At the same time, his brother, Warnie, had made India 'his country'. Gradually their literary tastes were combined and 'Animal-Land' and 'India' became 'Boxen'. As Lewis explained in **SBJ** I:

> The Animal-Land which came into action in the holidays when my brother was at home was a modern Animal-Land; it had to have trains and steamships if it was to be a country shared with him. It followed, of course, that the medieval Animal-Land about which I wrote my stories must be the same country at an earlier period; and of course the two periods must be properly connected ...
>
> Then Animal-Land had to be geographically related to my brother's India, and India consequently lifted out of its place in the real world. We made it an island, with its north coast running along the back of the Himalayas; between it and Animal-Land my brother rapidly invented the principal steamship routes. Soon there was a whole world and a map of that world.

Lewis added a very important caution in **SBJ** I about his juvenilia. 'For readers of my children's books,' he said, 'the best way of putting this would be to say that Animal-Land had nothing whatever in common with Narnia except the anthropomorphic beasts. Animal-Land, by its whole quality, excluded the least hint of wonder.'

II: The Great Boxonians

The Boxen stories are well stocked with memorable characters. Those the Lewis brothers seemed to love best, and which appear in most of the later stories, are **Lord Big** (a frog), the two kings under his control, **Benjamin VII** and **Hawki V** (the first a rabbit, and the other a man), and a young naval officer, **James Bar** (a bear). Boxen had a 'Damerfesk' or Parliament which had only a single chamber over which the kings presided. However 'effective control' of the Damerfesk was not in the hands of the kings, but in those of

> an all-important functionary known as the Littlemaster ... [who] was a Prime Minister, a judge, and if not always Commander-in-Chief ... certainly always a member of the General Staff ... The office was held at that time by ... a Frog – of powerful personality. Lord Big brought to his task one rather unfair advantage; he had been the tutor of the two young kings and continued to hold over them a quasi-parental authority. Their spasmodic efforts to break his yoke were, unhappily, more directed to the evasion of his enquiry into their private pleasures than to any serious political end. As a result Lord Big, immense in size, resonant of voice, chivalrous (he was the hero of innumerable duels), stormy, eloquent and impulsive, almost was the state (**SBJ** VI).

III: The Boxen Manuscripts

In 1927 Lewis went through the texts of the Animal-Land and Boxen stories and decided to write an 'Encyclopedia Boxoniana'. While this was never completed, the portion he wrote contains a 'Chronological Table' of Boxen history which runs from 1200 to 1909. It also provides the best guide we have to the number of stories which he was able to put his hands on in 1927. Some had been lost before it was written, and other stories were lost between 1927 and the time of Warnie Lewis's death in 1973. Those which survive comprise seven manuscripts from the 'Animal-Land' period, and six manuscripts from the late Boxen period.

(a) Animal-Land Stories

(1) The King's Ring
(2) Manx Against Manx
(3) The Relief of Murry
(4) History of Mouse-Land from Stone-Age to Bublish I
(5) History of Animal-Land
(6) The Chess Monograph
(7) The Geography of Animal-Land

(b) Boxen Stories

(1) Boxen: or Scenes from Boxonian Life
(2) The Locked Door and Than-Kyu
(3) The Sailor
(4) Tararo
(5) The Life of Lord John Big
(6) Littera Scripta Manet

Summary

I: The Animal-Land Histories and Stories

The Animal-Land manuscripts and the *Encyclopedia Boxoniana*, are all very short. (1) *The King's Ring*, a play about the theft of the crown jewels of Animal-Land by James Hit in the reign of Benjamin I, is the oldest text we have and it was probably written in 1906. (2) *Manx Against Manx* takes its name from the tailless cats of the Isle of Man. This story is about Sir Peter Mouse, a detective, and his search for a tailless mouse named 'Mr No-Tail'. (3) *The Relief of Murry* is also about Sir Peter Mouse albeit set in medieval Animal-Land. It concerns the siege of Murry by cats. (4) The *History of Mouse-Land from Stone-Age to Bublish I* begins with the Stone Age of Mouse-Land in 55 BC. The mouse tribes lose many of their people by fighting with one another. In 1216 they meet some Indians who, when asked 'how they got on without fighting each other's men' explain that 'they chose a man to rule them all and called him Rajah or king.'

(5) The *History of Animal-Land* retraces Animal-Land history from the very beginning up until present times and the birth of Lord Big. (6) *The Chess Monograph* describes what Lewis calls in the *Encyclopedia Boxoniana* 'the *risorgimento* of the Chess under Flaxman, and the foundation of the first Chessaries.' Until the founding of these 'chessaries' the Chessmen were 'few, scattered, unhoused, haunted, disliked, and penniless.' It

comes as a pleasant surprise to find the young Lewis comparing his Chessmen to the Jews. 'Just as the Jews were treated in England at the time,' he said, 'so were Chessmen treated, in Animal-Land, India, Dolfin-Land, Prussia, Pongee, and a great many more places, which I could mention, had I paper and time.' (7) *The Geography of Animal-Land* is a very short manuscript which provides details of the capital, the surface, the rivers and the thirteen provinces that make up Animal-Land.

II: The Boxen 'Novels'

With (1) *Boxen: or Scenes from Boxonian Life* we are miles from the early stories of Animal-Land, and Warren Lewis was right to describe them in his **Memoir** as 'a creditable performance for a boy not yet thirteen.' 'This narrative,' Lewis said in the *Encyclopedia Boxoniana*, 'in the form of a novel, deals primarily with the history of Orring's League in the early years of Hawki V and Benjamin VII, and the political rise of Polonius Green.'

The story opens with Lord Big, Benjamin and Hawki on the island of Fortressa. Lord Big learns that an elderly lizard named Orring, the Member of Parliament from the province of Piscia, is behind a plan to throw all the present 'Clique' or members of government out of office, and is using bribery to bring it about. Lord Big and the kings hurry back to Murry, the capital city of Boxen. There, as the tale of Orring's bribery unfolds, Lord Big encounters Polonius Green, 'a parrot of low birth, and the owner of a line of colliers.' Following a vote in Parliament, the old Clique is broken up and younger and more energetic members are elected – one of whom is Polonius Green.

(2) *The Locked Door and Than-Kyu. The Locked Door* is a sequel to *Boxen*, and it deals with the Tracity War. The story opens with Their Majesties having breakfast with Lord Big at the Palace Calcutta and this portrait of the threesome:

> The Little Master was a stout frog of massive build, and on the wrong side of 60. His expression was that of a naturally masterful person, given power by external circumstances, but slightly pompous and inclined to worry over small affairs: in appearance he was handsome, and was clad faultlessly in the fashion of thirty years ago. The Rajah was a young man of about 35, happy, careless, and humorous. The rabbit was like his fellow monarch but slightly stouter and not so agile (I).

In Parliament that morning the low-born Polonius Green infuriates the Little Master by proposing that there be a Chessman in the Clique. This race of people, which dates back to the early days of Animal-Land, no longer sounds like the Jews of the earlier story, but Germans. Their 'Frater Senior' is called Von Quinclë. Lord Big is infuriated with the suggestion and the Kings evict Polonius Green from the Clique.

Soon Boxen shipowners learn that their trading contracts with the Tracity Islands' Chessary have been cancelled and given to Polonius Green. It is now clear why he wanted a Chess in the Boxen Clique, and the anger of the nation is turned against him and the Chess. The government insists that the Chess honour their original agreement, but when they refuse Boxen prepares for war. Lord Big and the Kings, aboard the Gunboat *Thrush*, lead an expedition to the largest of the Tracity Islands. Von Quinclë refuses to reinstate the old trade regulation and war is declared. However, before it proceeds very far the Chess discover that Polonius Green had refused their offer of a trading monopoly. The war ends with Von Quinclë 'thoroughly reconciled to the Boxonians' (XIX).

(3) *Than-Kyu: A Sketch* relates an adventure of Lord Big on the island of Than-Kyu, an obscure and independent state between Turkey and Pongee. There, amidst the 'gleaming white domes and minarets', he manages to insult the island's most important people, and is forced to leave.

(4) *The Sailor: A Study* deals with the life of naval officers on *T.M.S. Greyhound*. It opens with the arrival in Murry of a young marine officer, Alexander Cottle, 'a strong and wiry young cat'. He is one of the officers and crew taking over the newly-built *Greyhound*. Immediately upon arrival he receives a summons to go ashore for a meeting with Oliver Vant, the First Lord of the Admiralty, Field Marshall Fortescue, head of the war office, and Lord Big. They believe the country needs 'reforming', and Lord Big thinks it should begin with the Navy, where the 'incompetency and immorality of individuals' is particularly bad. Young officers are being selected to reform the 'tone' of the ships and regiments, and Cottle has been chosen as their agent aboard the *Greyhound*.

Cottle begins his reforms just as the *Greyhound* sets off into freezing 'Clarendonian waters' in the northernmost part of the Animal-Land world. He soon makes an enemy of James Bar by causing his work load to be doubled, but even Bar comes to admire Cottle for his bravery, for during a storm he climbs out to the bridge to rescue a quick-firing gun before the water rises to the heights of the quick-firers.

We move next to Danphabel, near Murray, where we meet an owl named Viscount Puddiphat. He is the owner of numerous music halls, and he is very fond of James Bar. The Viscount meets Bar strolling arm in arm with Lt Cottle and he invites them to a party he is giving that evening. Bar explains that Cottle has reformed the navy and that 'we must decline your hospitality if it entails mixing with ... low actresses.' Besides this, the *Greyhound* is sailing that evening at midnight, and they must be on it. In reality, one of the *Greyhound*'s officers has persuaded Cottle to drop his idea of reform, but all agree that it is important when on shore to *appear* to be reformed. The two young friends go to the Viscount's supper party with the intention of staying a short time, but are 'held entranced by the conversation of the gay owl and his theatrical friends' and soon twelve o'clock has struck. That moment Lord Big and Marshall Fortescue are heard at the door. Bar and Cottle escape and board a train. They do not get far because of a strike on the railway but this works in their favour because many sailors missed the *Greyhound* because of it. Bar and Cottle are accepted back and we learn that they 'have since been good friends if not good officers and they manage to hit off a golden mean between Bar's desperate exploits and Cottle's absurd idealism.'

Reviews

Some reviewers were surprised that the Boxen tales are notably different from the Narnian stories, but nearly all were favourably impressed. Neil Philip wrote in *British Book News* (July 1985) pp. 437–8: 'This collection of juvenilia has three distinct interests. Firstly, it makes available to students of the writings of C.S. Lewis his earliest known works, about which much has been written by commentators on his work and by Lewis himself ... Secondly, to the ranks of published fiction by children it adds work of particular interest because it was produced by someone who – unlike, say, Daisy Ashford – grew up to be a writer. Thirdly, it allows free admission into an elaborate invented world, of great fascination to those interested in children's imaginative play ... As a child's view of the adult world of politics, the later "novels" offer a shrewd, witty and lively read.' Gregory Wolfe, in *Reflections*, 5 (Winter 1986), p.3, points out that while 'Most children's stories are written by adults trying to think like children; half the pleasure of reading the Boxen tales is that they were written by a child trying to be "grown up" ... The only surprise in *Boxen* is that the stories have no moral ... except, perhaps, that boys will be boys.'

POETRY

❧

Spirits in Bondage, Dymer,
Narrative Poems, Poems,
Collected Poems

SPIRITS IN BONDAGE:
A CYCLE OF LYRICS (1919)

Background

I: First Poems – 1915–17

Lewis's first ambition was to be a poet, and for many years he had his heart firmly set upon this. His poetic creativity seems to have begun shortly after he became a pupil of W. T. Kirkpatrick* in 1914. Mr Kirkpatrick, living in semi-retirement in Great Bookham, Surrey, was described by Lewis in **SBJ** as a 'purely logical entity' (IX), who had left Christianity years before for rationalism. Lewis had already lost the faith before he went to be crammed for Oxford by him, but one of the effects of being tutored by this remarkable man was that Lewis soon found 'the two hemispheres' of his mind in the sharpest contrast. 'On the one side a many-islanded sea of poetry and myth; on the other a glib and shallow "rationalism"' (**SBJ** IX).

When he arrived home at Easter 1915 for his first holiday he turned to his great love, verse, and devoted nearly all his hours to the craft of poetry and its wide variety of metrical forms. It was during this fortnight in Belfast that he wrote two of the romantic lyrics which were to appear in *Spirits in Bondage*. In one of them called 'The Hills of Down' he expresses his love for

> the green hills of Down.
> The soft low hills of Down.

From this time onwards until he went up to Oxford in 1917, Lewis spent much of every holiday writing verse. Fifty-two of the poems written during this two-year period were copied into a notebook bearing the title *The Metrical Meditations of a Cod*, 'Cod' being an Ulster expression of 'humorous and insincere self-deprecation' ('Amn't I the quare oul' cod to be doin' so and so' **LP** IV: 306).

II: Poems Written in Oxford

When Lewis arrived at University College,‡ Oxford, on 26 April 1917 he knew he would soon be in the war, and he had left his *Metrical Meditations* in the safekeeping of Arthur Greeves.* Most of the colleges were being used as hospitals or for billeting cadets, and as soon as he arrived there Lewis joined the Officers' Training Corps. Their military duties were light at the time, and in his spare time he turned to poetry. The poems he wrote during the next few months in Oxford were copied into a notebook he and Arthur were later to refer to as the 'reddy-brown MS book containing "Lullaby" and several other poems'.

On 7 June Lewis joined a cadet battalion and moved into Keble College. 'I am in a strangely productive mood,' he wrote to Arthur on 10 June, 'and spend my few moments of spare time in scribbling verse ... I propose to get together all the stuff I have perpetrated and see if any kind publisher would like to take it. After that, if the fates decide to kill me at the front, I shall enjoy a 9-days' immortality while friends who know nothing about poetry imagine that I must have been a genius' (**TST**).

III: War and Pessimism

There was not enough time for this. After three months of training Lewis went to France as a Second Lieutenant in the Somerset Light Infantry. He arrived at the front lines on 29 November 1917. In December the 1st Somerset Light Infantry was located near Monchy-Le-Preux, and it was while opposing guns sounded around them that Lewis probably composed his 'French Nocturne (Monchy-Le-Preux)'. One stanza of that poem is sufficient to illustrate how the voice of the poet had changed:

> What call have I to dream of anything?
> I am a wolf. Back to the world again,
> And speech of fellow-brutes that once were men
> Our throats can bark for slaughter: cannot sing.

His battalion spent Christmas and New Year under heavy enemy fire at Woringhem. It was almost certainly here that Lewis began writing his 'Apology' and the 'Ode for New Year's Day'. In the first he explains to the goddess, Despoina, why he cannot 'build a heaven of dreams in *real* hell'. The dejection in his 'Ode for New Year's Day' is even greater than that of the 'Apology' because Lewis now sees that the evil God who allows all this destruction is not the same as the 'Good'. In fact, 'Good' itself is only a 'phantom' created by 'our own hearts'.

Lewis was wounded in the Battle of Arras on 15 April 1918. Later, in a hospital in Etaples, he returned to poetry and quite a new interest for him – Philosophy. He was very impressed by John Locke' s *Essay Concerning Human Understanding*, in which the author insists that pure reality cannot be grasped by the human mind, that substance is 'an uncertain supposition of we know not what'. During his years with Mr Kirkpatrick, Lewis had not thought much about God but now, with so many of his friends either killed or missing, his outlook changed. 'You'll be surprised to hear that my views at present are getting almost monastic about the lusts of the flesh,' he wrote to Arthur on 23 May. 'They seem to me to extend the domination of matter over us: and out here where I see spirit continually dodging matter (shells, bullets, animal fears, animal pains) I have formulated my equation Matter = Nature = Satan. And on the other side Beauty, the only spiritual and non-natural thing I have yet found' (**TST**).

IV. 'Spirits in Bondage' Takes Shape

Later that month Lewis was moved to Endsleigh Palace Hospital in London. On 3 June he asked Arthur to send him the 'reddy-brown MS book' because 'I have decided to copy out all my work ... as a step towards possible publishing.' 'I believe in no God,' he reminded him, 'but I do believe that I have in me a spirit, a chip, shall we say, of universal spirit; and that, since all good and joyful things are spiritual and non-material, I must be careful not to let matter ... get too great hold on me, and dull the one spark I have' (**TST**). At the end of June he was moved to Ashton Court, near Bristol, where he was to be for nearly four months. It was here that his collection of poems took shape. It was sent to William Heinemann in London who said he was 'pleased to be its publisher'. In a letter to Arthur Greeves of 12 September 1918 Lewis said that his volume of poems, *Spirits in Bondage*, was 'mainly strung round the idea ... that nature is wholly diabolical and malevolent and that God, if He exists, is outside of and in opposition to the cosmic arrangement' (**TST**).

Mr Heinemann and his General Manager, Charles Sheldon Evans, asked Lewis to make a number of small alterations in his poems as well as to send substitutes for those they thought not on a level with the poet's 'best work'. None of the three notebooks the poems were written in has survived, and it is impossible to say exactly which of them each of the poems in *Spirits in Bondage* came from. However, we know that *Spirits in Bondage* contains fourteen poems from *The Metrical Meditations of a Cod* (of which 'Victory', 'Noon', 'Night', 'Star Bath', and 'Sonnet' are the only ones we know by name); one at least, 'Lullaby', is from the 'the reddy-brown MS book'; and the rest are from the notebook of poems written in France and the hospital. Lewis considered a number of possible pseudonyms before deciding on 'Clive Hamilton' – his own first name and his mother's family name.

The War ended on 11 November, and Lewis arrived home on 27 December 1918 to be fêted with champagne by his father* and brother, Warren.* He had been away since October 1917. Following a pleasant Christmas with his family, he returned to Oxford on 13 January 1919. Some months earlier John Galsworthy had seen a typescript of the book, and during his first term back in Oxford one of the poems, 'Death in Battle', appeared in Galsworthy's new periodical, *Reveille*, No 3 (February 1919).

For a long time now Lewis had tried to hide his atheism from his father and brother. Neither was deceived, however, and as they waited for the book to be published they exchanged thoughts about it. Warren complained to his father in a letter of 28 January 1919 that while he knew that his brother's atheism was 'purely academic' no 'useful purpose is served by endeavouring to advertise oneself as an Atheist' (**LP** VI:84). Mr Lewis took a more moderate view, and writing to Warren on 9 March he said, 'He is young and he will learn in time that a man has not absolutely solved the riddle of the heavens above and the earth beneath and the waters under the earth at twenty. I am not going to slop over but I do think that if Oxford does not spoil him … he may write something that men would not willingly let die' (**LP** VI:98). *Spirits in Bondage: A Cycle of Lyrics* by 'Clive Hamilton' was published on 20 March 1919.

Summary

The book opens with a Prologue in which, comparing himself to 'old Phoenician men, to the Tin Isles sailing', Lewis says:

> In my coracle of verses I will sing of lands unknown,
> Flying from the scarlet city where a Lord that knows no pity
> Mocks the broken people praying round his iron throne,
> – Sing about the Hidden country fresh and full of quiet green,
> Sailing over seas uncharted to a port that none has seen.

The volume is divided into three Parts, the first of which is entitled 'The Prison House'. The twenty-one poems which it contains include some light-hearted ones written before Lewis went to France, but most reflect the poet's hatred of the 'Lord that knows no pity'. The poem entitled 'Apology' reflects quite accurately Lewis's beliefs at that time. In it he addresses Despoina – better known as Persephone, the goddess of the underworld :

> Apology
> If men should ask, Despoina, why I tell
> Of nothing glad nor noble in my verse
> To lighten hearts beneath this present curse
> And build a heaven of dreams in real hell ...
>
> How should I sing of them? Can it be good
> To think of glory now, when all is done,
> And all our labour underneath the sun
> Has brought us this – and not the thing we would? ...
>
> But now we wake. The East is pale and cold,
> No hope is in the dawn, and no delight.

'Part II: Hesitation' contains three poems, and in them Lewis writes with admiration, and probably envy, of those things and people who seem untouched by the pessimism he feels. This section contains what is almost certainly one of his finest poems, 'In Praise of Solid People', which begins:

> Thank God that there are solid folk
> Who water flowers and roll the lawn,
> And sit and sew and talk and smoke,
> And snore all through the summer dawn.

In 'Part III: The Escape', which consists of sixteen poems, it is clear that while Lewis is not one of those 'solid folk', he can nevertheless find consolation in those things diabolical Nature and the pitiless Lord have not stripped him of. One of the poems that expresses this best is 'Oxford' which begins:

> It is well that there are palaces of peace
> And discipline and dreaming and desire,
> Lest we forget our heritage and cease
> The Spirit's work – to hunger and aspire.

In the final poem, 'Death in Battle', the poet returns to that escape hinted at in the Prologue. The best thing of all about dying in battle would be that one would finally be – alone. 'Ah, to be ever alone,' he says, and especially if one could wake to find oneself in the 'Country of Dreams'

> Beyond the tide of the ocean, hidden and sunk away,
> Out of the sound of battles, near to the end of day,
> Full of dim woods and streams.

Reviews

Spirits in Bondage received only a few anonymous reviews when it appeared, and included below are the three Albert Lewis preserved in his copy of the poems. The first is from the *Glasgow Herald* (24 March 1919): 'Part of this book voices in a minor key the unrest of man pent in the prison-house of life. Malignant natural powers surround him; if there be any God above he hears not and cares not. All is vanity and vexation of spirit. It is an age-old complaint of man, and, though Mr Holland's [sic] verse is all good, we do not find here any novelty of statement or setting. The other two parts are brighter in outlook, but there is too much general dream-stuff in them. Four poems "In Praise of Solid People", the song on page 73, the delightful verses on "The Ass", and the opening stanzas of "Our Daily Bread" bring us closer to earth, and it is a pleasure to come on these while wandering through a somewhat monotonous world of poetic romance and faerie.'

From *The Times Literary Supplement* (27 March 1919): 'These lyrics are always graceful and polished, and their varied themes are chosen from those which naturally attract poets – the Autumn Morning, Oxford, Lullaby, The Witch, Milton Read Again, and so on. The thought, when closed with, is found rather often not to rise above the commonplace. The piece which most arrested us was "The Satyr".'

From *The Scotsman* (31 March 1919): 'Desperate enough in its opening section, the verses in which play with Satanism in a not uninteresting way [sic], this eloquent, if often bitter, book of lyrical poems takes on a more hopeful tone as it goes on, and, after having found room for pieces in praise of Milton and of Oxford as "The Spirit's Stronghold", celebrates "Death in Battle" as opening the gates upon a "country of dreams" that can give relief to the troublesome thoughts and aspirations touched on in the prior songs. With all its emotional glooming and dissatisfaction, the work is strongly imagined, and never unhealthy, trifling, or affected.'

DYMER (1926)

Background

I: The Prose 'Dymer' of 1916

Lewis left more information about the writing of this poem than he did about any other of his works. In the Preface to the 1950 edition of *Dymer*, which is reprinted in his *Narrative Poems*, he said:

> What I 'found', what simply 'came to me', was the story of a man who, on some mysterious bride, begets a monster: which monster, as soon as it has killed its father, becomes a god. This story arrived, complete, in my mind somewhere about my seventeenth year.

Lewis began writing a prose version of this story during Christmas 1916. He was still a pupil of W.T. Kirkpatrick* and this first version of *Dymer* coincides with the writing of the earliest of the poems in *Spirits in Bondage*. Writing to Arthur Greeves* from Mr Kirkpatrick's house in Surrey, he said on 28 January 1917: 'I can see my way clear to the end of "Dymer" now and will let you have an instalment next Sunday: three more will finish him.'

II: 'Dymer' in Verse: 1918–1920

The prose version of *Dymer* has not survived, but he seems to have finished it before the War intervened and he went off to France with the Somerset Light Infantry. As already noted in the Background to *Spirits in Bondage*, Lewis was wounded in the Battle of Arras in April 1918, and after he returned to England in the next month he convalesced at a number of hospitals. Besides completing *Spirits in Bondage*, his new ideas caused him to begin a revision of *Dymer*. While he was at Perham Down Camp on Salisbury Plain during October and part of November 1918, he began reading Henri Bergson's *L'Évolution Créatrice* and *Energie Spirituelle*. It had, he said in **SBJ** XIII:

> a revolutionary effect on my emotional outlook. Hitherto my whole bent had been toward things pale, remote, and evanescent; the water-colour world of Morris, the leafy recesses of Malory, the twilight of Yeats. The word 'life' had for me pretty much the same associations it had for Shelley in *The Triumph of Life* ... Bergson ... did not abolish my old loves, but he gave me a new one. From him I first learned to relish energy, fertility, and urgency; the resource, the triumphs, and even the insolence of things that grow.

Writing to Arthur from a hospital in Eastbourne on 2 December 1918, he told him about a new version of *Dymer* in verse:

> I have just finished a short narrative, which is a verse version of our old friend 'Dymer', greatly reduced and altered to my new ideas. The main idea is that of development by self-destruction, both of individuals and species (as nature produces man only to conquer her [sic], and man produces a future and higher generation to conquer the ideals of the last, or again as an individual produces a nobler mood to undo all that today's has done). The background proceeds on the old assumption of good *outside and opposed to* the cosmic order. It is written in the metre of Venus and Adonis: 'Dymer' is changed to 'Ask' (you remember Ask and Embla in the Norse myths) and it is in the third person under the title of 'The Redemption of Ask' (**TST**).

Lewis returned to Oxford in January 1919 and took up residence in University College.‡ Though he was very busy reading Classical Moderations‡ and *Literae Humaniores*,‡ he still found time for poetry. He later drew up a chronological account of the creation of *Dymer* which is published as Note I of *Narrative Poems* (1969). Although none of the early versions has survived, we learn that after the prose version of 1916, and the verse version he wrote to Arthur about in December 1918, *Dymer* became a ballad called 'The Red Maid' in 1920. After this he had no more to say about the story for two years.

III: 'Dymer' The Final Version 1922–26

On 1 April 1922 Lewis began keeping a diary – *All My Road Before Me* (**AMR**) – and suddenly he has begun a new version of *Dymer*. On 2 April 1922 he wrote in his diary:

I sat in my own bedroom by an open window in bright sunshine and started a poem on 'Dymer' in rhyme royal.

There are numerous references to the poem in **AMR**, which Lewis kept during 1922–27 when he was much occupied with writing this final version of *Dymer*. It is one of the main sources of information about the day-to-day development of the poem. Of great importance, too, is the Preface Lewis wrote for the 1950 reprint of *Dymer*, hereafter called 'the Preface'. The poem itself was to undergo numerous revisions during 1922–26, but the story itself, that of 'a man who, on some mysterious bride, begets a monster: which monster, as soon as it has killed its father, becomes a god', did not change.

The first canto of *Dymer* was completed on 30 April 1922, and clarifying certain ideas about this Canto in the Preface, he said:

The Platonic and totalitarian state from which Dymer escapes in Canto I was a natural invention for one who detested the state in Plato's *Republic* as much as he liked everything else in Plato, and who was, by temperament, an extreme anarchist. I put into it my hatred of my public school and my recent hatred of the army. But I was also critical of my own anarchism. There had been a time when the sense of defiant and almost drunken liberation which fills the first two acts of *Siegfried* had completely satisfied me. Now, I thought, I knew better. My hero therefore must go through his Siegfried moment in Cantos I and II, and find in Canto IV what really comes of that mood in the end. For it seemed to me that two opposite forces in man tended equally to revolt. The one criticizes and at need defies civilization because it is not good enough, the other stabs it from below and behind because it is already too good for total baseness to endure. The hero who dethrones a tyrant will therefore be first fêted and afterwards murdered by the rabble who feel a disinterested hatred of order and reason as such.

During Lewis's undergraduate years Arthur Greeves had been replaced as a judge of his poetry by friends in Oxford, namely Owen Barfield* and

Cecil Harwood,* and both had read Canto I by the time Lewis ran into Barfield on 24 May 1922. Writing about their meeting in his diary, he said:

> We walked to Wadham gardens and sat under the trees. We began with Christina dreams: I condemned them – the love dream made a man incapable of real love, the hero dream made him a coward. He took the opposite view and a stubborn argument followed.

Amongst the books Lewis was reading at this time were Freud's *Introductory Lectures*, Havelock Ellis's *World of Dreams*, and Jung's *Analytical Psychology*. This new psychology, he said in his Preface, had 'joined forces with the fact that we felt ourselves (as young men always do) to be escaping from the illusions of adolescence, and as a result we were much exercised about the problem of fantasy or wishful thinking.' He goes on to say:

> The 'Christina Dream', as we called it (after Christina Pontifex in Butler's novel), was the hidden enemy whom we were all determined to unmask and defeat. My hero, therefore, had to be a man who had succumbed to its allurements and finally got the better of them ... By the time I wrote *Dymer* I had come under the influence of our common obsession about Christina Dreams, into a state of angry revolt against that spell.

In *Surprised by Joy* Lewis wrote about the central part 'Joy'§ or extreme longing had played in his life. In the early days that longing had been mediated to him by 'the water-colour world of Morris, the leafy recesses of Malory, the twilight of Yeats.' These were now the very images he 'spat upon' because of their encouragement of 'Christina Dreams'. Another early attraction had been the 'Occult'. This had come mainly through the works of Maeterlinck and the early poetry of W.B. Yeats. Lewis had been overawed by Yeats when he met him twice during March 1921. However, by the time he came to write *Dymer* this attraction for the Occult had been lost. 'I was now quite sure,' he said in the Preface, 'that magic or spiritism of any kind was a fantasy and of all fantasies the worst.' Besides this, Lewis had also become, in philosophical terms, an Idealist, and all supernaturalisms were 'equally illusions'. His hero, as he says in the Preface, 'was to be a man escaping from illusion', and he supplies us with this short summary of the poem:

He begins by egregiously supposing the universe to be his friend and seems for a time to find confirmation of his belief. Then he tries, as we all try, to repeat his moment of youthful rapture. It cannot be done; the old Matriarch sees to that. On top of his rebuff comes the discovery of the consequences which his rebelling against the City had produced. He sinks into despair and gives utterance to the pessimism which had, on the whole, been my own view about six years earlier. Hunger and a shock of real danger bring him to his senses and he at last accepts reality. But as he is setting out on the new and soberer life, the shabbiest of all bribes is offered him; the false promise that by magic or invited illusion there may be a short cut back to the one happiness he remembers. He relapses and swallows the bait, but he has grown too mature to be really deceived. He finds that the wish-fulfilment dream leads to the fear-fulfilment dream, recovers himself, defies the Magician who tempted him, and faces his destiny.

Summary

Canto I opens with a description of the Perfect City's effect on Dymer and the other citizens of the place:

> At Dymer's birth no comets scared the nation,
> The public crêche engulfed him with the rest,
> And twenty separate Boards of Education
> Closed round him. He was passed through every test,
> Was vaccinated, numbered, washed and dressed,
> Proctored, inspected, whipt, examined weekly,
> And for some nineteen years he bore it meekly. (6)

Then, without warning, a 'ripple of rude life' (7) caused Dymer to wake from his imprisonment. Swinging his right arm he strikes his lecturer dead. The rest of the class is dazed as Dymer leaves the school and strikes for the open country. There in a field he strips off his regulation clothes and rises up 'mother-naked' (16). By evening, however, he is 'Hungry and cold' (18) and lost in the darkness. The sound of music attracts him, and he seeks the source of it. Eventually, finding 'some pile of building' (30) from which it came, Dymer goes in.

In **Canto II** Dymer, in the palace, discovers many fine clothes. He puts them on and is soon imagining what a figure he will cut when he returns to the Perfect City to free the others. Venturing further into the house he finds a table set. Having a 'hunger in him that was worth/ Ten cities' (13) he eats and drinks with abandon. Then, seeing a 'curtained and low lintelled door' (27) he passes through it into a cool, dark place. He is outside, and finding some pillows on the ground, he lies down. In this darkness a hand suddenly touches his own. He opens wide his arms and 'The breathing body of a girl/ Slid into them' (32).

In **Canto III** Dymer awakes in the forest to find the girl gone. While looking for her he comes upon a palace. Is this the one he was in last night? He attempts to get in but at the top of a stairway a 'dark mass' (11) bars his way. It has 'pale hands of wrinkled flesh,/ Puckered and gnarled with vast antiquity' (12). He tries doorway after doorway in an attempt to find his lover, but whichever way he goes he encounters the old woman, the 'old, old matriarchal dreadfulness' (23).[1] In the end he turns away into the forest.

In **Canto IV** Dymer comes across a dying man and from him he learns that he has been the cause of a rebellion in the Perfect City. 'All in one day,' he says, 'one man and at one blow/ Brought ruin on us all' (16). The initial damage having been caused by Dymer, he tells him about their leader, Bran, whose eyes were 'like a prophet's' and whose 'tongue was never still'. As the dying man recounts the horrors let loose by Bran, Dymer is horrified to learn that he has been the cause of so much murder and madness.

In **Canto V** Dymer wakes the next morning 'Heart-sick with desolation' (7). He cries as he thinks of the 'deeds of Bran' (8). His 'store of happy hours' (9) has vanished, and he believes that his 'whole wealth' has

---

[1] Readers have often wondered what Lewis meant by the 'matriarchal dreadfulness'. Lewis loved the *Nibelungenlied*, a German poem of the 13th century, which embodies the ancient Norse Eddas. He had a particular admiration for Richard Wagner's retelling of it in his opera *The Nibelung's Ring*, and in 1914 he tried writing a poem on the subject (see **TST**, 6 October 1914).

On 23 June 1924 Lewis heard the second part of the opera, *The Valkyrie*, with Cecil Harwood,* who had been reading *Dymer* as it was being written. In the story, which he had read in many versions, Fricka (or Frigg), the wife of Wotan, often disagrees with her husband and she often succeeds in defeating his will. Writing about *The Valkyrie* in his diary of 23 June 1924, Lewis said: 'It is wonderful how in all the long scenes between Wotan and Brynhild or Wotan and Fricka … he really gives us the feeling of assisting at the debates of the gods … In answer to a question of Harwood's about the plot I explained that Fricka was my 'old, old matriarchal dreadfulness' (**AMR**).

passed. In **Canto VI** Dymer, deeply humbled, continues his journey until
he comes to 'an old house, folded round with billowy piles/ Of dark yew
hedge' (5). He sees walking on the green

> a mighty man whose beardless face
> Beneath grey hair shone out so large and mild
> It made a sort of moonlight in the place (7).

This Master Magician – whose physical appearance Lewis says in the
Preface 'owes something to Yeats as I saw him' – invites Dymer in for a
meal. His talk was 'of magic words/ And of the nations in the clouds
above' (15), and he goes on:

> till he had stolen quite away
> Dymer's dull wits and softly drawn apart
> The ivory gates of hope that change the heart (16).

The Magician urges Dymer to tell his story, after which, as Lewis said,
'the shabbiest of all bribes is offered him; the false promise that by magic
or invited illusion there may be a short cut back to the one happiness he
remembers'. 'For broken dreams,' says the Magician, 'the cure is, Dream
again/ And deeper' (24). Dymer 'relapses and swallows the bait', as
Lewis said in the Preface, and drinks from the magic cup.

We learn in **Canto VII** that the Magician is tormented by the stimulant
he has given Dymer, and is rarely able to sleep. Even so, like 'the dog
returning to its vomit' (7) he continues taking it. When Dymer awakes
from his sleep he is pallid with anger. Even though the wild things he met
there whispered 'of Eden-fields long lost by man' (16) he knew even at the
time they were part of his own imagination. He met the girl in his dream
'But every part/ Was what I made it – all that I had dreamed – / No more,
no less: the mirror of my heart' (20). And when Dymer saw that the girl
of his dreams cared nothing whatever about him except for sex 'that
moment snapped the spell' (25). Dymer defies the Magician, and as he
runs from his house there is a 'gun-crack' (33) and he is wounded.

In **Canto VIII** the bleeding Dymer is befriended by the 'bride' he has
longed for. As he reviews his life he realizes he has, all along, loved in
vain: what he loved was not a real woman but a spirit.[2] He looks round to

---

[2] Lewis returned to this theme in the novel he was writing at the time of his
death. In *After Ten Years* (in **OROW=OS**) Menelaus is given a choice between the
beautiful Helen of his dreams, and the faded, but real, Helen he married.

find the woman gone. After this he struggles on until he comes to 'An old lych-gate before a burial yard' (25). In **Canto IX** as Dymer lies dying in the graveyard his spirit ascends and 'Suddenly all round him he could hear/ Sad strings that fretted inconsolably/ And ominous horns that blew far and near/ There broke his human heart' (2).

> And here the well-worn fabric of our life
> Fell from him. Hope and purpose were cut short,
> – Even the blind trust that reaches in mid-strife
> Towards some heart of things. Here blew the mort
> For the world spirit herself. The last support
> Was fallen away – Himself, one spark of soul,
> Swam in unbroken void. He was the whole (4).

In the heavens Dymer meets an armed sentry whose responsibility it is to protect mankind from the 'beasts of the upper air' (8) and in particular a monster who threatens him. Dymer answers that while his own course is run there may be 'some deed still waiting to be done' (10). The sentry, not knowing he is talking to Dymer, relates how on earth 'one swollen with youth' lay with a lady who had 'Made glad the sons of heaven' (13). From this union of mortal with immortal the monster, the 'walker-in-the-night' (13), was born. 'Dymer's the name,' says the sentry, 'This spectre is his son' (14).

Dymer insists on relieving the sentry, and putting on his armour he confronts his offspring – a 'heavy brute ... full of eyes, clinking in scaly rind' (27). The monster succeeds in killing Dymer, and as soon as this happens it becomes a god. That same moment the earth is reborn, and the sentry runs forward to see what has happened. There is Dymer 'dead among the flowers and pinned beneath/ The brute' (33) but the next moment the sentry holds his breath –

> For when he had gazed hard with steady eyes
> Upon the brute, behold, no brute was there,
> But someone towering large against the skies,
> A wing'd and sworded shape, whose foam-like hair
> Lay white about its shoulders, and the air
> That came from it was burning hot. The whole
> Pure body brimmed with life, as a full bowl (34).

And from the distant corner of day's birth
He heard clear trumpets blowing and bells ring,
A noise of great good coming into earth
And such a music as the dumb would sing
If Balder had led back the blameless spring
With victory, with the voice of charging spears,
And in white lands long-lost Saturnian years (35).

Reviews

Lewis noted wryly in the Preface to the edition of 1950 that 'At its original appearance in 1926, *Dymer*, like many better books, found some good reviews and almost no readers.' One of the first, and most perceptive, good reviews was that by Dilys Powell in *The Sunday Times* (19 September 1926) p. 9: 'Mr Clive Hamilton's long allegorical poem "Dymer", she said, 'is executed with a consistent craftsmanship which excites admiration even where criticism is readiest to speak. The voyage of the soul in search of the spirit, its struggles with fear, with the listlessness of dreams, and its final triumph, are set forth with an unusual sureness. Of felicitous phrases there are many ... And yet it seems to us that Mr Hamilton has mistaken his opportunity. The idea was not one for treatment in verse. The exigencies of the poetic line prevent such an easy sequence as the allegory demands; but as a prose tale how splendidly it would have flowed!'

C. Henry Warren reviewing it in *The Spectator* (30 October 1926) p. 758, said: 'Mr Hamilton objectifies his theme so effectively and dramatically that it is not until the moving events are all done that we realize the full purport of what we have been reading. Here is a little epic burnt out of vital experience and given to us through a poet's eye.' The reviewer for *The Poetry Review*, XVII, 6 (November-December 1926), p. 442, said: 'One is little impressed by the allegory that is hard to understand, amazed at the alternate flashes of brilliance and dullness in the style of writing, and wholly delighted by the lyrical quality of many of the lines.'

NARRATIVE POEMS: DYMER, LAUNCELOT, THE NAMELESS ISLE, THE QUEEN OF DRUM: A STORY IN FIVE CANTOS (1969)

Background

I: The Failure of 'Dymer'

Lewis had offered *Dymer* (see above) to the publishers of his first work, *Spirits of Bondage*, and on 5 March 1926 they turned it down. He was deeply hurt, and without waiting to find out if another publisher would take it he analysed his disappointment in the pages of his diary. In this entry of 6 March 1926, which is included with a letter to Arthur Greeves* of 18 August 1930 in **TST**, he said:

> I have flattered myself with the idea of being among my own people when I was reading the poets and it is unpleasing to have to stand down and take my place in the crowd. Such a desire is contrary to my own settled principles: the very principles which I expressed in Dymer. It is fair to say that I had already gone some way towards repressing it ... when the completion of the poem ... and the sending off to a publisher threw me back into a tumult of self-love that I thought I had escaped. The cure of this disease is not easy to find – except the sort of violent, surgical cure which Reality itself may be preparing for me.

Reality did indeed deal violently with Lewis's ambitions as a poet. Following the brief success of *Dymer*, he turned to short poems which he duly sent off, one after the other, to periodicals. During the 1920s only one was accepted for publication. His friend Owen Barfield* was assisting the Editor of the literary periodical, *The Beacon*, during the twenties, and he accepted Lewis's 'Joy' for the issue of May 1924. This was fortunate because it was Lewis's first attempt to explain that 'intense longing' which he came to write about in *Surprised by Joy* as the 'central' experience of his life (See **Joy§**).

In the letter to Arthur Greeves of 18 August 1930 he said: 'The side of me which longs, not to write, for no one can stop us doing that, but to be approved as a writer, is not the side of us that is really worth much. And depend upon it, unless God has abandoned us, he will find means to cauterize that side somehow or other' (**TST**). God did indeed cauterize that side, but the story of how this happened is told in the *Background* section of *Poems*.

II: The End of the Narrative Poem

In his diary of 2 June 1923 Lewis records a conversation about poetry with Nevill Coghill. 'I said,' he told Coghill, 'my own line was chiefly narrative' (**AMR**). This taste was to remain with him all his life. However, the times were against him: narrative poems were out of fashion then, and they have continued so ever since. Quite apart from the failure of *Dymer*, Lewis was deeply saddened that no one would take the time to read long poems. Nowhere is this disappointment more clearly expressed than in a letter to his brother, Warnie,* of 2 August 1928, where he said:

> It sounds astonishing but English poetry is one of the things that you can come to the end of. I don't mean of course that I shall ever have read everything worth reading that was ever said in verse in the English language. But I do mean that there is no longer any chance of discovering a new long poem in English which will turn out to be just what I want and which can be added to the *Faerie Queene*, *The Prelude*, *Paradise Lost*, *The Ring and the Book*, the *Earthly Paradise*, and a few others – because there aren't any more (**L**).

III: 'Launcelot' and 'The Nameless Isle'

Despite the failure of *Dymer* and his conviction that he had come to the end of English poetry, Lewis wrote three more narrative poems. They were written purely because of the pleasure the writing gave him, and there is no indication that he ever attempted to publish any of them.

What was probably the first of these, *Launcelot*, was written in the early 1930s and we know little about it except that it is found in one of the notebooks which contains some of Lewis's lecture notes. Lewis always claimed to know very little about the story of King Arthur and the Grail Legend, and there is a confirmation of it in a letter to Father Peter Milward SJ of 9 May 1956. 'You need not be afraid,' he said, 'of telling me "only what I know already" about the Grail legend, for indeed I know very little' (L). Even so, for those who are interested in Lewis's writings about the Matter of Britain, they are considerable. He wrote extensively on the Arthurian romances of Chrétien de Troyes (*fl.* 1170–90) and *Sir Gawain and the Green Knight* in *The Allegory of Love*, and he published two essays on Sir Thomas Malory's *Le Morte D'Arthur*: 'The *Morte Darthur*' and 'The English Prose *Morte*'. Lewis also provided a Commentary to the Arthurian poems of Charles Williams* in *Arthurian Torso*, and in 'The Anthropological Approach' he warned of finding things in Arthurian literature that are not there. Best of all, he made Merlin a chief character in *That Hideous Strength*.

The Nameless Isle was fair-copied into one of Lewis's notebooks and dated 'August 1930'. It is headed by a short introduction on the Alliterative Line, and this is published as Note 2 in *Narrative Poems*. Alliteration means 'repeating and playing upon the same letter', and in Note 2 Lewis provides a succinct definition of Alliterative Verse (by 'verse' he means a single line of metrical writing):

> Every verse contains two half-verses. Each half-verse contains two beats or accents: and two dips which may consist of any number of unaccented syllables.

Alliterative Verse is a very old device and is the standard form of verse in Old English poems, such as *Beowulf*, and up to the 11th century. Lewis was later to devote a whole essay to 'The Alliterative Metre', and he there suggests the reader 'work his ear in' with the following illustration:

> We were TALKing of DRAGONS, | TOLkien and I
> In a BERKshire BAR. | The BIG WORKman
> Who had SAT SILent | and SUCKED his PIPE
> ALL the EVEning, | from his EMPTy MUG
> With GLEAMing EYE | GLANCED toWARDS us;
> 'I SEEN 'em mySELF,' | he SAID FIERCEly.

IV: 'The Queen of Drum'

There is, finally, *The Queen of Drum*, a particularly fine poem written between 1918 and 1938, which spans both Lewis's atheist and his Christian years. It began with a poem entitled 'Hippolytus' which he began in 1918. As no completed copy of the poem exists it is impossible to say much about it. However, it seems likely that it was based on the Greek tragedy of that title. Lewis was well-read in Classical mythology, and he attempted many re-tellings of ancient myths, viewing them from an unusual angle. Those he succeeded best with are *Till We Have Faces* and the incomplete *After Ten Years*. On 15 February 1917 he wrote to Arthur Greeves* about a poem he was writing on 'The Childhood of Medea' in which he described 'her lonely, frightened childhood away in a castle with the terrible old king her father and how she is gradually made to learn magic against her will' (**TST**).

'Hippolytus' probably began as a 're-telling' of the ancient story of that name, and it is worthwhile reviewing it. In the Greek tragedy, Hippolytus (which means 'loosed horse', 'wild driver or rider') is the illegitimate son of Theseus and the Amazon Hippolyte. He is a young man of perfect purity, devoted to the chase, who worships the goddess Artemis. Following the death of Hippolyte, Theseus marries Phaedra. While Theseus is away, Phaedra conceives a passion for Hippolytus. He rejects her advances, and in resentment Phaedra hangs herself after writing a letter accusing him of having seduced her. Theseus invokes the wrath of Poseidon on his son and banishes him. As Hippolytus is driving away Poseidon sends a sea-monster which frightens his horses. He is thrown from his chariot and dragged to death. Theseus learns of his error when it is too late.

It is impossible to say how Lewis's poem is related to the original, but one guess is that Hippolytus's way of dealing with his step-mother's advances is to escape to Fairyland. We know Lewis finished one version of 'Hippolytus', for in a letter to Arthur Greeves* of 18 September 1919 he mentions sending it off 'to the Odds and Ends Magazine' (**TST**). It is impossible to say whether it was ever published. In any event, Lewis continued to work on the poem, and in 1920 it was rewritten as 'Wild Hunt'. When he was compiling the *Lewis Papers*‡ in 1933-34, Warren Lewis* copied into Volume VIII 96 lines of a draft of a poem, now renamed 'Hippolytus', which he dated about 1923. It begins:

> Hippolytus woke shrieking in a gloom
> That staggered like a ship: the clothes were blown

> Out of his clutching hand ...
>   In haste he passed
> Forth on the street. None stirred. As clear as noon
> Showed every stone and tile. That night the moon
> Had slipt her moorings and with one huge eye
> Through headlong clouds flooded the ruined sky ...
>   And now his feet
> Fell on cool grass; wide fields before him lay ...
> The great hill-voice was calling everywhere
> Breathing sharp strength upon him. Now each limb
> Ran riot, charged with god ... (LP VIII:165–6).

In another version of part of the poem we learn that Hippolytus becomes
the King of Drum:

>   Whisper it not in Drum
> How Majesty stands breechless, blown away
> Like washing from the line: up past the grey
> And niggard grass of the heights ...
>   There suddenly
> Crowding the nine leagues ridge, the king could see
> Innumerable hordes – beast, woman, man.
> Nuzzling his feet, tongues out, the foxes ran,
> Wings lashed him in the face. Often he felt
> The wheezy mountain bear with icy pelt
> Brushing his side. But the men – alas for Drum.
>
> Why should my lord Archbishop home hither come
> Showing his teeth so yellow, and except
> His mitre, bare as an egg? (LP VIII:167).

The next mention of the poem occurs in Lewis's diary (AMR) of 16
January 1927 after which it is mentioned nearly every few days during
January and February 1927:

[16 January] I ... worked on the first chunk of the 'King of Drum' ...
This chunk is a new version of a piece I began writing about two
years ago, which itself was a re-writing of the 'Wild Hunt' (about
1920), which in its turn was based on something I started at Bristol
in 1918.

[18 January] Was thinking about imagination and intellect and the unholy muddle I am in about them at present: undigested scraps of anthroposophy‡ and psychoanalysis jostling with orthodox idealism over a background of good old Kirkian [see W.T. Kirkpatrick*] rationalism. Lord what a mess! And all the time ... there's the danger of falling back into most childish superstitions, or of running into dogmatic materialism to escape them. I hoped the 'King of Drum' might write itself so as to clear things up – the way 'Dymer' cleared up the Christina Dream business.

On 6 February he recorded, 'I spent the whole morning writing, got over the King's first interview with the Queen and made a start on the "College meeting".' A few entries later and, suddenly, the *Queen* of Drum begins to become the major character in the poem:

[27 February] Tried desperately hard to re-write the Queen's speech in the 'Drum' poem, all morning, without the slightest success. The old difficulty of smelting down a nasty little bit of factual stuff (the Queen's *conviction* of the others) into poetry: one only succeeds in expanding it into rhetoric.

By the time we hear any more of the poem Lewis had become a Christian, and that version of the poem which appears in *Narrative Poems* may certainly be described as a Christian poem. The final revision of the poem was probably begun in about 1933–34 when the *Führer* of the Nazis was still a less familiar figure than the *Duce* of the Fascists. The fate of the Queen was almost certainly modelled on the thirteenth-century poem *Thomas Rymer* by Thomas of Erceldoune. 'In *Thomas Rymer*,' Lewis said in *The Discarded Image* (VI), 'it will be remembered, the Fairy brings Thomas to a place where the road divides into three, leading respectively to Heaven, Hell, and "fair Elfland". Of those who reach the latter some will finally go to Hell, for the Devil has a right to 10 per cent of them every seventh year.' One of the several versions of *Thomas Rymer* ends with the Queen of Elfland leading him to his final decision:

> O see not ye yon narrow road
>   So thick beset wi thorns and briers?
> That is the path of righteousness,
>   Tho after it but few enquires.

> And see not ye that braid braid road,
>> That lies across yon lillie leven [field]?
> That is the path of wickedness,
>> Tho some call it the road to Heaven.
>
> And see not ye that bonny road
>> Which winds about the fernie brae?
> That is the road to Elfland,
>> Whe[re] you and I this night maun go.[3]

In the spring of 1938 Lewis sent the poem to John Masefield (the Poet Laureate) for his comments. In the first of several undated letters (which make up Note 3 in **NP**), Masefield said:

> Let me say now, that I have greatly enjoyed it, and feel an extraordinary beauty in the main theme – the escape of the Queen into Fairyland.
>
> At present, I cannot help feeling, that the design is encumbered. I think that I see your intention, but, as a showman, I find that the second canto, the long talk with the Archbishop and the martyrdom of the Archbishop, are sagas in themselves, and diminish the poignancy of your main theme. Whenever your Queen appears, there is imagination, beauty and tension.

Masefield went on to say, in another letter, 'Of course, we want the *Queen of Drum* in the Diversions. It is a very fine thing, and very beautiful; but the great difficulty is one of length.' The year before John Masefield and Nevill Coghill had organized the first of the 'Oxford Summer Diversions', which consisted of a programme of ballet, music and spoken verse. The programme for 4 August 1938 included *A Letter from Pontus* by Masefield and *The Queen of Drum* 'Spoken by the Author, C. S. Lewis'.

Summaries

Launcelot, which is a fragment, tells how during Advent – a period of 'saving and calamity' (3) – Sir Launcelot and the other knights of King Arthur's court go in quest of the Holy Grail. Nothing is heard from them

---

[3] *The English and Scottish Popular Ballads*, ed. F.J. Child (Boston: 1882–98), Vol. I, p. 324.

for over a year. Finally, as they arrive home, they have about them the 'dim disquiet of defeated men' (53), for none has managed to finish the quest. Queen Guinevere waits anxiously for over two years for word of Sir Launcelot, and then she is shocked to discover that he has been back three days without telling her. She urges him to come and see her, and Launcelot recounts the story of their quest for the Holy Grail. After leaving Camelot, he passed through ruined, 'barren countries' (128). When he asks a hermit 'How all this countryside has fallen into decay' (148), the answer is based on Chrétien de Troyes's *Conte du Graal*. He says:

> Nine broad realms in this distress
> Are lying for the sake of one man's heedlessness
> Who came to the King Fisherman, who saw the Spear
> That burns with blood, who saw the Sangrail drawing near,
> Yet would not ask for whom it served. Until there come
> The Good Knight who will kneel and see, yet not be dumb,
> But ask, the Wasted Country shall be still accursed
> And the spell upon the Fisher King be unreversed,
> Who now lies sick and languishing and near to death (153–60).

Launcelot goes off in hope of finding the Fisher King – the source of Ransom's new name in *That Hideous Strength* – and achieving the Grail. After leaving the Wasted Country he enters a 'warm green country' (180) where he meets a 'damosel, all clothed in bright' (197). She tells him that a tomb has been built there in which 'The three best knights of Christendom shall come to lie' (206). Expecting to hear himself named, he asks who they are. From on high comes a voice:

> 'A grave for Bors,' it cried, 'a grave
> For Percival, a grave for Galahad: but not
> For the Knight recreant of the Lake, for Launcelot!' (214–16).

He adventures on until he comes to a little Roman manor house where he meets the Queen of Castle Mortal, who seemed to Launcelot 'Somewhat like Morgan the enchantress, and somewhat/ Like Guinevere' (227–28). Invited to rest there, he visits the chapel that evening and discovers 'three coffins all of new cut stone' (266). When he asks who is to fill the coffins, the Queen tells him that they are for the 'three best knights of earth' (274) – Sir Lamorake, Sir Tristram, and Sir Launcelot du Lake. When he asks when they are expected to die, she reveals that she intends to entomb

their bodies there before they die. The fragment ends with the Queen of
Castle Mortal saying that it is her plan to decapitate the three knights in
order to make

> Their sweetness mine beyond recovery and to take
> That joy away from Morgan and from Guinevere
> And Nimue and Isoud and Elaine, and here
> Keep those bright heads and comb their hair and make them lie
> Between my breasts and worship them until I die (292–6).

The Nameless Isle is told in the first person by the 'master mariner' of a
small ship that is lost in a storm and wrecked on the 'Nameless Isle'.
There he meets the witch-queen of the island, surrounded by all manner
of beasts who feed from her breasts. Her daughter has been taken away
by an enchanter or wizard, and she promises a reward to anyone who can
bring her back. Her fear is that her daughter will be given a 'Heart-
changing draught' that will turn her into stone (218). The wizard has also
stolen her golden flute, which she is anxious to recover. The mariner
accepts the challenge and sets out to find the girl:

> Over hedge, over ditch, over high, over low,
> By waters and woods I went and ran,
> And swung the sword as I swung my legs.
> Laughing loudly, alone I walked,
> Till many a mile was marched away (254–8).

In the long grasses by a brook's margin he comes across the golden flute
and puts it in the bag he carries. Eventually he comes to a circle of
standing stones. There he finds a hunched and hairy dwarf who is
'grubby as if he had grown from the ground, plantlike, / Big of belly,
and with bandy legs' (309–10). He is the only living survivor of a
shipwreck. All the other members of the crew had been turned into
stone by the wizard. The mariner learns that the Queen 'Is the second
fear in this strange country' (350), and able to change men into brute
beasts. However, he does not believe this and he forces the dwarf to lead
him to the lair of the wizard. First he comes across the beautiful
daughter of the Queen, upon whom the wizard has already performed
his magic:

> Queen-like there stood
> A marble maid, mild of countenance,

Her lips open, her limbs so lithe
Made for moving, that the marble death
Seemed but that moment to have swathed her round (388–92).

The wizard turns out to be of very noble mien, and he soon explains why the mariner too should drink his magic cup and join the lady as a marble statue. The senses, those 'blind servants/ Five' (436–7), he says, cause us always to be in fear of death, and for this reason the passionless life of a statue is to be preferred to 'perishing perpetually' (446). The wizard reveals that he is the husband of the Queen, the rightful lord of the island, and the father of the beautiful stone girl. The golden flute had been made for their daughter, but after her mother used it to destroy men, the girl threw it away.

Convinced that only by accepting the magic cup can he ever know the girl, the young mariner decides to drink. However, as he puts this 'chalice of peace' (460) to his lips the dwarf appears and stops him. The dwarf pulls the golden flute from the bag and plays it. As he plays his appearance begins to change. The shaggy hair falls off, the humps on his shoulders disappear, and he goes on changing until

He was the fairest thing
That ever was on earth. Either shoulder
Was swept with wings; swan's down they were,
Elf-bright his eyes (535–8).

As he goes on playing all his mates whom the wizard had turned into stone begin to stir. They turn back into men, except that they are 'Fair in feature and of form godlike' (552). The flute soon wakes the maiden. 'The marble maid, under mask of stone, / Shook and shuddered. As a shadow streams/ Over the wheat waving, over the woman's face/ Life came lingering' (561–4). The 'wing'd wonder' (576) who had been a dwarf takes the woman to the mariner, and they are wed.

As they move back to the land of the wizard they hear the thunder of hoofs, and soon they are met by an army of magnificent creatures. The transformation of the dwarf's shipmates did not stop at turning from stone into flesh. When they are finally 'Unenchanted' they are centaurs. On the back of one of them is the 'lady of the land' who is now 'gentle and rejoicing' (632–3). She and the wizard are reconciled. A ship is prepared, and the elf, the mariner and the maiden sail away.

The Queen of Drum opens with a hurried conversation between two people. The dawn is about to break, and one of them must get inside before the doors are closed. Shortly afterwards, in the Castle of Drum, 'Gentlemen, pages, lords, and flunkey things' (I:17) attend the elderly King of Drum. He arises from his bed

> Rubbing his bleary eyes, muttering between dry gums
> 'Gi' me my teeth … dead tired … my lords – 't all comes
> From living in the valley. Too much wood.
> Sleep the clock round in Drum and get no good' (I:23–6).

On the appearance of his young Queen, the King accuses her of having been out all night. She refuses to answer. Later that morning there is a meeting of the Council in the sleepy, dark little country of Drum where 'Men work by lamplight in the month of June' (I:84). The meeting includes the King, the General, the Chancellor, and the Lord Archbishop. As has happened often, the question comes up 'What's wrong with Drum?' (I:114). They are startled when someone answers 'The Queen' (I:116). With this finally out in the open, the Chancellor says it is 'inhuman' for a Queen 'to expose a teeming nation's care/ And Princes yet unborn, to the damp air/ Of middle night.' Besides this, the people of Drum know because 'Always some chattering dame has seen her go … Out hill-wards' (I:141–50).

The General booms out: 'Have a wife and rule a wife./ Woman – they say – and dog – and walnut tree – / More you beat'm – better they be – '(I:182–4). Then, all at once the Queen is there, confronting them. She asks how they dare forbid her wandering by night outside the Castle when they wander in very strange places by themselves. Addressing the General, she asks:

> Five hours ago,
> Where were you? – and with whom? – how far away?
> Borrowing what wings of speed when break of day
> Recalled you, to be ready, here, to rise
> In the nick of time, and with your formal eyes
> And grave talk, to belie that other face
> And voice you've shown us in a different place? (I:225–31).

What the Queen is accusing them of is not dreaming, but actually being in some 'different place' while they sleep. However, unlike her, she says they return to the waking world with no memory of what they have been doing. She breaks down and is led away by the Archbishop, the only member of the Council with sympathy for her.

Canto II opens with a conversation between the King and the Chancellor about the Queen. They are worried because they have suspected all along that there are 'undiscovered wings' (II:52) and 'dark vacancies' (II:53) somewhere in the world we all inhabit. Now the Queen has 'opened all the doors' (II:96) and 'broken in the dams' (II:99) that protected us from those 'dark vacancies'. The Chancellor is worried that the Queen and the Archbishop are friendly, for he suspects that the Archbishop

>   guesses well enough
> That back there on the borderland there's stuff
> Not marked on any map ...
>   that this World in which we draw
> Our salaries, make our bows, and keep the law,
> This legible, plain universe we use
> For waking business, is a thing men choose
> By leaving out ... some larger thing (II: 119–29).

One difference between the Queen and the others is that, whereas she is able 'To keep the memory of her nights alive' (II:147) by going bodily to the 'dark vacancies' in the world, they have no memory of where they go in their dreams. This is all the more alarming because they come back from their nocturnal travels with aching knees and bruised shins. Then, remembering a 'fortune-telling man' (II:160) who was put in the Castle dungeons twenty years ago, the King and the Chancellor go to search for him.

In **Canto** III we find the Archbishop with the Queen. The Queen is angry that the Archbishop supposed her to be lying about being outside 'hunting on the hills' (III:35) while the rest of the Castle is asleep. He assumed she dreamed these things, but she reminds him that they have *met* up there in the woods and hills. 'Have I been in that place?' (III:43) he asks, 'I do not know./ Sometimes I think I have. I am uncertain' (III:44–5). As he continues to talk it is revealed that the country under discussion – the place the Queen actually visits – is fairy land. 'Child,' he says,

>   How can it profit us to talk
> Much of that region where you say you walk.
> We are not native there: we shall not die
> Nor live in elfin country, you and I.
> Greatly I fear lest, wilfully refusing
> Beauty at hand, you walk dark roads to find it,

> Impatient of dear earth because behind it
> You dream of phantom worlds, forever losing
> What is more wonderful ...' (III:59–67).

The Queen replies that she has an 'unbounded appetite for larger bliss' older than her mortal birth (III:75). Unlike the Archbishop, she finds this world such a 'threadbare vanity of days' (III:81) that she would hang herself rather than lose 'The air that breathes across it from the land I've seen' (III:83). To this he replies that there are 'two sorts of the unseen,' and that the one he knows best is the 'chaos vast' that 'Works in the cellarage of the soul' (III:104–10).

'You have described the downward journey well,' she says, 'But of the realm of light, have you no word?' (III: 122–3). The Archbishop admits sadly that he has lived all his life 'far deeper skilled/ In nice discriminations of old wine/ Than in those things for which God's blood was spilled' (III: 132–4). However, he goes on to say that, despite his ignorance of saints and sanctity, despite the fact that he is a 'Doctor of nescience' (III: 153) –

> I yet believe ...
> That from the place beyond all ken
> One only Word has come to men,
> And was incarnate and had hands
> And feet and walked in earthly lands
> And died, and rose ...
>   And to obey
> Is better than the hard assay
> Of piercing anywhere besides
> This mortal veil ...
>   all my counsel is no other
> Than this, now given at bitterest need;
> – Go, learn your catechism and creed (III:160–81).

Before the Queen can say much more, she is interrupted by a servant who tells them that the Queen has a new master in the 'Leader', as the General now calls himself.

In **Canto IV** the Queen and the Archbishop are escorted to the castle hall to meet the 'Leader', who has murdered the King and taken over Drum. He tells the Queen that she has nothing to fear from him 'provided that I get my way' (IV:97). He says he is not a jealous man and will leave her free except in one thing only: there must be 'No more night wandering nor no talk of them', and that she must share his bed. The

Queen, playing for time, asks if she may withdraw to her tower where she will promise to await him.

Turning his attention to the Archbishop, the General says that for some time now 'a certain somnolence has come/ To be the hall mark of the Church of Drum' (IV:174–5). He wants the Archbishop to contrive a 'state religion' which will be 'A Drummian kind of Christianity' (IV:183). To this the Archbishop replies: 'I cannot tell them more than I believe./ I dare not play with such immeasurables' (IV:210–11).

The General is surprised by this show of courage and offers, in return for obedience, to build cathedrals and whatever else the Church needs. When the Archbishop still refuses the General shouts 'You never talked like this before today' (IV:225). As the Archbishop is taken away to be beaten, the Queen has managed to lead the boy guarding her to a terrace between her tower and the great hall. Then with her heavy gold bracelet she strikes him, and makes her escape.

The Archbishop, tied to the wall, is flogged mercilessly in an attempt to make him accept the Leader's offer. Despite all, he will not give in, and the Canto ends:

> Ever he calls to Christ to be forgiven ...
> > His sides and all his ribs are riven,
> His guts are scattered and his skull is cloven,
> The man is dead. God has his soul to heaven (IV:297–304).

In **Canto V** the Queen is running among the woodlands overlooking Drum-land. The General pursues her with horses and hounds, helped by the bright moonlight. Exhausted with running, the Queen suddenly finds beside her a horse and rider. The horse is 'More beautiful and larger' than their earthly counterparts, and the 'elfin' knight riding him urges her to 'Keep, keep,'

> > 'On the midmost moss-way,
> Seek past the cross-way to the land you long for.
> Eat, eat,' he gave her of the loaves of faerie.
> 'Eat the brave honey of bees no man enslaveth.
> Heed not the road upon the right – 'twill lead you
> To heaven's height and the yoke whence I have freed you;
> Nor seek not to the left, that so you come now
> Through the world's cleft into that world I name not.
> Keep, keep the centre! Find the portals
> That chosen mortals at the world's edge enter.

> Isles untrampled by the warring legions
> Of Heaven and Darkness – the unreckoned regions
> That only as fable in His world appear
> Who seals man's ear as much as He is able ...
> Many are the ancient mansions,
> Isles His wars defile not,
> Woods and land unwounding
> The want whereof did haunt you' (V:199–216).

As she tries to decide what to do, there rises up before her 'A face to which she could have given a name' (V:250), and which she knows is speaking 'from among the dead' (V:254). He says:

> 'Quick. The last chance. Believe not the seducing elf.
> Daughter, turn back, have pity yet upon yourself
> Go not to the unwintering land where they who dwell
> Pay each tenth year the tenth soul of their tribe to Hell.
> Hear not the voice that promises, but rather hear
> His who commands, and fear. We have all cause to fear.
> Oh draw not down the anger, which is far away
> And slow to wake. Turn homeward ere the end of day (V:255–62).

The young Queen urges the spirit to go away. Then turning neither to the left nor the right, she goes straight on, and the poem ends:

> She had tasted elven bread.
> And so, the story tells, she passed away
> Out of the world: but if she dreams today
> In fairy land, or if she wakes in Hell,
> (The chance being one in ten) it doesn't tell (V:290–5).

Reviews

Norman Nicholson in the *Church Times* (24 December 1969) said: 'There is enough ... to show that Lewis had the instincts of a poet, if only he could have let himself go the way the stream was flowing instead of struggling stubbornly against it. As it was, even in a comparatively effective poem like 'The Queen of Drum', one keeps thinking, again and again, how much better he would have done it in prose.' The reviewer for *The Press* (21 February 1970) thought *The Queen of Drum* 'the finest' of the poems:

'"The Queen of Drum" is a magnificent poem which must not be allowed to be dragged into obscurity through the mediocrity of Lewis's other verse; as a story it will fascinate the casual reader, and as a complex piece of artistry it invites careful analysis.' The reviewer in *The Times Literary Supplement* (31 July 1970), p. 854, said: 'One can read [the poems] with pleasure but does not feel compelled to go on reading ... wishes again, not that Lewis had lost his boyishness, but that he had grown up just a little more.'

POEMS (1964) AND COLLECTED POEMS (1994)

Background

I: 'Metrical Poetry on Sane Subjects'

In between writing *Spirits in Bondage* and *Dymer* Lewis and his undergraduate friend Leo Baker* began putting together an Anthology of poems to be called 'The Way's the Way'. When the poets realized they would have to raise the money to have it printed, it was abandoned. However, while it was still being planned, Lewis explained to his father in a letter of 6 June 1920 why he and a few others were disillusioned with most modern poetry, and what they hoped to accomplish:

> It is being got up as a kind of counterblast to the ruling literary fashion here, which consists in the tendencies called 'Vorticist'. Vorticist poems are usually in *vers libre* (which means they are printed like verse, but neither rhyme nor scan, a line ending wherever you like). Some of them are clever, the majority merely affected, and a good few – especially among the French ones – indecent: not a sensuous indecency, but one meant to nauseate, the whole genus arising from the 'sick of everything' mood. So some of us others who are not yet sick of everything have decided to bring out a yearly collection of our own things in the hope of persuading the gilded youth that the possibilities of metrical poetry on sane subjects are not yet quite exhausted because the Vorticists are suffering from satiety (L).

The Vorticist movement, begun by Wyndham Lewis in about 1912, published two issues of *Blast: The Review of the Great English Vortex* in 1914 and 1915. Some of the early poems of T.S. Eliot* and Ezra Pound appeared in it, but this movement, like so many of its kind, soon ended. Still, 'metrical poetry on sane subjects' was not in fashion, being overtaken by free verse on subjects Lewis would have regarded as trivial if not insane.

As already mentioned in the Background to *Dymer*, with the writing of that long poem during the 1920s and all his other work he had little time for much else. Now and then he would send a short poem to a journal, but no one was interested. Of course *Dymer* was eventually published, but no one paid it much attention and Lewis was very disappointed. He blamed most of what had happened on the modern poets with whom he had almost no sympathy. Writing about this in his diary (**AMR**), he said on 20 May 1926 that his pupil Henry Yorke (later Henry Green, the novelist)

> tells me he met Siegfried Sassoon and other literary men during the strike. Siegfried spoke of the civil war which (he said) would begin, and then, sitting down on a tub in which a tree grew, laid his head against the tree, shut his eyes, and agonized in silence.
>
> Are all our modern poets like this? Were the old ones so? It is almost enough to prove R. Graves' contention that an artist is like a medium: a neurotic with an inferiority complex who gets his own back by attributing to himself abnormal powers.

Not long afterwards he began writing about the modern poet who was, and remained, the incarnation of what he most hated in modern poetry. Although he came to like T.S. Eliot himself very much in later life (see **LIFE** XXXI), he was infuriated by all the poems by Eliot he had seen, notably those he had come across in the American poetry journal, *The Dial*, and the very influential *Criterion* that Eliot edited.

He found Eliot's poems hopelessly obscure. Besides this, Eliot offended against proper **Stock Responses**,§ by which Lewis meant a deliberately organized response to such things as love, friendship, loyalty, as opposed to 'the direct free play of experience' (**PPL** VIII). An illustration he brought out often was a line from Eliot's 'Love Song of J. Alfred Prufrock' in which he describes evening as being 'Like a patient etherized upon a table'. Beginning on 9 June 1926 there are numerous entries in his diary about his plan for exposing Eliot's poetry through his own mock 'Eliotic' verse. 'I then wrote to [William Force] Stead,' he said on 9 June,

> enclosing for his criticism a parody of T.S. Eliot which I had just scribbled off: very nonsensical, but with a flavour of dirt all through. My idea is to send it up to his paper [*The Criterion*] in the

hope that he will be taken in and publish it: if he falls into the trap I will then consider how best to use the joke for the advancement of literature and the punishment of quackery. If he doesn't I shall have proved that there is something more than I suspected in this kind of stuff.

[10 June] Yorke [came] and ... I broached to him the idea of my literary dragonnade ... We both looked into T.S. Eliot's poems (which Betjeman* had lent me) and Yorke was pleased with the idea. He struck out a good opening line 'My soul is a windowless façade': then we hunted for a rhyme and of course 'de Sade' turned up, with the double merit of being irrelevant and offensive. We decided to bring Coghill* into the scheme.

[15 June] Coghill came for dinner ... After coffee we ... were joined by Yorke and later by [W.F.R.] Hardie. We all read our Eliotic poems and discussed plans of campaign. Coghill thought that if we succeeded it would always be open to Eliot to say that we had meant the poems seriously and afterwards pretended they were parodies: his answer to this was to make them acrostics and the ones he had composed read downwards 'Sham poetry pays the world in its own coin, paper money.'

Then came the brilliant idea that we should be a brother and sister, Rollo and Bridget Considine ... We rolled in laughter as we pictured a tea party where the Considines meet Eliot: Yorke would dress up for Bridget and perhaps bring a baby. We selected as our first shot, my 'Nidhogg' (by Rollo) and Hardie's 'Conversation' and Yorke's 'Sunday' (by Bridget).

The Considines were never able to meet Eliot or get their poems in *The Criterion*. Despite this, Lewis does not seem to have concluded that 'there is something more than I suspected in this kind of stuff.'

II: Resignation and Conversion

Lewis became a Theist in 1929, and with his conversion to Christianity in 1931 a totally unlooked-for watershed had been reached. It is tempting to say also that his watershed as a poet had been reached, but that would be to divide the man up, and that is certainly not what happened. The most noticeable effect of Lewis's conversion was the death of his old ambition as a poet and the emergence of a man never thereafter at a loss for the right words.

His old friend Arthur Greeves had a bitter disappointment of his own in the summer of 1930 when a book he had been working on for years was turned down. Lewis wrote on 18 August to say that they were both in the same boat because God was being merciful in not allowing them a literary success later to be revealed as 'dust and ashes'. It is tempting, he said, to suppose that it would be 'ample bliss' if your book was published even if it was read only by your friends. 'This is an *absolute delusion* ... I am *still* as disappointed an author as you. From the age of sixteen onwards I had one single ambition, from which I never wavered, in the prosecution of which I spent every ounce I could, on which I really and deliberately staked my whole contentment: and I recognise myself as having unmistakably failed in it ... Depend upon it, unless God has abandoned us, He will find means to cauterize that side somehow or other' (**TST**).

In his next letter, of 28 August 1930, Lewis admitted that now that he no longer regarded himself 'officially as an author' ideas had begun to 'bubble and simmer'. 'It is a very remarkable thing,' he said, 'that in the few religious lyrics which I have written during the last year, in which I had no idea of publication and at first very little idea even of showing them to friends, I have found myself impelled to take infinitely more pains, less ready to be contented with the fairly good and more determined to reach the best attainable, than ever I was in the days when I never wrote without the ardent hope of successful publication' (**TST**). Seventeen of these religious lyrics were sent to Owen Barfield during the summer of 1930, with the title 'Half Hours with Hamilton'.

They are some of the most beautiful poems Lewis wrote. Sixteen were to appear a few years later in *The Pilgrim's Regress* (1933), and these were always Lewis's favourites of his own poems. During the early 1930s he copied thirty-eight poems into his notebook of religious lyrics. One of these, first published in *Poems*, is the one entitled 'Reason' in which he says that when imagination and reason agree in him he will be able to say 'I BELIEVE'.

In that entry of his diary for 6 April 1926, which he sent to Arthur, Lewis said: 'I should like and like greatly to be known (and praised) by one or two friends and good judges: but I hold this as a refinement of pleasure easily foregone. If it went by another's name, so long as it was read and liked, I should be quite content' (**TST**). This really is what happened. Lewis wrote a good many poems over the next thirty years, but few saw them. He always sent a copy of his latest poem to Owen

Barfield, with a note saying 'Any good?', 'Will this do?' His chief enjoyment lay in the *writing* of poetry. Most of Lewis's prose came from his head almost exactly as it appears on the printed page, with only an occasional word being changed. It was not like this with his poems. Most went through endless revisions, the best examples of which are those religious lyrics of 1930 which he was still revising up to the time he died.

A few appeared under his own name but, from 1934 through to 1957, most of his poems were published in *The Oxford Magazine* or *Punch* under the pseudonym Nat Whilk (Anglo-Saxon for 'I know not whom') or 'N.W.' '"Poetry" with the Eliots and Audens has become such a horror,' he wrote to his brother on 20 July 1940, 'that the real thing now mainly survives in verse not intended to be fully serious – e.g. there is more real poetry in *Punch* now than in the high-brow periodicals.'

III: The Collecting and Editing of Lewis's *Poems*

Shortly after he was made Professor of Medieval and Renaissance English at Cambridge in 1954, Lewis began collecting his poems, published and unpublished, towards eventual publication in a volume to be called *Young King Cole, and other Pieces*. He began going through the three notebooks of poems written in the thirties, forties and fifties, and revising some of them extensively.

Following his marriage to Joy Gresham* in 1957, and during their three years together, he gave up copying poems into a notebook, and he published only two. It was, however, the bittersweet years with Joy which led him to write those poignant love poems 'Joys That Sting', 'Old Poets Remembered', and 'As the Ruin Falls'. In 1963 he returned to *Young King Cole*. He was still a long way from completing the task, but he got as far as writing an 'Introductory Letter' which he planned to use as a Preface. This 'Introductory Letter' is in the form of a letter to the editor of a literary periodical, and publication of it was delayed until 1994, when it was included in *Collected Poems*.

Following Lewis's death in 1963, Walter Hooper began the task of collecting and editing his poems for a volume entitled *Poems* (1964). This volume contains nearly all the poems from the 'Half Hours with Hamilton' and most of those written and published up until Lewis's death. It numbers 110 poems and 17 Epigrams and Epitaphs.

IV: Collected Poems

The *Collected Poems* of Lewis consists, with the exception of the *Narrative Poems*, of all his poetry that has come to light. It is made up of *Spirits in Bondage* (1919), *Poems* (1964) and a 'Miscellany' of 17 unpublished poems covering the years 1916 to 1963. Ten of these are from a collection of poems written between 1915–17 and which Lewis called 'Metrical Meditations of a Cod'. The others include a poignant one about Warren Lewis's* final leave-taking of Little Lea.‡ The Lewis brothers' father, Albert Lewis,* died in 1929 while Warren was on duty in China. After his return to England the brothers decided to sell the family home in Belfast. As Warren prepared to make his final visit to 'Little Lea' in June 1930, Lewis composed and sent him 'Leaving For Ever the Home of One's Youth'.

Another which should be mentioned is the 'Epitaph for Helen Joy Davidman'. Sometime before his marriage Lewis wrote two versions of an 'Epitaph'. The one he planned to use in *Young King Cole* appears as Epitaph 17 at the end of *Poems*. When Joy read this poem she knew she was dying, and she asked that it be used as her epitaph. In July 1963 Lewis revised the epitaph with her in mind and arranged for it to be cut into marble and placed in the Oxford Crematorium.

Summary

The book contains 110 short poems and 17 Epitaphs and Epigrams. It is divided into five parts. Part I, 'The Hidden Country', opens with 'A Confession' which Lewis revised after it had been published originally in *Punch* (1 December 1954) under the title *Spartan Nactus*. It contains in miniature his thoughts on 'Poetic Diction', and it is an answer to Eliot on what Lewis himself regarded as appropriate Stock Responses.§ After admitting that he is unable to see why evening would suggest Eliot's 'patient etherized upon a table', he admits that

> To me each evening looked far more
> Like the departure from a silent, yet a crowded, shore
> Of a ship whose freight was everything, leaving behind
> Gracefully, finally, without farewells, marooned mankind.

However, as one soon discovers, the 'Hidden Country' refers to those things which Lewis had a particular fondness for, or which simply gave him pleasure. Lovers of Narnia will particularly like his 'Narnian Suite' which includes a 'March for Strings, Kettledrums, and Sixty-three Dwarfs' and a 'March for Drum, Trumpet, and Twenty-one Giants'. One of the most poignant of the poems in this section is 'The Late Passenger' which explains how the Unicorn came to be left out of the Ark.

Part II, 'The Backward Glance', is openly nostalgic. It opens on a delightfully funny note with Lewis's 'Evolutionary Hymn' in which he was obviously enjoying himself. It begins:

> Lead us, Evolution, lead us
>   Up the future's endless stair:
> Chop us, change us, prod us, weed us,
>   For stagnation is despair:
> Groping, guessing, yet progressing,
>   Lead us nobody knows where.

Readers of Lewis's interplanetary novels will enjoy his 'Science-fiction Cradlesong' in which he prophesies that 'By and by Man will try/ To get out into the sky', with the result that being 'Closed in steel', man will feel no closer to Heaven than he already does on Earth.

Part III, 'A Larger World', refers to those subjects which are of more universal interest. They include some of the early theological poems first published in *The Pilgrim's Regress*. It is doubtful if we will find a greater compression of the Seven Deadly Sins than the poem entitled 'Deadly Sins' in which there is this definition of the deadliest of all:

> Pride, that from each step, anew
> Mounts again with mad aspiring,
> Must find all at last, save you,
> Set too low for her desiring.

This section contains three unpublished poems of great tenderness which were written either just before or just after Lewis's wife died. They compress into a small space *A Grief Observed*.

Part IV, 'Further Up and Further In' are the words uttered by Jewel the Unicorn in the penultimate chapter of *The Last Battle*, after he has discovered that the further he goes into the Narnia beyond the Stable the more like home it becomes. This section includes the five 'Sonnets' in which Lewis took some pride.

In Part V, 'Epigrams and Epitaphs', one finds a wealth of thoughts which could hardly be said better in prose. Number 11 is a good example:

> She was beautifully, delicately made,
> So small, so unafraid,
>   Till the bomb came.
>   Bombs are the same,
> Beautifully, delicately made.

Reviews

The reviewer in the *Church Times* (20 November 1964), ix, said: 'Except for the most poignant, "A Grief Observed" ... Lewis kept so strict a control over his personal emotions that a hasty reader might suppose he thought in depth but felt rather on the surface. The poems show how utterly mistaken that impression was. Lewis was an emotional person who wrote of his true heart with classical economy.' The reviewer for *The Times Literary Supplement* (7 January 1965), p. 2, said: 'Lewis's verse is not without talent or dexterity, and certainly not without feeling; but it is written in a variety of obsolescent modes ... His real talent was not here – it was for narrative, in which he is always immensely skilful and happily at home.'

American reviewers were much more sympathetic. Thomas Howard in 'Plucking Pizzicato', *Christianity Today*, 9 (18 June 1964), p. 30, said: 'This is the best – the glorious best – of Lewis. For here, with the gemlike beauty and hardness that poetry alone can achieve, are his ideas about the nature of things that lay behind all of his writings. One passes from poem to poem, thunderstruck with beauty, wanting to shout, "Oh this is true, this is a thousand times true, this is Truth."' The founder of the Wade Center,‡ Clyde S. Kilby, said in *The New York Times Book Review* (23 January 1966), p. 34: 'As might be expected, these are idea poems which reiterate themes known to have occupied Lewis's ingenious and provocative mind ... The music is often on the brittle side, something like the crackle of a bitten apple, as though Lewis wishes to discourage a reader from being lulled by mere cadence into unthoughtfulness. But again there is poetry smooth as a flower's petal or the sinuosity of a flowing stream. I think we have here a book that will take an important place in the Lewis canon.'

AUTOBIOGRAPHICAL

&

The Pilgrim's Regress,
Surprised by Joy,
A Grief Observed

THE PILGRIM'S REGRESS: AN ALLEGORICAL APOLOGY FOR CHRISTIANITY, REASON AND ROMANTICISM (1933)

Background

Lewis's first prose work, *The Pilgrim's Regress*, was an attempt to explain the elusive experience he called Joy§ and the part it played in his conversion. 'The central story of my life is about nothing else,' he stated firmly in *Surprised by Joy* I. However, before proceeding to *The Pilgrim's Regress* it is important that the reader have some idea of how Lewis defined what he meant by Joy. The clearest definition comes from **SBJ** I. He says that when he was about six the memory of a toy garden gave him a sensation of 'enormous bliss', a desire for he knew not what. There were to be similar experiences over the years, in which the quality common to all of them was 'an unsatisfied desire which is itself more desirable than any other satisfaction'. He was not to understand the *object* of this 'unsatisfied desire' until he became a Christian.

His earliest surviving attempts at a description of 'Joy' are found scattered throughout the diary he kept between 1922 and 1927 and which is published as *All My Road Before Me* (1991). We learn from it that as early as April 1922, when he was still an atheist, he wrote a poem about it. That poem, 'Joy,' was published a couple of years later, and it reveals how different his understanding of Joy was at that time from what it was to become. 'Joy' is very valuable in the history of Lewis's thought and it is reprinted in his *Collected Poems*.

Shortly after becoming a Theist, he attempted another explanation of what he meant by 'Joy'. This unpublished account is in prose, and consists of 58 pages in one of his notebooks. This 'Early Prose Joy', to give it a name, was written in 1930 and there is a copy of it in the Bodleian Library.‡ 'In this book,' he begins, 'I propose to describe the process by which I came back, like so many of my generation, from materialism to a belief in God.' He goes on to say that although the religious revival of that time was tending towards 'classicism in art, royalism in politics, and Catholicism in religion', he believed there to be 'a *via media* between syllogisms and psychoses', and that 'Thomas Aquinas and D.H. Lawrence do not divide the universe between them.' 'There are many ways back to the truth,' he said, and 'no way, faithfully followed, can lead anywhere, at last, except to the centre.' Lewis never attempted to publish this account of his conversion. Still, what makes it of particular interest is that he knew 'Joy' was not peculiar to him, but a universal experience.

He tried once more, in the Spring of 1932, to tell the story of Joy in verse, but did not get far. Then, as so often, inspiration came unlooked for. During a two-week holiday in Ireland with Arthur Greeves* in August 1932 he wrote the whole of *The Pilgrim's Regress*. At the time he was also engaged in writing *The Allegory of Love*, and the definition of Allegory he gives in Chapter II of that book is very useful in understanding the *Regress*. In Allegory, he said, 'you start with an immaterial fact, such as the passions which you actually experience, and ... then invent *visibilia* [visible things] to express them' (see **Allegory§**).

Summary

The central character is a kind of 'Everyman' called John who is born on the western side of the Eastern Mountains in Puritania. He grows up in fear of an unseen Landlord who is portrayed as a moral despot. At the same time, the young man has visions of an Island, which is both the cause and the object of his intense longing, or 'Joy'. He makes his first mistake in supposing the Island to be a disguise for Lust. When this deception is unmasked he sets off again to find the Island. Along the way he meets people who are allegorical personifications of ideas and schools of thought Lewis himself had encountered over the years. They include such characters and experiences as Mr Enlightenment (Nineteenth-century Rationalism), the 'Modern' literary movement, and Freudianism.

Eventually John is captured by the Spirit of the Age. Those passages dealing with the Pilgrim's imprisonment (III: 6–9) are some of the most astute in the book, and most likely to appeal to the modern reader. The Spirit of the Age is portrayed as a Giant whose eyes make everything he looks at transparent. Thus his glance at John makes it possible for the young man to see his own insides (lungs, intestines, etc.). The Giant attempts to convince him that this is *all* that a man is. John is rescued by Reason, who leads him as far as the Grand Canyon, on the other side of which is the continuation of the Main Road.

While wondering how to cross, John meets Mother Kirk (the Church). She gives him an allegorical account of the Sin of Adam (the Grand Canyon), explaining that she is the only one who could carry him across the canyon safely. John decides instead to go a long way around. Because Catholics speak of the Catholic Church as 'Mother Church', many assumed that Lewis was using the expression to mean the Catholic Church. But by 'Mother Kirk' Lewis really meant 'Traditional Christianity'.

Turning North he meets 'cerebral' men such as Mr Sensible (cultured Worldliness), Mr Neo-Angular and Mr Humanist. These men talk, Lewis explains in the running headlines to the book, as if 'they had "seen through" things they have not even seen' (VI: 3). Finding he cannot get to the Main Road this way, John turns South. There he meets, amongst others, Mr Broad who represents 'a modernizing religion which is friends with the World and goes on no pilgrimage'. Finally John reaches the house of Wisdom, and from him he learns the inadequacy of many of the philosophies Lewis had found attractive at one time: Idealist Philosophy, Materialism, and Hegelianism. Even if the reader never encounters these as living philosophies, he will get some idea of their effect on Lewis and his generation.

Upon leaving Wisdom's house, John is helped at one point by a 'Man' (Christ), and from this he learns that he must accept Grace or die. Then, having accepted Grace, John feels bound to acknowledge God's existence. There follows a chapter entitled 'Caught' in which Lewis repeats almost word for word what he gave in the 'Early Prose Joy' as his main reason for not wanting to be a Christian. More than anything, he wanted to call his soul his own. John realizes that in acknowledging the Lord he is 'never to be alone; never the master of his own soul, to have no privacy, no corner whereof you could say to the whole universe: This is my own, here I can do as I please.'

Continuing his journey, John stops for a while with History. In the chapter called 'History's Words' we find some of the most valuable ideas in the book. John is told that although not all men have the 'picture' of an Island, such as he has had, to lead them to the Landlord (God), they are nevertheless given 'pictures' which serve the same purpose. 'The best thing of all is to find Mother Kirk at the very beginning,' says History. He then explains that when Pagans don't have the benefit of the Church, the Landlord 'sends them pictures and stirs up sweet desire and so leads them back to Mother Kirk.'

In the chapter entitled 'Archetype and Ectype' John asks Wisdom about the thing that had quite terrified Lewis when he realized he would have to obey God. 'I am afraid,' says John, 'that the things the Landlord really intends for me may be utterly unlike the things he has taught me to desire.' 'They will be very unlike the things you imagine,' replies Wisdom. 'But you already know that the objects which your desire imagines are always inadequate to that desire. Until you have it you will not know what you wanted.'

John struggles to withdraw, but Reason will not let him, and he returns to Mother Kirk. In the chapter called *'Securus Te Projice'* ('Throw yourself away without care') she tells him to dive down to the bottom of a pool of water and come up on the other side. When he replies that he has never learned to dive, Mother Kirk says, 'The art of diving is not to do anything new but simply to cease doing something. You have only to let yourself go.' This incident is perhaps the most autobiographical in the book. In his letter to Arthur Greeves of 8 July 1930 Lewis mentions that Owen Barfield had just taught him to dive. It had enormous religious consequences for him, and at the end of the 'Early Prose Joy' he recalls this first dive and says, 'Nothing is simpler than this art. You do not need to do anything, you need only to stop doing something – to abstain from all attempt at self-preservation – to obey the command which Saint Augustine heard in a different context, *Securus te projice.'*

John at last finds the Island of his dreams, and discovers that it is the other side of the Eastern Mountains he had known all his life, the home of God. In the final part of the work, called 'The Regress', John is shown, as Lewis tells us in the running headlines, 'the real shape of the world we live in' and 'How we walk on a knife-edge between Heaven and Hell.' The 'regress' consists mainly in un-learning many of the things John had picked up over the years, and in this section Lewis attempts to answer many of the questions which had plagued him, such as the purpose of Hell. This last part of the book also contains most of the earliest, and best, of Lewis's religious poems.

Reviews

This work has received many excellent reviews over the years. One of the first was in *The Times Literary Supplement* (6 July 1933), p. 456, where the reviewer said: 'It is impossible to traverse more than a few pages of the allegory without recognizing a style that is out of the ordinary; and "Oxford" should be diagnosed from the neatness with which the extravagances of psycho-analysis are hit off in the eighth chapter of the third Book, and the essentials of Hegelianism packed into a nutshell in the last four chapters of the seventh. Moreover when John, the pilgrim-hero of this "Regress", begins to find the way to salvation he is inspired to break into fragments of song ... revealing a poetic gift that may rightly be called arresting.'

George Sayer* reviewing it in *Blackfriars*, 17 (4 January 1936), pp. 69–70, says: 'Thanks to a mind of quite remarkable acuity he is able to expose, often in only a few lines, the most essential weakness of almost every contemporary doctrine ... Perhaps the best of the destructive chapters are those on the psychologists ... showing that such doctrines as the wish-fulfilment can work both ways and that a man cut open (so that the ugliness of his internal organs can be seen) is no longer a man, and that conclusions derived from examining him don't apply to living men.' Another Catholic journal, the *Downside Review*, 54 (January 1936), pp. 138–9, under the impression that Lewis was a Catholic, said: 'The author ... hails from Northern Ireland, but he has not allowed this incident of environment to cramp his literary style ... This book has something of the humour of James Stephens in *The Crock of Gold* ... something of the satirical irony of Dean Swift ... Mr Lewis is always refreshingly himself. He has made a notable contribution to Catholic literature.'

W. Norman Pittenger, who also assumed Lewis was a Catholic, said in *The Living Church* (11 January 1936): 'Mr Lewis has written an amusing allegory, suggested by Bunyan's classic, but done with a delightful lightness and wit ... The "Pilgrim" ... lands up in the end in a resting-place which we fancy is none other than the Church of Rome. Anglicans may wish that he had come their way, but Mr Lewis, who is a Roman Catholic, does not see it so.'

SURPRISED BY JOY:
THE SHAPE OF MY
EARLY LIFE (1955)

Background

An early reference to this autobiography is found in Warnie Lewis's* diary of 25 March 1948 (**BF**): 'Much talk of old days, apropos of J's autobiography, which promises to be first rate – though of course there could hardly be anyone less competent to criticize the early chapters of such a work than I am.' By that summer Lewis had reached the end of World War I. In the end he worked on the book intermittently for another seven years. It was sent to the publishers in March 1955 and was published in September of that year. One of the things that caused him to take so long over it was the sudden burst of inspiration which led to the writing of the *Chronicles of Narnia*. Lewis also fulfilled a long-standing obligation to write his mammoth *English Literature in the Sixteenth Century* for the Oxford University Press.

It will be remembered that he had been trying since the early 1920s to tell the story of 'Joy', and *The Pilgrim's Regress* was written to show its relation to God. Now it probably seemed to Lewis that the best way to throw further illumination on the subject of Joy was by a full account of his conversion. 'This book is written,' he said in the Preface, 'partly in answer to requests that I would tell how I passed from Atheism to Christianity, and partly to correct one or two false notions that seem to have got about. How far the story matters to anyone but myself depends on the degree to which others have experienced what I call "joy" ... The book aims at telling the story of my conversion and is not a general autobiography.'

Summary

The title of the book comes, not from the author's friend Joy Gresham,* but as shown on the title page, from a poem by Wordsworth which begins:

> Surprised by Joy – Impatient as the Wind
> I turned to share the transport – Oh! with whom
> But Thee, deep buried in the silent tomb.

Chapter I, 'The First Years', opens with Lewis's birth on the outskirts of Belfast in 1898 and his early years with his parents and his brother. His father, Albert Lewis,* was a police court solicitor in Belfast, and he married Florence Augusta Hamilton,* a B.A. of Queen's College, Belfast, and the daughter of the parish priest. The family were members of the Church of Ireland, part of the Anglican Communion. Their only other child was Warren ('Warnie') Hamilton Lewis,* born in 1895. The chapter contains a warm and affectionate picture of domestic life in a roomy house. 'What drove me to write,' he said, 'was the extreme manual clumsiness from which I have always suffered.' When he was about six he invented his imaginary world of 'Animal-Land'.

He then describes those experiences which mediated the experience of Joy. The first 'glimpse' came when he was about six. Standing beside a flowering currant bush, he remembered an earlier morning years before when his brother had brought his toy garden into the nursery. 'It is difficult to find words strong enough for the sensation which came over me; Milton's "enormous bliss" of Eden … comes near it.' The second glimpse came through Beatrix Potter's *Squirrel Nutkin*. 'It troubled me,' he said, 'with what I can only describe as the Idea of Autumn.' The third glimpse came when he opened Longfellow's poem, *Tegner's Drapa*, and read

> I heard a voice that cried,
> Balder the beautiful
> Is dead, is dead –

'The reader,' he says, 'who finds these three episodes of no interest need read no further, for in a sense the central story of my life is about nothing else … The quality common to the three experiences is that of an unsatisfied desire which is itself more desirable than any other satisfaction. I call it Joy.' Lewis was deeply attached to his mother, and the first chapter ends with the agony caused by her death when he was nine.

Chapter II, 'Concentration Camp', is about the boarding school in England where Lewis was sent after the death of his mother. He disguises the name of Wynyard School‡ in Watford, Hertfordshire, as 'Belsen', after the concentration camp. Warren had gone there two years before, and by the time his brother joined him in 1908 the school was declining rapidly. The headmaster was insane, and Lewis made his escape when the school collapsed in 1910. Robert Capron* ('Oldie'), the headmaster, was committed to an asylum. The one good to come from 'Belsen' was the Anglo-Catholic church the boys attended on Sundays. 'There,' he said, 'I first became an effective believer ... What really mattered was that I here heard the doctrines of Christianity (as distinct from general "uplift") taught by men who obviously believed them.'

Chapter III, 'Mountbracken and Campbell', tells of his return to Belfast when he was 12. We are given a glimpse of his mother's side of the family. 'Mountbracken' is his name for Glenmachan House, the home of Mrs Lewis's cousin and dearest friend, Lady Ewart, the wife of Sir William Quartus Ewart. They had three daughters, and all opened their hearts and their home to the orphaned brothers. Warren was now at Malvern College,‡ and Lewis was allowed to continue his education at Campbell College‡ in Belfast. He would have been content if he had not fallen ill during his first term.

Chapter IV, 'I Broaden My Mind', opens with Lewis accompanying Warnie back to England in January 1911. Warnie was at Malvern College and 'Jack', as C.S. Lewis was known to his friends, was at a preparatory school overlooking it. 'Chartres' is his name for Cherbourg House,‡ and here, he said, 'my education really began'. While there he ceased being a Christian. One of the causes was the School Matron. 'She was floundering in the mazes of Theosophy, Rosicrucianism, Spiritualism; the whole Anglo-American Occultist tradition ... She loosened the whole framework, blunted all the sharp edges, of my belief.' Another assault on his faith came from the classics. 'Here, especially in Virgil, one was presented with a mass of religious ideas; and all teachers and editors took it for granted from the outset that these religious ideas were sheer illusion. No one ever attempted to show in what sense Christianity fulfilled Paganism or Paganism prefigured Christianity ... I became an apostate, dropping my faith with no sense of loss but with the greatest relief.'

Lewis also fell under the spell of a young master called 'Pogo' who was a wit, and a dressy man. 'A new element,' said Lewis, 'had entered my life: Vulgarity. Up till now I had committed nearly every other sin and folly within my power, but I had not yet been flashy.' It was also at

'Chartres' that Lewis 'underwent a violent, and wholly successful, assault of sexual temptation.'

Chapter V, 'Renaissance', is set at 'Chartres'. In the spring of 1912 Lewis was overwhelmed by Wagner's *Siegfried and the Twilight of the Gods*, with Arthur Rackham's illustrations. 'Pure "Northernness" engulfed me,' he said. 'A vision of huge, clear spaces hanging above the Atlantic in the endless twilight of Northern summer, remoteness, severity ... and almost at the same moment I knew that I had met this before, long, long ago ... in *Tegner's Drapa*, that Siegfried ... belonged to the same world as Balder and the sunward-sailing cranes. And with that plunge back into my own past there arose at once, almost like heartbreak, the memory of Joy itself ... I knew (with fatal knowledge) that to "have it again" was the supreme and only important object of desire.' At the same time he fell in love with the music to Wagner's *Das Rheingold*. From this point on he seemed to be living two separate lives: an 'inner' life of the imagination 'starving for Joy', and an 'outer' one full of bustle.

In 1913 Lewis won a scholarship to Malvern, and Chapters VI and VII, 'Bloodery' and 'Light and Shade,' cover the year spent there. The name of the school is disguised as 'Wyvern', but most readers knew it was Malvern, and Lewis has been criticized for his treatment of it. His brother was especially censorious about the description of Malvern as a veritable nightmare of fagging and homosexuality. Besides these things, Lewis loathed 'playing games'. 'To lie down,' he ends Chapter VI, 'to be out of the sound of voices, to pretend and grimace and evade and slink no more, that was the object of all desire.' Chapter VII is mainly about Lewis's expanding taste in English Literature. He recalls the 'perilous transition' from what had been his unconscious love of books into 'the right taste'. 'The moment good taste knows itself,' he concludes, 'some of its goodness is lost.' Two blessings at Malvern 'that wore no disguise' were 'Smewgy', the English master, and the school library.

Chapter VIII, 'Release', contains a very funny description of Lewis's father and his 'special labyrinthine operation' of 'reading between the lines'. With the loss of their mother at such an early age, Mr Lewis felt it necessary to be pals with his sons. Jack found this oppressive, and visits home became a penance. By a happy chance he met a boy who lived across the road, Arthur Greeves,* who shared his love for things Norse. He too had been 'stabbed' by Joy, and they became best friends. His father allowed Jack to leave Malvern, and he followed Warren to Bookham in Surrey for tutoring with W.T. Kirkpatrick* – 'The Great Knock'.

Chapter IX, 'The Great Knock', is the most joyful in the book. Mr Kirkpatrick had been Albert Lewis's headmaster at Lurgan College, Co.

Armagh, many years previously, and he was retired and living in Great Bookham, Surrey, where he gave private tuition. Lewis described him as almost 'a purely logical entity'. 'The idea,' he said, 'that human beings should exercise their vocal organs for any purpose except that of communicating or discovering truth was to him preposterous.' Mr Kirkpatrick was an atheist, and a rationalist. 'My own Atheism and Pessimism were fully formed before I went to Bookham,' Lewis reminds us. 'What I got there was merely fresh ammunition for the defence of a position already chosen.'

In Chapter X, 'Fortune's Smile', Lewis says, 'At the same time that I exchanged Wyvern for Bookham I also exchanged my brother for Arthur as my chief companion.' Arthur infected Lewis with a taste for the classic English novelists, and the 'Homeliness' which attaches books to simple experiences of 'weather, food, the family, the neighbourhood'. Hitherto his feelings for nature had been 'too narrowly romantic', and he picked up Arthur's love of the 'homely' in nature. Thus began a delight in walks through the 'bleak' countryside of County Down. Lewis says that his unhappy relationship with his father explained one of the worst acts of his life: 'I allowed myself to be prepared for confirmation, and confirmed, and to make my first Communion, in total disbelief, acting a part, eating and drinking my own condemnation.'

Chapter XI, 'Check', is mainly about Joy. In his attempt to imprison Joy he had become a scholar of the Norse literature which had mediated it. 'I woke,' he said, 'from building the temple to find that the God had flown … I was in the Wordsworthian predicament, lamenting that "a glory" had passed away.' He got 'stabs' of Joy through music, books and walks, but when Joy would not come through them he became worried, failing to see that 'the very moment when I longed to be so stabbed again, was itself again such a stabbing.' 'It is not blasphemous,' he said, 'to compare the error which I was making with that error which the angel at the Sepulchre rebuked when he said to the women, "Why seek ye the living among the dead? He is not here, He is risen" … Instead, I concluded that it was a mood or state within myself which might turn up in any context. To "get it again" became my constant endeavour.' He learned by experience that Joy 'is not a substitute for sex'.

The 'two hemispheres' of his mind were in the sharpest contrast. 'On the one side a many-islanded sea of poetry and myth; on the other a glib and shallow "rationalism". Nearly all that I loved I believed to be imaginary; nearly all that I believed to be real I thought grim and meaningless.' The chapter concludes with an account of his discovery of George MacDonald's *Phantastes* which 'baptized' his imagination.

Chapter XII, 'Guns and Good Company', begins with the winning of a scholarship to Oxford and his first term at University College‡ in 1917. He joined the Officers' Training Corps, was commissioned a Second Lieutenant in the Somerset Light Infantry, and arrived in France in November 1917. 'I am surprised,' he said, 'that I did not dislike the Army more ... Every few days one seemed to meet a scholar, an original, a poet, a cheery buffoon, a raconteur, or at the least a man of good will.' He read G.K. Chesterton and concluded, 'I did not know what I was letting myself in for. A young man who wishes to remain a sound Atheist cannot be too careful of his reading.' He describes some of the friends he made and the war itself. He was wounded at Mount Bernenchon in April 1918.

In Chapter XIII, 'The New Look', Lewis describes his first reading of Bergson – 'From him I first learned to relish energy, fertility, and urgency; the resource, the triumphs, and even the insolence, of things that grow.' After his return to Oxford in January 1919 he resumed his studies at University College.‡ He writes of the contributions made by his friends A.K. Hamilton-Jenkin,* Owen Barfield* and A.C. Harwood.* Following his reading of Classical Honour Moderations‡ and Greats‡, he met two men who caused him to retreat from the occult and romanticism in 'almost a panic-stricken fright'. One was 'an old, dirty, gabbling, tragic, Irish parson who had long since lost his faith'. The other had gone mad from flirting with 'Theosophy, Yoga, Spiritualism, Psychoanalysis, what not?' As the new Psychology swept through Oxford Lewis began to regard romantic images as 'wishful thinking', and he labelled Joy 'aesthetic experience'. He was 'hideously shocked' when Barfield and Harwood 'embraced the doctrines of Rudolf Steiner and became Anthroposophists.' (see **Anthroposophy‡**). But Barfield made short work of Lewis's 'chronological snobbery'.§ He accepted philosophical Idealism, and admitted 'that the whole universe was, in the last resort, mental; that our logic was participation in a cosmic *Logos*.'

Chapter XIV, 'Checkmate', describes the 'compulsion' of God which led him to become a Theist. It begins in 1922 with Lewis reading his third university subject, English Language and Literature.‡ He was still trying hard to keep God out of his life when he made friends with Nevill Coghill* 'and had the shock of discovering that he ... was a Christian and a thoroughgoing supernaturalist.' Those writers 'who did not suffer from religion ... all seemed a little thin.' On the other hand, the writers Lewis liked, such as Langland, Thomas Browne and George Herbert, were Christians. Lewis was elected a Fellow of Magdalen College‡ in 1925, and came to meet two other Christian friends, H.V.D. Dyson* and J.R.R. Tolkien.*

A reading of Samuel Alexander's *Space, Time and Deity*, with its theory of 'Enjoyment' and 'Contemplation', led him to see 'that all my waiting and watching for Joy, all my vain hopes to find some mental content on which I could, so to speak, lay my finger and say, "This is it", had been a futile attempt to contemplate the enjoyed.' The images and sensations which he had associated with Joy 'if idolatrously mistaken for Joy itself, soon honestly confessed themselves inadequate.' All said, in the last resort: '"It is not I. I am only a reminder. Look! Look! What do I remind you of?"'

He read Chesterton's *Everlasting Man* 'and for the first time saw the whole Christian outline of history set out in a form that seemed to ... make sense.' Shortly after this 'the hardest-boiled of all the atheists I ever knew sat in my room on the other side of the fire and remarked that the evidence for the historicity of the gospels was really surprisingly good ... If he, the cynic of cynics, the toughest of the toughs, were not – as I would still have put it – "safe", where could I turn?' He describes the next three years as ones in which, though he was offered a free choice, 'God closed in'. The chapter ends with perhaps the most famous passage in all his books – the account of his conversion to Theism.

In the concluding Chapter XV, 'The Beginning', Lewis says that because his conversion 'involved as yet no belief in a future life' he was 'permitted for several months, perhaps for a year, to know God and to attempt obedience without even raising that question.' He believed that 'God is such that if (*per impossibile*) his power could vanish and His other attributes remain, so that the supreme right were for ever robbed of the supreme might, we should still owe Him precisely the same kind and degree of allegiance as we now do.' He admitted that 'the transition from mere Theism to Christianity' was the 'one on which I am now least informed' (see the letter to Arthur Greeves of 18 October 1931 in **TST**).

There follows an account of what he calls the 'final step' to his conversion, when he was driven to Whipsnade Zoo (28 September 1931) in the side-car of Warnie's motor cycle. 'When we set out,' he says, 'I did not believe that Jesus Christ is the Son of God, and when we reached the zoo I did ... It was ... like when a man, after long sleep, still lying motionless in bed, becomes aware that he is now awake.' 'But what, in conclusion, of Joy?' he asked. In the end he saw that 'it never had the kind of importance' he once gave it, but 'was valuable only as a pointer to something other and outer.'

Reviews

Dorothy L. Sayers* said in her review in *Time and Tide*, 36 (1 October 1955), pp. 1263–4: 'Professor Lewis writes with delightful and humorous candour, and shows all his accustomed skill in translating complex abstractions into vivid concrete imagery. The limpidity of these waters may disguise their depth, so clearly do they reveal the bottom. But any illusion about this can be quickly dispelled by stepping into the river.' The reviewer for *The Times Literary Supplement* (7 October 1955), p. 583, said: 'The story ... lacks the appalling, double-you-for-damnation sense of crisis which hangs over, say, that of Bunyan. Yet the tension of these final chapters holds the interest like the close of a thriller. Nor is this lessened by the fact that the spiritual experiences here recorded follow – intellectually, at least – no common pattern. Few other Christians can have been convinced by just such strategy; few ever could be. God moves, indeed, in a mysterious way, and this book gives a brilliant account of one of the oddest and most decisive end-games He has ever played.'

Anne Fremantle said in *Commonweal*, 63 (3 February 1956), pp. 464–5: 'This is an almost agonizingly personal book: it is the conversion of a pure romantic, and it is as completely convincing as are the conversion stories of Augustine and Newman.' Theodore A. Gill wrote in *The Christian Century*, 73 (9 May 1956), p. 585: 'It is one long chat with a witty, wise, sophisticated scholar. It has eloquence and humour and startling insights. It has some of the most perceptive theology Lewis has written, done up more beguilingly than ever before. Here is a man you would be lucky to know – this engaging 'snob in Christ' ... You can watch the I.B.M. mind of C.S. Lewis schematizing, rationalizing, explaining, understanding everything so splendidly ... If a good book is one that says more than the author wrote, this one is right up in there.'

A GRIEF OBSERVED (1961)

Background

I: N.W. Clerk

A Grief Observed, the title which Lewis chose for this short book, precisely describes its nature. It is an observation of the grief that he suffered at the loss of his wife following her death in 1960, and also of the effect that this grief had on him and on his thinking. It was not initially intended for publication at all, but was his way of fighting back against the overwhelming emotional pressure of his bereavement. In times of crisis it was always his habit to turn to pen and ink in order to address his problems. This book, which has proved to be such an invaluable source of help for those experiencing great loss, is really the result of a brave man turning his attention towards his own pain and carefully observing what it was doing to him.

The book was written in the days immediately following the death of his wife in July. When Roger Lancelyn Green* came to visit Lewis at The Kilns in the first week of September, Lewis showed him the manuscript, and the two friends discussed the possibility of its publication, Green being bound to secrecy. Lewis did not wish to embarrass or upset his friends, and decided to publish the work under a pseudonym. Showing it to his literary agent Spencer Curtis Brown, he submitted it under the name *Dimidius*, Latin for 'Halved', a revealing statement of the unity of two people which his marriage had meant to him. Curtis Brown, in order to maintain the anonymity of the author, sent the book to Faber, who had not previously published any of Lewis's work. One of the directors of that company at the time was T.S. Eliot who found the book intensely moving, and having at once guessed the identity of the author, suggested that if Lewis was serious about maintaining his anonymity he should use a plausible English pen name rather than one which in itself would attract attention.

Lewis saw the sense of this and selected the name N. W. Clerk, thus combining a pen name he had used before, Nat Whilk (Anglo-Saxon for I know not whom) and Clerk meaning scholar or writer. The book was published by Faber in 1961 as by N.W. Clerk.

Ironically very few people recognized the identity of the author of *A Grief Observed* other than those he had in mind when he chose to remain anonymous. It is certain that any reader who knew him would immediately recognize his "voice" in this superbly clear and economical little book. Sister Penelope* was one who guessed correctly and was congratulated by Lewis but asked to keep the fact a secret. However the ruse performed its function in that those of his friends who did recognize his hand were protected from having to remark on it or discuss it with him, as they would have felt compelled to do had it been under his own name.

II: Clerk or Lewis?

When *A Grief Observed* was published, it found few reviewers, but many very grateful readers. Some indeed found this work by N.W. Clerk so helpful that they sent copies to C. S. Lewis, in the hope that it might be as helpful to him as it had been to them. And although he always acknowledged such gifts, he did not reveal that he himself was the author. The book did not become widely known, and it is conceivable that had it not eventually been published under his own name, it might not be in print today. However, shortly after Lewis died, Faber and Faber approached his trustees, Owen Barfield and Cecil Harwood, requesting permission to re-publish the book as by C.S. Lewis. Barfield and Harwood did not take this decision lightly, as they recalled the very serious point which Lewis had made in *The Personal Heresy*:

> The poet is not a man who asks me to look at him; he is a man who says 'look at that' and points; the more I follow the pointing of his finger, the less I can possibly see of him ... I must make of him not a spectacle but a pair of spectacles.

Were they to publish the book under his real name after it had already been published as by N.W. Clerk, they risked making him a spectacle, but at the same time might enable and encourage far more people to use it as a pair of spectacles through which to come to a better understanding of grief. Finally, they decided to run the risk, a decision for which many thousands of people have reason to be very grateful, and the book came out under the name C.S. Lewis in 1964.

Summary

A Grief Observed is unlike anything else by Lewis, in that it was not written with publication in mind, and thus, while it bears all that clarity which is his hallmark, it was neither consciously planned nor calculatedly structured. It is rather, the raw emotions of a man in an agony of bereavement, starkly recorded together with his observations of those emotions. It is this blatant honesty of approach which gives the book its power to move and in many cases to heal its readers. Lewis thought the fact that he did not craft the piece would disguise its true authorship. Plainly enough, any honest description of the desperation of grief and its wounds will be found to have similarities to *A Grief Observed*, but that lies in the nature of grief and not the skills of the writer.

Part I. The trough of despair

The first chapter of the book is a cry from the heart, being concerned almost exclusively with Lewis's own state in bereavement. It is the epitome of the very self-centredness of grief, as he describes his own feelings. 'No one ever told me that grief felt so like fear' and 'it feels like being mildly drunk' he says as he explores the physical attributes of his emotional state. But inevitably the object of his grief, his dead wife, referred to as 'H' for Helen, Joy's first (though never used) name, begins to intrude. As he progresses down into the emotional trough he is repeatedly surprised at what he feels. He passes through stages when he feels that he doesn't 'really mind so much' but this is soon followed by tears and pathetic wallowing in the spurious pleasure of his self-pity, which he finds both disturbing and disgusting.

And 'meanwhile, where is God?' Lewis seems to find that when in desperation he turns to God all he finds is 'A door slammed in your face …' and 'After that, silence'. He wonders why he has felt the presence of God in the happy times, and asks where He is now when He is needed? Lewis makes plain that his marriage was the completion of him as a man, and with the honesty for which his writing is renowned describes his relationship and its meaning to him.

'For those few years H and I feasted on love; every mode of it – solemn and merry, romantic and realistic, sometimes as dramatic as a thunderstorm, sometimes as comfortable and unemphatic as putting on your soft slippers. No cranny of heart or body remained unsatisfied.'

He has begged for assurance that H continues to exist somewhere, but there is no answer. He writes of his awareness of the embarrassment of those he meets as they try to avoid talking about his loss, or bravely face the issue at once. He goes on to speak of the danger not of ceasing to believe in God but of believing His absence is deliberate. He comes to the realization that all loving human relationships will end in separation; that we all go alone into the unknown.

This first chapter is a virtual descent into Hell. H's death is irrevocable and irreversible. He has difficulty in remembering her face. 'But her voice is still vivid ... that can turn me at any moment to a whimpering child.'

Part II. Beginning the climb

Lewis admits to being appalled when he reads the notes he has written, for he says, 'From the way I have been talking anyone would think that H's death mattered chiefly for its effect on myself', and thus faces up squarely to the solipsism of grief. He decides that he must 'think more about H' and less about himself. But here again he encounters a trap, that of creating in his mind a more and more imaginary woman who will eventually supplant the real person whom he has lost. Having found in her the reality which he had always sought, he now faces the possibility of that reality fading into an unreal artifice of his own creation. As the chapter progresses we find the raw emotions beginning to be replaced by reason, but reason still driven by the agony of his loss. His concern now is for H. He is told she is 'in God's hands' but that is no comfort. A supposedly loving God allowed her to suffer in this life; may He not continue to hurt her after death? In a moment of almost utter despair he finds himself making what is tantamount to a vicious attack on the nature of God.

'Sometimes it is hard not to say, "God forgive God." Sometimes it is hard to say so much. But if our faith is true, He didn't. He crucified him.' And:

'Supposing the truth were "God always vivisects"?'

This passage is then followed by the admission:

'I wrote that last night, it was a yell rather than a thought.'

He then proceeds to work through the whole concept of the possibility of an evil God, and in the end shows that such thoughts to which he has been tempted, are nonsense. Yet the grief, the emptiness are still there. Chapter II ends with what is almost a prose poem defining the nature of love, loss and bereavement, the pain, the fear, and at the very last the hope ...

'One flesh. Or, if you prefer, one ship. The starboard engine has gone. I, the port engine, must chug along somehow till we make harbour. Or rather, till the journey ends. How can I assume a harbour? A lee shore, more likely, a black night, a deafening gale, breakers ahead – and any lights shown from the land probably being waved by wreckers. Such was H's landfall. Such was my mother's. I say their landfalls; not their arrivals.'

Part III. A slow ascent

Part III begins with the observation of how flat and dull everything seems since H left him, as if by her very going she had somehow taken the value of all else with her, leaving the world drained of life and colour.

'Does grief finally subside into boredom tinged by faint nausea?' he asks, and then promptly and with an evident effort, turns away from emotion to apply thought instead. Thought in its turn brings him to a long and searching look at himself and the faith that he had always considered himself to have had, and he finds it wanting. Lewis likens his faith to a house of cards, for it seems to have collapsed at one blow. If it was so fragile, so easily dislodged, did it have any reality, any substance in the first place?

Looking back to 'a week ago' he compares his thoughts of then and the present, and begins to come to the realization that what he is going through is just that, a passage through a process, his raging at God was part of this journey which has put him through torment, his abuse more telling God what he wanted Him to hear out of anger and pain than a true expression of thought. But he still fears for H at God's hands, for he knows she was not perfect. He likens her to a stained sword that has to be scoured by God, and makes a heart-rending plea for her to be treated tenderly. He would bear her suffering if he could and wonders if it is ever allowed. And then comes a statement of renewed faith:

It was allowed to One, we are told, and I find I can now believe again, that He has done vicariously whatever can be so done.

In himself Lewis is calmer. He begins to feel that the door is no longer locked. God is there somewhere, and he wonders if it was not his own roaring, shouting need that deafened him to God's replies. Now that he has ceased to worry that his memory of H might become false he receives a sense of her, not physically, not emotionally, but

> a sort of unobtrusive but massive sense that she is, just as much as ever, a fact to be taken into account.

Lewis begins to understand what he had hitherto only been able to feel. He relates his loss to that of an amputee. Never again will he be a whole man in the sense that he was before, but with the realization of this also comes the ability to at least begin to accept it. Then comes the slide back as he tells of the experience common to most bereavements, of feeling guilty about the slow but sure easing of pain.

> Still, there's no denying that in some sense I 'feel better', and with that comes at once a sort of shame, and a feeling that one is under a sort of obligation to cherish and foment and prolong one's unhappiness ... I am sure that H wouldn't approve of it. She'd tell me not to be a fool. So I'm pretty certain, would God.

He then examines this phenomenon and soon cuts through to the heart of the matter, finding that the pain of parting is a part of the loving relationship. The marriage has simply moved on to a further phase of its eternal development. Just as he seems to be gaining the upper hand over his grief, it suddenly all comes undone, and the pain comes crashing in again. The chapter ends unexpectedly with another cry of agony, but not, this time, of despair.

> One keeps emerging from a phase but it always recurs. Round and round. Everything repeats. Am I going in circles, or dare I hope I am on a spiral? But if a spiral, am I going up or down? ... They say, 'The coward dies many times'; so does the beloved. Didn't the eagle find a fresh liver to tear in Prometheus every time it dined?

Part IV. And into the dawn

The short fourth chapter of A Grief Observed displays the beginnings of a real understanding of grief as a process rather than a state. By this time Lewis is aware of the nature of grief and the temptations and traps that it extends. He describes how his loss has taken from him even much of his pre-H past along with his present, and, as far as he can see it, his future. Yet he can say,

Still there are two enormous gains – I know myself too well now to call them 'lasting'. Turned to God, my mind no longer meets that locked door; turned to H, it no longer meets that vacuum – nor all that fuss about my mental image of her.

Looking over his jottings he sees that he never thought to praise either H or God, the route that would have lifted him up, for 'Praise is the mode of love which always has some element of joy in it.' And now, when he thinks of H in God's hands, he thinks of her as a weapon God can use and delight in. As he ponders the mysteries of the fruition of God and reunion with the dead, he knows he cannot know the answers, but now he has the intuition that they may be shatteringly simple. And he has experienced an even stronger sense of H's presence, which he describes as 'the impression of her *mind* momentarily facing my own', 'an extreme and cheerful intimacy ... that had not passed through the senses or the em-otions at all.' This results in what he calls 'a sort of spring cleaning in his mind', as he realizes the dead could be sheer intellects and that one must rethink one's concepts of their state of being. But he also realizes that it is useless to speculate. He has now reached the end of his journey and admits his inability to comprehend,

But I mustn't, because I have come to misunderstand a little less completely what a pure intelligence might be, lean over too far. There is also, whatever it means, the resurrection of the body. We cannot understand. The best is perhaps what we understand the least.

Didn't people dispute once whether the final vision of God was more an act of intelligence or of love? That is probably another of the nonsense questions.

How wicked it would be if we could call the dead back! She said not to me but to the Chaplain, 'I am at peace with God.' She smiled, but not at me.

Reviews

A reviewer for *The Church Times*, CXLIV (3 November 1961), p. 4, said: '[The book] is published in the hope that it may help others who have suffered in the same kind of way as Mr Clerk to find the same kind of relief as he has done.' *The Times Literary Supplement* (10 November 1961), p. 803: 'Begun after his wife's death from a long and painful illness the journal might itself have been an instrument of escape. But its honest dissection is the negation of self-pity. Honest it is; but too complex, intellectualized and indeed well-written to be artless in the sense of naïve. Drawing firmly back from each conventional posture of the mourner, Mr Clerk invites not sympathy but co-operation in his attempt to argue out a grief.'

Erika Fallaux reviewing *A Grief Observed* in *Life of the Spirit*, XVI (May 1962), pp. 498–9, said: 'I cannot remember a document more poignant and more moving – not only about dying, but about married love as well ... The Christian – whether he be a Catholic like ourselves or, like the author, so very close to being one (if he will allow me to say this without impertinence) – who in a moment of pain and panic asks himself these questions, is faced by a far more profound problem than the non-believer who knows he doesn't yet know all the answers, but narrows his cosmos to such an extent that he excludes all contradictions. The Christian has to learn to come to terms with a God he must believe is Love, yet who can at times look nightmarishly like a cosmic sadist.'

NOVELS

❧

Out of the Silent Planet,
The Dark Tower, Perelandra,
That Hideous Strength,
Till We Have Faces

OUT OF THE SILENT
PLANET (1938)

Background

I: An Early Interest in Science Fiction

Lewis's enjoyment of science fiction began as a boy when two of his favourite authors were H.G. Wells and Jules Verne. They inspired him to write, when he was six, a story entitled 'To Mars and Back'. It was not, however, mere *stories* of the heavens that he liked. He and his brother were given a telescope when 'Jack' Lewis was eleven, and this opened up a lifetime interest in the heavenly bodies. Later, as an Oxford undergraduate, he wrote to Arthur Greeves* about his poem on the goddess Venus. It was based upon, he said on 5 May 1919, 'a very curious legend about Helen' whom the magician Simon Magus takes up into the heavens. On the way, 'they had to fight "the Dynasties" or planets – the evil powers that hold the heaven, between us and something really friendly beyond' (**TST**). He did not finish the poem, but the theme was to reappear in the struggle of the *Oyéresu* to free the Silent Planet from the 'Bent One'.

'The idea of other planets exercised upon me,' he said in **SBJ** II, 'a peculiar, heady attraction, which was quite different from any other of my literary interests. The interest, when the fit was on me, was ravenous, like a lust ... My own planetary romances have been not so much the gratification of that fierce curiosity as its exorcism.'

II: The Influence of Lindsay, Stapledon and Haldane

In about 1935 Lewis came across a book that was to have a powerful influence on him, David Lindsay's *Voyage to Arcturus* (1920). The author's style was crude and his subject matter nearly diabolical. However, as Lewis said in a letter to Ruth Pitter* of 4 January 1947, 'From Lindsay I first learned what other planets in fiction were really good for: for *spiritual* adventures.' He was to mention this 'shattering, intolerable and irresistible work' years later in his essay **On Science Fiction** in which he makes the valuable distinction that good novels are 'comments on life', while good stories like *Voyage to Arcturus* are 'actual additions to life. They give, like certain rare dreams, sensations we never had before, and enlarge our conception of the range of possible experience.'

Lewis could tolerate David Lindsay's philosophy because his novels never pretended to be anything more than holiday-literature. On the other hand, there were others who were deadly serious about carrying their poisonous philosophy to other planets. In a letter to Roger Lancelyn Green* on 28 December 1938 he said:

> What actually spurred me to write was Olaf Stapledon's *Last and First Men* [1930] and an essay in J.B.S. Haldane's *Possible Worlds* [1927], both of which seemed to take the idea of such travel seriously and to have the desperately immoral outlook which I try to pillory in Weston.

The 'Last Men' in Stapledon's book are those pioneers in space who, in their effort to survive, slaughter the inhabitants of Mars and Venus. They eventually evolve from a 'super-brain' into the 'cosmic ideal' of a kind of world soul – or 'Soul of All' (XI). Professor Haldane, a well-known biochemist, biologist and Marxist, summed up what Lewis found so distasteful about colonizing space. Haldane hated Christianity, and in his 'Last Judgement', in *Possible Worlds*, he imagines how, just before the Earth is destroyed, some men might journey to Venus and conquer it. He believed that 'man should live for ever', and on Venus his ideal man is 'somewhere in between' an ant-heap mentality and a race 'absorbed in the pursuit of individual happiness'. Haldane expected man to jettison anything remotely ethical for, as he said, 'God's ways are not our ways'.

Lewis and Haldane never met but, following the publication of Lewis's trilogy, a review by Haldane entitled 'Auld Hornie [The Devil] F.R.S.' appeared in the *Modern Quarterly* (Autumn 1946). He paid Lewis the compliment of comparing his celestial landscapes and the human and non-human behaviour to the work of Dante and Milton, but he nevertheless took the novels to be an attack on Science. Because so many have made this mistake, it is fortunate that we have Lewis's **Reply to Professor Haldane** in which he disputes this.

Out of the Silent Planet was not, he insisted, an attack on Science, but 'on something which might be called "scientism" – a certain outlook on the world which is casually connected with the popularization of the sciences, though it is much less common among real scientists than among their readers. It is, in a word, the belief that the supreme moral end is the perpetuation of our own species, and that this is to be pursued even if, in the process of being fitted for survival, our species has to be stripped of all those things for which we value it – of pity, of happiness, and of freedom. I am not sure that you will find this belief formally asserted by any writer: such things creep in as assumed, and unstated, major premisses' (see **Science and Scientism**§*).

III: The Invention of a Christian Mythology

In Michaelmas Term 1928 Lewis began a series of public lectures on 'The Romance of the Rose and its Successors'. A few years later he began another series on the 'Prolegomena to Medieval Poetry'. In time they were brought together as the 'Prolegomena to the Study of Medieval and Renaissance Literature'. In them he discussed the Ptolemaic model of the universe and the astrological personifications of Mars, Venus and the other planets. These lectures formed the basis of other ones he gave at Cambridge, and together they became the core of his last book, *The Discarded Image*, which provides an invaluable background to the interplanetary novels.

One of the books discussed in the 'Prolegomena' lectures was a little-known work by a twelfth-century Platonist, Bernardus Silvestris. His *De Mundi Universitate*, edited by Carl Sigmund Barach and Johann Wrobel (Innsbruck, 1876), which Lewis finished reading for the first time on 4 August 1930, was to have an enormous influence on his trilogy. In Appendix I on 'Genius and Genius' in *The Allegory of Love*, Lewis distinguished between Genius A which means 'the universal god of generation' and Genius B which means the 'tutelary spirit, or "external soul" of an individual man'. In Bernardus Silvestris he had come across the term *Oyarses* which a colleague at Magdalen College, C.C.J. Webb, pointed out to him in a letter of 31 October 1931, was a corruption of οὐσιάρχης or *Ousiarches* ('ruling essence') from Pseudo-Apuleius's *Asclepius* (XIX). This was a very important discovery. The passage in Bernardus that was to play such an important part in his interplanetary trilogy was:

Illic Oyarses quidem erat et genius in artem et officium pictoris et figurantis addictus. In subteriacente enim mundo rerum facies universa caelum sequitur sumptisque de caelo proprietatibus ad imaginem quam conversio contulit figuratur. Namque impossibile est formam unam quamque alteri simillimam nasci horarum et climatum distantibus punctis. Oyarses igitur circuli quem pantomorphon Graecia, Latinitas nominat omniformem, formas rebus omnes omnibus et associat et ascribit (Liber Secundus, III, 91–100).

In *The 'Cosmographia' of Bernardus Silvestris*, translated by Winthrop Wetherbee (Columbia University Press, 1973), the passage is translated:

For the Usiarch here was that Genius devoted to the art and office of delineating and giving shape to the forms of things. For the whole appearance of things in the subordinate universe conforms to the heavens, whence it assumes its characteristics, and it is shaped to whatever image the motion of the heavens imparts. For it is impossible that one form should be born identical with another at points separate in time and place. And so the Usiarch of that sphere which is called in Greek Pantomorphos, and in Latin Omniformis, composes and assigns the forms of all creatures ('Microcosmos', chapter III, p. 96).

This was ideal for Lewis's purpose. He followed Bernardus in making an *Oyarses* or *Oyarsa* (plural *Oyéresu*) not only the 'ruling essence', the 'Genius devoted to the art and office of delineating and giving shape to the forms of things', but also something like an archangel. His 'silent planet myth' was beginning to take shape. In 1935 he published a poem on 'The Planets' in which he went beyond his medieval models in describing the essential qualities of those heavenly bodies. Now he went further. Having decided, as he told Ruth Pitter, that the other planets were good for '*spiritual* adventures', he renamed the planet Mars 'Malacandra' and provided it with an *Oyarsa* to rule it. In the letter to Roger Lancelyn Green of 28 December 1938, he said he had a particular motive in mind when writing *Out of the Silent Planet*: 'I like the whole interplanetary idea as a *mythology* and simply wished to conquer for my own (Christian) point of view what has always hitherto been used by the opposite side.'

One of the first to write a letter of appreciation for *Out of the Silent Planet* was Sister Penelope* of the Community of St Mary the Virgin. Replying to her on 9 August 1939, he said:

What set me about writing the book was the discovery that a pupil of mine took all that dream of interplanetary colonization quite seriously, and the realization that thousands of people, in one form or another, depend on some hope of perpetuating and improving the human species for the whole meaning of the universe – that a 'scientific' hope of defeating death is a real rival to Christianity ...

You will be both grieved and amused to learn that out of about sixty reviews, only two showed any knowledge that my idea of the fall of the Bent One was anything but a private invention of my own! But if only there were someone with a richer talent and more leisure, I believe this great ignorance might be a help to the evangelization of England: any amount of theology can now be smuggled into people's minds under cover of romance without their knowing it (**L**).

Theology, it may be said, with a look beyond our world. Lewis had long noticed, as he said in **Unreal Estates**, that 'Most of the earlier stories start from the ... assumption that we, the human race, are in the right, and everything else is ogres. I may have done a little towards altering that.' In *Out of the Silent Planet* he turned the tables on the traditional view that 'everything else is ogres'. He had not written anything about the possible inhabitants of other planets before *Out of the Silent Planet* appeared, but in later years he expressed the thoughts that he held when writing his interplanetary trilogy. These beliefs first found expression in *Miracles* VII, and then **Religion and Rocketry** but a passage from **The Seeing Eye** will serve us well here. In essence, he thought that if we reached other planets,

We might ... find a race which was, like us, rational but, unlike us, innocent – no wars nor any other wickedness among them; all peace and good fellowship. I don't think any Christian would be puzzled to find that they knew no story of an Incarnation or Redemption, and might even find our story hard to understand or accept if we told it to them. There would have been no Redemption in such a world because it would not have needed redeeming ... We should have much to learn from such people and nothing to teach them. We'd find some reason for exterminating them.

Summary

The novel opens with Dr Elwin Ransom, a middle-aged Philologist of Cambridge University, on a walking tour. He is kidnapped by two men, Dick Devine and Dr Weston, a mad physicist who wants to extend humanity to other planets. They force Ransom aboard their spaceship and fly to the planet Malacandra (Mars), where they hope to find gold. Although a captive, Ransom relishes the voyage through the heavens, and the description of it as seen through his eyes is one of the finest things in the book. 'The very name "Space" seemed a blasphemous libel for this empyrean ocean of radiance in which they swam. He could not call it "dead"; he felt life pouring into him from it every moment. How indeed should it be otherwise, since out of this ocean the worlds and all their life had come? ... He saw now that it was the womb of worlds, whose blazing and innumerable offspring looked down nightly even upon the earth with so many eyes – and here, with how many more! No: Space was the wrong name. Older thinkers had been wiser when they named it simply the heavens' (5).

During the voyage Ransom, overhearing Weston and Devine, learns that he has been brought along as a sacrifice to creatures called *sorns*. On arrival in Malacandra Ransom is struck by the 'bright, still, sparkling, unintelligible landscape – with needling shapes of pale green, thousands of feet high, with sheets of dazzling blue soda water, and acres of rose-red soapsuds' (7). However, when they spot a group of sorns – 'spindly and flimsy things, twice or three times the height of a man' (7) – he is terrified and manages to escape.

In hiding he encounters another of the three species of beings on Malacandra. It is a *hross* who has a sleek, black body very like that of a seal or an otter. The *hross* begins talking and Ransom gradually picks up the language of Malacandra. It is 'Old Solar', the language spoken before the Fall of Man. Ransom has several losses of confidence in dealing with the *hross*. 'They arose when the rationality of the *hross* tempted you to think of it as a man. Then it became abominable – a man seven feet high, with a snaky body, covered, face and all, with thick black animal hair, and whiskered like a cat. But starting at the other end you had an animal with everything an animal ought to have – glossy coat, liquid eye, sweet breath and whitest teeth – and added to all these, as though Paradise had never been lost and earliest dreams were true, the charm of speech and reason. Nothing could be more disgusting than the one impression; nothing more delightful than the other. It all depended on the point of view' (9).

Hyoi – the *hross* who befriends Ransom – takes him to the valley where his people live. Ransom is delighted with their simple agricultural life, and especially the *hross* cubs to whom he appears a 'hairless goblin'. Their only art is a combination of poetry and music. Ransom discovers that there are two other rational species on Malacandra: the *sorns* or *séroni*, tall, lean creatures like elongated men, their legs covered with feathers, who are devoted to scientific research; and the *pfifltriggi*, frog-like creatures who work as miners and artisans.

After becoming fluent in Old Solar, Ransom learns that on Malacandra the Earth is called Thulcandra – the 'silent planet'. The nearest Mala-candrian equivalent to 'evil' is 'bent'. When they learn that Ransom's 'bent companions' tried to kill him the *hrossa* tell him he must go to the Oyarsa. All he can learn of the Oyarsa is that he has always lived at Meldilorn, that he knows everything and rules everyone. When he inquires if the Oyarsa made the world, the *hrossa* are surprised. 'Did people in Thulcandra,' they ask, 'not know that Maleldil the Young had made and still ruled the world?' (11). Before Ransom has realized who Maleldil the Young is, and is about to undertake the religious instruction of the *hrossa*, he finds himself being treated as if *he* were the savage. They give him a first sketch of civilized religion (11).

The three species of *hnau* are not the only inhabitants of Malacandra. There are also spiritual beings called the *eldila* (singular *eldil*) who are visible to Ransom only as a faint movement of light. They are present throughout the planet and take a benevolent interest in the life of the Malacandrians. They inform the *hrossa* that the Oyarsa has sent for Ransom. However, just before Ransom leaves there is the crack of an English rifle and Hyoi lies dead at his feet. Weston and Devine are on to him. Ransom is heartbroken and ashamed of his race. The *hrossa* show him the way to Meldilorn where he is to meet the Oyarsa.

The *séroni* live at the top of the steep Malacandrian mountain, and Ransom meets this species next. The *sorn* 'Augray' acts as his host and explains many things to him. He tells him more about the *eldila* than the *hrossa* were able to do, and Ransom learns that the Oyarsa is himself the *eldil* who from the time Malacandra was made was put in charge of the planet. On the way to Meldilorn, Augray and the *sorns* have many questions for Ransom about Thulcandra. When Augray hears about man's wars, slavery and prostitution he thinks it must be 'because every one of them wants to be a little Oyarsa himself' (16). They are surprised that there is only one rational species on Earth and suppose 'this must have far-reaching effects in the narrowing of sympathies and even of thought' (ibid.).

Meldilorn is an island of pale red set in the middle of a lake. On the island is a grove of trees rising up to great heights like the spires of a cathedral and flowering at the top. After they cross over to it, Ransom meets some of the *pfifltriggi* who are carving pictures of history and mythology. Ransom notices that in their carving of the solar system the Earth is the only planet shown as having the representation of its Oyarsa erased.

Following a night there Ransom is taken to the Oyarsa of Malacandra. He cannot see him, but as the Oyarsa passes near him Ransom feels 'a tingling of his blood and a pricking on his fingers as if lightning were near him; and his heart and body seemed to him to be made of water' (18). He learns from him the story of his planet as it is known throughout the solar system. The Oyarsa explains that the Earth, like all the planets, once had an Oyarsa. After he became 'bent' 'it was in his mind to spoil other worlds besides his own.' To prevent this Maleldil drove him out of the heavens and bound him in the air of his own planet. It thus became silent. The Oyarsa goes on to speak of what Ransom recognized as the Incarnation. 'There are stories among us,' the Oyarsa says, that Maleldil 'dared terrible things, wrestling with the Bent One in Thulcandra' (ibid.). He asks Ransom to tell him more of what Maleldil did on earth.

Before this can happen they are interrupted by the arrival of a group of *hrossa* who are carrying the bodies of three of their companions and escorting Weston and Devine who, of course, killed the *hrossa*. Oyarsa demands to know why they did this. Weston makes the mistake of supposing the Malacandrians the most primitive type of creatures. He blusters about his ability to blow everyone up 'Pouff! Bang!' and dangles beads before their eyes – 'Pretty, pretty! See! See!' They have never seen anything so comical. All Meldilorn shakes with laughter.

Weston, completely misunderstanding what a fool he is seen to be, tells Oyarsa that he is there on behalf of 'Life' and that he and others intend to 'march on, step by step ... claiming planet after planet, system after system, till our posterity – whatever strange form and yet unguessed mentality they have assumed – dwell in the universe where the universe is habitable' (20). Weston has difficulty with Old Solar, so Ransom acts as a translator for him. This provides for some delightful irony, as in the following:

'I may fall,' said Weston. 'But while I live I will not, with such a key in my hand, consent to close the gates of the future on my race. What lies in that future, beyond our present ken, passes imagination to conceive: it is enough for me that there is a Beyond.' 'He is saying,' Ransom translates, 'that he will not stop trying to do all this unless you kill him. And he says that though he doesn't know what will happen to the creatures sprung from us, he wants it to happen very much' (ibid.).

When Weston protests his love for mankind, Oyarsa says 'What you really love is no completed creature but the very seed itself: for that is all that is left' (ibid.). Oyarsa realizes that Weston and Devine are, like the Oyarsa of Thulcandra, so 'bent' that they are beyond his help. As a penalty he orders their space ship back to Earth. Ransom, who is protected by the *eldila*, goes with them. Oyarsa has given orders that their ship will explode in ninety days, and they barely make it back to Earth in time.

In chapter 22 Lewis enters the story himself and the rest is told by him. He explains how, after Ransom's return from Mars, he wrote to him about Bernardus Silvestris's use of the word *Oyarses*. When they meet Ransom tells him of his trip to Malacandra and the threat to mankind from Weston. They decide that Lewis should write the story of Ransom's journey, making it sound like a work of fiction lest Weston sue for libel.

Lewis hoped that his readers would understand the theology of *Out of the Silent Planet* without having to be told. However, when asked, he did not mind explaining the meaning of *Maleldil*. Victor Hamm was one of the many who speculated about the exact meaning of the word, and after sending Lewis a copy of his article, 'Mr Lewis in Perelandra', *Thought* 20 (June 1945), Lewis replied on 11 August:

> MAL- is really equivalent to the definite article in some of the definite article's uses. ELDIL means a lord or ruler, Maleldil *'The Lord'*: i.e. it is, strictly speaking, the Old Solar not for DEUS but for DOMINUS.

For the sake of clarity, we may note that the 'Old One' is God the Father; the 'Bent One', or Bent Oyarsa of Thulcandra, is Satan; and the *eldila* are angels.

Reviews

Out of the Silent Planet received many favourable reviews, but most readers were unsure what the author meant by it. The reviewer for *The Times* (30 September 1938), p. 7, described it as 'a first novel ... of the kind to do with adventure beyond our Earth to which Mr Wells long ago accustomed us ... The world on which the three travellers alight differs from those of Mr Wells in being beautifully coloured and shaped, with inhabitants who are terrible only so long as they are unfamiliar. Here three species of rational beings live in amity together, ruled by a genie who is a kind of governor-general for the universal spirit.' The reviewer for *The Times Literary Supplement* (1 October 1938), p. 625, thought it much inferior to Wells and said: 'Alas! and alas! that ... a capable writer with an excellent basic notion, did not attend longer upon and learn more from his evident teacher ... it lacks too much of Mr Wells's special gift of dramatic sharpening, and above all of running characterization, other-worldly exposition and vivid incident in triple harness.'

One of the very few who saw what Lewis was doing was the Anglican divine, E.L. Mascall, who in *Theology* (April 1939), p. 304, said: 'This is an altogether satisfactory story, in which fiction and theology are so skilfully blended that the non-Christian will not realize that he is being instructed until it is too late. It is excellent propaganda and first-rate entertainment.'

Horace Reynolds writing in *The New York Times Book Review* (3 October 1943), p. 16, said: 'Everyone says a new world is just around the corner, but everyone is pretty vague about just what it is to be. The plain truth of the matter is that man has to imagine this new order before it can be realized. Mr Lewis's romance is one step forward in the preliminary dreaming, the discovery of the Mystery.'

THE DARK TOWER (1977)

Background

This story does not form part of the Trilogy because it exists only in a fragment and was not published until some years after Lewis's death. The manuscript, in the Bodleian Library,‡ consists of 62 pages. Pages 11 and 49 are missing, and it is not known whether Lewis finished the tale or abandoned it about halfway through. However, what survives appears to have been intended as a sequel to *Out of the Silent Planet*. That book ended with a Postscript in the form of an imaginary 'letter' from Ransom, of which the last sentence is: 'Now that "Weston" has shut the door, the way to the planets lies through the past; if there is to be any more space-travelling, it will have to be time-travelling as well ... !'

The first words of *The Dark Tower* pick up exactly where *Out of the Silent Planet* leaves off: '"Of course," said Orfieu, "the sort of time-travelling you read about in books – time-travelling in the body – is absolutely impossible."' Lewis was almost certainly referring to *The Dark Tower* when, in his letter to Sister Penelope* of 9 August 1939, he said, 'The letter at the end' of *Out of the Silent Planet* 'is pure fiction and the "circumstances which put the book out of date" are merely a way of preparing for a sequel' (L).

The fragment was probably written sometime in 1938–39 for one of the characters in chapter 1 mentions with wryness the 'remarkable discovery' 'that a man in 1938 can't get to 1939 in less than a year.' One of the Inklings, Father Gervase Mathew OP,* recalled hearing the first four chapters of the story read aloud at a meeting of the Inklings‡ in 1939 or 1940, and he remembered that the discussion was about time and memory.

There are two books mentioned in *The Dark Tower* which deal with time and memory, and they may be usefully read in conjunction with Lewis's story. The first is *An Adventure* (1911) by 'Elizabeth Morison' and 'Frances Lamont' – pseudonyms for Charlotte Anne Elizabeth Moberley and Eleanor Frances Jourdain. These ladies were both Principals of St Hugh's College, Oxford, and they claim that, on a visit to the Petit Trianon near Paris in 1901, they saw the palace and gardens exactly as they would have appeared to Marie Antoinette in 1792. The book was a sensation in Oxford. The other work is John William Dunne's *An Experiment with Time* (1927). Dunne was an aeronautical experimenter and the exponent of Serialism, and in Chapter III of his *Experiment* – the one most relevant to *The Dark Tower* – he suggests that all dreams are composed of images of past experience and images of future experience blended together in approximately equal proportions. This was to play a valuable part in this ingenious fragment.

Summary

The story, which is told in Lewis's voice, begins with five men meeting in Dr Orfieu's rooms in a Cambridge college.

> 'Of course,' said Orfieu, 'the sort of time-travelling you read about in books – time-travelling in the body – is absolutely impossible.'
>
> There were four of us in Orfieu's study. Scudamour, the youngest of the party, was there because he was Orfieu's assistant. Macphee had been asked down from Manchester because he was known to us all as an inveterate sceptic, and Orfieu thought that if once he were convinced, the learned world in general would have no excuse for incredulity. Ransom, the pale man with the green shade over his grey, distressed-looking eyes, was there for the opposite reason – because he had been the hero, or victim, of one of the strangest adventures that had ever befallen a mortal man. I had been mixed up with that affair – the story is told in another book – and it was to Ransom I owed my presence in Orfieu's party.

There follows a discussion about time-travel and the impossibility of a body occupying two places in different times at once. 'Where will the particles that compose your body be five hundred years hence?' asks Orfieu. 'They'll be all over the place – some in the earth, some in plants and animals, and some in the bodies of your descendants, if you have any. Thus to go to the year AD 3000 means going to a time at which your body doesn't exist.'

Orfieu then introduces his friends to the 'Chronoscope', which resembles a cinema projector. We learn that it catches an apparently arbitrary time-sequence, and reflects it on a screen. The friends suddenly find themselves looking into the interior of a Dark Tower at which a man sits completely still. He fills them with horror because of a poisonous sting projecting from his forehead. They watch as he stabs this 'sting' into the spine of human victims who are brought to him, after which they are dehumanized and leave as automata or 'Jerkies'. The chapter ends with the Stinging-man looking unblinkingly into the Chronoscope at Orfieu and his friends.

After watching for some time they realize that in this 'Othertime' the Dark Tower is a copy of the University Library which had just been built in Cambridge. Among those in the Tower they see a man who is Scudamour's exact double, and they watch with horror as he becomes a Stinging-man with a unicorn horn. Then they see a girl exactly like Scudamour's fiancée, Camilla Bembridge, brought in to be stung by him. In a moment of passion the real Scudamour flings himself into the Chronoscope. In doing so he wrecks it, and as he passes through it into Othertime his exact double jumps through into our world. Ransom concludes from this that the 'Othertime Scudamour' had exactly the same body as the Scudamour they know. 'I mean,' says Ransom, 'that the very same matter which made up Scudamour's body in 1938 made up that brute's body in Othertime … The Othertime occupant of that body is caught off his guard – simply pushed out of his body – but since that identical body is waiting for him in 1938, he inevitably slips into it and finds himself in Cambridge' (4).

The rest of the fragment, chapters 5–7, consists of a third-person account by Scudamour of his adventures in Othertime, following his return. Lewis handles the language difficulty with his usual adroitness. 'When Scudamour's consciousness entered the Othertime world it acquired no new knowledge in the strict sense of "knowledge", but it found itself furnished with a pair of ears and a tongue and vocal chords that had been trained for years in receiving and making the sounds of the Othertime language, and a brain which was in the habit of associating those sounds with certain ideas. He thus simply found himself using a language which, in another sense, he did not "know"' (chapter 5). Scudamour thus manages to pass himself off as the other man. It is not long before he meets there the double of Camilla who remembers him as someone called Michael. 'She looked at him with eyes full of love. He thought to himself that Camilla had not loved him so well in the old world' (ibid.). Scudamour finds her far more likeable than the one he left in Cambridge: 'The real Camilla Bembridge was what is called "modern". She was so free to talk about the things her grandmother could not mention that Ransom once said he wondered if she were free to talk about anything else ... And Scudamour, one gathers, had taken his tone from her. But here he felt different. Perhaps he had never been so very "modern" in his heart' (chapter 6).

In chapter 6 we also learn about what the others do in Othertime. The servants are called Drones, and they attempt to produce stings, hoping thereby to unseat the Stinging Man. In chapter 7 Scudamour has penetrated into the library of the Dark Tower, which is filled with numerous scientific and historical works. He learns that the Othertime aliens take for granted not only a backwards-forwards direction, but what they call a 'eckwards-andwards' direction. As a consequence, they are able to enjoy a kind of immortality. From other books he discovers how the aliens are able to 'exchange' the personality of one of their people for that of its Earthly double. They were able to make this 'time attraction' work, one writer recalled, when they took an earthly child 'of the same age and sex, and as nearly as possible, of the same physical type, and caused it to become conscious of its Othertime counterpart ... At the same time, he treated it with the greatest severity. Having thus produced in its mind a strong wish to change places with the Othertimer, he juxtaposed them, while the latter was asleep, and simply ordered the this-time child to escape him if it could.'

The reader will, doubtless, conclude that this is what happened with Camilla. But we can never be sure, nor can we discover how this might have affected the story because the manuscript breaks off at this point.

Reviews

The Dark Tower received favourable reviews in England. Tim Lenton, writing in the *Church of England Newspaper* (7 April 1977), p. 809, said: '"The Dark Tower" ... is as good as anything he wrote, and it is a tragedy for Lewis-addicts that it is incomplete. Even so, it is well worth reading for its original ideas on time and memory, and for sheer enjoyment for the clear, compelling style which was the author's hallmark.' Ian Stewart in *The Illustrated London News*, 265 (April 1977), p. 59, said: 'The best of these stories, *The Dark Tower*, is also the longest, though left unfinished ... Lewis takes his readers from the cosy world of speculative talk into the lurid realm of science fiction ... we ... can only regret that so inventive a storyteller did not complete his tale.' The Spenser scholar, Dr Alastair

Fowler, wrote in *The Times Literary Supplement* (1 July 1977), p. 795, 'In its present state "The Dark Tower" has flaws of clumsiness that would doubtless have been removed in a final draft. Yet it has the same holding power, the same compulsive readability, as the other parts of what I suppose we should now call the interplanetary tetralogy ... "The Dark Tower" is the least literary of all Lewis's fictions. Certainly it is the farthest from allegory and even from paraphrasable meaning. Consciously or unconsciously it approaches an area of mysteriously strong negative feelings and conflicts, untouched elsewhere in his work. Finished, it might have been his best.'

PERELANDRA (1943)

Background

I: Inspiration

In a piece written for children entitled **It All Began with a Picture ...**
Lewis said: 'All my seven Narnian books, and my three science fiction
books, began with seeing pictures in my head. At first they were not a
story, just pictures.' He expanded on this in a conversation with Kingsley
Amis and Brian Aldiss, **Unreal Estates**, in which he said:

> The starting point for my second novel, *Perelandra*, was my mental
> picture of the floating islands. The whole of the rest of my labours
> in a sense consisted of building up a world in which floating
> islands could exist. And then of course the story about an averted
> fall developed. This is because, as you know, having got your
> people to this exciting country, something must happen.

We don't know how long this 'mental picture' had been in Lewis's mind
before he wrote this undated fragment of verse, but it was almost
certainly the first thing he put on paper about *Perelandra*:

> The floating islands, the flat golden sky
> At noon, the peacock sunset: tepid waves
> With the land sliding over them like a skin:
> The alien Eve, green-bodied, stepping forth
> To meet my hero from her forest home,
> Proud, courteous, unafraid; no thought infirm
> Alters her cheek –

As these were the only lines of verse he appears to have written about the floating islands, he may have turned instantly to the prose work, *Perelandra*, which is arguably Lewis's most perfect book. It was, with *Till We Have Faces*, his favourite of his own works.

II: Influences

He had been lecturing in the University on Milton's *Paradise Lost* since 1937 and this, doubtless, furnished him with the basic plot of *Perelandra*. The story itself is taken, as was *Paradise Lost*, from Genesis 1–3. What Lewis does is to re-imagine the story of the Fall of Man and give us the story of Paradise Retained. An excellent introduction to Lewis's ideas on the Fall itself is his *Preface to 'Paradise Lost'*. In the chapter entitled 'The Fall' he said:

> What would have happened if instead of his 'compliance bad' Adam had scolded or even chastised Eve and then interceded with God on her behalf, we are not told. The reason we are not told is that Milton does not know ... This ignorance is not without significance. We see the results of our actions, but we do not know what would have happened if we had abstained. For all Adam knew, God might have had other cards in His hand; but Adam never raised the question, and now nobody will ever know. Rejected goods are invisible.

In his letter to Mrs Hook of 29 December 1958 Lewis explained that whereas Aslan was 'an invention giving an imaginary answer to the question, "What might Christ become like if there really were a world like Narnia and He chose to be incarnate and die and rise again in *that* world as He actually has done in ours?" ... So in "Perelandra". This also works out a *supposition*. ("Suppose, even now, in some other planet there were a first couple undergoing the same that Adam and Eve underwent here, but successfully")' (L).

Besides the biblical parallel there is a good deal of recognizable borrowing in the book. Apart from his mental picture of floating islands, he would have remembered the following passage in Olaf Stapledon's *Last and First Men* (chapter 13, Section I): 'In early days on Venus men had gathered foodstuffs from the great floating islands of vegetable matter ... ' From the first Lewis found it natural to picture the 'Adam' and 'Eve' of Perelandra as green. The idea came, he said, from a passage in Richard Burton's *Anatomy of Melancholy* (1621). Writing in Part 2, Section 2, Mem. 3

about the inhabitants of other planets Burton mentions: 'those two green children which Nubrigensis speaks of in his time, that fell from heaven.'

Of much greater importance is what Lewis called his 'Norse complex'. One of his most perceptive critics, Charles A. Brady, a Professor of English at Canisius College in Buffalo, New York, published two articles entitled 'Introduction to Lewis' and 'C.S. Lewis: II' in *America*, 71 (27 May and 10 June 1944). After reading them Lewis wrote to the author on 29 October 1944, saying: 'Obviously one ought never to thank a critic for praise: but perhaps one can congratulate a fellow scholar on the thoroughness of his work even if the subject of his work happens to be oneself. You are the first of my critics so far who has really read and understood *all* my books and "made up" the subject in a way that makes you an authority.' But, he said,

> you just missed tapping my whole Norse complex – Old Icelandic, Wagner's *Ring* and (again) Morris. The Wagner is important: you will also see, if you look, how *operatic* the whole building up of the climax is in *Perelandra*. Milton I think you possibly over-rate: it is difficult to distinguish him from Dante and St Augustine. (Tinidril at her second appearance owes something to Matilda at the end of *Purgatorio*) (L).

Richard Wagner's *Ring of the Nibelung* is a series of four music dramas based on the thirteenth-century *Nibelungenlied*. From the time he discovered it in 1911 it was Lewis's favourite story of all stories, and he never lost a chance of hearing the operas performed. He first read Wagner's libretto in *The Rhinegold and The Valkyrie* (1910) and *Siegfried and The Twilight of the Gods* (1911), translated by Margaret Armour, with illustrations by Arthur Rackham. They were two of his most treasured books.

In a paper read to the Oxford University C.S. Lewis Society‡ on 9 May 1995, 'In the Hall of the Fisher King: C.S. Lewis's Cosmic Trilogy as Arthurian Romance', Father Jerome Bertram pointed out that 'It is through the *Ring* that we can discover firstly what was Lewis's main theme in *Perelandra* ... The question is ... how can a totally free person, without unfair manipulation by God, spontaneously carry out what God most desires, and find for herself a destiny which God fully intends.' He went on to explain that:

> the Woman needs to make her own free and spontaneous choice to do the Will of God, without being unduly influenced by God.

Ransom, as another free agent, can help, but will not himself receive undue help. The greatest part of the long drama of *Perelandra* deals with this question, which in the end is unresolved, just as it is unresolved in Wagner. At one point Ransom himself asks why isn't Maleldil doing anything, only to be answered by the fact that his own remarkable voyage to Venus is a pretty considerable contribution – 'he himself was the miracle' (chapter 11). His long struggle with the Unman, and his final victory leaves the Woman free to make her own discovery of why she wants to obey God's will, and gives the cue for a magnificent operatic chorus to celebrate the victory. But we are not much wiser about the problem of grace and free-will: in the *Ring* everything goes wrong despite the fulfilment of the conditions, in *Perelandra* everything comes out all right despite the considerable amount of poison that the Unman has whispered into the Woman's ears, and the introduction of Death into her planet at the hands of Ransom, of all people.

Lewis devoted a chapter to 'Milton and St Augustine' in his *Preface to 'Paradise Lost'*. It is primarily a discussion of St Augustine's *The City of God*, Book XIV of which is concerned with the disobedience of Adam (see chapter xi).

Matilda, an attendant and friend of Beatrice, appears in *Purgatorio* XXVIII. The scene is Dante's Earthly Paradise. Dorothy L. Sayers* says in her translation of Dante's *Purgatory* (1955), Commentary to Canto XXVIII, p. 293: 'In the *allegory*, the Earthly Paradise is the state of *innocence*. It is from here that Man, if he had never fallen, would have set out upon his journey to the Celestial Paradise which is his ultimate destination ... Some commentators have seen in [Matilda] the "one permanent resident" of the Earthly Paradise, and supposed her to be the image of Empire, Philosophy or Natural Perfection.' The meeting between Dante and Matilda, which has a striking resemblance to that between Ransom and Tinidril, begins in Canto XXVIII, line 37:

> And there appeared to me – as when the intrusion
> Of some new wonder takes one unaware
> And throws all one's ideas into confusion –
>
> A lady all alone, who wandered there
> Sighing and plucking flower on floweret gay,
> With which her path was painted everywhere.

After they have come together the Lady begins to speak (line 76):

> 'You are newcomers here, and, as I guess,'
>   Said she, 'my smiling in this spot elect
>   To be the cradle of the human race
>
> May make you wonder, and perchance suspect;
>   But the psalm *Delectasti* gives you light
>   To illuminate your clouded intellect.
>
> And thou in front, who didst my approach invite,
>   Wouldst know more, ask on; I came prepared
>   To answer questions and content thee quite.'
>
> I said: 'The water, and the forest stirred
>   To music, seem to contradict what I
>   Had come to think, from what I lately heard.'
>
> She therefore: 'I will tell the reason why
>   These things are so, which cause perplexities,
>   And thus I'll make the offending mists to fly.
>
> The most high Good, that His sole self doth please,
>   Making man good, and for good, set him in
>   This place as earnest of eternal peace.'

III: The Writing of 'Perelandra'

The first we hear of the novel comes in a letter to Sister Penelope* of 9
November 1941, in which Lewis mentions the difficulty of creating an
unfallen 'Eve' for his story: 'I've got Ransom to Venus and through his
first conversation with the "Eve" of that world: a difficult chapter. I hadn't
realized till I came to write it all the *Ave-Eva* business. I may have
embarked on the impossible. This woman has got to combine
characteristics which the Fall has put poles apart – she's got to be in some
ways like a Pagan goddess and in other ways like the Blessed Virgin. But
if one can get even a fraction of it into words it is worth doing' (L).

On 23 December 1941 he wrote to Arthur Greeves:* 'I'm engaged on a
sequel to *The Silent Planet* in which the same man goes to Venus. The idea
is that Venus is at the Adam-and-Eve stage: i.e. the first two rational

creatures have just appeared and are still innocent. My hero arrives in
time to prevent their "falling" as *our* first pair did' (**TST**). On 11 May 1942
Lewis told Sister Penelope that: 'The Venus book is just finished, except
that I now find the two first chapters need re-writing.' The book was sent
to the publishers soon afterwards, and it came out in April 1943.

Summary

Perelandra opens with Lewis being summoned to Ransom's cottage near
Worchester. Ever since he'd been told about the eldila Lewis had been
very afraid of meeting one and he becomes more frightened as he goes
along. In the cottage, while waiting for Ransom, he senses that he is in the
presence of the Oyarsa of Malacandra. Ransom returns and explains that
he has been ordered to Perelandra (Venus) because it is rumoured that the
Black Oyarsa of Thulcandra (Satan) is meditating an attack on it. Lewis
helps Ransom into a box rather like a coffin, and he is transported to
Perelandra by the Oyarsa of Malacandra. About a year later he returns,
and Lewis and a doctor friend hurry to the cottage to hear his story, which
is told to the reader by Lewis.

Perelandra is a young world of floating islands, and the casket Ransom
lands in is dissolved. 'The sky was pure, flat gold like the background of a
medieval picture. It looked very distant – so far off as a cirrus cloud looks
from earth. The ocean was gold too, in the offing, flecked with innumerable shadows. The nearer waves, though golden where their
summits caught the light, were green on their slopes: first emerald, and
lower down a lustrous bottle green, deepening to blue where they passed
beneath the shadow of other waves' (3). Ransom climbs on to one of the
islands and finds himself in a world of such exquisite colours and other
sensuous delights that, in speaking of it later, he complained of it being
'too *definite* for language' (ibid.). The islands are moving with the waves
and Ransom finds it rather like walking aboard a moving ship. He comes
across a 'bubble-tree', the fruit of which 'was like the discovery of a totally
new genus of pleasures', but so complete and satisfying that to take more
than he needed 'would be a vulgarity – like asking to hear the same
symphony twice in a day' (ibid.).

The next day Ransom finds himself in the company of a small and
friendly dragon. This causes him to wonder if all the things which
appeared as mythology on earth were scattered through other worlds as
realities. He next meets the naked woman he calls the 'Green Lady'
because she looks like a goddess carved out of green stone. She is

surrounded by innumerable beasts who delight in her presence. Although Ransom is able to converse with her in Old Solar, the language spoken before the Fall, he finds it very difficult to understand her: 'Never had Ransom seen a face so calm, and so unearthly … a calm which no storm had ever preceded' (4). For her part, the Lady is puzzled by Ransom's self-consciousness: 'I have never done it before,' she says, 'stepping out of life into the Alongside and looking at oneself living as if one were not alive' (5). She is even more puzzled when Ransom asks about her mother. 'What do you mean?' she says, 'I *am* the Mother' (ibid.). Ransom gradually learns that she and the King, who does not appear until the end of the book, are the only inhabitants of Perelandra, the unfallen 'Adam' and 'Eve' of that planet. They are in unbroken communion with Maleldil, who speaks directly to them. Ransom begins to feel worried as the Lady picks up a little of the psychology of his race. 'What you have made me see,' she tells him, 'is as plain as the sky, but I never saw it before … One goes into the forest to pick food and already the thought of one fruit rather than another has grown up in one's mind … You could send your soul after the good you had expected, instead of turning it to the good you had got' (ibid.).

The Lady allows Ransom to accompany her to the 'Fixed Land' of Perelandra – the one part of it that doesn't float. Ransom learns that while Maleldil allows the Lady and the King to go there whenever they please, he has forbidden them to spend the night on it. Ransom and the Lady see something fall on the Fixed Land, and Ransom is horrified to find that his old enemy, Dr Weston, has arrived in a space ship. He is a physicist who is possessed of 'the wild dream that planet after planet, system after system, in the end galaxy after galaxy, can be forced to sustain, everywhere and for ever, the sort of life which is contained in the loins of our own species – a dream begotten by the hatred of death upon the fear of true immortality' (6). 'So, that,' Ransom thinks, 'is why I have been sent here. He failed on Malacandra and now he is coming here. And it's up to me to do something about it' (ibid.).

Weston, as always, is obsessed with finding new territory for man to spread himself. 'Man in himself,' he says, 'is nothing. The forward movement of Life – its growing spirituality – is everything … To spread spirituality, not to spread the human race, is henceforth my mission' (7). When Ransom mentions that the Devil is a spirit, Weston says, '*Your* Devil and *your* God are both pictures of the same Force … The next stage of emergent evolution beckoning us forward, is God; the transcended stage behind, ejecting us, is the Devil' (ibid.). Moments later Weston shouts, 'I call that Force into me completely' (ibid.). The next instant he is seized by a convulsion which leaves the Devil in possession of his body. Ransom is unsure whether the man he knew as Weston still exists in the body he once inhabited, and from this point on he calls him the 'Un-man'. Ransom is further disquieted by hearing the Un-man speaking fluent Old Solar.

It is now evident that Weston is bent on tempting the Lady to disobey Maleldil by spending the night on the Fixed Land. When the Lady reminds the Un-man that Maleldil has forbidden them from dwelling on the Fixed Land, he replies, 'But He has never forbidden you to think about it' (8). This is followed by the suggestion that Maleldil would be *pleased* by her disobedience: it would make her 'a full woman' like the women on Earth who 'do not need to wait for Him to tell them what is good, but know it for themselves as He does' (ibid.).

Watching the corpse of the Un-man shuffle about, Ransom realizes that 'Weston's body, travelling in a space-ship had been the bridge by which something else had invaded Perelandra – whether that supreme and original evil whom in Mars they call The Bent One, or one of his lesser followers' (9). Despite his attempts to counter the Un-man's arguments, the Un-man twists everything, telling the Lady that Ransom 'wants to keep you young. He does not want you to go on to the new fruits that you have never tasted before' (ibid.). No matter what she says about fidelity to Maleldil, the Un-man has an answer: 'The wrong kind of obeying itself can be a disobeying' – 'There might be a commanding which He wished you to break' – 'It is forbidding for the mere sake of forbidding' – 'He longs to see His creature become fully itself, to stand up in its own reason and its own courage even against Him. But how can He *tell* it to do this?' (ibid.).

In the rest of the ninth chapter the argument shifts to a great theological issue. In the fourth century St Augustine gave classical formulation to the Church's belief that Adam's Fall brought more good than evil. His expression *Felix peccatum Adae* is rendered 'O happy fault, O necessary sin of Adam' in the Easter liturgy of the Catholic Church. The Un-man tells the Lady that only by disobeying Maleldil will she go from her present 'smallness' into 'Deep Life, with all its joy and splendour and hardness.' Ransom mentions the result of Eve's disobedience: 'All love was troubled and made cold, and Maleldil's voice became hard to hear ... and the woman was against the man and the mother against the child.' This only leads the Un-man to make disobedience seem noble and disinterested: 'Because there was not always food enough, a woman could give the only fruit to her child or her husband and eat death instead – could give them all, as you in your little narrow life of playing and kissing and riding fishes have never done, nor shall do till you break the commandment.'

Ransom thinks to himself: 'How if the enemy were right after all?' He rouses himself and helps the Lady to see that 'Whatever you do, He will make good of it. But not the good He had prepared for you if you had obeyed Him. That is lost for ever.' Turning on the Un-man, Ransom shouts, 'Tell her all. What good came to you? Do *you* rejoice that Maleldil became a man?' The remembrance of what the Incarnation still meant to the Un-man causes him to howl like a dog, and he abandons the temptation for the moment.

Ransom is exhausted, but the Un-man does not require sleep. As a result Ransom often wakes to hear him going on and on with his temptation. Where, wonders Ransom, is Maleldil's 'representative'? Why doesn't he *stop* this? He is stunned to realize that *he* is that representative. 'What had happened on Earth, when Maleldil was born a man at Bethlehem, had altered the universe for ever. The new world of Perelandra was not a mere repetition of the old world Tellus ... When Eve fell, God was not Man. He had not yet made men members of His body: since then He had, and through them henceforward He would save and suffer. One of the purposes for which He had done all this was to save Perelandra not through Himself but through Himself in Ransom' (11). Ransom expects to fail, but he nevertheless sets out to destroy the body of the Un-man, and he chases him to the Fixed Land.

They are swept by the ocean into the bowels of the Fixed Land. In caverns lit by subterranean fires Ransom and the Un-man battle, and in the end Ransom destroys the body of Weston. Ransom is afterwards washed out of the mountain by an underground stream. He lies exhausted for a long time on the outside, nourished by the plants which grow at the entrance to the underground caverns. When he is well enough to travel, he finds a bleeding wound in his heel, caused by a bite from the Un-man.

The last two chapters of *Perelandra* are very beautiful. In a valley between two mountains of the Fixed Land Ransom is greeted by the Oyarsa of Malacandra and the Oyarsa of Perelandra. In tribute to him they assume human shapes, thus allowing Ransom to see the classical shapes of Mars and Venus. He understands better than ever why we call one masculine and the other feminine. 'The Oyarsa of Mars shone with cold and morning colours, a little metallic – pure, hard, and bracing. The Oyarsa of Venus glowed with a warm splendour, full of the suggestion of teeming vegetable life' (16).

A multitude of animals pour into the valley, followed by Tor and Tinidril, the King and his Lady – 'Paradise itself in its two Persons, Paradise walking hand in hand, its two bodies shining in the light like emeralds' (ibid.). They thank Ransom for his part in Perelandra's preservation, after which he sees Perelandra hand over the governance of the planet to the King. Ransom is almost overwhelmed by the sight of Tor, the King, because of his physical magnificence and his likeness to Christ. The King explains to Ransom that during the Lady's temptation he had been driven away to learn of good and evil. 'We have learned of evil,' he says, 'though not as the Evil One wished us to learn. We have learned better than that, and know it more, for it is waking that understands sleep and not sleep that understands waking' (ibid.).

Lewis takes the prediction of the Second Coming from Matthew 24: 29–31 and incorporates his own myth into it. Echoing the biblical 'the moon shall not give her light' from Matthew 24:29, Tor explains the part he and other unfallen creatures will take in this: 'We will fall upon your moon, wherein there is a secret evil, and which is as the shield of the Dark Lord of Thulcandra ... We shall break her. Her light will be put out' (ibid.). After many months Ransom is returned to Earth in such a casket as he came in.

Reviews

This time the reviewers were in little doubt of what Lewis intended, and many who disagreed with his Christian orthodoxy nevertheless liked the book. Leonard Bacon, writing in the *Saturday Review of Literature*, 29 (25 May 1946), pp. 13–14, said: '"Perelandra" is the result of the poetic imagination in full blast and should never have been written in prose, however excellent ... The reader is taken into an Eden with the dew on it, where not unnaturally the only rational inhabitants are a thoroughly interesting Eve and perhaps the only endurable Adam in literature.'

After being told so often that his poetry would have been better as prose, Kate O'Brien insists in *The Spectator*, 170, (14 May 1943), p. 458, that the opposite would be true of *Perelandra*: 'Bravely as Mr Lewis has assaulted the high and mighty symbols of human hope, serious and imaginative as is his purpose, the things he intends ... cannot be done at the pace and within the structure of narrative prose. It is a subject for verse, and verse at its most immense ... Passages in this book which tremble near the absurd because they have to be so much explained, might well have been majestic and beyond question in the simple, inevitable dress of poetry.'

John Gilland Brunini said in *The Commonweal*, 40 (2 May 1944), pp. 90–1: 'The book can be ranked high in the fields of creative imagination, speculative theology and engrossing adventure ... It is writing of the highest order. Definitely in the Wellsian vein, "Perelandra" is, from all standpoints, far superior to other tales of interplanetary adventures.' Victor M. Hamm in an essay entitled 'Mr Lewis in Perelandra' published in *Thought*, 20 (June 1945), pp. 271–90, singled out the description of the Oyarsa of Mars and the Oyarsa of Venus for particular praise: 'The substance of this wonderful scene ... which culminates in a grand chorus of praises to Maleldil [is] an inspired litany of love and homage. Blake should sound like this, in the *Prophetic Books*, but somehow he never does; there is in them too much of the Ossianic vagueness and verbiage. Keats does, in *Hyperion*, but his allegory is unintelligible. Dante is the man: in the sweep through the gyres of Heaven, to the crowning visit of God as the point that moves the sun and all the stars, he is loftier, of course, and more sustained, and he writes poetry instead of prose; but read and see whether the prophetic imagination is not in Lewis too, and something of the high style as well.'

THAT HIDEOUS STRENGTH:
A MODERN FAIRY-TALE FOR
GROWN-UPS (1945)

Background

I: The New Tower of Babel

This novel has been described as 'a Charles Williams* novel by C.S. Lewis'. This is because it is set, like Williams's 'spiritual shockers', not on a distant planet, but in everyday surroundings among ordinary people. However, following a number of bad reviews, Lewis said, in a letter to Dorothy L. Sayers* of 6 December 1945: 'Apparently reviewers *will not* tolerate a mixture of the realistic and the supernatural. Which is a pity, because (a) It's just the mixture I like, and (b) We have to put up with it in real life.'

He probably began the writing of this last adventure of Dr Ransom soon after he finished *Perelandra*, but some of the ingredients go further back than that. Sometime before the First War he had read about an attempt by a German scientist to keep all the functions of a human head alive after it had been severed from its body (mentioned by Grace Ironwood in **THS** (9:iv). It was still in his memory a few years later when, as he says in his diary of 29 May 1923, he and A.J. Hamilton Jenkin* discussed

> the horror play in which we were thinking almost seriously of collaborating. It is to turn on the idea of a scientist who discovers a means of keeping the brain and motor nerves alive in a corpse by means of injections (**AMR**).

Lewis seems to have been pretty far along with the book when he wrote to E.R. Eddison on 30 December 1942 for advice on the nuptial practices of bears: 'I have brought in a beare in the book I now write and it shall to bedde at the end with the other.' He wrote to Eddison again on 29 April 1943 to say that he had finished '300 sheets' of the book. *That Hideous Strength* was almost certainly completed a few months later because the Preface is dated by Lewis (in the American edition only) 'Christmas Eve, 1943'. On the title page Lewis gives the source of the book's title:

> The Shadow of that hyddeous strength
> Sax myle and more it is of length.

'The shadow of that hideous strength, six miles and more it is of length' is a description of the shadow of the Tower of Babel, and in Lewis's novel it is represented by the National Institute of Co-ordinated Experiments (N.I.C.E.) at Belbury. The description comes from the Scottish poet Sir David Lyndsay's *Ane Dialog betwix Experience and ane Courteor*, better known as *The Monarchie* (1554). Writing about Lyndsay (1486–1555) in EL (Book I, 1, p. 104), Lewis describes *Ane Dialog* as 'A metrical homily on world history.' 'In poems of this type,' he said, 'we do not look for "jewels five words long" nor for any great originality of conception. Their attraction lies in the perennial interest of the matter and in those local variations which it elicits from authors happily ignorant of archaeology and therefore compelled to see the past as if it were part of their own present ... I learn ... that when the building of the tower of Babel was abandoned the *schaddow of that hidduous strength* was already six miles long' [Book II, lines 1751–2].' Of course Lyndsay and Lewis both had in mind the passage from Genesis 11:4–9:

> Then they said, 'Come, let us build ourselves a city, and a tower with its top in the heavens, and let us make a name for ourselves, lest we be scattered abroad upon the face of the whole earth.' And the Lord came down to see the city and the tower, which the sons of men built. And the Lord said, 'Behold, they are one people, and they have all one language; and this is only the beginning of what they will do; and nothing that they propose to do will now be impossible for them. Come, let us go down, and there confuse their language, that they may not understand one another's speech.' So the Lord scattered them abroad from there over the face of all the earth, and they left off building the city. Therefore its name was called Babel, because there the Lord confused the language of all the earth (RSV).

II: Arthurian Elements

There is probably not any single version of the story of King Arthur that conforms to all its ingredients in Lewis's novel. He took a very free hand and the result is his own valuable contribution to Arthurian literature. From the 'Matter of Britain' he borrowed a number of elements, such as the Fisher King, the Pendragon, Logres, and Merlin, and used them in a violent conflict between a modern totalitarian state and the spiritual kingdom of Logres.

In giving Ransom the name of 'Mr Fisher-King', the head of the company of Logres, Lewis meant to draw our attention to the Arthurian Legend and the healing of the Wasteland created, in this instance, by the N.I.C.E. Years before Lewis had brought the Fisher King into his Arthurian poem, *Launcelot* (see pp. 160–1), but in *That Hideous Strength* the version of the Fisher King story he had in mind was *Perceval* or *Le Conte du Graal* by Chrétien de Troyes (*fl.* 1170–90). An excellent summary of it is found in Charles Williams's *The Figure of Arthur* (V), which Lewis included in *Arthurian Torso*. Williams tells how a youth named Perceval achieved knighthood under the instruction of an old knight, Gournemant, who gave him three pieces of advice: 'to be slow to speak, to be slow to ask questions, and to be slow to quote his mother's saying on all occasions.' In his adventures Perceval

came to a river where two men were fishing from a boat. One of them directed him to a castle close by. There Perceval was taken into a hall, where were four hundred men sitting round a fire, and an old man lying on a couch. The old man gave him a sword on which was an inscription that it was to break only in one peril, and that known only to the maker. Presently a squire entered, bearing a lance from the point of which a drop of blood continually ran down; then came two more squires, each carrying a ten-branched candlestick; and after them a damsel bearing 'a grail'. What the grail was is not defined; only it is said that the light which shone from it wholly abolished the blaze of the candles which preceded it. After it came another damsel carrying a silver plate. The pageant passed between the couch and the fire and went out. Perceval, remembering Gournemant's advice, did not venture to ask any question. Supper was served in the hall, and with each course the grail was brought in and carried to an inner room where some unknown person was fed with a Host from it. Perceval still asked nothing. He was taken to his chamber; the next morning he found the castle deserted and his horse waiting, ready saddled, outside it. Riding away, he presently came to a place where a knight was lying dead and a girl weeping over him. It was from her that he now learned that the Fisherman and the old man of the castle were the same person – a king who had been mysteriously wounded by a spear through the thigh. If only (she went on) Perceval had asked what was the meaning of the pageant he had seen, the king would have been healed and the land should have had great good.

In the novel we find Ransom, the Fisher King, suffering almost continuously from the wound he received in his struggle with the Un-man in Perelandra. No doubt Lewis had in mind the 'Dolorous Blow' dealt by Sir Balyn with his sword to King Pelles in Book II of Malory's *Morte D'Arthur*. Sir Balyn's sword was the one Longinus used to pierce Christ's side, and it was brought to England by Joseph of Arimathea. But besides being the 'Fisher King', Ransom is also the 'Pendragon of Logres'. In Malory, Uther Pendragon was the father of King Arthur, and Pendragon is usually taken to mean the successor of Arthur. 'Logres' is a translation of the Welsh word for England, *Lloegyr*, and from Chrétien de Troyes onwards it has been the usual term for Arthur's kingdom. These things emerge gradually as the novel unfolds. In **THS** (17:iv) Dr Dimble explains to the company which has gathered round the Fisher King:

> It all began ... when we discovered that the Arthurian story is mostly true history. There was a moment in the sixth century when something that is always trying to break through into this country nearly succeeded. Logres was our name for it – it will do as well as another. And then ... gradually we began to see all English history in a new way. We discovered the haunting ... How something we may call Britain is always haunted by something we may call Logres. Haven't you noticed that we are two countries? After every Arthur, a Mordred; behind every Milton, a Cromwell; a nation of poets, a nation of shopkeepers; the home of Sidney – and of Cecil Rhodes. Is it any wonder they call us hypocrites? But what they mistake for hypocrisy is really the struggle between Logres and Britain ...
>
> Ransom was summoned to the bedside of an old man then dying in Cumberland ... That man was the Pendragon, the successor of Arthur and Uther and Cassibelaun. Then we learned the truth. There has been a secret Logres in the very heart of Britain all these years; an unbroken succession of Pendragons. That old man was

the seventy-eighth from Arthur: our Director received from him the office and the blessings.

Immediately after writing the novel Lewis contributed to a symposium entitled 'What France Means to You' in *La France Libre*, Vol. VII, No. 42 (15 April 1944). The magazine was published in London with the intention of helping our allies in France. In his contribution Lewis said France meant to him 'the Crusades, the Song of Roland, Chartres Cathedral, the Arthurian cycle, the University of Paris.' Then, without using the word 'Logres', he implies that France has one too: 'It seems to me that your being is double. No doubt it's the same with all nations ... Behind Sidney's England, I can see (unfortunately) that of Cecil Rhodes ... For you as for us, the Devil is truly the obverse of our authentic being; he incites Shelley's citizens to Tyranny, as he incites Abelard's to Stupidity. The future depends, for each of our two countries, on the choice we make between our good and our evil genius. Is it too late to find that other France, that other England?'[1] The same idea appeared in *The Last Battle* (16) where in the *real* Narnia beyond the 'Shadowlands' the children see 'the England within England', and Mr. Tumnus explains that 'All the *real* countries – are only spurs jutting out from the great mountains of Aslan.'

The story of Merlin was first set out in Geoffrey of Monmouth's *Vita Merlini* (c. 1150). He was the magician who guided the destinies of Arthur and his predecessors and he belongs, like the real Arthur, to the Fifth Century. Dr Dimble explains in **THS** (13:iv) that he is at the opposite extreme of the N.I.C.E.:

> He is the last vestige of an old order in which matter and spirit were, from our modern point of view, confused. For him every operation on Nature is a kind of personal contact, like coaxing a child or stroking one's horse. After him came the modern man to whom Nature is something dead – a machine to be worked, and taken to bits if it won't work the way he pleases.

Finally, Lewis notes in his Preface that 'This is a "tall" story about devilry, though it has behind it a serious "point" which I have tried to make in my *Abolition of Man*.' That book is about objective right and wrong, Natural Law,§ and the reader would be wise to read the summary of it before reading the summary of this novel.

[1] The French text as well as a translation of Lewis's part in 'What France Means to You' is found in *The Canadian C.S. Lewis Journal*,‡ No. 87 (Spring 1995).

Summary

When the story opens Jane and Mark Studdock have been married for six months, and Jane is sitting in their flat and reflecting that marriage 'had proved to be the door out of a world of work and comradeship and laughter and innumerable things to do, into something like solitary confinement' (1:i). She picks up that morning's paper and sees a picture of the brilliant French scientist, Alcasan, who has just been guillotined for poisoning his wife. She remembers her dream of the night before when she saw and overheard Alcasan talking to another man. The other man twists Alcasan's head off and takes it away. She then sees people digging up 'a sort of ancient British, druidical kind of man' who, before they get to him, comes to life. It disturbs Jane that she had seen Alcasan in her dream before she saw his photograph in the paper.

Mark is a Fellow of Sociology at Bracton College in Edgestow University in the small midlands town of Edgestow. We learn that in Mark's mind 'hardly one rag of noble thought, either Christian or Pagan, had a secure lodging. His education had been neither scientific nor classical – merely "Modern". The severities both of abstraction and of high human tradition had passed him by ... He was a ... glib examinee in subjects that require no exact knowledge' (9: ii). Ever since he arrived at Bracton he has been trying desperately to get into its 'inner ring'.

Jane, too, has ambitions. She had always intended to continue her own career as a scholar after she was married: that was one of the reasons why they were to have no children. However, perhaps because she is 'not a very original thinker' she finds herself frustrated. Her doctoral thesis is on John Donne's 'triumphant vindication of the body' but she can't force herself to get on with it.

Lewis has so often been accused of being anti-feminist in writing about Jane that it might be as well to mention this objection. An early manuscript shows that he had originally made Jane a biochemist. However, he knew too little about that subject to make his character convincing, and he made her instead a student of English Literature. When Daphne and Cecil Harwood* complained about Jane's not being 'a very original thinker', Lewis replied on 11 September 1945:

> Rê Jane, she wasn't meant to illustrate the problem of the married woman and her own career in general: rather the problem of everyone who follows an *imagined* vocation at the expense of a real one. Perhaps I should have emphasized more the fact that her thesis on Donne was all derivative bilge. If I'd been tackling the

problem which Cecil thinks I had in mind, of course I'd have taken
a woman capable of making a real contribution to literature.

Since his election five years ago, Mark has cared desperately about
being in the 'progressive element' of his college. On the same day that
his wife wakes from her nightmare about Alcasan, he is invited by an
important member of the progressive element, the sub-warden, Curry, to
meet Lord Feverstone. It turns out that Lord Feverstone is the same Dick
Devine who went with Dr Weston to Malacandra in **OSP**. That evening at
a college meeting the Progressive Element manages to force the college
into selling Bragdon Wood, which lies in the centre of their grounds. The
Wood contains 'Merlin's Well', a well of British-Roman date, and the
purchaser is the National Institute of Co-ordinated Experiments –
'the first-fruits of that constructive fusion between the state and the
laboratory on which so many thoughtful people base their hopes of a
better world' (1:iv).

From this point on the story switches back and forth from the doings
of Jane to those of Mark. Jane had been so frightened by her dream that
she calls Mrs Dimble, whose husband had been Jane's tutor in North-
umberland College and who is an authority on the Arthurian legend.
When the Dimbles hear of Jane's dream they conclude that she should
seek help from a friend who lives in the manor house of 'St Anne's on the
Hill'.

Mark meanwhile meets Lord Feverstone, a member of the N.I.C.E.,
who suggests Mark apply for a job there. In explaining the purpose of the
N.I.C.E. he says, 'Man has got to take charge of Man. That means,
remember, that some men have got to take charge of the rest – which is
another reason for cashing in on it as soon as one can' (2:i). A thrill runs
through Mark as he discovers that this involves sterilization of the unfit,
liquidation of backward races, selective breeding, pre-natal education,
vivisection, biochemical conditioning of the brain, and eventually the
elimination of organic life altogether, to be replaced by the chemical.
Feverstone invites Mark to come out to Belbury and meet John Wither
who is Deputy Director of the N.I.C.E.

The next day, Mark and Lord Feverstone make their way to Belbury, a
few miles south of Edgestow, while Jane is on a train going north to the
little village of St Anne's to see Miss Ironwood, a doctor, about her
dreams. From this point onwards, as the story unfolds, they see very little
of one another. At St Anne's, Jane finds it easy to like the inhabitants, but
she is horrified to discover that she has the hereditary power of dreaming
realities. Miss Ironwood and the Dimbles urge her to join their 'side'.

At Belbury Mark accepts a job with the N.I.C.E., and this is the beginning of a long befuddlement as to whether he is ever in or out of the organization's 'inner ring'.§ Three of those who befriend Mark are a lesbian called 'Fairy' Hardcastle, Chief of the Institutional Police, an Italian physiologist, Professor Filostrato, and a mad Anglican parson, Mr Straik, who believes that the N.I.C.E. is realizing the Kingdom of God in this world. They are receiving the assistance of higher beings called 'macrobres' which, unknown to them, are really the dark eldila, or devils, of Earth.

While Jane continues to dream frightening realities, Mark finds himself unable to leave the N.I.C.E. because a murder charge is devised to keep him there. As he is drawn into the workings of the N.I.C.E. the distinction between truth and falsehood begins to disappear. Eventually, Filostrato and Straik decide to introduce Mark to the real 'Head' of the N.I.C.E. The young man's excitement mounts when they go on to explain that it is not Man in the abstract that will be given power over other men, but a single man. This excitement quickly turns to horror when Mark meets the 'Head' of the Institute, which turns out to be the actual *head* of Alcasan, kept alive by infusions of blood.

Jane comes to love the people at St Anne's and when they are certain of her loyalty they introduce her to their 'Head'. This is Ransom who has not aged since he came back from Perelandra, but who is in great pain from the wound on his foot – where he was bitten by the Un-man. Ransom is revealed to be the new Pendragon of Logres. Jane is to be their 'seer' and tell them what the N.I.C.E. is doing. Another addition to the Arthurian legend concerns the old man whom Jane 'sees' the N.I.C.E. digging up from Bragdon Wood. This turns out to be Merlin, whose magic the N.I.C.E. needs. Merlin wakes before anyone can get to him, and finding a tramp he takes his clothes, and joins the company at St Anne's. He recognizes Ransom as the rightful Pendragon. The moment, however, Merlin lays eyes on Jane he calls her 'the falsest lady of any at this time alive' (13:iii). 'It was the purpose of God,' he explains to Ransom, 'that she and her lord should between them have begotten a child by whom the enemies should have been put out of Logres for a thousand years.' Merlin knows that Jane and Mark have been using contraceptives, and he says, 'Be assured that the child will never be born, for the hour of its begetting is past. Of their own will they are barren.' Ransom, however, knows that Jane is now a Christian, and that she and Mark will have a child who will become the next Pendragon.

The N.I.C.E., upon finding the tramp, assume that he is Merlin and they take him to Belbury where they try talking with him in Latin. When they can get nothing from him, they advertise for a Celtic scholar. Meanwhile, the N.I.C.E. discover Mark trying to leave their side, and they confine him to Belbury. They leave him to look after 'Merlin', whom they dress in a doctor's gown in order that he can attend a great N.I.C.E. banquet. The tramp understands little of what is happening, but he trusts Mark and lets him know that he is not Merlin.

Even though he knows it will end with his death, Merlin is prepared to confront the powers of Hell by receiving into his body the *Oyéresu* of the Planets. Ransom then sends him to Belbury as a specialist in Celtic. He attends the great banquet as the tramp's 'interpreter'. In a splendid and spectacular scene, which is meant to echo the fall of the Tower of Babel with its resultant confusion of languages, Wither and the other speakers find themselves babbling nonsense. As the numerous caged animals are liberated from the laboratories, where they were to be vivisected, Merlin arranges for Mark and the tramp to escape before the full curse of Babel is loosed upon the N.I.C.E.

As he makes his way to St Anne's, Mark turns back to see Belbury destroyed by an earthquake. With this danger to Britain averted, Ransom's work as the Pendragon is complete. Mark and Jane are united, and after saying goodbye to his friends Ransom is taken by the eldila to Perelandra where he will be healed of his wound.

Reviews

Graham Greene said in the *Evening Standard* (24 August 1945), p. 6: 'Mr Lewis writes admirably and excitingly when he is describing the Institute, with its sinister muffled life under a Deputy Director who talks as a crab walks, but I found Professor Ransom and the "good" characters peculiarly unconvincing. The allegory becomes a little too friendly, like a sermon at a children's service, or perhaps like a whimsical charade organized by a middle-aged bachelor uncle.'

The Times Literary Supplement (25 August 1945), p. 401 complained that: 'In its central theme, and its occult circumstances, this novel has a close affinity with the novels of the late Charles Williams and with his poem "Taliessin Through Logres" ... In imaginative quality it suffers from the comparison which it provokes, particularly in Mr Lewis's characters, who tend to be caricatures or at best personifications of certain mental or moral attitudes he is concerned to present.'

H.P.E. [Mrs H.P. Edens] wrote in *Punch* (29 August 1945), p. 191: 'Here, speeded up in imagination, as the atomic bomb has speeded it up in fact, is the death-grapple of technocracy – and the devil, with nature – and nature's God ... Behind N.I.C.E. are the powers of darkness. Behind Dr

Ransom and a handful of Christians are God and His angels. In everything created this opposition is manifest; but it is Mr Lewis's triumph to have shown, with shattering credibility, how the pitiful little souls of Jane and Mark Studdock become the apocalyptic battlefield of Heaven and Hell.'

Orville Prescott said in *The New York Times* (21 May 1946): '*That Hideous Strength* is a parable on much the same theme as was Aldous Huxley's *Brave New World* – the degeneration of man which inevitably follows a gross and slavish scientific materialism which excludes all idealistic, ethical and religious values. But when Mr Huxley wrote his bitter books his mood was one of cynical despair. Mr Lewis, on the contrary, sounds a militant call to battle.' The reviewer in *Time*, XLVII, No. 23 (10 June 1946), p. 36, wrote: 'For Christian readers, Lewis's allegory adds up to an elaborate modern version of an old story which atomic man may well paste in his hat: *The Tower of Babel.*'

Leonard Bacon said in *The Saturday Review of Literature*, 29 (25 May 1946), pp. 13–4: 'When Mr Lewis, harking back to the world of Merlin, says that the mysterious Land of Logres, or "Lancelot, or Pelleas, or Pellenore", far away in the beginning of time, is what keeps England from degenerating into Great Britain, he says what is fundamentally true and so magnificently full of important implications that it would take common clay a month to ferret out the full bearing of the observation.' Joseph McSorley reviewing it in *The Catholic World*, 163 (June 1946), pp. 277–8, wrote: 'The plain fact is that Mr Lewis has too many exceptional gifts. They sprout all over his latest work, draining away strength from a story which drastic pruning could have made timely and rousing.'

A note on the Variant Texts of That Hideous Strength

In 1989 Dr David Lake of the University of Queensland published a valuable article entitled 'The Variant Texts of *That Hideous Strength*' in *The Ring Bearer*, Journal of the Mythopoeic Literature Society of Australia, vol. 7, No. 1 (Winter 1989), which goes into considerable detail about the differences between the various editions of *That Hideous Strength*. For our purposes, a brief analysis will have to do.

There are three editions of the book:

(1) That of Bodley Head in 1945 (hitherto **B**);
(2) That of Macmillan in 1946 (hitherto **M**);
(3) That of Avon Books of New York in [1946] who altered the title to *The Tortured Planet* (hitherto **A**).

The first major distinction is that between **B** and **M**. These two texts differ, Dr Lake notes, in some two dozen substantive readings, as well as several places in which the paragraphing is different. Because **B** is clearly superior to **M** it seems that either Lewis or, more likely, a copy editor at Bodley Head, revised that edition before it was published, whereas the **M** edition seems to have been printed from Lewis's original handwritten manuscript or a typescript of it. What follows are just a few of the variations between **M** and **B**:

M		**B**	
page		page	
viii	*Christmas Eve 1943*	8	(deleted)
20	(deleted)	29	He stared ... Feverstone
278	1st of October	293	14th of October
313	*ut tibi ... molestior essem*	329	*tibi ... molestum esse*
318	*causam veneris*	334	*causam venenis*
379	The whole house	395	All the house
379	The bottom of the universe	396	The base of the universe
404	He also disliked to be kept waiting.	422	(deleted)

Lewis was always frugal with paper but as *That Hideous Strength* was published during the war, he was more than usually so. For instance, what is one paragraph on page 46 of **M** is divided into five paragraphs on page 56 of **B**; what is one paragraph on page 185 of **M** is divided into six paragraphs on pages 197–8 of **B**; and what is one paragraph on page 384 of **M** is divided into eleven paragraphs on pages 400–1 of **B**. These very long paragraphs in **M** do not affect the sense of the book, but breaking them up makes for easier reading.

What is more serious are the deletions of whole sentences from one of the editions. For instance, in chapter 1, part 4 (p. 20 of **M** and p. 28 of **B**) Canon Jewel is described as 'blind'. Two paragraphs later **B** says 'He stared with puzzled eyes in the direction of Feverstone.' Perhaps someone at Macmillan spotted this because that last sentence was deleted from **M**.

Sometime in the 1940s Macmillan leased the paperback rights in the three science fiction novels to Avon Publishing Co. of New York, and either Macmillan or Avon, but probably Avon, asked Lewis to abridge *That Hideous Strength*. He did, and the result was **A** which was published by Avon in [1946] under the title *The Tortured Planet* which is about a third shorter than **B** and **M**. Interestingly, **A** was abridged, not from **M**, but from **B**. Lewis obviously took great care in pruning the book, and he said in the Preface to **A**, 'In reducing the original story to a length suitable for this edition, I believe I have altered nothing but the tempo and the manner.' Even so, he could not help but revise the book to some extent, and those revisions were carefully made. It would appear that after this Avon asked Lewis to do the same with *Perelandra* because there exists from Lewis's library a copy of *Perelandra* which is abridged in his own hand. He seems to have had in mind shortening this book by about a quarter. In any event, the abridgement was never used, and on the title page he wrote 'With excisions for an abridgement which was to have been made (but, I think, was not) in a cheaper American edition.' Lewis was probably relieved that the excisions were never published because, as he said in the Preface to **A**, 'I myself prefer the more leisurely pace.' The next thing that happened is that Pan Books of London reprinted the abridgement of *The Tortured Planet* (**A**) in 1955, at the same time restoring its original title of *That Hideous Strength*.

In **A**, Lewis caught a number of what were probably typographical errors in **B**. For instance, for 'that lovely afternoon' on page 199 of **B** we have 'this lovely afternoon' in **A**. He found a more serious one on page 334 of **B** where Ransom says to Merlin '*dic mihi qui sis et quam ob causam venenis*' ('Tell me who you are and why you come'.) '*Venenis*' is a printer's error for '*veneris*', the subjunctive perfect of *venire*. It was corrected in **M**. However, in **A** Lewis turned it into better Latin by using the subjunctive '*venias*'. In chapter 17, part vi of **A** Lewis added a sentence to make something clearer. In **B** (p. 468) and **M** (p. 450) he had simply put: '"What's the matter with that jackdaw?" said Dr Dimble.' As there had been no reference to the jackdaw, Lewis added in **A** the sentence, 'The bird had hitherto been asleep on Ransom's shoulder.'

In 1965 Macmillan of New York published a paperback of their edition of **M**, which paperback is henceforth called **P**. **P** is exactly the same as **M**, and in fact is an offprint of it. The curious thing about this is that when Pan of London replaced **A** with an unabridged paperback in 1983 it was not an offprint of **B**, but of **M**. This means that in England one could buy both the original editions: the hardback **B** and the paperback **P**.

None of the errors in these editions is major, and there is no reason why they should spoil the book for anyone. Nevertheless, when a critical edition of *That Hideous Strength* is produced it should make use of the corrections and improvements found in the Abridged Edition.

TILL WE HAVE FACES:
A MYTH RETOLD (1956)

'I am so glad you both liked **TWHF**,' Lewis wrote to the children, Anne and Martin Kilmer, on 7 August 1957. 'I think it much my best book but not many people agree' (**LTC**). Lewis described this book to Charles Wrong on 8 August 1959 as the 'favourite of all my books'. It was, nevertheless, he told him, 'A complete flop. The worst flop I've ever had' ('A Chance Meeting', **ABT**). 'You gave me much pleasure by what you said about *Till We Have Faces*,' he wrote to Anne Scott on 26 August 1960, 'for that book, which I consider far and away the best I have written, has been my one big failure both with the critics and with the public' (**L**).

The main charge against the novel when it first appeared was obscurity. 'What is he trying to say?' However, in recent years there has been a serious re-assessment of the book, almost an about-face in criticism, and it is generally regarded, not only as Lewis's best book, but as a very great book. One can go directly to a summary of the book, but what some regard as causing the story to be obscure might be cleared up by the *Background* given here.

Background

I: A 'Re-interpretation of an old story'

In the first English edition of the book Lewis said: 'This re-interpretation of an old story has lived in the author's mind, thickening and hardening with the years, ever since he was an undergraduate. That way, he could be said to have worked at it most of his life. Recently, what seemed to be the right form presented itself and themes suddenly interlocked: the straight tale of barbarism, the mind of an ugly woman, dark idolatry and pale enlightenment at war with each other and with vision, and the havoc which a vocation, or even a faith, works on human life.'

He realized that many would not be familiar with the Greek and Roman mythologies he grew up with, and in a 'Note' appended to the first American edition of the novel he summarized the 'old story' he was re-interpreting. It is the story of Cupid and Psyche from the *Metamorphoses* or *The Golden Ass* of Lucius Apuleius Platonicus (usually known as Apuleius), who was born about AD 125. Many have enjoyed *Till We Have Faces* without having even heard of Apuleius, but Lewis's novel will be much clearer if the reader has some notion of the story he was re-interpreting. What follows is Lewis's summary of Apuleius's tale of Cupid and Psyche:

II: A Summary of Apuleius's 'Metamorphoses'

A king and queen had three daughters, of whom the youngest was so beautiful that men worshipped her as a goddess and neglected the worship of Venus for her sake. One result was that Psyche (as the youngest was called) had no suitors; men reverenced her supposed deity too much to aspire to her hand. When her father consulted the oracle of Apollo about her marriage he received the answer: 'Hope for no human son-in-law. You must expose Psyche on a mountain to be the prey of a dragon.' This he obediently did.

But Venus, jealous of Psyche's beauty, had already devised a different punishment for her; she had ordered her son Cupid to afflict the girl with an irresistible passion for the basest of men. Cupid set off to do so but, on seeing Psyche, fell in love with her himself. As soon as she was left on the mountain he therefore had her carried off by the West-Wind (Zephyrus) to a secret place where he had prepared a stately palace. Here he visited her by night and enjoyed her love; but he forbade her to see his face. Presently she begged that she might receive a visit from her two sisters. The god reluctantly consented and wafted them to her palace. Here they were royally feasted, and expressed great delight at all the splendours they saw. But inwardly they were devoured with envy, for their husbands were not gods and their houses not so fine as hers.

They therefore plotted to destroy her happiness. At their next visit they persuaded her that her mysterious husband must really be a monstrous serpent. 'You must take into your bedroom tonight,' they said, 'a lamp covered with a cloak and a sharp knife. When he sleeps uncover the lamp – see the horror that is lying in your bed – and stab it to death.' All this the gullible Psyche promised to do.

When she uncovered the lamp and saw the sleeping god she gazed on him with insatiable love, till a drop of hot oil from her lamp fell on his shoulder and woke him. Starting up, he spread his shining wings, rebuked her, and vanished from her sight.

The two sisters did not long enjoy their malice, for Cupid took such measures as led both to their death. Psyche meanwhile wandered away, wretched and desolate, and attempted to drown herself in the first river she came to; but the god Pan frustrated her attempt and warned her never to repeat it. After many miseries she fell into the hands of her bitterest enemy, Venus, who seized her for a slave, beat her, and set her what were meant to be impossible tasks. The first, that of sorting out seeds into separate heaps, she did by the help of some friendly ants. Next, she had to get a hank of golden wool from some man-killing sheep; a reed by a river bank whispered to her that this could be achieved by plucking the wool off the bushes. After that, she had to fetch a cupful of the water of the Styx, which could be reached only by climbing certain impracticable mountains, but an eagle met her, took the cup from her hand, and returned with it full of the water. Finally she was sent down to the lower world to bring back to Venus, in a box, the beauty of Persephone, the Queen of the Dead. A mysterious voice told her how she could reach Persephone and yet return to our world; on the way she would be asked for help by various people who seemed to deserve her pity, but she must refuse them all. And when Persephone gave her the box (full of beauty) she must on no account open the lid to look inside. Psyche obeyed all this and returned to the upper world with the box; but then at last curiosity overcame her and she looked into it. She immediately lost consciousness.

Cupid now came to her again, but this time he forgave her. He interceded with Jupiter, who agreed to permit his marriage and make Psyche a goddess. Venus was reconciled and they all lived happily ever after.

III: Lewis's first attempt to Re-tell the Story

Lewis said his 're-interpretation' had been in his mind since he was an undergraduate. Fortunately, we can be specific. When he was twenty-three years old, an undergraduate at Oxford, he wrote in his diary of 23 November 1922: 'After lunch I went out for a walk up Shotover, thinking how to make a masque or play of Psyche and Caspian' (**AMR**). About a year later, 9 September 1923, he said: 'My head was very full of my old idea of a poem on my own version of the Cupid and Psyche story in which Psyche's sister would not be jealous, but unable to see anything but moors when Psyche showed her the Palace. I have tried it twice before, once in couplet and once in ballad form.'

Fortunately, fragments of these attempts to re-tell the story were copied by his brother, Warnie,* into the **Lewis Papers** VIII: pp. 163–4. There are 78 couplets in all. They begin:

> The tale of Psyche is unjustly told
> And half of the truth concealed by all who hold
> With Apuleius …

What 'drove them to this thing' was:

>   but summer rains
> Withheld and harvest withering on the plains.
> The streams were low, and in the starving tribe
> Ran murmurs that of old a dearer bribe
> Had charmed the rain. Forgotten customs then
> Stirred in their sleep below the hearts of men
> Thrusting up evil heads.

He insists that the jealousy of Psyche's two sisters is 'slander'. The story of what really happened has been 'told amiss':

>   for across the tale, they bring
> Two ugly elder daughters of the king,
> Two Cinderella's sisters, who must come
> To visit Psyche in her secret home
> And envy it: and for no other cause
> Tempt her to break that fairy country's laws –
> Which leads to her undoing. But all this
> Is weighted on one side and told amiss.

It's like the work of some poetic youth,
Angry, and far too certain of the truth,
Mad from the gleams of vision that claim to find
Bye ways to something missed by all mankind.
He thinks that only envy or dull eyes
Keep all men from believing in the prize
He holds in secret. In revenge he drew
– For portrait of us all – the sisters two,
Misunderstanding them: and poets since
Have followed.
　　　　　Now I say there was a prince
Twin brother to this Psyche, fair as she,
And prettier than a boy would choose to be,
His name was Jardis. Older far than these
Was Caspian who had rocked them on her knees,
The child of the first marriage of the king.

In another version of the last six lines he expands on Psyche's twin – Jardis. 'On my life,' says Lewis:

I'll guess it's he that taught
The story, as we have it, to the world.

IV: The Prose Version

Lewis was to go on attempting to tell the story in verse, but none of the other attempts has survived. Then, in the spring of 1955 he understood exactly what he wanted to say and the final version in prose was written with considerable ease. During a weekend at The Kilns, he and Warnie entertained Joy Gresham* and it was during her visit, and because of her, that he discovered how the story should develop. In a letter to William Gresham of 23 March 1955, Joy said that Jack 'was lamenting that he couldn't get a good idea for a book.' They settled into comfortable chairs and 'kicked a few ideas around till one came to light. Then we had another whisky each and bounced it back and forth between us.' The next day, said Joy, 'without further planning, he wrote the first chapter! I read it and made some criticisms.' Lewis then 'did it over and went on with the next.' Writing to her husband again on 29 April, Joy said that while she could not 'write one-tenth as well as Jack', she could nevertheless 'tell him how to write more like himself! He is now about three-quarters of the

way through the book ... and says he finds my advice indispensable.'
(**AGCI**, chapter 4, pp. 116–7).

V: What Lewis Attempted in *Till We Have Faces*

Several of his friends, including his publishers, did not at first understand
what Lewis was attempting even in prose. For this reason, it may be wise
to be specific about certain alterations he was making in the myth of
Cupid and Psyche.

(A) The 'central alteration' in Lewis's version
In the remaining part of the 'Note' he wrote for the American edition he
said:

> The central alteration in my own version consists in making
> Psyche's palace invisible to normal, mortal eyes – if 'making' is not
> the wrong word for something which forced itself upon me, almost
> at my first reading of the story, as the way the thing must have
> been. This change of course brings with it a more ambivalent
> motive and a different character for my heroine, and finally
> modifies the whole quality of the tale. I felt quite free to go behind
> Apuleius, whom I suppose to have been its transmitter, not its
> inventor. Nothing was further from my aim than to recapture the
> peculiar quality of the *Metamorphoses* – that strange compound of
> picaresque novel, horror comic, mystagogue's tract, pornography
> and stylistic experiment. Apuleius was of course a man of genius:
> but in relation to my work he is a 'source', not an 'influence' nor a
> 'model'.
>
> His version has been followed pretty closely by William Morris
> (in *The Earthly Paradise*) and by Robert Bridges (*Eros and Psyche*).
> Neither poem, in my opinion, shows its author at his best. The
> whole *Metamorphoses* was last translated by Mr Robert Graves
> (Penguin Books, 1950).

(B) Telling the story from a Christian perspective
Lewis was an atheist when he tried telling the story in 1923. After his
conversion in 1931 he saw everything from a Christian perspective, and it
was this which caused him to see two changes in the Cupid and Psyche
story with absolute clarity. (1) Psyche has two half-sisters, but the story is
told by Orual (or 'Maia' as Psyche calls her), who, when visiting Psyche,
cannot see her palace; (2) Lewis now knows *why* the palace is invisible to

Orual. This very important 'why' he explained in a letter to his friend, Katharine Farrer* of 2 April 1955, when he was writing the story:

> [In] my version of Cupid and Psyche Apuleius got it all wrong. The elder sister (I reduce her to one) couldn't *see* Psyche's palace when she visited her. She saw only rock and heather. When P. said she was giving her noble wine, the poor sister saw and tasted only spring water. Hence her dreadful problem: 'Is P. mad or am I blind?' As you see, though I didn't start from that, it is the story of every nice, affectionate agnostic whose dearest one suddenly 'gets religion', or even every luke-warm Christian whose dearest gets a Vocation. Never, I think, treated sympathetically by a Christian writer before. I do it all through the mouth of the elder sister. In a word, I'm very much 'with book'.

This difficulty caused by one's dearest 'getting religion' was later expanded in a letter to Clyde S. Kilby (see **Wade Center‡**) of 10 February 1957:

> Orual is (not a symbol but) an instance, a 'case', of human affection in its natural condition: true, tender, suffering, but in the long run, tyrannically possessive and ready to turn to hatred when the beloved ceases to be its possession. What such love particularly cannot stand is to see the beloved passing into a sphere where it cannot follow. All this, I hoped, would stand in a mere story in its own right. But ...
>
> Of course I had always in mind its close parallel to what is probably at this moment going on in at least five families in your own town at this moment. Someone becomes a Christian, or, in a family nominally Christian already, does something like becoming a missionary or entering a religious Order. The others suffer a sense of outrage. What they love is being taken from them! The boy must be mad! And the conceit of him! Or is there something in it after all? Let's hope it is only a phase! If only he'd listen to his natural advisers! Oh come back, come back, be sensible, be the dear son we used to know. Now I, as a Christian, have a good deal of sympathy with these jealous, puzzled, suffering people (for they do suffer, and out of their suffering much of the bitterness against religion arises). I believe the thing is common. There is very nearly a touch of it in Luke 2:48, 'Son, *why hast thou* so dealt with us?' And is the reply easy for a loving heart to bear? (**L**).

(C) Why Orual's love can turn to hatred

Lewis was soon to write *The Four Loves*, and one point made repeatedly in that book is that each of the three natural loves (Affection, Friendship, Eros) *left to itself* easily becomes a demon. As he said in the Introduction to *The Four Loves*:

> St John's saying that God is love has long been balanced in my mind against the remark of a modern author (M. Denis de Rougemont) that 'love ceases to be a demon only when he ceases to be a god'; which of course can be re-stated in the form 'begins to be a demon the moment he begins to be a god.' This balance seems to me an indispensable safeguard. If we ignore it the truth that God is love may slyly come to mean for us the converse, that love is God.
>
> I suppose that everyone who has thought about the matter will see what M. de Rougemont meant. Every human love, at its height, has a tendency to claim for itself a divine authority. Its voice tends to sound as if it were the will of God Himself. It tells us not to count the cost, it demands of us a total commitment, it attempts to over-ride all other claims and insinuates that any action which is sincerely done 'for love's sake' is thereby lawful and even meritorious. That erotic love and love of one's country may thus attempt to 'become gods' is generally recognized. But family affection may do the same.

To this we might add a comment about the book which Lewis made to his former pupil, Father Peter Milward SJ, on 24 September 1959:

> The main themes are (1) Natural affection, if left to mere nature, easily becomes a special kind of hatred, (2) God is, to our natural affections, the ultimate object of jealousy.

(D) The difficulty of creating Psyche

Just as years before Lewis had difficulties creating the unfallen Lady in *Perelandra*, so he was now having similar difficulties creating Psyche. By the time he wrote to Mrs Farrer again, on 9 July 1955, the book was written, and she had read it. She had, however, failed to see what he was trying to do with Psyche, and in replying to her criticism he said:

> About Psyche herself your *diagnosis* is wrong, but that only shows I have failed to get across what I intended. Pin-up girl, nothing! The attempt was precisely to show the biddable ideal daughter, Maia's

little pet (the ideal object for a devouring maternal love, the live doll), turning into the, sometimes terrifying, sometimes maternal, goddess. I'll try to mend it, but not, I think, in the directions you suggest. I think she must have the same deep voice as Orual: for 'you also are Psyche'. The whole thing is very tricky, though. The numinous breaking through the childish mustn't be made just like the mature breaking through the juvenile; the traits of eternal *youth* have to come in.

Another friend to whom he showed the manuscript was Christian Hardie (wife of Colin Hardie*). He wrote to her on 31 July 1955:

The idea of re-writing the old myth, with the palace invisible, has been in my mind ever since I was an undergraduate and it always involved writing through the mouth of the elder sister. I tried it in all sorts of verse-forms in the days when I still supposed myself to be a poet. So, though the version you have read was very quickly written, you might say I've been at work on Orual for 35 years. *Of course in my pre-Christian days she was to be in the right and the gods in the wrong* (emphasis added).

In the letter to Clyde S. Kilby of 10 February 1957 he said of Psyche:

Psyche is an instance of the *anima naturaliter Christiana* making the best of the Pagan religion she is brought up in and thus being guided (but always 'under the cloud', always in terms of her own imagination or that of her people) towards the true God. She is in some ways like Christ not because she is a symbol of Him but because every good man or woman is like Christ. What else could they be like? But of course my interest is primarily in Orual (L).

One of the clearest statements about what Lewis was doing with the three sisters comes in a letter to the children, Anne and Martin Kilmer, of 7 August 1957. Asked whether Psyche, Orual and Redival are 'goddesses', Lewis said:

They're just human souls. Psyche has a vocation and becomes a saint. Orual lives the practical life and is, after many sins, saved. As for Redival – well, we'll all hope the best for everyone! (**LTC**).

VI: What the Title of the Book Means

Lewis's own first choice for a title was *Bareface*. His publisher, Jocelyn Gibb,* objected strongly to this and warned Lewis that it might be mistaken for a 'Western'. 'I don't see why people ... would be deterred from buying it if they *did* think it a Western,' Lewis replied on 16 February 1956. 'Actually, I think the title cryptic enough to be intriguing. (The point, of course, is that Orual after going bareface in her youth, is made really and spiritually bareface, to herself and all the dead, at the end.)'

Then, on 29 February he wrote to Gibb, 'One other possible title has occurred to me: *Till We Have Faces*. (My heroine says in one passage, "How can the gods meet us face to face till we have faces?")' Many have been puzzled by those words but their meaning becomes clearer when we see how they are used. In the last chapter Orual recalls her Greek tutor saying to her 'To say the very thing you really mean, the whole of it, nothing more or less or other than what you really mean; that's the whole art and joy of words.' She goes on to say:

> When the time comes to you at which you will be forced at last to utter the speech which has lain at the centre of your soul for years, which you have, all that time, idiot-like, been saying over and over, you'll not talk about joy of words. I saw well why the gods do not speak to us openly, nor let us answer. Till that word can be dug out of us, why should they hear the babble that we think we mean? How can they meet us face to face till we have faces?

One of those who was still puzzled by what Lewis meant by the title was Dorothea Conybeare, who asked him to explain it. On receiving a reply, she passed it on to Rose Macaulay, who had also been puzzled, and the letter is quoted in *Letters to a Sister from Rose Macaulay*, ed. Constance Babington Smith (1964), p. 261. Lewis said:

> How can they (i.e. the gods) meet us face to face till we have faces? The idea was that a human being must become real before it can expect to receive any message from the superhuman; that is, it must be speaking with its own voice (not one of its borrowed voices), expressing its actual desires (not what it imagines that it desires), being for good or ill itself, not any mask, veil or *persona*.

Further clarification is found in a poem Lewis was writing at the same time as the book. It is 'Legion' and was published in *The Month*, XIII

(April 1955). In this poem 'voices' means much the same as 'faces'. Addressing God, the petitioner says:

> Lord, hear my voice, my present voice I mean,
> Not that which may be speaking an hour hence ...
> for if all
> My quarrelling selves must bear an equal voice,
> Farewell, thou has created me in vain.

VII: Pagan and Greek Religion

In his piece on 'The Re-Interpretation of an old Story' Lewis spoke of this book as a tale of 'dark idolatry and pale enlightenment at war with each other.' What he had in mind had been expressed earlier in his essay on **Christian Apologetics** in which he said:

> We may ... divide religions, as we do soups, into 'thick' and 'clear'. By Thick I mean those which have orgies and ecstasies and mysteries and local attachments: Africa is full of Thick religions. By Clear I mean those which are philosophical, ethical and universalizing: Stoicism, Buddhism and the Ethical Church are Clear religions. Now if there is a true religion it must be both Thick and Clear: for the true God must have made both the child and the man, both the savage and the citizen, both the head and the belly ... Christianity breaks down the wall of the partition. It takes a convert from central Africa and tells him to obey an enlightened universalist ethic: it takes a twentieth-century academic prig like me and tells me to go fasting to a Mystery, to drink the blood of the Lord. The savage convert has to be Clear: I have to be Thick. That is how one knows one has come to the real religion.

In the book Lewis tried to show a contrast between the 'Thick' dark idolatry of Ungit and the 'Clear' pale enlightenment represented by Greek thought and religion during that period. To make the contrast sharper still, he asked his publisher, Jocelyn Gibb, to design a cover for the book that would reflect the two. The cover was to show a Stone representing Ungit and a Statue representing Psyche. In a letter to Gibb of 11 April 1956 he said the Stone should be 'Billowy, Indefinite, Ugly, Suggestive of life, Dark, Sexy, Old and Barbarous' while the Statue should be 'Rigid, Definite, Pretty-pretty, Dead as a Dutch doll, Light, New, Thinks itself very civilized and Up-to-date.' The artist attempted this on the cover of the English edition, but the result was not entirely satisfactory.

Summary

Part I

I. This chapter provides a setting for the story. It takes place in the land of Glome which is, as Lewis said in his letter to Clyde S. Kilby of 10 February 1957, 'a little barbarous state on the borders of the Hellenistic world with Greek culture just beginning to affect it' (L). The time is sometime between the death of Socrates in about 399 BC and the birth of Christ. The story is told by Orual, the step-sister of Psyche, looking back on her life when she is an old woman. 'I will write in this book,' she says,

> what no one who has happiness would dare to write. I will accuse the gods; especially the god who lives on the Grey Mountain. That is, I will tell all he has done to me from the very beginning, as if I were making my complaint of him before a judge ... I was Orual the eldest daughter of Trom, King of Glome. The city of Glome stands on the left hand of the river Shennit to a traveller who is coming up from the south-east, not more than a day's journey above Ringal, which is the last town southward that belongs to the land of Glome ... The god of the Grey Mountain, who hates me, is the son of Ungit, but Ungit sits there alone. In the furthest recess of her house where she sits it is so dark that you cannot see her well, but in summer enough light may come down from the smoke-holes in the roof to show her a little. She is a black stone without head or hands or face, and a very great goddess. My old master, whom we called the Fox, said she was the same whom the Greeks call Aphrodite.

It gradually unfolds that the Queen of Glome has just died, and Orual and her sister, Redival, have had their hair cut off as a sign of mourning. Soon afterwards the King buys a Greek slave he calls the 'Fox'. Orual and Redival are brought to meet him, and the King says to the slave: 'Now, Greekling, I trust to beget a prince one of these days and I have a mind to see him brought up in all the wisdom of your people. Meanwhile practise on *them*.' Orual takes to him at once, and from him she begins to learn Greek mythology and philosophy. Having failed to get a son from his first wife, it is not many months before the King marries a daughter of the King of Caphad.

II. The young queen dies after giving birth to a girl – Psyche. The King is furious at not having a son. In his anger he kills a slave and taunts Orual for her ugliness. He threatens to send the Fox to the mines, but he gradually realizes that he is useful in writing Greek and as an adviser. Over time Psyche grows up to be so beautiful that the Fox says: 'Old fool that I am, I could almost believe that there really is divine blood in your family. Helen herself, new-hatched, must have looked so.' Orual, who is like a mother to Psyche, says of her: 'I wanted to be a wife so that I could have been her real mother. I wanted to be a boy so that she could be in love with me. I wanted her to be my full sister instead of my half-sister. I wanted her to be a slave so that I could set her free and make her rich.'

III. Redival ends the good time they were having. Their old nurse Batta catches her 'kissing and whispering love-talk' to a young officer of the guard named Tarin. The King has him castrated and sold at Ringal. He insists that from now on the Fox never let Redival out of his sight. As a result, the pleasure Orual, Psyche and the Fox had found in one another's company is ruined by Redival's presence. Other things go wrong as well. Glome has a very bad harvest, the King is unable to wed into another royal house, and Orual becomes afraid for Psyche's sake when people begin to treat her as if she were a goddess. A rebellion caused by Tarin's father is followed by a plague, during which the Fox nearly dies. During his illness, Orual assists her father in the Pillar Room of the Palace with affairs of state.

The Fox is nursed back to health by Psyche, and when news of this gets out people begin to come to the Palace to be healed by her. The King, afraid that they will turn on him if his daughter stops healing, encourages her to mix among them. Eventually, Psyche falls ill of the fever herself.

IV. When the granaries of the city become empty, the King is put under constant pressure to feed the people. After she is well Psyche goes among the people, but it is clear now that the adoration of her has ended. Many call her the 'Accursed', and the King feels trapped.

V. The Priest of Ungit visits the Palace. One by one he lays at the feet of the King the woes which have fallen upon Glome. In the past, he says, the only thing that won favour with Ungit and expiated the sins of Glome was a 'Great Offering' to Ungit's son, the god of the Mountain, the 'Brute', as he is called. He was seen recently on the Mountain – 'very black and big, a terrible shape'. He must be given a victim, the Accursed.

The Great Offering must be given to the Brute, the Priest says, 'For the Brute is, in a mystery, Ungit herself or Ungit's son, the god of the Mountain: or both. The victim is led up the mountain to the Holy Tree, and bound to the Tree and left. Then the Brute comes ... In the Great Offering the victim must be perfect. For in holy language a man so offered is said to be Ungit's husband, and a woman is said to be the bride of Ungit's son. And both are called the Brute's Supper. And when the Brute is Ungit it lies with the man, and when it is her son it lies with the woman. And either way there is a devouring ... Some say the loving and the devouring are all the same thing.'

The King is terrified that *he* has been chosen to be the Victim, and while he pretends otherwise, he is relieved when he learns that it is Psyche. Orual is beside herself, and begs the King to save Psyche. In his anger he beats her savagely, and agrees to sacrifice Psyche.

VI. It is obvious to Orual and the Fox that the King is sheltering behind his own daughter. Meanwhile, Psyche is imprisoned in the palace, awaiting the Great Offering. Bardia, who is guarding the door, allows Orual a few minutes with her so that she can comfort her.

VII. Orual is disappointed to find Psyche so resigned. She thinks the gods cannot be real because they are said to be so vile. 'Or else,' suggests Psyche, 'they are real gods but don't really do these things. Or even – mightn't it be – they do these things and the things are not what they seem to be?' She reveals that when she has been on the Grey Mountain she has felt a great 'longing', which she now thinks may be a longing for death. Orual is appalled. 'Oh, cruel, cruel!' she says. 'Is it nothing to you that you leave me here alone? ... Did you ever love me at all?'

VIII – IX. Still bruised from her father's beating, Orual is unable to prevent Psyche, drugged and painted, being taken to the Mountain. There she is left tied to the sacred Tree. While waiting for the right time to go to the Mountain and give Psyche a proper burial, Orual asks Bardia to give her lessons in swordsmanship. He is surprised how good she is. On their return to the Mountain and the Tree, they find the chains in place, but no sign of Psyche. Then, going past the Tree, down to a stream beyond which lies a beautiful valley, they receive a shock: on the other side of the stream is Psyche.

X. 'Oh, Maia,' Psyche says, 'I have longed for this ... I knew you would come.' While Bardia stays on the other side, Orual is helped across the stream by Psyche, who is happier than she has ever been. Sitting on the warm heather, she relates the story of how she was rescued by the Westwind, who took her to a Palace. Invisible female servants ministered to her, but she felt ashamed when she took off her clothes. But why, asked Orual, did she feel ashamed in front of women?

'This shame,' explained Psyche, 'has nothing to do with He or She. It's the being mortal; being, how shall I say it? ... insufficient ... And then ...

the night came – and then – he … The Bridegroom … the god himself.'
She says her Bridegroom, who only comes at night, never shows his face.
When Orual asks to be conducted to Psyche's Palace, Psyche asks what
she means. 'Where is the Palace?' says Orual. 'How far have we to go to
reach it?' 'But,' says Psyche, '*this* is it, Orual! It is here! You are standing
on the stairs of the great gate.'

XI. Orual suspects her sister is mad and is anxious to get her away.
Psyche has never seen the Bridegroom, but she will not leave him. 'This is
my home,' she insists. 'I am a wife.' Orual is confused because her sister
has never looked healthier. Even so, she believes that she is mad and she
pleads with her to come with her away from the Mountain.

XII. Bardia comes forward, when called, and he and Orual camp on the
other side of the stream. That night when Orual goes to the stream for a
drink she looks across:

> There stood the palace; grey, as all things were grey in that hour
> and place, but solid and motionless, wall within wall, pillar and
> arch and architrave, acres of it, a labyrinthine beauty.

As she prepares to cross the stream, she looks again. The palace has
vanished. Orual's heart tells her that Psyche 'is ten times happier, there in
the Mountain, than you could ever make her. Leave her alone. Don't spoil
it.'

XIII. After her return to Glome, Orual tells the Fox what she has seen.
He is a Greek rationalist and, partly because Orual does not tell him about
her glimpse of Psyche's palace, he believes that Psyche was probably
freed by a 'robber or runaway' who pretends to be a god's messenger, and
comes to her in the night as the Bridegroom. Orual decides that she must
return to the Mountain and kill Psyche.

XIV. Taking with her Bardia, a lamp, some bandages, and a dagger, she
returns to the Mountain. She visits Psyche alone and tries to persuade her
that her husband is either a monster or a felon. By stabbing her own arm,
she forces Psyche to agree to look at her husband's face when he is asleep.
'You are indeed teaching me about kinds of love I did not know,' says
Psyche. 'It is like looking into a deep pit. I am not sure whether I like your
kind better than hatred. Oh, Orual – to take my love for you … and then
to make of it a tool, a weapon, a thing of policy and mastery, an
instrument of torture … I begin to think I never knew you.'

That night Orual sees a light flare up. Then a 'great voice' rises up in
'implacable sternness'. She hears Psyche weeping as a storm lays waste
the valley. A god – the Bridegroom – appears to Orual. His beauty is such

that she can hardly look at him. She realizes that she knew all along that Psyche's lover was a god, that she has blown dust in her own eyes in an attempt to hide from the truth. 'Now Psyche goes out in exile,' says the god. 'Now she must hunger and thirst and tread hard roads. Those against whom I cannot fight must do their will upon her. You, woman, shall know yourself and your work. You also shall be Psyche.'

XVI – XX. Deeply shamed, Orual returns to Glome. She tells neither Bardia nor the Fox of the conversation she had with Psyche. From this time on Orual hides her ugliness with a veil, which she wears all the time. Shortly afterwards the King is injured in a fall, and after defying her father Orual loses her fear of him. As she continues to train with the sword, Orual begins to repress her identity. 'My aim,' she said, 'was to build up more and more that strength, hard and joyless, which had come to me when I heard the god's sentence; by learning, fighting and labouring, to drive all the woman out of me' (XVI).

Soon the King and the Priest are mortally ill, and pressure falls upon Orual to take over. Bardia and the Fox negotiate with Arnom, who will become the new priest, to support her. But she must be able to defend the country as well. Trunia, the rightful heir to the throne of Phars, turns up and asks for help against his brother Argan. Orual is an experienced swordsman, and as she prepares to face Argan in combat, her father dies. She solidifies her position as Queen by killing Argan, and her reign begins at this point. She finds that her strength lies in two things: the Fox and Bardia as counsellors, and her veil. She continues the attempt to erase her identity: 'One little stairway led me from feast to council, all the bustle and skill and glory of queenship, to my own chamber to be alone with myself – that is, with a nothingness' (XX). She erects a new statue of Ungit alongside the old one in the House of Ungit. It was made in Greece, and in comparison to the old Ungit was beautiful and lifelike.

XXI. After years of hard work, Queen Orual has put the country in good order, and she decides to go on a progress and travel in other lands. She takes with her Bardia's son, Ilerdia, and a number of others. After a stop in Phars to visit Trunia and Redival, she goes on to Essur. While the others are busy with the camp, Orual wanders into the woods. There she comes across a temple built in the Greek style.

On the altar is the image of a goddess, made of pale wood. It is marred by a band of black cloth tied round the head – so as to hide its face. A priest tells her the story of this goddess – Istra – which is very like that of Orual and Psyche, except that in the story both of Istra's sisters visit her, and both see her palace. 'They *saw* the palace?' Orual asks the priest. 'Of course they saw the palace,' he answers. 'They weren't blind.' 'Why did she – they – want to separate her from the god,' Orual asks, 'if they had seen the palace?' 'They wanted to destroy her *because* they had seen her palace.' 'But why?' she asked. 'Because they were jealous. Her husband and her house were so much finer than theirs.'

For years Orual's old quarrel with the gods had slept, but now she is resolved to state her case against them. 'Jealous! I jealous of Psyche?' she says to herself. She then hurries back to Glome to write her accusation against the gods. That accusation is what we have been reading so far – the first twenty-one chapters of *Till We Have Faces*. At the end of chapter XXI she reviews her charges. The gods took Psyche from her; they put her in a position where it hung upon her word as to whether Psyche should 'continue in bliss or be cast out into misery'; they would not tell her 'whether she was the bride of a god, or mad, or a brute's or villain's spoil'; they would give her no 'clear sign', though she begged for it. Finally, they have 'sent out a lying story in which I was given no riddle to guess ... and of my own will destroyed her, and that for jealousy.' If the gods do not answer these charges, might it be 'because they have no answer?'

Part II

I. Orual has not finished her Case Against the Gods. What follows in this Part of *Till We Have Faces* is similar to the tasks Venus gave Psyche in Apuleius's *Metamorphoses*. Orual is to undertake tasks which will force her to see herself as she really is.

From Tarin she learns how lonely Redival was after she turned from her to the Fox and Psyche. Soon afterwards she discovers that Bardia is ill, and as she prepares to visit him Arnom stops her. He says Bardia's loyalty would drive him to do whatever she wanted, but he is an old man who should be allowed to 'drowse and dream'. When Bardia's wife, Ansit, meets the Queen she reproves her for taking Bardia from her. 'What mad thought is in your mind?' says Orual. 'Oh, I know well enough,' answered Ansit, 'that you were not lovers. You left me that ... When you had used him, you would let him steal home to me; until you needed him again.' Orual is forced to admit that she has always been in love with Bardia. Lewis's publisher, Jocelyn Gibb,* had not realized this, and in a letter of 16 February 1956, Lewis said:

> Am I to understand that you ... got as far as O's scene with Bardia's widow without having yet realized that O was, in a most perfectly ordinary, jealous, ravenous, biological fashion, in love with Bardia?

II. Shortly after the visit with Ansit, Orual takes part in the rite of the Year's birth. The Priest is shut up in the house of Ungit from sunset, and on the following morning fights his way out and is said to be born. The fight is staged with wooden swords, and wine is poured over the combatants instead of blood.

As Queen, Orual must sit in Ungit's house and await the birth of the new year. Sitting there, she looks closely at Ungit herself, a shapeless, uneven, lumpy, furrowed stone, covered with blood. She detects on Ungit 'a face such as you might see in a loaf, swollen, brooding, infinitely female.' 'Who is Ungit?' she asks Arnom. 'She signifies the earth,' he says, 'which is the womb and mother of all living things.' When Orual notices that the people prefer the old shapeless Ungit to the beautiful new Greek statue, she asks one why this is. 'That other, the Greek Ungit, she wouldn't understand my speech. She's only for nobles and learned men. There's no comfort in her.'

At home Orual has a dream in which her father appears. He takes her into the Pillar Room where he forces her to dig a hole. Descending deeper and deeper, they come to a Pillar Room far below the Palace. And there the King forces Orual to look into a mirror. She has the face of Ungit. 'It was I who was Ungit,' Orual writes. 'That ruinous face was mine. I was that Batta-thing, that all-devouring, womblike, yet barren, thing. Glome was a web; I the swollen spider, squat at its centre, gorged with men's stolen lives.' After facing this truth Orual tries to commit suicide, but is prevented by a god. 'Do not do it,' he says. 'You cannot escape Ungit by going to the deadlands, for she is there also. Die before you die. There is no chance after.'

III. Orual is determined to die to herself and achieve beauty of soul. 'To say that I was Ungit,' she explains, 'meant that I was as ugly in soul as she; greedy, blood-gorged. But if I practised true philosophy, as Socrates meant it, I should change my ugly soul into a fair one. And this, the gods helping me, I would do.' This was not as easy as she imagined. Although she set out every morning 'to be just and calm and wise' in all her thoughts and acts, it was not long before she was back 'in some old rage, resentment, gnawing fantasy, or sullen bitterness.'

In another dream she attempts to catch the golden fleece from the rams of the gods so that she can become beautiful with the gods' beauty. But she ends up being trampled by the rams, not because of anger, but because the rams were like the gladness of the Divine Nature which 'wounds and perhaps destroys us merely by being what it is.' She spots another woman calmly collecting the golden fleece from a hedge. What Orual sought in vain, she took at her leisure. In compensation, Orual says to herself 'However I might have devoured Bardia, I had at least loved Psyche truly.'

In another dream, imagining herself to be Ungit's slave, she walks over burning sands with an empty bowl which she must fill with the water of death and bring back for Ungit. However, she soon finds herself in a courtroom, the bowl having turned into a book – her complaint against the gods. In her rage against them she claims Psyche as her own. 'The girl was mine. What right had you to steal her away into your dreadful heights? ... I was my own and Psyche was mine and no one else had any right to her. Oh, you'll say you took her away into bliss and joy and such as I could never have given her, and I ought to have been glad of it for her sake. Why? What should I care for some horrible, new happiness which I hadn't given her and which separated her from me? ... She was mine. *Mine*; do you not know what the word means? Mine!'

The Judge stops her, and Orual realizes that she has been reading this same thing over and over, 'starting the first word again almost before the last was out of my mouth ... There was given to me a certainty that this, at last, was my real voice.' 'Are you answered?' asked the Judge. 'Yes,' said Orual.

IV. To have heard herself making the complaint was to be answered. Orual recalls the Fox saying that the 'whole art and joy of words' was to 'say the very thing you really mean.' And now, using the words that became the title of the book, Orual sees why it is so important to utter the speech at the centre of one's soul:

> I saw well why the gods do not speak to us openly, nor let us answer. Till that word can be dug out of us, why should they hear the babble that we think we mean? How can they meet us face to face till we have faces?

The trial having ended, the Fox approaches. He shows her a series of living pictures in which Psyche undertakes four tasks. She is able to do the first three easily because Orual, as it turns out, has borne the anguish for her. However, in the last picture Orual is horrified to see a woman like herself – it was herself – holding out her hands to Psyche, her left arm dripping with blood (from the attempt to force Psyche to light the lamp in order to see her husband). 'Oh, Psyche,' it wailed. 'Oh, my own child, my only love. Come back. Come back. Back to the old world where we were happy together. Come back to Maia.'

'Did we really do these things to her?' Orual asks the Fox. 'Yes,' he answers, 'we did.'

She had no more dangerous enemies than us. And in that far distant day when the gods become wholly beautiful, or we at last are shown how beautiful they always were, this will happen more and more. For mortals, as you said, will become more and more jealous. And mother and wife and child and friend will all be in league to keep a soul from being united with the Divine Nature.

Voices are now heard proclaiming the return of Psyche from the land of the dead. She has returned with the casket of beauty that Ungit commanded her to bring. 'Oh, Psyche, oh, goddess,' said Orual. 'Never again will I call you mine.' She is reunited with Psyche, and as they talk word arrives that the god is coming to judge Orual. As Orual and Psyche stand across a pool of water from the god they see reflected in the water two Psyches – both beautiful beyond all imagining. 'You also are Psyche,' comes the voice of the god.

The vision ends, and Orual is soon afterwards found in the garden of her Palace, the book of accusations against the gods in her hand. 'The old body,' she realizes when she comes round, 'will not stand many more such seeings; perhaps (but who can tell?) the soul will not need them.' Arnom the priest tells her she is near her death. Four days later she picks up the pen again and writes her last words –

I ended my first book with the words *No answer*. I know now, Lord, why you utter no answer. You are yourself the answer. Before your face questions die away. What other answer would suffice? Only words, words; to be led out to battle against other words. Long did I hate you, long did I fear you. I might –

Reviews

Most reviewers had difficulty understanding the book. T.H. White, reviewing it in *Time and Tide*, 37 (13 October 1956), pp. 1227–8, said: 'Although this is a satisfactory novel, I do not wholly agree with its apparent moral – or perhaps with the way it is constructed to convey that moral … I think Queen Orual was possessively jealous of Psyche, whose life she wrecked for that reason – how rightly does the Queen's old teacher remark, "You must obey the god within you, not the god within me" … and I think her philosopher could have told her so from the start, in plain terms, without the author having to resort to the metaphysical mumbo-jumbo of the final section.'

Gerard Meath O.P. in *Blackfriars*, 38 (December 1957), p. 536, said: 'This story is more convincing and real to us than that of Apuleius himself ... [Orual] sees the possessiveness and jealousy that lurked in her love of Psyche; all this and much more she sees in her complaint to the gods in the end, and when all this truth is revealed to her in her own speech then she is ready to be transformed into yet another Psyche. Presumably one may see here also the destroying of the sinful self and think of St Paul and Jung and so on and on endlessly. But the further one takes these interpretations the greater the danger of ruining the story. Best to read it and enjoy it, and if you insist on being done good to let the story do its own work.'

Chad Walsh* said in *The New York Herald Tribune Book Review* (20 January 1957), p. 3: 'It is rare that dust jackets make critical judgements which future critics affirm, but there is a sober chance that C.S. Lewis's *Till We Have Faces* is indeed "the most significant and triumphant work he has yet produced".' Charles J. Rolo in the *Atlantic Monthly*, 199 (February 1957), pp. 84–5, thought that while the book was 'a brilliant reworking of the legend of Cupid and Psyche ... A single reading left some of the novel's meanings obscure; from the standpoint of interpretation, it is a difficult book. But on the narrative level, its eloquence, vividness, and intensity weave a seductive spell.' Riley Hughes in *Catholic World*, 184 (March 1957), p. 472, thought '*Till We Have Faces* should prove to be the most widely read, as it is the most brilliant, of Mr Lewis's four novels.' Ben Ray Redman wrote in *The Saturday Review*, 40 (12 January 1957), p. 15: 'The religious allegory is plain to read. In Mr Lewis's sensitive hands the ancient myth retains its fascination, while being endowed with new meanings, new depths, new terrors.'

THEOLOGICAL FANTASIES

❧

The Screwtape Letters
(with *Screwtape Proposes a Toast*),
The Great Divorce

THE SCREWTAPE
LETTERS (1942)

Background

I: The Conception of 'The Screwtape Letters'

Lewis provides us with the actual moment of the book's conception. In May 1940 Warnie Lewis* had been evacuated from Dunkirk and was at Wenvoe Camp in Cardiff, Wales, when his brother wrote to him on Saturday evening, 20 July. The night before he and Dr R.E. 'Humphrey' Havard* had listened to Hitler speaking over the radio. 'I don't know if I'm weaker than other people,' he said, 'but it is a positive revelation to me how *while the speech lasts* it is impossible not to waver just a little. I should be useless as a schoolmaster or a policeman. Statements which I *know* to be untrue all but convince me, at any rate for the moment, if only the man says them unflinchingly.'

The next day, Sunday, 21 July 1940, Lewis was possibly still thinking of Hitler's momentary persuasiveness when he went to Holy Trinity Church, Headington Quarry, for the Communion service. That afternoon he continued the letter to Warnie:

> Before the service was over – one could wish these things came more seasonably – I was struck by an idea for a book which I think might be both useful and entertaining. It would be called *As one Devil to Another* and would consist of letters from an elderly retired devil to a young devil who has just started work on his first 'patient'. The idea would be to give all the psychology of temptation from the *other* point of view.
>
> E.g. 'About undermining his faith in prayer, I don't think you need have any difficulty with his intellect, provided you never say the wrong thing at the wrong moment. After all, the Enemy [God]

will either answer his prayers or not. If He does *not*, then that's simple – it shows prayers are no good. If He *does* – I've always found that, oddly enough, this can be just as easily utilized. It needs only a word from you to make him believe that the very fact of feeling more patient after he's prayed for patience will be taken as a proof that prayer is a kind of self-hypnosis. Or if it is answered by some external event, then since that event will have causes which you can point to, he can be persuaded that it would have happened anyway. You see the idea? Prayer can always be discredited either because it works or because it doesn't.' Or again, 'In attacking faith, I should be chary of argument. Arguments only provoke answers. What you want to work away at is the mere unreasoning *feeling* that "that sort of thing can't really be true"' (L).

II: Lewis's Beliefs about God and the Devil

We don't know how long it took Lewis to write *The Screwtape Letters*, but it was probably written by Christmas 1940. This means that *Screwtape* was in existence before he began any of the four series of broadcasts which make up *Mere Christianity*. In the broadcast entitled 'The Invasion' Lewis explained what Dualism meant and why we cannot believe it. However, in the original Preface to *Screwtape* Lewis had said very little about devils except that

> There are two equal and opposite errors into which our race can fall about the devils. One is to disbelieve in their existence. The other is to believe, and to feel an excessive and unhealthy interest in them. They themselves are equally pleased by both errors and hail a materialist or a magician with the same delight.

Still, some readers of *Screwtape* came away with the impression that God and Satan were equal and independent powers, and some years later, in the additional new Preface (hereafter: 'New Preface') he wrote for *The Screwtape Letters and Screwtape Proposes a Toast* (1961), Lewis answered a number of questions raised about *The Screwtape Letters*. He said that 'Though I had never written anything more easily, I never wrote with less enjoyment ... Though it was easy to twist one's mind into the diabolical attitude, it was not fun, or not for long. The strain produced a sort of spiritual cramp. The world into which I had to project myself while I spoke through Screwtape was all dust, grit, thirst, and itch. Every trace of beauty, freshness and geniality had to be excluded.' He mentions, too, a debt to Stephen McKenna's *Confessions of a Well-Meaning Woman* (1922) which contains 'the same moral inversion – the blacks all white and the whites all black – and the humour which comes of speaking through a totally humourless *persona.'*

On the question of whether he 'believed in the Devil', Lewis said in the New Preface:

Now if by 'the Devil' you mean a power opposite to God and, like God, self-existent from all eternity, the answer is certainly 'No'. There is no uncreated being except God. God has no opposite. No being could attain a 'perfect badness' opposite to the perfect goodness of God; for when you have taken away every kind of good thing (intelligence, will, memory, energy and existence itself) there would be none of him left.

The proper question is whether I believe in devils. I do. That is to say, I believe in angels and I believe that some of these, by the abuse of their free will, have become enemies to God and, as a corollary, to us. These we may call devils. They do not differ in nature from good angels, but their nature is depraved. *Devil* is the opposite of *angel* only as Bad Man is the opposite of Good Man. Satan, the leader or dictator of devils, is the opposite not of God but of Michael.

In the same work he also explained why he chose to give Hell the ethos of a bureaucracy:

I live in the Managerial Age, in a world of 'Admin.' The greatest evil is not now done in those sordid 'dens of crime' that Dickens loved to paint. It is not done even in concentration camps and labour camps ... It is conceived and ordered ... in clean, carpeted, warmed and well-lighted offices, by quiet men with white collars and cut fingernails and smooth-shaven cheeks who do not need to raise their voice. Hence, naturally enough, my symbol for Hell is something like the bureaucracy of a police state or the offices of a thoroughly nasty business concern.

Summary

The Screwtape Letters consists of thirty-one letters from Screwtape, an elderly devil in Hell's civil service, to a younger devil, Wormwood, on the art of temptation. Wormwood has been put in charge of a young man – the 'Patient' – whose soul he is trying to secure. The purpose of the book is to show how the life of man looks from the viewpoint of Hell, and to throw light on Heaven from this unusual perspective. The events in the life of the 'Patient' are not meant to be of great interest: the main interest is meant to be the immortal consequences of seemingly small and insignificant choices in the every-day life of Everyman.

In **Letter** I Screwtape repeats what had come into Lewis's head at church on 21 July 1940: 'In attacking faith, I should be chary of argument. Arguments only provoke answers. What you want to work away at is the mere unreasoning *feeling* that "that sort of thing can't really be *true*".' It is best if the Patient, instead of reading science, has a grand general idea about 'the results of modern investigation'. In **II** the Patient has become a Christian, and Screwtape explains how the church itself might cure him of this. 'Provided that any of those neighbours sing out of tune, or have boots that squeak, or double chins, or odd clothes, the patient will quite easily believe that their religion must therefore be somehow ridiculous.'

III is advice on building up 'daily pinpricks' between the Patient and his mother. Here are two: (1) If the Patient keeps his mind 'on the inner life' and 'off the most elementary duties' he will be able to 'practise self-examination for an hour without discovering any of those facts about himself' obvious to everyone else. (2) As 'domestic hatred' expresses itself by saying things which would appear harmless on paper, the Patient 'must demand that all his own utterances are to be taken at their face value' while judging his mother's utterances 'with the fullest and most over-sensitive interpretation'.

IV is about Prayer. If the Patient insists on praying, he should be encouraged to 'produce in himself a vaguely devotional *mood* in which real concentration of will and intelligence have no part.' He should turn his gaze 'away from Him' and towards himself, at the same time 'watching' his own mind in an effort to 'produce *feelings*' by an effort of the will. The Enemy will not be idle. 'Wherever there is prayer, there is danger of His own immediate action.' In **V** Screwtape is annoyed to find Wormwood 'delirious with joy' over the outbreak of war. 'Men are killed in places where they knew they might be killed and to which they go, if they are at all of the Enemy's party, prepared. How much better for us if *all* humans died in costly nursing homes amid doctors who lie, nurses who lie, friends who lie, as we have trained them, promising life to the dying.'

In **VI** Wormwood is advised to direct the Patient's malice 'to his immediate neighbours whom he meets every day and to thrust his benevolence out to the remotest circumference, to people he does not know.' In **VII** Screwtape considers whether to keep the Patient ignorant of Wormwood's existence. 'The fact that "devils" are predominantly *comic* figures in the modern imagination will help you. If any faint suspicion of your existence begins to arise in his mind, suggest to him a picture of something in red tights, and persuade him that since he cannot believe in that ... he therefore cannot believe in you.'

VIII is on the nature of Man. Because Man is 'half spirit and half animal' he will go through a 'series of troughs and peaks' in which 'periods of emotional and bodily richness and liveliness will alternate with periods of numbness and poverty.' What does the Enemy make of this? 'One must face the fact that all the talk about His love for men, and His service being perfect freedom, is not ... mere propaganda ... He really *does* want to fill the universe with a lot of loathsome little replicas of Himself.'

The 'Irresistible and the Indisputable' are, says Screwtape, weapons which the Enemy never uses. 'He cannot ravish. He can only woo.' On the other hand,

> Our case is never more in danger than when a human, no longer desiring, but still intending, to do our Enemy's will, looks round upon a universe from which every trace of Him seems to have vanished, and asks why he has been forsaken, and still obeys.

IX is about Pleasure, and Screwtape says, 'Never forget that when we are dealing with any pleasure in its healthy and normal and satisfying form, we are, in a sense, on the Enemy's ground. I know we have won many a soul through pleasure. All the same, it is His invention, not ours. He made the pleasures: all our research so far has not enabled us to produce one. All we can do is to encourage the humans to take the pleasures which our Enemy has produced, at times, or in ways, or in degrees, which He has forbidden.' In **X** Wormwood is urged to warn the Patient that a careful choice of friends and the encouragement of virtue is 'Puritanism'. 'The value we have given to that word is one of the really solid triumphs of the last hundred years. By it we rescue annually thousands of humans from temperance, chastity, and sobriety of life.'

In **XI** the 'causes of human laughter' are divided into Joy, Fun, the Joke Proper and Flippancy. Joy is found among 'friends and lovers reunited on the eve of a holiday'; Fun is 'a sort of emotional froth arising from the play instinct.' The Joke Proper 'which turns on sudden perception of incongruity', is more promising for Hell. This is because humans are divided into two kinds: 'The first sort joke about sex because it gives rise to many incongruities: the second cultivate incongruities because they afford a pretext for talking about sex.' Hell uses Jokes or Humour as a 'means of destroying shame'. Flippancy is better than anything because among flippant people the Joke is always assumed to have been made. They talk '*as if* virtue were funny'.

In **XII** the Patient begins to drift away from the Enemy, and Screwtape notes that anything or nothing is sufficient to attract his wandering attention. 'Nothing' itself, he says, 'is very strong: strong enough to steal away a man's best years not in sweet sins but in a dreary flickering of the mind over it knows not what and knows not why, in the gratification of curiosities so feeble that the man is only half aware of them.' This is followed by one of the most admirable passages in the book:

> It does not matter how small the sins are provided that their cumulative effect is to edge the man away from the Light and out into the Nothing. Murder is no better than cards if cards can do the trick. Indeed the safest road to Hell is the gradual one – the gentle slope, soft underfoot, without sudden turnings, without milestones, without signposts.

In **XIII** Screwtape says innocent pleasures such as a walk through the country, stamp-collecting, books, contribute to a man's self-forgetfulness. Hell, on the other hand, wants a man to 'abandon the people or food or books he really likes in favour of the "best" people, the "right" food, the "important" books.' In **XIV** the Patient has become Humble, and Screwtape is keen to corrupt him. 'Let him think of [Humility] not as self-forgetfulness but as a certain kind of opinion (namely, a low opinion) of his own talents and character. Some talents, I gather, he has. Fix in his mind the idea that humility consists in trying to believe those talents to be less valuable than he believes them to be … thus introducing an element of dishonesty and make-believe into the heart of what otherwise threatens to become a virtue.'

In **XV** the subject is Time. Because human beings live in time, but are destined for eternity, the Enemy 'wants them to attend chiefly to two things, to eternity itself, and to that point of time which they call the Present.' Hell, on the other hand, wants man to 'live in the Future' because it is 'the thing *least like eternity* … the most completely temporal part of time.' The Enemy wants men to think of the Future too 'just so much as is necessary for *now* planning the acts of justice or charity which will probably be their duty tomorrow.' Hell wants 'a man hag-ridden by the Future ... a whole race perpetually in pursuit of the rainbow's end, never honest, nor kind, nor happy *now*, but always using as mere fuel wherewith to heap the altar of the future every real gift which is offered them in the Present.'

In **XVI** Screwtape considers what is a 'suitable' church for the Patient. There is, on the one hand, the 'low-church' vicar 'who has been so long engaged in watering down the faith to make it easier for a supposedly incredulous and hard-headed congregation that it is now he who shocks his parishioners with his unbelief.' On the other hand, there is 'high-church' Father Spike who 'cannot bring himself to preach anything which is not calculated to shock, grieve, puzzle, or humiliate his parents and their friends.' Hell has 'removed from men's minds what that pestilent fellow Paul used to teach about food and other unessentials – namely, that the human without scruples should always give in to the human with scruples.' **XVII** is about Gluttony. No one hears sermons preached about Gluttony any more because Hell has been 'concentrating ... on gluttony of Delicacy, not gluttony of Excess.' The devil Glubose is training an old woman in the 'All-I-want' state of mind. 'She is always turning from what has been offered her to say with a demure little sigh and a smile "Oh please, please ... *all* I want is a cup of tea, weak but not too weak, and the teeniest weeniest bit of really crisp toast."'

In **XVIII** Screwtape reveals Hell's intention of making '"being in love" ... the only respectable ground for marriage.' Whereas the Enemy promises love as a *result* of 'fidelity, fertility and good will', Hell seeks to make mutual help, chastity and the transmission of life 'something lower than a storm of emotion'. In **XIX** Screwtape gives Hell's account of how Satan was thrown out of Heaven: 'Our Father's disgust at such an unprovoked lack of confidence caused him to remove himself an infinite distance from the Presence with a suddenness which has given rise to the ridiculous enemy story that he was forcibly thrown out of Heaven.' In **XX** he discusses the Lowerarchy's 'general misdirection of what may be called sexual "taste".' 'Hell has discovered that a man is 'haunted by ... a terrestrial and an infernal Venus, and that his desire differs qualitatively according to its object. There is one type for which his desire is such as to be naturally amenable to the Enemy – readily mixed with charity, readily obedient to marriage ... there is another type which he desires brutally, and desires to desire brutally, a type best used to draw him away from marriage.'

In **XXI** Wormwood is told to guard in the Patient's mind the assumption 'My time is my own' so that he will feel 'as a grievous tax that portion of his property which he has to make over to his employers, and as a generous donation that further portion which he allows to religious duties.' Such claims to ownership 'sound equally funny in Heaven and Hell'.

In **XXII** Screwtape is furious that the Patient is in love with a Christian, and he complains that the Enemy is 'a hedonist at heart' and that 'Everything has to be *twisted* before it's any use to us.' In **XXIII** Screwtape reveals Hell's success in encouraging conceptions of a 'historical Jesus'. 'In the last generation we promoted the construction of such a "historical Jesus" on liberal and humanitarian lines; we are now putting forward a new "historical Jesus" on Marxian, catastrophic, and revolutionary lines ... they all tend to direct men's devotion to something which does not exist, for each "historical Jesus" is unhistorical.' As the Patient grows closer to Christian friends Screwtape reveals in **XXIV** how this friendship can be twisted into an 'Inner Ring'.§ In **XXV** he finds the trouble with the Patient and his friends is that they are '*merely* Christian'. 'What we want, if men become Christians at all, is to keep them in the state of mind I call "Christianity And". You know – Christianity and the Crisis, Christianity and the New Psychology ... If they must be Christians let them at least be Christians with a difference.' **XXVI** reveals how Unselfishness can be corrupted by the 'Generous Conflict Illusion': 'Something quite trivial like having tea in the garden, is proposed. One member takes care to make it quite clear ... that he would rather not but is, of course, prepared to do so out of "Unselfishness". The others instantly withdraw their proposal, ostensibly through their "Unselfishness", but really because they don't want to be used as a sort of lay figure on which the first speaker practises petty altruisms ... Passions are roused. Soon someone is saying "Very well then, I won't have any tea at all!", and a real quarrel ensues.'

Letter **XXVII** concerns the 'heads I win, tails you lose' argument about Prayer. 'If you tried to explain to him,' says Screwtape, 'that men's prayers today are one of the innumerable co-ordinates with which the Enemy harmonizes the weather of tomorrow, he would reply that then the Enemy always knew men were going to make those prayers and, if so, they did not pray freely but were predestined to do so.' The Enemy, explains Screwtape, 'does not *foresee* the humans making their free contributions in a future, but *sees* them doing so in His unbounded Now. And obviously to watch a man doing something is not to make him do it.'

As the war worsens Screwtape reveals in **XXVIII** that Hell does not want the Patient killed by a bomb. 'If only he can be kept alive, you have time itself for your ally.' Why? Because 'The long, dull, monotonous years of middle-aged prosperity or middle-aged adversity' are Hell's best 'campaigning weather'. 'It is so hard for these creatures to *persevere*. The routine of adversity, the gradual decay of youthful loves and youthful hopes, the quiet despair ... all this provides admirable opportunities of wearing out a soul by attrition.' In **XXIX**, when it looks certain the Germans will bomb the Patient's town, Wormwood tries to encourage cowardice in him. The Enemy permits wars because 'moral issues really come to the point' in a dangerous world. 'He sees as well as you do,' says Screwtape, 'that courage is not simply *one* of the virtues, but the form of every virtue at the testing point, which means, at the point of highest reality. A chastity or honesty, or mercy, which yields to danger will be chaste or honest or merciful only on conditions. Pilate was merciful till it became risky.' In **XXX** Screwtape is furious because, in a raid, the Patient was frightened 'and thinks himself a great coward'. As the war provides no material for an *intellectual* attack on the man's faith, Screwtape advises an attack on his emotions. 'It turns on making him *feel*, when first he sees human remains plastered on a wall, that this is "what the world is *really* like" and that all his religion has been a fantasy.'

XXXI opens with Screwtape's promise to consume Wormwood in Hell because the Patient has been killed. 'You have let a soul slip through your fingers.' He describes the Patient at the moment of his death: 'There was a sudden clearing of his eyes ... as he saw you for the first time ... Just think (and let it be the beginning of your agony) what he felt at that moment; as if a scab had fallen from an old sore, as if he were emerging from a hideous, shell-like tether, as if he shuffled off for good and all a defiled, wet, clinging garment.' To cause Wormwood further pain, Screwtape explains exactly what the Patient saw in his dying moments:

> He saw Him. This animal, this thing begotten in a bed, could look on Him. What is blinding, suffocating fire to you, is now cool light to him, is clarity itself, and wears the form of a Man ... Pains he may still have to encounter, but they *embrace* those pains. They would not barter them for any earthly pleasure ... He is caught up into that world where pain and pleasure take on transfinite values and all our arithmetic is dismayed ... If only we could find out what He is really up to!

Reviews

The Times Literary Supplement (28 February 1942), p. 100, said: 'A reviewer's task is not to be a prophet, and time alone can show whether it is or is not an enduring piece of satirical writing. In any case that is a minor matter. It is much more to the point that in so readable a fashion Mr Lewis has contrived to say much that a distracted world greatly requires to hear.' 'Artifex' in the *Manchester Guardian* (24 February 1942), p. 3, said: 'The book is sparkling yet truly reverent, in fact a perfect joy, and should become a classic.' A reviewer in *The Guardian‡* (13 March 1942), p. 86 – in which the *Letters* were first published – said: '[Lewis] is in earnest with his belief in devils, and as anxious to unmask their strategy against souls as our intelligence department to detect the designs of Hitler.'

L.P. Jacks, in *The Hibbert Journal*, XL, No. 4 (July 1942), pp. 395–8, said: 'To entrust the ruin of souls to unqualified practitioners like Wormwood is surely a mistake. This will be a comforting thought to some of us, who would be hopelessly undone if a Screwtape had the management of our temptations, but which have a fair chance of slipping through into heaven if the fiend charged to accomplish our damnation were a bungler like Wormwood ... It is to be hoped that neither Mr Lewis's book, nor *The Hibbert Journal* containing this review, will find its way into those regions to apprise the infernal authorities of their mistake.' One of the book's most trenchant reviewers was C.E.M. Joad who admitted in the *New Statesman and Nation*, 23 (16 May 1942), p. 324, that: 'Mr Lewis possesses the rare gift of being able to make righteousness readable, and has produced a pretty piece of homily lit by flashes of insight.'

Charles Williams* said in *The Dublin Review*, No. 423 (October 1942), pp. 170–1: 'I allow that Mr Lewis's Screwtape is highly intelligent, almost too intelligent for a devil, everywhere except in the centre. One of the pleasantest things in the book is his failure there, his incapacity to understand what the Enemy "is really up to".' And Leonard Bacon, in *The Saturday Review of Literature*, 26 (17 April 1943), p. 20, called it 'this admirable, diverting, and remarkably original work ... There is a spectacular and satisfactory nova in the bleak sky of satire.'

SCREWTAPE PROPOSES
A TOAST (1959)

Background

Lewis was often asked to write more Screwtape letters, but he felt no inclination to do so. In the New Preface to *Screwtape Letters and Screwtape Proposes a Toast* he said, 'The idea of something like a lecture or "address" hovered vaguely in my mind, now forgotten, now recalled, never written. Then came an invitation from *The Saturday Evening Post*, and that pressed the trigger.' The result was 'Screwtape Proposes a Toast', a toast by Screwtape at the 'annual dinner of the Tempter's Training College for young Devils'. It was published in *The Saturday Evening Post*, CCXXXII (19 December 1959), pp. 36, 88–9.

Summary

Screwtape begins his 'Toast' by pointing out that the dinner has consisted of human souls. He complains, however, that even their best cookery could not prevent them from being 'insipid'. 'Oh, to get one's teeth again into a Farinata, a Henry VIII or even a Hitler! ... Instead of this ... There was a municipal authority with Graft sauce ... Then there was the lukewarm Casserole of Adulterers ... Gastronomically, all this is deplorable.' However, the dinner is nevertheless 'full of hope and promise' because (1) Hell has never had souls 'in more abundance', and (2) while the souls are of poor quality, Hell has managed to raise them to a 'level of clarity and deliberateness at which mortal sin becomes possible.'

He traces the stages in this 'triumph'. Following the nineteenth-century movements towards liberty and equality, there was much religious toleration. There was also a good deal of Atheism about, and Hell believed it should be encouraged. But the Enemy 'perverted' it to His own ends, and Christian Socialism was rampant. 'The rich were increasingly giving up their powers, not in the face of revolution and compulsion, but in obedience to their own consciences.' Then came 'Our Father Below's' counterattack. 'Hidden in the heart of this striving for Liberty there was also a deep hatred of personal freedom. That invaluable man Rousseau first revealed it. In his perfect democracy ... only the state religion is permitted, slavery is restored, and the individual is told that he has really willed ... whatever the Government tells him to do. From that starting point, via Hegel ... we easily contrived both the Nazi and the Communist state.'

'*Democracy*,' Screwtape says, is the word with which the devils are to lead men by the nose. 'It will never occur to them that *democracy* is properly the name of a political system ... Nor must they ever be allowed to raise Aristotle's question: whether "democratic behaviour" means the behaviour that democracies like or the behaviour that will preserve a democracy.' Because men venerate democracy, devils are to move their minds from the political ideal that men should be 'equally treated' to a factual belief that 'all men are equal'. By the word 'democracy' men can be led 'to practise, not only without shame but with a positive glow of self-approval, conduct which, if undefended by the magic word, would be universally derided.' By the feelings which prompt men to say '*I'm as good as you*,' Hell can cause a man to 'enthrone at the centre of his life a good solid, resounding lie.'

The Tempters are urged to fix their attention on the 'vast, overall movement towards the discrediting, and finally the elimination, of every kind of human excellence – moral, cultural, social, or intellectual.' Screwtape admits that his own experience has been in the 'English sector' and that each Tempter 'must labour to make the country you are dealing with more like what England already is.' He traces Hell's use of 'the spirit of *I'm as good as you*' in several areas of human life. (1) In the educational system the 'basic principle of the new education is to be that dunces and idlers must not be made to feel inferior to intelligent and industrious pupils.' (2) Concerning the national government, Hell would welcome the disappearance of democracy 'in the strict sense of the word'. (3) The spirit of '*I'm as good as you*' is to be used on the individual human 'as a state of mind which, necessarily excluding humility, charity, contentment, and all the pleasures of gratitude or admiration, turns a human being away from almost every road which might finally lead him to Heaven.'

THE GREAT DIVORCE:
A DREAM (1945)

Background

I: The 'Refrigerium'

The idea for this book was to mature in Lewis's mind for a long time before it came to fruition. In August and September 1931 he read the works of the seventeenth-century Anglican divine, Jeremy Taylor. In Taylor's sermon on 'Christ's Advent to Judgement' he came across the idea of the *Refrigerium*. 'The church of Rome amongst other strange opinions,' said Taylor,

> hath inserted this one into her public offices; that the perishing souls in hell may have sometimes remission and refreshment, like the fits of an intermitting fever: for so it is in the Roman missal printed at Paris, 1626, in the mass for the dead; *Ut quia de ejus vitae qualitate diffidimus, etsi plenam veniam anima ipsius obtinere non potest, saltem vel inter ipsa tormenta quae forsan partitur, refrigerium de abundantia miserationum tuarum sentiat* (*Whole Works*, ed. R. Heber (London, 1822), Vol. V, p. 45).

which may be translated:

> And since we are unsure about the character of his life, even if his soul is unable to obtain full remission, let him at least feel some relief, through the abundance of thy great mercies, among whatever crushing sufferings he endures.

In the same sermon Taylor mentions another source of the *Refrigerium* – the fourth-century Latin poet and hymn-writer, Prudentius Aurelius Clemens. In his 'Hymn for the Lighting of the Lamp', found in his

Liber Cathemerinon, he says: 'Often below the Styx holidays from their punishments are kept, even by the guilty spirits ... Hell grows feeble with mitigated torments and the shadowy nation, free from fires, exults in the leisure of its prison; the rivers cease to burn with their usual sulphur.'

The idea took hold, and in his diary for 16 April 1933 Warnie Lewis* said: 'J[ack] has a new idea for a religious work, based on the opinion of some of the Fathers, that while punishment for the damned is eternal, it is intermittent: he proposes to do sort of an infernal day excursion to Paradise. I shall be very interested to see how he handles it' (**BF**).

The translation given above of the passage said to come from a Parisian Missal of 1626 was made by Father Jerome Bertram of the Oxford Oratory, who says: 'In *The Great Divorce* Lewis is making use of the old tradition of the Refrigerium or Holiday from Hell. He would have been aware of this from his earliest student days from the tenth-century Anglo-Saxon poem *The Seafarer*, where the hero meets Judas during one of his occasional days off. The idea is older than that, and is usually considered to date from the apocryphal *Apocalypse of Paul* dating from the late fourth century, in which Christ grants a day and a night's refreshment for ever on Easter day (M.R. James, *The Apocryphal New Testament*, p. 548). It became something of a commonplace in late first-millennium tradition, though the Church never gave any official countenance to the idea.

'The actual word *refrigerium* is Scriptural, occurring in the Vulgate six times, most notably in Psalm 65:12, *eduxisti nos in refrigerium*, thou has brought us out to a place of rest. The meaning is consistently rest or repose after the heat and turmoil of life, hence it is appropriately used in the Mass *locum refrigerii, lucis et pacis* a place of rest, light and peace, for the faithful departed. In none of these texts, however, is there any suggestion of repose from damnation. In early Christian tradition *refrigerium* meant a commemorative celebration at a grave, naturally including prayers for the repose of the soul of the departed.

'Lewis cites Jeremy Taylor who claims to have found the idea of repose from Hell in an early seventeenth-century Parisian Missal which has not been traced. However, a feature of early Gallican missals was a Mass for one whose soul was in doubt, *Missa pro cuius anima dubitatur*, for which various formulae are cited. This Mass found its way into Italian missals in the late fifteenth century, but was eliminated in the 1570 reform of the Roman Missal. The common theme is a prayer, if possible for the salvation of the deceased, but failing that at least for some mitigation of Hell. Some colour to this aspiration is given by an ambiguous passage in St Augustine, which may refer either to Hell or Purgatory (see Dom A.

Cabassut, 'La Mitigation des peines de l'enfer d'après les livres liturgiques' in *Revue d'Histoire Ecclesiastique* 23 (1927), pp. 65–70.)'

II: God Cannot Overrule Freewill

It was to be eleven years before Lewis began his *Refrigerium* story, but the thought behind it was there before he read Jeremy Taylor. In between his conversion to Theism (1929) and his conversion to Christianity (1931), Lewis composed the two poems entitled 'Divine Justice' and 'Nearly They Stood' in *Poems*, and which appeared in *The Pilgrim's Regress* (X, pp. 3–4) in 1933.

The poems and the chapter entitled 'The Black Hole' (X, p. 4) contain three of the powerful ideas that were to figure in *The Great Divorce*: (1) you cannot fix a point beyond which a man is unable to repent and be saved but 'there will be such a point somewhere'; (2) even God cannot overrule free will because 'It is meaningless to talk of forcing a man to do freely what a man has freely made impossible for himself'; (3) 'evil is fissiparous and could never in a thousand eternities find any way to arrest its own re-production', and Hell was created as a 'tourniquet' to stop the lost soul's downward progression.

The next stage in Lewis's thinking comes in *The Problem of Pain*. In the chapter on 'Hell' he imagines a 'jolly, ruddy-cheeked man, without a care in the world, unshakeably confident to the very end that he alone has found the answer to the riddle of life.' Lewis's most distinctive gift was a colossal enjoyment of things outside himself. It comes, then, as no surprise that to Lewis the most pathetic feature of this jolly man will be his loss of 'The taste for the *other*', and that Hell will mean 'to live wholly in the self and to make the best of what he finds there.' A pretty accurate précis of his thoughts about the matter is found in a letter Lewis wrote to his brother on 28 January 1940: 'I begin to suspect that the world is divided not only into the happy and the unhappy, but into those who *like* happiness and those who, odd as it seems, really don't.'

III: Discussion by The Inklings

We learn that *The Great Divorce* is being written from J.R.R. Tolkien's* letter to Christopher Tolkien* of 13 April 1944. He says that at the Inklings meeting on the 13th, 'The best entertainment proved to be a chapter of Major Lewis's projected book – on ... the court of Louis XIV' and 'the concluding chapter of C.S.L.'s new moral allegory or "vision", based on the medieval fancy of the *Refrigerium*, by which lost souls have an occasional holiday in Paradise.' At this time Lewis's book was called *Who Goes Home?* – a cry shouted by the policeman on duty through the corridors of the House of Commons after it has concluded its sitting and is about to close its doors.

Tolkien wrote to his son again on 14 May to say that he had just heard two chapters of Lewis's '*Who Goes Home?* – a new allegory on Heaven and Hell'. And in his letter to Christopher Tolkien of 31 May he said that 'the chief entertainment' at the Inklings meeting on 25 May 'was provided by a chapter of Warnie Lewis's book on the times of Louis XIV (very good I thought it); and some excerpts from C.S.L.'s *Who Goes Home?* – a book on Hell, which I suggested should have been called rather "Hugo's Home"' [after Hugo Dyson*] (**LJRRT**). Lewis had finished the book by the end of the summer of 1944.

Summary

In the **Preface** Lewis remarked that William Blake's *Marriage of Heaven and Hell* is one of many attempts to make us believe such a 'marriage' possible: that 'reality never presents us with an absolutely unavoidable "either-or".' That is, he said, a 'disastrous error'. We do not live in a world where all roads meet at the centre, but one 'where every road, after a few miles, forks into two, and each of those into two again, and at each fork you must make a decision.' Good becomes continually more different not only from evil but from other good.

Not all who choose the wrong road perish, but their rescue consists in being put back on the right road, never in just 'going on'. 'If we insist on keeping Hell (or even earth) we shall not see Heaven: if we accept Heaven we shall not be able to retain even the smallest and most intimate souvenirs of Hell.' Earth, if chosen instead of Heaven, will turn out to be a region of Hell: if put second to Heaven, it will be found to be 'the beginning of a part of Heaven itself.' Lewis urged his readers to remember that his book is a 'fantasy', and not even a 'guess or a speculation at what may actually await us.'

In chapter **I** Lewis is one of many standing at a bus queue in a 'long mean street' in the rain as evening closes in. The 'grey town' is full of dingy lodging houses and the others in the queue argue bitterly until a bus 'blazing with gold light' and 'heraldically coloured' appears. Lewis boards the bus with the others, and they leave the town. In **II** he talks to someone about the 'grey town'. Because everyone is continually quarrelling with his neighbours, there is constant moving to the edge of town. Because the grey town goes on expanding, some people spend centuries travelling to the bus station. The inhabitants of the grey town live under the continual fear of the twilight turning into night. Outside the bus the light is growing brighter.

In III they arrive at the top of a 'level, grassy country through which there ran a wide river'. After leaving the bus, Lewis notices that the other passengers appear transparent when in the light, 'smudgy and imperfectly opaque when ... in the shadow of some tree'. The grass does not bend beneath their feet and Lewis is unable to pluck a daisy because it is as hard as a diamond. He sees the grass *through* his feet, and he knows that he is a phantom like the others. Soon the earth shakes as a great many people advance to meet them. 'Some were naked, some robed. But the naked ones did not seem less adorned, and the robes did not disguise in those who wore them the massive grandeur of muscle and the radiant smoothness of flesh.'

In IV he witnesses a conversation between one of the 'bright' or 'solid' people and 'the Big Man' or the 'Big Ghost' from the grey town. The Ghost resists all offers of 'Bleeding Charity' because he insists on his 'rights'. In V Lewis overhears a conversation between a Spirit named Dick and a Ghost who is an Anglican bishop. Dick had been a clergyman, and the Bishop chides him with having become 'rather narrow-minded' towards the end of his life. 'Why, my dear boy, you were coming to believe in a literal Heaven and Hell!' 'But wasn't I right?' asked the Spirit. The Bishop is shocked to find him calling the grey town 'Hell'. 'You have been in Hell,' says Dick, 'though if you don't go back you may call it Purgatory.' The Bishop insists that his opinions were honest and heroic. 'When the doctrine of the Resurrection ceased to commend itself to the critical faculties which God had given me, I openly rejected it. I preached my famous sermon.' Dick asks, 'When, in our whole lives, did we honestly face, in solitude, the one question on which all turned: whether after all the Supernatural might not in fact occur?' He insists that they had both allowed themselves to 'reach a point where we no longer believed the Faith.' When Dick asks the Bishop to 'repent and believe' he insists that for him 'there is no such thing as a final answer ... to travel hopefully is better than to arrive.' The Bishop refuses to stay and 'thicken up' because he is keen to get back to the grey town where he will be giving a theological paper. 'I'm going to point out how people always forget that Jesus ... was a comparatively young man when he died. He would have outgrown some of his earlier views, you know, if he'd lived. As he might have done, with a little more tact and patience. I am going to ask my audience to consider what his mature views would have been ... What a different Christianity we might have had if only the Founder had reached his full stature!'

In **VI** a Ghost lifts with enormous difficulty an apple from one of the heavenly trees. As he attempts to get it back to the bus, he is stopped by an angel. 'Fool,' it said, 'put it down ... There is not room for it in Hell. Stay here and learn to eat such apples.' The Ghost continued dragging the apple to the bus. In **VII** Lewis gets into conversation with a Ghost who insists that the encouragement to stay here 'is only an advertisement stunt' run by the 'same firm' as those who trap tourists into going to other places. He refuses to be 'taken in'.

In **VIII** Lewis observes a Spirit trying to persuade a female Ghost to let him help her walk to the Mountains. She is trying to hide from these Bright People. 'How *can* I go out like this among a lot of people with solid bodies?' The Spirit answers, 'An hour hence and you will not care ... Don't you remember on earth – there were things too hot to touch with your finger but you could drink them all right? Shame is like that. If you will accept it – if you will drink the cup to the bottom – you will find it very nourishing: but try to do anything else with it and it scalds.'

In **IX** we meet the writer George MacDonald. As Virgil was Dante's guide in *The Divine Comedy*, so MacDonald is Lewis's guide in this 'Valley of the Shadow of Life'. 'Here,' said Lewis, 'was an enthroned and shining god, whose ageless spirit weighed upon mine like a burden of solid gold.' He addresses a number of questions to his mentor.

(1) 'Is judgement not final?' 'Is there really a way out of Hell into Heaven?' MacDonald replies: 'To any that leaves it, it is Purgatory ... And yet to those who stay here it will have been Heaven from the first ... but to those who remain there they will have been in Hell even from the beginning.' MacDonald explains that 'good and evil, when they are full grown, become retrospective.' 'That is what mortals misunderstand,' he explains. 'They say of some temporal suffering, "No future bliss can make up for it", not knowing that Heaven, once attained, will work backwards and turn even that agony into a glory. And of some sinful pleasure they say "Let me but have *this* and I'll take the consequences": little dreaming how damnation will spread back and back into their past and contaminate the pleasure of the sin. Both processes begin even before death.'

(2) MacDonald says that when the sun arises in the Valley of the Shadow of Life, and the twilight turns to blackness in the grey town, the 'Blessed will say, "We have never lived anywhere except in

Heaven", and the Lost, "We have always been in Hell."'

(3) But, asks Lewis, is it not true that Heaven and Hell are only 'states of the mind'? 'Hell,' answers MacDonald, 'is a state of mind ... But Heaven is reality itself. All that is fully real is Heavenly.'

(4) Is there a choice after death? 'My Roman Catholic friends,' says Lewis, 'would be surprised, for to them souls in Purgatory are already saved. And my Protestant friends would like it no better, for they'd say that the tree lies as it falls.' 'Ye cannot fully understand the relations of choice and Time,' answers MacDonald, 'until you are beyond both. And ye were not brought here to study such curiosities. What concerns you is the nature of the choice itself.'

(5) Lewis asks, 'What do they choose, these souls who go back? ... And how *can* they choose it?' 'Milton was right,' answers MacDonald. 'The choice of every lost soul can be expressed in the words "Better to reign in Hell than serve in Heaven." There is always something they prefer to joy – that is to reality.'

(6) Is anyone lost, asks Lewis, through mere sensuality? 'Some are, no doubt,' says MacDonald. The sensualist begins with a real pleasure but as time goes on 'though the pleasure becomes less and less and the craving fiercer and fiercer, and though he knows that joy can never come that way, yet he prefers to joy the mere fondling of unappeasable lust.'

(7) If the Solid People are so full of love, Lewis says, 'Why not go down into Hell to rescue the Ghosts?' The Solid People, replies MacDonald, live only to journey further and further into the mountains. Even though they have interrupted their journey to meet the Ghosts on the plain 'it would be no use to come further even if it were possible.'

(8) 'But what of the poor Ghosts,' asks Lewis, 'who never get into the omnibus at all?' 'Everyone who wishes it does,' answers MacDonald. 'There are only two kinds of people in the end: those who say to God, "Thy will be done", and those to whom God says, in the end, "*Thy* will be done" ... Without that self-choice there could be no Hell.'

In **X** Lewis and his Teacher listen to a monologue from a female Ghost who had been married to Robert. Her nagging had driven him to a nervous breakdown and in Heaven she wants him back. 'I must have someone to – to do things to,' she tells a Spirit. 'It's simply frightful down there ... I can't alter them.'

No **XI** consists of a conversation between a Ghost and her brother, now a Spirit. The Ghost wants to see her son, Michael, who is also in Heaven, but this is impossible until she can 'learn to want someone else besides Michael'. She complains that Mother-love is the 'highest and holiest feeling in human nature', and the Spirit says: 'No natural feelings are high or low in themselves. They are all holy when God's hand is on the rein. They all go bad when they set up on their own and make themselves into false gods.'

Lewis and MacDonald listen to a conversation between a Spirit and a Ghost whose life has been ruined by lust. That lust, in the form of a Lizard, now sits on his shoulder 'whispering things in his ear'. When the Ghost permits the Spirits to kill the Lizard the Ghost is transformed into 'an immense man, naked, not much smaller than the Angel', and the Lizard is transformed into a great stallion. The man mounts the stallion and rides away. 'Lust,' observes MacDonald, 'is a poor, weak, whimpering, whispering thing compared with that richness and energy of desire which will arise when lust has been killed.'

In chapters **XII** and **XIII** Lewis and MacDonald watch a procession of Bright Spirits, followed by young boys and girls. There follows the Lady in whose honour all this was being done. Lewis asks if she is the Blessed Virgin. 'It's someone ye'll never have heard of,' answers MacDonald. 'Her name on earth was Sarah Smith and she lived at Golders Green.' The Lady is in sharp contrast to the mother Ghost in chapter **XI**. Lewis learns that, while Sarah Smith had no children, 'Every young man or boy that met her became her son … Every girl that met her was her daughter … Her motherhood was of a different kind. Those on whom it fell went back to their natural parents loving them more. Few men looked on her without becoming, in a certain fashion, her lovers. But it was the kind of love that made them not less true, but truer, to their own wives.'

The procession stops and the Lady is approached by two Ghosts, a Dwarf who is holding by a chain a tall, theatrical man much bigger than himself. The Dwarf, named Frank, was Sarah's husband on Earth. The tall Ghost – the 'Tragedian' – is that part of Frank who has struck so many poses that he has become a separate self. He is so desperate to be needed, so ready to use blackmail for the sake of what he calls love, that it is now nearly all that is left of the real Frank. '"And now!" said the Tragedian with a hackneyed gesture of despair. "Now, you need me no more?" "But of course not!" said the Lady … "What needs could I have," she said, "now that I have all? I am full now, not empty. I am in Love Himself, not lonely. Strong, not weak. You shall be the same. Come and see. We shall have no *need* for one another now: we can begin to love truly."' In the end the Dwarf loses his 'struggle against joy', and growing smaller and smaller he disappears altogether. 'I cannot love a lie. I cannot love the thing which is not', says the lady as she moves away with the procession.

Lewis asks MacDonald questions which solicit some of the most profound statements in the book.

(1) Does not 'the final loss of one soul give the lie to all the joy of those who are saved?' MacDonald replies that while this 'sounds very merciful', what lies behind it is 'The demand of the loveless and the self-imprisoned that they should be allowed to blackmail the universe: that till they consent to be happy (on their own terms) no one else shall taste joy: that theirs should be the final power; that Hell should be able to *veto* Heaven.' 'Son, son,' he says, 'it must be one way or the other. Either the day must come when joy prevails and all the makers of misery are no longer able to infect it: or else for ever and ever the makers of misery can destroy in others the happiness they reject for themselves. I know it has a grand sound to say ye'll accept no salvation which leaves even one creature in the dark outside. But watch that sophistry or ye'll make a Dog in the Manger the tyrant of the universe.'[1]

(2) Lewis asks if Pity dies. MacDonald answers that one must distinguish the '*Action* of Pity' and the '*Passion* of Pity.' He defines the Passion of Pity as 'the pity we merely suffer, the ache that draws men to concede what should not be conceded and to flatter when they should speak truth.' The Action of Pity, on the other hand, 'leaps quicker than light from the highest place to the lowest to bring healing and joy, whatever the cost to itself ... But it will not, at the cunning tears of Hell, impose on good the tyranny of evil.'

(3) Lewis is troubled that the Lady did not go down with Frank into Hell. MacDonald shows Lewis a very small crack in the soil and explains that this is the crack the bus came through. 'All Hell is smaller than one pebble of your earthly world ... Look at yon butterfly. If it swallowed all Hell, Hell would not be big enough to do it any harm or to have any taste.'

(4) Lewis asks whether Our Lord will ever go down into Hell again. MacDonald replies that 'All moments that have been or shall be were, or are, present in the moment of His descending. There is no spirit in prison to Whom He did not preach.'

(5) Lewis reminds MacDonald that on Earth he was a Universalist who talked as if all men would be saved. MacDonald replies 'Any man may choose eternal death. Those who choose it will have it. But if ye are trying to leap on into eternity, if ye are trying to see the final state of things as they *will* be ...when there are no more possibilities left but only the Real, then ye ask what cannot be answered to moral ears.'

---

[1] A 'dog in the manger' is a churlish person who will neither use a thing nor allow anyone else to do so.

In **XIV** Lewis sees a number of gigantic forms standing about a little table on which are figures like chessmen. They are the puppet representations of the great forms that stood by, and they act out on the board the inmost natures of these giant masters. 'These conversations between the Spirits and the Ghosts,' says Lewis, 'were they only the mimicry of choices that had really been made long ago?' MacDonald replies that Lewis has seen only 'the choices a bit more clearly than ye could see them on earth: the lens was clearer.'

MacDonald warns Lewis he is only dreaming and that 'if ye come to tell of what ye have seen, make it plain that it was but a dream ... Give no poor fool the pretext to think ye are claiming knowledge of what no mortal knows.' The East is behind Lewis as he stands facing MacDonald. Suddenly his Teacher's face and everything else is flush with the light of the rising Sun. He hears the chorus of bird noises, hounds and horns, and above all the voices of ten thousand men and woodland angels, all beginning to sing. 'The morning! The morning!' he cries, realizing that, as the sun rises here, the twilight will turn to blackness in the grey town. 'I am caught by the morning and I am a ghost,' he screams. 'I awoke,' he said, 'in a cold room, hunched on the floor beside a black and empty grate, the clock striking three, and the siren howling overhead.'

Reviews

Roger Lloyd in *Time and Tide*, 27, No 3 (19 January 1946), p. 60, said: 'Mr Lewis has a horrifyingly accurate knowledge of all the darker spots in our nature, and he will not let them alone. Nor will the God of the Christian religion ... How should it be otherwise with us who make our social orders, our very history, out of our scarcities, not out of our joys?' A.C. Deane in *The Spectator*, No 6135 (25 January 1946), p. 96, complained: 'Even when he insists on the truths Mr Lewis wishes to enforce – the inexorable working of the moral law – it should never be without reserve, without tenderness, without consciousness of infinite love and supernatural redemption behind that law. It is hard to find any such feeling in these glittering yet distasteful pages.'

The Times Literary Supplement (2 February 1946), p. 58, said: 'The book succeeds because its readers will forget that it is a work of art, and remember not so much what happened in it as what it made them think ... *The Great Divorce* will be read to the end, with steady interest and mounting excitement, by those who have already some sense of the nature of transcendent reality. Those who find themselves in agreement with the arguments put up by the Ghosts for not being saved will be unlikely to finish the book.' *The New Yorker* (16 March 1946) said: 'If wit and wisdom, style and scholarship are requisites to passage through the pearly gates, Mr Lewis will be among the angels.'

THEOLOGY

❀

*The Problem of Pain, Mere Christianity,
The Abolition of Man, Miracles, Reflections
on the Psalms, The Four Loves,
Letters to Malcolm*

THE PROBLEM OF PAIN (1940)

Background

I: 'The Good is dead'

When he was seventeen Lewis informed Arthur Greeves* in a letter of 12 October 1916 that he regarded Christianity as 'one mythology of many' and that he was not returning to 'the bondage of believing in any old ... superstition' (TST). But didn't it make him 'sad' not to believe in God? asked Greeves. 'No,' Lewis replied on 18 October:

> No; strange as it may appear I am quite content to live without believing in a bogey who is prepared to torture me for ever and ever if I should fail in coming up to an almost impossible ideal (TST).

Two years later when he was in the trenches of France, Lewis wrote many of the poems which went into *Spirits in Bondage* (1919). In some he railed at God for not being *good*. No, he complained in *'De Profundis'*, 'The good is dead' and the 'ancient hope' of there being 'a just God that cares for earthly pain' is merely a 'dream'. Thus began his full-scale rebellion against God.

However, with his conversion in 1931, *God* and the *Good* were again seen as one and the same, and from this time on Lewis's apologetical works were written in defence of doctrines that he had rejected in his youth. From the first, he would have nothing to do with what he called 'Christianity-and-water', always defending a full-blooded orthodoxy. 'I am,' he said in 'On Ethics', a 'dogmatic Christian untinged with Modernist reservations and committed to supernaturalism in its full rigour.'

II: The Christian Challenge Series

Ashley Sampson was the owner of a small publishing firm in London called the Centenary Press. In about 1930 he was bought out by another publisher, Geoffrey Bles.* The two firms were combined and, though Sampson was working for Bles, some of their titles continued to carry the imprint of 'The Centenary Press'.

Sampson had been greatly impressed by the only two works of Lewis's generally known to Christians, *The Pilgrim's Regress* (1933) and *Out of the Silent Planet* (1938), and he felt he was exactly the man to write a book on pain for his 'Christian Challenge' series. He had begun this series with the purpose of introducing the Christian faith to people outside the Church, and by the beginning of the War the series contained over twenty titles on different aspects of the Faith, including *The Doctrine of the Incarnation* by J.K. Mozley, *The Origins of Religion* by E.O. James, and *The Christian Hope of Immortality* by A.E. Taylor.

At first Lewis refused to have the book published under his own name. He was not a clergyman, and he felt presumptuous in talking about a subject he was certainly not brave about. He said in the Preface:

> When Mr Ashley Sampson suggested to me the writing of this book, I asked leave to be allowed to write it anonymously, since, if I were to say what I really thought about pain, I should be forced to make statements of such apparent fortitude that they would become ridiculous if anyone knew who made them. Anonymity was rejected as inconsistent with the series; but Mr Sampson pointed out that I could write a preface explaining that I did not live up to my own principles! ... There is one criticism which cannot be brought against me. No one can say, 'He jests at scars who never felt a wound', for I have never for one moment been in a state of mind to which even the imagination of serious pain was less than intolerable ... If any parts of the book are 'original', in the sense of being novel or unorthodox, they are so against my will and as a result of my ignorance.

For whatever reason, an advertisement by the Centenary Press of the Christian Challenge Series in *The Church Times* of 15 November 1949 gave Lewis's name as 'C.S. Lewis, M.D.'

III: Read to The Inklings

The book, the first 'straight' work of Christian apologetics that Lewis wrote, was begun in the summer of 1939. As it was being written, he read it in instalments to the Inklings,‡ to whom it was dedicated. Warren 'Warnie' Lewis* was in France when his brother wrote to him on 11 November 1939 saying that at a recent meeting of the Inklings 'The bill of fare ... consisted of a section of the new Hobbit book from Tolkien,* a nativity play from [Charles] Williams* ... and a chapter out of the book on *The Problem of Pain* from me' (L).

He read some more of it to Tolkien on 30 November when they met in the latter's house. Writing about this meeting to Warnie on 3 December, he said:

> If you are writing a book about pain and then get some actual pain as I did from my rib, it does *not* either, as the cynic would expect, blow the doctrine to bits, nor, as a Christian would hope, turn into practice, but remains quite unconnected and irrelevant, just as any other bit of actual life does when you are reading or writing (L).

The book was finished by the spring of 1940, by which time Lewis realized, as he put it in chapter VI, that 'All arguments in justification of suffering provoke bitter resentment against the author.' There had been no resentment from Charles Williams, but in the Preface to **EPCW** Lewis remembered his observation that God's displeasure had not been directed at the weak and impatient Job, but at

> the 'comforters', the self-appointed advocates on God's side, the people who tried to show that all was well – 'the sort of people,' he said, immeasurably dropping his lower jaw and fixing me with his eyes – 'the sort of people who wrote books on the Problem of Pain.'

IV: The Preface to the French Edition

C.S. Lewis wrote several books with his fellow Anglicans in mind, but rarely did he include in any of his works beliefs that were not common to nearly all Christians. From the time of his conversion, he seems to have made up his mind to speak only of those things which unified Christians. We see him arguing for this 'mere Christianity' position as early as August 1933 when, writing to his pupil Dom Bede Griffiths,* who had become a Catholic, he said: 'When all is said ... about the divisions of Christendom, there remains, by God's mercy, an enormous common ground.'

In the Preface to *The Problem of Pain* he made his position on this 'common ground' very clear. 'I have tried to assume nothing,' he said, 'that is not professed by all baptized and communicating Christians.' After the book had been translated into French by Marguerite Faguer, the publishers, Desclée de Brouwer of Paris, asked Lewis to say something about himself to their predominantly Catholic readers. The following translation of Lewis's Preface to *La Problème de la Souffrance* (1950)[1] sheds a great deal of light on what he regarded as the 'common ground' of 'Mere Christianity'.§ English readers are unlikely to come across the Preface, and a translation by Eliane Tixier and Victoria Hobson is given below:

> I was asked to write a few words of introduction to this book for French readers, who might at first find something ambiguous in my position. Who, one might ask, is this Anglican layman, translated and introduced by Catholics, who, on the frontispiece of *The Screwtape Letters*, brings together a quotation from Sir Thomas More and one from Martin Luther? Is he unaware of the differences between Christians, or does he consider them unimportant? By no means. As a Christian, I am very much aware that our divisions grieve the Holy Spirit and hold back the work of Christ; as a logician I realize that when two churches affirm opposing positions, these cannot be reconciled.
>
> But because I was an unbeliever for a long time, I perceived something which perhaps those brought up in the Church do not see. Even when I feared and detested Christianity, I was struck by its essential unity, which, in spite of its divisions, it has never lost. I trembled on recognizing the same unmistakable aroma coming

[1] The French edition also contains a footnote (chapter ix, p. 163) written specially for it by Lewis. It occurs in chapter IX, 'Animal Pain', para. 6. In a discussion about the Incarnation, Lewis had written: 'I certainly think that Christ, in the flesh, was not omniscient – if only because a human brain could not, presumably, be the vehicle of omniscient consciousness, and to say that Our Lord's thinking was not really conditioned by the size and shape of His brain might be to deny the real incarnation and become a Docetist.' After the word 'Docetist' there follows a footnote saying: 'I now consider the conception of the Incarnation implied in this paragraph as gross and the result of ignorance.'

from the writings of Dante and Bunyan, Thomas Aquinas and William Law.

Since my conversion, it has seemed my particular task to tell the outside world what all Christians believe. Controversy I leave to others: that is the business of theologians. I think that you and I, the laity, simple soldiers of the Faith, will best serve the cause of reconciliation not so much by contributing to such debates, but by our prayers, and by sharing all that can already be shared of Christian life.

If the unity of charity and intention between us were strong enough, perhaps our doctrinal differences would be resolved sooner; without that spiritual unity, a doctrinal agreement between our religious leaders would be sterile.

In the meantime, it will be apparent that the man who is most faithful in living the Christian life in his own church is spiritually the closest to the faithful believers in other confessions: because the geography of the spiritual world is very different from that of the physical world. In the latter, countries touch each other at their borders, in the former, at their centre. It is the lukewarm and indifferent in each country who are furthest from all other countries.

Summary

Chapter I, 'Introductory', opens with the arresting words 'Not many years ago when I was an atheist … ' One of the reasons for his atheism was that since the greater part of the universe consisted of empty space it seemed 'improbable that any planet except the Earth sustains life.' He concluded that 'Either there is no spirit behind the universe, or else a spirit indifferent to good and evil, or else an evil spirit.' On the other hand, 'If the universe is so bad, or even half so bad, how on earth did human beings ever come to attribute it to the activity of a wise and good Creator?' Lewis goes on to describe the origin of religion, beginning with the 'experience of the Numinous'. This is a special kind of fear which excites awe, is as old as humanity itself, and is 'a direct experience of the really supernatural, to which the name Revelation might properly be given.'

In chapter II, 'Divine Omnipotence', he argues that 'Omnipotence means power to do all that is intrinsically possible, not to do the intrinsically impossible. You may attribute miracles to Him, but not nonsense.' 'Not even Omnipotence,' he says, 'could create a society of free souls without at the same time creating a relatively independent and "inexorable" Nature.' But if matter has a 'fixed nature and obeys constant laws' not all states of matter will be equally beneficial to everyone. Thus if God intervened every time men were abusing their free will 'so that a wooden beam became soft as grass when it was used as a weapon' freedom of the will would be void. While Christians believe that God works miracles, 'the very conception of a common, and therefore, stable, world, demands that these occasions should be extremely rare.'

Chapter III on 'Divine Goodness' opens with the dilemma that if God is wiser than we are His judgements must differ from ours on many things. Thus, 'What seems to us good may therefore not be good in His eyes, and what seems to us evil may not be evil.' While arguing that Divine goodness 'differs from ours not as white from black but as a perfect circle from a child's first attempt to draw a wheel', he makes a distinction that was to appear in a number of his works. By 'goodness' God means Love and we mean Kindness. 'What would really satisfy us would be a God who said of anything we happened to like doing, "What does it matter so long as they are contented?" We want ... not so much a Father in Heaven as a grandfather in heaven – a senile benevolence who, as they say, "liked to see young people enjoying themselves".' 'When Christianity says that God loves man,' he insists, 'it means that God *loves* man: not that He has some "disinterested", because really indifferent, concern for our welfare, but that, in awful and surprising truth, we are the objects of His love ... God intends to give us what we need, not what we think we want.'

Chapter IV on 'Human Wickedness' contains the first expression of an argument which was to become familiar in Lewis's apologetics. To the question, 'Why is it so hard to convince modern man that he needs to change?' he replies: 'When the apostles preached, they could assume even in their Pagan hearers a real consciousness of deserving the Divine anger ... It was against this background that the Gospel appeared as good news. It brought news of possible healing to men who knew they were mortally ill. But all this has changed. Christianity now has to preach the diagnosis – in itself very bad news – before it can win a hearing for the cure.'

We have so concentrated on one of the virtues – "kindness" or mercy – that most of us do not feel anything except kindness to be really good or anything but cruelty to be really bad. Another cause is the effect of psychoanalysis with its doctrine of repressions and inhibitions. There follow eight 'considerations' to help us perceive our badness. (1) 'We are deceived by looking on the outside of things.' (2) As wholesome as the *social* conscience is 'Beware lest you are making use of the idea of corporate guilt to distract your attention from those hum-drum, old fashioned guilts of your own.' (3) 'We have a strange illusion that mere time cancels sin.' (4) 'We must guard against the feeling that there is "safety in numbers".' (5) 'From considering how the cruelty of our ancestors looks to us, you may get some inkling how our softness, worldliness, and timidity would have looked to them, and how both must look to God.' (6) We have become increasingly cruel 'in the attempt to reduce all virtues to kindness.' (7) 'The moral law may exist to be transcended: but there is no transcending it for those who have not first admitted its claims upon them.' (8) 'Many schools of thought encourage us to shift the responsibility for our behaviour from our own shoulders to some inherent necessity in the nature of human life, and thus, indirectly, to the Creator.'

In chapter V on 'The Fall of Man' we are warned about the sub-Christian theories of evil, Monism and Dualism. Lewis restates the classical doctrine of Original Sin from St Augustine, which is that we sin 'in Adam'. He argues that while it may have been possible for God to have removed the results of Adam's sin 'this would not have been much good unless He was prepared to remove the results of the second sin, and of the third, and so on forever.' After defining the 'great sin' of Pride, he provides a 'myth' in the Socratic sense, of what he thinks could have happened when Man fell. 'Human spirit,' he concludes, 'from being the master of human nature became a mere lodger in its own house.' He warns against speculating about 'what might have happened' if man had remained innocent. Whenever we talk of what might have happened we do not really know what we are talking about.

Chapter VI entitled 'Human Pain' begins with the premise that 'The proper good of a creature is to surrender itself to its Creator ... When it does so, it is good and happy ... In the world as we now know it, the problem is how to recover this self-surrender.' Lewis believed that to render back to God what we have so long claimed as our own 'is in itself ... a grievous pain', and he defines three good results of physical pain. (1) 'God whispers to us in our pleasures, speaks in our conscience, but shouts in our pains: it is His megaphone to rouse a deaf world.' (2) Pain 'shatters the illusion that what we have, whether good or bad in itself, is our own and enough for us.' God allows misfortune to fall upon decent, inoffensive people by way of warning them 'of an insufficiency that one day they will have to discover.' (3) Pain is inherent in the act of choosing. After comparing Kant and Aristotle on the motivation of moral acts, Lewis agrees with Kant in thinking 'self-surrender' unpleasant, but agrees with Aristotle in believing that 'the more virtuous a man becomes the more he enjoys virtuous actions.' He goes on to discuss 'whether God commands certain things because they are right, or whether certain things are right because God commands them', and concludes that we should embrace the first alternative (see **Natural Law**§ IV: 'The Euthyphro Dilemma').

After admitting that he 'would crawl through sewers' to find an escape from pain, Lewis gives two reasons why the Christian doctrine of being made 'perfect through suffering' is not incredible. (1) Even if pain had no spiritual value it 'would have to exist in order that there should be something to be feared and pitied.' (2) We must be careful to distinguish the pain we know from that we imagine.

Chapter VII called 'Human Pain, cont.' consists of six propositions necessary to complete the account of human suffering. (1) While suffering is not good in itself, any painful experience can be good if the sufferer submits to the will of God. (2) If tribulation is necessary to our redemption we must expect that it will not end until God sees the world to be either redeemed or no further redeemable. (3) The doctrine of self-surrender and obedience is a purely theological, not a political, doctrine. (4) God withholds the settled happiness and security we desire: but joy, pleasure and merriment 'He has scattered broadcast.' (5) We should not make the problem of pain worse than it is by vague talk about the 'unimaginable sum of human misery'. No one can experience 'the total amount of pain'. (6) Unlike other evils, pain has no tendency, in its own right, to proliferate. When it is over, it is over, and the natural sequel is joy.

In chapter VIII on 'Hell' we are reminded that the doctrine of Hell has the support of Scripture, of Our Lord's own words, it has always been held by Christendom, and it has the support of Reason. While admitting that Hell cannot be made a 'tolerable' doctrine, Lewis attempts to show why it is moral by a criticism of the objections ordinarily made against it. (1) Many object to retributive punishment as such, but 'the demand that God should forgive such a man while he remains what he is, is based on a confusion between condoning and forgiving. To condone an evil is simply to ignore it, to treat it as if it were good.' (2) To the objection that a man is not given a 'second chance', he argues that if a million chances were likely to do good they would be given, but only omniscience can know when to stop. (3) To the objection about the intensity of the pains of hell, he argues that it could be, not the pains of Hell, but its pleasures that would 'send any soul, not already damned, flying to its prayers in nightmare terror.' (4) An objection, later to show up in *The Great Divorce*, is that no charitable man could himself be blessed in heaven while he knew that even one human soul was still in Hell. 'I willingly believe that the damned are, in one sense, successful, rebels to the end; that the doors of Hell are locked on the *inside*.'

Chapter IX on 'Animal Pain' attempts to answer three questions. (1) 'What do animals suffer?' Quite simply, we don't know. Some animals have nervous systems like our own, but some may be sentient without consciousness. We may be 'reading into the beasts a self for which there is no real evidence.' (2) 'How did disease and pain enter the animal world?' It is a 'reasonable supposition' that Satan may have corrupted the animal world before man appeared, thus causing animals to slip back into the behaviour proper to vegetables. (3) 'How can animals' suffering be reconciled with the justice of God?' Man was appointed by God to have dominion over the beasts, and it seems possible that certain animals may have an immortality, 'not in themselves, but in the immortality of their masters.'

Chapter X on 'Heaven' is a corrective for those who imagine Lewis to have been obsessed with sin. Perhaps his most outstanding gift was that of making Heaven desirable, as he had done once before in his sermon 'The Weight of Glory'. He begins with St Paul's words: 'I reckon that the sufferings of this present time are not worthy to be compared with the glory that shall be revealed in us.' If this is true, he says, 'a book on suffering which says nothing of heaven, is leaving out almost the whole of one side of the account' and no solution of the problem of pain which does this 'can be called a Christian one.' To the question as to whether it is 'mercenary' to desire heaven, he answers that 'It is safe to tell the pure in heart that they shall see God, for only the pure in heart want to.' A desire of heaven is so ingrained in us he wonders if 'in our heart of hearts, we have ever desired anything else.' We must not make the mistake of imagining that we have actually *had* what we are born desiring. 'All the things that have ever deeply possessed your soul have been but hints of it – tantalising glimpses ... It is the secret signature of each soul, the incommunicable and unappeasable want, the thing we desired before we met our wives or made our friends or chose our work, and which we shall still desire on our deathbeds ... If we lose this, we lose all.'

Every soul, he insists, is unique. 'It is not humanity in the abstract that is to be saved,' he says, 'but you – you, the individual reader, John Stubbs or Janet Smith ... Your place in heaven will seem to be made for you and you alone, because you were made for it – made for it stitch by stitch as a glove is made for a hand.' The closer we draw to the centre the more the sufferings of the present time disappear until they finally drop out of sight. We must remember that heaven 'does not exist for us, but we for it.'

Reviews

W.G. de Burgh said in *The Guardian*‡ (22 November 1940), p. 560: 'This is a strong book: strong in its background of sound scholarship never obtruded on the reader, but evident to the discerning eye, strong in its frank admission of mysteries and unpalatable facts, strong above all in its uncompromising affirmation of the Christian revelation.' *The Church Times*, CXXIII (29 November 1940), p. 752 commented: 'Here is a book that no thoughtful person can afford to miss, a really constructive message for the times ... Unlike some other defenders of the Faith, he carries the reader along by the clarity and sparkle of his style. He need not apologize for being a layman, for his knowledge of St Augustine and Hooker is considerably deeper than that of most ecclesiastics, and the independence of the layman is an asset to the defender of the Faith. That he comes to the Catholic position from atheism ensures that he can sympathize with the difficulties of the average man who is troubled by doubts.'

Benet O'Driscoll O.P., in *Blackfriars*, XXI (December 1940), pp. 718–20, said: 'His thesis that the possibility of pain and death resulted from the first sin is in line with Catholic doctrine, and the tentative account he gives of the Fall has much in common with the accepted Catholic teaching. But for many people the very terms of the problem have become words almost empty of meaning, and perhaps the most valuable chapters are those in which an attempt is made to lead the reader to appreciate the meaning of the Divine Goodness, and to a sense of personal sin.'

Edwyn Bevan in *The Spectator* (25 October 1940), p. 422, said: 'It says so many things which seem to me to need saying today, and traverses so many glibly repeated modern opinions that it will help many people, I think, to revise what they have taken for granted and face possibilities which had not occurred to them.' Charles Williams* said in *Theology*, XLII (January 1941), pp. 62–3: 'Mr Lewis's ... style is what style always is – goodness working on goodness, a lucid and sincere intellect at work on the facts of life or the great statements of other minds ... The chapter on Animal Pain is perhaps especially valuable, as that of Hell is especially terrifying, and that on Divine Omnipotence especially lucid. It is good to be reminded that "nonsense remains nonsense even when one talks it about God." Meaning by nonsense, nonsense.'

MERE CHRISTIANITY A REVISED AND AMPLIFIED EDITION, WITH A NEW INTRODUCTION, OF THE THREE BOOKS 'BROADCAST TALKS', 'CHRISTIAN BEHAVIOUR' AND 'BEYOND PERSONALITY' (1952)

Background

I: The First Series of Radio Talks – 'Right and Wrong'

Mere Christianity is a combination of three books which were originally four series of radio broadcasts. The books may be read separately. However, because Lewis revised them, and added new chapters, we will look at *Mere Christianity* in its final form.

It began on 7 February 1941 when J.W. Welch, Director of the BBC's Religious Broadcasting Department, wrote to thank Lewis for the help he had been given by *The Problem of Pain*, and asking him to help them 'in our work of religious broadcasting'. He made two suggestions:

(1) You might be willing to speak about the Christian, or lack of Christian, assumptions underlying modern literature, treating modern writers as those who feel they have something they must say and which expresses, sometimes in advance, the mood and values of our people, passing from description and analysis to something more positive and helpful.

(2) A series of talks on something like 'The Christian Faith as I See It – by a Layman'; I am sure there is need of a positive restatement of Christian doctrines in lay language.

Lewis was not an avid reader of modern literature, and, in any event, their assumptions worried him less than a general ignorance of the Christian Faith. Writing to Dr Welch on 10 February 1941, he said:

> Modern literature would not suit me. I think what I mainly want to talk about is the Law of Nature, or objective right and wrong. It seems to me that the N.T., by preaching repentance and forgiveness, always *assumes* an audience who already believe in the law of Nature and know they have disobeyed it. In modern England we cannot at present assume this, and therefore most apologetic begins a stage too far on. The first step is to create, or recover, the sense of guilt.

Lewis next heard from Eric Fenn who had joined the BBC in 1939 as assistant head of religious broadcasting.[2] Fenn, a Presbyterian, wrote to Lewis on 14 February 1941 saying:

> I wonder whether you would care to consider a series of four Wednesday evening talks (7.40–8.00 P.M.) in August, or, alternatively, September?
> If so we should be grateful for draft scripts a month in advance of the broadcasts so as to have time to discuss these with you and to arrange a microphone rehearsal and things of that kind. The process of getting a series of talks 'on the air' is rather more laborious than it appears from the other side of the microphone.

Lewis gave Fenn luncheon in Magdalen College shortly afterwards and they arranged for a microphone rehearsal. It was the first time Lewis had heard a recording of his voice, and when he wrote to Arthur Greeves* on 25 May 1941 he said: 'I was unprepared for the total unfamiliarity of the voice; not a trace, not a hint, of anything one could identify with oneself –

---

[2] Eric Fenn was born on 3 June 1899, and in 1917, refusing military service, he went to Wormwood Scrubbs because of his pacifist convictions. After the war he took a degree at the Imperial College, and then trained for the ministry at Westminster College, Cambridge. In 1926 he began working with the Student Christian Movement, and he helped set up the Oxford Conference in 1937 on Church, Community and State. He was with the BBC 1939–1945, after which he broadcast regularly on the programme 'Think on These Things'. From 1957 until his retirement in 1968 he was Professor of Christian Doctrine at the Selly Oak College, Birmingham. He died on 21 June 1995.

one couldn't possibly guess who it was' (**TST**). Lewis had sent the first series of four talks to Eric Fenn on 17 May. 'Will this do?' he asked. 'I find the more colloquial you are in the actual talks the harder it is to make a close précis.' But Lewis soon learned the knack.

Severe restrictions were imposed on all broadcasters during the War by the official Censor, after which they had to be rigidly adhered to. No silence was permitted lest the British traitor 'Lord Hawhaw' fill the gap with propaganda radioed from Germany. Lewis would send his radio scripts to the BBC who, after the necessary censorship examination, typed several copies, one of which was sent to Lewis to practise with. At that time nearly all programmes were given 'live', and Lewis's talks, entitled **Right or Wrong: A Clue to the Meaning of the Universe**, were given over the air every Wednesday evening in August 1941 from 7.45 to 8.00 p.m. The subject of these talks was what is generally known as Natural Law§ but which Lewis called in the first talk 'The Law of Human Nature'.

The discipline forced upon Lewis by the BBC almost certainly contributed to his remarkable talent for distilling things of great moment into few words. The talks were given 'live', not recorded, but the BBC has preserved on microfilm the typed scripts. Comparing these with what was finally published, we can see how much trouble he was willing to take over his remarkably vivid analogies and metaphors. For instance, in the fourth talk he had originally written 'If there was a controlling power outside the universe, it could not show itself to us as one of the facts inside the universe – no more than the author of a play could walk in as one of the characters *in* the play.' The analogy was altered on the script to ' ... no more than the operator in a cinema could himself appear on the screen.' This was finally replaced by the one in the book: ' ... no more than the architect of a house could actually be a wall or staircase or fireplace in that house.'

The talks were enormously popular, and Lewis was overwhelmed with letters both from an adoring and an irate public. The BBC persuaded him to return to the microphone on 6 September 1941 to give a talk on 'Answers to Listeners' Questions', which was later redrafted and included in the published work as 'Some Objections'. Thus began that vast correspondence that was to be Lewis's lot for the rest of his life. 'As the aftermath of those Broadcast Talks I gave early last summer,' he wrote to Arthur Greeves on 23 December 1941,

I had an enormous pile of letters from strangers to answer. One gets funny letters after broadcasting – some from lunatics who sign themselves 'Jehovah' or begin 'Dear Mr Lewis, I was married at the age of 20 to a man I didn't love' – but many from serious enquirers whom it was a duty to answer fully (**TST**).

II: The Second Series – 'What Christians Believe'

Before the first series of the talks was over the BBC had asked for a second series of five talks, fifteen minutes each. Lewis agreed, and his talks on **What Christians Believe** were scheduled to be broadcast from 4.45 to 5.00 p.m. on 11 and 18 January and 1, 8 and 15 February 1942. The scripts were finished in November 1941, and after reading them Fenn wrote to Lewis on 5 December:

> I have at last had time to read your scripts. I think they are quite first class – indeed I don't know when I have read anything in the same class at all. There is a clarity and inexorableness about them, which made me positively gasp!

This set of talks were also given 'live'. Lewis could not assume that those listening to this series had heard his first one, and he began his broadcast on 11 January 1942 with this introduction, later removed from the published talk:

> It's not because I'm anybody in particular that I've been asked to tell you what Christians believe. In fact it's just the opposite. They've asked me, first of all because I'm a layman and not a parson, and consequently it was thought I might understand the ordinary person's point of view a bit better. Secondly, I think they asked me because it was known that I'd been an atheist for many years and only became a Christian quite fairly recently. They thought that would mean I'd be able to see the difficulties – able to remember what Christianity looks like from the outside. So you see, the long and the short of it is that I've been selected for this job just because I'm an amateur not a professional, and a beginner, not an old hand. Of course this means that you may well ask what right I have to talk on the subject at all.
>
> Well, when I'd finished my scripts I sent them round to various people who *were* professionals: to one Church of England theologian, one Roman Catholic, one Presbyterian, and one Methodist. The Church of England man and the Presbyterian

agreed with the whole thing. The Roman Catholic and the Methodist agreed in the main, but would have liked one or two places altered. So there you've got all the cards on the table.

What I'm going to say isn't *exactly* what all these people would say; but the greater part of it is what all Christians agree on. And the main reason why I couldn't alter it so as to make them agree completely was that I've only got 15 minutes for each talk. That doesn't give you time to make many subtle distinctions. You've got to go at it rather like a bull in a china shop or you won't get through.

One thing I can promise you. In spite of all the unfortunate differences between Christians, what they agree on is still something pretty big and pretty solid: big enough to blow any of us sky-high if it happens to be true. And if it's true, it's quite ridiculous to put off doing anything about it simply because Christians don't fully agree among themselves. That's as if a man bleeding to death refused medical assistance because he'd heard that some doctors differed about the treatment of cancer. For if Christianity is true at all, it's as serious as that. Well, here goes ...

It is not known who the Anglican clergyman who read the scripts was but it might possibly have been Lewis's friend, Austin Farrer,* who at the time was Chaplain of Trinity College, Oxford. Dom Bede Griffiths* was the Roman Catholic; the Rev. Joseph Dowell, a Padre with the RAF, was the Methodist; Eric Fenn was the Presbyterian.

Dom Bede's letters to Lewis have not survived, but we get some idea of the complexity of the problems involved if we look at Lewis's letter to Dom Bede of 21 December 1941. It is about the meaning of the Atonement which Lewis discussed in the talk on 'The Perfect Penitent':

About the scripts ... I think I gave the impression of going further than I intended, in saying that all theories of the Atonement were 'to be rejected if we don't find them helpful.' What I meant was 'need not be used' – a very different thing. Is there, on your view, a real difference here: that the Divinity of Our Lord *has to be* believed whether you find it a help or a 'scandal' (otherwise you're not a Christian at all) but the Anselmic theory of Atonement is *not* in that position. Would you admit that a man was a Christian (and could be a member of your church) who said, 'I believe that Christ's death redeemed man from sin, but I can make nothing of any of the theories as to *how*'? ... It therefore doesn't much matter what you think of my *own* theory because that is advanced only as my own. But I'd like to be able to meet you on the other point – how far *any* theory is *de fide*. The Council of Trent 'made satisfaction' seems to be the real hitch. What was the contest? What error was it directed against? Still, don't bother, for I fear I shall have to give up my original hope. I think I could get something you and your friends would pass, but not without making the talk either longer or shorter: but I'm on the Procrustes' bed of neither more nor less than 15 minutes (**L**).

One of the most substantial alterations Lewis made in this series of talks concerned the famous passage in 'The Shocking Alternative' about whether Jesus was 'either God or a good man'. The original explanation over the air was much longer than that pared down for the book, and to give the reader some idea of how much more trenchant Lewis made it (see the Summary below), the words he later removed are given below in italics:

I'm trying here to prevent you from saying the really silly thing that people often say about him: 'I'm ready to accept Jesus as a great moral teacher, but I don't accept his claim to be God.' That's the one thing you mustn't say. A man who was merely a man and said the sort of things Jesus said wouldn't be a great moral teacher. He'd either be a lunatic – on a level with the man who says he's a poached egg – or the Devil of Hell. *Of course you can take the line of saying He didn't say these things, but His followers invented them. But that's only shifting the difficulty. They were Jews too: the last people who would invent such a thing, the people who had never said anything of the sort about Moses or Elijah. That theory only saddles you with twelve inexplicable lunatics instead of one. We can't get out of it that way.* You must make your choice. Either this man was, and is, the Son of God: or else a madman: or something worse. You can shut Him up for a fool: you can spit at him and kill him as a demon: or you can fall at His feet and call Him Lord and God. But don't come to Him with any patronizing nonsense about His being a great human teacher. He hasn't left that open to you. He didn't intend to.

As before, Lewis was overwhelmed with letters before the series ended on 15 February 1942. He knew the BBC had their own periodical, *The Listener,* and when he wrote to Eric Fenn on 23 February he said:

I'm still wading through the correspondence caused by the talks: if you *could* have seen your way to putting them in *The Listener* it would have made all the difference to me. I wrote 35 letters yesterday: all out of working hours ...

Yes, I'll try to do a series in the Autumn if you like and look forward to seeing you here to discuss it when convenient.

Geoffrey Bles* had just brought out *The Screwtape Letters* and it was sell-ing so well – it was reprinted eight times in 1942 – that they were delighted to publish the two series, 'Right and Wrong' and 'What Christians Believe' as *Broadcast Talks*. The talks in this book are almost exactly as they were given over the air. Lewis adapted the introductory remarks of that broadcast of 11 January 1942 – given above – for a brief Preface which he dated 6 April 1942, and *Broadcast Talks* was published in July 1942.

III: The Third Series – 'Christian Behaviour'

Lewis had thought Fenn asked him to write eight fifteen-minute talks for a series to be broadcast on Sunday afternoons from 20 September to 8 November 1942, at 2.50–3.00 p.m. He wrote to Fenn on 28 June 1942 with a proposal of what the talks might include, and the finished scripts were sent on 29 July. Lewis was in Cornwall addressing the RAF when Fenn wrote to him there on 15 September to say that Lewis had obviously misunderstood him. This time the talks were to be, not fifteen minutes each, but ten!

Lewis carried out a blitz on the typed scripts, deleting whatever he could to bring the talks down by five minutes. Fenn had been worried about several points in the talk on 'Sexual Morality' and Lewis had to write this script out again. The original of that script in Lewis's hand is preserved in the BBC's Written Archives Centre, and there is a photograph of it in the Anniversary Edition of *Mere Christianity* (New York: Macmillan, 1981).

Lewis afterwards restored the talks to what they had been before he had to do any cutting. He added four new chapters, on 'The Cardinal Virtues', 'Christian Marriage', 'Charity' and 'Hope' and they were published as *Christian Behaviour* by Geoffrey Bles in April 1943.

IV: The Fourth Series – 'Beyond Personality'

The first we hear of this series came in a letter Eric Fenn wrote to Lewis on
11 June 1943:

> Have you thought any further about the series of more theological
> talks you were inclined to when I last saw you? We have been
> considering lately a suggestion made at an informal conference on
> religious broadcasting, which we held recently – namely, the need
> for a series of talks which would take some of the more abstruse
> theological doctrines and show what sort of difference they make,
> both to thought and to conduct.

When Lewis replied on 16 June he already had a good idea of what it
would take to complete his apology for Christianity:

> Yes, I should like to give the sort of series you suggest. Something
> of this sort.
>   1. The doctrine of the Trinity
>   2. The doctrine of the Trinity
>   3. Creation
>   4. The Incarnation
>   5. The Two Natures
>   6. The Resurrection
>   7. The Ascension.
> Not by these titles. (Perhaps 1. and 2. Has God a Picture? 3. Creation.
> 4. and 5. The Human element in God. 6. The defeat of death. 7. The
> promotion of Man.) Would this at all suit?

The talks were scheduled for Tuesday evenings from 22 February to 4
April 1944. Lewis had the scripts finished by 10 December, but he could
not find anyone to type them, and had to wait until 22 December for a
friend to take them to London for him.

Fenn wrote to him on 22 December saying 'I like them immensely, and
think that, as usual, you have achieved a quite astonishing degree of
clarity in a very difficult subject.' However, he went on to say that this
time Lewis had made the mistake of working 'to a 10-minute script, and
not a 15-minute' one.

'I could kick myself for not having used my 15 minutes to the full,'
replied Lewis on 27 December 1943:

I *could* add to them, but it would probably break the unity of each ... Of course your threatened 'scrutiny' of some of my analogies (the very word has a sinister sound suggesting Scrooge, Screws, Screwtape, scraping and Inland Revenue) may lead to at least 600 additional words in some cases. But, as you know, I'm very biddable when it comes to the point ... You'd better come to dine and spend the night for your Screw-tiny, hadn't you?

Fenn's 'Screw-tiny' took the form of a long letter of 29 December 1943 in which he criticized a number of points in these scripts. During all the time they worked together Fenn seems to have been worried that Lewis was making Christianity a solitary thing. Now he was worried about the original version of the talk called 'Let's Pretend', and he asked:

If this might not be the place to say a bit more about the Christian community? With the exception of one or two references, you don't seem to mention that at all, and the scripts give, therefore, an impression of a purely individualistic approach ... You are thinking all the time about one man in relation to God, and not at all about the connection this always establishes with other men. I do think it would strengthen the series to say something more about the Church.

Fenn was not the only one who criticized Lewis's reluctance to say anything about the Church. His near avoidance of this issue came in for particular criticism from Catholics. We get some idea of why Lewis was so reluctant from his reply to Fenn of New Year's Eve 1943: 'The Church – 'he said, 'it's difficult to go on long about that without raising the denominational question. But I'll peg away.' We don't have Lewis's original draft of 'Let's Pretend', but it's a safe bet that the part Fenn persuaded him to add to this broadcast was the passage:

Men are mirrors, or 'carriers' of Christ to other men. Sometimes unconscious carriers. This 'good infection' can be carried by those who haven't got it themselves. People who weren't Christians themselves helped me to Christianity. But usually it's those who know Him that bring Him to others. That's why the Church, the whole body of Christians showing Him to one another, is so important. You might say that when two Christians are following Christ together there's not twice as much Christianity as when they're apart, but sixteen times as much.

Apart from the talk on 'Sexual Morality' in Lewis's hand, which is in the BBC Written Archives Centre, the only other portion of Lewis's original scripts that have survived is in the Bodleian Library.‡ It consists of four sheets which contain most of Lewis's talk on 'The Obstinate Toy Soldiers' and the first page of 'Let's Pretend'. On the back of these pages Lewis had written a talk on **Christian Reunion** which was not published until after his death.

Lewis finished his abridgements and posted them to Fenn on 5 January 1944. The next news from Fenn was disconcerting. The BBC was having to re-schedule the talks for 10.20 at night. He said he

> explained to the powers that be that this was extremely awkward for you, and attempted to get permission to broadcast from Oxford, but on security grounds, outside broadcasts of that kind have been cut down drastically ... We don't like recording talks, and it always drops the temperature in the audience when they hear that it is a recording, but this may be the only thing left to be done.

'Pox on your "powers"!' Lewis replied on 10 February:

> Who the devil is going to listen to anything at 10.20? If it is possible (but I suppose you'd have anticipated my suggestion if it were) cancel the whole thing for this spring and put it on later in the year. If not – I can't spend any Tuesday nights in town, as a talk at 10.20 means catching the midnight train and getting to bed about 3 o'clock. Well, I'll give *three* under those conditions. The rest you'll have to record. I don't mind which.
>
> If you know the address of any reliable firm of assassins, nose-slitters, garotters and poisoners I should be grateful to have it.
>
> I shall write a book about the BBC – you see if I don't! Gr-r-r-r!!

As it turned out, Lewis recorded talks 2 ('The Three-Personal God'), 6 ('Nice People or New Men') and 7 ('The New Men') on to gramophone discs. Unfortunately, the only one of these recordings to survive is the last one – 'The New Men'. It was recorded on 21 March 1944 and is 14.12 minutes long. In 1982 the Episcopal-Radio TV Foundation of Atlanta, Georgia, included 'The New Men' in a nine-cassette album of Michael York reading *Mere Christianity*. For more details see **Recordings of C.S. Lewis.**‡

This was the only series to appear in *The Listener*. It came out in weekly instalments between 24 February and 6 April 1944, details of which are found in the BIBLIOGRAPHY. By the time *Beyond Personality* was published in October 1944 Lewis had added a number of minor additions and four new chapters.

Before this last series of broadcasts was over Eric Fenn wrote to Lewis on 23 March about a report from the BBC's 'Listener Research'. It was about the effect produced on people by the second talk in Lewis's last series:

> The single most important fact is the sharp division you produced in your audience. They obviously either regard you as 'the cat's whiskers' or as beneath contempt, which is interesting, and ought, I feel, to teach us something, but I can't think what!

But Lewis knew, and in his reply of 25 March he said:

> Thanks for the suitable lenten reading which I return ... The two views you report (Cat's Whiskers and Beneath Contempt) aren't very illuminating about *me* perhaps; about my subject matter, it is an old story, isn't it? They love, or hate.

Summary

Book I: 'Right and Wrong as a Clue to The Meaning of the Universe'

Chapter 1 'The Law of Human Nature' is about what is traditionally known as Natural Law.§ Lewis regarded the subject as immensely important and he treated it in *The Abolition of Man* as well as the essay, 'The Poison of Subjectivism'. In the discussion here he begins by distinguishing between the 'Law of Human Nature' and the 'Laws of Nature' such as gravitation. For instance, if you leave a body unsupported in the air it 'has no more choice about falling than a stone has' but 'a man could choose either to obey the Law of Human Nature or to disobey it.' People have always understood the Law of Human Nature and there is a great unanimity of belief in all cultures about morality.

Chapter 2, 'Some Objections', answers some of those occasioned by the broadcasts. (1) You may feel an instinct to help a man in danger as well as an instinct to run away. The feeling that you *ought* to help, which judges the two instincts, is separate from them. (2) 'We are not acting *from* instinct when we set about making an instinct stronger than it is' – this third thing is the Moral Law. (3) 'The Moral Law is not any one instinct or any set of instincts: it is something which makes a kind of tune (the tune we call goodness or right conduct) by directing the instincts.' Thus, there is one standard that measures nearly all the others. Otherwise it would make no sense to prefer 'Christian morality' to 'Nazi morality'. Chapter 3, 'The Reality of the Law', contrasts the Laws of Nature with those of Human Nature, and the conclusion is reached that 'There is something above and beyond the ordinary facts of men's behaviour ... a real law, which none of us made, but which we find pressing on us.'

In Chapter 4, 'What Lies Behind the Law', he argues that while 'Science works by experiments' and 'watches how things behave', the power that made the universe 'would be not one of the observed facts but a reality which makes them.' 'If there was a controlling power outside the universe, it could not show itself to us as one of the facts inside the universe – no more than the architect of a house could actually be a wall or staircase or fireplace in that house.' Chapter 5, 'We Have Cause to be Uneasy', answers the objection that in introducing 'somebody or something from beyond the material universe' the author was setting the clock back with one more 'religious law'. (1) 'Progress means getting nearer to the place where you want to be ... If you are on the wrong road, progress means doing an about-turn.' (2) The evidence we have of 'Somebody' behind the universe is the universe itself, and the Moral Law which 'is more like a mind than it is like anything else.' (3) Christianity tells people to repent and promises forgiveness. 'When you know you are sick, you will listen to the doctor.'

Book II: 'What Christians Believe'

Chapter 1, 'The Rival Conceptions of God', opens with the assertion that 'If you are a Christian you do not have to believe that all the other religions are simply wrong all through ... Even the queerest ones contain at least some hint of the truth.' Humanity is divided into the majority who believe in some kind of God or gods, and the minority who do not. Believers can be divided between (1) those who believe God is beyond good and evil – such as the Pantheists who believe 'the universe almost *is* God', and (2) the Christians who 'think God invented and made the universe'. Christianity is 'a fighting religion', an effort to put things right. Atheism is 'too simple' because 'If the whole universe has no meaning, we should never have found out that it has no meaning.'

Chapter 2, 'The Invasion', opens with a dismissal of 'Christianity-and-water', the view that 'there is a good God in Heaven and everything is all right – leaving out all the difficult and terrible doctrines about sin and hell and the devil, and the redemption.' There are only two views that face the facts: (1) The Christian view which is 'that this is a good world that has gone wrong, but still retains the memory of what it ought to have been'; (2) Dualism which is 'the belief that there are two equal and independent powers at the back of everything, one of them good and the other bad, and that this universe is the battlefield in which they fight out an endless war.' If we believe there is a Good Power and a Bad Power, we (a) are merely saying we prefer one to the other, or (b) we are saying that whatever one we like, 'one of them is actually wrong ... in regarding itself as good.'

Good means 'what you ought to prefer quite regardless of what you happen to like.' The moment you grant this 'you are putting into the universe a third thing in addition to the two Powers' which is 'further back and higher up than either of them' and which 'will be the real God'. The devil is a fallen angel who gets his power even to be evil from goodness itself. Because he is merely a rebel and not an independent power, the battle going on is 'a civil war, a rebellion' and 'we are living in a part of the universe occupied by the rebel'.

Chapter 3, 'The Shocking Alternative', is about Free Will. 'A world of automata,' he insists, 'would hardly be worth creating. The happiness which God designs for His higher creatures is the happiness of being freely, voluntarily united to Him and to each other in an ecstasy of love and delight compared with which the most rapturous love between a man and woman on this earth is mere milk and water. And for that they must be free.' We fell because Satan put into the heads of our remote ancestors that 'they could "be like gods" – could set up on their own as if they had created themselves ... invent some sort of happiness for themselves outside God.'

Because God 'cannot give us a happiness and peace apart from Himself' He (1) left us a conscience, the sense of right and wrong'; (2)'sent the human race ... good dreams ... those queer stories scattered all through the heathen religions about a god who dies and comes to life again'; (3) selected 'one particular people [the Jews] and spent several centuries hammering into their heads the sort of God He was'; (4) finally, sent His Son, Jesus. Following a discussion about Jesus's behaviour, notably that of forgiving sins committed against *other people*, Lewis concluded with the most famous passage in the book. It concerns the age-old question of whether Jesus was 'God or a good man' or, as Lewis put it, either 'a great moral teacher' or 'God': 'A man who was merely a man and said the sort of things Jesus said would not be a great moral teacher. He would either be a lunatic ... or else he would be the Devil of Hell ... You must make your choice.'

Chapter 4, 'The Perfect Penitent', is about the Atonement. Lewis had difficulty in writing this chapter because even within orthodox Christianity there is no official formulation, and he had as well to consider the various emphases given to doctrines of the Atonement by the different denominations. His answer was to admit that while 'different theories have been held as to how it works', all agree with 'the central Christian belief' that 'Christ's death has somehow put us right with God and given us a fresh start'. 'We are told,' he says, 'that Christ was killed for us, that His death has washed out our sins, and that by dying He disabled death itself. That is the formula. That is Christianity. That is what has to be believed.'

His answer as to why Christ's death has 'put us right with God' has aroused the animosity of some people, yet it is generally accepted as a brilliant way of putting the truth across. Man got himself into a 'hole' by trying 'to set up on his own' and behaving 'as if he belonged to himself.' He is 'a rebel who must lay down his arms.' His need for repentance, however, meets with the 'catch' that while only bad people need to repent 'only a good person can repent perfectly.'

Repentance is 'not something God demands of you before He will take you back and which He could let you off if He chose: it is simply a description of what going back to Him is like.' But again we come up against the 'catch'. How can this take place? 'Supposing God became a man – suppose our human nature which can suffer and die was amalgamated with God's nature in one person ... We cannot share God's dying unless God dies; and He cannot die except by being a man. That is the sense in which He pays our debt, and suffers for us what He Himself need not suffer at all.'

Chapter 5, 'The Practical Conclusion', discusses the methods God has chosen to spread the 'new life'. It is spread by 'baptism, belief, and that mysterious action which different Christians call by different names – Holy Communion, the Mass, the Lord's Supper.' Lewis answers some of the most perennial objections to this aspect of Christianity. (1) We are to believe these things on Christ's authority. 'A man who jibbed at authority in other things as some people do in religion would have to be content to know nothing all his life.' (2) The Christian 'does not think God will love us because we are good, but that God will make us good because He loves us.' (3) The Christian is not to be 'more spiritual than God.' We are not to shun 'bodily acts' such as baptism and Holy Communion because they strike us as crude and unspiritual. 'God does not: He invented eating. He likes matter.' (4) 'Is it not frightfully unfair that this new life should be confined to people who have heard of Christ and been able to believe in Him?' Lewis answered that 'We do know that no man can be saved except through Christ; we do not know that only those who know Him can be saved through Him.' (5) If these things are so important, why doesn't God land in force and undermine the devil? The promised 'invasion' by God will surely come but for the time being 'He wants to give us the chance of joining His side freely.'

Book III: 'Christian Behaviour'

Chapter 1, 'The Three Parts of Morality', is about Morality as opposed to 'ideals' of our own. Morality is concerned with: (1) fair play and harmony between individuals; (2) 'harmonizing the things inside each individual'; and (3) the 'general purpose of life as a whole: what man was made for.' The chapter ends with something Lewis never allowed his readers to forget and which appears also in 'The Weight of Glory' and 'Man or Rabbit?' 'Christianity asserts,' he says, 'that every individual human being is going to live for ever ... There are a good many things which would not be worth bothering about if I were going to live only seventy years, but which I had better bother about very seriously if I am going to live for ever.'

In chapter 2, '"The Cardinal Virtues"', Lewis distinguishes between the 'Theological' virtues which only Christians know about, and the 'Cardinal' ones which 'all civilized people recognize'. (1) **Prudence** means 'practical common sense, taking the trouble to think out what you are doing and what is likely to come of it.' Lewis put some Christian 'meat' on to this by assuring us that when Christ 'told us to be not only "as harmless as doves", but also "as wise as serpents", He wants a child's heart, but a grown-up's head.' (2) **Temperance** has picked up the meaning 'teetotalism', but when christened a 'cardinal' virtue it 'referred not specially to drink, but to all pleasures; and it meant not abstaining, but going the right length and no further.' The unfortunate thing about restricting Temperance to drink is that 'it helps people to forget that you can be just as intemperate about lots of other things.' (3) **Justice** 'is the old name for everything we should now call "fairness"; it includes honesty, give and take, truthfulness, keeping promises, and all that side of life.' (4) **Fortitude** or 'Guts' includes the kind of courage 'that faces danger as well as the kind that "sticks it" under pain.' Lewis emphasized that virtues are not the *actions* themselves, but 'a certain quality of character' acquired by those who practise them. 'The point is not that God will refuse you admission to His eternal world if you have not got certain qualities of character; the point is that if people have not got at least the beginnings of those qualities inside them, then no possible external conditions could make a "Heaven" for them.'

Chapter 3, 'Social Morality', makes two points about morality. (1) Christ 'did not come to preach any brand new morality', and the main job of moral teachers 'is to keep on bringing us back, time after time, to the old simple principles which we are all so anxious not to see.' Lewis found this perfectly stated by Dr Johnson: 'People need to be reminded more often than they need to be instructed.' (2) 'Christianity has not, and does not profess to have, a detailed political programme for applying "Do as you would be done by" to a particular society at a particular moment ... It is meant for all men at all times and the particular programme which suited one place or time would not suit another.'

Chapter 4, 'Morality and Psychoanalysis', considers how Christians are to apply 'do as you would be done by', and become the sort of people who really would apply it if they saw how. Because Christian morality and psychoanalysis both claim to be a 'technique for putting the human machine right' it is important to distinguish between the actual medical theories of the world of Freud and its general philosophical view of the world. Two things are involved in a moral choice. One is the act of choosing, and the other is the feelings and impulses which are the 'raw material' of his choice. The 'raw material' may be normal or abnormal: the fear of things really dangerous is normal, but an irrational fear of cats or spiders is abnormal. Morality is concerned with the free choice each is making because every time you make a choice 'you are turning the central part of you, the part of you that chooses, into something a little different from what it was before. And taking all your life as a whole you are slowly turning this central thing either into a heavenly creature or into a hellish creature.' There follows an analogy about sleep versus waking that was to appear again with great force in *Perelandra* (17). 'When a man is getting worse, he understands his own badness less and less. A moderately bad man knows he is not very good: a thoroughly bad man thinks he is all right.'

Chapter 5, 'Sexual Morality'. 'Chastity,' said Lewis in one of his most challenging chapters, 'is the most unpopular of the Christian virtues. There is no getting away from it: the Christian rule is, "Either marriage, with complete faithfulness to your partner, or else total abstinence." Now this is so difficult and so contrary to our instincts, that obviously either

Christianity is wrong or our sexual instinct, as it now is, has gone wrong. One or the other. Of course, being a Christian, I think it is the instinct which has gone wrong.' There follows a delightful example of what it would be like if we gave the appetite for food the exaggerated importance we give the appetite for sex.

Lewis denied that Christians claim that sex, or the body, or pleasure, were bad in themselves. Indeed, Christianity 'is almost the only one of the great religions which thoroughly approves of the body – which believes that matter is good, that God Himself once took on a human body.' It is difficult for us to desire, or achieve, complete chastity because: (1) 'Our warped natures, the devils who tempt us, and all the contemporary propaganda for lust, combine to make us feel that the desires we are resisting are so "natural", so "healthy", and so reasonable, that it is almost perverse and abnormal to resist them.' (2) Many people are deterred from attempting Christian chastity because they imagine it to be impossible, but 'You must ask for God's help ... Very often what God first helps us towards is not the virtue itself but just this power of always trying again.' (3) People often misunderstand the difference between 'repression', which means thrusting things into the subconscious so that it is difficult to recognize them, and 'suppression', which means denying or resisting something. The centre of Christian morality is not chastity; the sins of the flesh are the least bad of all sins. The 'Diabolical Self' is worse than the 'Animal Self' and this is why 'a cold, self-righteous prig who goes regularly to church may be far nearer to Hell than a prostitute. But, of course, it is better to be neither.'

Chapter 6, 'Christian Marriage', is about what Christ means when He says that a man and wife are to be regarded as a single organism. 'The male and the female, were made to be combined together in pairs, not simply on the sexual level, but totally combined ... The monstrosity of sexual intercourse outside marriage is that those who indulge in it are trying to isolate one kind of union (the sexual) from all the other kinds of union which were intended to go along with it and make up the total union.' We are urged to realize that the thrill of 'being in love' is very short lived, and that 'it is just the people who are ready to submit to the loss of the thrill and settle down to the sober interest, who are then most likely to meet new thrills in some quite different direction.'

Two questions arise about the biblical question of the 'headship' of the man in a marriage. (1) While it is to be hoped that disagreements will never arise, if they do 'one or other party must, in the last resort, have the power of deciding the family policy.' (2) If there must be a head, why the man? 'There must be something unnatural,' he answers, 'about the rule of wives over their husbands, because the wives themselves are half ashamed of it and despise the husbands whom they rule.' He goes on to distinguish between the 'Foreign Policy' and the 'Domestic Policy' in a marriage. 'The relations of the family to the outer world – its foreign policy – must depend, in the last resort, upon the man, because he always ought to be, and usually is, much more just to the outsiders. A woman is primarily fighting for her own children and husband against the rest of the world. Naturally, almost, in a sense, rightly, their claims override, for her, all other claims. She is the special trustee of their interests.'[3]

Chapter 7, 'Forgiveness', opens with the usual need of distinguishing between the sinner and sins. Lewis's unique contribution to this lies in pointing out that 'loving your neighbour' does not mean finding him 'attractive'. After all, he says, 'that is not why I love myself ... my self-love makes me think myself nice, but thinking myself nice is not why I love myself. So loving my enemies does not apparently mean thinking them nice either. That is an enormous relief.' We must be sure to make that distinction. Suppose one reads a story which makes our enemies seem very bad, and then we learn that the story is untrue. The wish to 'cling to the first story for the sheer pleasure of thinking your enemies as bad as possible' will cause you to eventually 'wish to see grey as black, and then to see white itself as black.'

Chapter 8, 'The Great Sin', is one of the best-known in the book. Lewis insists that the 'centre' of Christian morals lies in Pride – 'the essential vice, the utmost evil', 'the complete anti-God state of mind.' It is *essentially* competitive, while other vices are competitive only by accident. 'We say that people are proud of being rich, or clever, or good-looking, but they are not. They are proud of being richer, or cleverer, or better-looking than others. If every one else became equally rich, or clever, or good-looking there would be nothing to be proud about. It is the comparison that makes you proud.' In God we come up against something which is immeasurably superior to us, and it is the proud person's refusal to acknowledge this which means enmity to God. The other vices come to us from the devil 'working through our animal nature', but Pride is 'direct from Hell.'

Four misunderstandings are cleared up. (1) 'Pleasure in being praised is not Pride.' The difference between Vanity and Pride is that whereas the

---

[3] J.R.R. Tolkien* took exception to a number of things in the chapters on 'Sexual Morality' and 'Christian Marriage' of the 1943 edition of *Christian Behaviour*. His comments are found in the draft of a letter to Lewis, published as item number 49 in **LJRRT**, pp. 59–62.

vain person cares too much what people think of him, the proud one looks down on the opinion of others. (2) Admiration is not the same as Pride. When we say 'that a man is "proud" of his son, or his father, or his school, or regiment' we really mean that he has 'a warm-hearted admiration' for them. (3) God does not forbid Pride because 'He is offended at it', and he does not demand Humility because He thinks it is 'due to His own dignity'. God wants us to know Him, and give us Himself, but this is impossible unless we 'take off a lot of silly, ugly, fancy-dress in which we have all got ourselves up and are strutting about like the little idiots we are.' (4) A really humble man will not be what most people call 'humble' nowadays. Instead of being a 'greasy, smarmy person' probably all you will think about him 'is that he seemed a cheerful, intelligent chap who took a real interest in what *you* said to *him.*'

Chapters 9–12 are about the 'Theological Virtues': In chapter 9, 'Charity', Lewis provides instant relief by pointing out that this Love in the Christian sense 'does not mean an emotion.' It is a state 'not of the feelings but of the will.' Being 'cold' by temperament is 'no more a sin than having a bad digestion.' 'The rule for all of us,' he says, 'is perfectly simple. Do not waste time bothering whether you "love" your neighbour; act as if you did. As soon as we do this we find one of the great secrets. When you are behaving as if you loved someone, you will presently come to love him.' If we find that we have no love for God 'Do not sit trying to manufacture feelings. Ask yourself, "If I were sure that I loved God, what would I do?" When you have found the answer, go and do it.'

In chapter 10, 'Hope', Hope is defined as 'a continual looking forward to the eternal world' rather than a form of 'escapism or wishful thinking.' Lewis explains why most of us find it difficult to want Heaven. (1) 'The Fool's Way' is to blame things themselves – holidays, wives, hobbies – because he supposes that 'the mysterious something we are all after' lies in them. (2) 'The Way of the Disillusioned "Sensible Man"' – who decides the 'mysterious something' is really 'moonshine' and settles down and learns that he should not expect much. (3) 'The Christian Way' – which is one of Lewis's finest explanations of the 'Joy' written about in *The Pilgrim's Regress* and *Surprised by Joy*. The Christian explains Hope thus:

Creatures are not born with desires unless satisfaction for those desires exists ... If I find in myself a desire which no experience in this world can satisfy, the most probable explanation is that I was made for another world. If none of my earthly pleasures satisfy it, that does not prove that the universe is a fraud. Probably earthly pleasures were never meant to satisfy it, but only to arouse it, to suggest the real thing.

Chapter 11, 'Faith'. 'Faith' is used by Christians in two senses. (1) 'It means simply Belief – accepting or regarding as true the doctrines of Christianity.' What is there moral or immoral about believing or not believing a set of statements? Prior to an operation, your reason tells you that anaesthetics don't smother you and the surgeon won't start operating until you are unconscious. Still, once on the table, 'panic begins' and you lose your faith in anaesthetics. It wasn't reason that was taking away the faith, because faith is based on reason. 'The battle is between faith and reason on one side and emotion and imagination on the other.' Thus, faith 'is the art of holding on to things your reason has once accepted, in spite of your changing moods.'

(2) Faith in the other sense means the effort, after you've discovered that you're proud, 'to make some serious attempt to practise the Christian virtues.' Lewis predicted that for most of us things will go well for the first week, but that by six weeks we will have 'fallen lower than the point we began from.' 'Only those who try to resist temptation know how strong it is ... Christ, because He was the only man who never yielded to temptation, is also the only man who knows to the full what temptation means – the only complete realist.'

Chapter 12, which is also called 'Faith', begins with a reminder that what God mainly cares about is 'not exactly our actions' but that 'we should be creatures of a certain kind or quality.' There follows one of Lewis's most famous analogies. 'Christians,' he says, 'have often disputed as to whether what leads the Christian home is good actions, or Faith in Christ.' That, he says, is 'like asking which blade in a pair of scissors is most necessary.'

Book IV: 'Beyond Personality: or First Steps in the Doctrine of the Trinity'

Chapter 1, 'Making and Begetting', begins with the warning that 'you will not get eternal life by simply feeling the presence of God in flowers or music', and that the Christian should know some Theology. We then go to the statement of the Nicene Creed about Christ being 'begotten not created' 'before all worlds.' To beget means 'to beget something of the same kind as yourself', such as beavers begetting little beavers. For a man to make something, such as a statue, he makes something 'of a different kind' from himself. Similarly, 'What God begets is God' and what He *creates* 'is not God.' The difference between man and God is that what man 'in his natural condition, has not got, is Spiritual life.'

Chapter 2 – 'The Three-Personal God' – is about the Trinity, and includes this illustration of how the Father, the Son and the Holy Spirit operate in the life of a Christian:

> An ordinary simple Christian kneels down to say his prayers. He is trying to get in to touch with God. But if he is a Christian he knows that what is prompting him to pray is also God: God, so to speak, inside him. But he also knows that all his real knowledge of God comes through Christ, the Man who was God – that Christ is standing beside him, helping him to pray, praying for him ... God is the thing to which he is praying – the goal he is trying to reach. God is also the thing inside him which is pushing him on – the motive power. God is also the road or bridge along which he is being pushed to that goal. So that the whole threefold life of the three-personal Being is actually going on in that ordinary little bedroom.

Chapter 3, 'Time and Beyond Time', is about what Time is to God, and of how 'If a million people are praying to Him at ten-thirty tonight, He need not listen to them all in that one little snippet which we call ten-thirty.' This is because God is not 'hurried along in the Time-stream of this universe' any more than a character in a novel is hurried along by the Time-stream created by a novelist.

A difficulty for some Christians is the supposition that if God *foresees* our acts how we can still be free not to do them. But all God's days 'are "Now" for Him ... He does not "foresee" you doing things tomorrow; He simply sees you doing them: because, though tomorrow is not yet there for you, it is for Him ... He does not know your action till you have done it: but then the moment at which you have done it is already "Now" for Him.'

Chapter 4, 'Good Infection', is about the part of the Holy Spirit in the life of the Church. Lewis says we are likely to find Him 'vaguer or more shadowy' than the Father and the Son because 'In the Christian life you are not usually looking *at* Him: He is always acting through you.' The importance of all this for the Christian is that this 'three-Personal life is to be played out in each one of us ... each one of us has got to enter that pattern, take his place in that dance.' From our parents we receive *Bios*, or biological life, but from God only can we receive *Zoe*, or spiritual life.

There follows a brilliantly clear and concise summary of what it means to
be a Christian:

> The whole offer which Christianity makes is this: that we can, if we
> let God have His way, come to share in the life of Christ ... If we
> share in this kind of life we also shall be sons of God. We shall love
> the Father as He does and the Holy Ghost will arise in us ... Every
> Christian is to become a little Christ. The whole purpose of
> becoming a Christian is simply nothing else.

Chapter 5 – 'The Obstinate Toy Soldiers' – is about the Incarnation, the
Resurrection, and how a Christian can be drawn up into the spiritual life
of Christ. On the *descent* involved in the Incarnation, Lewis says: 'The
Eternal Being, who knows everything and who created the whole
universe, became not only a man but (before that) a baby, and before that
a *foetus* inside a Woman's body. If you want to get the hang of it, think
how you would like to become a slug or a crab.' Lewis then brings in one
of his favourite themes, that of 'Transposition', by pointing out that 'The
natural human creature in Him was taken up fully into the divine Son.'

  Chapter 6, 'Two Notes', arose out of two objections to Chapter 5. (1)
Why did not God begin by begetting many sons at the outset and so avoid
the difficult and painful process of bringing us to life? 'The process of
being turned from a creature into a son would not have been difficult or
painful if the human race had not turned away from God.' (2) Are real
people less important than 'collective things like classes, races, and so
forth'?   Christianity 'thinks of human individuals not as mere members
of a group or items in a list, but as organs in a body ... If you forget that
[another Christian] belongs to the same organism as yourself you will
become an Individualist. If you forget that he is a different organ from
you, if you want to suppress differences and make people all alike, you
will become a Totalitarian. But a Christian must not be either a
Totalitarian or an Individualist.'

  In chapter 7, 'Let's Pretend', it is suggested that if we don't feel friendly
towards someone 'the best thing you can do ... is to behave as if you were
a nicer person.' Rather than wait to feel like a son of God, we should
assume that we are, and begin to act like it. The young Christian will then
'be alarmed not only about what we do, but about what we are.' This will
make us see that everything must be done by Christ.

  In chapter 8, 'Is Christianity Hard or Easy?', Lewis answers that it is
'harder and easier' than aspiring for merely 'decent behaviour.' This is
because Christ says, 'Give me All. I don't want so much of your time and

so much of your money and so much of your work: I want You.' Christ 'never talked vague, idealistic gas. When he said, "Be perfect", He meant it ... The Church exists for nothing else but to draw men into Christ, to make them little Christs. If they are not doing that, all the cathedrals, clergy, missions, sermons, even the Bible itself, are simply a waste of time.'

Chapter 9, 'Counting the Cost', continues the discussion of Christ's command 'Be ye perfect.' The reason for 'counting the cost' is because Christ means 'Whatever suffering it may cost you in your earthly life, whatever inconceivable purification it may cost you after death, whatever it costs Me, I will never rest, nor let you rest until you are literally perfect.'[4] Lewis emphasizes that these seemingly impossible demands are put upon us because, with Christ's help, they are possible. Christ means, says Lewis, that whereas 'You thought you were going to be made into a decent little cottage ... He is building a palace. He intends to come and live in it Himself.'

Chapter 10, 'Nice People or New Men', answers the question 'If Christianity is true why are not all Christians obviously nicer than all non-Christians?' Some of the world's demands about 'results' Lewis considers illogical. (1) As in nearly everything he wrote, he discouraged the notion of judging humanity in the mass. It is not a case of the world consisting of '100 per cent Christians and 100 per cent non-Christians' but Christians 'who are slowly ceasing to be Christians but who still call themselves by that name: some of them clergymen', some who are becoming Christians, and others who belong to Christ without knowing it. (2) It does not follow that Christians will be 'nicer' than non-Christians. 'Christian Miss Bates,' he says, 'may have an unkinder tongue than unbelieving Dick Firkin', but this in itself doesn't tell us whether Christianity works. The question is what Miss Bates's tongue would be like if she were not a Christian, and what Dick's would be like if he became one.' No one can help his upbringing or the temperament he was born with. 'What is being managed in Dick Firkin's case is much "nicer" than what is being managed in Miss Bates's.'

(3) Christ wants much more than to 'pull Miss Bates up to the same level on which Dick has been all along.' The real question is: 'Will they turn to Him and thus fulfil the only purpose for which they were created? Their free will is trembling inside them like the needle of a compass. But this is a needle that can choose. It *can* point to the true

---

[4] The words 'whatever purification it may cost you after death' are Lewis's first reference to Purgatory. This was to be a main theme of *The Great Divorce*. See the passage about Purgatory in Letter xx of *Letters to Malcolm*.

North; but it need not. Will the needle swing round, and settle, and point
to God?' Lewis goes on to interpret Christ's words about 'Blessed are the
poor' and 'How hard it is for the rich to enter the Kingdom' as meaning
more than the economically poor and the economically rich, but other
kinds of riches and poverty as well. The danger of riches is that 'you may
forget that you are at every moment totally dependent on God' and
because 'people who have all these natural kinds of goodness cannot be
brought to recognize their need for Christ at all until, one day, the natural
goodness lets them down.'

Chapter 11, 'The New Men', contrasts the popular idea of the 'Next
Step' as one of Evolution from men into Supermen who can master the
planet with the Christian view of the Next Step as something that has
already happened and which means 'a change from being creatures of
God to being sons of God.' We are still 'the early Christians' because,
compared with the development of man on this planet, 'the diffusion of
Christianity over the human race seems to go like a flash of lightning – for
two thousand years is almost nothing in the history of the universe.'   Of
course the world has again and again thought Christianity was dying, but
every time it has been disappointed. Its first disappointment was over the
crucifixion, but 'The Man came to life again' and 'it has been happening
ever since.'

Lewis illustrates his remarkable gift for imagining Goodness by
suggesting how holy people who acquire 'the mind of Christ' in this
world will differ from our usual notion of 'religious people'. 'Their very
voices and faces are different from ours ... stronger, quieter, happier, more
radiant. They begin where most of us leave off ... They love you more
than other men do, but they need you less.' The analogy chosen to
illustrate how holy people will be more, rather than less, 'themselves' as a
result of surrendering to Christ, is one of his best. 'Suppose a person who
knew nothing about salt. You give him a pinch to taste and he experiences
a particular strong, sharp taste. You then tell him that in your country
people use salt in all their cookery. Might he not reply "In that case I
suppose all your dishes taste exactly the same: because the taste of that
stuff you have just given me is so strong that it will kill the taste of
everything else." But you and I know that the real effect of salt is exactly
the opposite ... It is something like that with Christ and us. The more we
get what we now call "ourselves" out of the way and let Him take us over,
the more truly ourselves we become.' This explains why, apart from God,
natural men, even 'great tyrants and conquerors', end up being much the
same, while the saints are 'gloriously different.'

He concludes with one of his most magnificent pieces of writing. After urging his listeners and readers to believe that they will never have a 'personality' until they forget about trying and turn to God, he says, 'Look for yourself, and you will find in the long run only hatred, loneliness, despair, rage, ruin, and decay. But look for Christ and you will find Him, and with Him everything else thrown in.'

Reviews

Broadcast Talks: It was highly praised in *The Tablet*, 180 (18 July 1942), p. 32: 'We have never read arguments better marshalled and handled so that they can be remembered, or any book more useful to the Christian, in the Army or elsewhere, who finds himself called upon to argue briefly from first premises, to say why morality is not herd-instinct, why there is a special and unique character attached to the sense of obligation, why the conviction that there is a law of right and wrong and a transcendent morality is only intelligible if there is a God.' *The Times Literary Supplement* (19 September 1942), p. 460, said: 'No writer of popular apologetics today is more effective than Mr C.S. Lewis. He is a layman and for many years was not a Christian believer, and is therefore not only entirely unprofessional in manner, but also keenly aware of the difficulties commonly levelled against the Christian faith.'

Martin Tindal said in *Time and Tide*, 23 (19 September 1942), p. 744: 'Mr C.S. Lewis has made the kind of public return to the ancient faith which infuriates other intellectuals. If only these undeniably intelligent laymen had kept quiet about their change of direction, they might have been endurable. But they have not kept quiet … An uncompromising, tonic little book.' G.D. Smith wrote in *The Clergy Review*, XXII (December 1942), pp. 561–3: 'The author shows himself a master in the rare art of conveying profound truths in simple and compelling language.'

Christian Behaviour: *The Guardian* reviewer said (21 May 1943), p. 170: 'His learning is abundantly seasoned with common sense, his humour and his irony are always at the service of the most serious purposes, and his originality is the offspring of enthusiastically loyal orthodoxy.' Robert Speaight said in *The Tablet*, 181 (26 June 1943), p. 308: 'Mr Lewis is that rare being – a born broadcaster; born to the manner as well as to the matter. He neither buttonholes you nor bombards you; there is no false intimacy and no false eloquence. He approaches you directly, as a rational person only to be persuaded by reason. He is confident and yet humble in his possession and propagation of truth. He is helped by a speaking voice of great charm and a style of manifest sincerity.'

Beyond Personality: A reviewer said in *The Times Literary Supplement* (21 October 1944), p. 513: 'Mr Lewis has a quite unique power of making theology an attractive, exciting and (one might almost say) an uproariously fascinating quest ... Those who have inherited Christianity may write about it with truth and learning, but they can scarcely write with the *excitement* which men like Maritain and C.S. Lewis show, to whom the Christian faith is the unlooked-for discovery of the pearl of great price.'

G.D. Smith wrote in *The Clergy Review*, XXV (February 1945), pp. 62–9: 'To the task of expounding the Christian religion Mr C.S. Lewis brings uncommon gifts of lucid statement, apt illustration, and forceful expression, talents which cause his broadcast talks on Christianity to be heard with attention by millions of listeners and have earned for his recent books on religious subjects a very wide popularity.' H.C.L. Heywood said in *Theology*, XLVIII (March 1945), pp. 66–8: 'Most of us know quite a lot of people who ought to read this book.'

THE ABOLITION OF MAN
OR REFLECTIONS ON
EDUCATION WITH SPECIAL
REFERENCE TO THE TEACHING
OF ENGLISH IN THE UPPER
FORMS OF SCHOOLS (1943)

Background

I: 'The Hegemony of Moral Values'

During his undergraduate and postgraduate years at Oxford, Lewis was much occupied with Philosophy. He was hoping to gain a Fellowship in that subject at one of the Colleges, and in his diary (**AMR**) of 6 July 1922 he mentions writing a dissertation on 'the hegemony of moral value'. 'Hegemony' means 'leadership' or 'predominance', and while Lewis did not then associate morals with God, he nevertheless believed in what the philosophers called the 'Absolute'.

This was a long way from being a Christian, but during the 1920s, when Lewis expected to be a philosopher, he was convinced there was an 'Absolute' or 'One' or 'The Whole', and that morals were of great 'value'. In October 1924, while temporarily employed at University College,‡ he began a series of lectures on 'The Good, its position among the values'. In March of that year he read a paper on 'The Hegemony of Moral Values' to the Philosophical Society. It is unfortunate that it has not survived, but we know that he accepted the primacy of a spiritual reality, which was essentially one of divine immanence rather than transcendence – the spirit within man and all reality, rather than a personal Father above him. 'I distinguished,' said Lewis in **SBJ** XIV, 'this philosophical "God" very sharply ... from "the God of popular religion."'

In 1929 a 'wholly new situation' developed, as Lewis explained in **SBJ** XIV:

As the dry bones shook and came together in that dreadful valley of Ezekiel's, so now a philosophical theorem, cerebrally entertained, began to stir and heave and throw off its gravecloths, and stood upright and became a living presence. I was to be allowed to play at philosophy no longer.

II: The Riddell Memorial Lectures

After the University of Durham asked Lewis to deliver the three Riddell Memorial Lectures (founded in memory of Sir John Buchanan Riddell, 1849–1924), Lewis immersed himself in the *Encyclopaedia of Religion and Ethics*, ed. James Hastings (Edinburgh: 1908–26), the main source of his examples for what he calls the 'Tao'. He had already mentioned the universality of agreement about Natural Law§ in *Mere Christianity*, and in his essay **On Ethics** of about 1942 he insisted that 'In triumphant monotony the same indispensable platitudes will meet us in culture after culture.'

On 8 February 1943, a few weeks before he went up to Durham to deliver his lectures, he addressed the Socratic Club‡ on the question 'If We Have Christ's Ethics Does the Rest of the Christian Faith Matter?' In this paper, by way of complementing what he was going to say in Durham, his subject was the relationship between Natural Law and Christianity. A précis of that paper, found in the *Socratic Digest* (No 1, p. 23), is an invaluable addition to his writings on Natural Law and is quoted in full:

> Mr Lewis first demonstrated the existence of a massive and immemorial moral law by listing precepts from Greek, Roman, Chinese, Babylonian, ancient Egyptian and Old Norse sources. By this account of the immutable laws of general and special beneficence, duties to parents and to children, of justice, good faith and of the law of mercy, three illusions were dispelled: first, that the expression 'Christian moral principles' means anything different from 'moral principles'; secondly, the anthropological illusion that the crude and barbarous man is the natural and normal man; and, thirdly, that the great disease of humanity is ignorance and the great cure, education. On the contrary, it is only too obvious that while there is massive and immemorial agreement about moral law, there is also a massive and immemorial inability to obey it.

In considering the remedy for the cleavage between human nature and generally accepted moral law, Mr Lewis first separated from normal humanity those faddists, whether Epicureans, Communists, or H.G. Wells, whose indefensible naïvety forbade them to understand the actual condition of Man. The remainder of humanity would be divided into the ordinary mass of pagan mankind and Christians. Both these classes of men know the moral law and recognize their own inability to keep it. Both endeavour to deal with this tragic situation. The pagan mysteries and Christianity are two alternative solutions, and whatever falls outside these two is simply naïve. Now the *differentia* of Christianity, as against pagan mystery religions, lies in its survival, its historical core, its combination of the ethical and the sacramental, its ability to produce that 'new man' which all rites of initiation premise, and finally its restraining effect upon a community under its domination.

The datum is the complete cleavage between human behaviour and the code of morals which humanity acknowledges. And Christianity is the cure for this particular disease. For 'excellent instructions' we have always had; the problem is how to obey them. To ask whether the rest of the Christian Faith matters when we have Christ's ethics presupposes a world of unfallen men with no need of redemption. 'The rest of the Christian Faith' is the means of carrying out, instead of merely being able to discourse on the ethics we already know.

In his diary, *Brothers and Friends* (22–24 February 1943), Warren Lewis described the visit he made with his brother to the University of Durham. They arrived there on 24 February, after which they journeyed a few miles north to Newcastle-upon-Tyne where the three Riddell Memorial Lectures were given on the evenings of 24, 25 and 26 February.

Summary

I: The Problem

Chapter I, 'Men Without Chests', opens with a discussion of two textbooks for pupils in the upper forms of school. The books had not long been published, and Lewis conceals their titles and authors under fictitious names. In reality, what he calls *The Green Book* by 'Gaius and

Titius' is *The Control of Language* (1940) by Alex King and Martin Ketley; the book by 'Orbilius' is *The Reading and Writing of English* (1936) by E.G. Biaggini. In their book Gaius and Titius mention the story of Coleridge at the waterfall. One tourist calls the waterfall 'sublime' and the other 'pretty'. Coleridge, Lewis tells us, 'endorsed the first judgement and rejected the second with disgust.' Gaius and Titius comment: 'When the man said *That is sublime*, he appeared to be making a remark about the waterfall ... Actually ... he was not making a remark about the waterfall, but a remark about his own feelings. What he was saying was really *I have feelings associated in my mind with the word "Sublime"*, or shortly, *I have sublime feelings*.' Lewis says:

> Even if it were granted that such qualities as sublimity were simply and solely projected in to things from our own emotions, yet the emotions which prompt the projection are the correlatives, and therefore almost the opposites, of the qualities projected. The feelings which make a man call an object sublime are not sublime feelings but feelings of veneration ... If the view held by Gaius and Titius were consistently applied it would lead to obvious absurdities. It would force them to maintain that *You are contemptible* means *I have contemptible feelings*: in fact that *Your feelings are contemptible* means *My feelings are contemptible*.

He concludes that those who read *The Green Book* will believe (1) 'that all sentences containing a predicate of value are statements about the emotional state of the speaker' and (2) 'that all such statements are unimportant.' Thus, while Gaius and Titius teach the pupil nothing about letters, they have 'cut out of his soul, long before he is old enough to choose, the possibility of having certain experiences which thinkers of more authority than they have held to be generous, fruitful and humane.'

II: The Educational Predicament

'Until quite modern times,' said Lewis, 'all teachers and even all men believed the universe to be such that certain emotional reactions on our part could be either congruous or incongruous to it – believed, in fact, that objects did not merely receive, but could *merit*, our approval or disapproval, or reverence, or our contempt.' In support, he quotes Coleridge, Shelley, Traherne, St Augustine, Aristotle, Plato and the Chinese *Tao* which is the 'reality beyond all predicates ... the Way in which things everlastingly emerge.' What is common to all these civilizations is 'the doctrine of objective value, the belief that certain attitudes are really true, and others really false.'

More and more educators are like Gaius and Titius in debunking proper sentiments as 'merely propaganda', and Lewis argues that only by training emotions into 'stable sentiments' can the Chest – Magnanimity – Sentiment – act as the 'indispensable liaison officers between cerebral man and visceral man.' Meanwhile, he says:

> In a sort of ghastly simplicity we remove the organ and demand the function. We make men without chests and expect of them virtue and enterprise. We laugh at honour and are shocked to find traitors in our midst. We castrate and bid the geldings be fruitful.

In chapter II, 'The Way', Lewis maintains that 'The practical result of education in the spirit of *The Green Book* must be the destruction of the society which accepts it.' But even while educators such as Gaius and Titius claim that all traditional values are subjective they nevertheless show 'by the very act of writing *The Green Book* that there must be some other values about which they are not subjective at all.' They write 'in order to produce certain states of mind in the rising generation ... because they think them to be the means to some state of society which they regard as desirable.'

III: 'Real' or 'Basic' Values

Having cut away traditional morality in order that the supposedly 'real' or 'basic' values may emerge, how will the Innovator defend dying for a good cause if he believes that altruism is no more 'rational' nor 'intelligent' than selfishness? Lewis answers:

> From propositions about fact alone no practical conclusion can ever be drawn. *This will preserve society* cannot lead to *do this* except by the mediation of *society ought to be preserved*. *This will cost you your life* cannot lead directly to *do not do this*: it can lead to it only through a felt desire or an acknowledged duty of self-preservation. The Innovator is trying to get a conclusion in the imperative mood out of premises in the indicative mood: and though he continues trying to all eternity he cannot succeed, for the thing is impossible. We must therefore either extend the word Reason to include what

our ancestors called Practical Reason and confess that judgements such as *society ought to be preserved* ... are not mere sentiments but are rationality itself: or else we must give up at once, and for ever, the attempt to find a core of 'rational' value behind all the sentiments we have debunked.

IV: An Appeal to 'Instinct'

The Innovator is more likely to give up the quest for a 'rational' core and to seek for some other ground even more 'basic' and 'realistic'. If he feels that he has found this in 'Instinct', the answer is that such things as the preservation of society or our species are 'ends that do not hang on the precarious thread of Reason' but 'are given by Instinct'. On the other hand, we do *not* have an instinctive urge to keep promises or to respect individual life, and this is why 'scruples of justice and humanity – in fact the *Tao* – can be properly swept away when they conflict with our real end, the preservation of the species.' The Innovator, wishing to get rid of the old sexual morality, expects to find one in Instinct.

V: How Does Instinct Help Us Find 'Real' Values?

If Instinct is something we *must* obey why are such works such as *The Green Book* written? 'Why this stream of exhortation to drive us where we cannot help going?' If we are facing death, he answers, and if death cuts off every possible satisfaction, and if we have an instinctive desire for the good of posterity, then this desire, by the very nature of the case, can never be satisfied, since its aim is achieved, if at all, when we are dead. 'It looks very much as if the Innovator would have to say not that we must obey instinct, nor that it will satisfy us to do so, but that we *ought* to obey instinct.'

VI: *Which* Instinct Should We Obey?

The Innovator says we should obey instinct. Why? 'Is there another instinct of a higher order directing us to do so, and a third of a still higher order directing us to obey *it*? – an infinite regress of instincts?'

Telling us to obey instinct is like telling us to obey 'people'. People say different things: so do instincts. Our instincts are at war. If it is held that the instinct for preserving the species should always be obeyed at the expense of other instincts, whence do we derive this rule of precedence? To listen to that instinct speaking in its own cause and deciding in its own favour would be rather simple minded. Each instinct, if you listen to it, will claim to be gratified at the expense of all the rest. By the very act of listening to one rather than to others we have already prejudged the case. If we did not bring to the examination of our instincts a knowledge of their comparative dignity we could never learn it from them. And that knowledge cannot itself be instinctive: the judge cannot be one of the parties judged: or, if he is, the decision is worthless and there is no ground for placing the preservation of the species above self-preservation or sexual appetite.

VII: Where Is There An Instinct To 'preserve the species'?

Lewis answers that 'Only people educated in a particular way have ever had the idea "posterity" before their minds at all ... No parents who were guided by this instinct would dream for a moment of setting up the claims of their hypothetical descendants against those of the baby actually crowing and kicking in the room.' Again, *which* instinct should the Innovator follow? The truth becomes apparent that 'neither in any operation with factual propositions nor in any appeal to instinct' can the Innovator find the basis for a system of values.

The principles the Innovator is looking for are found elsewhere than instinct. 'All within the four seas are his brothers', says Confucius; 'Do as you would be done by', says Jesus; 'Humanity is to be preserved', says Locke. 'All the practical principles behind the Innovator's case for posterity, or society, or the species, are there from time immemorial in the *Tao*.'

> But they are nowhere else. Unless you accept these without question as being to the world of action what axioms are to the world of theory, you can have no practical principles whatever. You cannot reach them as conclusions: they are premises.

VIII: The *Tao* the Sole Source of All Value Judgements

The Innovator has been attacking traditional values in defence of what he supposed to be 'rational' or 'biological' values. But all values, the ones he attacks and the ones he defends, are derived from the *Tao*. No attempt to find values 'outside traditional values' can advance the Innovator one inch towards the conception that a man should die for the community or work for posterity. The *Tao*, or Natural Law, or Traditional Morality, or the First Principles of Practical Reason, or First Platitudes, is not one among a series of value judgements. 'It is the sole source of all value judgements. If it is rejected, all value is rejected. If any value is retained, it is retained.'

> What purport to be new systems or ... 'ideologies', all consist of fragments from the *Tao* itself, arbitrarily wrenched from their context in the whole and then swollen to madness in their isolation ... The rebellion of new ideologies against the *Tao* is a rebellion of the branches against the tree: if the rebels could succeed they would find that they had destroyed themselves. The human mind has no more power of inventing a new value than of imagining a new primary colour, or, indeed, of creating a new sun and a new sky for it to move in.

IX: Is Progress in Values Possible?

Lewis distinguishes between 'development' and 'innovation'. 'From the Confucian "Do not do to others what you would not like them to do to you" to the Christian "Do as you would be done by" is a real advance.' The morality of Nietzsche who scraps traditional morality altogether is a 'mere innovation'. Those who understand the spirit of the *Tao* are the only ones who know how to modify it. This is because, he says, 'Only those who are practising the *Tao* will understand it.'

Chapter III, 'The Abolition of Man', begins with a consideration of what is meant by 'Man's conquest of Nature'. Lewis believed that such a 'conquest' has not been without its benefits to man. He considers three typical examples of 'conquest': the aeroplane, the radio, and the contraceptive. Regarding the first two, he believes man to be 'as much the patient or subject as the possessor, since he is the target both for bombs and for propaganda.' Contraception, he argues, is a much more serious matter because of the 'paradoxical, negative sense in which all possible future generations are the patients or subjects of a power wielded by those already alive':

> By contraception simply, they are denied existence; by contra-
> ception used as a means of selective breeding, they are, without

their concurring voice, made to be what one generation, for its own reasons, may choose to prefer. From this point of view, what we call Man's power over Nature turns out to be a power exercised by some men over other men with Nature as its instrument.

X: The Power of Earlier Generations Over Later Ones

Lewis found that those who write on social matters usually forget to include Time among the dimensions. To understand its application, we must imagine the race extended in time from its beginning to its extinction. The picture sometimes painted is one of 'a progressive emancipation from tradition and a progressive control of natural processes resulting in a continual increase of human power.' In reality, he says, what any one age really attains, by eugenics and scientific education, is 'the power to make its descendants what it pleases' because 'all men who live after it are the patients of that power':

> There is therefore no question of a power vested in the race as a whole steadily growing as long as the race survives. The last men, far from being the heirs of power, will be of all men most subject to the dead hand of the great planners and conditioners and will themselves exercise least power upon the future ... Man's conquest of Nature, if the dreams of some scientific planners are realized, means the rule of a few hundreds of men over billions upon billions of men. There neither is nor can be any simple increase of power on Man's side. Each new power won *by* man is a power *over* man as well. Each advance leaves him weaker as well as stronger. In every victory, besides being the general who triumphs, he is also the prisoner who follows the triumphal car.

XI: Moulding the New Men

The power of some men to make other men what *they* please has always been with us, but there will be some differences. (1) The 'man-moulders' of the new age will be armed 'with the powers of an omnicompetent state and an irresistible scientific technique.' (2) In former systems the kind of men teachers were trying to produce, and the teachers' motives for producing them, were prescribed by the *Tao*. They were handing on what they had received. In the new age Values are 'mere natural phenomena' and Judgements of Value 'are to be produced in the pupil as part of the conditioning.' If there is any of the *Tao* in this, it will be the product, and not the motive, of education. In this last stage of Man's struggle with Nature, the Conditioners will *produce* the kind of conscience they decide on – and Human Nature will have been conquered.

XII: What Motivates the New Creators of Motives?

The new Conditioners will probably see themselves as 'servants and guardians of humanity' who believe they have a duty to do it 'good'. Will they so condition the rest of us that we go on having 'the old idea of duty and the old reactions' to it? If 'duty' itself is on trial, how can duty help them to decide? They can't make one of the things compared the standard of comparison.

Lewis thinks some will ask why he supposes the Conditioners to be 'bad men'. But 'good' and 'bad' to the Conditioners are words without content. It is *from* them that the content of these words is to be derived. But do we not all want more or less the same things out of life? It is false, says Lewis, to say that we do. What *motive* will the Conditioners have for trying to give us what we want? Duty? The preservation of the species? These things come from the *Tao*, which cannot be valid for the Conditioner. They are not men at all, says Lewis:

> Stepping outside the *Tao*, they have stepped into the void. Nor are their subjects necessarily unhappy men. They are not men at all: they are artefacts. Man's final conquest has proved to be the abolition of Man.

XIII: The Rule of Nature

As all values are subjective to the Conditioners, and as 'good' is debunked, probably the strongest motivation to them will be 'simply their own pleasure'. 'Those who stand outside all judgements of value cannot have any ground for preferring one of their own impulses to another except the emotional strength of that impulse.' It would seem, then, that our hope of a 'conditioned' happiness rests on 'chance' – the chance that benevolent impulses may be predominant in our Conditioners. 'And Chance here means Nature. It is from heredity, digestion, the weather, and the association of ideas, that the motives of the Conditioners will spring.'

Thus, 'Man's victory over Nature' progresses from (1) Man's emancipation from the *Tao*, (2) the reduction of the *Tao* to a mere natural product, (3) by freedom from the *Tao*, the subjection of the whole of the race to some individual men, (4) the subjection of those individual men to their irrational impulses (the purely 'natural'), (5) obedience to these irrational impulses or Chance and, finally, and as a result (6) Nature's conquest of Man:

> Every victory we seemed to win has led us, step by step, to this conclusion. All Nature's apparent reverses have been but tactical withdrawals. We thought we were beating her back when she was luring us on. What looked to us like hands held up in surrender was really the opening of arms to enfold us for ever. If the fully planned and conditioned world (with its *Tao* a mere product of the planning) comes into existence, Nature will be troubled no more by the restive species that rose in revolt against her so many millions of years ago, will be vexed no longer by its chatter of truth and mercy and beauty and happiness ... If the eugenics are efficient enough there will be no second revolt, but all snug beneath the Conditioners, and the Conditioners beneath her, till the moon falls or the sun grows cold.

XIV: How Man Brings About His Subjection to Nature

Nature is a word of varying meanings. (1) By 'the Natural' we usually mean the *opposite* of 'the Artificial, the Civil, the Human, the Spiritual, and the Supernatural'. Thus Nature is the 'world of quantity, as against the world of quality', of 'objects against consciousness', of 'that which knows no value as against that which both has and perceives value', of 'efficient causes as against final causes'.

(2) When we understand a thing analytically and then dominate and use it for our own convenience we reduce it to the level of 'Nature' in the sense that we suspend our judgements of value about it. We are using 'Nature' in this sense when we *repress* elements in what would otherwise be our total reaction to it. This is what we do when we find it necessary, for instance, to cut up a dead man or a live animal in a dissecting room. The dead man and the live animal are objects which *resist* the movement of the mind whereby we 'thrust them into the world of mere Nature'.

A similar price is exacted for our analytical knowledge and manipulative power. For instance, we lose something when we cease to see trees as Dryads or as beautiful objects while we cut them into beams, and the stars lose their divinity when we think of them only as quantity, gases and the like. 'The great minds know very well that the object, so treated, is an artificial abstraction, that something of its reality has been lost.'

It is by reducing things to *mere Nature* that Man is able to conquer Nature. However, this wresting of powers *from* Nature is also the surrendering of things *to* Nature, and the final stage of surrender is reached when we reduce our own species – Man himself – to the level of a mere 'natural object'. Thus, 'the being who stood to gain and the being who has been sacrificed are one and the same.'

XV: From Science the Cure Might Come

People write 'as if Magic were a medieval survival and Science the new thing that came in to sweep it away.' Actually, the 'serious magical endeavour and the serious scientific endeavour are twins: one was sickly and died, the other strong and throve.' Magic and applied science are united by the fact that both are separated from the 'wisdom' of earliest ages:

> For the wise men of old the cardinal problem had been how to conform the soul to reality, and the solution had been knowledge, self-discipline and virtue. For magic and applied science alike the problem is how to subdue reality to the wishes of men.

A 'regenerate science' would explain things without explaining them away. 'When it spoke of the parts it would remember the whole. While studying the *It* it would not lose what Martin Buber calls the *Thou*-situation. The analogy between the *Tao* of Man and the instinct of an animal species would mean for it new light cast on the unknown thing, Instinct, by the inly known reality of conscience and not a reduction of conscience to the category of Instinct ... In a word, it would conquer Nature without being at the same time conquered by her and buy knowledge at a lower cost than that of life.'

The book ends with an Appendix of 'Illustrations of the *Tao*' which are collected from many cultures.

Reviews

One of the few letters Lewis saved was one Owen Barfield* wrote about the book on 22 January 1944: 'It is a real triumph. There may be a piece of contemporary writing in which precision of thought, liveliness of expression and depth of meaning unite with the same felicity, but I have not come across it.' Philip Leon said in *The Hibbert Journal* 42 (April 1944), pp. 280–2: 'Mr Lewis's is a finely philosophical mind which makes dialectic rings round unphilosophical and, indeed, mindless minds ... No summary can do justice to the fineness of Mr Lewis's thought.'

L.W. Grensted in *Theology*, XLVII (May 1944), pp. 117–8, said: 'He is really concerned with the vindication of the Natural Law, not as demonstrable but as absolute, standing in its own right ... If all our education is to be a system of "conditioning" and science holds out the hope that man can be wholly bent to any purpose that the "conditioners" require, what is to determine the Conditioners themselves? It is Karl Mannheim's problem over again. Mannheim found no solution. Mr Lewis shows, paradoxically and shrewdly enough, that the only end is the abolition of man.' W.G.L., reviewing it in *The Churchman*, LVIII (July–September 1944), p. 144, said: 'This is a most thought-provoking book, and deserves the attention and study of all those interested in the education of the young.'

One of those who seemed to understand the book best was Chad Walsh* who wrote in the *New York Herald Tribune Book Review* (13 April 1947), p. 5: 'This quiet little book is uniquely calculated to infuriate John Dewey's disciples and all other moralists who want to pick and choose from among the scraps of universal morality, who want to have their cake and eat it too. The final chapter will horrify the people who share Mr Lewis's views, for it presents an all-too-plausible picture of man's destiny after the concept of absolute values has gone out the window ... In 1947 we still believe our "realism" is directed toward some desirable goal. Unless humanity makes an abrupt about-face, it seems likely that our grandchildren will have no goals. They will love or hate, caress or kill, as irrational nature dictates, and no one will use the words "good" or "bad", "social" or "anti-social", or even "expedient" or "inexpedient".'

MIRACLES:
A PRELIMINARY STUDY (1947)

Background

I: An Early Interest in Miracles

On 26 November 1942 Lewis preached a sermon on *'Miracles'* at the Church of St Jude on the Hill, London, which opened with a statement of what he believed was the chief modern problem about miracles. He was later to use it almost word for word as the opening paragraph of this book. He said:

> I have known only one person in my life who claimed to have seen a ghost. It was a woman; and the interesting thing is that she disbelieved in the immortality of the soul before seeing the ghost and still disbelieves after having seen it. She thinks it was a hallucination. In other words, seeing is not believing. This is the first thing to get clear in talking about miracles. Whatever experiences we may have, we shall not regard them as miraculous if we already hold a philosophy which excludes the supernatural.

The traditional Christian view of miracles was stated by St Athanasius (c. 296–373) in the eighteenth section of his famous *De Incarnatione*. Lewis quotes that section in his sermon: 'Our Lord took a body like to ours and lived as a man in order that those who had refused to recognize Him in his superintendence and captaincy of the whole universe might come to recognize from the works He did here below in the body that what dwelled in this body was the Word of God.' And this, said Lewis, 'accords exactly with Christ's own account of His miracles: "The Son can do nothing of Himself, but what He seeth the Father do."' Following in the same tradition, St Thomas Aquinas (c. 1225–74) said 'those happenings are properly called miraculous which are done by divine agency outside the commonly observed order of things.'

By the time Lewis turned his mind to miracles most theologians had stopped believing in the same way as Athanasius and Aquinas. The belief in the improbability of miracles was mainly a result of the rise of modern science in the seventeenth and eighteenth centuries, which increasingly saw the world as a closed system subject to the laws of Nature. Lewis himself, in his atheist years, had learned much of his scepticism from David Hume's famous *Essay on Miracles* (1748) and the writings of philosophers such as G.W.F. Hegel who identified God with the Law of Nature. Lewis knew from the beginning that a defence of the miracles recorded in the New Testament would have to begin with a philosophical attack on unbelief. That explains why so large a part of his book was devoted to that.

That little sermon at St Jude's – a shorter version of which had appeared in *The Guardian*‡ on 2 October 1942 – was a miniature version of his book on *Miracles*. A few months later he followed it with a two-part essay on 'Dogma and the Universe' in *The Guardian* on 19 and 26 March 1943. 'It is a common reproach against Christianity,' he said, 'that its dogmas are unchanging, while human knowledge is in continual growth.' But he goes on to argue that 'the positive historical statements made by Christianity have the power, elsewhere found chiefly in formal principles, of receiving, without intrinsic change, the increasing complexity of meaning which increasing knowledge puts into them.'

II: Dorothy L. Sayers Offers Encouragement

On 13 May 1943 Dorothy L. Sayers* wrote to thank Lewis for *The Screwtape Letters*. In her light-hearted letter she complained about an atheist who was bothering her about various problems connected with Christianity, including Miracles. 'Anyhow,' she said –

there aren't any up-to-date books about Miracles. People have stopped arguing about them. Why? Has Physics sold the pass? Or is it merely that everybody is thinking in terms of Sociology and international Ethics? Please tell me what to do with this relic of the Darwinian age who is wasting my time, sapping my energies and destroying my soul.

This was exactly the encouragement Lewis needed, and when he wrote to Miss Sayers on 17 May he said, 'I'm starting a book on Miracles.' We next hear of it in a letter to Sister Penelope.* On 24 September 1943 he said, 'I've written about 6 chapters of the book on Miracles. Did I tell you that the attempt to write on the Supernatural has turned many chapters into sorts of hymns on Nature! One never knows what one's in for when one starts thinking.' In another letter of 5 October 1943, he reported that the 'MS on Miracles is still a long way from completion.'

A year later a brief version of the chapter entitled 'Horrid Red Things', on the difference between 'thought' and 'imagination', appeared in *The Church of England Newspaper* on 6 October 1944. A further chapter from the book on 'The Grand Miracle', the Incarnation, appeared in an abbreviated form in *The Guardian* of 27 April 1945. A month later – 28 May 1945 – Lewis was able to tell Sister Penelope 'The Miracle book is finished but will not come out till next year' (L). For some reason publication was delayed until May 1947.

Summary

Miracles is a closely-reasoned philosophical defence of the supernatural, and of the miracles of the Old and New Testaments in particular. Chapter I on 'The Scope of This Book' opens with the story of the woman who, after seeing a ghost, did not believe her eyes. 'If immediate experience cannot prove or disprove the miraculous, still less can history do so.' This is because history never provides the same sort of demonstrable evidence as we find in mathematics. Lewis's book is intended 'as a preliminary to historical inquiry' but he warns that 'Those who assume that miracles cannot happen are merely wasting their time by looking into the texts: we know in advance what results they will find for they have begun by begging the question.'

Chapter II, 'The Naturalist and the Supernaturalist', opens with the assertion that 'miracle' means 'an interference with Nature by supernatural power.' 'Some people believe that nothing exists except Nature; I call these people *Naturalists*. Others think that, besides Nature, there exists something else: I call them *Supernaturalists*.' There follows a careful attempt at defining what each believes. In brief, a Naturalist believes that 'Nature' is 'everything' or 'the whole show', 'that the ultimate Fact, the thing you can't go behind, is a vast process in space and time which is *going on of its own accord*. Inside that total system every particular event (such as your sitting reading this book) happens because some other event has happened; in the long run, because the Total Event is happening.' 'The Supernaturalist agrees with the Naturalist that there must be something which exists in its own right; some basic Fact whose existence it would be nonsensical to try to explain because this fact is itself the ground or starting point of all explanations. But he does not identify this Fact with "the whole show".'

In Chapter III, 'The Self-Contradiction of the Naturalist', Naturalism is defined as 'the doctrine that only Nature – the whole interlocked system – exists.' While 'older scientists' believed that 'the smallest particles of matter moved according to strict laws' some 'modern scientists' believe that the individual unit of matter 'moves in an indeterminate or random fashion'. If the latter are right in admitting that something 'outside' Nature exists, this 'something' could be called 'the Subnatural'. Does Nature also have a door opening on to the Supernatural? Everything we know, beyond our own immediate sensations, 'is inferred' from those sensations. When we are presented with colours, shapes, sounds, pleasures and pains we cannot 'perfectly predict or control', we infer that there must be something besides ourselves, and we infer that it 'must be systematic'.

The claim is made that 'All possible knowledge, then, depends on the validity of reasoning.' If the certainty we express by words like 'must be' and 'therefore' and 'since' is a real perception of how things outside our own minds really 'must be', we have admitted human reasoning. But if this certainty is 'merely a feeling *in* our own minds and not a genuine insight into realities beyond them', it only illustrates how our minds work. It follows that 'A theory which explained everything else in the whole universe but which made it impossible to believe that our thinking was valid, would be utterly out of court.'

We may, however, believe in the validity of thought under certain conditions. Consider these sentences: (1) 'He thinks that dog dangerous because he has often seen it muzzled and he has noticed that messengers always try to avoid going to that house.' (2) 'He thinks that dog dangerous because it is black and ever since he was bitten by a black dog in childhood he has always been afraid of black dogs.' We must conclude that while one explanation substantiates the validity of his thought the other discredits it. The difference is that the first man's 'belief is caused by something rational (by argument from observed facts)' while the other man's belief 'is caused by something irrational (association of ideas).'

We may 'state it as a rule that *no thought is valid if it can be fully explained as the result of irrational causes.*' Naturalism is a theory precisely of this sort.

It believes that the mind itself is 'simply the product of the Total System', that all thoughts whatever are the results of irrational causes. The simplest form of this argument is found in J.B.S. Haldane's *Possible Worlds*:

> If my mental processes are determined wholly by the motions of atoms in my brain, I have no reason to suppose that my beliefs are true ... and hence I have no reason for supposing my brain to be composed of atoms.

The Naturalist contradicts himself when he argues that all thoughts are the result of irrational causes *except* the thoughts which constitute the proof itself. You must assume that inference is valid before you begin an argument for its validity.

The Argument with Miss Anscombe over Chapter III

On 2 February 1948 Miss G.E.M. Anscombe,* a Research Fellow of Somerville College, Oxford, gave a paper to the Socratic Club‡ entitled 'A Reply to Mr C.S. Lewis's Argument That "Naturalism" Is Self-Refuting'. It was published in the *Socratic Digest*, No 4 [1948], and is reprinted in Vol. II of her Collected Philosophical Papers, *Metaphysics and the Philosophy of Mind* (1981). The crucial points of her argument will be found under her name in the **WHO'S WHO** section of this book. Lewis believed Miss Anscombe had misunderstood his argument, and he published a 'Reply' in the *Socratic Digest*, No 4 [1948]. He accepted, however, that he was unclear about a certain point and he revised Chapter III of *Miracles*, giving it the new title 'The Cardinal Difficulty of Naturalism', for the edition which Collins-Fontana (London) published in 1960, and Macmillan of New York in 1978.

The first six paragraphs of the revised chapter are exactly as in the original chapter, and the last five pages of the old chapter are replaced by ten pages of the new. Lewis began the new part by distinguishing between 'the Cause-Effect *because*' and the 'Ground-Consequent *because*', where before he had spoken of 'irrational causes'. The two senses of 'because' are illustrated. 'We can say, "Grandfather is ill today *because* he ate lobster yesterday." We can also say, "Grandfather must be ill today *because* he hasn't got up yet (and we know he is an invariably early riser when he is well)." In the first sentence *because* indicates the relation of Cause and Effect: The eating made him ill. In the second, it indicates the relation of what logicians call Ground and Consequent. The old man's late rising is not the cause of his disorder but the reason why we believe him to be disordered.'

'If what we think at the end of our reasoning is to be true,' he says, 'the correct answer to the question, "Why do you think this?" must begin with the Ground-Consequent *because*.' On the other hand, every event in Nature must be connected with previous events in the Cause-Effect relation. 'Unfortunately,' he says, 'the two systems are wholly distinct ... But even if grounds do exist, what exactly have they got to do with the actual occurrence of the belief as a psychological event?' The only possible answer seems to be that 'being a cause and being a proof ... coincide.' This, he says, is 'clearly untrue', and an explanation follows. In conclusion, 'Any thing which professes to explain our reasoning fully without introducing an act of knowing thus solely determined by what is known, is really a theory that there is no reasoning.'

In chapter IV, 'Nature and Supernature', the argument is made that a man's reason cannot be the source of his 'imperfect and intermittent' rationality, but that each human mind 'has its tap-root in an eternal, self-existent, rational being, whom we call God.' God is not a 'cosmic consciousness' growing out of Nature, nor independent of it, but the creator of Nature. In Chapter V, 'A Further Difficulty in Naturalism', Lewis argues that when we make moral judgements such as 'This is good' and 'This is evil' we are employing some power different from Reason. We 'just see' that there is no reason why our neighbour's happiness should be sacrificed to our own. The Naturalist attempts to explain why we make moral judgements by saying that the 'chemical conditions' which produce life cause us to make them, but he is unable to explain how we could be 'right' in doing so. In a world of Naturalists all moral judgements would be statements about the speaker's feelings, mistaken by him for statements about the moral quality of actions which he has already admitted does not exist. 'Do they remember while they ... tell us we "ought to make a better world" the words "ought" and "better" must, on their own showing, refer to an irrationally conditioned impulse which cannot be true or false any more than a vomit or a yawn?' In making moral judgements we must believe that the conscience is not a product of Nature.

In chapter VI, 'Answers to Misgivings', the author admits that Rational Thinking 'can be shown to be conditioned by its exercise by a natural object (the brain).' Thus, 'It is temporarily impaired by alcohol or a blow on the head. It wanes as the brain decays and vanishes when the brain ceases to function. In the same way the moral outlook of a community can be shown to be closely connected with its history, geographical environment, economic structure, and so forth.' Far from constituting a difficulty, this is exactly what we should expect. 'A man's Rational thinking is *just so much* of his share in eternal Reason as the state of his brain allows to become operative: it represents, so to speak, the bargain struck or the frontier fixed between Reason and Nature at that particular point. A nation's moral outlook is just so much of its share in eternal Moral Wisdom as its history, economics, etc., lets through.' The second misgiving is that an argument for the Supernatural should be needed at all. 'If so stupendous a thing exists, ought it not to be obvious as the sun in the sky?' The next thing to be considered is whether Supernature ever produces 'particular results in space and time *except* through the instrumentality of human brains acting on human nerves and muscles.'

Chapter VII, 'A Chapter of Red Herrings', considers two 'red herrings' about Miracles. (1) Miracles can't happen because the 'laws of Nature' exclude them. They are regarded as a 'scientific impossibility'. But a miracle is, by definition, an 'exception' to the laws of Nature. Those who believe in them do not deny that the 'laws' exist, only that they can be suspended. The idea that miracles are a 'scientific impossibility' is bound up with the notion that the early Christians didn't know the laws of Nature. This is not at all what you find in the New Testament. When Joseph discovered that his fiancée was going to have a baby he decided to repudiate her. He knew as well as a modern gynaecologist that in the ordinary course of nature women don't have babies unless they have lain with men.

(2) There is also the notion that people believed in miracles 'in olden times' because they thought the Earth was the largest thing in the universe and Man the most important creature. The immensity of the universe is not a recent discovery. In the second century AD Ptolemy taught that in relation to the distance of the fixed stars the whole Earth must be regarded as a point with no magnitude. A more important question is why the spatial insignificance of the Earth has in modern times been set up as a stock argument against Christianity. (a) 'If the universe is teeming with life other than ours, then this, we are told, makes it quite ridiculous to believe that God could be so concerned with the human race as to "come down from Heaven" and be made man for its redemption.' (b) 'If, on the other hand, our planet is really unique in harbouring organic life, then this is thought to prove that life is only an accidental bye-product in the universe and so again we disprove our religion.'

By the time he wrote this chapter Lewis had published his science fiction novels and had thought carefully what effect, if any, the presence of rational creatures on other planets would have on our redemption. He said we must first know (1) whether there are rational creatures on other bodies in space; (2) whether they are in need of redemption; (3) whether their redemption would take the same mode as ours; (4) and whether redemption has been withheld from them. He goes on to counter the belief that the *size* of a world or a creature would somehow affect its value. Earlier, in **OSP** 18, the Oyarsa told Ransom that his people were told never to speak of size or numbers to human beings because 'it makes you do reverence to nothings and pass by what is really great.' Nevertheless, Lewis repeats in this chapter what he had said earlier in **Dogma and the Universe** about the effect of size on the human imagination. 'If the vastness of Nature ever threatens to overcrowd our spirits we must remember that it is only Nature spiritualized by human imagination which does so.' Ancient and medieval men were awed by the brightness of the planets, but modern men by bigness. 'Taken as a serious philosophical argument both are ridiculous.'

Chapter VIII, 'Miracles and the Laws of Nature', begins with a consideration of three concepts of the 'Laws' of Nature: (1) That they are brute facts with no discoverable rhyme or reason about them; (2) That they are applications of the law of averages; (3) That the fundamental laws of Physics are really 'necessary truths' like the truths of mathematics. But these 'laws' do not cause events: they state the pattern to which every event must conform. The laws of Nature leave out precisely what makes up 'true history'. 'To think the laws can produce it is like thinking that you can create real money by simply doing sums.'

We come now to Lewis's definition of a miracle. It is inaccurate to define a miracle as something that 'breaks the laws of Nature'. 'If I knock out my pipe I alter the position of a great many atoms: in the long run, and to an infinitesimal degree, of all the atoms there are. Nature digests or assimilates this event with perfect ease and harmonizes it in a twinkling with all other events ... If God creates a miraculous spermatozoon in the body of a virgin, it does not proceed to break any laws. The laws at once take it over. Nature is ready. Pregnancy follows, according to all the normal laws, and nine months later a child is born.' Whenever an event 'invades' her, Nature 'will rush to the point where she is invaded ... and there hasten to accommodate the newcomer.' Thus, 'the divine art of miracle is not an art of suspending the pattern to which events conform but of feeding new events into that pattern.'

In chapter IX, 'A Chapter Not Strictly Necessary', Lewis says he was held back from accepting Supernaturalism because of a repugnance to the view that Nature was created by God, and could be altered by Him. He preferred a Nature that was simply 'there'. The reason for this is that for the Naturalist, 'Nature' is 'everything'. 'And Everything is not a subject

about which anything very interesting can be said or (save by illusion) felt
... But everything becomes different when we recognize that Nature is a
creature, a created thing, with its own particular tang or flavour. There is
no need any longer to select and slur.'

Chapter X, 'Horrid Red Things', is a defence of metaphorical language
in the New Testament. It begins with modern objections to statements of
Christian doctrine which seem to give a 'savage' and 'primitive' picture of
the universe such as a local 'Heaven', a flat earth, and a God who can
have children. Still, even when you scrape Christianity clear of in-
essentials, the 'core' of it remains 'entirely miraculous and supernatural'. Lewis gives three examples of metaphorical thinking. (1) When
he thinks about London he sees a mental picture of Euston Station.
'Though I have the image while I am thinking about London, what I think
or say is not *about* that image, and would be manifest nonsense if it were.'
To think is one thing, and to imagine is another. (2) A child knew that if
you ate too many aspirin tablets they would kill you, but imagined this
was because they contained a red-coloured poison or 'Horrid Red
Things'. Thus, 'thinking may be sound in certain respects where it is
accompanied not only by false images but by false images mistaken for
true ones.' (3) When a man says he 'grasps' an argument he is not
thinking he can seize it like a gun. If he tries to be clearer by saying 'I see
your point' he does not mean that a pointed object has appeared before
him. If we are going to talk at all about things which are not perceived by
the senses, we are forced to use language metaphorically.

We are given three guiding principles: (1) thought is distinct from the
imagination which accompanies it; (2) thought may be sound even when
the false images that accompany it are mistaken for true ones; (3) anyone
who talks about things that cannot be seen, or touched, or heard, or the
like, must inevitably talk as *if they could be* seen or touched or heard. The
early Christians did not raise questions about 'primitive' and 'naïve'
language because they were not trying to satisfy speculative curiosity.
Once they recognized the need for philosophical definiteness 'Christianity decides quite clearly that the naïve images are false.' The Christian
doctrines 'have always been statements about spiritual reality, not
specimens of primitive physical science.'

In chapter XI, 'Christianity and "Religion"', Lewis says Christians find
themselves opposed 'not to the irreligion of our hearers but by their real
religion.' 'Speak about beauty, truth and goodness, or about a God who is
simply the indwelling principle of these three ... and you will command
friendly interest. But the temperature drops as soon as you mention a God
who has purposes and performs particular actions, who does one thing

and not another, a concrete, choosing, commanding, prohibiting God with a determinate character.' The popular 'religion', which is none other than Pantheism, excludes miracles because it excludes the 'living God' of Christianity.

The difference between the two is often misunderstood by those who compare an adult knowledge of Pantheism with a knowledge of Christianity acquired in childhood. To Pantheists God is everywhere because their minds are dominated by the picture of a gas, or fluid, or space itself. Christians, on the other hand, must always appear to deal in negatives because they deal with facts. As statements about God are either true or false, they must affirm some and deny others. In accepting God as He shows Himself to be we accept a God who performs miracles. But man's taproot in Pantheism goes very deep. This is because his God 'is there if you wish for him, like a book on a shelf.' 'But God Himself, alive, pulling at the other end of the cord, perhaps approaching at an infinite speed, the hunter, king, husband – that is quite another matter. There comes a moment when the children who have been playing at burglars hush suddenly: was that a *real* footstep in the hall? There comes a moment when people who have been dabbling in religion ("Man's search for God"!) suddenly draw back. Suppose we really found Him? We never meant it to come to *that*! Worse still, supposing He had found us?'

In chapter XII, 'The Propriety of Miracles', the question is asked, not if God can work miracles, but '*Would* He?' To many, miracles seem an interruption to 'the steady development of Nature'. To a stupid schoolboy the abnormal hexameters in Virgil and the half-rhymes in English poets are due to incompetence. In reality, they break the superficial regularity of the metre in obedience to a higher and subtler law. 'The extent to which one can distinguish a just "licence" from a mere botch or failure of unity depends on the extent to which one has grasped the real and inward significance of the work as a whole.' If miracles occur we may be sure that *not* to have wrought them would be the real inconsistency.

Chapter XIII, 'On Probability', opens with a discussion of David Hume's *Essay on Miracles* in which 'probability rests on what may be called the majority vote of our past experiences. The more often a thing has been known to happen, the more probable it is that it should happen again; and the less often the less probable.' Probabilities of the kind that Hume concerns himself with hold 'inside the framework of an assumed Uniformity of Nature'. If we hold to this kind of probability we get a complete deadlock because the only kind Hume allows holds exclusively 'within the frame of uniformity'. When, however, uniformity itself is in question, this kind of probability is suspended. We should judge the probability of miracles by our 'innate sense of the fitness of things'.

With chapter XIV, 'The Grand Miracle', we reach the heart of the book. It is carefully laid out. (1) The 'Grand Miracle' is the Incarnation, the fact of God becoming Man. 'Every other miracle prepares for this, or exhibits this, or results from this. Just as every natural event is the manifestation at a particular place and moment of Nature's total character, so every particular Christian miracle manifests at a particular place and moment the character and significance of the Incarnation.' (2) The Incarnation has happened only once and so is, by Hume's standards, infinitely 'improbable'. But, then, 'the whole history of the Earth has also happened once.' (3) The 'fitness' of the Incarnation is illustrated by an analogy. We are to imagine that we possess parts of a novel or a symphony. If someone offers us what he claims is the 'missing part of the work' our business would be to fit it into the whole and find out if it illuminates all the parts and can be seen to 'pull them together'. It is far less important that the doctrine of the Incarnation be fully comprehensible than that 'it illuminate and integrate the whole mass'.

(4) What is actually *meant* by 'God becoming Man'? We get some idea of 'the Supernatural descending into the Natural' by our own experience as a rational animal. We cannot conceive how the Divine Spirit dwelled within the human spirit of Jesus, but neither can we conceive how the human spirit of any man dwells in a natural organism. The Incarnation is compared to a diver who goes down 'into the death-like region of ooze and slime and old decay; then up again, back to colour and light, his lungs almost bursting, till suddenly he breaks surface again, holding in his hand the dripping, precious thing that he went down to recover.' This is a repetition of a familiar pattern, in vegetable as well as animal life. 'There is descent from the full and perfect organisms into the spermatozoon and ovum, and in the dark womb a life at first inferior in kind to that of the species which is being reproduced: then the slow ascent to the perfect embryo, to the living, conscious baby, and finally to the adult.'

(5) In asking if this doctrine is not 'fitting in too well', Lewis introduces a theme which played a large part in his conversion. There have been many religions in which the annual drama was not only that of the annual corn crop, but that of a 'corn-king' – Adonis, Osiris, and others – who died and rose again the following year. In the case of Christianity this is *'actually true'* of a Man who was executed under a Roman magistrate in a known year, and who before His death took bread (corn) in his hands and said 'This is my body.' In this instance it happened to a people, the Jews, in which there was no trace of Nature-religion. The 'double character' of

Jahweh is this. He is the God of Nature, 'Bacchus, Venus, Ceres all rolled into one'; but He is not a Nature-God who dies and comes to life every year as a true Corn-king. 'He is not a nature-God, but the God of Nature – her inventor, maker, owner, and controller.'

(6) To the modern mind, Democratic in birth and education, the idea of a 'chosen race' is repulsive. We should prefer to think that all nations and individuals start level in the search for God, but when we look into the Selectiveness which the Christians attribute to God we find none of the 'favouritism' we were afraid of. 'The "chosen" people are chosen not for their own sake ... but for the sake of the unchosen ... That nation has been chosen to bear a heavy burden. Their sufferings are great: but, as Isaiah recognized, their sufferings heal others.' (7) Most religions, when brought face to face with the facts of Nature, either give Nature a 'transcendent prestige' or promise a release from her. Christianity does neither. Anyone approaching it with the idea that 'because Jahweh is the God of fertility our lasciviousness is going to be authorized ... he will be stunned and repelled by the inflexible Christian demand for chastity, humility, mercy and justice.' On the other hand, if we come to it regarding the death which precedes every re-birth as the 'mere odious necessity of an evil cosmos' from which we hope to be delivered we shall be equally disappointed. We are told, instead, of the need for self-surrender and the willing sacrifice of self to others.

(8) In *Perelandra* Lewis raised the question of whether or not the Fall of Man could justly be called the *felix peccatum Adae* – the 'fortunate sin of Adam'. He makes it clear here that more was *gained* by the Fall than lost. 'Redeemed humanity is to be something more glorious than unfallen humanity would have been, more glorious than any unfallen race now is ... The greater the sin, the greater the mercy: the deeper the death, the brighter the re-birth. And this super-added glory will, with true vicariousness, exalt all creatures and those who have never fallen will thus bless Adam's fall.'

(9) The Christian doctrine of Death adopts neither the view that Death 'doesn't matter' nor that it is the greatest of all evils. Man was originally immune to it, and when he is called into a new life he will be immune to it again. This doctrine would be nonsensical if man were nothing more than a natural organism. (10) Man is a 'composite being – a natural organism tenanted by, or in a state of *symbiosis* with, a supernatural spirit.' The supernatural spirit and the natural organism in Man have 'quarrelled' but their quarrel is not one of 'mutual destruction'. If Nature is allowed to dominate she wrecks spiritual activities, but Spirit confirms

and improves natural activities. 'The brain,' for instance, 'does not become less a brain by being used for rational thought.'

(11) Death is the 'means of redemption from sin', the very means whereby sin is defeated. How is this so? Satan persuaded Man to rebel against God, and in so doing Man lost control of the 'rebellion' between the organic and the spiritual. Satan thus produced human death. In creating Man, God gave him such a constitution that if the highest part rebelled against God, Man would lose control over the lower part as well. God provided this 'safety device' because 'once Man has fallen, natural immortality would be the one utterly hopeless destiny for him.' He could, for instance, except for this 'safety device', 'progress from being merely a fallen man to being a fiend, possibly beyond all modes of redemption.' To convert this 'penal code' into a means of 'eternal life' it is necessary that Humanity 'embrace death freely ... drink it to the dregs.' Only one who was perfectly a Man could perform this 'perfect dying', and the 'volunteer' for this is Christ. Thus it is that the miracle of the Incarnation, far from denying what we already know of reality, 'writes the comment which makes that crabbed text plain: or rather, proves itself to be the text on which Nature was only the commentary. In science we have been reading only the notes to a poem; in Christianity we find the poem itself.'

In chapter XV, 'Miracles of the Old Creation', the miracles of Christ are classified in two ways. The first system yields the classes: (1) Miracles of Fertility; (2) Miracles of Healing; (3) Miracles of Destruction; (4) Miracles of Dominion over the Inorganic; (5) Miracles of Reversal; (6) Miracles of Perfecting or Glorification. The second system yields two classes: (1) Miracles of the Old Creation; and (2) Miracles of the New Creation. In all of them 'the incarnate God does suddenly and locally something that God has done or will do in general.' Miracles 'do close and small and, as it were, in focus what God at other times does so large that men do not attend to it.'

Miracles of the Old Creation are those in which we see 'the Divine Man focusing for us what the God of Nature has already done on a larger scale.' The earliest Miracle of *Fertility* was the conversion of water into wine at the wedding feast in Cana. 'Every year, as part of the Natural order, God makes wine. He does so by creating a vegetable organism that can turn water, soil, and sunlight into a juice which will, under proper conditions, become wine ... Once, and in one year only, God, now incarnate, short-circuits the process: makes wine in a moment.' In the Miracles of *Healing* 'The Power that always was behind all healings puts on a face and hands.' The single Miracle of *Destruction* is the withering of the fig tree and is 'an acted parable, a symbol of God's sentence on all that is "fruitless".'

Chapter XVI, 'Miracles of the New Creation', opens with the statement that from the time of the Apostles 'to preach Christianity meant primarily to preach the Resurrection.' The 'Resurrection' to which they bore witness was 'not the action of rising from the dead but the state of having risen.' This 'Termination of the period is important, for ... there is no possibility of isolating the doctrine of the Resurrection from that of the Ascension.'

Although the Resurrection is often regarded today as evidence of 'survival', it did not mean that to the New Testament writers. To them the Risen Lord is the 'pioneer of life' who has 'forced open a door that has been locked since the death of the first man. He has met, fought, and beaten the King of Death.' We expect them to tell of a risen life which is 'purely "spiritual" in the negative sense of that word.' But Jesus has constantly to assure the disciples that he is not a 'ghost'. He asserts that he is corporeal and eats broiled fish. At the same time, His risen body is like, and yet unlike, the body His friends knew before the execution.

On the Ascension, the gospel writers say that the Ascended Lord 'was caught into the sky and sat down at the right hand of God', and that 'He was lifted up and a cloud cut Him off from their sight.' We cannot get rid of these 'embarrassing passages' by dropping the story because 'an objective entity must go somewhere – something must happen to it.' The records represent Christ as passing after death neither into a purely 'spiritual' mode of existence nor into a 'natural' life such as we know, but 'into a life which has its own, new Nature.' It is the picture of a new human nature: not a picture of 'unmaking but of remaking.' 'The old field of space, time, matter and the senses is to be weeded, dug, and sown for a new crop. We may be tired of that old field: God is not.'

We go on to consider the 'miracles of the New Creation', which 'anticipate' the Resurrection. (1) In the Walking on the Water 'we see the relations of Spirit and Nature so altered that Nature can be made to do whatever Spirit pleases.' (2) The Raising of Lazarus differs from the Resurrection of Christ because Lazarus 'was not raised to a new and more glorious mode of existence but merely restored to the sort of life he had had before.' (3) The Transfiguration of Jesus is also 'an anticipatory glimpse of something to come.' The New Nature is interlocked at some points with the Old and because of this interlocking 'some facts about it come through into our present experience in all their literal facthood.'

This New Nature, which is 'supernatural' in relation to the world of our five senses, but 'natural' from its own point of view, is shocking to a certain philosophical preconception. This New Nature is compared to a skyscraper with several floors. We are prepared for the sort of 'one floor' reality Naturalists believe in, and we are prepared for a 'ground floor' reality as 'religion' conceives it, but we are not prepared for anything in between. 'We feel quite sure that the first step beyond the world of our present experience must lead either nowhere at all or else into the blinding abyss of undifferentiated spirituality.'

Reviews

C.E. Raven writing in *The Spectator*, 178 (16 May 1947), p. 566 said: 'Probably none of his books so clearly reveals his own religious outlook or gives him so congenial a scope. There are in it passages of great beauty like the description of the Incarnation and of fine insights like the affirmation of the basic actuality of God: there are also passages in which he almost reminds us of the gaiety and vigour of G.K. Chesterton.' A.C. Supholme said in *Theology*, L (October 1947), pp. 395–7: 'One of Pascal's contemporaries quaintly says that the author of the Provincial Letters vexed the Jesuits by writing theology which even women could read. Dr Lewis performs a similar service for English theology. He makes it readable. The rather rare combination of the gifts of poet, philosopher and theologian is quite irresistible.'

G.C. Atkins in *Christian Century*, 64 (3 December 1947), p. 1486, said: 'The arresting quality of the book is not so much in the line of argument ... as in the author's way of doing it. In an unusual way, the style is the book, and the style is beyond characterization in the space here permitted. Epigram, paradox, bravura, analogies and audacities – a *tour de force* of the *joie d'écrire*.'

REFLECTIONS ON
THE PSALMS (1958)

Background

I: The Psalter

The practice of saying prayers at fixed hours of the day or night was general among the Jews, and it is from them that the primitive Church took it over. By the Middle Ages priests and religious were required to say what is called the 'Divine Office'. This includes the 'Night Office' (or 'Matins'), and the 'Day Offices' – Lauds, Prime, Terce, Sext, None, Vespers and Compline. These eight 'hours' are principally made up of the Scriptures, the Psalms and prayers. Over time the Offices were revised so that they could be fitted into the actual hours of people's daily lives. For instance, in the Divine Office of the Catholic Church the 150 Psalms which make up the Psalter are recited every month – but not in the order in which they appear in the Bible. All priests are required to do this, but many laymen recite the Divine Office as well.

At the Reformation the place of the eight Offices was taken in the Anglican Church by the two offices of Morning and Evening Prayer, both of which are found in the *Book of Common Prayer*.‡ Morning Prayer derives from the Office of Matins and Lauds, while Evening Prayer or Evensong is derived from the Office of Vespers and Compline. Each includes prayers, Scripture and the Psalms. All Anglican clergymen recite the Psalter every month, and many laymen do this as well. As in the Divine Office, the Prayer Book chooses particular psalms for special days such as Christmas and Easter.

II: Lewis's Use of the Psalter

In **SBJ** XV Lewis said, 'As soon as I became a Theist I started attending my parish church on Sundays and my college chapel on weekdays.'

Adam Fox,* the Dean of Magdalen College‡ for many years, wrote in 'At the Breakfast Table' (**ABT**) of Lewis's regular attendance at the College Chapel. And Richard Ladborough* mentions in his 'In Cambridge' (**ABT**) that 'the chapel was the centre of his life in college. He daily attended weekday Matins at 8 o'clock.' By a constant reading of the Psalter, Lewis came to know the Psalms almost by heart. Sometimes he read the Bible on its own, but it was through the continuous reading and praying of Morning and Evening Prayer that he came to know the Bible and the Psalms so well.

The Psalms were written in Hebrew, but as Lewis was not a Hebraist he used the translation of the Psalms found in the Book of Common Prayer. It was the work of Miles Coverdale (1488–1568) who produced the first complete English Bible. There is a good deal about Coverdale as a translator in *English Literature in the Sixteenth Century*. Coverdale, Lewis pointed out in the Introduction to *Reflections on the Psalms*, is 'by no means the most accurate' of translators, but 'in beauty, in poetry, he, and St Jerome, the great Latin translator, are beyond all whom I know.'

The book was written during the autumn of 1957 and it was published in September 1958. The next month Lewis was invited by the Archbishop of Canterbury to become a member of the 'Commission to Revise the Psalter' whose purpose was 'To produce for the consideration of the Convocations a revision of the text of the Psalter designed to remove obscurities and serious errors of translation yet such as to retain, as far as possible, the general character in style and rhythm of Coverdale's version and its suitability for congregational use.' Lewis accepted and for information on his work with the Commission see the **LIFE** XXXI ff.

Summary

In the Introductory chapter Lewis explains that his book is 'not a work of scholarship'. He is writing 'as one amateur to another, talking about difficulties I have met, or light I have gained, when reading the Psalms, with the hope that this might at any rate interest, and sometimes even help, other inexpert readers.' 'I am,' he says, '"comparing notes", not presuming to instruct.' (1) We must first note that the Psalms are 'not sermons', but poems written by many poets at many different dates, which were meant to be sung.

Another characteristic of them is (2) Parallelism. This is the practice of saying the same thing twice in different words, an example of which is 'He that dwelleth in heaven shall laugh them to scorn: the Lord shall have them in derision' (2:4). Our Lord, who was soaked in the poetic tradition of his country, used parallelism often. As, for instance, when He said 'For with what judgement ye judge, ye shall be judged, and with what measure ye mete, it shall be measured to you again' (Matthew 7:2).

Chapter II introduces the theme of 'Judgement in the Psalms'. If there is any thought at which a Christian trembles it is certainly at the thought of God's 'judgement'. And this note of judgement, Lewis reminds us, goes back to the teaching of Our Lord Himself, especially in the terrible parable of the Sheep and Goats. Judgement in the Psalms is found to be 'an occasion of universal rejoicing' as in 35:24 where the Psalmist says 'Judge me, O Lord my God, according to Thy righteousness.' The reason for this is that to the ancient Jews, God's judgement was thought of in terms of an earthly court of justice. The difference between the Christian and the ancient Jew is that, whereas the Christian sees himself tried in a criminal case, the Jew pictures a civil case with himself as the plaintiff.

While it is true that the Christian picture of God's judgement is 'far more profound and far safer for our souls than the Jewish', the Jewish concept 'supplements the Christian picture in one important way.' The alarming thing about the Christian picture is the infinite purity of the standard against which our actions will be judged: we are all in the same boat. On the other hand, the Jewish picture of a civil action reminds us that 'perhaps we are faulty not only by the Divine standard ... but also by a very human standard which all reasonable people admit and which we ourselves usually wish to enforce upon others.' We should beware of a tyrannous 'sensitivity'.

In chapter III, 'The Cursings', Lewis admits that 'the spirit of hatred' we find in some of the Psalms 'strikes us in the face ... like the heat from a furnace mouth.' Others cease to be frightful only by becoming, to the modern mind, 'almost comic' in their naïvety. Some of the worst of the cursings are found in Psalm 109. One way of dealing with these Psalms is to 'leave them alone'. But this is not easily done because the bad parts are often 'intertwined with the exquisite things'. We must remember that if 'all Holy Scripture is "written for our learning" or that the age-old use of the Psalms in Christian worship was not entirely contrary to the will of God, and if we remember that Our Lord's mind and language were clearly steeped in the Psalter, we shall prefer, if possible, to make some use of them.' What use?

(1) We see in the Psalms hatred in its 'wild' or 'natural' condition. Although we, unlike the ancient Jews, do not live in a world of so much massacre and violence and blood sacrifice, another difference between us is that we are 'far more subtle than they in disguising our ill will from others and from ourselves.' For all our attempts to hide our real feelings,

we are, nevertheless, 'blood brothers to these ferocious, self-pitying, barbaric men.' (2) Another use of these Psalms is in seeing 'hatred undisguised'. Those we hurt may succeed in resisting the temptation to hate, but the question is 'How do I, who provoked that hatred, stand?'

(3) It is tempting to excuse the cursings on the grounds that the Jews were not Christians and so 'knew no better'. This defence does not go far because Judaism contained the 'corrective' to this natural reaction to cruelty. Among other passages in the Old Testament, we come across in Leviticus (19:17, 18) 'Thou shalt not hate thy brother in thine heart ... thou shalt not avenge or bear any grudge against the children of thy people, but thou shalt love thy neighbour as thyself.' The more one looks into these passages, the more one sees 'what a tissue of quotations from it the New Testament is, how constantly Our Lord repeated, reinforced, continued, refined, and sublimated, the Judaic ethics, how seldom He introduced a novelty.' (4) If you compare the Psalms with Pagan literature, one's first impression is that 'the Jews were much more vindictive and vitriolic than the Pagans.'

Chapter IV, 'Death in the Psalms', opens with several examples of how Christians have read into the Psalms and other parts of the Old Testament a belief in the afterlife which did not exist. In most parts of the Old Testament there is little or no belief in a future life. They believed that the dead went into 'Sheol', the state for the good and the bad alike. To the ancient Jews, the dead were simply dead. By Our Lord's time, however, Judaism had changed in this respect. How this new belief crept in we are not told. Lewis admits that he is 'more concerned to try to understand the absence of such a belief, in the midst of intense religious feeling, over the earlier period.'

It is possible for men to be too much concerned with their eternal destiny, and it seems clear that God did not want the Chosen People to follow the example of the Egyptians whose main business in life was the attempt to secure the well-being of the dead. Happiness or misery beyond death, simple in themselves, 'are not even religious subjects at all.'

Chapter V, on '"The Fair Beauty of the Lord"', is about that 'delight in God which made David dance.' This delight is centred on the Temple, and 'We get nearest to their state of mind if we think of a pious modern farm labourer at church on Christmas Day or at the harvest thanksgiving.' For both the farm labourer and the ancient Jew all these things are one in his mind. The ancient Jew 'had never heard of music, or festivity, or agriculture as things separate from religion, nor of religion as something separate from them. Life was one.' But when the mind becomes more capable of abstraction it becomes possible to distinguish the rite from the vision of God. If the rite becomes a 'substitute' for, and a 'rival' to God Himself, 'it may take on a rebellious, cancerous life of its own.'

A parallel situation occurred at some time in Judaism. The unity fell apart: the sacrificial rites became distinguishable from the meetings with God, and this is what is referred to in Psalm 50 where God tells His people that all this Temple worship, considered in itself, 'is not the real point at all.' God does not need to be fed with roast meat: 'If I were hungry,' he says in 50:12, 'do you think I would apply to *you*?' Even so, it is the 'joy and delight in God which meets us in the Psalms' that is 'the living centre of Judaism.'

In chapter VI, '"Sweeter than Honey"', Lewis discusses a characteristic of the Psalms which he found 'bewildering' at first. It is the Psalmist's praise for the *Laws* of God, that is, the Ten Commandments and all the whole complex legislation contained in Leviticus, Numbers and Deuteronomy. One of many examples is 'More to be desired are they than gold, yea than much fine gold: sweeter also than honey and the honeycomb' (19:10). How could all these 'Laws', 'statutes', 'commandments' be regarded as *sweet*? Scholars believe that what the Psalmist meant by 'delighting in the Law' is not obeying it – though he could mean that too – but 'studying' it. It is 'very like what one of us would mean if he said that somebody "loved" history, or physics, or archaeology.' However, when even righteousness 'shrinks into insignificance' under the 'vast overgrowth' of the Jewish Law, it can 'take on a cancerous life of its own and work against the thing for whose sake it existed.' It is about *this* abuse that Our Lord uttered some of His sternest words against the scribes and Pharisees.

Next we meet a theological controversy raised often in Lewis's writings. 'There were,' he said, 'in the eighteenth century terrible theologians who held that "God did not command certain things because they are right, but certain things are right because God commanded them." To make the position perfectly clear, one of them even said that though God has, as it happens, commanded us to love Him and one another, He might equally well have commanded us to hate Him and one another, and hatred would then have been right.' (see **Natural Law**§ V: 'The Euthyphro Dilemma'). The answer is that the Jews never discussed this in abstract and philosophical terms, but at once assumed the right view: 'They know that the Lord (not merely obedience to the Lord) is "righteousness" and commands "righteousness" because He loves it (11:8). He enjoins what is good because it is good, because He is good.'

In chapter VII, 'Connivance', we are told that many Psalms speak not only of the evil we do ourselves but God's blame for those who have 'dwelled with' or been on intimate terms with those who are 'vain'. Thus we find in Psalm 119 the question 'Don't I hate those who hate thee, Lord? ... Why, I hate them as if they were *my* enemies!' The several pages he spends on this are worth a careful study. (1) What should be our conduct towards those in high public position, whether newspaper editors, politicians or celebrities, who lie and behave abominably? Lewis laments that there seems 'no medium between hopeless submission and full-dress revolution' to this evil. (2) 'How ought we to behave in the presence of very bad people?' Our primary example must be Christ Himself in his relation to the Samaritan woman at the well, the woman taken in adultery, and His own dining with publicans. A Christian should 'avoid, where he decently can, any meeting with people who are bullies, lascivious, cruel, dishonest, spiteful and so forth.' Not because we are 'too good' for them, but because we are not good enough. Our temptation, like that of the Psalmist, would be to 'condone' or 'connive' or 'consent' to such evil, and the best thing is to avoid such company. When it is unavoidable, we can always resort to silence.

In chapter VIII on 'Nature', we begin with the two factors which determine the Psalmists' approach to Nature. (1) The ancient Jews were chiefly a nation of peasants. Where towns were few, no one was aware of what we call 'the country', nor was there anything we would recognize as 'nature poetry'. On the other hand, what they give us 'far more sensuously and delightedly' than anything even in Greek, is 'the very feel of weather ... enjoyed almost as a vegetable might be supposed to enjoy it.'

(2) The ancient Jew believed in one God, maker of heaven and earth, and so for him Nature and God were distinct. This relation may be for us a platitude, but Creation, in any unambiguous sense, seems to have been a rare doctrine in Paganism, and where it does occur it is often religiously unimportant. The exception is Plato in whom we find 'a clear Theology of Creation in the Judaic and Christian sense'. What makes the belief 'peculiar' in Jewish thought is that 'To say that God created Nature, while it brings God and Nature into relation, also separates them. What makes and what is made must be two, not one.'

Thus the doctrine of Creation (a) 'empties Nature of divinity'. We find an example of this in Job 31:26–28 where, conscious of an utterly spontaneous impulse to pay some reverence to the sun or moon, he knows it would have been iniquity: 'If I beheld the sun when it shined, or the moon walking in brightness; and my heart hath been secretly enticed, or my mouth kissed my hand; this also would be an iniquity.' And (b) the same doctrine makes Nature 'an index', a symbol, a manifestation, of the

Divine.' Yet another result of the doctrine is (c) 'to see Nature not as a mere datum but as an achievement.' 'All His works are *faithful* – He spake and it was done, He commanded and it stood fast' (33:4, 9).

In chapter IX, 'A Word About Praising', Lewis admits that at one time he found a stumbling block in the demand 'so clamorously made by all religious people that we should "praise" God; still more in the suggestion that God Himself demanded it.' (1) This demand does not sound ludicrous when we think of what it means to feel 'admiration' for a picture. A picture 'deserves' or 'demands' admiration when that is 'the correct, adequate or appropriate response to it.' God not only 'demands' praise 'as the supremely beautiful and all-satisfying Object' but also 'as lawgiver.' (2) Another reason for praising God is that, as we find in a world which 'rings with praise' of various things, 'praise almost seems to be inner health made audible.' Thus, 'praise not merely expresses but completes the enjoyment; it is its appointed consummation.'

Chapter X, on 'Second Meanings', begins by pointing out that Christians have believed the Psalms 'to contain a second or hidden meaning, an "allegorical" sense, concerned with the central truth of Christianity, with the Incarnation, the Passion, the Resurrection, the Ascension, and with the Redemption of man.' What are we to make of it? There are many illustrations of what appears prophetic knowledge about Christ in classical literature. In the *Republic* (II, 361) Plato imagines a 'just man' who 'is bound, scourged, and finally impaled.' Is this a lucky coincidence? The answer is that if Plato, starting from one example and from his insight into the nature of goodness and the nature of the world, was led on to see the possibility of a perfect example, and thus to depict something extremely like the Passion of Christ, 'this happened not because he was lucky but because he was wise.'

But what 'are we to say of those gods in various pagan mythologies who are killed and rise again and who thereby renew or transform the life of their worshippers or of nature'? Such Pagan Christs§ were a favourite theme with Lewis. 'It is not accidental,' he says. 'In the sequence of night and day, in the annual death and rebirth of the crops, in the myths which these processes give rise to, in the strong, if half-articulate, feeling ... there is already a likeness permitted by God to that truth on which all depends.'

Chapter XI, on 'Scripture', will interest those who want Lewis's own views on Scripture. He makes the following points: (1) He has been suspected of being a Fundamentalist because he has never regarded 'any narrative as unhistorical simply on the ground that it includes the miraculous.' 'I have to decide on quite other grounds,' he answers, 'whether a given narrative is historical or not.' His main reason for supposing the Book of Job to be unhistorical is because 'the author quite obviously writes as a story-teller not as a chronicler.' (2) He has no difficulty in accepting the view of those scholars who 'tell us that the account of Creation in Genesis is derived from earlier Semitic stories which were Pagan and mythical.' This is because 'no good work is done anywhere without aid from the Father of Lights' and thus, 'When a series of such re-tellings turns a creation story which at first had almost no religious or metaphysical significance into a story which achieves the idea of true Creation and of a transcendent Creator ... nothing will make me believe that some of the re-tellers, or some one of them, has not been guided by God.' (3) The total result is that the Bible is not 'the Word of God' in the sense that every passage, in itself, gives impeccable science or history. 'It carries the Word of God; and we ... receive that word from it not by using it as an encyclopedia or an encyclical but by steeping ourselves in its tone or temper and so learning its overall message.' (4) There is 'no imperfection' in the teaching of Our Lord, but what is not given us 'is that cut-and-dried, fool-proof, systematic fashion we might have expected or desired.' We cannot reduce His utterances to a 'system': 'He preaches but He does not lecture.'

The Old Testament is 'God's word' because (1) If it has been 'made the vehicle of what is more than human, we can of course set no limit to the weight or multiplicity of meanings which may have been laid upon it.' (2) 'We are committed to it in principle by Our Lord Himself. On that famous journey to Emmaus He found fault with the two disciples for not believing what the prophets had said ... In the predictions of His Own Passion which He had previously made to the disciples ... He accepted – indeed He claimed to be – the second meaning of Scripture.'

Chapter XII, 'Second Meaning in the Psalms', deals with one of the most complex subjects in the book. We begin by observing that 'Our Lord's interpretation of the Psalms was common ground between Himself and His opponents.' For instance, two figures meet us in the Psalms: that of the Sufferer and that of the conquering and liberating King. The Sufferer was generally identified with the whole nation of Israel, and the King was the successor of David, the coming Messiah. Our Lord identified Himself with both these characters.

Interpretations, such as these, which were already established in the New Testament naturally have a special claim on our attention. We should note that the Prayer Book appoints Psalms 19, 45 and 85 to be read during Morning Prayer, and Psalms 89, 110 and 132 to be read during Evening Prayer on Christmas Day. (The Divine Office uses most of the same ones for this feast.) Psalm 110 is particularly appropriate for

Christmas Day because two things attach it to Christ: He has already told us that He it is who is referred to in the first line, 'The Lord said unto my Lord'; He is also referred to in the fourth line 'Thou art a Priest for ever after the order of Melchizedech.'

Another thing that makes Psalm 110 appropriate for Christmas Day is that these second meanings removed a difficulty for the Jewish convert to Christianity: 'He might be brought up to see how Christ was the successor of David ... He was, in a similar sense, the successor of Aaron. The idea of His priesthood therefore involved the recognition of priesthood independent of and superior to Aaron's. Melchizedek was there to give this conception the sanction of the Scriptures.' For gentile Christians it works the other way round. 'We are more likely to start from the priestly, sacrificial and intercessory character of Christ, and under-stress that of king and conqueror.' But this however is corrected by Psalm 45 where there is an almost 'threatening tone': 'Gird thee with thy sword upon thy thigh, O thou most mighty ... thine arrows are very sharp' (4:6). For those who first read these Psalms as poems about the birth of Christ,

> that birth primarily meant something very militant; the hero, the 'judge' or champion or giant-killer, who was to fight and beat death, Hell and the devils, had at last arrived, and the evidence suggests that Our Lord thought of Himself in those terms.

We turn next to the identification in Psalm 45 of the Bridegroom with Christ and the Bride with the Church, an identification also found in the Song of Songs. 'No one ... who accepts that spiritual or second sense is denying, or saying anything against, the very plain sense which the writers did intend. The Psalm remains a rich, festive Epithalamium, the Song remains fine, sometimes exquisite, love poetry.'

We conclude with what is probably the most interesting feature of 'second meanings'. Lewis combines Psalm 84:10 – 'For one day in thy courts is better than a thousand' – with 2 Peter 3:8 – 'one day is with the Lord as a thousand years, and a thousand years as one day.' Ever afterwards, he says, 'the "one day" in God's courts which is better than a thousand, must carry a double meaning. The Eternal may meet us in what is, by our present measurements, a day, or (more likely) a minute or a second; but we have touched what is not in any way commensurable with length of time, whether long or short. Hence our hope finally to emerge, if not altogether from time ... at any rate from the tyranny, the unilinear poverty, of time, to ride it not to be ridden by it, and so cure that always aching wound ... which mere succession and mutability inflict on us, almost equally when we are happy and when we are unhappy.'

Reviews

The reviewer for *The Times Literary Supplement* (12 September 1958), p. 517, said: 'This book may not tell the reader all he would like to know about the Psalms, but it will tell him a good deal he will not like to know about himself.' The reviewer for *The Church Times*, CXLI (12 September 1958), p. 5, said: 'This is a brilliant book, not least in its powerful simplicity. The Psalms are not the easiest thing in the Bible to use or to understand. Here is a touch of magic interpretation ... which can do more than all the learned commentaries to make the reading of the Psalms an open door into the world of the Kingdom and the glory of the Lord.'

Gregory Murray wrote in *The Tablet*, 212 (20 September 1958), pp. 237–8: 'I know of no book on the Psalms that can compare with this for interest and stimulating helpfulness.' Dom Augustine James in *The Downside Review*, 78 (September 1958), pp. 131–4, wrote: 'C.S. Lewis's books are always delectable. One gets the impression as one reads them, that he is sitting on the other side of the hearth and conversing familiarly and yet with great enthusiasm on some subject of inspiring interest. One listens, spell-bound, as he unravels one knotty problem after another, always in language understandable to those who do not possess a fraction of his learning, charmed by the flashes of wit with which he illuminates his meanings. *Reflections on the Psalms* forms the subject of one of the happiest of such conversations.'

Fr Joseph Bourke O.P., in *Blackfriars*, XL (September 1959), pp. 389–91, said: 'One feels that what he is saying, though always said beautifully and worth hearing, has only the most tenuous connection with the psalms ... A little more technical equipment could have been engaged, one feels, without impairing the refreshing sympathy of the author's approach.'

THE FOUR LOVES (1960)

Background

In January 1958 Lewis received a request from the Episcopal Radio-TV Foundation of Atlanta, Georgia, to make some tape-recordings to be played over the air. The subject was left up to him, and when he replied on 5 January 1958 he said: 'The subject I want to say something about in the near future in some form or other is the four loves – Storge, Philia, Eros and Agape. This seems to bring in nearly the whole of Christian ethics.'

A more detailed account of the writing and recording of his *Four Talks on Love* is found in the **LIFE XXX**. It is enough to say here that Lewis finished his scripts in the summer of 1958 and recorded them in London 19–20 August. An hour was devoted to each of the Loves, and the recordings were later heard over various radio stations in the United States. Since 1970 the Foundation has been selling cassettes of the *Four Talks on Love* (see **Recordings of C.S. Lewis‡**). Lewis afterwards used the scripts as the basis for his book *The Four Loves* which was completed in June 1959 and published in March 1960.

Although Lewis disliked writing what he called 'blurbology', his publisher, Jocelyn Gibb, * prevailed upon him to write the blurb which appeared on the dustcover of the original English edition. It is the best summary of what he set out to do:

The four loves are, of course, Affection, Friendship, Eros and Charity. They have often been dealt with separately by authors as different as Ovid, St Bernard and Stendhal: and usually one or other of them is treated as the only love worth much consideration. Dr Lewis is more a map-maker than a partisan. He marks frontiers and trade-routes and tries to do justice to all.

Three quotations used by the author indicate the principles that govern his survey: from St John, 'God is Love', from Donne, 'That our affections kill us not, nor dye' and from Denis de Rougemont, 'Love ceases to be a demon when he ceases to be a god.'

On the three natural loves much demolition and reconstruction has proved necessary. Affection had to be disentangled from a suffocating over-growth of sentimentality, and Eros from some misplaced solemnities. Friendship needed defence against modern neglect and even suspicion.

Dr Lewis's power of expressing easily thoughts not very easy in themselves has never been more fully exhibited.

Summary

In chapter I, the 'Introduction', Lewis distinguished between *Gift-love* ('that love which moves a man to work and plan and save for the future well-being of his family which he will die without sharing or seeing') and *Need-love* ('that which sends a lonely or frightened child to its mother's arms'). It seemed obvious to him that Divine Love is Gift-love: 'The Father gives all He is and has to the Son. The Son gives Himself back to the Father, and gives Himself to the world, and for the world to the Father, and thus gives the world (in Himself) back to the Father too.' Need-love he defined as 'The accurate reflection in consciousness of our actual nature. We are born helpless. As soon as we are fully conscious we discover loneliness. We need others physically, emotionally, intellectually; we need them if we are to know anything, even ourselves.'

The more he thought of it the more complex it seemed, and he concluded: (1) We do violence to most languages if we do *not* call Need-love 'love'; (2) We must be cautious about calling Need-love 'mere selfishness'. All our indulgences can be selfishly indulged, but no one calls a child selfish because it turns for comfort to its mother; (3) A man's spiritual health is exactly proportional to his love for God, and what is man's love for God, but very largely, and often entirely, Need-love? And God will have it so. 'He addresses our Need-love: "Come unto me all ye that travail and are heavy-laden", or, in the Old Testament, "Open your mouth wide and I will fill it."'

Another distinction may be made between two kinds of 'nearness to God'. (1) One is 'nearness by likeness'. Man is near God in this sense in that he shares divine attributes such as activity, strength, fecundity, rationality. (2) There is also 'nearness by approach'. Man is near God when he is closest to that union with God, that vision and enjoyment of God, which one day will be his final resting place. This last distinction seemed necessary because St John's statement that 'God is love' had long been balanced in his mind against the remark of Denis de Rougemont's in *Love in the Western World* (1940) that 'love ceases to be a demon only when he ceases to be a god.' Our human loves are only likely to become gods to us when they are in their best, most elevated conditions, when they are most like Gift-love. It is then that we may say, and say quite truly, that those who love greatly are 'near' to God.

In chapter II, 'Liking and Loves for the Sub-human', Lewis said most of his generation were reproved as children for saying that they 'loved' strawberries, and that some people take a pride in the fact that English has the two verbs *love* and *like* while French has to get on with *aimer* for both. But the truth is that there is a 'continuity' between our elementary likings for things and loves for people. Pleasures may be divided into two classes: (1) Need-pleasures such as we get by drinking a glass of water when thirsty, and (2) Appreciative-pleasures such as an unexpected aroma of sweet-peas meeting us on a morning walk. Need-pleasures die on us pretty quickly. The tap and the glass will lose interest for us after we have quenched our thirst. On the other hand, Pleasures of Appreciation do not merely gratify our senses; they claim our appreciation by right.

From pleasures, we turn to two types of love for the non-personal. (1) Love of nature, not of particularities (as a botanist may love flowers), but of nature's fullness, her 'moods', her 'spirits', the sort of nature Wordsworth talked about as a poet. For some, love of nature in this sense has been an indispensable initiation into the journey towards God, and not, on Christian premises, by accident. The creation derives from the Creator and in some fashion reflects Him. But only reflects. Nature does not *teach*. The attempt to set love of Nature up as a religion 'will lead us to a great deal of nonsense'. (2) When rulers need to nerve their subjects to defend their home-land, there should be no shame in appealing to patriotic motives, and no need to pretend that somehow it is 'justice' or 'civilization' or 'humanity' that is being defended. 'I may without self-righteousness or hypocrisy think it just to defend my house by force against a burglar; but if I start pretending that I blacked his eye purely on moral grounds – wholly indifferent to the fact that the house in question was mine – I become insufferable.' There should be no false transcendence given to things that are very much of this world.

Chapter III is on 'Affection', the first of the loves. The name comes from the Greek word *storge* which is defined as 'affection, especially of parents to offspring' and also of offspring to parents. It is the 'humblest and most widely diffused of loves, the love in which our experience seems to differ least from that of the animals.' A useful image is that of 'a mother nursing a baby, a bitch or a cat with a basketful of puppies or kittens; all in a squeaking, nuzzling heap together; purrings, lickings, baby-talk, milk, warmth, the smell of young life.' Almost anyone can become an object of affection; the ugly, the stupid, even the exasperating. But its objects have to be familiar. Indeed, affection usually arises between people who take each other for granted.

We must remember that Affection does not exist apart from the other loves. 'As gin is not only a drink in itself but also a base for many mixed drinks, so Affection, besides being a love itself, can enter into the other loves and colour them all through and become the very medium in which from day to day they operate.' For instance, Affection overlaps with Eros in two significant areas. The first is the kiss. Of course, the kiss of Affection is different from the kiss of Eros, but not all kisses between lovers are erotic kisses. Secondly, both these loves tend to use 'baby-talk': the language of the earliest tenderness we have ever known is recalled to do duty for the new sort.

There are dangers to be guarded against. (1) This disinterested facet of Affection might lead us to suppose that it is a very high form of love, as Victorian novelists believed. But it is not; all its characteristics are ambivalent, providing opportunities for ill as well as for good. For instance, we may feel Affection for someone far beyond his deserts. But it is possible to draw from this fact the ludicrous conclusion that, though we may be without desert ourselves, we yet have a right to Affection from other people. (2) Another ambivalent quality of Affection is its ease or informality. It allows us to take liberties with each other which would be ill-bred if we took them with strangers. But if we are not careful, it will allow us simply to take liberties.

(3) A third danger is jealousy and it is closely connected with Affection's reliance on what is old and familiar. We come to value the old ways so highly for the Affection they give rise to that we do not wish to see them changed, even for the better. Change is a threat to Affection. The jealousy may take two forms. It may ridicule the change or it may begin to fear that there really is something worth having in the change after all, and that it is unfair that the change hasn't come to us. 'Why him?'

All these perversions are connected with Affection as a Need-love. But Affection as a Gift-love has its perversions too. Take the maternal instinct. This is a Gift-love, but one that needs to give; therefore 'needs to be needed'. But the proper aim of giving is to put the recipient in a state where he no longer needs our gift. Such a love must 'work towards its own abdication ... The hour when we can say "They need me no longer" should be our reward.' Only if something more, and other, than Affection, is added, will Affection keep from going bad. You need 'common sense', 'give and take', 'decency' and the continual intervention of a far higher sort of love than Affection in itself can ever be.

Chapter IV is on 'Friendship'. 'When either Affection or Eros is one's theme, one finds a prepared audience ... But very few modern people think Friendship a love of comparable value or even a love at all.' The most obvious reason for this low esteem must be that few people now experience real Friendship. Friendship is the least necessary, biologically speaking, of the loves. 'Friendship is – in a sense not at all derogatory to it – the least *natural* of loves; the least instinctive, organic, biological, gregarious and necessary.'

It was this 'non-natural' quality in Friendship that caused it to be exalted in ancient and medieval times. 'Affection and Eros were too obviously connected with our nerves, too obviously shared with the brutes ... But in Friendship – in that luminous, tranquil, rational world of relationships freely chosen – you got away from all that. This alone, of all the loves, seems to raise you almost to the level of gods or angels.' If a man believes that the old estimate of Friendship was the correct one, Lewis can hardly write a chapter on it except as a 'rehabilitation'.

Lewis begins his rehabilitation by demolishing the idea that any Friendship between people of the same sex must be unconsciously homosexual. 'It has actually become necessary in our time to rebut the theory that every firm and serious friendship is really homosexual.' The very lack of evidence of homosexuality is treated as evidence; the absence of smoke proves that the fire is very carefully hidden. Yes, if it exists at all. But we must first prove its existence. 'Otherwise,' he says, 'we are arguing like a man who should say, "If there were an invisible cat in that chair, the chair would look empty; but the chair does look empty; therefore there is an invisible cat in it."'

In some ways, nothing is less like a love-affair than a Friendship. 'Lovers are always talking about their love; Friends hardly ever about their Friendship. Lovers are normally seen face to face, absorbed in each other; Friends, side by side, absorbed in some common interest.' Moreover, unlike Eros, Friendship does not necessarily limit itself to two people. We require other lights than our own to show us all the facets of a friend.

Simply being with other people is not Friendship. Companionship or clubbableness is only 'the matrix of Friendship'. It is only when two companions discover that they have in common some interest or insight which the others do not share that Friendship arises: 'It is when two such persons discover one another, when ... they share their vision – it is then that Friendship is born. And instantly *they stand together* in an immense solitude.'

The good offices that our friends may perform for us in times of need are not the stuff of Friendship, but another by-product. What, after all, do such things have to do with the question at the heart of Friendship, *Do you see the same truth*? The things our friends do, their previous history, their families, are in a way irrelevant to Friendship. 'Eros will have naked bodies; Friendship naked personalities.' At its best, though, Friendship is a love that is free from instinct, from jealousy, from the need to be needed and from all duties but those which love has freely assumed. 'Have we here found a natural love, which is Love itself?'

(1) The first thing that can be said against Friendship is often voiced by those in Authority: 'Every real Friendship is a sort of secession, even a rebellion ... Men who have real Friends are less easy to "get at"; harder for good Authorities to correct or for bad Authorities to corrupt.' The shared insight that ignites the Friendship may be as harmless as stamp-collecting but when the shared insight is something bad, the situation is even worse. (2) Another thing that can be said against Friendship is that a vacuum may be created around the circle of friends across which no voice can carry. Though individual friends may be perfectly humble within the circle, a corporate pride may develop, be it Olympian, Titanic or just plain vulgar, leading to the labelling of the circle as a clique or a coterie.

The susceptibility of Friendship to pride is perhaps a good indication of its value. Only a high spiritual love would be liable to such a spiritual danger. And this may be 'why Scripture uses Friendship so rarely as an image of the highest love.' It is already too spiritual to be a good symbol of spiritual things. God can safely represent Himself to us as Father and Husband because only an idiot would think that He is physically either of those things.

Chapter V, on 'Eros', opens with the words, 'By *Eros* I mean of course that state which we call "being in love", or that kind of love which lovers are "in".' We are warned, however, that the chapter is not going to be concerned with human sexuality as such: 'Sexuality makes part of our subject only when it becomes an ingredient in the complex state of "being in love".' The sexual experience can occur without Eros, without 'being in love' and for this reason Lewis calls the 'carnal or animally sexual element within Eros' *Venus.*

He does not subscribe 'to the popular idea that it is the absence or presence of Eros which makes the sexual act "impure" or "pure", degraded or fine, unlawful or lawful.' The times and places in which marriage depends on Eros are in a small minority. Most of our ancestors 'were married off in early youth to partners chosen by their parents on grounds that had nothing to do with Eros. They went to the act with no other "fuel", so to speak, than plain animal desire. And they did right.' Conversely, 'this act, done under the influence of a soaring and iridescent Eros which reduces the role of the senses to a minor consideration, may yet be plain adultery, may involve breaking a wife's heart, deceiving a husband, betraying a friend, polluting hospitality and deserting your children. It has not pleased God that the distinction between a sin and a duty should turn on fine feelings.'

Eros makes a man want, not a woman, but one particular woman; not Venus, but the Beloved. Eros thus wonderfully transforms what is *par excellence* 'a Need-pleasure into the most Appreciative of all pleasures'. It is the nature of a Need-pleasure to show us the object solely in relation to our need, even our momentary need. But in Eros, a Need, at its most intense, sees the object most intensely as a thing admirable in herself, important far beyond her relation to the lover's need.

St Paul, dissuading his converts from marriage, says nothing about a surrender to the senses. What he fears 'is the preoccupation, the need of constantly "pleasing" – that is, considering – one's partner, the multiple distractions of domesticity.' Thus, it is the marriage itself – not the marriage bed – that will be likely to hinder us from waiting uninterruptedly on God. Meanwhile, Lewis says, 'we are all being encouraged to take Venus too seriously; at any rate, with a wrong kind of seriousness. All my life a ludicrous and portentous solemnization of sex has been going on.' Even advertisements at their sexiest 'paint the whole business in terms of the rapt, the intense, the swoony-devout; seldom a hint of gaiety.' What is needed is

> a roar of old-fashioned laughter ... In Eros at times we seem to be flying; Venus gives us the sudden twitch that reminds us we are really captive balloons. It is a continual demonstration of the truth that we are composite creatures, rational animals, akin on one side to the angels, on the other to tom-cats.

Of all possible views of the human body, the best is that of St Francis, who called his body 'Brother Ass'. The term is exquisitely right because no one in his senses can either revere or hate a donkey. It is both beautiful and stupid; lovable and infuriating. So with the flesh, there are certain moments of soaring poetry, but also an irreducible element of ludicrous and obstinate un-poetry. There is comic relief within Eros as well as great drama.

In a certain attitude which Venus can evoke, lovers are not merely themselves, but become representatives, symbols of 'the Pagan sacrament' in sex. 'In us all the masculinity and femininity of the world ... are momentarily focused. The man does play Sky-Father and the woman Earth-Mother; he does play Form, and she Matter.' But *play* is the operative word. If these roles were to be assumed literally, they would become idolatrous on the woman's part and blasphemous on the man's. Nevertheless, what cannot lawfully be yielded or claimed can be lawfully enacted. It may be so within the rite or drama of Venus.

Lewis dare not mention this Pagan sacrament without recognizing the biblical view of marriage. 'The husband here is the head of the wife just in so far as he is to her what Christ is to the Church. He is to love her as Christ loved the Church – read on – and *gave his life for her* (Ephesians 5:25). This headship, then, is most fully embodied in him whose marriage is most like a crucifixion; whose wife receives most and gives least.' 'The sternest feminist,' Lewis added, 'need not grudge my sex the crown offered to it either in the Pagan or in the Christian mystery. For the one is of paper and the other of thorns.'

Eros does not aim at happiness; only at being with the beloved: 'Better to be miserable with her than happy without her.' This is the terror and the grandeur of love, and it is here that the seeds of danger are concealed. Eros 'has spoken like a god', and Eros unreservedly honoured becomes a demon. It seems to sanction all sorts of betrayals and sacrifices that the lovers concerned would not otherwise have dared to commit. 'The votaries may even come to feel a particular merit in such sacrifices; what costlier offering can be laid on love's altar than one's conscience?' But Eros is not a permanent presence. The selfless liberation that he calls lovers to is at best intermittent. Like a godparent, he makes the vows; it is *we* who must keep them. And all good Christian lovers know that the vows cannot be kept except by humility, charity and divine grace; that it is indeed the whole Christian life seen from one particular angle. Thus Eros, like the other loves, dies or becomes a demon unless it obeys God.

Chapter VI, on 'Charity', begins: 'William Morris wrote a poem called *Love is Enough* and someone is said to have reviewed it briefly in the words "It isn't". Such has been the burden of this book ... The natural loves are not self-sufficient. Something else, at first vaguely described as "decency and common sense", but later revealed as goodness, and finally as the whole Christian life in one particular relation, must come to the help of the mere feeling if the feeling is to be kept sweet.'

Why have we waited until now to recognize that all our natural loves are 'rivals to the love of God'? (1) It is dangerous to press upon a man the duty of getting beyond earthly love when his real difficulty lies in getting so far. (2) Properly understood, the earthly loves are not rivals to God's love in any case. When obedient to Him there is no rivalry. And when disobedient there is no rivalry either, because without His help they cannot even remain themselves and do what they promise to do. They either vanish or become demons.

Augustine suggests that the sorrow we feel when our human loves come to an end is a proof that they were misdirected. This is good sense, and appeals to the safety-first temperament. Who would not wish to avoid the pain of bereavement or separation from our beloved fellow creatures? But loving them less is surely not the answer. 'We follow One who wept over Jerusalem and at the grave of Lazarus, and, loving all, yet had one disciple whom, in a special sense, he "loved"'. And even if it were granted that insurances against heart-break were our highest wisdom, does God Himself offer them? Apparently not. We draw nearer to God, then, not by trying to avoid the sufferings inherent in all loves, but by accepting them and offering them to Him. To love at all is to be vulnerable. 'If our hearts need to be broken, and if God chooses this as the way in which they should break, so be it.'

All natural loves can be inordinate, but it is the smallness of our love for God, not the greatness of our love for man, that constitutes the inordinacy. The real question is, which do you serve, or put first, when the alternative comes? Our Lord said, 'If any man come to me and hate not his father and mother and wife ... and his own life also, he cannot be my disciple' (Luke 14:26). But how are we to understand the word 'hate'? 'Our Lord, in the sense here intended, "hated" Peter when he said, "Get thee behind me." To hate is to reject, to set one's face against, to make no concession to, the Beloved when the Beloved utters, however sweetly and however pitiably, the suggestions of the Devil.'

Finally, we must try to relate the 'loves' to that Love which is God a little more precisely: (1) God is love, and God, admitted to the human heart, transforms both our natural Gift-love (by enabling us to love the unlovable) and our natural Need-love (by enabling us to accept love even when we are unlovable). (2) God may require a natural love not to be transformed, but to be renounced. Eros, directed to a forbidden object, may have to be sacrificed. (3) Even where a natural love is allowed to continue, it must be perfected. 'As God becomes Man "Not by conversion of the Godhead into flesh, but by taking of the Manhood into God", so here; Charity does not dwindle into merely natural love but natural love is taken up into, made the tuned and obedient instrument of, Love Himself.' The necessity for this conversion of our natural loves is inexorable; at least, if they are to enter Heaven. In Heaven, a love that had never embodied Love Himself would be irrelevant. Nature will have passed away. 'All that is not eternal is eternally out of date.'

We must not suppose that reunion with the beloved dead is the goal of the Christian life. 'Heaven can give heavenly comfort; no other kind. And earth cannot give earthly comfort either. There is no earthly comfort in the long run.' We were made for God. Only by being in some respect like Him, only by being a manifestation of His beauty, wisdom or goodness, has any earthly Beloved excited our love. 'When we see the face of God we shall know that we have always known it ... All that was true love in them was, even on earth, far more His than ours, and ours only because His.'

Reviews

Christopher Derrick in *The Tablet*, 214 (9 April 1960), pp. 346–7, said: 'Anything new by Dr Lewis is a treat, if only because of the almost muscular response of pleasure which his writing provokes, in its utter courtesy and clearness, whatever the subject may be: here, we feel, is one who could delight us, if he chose, with economics – nay, with golf ... Few will dissent from his expert charting of the various corruptions towards which natural love necessarily tends, but most people will feel that he exaggerates the pace and the actual effect of this tendency; and after all, natural love, imperfect, self-deceiving and temporary though it is, is a great improvement on honest natural bloody-mindedness.'

Edmund Fuller in *The Chicago Sunday Tribune* (31 July 1960), p. 6, said: 'The author's fertile mind has found an amazing wealth of aspects and achieved a depth of insight into the four loves that make this a book for reading and re-reading, to ponder. He is extremely good and fresh, often funny, on the troubled issue of Eros, particularly touching the 'ludicrous and portentous solemnization of sex' in everything from fiction to marriage manuals. The chapter on charity is perhaps the most needed.' Michael Novak in *Commonweal*, 72 (19 August 1960), p. 430: 'Mr Lewis writes with one of the most self-effacing and congenial pens in the language, but his is a mind of ranging perspective ... The image of Christian life which [he] is quietly sketching is a beautiful thing.' Martin

D'Arcy S.J. said in *The New York Times Book Review* (31 July 1960), p. 4: *The Four Loves* 'deserves to become a minor classic as a modern mirror of souls, a mirror of the virtues and failing of human loving. Lewis combines a novelist's insights into motives with a profound religious understanding.'

LETTERS TO MALCOLM:
CHIEFLY ON PRAYER (1964)

Background

I: The First Attempt

This was Lewis's last book, written about six months before he died. It had behind it at least one false start. He was writing a book on prayer in December 1952 for, in a letter to Don Giovanni Calabria* of 5 January 1953, he said: 'I invite your prayers about a work which I now have in hand. I am trying to write a book about private prayers for the use of the laity, especially for those who have been recently converted to the Christian faith and so far are without any sustained and regular habit of prayer. I tackled the job because I saw many no doubt very beautiful books written on this subject of prayer for the religious but few which instruct tiros and those still babes (so to say) in the Faith. I find many difficulties nor do I definitely know whether God wishes me to complete this task or not.' He mentioned it again on 17 March 1953: 'I am still working on my book on Prayer'(**LDGC**). However, when he wrote to Sister Penelope* on 15 February 1954 he said: 'I have had to abandon the book on prayer; it was clearly not for me.'

We cannot say how far he got before the work was abandoned. However, a 45-page manuscript of this early attempt has survived, and the opening paragraphs provide some idea of the kind of book he wanted to write:

Many of the things we learned at school were first explained to us successfully not by masters but by other boys. One inky fourth former can make another inky fourth former understand what an adult cannot make him understand. The two boys speak the same language and have the same difficulties. The boy at your elbow knows your difficulty because it was his difficulty yesterday or perhaps half an hour ago. The master very often does not. When you ask him for an explanation he often explains very clearly and at great length all the things you understand already and leaves out the thing you wanted to have explained. The reason usually is that your difficulty about that one thing arises from a mis-understanding so elementary that he never suspected it. There are, in fact, certain kinds of help you can get only from a person on your own level. That is my only excuse for writing a book on prayer.

Lewis appears to have got stuck soon after he began and found no way out of his difficulties. A book usually came straight from his head on to paper with very few corrections, but in this fragment, in which there is a great deal of re-writing, he three times began a paragraph: 'I now turn from prayer considered as Request to prayer considered as Adoration.'

Some of the ideas he was most passionate about – such as Praise – found their way into *Reflections on the Psalms*, others into *The Four Loves*. There are, however, a few passages that are not duplicated anywhere. The reviewer of *Letters to Malcolm* for *The Times Literary Supplement* of 27 February 1964 noted that the 'secret' of Lewis's power 'probably lay in the fact that he had himself found the way to Christian belief with great difficulty; he genuinely knew what it was like not to believe; he could never therefore quite see himself in the position of someone who, untroubled by doubts, simply hands out the Faith.' We find a fine illustration of this in what remains of the original attempt to write about prayer. Discussing the 'Agnostic's view of prayer', he said:

> The modern man who has come to Christianity as an adult may begin to feel uncomfortable. Are we not making our relation to our Creator far too Personal? ... And if this is so, is it not really 'putting back the clock' to re-introduce a crudely personal approach on the highest level of all? Is not prayer simply the last survival of savage, pre-philosophical, thinking?
>
> Now for certain people at certain moments this objection is positively a healthy one. Some who have always been Christians, and whose adult prayers are still much too like the prayers they made in childhood, who still in their heart of hearts think of God only as a Big Man in the sky, may easily take the idea of prayer far too much for granted. The possibility of personal intercourse between the little, hairless bipeds called Men and the in-conceivable, self-existent Being which underlies all phenomena

and all space and time, may seem to such people nothing surprising, nothing that we had not a right to expect. If the fact that it appears outrageous to those who have had a purely scientific upbringing startles any such Christian into the realization that, in a sense, it really is outrageous, not to be thought of without amazement and trembling, then it will have done him good. There is a certain type of Christian (I suspect I am of that type myself) who often needs to learn reverence from a certain type of Agnostic.

II: 'Malcolm' to the Rescue

Lewis knew he had not found the right Form for what he had to say about Prayer until, in the spring of 1963, the idea came to him of an imaginary correspondence between himself and a friend, 'Malcolm'. With very little re-writing, *Letters to Malcolm*, now regarded as one of his most outstanding works on Christian apologetics, fairly gushed from his pen during March and April 1963. When he wrote to Mary Willis Shelburne on 22 April 1963 he said, 'I've finished a book on Prayer. Don't know if it is any good' (**LAL**). On 16 May he informed Jocelyn Gibb* that the book was with the typist, and when Gibb received it a few weeks later he wrote on 13 June to say: 'Respect and admire you as I do, this *Letters to Malcolm* ... has knocked me flat. Not quite; I can just sit up and shout hurrah, and again, hurrah. It's the best you've done since *The Problem of Pain*. By Jove, this is something of a present to a publisher!' When Gibb asked him for help in writing a blurb for the book Lewis replied on 28 June:

> I'd like you to make the point that the reader is merely being allowed to listen to two ordinary laymen discussing the practical and speculative problems of prayer as these appear to them; i.e. the author does *not* claim to be teaching.
>
> Would it be good to say 'Some passages are controversial but this is almost an accident. The wayfaring Christian cannot quite ignore recent Anglican theology when it has been built as a barricade across the high road' [?]

Number XII of the *Letters to Malcolm* is probably as good an explanation as any as to why the first attempt at writing on prayer did not succeed and why the second succeeded so well. 'However badly needed a good book on prayer is,' he said to Malcolm, 'I shall never try to write it. Two people on the foothills comparing notes in private are all very well. But in a book one would inevitably seem to be attempting, not discussion, but instruction. And for me to offer the world instruction about prayer would be impudence.'

It was Lewis who decided that the fictitious Malcolm was to be treated as though he were an old friend with a wife named 'Betty' and a son called 'George'. From the beginning readers have wondered who Malcolm was. Lewis seemed so genuinely surprised by how well the ruse worked that when a friend, who read the book in manuscript, asked who his correspondent was, he said in astonishment 'What! *You* too!!' Still, the fact that most people assume a real Malcolm suggests that his ability to feign was as robust as it was twenty-three years earlier when he assisted Screwtape with his correspondence.

Summary

Letters to Malcolm comprises twenty-two epistles to the imaginary correspondent, chiefly on the subject of prayer. To reinforce the idea that Malcolm is a real man Lewis began section I by allowing Malcolm to choose the topic they will discuss: 'I am all in favour of your idea that we should go back to our old plan of having a more or less set subject – an *agendum* – for our letters. When we were last separated the correspondence languished for lack of it. How much better we did in our undergraduate days with our interminable letters on the *Republic*, and classical metres, and what was then the "new" psychology!'

'There is no subject in the world,' he warns Malcolm, 'on which I have less to say than liturgiology ... To judge from their practice, very few Anglican clergymen take this view. It looks as if they believed people can be lured to go to church by incessant brightenings, lightenings, abridgements, simplifications and complications of the service.' He deplores Novelty in the liturgy and he wishes clergymen would remember that 'the charge to Peter was Feed my sheep; not Try experiments on my rats, or even, Teach my performing dogs new tricks.' Lewis lived all his life with the 1662 *Book of Common Prayer*‡ but he knew that the Liturgical Commission of the Church of England set up in 1955 was planning to authorize new services for experimental use. He hoped things would proceed much slower than they have. While admitting that 'No living language can be timeless', he hoped changes would occur 'gradually and ... imperceptibly; here a little and there a little; one obsolete word replaced in a century.' As it turned out 'Series II' (the first new Anglican eucharistic liturgy since the Prayer Book of 1928) was introduced in 1967, and the complete *Alternative Service Book* was published in 1980.

In II he debates the relative merits of 'ready-made' and 'home-made' prayers. His personal preference is for a staple diet of home-made prayers, for the reason that no other creature is identical with him and no other situation identical with his. Indeed, he himself and his situation are in continual change and so a ready-made form would no more serve for his intercourse with God than it would serve for his correspondence with Malcolm. Nevertheless, he likes to use ready-made prayers at times. They keep him in touch with 'sound doctrine'; they remind him 'what things I ought to ask'; and they also provide an element of the ceremonial.

In III he insists that there is a theological defence for devotions to the saints: 'If you can ask for the prayers of the living, why should you not ask for the prayers of the dead?' But he hopes there will be no scheme for canonizations in the Church of England because it would cause division. On the other hand, praying *with* the saints he considered a less controversial matter and one which he said he has recently come to understand and practise. He hopes that the voice of the great saints and 'our own dear dead' may drown some of the uglier qualities and set off any tiny value which his own prayers might have.

He advises against praying last thing at night: sleepiness is too great a danger. He would rather pray on a crowded train than put it off till midnight. Also, he finds prayer easier on a park bench or pacing up and down a back street than in an empty church. Churches are usually too cold, or else the organist is practising or the cleaner is at work. He favours kneeling because 'The body ought to pray as well as the soul.' On the other hand, 'a concentrated mind and a sitting body make for better prayer than a kneeling body and a mind half asleep.'

In IV he examines the verse in Philippians 4:6 about 'making your requests known to God.' Does God not know our needs? If He knows them, do we have to select the needs which merit His attention? He answers the first question by stating that we are always and therefore equally known to God, just as cabbages and earthworms are known. 'But when we (a) become aware of the fact – the present fact, not the generalization – and (b) assent with all our will to be so known, then we treat ourselves, in relation to God, not as things but as persons.' It is a process of 'unveiling'; a change in us, not in God; and only by the Holy Spirit can we do it.

We must lay before God what is in us, not what ought to be in us. Our various concerns may be misplaced or disproportionate, but where they are sinful they must be laid before God in repentance, and where they are innocent they must, in simple honesty, be laid before the One who will help us to moderate our excesses. 'The ordinate frame of mind (loving things according to their real value) is one of the blessings we must pray for, not a fancy dress we must put on when we pray.' Lastly, those who do not turn to God in petty matters will have no habit or such resort to help them when the great trials come. We may be deterred from praying by a sense of *our* dignity rather than of God's.

In V he writes of his habit of 'festooning' his prayers with private overtones. He illustrates this with phrases in the Lord's Prayer. *Thy kingdom come*: 'That is, may your reign be realized here, as it is realized there.' Lewis gives *Heaven* three meanings: the beauty of the natural, sinless world of stars and sunrise and water; the goodness of really good human families or religious houses; and, of course, the usual sense, the place of the blessed dead. *Earth* can be given a whole host of overtones, but we must remember not to address God as if He were a public meeting.

Thy will be done: At first he festooned this only as a plea for the spirit of submissiveness to God's will. Lately, he has learned to say it as 'Thy will be *done* – by me – now.' The phrase thus becomes, in the long run, a request to be given 'the same mind which was also in Christ.' There is also a third festoon the words can bear: a request for the spirit of submissiveness not only towards possible future afflictions but also towards possible future blessings. We should be ready to accept new blessings, not just repetitions of old ones. If there is a prayer that God never grants, the 'strongest candidate is the prayer we might express in the single word *encore*. And how should the Infinite repeat Himself? All space and time are too little for Him to utter Himself in them *once*.'

Our daily bread: One of its uses is to remind him daily that the 'naïve' view of prayer is firmly built into Our Lord's teaching. *Forgive us ... as we forgive*: 'To forgive for the moment is not difficult. But to go on forgiving, to forgive the same offence again every time it recurs to the memory – there's the real tussle. My resource is to look for some action of my own which is open to the same charge as the one I'm resenting.'

Lead us not into temptation: He reminds Malcolm that the Greek word for 'temptation' means 'trial' or 'trying circumstance' and so is a larger word than English 'temptation'. The petition means: 'Make straight our paths. Spare us, where possible, from all crises, whether of temptation or affliction.' He does not often use *the kingdom, the power, and the glory*, but when he does 'I have an idea of the *kingdom* as sovereignty *de jure*; God, as good, would have a claim on my obedience even if He had no power. The *power* is the sovereignty *de facto* – He is omnipotent. And the *glory* is –

well, the glory; the "beauty so old and new", the "light from behind the sun".'

In VI he says there is a danger in the concept of 'religion' because it carries the suggestion that it is one more department of life, like the social or the intellectual. In fact, religion is either an illusion or our whole life falls under it. 'We have no non-religious activities; only religious and irreligious.' A love of religious observances is a merely natural taste and it is possible that a man's most genuinely Christian actions fall entirely outside that part of his life which he calls 'religious'. But to say that 'religion' as a department has no right to exist should not be misunderstood. It does not necessarily mean that the department ought to be abolished. Nor does it mean that it should cease being departmental by being extended to the whole of life.

Lewis is in total disagreement with those modern psychologists who always diagnose guilt feelings as purely pathological. There are people who feel guilty, but are not; people who are guilty, but don't feel it; and people who both feel guilty and are guilty. But it is a mistake to be overly concerned about feelings.

VII is about petitionary prayer. Our Lord's prayer in Gethsemane was a petition. His reservation – 'not my will but thine' – makes an enormous difference, but it does not remove from the prayer its petitionary character. He insists that Determinism is not a good argument against petitionary prayer. After all, Determinists will, like everyone else, ask you to hand them the salt; they will just attribute the request to some cause outside themselves. Likewise, if a strict Determinist believed in God, petitionary prayer would be no more irrational in him than in anyone else. Another argument put up against petitionary prayer is that, if God alters the course of events in answer to our requests, then the world will become unpredictable and man will have lost the freedom to plan ahead. Lewis rebuts this by stating that the world is already unpredictable, whether or not petitionary prayer is possible, and that, nevertheless, we see planned and purposive action going on around us every day.

In VIII we learn that Malcolm's son, George, is seriously ill. This makes their previous discussion on prayer seem unreal. 'The distance between the abstract, "Does God hear petitionary prayers?" and the concrete, "Will He – can He – grant our prayers for George?" is apparently infinite.' Prayers in this anguished situation are themselves a form of anguish. Such desperate emotions are not to be regarded as defects in faith. Like all afflictions, they are, if we can so take them, our share in the Passion of Christ. We all try to accept with some sort of submission our afflictions when they actually arrive. But the prayer in

Gethsemane shows that the preceding anxiety is equally God's will and equally part of our human destiny. The perfect Man experienced it, and the servant is not greater than the Master. This apparent desertion by God may be due to the fact that to be created is, in a sense, 'to be ejected or separated'.

He states in IX that, if our prayers are granted at all, they must be granted from the foundation of the world, for God and His acts are not in time. Intercourse between God and man occurs at particular moments for the man, but not for God. It follows therefore that our prayers are heard not only before we make them but before we are made ourselves. How then can our prayers be said to be 'acting upon' God? A cause and effect explanation of prayer is inadequate to account for what happens when we pray and, indeed, for whatever happens at the Frontier between man and God. One attempt to define causally what happens there has led to the whole puzzle about Grace and Free Will. But Scripture just sails over the problem. 'Work out your own salvation in fear and trembling' – pure Pelagianism. Why? 'For it is God who worketh in you' – pure Augustinianism. It seems that 'God did this' and 'I did this' need not be seen as mutually exclusive statements.

In X he acknowledges his reservations about Pascal's magnificent dictum: 'God has instituted prayer so as to confer upon His creatures the dignity of being causes.' But he has two disagreements. (1) He thinks that Pascal 'suggests a far too explicit agent-and-patient relation, with God as the patient.' (2) He thinks that viewing prayers as just 'causes' suggests that the whole importance of petitionary prayer lies in the 'achievement of the thing asked for'. In reality, the petitioner wants his prayer to be 'heard' perhaps even more than he wants it to be granted. We can bear to be refused but we cannot bear to be ignored.

A refusal is an 'apparent stone', but it will be bread to us if we believe that a Father's hand put it into ours. But if, having prayed for our heart's desire and got it, we then become convinced that this was a mere accident or by-product of some quite different providential design, then the apparent bread would become a stone. There are no by-products with God. With Him, every providence is a special providence; He does not work by 'general laws'. One of the purposes for which God instituted prayer may have been to 'bear witness that the course of events is not governed like a state but created like a work of art to which every being makes its contribution and (in prayer) a conscious contribution, and in which every being (and every prayer) is both an end and a means.'

Letter XI tackles the 'embarrassing' New Testament promise that 'what we pray for with faith we shall receive' (Mark 11:24). Lewis wants to know how this astonishing promise can be reconciled (a) with the observed facts; and (b) with the prayer in Gethsemane, and the universally accepted view that we should ask everything with a reservation ('if it be Thy will'). No evasion is possible. Every war, every famine and plague is a monument to a petition that was not granted. Logically speaking, it is easy to see that many petitions ask for what is not good for us or for others, or not even intrinsically possible. But why are such lavish promises made about prayer in the first place?

He suggests that the promises refer to a degree or a kind of faith which most believers never experience. Most of us are plain suitors when it comes to prayer; we do not often rise to the level of servant, let alone the level of a friend who is in his master's secrets. And although we may be ashamed of the admission, it must be borne in mind that it is no sin to be a suitor. 'Our Lord descends into the humiliation of being a suitor, of praying on His own behalf, in Gethsemane. But when He does so the certitude about His Father's will is apparently withdrawn.'

In XII the subject is Mysticism. A view is gaining ground, he says, which states that mystics, be they Christian, Buddhist, Hindu or other, all 'find the same things'. He doubts this. But even where similarities are undeniable, it is possible that it is only the means that are similar, not the ends. All mystics experience the 'temporary shattering of our ordinary spatial and temporal consciousness and of our discursive intellect.' So what? Everyone who leaves land and puts to sea will 'find the same things', be they tourists, pirates or missionaries. The merits of the mystical voyage depends not at all on its being mystical – that is, on its being a departure, but on the motives, skills and constancy of the voyager, and most certainly on the grace of God. Departures are all alike; 'it is the landfall that crowns the voyage.'

Lewis wonders why it is easier to pray for other people than for himself and he makes two suggestions. (1) While one is praying for others, one needn't have the bother of actually *doing* anything for them. (2) When he is praying for another person (in this instance, Malcolm) he is giving all the spiritual work to Malcolm and to God, and none to himself as he would do if he was praying about his own besetting sins. It may be for this reason that one fights shy of admitting an act to be a sin in the first place.

He begins Letter XIII by saying that he has found 'in an old notebook a poem, with no author's name attached, which is rather relevant to something we were talking about a few weeks ago – I mean, the haunting fear that there is no one listening, and that what we call prayer is a soliloquy.' He goes on to criticize the poem. This is a pleasant touch because the poem is Lewis's, and it is reprinted under the title 'Prayer' in

Poems and *Collected Poems*. However, the point he is making is that the two statements 'God did it' and 'I did it' might both be true of the same thing. In that sense, prayer could be described as God speaking to God, for it is only by the Holy Spirit that we pray.

What then, of liars and blasphemers? Is God speaking through them too? In one sense, almost Yes. Apart from God they could not speak at all. But it is a distortion of His speech. 'We poison the wine as He decants it into us; murder a melody He would play with us as the instrument. Hence all sin, whatever else it is, is sacrilege.' But why should God bother to speak to Himself through man? You might as well ask why He should create in the first place, for creation seems to be only 'delegation through and through'.

He ends with a distinction between Pantheism and Christianity, and the finest definition of the Incarnation in the whole of his works. 'In Pantheism,' he says, 'God is all.' But, he says, 'the whole point of creation surely is that He was not content to be all. He intends to be 'all *in all*'. In creation God makes – invents – a person and 'utters' – injects – him into the realm of Nature:

> In the Incarnation, God the Son takes the body and human soul of Jesus, and, through that, the whole environment of Nature, all the creaturely predicament, into His own being. So that 'He came down from Heaven' can almost be transposed into 'Heaven drew earth up into it' … The pure light walks the earth; the darkness, received into the heart of Deity, is there swallowed up. Where, except in uncreated light, can the darkness be drowned?

In XIV he is anxious to maintain a balance or a tension between the Pantheists (to whom one must emphasize the distinctness, and relative independence, of God's creatures) and the Deists (to whom one must emphasize the divine presence in my neighbour, my dog, my cabbage-patch). What corroborates his belief that God 'walks everywhere *incognito*' is the fact that an awareness of God's presence has so often been unwelcome. When he finally gets around to calling upon God the reply comes back, 'But you have been evading me for hours.'

In XV he explains the moves he makes before praying. He tries to banish his idea of God as a 'bright blur'; he remembers that the four walls of the room are but matter, something totally unimaginable and only mathematically describable; and he acknowledges that what he calls himself is mostly unknown to him. The only thing of which he can be certain when he prays is that a momentary confrontation between subject and object is occurring. There is no question of a God 'up there' or 'out there'; rather, the question is of the present operation of God 'in here' as the ground of his own being, and God 'in there' as the ground of the matter that surrounds him, and God embracing both and uniting both in the daily miracle of finite consciousness.

The 'moment of prayer' involves for him the awareness, the re-awakened awareness, that this 'real world' and 'real self' are very far from rock-bottom realities, they are but a sort of stage set and a kind of actor. 'And in prayer this real I struggles to speak, for once, from his real being, and to address, for once, not the other actors, but – what shall I call Him? The Author, for He invented us all? The Producer, for He controls all? Or the Audience, for He watches, and will judge, the performance?'

In XVI Lewis considers the use of images as an aid to prayer. Physical images he finds of use only in so far as a focus for visual concentration symbolizes, and promotes, mental concentration. This leads him to discuss Ignatius Loyola's *Spiritual Exercises*, and his use of mental images, such as picturing in one's mind the Nativity or the Marriage at Cana. This does not work for Lewis because, as he says, 'If I started with a *composito loci* I should never reach the meditation. The picture would go on elaborating itself indefinitely and becoming every moment of less spiritual relevance.' Even picturing the Crucifixion, a scene unlikely to lure him into trivialities, is of limited value. 'Compunction, compassion, gratitude – all the fruitful emotions – are strangled. Sheer physical horror leaves no room for them ... Even so, the image ought to be periodically faced.'

XVII is about the prayer of worship or adoration and the principle Lewis starts with is 'Begin where you are', that is, do not try to summon up what you believe about the goodness and greatness of God, but simply become aware of whatever is good in your immediate surroundings and of whatever lawful pleasure may be derived from them. Pleasures are 'shafts of the glory as it strikes our sensibilities'. He tries both to receive pleasures and recognize their divine source in a single experience. Inattention, or greed, or conceit, or a tendency to subjectify pleasures as an event in one's own nervous system, may ruin the experience. But when one avoids these pitfalls, one knows that one is being touched by a finger of that right hand at which there are pleasures for evermore. Almost every day furnishes us with such experiences. They give us new 'bearings' on God: He becomes brighter and less blurry as a result. We see something of that 'game' which is Heaven, and realize that it may, after all, be worth the candle which is creation and our present sufferings.

Letter XVIII tackles the subject of penitential prayers. At the lowest level there is simply the attempt to placate a supposedly angry power. At the highest level, the attempt is rather to restore an infinitely valued and vulnerable personal relation, and if forgiveness, in the 'crude' sense of remission of penalty, comes in, this is valued chiefly as a symptom or seal of the reconciliation. God's wrath is as fierce as His love. It is a just, generous, scalding indignation which passes (in forgiveness) into embracing, exultant, re-welcoming love. 'Hot wrath, hot love. Such anger is the fluid love bleeds when you cut it.' 'Turn God's wrath into mere enlightened disapproval, and you also turn His love into mere humanitarianism.' It comes of being high-minded.

He has found 'that the degrees of shame and disgust which I actually feel at my own sins do not at all correspond to what my reason tells me about their comparative gravity ... Similarly, I have confessed ghastly uncharities with less reluctance than small unmentionables.' He suggests that our *emotional* reactions to our own behaviour are of limited ethical significance.

In XIX Lewis writes more about Holy Communion than he does anywhere else. This is because 'people draw conclusions even from silence. Someone said in print the other day that I seemed to "admit rather than welcome" the sacraments.' He regrets that definitions have been felt to be necessary because he says 'This light has been withheld from me. I do not know and can't imagine what the disciples understood Our Lord to mean when, His body still unbroken and His blood unshed, He handed them the bread and wine, saying *they* were His body and blood.' 'I find "substance" (in Aristotle's sense),' he says, 'when stripped of its own accidents and endowed with the accidents of some other substance, an object I cannot think.'[1] On the other, he can get on no better 'with those who tell me that the elements are mere bread and mere wine, used symbolically to remind me of the death of Christ.' At the same time he finds 'no difficulty in believing that the veil between the worlds, nowhere else (for me) so opaque to the intellect, is nowhere else so thin and permeable to divine operation.'

[1] Lewis is referring to the definition by Thomas Aquinas of the Catholic doctrine of Transubstantiation, whereby the bread and wine used in the Eucharist are changed into the Body and Blood of Christ, only the 'accidents' (i.e. the appearances of the bread and wine) remaining. St Thomas said in the *Summa Theologica*, Part III, Question 75, Article 4: 'The whole substance of the bread is changed into the whole substance of Christ's body, and the whole substance of the wine into the whole substance of Christ's blood. Hence this is not a formal, but a substantial conversion; nor is it a kind of natural movement: but, with a name of its own, it can be called *transubstantiation*.'

For him the value of the 'magical element' in Christianity is that it is a 'permanent witness' to the 'realm of objective facts – hard, determinate facts, not to be constructed *a priori*, and not to be dissolved into maxims, ideals, values and the like.' Enlightened people want to get rid of this 'magical element' in favour of some 'spiritual' or 'psychological' or 'ethical' element, and he is grateful that –

> The command, after all, was Take, eat: not Take, understand. Particularly, I hope I need not be tormented by the question 'What is this?' – this wafer, this sip of wine. That has a dreadful effect on me. It invites me to take 'this' out of its holy context and regard it as an object among objects, indeed as part of nature. It is like taking a red coal out of the fire to examine it: it becomes a dead coal.

In Letter XX he concerns himself with prayers for the dead. 'Of course,' he says to Malcolm, 'I pray for the dead. The action is so spontaneous, so all but inevitable, that only the most compulsive theological case against it would deter me. And I hardly know how the rest of my prayers would survive if those for the dead were forbidden. At our age the majority of those we love best are dead. What sort of intercourse with God could I have if what I love best were unmentionable to Him?'

On the traditional Protestant view, of course, there is no point in praying for the dead because they are either damned or saved and nothing more can be done for them either way. But Lewis says he believes in Purgatory, a doctrine he had been defending since he wrote about it in *The Great Divorce*. He is quick to point out that he does not mean '"the Romish doctrine concerning Purgatory" as that Romish doctrine had then become' in the sixteenth century (a reference to Article XXII on Purgatory, one of the Thirty-Nine Articles in the *Book of Common Prayer*‡). While he loved Dante's *Purgatorio*, he cannot accept the teaching on Purgatory by the sixteenth-century martyrs, Thomas More and John Fisher. 'The right view,' he says, 'returns magnificently in Newman's *Dream [of Gerontius]*. There, if I remember it rightly, the saved soul, at the very foot of the throne, begs to be taken away and cleansed. It cannot bear for a moment longer "With its darkness to affront that light." Religion has reclaimed Purgatory.'

There follows Lewis's famous definition of Purgatory. 'My favourite image on this matter,' he says, 'comes from the dentist's chair. I hope that when the tooth of life is drawn and I am "coming round", a voice will say, "Rinse your mouth out with this." *This* will be Purgatory. The rinsing may take longer than I can now imagine. The taste of *this* may be more fiery and astringent than my present sensibility could endure. But More and Fisher shall not persuade me that it will be disgusting and unhallowed.'

As for the other contention that the dead cannot be prayed for because they are not in time, Lewis again begs to differ. 'The dead might experience a time which was not quite so linear as ours – it might, so to speak, have thickness as well as length.' He feels that timelessness for the dead would be somehow 'inconsistent with the resurrection of the body'. Indeed, whether we are dead or alive, the mode of succession which we call time might be the only way we, with our creaturely limitations, can experience what is a fundamentally timeless reality. Our prayers are granted, or not, in eternity, and we ourselves are eternal in God's eyes; that is, in our deepest reality. So the question is not whether the dead are part of 'timeless reality'. They are; so is a flash of lightning. The question is whether they share the divine perception of timelessness.

The penultimate letter points out that the frequent irksomeness of praying is no proof that we are doing something which we were not created to do. All good actions are variously impeded by evil in ourselves or in others. Not to practise them is to abandon our humanity. To practise them spontaneously and delightfully is not yet possible. This situation creates the category of duty, the whole specifically moral realm. Occasionally one experiences a rich moment in prayer. But Lewis doesn't set much store by these moments. He has a notion that what seem our worst prayers (those least supported by devotional feeling and which contend with the greatest disinclination) may really be, in God's eyes, our best.

Lewis begins his final letter (XXII) with an analysis of 'liberal Christians' and why he thinks they 'genuinely believe that writers of my sort are doing a great deal of harm.' While admitting that those who believe in a supernatural Christianity 'do in some measure queer their pitch', he says 'they make no similar contribution to the forces of secularism.' 'Is it possible,' he asks, that 'many "liberals" have a highly illiberal motive for banishing the idea of Heaven? They want the gilt-edged security of a religion so contrived that no possible fact could ever refute it. In such a religion they have the comfortable feeling that whatever the real universe may be like, they will not have "been had" or "backed the wrong horse". It is close to the spirit of the man who hid his talent in a napkin – "I know you are a hard man and I'm taking no risks." But surely the sort of religion they want would consist of nothing but tautologies?'

His ideas about the resurrection of the body have nothing to do with 'the old picture of the soul reassuming the corpse.' The image he has is of a memory-like power of raising dead sensations from their graves. He doesn't mean that the blessed dead will have excellent memories of their sensuous experiences on earth. He means that memory as we now know it is a dim foretaste of a power which the soul will exercise hereafter. At present we tend to think of the soul as somehow 'inside' the body. But the glorified body of the resurrection as Lewis conceives it – the sensuous life raised from its death – will be inside the soul. 'As God is not in space but space is in God.'

We are not here concerned with matter as such at all. 'Matter enters our experience only by becoming sensation (when we perceive it) or conception (when we understand it). That is, by becoming soul.' And that element in the soul which it becomes will, in Lewis's view, be raised and glorified. 'I don't say the resurrection of this body,' he says, 'will happen at once. It may well be that this part of us sleeps in death, and the intellectual soul is sent to Lenten lands where she fasts in naked spirituality ... Then the new earth and sky, the same yet not the same, will rise in us as we have risen in Christ ... Guesses, of course, only guesses. If they are not true, something better will be. For "we know that we shall be made like Him, for we shall see Him as He is."'

Reviews

The reviewer for *The Times* (30 January 1964), p. 15, spoke for many when he said 'Only Screwtape will be glad that Mr Lewis has written his last letter.' The reviewer for *The Church Times*, CXLVII (31 January 1964), p. 5, wrote: 'With the death of C.S. Lewis, a glory departed. But regret must then immediately give place to gratitude for so generous a legacy as this. Here is a book which ... is as good as anything he ever wrote ... It is splendid, glorious stuff, the product of a luminous and original mind, tough and honest in facing the agonizing questions raised inevitably by any consideration of prayer, and yet endowed with an extraordinary sensitivity and tenderness for the fears and foibles of men.'

Fr Illtud Evans O.P. said in *The Tablet*, 218 (1 February 1964), p. 128: 'The prose he *wrote*, we must learn to say, for this is the last of his books. The return, at the end, to the writing that brought him greatest fame, must still the speculations of those who assumed that the long years of spiritual silence since *Screwtape* and *Mere Christianity* meant some slackening of the strength of an apologetic that had no English parallel.'

Nathan A. Scott Jr said in *Saturday Review* (7 March 1964), p. 41: 'Apart from *The Screwtape Letters*, it may well prove to be the profoundest of C.S.

Lewis's many essays in theological apologetic: it is, in any event, a fine capstone to this side of his literary career.' The reviewer for *The Times Literary Supplement* (27 February 1964), p. 173, wrote: 'The reader feels not so much that he is listening to what C.S. Lewis has to say but that he is making his own search with a humorous, sensible friend beside him. That is writing that requires very great literary skill, and it is a skill that probably could not be compassed at all if it did not come from a mind that was sincerely concerned to do just that. That this should be the last book that we have from C.S. Lewis is a matter for genuine regret.' George Scott-Moncrieff said in *The Month*, 31 (May 1964), p. 310: 'In this posthumously published book C.S. Lewis might be described as being concerned not only with prayer but also taking the protest out of Protestantism. His "letters" are full of practical ecumenism ... He can see no grounds for a disbelief in Purgatory, only rejecting some of the later medieval accretions to the doctrine. His rejection of these and of other elaborations and abuses in Catholic attitudes are all just and fair enough, and temperately made. His humility is deeply impressive.'

THE CHRONICLES
OF NARNIA

The Magician's Nephew,
The Lion, the Witch and the Wardrobe,
The Horse and His Boy, Prince Caspian,
The Voyage of the 'Dawn Treader',
The Silver Chair, The Last Battle

THE CHRONICLES OF NARNIA

I: A Defence of the Fairy Tale

There was some surprise when Lewis, very popular at the end of the 1940s for both his literary criticism and his theological writings, turned to writing fairy tales. As they became better known, he was asked how he came to write them. Nearly all that he had to say about the Narnian stories and fairy tales in general is found in his *Letters to Children* and in three essays found in *Of This and Other Worlds* (US: *On Stories and Other Essays on Literature*): **On Three Ways of Writing for Children (Three Ways** for short), **Sometimes Fairy Stories May Say Best What's to be Said** (or **Sometimes Fairy Stories**), and **It All Began with a Picture ...**

In **Three Ways** he defended the fairy tales with four propositions. (1) 'Critics who treat *adult* as a term of approval,' he said, 'instead of a merely descriptive term, cannot be adult themselves. To be concerned about being grown up, to admire the grown up because it is grown up, to blush at the suspicion of being childish; these things are the marks of childhood and adolescence ... When I was ten, I read fairy tales in secret and would have been ashamed if I had been found doing so. Now that I am fifty I read them openly. When I became a man I put away childish things, including the fear of childishness and the desire to be very grown up.' (2) The modern view, he believed, involves a false conception of growth, and to the charge of 'arrested development' he replied:

> Surely arrested development consists not in refusing to lose old things but in failing to add new things? I now like hock, which I am sure I should not have liked as a child. But I still like lemon-squash. I call this growth or development because I have been enriched: where I formerly had only one pleasure, I now have two. But if I had to lose the taste for lemon-squash before I acquired the taste for

hock, that would not be growth but simple change ... A tree grows because it adds rings: a train doesn't grow by leaving one station behind and puffing on to the next ... I think my growth is just as apparent when I now read the fairy tales as when I read the novelists, for I now enjoy the fairy tales better than I did in childhood: being now able to put more in.

(3) He believed the association of fairy tale and fantasy with childhood to be local and accidental. How did fairy tales become associated with children? For the answer to this Lewis always referred to J.R.R. Tolkien's* essay **On Fairy Stories** (in Tolkien's *Tree and Leaf, including the poem 'Mythopoeia'*, ed. Christopher Tolkien, 1988) in which he said:

In describing a fairy story which they think adults might possibly read for their own entertainment, reviewers frequently indulge in such waggeries as: 'this book is for children from the ages of six to sixty.' But I have never yet seen the puff of a new motor-model that began thus: 'this toy will amuse infants from seventeen to seventy' ... The association of children and fairy stories is an accident of our domestic history. Fairy stories have in the modern lettered world been relegated to the 'nursery', as shabby or old-fashioned furniture is relegated to the play-room, primarily because the adults do not want it, and do not mind if it is misused. Children as a class – except in a common lack of experience they are not one – neither like fairy stories more, nor understand them better than adults do.

(4) Lewis believed that no literature gives children less of a 'false impression' of the world than fairy tales. He believed that 'realistic' stories for children were more likely to deceive than the fairy tale. While 'realistic' stories may contain adventures and successes that are possible, they are 'almost infinitely improbable' and thus raise 'false impressions'.

A similar observation about books for grown-ups was made in *An Experiment in Criticism*. In the chapter 'On Realisms' he distinguished between 'realism of presentation' which involves 'true to life' details about things that can be seen or heard or touched, and 'realism of content', which involves the probability of something actually happening. A story could be a masterpiece of realistic detail, and at the same time unrealistic in content. The school story is, thus, more likely than the fairy tale to raise 'false expectations'. Besides this, the school story is 'compensatory' and we 'run to it from the disappointments and humiliations of the real world', only to be sent 'back to the real world undivinely discontented' for it is 'all flattery to the ego.'

A child's longing for fairy land is very different: 'Does anyone suppose that he really and prosaically longs for all the dangers and discomforts of a fairy tale?' he asks, 'really wants dragons in contemporary England?' 'It would be much truer to say that fairy land arouses a longing for he knows not what. It stirs and troubles him (to his life-long enrichment) with the dim sense of something beyond his reach and, far from dulling or emptying the actual world, gives it a new dimension of depth. He does not despise real woods because he has read of enchanted woods: the reading makes all real woods a little enchanted.'

(5) To the charge that fairy tales 'frighten' children, he replied that we must not do anything that would give children 'those haunting, disabling, pathological fears against which ordinary courage is helpless: in fact, *phobias*.' On the other hand, he did not agree with the notion 'that we must try to keep out of his mind the knowledge that he is born into a world of death, violence, wounds, adventure, heroism and cowardice, good and evil.' 'If they mean the first,' he said, 'I agree with them: but not if they mean the second':

> There is something ludicrous in the idea of so educating a generation which is born to the Ogpu and the atomic bomb. Since it is so likely that they will meet cruel enemies, let them at least have heard of brave knights and heroic courage ... I side impenitently with the human race against the modern reformer. Let there be wicked kings and beheadings, battles and dungeons, giants and dragons, and let villains be soundly killed at the end of the book. Nothing will persuade me that this causes an ordinary child any kind or degree of fear beyond what it wants, and needs, to feel. For, of course, it wants to be a little frightened.

II: Lewis: The Author and the Christian

In **Sometimes Fairy Stories** he distinguished between (a) 'an author as author' with his reasons for writing as he does, and (b) 'the author as man, citizen, or Christian' who has his reasons for saying certain things. Lewis claimed that in his capacity of 'author as author' he fell in love with the Form of the fairy tale because of 'its brevity, its severe restraints on description, its flexible traditionalism, its inflexible hostility to all analysis, digression, reflections and "gas".' In his capacity as a Man who is also a Christian Lewis gave this as his reason for writing the Narnian stories:

> I thought I saw how stories of this kind could steal past a certain inhibition which had paralysed much of my own religion in childhood. Why did one find it so hard to feel as one was told one ought to feel about God or about the sufferings of Christ? I thought the chief reason was that one was told one ought to. An obligation to feel can freeze feelings. And reverence itself did harm. The whole subject was associated with lowered voices; almost as if it were something medical. But supposing that by casting all these things into an imaginary world, stripping them of their stained-glass and Sunday School associations, one could make them for the first time appear in their real potency? Could one not thus steal past those watchful dragons? I thought one could.

III: The Inspiration of Narnia

Many hundreds of children, who still do not know that Lewis is dead, write to thank him for the Narnian stories. Nearly all ask: 'What *inspired* you to write them?' We learn a great deal about his 'inspiration' from the *Letters to Children* and the essays mentioned above. **It All Began with a Picture ...** was written especially for children, and he says there that 'you must not believe all that authors tell you about how they wrote their books', not because they mean to lie, but because 'a man writing a story is too excited about the story itself to sit back and notice how he is doing it. In fact, that might stop the works; just as, if you start thinking about how you tie your tie, the next thing is that you find you can't tie it. And afterwards, when the story is finished, he has forgotten a good deal of what writing it was like.'

In **Sometimes Fairy Stories** he dismisses one notion sometimes ascribed to him. 'Some people,' he says, 'seem to think that I began by asking myself how I could say something about Christianity to children; then fixed on the fairy tale as an instrument, then collected information about child psychology and decided what age group I'd write for; then drew up a list of basic Christian truths and hammered out "allegories" to embody them. This is all pure moonshine. I couldn't write in that way. It all began with images; a faun carrying an umbrella, a queen on a sledge, a magnificent lion. At first there wasn't even anything Christian about them; that element pushed itself in of its own accord.' In **It All Began with a Picture ...** he enlarges on the 'images' with which Narnia began:

> All my seven Narnian books, and my three science-fiction books, began with seeing pictures in my head. At first they were not a story, just pictures. The *Lion* all began with a picture of a Faun carrying an umbrella and parcels in a snowy wood. This picture had been in my mind since I was about sixteen. Then one day, when I was about forty, I said to myself: 'Let's try to make a story about it.'
>
> At first I had very little idea how the story would go. But then suddenly Aslan came bounding into it. I think I had been having a good many dreams of lions about that time. Apart from that, I don't know where the Lion came from or why He came. But once He was there He pulled the whole story together, and soon He pulled the six other Narnian stories in after Him.

He contributes another element to the explanation of his inspiration in **Three Ways**. He compared the 'pictures' he saw in his mind to 'bird-watching':

> Some of these pictures have a common flavour, almost a common smell, which groups them together. Keep quiet and watch and they will begin joining themselves up. If you were very lucky (I have never been as lucky as all that) a whole set might join themselves so consistently that there you had a complete story; without doing anything yourself. But more often (in my experience always) there are gaps. Then at last you have to do some deliberate inventing, have to contrive reasons why these characters should be in these various places doing these various things.

IV: The Writing of the Narnias

Shortly before Britain declared war on Germany (3 September 1939) many children were evacuated from London, and Lewis and Mrs Moore* agreed to have some of them at The Kilns.‡ Warnie Lewis* had been recalled into active service, and on 2 September 1939 Lewis wrote to tell him that 'Our schoolgirls have arrived and all seem to me – and what's more to Minto [Mrs Moore] – to be very nice, unaffected creatures and all most flatteringly delighted with their new surroundings' (L). He wrote to his brother again on 10 September to say that the day before 'they met me in the avenue, jumping with joy, to tell me "War has been declared" – and one added "Perhaps there'll be an air raid *tonight*!!" Lewis and Mrs Moore greatly enjoyed the many children who were at The Kilns during the war. It seems likely that the presence of some of these children caused Lewis to pen what may have been his first words about Narnia. On the back of the manuscript of *The Dark Tower*, probably written in 1939, he wrote the words:

> This book is about four children whose names were Ann, Martin, Rose and Peter. But it is mostly about Peter who was the youngest. They all had to go away from London suddenly because of the Air Raids, and because Father, who was in the army, had gone off to the war and Mother was doing some kind of war work. They were sent to stay with a relation of Mother's who was a very old Professor who lived by himself in the country.

Three of the names of the children are different, but the paragraph is certainly close to the opening paragraph of *The Lion, the Witch and the Wardrobe*. After this, we learn no more about the story until Chad Walsh* visited Lewis in the summer of 1948. Walsh was a professor of English at Beloit College in Wisconsin who was writing a book about Lewis. In his *C.S. Lewis: Apostle to the Skeptics* (1949), he said that during the visit Lewis talked 'vaguely of completing a children's book which he has begun "in the tradition of E. Nesbit"' (p. 10).

The next thing we hear comes from Lewis's friend, Roger Lancelyn Green.* He read all the books in manuscript, and his account of them is found in *C.S. Lewis: A Biography* (X). Green dined with Lewis in Magdalen College on 10 March 1949, and writing about it in his diary he said that he and Lewis had a 'wonderful talk until midnight: he read me two chapters of a story for children he is writing – very good indeed, though a trifle self-conscious.' He assumed that the *Lion* was finished.

Shortly afterwards he ran into J.R.R. Tolkien.* He too had read the *Lion* in manuscript, and he said to Green: 'I hear you've been reading Jack's children's story. It really won't do, you know! I mean to say: "*Nymphs and their Ways, The Love-Life of a Faun*." Doesn't he know what he's talking about?' Tolkien had very severe standards, and he probably thought the Narnian stories too hastily written, and containing too many inconsistencies.

Sometimes, Lewis said, when the 'pictures' didn't group themselves to form a complete picture he had to do 'some deliberate inventing', and as evidence of this we might note this example from one of his notebooks:

Plots

SHIP. Two children somehow got on board a ship of ancient build. Discover presently that they are sailing in time (backwards): the captain will bring them to islands. Attack by enemies. Children captured. Discover that the first captain was really taking them because his sick king needs blood of a boy in the far future. *Nevertheless* prefer the Captain and his side to their *soi-disant* rescuers. Escape and return to their first hosts. The blood giving, not fatal, and happy ending. Various islands (of Odyssey and St Brendan) can be thrown in. Beauty of the ship the initial spell. To be a very green and pearly story.

PICTURE. A magic picture. One of the children gets through the frame into the picture and one of the creatures gets out of the picture into our world.

INVERTED. Ordinary fairy tale K., Q. and court, *into* which erupts a child from our world.

SEQUEL TO L.W.W. The present tyrants to be Men. Intervening history of Narnia told nominally by the Dwarf but really an abstract of his story which amounts to telling it in my own person.

This is probably a rough sketch of *The Voyage of the 'Dawn Treader'* which was to be the 'Sequel to *The Lion, the Witch and the Wardrobe*'. It did not work out that way, but many of the ideas found their way into other stories. For instance, the 'intervening history of Narnia told nominally by the Dwarf' comes, not in the '*Dawn Treader*', but in *Prince Caspian*.

When Roger Lancelyn Green visited Lewis on 14 June 1949 Lewis read aloud two chapters of a new story. This was **The Lefay Fragment**, as it is called, and it is about a boy named Digory who lives with his Aunt Gertrude because his parents are dead. He is able to understand what animals and trees say, and he is friends with the big Oak in his garden, and a squirrel called Pattertwig who lives there. One day the girl next door, Polly, persuades him to cut a limb off the big Oak so that they can make a raft. From that moment on he is deeply saddened because by this act he loses his ability to talk with the trees and animals. The next day Digory has a visit from his Godmother, Mrs Lefay, whom he doesn't remember seeing before. She is 'the shortest and fattest woman' he had ever seen, and her black dress is covered with snuff. When he says 'How do you do, Godmother?' the spry old lady says 'I won't ask how *you* do, because I see you do very badly.' She tells him that he looks 'exactly like what Adam must have looked five minutes after he'd been turned out of the Garden of

Eden.' There are indications that she understands the problem and is able to help him, but here the story ends. After introducing the Narnian equivalent of the Fall, Lewis could not decide how to go on.

Portions of the **Lefay Fragment** are found in other Narnian stories. The description of Aunt Gertrude sounds almost exactly like the Head of Experiment House in *The Silver Chair*, and Pattertwig shows up in *Prince Caspian*. The reader will find the whole of the **Lefay Fragment** and the few other Narnian manuscripts in Walter Hooper's *Past Watchful Dragons* (New York: Macmillan, 1979; London: Fount Paperbacks 1980). After abandoning the fragment, Aslan 'pulled the six other Narnian stories in after Him', and Lewis wrote the sequel to the *Lion*. This was *Prince Caspian* which was finished by the beginning of December 1949 and ready for Roger Lancelyn Green to see. By the end of February 1950 the manuscript of *The Voyage of the 'Dawn Treader'* was ready for Green to read and report on.

Green recorded in his diary that, when he joined Lewis and the other Inklings in the 'Bird and Baby' pub‡ on 22 June 1950, they were handing around the proofs of the *Lion*. Then on 26 July Lewis had *The Horse and His Boy* ready for him to read. By 13 November 1950 Lewis had written several chapters of what was first called *Night Under Narnia*, and then *The Wild Waste Lands* and finally *The Silver Chair*, and when Green saw Lewis again at the beginning of March 1951 he was able to read the rest of it. Green had made notes for some possible alterations to *The Silver Chair*, and the letter Lewis wrote to Green on 6 March mentions exactly the sort of problem he occasionally ran into: 'You are quite right about a wood fire,' he said. 'Wood keeps on glowing red again in the places you have already extinguished – phoenix-like. Even the large webbed feet of a Marshwiggle couldn't do it. Yet it must be a flat hearth, I think. *Does* peat go out easily by treading? As an Irishman I ought to know, but don't. I think it will have to be a coal fire in a flat hearth. After all, Underland might well use coal, whereas wood or charcoal would have to be imported.'

We should note that between the summer of 1948 and March 1951 Lewis had written five of the Chronicles of Narnia. After this he turned back to the beginning of Narnia, as he had once before in the **Lefay Fragment**, and began *The Magician's Nephew*. The names 'Digory' and 'Polly' are retained from the **Lefay Fragment** and the story is set in the days when 'Mr Sherlock Holmes was still living in Baker Street and the Bastables were looking for treasure in the Lewisham Road.' When Roger Lancelyn Green was staying with Lewis at Magdalen College 31 May–1 June 1951 he found that a little under half of this new story had been written. When he was there again on 31 October and 2 November 1951 about three-quarters was written. Green was unhappy about one section of the story: in this section Digory paid several visits to the dying world of Charn, during which he stayed in a farm cottage with an old countryman called Piers and his wife. Green thought they spoke with too laboured a 'Loamshire' accent, and the whole part seemed to him 'too simple and honest and far too long-winded' but most of all 'seemed to him quite out of harmony with the rest of the book'. Lewis was not convinced, but he set the book aside for the moment.

While thinking about what next to do with *The Magician's Nephew*, Lewis was very busy. Over the next year and a half he completed one of his finest books, *English Literature in the Sixteenth Century*. He then returned with renewed interest to Narnia. However, instead of solving the problems in *The Magician's Nephew*, he wrote the whole of *The Last Battle*. Green read the first half of this in February 1953, and on 11 March Lewis wrote to his publisher, Geoffrey Bles, to say 'You will hear with mixed feelings that I have just finished the seventh and really the last of the Narnian stories.' He then revised *The Magician's Nephew*, and after Green read it in February 1954 he noted in his diary: 'It seems the best of the lot ... and is certainly vastly improved by the omission of the long section about Piers the Plowman – which I take some credit for persuading Jack to cut out. It's a single unity now, and irresistibly gripping and compelling.'

V: Illustrations by Pauline Baynes*

While the Narnian stories were being written, the publishers were busy in the background. The letters that passed between Lewis and his publisher, Geoffrey Bles,* are evidence of the many editorial decisions which needed to be made. Bles raised the interesting question of the gender of some of the creatures in Narnia, and Lewis replied: 'My view about *He* and *It* was that the semi-humanity would be kept before the imagination by an unobtrusive mixture of the two. Your reaction, however, shows that either such a mixture would not be unobtrusive or else that I, at any rate, could not make it so.' Lewis nearly always had difficulty over titles, and when he wrote to Bles on 13 April 1953 about one of the stories, he said: 'What are your reactions to any of the following? *The Horse and the Boy* (which might allure the "pony-book" public) – *The Desert Road to Narnia* – *Cor or Archenland* – *The Horse Stole the Boy* – *Over the Border* – *The Horse Bree*. Suggestions will be welcomed.' Bles replied: 'I like best *The Horse and the*

Boy, but what about *The Horse and His Boy*, which is a little startling and conveys the idea of your other title *The Horse Stole the Boy*?'

There had from the first been the momentous decision of choosing an illustrator for the books, a choice which lay with Lewis. About the time that the manuscript of *The Lion* was sent to Bles in 1949, Professor Tolkien was showing his friends the illustrations an almost unknown young woman had drawn for his *Farmer Giles of Ham*. Lewis liked them so much that he wanted the same artist for his stories. In a letter to his publishers of 16 March 1949 Tolkien said: 'Miss Baynes' pictures ... are more than illustrations, they are a collateral theme. I showed them to my friends whose polite comment was that they reduced my text to a commentary on the drawings' (LJRRT). Lewis met Pauline Baynes for the first time when he gave her a luncheon party in Magdalen College on 31 December 1949.

Later, when asked how she came to be chosen as the illustrator of Narnia, Pauline Baynes said: 'C.S. Lewis told me that he had actually gone into a bookshop and asked the assistant there if she could recommend someone who could draw children and animals. I don't know whether he was just being kind to me and making me feel that I was more important than I was or whether he'd simply heard about me from his friend Tolkien' (PWD 6). She and Lewis were to meet several times to discuss the illustrations, and there seems unanimous agreement that the choice of an illustrator for Narnia was perfect. In a letter of 15 August 1967 Miss Baynes described her work on the books:

> Dr Lewis and I hardly corresponded at all over the illustrations to his books: he was, to me, the most kindly and tolerant of authors – who seemed happy to leave everything in my completely inexperienced hands! Once or twice I queried the sort of character he had in mind – as with Puddleglum – and then he replied, but otherwise he made no remarks or criticisms, despite the fact that the drawings were very far from perfect or even, possibly, from what he had in mind. I had rather the feeling that, having got the story written down and out of his mind, the rest was someone else's job, and that he wouldn't interfere. As I remember, he only once asked for an alteration – and then with many apologies – when I (with my little knowledge) had drawn one of the characters rowing a boat facing the wrong direction! [*Prince Caspian* 3].
>
> When he *did* criticize, it was put over so charmingly, that it wasn't a criticism, i.e., I did the drawings as best as I could – (I can't have been much more than 21 and quite untrained) and didn't realize how hideous I had made the children – they were as nice as

I could get them – and Dr Lewis said, when we were starting on the second book, 'I know you made the children rather plain – *in the interests of realism* – but do you think you could possibly pretty them up a little now?' – was not that charmingly put?

We had very few meetings – one, I think, in Geoffrey Bles' office, once over lunch at the Charing Cross Hotel [1 January 1951] – (rather a hectic affair with him watching the clock for his train) – and once when he invited me to lunch at Magdalen [31 December 1949] with an imposing collection of fellow guests, including Ruth Pitter.* On all these occasions, being a self-conscious and stupidly introverted girl, all I could think of was whether I was saying and doing the right thing, so that I didn't really register the important things like what Dr Lewis said and did! He was invariably friendly and kind to me, but I suppose inevitably, I always felt overawed. I distinctly remember him picking the chestnuts out of the brussels sprouts with his fingers and saying it was a pity to waste them at the end of the Magdalen lunch! ...

One remark he made somehow made a big impression on me – but I don't really see why it should have done so. At the time of the Charing Cross Hotel lunch, he looked through some of the drawings I had done – and it was of bears – and he said 'This one is particularly nice – you have got the right feel' – and I said 'How funny, I find bears no trouble at all, very easy to draw' – whereupon he answered – 'Things one finds easy are invariably the best.' This took a lot of thinking about, for though it is of course logical, up till then I had thought that nothing could be worthwhile that had not been a battle, a difficulty overcome, and that good things could only come after a lot of hard work and rubbing out. Of course he was right: if one knows about something so that you can draw it effortlessly it will be fluent and direct [**PWD** 6].

As Miss Baynes said, Lewis hoped she would 'pretty' the human faces up a little. His letter to her of 21 January 1954 is evidence of how his enthusiasm increased from book to book:

I lunched with Bles yesterday to see the drawings for *The Horse* and feel I must write to tell you how very much we both enjoyed them. It is delightful to find (and not only for selfish reasons) that you do each book a little bit better than the last – it is nice to see an artist growing. (If only you could take six months off and devote them to anatomy, there's no limit to your possibilities.)

Both the drawings of Lasaraleen in her litter were a rich feast of line and of fantastic-satiric imagination: my only regret was that we couldn't have both. Shasta among the tombs (in the new technique, which is lovely) was exactly what I wanted. The pictures of Rabadash hanging on the hook and just turning into an ass were the best comedy you've done yet. The Tiscoc was superb: far beyond anything you were doing five years ago. I thought that your human faces – the boys, King Lune etc. – were, this time, really good. The crowds are beautiful, realistic yet also lovely wavy compositions: but your crowds always were. How did you do Tashbaan? We only got its full wealth by using a magnifying glass! The result is exactly right. Thanks enormously for all the intense work you have put into them all. And more power to your elbow: congratulations.

Lewis paid quite careful attention to details. When the illustrations to *The Magician's Nephew* were sent to him, he wrote to Pauline Baynes on 2 October 1954: 'I say! You *have* learned something about animals in the last few months ... This Horse, whether charging with his hansom, or growing his wings, or flying, is the real thing ... I was very sorry to lose Aunt Letty mending the mattress – a nice, homely scene – but doomed her in the end because she is dressed more in the style of the 1860s than in that of the 1900s. (The difference naturally seems more to me than to you!).' However, after Aunt Letty's dress had been suitably altered it did find its way into chapter 7.

When *The Last Battle* won the Carnegie Medal for the best children's book of 1956, Miss Baynes wrote at once to congratulate Lewis. He refused to take all the credit, and replied on 4 May 1957: 'Is it not rather "our" Medal? I'm sure the illustrations were taken into consideration as well as the text.'

VI: Summaries of the Chronicles of Narnia

The summaries given below follow the sequence in which Lewis meant for them to be read. However, it will be useful for the reader to keep in mind the order in which the books were published, which is as follows: *The Lion, the Witch and the Wardrobe* (1950); *Prince Caspian* (1951); *The Voyage of the 'Dawn Treader'* (1952); *The Silver Chair* (1953); *The Horse and His Boy* (1954); *The Magician's Nephew* (1955); *The Last Battle* (1956).

1. The Magician's Nephew

This story is set in the days when 'Mr Sherlock Holmes was still living in Baker Street and the Bastables were looking for treasure in the Lewisham Road.' Digory Kirke's father is in India and his mother is so ill she may be dying. They live in a terraced house with his aunt and his Uncle Andrew who is an amateur magician. Next door is a girl named Polly Plummer. Digory and Polly stumble into Uncle Andrew's study by accident, and by the use of Uncle Andrew's Magic Rings they journey to the dying world of Charn.

Digory gives way to temptation, and this causes the wicked Queen of Charn, Jadis (later the White Witch), to wake from a charmed sleep. She has destroyed the land of Charn, and Digory and Polly attempt to escape by the use of the Rings. Queen Jadis, because she was touching the children when they put on a Ring, manages to accompany them to London. Uncle Andrew is besotted by Jadis, who makes plans to conquer our world. Digory and Polly, in an attempt to take her back to Charn, accidentally take with them, not only Jadis, but Uncle Andrew, and a friendly cabby and his horse, Strawberry. By another accident, they arrive, not in Charn, but in Narnia at the moment of its creation by Aslan.

Following the creation of the animals and other creatures, Aslan chose two of every species. Them he breathed on, saying: 'Narnia, Narnia, Narnia, awake. Love. Think. Speak. Be walking trees. Be talking beasts. Be divine waters' (9). One of the animals given the gift of speech is Strawberry. Aslan warns the Talking Beasts that it is their responsibility to look after the Dumb Beasts, and that unless they treat them gently they will return to being dumb themselves.

Aslan then turns to the humans. He knows that Digory is responsible for the witch, Jadis, being there, and he says, 'As Adam's race has done the harm, Adam's race shall help to heal it.' The wife of Frank, the cabby, is called from the Earth into Narnia, and Frank is told: 'You shall rule and name all these creatures, and do justice among them, and protect them from their enemies when enemies arise. And enemies will arise, for there is an evil Witch in this world.' Strawberry is made a flying horse and given the new name Fledge. He takes Digory and Polly to the far-off Western Wild in order to bring back an apple from a tree in the garden there. Digory is told he must pluck the apple.

When they arrive, Digory is sorely tempted because he has hoped all along to find a magical apple that will heal his mother. But over the gate of the garden is the verse:

Come in by the gold gates or not at all,
Take of my fruit for others or forbear,
For those who steal or those who climb my wall
Shall find their heart's desire and find despair.

Inside the garden they find the Witch having already eaten some of the fruit, the mouth of her 'deadly white' face stained by it. She urges Digory to eat the apple of youth which grows there so that they can both live for ever as King and Queen of Narnia. This he refuses, but it's not so easy to resist the temptation she whispers to him that the fruit will heal his mother. However, in the end he refuses to steal it, and he takes the Apple back to Aslan.

'No hand but yours shall sow the seed of the Tree that is to be the protection of Narnia,' Aslan says to Digory, as he has him plant the Apple by the river. While it grows, they proceed with the Coronation of King Frank of Narnia and Helen his Queen. When the time comes for them to go home the Tree is full grown, and Aslan talks to Digory about what would have happened if he had stolen the fruit for his mother. 'It would have healed her,' he said, 'but not to your joy or hers. The day would have come when both you and she would have looked back and said it would have been better to die in that illness.' 'That is what *would* have happened,' Aslan adds in a whisper, 'with a stolen apple. It is not what will happen now.' He then bids Digory pluck one of the Apples for his mother.

Uncle Andrew and the children are returned to this world, and Digory at once takes the Narnian fruit to his mother. 'The smell of the Apple of Youth was as if there was a window in the room that opened on Heaven.' The Apple heals Digory's mother, after which Father returns from India. His 'Old Great-Uncle Kirke' has died and left them very rich, with a great house in the country. Meanwhile, in London, a tree grows from the core of the Apple brought back from Narnia. Years later, when it is blown down by a storm, Professor Digory Kirke, as he has become, uses its wood to build a Wardrobe for his house in the country.

2. The Lion, the Witch and the Wardrobe

This story opens with the four Pevensie children, Peter, Susan, Edmund and Lucy, being sent away from London during the War because of the air raids. They go to the large house of old Professor Kirke who lives in the country. While there, Lucy hides in the Wardrobe in the spare room and discovers it to be an entrance into Narnia. She meets Mr Tumnus, the faun, and learns that Narnia is ruled by the White Witch (Jadis) who has cast the country into perpetual winter. Later, Edmund finds his way into Narnia and meets the Witch. She promises to make him a Prince if he will bring his brother and sisters to her.

After this all four children go through the Wardrobe into Narnia. They find Mr Tumnus's home destroyed and Mr Tumnus taken prisoner by the White Witch. In the cave is a letter charging him with high treason. It is signed by 'Maugrim, Captain of the Secret Police' (6). The children are befriended by Mr and Mrs Beaver, and it is from them that they first hear of Aslan. 'At the name of Aslan each one of the children felt something jump in its inside' (7). Aslan, the Beavers explain, is the great Lion and 'king of the Wood and the son of the great Emperor-beyond-the-Sea' (8) who has returned to Narnia after a long absence. He wants to meet the children at the Stone Table. Behind this there is an ancient prediction that the White Witch will be overthrown when four 'sons of Adam and daughters of Eve' sit on the four thrones of Cair Paravel.

While they are talking, Edmund slips away to the White Witch. In her castle he learns what she is really like. She sets off with Edmund and her devilish forces in an attempt to prevent the other children from reaching Aslan. The sudden Spring begins to melt the ice and snow, thus forecasting her doom.

The children join forces with those Narnians loyal to Aslan, and they fight the army of the White Witch. Peter fights and kills the wolf, Maugrim, and is knighted 'Sir Peter Wolf's-Bane' (12). The Witch then prepares to kill Edmund in an attempt to overturn the prophecy about the four thrones. At this point Aslan intervenes. 'Tell us of this Deep Magic,' he says. 'Tell you?' she says. 'Tell you what is written on that very Table of Stone which stands beside us? Tell you what is written in letters deep as a spear is long on the fire-stones of the Secret Hill? ... You know that every traitor belongs to me as my lawful prey and that for every treachery I have a right to a kill.'

Aslan then offers his life for Edmund's, thus satisfying the Magic which the Emperor-Over-Sea put into Narnia at the beginning. Susan and Lucy are hiding nearby and witness as Aslan is slain on the Stone Table with the Stone Knife. While they grieve for him the Table is cracked, and Aslan, resurrected from the dead, returns. He tells them of the 'Deeper Magic from before the dawn of Time' (15): if a willing victim who had committed no treachery is killed in a traitor's place, the Table shall crack and Death itself begins to work backwards. The four children and the loyal Narnians join Aslan in defeating the White Witch and her forces. The children are crowned Kings and Queens of Narnia at Cair Paravel. They reign for many years, until one day, while following the White Stag, they chase him into a thicket past the Lamp Post and – come tumbling out of the Wardrobe into this world.

A Note on the Differences between the
English and American Editions of
The Lion, the Witch and the Wardrobe,
and *The Voyage of the 'Dawn Treader'*

Lewis made several significant changes in the American editions of *The Lion, the Witch and the Wardrobe* and *The Voyage of the 'Dawn Treader'*. Those made in *The Lion* are as follows: (1) In chapter 6 of the English edition the Captain of the Secret Police is called 'Maugrim': in the American edition this is changed to 'Fenris Ulf'. The name 'Maugrim' had probably been suggested by 'maugre' or ill-will. The name 'Fenris' is taken from Norse mythology. In that mythology Loki is a kind of Scandinavian Mephistopheles who is plotting to hasten the downfall of the gods. He spawns three monster children, one of whom is a great and terrible wolf named Fenris. (2) To be consistent it was necessary that in chapter 12 Peter's title be changed from 'Sir Peter Wolf's-Bane' to 'Sir Peter Fenris-Bane'.

(3) In chapter 13 of the English edition there is an exchange between Aslan and the White Witch about the 'Deep Magic from the Dawn of Time' which allows every traitor to become the Witch's 'lawful prey'. We would probably be right in saying that the Deep Magic 'put into Narnia at the very beginning' is the moral order, the Moral or Natural Law§ of Narnia. As Lewis says of Natural Law in **AOM** (1): 'It is Nature, it is the Way, the Road. It is the Way in which the universe goes on.' Lewis believed that 'God commands certain things because they are right', not 'certain things are right because God commands them' (**PP** 6). Thus, while God is the origin of the Moral Law, He commands it not because it originated with Him but because it is right. It would follow that Aslan is one with the moral order of Narnia. 'Do you think I wouldn't obey my own rules?' he asks Lucy in **VDT** 10.

When Aslan suggests that the Witch 'Tell us of this Deep Magic', she mentions the three places this Deep Magic can be found. 'Tell you,' she says, 'what is written on that very Table of Stone which stands beside us? Tell you what is written in letters deep as a spear is long on the fire-stones of the Secret Hill? Tell you what is engraved on the sceptre of the Emperor-Over-Sea?' In the American edition the sentence containing 'the fire-stones of the Secret Hill' is changed to 'Tell you what is written in letters deep as a spear is long on the *trunk of the World Ash Tree* [emphasis added]?'

There is no exact equivalent in Christian history, but the 'Table of Stone', 'fire-stones' and 'Secret Hill' are obviously intended as the Narnian equivalent of Calvary. In the American edition of *The Lion* Lewis gave the Norse imagery additional emphasis. The 'World Ash Tree' is meant to recall the great World Ash Tree, or 'Yggdrasil', which has a central place in Norse mythology. In Teutonic myth the gods live in Asgard, men live in Midgard, and below this is the realm of the dead, Niflheim. The branches of the ever-green Yggdrasil stretch into all these regions, nourishing and sustaining all spiritual and physical life. Odin, the chief deity of Norse mythology, is the god of wisdom. He is also the inventor of runes – the earliest alphabet used by northern nations, whose characters sometimes have magical influence and were used for divination. A story which had great appeal to Lewis is that of Odin's self-sacrifice. He hung upon the sacred tree Yggdrasil for nine days and nights, self-wounded by his spear. 'Nine nights I hung upon the Tree, wounded with the spear as an offering to Odin, myself sacrificed to myself' (*Hávamál*), Lewis quoted in *Dymer*. When he had mastered the wisdom he sought, Odin cut magic runes in three places: upon his spear Gungnir, upon the teeth of his horse Sleipnir, and upon the claws of the bear. Lewis clearly had these events in mind when he composed the similar episode in Narnia.

The principal change made in *The Voyage* occurs in chapter 12. As King Caspian and the crew of the 'Dawn Treader' emerge from the black cloud over the Dark Island, the English edition says: 'In a few moments the darkness turned into a greyness ahead, and then, almost before they dared to begin hoping, they had shot out into the sunlight and were in the warm, blue world again. And all at once everybody realized that there was nothing to be afraid of and never had been. They blinked their eyes and looked about them. The brightness of the ship ...' This was altered in the American edition to read: 'In a few moments the darkness turned into a greyness ahead, and then, almost before they dared to begin hoping, they had shot out into the sunlight and were in the warm, blue world again. And just as there are moments when simply to lie in bed and see the daylight pouring through your window and to hear the cheerful voice of an early postman or milkman down below and to realize that *it was only a dream: it wasn't real*, is so heavenly that it was very nearly worth having the nightmare in order to have the joy of waking, so they all felt when they came out of the dark. The brightness of the ship ...'

These and a few other changes are given in detail by Paul F. Ford in his *Companion to Narnia* (San Francisco: HarperCollins, 1980; fourth impression 1994). Lewis allowed these differences in the American edition to remain. However, when the new American impressions of the Chronicles were published by HarperCollins of New York in 1994 the differences were removed, and now all editions conform to the original English editions.

3: The Horse and His Boy

This story is set in the reign of Peter, Edmund, Susan and Lucy, as described in *The Lion*, and is thus a story within a story. It tells how the boy Shasta of Calormen runs away to avoid being sold as a slave. He is assisted in his escape by Bree, a Talking Horse of Narnia. They are joined by a girl, Aravis, and her talking horse Hwin, who are also trying to leave Calormen. In Tashbaan, the capital of Calormen, Shasta is mistaken for Prince Corin of Archenland who is there with King Edmund and Queen Susan, who are on a state visit from Narnia. Queen Susan had earlier had a proposal from Prince Rabadash, but she tells her brother that she would not marry him 'for all the jewels in Tashbaan' (4).

Meanwhile, in the palace of the Tisroc, Aravis discovers a plot by Prince Rabadash to invade Archenland and Narnia. While Edmund and Susan sail home on their ship, Shasta and Aravis escape with the horses across the desert towards Archenland, in order to warn King Lune of Rabadash's plan. They are hurried along by a lion, who is really Aslan. Aravis is wounded and is tended by the Hermit of the Southern Marches, and Shasta, again forced on by Aslan, reaches Archenland in time to warn King Lune of Prince Rabadash's plot. The Narnians are able to defeat the Calormen army, and Aslan teaches Rabadash an important lesson by turning him into an Ass. Shasta discovers that he is really the twin brother of Prince Corin of Archenland. In time he succeeds his father as King of Archenland and marries Aravis.

4. Prince Caspian: The Return to Narnia

This tale opens with the same four Pevensie children waiting on a station platform one year after the adventure recounted in *The Lion*. They are suddenly drawn into Narnia and find themselves in the ruins of Cair Paravel. Centuries have passed since their previous visit, and after rescuing Trumpkin the Dwarf they learn that the Telmarines now rule Narnia. The word *Tellus* comes from the Latin and in Roman mythology means the goddess of the *Earth*. It is also a name for the Earth and its inhabitants. *Mare* in Latin means *sea*, and it is from this word that we get *marine*. 'Telmar', thus, means *earth-sea*, and 'Telmarines' are 'Sailors from the Earth' or 'Earthly sailors', as explained by Aslan at the end of the book.

Trumpkin goes on to tell the children that Prince Caspian, who needs their help, was raised by his uncle, Miraz, king of Narnia, and his wife Queen Prunaprismia. Caspian was educated by a kindly old tutor named Doctor Cornelius, who, sensing the young man's love for the 'Old Things', tells him things Miraz does not want spoken of. Narnia, he explains, was not originally the world of Men, but 'the country of Aslan, the country of the Waking Trees and Visible Naiads, of Fauns and Satyrs, of Dwarfs and Giants, of the Gods and the Centaurs, of Talking Beasts.' Prince Caspian's family comes from a race who are not 'native Narnians' at all, but 'Telmarines' from 'the Land of Telmar, far beyond the Western Mountains' (4). Caspian the First and his followers conquered the country and drove the native Narnians into hiding. Now Miraz is 'trying to cover up even the memory of them.' The Telmarines are 'in deadly fear of the sea' and will not go near it because of their quarrel with the trees and because Aslan's land lies beyond the sea at the eastern end of the world.

Caspian eventually realizes that the odd-looking Doctor Cornelius is not a man, but a combination of Dwarf and Telmarine. Doctor Cornelius reveals that Caspian is the true King of Narnia, and that Miraz usurped the throne from his late father, Caspian the Ninth. In an attempt to rid himself of those faithful to him, Miraz persuaded seven noble lords, who alone among the Telmarines did not fear the sea, to sail away looking for new lands beyond the Eastern Sea. They have never returned.

Not long after this conversation Queen Prunaprismia has a child, and now that he has an heir, Miraz plans to kill Prince Caspian. Doctor Cornelius helps him escape, and takes him to the Narnians who have been in hiding all this time. Caspian leads them to Aslan's How, which covers the ancient Stone Table. All is not well with these ancient creatures because the Black Dwarf, Nikabrik, has gone bad. As those faithful to Prince Caspian prepare to meet Miraz and his army in battle, the Prince blows Susan's Horn to summon help.

The children realize that it was the winding of the Horn which pulled them into Narnia, and they rush with Trumpkin towards Aslan's How to help the old Narnians. They get lost and are helped along the way by Aslan. As they move towards Aslan's How the Lion rouses all faithful Narnians, who follow him. Meanwhile, Nikabrik had been maintaining that Aslan no longer exists, and has counselled the others to use black sorcery and raise up the White Witch. Aslan and the others destroy them. Peter then challenges Miraz to single combat. At this point we meet Reepicheep, the valiant Mouse (13). Before Peter can defeat Miraz he is killed by his own men, who accuse the Narnians of treachery.

Miraz's army is then defeated, and afterwards peace and order are brought to Narnia.

Aslan explains to the Telmarines that they do not 'belong to this world at all.' 'You came hither,' he said, 'certain generations ago, out of that same world to which the High King Peter belongs ... You, Sir Caspian, might have known that you could be no true King of Narnia unless, like the Kings of old, you were a son of Adam and came from the world of Adam's sons' (15). He tells how a shipload of earthly pirates and their captives dropped right through 'one of the chinks or chasms between that world and this', and found themselves in the Land of Telmar. Before that chasm is closed for ever, Aslan compels the Telmarines either to accept the restitution of Narnia or return to the Earth. Some stay and some leave. Finally, the children are returned to their own world.

5: The Voyage of the 'Dawn Treader'

We are introduced to a new character from our world, the unpleasant Eustace Clarence Scrubb, who is receiving a visit from his cousins Edmund and Lucy Pevensie. They are drawn into Narnia through a picture of a ship, and sail with the former Prince Caspian, now Caspian X, to search for the seven Narnian lords whom the wicked Miraz sent to explore the unknown Eastern Seas beyond the Lone Islands. Reepicheep, the valiant Mouse, hopes that by sailing to the eastern end of the world they will find Aslan's own country.

On one island Eustace gives way to greed and is turned into a dragon. After he has learned humility Aslan restores him to human form. They sail on to the island of the invisible Monopods. Lucy, daring the adventure of the Magician's Book, says the spell which causes them to recover visibility. By a hair's breadth they miss landing on the Dark Island. They are able to save Lord Rhoop from the Island, but he urges them to hurry away because 'This is an Island where Dreams come true'. 'That's the island I've been looking for this long time,' says one sailor unthinkingly. 'Fools!' says Lord Rhoop. 'This is where dreams – dreams, do you understand – come to life, come real. Not daydreams: dreams ... dreams that make you afraid of going to sleep again.' When they reach 'The Beginning of the End of the World' they discover the last three Narnian lords. They are in an enchanted sleep at the mystic table on which is lying the Stone Knife with which Aslan was slain by the White Witch. They are guarded by Ramandu, a retired star. Caspian X later marries Ramandu's daughter.

As they approach the End of the World, Reepicheep and the three children go forward. Then 'quivering with happiness' (16) Reepicheep gets in his little coracle and goes on alone to Aslan's Own Country. The children meet Aslan and, before he sends them home, he tells them that though Edmund and Lucy will never come back to Narnia they will know him better under a different name in their own world.

6: The Silver Chair

A few months after the adventures recounted in *The Voyage of the 'Dawn Treader'* Eustace and Jill Pole are called away from their horrible co-educational school into Narnia. Seventy Narnian years have passed, and Jill learns from Aslan that King Caspian X is now an old man and that his only son, Prince Rilian, was stolen from him many years before. 'I lay on you this command,' he says, 'that you seek this lost prince until either you have found him and brought him to his father's house, or else died in the attempt, or else gone back into your own world' (2). Aslan gives Jill four signs by which she and Eustace will be guided in their quest: they will meet an old friend whom they must greet at once; they must journey to the North till they come to the land of the giants and the City Ruinous; they will find a writing on the stone of that city which they are to follow; they can recognize Rilian because he will ask them to do something 'in the name of Aslan'.

After they bungle the first sign by Eustace's failure to recognize the aged Caspian, one of Lewis's most delightful creatures, Puddleglum the Marshwiggle, leads them into giants' country in the wild wastelands of the north. They meet the Lady of the Green Kirtle who directs them to the House of Harfang, which turns out to be the home of the King and Queen of the Giants. After discovering that they are to be eaten at the giants' Autumn Feast, they escape. They discover Underland where a Witch, the Lady of the Green Kirtle, has Prince Rilian in her power, and is preparing to invade Narnia with her army of Earthmen.

The Witch, by enchantment, brings them to a state in which they are almost ready to disbelieve Aslan's existence. By a great effort of the will, and faith in Aslan, Puddleglum breaks the enchantment. The Witch turns herself into a serpent, and she is killed by Prince Rilian. He escapes with the children and the Marshwiggle to Narnia, and they arrive just in time for the Prince to bid farewell to King Caspian X before the old man dies. Eustace and Jill are taken to the Mountains of Aslan overlooking Narnia, where they witness the resurrection of Caspian by the blood of Aslan. Caspian is allowed to step into our world for a few minutes in order that he and the children may give the bullies at the co-educational school a sound thrashing.

7: The Last Battle

This last chronicle recounts the end of Narnia two hundred years after Aslan was last seen moving visibly through the world. Shift the Ape dresses the simple ass, Puzzle, in the skin of a lion, and this way deceives the Talking Beasts and Dwarfs into thinking it is Aslan. By this deception the Calormenes, who worship the false god Tash and who have long wanted Narnia, are able to overrun the country.

Tirian, the last King of Narnia, is taken captive by the Calormenes. He watches as, night after night, the simple Narnians gather round the Stable. In the light of a bonfire, Shift brings Puzzle out in his lion's skin and passes him off as Aslan. The King prays to Aslan for help and cries out to those children of this world he has heard about. 'Children! Children! Friends of Narnia! Quick. Come to me. Across the worlds I call you' (4). Eustace and Jill are pulled into Narnia by the King's appeal. After freeing Tirian, they disguise themselves as Calormenes and, with the King and his unicorn friend Jewel, they steal Puzzle from the Stable.

The Stable now empty, the Calormenes are horrified to discover that it is soon occupied by the odious Tash – in whom they had lost faith. In a rare moment of peace for King Tirian and the children, Jill says, 'Our world is going to have an end some day. Perhaps this one won't. Oh Jewel – wouldn't it be lovely if Narnia just went on and on?' (8). Moments later Farsight the Eagle arrives with the news that the royal palace Cair Paravel is now filled with dead Narnians and living Calormenes. Roonwit the Centaur, as he lay dying of a Calormene arrow, sent a message to the King saying that 'all worlds draw to an end and that noble death is a treasure which no one is too poor to buy' (8).

Tirian and his followers hope that by exposing Shift's attempt to pass Puzzle off as Aslan they will undo the Ape's trickery. They are shocked to discover that Shift has become the mouthpiece of the Calormenes. As the crowds of simple Narnians continue to gather round the Stable, the Ape tells them that Puzzle, a 'Wicked Beast has ... dressed itself up in a lion-skin and is wandering about in these very woods pretending to be Aslan' (9). Shift tells them that 'Aslan – Tashlan – is angrier than ever. He says he's been a great deal too good to you, coming out every night to be looked at, see! Well, he's not coming out any more' (10). After daring them to look inside the Stable, Shift goes in and is gobbled up by the odious Tash. Tirian then leads the loyal Narnians in the Last Battle around the Stable. Those who are not killed are forced through the Stable door. There they find Tash, who instantly pounces upon the Calormenes. Aslan then appears and says, 'Begone, Monster, and take your lawful prey to your own place: in the name of Aslan and Aslan's great Father the Emperor-over-the-Sea' (12).

The next moment Tirian, still inside the Stable, finds himself greeted by all the Kings and Queens of Narnia, Peter, Edmund, Lucy, Digory, Polly – and those killed in the Last Battle – Eustace and Jill. When he asks after Susan he learns that she 'is no longer a friend of Narnia' (12). Although they are *in* the Stable they find themselves in a vast open space, and Jill points up the significance of this. 'In our world too,' she says, 'a stable once had something inside it that was bigger than our whole world' (13). Aslan comes to the Stable Door and holds his Last Judgement. Those who are worthy pass in, while those who are not pass into darkness. Narnia is then destroyed and the Stable Door is closed for ever.

Those inside the Stable find that they are in the *real* Narnia of which the other had been 'only a shadow or a copy of the real Narnia as our world, England and all, is only a shadow or copy of something in Aslan's real world' (15). Aslan leads them to the Garden of Paradise, where they are united with Reepicheep and all their friends. They see from that great height all that was worth saving from all worlds joined on to Aslan's Own Country.

VII: Outline of Narnian History so far as it is known

Lewis had no over-all outline of all seven stories in his head when he began. He worked from the 'pictures' as they came to him. Then, when the stories had been written, and published, he went back and reviewed them as a whole. It was then that he wrote, for his own convenience, the 'Outline of Narnian history so far as it is known' as given below. There are, all told, 2555 Narnian years between its Creation and its End, and only 52 Earthly years. There is, however, no Narnian equivalent of an earthly year. For instance, between 1940 and 1941 of our time 1303 Narnian years go by: between 1941 and 1942 of our time only 3 Narnian years go by.

This was no accident. Lewis loved the idea that different worlds might have different 'times', as for instance, in *The Dark Tower*. He also played with the idea that time might have 'thickness' as well as length. He returns to the theme again in *The Lion* (5) when the Professor says, 'I should not be at all surprised to find that the other world had a separate time of its own; so that however long you stayed there it would never take up any of *our* time.' But the most complete expression of the idea is found in *Letters to Malcolm* (XX) where he suggests:

The dead might experience a time which was not quite so linear as ours – it might, so to speak, have thickness as well as length. Already in this life we get some thickness whenever we learn to attend to more than one thing at once. One can suppose this increased to any extent, so that though, for them as for us, the present is always becoming the past, yet each present contains unimaginably more than ours.

Outline of Narnian History
so far as it is known

NARNIA Narnian years		ENGLAND English years	
		1888	Digory Kirke born
		1889	Polly Plummer born
1	Creation of Narnia. The Beasts made able to talk. Digory plants the Tree of Protection. The White Witch Jadis enters Narnia but flies into the far North. Frank I becomes King of Narnia	1900	Polly and Digory carried into Narnia by magic Rings
180	Prince Col, younger son of K. Frank V of Narnia, leads certain followers into Archenland (not then inhabited) and becomes first King of that country		
204	Certain outlaws from Archenland fly across the Southern desert and set up the new kingdom of Calormen	1927	Peter Pevensie born
		1928	Susan Pevensie born
300	The empire of Calormen spreads mightily. Calormenes colonize the	1930	Edmund Pevensie born

land of Telmar to the West of Narnia

302	The Calormenes in Telmar behave very wickedly and Aslan turns them into dumb beasts. The country lies waste. King Gale of Narnia delivers the Lone Islands from a dragon and is made Emperor by their grateful inhabitants	1932	Lucy Pevensie born
407	Olvin of Archenland kills the Giant Pire		
460	Pirates from our world take possession of Telmar		
570	About this time lived Moonwood the Hare		
898	The White Witch Jadis returns into Narnia out of the far North		
900	The Long Winter begins		
1000	The Pevensies arrive in Narnia. The treachery of Edmund. The sacrifice of Aslan. The White Witch defeated and the Long Winter ended. Peter becomes High King of Narnia	1940	The Pevensies, staying with Digory (now Professor) Kirke, reach Narnia through the Magic Wardrobe
1014	K. Peter carries out a successful raid on the Northern Giants. Q. Susan and K. Edmund visit the		

Court of Calormen. K.
Lune of Archenland
discovers his long-lost
son Prince Cor and
defeats a treacherous
attack by Prince Rabadash
of Calormen

1015 The Pevensies hunt the
      White Stag and vanish out
      of Narnia

1050 Ram the Great succeeds
      Cor as K. of Archenland

1502 About this time lived
      Q. Swanwhite of Narnia

1998 The Telmarines invade and
      conquer Narnia. Caspian I
      becomes King of Narnia

2290 Prince Caspian, son of
      Caspian IX, born. Caspian
      IX murdered by his brother
      Miraz who usurps the
      throne

2303 Prince Caspian escapes   1941 The Pevensies again
      from his uncle Miraz.   caught into Narnia by
      Civil War in Narnia. By   the blast of the Magic
      the aid of Aslan and of   Horn
      the Pevensies, whom
      Caspian summons with
      Q. Susan's magic Horn,
      Miraz is defeated and
      killed. Caspian becomes
      King Caspian X of
      Narnia

2304 Caspian X defeats the
      Northern Giants

2306–7	Caspian X's great voyage to the end of the World	1942	Edmund, Lucy and Eustace reach Narnia again and take part in Caspian's voyage
2310	Caspian X marries Ramandu's daughter		
2325	Prince Rilian born		
2345	The Queen killed by a Serpent. Rilian disappears		
2356	Eustace and Jill appear in Narnia and rescue Prince Rilian. Death of Caspian X	1942	Eustace and Jill, from Experiment House, are carried away into Narnia
2534	Outbreak of outlaws in Lantern Waste. Towers built to guard that region		
2555	Rebellion of Shift the Ape. King Tirian rescued by Eustace and Jill. Narnia in the hands of the Calormenes. The last battle. End of Narnia. End of the world	1949	Serious accident on British Railways

VIII: Allegory, Supposal and Symbolism

It is often asked if the Narnian stories are 'allegories'. The answer is 'No'. However, as the word 'allegory' is used so variously by different readers, it will be a good thing to see how Lewis defined the words 'allegory' and 'symbolism', and what he meant by a 'supposal'. The most concise definition he gave of Allegory is found in his letter to Mrs Hook of 29 December 1958 (L) in which he says:

By an allegory I mean a composition (whether pictorial or literary) in which immaterial realities are represented by feigned physical objects, e.g. a pictured Cupid allegorically represents erotic love (which in reality is an experience, not an object occupying a given area of space) or, in Bunyan, a giant represents Despair.

However, the fullest definition comes in chapter II of *The Allegory of Love*:

[ALLEGORY] Allegory, in some sense, belongs not to medieval man but to man, or even to mind, in general. It is of the very nature of thought and language to represent what is immaterial in picturable terms. What is good or happy has always been high like the heavens and bright like the sun. Evil and misery were deep and dark from the first ... This fundamental equivalence between the immaterial and the material may be used by the mind in two ways ... On the one hand you can start with an immaterial fact, such as the passions which you actually experience, and can then invent *visibilia* [visible things] to express them. If you are hesitating between an angry retort and a soft answer, you can express your state of mind by inventing a person called *Ira* [Anger] with a torch and letting her contend with another invented person called *Patientia* [Patience]. This is allegory.

Is Aslan an allegory? In explaining why Aslan was *not* an allegory Lewis usually made a sharp distinction between an Allegory or Representation and a 'Supposal'. For instance, in his letter to Mrs Hook of 29 December 1958 (L) he said:

If Aslan represented the immaterial Deity, he would be an allegorical figure. In reality however he is an invention giving an imaginary answer to the question, 'What might Christ become like if there really were a world like Narnia and He chose to be incarnate and die and rise again in *that* world as He actually has done in ours?' This is not allegory at all. So in *Perelandra*. This also works out a *supposition*. ('Suppose, even now, in some other planet there were a first couple undergoing the same that Adam and Eve underwent there, but successfully.')
     Allegory and such supposals differ because they mix the real and the unreal in different ways. Bunyan's picture of Giant Despair does not start from supposal at all. It is not a supposition but a *fact* that despair can capture and imprison a human soul. What is

unreal (fictional) is the giant, the castle and the dungeon. The Incarnation of Christ in another world is mere supposal: but *granted* the supposition, He would really have been a physical object in that world as He was in Palestine, and His death on the Stone Table would have been a physical event no less than his death on Calvary.

Again, writing to a schoolgirl, Sophia Storr, who asked about the writing of the books, Lewis mentioned (24 December 1959) both Aslan's part in the stories, and what he meant by Allegory:

When I started *The Lion, Witch and Wardrobe* I don't think I foresaw what Aslan was going to do and suffer. I think He just insisted on behaving in His own way. This of course I did understand and the whole series became Christian.

But it is not, as some people think, an *allegory*. That is, I don't say 'Let us represent Christ as Aslan.' I say, 'Supposing there was a world like Narnia, and supposing, like ours, it needed redemption, let us imagine what sort of Incarnation and Passion and Resurrection Christ would have there.' See? (L).

Because readers continue to ask if 'Aslan = Jesus' it is worth making the point even clearer by mentioning the answer Lewis gave to the Fifth Graders he wrote to on 29 May 1954. It is found in his *Letters to Children*:

You are mistaken when you think that everything in the books 'represents' something in this world. Things do that in *The Pilgrim's Progress* but I'm not writing in that way. I did not say to myself 'Let us represent Jesus as He really is in our world by a Lion in Narnia': I said 'Let us *suppose* that there were a land like Narnia and that the Son of God, as He became a Man in our world, became a Lion there, and then imagine what would have happened.' If you think about it, you will see that it is quite a different thing.

In **It All Began with a Picture** ... Lewis said that, once Aslan bounded into *The Lion*, he not only 'pulled' the story 'together', but he also 'pulled the six other Narnian stories in after him.' A very clear explanation of the central position of Aslan to Narnia, and the inter-relationship between the stories, is found in Lewis's letter to Anne of 5 March 1961:

What Aslan meant when he said he had died is, in one sense plain enough. Read the earlier book in this series called *The Lion, the Witch and the Wardrobe*, and you will find the full story of how he was killed by the White Witch and came to life again. When you have read that, I think you will probably see that there is a deeper meaning behind it. The whole Narnian story is about Christ. That is to say, I asked myself 'Supposing that there really was a world like Narnia and supposing it had (like our world) gone wrong and supposing Christ wanted to go into that world and save it (as He did ours) what might have happened?' The stories are my answers. Since Narnia is a world of Talking Beasts, I thought He would become a Talking Beast there, as He became a man here. I pictured Him becoming a lion there because (a) The lion is supposed to be the king of beasts; (b) Christ is called 'The Lion of Judah' in the Bible; (c) I'd been having strange dreams about lions when I began writing the work. The whole series works out like this.

The Magician's Nephew tells the Creation and how evil entered Narnia.

The Lion etc the Crucifixion and Resurrection.

Prince Caspian restoration of the true religion after a corruption.

The Horse and His Boy the calling and conversion of a heathen.

The Voyage of the 'Dawn Treader' the spiritual life (especially in Reepicheep).

The Silver Chair the continued war against the powers of darkness.

The Last Battle the coming of the Antichrist (the Ape). The end of the world and the Last Judgement.

Some of Lewis's young readers asked him if the Narnian stories contained 'symbols', and probably the clearest way of answering that is by showing what he meant by Symbolism and its relation to Allegory. The fullest definition of Symbolism is found in chapter II of *The Allegory of Love* where he says:

[SYMBOLISM] If our passions, being immaterial, can be copied by material inventions, then it is possible that our material world in its turn is the copy of an invisible world … The attempt to read that something else through its sensible imitations, to see the archetype in the copy, is what I mean by symbolism or sacramentalism … The allegorist leaves the given – his own passions – to talk of that which is confessedly less real, which is a fiction. The symbolist leaves the given to find that which is more real. To put the difference in another way, for the symbolist it is we who are the allegory ... Symbolism comes to us from Greece. It makes its first effective appearance in European thought with the dialogues of Plato.

The Narnian character closest to Lewis himself is the 'old Professor' we meet in *The Lion*, and who appears again as Lord Digory in *The Last Battle*. In the first instance he chides the children for not seeing that there might be more than one 'time' and that there might be more than one world. 'I wonder what they *do* teach them at these schools,' he exclaims (5). He was referring to the absence of the teaching of metaphysical thought in the new schools – especially as found in the Platonic Dialogues.

In *The Last Battle* (15) we find the most perfect example of Symbolism in all Lewis's work, and Plato named specifically. Those who fought in the Last Battle are now inside the world beyond the door of the Stable, and it too appears to be Narnia. Peter is mystified because 'Aslan told us older ones that we should never return to Narnia, and here we are.' 'Yes,' says Eustace, 'we saw it all destroyed.' 'And it's all so different,' says Lucy. There follows Lord Digory's explanation of how 'our material world in its turn is the copy of an invisible world':

> When Aslan said you could never go back to Narnia, he meant the Narnia you were thinking of. But that was not the real Narnia. That had a beginning and an end. It was only a shadow or a copy of the real Narnia which has always been here and always will be here: just as our world, England and all, is only a shadow or copy of something in Aslan's real world. You need not mourn over Narnia, Lucy. All of the old Narnia that mattered, all the dear creatures, have been drawn into the real Narnia through the Door. And of course it is different; as different as a real thing is from a shadow or as waking life is from a dream ... It's all in Plato, all in Plato: bless me, what *do* they teach them at these schools!

Because Plato is not taught much in schools it is important to mention his influence on the Narnian stories. It is from his Socratic Dialogues, such as the *Timaeus* (29), that Lewis derived the idea – strongly expressed in *The Last Battle* – that everything good and true in this material world is a 'copy' of something in the eternal world of 'Ideas' or 'Forms'. By grasping the eternal Forms and participating in them the soul attains its true well-being. Or as Lewis said in *The Allegory of Love* (II): 'All visible things exist just in so far as they succeed in imitating the Forms.'

Another very important idea in Lewis's work, particularly *The Last Battle*, and which found expression in the film *Shadowlands*,‡ comes from Plato's *Republic*. It is from this dialogue that Lewis derived the notion of Heaven as the unchanging reality behind this shifting changing world of *shadows*, or *shadowlands* as Lewis called it. In Book VII of the *Republic* Socrates is speaking to the young man Glaucon:

> Picture men dwelling in a sort of subterranean cavern with a long entrance open to the light on its entire width. Conceive them as having their legs and necks fettered from childhood, so that they remain in the same spot, able to look forward only, and prevented by the fetters from turning their heads. Picture further the light from a fire burning higher up and at a distance behind them, and between the fire and the prisoners and above them a road along which a low wall has been built, as the exhibitors of puppet shows have partitions between the men themselves, above which they show the puppets.
>
> All this I see, he said.
>
> See also, then, men carrying past the wall implements of all kinds that rise above the wall, and human images and shapes of animals as well, wrought in stone and wood and every material, some of these bearers presumably speaking and others silent.
>
> A strange image you speak of, he said, and strange prisoners.
>
> Like to us, I said. For, to begin with, tell me do you think that these men would have seen anything of themselves or of one another except the shadows cast from the fire on the wall of the cave that fronted them?
>
> How could they, he said, if they were compelled to hold their heads unmoved through life?
>
> And again, would not the same be true of the objects carried past them?
>
> Surely.
>
> If then they were able to talk to one another, do you not think that they would suppose that in naming the things that they saw they were naming the passing objects?
>
> Necessarily.
>
> And if their prison had an echo from the wall opposite them, when one of the passers-by uttered a sound, do you think that they would suppose anything else than the passing shadow to be the speaker?
>
> By Zeus, I do not, said he.

Then in every way such prisoners would deem reality to be nothing else than the shadows of the artificial objects.

Quite inevitably, he said.

Consider, then, what would be the manner of the release and healing from these bonds and this folly if in the course of nature something of this sort should happen to them. When one was freed from his fetters and compelled to stand up suddenly and turn his head around and walk and to lift up his eyes to the light, and in doing all this felt pain and, because of the dazzle and glitter of the light, was unable to discern the objects whose shadows he formerly saw, what do you suppose would be his answer if someone told him that what he had seen before was all a cheat and an illusion, but that now, being nearer to reality and turned toward more real things, he saw more truly?[1]

These ideas about Forms and Shadows were more than a merely literary device. Lewis believed with all his heart that the salvation of all that was good in our world would be part of the general Resurrection.

IX: Theology and Narnia – We Murder to Dissect

What have the Chronicles of Narnia and the Bible in common? How have the Bible and Christian theology 'influenced' the Narnian books? Are the Chronicles of Narnia works of theology?

To talk about 'influences' is dangerous for those readers who are under the mistaken notion that if you have found a biblical or literary 'influence' behind a work there is no more to be said about it. Thus, before saying anything more about 'influences' let us consider three cautions. (1) The first is from Lewis's essay **The Genesis of a Medieval Book**. For years scholars of the Arthurian Legend have asked what the Holy Grail *is*. Is it the Cup of the Last Supper, or a Celtic Cauldron of Plenty, or something else? And if it is one of these things, is it the *same thing* in all the stories in which it appears? In his essay Lewis could just as easily be answering a question about whether something in the Bible *is* the same thing in the Narnian stories. He says:

[1] The translation is by Paul Shorey and it is found in *The Collected Dialogues of Plato, Including the Letters*, ed. Edith Hamilton and Huntington Cairns (Princeton University Press, eleventh printing 1982).

The text before us, however it came into existence, must be allowed to work on us in its own way, and must be judged on its own merits … And while we are reading or criticizing we must be on our guard against a certain elliptical mode of expression which may be legitimate for some purpose but is deadly for us. We must not say that the Grail 'is' a Celtic cauldron of plenty, or that Malory's Gawain 'is' a solar deity, or that the land of Gome in Chrétien's *Lancelot* 'is' the world of the dead. *Within a given story any object, person, or place is neither more nor less nor other than what that story effectively shows it to be. The ingredients of one story cannot 'be' anything in another story, for they are not in it at all.* (Emphasis added.)

(2) The second 'caution' comes from Wordsworth's poem *The Table Turned* in which he says (the last sentence has been italicized):

> Our meddling intellect
> Mis-shapes the beauteous forms of things: –
> *We murder to dissect.*

Every time we spot something in the Narnian stories which we have also come across in the Bible, we should remember these cautions: 'The ingredients of one story cannot *be* anything in another story, for they are not in it at all', and we *murder* a literary work when we dissect it. Still, it is true that Lewis made a free use of the Bible without contradicting the truth of what he found there, and this poses an interesting theological problem.

(3) The third caution concerns a question about the relationship between Aslan and Christ. Before saying Aslan 'is' Christ let us keep in mind the advice Lewis gave to the Fifth Graders on 29 May 1954 (**LTC**): 'I did not say to myself "Let us represent Jesus as He really is in our world by a Lion in Narnia": I said "Let us *suppose* that there were a land like Narnia and that the Son of God, as He became a Man in our world, became a Lion there, and then imagine what would have happened."'

It is the 'supposing' and the 'imagining' that Lewis was so successful with. The Narnian stories are deeply Christian in that they are suffused throughout with much that came directly from the Gospel and, rooted in the soil of Narnia, bore fruit that was natural to it there. Much else simply arose 'inevitably', as Lewis said in **Three Ways of Writing for Children** 'from the whole cast of the author's mind.' The Narnian stories are the *fruits* of theology, and for this reason they are not meant to stand up to the same sort of clear theological analysis that an intended work of theology might be subjected to.

X: Aslan and the Incarnation

Having been warned about the danger of dissecting, it is nevertheless legitimate to think about the relation of Theology to the Narnian stories. Theology is an intellectual discipline, a 'science of God', a method of arranging and interpreting formally revealed truths about God. *Mere Christianity* was meant to do this for ordinary people. 'Doctrines are not God,' Lewis pointed out in **MC** IV:1, 'they are only a kind of map. But that map is based on the experience of hundreds of people who really were in touch with God – experiences compared with which any thrills or pious feelings you and I are likely to get on our own are very elementary and very confused ... If you do not listen to Theology, that will not mean that you have no ideas about God. It will mean that you have a lot of wrong ones' (IV:1).

One of the doctrines which Lewis wrote a great deal about, and which most would consider the central truth of the Gospel, is that of the Incarnation. This doctrine affirms that the eternal Son of God took human flesh from His human mother and that Jesus is at once fully God and fully man. A classical statement of the Incarnation is found in the Athanasian Creed – Lewis wrote of it in **On the Reading of Old Books** – in which it is said that Christ is:

> God and Man; God, of the Substance of the Father, begotten before the worlds: and Man, of the Substance of his Mother, born in the world; Perfect God, and Perfect Man ... Who although he be God and Man; yet he is not two, but one Christ; One, not by conversion of the Godhead into flesh: but by taking of the Manhood into God.

This means that in some mysterious way the eternal Son of God is united with a human Mother to become one person. It is the union, as is said in the Nicene Creed, of Perfect God and Perfect Man. The Christian account goes on to say that by his Incarnation Christ was able to taste death on behalf of the whole human race, and that by his rising to life again he restores us to everlasting life. He then ascends into Heaven in his glorified Manhood – which Manhood, the Creeds say, he keeps for all time.

Before considering the application of this to Aslan, let us note the appropriateness of Lewis's choice in choosing a Lion to be the incarnation of Christ in Narnia. As so many writers of animal stories before him, Lewis naturally thought of the Lion as the King among beasts. But he was borrowing from the Christian tradition as well, because the Lion had for long symbolized (as Lewis used the word) the Messiah. Aslan also appears at the end of *The Voyage of the 'Dawn Treader'* as a Lamb. The theologian Austin Farrer,* said this about Aslan:

> The Seer of Revelation is shown Christ as a Lamb, not a Lion. But it is to be observed that at his first appearance the Lamb-Christ is introduced as a paradoxical substitute for a Lion-Christ. 'One ... saith unto me, Weep not: behold, the Lion from the Tribe of Judah, the Scion of David, has conquered; he can open the Book ... And I saw in the midst of the Throne ... a Lamb standing as though slaughtered' (Revelation 5:5f). A Jewish seer of much the same date presents the straight picture of the royal Aslan: 'And I beheld, and lo, as it were a lion roused out of the wood roaring; and I heard him send forth a human voice ... This is the Messiah whom the Most High has kept unto the end of the days, who shall spring up out of the seed of David' (2 Esdras 11:37; 12:32). The Lion-Messiah of Jewish tradition derives from the Oracles of Jacob on his twelve sons. He praises Judah as the royal stem, a lion none does rouse, a hand from which the sceptre will never depart (Genesis 49:9). **PWD** 7.

The Lion having been chosen to represent Christ – surely the most appropriate choice in a land of Talking Beasts – we straightway run into difficulties when we attempt to apply the doctrine of the Incarnation to Aslan. We don't know if he was ever a cub suckled by a lioness. Indeed, He is not always found in the fashion of a Lion, although if chapter 14 of *The Horse and His Boy* were the only part of the stories we possessed we might be led to think so. In that chapter Lewis, interestingly, makes Bree the Horse guilty of the Gnostic heresy of Docetism (a tendency in the early Church to treat the humanity and sufferings of Christ as apparent but not real). Bree did not believe that Aslan's *lion* nature was genuine. 'No doubt,' he said –

> When they speak of him as a Lion they only mean he's as strong as a lion or ... as fierce as a lion. Or something of that kind ... It would be quite absurd to suppose he is a *real* lion. Indeed it would be disrespectful. If he was a lion he'd have to be a Beast just like the rest of us. Why! ... If he was a lion he'd have four paws and a tail, and *Whiskers*!

The next moment Aslan is standing in front of him, and he says:

> Now Bree ... you poor, proud, frightened Horse, draw near. Nearer
> still, my son. Do not dare not to dare. Touch me. Smell me. Here are
> my paws, here is my tail, these are my whiskers, I am a true Beast.

The episode was probably modelled on John's account of the risen Lord's
appearance to the doubting Thomas: 'Then said [Jesus] to Thomas, Reach
hither thy finger, and behold my hands; and reach hither thy hand and
thrust it into my side: and be not faithless, but believing' (John 20:27).

The passage from John and the passage from *The Horse and His Boy* are
similar, but they mean something quite different. Thomas had been with
Jesus for several years and he is saying (John 29:25) that only by handling
his physical body will he believe that Jesus is risen, and that the risen
Lord is the same person as the incarnate and crucified Jesus.

Bree, on the other hand, is like the Bishop in *The Great Divorce* (5) who
thought of Jesus as 'something purely spiritual'. Bree even denies that
Aslan has the body of an animal, for as he says, 'If he was a lion he'd have
to be a Beast just like the rest of us' (14). What Aslan makes very clear is
that he is not a man, nor a phantom, but – like Horses, Squirrels, Rabbits,
Dogs and so on – he is a true *Beast*. And that really is what Lewis meant
when he said 'Let us *suppose* that there were a land like Narnia and that
the Son of God, as He became a Man in our world, became a Lion there,
and then imagine what would have happened.'

There are many ways in which attempts to establish exact theological
equivalents between Christ and Aslan break down, but perhaps one more
example will suffice. The gospels represent Christ as passing after death
into a life that has its own new nature: He is still corporeal, can eat broiled
fish, but finds locked doors no obstacle for him (John 20:19) and can
ascend bodily into Heaven. He is related to Nature in such a way that
Spirit and Nature are fully harmonized. Or, to use Lewis's analogy from
Miracles: 'Spirit rides Nature so perfectly that the two together make
rather a Centaur than a mounted knight' (16). It is certainly difficult to
explain how (if at all) Aslan's pre-resurrection body differed from that
which he had after his death. In *The Lion* we see Aslan undergoing
something very like the Passion of Christ: 'But how slowly he walked!
And his great, royal head drooped so that his nose nearly touched the
grass. Presently he stumbled and gave a low moan' (14). What does it
mean? It means exactly what it says. Even so, it does not appear that any
physical change is caused by his resurrection: he was omniscient and
omnipotent both before and after the event. At this point it is enough to
accept the author's word that whatever change was needed was there
whether we could detect it or not. 'The Passion and Resurrection of

Aslan,' Lewis wrote to Patricia Mary Mackey on 8 June 1960, 'are the Passion and Resurrection Christ might be supposed to have had in *that* world – like those in our world but not exactly like' (**PWD**).

Before leaving the subject, let us step right out of the Narnian stories, and note Aslan's effect on *us*. In **Fern-seed and Elephants** Lewis remarked that the 'flavour of the personality' of Jesus is so strong that 'even while He says things which, on any other assumption than that of Divine Incarnation in the fullest sense, would be appallingly arrogant, yet we – and many unbelievers – accept Him *at His own valuation* when He says, "I am meek and lowly of heart"' (emphasis added). This is true of Aslan as well. Most readers of the Narnian stories, whether believers or unbelievers, find no difficulty in accepting Aslan 'at *his* own valuation'. Indeed, such is the personality of this Lion that the faith we have in him is very close to that faith the early disciples had in Jesus. The disciples believed Jesus – not this or that saying of His, keeping always the decision in their own hands – but *Him*. Readers of the Chronicles have a similar unreserved faith in Aslan.

XI: Aslan and Christ

Instead of thinking 'Aslan equals Jesus' we should really be thinking 'As the Son of God became a man when he came to Earth, so the Son of God became a Lion when he came to Narnia.' The Man and the Lion have in common the same point of origin but each incarnation is appropriate to the world the Son of God becomes a part of.

Is Aslan an 'appropriate' answer to what Christ would have been like if He had become incarnate in Narnia? Is he an appropriate 'development' of an imagined incarnation in Narnia? Put another way, if, let us say, St Paul were to read the Chronicles of Narnia would he say 'Yes, that *is* the way the Son of God would have behaved if there were such a world as Narnia'?

We have seen that it will not do to treat the Narnian stories as if they were systematic theology camouflaged as fairy tales. They were not meant to be that. It was, however, very important to Lewis that the 'supposal' of what the Son of God would be like in Narnia be very close to what He was like in this world. It appears that he tried hard to make the personality of Aslan as like that of Jesus as it was possible and reasonable to do. A good place to begin is a letter Lewis wrote to a former pupil on 26 March 1940 in which he said:

The truth is ... that the sweetly-attractive-human-Jesus is a product of the 19th-century scepticism, produced by people who were ceasing to believe in His divinity but wanted to keep as much Christianity as they could. It is not what an unbeliever coming to the records with an open mind will (at first) find there. The first thing you find is that we are simply not *invited* to speak, to pass any moral judgement on Him, however favourable: it is only too clear that He is going to do whatever judging there is: it is *we* who are *being* judged, sometimes tenderly, sometimes with stunning severity (**L**).

Again, in **Fern-seed and Elephants** Lewis says that 'If anything whatever is common to all believers, and even to many unbelievers, it is the sense that in the gospels they have met a personality.' Jesus, he goes on to say, is one of those characters whom, besides knowing them to be historical, we also 'know as we know real people.' We are not in the least perturbed by the contrasts within the character of Jesus

of peasant shrewdness, intolerable severity, and irresistible tenderness. So strong is the flavour of the personality that, even while he says things which, on any other assumption than that of divine Incarnation in the fullest sense, would be appallingly arrogant, yet we – and many unbelievers too – accept him at his own valuation when he says 'I am meek and lowly of heart'. Even those passages in the New Testament which superficially, and in intention, are most concerned with the divine, and least with the human nature, bring us face to face with the personality.

In *The Lion, the Witch and the Wardrobe* and all the other Chronicles, Lewis embodies in Aslan many of the qualities he found in Christ. Two of the most noticeable are the 'intolerable severity and irresistible tenderness'. Right from the beginning it is pointed out (**LWW** 8) – in anticipation of Aslan's 'intolerable severity' – that he is not 'safe'. 'Of course he isn't safe,' says Mr Beaver, 'but he's good.' In **LWW** 17 Mr Beaver tells the children that Aslan 'doesn't like being tied down'. 'You musn't press him,' he says. 'He's wild, you know. Not like a *tame* lion.' 'It's not as if he were a *tame* lion,' Coriakin says to Lucy after Aslan vanishes (**VDT** 11).

Following Aslan's resurrection, the author says, 'Then with a roar that shook all Narnia from the western lamp-post to the shores of the Eastern sea, the great beast flung himself upon the White Witch' (**LWW** 16). After Eustace is unable to shed his dragon skin, Aslan does it for him. The incident probably echoes Conversion. 'The very first tear he made was so deep that I thought it had gone right into my heart,' said Eustace. 'And when he began pulling the skin off, it hurt worse than anything I've ever felt' (**VTD** 7). When Jill asks Aslan to move so she can get to the stream for a drink 'The Lion answered this only by a look and a very low growl.' '"I have swallowed up girls and boys, women and men, kings and emperors, cities and realms," said the Lion. It didn't say this as if it were boasting, nor as if it were sorry, nor as if it were angry. It just said it' (**SC** 11). When it is vitally important that Aravis reach the Hermit of the Southern March 'the lion rose on its hind legs, larger than you would have believed a lion could be, and jabbed at Aravis with its right paw ... Aravis screamed and reeled in the saddle. The lion was tearing her shoulder' (**HHB** 10). When Rabadash persists in his war with Narnia he is turned into an ass (**HHB** 13).

Sometimes the severity is muted, but nevertheless clear. When Lucy begins to blame the others for what is her own fault 'From somewhere deep inside Aslan's body there came the faintest suggestion of a growl', and when pressed for news of 'what would have happened' in a certain circumstance 'Aslan said nothing' (**PC** 10). When Polly begs Aslan to help Uncle Andrew, Aslan tells her that he is unable to help 'this old sinner'. 'I cannot comfort him,' he says, 'he has made himself unable to hear my voice' (**MN** 14). This self-blinding happens to the Dwarfs as well. 'They have chosen cunning instead of belief,' says Aslan. 'Their prison is only in their own minds, yet they are in that prison; and so afraid of being taken in that they cannot be taken out' (**LB** 13). Finally, there is the final Judgement and the separation of the 'sheep and the goats' (Matthew 25:33). 'The creatures came rushing on ... But as they came right up to Aslan one or other of two things happened to each of them. They all looked straight in his face ... And when some looked, the expression of their faces changed terribly – it was fear and hatred ... And all the creatures who looked at Aslan in that way swerved to their right, his left, and disappeared into his huge black shadow ... But the others looked in the face of Aslan and loved him ... And all these came in at the Door, in on Aslan's right' (**LB** 14).

There are just as many instances of 'irresistible tenderness'. After he has restored Edmund – the betrayer – and before he dies on the Stone Table, the Lion talks to him in private. 'They saw Aslan and Edmund walking together ... There is no need to tell you (and no one ever heard) what Aslan was saying, but it was a conversation which Edmund never forgot' (**LWW** 13). After Aslan has brought all the animal statues back to life one of the lions rushed about saying 'Did you hear what he said? *Us*

Lions. That means him and me. *Us Lions*. That's what I like about Aslan. No side, no stand-off-ishness. *Us Lions*. That meant him and me' (**LWW** 16). When Peter admits his very serious fault, Aslan consoles him saying, 'My dear son' (**PC** 14). 'Sweetheart,' he addresses Gwendolen, and 'Dear Heart' he calls the poor, harried schoolmistress (**PC** 14). After Reepicheep has lost his tail – 'the honour and glory of a Mouse' – all the other Mice are willing to cut theirs off in order to help him 'bear the shame'. '"Ah!" roared Aslan. "You have conquered me. You have great hearts. Not for the sake of your dignity, Reepicheep, but for the love that is between you and your people ... you shall have your tail again"' (**PC** 15).

'Spying on people by magic is the same as spying on them in any other way,' Aslan tells Lucy. 'And you have misjudged your friend. She is weak, but she loves you. She was afraid of the older girl and said what she does not mean' (**VDT** 11). 'Courage, dear heart,' Aslan whispers to Lucy when he appears as an albatross and rescues them from the Dark Island (**VDT** 12). 'Oh, Aslan,' says Lucy at the end of their adventure, 'will you tell us how to get into your country from our world?' 'I shall be telling you all the time,' he says. 'But I will not tell you how long or short the way will be; only that it lies across a river.' As she and the others are returned to their world there is 'the feel of Aslan's mane and a Lion's kiss on their foreheads' (**VDT** 16). As Eustace and Jill weep over the body of the dead King Caspian 'Even the Lion wept: great Lion-tears, each tear more precious than the Earth would be if it was a single solid diamond' (**SC** 16).

'Tell me your sorrows,' Aslan says to the tired and dispirited Shasta. After this 'The High King above all kings stooped towards him. Its mane, and some strange and solemn perfume that hung about the mane, was all round him. It touched his forehead with its tongue. He lifted his face and their eyes met' (**HHB** 11). 'But please, please – won't you – can't you give me something that will cure Mother?' Digory says to Aslan. 'Up till then he had been looking at the Lion's great front feet and the huge claws on them; now, in his despair, he looked up at its face. What he saw surprised him as much as anything in his whole life. For the tawny face was bent down near his own and (wonder of wonders) great shining tears stood in the Lion's eyes ... "My son, my son," said Aslan. "I know. Grief is great. Only you and I in this land know that yet. Let us be good to one another"' (**MN** 12). 'You do not yet look so happy as I mean you to be,' Aslan says at the end of the stories. 'The term is over: the holidays have begun. The dream is ended: this is the morning' (**LB** 16).

Very rarely was Lewis required to defend Aslan as a 'supposal' of what the Son of God might have been like in Narnia. In 1955 a nine-year-old

American boy, Laurence Krieg, became worried that he was committing idol-worship by loving Aslan more than Jesus. His mother mentioned this to Lewis, who in his reply of 6 May 1955 explained why he was not worried about the resemblance:

> Laurence can't *really* love Aslan more than Jesus, even if he feels that's what he is doing. For the things he loves Aslan for doing or saying are simply the things Jesus really did and said. So that when Laurence thinks he is loving Aslan, he is really loving Jesus: and perhaps loving Him more than he ever did before. Of course there is one thing Aslan has that Jesus has not – I mean, the body of a lion. (But remember, if there are other worlds and they need to be saved and Christ were to save them – as He would – He may really have taken all sorts of bodies in them which we don't know about.) Now if Laurence is bothered because he finds the lion-body seems nicer to him than the man-body, I don't think he *need* be bothered at all. God knows all about the way a little boy's imagination works (He made it, after all) and knows that at a certain age the idea of talking and friendly animals is very attractive. So I don't think He minds if Laurence likes the Lion-body. And anyway, Laurence will find as he grows older, that feeling (liking the lion-body better) will die away of itself, without his taking any trouble about it. So he needn't bother (**LTC**).

It is worth noting that when Jane Douglass approached Lewis with the idea of making a cartoon version of *The Lion* for television, Lewis replied on 19 June 1954: 'I am sure you understand that Aslan is a divine figure, and anything remotely approaching the comic (above all anything in the Disney line) would be to me simple blasphemy.'

XII: The Narnian Trinity

If the Chronicles of Narnia have a theological weakness, it is possibly that the Trinity (Father, Son and Holy Spirit) is not properly represented. It might be that Lewis felt that picturing the Father and the Spirit was beyond his capacity, and it would be hard to argue with this except for his dizzyingly successful descriptions of the two planetary archangels, the *Oyéresu* of Perelandra and Malacandra in *Perelandra* 16.

In any event, we learn from the first that Aslan is the 'King of the wood and the son of the great Emperor-Beyond-the-Sea' (**LWW** 8).

'Aslan,' said Caspian, 'is the great Lion who comes from over the sea' (**PC** 4). 'Every story,' Doctor Cornelius tells Caspian, 'says that [Aslan] is the Son of the great Emperor-over-Sea, and over the sea he will pass' (**PC** 7). What is particularly important to notice is that in the first of the Chronicles, in the chapter entitled 'Deeper Magic from Before the Dawn of Time', Aslan is identified as the Son of the One with Whom the 'Deep Magic' originated. 'Tell you what is engraved on the sceptre of the Emperor-Beyond-the-Sea?' the White Witch screams at Aslan. 'You at least know the magic which the Emperor put into Narnia at the very beginning' (**LWW** 13). When Lucy discovers what this could involve for Aslan she says 'Oh, Aslan! ... Can't we do something about the Deep Magic? Isn't there something you can work against it?' '"Work against the Emperor's Magic?" said Aslan, turning to her with something like a frown on his face. And nobody ever made that suggestion to him again' (**LWW** 13). Later Aslan has to reprimand Lucy again. 'Do you think I wouldn't obey my own rules?' he asks (**VDT** 11).

By the 'Deep Magic' and Aslan's 'own rules' are meant the Narnian equivalent of God's plan of salvation – the only authentic wisdom – which is not accessible to rational speculation. Lewis probably had in mind 1 Corinthians 2:4–6: 'My speech and my message were not in plausible words of wisdom, but in demonstration of the Spirit and power, that your faith might not rest in the wisdom of men but in the power of God. Yet among the mature we do impart wisdom, although it is not a wisdom of this age or of the rulers of this age, who are doomed to pass away.'

Following Aslan's resurrection, Susan asks how he could be alive again. '"It means," said Aslan, "that though the Witch knew the Deep Magic, there is a magic deeper still which she did not know. Her knowledge goes back only to the dawn of Time. But if she could have looked a little further back, into the stillness and the darkness before Time dawned, she would have read there a different incantation. She would have known that when a willing victim who had committed no treachery was killed in a traitor's stead, the Table would crack and Death itself would start working backwards."' This, too, is probably a reference to 1 Corinthians 2:7–8: 'But we impart a secret and hidden wisdom of God, which God decreed before the ages for our glorification. None of the rulers of this age understood this; for if they had, they would not have crucified the Lord of glory.'

'Beyond-the-Sea' where the Emperor resides would appear to be the same as what is elsewhere called 'Aslan's Country'. 'Your Kings are in deadly fear of the sea,' Doctor Cornelius says to Caspian, 'because they

can never quite forget that in all stories Aslan comes from over the sea ...
They feel safer if no one in Narnia dares to go down to the coast and look
out to sea – towards Aslan's land and the morning and the eastern end of
the world' (**PC** 4). At the end of 'Dawn Treader's' voyage Reepicheep
sails off in his little coracle towards 'Aslan's country' which lies at the
end of the World (**VDT** 16). *The Silver Chair* begins and ends on 'the
Mountain of Aslan, high up above and beyond the end of that world in
which Narnia lies' (16). And finally in *The Last Battle* those who are
victorious and pass through the Stable Door find themselves in 'the real
Narnia'. Looking 'far out to sea' Lucy 'could discover the islands, island
after island to the end of the world, and beyond the end, the huge
mountain which they had called Aslan's country. But now she saw that it
was part of a great chain of mountains which ringed round the whole
world.'

The other Member of the Trinity, the Holy Spirit, is equally vague in
the Narnian books. Still, He is represented. 'Spirit' comes from the
Hebrew *ruach* and the Greek word πνεῦμα, which words mean *Breath*. As
with the 'Emperor-Over-Sea,' Lewis attempts no pictorial device to
represent the Holy Spirit, but we find Aslan incorporating into himself
the Second Person of the Trinity by the use of his breath and the sweet
fragrance of his person. The Christian will recall Jesus's appearance to the
Disciples after His resurrection: 'Jesus said to them again, "Peace be with
you. As the Father has sent me, even so I send you." And when he had
said this, he breathed on them, and said to them, "Receive the Holy
Spirit"' (John 20:22). When Aslan appears to Lucy and Susan after his
resurrection, Susan wonders if he is a ghost. 'You're not – not a – ?' she
says. 'Aslan stooped his golden head and licked her forehead. The
warmth of his breath and a rich sort of smell that seemed to hang about
his hair came all over her' (**LWW** 15). Aslan breathes on the statues to
bring them to life (**LWW** 16). 'His warm breath came all round' Lucy (**PC**
10). When he comforts her in the vicinity of the Dark Island with his voice
there is with it 'a delicious smell breathed in her face' (**VDT** 12).

In the Acts of the Apostles (2:2–4) it is recounted how, at Pentecost, the
Apostles are assembled waiting for the Spirit when 'Suddenly a sound
came from heaven like the rush of a mighty wind, and it filled all the
house where they were sitting. And there appeared to them tongues as of
fire, distributed and resting on each one of them. And they were all filled
with the Holy Spirit and began to speak in other tongues, as the Spirit
gave them utterance.' Following the creation of Narnia, Aslan confers on
those animals chosen to be Talking Beasts the gift of speech:

The Lion opened his mouth, but no sound came from it; he was breathing out, a long, warm breath; it seemed to sway all the beasts as the wind sways a line of trees. Far overhead from beyond the veil of blue sky which hid them the stars sang again: a pure, cold, difficult music. Then there came a swift flash like fire (but it burnt nobody) either from the sky or from the Lion itself, and every drop of blood tingled in the children's bodies, and the deepest, wildest voice they had ever heard was saying:

'Narnia, Narnia, Narnia, awake. Think. Speak. Be walking trees. Be talking beasts. Be divine waters.' (**MN** 9).

Perhaps the most moving representation of all *three* members of the Holy Trinity, is found in **HHB** 11. It is dark, and Shasta does not know who is walking beside him in the darkness, revealing many things about his life. 'Who *are* you?' Shasta asks.

'Myself,' said the Voice, very deep and low so that the earth shook: and again 'Myself,' loud and clear and gay: and then the third time 'Myself,' whispered so softly you could hardly hear it, and yet it seemed to come from all round you as if the leaves rustled with it … After one glance at the Lion's face he slipped out of the saddle and fell at its feet. He couldn't say anything but then he didn't want to say anything, and he knew he needn't say anything.

The High King above all kings stooped towards him. Its mane, and some strange and solemn perfume that hung about the mane, was all round him. It touched his forehead with its tongue. He lifted his face and their eyes met. Then instantly the pale brightness of the mist and the fiery brightness of the Lion rolled themselves together into a swirling glory and gathered themselves up and disappeared.

Lewis said two of the qualities he gave Aslan, the 'strange and solemn perfume' and the 'light', the 'gold' and 'brightness' of Aslan's mane were suggested by passages about the Holy Grail in Malory's *Morte D'Arthur* and Tennyson's *Idylls of the King*. Those passages are:

Then anon they heard racking and crying of thunder, that hem thought the place should all to-rive; in the midst of the blast entred a sunne beame more clear by seven times then ever they saw day, and all they were alighted of the grace of the holy Ghost … Then there entred into the hall the holy grale covered with white samite, but there was none that might see it, nor who beare it, and there was all the hall fulfilled with good odurs (*Morte* XIII, 7).

> And all at once, as there we sat, we heard
> A cracking and a riving of the roofs,
> And rending, and a blast, and overhead
> Thunder, and in the thunder was a cry.
> And in the blast there smote along the hall
> A beam of light seven times more clear than day:
> And down the long beam stole the Holy Grail
> All over cover'd with a luminous cloud,
> And none might see who bare it, and it past.
> (*Idylls*, 'The Holy Grail' 182–90).

XIII: Obvious and Embedded Christianity

One of those who has shed much light on the Narnian stories is Paul Ford. His *Companion to Narnia* (San Francisco: 1980) is a very valuable resource book on Narnia, and one of its many treasures is a whole section on 'Biblical Allusions'. He is careful to point out in that entry that 'In contrast to direct or explicit scriptural references, which are extremely rare, the numerous allusions are indirect hints of actual biblical phraseology or suggestions of biblical themes or scenes.' We might note two things about the biblical allusions:

(1) Sometimes they are obvious. When this happens they serve much the same purpose in Narnia as they do in this world. Lewis pointed this out to Sophia Storr in his letter of 24 December 1959, in which he said he imagined 'what sort of Incarnation and Passion and Resurrection Christ would have' in Narnia. 'I think this is pretty obvious,' he said, 'if you take all the seven Narnian books as a whole' –

In *The Magician's Nephew* Aslan creates Narnia. In *Prince Caspian* the old stories about Him are beginning to be disbelieved. At the end of the *'Dawn Treader'* He appears as the Lamb. His three replies to Shasta suggest the Trinity. In *The Silver Chair* the old king is raised from the dead by a drop of Aslan's blood. Finally in *The Last Battle* we have the reign of anti-Christ (the ape), the end of the world, and the Last Judgement (**L**).

Lewis was remarkably faithful to the Christian Faith in applying to Narnia not only what *has* happened in this world, but what Christ said *will* happen when we least look for it.

If those who reread the Narnias often need to take a deep breath before they return to *The Last Battle* this may be because the first eleven chapters, which take place in the old, familiar Narnia, are so extremely painful. Almost everything we have come to love is, bit by bit, taken from us. Our sense of loss is made more excruciating because we are allowed – indeed encouraged – to believe that things will eventually get back to 'normal'. We feel certain that the King, at least, will not be deceived by Shift's trickery: but he is. When Eustace and Jill arrive we know it will only be a matter of time until all is put right. Yet, despite their willingness to help, there is so little they can do without the help of Aslan. And where, by the way, *is* he? Our hearts warm within us as Jewel the Unicorn recounts the centuries of past happiness in which every day and week in Narnia had seemed to be better than the last:

> And as he went on, the picture of all those happy years, all the thousands of them, piled up in Jill's mind till it was rather like looking down from a high hill on to a rich, lovely plain full of woods and waters and cornfields, which spread away and away till it got thin and misty from distance. And she said:
> 'Oh, I do hope we can soon settle the Ape and get back to those good, ordinary times. And then I hope they'll go on for ever and ever and ever. *Our* world is going to have an end some day. Perhaps this one won't. Oh Jewel – wouldn't it be lovely if Narnia just went on and on – like what you said it has been?'
> 'Nay, sister,' answered Jewel, 'all worlds draw to an end; except Aslan's own country.'
> 'Well, at least,' said Jill, 'I hope the end of this one is millions of millions of millions of years away' (**LB** 8).

So do we all. Yet a few minutes later Farsight the Eagle brings word that Cair Paravel, the high seat of all the Kings of Narnia, has been taken by the Calormenes. And, as he lay dying, Roonwit the Centaur asked the King to remember that 'all worlds draw to an end and that noble death is a treasure which no one is too poor to buy' (**LB** 8).

Lewis's didactic purpose ought to be clear to those who are Christians. He uses his own invented world to illustrate what the Church has been teaching since the beginning, but which is becoming more and more neglected or forgotten. Namely, that this world will come to an end; it was never meant to be our real home – that lies elsewhere; we do not know, we cannot possibly know, when the end will come; and the end will come, not from within, but from without.

Most of the events in *The Last Battle* are based on Our Lord's apocalyptic prophecies recorded in Matthew 24, Mark 13 and Luke 21. The treachery of Shift the Ape was suggested by the Dominical words found in Matthew 24:23f:

> If any man shall say unto you, Lo, here is Christ, or there; believe it not. For there shall arise false Christs, and false prophets, and shall shew great signs and wonders; insomuch that, if it were possible, they shall deceive the very elect (AV).

The Ape almost – so very, very nearly – succeeds in deceiving even the most faithful followers of Aslan, first through trickery and later, when he becomes the tool of Rishda Tarkaan and Ginger the Cat, in confounding the true and the false, in the course of which he invents a synthetic religion: the confusion of Aslan with the demon Tash as 'Tashlan'. As the monkey Shift is a parody of a man, so his blasphemous new theology is a parody of the truth. We are prepared for ordinary wickedness in an adventure story, but with the advent of the 'new theology' we move into a new and dreadful dimension where ordinary courage seems helpless.

From this point on Lewis lets go the full power of his imagination, and we are carried relentlessly forward into what is truly the *last* battle of Narnia, in front of the Stable. There King Tirian, the children, and the remnant of faithful Narnians are either slain or make their way inside. As the Stable was the entrance of the incarnate Son into the world, so now it comes into use again as the way into his eternal world, Aslan's Country. Drawing out this brilliant piece of symbolism, Lewis has Lucy say: 'In our world too, a Stable once had something inside it that was bigger than our whole world' (**LB** 13).

There is an interesting piece of unravelling of the new synthetic religion near the end of the book. Numbered among the blessed in the real and eternal Narnia is Emeth the Calormene. The name was not chosen at random. *Emeth* is the Hebrew word for 'faithful, true', and he is quite surprised at finding himself there. Expecting that Aslan will kill him, he finds instead that

> the Glorious One bent down his golden head and touched my forehead with his tongue and said, Son, thou art welcome. But I said, Alas, Lord, I am no son of thine but the servant of Tash. He

answered, Child, all the service thou has done to Tash, I account as service done to me ... I ... said, Lord, is it then true, as the Ape said, that thou and Tash are one? The Lion growled so that the earth shook ... and said, It is false. Not because he and I are one, but because we are opposites, I take to me the services which thou has done to him. For I and he are of such different kinds that no service which is vile can be done to me, and none which is not vile can be done to him. Therefore if any man swear by Tash and keep his oath for the oath's sake, it is by me that he has truly sworn, though he know it not, and it is I who reward him. And if any man do a cruelty in my name, then, though he says the name Aslan, it is Tash whom he serves and by Tash his deed is accepted (**LB** 15).

Many have wondered how Lewis justified putting Emeth there, and the answer is that this is how Lewis imagined God might deal with the virtuous heathen. 'Is it not frightfully unfair,' he said in *Mere Christianity* II, 5, 'that this new life should be confined to people who have heard of Christ and been able to believe in Him? But the truth is that God has not told us what His arrangements about the other people are. We do know that no man can be saved except through Christ; we do not know that only those who know Him can be saved through Him.'

When asked about the salvation of Emeth, Lewis cited John 10:16:

And other sheep I have, which are not of this fold: them also I must bring, and they shall hear my voice; and there shall be one fold, and one shepherd.

With a terrible beauty that makes the heart ache, and which is perhaps only matched by Dante's *Paradiso*, Aslan goes to the Stable door and holds his Last Judgement. Those who are worthy pass in, the others turn away into darkness. Inside, the children watch as Aslan, fulfilling the apocalyptic prophecies of the New Testament, destroys Narnia by water and fire and closes the Stable door upon it for ever.

After this dazzling feat of the imagination, one might reasonably expect that Lewis could not help but let us down in 'unwinding' his story. He knew that the merest slip of the pen could have cast a shadow of incredulity over all that went before, and he proceeded very cautiously in opening the children's eyes to where they are. The question was how do you portray Heaven? How make it *heavenly*? How 'unwind' *upwards*. To see how he did this is worth reading all the books for.

(2) In many places the Christianity is embedded. When this occurs we cannot say absolutely that such and such a passage in a Narnian book *is taken from* or *equals* such and such a passage in the Bible. The biblical and classical sources blend into Lewis's stories, not like raisins in a cake, but like leaven in bread. It is difficult to say where they begin and where they end. Sometimes they run into one another, and always the stories are *about* something different from 'parallels' or 'sources'.

For instance, in **VDT** 13–14 the children find three Lords of Narnia asleep under an enchantment, round a table spread with exotic foods supplied by a beautiful Princess. On the table is the cruel-looking knife with which the White Witch killed Aslan. The Princess's father, Ramandu, appears but is unable to speak until a bird lays a live coal on his lips.

Apart from Lewis's imagination, there are a number of 'sources' for these elements. The reader of American literature, upon finding that the Lords of Narnia have slept so long their beards and hair looked like haystacks, will remember Rip Van Winkle. The Knife recalls both the Cross upon which Christ was killed, and King Pelles' sword which struck the Dolorous Blow in the Arthurian legends. And some student of the Bible, upon reading about the bird flying 'to the Old Man with something in its beak that looked like a ... live coal, which it ... laid ... in the Old Man's mouth', will recall Isaiah 6:6 and say '*Gotcha!*' For, yes indeed, Lewis was bound to have recalled, even if subconsciously, that very passage from Isaiah – 'Then flew one of the seraphims unto me, having a live coal in his hand, which he had taken with the tongs from off the altar: and he laid it upon my mouth.'

But we have not exhausted the meaning of a passage in a Narnian story when we lay claim to 'parallels' and 'sources'. Lewis himself says as much through the mouth of the Old Man. When Eustace says to him 'In our world a star is a huge ball of flaming gas', he replies, 'Even in your world, my son, that is not what a star is but only what it is made of' (**VDT** 14). And as Lewis said in a different context, but which certainly applies to the danger of source-hunting: 'It is like taking a red coal out of the fire to examine it; it becomes a dead coal' (**LTM** 19). The Bible, and many other things, some of which we will probably never know about, are *embedded* in the Narnian stories. But that is not what the stories *are*. They are themselves.

XIV: Some Notes Towards Appreciation

The best way to enjoy the Chronicles of Narnia is simply to read them. However, some points might be made towards a fuller appreciation of them. (1) Lewis said in **On Three Ways** that he did not write his Narnian stories with the specific purpose of teaching 'morals', but allowed his 'pictures' to 'tell you their own moral'. In an essay written sometime before 1939 and entitled **Christianity and Literature**, he made the point that

> 'Originality' in the New Testament is quite plainly the prerogative of God alone ... The duty and happiness of every other being is placed in being derivative, in reflecting like a mirror ... If I have read the New Testament aright, it leaves no room for 'creativeness' even in a modified or metaphorical sense. Our whole destiny seems to lie in the opposite direction, in being as little as possible ourselves, in acquiring a fragrance that is not our own but borrowed, in becoming clean mirrors filled with the image of a face that is not ours ...
>
> Applying this principle to literature, in its greatest generality, we should get as the basis of all critical theory the maxim that an author should never conceive himself as bringing into existence beauty or wisdom which did not exist before, but simply and solely as trying to embody in terms of his own art some reflection of eternal Beauty and Wisdom.

He went on to point out a difference between a Christian writer and one who is an unbeliever. 'The unbeliever,' he said, 'may take his own temperament and experience, just as they happen to stand, and consider them worth communicating simply because they are facts or, worse still, because they are his.' However, for the Christian writer 'his own temperament and experience, as mere fact, and as merely his, are of no value or importance whatsoever: he will deal with them, if at all, only because they are the medium through which, or the position from which, something universally profitable appeared to him.'

(2) While Lewis believed that 'When Christian work is done on a serious subject there is no gravity and no sublimity it cannot attain', he nevertheless deplored 'the fussy and ridiculous claims of literature that tries to be important simply as literature.' In another essay, **Christianity and Culture**, written in 1940, he made a point he would certainly have applied to his Narnian stories:

A great deal ... of our literature was made to be read lightly, for entertainment. If we do not read it, in a sense, 'for fun' and with our feet on the fender, we are not using it as it was meant to be used, and all our criticism of it will be pure illusion.

(3) Closely related to this is a point made in *An Experiment in Criticism* III. We should not begin with the idea that we have to 'do things' with books, bringing to works of art, such as the Narnian stories, our preconceptions about what *should be* in them. 'Real appreciation,' said Lewis, 'demands the opposite process':

We must not let loose our own subjectivity upon [them]. We must begin by laying aside as completely as we can all our own preconceptions, interests, and associations ... After the negative effort, the positive. We must use our eyes. We must look, and go on looking till we have certainly seen exactly what is there ... The first demand any work of any art makes upon us is surrender. Look. Listen. Receive. Get yourself out of the way.

(4) Fairy tales, he observed in **Sometimes Fairy Stories May Say Best What's to be Said**, 'can give us experiences we have never had and thus, instead of "commenting on life", can add to it.' Long before he turned to writing fairy tales Lewis observed in **Christianity and Culture** that 'The difficulty of converting an uneducated man nowadays lies in his complacency. Popularized science, the conventions or "unconventions" of his immediate circle, party programmes, etc., enclose him in a tiny windowless universe which he mistakes for the only possible universe. A cultured person, on the other hand, is almost compelled to be aware that reality is very odd and that the ultimate truth, whatever it may be, *must* have the characteristics of strangeness – *must* be something that would seem remote and fantastic to the uncultured.'

What kind of stories can best remove these obstacles? 'Each of us,' he said in the Epilogue to *An Experiment in Criticism*, 'by nature sees the whole world from one point of view with a perspective and a selectiveness peculiar to himself ... but ...

We want to see with other eyes, to imagine with other imaginations, to feel with other hearts, as well as with our own ... We demand windows ... One of the things we feel after reading a great work is 'I have got out.' Or from another point of view, 'I have got in' ...

In coming to understand anything we are rejecting the facts as they are for us in favour of the facts as they are. The primary impulse of each is to maintain and aggrandize himself. The secondary impulse is to go out of the self, to correct its provincialism and heal its loneliness. In love, in virtue, in the pursuit of knowledge, and in the reception of the arts, we are doing this. Obviously this process can be described either as an enlargement or as a temporary annihilation of the self. But that is an old paradox; 'he that loseth his life shall save it.'

(5) It is possible that all the Chronicles of Narnia will do for most readers is to provide them with some innocent fun. However, for those who 'demand windows' and who are able to 'get out' of their own 'windowless universes', Aslan may well do for them what he promised he would do for Lucy and Edmund at the end of *The Voyage of the 'Dawn Treader'*. When Aslan tells them that they are too old to come back to Narnia, they are heartbroken. 'It isn't Narnia, you know,' sobbed Lucy. 'It's *you*. We shan't meet *you* there. And how can we live, never meeting you?'

> 'But you shall meet me, dear one,' said Aslan. 'Are – are you there too, Sir?' said Edmund.
>
> 'I am,' said Aslan. 'But there I have another name. You must learn to know me by that name. This was the very reason why you were brought to Narnia, that by knowing me here for a little, you may know me better there.' (VDT 16).

Reviews

The Lion, the Witch and the Wardrobe: From *The Guardian* (23 February 1951): 'The whole air of the story is rich and strange and coherent; there is something of Hans Andersen's power to move and George MacDonald's power to create strange worlds, and it is, naturally, beautifully written.' The reviewer for *The Times Literary Supplement, Children's Book Section* (17 November 1950), p. vi, said: 'It never becomes that tiresome thing, allegory, which can be worked out like a code or a crossword puzzle; but awareness grows that the frozen kingdom thawing with the arrival of the wild and loving Lion, his death in exchange for Edmund's life, his return, his setting the statues free, emblazon in a fabulous and holy heraldry the theme of redemption.' For the 'Children's Christmas Number' of *Time and Tide* 31 (2 December 1950), children reviewed the new books for children.

The reviewer of *The Lion* said: 'I think that this book is very nice. It could not be better.' Thomas More Tickell (7½).

Prince Caspian: From *The Church Times, Christmas Book Supplement,* CXXXIV (30 November 1951), p. i: 'Let no one suppose that this volume ... is just pious precept. *Prince Caspian* is a first-rate story ... The adventures carry suspense. The talking animals and dwarfs are good and bad in a thoroughly whole-hearted way, and their fate is exactly right for the necessary poetic justice.' *Saturday Review*, 34 (10 November 1951), pp. 70–1 commented: 'Boys and girls who enjoyed the first book will find here the same reward: a good plot, convincing characters, and the graceful working that distinguishes this writer.' Chad Walsh* wrote in *The New York Times Book Review* (11 November 1951), p. 26: 'The cuteness and archness that mar so many books written for children is blessedly lacking here. The story is for boys and girls who like their dwarfs and fauns as solid as the traffic policeman on the corner.'

The Voyage of the 'Dawn Treader': Louise S. Bechtel said in *The New York Herald Tribune Book Review* (16 November 1952), pp. 2–3: 'The strange symbolism will not often be understood, but it is well worth that place at the back of the child's mind where it will linger until suddenly it is clear.' Chad Walsh, *The New York Times Book Review* (16 November 1952), p. 37, said: 'My favourite was the first book of the trilogy – indeed, it seems destined to become a modern fairy tale classic. The second was, by comparison, a let-down. The present book is better than its immediate predecessor, though perhaps not up to the very high level of *The Lion, the Witch and the Wardrobe*'. The reviewer in the *New Yorker*, 28 (6 December 1952), p. 194, said: 'A juvenile odyssey that in excitement and beauty surpasses even the preceding volumes.'

The Silver Chair: V. H. wrote in the *Horn Book*, 19 (October 1953), p. 177: 'Those who have accepted Mr Lewis's three earlier Narnia stories as favourites will find this one equally entrancing and it may be introduced as a first to any lover of make-believe. Adults reading it aloud will appreciate its distinction of style – the deft characterizations, colourful descriptions and playful bits of satire.' Louise S. Bechtel said in *The New York Herald Tribune Book Review* (15 November 1953), p. 28: 'The style is somewhat simpler, but still superior; the rich inventiveness, the vividly imagined weird places, the suspense, all are the same.' And Chad Walsh, in *The New York Times Book Review* (27 December 1953), p. 14, said: 'Mr Lewis's sardonic malice has free rein here, with results that should delight any adult who answers the universal plea, "Read me a story".'

The Horse and His Boy: The reviewer for *Kirkus*, 22 (1 August 1954), p. 484, said: 'A beautifully written tale ... in which C.S. Lewis's talents seem to flower more than ever.' Chad Walsh in *The New York Times Book Review* (17 October 1954), p. 44; said: 'Children, surfeited on un-imaginative tales of socially adjusted children learning socially useful processes, will welcome this story.' Louise S. Bechtel, *The New York Herald Tribune Book Review* (14 November 1954), p. 6: 'It is ... in style and imaginative power still far above other modern fairy tales.' From *Commonweal*, 61 (19 November 1954), p. 203: 'Children who loved the previous books about the magic land of Narnia will welcome these new adventures. But it is not necessary to know the other stories first.'

The Magician's Nephew: E. S. Lauterbach said in *The New York Herald Tribune Book Review* (25 September 1955), p. 8: 'There are magic happenings on every page of this book which will delight old and young lovers of fairy tales. Mr Lewis's prose is clear and simple, yet at times extremely subtle.' Chad Walsh said in *The New York Times Book Review* (30 October 1955), p. 40: 'I am happy to report that Narnia has now produced one of its best crops.'

The Last Battle: Chad Walsh said in *The New York Times Book Review* (30 September 1956), p. 46: 'This is one of the best ... The Christian symbolism is clear enough, but the book can stand on its own feet as a deeply moving and hauntingly lovely story apart from the doctrinal content.' H.P.M., writing in *Horn Book*, 32 (October 1956), p. 352, said: 'It is the culmination of an excellent series, and boys and girls who have loved the other books will find it very satisfying.' Edmund Fuller said in *Chicago Sunday Tribune* (11 November 1956), p. 34: 'The series known as "The Chronicles of Narnia" ... I believe to be the finest group of stories for children, Christian in theme, written in our times.'

Charles A. Brady, writing in *America* (27 October 1956), proclaimed it: 'The greatest addition to the imperishable deposit of children's literature since the *Jungle Books*. Narnia takes its place forever now beside the jasper-lucent landscapes of Carroll, Anderson, MacDonald and Kipling ... The child will not respond to these values at once, though they will awaken in his memory when the time comes for full realization. He will respond immediately, however, to the narrative sweep; to the evocation of the heroic mood; to the constant eliciting of the numinous. Very possibly this latter service is the most startling one Lewis renders contemporary childhood, contemporary Catholic childhood not least. He touches the nerve of religious awe on almost every page. He evangelizes through the imagination.'

Publication Record (England)

I: The Original Hardcover Books

All seven of the Chronicles of Narnia were originally published in London in hardback and all were illustrated by Pauline Baynes. (1) *The Lion, the Witch and the Wardrobe: A Story for Children* was published by Geoffrey Bles* on 16 October 1950; (2) *Prince Caspian: The Return to Narnia* was published by Geoffrey Bles on 15 October 1951; (3) *The Voyage of the 'Dawn Treader'* was published by Geoffrey Bles on 1 September 1952; (4) *The Silver Chair* was published by Geoffrey Bles on 7 September 1953; (5) *The Horse and His Boy* was published by Geoffrey Bles on 6 September 1954; (6) *The Magician's Nephew* was published by The Bodley Head on 2 May 1955; (7) *The Last Battle: A Story for Children* was published by The Bodley Head on 19 March 1956. The covers of all the books carry designs by Pauline Baynes, and *The Lion*, *Prince Caspian* and *The Horse and His Boy* have full-page illustrations on the frontispiece, the first two in colour.

These original Bles editions also contain a number of maps. Soon after Pauline Baynes was commissioned to illustrate *The Lion, the Witch and the Wardrobe*, Lewis sent her a map he had made of Narnia. It is now in the Bodleian Library‡ and it shows Narnia, bordered on the north by the 'Wild Lands of the North' and on the south by Archenland. With this and descriptions from the books to guide her, Pauline Baynes provided maps for four of the Chronicles: (1) 'A Map of Narnia and adjoining Lands' appeared on the end-papers of *Prince Caspian*. (2) A map of the Bight of Calormen and the Lone Islands of the Great Eastern Ocean is on the end-papers of *The Voyage of the 'Dawn Treader'*. (3) 'A Map of the Wild Lands of the North' appeared on the end-papers of *The Silver Chair*, and (4) the map on the end-papers of *The Horse and His Boy* shows the position of Tashbaan, the Desert and Archenland.

II: The First Paperbacks – 'Puffin Books'

The first paperbacks of the books were published as 'Puffin Books' by Penguin Books Ltd of Harmondsworth, Middlesex. (1) *The Lion, the Witch and the Wardrobe: A Story for Children* on 29 October 1959; (2) *Prince Caspian: The Return to Narnia* on 19 April 1962; (3) *The Magician's Nephew* on 27 June 1963; (4) *The Last Battle: A Story for Children* on 30 January 1964; (5) *The Voyage of the 'Dawn Treader'* on 25 March 1965; (6) *The Silver Chair* on 24 June 1965; and (7) *The Horse and His Boy* on 30 September 1965. The books were distinctive in having cover designs of the Narnian characters drawn especially for them by Pauline Baynes. The first boxed set of the Chronicles was produced by Penguin in a box that also featured designs by Pauline Baynes. All Pauline Baynes's maps mentioned above appear in these books with the exception of the one in *The Voyage of the 'Dawn Treader'*.

III: Collins takes over from Bles

The firm of Geoffrey Bles had been bought by William Collins* & Sons as far back as 1953. Although Collins began publishing the paperbacks of Lewis's works in 1955, the imprint of 'Geoffrey Bles Ltd' remained on the hardcover books until the retirement of the Managing Director of Bles, Jocelyn Gibb,* in 1974. That same year William Collins & Sons published hardback copies of the five Narnias previously published by Bles. The other two, *The Magician's Nephew* and *The Last Battle* continued to be published in hardback by The Bodley Head until 1989 when they, too, were published in hardback by Collins. All seven books appeared with new designs by Pauline Baynes, but none contained any of the four maps she had drawn for the Bles editions.

IV: Paperback Rights are acquired by Collins

In 1980 William Collins & Sons, having acquired the paperback rights to *The Magician's Nephew* and *The Last Battle* from The Bodley Head, issued the entire set of Chronicles as 'Fontana Lions'. The books had two distinctive features. The cover designs were by Stephen Lavis, and for the first time the books were given the order Lewis said they should be read in: (1) *The Magician's Nephew*; (2) *The Lion, the Witch and the Wardrobe*; (3) *The Horse and His Boy*; (4) *Prince Caspian*; (5) *The Voyage of the 'Dawn Treader'*; (6) *The Silver Chair*; (7) *The Last Battle*. All Pauline Baynes's maps mentioned in 'I: The Original Hardcover Books' appear in these books, with the exception of that in *The Voyage of the 'Dawn Treader'*.

V: Collins and Harper & Row become HarperCollins

In 1990 the publishers Harper & Row and William Collins & Sons were combined, and while some books continued to come out under the imprint 'Collins', the publishers of the Chronicles of Narnia are now HarperCollins.

In November 1992 HarperCollins published the Chronicles in a boxed set of paperback 'Lions'. The illustrations inside the books were the originals by Pauline Baynes. The covers were designed so that when the books are placed together the picture running along the spine forms a frieze of Cair Paravel. This was the thirty-first impression of *The Magician's Nephew*, the thirty-fifth impression of *The Lion, the Witch and the Wardrobe*, the twenty-sixth impression of *The Horse and His Boy*, the twenty-seventh impression of *Prince Caspian*, the twenty-fifth impression of *The Voyage of the 'Dawn Treader'*, and the twenty-sixth impression of *The Last Battle*. These 'Lions' contain the four maps by Pauline Baynes mentioned in 'I: The Original Hardcover Books'.

VI: Special Editions

Over the years there have been many Special Editions of *The Lion, the Witch and the Wardrobe*. (1) On 26 August 1965 Collins published a hardback edition of the book in the 'Evergreen Library'. (2) In 1981 Macmillan Publishing Company of New York brought out a lovely hardback edition illustrated by Michael Hague. (3) A hardback edition of the book was brought out by Collins Educational in the 'Cascades' series in 1983. (4) In 1986 Clio Press Ltd, Oxford, in arrangement with Collins, brought out hardback copies of all seven of the Chronicles in the 'Windrush Large Print Children's Books'. (5) A paperback 'television tie-in special edition' was published by Collins in September 1988, to go with the BBC Television production of *The Lion* between 13 November and 18 December. (6) On 10 October 1991 HarperCollins published a de luxe hardcover edition of *The Lion* containing, besides all the original illustrations, 18 additional full-page colour illustrations by Pauline Baynes as well as a full-page copy of her map of Narnia. (7) A hardback 'graphic novel' edition of *The Lion*, abridged and illustrated by Robin Lawrie, was published by HarperCollins in 1993.

Publication Record (United States)

I: The Original Hardcover Books

The seven books were published in New York by Macmillan Publishing Company as hardbacks: (1) *The Lion, the Witch and the Wardrobe: A Story for Children* 7 November 1950; (2) *Prince Caspian: The Return to Narnia* 16

October 1951; (3) *The Voyage of the 'Dawn Treader'* 30 September 1952; (4) *The Silver Chair* 6 October 1953; (5) *The Horse and His Boy* 5 October 1954; (6) *The Magician's Nephew* 4 October 1955; (7) *The Last Battle: A Story for Children* 4 September 1956. A good many of Pauline Baynes's illustrations were not included in these books, and they contain none of the maps which appeared in the end-papers of the Bles editions.

II: The First Paperbacks – 'Collier Books'

The seven books were published as a boxed set and individually in 1970 by Macmillan Publishing Company of New York as 'Collier Books'. The covers were illustrated by Roger Hane, and the books contained fewer of Pauline Baynes's illustrations than the Macmillan hard-cover books. Instead of the original illustrations the books contained 'pictures adapted from illustrations by Pauline Baynes'. In 1986 Macmillan brought out a new mass market paperback boxed set, redesigned and using Roger Hane's cover art in a new way. There were no changes in the content.

III: G.K. Hall Edition

In 1986 there was an edition of the seven Chronicles in large print format from G.K. Hall Publishers of Boston, in their Large Print Book Series. These are essentially photo-enlargements of the original 1950–56 Macmillan hardcovers.

IV: Macmillan Trade Hardcovers and Paperbacks

In 1988 Macmillan issued these lovely books, with fresh reproductions of Pauline Baynes's illustrations, in boxed sets. This new edition carried the line 'Reset and reissued 1988'. The cover art for these trade editions is that of Daniel Sans Souci. One of the greatest changes between these books and the original Collier Books is the Americanization of the spelling. The publishers also altered Lewis's delightfully inconsistent use of capitalization, reducing nearly everything to lower case.

V: From Macmillan to HarperCollins

In May 1994 the seven Chronicles of Narnia were published simultaneously in hardcover, trade paperback and mass market 'HarperTrophy' paperback, all in boxed sets, by HarperCollins of New York. They contain, with the exceptions of the frontispieces, all the illustrations and maps by Pauline Baynes that had appeared in the original Bles editions. *The Lion, the Witch and the Wardrobe* and *The Last Battle* contain Pauline Baynes's map of Narnia. The jackets of the hardcover and trade paperback editions were designed by Tom Starace with art by Chris Van Allsburg. Each of the 'HarperTrophy' paperbacks contain a 'Cast of Characters', with covers illustrated by Leo and Diane Dillon.

LITERARY CRITICISM

❧

A Preface to 'Paradise Lost',
English Literature in the Sixteenth Century,
An Experiment in Criticism,
The Discarded Image

A PREFACE TO
'PARADISE LOST' (1942)

Background

I: Milton and Charles Williams's Defence

In a scrap of diary Lewis wrote when he was nine years old he records on 5 March 1908 that 'I read "Paradise Lost", reflections there-on.' We do not know what his 'reflections' were, nor how much of the poem he read, but it was not many years before it had become a favourite of his.

A deep and abiding love for Milton began during 1914–17 when Lewis was a pupil of W.T. Kirkpatrick* in Surrey. He refers to Milton constantly in his letters to Arthur Greeves.* On 27 September 1916 he said 'I am now at "Comus", which is an absolute dream of delight,' and on 7 February 1917 he said 'I am now through the first two books of *Paradise Lost* and really love Milton better every time I come back to him' (**TST**). Shortly after this he composed a poem entitled 'Milton Read Again (in Surrey)' published in *Spirits in Bondage*, which begins:

> Three golden months while summer on us stole
> I have read your joyful tale another time,
> Breathing more freely in that larger clime
> And learning wiselier to deserve the whole.

Later, as a Fellow of Magdalen College,‡ Lewis's lectures in the English School were primarily about Medieval and Renaissance Poetry. Still, Milton remained one of his favourite poets, and in the Trinity Term of 1930 he gave a course on 'The Text of Milton's *Comus*' to B. Litt. Students. In Hilary Term 1937 he gave a series of lectures in the English School on 'Milton and the Epic Tradition', which lectures were repeated the following year.

It was not long after this that Charles Williams* came to live in Oxford, and Lewis arranged for him to lecture on Milton during Hilary Term of 1940. It was Williams's second lecture on 5 February 1940 that caused such excitement in Lewis and indeed in nearly everyone who heard the lecture. 'C.W. lectured nominally on *Comus*,' Lewis wrote to his brother on 11 February, 'but really on Chastity. Simply as criticism it was superb – because here was a man who really started from the same point of view as Milton and really cared with every fibre of his being about "the sage and serious doctrine of virginity" which it would never occur to the ordinary modern critic to take seriously' (L).

Shortly after this Williams contributed an Introduction to the 1940 edition of *The English Poems of John Milton*, ed. H.C. Beeching (Oxford University Press, World's Classic Edition, originally published 1913). It made a tremendous impression on Lewis and was certainly one of the factors which led to the writing of his *Preface*. Williams began his Introduction by explaining that for a long time the reputation of Milton had been under attack:

> The result of this attack, which has come from various sources otherwise not noticeably sympathetic with each other, has been to distract the orthodox defenders of Milton, and to compel the reconsideration everywhere of his power as a poet ...
>
> The general opposition resolved itself into four statements: (i) that Milton was a bad man; (ii) that Milton was, especially, a proud man and was continually writing approvingly about his own pride ...; (iii) that Milton's verse is hard, sonorous and insensitive; (iv) that Milton's subject was remote and uninteresting. This being almost exactly what the orthodox party had been, for centuries, saying with admiration, they were quite helpless when they found it said with contempt. The solemn rituals in praise of Milton were suddenly profaned by a change of accent, but the choruses had not altered; what then were the pious worshippers to do?
>
> There had been, of course, another possibility all along; it may be put very briefly by saying that Milton was not a fool. The peculiar ignorance of Christian doctrine which distinguished most of the academic Chairs and of the unacademic journalists who had been hymning Milton had not prevented them from arguing about the subtle theological point of the Nature of the Divine Son in *Paradise Lost*. The peculiar opposition to high speculations on the nature of chastity felt in both academic and unacademic circles had prevented any serious appreciation of that great miracle of the transmutation of the flesh promised in *Comus*. And the peculiar

ignorance of morals also felt everywhere had enabled both circles to assume that Milton might be proud and that yet he might not at the same time believe that pride was wrong and foolish. It was never thought that, if he sinned, he might repent, and that his repentance might be written as high in his poetry as, after another matter, Dante's in his. Finally, it was not supposed, in either of those circles, that Satan could be supposed to be Satan, and therefore a tempter; that Christ (in *Paradise Regained*) could be supposed to hold human culture a poor thing in comparison with the salvation of the soul.[1]

II: The Ballard Mathews Lectures

Lewis would probably have written his *Preface* in any event, but much of what he wrote was owing to Williams's Introduction. What set him to work was an invitation from University College of North Wales in Bangor. In a letter of 11 March 1941 the Principal of the College, the classicist, Emrys Evans, said, 'I am writing on behalf of the Senate of the College to extend to you an invitation to deliver the Ballard Mathews Lectures here next session ... We should be highly honoured if you could find it possible to give a short course of three lectures in the session 1941–42.' Lewis was unsure what reply to make. Only weeks before the Chaplain-in-Chief to the Royal Air Force, Maurice Edwards, had asked if he would accept a travelling lectureship in Theology to members of the RAF. Lewis had agreed, but as there was a possibility that the RAF lectureship would involve all his time, he mentioned this in his reply to Emrys Evans of 14 March:

> I am at present in the state of having promised to undertake some lecturing to the forces which may, or may not, develop into a full-time job. If it does, I do not know what my commitments will be. I am therefore in some doubt how to answer your invitation. It may be that almost everyone's plans are at present equally uncertain: if so, a conditional acceptance is a nuisance you may have to face from anyone, and if you choose to face it from me, I accept ... I await your decision.

[1] This Introduction is reprinted in Charles Williams's *The Image of the City and Other Essays*, Selected by Anne Ridler with a Critical Introduction (London: O.U.P., 1958).

In the end the travelling lectureship did not turn out to be full-time, and when Lewis wrote to the Principal on 30 October 1941 it appears that he had already finished his *Preface*:

> What I have to say about *Paradise Lost* turns out to be pretty bulky. I shall have no difficulty about selected high lights for three lectures, but I'm thinking of subsequent publication. May I take it that it would not be objectionable to your college if I publish (with any publisher I can get and with the subtitle "expanded from the B.M. Lectures 1941") a book much too long to have been actually delivered – say, 60 to 70 thousand words?

University College agreed, and immediately after Lewis completed the scripts of his talks on **What Christians Believe** – Book II of *Mere Christianity* – and sent them to the BBC, he travelled up to Bangor. His three lectures on *Paradise Lost* were delivered on the three successive evenings of 1–3 December 1941. The *Preface* was published by Oxford University Press the following year.

Summary

Chapter I on 'Epic Poetry' begins: 'The first qualification for judging any piece of workmanship from a corkscrew to a cathedral is to know *what* it is – what it was intended to do and how it is meant to be used. After that has been discovered the temperance reformer may decide that the corkscrew was made for a bad purpose, and the communist may think the same about the cathedral. But such questions come later ... The first thing the reader needs to know about *Paradise Lost* is what Milton meant it to be.'

Milton was writing 'epic poetry which is a species of narrative poetry' but neither the species nor the genus is very well understood at present. The modern reader, used to lyric poetry, expects 'good lines', 'little ebullient patches of delight'. Of the continuity of a long narrative poem, 'the subordination of the line to the paragraph and the paragraph to the Book and even of the Book to the whole, of the grand sweeping effects that take a quarter of an hour to develop themselves, he has no conception.' Thus, a study of *Paradise Lost* must begin with a study of the epic in general. Every poem must be considered in two ways: 'as what the poet has to say, and as a *thing* which he *makes*.' It has two parents: a mother who is 'the mass of experience, thought, and the like, inside the poet', and a father who is 'the pre-existing Form (epic, tragedy, the novel, or what not) which he meets in the public world.'

In chapter II, 'Is Criticism Possible?', Lewis takes T.S. Eliot* to task for saying that the best contemporary poets are the only 'jury of judgement' whose verdict on his own views of *Paradise Lost* he will accept. He was quoting Eliot's essay 'A Note on the Verse of John Milton' in *Essays and Studies*, Vol. XXI (1936). This is a vicious circle, he argues, and as unendurable as the doctrine which allows only dentists to say whether our teeth are aching, and only governments to tell us whether we are being well governed. However, if all Eliot means is that a good poet, other things being equal, is reasonably likely, in talking about the kinds of poetry he has himself written well and read with delight, to say something more worth hearing than another, then 'we need not deny it'.

Chapter III on 'Primary Epic' looks at such poems as those of Homer and the English *Beowulf*. Primary Epic is not to be identified with 'oral poetry of the heroic age' or even with 'oral court poetry'. It is one of the possible entertainments, 'marked off from the others, in Homer by the spontaneity and quasi-oracular character of the poet's performance, and in both Homer and *Beowulf* by tragic quality, by supposed historical truth, and by the gravity that goes with "true tragedy".' Homer's poems and *Beowulf* both have the oral technique, the repetitions and stylized diction of oral poetry, so that, if not oral themselves, they are at least clearly modelled on work that was. Both are in the tradition of Primary Epic.

Chapter IV, 'The Technique of Primary Epic', begins by pointing out just how much of oral poetry is made up of stock words, phrases or even whole lines. There is an obvious reason for this from the poet's point of view: such repetitions can be recited almost mechanically whilst the singer is subconsciously forming the next verse. But there are also reasons from the hearer's point of view. Unexpected lines tire an audience; they are harder to understand and enjoy than the expected; they also cause the next line to be lost. 'To look for single, "good" lines is like looking for single "good" stones in a cathedral.'

Epic language, therefore, must be *familiar* – not in the sense of being colloquial or commonplace – but in being the predictable mode of expression of poetic utterance. Homeric diction contains many recurrent phrases such as the *wine-dark sea*, the *rosy-fingered dawn*, which, by their very immutability and frequency of use, have the effect of emphasizing the 'unchanging human environment'. The result is that Homer's poetry is, in an unusual degree, believable, however extraordinary the foreground events.

In chapter V, 'The Subject of Primary Epic', the author notes that a distinguishing mark of Primary Epic is that it has a 'great subject' such as the life of Arthur or Jerusalem's fall. That notion enters the epic with Virgil. Homer's *Odyssey* has as its subject the fortunes of an individual. The fact that these adventures happened to Odysseus while he was returning from the Trojan War does not make that war the subject of the poem. The Trojan War is not even the subject of the *Iliad*. It is merely the background to a purely personal story – that of Achilles' wrath, suffering, repentance and killing of Hector. *Beowulf* is a little different. In this English poem the fundamental darkness comes out into the foreground and is partly embodied in the monsters. It is the characteristic theme of Northern mythology – the gods and men ranged in battle against the giants. To that extent the poem is more cheerful at heart, though not on the surface, and has the first hints of a Great Subject. But the truth is that Primary Epic neither had, nor could have, a great subject in the Virgilian sense.

Chapter VI, on 'Virgil and the Subject of Secondary Epic', opens with the view that Virgil altered the very meaning of the word 'epic'. He wanted the Romans to have a great poem to rival the *Iliad*, and the way he went about this was to take one single national legend and treat it in such a way as to make a vaster theme implicit in it. The radical differences between Virgil and Homer appear on the very first page of the *Aeneid*. Carthage is an ancient city, facing the Tiber's mouth a long way off. He is already spreading out his story both in time and space. The heroes whose adventures we are to follow are the remnant of some earlier order destroyed before the curtain rose, and they fight not for their own land like Homeric heroes; they are men with a vocation, men on whom a burden is laid. 'In making his legend symbolical of the destiny of Rome, he has, willy-nilly, symbolized the destiny of Man.' The merely heroic epic is now a spent force. It must go on from Virgil, and the only further development left is the explicitly religious subject.

In chapter VII, 'The Style of Secondary Epic', Lewis sees the Style of Virgil and Milton 'as the solution of a very definite problem'. It has to be grand or 'elevated' in order to achieve that epic exhilaration which Primary Epic partly achieved through its external aids. Milton's style is commonly spoken of as being like organ music. Lewis reverses this: 'It might be more helpful to regard the reader as the organ and Milton as the organist. It is on us he plays, if we will let him.'

The ostensible philosophical purpose of *Paradise Lost* (to justify the ways of God to Man) is here of quite secondary importance. The real function of the opening twenty-six lines is to give us 'the sensation *that some great thing is now about to begin.'* Like modern poets, Milton throws ideas together because of their emotional power, but, unlike modern poets, he provides a façade of logical connections between them. His 'learned allusions' are not done for show, but in order to guide the reader's imagination in to the channels where the poet wishes them to flow. And the learning which a reader requires in responding to a given allusion does not equal the learning Milton needed to find it. Once this is grasped even Milton's most severely criticized feature (the Latinism of his constructions) can be approached with understanding. Milton adopts this technique in order to keep the reader on the move.

Finally, how suitable is Milton's style to the subject he has chosen? How well, for instance, does *Paradise Lost* actually convey the idea of Paradise? In analysing the way Milton went about this Lewis might have been speaking of how he went about writing such works as *Perelandra*. Milton does not describe his own private image of the happy garden; instead of trying to capture a 'heavenly' atmosphere, as a bad poet would, he presents pictures which pull out the Paradisal Stop in each one of us.

In chapter VIII, 'Defence of this Style', Lewis defends Milton's style from the charges of Manipulation, Stock Responses§ and Grandiosity. First of all, manipulation is not necessarily vile. As Aristotle points out, intellect of itself 'moves nothing', the transition from thinking to doing needs to be assisted by 'appropriate states of feeling'. And just as Rhetoric, properly employed, calls on passions in support of reason to stimulate action, so Poetry calls on emotion for the sake of providing imaginative vision, and therefore, in the long run, for the sake of wisdom and spiritual health. 'The idea of a poetry which exists only for the poet – a poetry which the public rather overhears than hears – is a foolish novelty in criticism. There is nothing specially admirable in talking to oneself.'

Next comes the question of Stock Responses which, for critics such as Dr I.A. Richards, do not allow for 'the direct free play of experience'. This is discussed under **Stock Responses§** and so it is enough here to say that Lewis thought that the demise of stock themes and stock responses has not bettered the world, and he views Milton's poetry as more than ever necessary to us while we recover 'the lost poetic art of enriching a response without making it eccentric, and of being normal without being vulgar.'

Chapter IX, 'The Doctrine of the Unchanging Human Heart', addresses the question as to whether the things which separate one age from another are superficial. Lewis once held this view, but no more. He admits that if you remove from people those things which make them different, what is left must be the same, but he asserts that the search, in poetry, for the lowest common multiple, may well result in ignorance of what poems are really about.

This is a theme which appears throughout Lewis's literary criticism and about which he was passionate. Those who wonder what Lewis's response to 'Deconstructionism' might be will probably find it here. 'I had much rather know,' he says here, 'what I should feel like if I adopted the beliefs of Lucretius than how Lucretius would have felt if he had never entertained them. The possible Lucretius in myself interests me more than the possible C.S. Lewis in Lucretius.' He suggests the practice of imitating or inheriting the human hearts of previous ages so that readers almost become medieval knights while reading Malory, or become eighteenth-century Londoners while reading Johnson. 'Only thus will you be able to judge the work "in the same spirit that its author writ" and to avoid chimerical criticism.'

Chapter X, 'Milton and St Augustine', looks at Milton's version of the Fall, a version which is substantially that of St Augustine, which is that of the Church as a whole. The doctrines are as follows: (1) God created all things good; (2) what we call bad things are things deprived of or perverted from good things; (3) good and bad angels have the same Nature, happy when it adheres to God and miserable when it adheres to itself – hence those passages in Milton where the excellence of Satan's Nature is insisted on, in contrast to the perversion of his will; (4) though God has made all creatures good He foreknows that some will become bad. God observes that Satan 'shall pervert' man; (5) if there had been no Fall the human race would have been promoted to angelic status; (6) Satan attacked Eve rather than Adam because he knew she was less intelligent and more credulous; (7) Adam was not deceived, but yielded to Eve because of the bond between them; (8) the Fall consisted in disobedience not in any intrinsic importance pertaining to the apple; (9) the Fall resulted from Pride; (10) since the Fall consisted in man's Disobedience to his superior, it was punished by man's loss of Authority over his inferiors; that is, chiefly, over his passions and his physical organism; (11) this Disobedience of man's organism to man is specially evident in sexuality. Lewis hopes that this short analysis will illustrate the truth of Addison's observation that 'the great moral which reigns in Milton is the most universal and most useful that can be imagined, that Obedience to the will of God makes men happy and that Disobedience makes them miserable.' 'If you can't be interested in that,' says Lewis, 'you can't be interested in Paradise Lost.'

Chapter XI is on 'Hierarchy', another subject dear to Lewis's heart (see **Hierarchy§**). According to the conception of hierarchy which belongs to the tradition of European ethics stretching from Aristotle to Johnson, degrees of value are objectively present in the universe. 'Everything except God has some natural superior; everything except unformed matter has some natural inferior. The goodness and dignity of every being consists in obeying its natural superior and ruling its natural inferior.' Hierarchy is destroyed either by ruling or obeying natural equals or by failing to obey a natural superior or to rule a natural inferior. Milton makes this hierarchical principle explicit in two contrasted passages in *Paradise Lost*.

Chapter XII, on 'The Theology of *"Paradise Lost"*', looks at Denis Saurat's analysis of Milton's theological doctrines in his *Milton: Man and Thinker* (1925). Lewis divides Saurat's charges against the doctrines into four groups: (1) Doctrines which occur in *Paradise Lost*, but which are not heretical, for instance, 'that the Father is non-manifested and unknowable, the Son being His sole manifestation.' Saurat rightly quotes the passage where Milton tells us that the Father 'whom else no creature can behold' is made 'visible' in the Son. This merely proves that Milton had read in St Paul that Christ 'is the image of the invisible God'. (2) Doctrines 'which are heretical, but do not occur in Milton' – for instance, the doctrine of latent evil in God. (3) Doctrines which are heretical and occur in the *De Doctrina* but not in *Paradise Lost*. Only one doctrine falls under this heading: Milton's Arianism. (4) Doctrines which are 'possibly heretical and really do occur in *Paradise Lost*.' The examples Lewis deals with are that 'God includes the whole of Space' and 'Matter is a part of God', but, after four pages of close argument he concludes that 'the heresies of *Paradise Lost* … resolve themselves to something very small and rather ambiguous.'

Lewis begins Chapter XIII, on 'Satan', by pointing out that 'It is a very old critical discovery that the imitation in art of unpleasing objects or people may itself be a pleasing imitation.' Milton's Satan has never, until modern times, been thought anything other than a 'magnificent poetic achievement'. Whether he is also magnificent in the sense of being admirable and heroic as a character is another question. The aim in this chapter is not to convert those who admire Satan, but only to make it a little clearer what it is they are admiring.

(1) First of all, the Satanic predicament is suffering from a 'sense of injur'd merit'. Satan thought himself 'impaired'. 'This is a well known state of mind which we can all study in domestic animals, children, film-stars, politicians, or minor poets; and perhaps nearer home.' (2) He is self-contradictory: he wants hierarchy and he doesn't want hierarchy: 'Order

and Degrees Jarr not with liberty.' (3) He is a Liar, as when he says that the 'terror of his arm' has put God in doubt of 'His empire'. (4) He is nonsensical when he claims as a proof of his self-existence that 'he wasn't there to see it being done'. What we see in Satan is the 'horrible co-existence of a subtle and incessant intellectual activity with an incapacity to understand anything.' (5) He is not in control of himself: in Book IX he becomes by his own will a serpent; but in Book X he is a serpent whether he will or no.

It remains, of course, true that Satan is the best drawn of Milton's characters. Why is this? There follows one of Lewis's grandest insights into human nature and writing:

> In all but a few writers the 'good' characters are the least successful, and every one who has ever tried to make even the humblest story ought to know why. To make a character worse than oneself it is only necessary to release imaginatively from control some of the bad passions which, in real life, are always straining at the leash; the Satan, the Iago, the Becky Sharp, within each of us, is always there and only too ready, the moment the leash is slipped, to come out and have in our books that holiday we try to deny them in our lives. But if you try to draw a character better than yourself, all you can do is to take the best moments you have had and to imagine them prolonged and more consistently embodied in action ... We do not really know what it feels like to be a man much better than ourselves ... The Satan in Milton enables him to draw the character well just as the Satan in us enables us to receive it.

To admire Satan amounts to giving one's vote for 'a world of lies and propaganda, of wishful thinking, of incessant autobiography.'

Chapter XIV, 'Satan's Followers', is about the infernal debate by Satan's followers in Book II of *Paradise Lost*. Lewis attempts to point out the moral significance of each of the speeches in Pandemonium. (1) The kernel of *Moloch*'s speech is in the lines 54–8. Shall we sit 'lingering here' and 'accept this dark opprobrious den of shame'? No! The way out of these intolerable sensations for him is plain rage. He is the 'simplest of the fiends; a mere rat in the trap.' (2) The key to *Belial*'s approach comes at line 163, 'Is this the worst?' Was it not far worse when we fled 'pursued and strook' by 'Heav'n's afflicting thunder'? His policy is the very opposite of Moloch's, 'to be very, very quiet, to do nothing that might release the fierce energies of Hell.'

(3) *Mammon* goes one better. 'Nor want we skill or art from whence to raise Magnificence; and what can Heav'n show more?' (272). Those last five words reveal his desperate plan to make Hell a substitute for Heaven and to blind himself to the necessary discrepancies. The human analogues are here the most obvious and the most terrible of all – 'the men who seem to have passed from Heaven to Hell and can't see the difference.' (4) The voice of *Beelzebub* recalls the fiends to reality. Hell is their 'dungeon' not their 'safe retreat'. They cannot escape, nor can they hurt their enemy; but perhaps there is a chance of injuring someone else, man.

Chapter XV, 'The Mistake About Milton's Angels', looks at the mistake Johnson made when he said that Milton 'saw that immateriality supplied no images' and that he therefore 'invested' his angels with 'form and matter'. But Milton in fact inclined to the Platonic Theology which believed all created spirits to be corporeal. When his Archangel dined with Adam he did not simply appear to eat, nor was his eating a mere symbol – 'not seemingly … nor in mist'. The corporeality of his angels is not a poetic device. 'Milton put it there chiefly because he thought it was true.' Only in one passage does Milton seem to waver from this belief. In Book V Raphael seems to assume the modern or scholastic view. After explaining that it is a hard thing to relate 'the invisible exploits of warring spirits', he says that he will adapt his narrative to human sense 'by likening spiritual to corporal forms'. But 'throughout the rest of the poem Platonic Theology rules undisputed.'

Lewis confesses in chapter XVI, on 'Adam and Eve', that when he first came to *Paradise Lost* he expected the beauty of our first parents to be that of 'the primitive, the unsophisticated, the naïve'. Such expectations were due to his refusal to 'suspend disbelief'. The whole point about Adam and Eve is that they were never young or immature or undeveloped. Had they not fallen they would still have been alive in Paradise, and to that 'capital seat' all generations 'from all the ends of the Earth' would have come periodically to do their homage.

Adam's kingly manner is the 'outward expression of his supernatural kingship of earth and his wisdom.' When he received the homage of the beasts he instantaneously 'understood their Nature' and assigned their names. He has complete insight into the mysteries of the soul and can give Eve a full explanation of the phenomena of dreams. Royalty is less apparent in Eve, partly because her humility is often misunderstood. She thinks herself more fortunate than Adam, because she has him for her companion while he 'like consort to himself can nowhere find', and obeys his commands 'unargued'. This is becoming humility, which is not to say that Eve is unmajestic. She is also made 'so awful that with honour he may love.'

Which point brings us to chapter XVII, on 'Unfallen Sexuality'. The difficulty with Milton's depiction is that Eve exhibits sexual modesty. Her impulse on first meeting Adam is to turn back; she is led to the bridal bower 'blushing like the morn'; she yields to her lover's embraces with 'sweet, reluctant, amorous delay'. Although one can imagine a kind of innocent shame, the problem is that Milton's Eve displays modesty too exclusively in sexual contexts and his Adam does not exhibit it at all. 'Milton's love passages … are not consistent with what he himself believed about the world before the Fall.' Milton should not have touched the theme at all. He might have done better 'if he had said nothing about angelic love and treated the loves of Adam and Eve as remotely as those of the angels.' Even a protestation that he was approaching the unimaginable would have done much to save him. As it is, the poet hardly seems to be aware of the magnitude of his own undertaking and appears to think that by twice using the word 'mysterious' in this connection he excuses his very un-mysterious pictures.

Chapter XVIII, on 'The Fall', begins 'Eve fell through Pride'. Lewis is at his best with this subject. One by one he takes the statements made to Eve by Satan, explaining their effect upon her. She believes all that Satan tells her about her great beauty, how it deserves more spectators, how she should be served by angels, even be Queen of Heaven. She resolves to deny Adam the fruit if it means Divinity, but to share it with him if it means death – and hardly has she made this second decision but she is congratulating herself upon it as a singular proof of the tenderness and magnanimity of her love. 'I am not sure,' says Lewis, 'that critics always notice the precise sin which Eve is now committing, yet there is no mystery about it. Its name in English is Murder. If the fruit is to produce deity Adam shall have none of it: she means to do a corner in divinity. But if it means death, then he must be made to eat it.'

If the precise movement of Eve's mind at this point is not always noticed, he comments, that is because Milton's truth to nature is here almost too great, and the reader is involved in the same illusion as Eve herself: 'No man, perhaps, ever at first described to himself the act he was about to do as Murder, or Adultery, or Fraud, or Treachery, or Perversion; and when he hears it so described by other men he is (in a way) sincerely shocked and surprised … If you or I, reader, ever commit a great crime, be sure we shall feel very much more like Eve than like Iago.'

'Adam fell by uxoriousness.' 'If the reader,' says Lewis, 'finds it hard to look upon Adam's action as a sin at all, that is because he is not really granting Milton's premises. If conjugal love were the highest value in Adam's world, then of course his resolve would have been the correct one. But if there are things that have an even higher claim on a man, if the universe is imagined to be such that, when the pinch comes, a man ought to reject wife and mother and his own life also, then the case is altered, and then Adam can do no good to Eve ... by becoming her accomplice.' The effects of the Fall on him are quite unlike its effects on Eve. 'She had rushed at once into false sentiment which made murder itself appear proof of fine sensibility. Adam ... becomes a man of the world, a punster, an aspirant to fine raillery.'

What follows their Fall is 'one of Milton's failures'. Of course, Adam and Eve must now lust after each other, but Milton's poetry does not suffice to draw the distinction between their new appetites and their unfallen innocence. The best he does is Adam's cool statement that he has never been so ripe for 'play' as now. Adam would not have said that before he fell. 'Perhaps he would not have said "to enjoy thee".' Eve is becoming to him a *thing*. 'And she does not mind: all her dreams of godhead have come to that.'

Chapter XIX, 'Conclusion', gives a short estimate of the value of *Paradise Lost*. (1) On the debit side, the last two books constitute a grave structural flaw. Despite fine moments and a great recovery at the end, Dr Johnson might have said of the final sixth of the poem 'the story cannot possibly be told in a manner that shall make less impression on the mind.' (2) Milton's presentation of God the Father is unsatisfactory. When, for instance, the Father entertains the angels with 'rubied Nectar' served 'in Pearl, in Diamond, and massie Gold' we see Milton's failure 'to disentangle himself from the bad tradition ... of making Heaven too like Olympus.'

On the credit side, *Paradise Lost* is a great thing. 'Its story, as treated by Milton, fulfils the conditions of great story better perhaps than any other, for, more than any other, it leaves things where it did not find them ... *Paradise Lost* records a real, irreversible, unrepeatable process in the history of the universe.' Even for those who do not believe this, it embodies 'the great change in every individual soul from happy dependence to miserable self-assertion and thence either, as in Satan, to final isolation, or, as in Adam, to reconcilement and a different happiness.'

After Blake, Milton criticism became 'lost in misunderstanding', and the 'true line' was hardly found again until Charles Williams's Preface. Some critics may actually hate Milton through fear and envy. 'It is not rustic, naïve, or unbuttoned. It will therefore be unintelligible to those who lack the right qualifications, and hateful to the baser spirits among them.' *Paradise Lost* has been compared to the Great Wall of China, and the comparison is good: both are among the wonders of the world and both divide the tilled fields and cities of an ancient culture from the barbarians. 'We have only to add that the Wall is necessarily hated by those who see it from the wrong side, and the parallel is complete.' Another class of critic dislikes it because, for them, reality is 'the mere stream of consciousness'. 'In my opinion,' says Lewis, 'this whole type of criticism is based on an error. The disorganized consciousness which it regards as specially real is in fact highly artificial. It is discovered by introspection – that is, by artificially suspending all the normal and outgoing activities of the mind and then attending to what is left. In that residuum it discovers no concentrated will, no logical thought, no morals, no stable sentiments, and (in a word) no mental hierarchy' (see **Law of Inattention§**).

Finally, there are those who, like T.S. Eliot, are outside the Wall not because they are barbarians, but because they 'have gone out in order to fast and pray in the wilderness'. If this is done because the fashion of the world passes away, it should be honoured. But if it is done in the belief that poetry should only have the 'penitential qualities' of Eliot's best work, it is mistaken. 'As long as we live in merry middle earth it is necessary to have middle things.'

Reviews

Anne Ridler, writing in *Time and Tide*, 23 (7 November 1942), p. 892, said: 'His book is ... an indictment of our critical premises and methods of reading. Indeed it is a tract for the times, for what he condemns in our approach to Milton is implied by what he disapproves in our contemporary life: it is a showing up of contemporary Cant as much as was *The Screwtape Letters*, though it is concerned with literary effort.'

V.G. Turner SJ said in *The Tablet*, 181 (9 January 1943), p. 20: 'The book is one of very great moment indeed, and is, in fact, much more than an essay on Milton; it is above all the kind of criticism, of which it is an almost perfect instance, that is immensely valuable and important. What is this kind? It includes, but is not exhausted by, a serious effort to rethink a writer's thoughts with him, to understand and for the moment to share his presuppositions (by a suspension of disbelief, if need be), to get out of one's own skin by history and to get into his. This is already to be released in some degree from contemporaneity and the domination of fashion and party-cries. It is also to begin to understand, whether one approves of it or not, what has been the cultural achievement of Christianity in Europe.'

Naomi Royde Smith wrote in *The Dublin Review*, 212 (January 1943), pp. 90–1: 'C.S. Lewis ... more than any other critic now writing, adds wit, learning and enthusiasm to that ability to discuss rather than to destroy which is the prerequisite of the critic's true function ... Armed with this *Preface*, any lecturer on Literature might draw up the syllabus of a fresh and stimulating course for the study of any masterpiece in any language, or launch on a detailed and erudite development of some one of the ideas it offers.'

ENGLISH LITERATURE IN THE SIXTEENTH CENTURY, EXCLUDING DRAMA (1954)

Background

I: The Oxford History of English Literature

In 1935 the Delegates of the Oxford University Press conceived the idea of *The Oxford History of English Literature* and in March of that year they appointed as General Editors two distinguished scholars, F.P. Wilson (1889–1963) and Bonamy Dobrée (1891–1974). These men were to work for many years in close co-operation with Kenneth Sisam (1887–1971), who was Assistant Secretary to the Delegates of the Oxford University Press at this time, and Secretary from 1942 to 1948.

It was thought from the start that the series should consist of twelve volumes, and after a few months the Press was clear about the first three. Volume I was to be split between Anglo-Saxon and Middle English Literature; Volume II would cover Chaucer and the Fifteenth Century; and Volume III would be devoted to the Sixteenth Century. During these early months it was not certain who would be invited to write which volume, with the exception of Lewis. F.P. Wilson had been his tutor in English 1922–23, and as early as June 1935 he asked Lewis to write Volume III on the Sixteenth Century.

The Press made its first public announcement about the series in *The Times Literary Supplement* of 24 October 1935 (p. 665):

> The Oxford University Press announces that it has undertaken the production of *The Oxford History of English Literature* under the editorship of Professor F.P. Wilson, of Leeds University, and Mr Bonamy Dobrée. It is proposed to publish the work in twelve volumes, and as a rule each volume would be the work of a single author. The plan will thus be similar to that of the *Oxford History of*

England now in course of publication under the editorship of G.N. Clark.

Some years earlier the other great University press had published *The Cambridge History of English Literature* in fourteen volumes. This, however, was a composite work; each chapter of every volume was written by a different scholar. Part of the uniqueness of *The Oxford History of English Literature* lay in the fact that each volume would be written by a single author. To get some idea of the grandeur of what Oxford University Press had in mind we might look at the first complete plan for *The Oxford History of English Literature*. It is dated 11 September 1937 and it enumerated the following points:

Each volume will aim at giving, with a sufficient balance of sweep and detail, a rounded history of the literature of the period. While the main stress will be critical, attention will be paid to the relationship of our literature to other literatures, to philosophical, scientific, and political movements in so far as they impinge on literature, to the state of the language, to social background, and to the material conditions under which writers worked. For example, some account will be given of the general conditions of book publishing at the time and of the type of reader for various kinds of work; and, where significant, mention will be made of books, which, though little read now, were the staple reading of the public of those days ...

While the volumes will in the main begin and end at a definite date, care will be taken to lay emphasis on transition periods. This will require a certain degree of dovetailing, and authors are asked to consult with those writing the volumes on either side of them, and with the general editors, so as to avoid overlapping ... Each full volume is to consist of about 150,000 words of text, followed by a fairly extensive selective bibliography, a table of main dates of public events, writers and books ... and an index.

This same year – 1937 – Wilson, Dobrée, Sisam and others came up with a 'Final Scheme' of what (roughly) the series would consist of:

I. Medieval Literature to 1400
    ½ Anglo-Saxon
    ½ Middle English

II. Chaucer and the Fifteenth Century
   ½+ Chaucer and fifteenth-century poetry and prose
   ¼– The Religious Drama
   ¼– The Ballad
III. The Sixteenth Century
   From c. 1500 to c. 1600 including Spenser, Shakespeare and
   Marlowe (as poets) and omitting Donne
IV. The Elizabethan Drama
V. The Early Seventeenth Century
   From c. 1600 to c. 1660
VI. The Late Seventeenth Century
   From c. 1660 to c. 1700
VII. The Early Eighteenth Century
   From c. 1700 to c. 1740
VIII. The Mid-Eighteenth Century
   From c. 1740 to c. 1780
IX. The Romantic Period
   From c. 1780 to c. 1810
X. The Romantic Period
   1810–1830
XI. The Mid-Nineteenth Century
   From c. 1830 to c. 1890
XII. Modern Literature
   From c. 1850

By this time it was clear that Lewis was making Medieval and Renaissance English Literature his chosen field. After his election to a Fellowship at Magdalen College‡ in 1925 he began a series of University lectures on 'Some English Thinkers of the Renaissance (Elyot, Ascham, Hooker, Bacon).' In 1932 he began his very popular series of lectures on the 'Prolegomena to Medieval Poetry', and from 1928 to 1935 he was writing *The Allegory of Love,* a large part of which is devoted to Spenser. During the Lent Term of 1939 Lewis lectured twice weekly in Cambridge on the 'Prolegomena to the Study of Renaissance Poetry', which lectures were repeated at Oxford the following term, and thereafter for many years.

II: The Writing of 'O Hell!'

As mentioned earlier, the Delegates knew the individual volumes would 'require a certain degree of dovetailing' and it was up to the general editors to see there was no overlapping of periods. Douglas Bush was writing on 'The Early Seventeenth Century, From c. 1600 to c. 1660', and Wilson had to decide in a few instances which authors Lewis should write about and which Bush should have. He wrote to Lewis about some of the authors he was uncertain about, and Lewis replied on 25 January 1938:

My dear Wilson

No, I don't want Dunbar: and I don't cleave to Douglas even, if anyone wants him. And at the other end of the principle is a simple one – the sooner Bush can begin and I leave off, the better I shall be pleased. The O HELL lies like a nightmare on my chest ever since I got your specimen bibliography: I shan't try to desert – anyway, I suppose the exit is thronged with dreadful faces and fiery arms – but I have a growing doubt if I ought to be doing this.

Mind you, I'd sooner have Dunbar than Donne: sooner, in general, come early on the scene than linger late. Let the others choose … Do you think there's any chance of the world ending before the O HELL appears?

Yours, in deep depression …

Lewis was writing his lectures on the 'Prolegomena to the Study of Renaissance Poetry' when F.P. Wilson gave a 'progress report' on the series on 20 December 1938. By this time a good many of the volumes were under way, and Lewis is quoted in the report as saying:

I go on reading and write on each subject while it is fresh in mind. Out of these scattered sheets, perhaps after much correction, I hope to build up a book. The subjects so treated already are Platonism, Douglas, Lyndsay, Tottel, Mulcaster's Elementarie, Sir Thomas More, Prayer-book, Sidney, Marlowe (non-dramatic), Nashe, Watson, Barclay, Googe, Raleigh (poems), Shakespeare (poems), Webbe; and among other sources Petrarch and Machiavelli.

I am at present hard at work not directly on the book but on a lecture entitled 'Prolegomena to Renaissance Poetry': a similar Prolegomena to Medieval Poetry which I have and still give proved to be a useful buttress to the other book.

I can give no indication of when it will be done. I find the work to be got through is enormous and would be delighted for an honourable pretext to withdraw: excessive pressure from the delegates might come to constitute an honourable pretext.

In his reminiscences of Lewis (**LIFE XXXII**) Francis Warner explained what he meant when he said he wrote on various subjects while they were 'fresh in mind'. When he asked Lewis how he went about writing the OHEL volume, 'He replied,' said Dr Warner, 'that he tried to read every book in that century ... Every time he read an author he wrote himself an essay on the subject, dated it, and put it in a drawer for a year and a day. He would then take it out and mark it. Any essay falling below a clear alpha was sent back to be done again.'

It would seem, then, that a large portion of the book had been written by the time G.M. Trevelyan, Master of Trinity College, Cambridge, invited Lewis to give the Clark Lectures during Easter Term 1944. This consisted of four lectures entitled 'Studies in Sixteenth-Century Literature' given at the Mill Lane Lecture rooms on Wednesdays, 26 April, 3, 10 and 17 May.

From this point on and for the next nine years Lewis continued with the writing of what was to be Volume III of *The Oxford History of English Literature*, the initials of which yielded Lewis's favourite abbreviation – OHEL, pronounced 'O *Hell!*' Charles Wrong, who had been Lewis's pupil at Magdalen College, recalled a conversation he had with him about various things. Commenting on *English Literature in the Sixteenth Century*, Wrong remembers Lewis saying:

> When they asked me to do that, I was tremendously flattered. It's like a girl committing herself to marrying an elderly millionaire who's also a duke. In the end she finally has to settle down and live with the chap, and it's a hellish long time before he dies ('A Chance Meeting', **ABT**).

Another pupil, John Wain,* regarded the OHEL as Lewis's greatest book, and in 'A Great Clerk' (**ABT**) he said: 'As he worked on the book – and it took nine years – Lewis showed various chapters in typescript to friends who might advise him. I got, for some reason, "The Close of the Middle Ages in Scotland". I read it with nothing but admiration ... I laid it on his desk on one of my visits to him, without comment; and a year or two later, when the book came out, he complained half-comically, "I never got any criticism of that chapter I gave you." It was like his humility to bring work of that quality, so deeply pondered and so brilliantly written, to an insignificant young man in his twenties, completely unknown in the world of letters, and ask quite genuinely for "criticism".'

His chief relaxation during this time was, apart from the two-week jaunt in Ireland every summer, the writing of the first five 'Chronicles of Narnia'. Still, as time went on he spent every available minute in the Duke Humfrey

Library of the Bodleian reading the entire works of about two hundred authors. Lewis had been reading Shakespeare, Spenser, Sir Philip Sidney and other old favourites for years. But that was only a small part of it. For the section of the book on 'Religious Controversy and Translation' he read for the first time the *entire works* of Thomas More, Luther, Calvin, Tyndale and others. 'It's a brilliant piece of work. And work it was,' said Millar MacLure, reviewing the book in *Canadian Forum*, 35 (July 1955), p. 94:

> Think of it: to face anew those shelves in the Bodleian, full of the brown-and-gold meditations of our ancestors – on hunting, poetry, bishops, love, diet, Arthur of Britain, the returns of electors, Richard III, hawking, on Italian adultery, Greek pronunciation, import of wines, the soil of Derbyshire, Petrarch's metres, saving grace, a hue-and-cry in Norwich – and to set all that in order. Mr Lewis has earned his new chair at Cambridge.

Some of the weariness that overtook Lewis in the last stages of the writing is evident in a few of the letters he wrote to an American friend, Dr Warfield M. Firor, a surgeon in Baltimore (see **LIFE** XX–XXI). 'I am spending,' he wrote on 26 July 1950,

> most of my time at present ploughing through back numbers of learned periodicals less in the hope of fresh knowledge than in fear I've missed something. In your subject, which is experimental, I suppose one doesn't have to poke back too far, because everything before a certain date would be definitely superseded. With us literary blokes of course this absolutely decisive 'supersession' occurs only very rarely – say, as the result of a windfall like the discovery of a new MS, and views often disappear not because someone has proved them false but merely because they have gone out of fashion. In any forgotten article the really illuminating thing might lie hid: though about 90 to 10 against. So that I mostly pass the hours reading rubbish. The worst rubbish being the pseudo-scientific – the attempt to apply, or the pretence of applying, the methods of *your* discipline to *ours*.

Mrs Moore* died on 12 January 1951, and when he wrote to Dr Firor on 23 April, Lewis said:

> I have seized my new freedom to get that infernal book on the XVIth century done, or as nearly done as I can. The College is

giving me a year off to do it, but the work can be done only in England, and much less ambitious holidays than a jaunt to America will serve my turn.

Lewis's year off from College duties and teaching was from October 1951 to October 1952, and writing to Dr Firor on 20 December 1951 he said:

My year 'off' has been, as it was meant to be, so far a year of very hard work, but mostly congenial. The book really begins to look as if it might be finished in 1952 and I am, between ourselves, pleased with the manner of it – but afraid of hidden errors ... A mistake in a history of literature walks in silence till the day it turns irrevocable in a printed book and the book goes for review to the only man in England who would have known it was a mistake. This, I suppose, is good for one's soul: and the *kind* of good I must learn to digest (L).

His colleague on the English Faculty, Dame Helen Gardner (1908–86) said in her obituary of Lewis for the British Academy:

The merits of this book are very great indeed. It is, to begin with, a genuine literary history. It is perfectly apparent which poets and which poems Lewis thinks 'the best', and the book exemplifies again and again his gift for summing up the peculiar virtues of a work, and his genius for the brief, pregnant quotation that gives the quiddity of a writer. But he respected the nature of his commission and attempted to provide a continuous narrative history of literature in the century. The volume satisfies his own criterion of a good literary history: it tells us what works exist and puts them in their setting. The book is also brilliantly written, compulsively readable, and constantly illuminated by sentences that are as true as they are witty. Who else could have written a literary history that continually arouses delighted laughter?[1]

The book was finished and sent to the publishers in May 1952, and Lewis celebrated by motoring around Ulster with Arthur Greeves.* 'The OHEL is finished and gone to press,' he wrote to Sister Penelope* on 28 November 1952. '"Joy, joy, my task is done."'

---

[1] 'C.S. Lewis: 1898–1963,' *Proceedings of the British Academy*, LI (1965), pp. 12, 19.

III: The Present OHEL

Following the retirement of the original editors, John Buxton and Norman Davis were brought in to act as General Editors, and except for one volume, the Oxford History of English Literature is complete. In 1990 a number of the names of the original works were changed, one of which was *English Literature in the Sixteenth Century* which was given the new title *Poetry and Prose in the Sixteenth Century*. The series is made up of the following:

I. *Middle English Literature 1100–1400*, by J.A.W. Bennett,* edited and completed by Douglas Gray (1986)

II. *Chaucer and Fifteenth-Century Verse and Prose*, by H.S. Bennett (1947)

III. *Malory and Fifteenth-Century Drama, Lyrics, and Ballads*, by E.K. Chambers (1945). (Originally titled *English Literature at the Close of the Middle Ages*)

IV. *Poetry and Prose in the Sixteenth Century*, by C.S. Lewis (1954). (Originally titled *English Literature in the Sixteenth Century, Excluding Drama*)

V. *English Drama 1485–1585*, by F.P. Wilson, edited with a bibliography by G.K. Hunter (1969)

VI. *English Drama 1586–1642: Shakespeare and his Age*, by G. Hunter (forthcoming)

VII. *The Early Seventeenth Century 1600–1660: Jonson, Donne and Milton*, by Douglas Bush (1945). (Originally titled *English Literature in the Earlier Seventeenth Century 1600–1660*)

VIII. *Restoration Literature 1660–1700: Dryden, Bunyan and Pepys*, by James Sutherland (1969). (Originally titled *English Literature of the Late Seventeenth Century*)

IX. *The Early Eighteenth Century 1700–1740: Swift, Defoe and Pope*, by Bonamy Dobrée (1959). (Originally titled *English Literature in the Eighteenth Century, 1700–1740*)

X. *The Age of Johnson 1740–1789*, by John Butt, edited and completed by Geoffrey Carnall (1979). (Originally titled *The Mid-Eighteenth Century*)

XI. *The Rise of the Romantics 1789–1815: Wordsworth, Coleridge and Jane Austen*, by W.L. Renwick (1963)

XII. *English Literature 1815–1832: Scott, Byron and Keats*, by Ian Jack (1963)

XIII. *The Victorian Novel*, by Alan Horsman (1990)

XIV. *Victorian Poetry, Drama, and Miscellaneous Prose 1832–1890*, by Paul Turner (1989). (Originally titled *English Literature 1832–1900, Excluding the Novel*)

XV. *Writers of the Early Twentieth Century: Hardy to Lawrence*, by J.I.M. Stewart (1963). (Originally titled *Eight Modern Writers*)

Summary

Introduction: 'New Learning and New Ignorance'

This chapter is a rough outline of English literature in the sixteenth century. At its beginning it is 'still medieval in form and spirit'. The characteristic disease of late medieval poetry – metrical disorder – is healed, but replaced by a 'lifeless and laboured regularity'. The mid-century is an 'earnest, heavy-handed, commonplace age: a drab age'. Then, in the last quarter of the century, with a startling suddenness, 'Youth returns'. Sidney, Spenser, Shakespeare and Hooker 'display what is almost a new culture'. It lasted through most of the next century and 'enriched the very meaning of the words *England* and *Aristocracy*.'

What caused this sudden flowering of talent? Was it that *renascentia* – the recovery of Greek and the substitution of Augustan for medieval Latin? Lewis sees no close connection there. Did the new astronomy shock men's minds into new channels of thought – as Darwin shocked the Victorians and Freud Lewis's own age? Again, this is hard to assess. What proved important about the new astronomy was 'not the mere alteration in our map of space, but the methodological revolution which verified it.' The effects of empiricism on our thought and emotions were profound. Nature was emptied 'first of her indwelling spirit, then of her occult sympathies and antipathies, finally of her colours, smells and tastes.' Man with his new scientific powers became rich like Midas, 'but all that he touched had gone dead and cold.'

But in the sixteenth century these effects were still embryonic. Behind all the literature of this period lies the older conception of Nature not as a machine but as a festival, a ceremony, dancing and tingling with anthropomorphic life. This view of Nature is no mere metaphor or conceit, it is part of a system of thought about the universe which is radically different from our own. This genial cosmology, though it already contains the seeds of its own destruction, is not to be seen as alien to this age. Indeed, a passage from Campanella (1568–1639) shows how the new empiricism might give rise to a new sort of magic – how a concentration on man's inductive senses may lead him to conclude that the universe itself has such senses and how, if so, it might be possible to awaken these sleeping senses by *magia divina*.

Far from being a medieval 'survival', sixteenth-century magic was as characteristic of the period as exploration or the birth of secular drama. We view it as an anomaly only because we know that science succeeded and magic failed. But that event was still then uncertain. Stripping off our knowledge of it, we see that an early scientist such as Bacon had a close affinity with the magicians. Both sought knowledge for the sake of power, and both moved in a grandiose dream of days when Man shall have been raised to a performance of 'all things possible'. In the light of all this, Shakespeare's *Tempest* should be seen as his play on magic as *Macbeth* is his play on sorcery and the *Merchant* on usury.

The new geography excited much more interest than the new astronomy, especially among merchants and politicians, 'but the literary texts suggest that it did not stimulate the imagination so much as we might have expected.' The wonder and glory of exploration, though sometimes expressed by Hakluyt and the voyagers themselves, was seldom the theme of imaginative writers. Something of it is felt in the *Utopia*, but there are only casual references in Spenser, Shakespeare, Donne and others.

Lewis's treatment of Humanism is perhaps the most controversial part of the book. 'By a humanist,' he said, 'I mean one who taught, or learned, or at least strongly favoured, Greek and the new kind of Latin; and by Humanism, the critical principles and critical outlook which ordinarily went with these studies. Humanism is in fact the first form of classicism.' The humanists did two important things: (1) They 'recovered, edited and expounded a great many ancient texts in Latin, Greek and Hebrew.' (2) They also initiated that temper and those critical principles which have since come to be called 'classicism': we say, for example, that they substituted 'classical' for 'medieval' Latin. But of all the texts in humanists' Latin, it would be hard to think of a single one (apart from the *Utopia*) which is read for anything other than historical purposes today. That is not so with medieval Latin texts. They are still living, but the classical were 'still-born'. And it could hardly have been anything other than still-born since it was built on a negative conception of excellence in which it was better to omit a beauty than to leave in anything that might have the shadow of an 'unclassical' offence.

For the humanist the attraction of ancient literature lay in its order, discipline, weight and decorum. But this desire to be very 'adult' had some unfortunate consequences. Elevation and gravity of language are only admirable, or even tolerable, when they grow from elevation and gravity of thought. The reason why humanistic culture was overwhelmingly Latin was that Greek is too supple and sensitive to take the hard polish which was what the humanists principally cared for.

The chief negative characteristic of Humanism was a hatred of the Middle Ages and it is this that unites the humanist with the puritan. The two especial objects of their aversion were chivalrous romance and scholastic philosophy. But one most unfortunate exception to their rejection of the Middle Ages was the idea that every great poem is an allegory. The humanists could not bring themselves to believe that poets such as Virgil cared about shepherds, lovers, warriors, voyages or battles. 'They must be only a disguise for something more "adult".' So far as the common reader was concerned, the humanists' attack on romance was not, in the sixteenth century, very successful; but their attack on philosophy was far more serious. It was 'Philistinism', even 'obscurantist' – a New Learning which created a New Ignorance. In 1550 at Oxford books were publicly burned for containing 'barbarism, ignorance of Scripture, and much deceit.' Even so, we owe a debt to the humanists that can never be cancelled: 'if their manners were often like those of giants, so were their labours.'

By 'puritan' is meant Protestants who wished to abolish episcopacy and remodel the Church of England on the lines which Calvin had laid down for Geneva. 'Dicken's Mrs Clennam, trying to expiate her early sin by a long life of voluntary gloom, was doing exactly what the first Protestants would have forbidden her to do. They would have thought her whole conception of expiation papistical.' The Protestant doctrines were 'not of terror but of joy and hope', and those 'very troublesome problems and very dark solutions' familiar to the modern reader were 'astonishingly absent from the thought of the first Protestants.' (Lewis points out in a footnote that 'When Judas hanged himself he had not been reading Calvin.') They also laid a strong emphasis on justification by faith not merit. We might note the psychological similarity between the puritan's desire to smell out and condemn vestiges of Popery in the Church and the humanist's desire to smell out and condemn vestiges of 'barbarism' in his neighbour's Latin.

The 'original Protestant experience' of the Reformation is described as one of 'relief and buoyancy'. In England, Henry VIII 'wanting Anne Boleyn and therefore wanting his previous marriage annulled, quarrels with the Pope', and during 'this series of ecclesiastical revolutions and counter-revolutions England as a whole somehow changed her religion.' We must 'take care not to assume that a sixteenth-century man who lived through these changes had necessarily felt himself, at any stage, confronted with the clear issue which would face a modern in the same circumstances ... We may well believe that such a man, though baptized in the Old Religion and dying in the New, did not feel that he had, in any clear sense, either committed apostasy or undergone a conversion. He had only tried to do what he was told in a world where doing what he was told had been, according to all his Betters, the thing mainly demanded of him.'

Lewis speaks of the Divine Right of Kings rising slowly above the horizon while the medieval conception of Natural Law sinks in the west. Speaking of the views of Henry de Bracton (Bracton College in *That Hideous Strength* is named after him) and Thomas Aquinas on Natural Law, he said: 'For Aquinas, as for Bracton, political power ... is never free and never originates. Its business is to enforce something that is already there' (see **Natural Law§** and **Democracy§**). 'We must not suppose that the medieval conception of Natural Law vanished overnight ... On the contrary ... it reached its fullest and most beautiful expression when the tide of history had turned against it.' Lewis went on to show how Hooker, Calvin and Tyndale thought about Natural Law and the 'new order' which was coming in.

Poets as great as Spenser and Shakespeare became attached to the new order and 'pour out tranquil, golden poetry about the great chain of concord and the beauty of degree.' The repudiation of medieval principles goes farthest in Machiavelli's *The Prince* (1513). But it is as the father of a new type of villain that Machiavelli is most important to the literary historian. Kyd's Lorenzo and Shakespeare's Iago are both 'Machiavellian' villains, and the devil in Marlowe or Milton is not, as in medieval literature, 'an ass', but cunning, subtle and clever. Side by side with the new villain comes the old type in new guise. Tamburlaine is Grendel, Herod and Blunderbore all in one – and heroic to boot. 'The play is a hideous moral spoonerism: Giant the Jack Killer.' Other changes from medieval times include a new inhibition about male tears and a frankness about a hero's moral worthiness. The sixteenth-century man was to be a Stoic, independent of Fortune, 'gladly obedient' to anything 'the high and general cause' may lay on him.

'It may or may not have been noticed,' the author said in a passage he obviously enjoyed writing, 'that the word *Renaissance* has not yet occurred in this book.' The word 'has sometimes been used merely to mean the "revival of learning", the recovery of Greek, and the "classicizing" of Latin. If it still bore that clear and useful sense, I should of course have employed it. Unfortunately it has, for many years, been widening its meaning, till now "the Renaissance" can hardly be defined except as "an imaginary entity responsible for everything the speaker likes in the fifteenth and sixteenth centuries".' Thus, as commonly understood, the 'Renaissance', never existed (see **Renaissance§**).

The chapter concludes with a look at the social, political and economic conditions which affected the literature of the period. One particularly striking effect was that, during the century, the professional author in the modern sense, the man who writes for the booksellers, was coming into existence. As a whole, however, Lewis is loath to notice any particular effect or 'spirit' or 'meaning'. This is because the sixteenth century, like all periods, is confusing and heterogeneous. Alongside a quality of advent-urousness and expansion, for example, are many growing restrictions on liberty (Calvinism and Constellation both threatening free will, sovereignty threatening political freedom, Humanism constraining vocabulary and spontaneous emotion). Any pattern or significance imposed upon this mixture is like 'the pictures we see in the fire'.

Periods are, nevertheless, a 'methodological necessity', and the author explains what he means by the three periods into which he has divided his study. (1) 'The Late Medieval extends very roughly to the end of Edward VI's reign. The most obvious mark of Late Medieval poetry in England is its metrical irregularity; other marks, common to England and Scotland, are allegory and the predominance of rhyme royal ... Prose is usually simple and unartificial.' (2) The Drab Age begins before the Late Medieval has ended, towards the end of Henry VIII's reign, and lasts into the late seventies. *Drab* is not used as a dyslogistic term. 'It marks a period in which ... poetry has little richness either of sound or images ... Prose is now more artificial in some writers, more cumbersome in others.' (3) The Golden Age is what we 'usually think of first when "the great Elizabethans" are mentioned: it is largely responsible, in England, for the emotional overtones of the word *Renaissance*. The epithet *golden* is not eulogistic. It means, not simply good poetry, but poetry which is, so to speak, innocent or ingenuous.'

Book I: Late Medieval

Chapter I: The Close of the Middle Ages in Scotland

The author begins by mentioning the 'principal strands' of poetry behind the sixteenth-century poets, **Gavin Douglas** (1475?–1522) and **William Dunbar** (1456?–1513?): (1) The forthright narrative in octosyllabic couples as in Barbour's *Bruce*; (2) A large body of poems which combine rhyme and alliteration in various patterns; (3) Our knowledge of comic poetry, like our knowledge of the lyric, in this period depends mainly on the praiseworthy taste of some sixteenth-century Scotsmen for compiling anthologies; (4) We have few certain specimens of the pure lyric before Dunbar; (5) 'Finally, we have the full-blown high style, from which I am anxious, if I can, to remove the epithet "Chaucerian".'

The century opens with the appearance of the *Palice of Honour* by Gavin Douglas, a work whose quality was prodigality and whose vice was excess, and which addresses the problem 'Where does true Honour lie?' His allegory, *King Hart*, is as different as possible from the *Palice of Honour*, being composed in a simpler stanza, 'classically free from irrelevancies, and stern rather than luxuriant.' Its theme is morality and the inevitable shipwreck of all merely human hopes and pleasures. The *XIII Bukes of the Eneados* is Douglas's translation of the *Aeneid* and it is a 'great work'. The couplet in which most of the book is written is a happy mean between the severity of Pope and the rambling of Keats. 'Often it has the ring and energy of Dryden.' The poetical career of his older contemporary, William Dunbar, probably began earlier and ended later than Douglas's. He wrote court poems in the high style, petitionary poems, comic or rather 'abusive' verse, religious poetry (of the public and liturgical type). 'The most widely remembered of his poems come in the class which he himself would probably have called "moral". There is a real affinity between these and the *Odes* of Horace.'

David Lyndsay (1486–1555) was the 'last of the major medieval poets in Scotland', and his works are a fine example of the 'single talent well employed'. Decorum, discipline, a perfect understanding of his aim and of the means to that aim are his characteristics. His masterpiece is *Squire Meldrum*, a 'completely successful' poem 'which stands, as it were, at the triple frontier where the novel, the romance, and the biography all march together.' It was in his *Dialog betwix Experience and ane Courteour*, better known as the *Monarche*, that we come across that description of the building of the tower of Babel and the *schaddow of that hidduous strength*, which Lewis took for the title of the third book in his space trilogy, *That Hideous Strength*.

We are given a glance at some minor and anonymous poets and then at **Alexander Montgomerie** (1545?–1611?), the representative of the transition from the Late Medieval period. There are two obviously new elements in his work: he is a sonneteer, and in his miscellaneous poems there is a hint of stateliness 'which comes in when the classic model of the ode begins to mix with the native song in men's conception of lyric poetry.' What remains of Scottish poetry in this century amounts to not much more than the *Sevin Seages* and *Court of Venus* of **John Rolland** and a collection of Protestant hymns compiled and largely composed by the brothers Wedderburn. In **Alexander Hume**'s *Hymnes or Sacred Songs* 'we reach religious poetry proper as distinct from hymnody; and we also reach the point at which Scottish poetry is ceasing to be very noticeably Scots.'

Why the sudden extinction of this poetical literature? Historians whose sympathies are Roman attribute the catastrophe to the Reformation. If correct, this must have been some peculiarity of the Scottish Reformation 'for in England the old religion had had no such poetical glories to show and the new had many.' Lewis suspects that Scottish poetry, being essentially court poetry, could not live without a court. Whatever the cause, it should not be assumed that this branch of culture was not vital and healthy. 'Higher organisms are often conquered by lower ones ... An art, a whole civilization, may at any time slip through men's fingers in a very few years and be gone beyond recovery.'

The crop of sixteenth-century Scottish prose is plentiful and some of it can be classed as Late Medieval. John Gau's *The Richt Vay to the Kingdome of Hevine* (1533) 'has the distinction of being the first specimen of Protestant theology in Scots.' One of the most remarkable works of the century is the anonymous *Complaynt of Scotlande*, its form a dream allegory, its landscape painting indebted almost certainly to Dunbar and probably to Alanus ab Insulis. As for historians of the period, **Hector Boece** (1465?–1536) and **Johannes Major** (1479–1550) represent the humanistic and medieval conceptions of historical writing respectively. **John Lesley** (1526–96), a sounder historian than Boece, has a narrative style free from rhetoric and not very typical of either the medieval or the humanist kind of history. Lesley's great opposite on the Protestant side, **Robert Lindsay** of Pitscottie (1532–92), is a medieval not a Renaissance historian, and in his *History of Scotland* 'for the first and last time, Scots prose of medieval character achieves permanent value.'

Chapter II: The Close of the Middle Ages in England

In turning from the Scottish poetry of that age to the English 'we pass from civilization to barbarism' – at least as far as poetry is concerned. From the varied excellence of the fourteenth century to the work of the early sixteenth, the history of English poetry is one of decay – and the further south you go, the worse it has decayed. In Cheshire we find an alliterative poem, *Scotish Feilde*, which, given its provenance and title, has perhaps not surprisingly escaped this decay. Indeed, it is incomparably better battle poetry than England was to produce for many centuries. From the same region, at Chester, we have **Henry Bradshaw**'s *Lyfe of St Werburge* (1513) which, in a creditable sense, shows how bad medieval poetry could be. 'It could be as bad as this and no worse: that is, it could be dull and feeble, but not odious or perverse. Its badness is always an honest, innocent kind of badness: and at any moment there may come a gleam of imagination.' *St Werburge* is a good example of another perplexing and repellent defect of Late Medieval poetry in England, its metre.

Of the bad poets who wrote at this time we meet first **Stephen Hawes** (1475?–1511) – the 'most completely medieval' poet. His *Example of Virtue* (1504) and *The Pastime of Pleasure* (1505) have a not unimportant place in the history of English allegory and it is probable that Spenser had read the *Pastime*. Next comes **Alexander Barclay** (1475?–1552), with whom 'we touch rock bottom'. His poetry has no intrinsic value and the opening exhortation of the *Castell of Labour* (1503), 'Subdue you to payne to rede this tretyse' is fully justified and might as well refer to any of his poems. All Barclay's works are outweighed in value by the few poems which Thomas More wrote in his youth.

When all's said **John Skelton** (1464?–1529) is the only poet of the age who is still read for pleasure. Skelton was a translator, tutor to Henry VIII, a satirist, and a jest-book hero in Elizabethan tradition. In his earliest surviving pieces, he appears as a typical poet of the late Middle Ages: no better than Barclay and inferior to Hawes. A characteristic feature of his later work is the absence of metre and rhyme scheme in the strict sense. The resulting style was Skelton's own invention. *Philip Sparrow*, a mock-heroic poem about a pet bird, is a perfect little light bubble and well-suited to Skelton's childishness and artlessness. 'We should not, I think, refuse to call this poem great; perfection in light poetry, perfect smallness, is among the rarest of literary achievements.' Similarly tender and playful is the *Garland of Laurel* where he returns to the 'broad highway of medieval poetry'. Such extreme unpretentiousness is without parallel in English literature. 'No student of the early sixteenth century comes away from Skelton uncheered. He has no real predecessors and no important disciples; he stands out of the streamy historical process, an unmistakable individual, a man we have met.'

Miles Coverdale's *Goostly Psalmes and Spirituall Songs* (before 1539) is on the border line between the Late Medieval and the Drab. 'He is prosaic and of no literary importance.' **John Heywood** (1497–1578), on the other hand, is a far more interesting transitional poet, if for nothing other than the fact that he wrote good Drab poetry before writing Late Medieval poetry. One of his best poems is a 'Description of a Most Noble Lady'. His characteristic output consists of anecdotes, epigrams, proverbs, cautionary tales, fables. His endless *bon mots* are 'unendurable', but, ironically, Heywood's best title to fame is the joke he cracked on his deathbed; that, and the refrain: 'All a green willow, willow/All a green willow is my garland.'

Finally, we look at prose writers. Vernacular prose history at this period is just beginning to branch off from the records of the city of London. *Arnold's Chronicle*, the folio of 1502, contains articles, charters, ordinances, oaths. *Nut Brown Maid* is 'like a gold ring found lying in an old drawer of odds and ends.' Comic prose is represented by two works of very different merit, the *Hundred Merry Tales* and the *Howleglass*. The latter is a collection of (fairly obvious) practical jokes; the former a group of stories with humorous morals appended. Neither book has deserved so well of posterity as the writing of **Sir John Bourchier, Lord Berners** (1469–1533), the last of the great medieval translators. Our debt to him for having given us Froissart is huge. 'He was probably omnivorous, and his taste was excellent as long as he did not think about it. To the present day one meets men, great readers, who write admirably until the fatal moment when they remember that they are writing.'

Book II: 'Drab'

Chapter I: Drab Age Prose –
Religious Controversy and Translation

'In England, as elsewhere,' we are told, 'the Reformation was a process that occurred on three planes: firstly in the thought and conscience of the individual, secondly in the intertangled realms of ecclesiastical and political activity, and thirdly on the printed page. All are connected but only the third is our direct concern. We are to consider what men wrote, and our judgement on it must, of course, attempt to be literary, not theological.' Despite the limitation Lewis had to set on his subject, this chapter would appeal strongly to those interested in his theological books.

The first author to be considered is **John Colet** (1467?–1519), a 'Platonist at heart' who 'has really little interest in the temporal and mutable world below the moon.' Because he was a 'cloistered perfectionist' and a rhetorician, he 'often says, not exactly more than he means, but more than he understands.' Still, he has an important place in the history of biblical studies. He helped to banish the old allegorical methods of interpretation, at least as regards the New Testament, and made some attempt to see the Pauline epistles in their real historical setting. He saw marriage as nothing more than a remedy against fornication, and when he founded St Paul's School, he forbade all use of medieval Latin on the grounds that it was corrupting and more 'blotterature than literature'.

The same ascetic strain is to be found in **John Fisher** (1459–1535), the martyr Bishop of Rochester, famous for preaching against Luther in 1521. His style is 'grave and a little diffuse, never comic ... mildly rhetorical, and at times really eloquent ... Many of his comparisons, such as that of the Blessed Virgin to morning ... or of faith and works to the sunbeams ... are ingeniously beautiful and, if compressed and versified, would be exactly what we call "metaphysical" poetry. His chief weakness is that he is too leisurely: he is in no hurry to end a sentence or to let an idea go.' A medieval sweetness and richness hangs about his prose and one merit that he can claim (very unusual in that age) is that he is hardly at all scurrilous. Compared with More and Tyndale, Fisher's theological attacks are almost courteous.

Thomas More (1478–1535) has, in recent years, been restored to his rightful place as a major English author. His non-poetic works fall into three classes: those of 'pure' literature; controversies; and moral and devotional treatises. Outstanding within the first class is his *Utopia*. 'It becomes intelligible and delightful as soon as we take it for what it is – a holiday work, a spontaneous overflow of intellectual high spirits, a revel of debate, paradox, comedy and (above all) of invention, which starts many hares and kills none. It is written by More the translator of Lucian and friend of Erasmus, not More the chancellor or the ascetic. Its place on our shelves is close to *Gulliver* and *Erewhon*, within reasonable distance of Rabelais, a long way from the *Republic* or *New Worlds for Old*.'

More's polemical writings are, in contrast, not a labour of love, but a duty, commissioned as they were by the Bishop of London. Two works stand apart from the rest. First, the *Dialogue of Comfort against Tribulation* (1528), which is not great theology, but perhaps the best specimen of Platonic dialogue ever produced in English. The other is the *Supplication of Souls* (1529) in which Purgatory has been degraded into a department of Hell, 'black, salt, macabre'. 'In Fisher the pain has been separated from any spiritual purification, but the torments had at least been inflicted by angels. In More this last link with heaven is severed' (see the discussion of Purgatory in *Letters to Malcolm* XX). As specimens of the art of controversy these works are not great. 'How to throw the grand arguments into bold relief and to condense the lesser, how to decline small points and to answer others while seeming to decline them, where to refresh the reader with some eloquent assault over the ruins of a lately demolished fortification – of all this More has no opinion.'

It is with relief, then, that we turn to More's devotional works. *The Dialogue* is 'the noblest of all his vernacular writings.' It was written in the Tower while More waited for death, and it should be on everyone's shelves. The *Treatise on the Passion* is less good, containing passages of exquisite pathos and insight balanced by plenty of errors. Of his English prose as a whole, great claims are not in order. It is neither concise nor full; it has neither lightning thrusts nor a swelling tide of thought and feeling. 'As for his sanctity, to live and die like a saint is no doubt a better thing than to write like one, but it is not the same thing; and More does not write like a saint.'

The theological works of **William Tyndale** (?–1536) are repetitious, and we are not given a detailed account of them one by one. However, it is worth pausing at *The Obedience of a Christian Man*, interesting for its political philosophy – one which is almost identical to Shakespeare's. Elsewhere Tyndale attacks the 'theological hedonism' of the Church of Rome; talks of the 'thunder' of the Law and the 'rain' of the Gospel; and extols the spiritual transition that comes by 'the gift of faith'. As a writer he is inferior to More in his use of humour, but superior in overall style. 'He is, beyond comparison, lighter, swifter, more economical. He is very unadorned ... but not at all jejeune.' In Tyndale there is not the manysidedness, the elbow-room of More's mind; but in More we miss the joyful, lyric, poetic quality of Tyndale.

This section of the chapter ends with a look at some minor religious controversialists of the day. **Hugh Latimer** (1485?–1555?), another martyr, and a man of 'real genius', wrote sermons that may not have been literature, 'but the mere strength and pith and urgency of his sentences, in that age so given to verbiage, is a literary virtue.' As importunate as Hazlitt, he would have been a fine broadcaster. **Thomas Cranmer's** (1489–1556) great achievements as a translator are 'sunk in the corporate anonymity of *The Book of Common Prayer*.‡' The rest of his work is 'flat and official'. **John Knox** (1505–72) was a self-ignorant man, the 'most embarrassing' of whose works is the *First Blast of the Trumpet against the Monstrous Regiment of Women*. To the end of his days he could not understand why Queen Elizabeth disliked it.

The second section of the chapter deals with the English Bible and the *Book of Common Prayer*, 'achievements of much more lasting value than the original works of More and Tyndale.' The story of the English Bible is best seen in three streams: the group of translators led by Tyndale and then Coverdale who make up the 'central Protestant tradition'; the Protestant 'irregulars' (Richard Taverner, John Cheke, etc.); and the 'popish versions, the Rheims New Testament and later the Douay.' All these groups affected one another and all affected the Authorized Version. Tyndale is to be praised for phrases such as 'The Lord's Anointed', 'flowing with milk and honey', 'filthy lucre', and for many of his coinages ('peacemakers', 'passover', 'long-suffering', 'scapegoat'); Coverdale for 'tender mercies' and 'lovingkindness'. Of the Protestant irregulars, Lewis confines himself to a discussion of the Geneva Bible of 1560. Some of its most felicitous turns have gone into the Authorized Version: 'smite them hip and thigh', 'vanity of vanities', 'except a man be born again'. The Roman tradition in the Rheims version inclined towards a very literal translation of the Latin, whereas Tyndale inclined towards paraphrase.

The *Prayer Book* is the 'one glory of the Drab age', so glorious that it would throw doubt on the justice of the epithet 'Drab' if we forgot that it was principally a work of translation. There is no such sharp break between it and earlier liturgical prose as there is between Tyndale and the medieval translators of Scripture. 'It is an anonymous and corporate work in which Cranmer bore the chief part, and it is almost wholly traditional in matter, though some of the excellencies of its style are new.' It dreads excess. 'It has almost an Augustan shrinking, not from passion, but from what came to be called enthusiasm', and is as sparing as the gospels themselves of references to wounds, hearts, flames, blood and tears. 'The difference here does not exactly coincide with that between Roman and Anglican piety, though it comes near to doing so.' While it offers little and concedes little to merely natural feelings, even religious feelings, it will not heighten till it has first sobered them. 'But at its greatest it shines with a white light hardly surpassed outside the pages of the New Testament itself.'

Chapter II: Drab Age Verse

This section begins by looking at the lyric. When read merely as poems many of these lyrics, with their simple rhymes, repeated refrains, short lines and plain language, seem dull. Others seem fresh and ingenuous. Both types were written not to be read but to be sung, 'hence purely literary judgement ... may be as unfair as the study-criticisms we make about plays we never saw acted.' The *Nut Brown Maid* is one of the best specimens of the early Tudor lyric; and all that is finest in **Sir Thomas Wyatt** (1503–42) is rooted in this poetry. As the first of our Italianate poets he has an important part to play in the process of evolution that led to the

Elizabethan sonnet. But his permanent value is to be found in his Drab lyrics. Here, his strengths and his weaknesses are connected alike with his unadorned style. 'When he is bad, he is flat or even dull. And when he is good he is hardly one of the irresistible poets.'

Henry Howard, Earl of Surrey (1517–47), admired Wyatt both as a man and as a poet. To him Wyatt was not so much the 'technical master as the man who had suggested new possibilities, who had claimed and partly shown, that the new-fashioned continental poetry could be naturalized in England.' Surrey's work was less related to music than Wyatt's and less given to refrain. It follows what was newest (and worst) in Wyatt, his poulter's measure. But Surrey is more up-to-date in temper: with him the Drab Age is fully established.

Surrey's Petrarchan pieces are more accomplished and useful than Wyatt's. 'His love poetry is usually best when it is least about love. He takes every opportunity of bringing in external nature, or narrative, as if to take a holiday from the erotic treadmill.' If as a love poet he is 'correctly cold and regularly low', he can express real feelings, especially on friendship – a good example being the poem on his imprisonment at Windsor. His greatest exploration was that which led him to translate two books of the *Aeneid* in blank verse. It is a poor translation, but contains good verses – for a blank verse pioneer, astonishingly good. It raises the 'utility' of Surrey above Chaucer and Milton and perhaps even Shakespeare. 'By any same standard, however, he is merely a man who served his generation well and has left one or two poems of permanent, though moderate value.'

'The grand function of the Drab Age poets was to build a firm metrical highway out of the late medieval swamp.' In **Richard Tottel**'s *Miscellany* (1557), a collection of 310 poems by Surrey, Wyatt, Grimald and 'Uncertain Auctors', we can see this highway being constructed and, perhaps more interestingly, discover traces of one or two uncompleted roads – systems of metre that were never worked out. However, we must not treat this anthology as if it were Golden Age poetry in embryo. It has its own merits, and these are demonstrated not by departing from plainness, sententiousness or brevity, but by somehow sublimating these qualities into dignity and force. In 'The plage is great' are two simple lines: 'The cause of things I will not blame/Lest I offend the prince of peas.' This sort of severity, neatness and precision bring Drab Age poetry much closer to the Augustans than to Sidney, Spenser and Shakespeare.

After Tottel the greatest composite monument of the Drab Age is the *Mirror for Magistrates*, but no one lays it down without a sense of relief. Like Tottel it did useful work in re-establishing metrical regularity, and an immense amount of serious thought and honest work went into its composition, but its influence on succeeding poets was mainly bad, not least for encouraging a taste for heavily doctrinal history in verse.

Much of the most characteristic work of the Drab Age is to be found in its copious translations from the Latin. Their metres mark them off from medieval work; their clumsiness and their diction from the Golden Age. **Thomas Phaer** (1510–60), the earliest of these translators, is much the best. Anyone who cares for epic and cannot master either Virgil's Latin or Douglas's Scots will be 'tolerably safe' with Phaer's *Seven first books of the Eneidos*. Other translators and translations are described by Lewis as 'very bad', 'beneath criticism', 'few books less repay perusal', 'unhappy', 'execrable', 'very, very bad'. **John Studley**, however, is to be thanked for giving Lewis the name of one of his best-loved Narnian characters: he 'uses more often than his fellows' that diction which, whether 'low' in his own day or not, cannot now be read without a smile – 'frostyface', 'topsy turvy' and he translates the words *Tacitae Stygis* in *Hippolytus* 625 as '*Stygian puddle glum*'.

We now turn to the original poets of the Drab Age of which there is little to be said by way of commendation. To turn from most Drab poetry to *A Handful of Pleasant Delights* by **Clement Robinson** 'and divers others' is like 'passing from a gimcrack parlour into sweet open air'. It is difficult to make a literary and non-musical judgement of such work. Many of the pieces in the *Handful* hardly exist without the music; 'even Greensleaves, if we could forget the tune, would die in print.'

This was not a period during which the genial spring of 'Renaissance' gradually ripened poetry towards its Golden summer. In this age there was no such advance; save in metrical smoothness there was a decline. 'If our knowledge of literature ended with these poets there would be nothing to suggest that English poetry was soon, or ever, going to rise again.' The suggestion that Henry VIII was responsible for the Drab Age by cutting off the heads of scholars and poets, is false. Who (save Surrey) were the promising poets that he killed? 'It is not clear that our poetry would be much the poorer if he had beheaded nearly every writer mentioned in this chapter.'

Chapter III: Drab and Transitional Prose

Some of the prose considered in an earlier chapter was 'applied' prose, such as never owed much to conscious artistry. In this chapter we consider 'picked prose' and 'adorned prose', and we begin with **Sir Thomas Elyot** (1490?–1546). His *Dictionary* 'is probably the most useful thing he did', but as an English author he is chiefly remembered for the

Book of the Governor, a sort of blue-print for the education of the aristocracy. His love of long words is a constant trait and he is a convinced neologist ('for the augmentation of the language'). But the important thing about Elyot is that he is aware of prose as an art. His sentences do not simply happen, they are built. The same impulse towards a more formal prose appears in the historian **Edward Hall** (d. 1547). His *Union of the Two Noble and Illustre Families of Lancaster and York* is, after More's *Richard III*, 'the first English attempt at history in the grand manner.' There is nothing about him that excites love: we praise the writer, but feel the man may have been little better than a government tool.

Roger Ascham (1515–68), on the other hand, is 'everyone's friend ... His delightful, and delighted, temperament has flowed into his writing.' His *Toxophilus* (1545) is 'one of the most genial and winning books that had yet appeared in English.' *The Schoolmaster* is a protest against cruelty in teaching. He is interested in everything: the optical illusions produced by broken ground, an unlucky archer 'crying after the shafte', the precision with which a cook chops herbs. And his style is good too. He is against neologisms (or 'ink-horn' terms); he would rather write 'faule of the leafe' than 'Autumn'. And although his verbal tricks are refined, they are not used so sententiously as to be called euphuism.

Ascham's friend **John Cheke** (1514–58) had a bee in his bonnet about 'pure and unmixed' English. His translation of St Matthew makes 'lunatic' *moond*, 'proselyte' *freshman*, and 'crucified' *crossed*. Elsewhere, his style is much less visibly artful than Elyot's or Hall's. **Thomas Starkey** (1499?–1538) uses a style less artificial than either of those two men. His *Dialogue* of 1534 is interesting for its passionate love of urban life, but as a writer of dialogue itself he 'does not rank very high'.

We now move among the crowd of sixteenth-century prose writers. More than a score of them are evaluated, of whom four stand out in particular. **John Foxe** (1517–87) among Protestants soon acquired and long retained almost scriptural authority, and his enormous influence is curiously out of proportion to his actual status as an English man of letters, for Latin was the medium he preferred. **Raphael Holinshed** (d. ?1580) headed a team of historians who published their *Chronicles* 1577 and 1587 – famous more for the use Shakespeare made of them than for any intrinsic merit. **Anne Lady Bacon** (1528–1610), the first female writer to have been mentioned in this chapter, is 'the best of all sixteenth-century translators', if 'quality without bulk were enough'. And **William Harrison** (1534–93), one of Holinshed's colleagues, supplied in his own *Description of Britain* a work whose style emerges quite clearly from the Drab Age. Most Drab prose writers sound 'middle-aged' but in Harrison is evident 'that spirit of youthfulness which is often characteristic of the "Golden" period.'

Finally, we come to **John Lyly** (c.1553–1606), 'an author once unjustly celebrated for a style which he did not invent, and now inadequately praised for his real, and very remarkable, achievement.' If Lyly had never written *Euphues* he would have been placed among the 'Golden' writers: that 'fatal success' ties him down to the transitional category. Euphuism gradually emerged as a structural decoration alternative to the 'ink-horn decoration of vocabulary'. Its elements – antithesis, alliteration, balance, rhyme and assonance – were not new. The novelty was the excess with which they were employed, and the credit (or discredit) for keeping the thing up for whole pages 'or decades of pages' at a stretch, must be given to Lyly. *Euphues* is worst where it is least euphuistic. 'In the dialogue between Euphues and Atheos euphuism is almost wholly abandoned, and it is here that the confident fatuity of Lyly's thought becomes most exasperating.' Euphuism shows its real value in Lyly's plays (*Endimion, Love's Metamorphosis*, etc.). In a theatre which had too much of belly laughter and graphic abuse, Lyly's lightness of touch, his delicacy and blessed unreality are 'real advances in civilization'. It is on these comedies that Lyly's fame must rest: they are good, not despite, but because of, his style. It is the perfect instrument for his essentially poetic genius and purpose. Here is the 'Golden' literature at last.

Book III: 'Golden'

Chapter I: Sidney and Spenser

The chapter opens with a look at certain defences of poetry. The neo-Platonic conception of art is the one demanded by most Golden poetry. Sidney himself opined that the poet, unlike the historian, is not 'captiued to the trueth of a foolish world' but can 'deliuer a golden'. To improve on Nature and paint what might be or ought to be was not to retreat from reality into a merely subjective refuge; it was the poet's duty and joy so to reascend from this 'foolish world' and assert his divine origin.

Sir Philip Sidney (1554–86) is 'dazzling'. 'He is that rare thing, the aristocrat in whom the aristocratic ideal is really embodied.' His life as scholar, soldier, statesman, is as interesting as his art, which is no small achievement. His sonnet sequence, *Astrophel and Stella*, with all its faults, 'towers above everything that had been done in poetry, south of the Tweed, since Chaucer died.' His *Arcadia* of 1593 assumes in its readers an agreed response to a certain ideal of virtue, honour, friendship and magnanimity. It is a kind of touchstone. 'What a man thinks of it, far more than what he thinks of Shakespeare or Spenser or Donne, tests the depth of his sympathy with the sixteenth century.' It gathers up what a whole generation wanted to say. 'The very gallimaufry that it is – medieval, Protestant, pastoral, Stoical, Platonic – makes it the more characteristic and, as long as that society lasted, more satisfactory.'

The heart of the *Arcadia* is 'its nobility of sentiment'. He has the right Stock Responses§. Sidney's conception of love 'is a Platonic elaboration of medieval *Frauendienst* – the theory … that erotic love can be a sensuous appetite of intelligible good.' There is no notion that 'love has a right to override all claims … It leaves the laws of friendship sacred. "Life of my desires," says Musidorus to Philoclea, "what is mine euen to my soule is yours; but the secret of my friend is not mine."' Theoretically, everyone is a pagan in *Arcadia*, but Christian theology is always breaking in. Thus a single phrase like 'Since neither we made ourselves nor bought ourselves' casually and perhaps unconsciously lets in the whole doctrine of the Redemption. Pamela's prayer is Christian in all but name. This superficial discrepancy does no harm. The convention was well understood and very useful. In such works the gods are all God *incognito* and everyone is in the secret. 'Paganism is the religion of poetry through which the author can express, at any moment, just so much or so little of his real religion as his art requires.'

Sidney's *Defence of Poesie* is 'the best critical essay in English before Dryden'. His central doctrine, that the poet is a 'second Creator producing a second Nature', is taken from Scaliger. The basis of this position is 'the *de jure* superiority of Man in the natural universe.' He is set 'beyond and over' it. Nothing shows both that superiority and its loss (*de facto*) by the Fall so clearly as poetry. For in it we surpass Nature; our 'erected wit' still enabling us to conceive perfection though our 'infected wil' hinders us from achieving it in action. Poetry entices Passion to virtue and, for Sidney, if poetry does not ravish, it is nothing. Poetic images of virtue are no mere *moralitas*, no powder hidden under jam. They are the final sweetness of that sweet world, 'the form of goodness, which seen we cannot but love.' The assumption that the ethical is the aesthetic *par excellence* is so basic to Sidney that he never argues it. He thought we would know.

Where Sidney's work rises out of the contemporary Drab like a rocket, that of **Edmund Spenser** (1552–99) climbs out slowly and painfully, 'like Christian from the slough'. While this history considers all his writings, the greater part of it is given to the poet's life's work, *Faerie Queene*, the first three books of which were published in 1590. Everything else either led up to or was a digression from that central achievement. 'All his life,' we are told, 'he was in the position of a painter who, while engaged on some great work, frequently has visitors in the studio. They have to be entertained … with anything he can lay his hands on. Old canvases that he himself cares nothing about will be brought forward. Worse still, they must be shown the great work itself in various stages of incompleteness. This helps to explain the extraordinary disparity in value between the *Faerie Queene* and nearly all the minor poems. Virgil without the *Aeneid*, Milton without *Paradise Lost*, Goethe without *Faust*, would still rank as great poets. But if Spenser were shorn of the *Faerie Queene*, though the *Epithalamion* … would appear in anthologies, the rest of his work would be known only to professional scholars.' Apart from one or two faults it is perfection – 'the Drab has been completely purged away.'

Formally considered, the *Faerie Queene* is the fusion of two kinds, the medieval allegory and the more recent romantic epic of the Italians. Because it is allegory – neither strictly religious nor strictly erotic, but universal – every part of the poet's experience can be brought in. 'Fairy land' provides the unity, a unity not of plot but of milieu. 'Few poems have a greater harmony of atmosphere. The multiplicity of the stories, far from impairing the unity, supports it: for just that multiplicity, that packed fullness of "vehement adventures", is the quality of Faerie Land; as tragedy is the quality of Hardy's Wessex.'

Lewis tells us that when he wrote about the *Faerie Queene* in *The Allegory of Love*, 'I do not think I sufficiently emphasized the originality and fruitfulness of this structural invention.' In the absence of the biographical novel, the *Faerie Queene* was really the only way for Spenser to talk about, in a single work, all the things that interested him. The 'primary structural idea' is reinforced by two others: an 'allegorical core' to each book: and, striding across from book to book, the quest of Arthur for Gloriana. Gloriana is both Queen Elizabeth and 'the idole of her Maker's great magnificence'. 'Arthur is an embodiment of what Professor Nygren calls "Eros religion", the thirst of the soul for the Perfection beyond the created universe.' The best parallel to Arthur's quest is the repeated (and always disappointed) belief of the Trojans in the *Aeneid* that they have already found the *mansuram urbem*. 'It is the very nature of the Platonic quest and the Eros religion that the soul cannot know her true aim till she has achieved it.'

Some scholars believe that in part of the *Faerie Queene* Spenser was expounding the doctrines of a school. 'In general he is concerned with agreements, not differences … He never dreamed of expounding something he could call "his philosophy". His business was to embody in moving images the common wisdom.' In this respect, Spenser was like Shakespeare. 'I do not think Shakespeare wrote a single line to express "his" ideas. What some call his philosophy, he would have called common knowledge.'

This tranquillity is the fruit of Spenser's very un-Existential approach to life. He feels no *Angst* because he thinks that man's nature is given, discoverable and discovered. As an inheritor of the Platonic and Christian dualism, he 'tolerates the indignities of time', refusing to be deceived by them, recognizing them as truths indeed but only truths of 'a foolish world'. 'He would not have called himself "the poet of our waking dreams": rather the poet of our waking.'

Chapter II: Prose in the 'Golden' Period

In the last quarter of the sixteenth century there was a greatly increased output in this literature. There was also a remarkable improvement in quality; but even if this had not been so, the mere quantity would be striking. Part of the explanation is that literature was finding its feet as a commercial art and printers were eager for copy. Part of it is due to that 'academic overproduction' that was so deprecated by Spenser's tutor, Richard Mulcaster. Among the forms which prose took at this time *fiction* holds a very important place. 'The truth is that Elizabethan fiction points only rarely and uncertainly towards the novel properly so called.' Another dominant form was the pamphlet, which might also have served for fiction. The difference is that 'the taste for confessed fiction was then (as it still is) rarer than the taste for sensational reading which claims to be "news". The lowest sort of reader wants to be assured ... that what he reads is true.'

Stephen Gosson (1554–1624) and his *School of Abuse* (1579) are remembered because in that pamphlet he contributed to what some have called the puritan attack on the theatre. But the pamphlet was not much more than a rhetorical display, and Gosson no more deserves a place in the history of English criticism than does **Thomas Lodge** (1558?–1625) who replied to Gosson with *Honest Excuses*, a rhetorical, sometimes euphuistic, sometimes biblical, unreliably learned work. Only **Philip Stubbes** (c. 1555–1610+) is of permanent interest in the controversy over the theatre. His *Anatomy of Abuses* is like something by Cobbett in its hot, compassionate and somewhat undiscriminating tone. His preoccupation with theatrical dress should be connected with his statement that Pride is his 'chiefest argument'. That is not the only point at which Stubbes, despite his Protestant theology, strikes a medieval note. 'The whole layout of the *Anatomy*, with its inset stories of dreadful judgement, would have commended itself to Chaucer's Pardoner.'

The immense contemporary popularity of **Robert Greene** (1560?–92), his early death, his miseries, his heavily publicized but not therefore insincere repentance, made him in some sort the hero and spokesman of the many commercial writers mentioned in this chapter. '**Martin Marprelate** gentleman' – the name assumed by the authors of some anonymous tracts – also deserves attention, not as a theologian but as a writer. By 1588 the bishops, what between their control of the press and the powers of the detested High Commission established in 1582, had reduced their puritan critics to silence. At that moment there appeared the first of seven pamphlets by Martin Marprelate. The 'racy, fleering, cockney manner' he used in *Oh read over D. John Bridges* was something of a novelty. He is not to be condemned for introducing scurrility into a theological debate because 'debate was precisely what the bishops had suppressed'. While he displayed a new manner in controversy, it cannot be claimed that he attained excellence.

Thomas Nashe (1567–1601) was the greatest of the Elizabethan pamphleteers, 'the perfect literary showman, the juggler with words who can keep a crowd spell-bound by sheer virtuosity.' There is little need for the modern reader to understand the issues being addressed in his work: the liveliness of the style is enough. His name-calling is particularly good and confers a grievous immortality on its victims. If asked what Nashe 'says' the answer would have to be 'Nothing'. He maintains no attitude, expresses no thought, but simply thrives on producing ludicrous, incoherent and violent images. He is something of a cross between Picasso, Thurber and Lewis Carroll. Although, within the century, Nashe had no successor of stature comparable to his own, the general standard of prose, even in the works with little or no literary pretension, is markedly better than in the Drab Age. 'Somehow or other during the latter part of the sixteenth century Englishmen learned how to write.'

In the second section of the chapter we look at prose fiction which it would be a mistake to call 'the novel'. It may be divided into three classes: the romantic, the realistic, and a type of writing in which we 'are expected to be interested not in what the characters were or felt or did, but in what they said.' **John Grange**'s *Golden Aphroditis* (1577) and Lyly's *Euphues* (1578) are the earliest specimens of this third kind. Neither deserves, as some critics assert, to be called 'the first English novel', for the group to which they belong 'is further from the true novel than medieval romance had been'. They are somewhere between a novel and a colloquy. It is 'a static and declamatory school of fiction.'

There is a more direct line of descent to the genuine novel from the romances. These may be just as rhetorical or euphuistic as the previous genre, but they possess real narrative interest. The authors aim at arousing curiosity, pity, terror and admiration. There is often a complete plot, reminiscent of chivalric or Greek romance. High sentiment and florid description of nature are not uncommon. Greene's *Pandosto* and Lodge's *Rosalynde* are the prime examples of the type, both having superadded interest to the modern reader by virtue of being sources for the *Winter's Tale* and *As You Like It*, respectively.

As for the realistic stories, the adjective is used mainly in a negative sense. They are 'realistic' only in so far they 'generally avoid rhetoric and the supernatural, write their dialogue in "language such as men do use", and deal chiefly with the life of humble people.' Greene's *Groats-Worth of Wit* is remembered mostly for its description of Shakespeare as an 'upstart crow'. Nashe's *Unfortunate Traveller* is better for being 'full-blooded'. Compared with Nashe, **Thomas Deloney** (who died about 1600), may appear almost tame. His *Jacke of Newbury* (1597) comes the nearest of his works to the shape of a true novel. His works excel in their dialogue, but 'the comic parts are often too coprological or violent: I can hardly regard burying a man alive (even if he was a "massing priest") as a "mad pranke".'

We next turn to literary critics, travellers and theologians. The *Schort Treatise conteining some rewlis and cautelis ... in Scottis Poesie* by **King James VI of Scotland** (1566–1625) would still give someone a grounding in English prosody. The *Art of English Poesy* by **George Puttenham** (c.1529–91) contains more sense about poetry than was written by any man of his age. **Richard Hakluyt** (1552–1616), editor of the three-volume *Principal Navigations ... of these 1600 years* (1589), provided one of the 'most useful and delightful publications of the century'. His authors differ widely in merit; but Hakluyt himself, though usually behind the scenes, records the day and hour which first kindled his lifelong passion for geography in 'a passage that warms the heart'.

The two theologians who deserve most attention from a literary historian are **Cardinal William Allen** (1532–94) on the Roman side and **Richard Hooker** (1554?–1600) on the Protestant. Allen will appeal most easily to moderns in the *Apology of the English Seminaries* (1581), and the *True, Sincere and Modest Defence* (1584) 'gives him a higher place as a vernacular writer than our older critical tradition recognized. Like Hooker, he rises above the usual controversial methods of the time; he neither carps nor snarls and trusts more to a steady exposition of what he believes to be the truth than to a fussy detection of errors. This makes him in the long run more formidable.' It is significant that he writes not only to refute but also 'for the stirring vp of the feare of God in myself.' Purgatory is for him essentially a balancing of accounts, a 'satisfaction of God's iustice' where sin is 'recompensed' by 'payne'. 'There is light as well as gloom in his theology, as we see in his beautiful chapters on heaven.' The staple of Allen's prose style 'is the long sentence', not braced with a latinized structure, but rather 'spreading like a pool.' His real merit lies in the trenchancy of the short sentences with which he varies his style and partly in the fact that he comes as near as any man could to succeeding in that type of long sentence.

'Up till now,' we are told, 'there had ... been no work on the Anglican side which could be called a resounding success: but a far stronger champion was at hand.' Richard Hooker, Lewis's favourite theologian, caused the puritans the darkest suspicions with his passionate sermon *Of Justification* in which he said of our Catholic ancestors, 'God, I doubt not, was merciful to save thousands of them.' He had bidden his hearers 'Beware lest we make too many ways of denying Christ.' There is an 'agonized charity which vibrates in sentence after sentence.'

Wholly different in tone is his *Laws of Ecclesiastical Polity*. Its 'mellow gold' is not merely 'the natural overflow of a mild eupeptic who has good reason to be pleased with the *status quo*'. It is the work of prudence, of art, of moral virtue and of Grace. There are two elements in Hooker's thought which must be grasped before we can understand anything else about him. (1) Though he is 'not writing to defend the freedom of the individual, he is certainly writing to defend the freedom of Man from what he believes to be a false conception of supernatural authority.' (2) Hooker 'never heard of a religion called Anglicanism. He would never have dreamed of trying to "convert" any foreigner to the Church of England. It was to him obvious that a German or Italian would not belong to the Church of England, just as an Ephesian or Galatian would not have belonged to the Church of Corinth. Hooker is never seeking for "the true Church" ... He is not, save accidentally, preaching "a religion"; he is discussing the kind and degree of liberty proper to national churches within the universal, visible Church.'

Chapter III: Verse in the 'Golden' Period

In the final chapter we begin by looking at the poets who lag behind the Golden Age: 'the belated, or vestigial, poetry.' The *Fig for Fortune* (1596) of **Anthony Copley** (1567–1607?) is 'unmistakably Late Medieval'. This dream allegory deserves to be remembered if only for the delightful verb 'to cravin-cockadoodle it'. The 'dismal fourteeners' of *Pelops and Hippodamia* by **Matthew Grove** should be remembered if only to 'throw into bolder relief the transcendent novelty of all the Golden *ephyllia*.' Grove's single moment of interest is his anticipation of Donne when he wishes that 'Jove would him convert' into a 'black flea' in his lady's bed.

In this period are many Drab passages, or whole poems, by writers who also produced Golden work – **Michael Drayton**, for instance. The Golden poets are chiefly those who write for their living and have to face frank criticism: courtiers who versified in odd moments tended to be Drab. The Queen herself had been a minor Drab poetess; **Puttenham's** taste was for the Drab; and **Walter Raleigh**, the most distinguished courtier poet of the period, wrote more Drab than anything else.

We turn next to satires, of which there were quite a crop in the 1590s. They were imitations of the satires of the Romans, and either Lodge or Donne led the pack in their successful execution. Lodge's *Fig for Momus* has little real satiric power, but is of fascinating interest to the literary historian. His perfectly end-stopped heroic couplets and the internal structure of the line often anticipates Augustan practice, and Epistle V even contains the line 'Wit shines in Vertue, Vertue shines in Wit' – which almost exactly prefigures a line in Pope.

John Donne, on the contrary, deliberately avoids smoothness and there is in his work a complete absence 'of that cheerful normality which in Horace, or that occasional grandeur which in Juvenal, relieves the monotony of vituperation.' **Joseph Hall** and **John Marston**, **William Rankin** and **Thomas Middleton** are two more pairs of 'Jacob and Esau' in their approaches to satire. **Samuel Rowland** is funny; **Cyril Tourneur** is freakish. In the aggregate they are all a weariness, for 'the shapeless Roman model was a fatal encouragement to the Elizabethan love of facile moral ferocity.'

And now we come to the Golden poetry proper. **Thomas Watson** (1557?–92) has the distinction of being the earliest of the poets who are Golden from their first word, and as pure an example as we can find of the 'Renaissance' poet. He is also a very minor poet indeed, and we may welcome this fact as a further safeguard against the tendency to make 'Golden' a eulogistic term. Perhaps one line of Watson's deserves to be remembered: 'In all this world I think none loues but I.'

Eulogy is quite in order, however, when it comes to **Christopher Marlowe** (1564–93) and his *Hero and Leander*. 'This is a more perfect work than any of his plays, not because their poetry is always inferior to it but because in it the poetry and the theme are at one. Here, and here only, he found matter to which his genius was entirely adequate. For Marlowe is our great master of the material imagination; he writes best about flesh, gold, gems, stone, fire, clothes, water, snow and air. It is only in such concretes that his imagination can fix itself.' The honey-sweetness which appears as one element among many in the *Faerie Queene* or the *Arcadia* is here 'the substance of the whole poem'. It was an obvious project, but one difficult to carry off successfully, as Shakespeare's *Venus and Adonis* shows. We do not see the 'frenzy' of Hero and Leander 'from outside as we see that of Shakespeare's Venus. We are at the centre and see the rest of the universe transfigured by the hard, brittle splendour of erotic vision.' The great thing about Marlowe's poem is its honesty – there is no nonsense, no pretence that appetite is anything other than appetite.

Remembering that this book does not deal with drama, we come to the poet responsible for the very best of 'good Golden': **William Shakespeare** (1564–1616). *Venus and Adonis*, if it were his only work, might not now be highly praised; *The Rape of Lucrece* might stand higher if it stood alone and were compared solely with other Elizabethan products. As it is, it sinks almost to nothing in comparison with Shakespeare's sonnets which 'are the very heart of the Golden Age, the highest and purest achievement of the Golden way of writing.' What we find in these poems is a patience, an anxiety, to find excuses for the beloved, a 'transference of the whole self into another self without the demand for a return', which 'have hardly a precedent in profane literature.' 'In certain senses of the word "love", Shakespeare is not so much our best as our only love poet.'

But the sonnets are not dramatic: 'the end of each is clearly in view from the beginning, the theme already chosen.' Instead of a thought or emotion growing and changing in the heat of a situation we get an 'arrangement' – a pattern or minuet – of thoughts and images. Shakespeare left it to his created persons, his Lears and Othellos, to pour out 'raw experience'. In his own person he does not do so. He sings from above, 'moved and yet not moved; a Golden, Olympian poet.'

The most secret of his poems is *The Phoenix and the Turtle*. Its supreme invention was the introduction of Reason as the principal speaker. The words which sum up Shakespeare's doctrine, 'Love hath reason, reason none', owe all their importance to the fact that it is Reason who utters them. In the mouth of a lover or a mourner they would be the 'stalest claptrap, one more expression of "will" revolting against "wit".' However, it is Reason who sees rational categories overthrown, who confesses that neither truth nor beauty is the highest good. It is Reason who 'exalts love above reason'.

In 1598 **George Chapman** (1559–1634) achieved that work he was born to do, which was not, as he imagined, translating Homer, but finishing

Hero and Leander. Except for academic purposes, the two parts of this poem, Marlowe's and Chapman's, should always be read together. Between them a great story is greatly told and the introduction of Chapman's *Ceremonie* (his equivalent of Spenser's Concord and Shakespeare's Degree) makes his part of the poem quintessentially Elizabethan. Thus the completed work unconsciously tells an important chapter in the history of poetry too.

Golden poetry has limitations which become vices when it attempts matter beyond its reach. The style of Homer, Dante or Chaucer could handle anything, but the Golden style not only fails but becomes ludicrous, even odious, when it attempts to present heroic action occurring in the real world. A good illustration is found in the work of **Gervase Markham**, but it is a 'defect visible in the battle poetry of Drayton, Spenser, and even Shakespeare'. With the work of **Michael Drayton** (1563–1631) we come to the close of the chapter. Although only 'half Golden', he 'began with Drab, constantly relapsed into it, and in his old age, when the Golden period was over, at last produced his perfect Golden work, so pure and fine that no English poet has rivalled it.' His *Shepherd's Sirena* (1627) and *Muses Elizium* (1630) are finer, more rarefied, than anything that foregoes them. In them we find the 'ultimate refinement of Golden poetry: Gold "to ayery thinnesse beate", without weight, ready to leave the earth.'

Epilogue: New Tendencies

The Epilogue falls into three parts: one deals with prose; the others deal respectively with the two different directions in which verse passed out of its Golden phase. The part dealing with prose must, historically, be the least interesting of the three. The end of the sixteenth century does not even approximately mark the end of Golden prose: Thomas Browne, Jeremy Taylor, John Milton and Thomas Traherne are still to come. The real break is later when men like John Tillotson and John Dryden taught English prose to live on a sparer diet. And so Lewis mentions only two writers, Henry Smith and Francis Bacon, who are already moving 'towards that drier and more utilitarian manner'.

One path which poetry took away from the Golden was that which led towards the Metaphysical. The novelty of Metaphysical poetry, like most literary novelties, consisted in doing more continuously or to a higher degree, something that had been done before. The yoking together of disparate images had been practised as far back as Ovid and Lucretius: Donne, Herbert and their school yield images more disparate and do so more often. However, their whole approach rested on the fact that most poetry, contemporary and historical, did not possess such violent clashes of imagery. It was that very immemorial standard of decorum – against which the Metaphysicals 'offend' – which gave them their point, their wit. God is asked to 'batter' a heart, Christ's 'stretched sinews' become fiddlestrings, cherubs have breakfasts, stars are a patrol, snow puts a periwig on bald woods. 'We may thus describe Metaphysical poetry either as being "parasitic" (it lives on other, non-Metaphysical poetry) or as being of a "higher" logical order (it presupposes other poetry).' The second path out of Golden poetry had two destinations. One was the Augustan, to which the satires of Lodge and Donne's *Elegy* XVII lines 26–59 distantly point. The other was the 'counterpoint' technique as represented by Milton and Thomas Campion.

Lewis looks back on the sixteenth century in surprise. Somehow the 'upstart' Tudor aristocracy produced a Sidney and became fit to patronize a Spenser, an Inigo Jones, an early Milton. Somehow such an apparent makeshift as the Elizabethan church became the church of Hooker, Donne, Andrewes, Taylor and Herbert. He also observes one great loss suffered by poetry. The Golden style became too rich, the Metaphysical too subtle, to tell a plain tale, and hence, between the two, huge territories that had once flourished under the rule of poetry were in effect ceded to prose. They have not been recovered. 'I do not suppose that the sixteenth century differs in these respects from any other arbitrarily selected stretch of years. It illustrates well enough the usual complex, unpatterned historical process; in which, while men often throw away irreplaceable wealth, they not infrequently escape what seemed inevitable dangers, not knowing that they have done either nor how they did it.'

The text of the book is followed by a Chronological Table in which each year of the sixteenth century is followed by some 'Public Events', 'Private Events', 'English and Scottish Texts', and 'Greek, Latin and Continental Vernaculars'; a Bibliography; and an Index.

Reviews

The Times Literary Supplement (17 September 1954), p. 592, said: 'Mr Lewis … knows how to make his learning *felt* – you feel, reading him, that he has read what he is talking about. Even so, what is best in his book, perhaps, is the lively, individual quality of it.' John Wain* in *The Spectator*, 193 (1 October 1954), pp. 403–5, said: 'Mr Lewis is today the only major critic of English literature who makes a principle of telling us which authors he thinks we shall *enjoy*: this may not sound much, but most dons have moved a long way from any recognition that literature is something that people used to read for fun. Mr Lewis, now as always, writes as if inviting us to a feast.' Roger Sharrock wrote in *The Tablet*, 204 (16 October 1954), p. 369: 'What he gives us is a highly personal and characteristic critical essay which skilfully contrives to embrace among its judgements and epigrams all the information requisite to a work of this kind.'

Helen Gardner said in *The New Statesman and Nation*, 48 (30 October 1954), p. 546: 'Mr Lewis's volume ... leaves an overwhelming impression of three things. First, the range of the author's learning ... Second, there is his conscientiousness. Third, and by far the most important, there is the strength of his capacity for enjoyment. This enables him to write with astonishing freshness on subjects which might be thought to be exhausted.'

J.B.L. reviewing in *The Oxford Magazine*, LXXIII (2 December 1954), p. 134, said: 'I have often heard [Lewis's] excursions into what has been called popular theology adversely commented upon, and sometimes even with the suggestion that he was neglecting his proper business. I will express no opinion upon these activities, but I will insist that this book is not only a triumphant refutation of the view that they have been a mere distraction, but a triumphant justification of the interests and studies that have laid behind them.'

Donald Davie said in *Essays in Criticism*, 5 (1955), pp. 159–64: 'The great virtue of this book is ... the critic's ability to enter sympathetically into literary conventions so alien to a modern temper that one had thought them irrecoverably lost ... This is a very good book, far and away the best piece of orthodox literary history that has appeared for many a long year.' Christopher Devlin said in *The Month*, 199 (June 1955), pp. 373–4: 'There is a generosity about Professor Lewis's conception of literature which combines scientific thoroughness with high reasoning as well as with sensitive appreciation. Such an unusual combination is particularly helpful with the greater poets; the pages on the sonnets of Shakespeare and the lyrics of Thomas Campion are a joy to read. But what is perhaps even more to be praised is that the acres of *dull* poetry, which he has to cover, become full, under his skilled hand, of entertainment as well as of information.'

AN EXPERIMENT IN CRITICISM (1961)

Background

I. High Brows and Low Brows

Lewis's 'experiment' consists in mounting the usual method of literary judgements back to front. Instead of classifying books, he classifies readers and how they 'use' or 'receive' books. This approach will be easier to understand if we look at the way Lewis went about literary criticism before he put things back to front. Of particular relevance is his essay **High Brows and Low Brows**, in which Lewis mentions a school 'where the library regulations divide the contents of the library into two classes: Good Books and Books. The boys are allowed to take out two Good Books for every one Book. To read a Good Book is meritorious, to read a Book only tolerable.' He asks whether 'lowbrow' books are the same as 'bad' books and, if not, whether the distinction between 'high' and 'low' brow is useful in some other way.

'As soon as we approach the first question,' he says, 'we notice that even if all lowbrow books … are in fact bad, even so the distinction between low- and highbrow … will not coincide with the distinction between bad books and good books, for the very obvious reason that [highbrow books] may also be bad.' *Gorboduc*, a very serious and very literary work by Thomas Norton and Thomas Sackville, would be classified by the school library as a 'Good Book' but most would agree that it is bad. On the other hand, Rider Haggard's *She* is a perfect example of a 'lowbrow' book that most would agree is certainly very good.

Casting about for another definition of highbrow and lowbrow, he looks at and disregards the following pairings: weighty and trivial; stylish and unstylish; artistic and popular; difficult and easy; refined and vulgar; noble and debased. He concludes that the distinction between high- and lowbrow rests upon a confusion between *degrees of merit* and *differences of kind*. 'Our map of literature has been made to look like an examination list – a single column of names with a horizontal line drawn across it, the honour candidates above that line, and the pass candidates below it.' He would prefer a whole series of vertical lines 'representing different kinds of work, and an almost infinite series of horizontal lines crossing these to represent the different degrees of goodness in each kind. Thus "Simple Adventure Story" is a vertical column with the *Odyssey* at the top and Edgar Wallace at the bottom. Rider Haggard, R.L. Stevenson, Scott, William Morris will be placed on horizontal lines crossing "Adventure Story" at such heights as we may decide. "Psychological Story" is a separate column, with its own top (Tolstoy or another) and its own bottom.'

Unless the second map is preferred to the first, Lewis foresees a time when readers and students will view good literature as an accomplishment rather than a delight. For them a good critic will be, as the theologians say, a 'twice-born' critic, one who is regenerate and washed from his Original Taste. 'As they will be contemptuous of popular books, so they will be naïvely tolerant of dullness and difficulty in any quack or sloven who comes before them with lofty pretensions; *all* literature having been as hard to them as that, so much an acquired taste, they will not see the difference. They will be angry with a true lover of literature who does not take pains to unravel the latest poetical puzzle, and call him a *dilettante*. Having obtained the freedom of Parnassus at a great price, they will be unable to endure the nonchalance of those who were free-born.'

II: Literature as Religion

One reason Lewis was such a 'true lover of literature' and could be so self-forgetful while reading was because he sought in books (as he called it here) an 'enlargement of his being'. What the reader gets from reading, he argued in *The Personal Heresy* (I), is 'a voyage beyond the limits of his personal point of view, an annihilation of the brute fact of his own particular psychology rather than its assertion.' And in *A Preface to 'Paradise Lost'* (IX) he claimed: 'I had much rather know what I should feel like if I adopted the beliefs of Lucretius than how Lucretius would have felt if he had never entertained them ... There is in G.K. Chesterton's *Avowals and Denials* a wholly admirable essay called *On Man: Heir of All the Ages*. An heir is one who inherits and "any man who is cut off from the past … is a man most unjustly disinherited". To enjoy our full humanity we ought, so far as possible, to contain within us potentially at all times, and on occasion to actualize, all the modes of feeling and thinking through which man has passed. You must, so far as in you lies, become an Achaean chief while reading Homer, a medieval knight while reading Malory, and an eighteenth-century Londoner while reading Johnson. Only thus will you be able to judge the work "in the same spirit that its author writ" and to avoid chimerical criticism.'

This desire to get 'out of himself', to 'see through other eyes', was beautifully matched by his undeniably Christian view of literature. In **Christianity and Literature** he maintained that 'Originality' is 'the prerogative of God alone'. Applying this to literature, he said the basis of all critical theory should be 'the maxim that an author should never conceive himself as bringing into existence beauty or wisdom which did not exist before, but simply and solely as trying to embody in terms of his own art some reflection of eternal Beauty and Wisdom.'

'Our criticism,' he went on, 'would therefore from the beginning group itself with some existing theories of poetry against others. It would have affinities with the primitive or Homeric theory in which the poet is the mere pensioner of the Muses. It would have affinities with the Platonic doctrine of a transcendent Form partly imitable on earth; and remoter affinities with the Aristotelian doctrine of [mimesis] and the Augustan doctrine about the imitation of Nature and the Ancients. It would be opposed to the theory of genius as, perhaps, generally understood; and above all it would be opposed to the idea that literature is self-expression.'

To the Christian 'his own temperament and experience, as mere fact, and as merely his, are of no value or importance whatsoever: he will deal with them, if at all, only because they are the medium through which, or the position from which, something universally profitable appeared to him.' Comparing the 'expressionist' and the Christian attitudes towards the self or temperament, he said, 'St Augustine and Rousseau both wrote *Confessions*; but to the one his own temperament is a kind of absolute (*au moins je suis autre*), to the other it is "a narrow house too narrow for Thee to enter – oh make it wide. It is in ruins – oh rebuild it"… It is not hard to argue that all the greatest poems have been made by men who valued something else much more than poetry … The real frivolity, the solemn vacuity, is all with those who make literature a self-existent thing to be valued for its own sake.'

Lewis does not name F.R. Leavis in his *Experiment* as one who did most to make literature a 'self-existent thing', but he certainly had him in mind when, in chapter XI, he describes the 'Vigilant School' of critics whose seriousness about literature causes them to act as 'watchdogs or detectives'. While many continue to be liberated by *Experiment in Criticism*, it was loathed by the Vigilant School. Lewis loved Cambridge but he deplored the effect the Vigilants were having – not only there but in many other places as well.

'Matthew Arnold made the horrible prophecy,' he said in **Unreal Estates** (1962), 'that literature would increasingly replace religion. It has, and it's taken on all the features of bitter persecution, great intolerance, and traffic in relics. All literature becomes a sacred text. A sacred text is always exposed to the most monstrous exegesis: hence we have the spectacle of some wretched scholar taking a pure *divertissement* written in the seventeenth century and getting the most profound ambiguities and social criticisms out of it, which of course aren't there at all ... It's the discovery of the mare's nest by the pursuit of the red herring.'

John Wain's* review of *An Experiment in Criticism* sheds so much light on Cambridge and the Vigilant School of Criticism as it was during Lewis's time there, that rather than save it to the end it is better to have it here. Describing the Vigilants in *The Observer* (22 October 1961), he said:

As we all know, this orthodoxy is puritan in character. Its main tenet is that literary study is not an amusement, nor a means of investigating the variety of human characters, nor an historical inquiry; it is a moral activity, whose object is to brace the reader up to a state of moral alertness which will enable him to face the great issues of life. Reading of this kind should be deep rather than wide; a few masterpieces, incessantly pored on, contain everything necessary to salvation.

In putting out this book, which contains a number of sharp challenges to the Cambridge party line, Mr Lewis has shown a courage that can best be appreciated by anyone who has ever spent an evening in the company of a group of youths who have been through the discipline ... To admire, or even to show a tolerant interest in, any author not on the small (and dwindling) list of sacred names is to convict oneself of frivolity ... It is this orthodoxy, with its insistence that there can be no matters of opinion in literature, and therefore no room for toleration or gentleness, that has banished, seemingly for ever, all trace of geniality and breadth, let alone any politeness, from the academic-literary arena. Under its influence, men who might otherwise be capable of imaginative sympathy with a point of view not their own have degenerated into Yahoos who make literary controversy hideous with their howls of denunciation. Moral indignation, which the rest of us know as a dangerous indulgence, is to them the very ink in their fountain-pens (p. 31).

Summary

In chapter I, 'The Few and the Many', Lewis explains the meaning of his 'experiment': 'Literary criticism is traditionally employed in judging books. Any judgement it implies about men's reading of books is a corollary from its judgement on the books themselves. Bad taste is, as it were by definition, a taste for bad books. I want to find out what sort of picture we shall get by reversing the process. Let us make our distinction between readers or types of reading the basis, and our distinction between books the corollary. Let us try to discover how far it might be plausible to define a good book as a book which is read in one way, and a bad book as a book which is read in another.'

He begins by defining the difference between 'the unliterary' majority (the 'Many') and 'the literary' minority (the 'Few'). (1) The first mark of the majority is that they never read anything twice ... The minority, however, who read great works, 'will read the same work ten, twenty or thirty times during the course of their life;' (2) The majority do not set much store on reading, but turn to it only as a last resource ... 'But literary people are always looking for leisure and silence in which to read' and feel 'impoverished' when they are denied the time; (3) The first reading of some literary work is often, to the literary, 'an experience so momentous that only experiences of love, religion or bereavement can furnish a standard of comparison.' There is no sign of this among the unliterary.

These two approaches to literature are so different that to say that the first group *likes* one sort of book and the second group *likes* another kind of book is to leave out nearly all the facts. It is therefore incorrect to define 'good taste' as the taste of the few. If that were so there would be no 'bad taste', for the inclination which the unliterary have to their sort of reading 'is not the same thing and, if the word were univocally used, would not be called taste at all.'

In chapter II, 'False Characterizations', he refines and develops the definitions used in chapter I. The unliterary 'many' are not, necessarily, illiterate, crass, crude or barbarous. The literary 'few' may well be ignorant, caddish, warped and truculent. Nor are the two groups cut off by immovable barriers. Individuals can move from one camp to the other, and some people who may be deeply appreciative of one art (music, say) may yet have a trivial attitude to poetry. More surprising still, those who might be expected *ex officio* to have a profound love of literature – scholars and writers – may in reality have nothing of the sort. Fashion followers and status seekers are obviously not members of 'the few'. But neither is the person who reads 'to improve himself ... to become a more complete man.' This attitude fixes attention on oneself and makes reading into little more than 'therapy'.

Chapter III is entitled 'How the Few and the Many Use Pictures and Music'. The Many 'use' or 'do things with' pictures, treating them almost as hieroglyphs – triggers to emotion or imagination. This is why those pictures which, in reproduction, are popular are of things which in reality would please or amuse or excite or move those who admire them. This sort of attitude *uses* the picture to stimulate an emotional reaction, in the same way that a toy or an ikon is used. The emotion may be good or bad, and the same picture may be used for either end, but it is not real appreciation.

Real appreciation *receives* the art of the painter in an act of surrender. This does not make the spectator passive, for his reaction is to be one of active imagination – but it must be 'obedient'. The true critic seems passive at first only because he is making sure of his orders. 'We sit down before the picture in order to have something done to us, not that we may do things with it. The first demand any work of art makes upon us is surrender. Look. Listen. Receive.'

Music too can be *used* or *received*. To *use* music is both to join in with it (to sing, hum, beat time, sway) and also to beget emotion upon it. 'Dim ideas of inconsolable sorrows, brilliant revelry, or well-fought fields, arise.' But to *receive* music is to grasp the total structure of the work, to admit into one's aural imagination the composer's whole invention, to attend fully to the actual sounds being made, not just the 'tune'. Such a reception may evoke emotion, but it will be an emotion 'impregnated with intelligence'.

In chapter IV, 'The Reading of the Unliterary', we look at five characteristics of the reading of the unliterary and their *use* of art: (1) 'They never, uncompelled, read anything that is not narrative'; (2) 'They have no ears. They read exclusively by the eye. The most horrible cacophonies and the most perfect specimens of rhythm and vocalic melody are to them exactly equal'; (3) 'Not only as regards the ear but also in every other way they are either quite unconscious of style, or even prefer books which we should think badly written'; (4) 'They enjoy narratives in which the verbal element is reduced to the minimum'; (5)

'They demand swift-moving narrative. Something must always be "happening".'

The kinds of 'Event' enjoyed by the unliterary fall into three categories: the thriller; the mystery; the romance. Each genre satisfies something inside each one of us. We speak of some readers as 'unliterary, not because they enjoy stories for the reasons mentioned, but because they enjoy them for no other.' 'Not what they have but what they lack cuts them off from the fulness of literary experience.'

Chapter V, 'On Myth', deals with a subject always close to Lewis's heart (see **Myth§**). The Orpheus myth has a powerful effect on us even in summarized form, and this is because of its 'extra-literary' quality. 'It is true that such a story can hardly reach us except in words. But this is logically accidental. If some perfected art of mime or silent film or serial pictures could make it clear with no words at all, it would still affect us in the same way.' The pleasures of the story of Orpheus depend upon a peculiar flavour, not upon such attractions as suspense or surprise. And, like all myths, it is fantastic, it deals with impossibles and preternaturals; it is not comic; it is numinous; and human sympathy for the characters of the story *as individuals* is at a minimum.

The degree to which any story is a myth depends largely on the person who hears or reads it. For instance, not all literary people have a taste for myth, but the unliterary never have it. This is because the core of a myth is not much more than an 'Event'. Besides this, the fantastic elements it contains mean it provides little in the way of vicarious pleasures. The literary person, on the other hand, will let his imagination feed on the myth continually. Attempts to allegorize it will not eradicate the myth's power nor the feeling that it communicates something momentous. There are a number of mythical elements in the work of such modern writers as Kafka, Stevenson, Mervyn Peake, Rider Haggard and J.R.R. Tolkien.*

In chapter VI, 'The Meanings of "Fantasy"', we are told that the word *fantasy* is both a literary and a psychological term. 'As a literary term a fantasy means any narrative that deals with impossible and preternaturals. *The Ancient Mariner, Gulliver, Erewhon, The Wind in the Willows* ... are fantasies.' As a psychological term *fantasy* has three meanings: (1) 'An imaginative construction which in some way or other pleases the patient and is mistaken by him for reality'; (2) 'A pleasing imaginative construction entertained incessantly, and to his injury, by the patient'; (3) 'The same activity indulged in moderately and briefly as a temporary holiday or recreation, duly subordinated to more effective and outgoing activities.'

We next enquire into the relation between 'castle-building and reading'. One kind of story dear to the unliterary 'is that which enables them to enjoy love or wealth or distinction vicariously through the characters.' For instance, some of them like 'comic stories', not because they imagine that they are *there* in the story, but because they like being 'spectators'. They like stories of ghosts and other horrors because 'the reader sees himself in the role of the courageous and resourceful hero.' However, the favourite reading of the unliterary is 'castle-building' and that because it 'takes them least out of themselves, confirms them in an indulgence which they already use too much, and turns them away from most of what is most worth having both in books and life.'

In chapter VII, 'On Realisms', a distinction is drawn between *Realism of Content* and *Realism of Presentation*. The former is to be found in fiction that is probable or true to life, such as Constant's *Adolphe*. The latter is to be found in, for example, medieval romance where improbable or even impossible sets of circumstances are nevertheless rendered in a realistic fashion. Both realisms together are seen in *War and Peace*. Both are absent in *Rasselas* and *Candide*.

The two realisms are quite independent, and the modern taste is for realism of *Content*, usually coupled with realism of *Presentation*. 'True to life' overrides all other considerations. But earlier audiences would not have seen the point of such stories as *Middlemarch* or *Vanity Fair* where everything is ordinary and every-day. In past times, tales such as that of *Oedipus* were told just because they were exceptional and atypical, and because attention was fixed on 'the more than ordinary terror, splendour, wonder, pity or absurdity of a particular case. These, not for any light they might throw thereafter on the life of man, but for their own sake, are what matters.' When such stories are done well we usually get 'hypothetical probability – what would be probable if the initial situation occurred.' The attempt to force such stories as *Oedipus* into a 'radically realistic theory of literature' is perverse. 'The strange events are not clothed with hypothetical probability in order to increase our knowledge of real life by showing how it would react to this improbable test. It is the other way round. The hypothetical probability is brought in to make the strange events more fully imaginable.'

But is this not *escapism*? Not necessarily. All reading, even of realistic novels, is an escape of some kind, and 'childish' is only a pejorative term if it refers to something intrinsically defective associated with childhood:

Who in his senses would not keep, if he could, that tireless curiosity, that intensity of imagination, that facility of suspending disbelief, that unspoiled appetite, that readiness to wonder, to pity, and to admire? The process of growing up is to be valued for what we gain, not for what we lose. Not to acquire a taste for the realistic is childish in the bad sense; to have lost the taste for marvels and adventures is no more a matter for congratulation than losing our teeth, our hair, our palate, and finally, our hopes.

Chapter VIII, 'On Misreading by the Literary', is concerned with confusions between art and real life. The uneducated, unliterary person is usually safe from such confusions. His view of art is not high enough to make him expect anything more from art than entertainment and relaxation. But the ignorant, the youthful and the egoistic castle-builder may well let art inform their view of real life more than is appropriate. And so may the literary – those, for instance, who value Tragedy because they think it gives them some sort of 'philosophy' of 'life'. Life is much more tragic than any play, and sublime and satisfying endings occur on stage, not because they are characteristic of human misery, but because they are necessary to good drama. Contrariwise, comic works of art are usually funnier than real life, which is why people feel that they cannot acknowledge the humour of a real situation more emphatically than by saying 'It's as good as a play'.

Of course, a great play or narrative will suggest to us many interesting reflections. They are complex and carefully made objects. 'Attention to the very objects they are is our first step. To value them chiefly for reflections which they may suggest to us or morals we may draw from them, is a flagrant instance of "using" instead of "receiving".' It is the function of the 'literature of knowledge' to change our opinions. However, 'In reading imaginative work ... we should be much less concerned with altering our own opinions ... than with entering fully into the opinions, and therefore also the attitudes, feelings and total experience, of other men.'

Lewis goes on to protest against 'the increasing importance' of 'English Literature as an academic subject', by which he chiefly means the school of F.R. Leavis at Cambridge (see **LIFE XXVII, XXXVI**). This school 'directs to the study of literature a great many talented, ingenious and diligent people whose real interests are not specifically literary at all. Forced to talk incessantly about books, what can they do but try to make books into the sort of things they can talk about? Hence literature becomes for them a religion, a philosophy, a school of ethics, a psychotherapy, a sociology – anything rather than a collection of works of art.' To them *divertissements* 'are either disparaged or misrepresented as being really far more serious than they look.' But to a real lover of literature, an exquisitely made *divertissement* is a more respectable thing than some 'philosophies of life' which are foisted upon the great poets. Critics who extract such philosophies will produce work commensurate with their own calibre. They may be compared to the long succession of divines who have 'based edifying and eloquent sermons on some straining of their texts.' The sermon, though bad exegesis, 'was often good homilectics in its own right.'

Chapter IX, 'Survey', sums up what has so far been said. (1) Art can either be 'used' or 'received'. 'When we "receive" it, we exert our senses and imagination and various other powers according to a pattern invented by the artist. When we "use" it we treat it as assistance for our own activities.' (2) When the art in question is literature a complication arises: 'to "receive" significant words is always, in one sense, to "use" them, to go through and beyond them, to an imagined something which is not itself verbal.' The 'user' wants to use this *content* 'as a help to castle-building, or perhaps as a source for "philosophies of life".' The 'receiver' wants to 'rest in it'. (3) The 'user' never makes a full use of the words, and prefers those of which no really full use can be made. 'Words are to him mere pointers or signposts.' For the 'receiver words do something 'for which "pointing" is far too coarse a name. They are exquisitely detailed compulsions on a mind willing and able to be so compelled.' (4) 'Because good words can thus compel, thus guide us into every cranny of a character's mind or make palpable and individual Dante's Hell or Pindar's gods'-eye view of an island, good reading is always aural as well as visual.' (5) 'What bad reading wholly consists in may enter as an ingredient into good reading. Excitement and curiosity obviously do. So does vicarious happiness; not that good readers ever read for the sake of it, but that when happiness legitimately occurs in a fiction they enter into it.'

Lewis discourages the practice of literary criticism in schools. 'The necessary condition of all good reading is "to get ourselves out of the way"; we do not help the young to do this by forcing them to keep on expressing opinions.' Children must be taught to see through sophistry and propaganda, but forewarning them against the bad may end up making them suspicious of and impervious to the good. 'The best safeguard against bad literature is a full experience of the good; just as a real and affectionate acquaintance with honest people gives a better protection against rogues than a habitual distrust of everyone.'

In chapter X, on 'Poetry', the author confesses that such a subject hardly deserves mention in the current study because the unliterary do not read poetry. There is a 'little trickle or puddle still left in the dry bed where ballad and nursery rhyme and proverbial jingle once flowed. But it is now so tiny that it hardly deserves mention in a book on this scale.' Indeed, many of the literary do not read it, especially if it is modern poetry.

Lewis saw the difficulty of reading modern poetry as an inevitable consequence of poetic diction's move away from prose. 'When the art of reading poetry requires talents hardly less exalted than the art of writing it, readers cannot be much more numerous than poets.' He is neither one of those who hopes modern poetry will perish, 'asphyxiated in the vacuum of its own purity', nor one of those who hopes that, by 'culture', the laity may be raised to the level of the *cognoscenti*. He is haunted by the possibility that poetry, like the ancient art of Rhetoric, will live on in a scholastic and academic form long after its original artistic life has come to an end.

But even though poetry is read only by the literary it is none the less open to merely subjective readings. We should resist this temptation. One's personal interpretation of a poem may be enjoyable, but why not have structure, learn how to pronounce the words, and then, once you have received what the author intended, see which reading is the better. One will never quite get inside the poet's skin, but the attempt is worth the effort.

In chapter XI we reach 'The Experiment' itself. The apparatus has been assembled: now is the time to apply the theory that good literature is that which 'permits, invites or even compels good reading', and bad literature is that which does the same for bad reading. The definition has three main points in its favour. (1) 'It fixes our attention on the act of reading. Whatever the value of the literature may be, it is actual only when and where good readers read.' (2) 'The proposed system puts our feet on solid ground, whereas the usual one puts them on a quicksand.' It removes the curse of fashion from literary judgements and places criticism on the firmer ground of empirical evidence: how real people read real books. This results in the third advantage. (3) 'It would make critical condemnation a laborious task.' Condemnations can never be quite final. The case can always be re-opened as long as there are people, or even only one person, who well and truly reads, and re-reads, and loves for a lifetime, a book that everyone else had thought bad.

'One result of my system,' Lewis says, 'would be to silence the type of critic for whom all the great names in English literature ... are so many lamp-posts for a dog. And this I consider a good thing. These dethronements are a great waste of energy. Their acrimony produces heat at the expense of light ... The real way of mending a man's taste is not to denigrate his present favourites but to teach him how to enjoy something better.' The snag in this system is 'the fact that the same book may be read in different ways.' Fine love poetry, for example, may be used by some as pornography. Therefore, for clarification, it ought to be said that what damns a book is 'not the existence of bad readings, but the absence of good ones.' 'Ideally, we should like to define a good book as one which "permits, invites, or compels" good reading.'

'I want to convince people,' says Lewis, 'that adverse judgements are always the most hazardous ... A negative proposition is harder to establish than a positive. Once glance may enable us to say there is a spider in the room; we should need a spring-cleaning (at least) before we could say with certainty that there wasn't. When we pronounce a book good we have a positive experience of our own to go upon ... In calling the book bad we are claiming not that it can elicit bad reading, but that it can't elicit good. This negative proposition can never be certain.'

Bearing this in mind, evaluative criticism is an undertaking of restricted utility. The critic's job is to describe, almost to define, a work's character and then leave the world to its own (now better informed) reactions. The critic is to have the character that George MacDonald attributed to God: 'easy to please, but hard to satisfy.' He exists in order 'to multiply, safeguard, or prolong those moments when a good reader is reading well a good book.'

Lewis wonders whether he can say with certainty 'that any evaluative criticism has ever actually helped me to understand and appreciate any great work of literature or any part of one.' After much thought about the kinds of help he has received, he says: (1) 'At the top comes Dryasdust. Obviously I have owed, and must continue to owe, far more to editors, textual critics, commentators, and lexicographers than to anyone else. Find out what the author actually wrote and what the hard words meant and what the allusions were to, and you have done far more for me than a hundred new interpretations or assessments could ever do.' (2) 'I must put second that despised class, the literary historians ... They have helped me, first of all, by telling me what works exist. But still more by putting them in their setting; thus showing me what demands they were meant to satisfy.' (3) 'Thirdly, I must in honesty place various emotive critics who, up to a certain age, did me very good service by infecting me with their own enthusiasms and thus not only sending me but sending me with a good appetite to the authors they admired.' (4) 'The evaluative critics come at the bottom of the list.' He is not sure that he can claim that his 'appreciation of any scene, chapter, stanza or line has been improved' by them.

Finally, we come to 'the Vigilant school of critics', and the heart of his disagreement with F.R. Leavis and his disciples. The Vigilants

> see all clear thinking, all sense of reality, and all fineness of living, threatened on every side by propaganda, by advertisement, by film and television ... The printed word is most subtly dangerous, able 'if it were possible, to deceive the very elect', not in obvious trash beyond the pale but in authors who appear ... to be 'literary' and well within the pale ... Against this the Vigilant school are our watchdogs or detectives ... They are entirely honest, and wholly in earnest. They believe they are smelling out and checking a very great evil. They could sincerely say like St Paul, 'Woe to me if I preach not the Gospel': 'Woe to me if I do not seek out vulgarity, superficiality, and false sentiment, and expose them wherever they lie hidden ... '

The all-important conjunction (Reader Meets Text) is as necessary for the critic as for the ordinary reader. Both must surrender; both must receive; both must welcome good literature's embrace with openness, obedience and a whole heart.

The book ends with an 'Epilogue' in which Lewis answers the question: 'What makes this sort of surrender good?' A work of literature can be considered in two lights. 'It both *means* and *is*. It is both *Logos* (something said) and *Poiema* (something made). As Logos it tells a story, or expresses an emotion, or exhorts or pleads or describes or rebukes or excites laughter. As Poiema, by its aural beauties and also by the balance and contrast and the unified multiplicity of its successive contrast and the unified multiplicity of its successive parts, it is an *objet d'art*, a thing shaped so as to give great satisfaction.'

The mark of strictly literary reading, as opposed to scientific or otherwise informative reading, 'is that we need not believe or approve the Logos'. We do not believe, for instance, that Dante's universe is like the real one. Besides this, none of us can accept simultaneously the views of writers so different as Housman and Chesterton. Why occupy our hearts with stories of things that never happened? What is the point of entering vicariously into feelings which we should try to avoid actually having? Of fixing our eye on things that can never exist?

There is no use trying to avoid the question 'by locating the whole goodness of a literary work in its character as Poiema, for it is out of our various interests in the Logos that the Poiema is made.' And here we reach what may be called the centre of Lewis's belief about the good of literature. 'The nearest I have yet got,' he says, 'to an answer is that we seek *an enlargement of our being. We want to be more than ourselves'* (emphasis added). Each of us sees the whole world from one point of view, with a perspective and a selectiveness peculiar to himself. And when we build disinterested fantasies, they are saturated with, and limited by, our own psychology. 'We want to see with other eyes, to imagine with other imaginations, to feel with other hearts, as well as with our own ... One of the things we feel after reading a great work is "I have got out". Or from another point of view, "I have got in".'

Readers of *Mere Christianity* will hopefully recall the last paragraph of that book in which Lewis said: 'Christ will indeed give you a real personality: but you must not go to Him for the sake of that. As long as your own personality is what you are bothering about you are not going to Him at all. The very first step is to try to forget about the self altogether. Your real, new self ... will not come as long as you are looking for it. It will come when you are looking for Him.' His beliefs about literature involve something of the same kind of sacrifice. 'The primary impulse of each,' he says, 'is to maintain and aggrandize himself. The secondary impulse is to go out of the self, to correct its provincialism and heal its loneliness ... Obviously this process can be described either as an enlargement or as a temporary annihilation of the self. But that is an old paradox; "he that loseth his life shall save it".'

The book ends in a magnificent passage which explains not only the pleasure Lewis got from reading but the main reason he spent his life as a teacher of literature:

> My own eyes are not enough for me, I will see through those of others. Reality, even seen through the eyes of many, is not enough. I will see what others have invented. Even the eyes of all humanity are not enough. I regret that the brutes cannot write books. Very gladly would I learn what face things present to a mouse or a bee ... Literary experience heals the wound, without undermining the privilege, of individuality. There are mass emotions which heal the wound; but they destroy the privilege. In them our separate selves are pooled and we sink back into sub-individuality. But in reading great literature I become a thousand men and yet remain myself ... Here, as in worship, in love, in moral action, and in knowing, I transcend myself; and am never more myself than when I do.

Reviews

Bernard Bergonzi reviewing it in *The Spectator*, 207 (17 November 1961), pp. 718, 720, said: 'Professor Lewis's motive is admirable, since he would like all books to have a chance, and he is right to oppose the kind of criticism which regards a work with the air of a suspicious frontier guard examining the passport of an unfriendly alien.' *The Church Times*, CXLIV (24 November 1961), p. vii, said: 'Professor Lewis is at one and the same time provocative, tactful, biased, open-minded, old-fashioned, far-seeing, very annoying and very wise. He believes that literature exists for the joy of the reader, and that all who come between the reader and his joy – whether Cambridge critics, conscientious schoolmasters, or (God forgive him!) painstaking reviewers – may kill the very art which they seek to protect.'

Christopher Derrick in *The Tablet*, 215 (16 December 1961), pp. 1208–9, said: 'This is a plea for a resolutely low-church attitude to criticism, and already it has drawn some angry gunfire from representatives of the high and powerful priesthood which it threatens. The point is that this cultural priesthood not only offers ... something rather like a surrogate religion, but also creates in its observants an habitual attitude of anxious prickly suspicion towards books, and even towards life and the universe at large. Dr Lewis insists that this is a bad thing, that imaginative literature offers an immensely valuable "enlargement of our being"... He is wonderfully right; for those in favour of happiness but distrustful of politics and the elevated disapproving mind, his book is a charter and a liberation.'

THE DISCARDED IMAGE: AN INTRODUCTION TO MEDIEVAL AND RENAISSANCE LITERATURE (1964)

Background

I: Lectures at Oxford and Cambridge

This book is based on several series of lectures given at Oxford over many years, some of which were repeated many times. We might begin by noting the various series of twice-weekly courses which, directly and indirectly, became *The Discarded Image*. There was first a course of lectures in Michaelmas Term 1926 entitled 'Some Thinkers of the Renaissance (Elyot, Ascham, Hooker, Bacon).' These were repeated in Hilary Term 1929 and Michaelmas Term 1930. Then in Michaelmas Term 1928 Lewis gave for the first time a twice-weekly course on 'The Romance of the Rose and its Successors', much of which later went into *The Allegory of Love: A Study in Medieval Tradition* (1936). It was in the Hilary Term of 1932 that he gave a course of lectures directly related to *The Discarded Image*, the highly celebrated series entitled 'Prolegomena to Medieval Poetry'. This 'Prolegomena' or 'Introduction' consisted of two lectures per week. A continuation of the course was delivered during the Trinity Term of 1932. Thereafter this series was delivered almost every year from 1933 until he went to Cambridge in 1954.

In the Lent Term of 1939 Lewis gave at Cambridge, for the first time, another very popular series, his 'Prolegomena to the Study of Renaissance Poetry'. This was repeated in Oxford shortly afterwards and every two or three years until he left Oxford for Cambridge. In Michaelmas Term 1944 Lewis added to his schedule a twice-weekly 'Introduction to Renaissance Literature', and in the Trinity Term of 1954 he gave for the first time a 'Prolegomena to Medieval Literature'.

While still at Oxford, in Trinity Term 1943, Lewis gave another course which was to find its way into both *The Discarded Image* but mainly into

English Literature in the Sixteenth Century. It was entitled 'Some Sixteenth-Century Writers'. Of particular relevance to *The Discarded Image* was a course given in Michaelmas Term 1949 on 'The Earlier Sixteenth Century'. Finally, there were the lectures Lewis gave in Cambridge on 'English Literature 1300–1500'. This consisted of two lectures every week delivered every Michaelmas Term during the years 1956 through to 1961, and for the last time during Michaelmas Term 1962.

II: Lewis the Lecturer

A bare summary of *The Discarded Image* cannot possibly convey the impression given to those students who *heard* Lewis. Not even *The Discarded Image* itself can do that. Still, there are those who have left reminiscences of his lectures, and at least one who kept detailed notes. The late William Arthur Walter Jarvis matriculated at St Edmund Hall in 1935, where he read English. He attended Lewis's 'Prolegomena to Medieval Poetry' in 1936 and his notes are very clear and detailed, and contain several charming sketches which illustrate the lectures. (They are in the Bodleian Library‡ under the catalogue number 'MS. Eng. d. 2567.') But perhaps the best description we have of Lewis the lecturer comes from his friend Roger Lancelyn Green* who in *C.S. Lewis: A Biography* (VI) said:

> Lewis lectured almost entirely from a written text; but he would add to this, both during the lectures with additional examples or explanations, and in the basic text before delivering the course again where further research or later criticism made this desirable. There were also the lighter moments: good laughs which he timed with all an actor's skill, and knew from previous experience when to expect so that he could build up to them. Thus in the 'Prolegomena to Medieval Studies' ... in describing the various types of men born under the different planetary influences, when he came to Jupiter: 'the Jovial character is cheerful, festive; those born under Jupiter are apt to be loud-voiced and red-faced – it is obvious under which planet *I* was born!' always produced its laugh.
>
> On one occasion during the war, when the audience at his lectures came to consist predominantly of women, and these tended more and more to come without their academic gowns (which were still statutory wear at lectures), Lewis strode into the Hall at his usual speed, but did not begin to lecture when he had

deposited his notes on the lectern. Instead, he gazed slowly up and down the crowded tables with a blank stare until, like Mr Puff, he produced 'a proper expectation in the audience'; then, with his usual perfect timing, he exclaimed, 'Oh! I must apologize for wearing a *gown*!' At the next lecture gowns were in fashion again.

Whether one had read any of his works or not, the first sight of C.S. Lewis was always a surprise. One undergraduate just initiated to lecturers as varied as Tolkien,* Edmund Blunden and Lascelles Abercrombie, remembers the shock as he sat for the first time in the Hall at Magdalen in October 1938 and there strode in a big man with a large red face and shabby clothes, looking like nothing so much as a prosperous butcher, who began addressing his audience in a loud, booming voice and with tremendous gusto.

Of course one soon got over this first impression when Lewis began lecturing. It was obvious even in such utilitarian lectures as his two 'Prolegomena' series (to 'Medieval' and 'Renaissance Literature') that one was listening not merely to a scholar of immense erudition, but to a lover of literature who had read every text he mentioned, had enjoyed most of them, and was eager to share both his knowledge and his enthusiasm with anyone whom he could persuade to do so ...

Perhaps the impression of not wasting more time than was absolutely necessary was given by the fact that Lewis did indeed seek to exemplify Kipling's dictum about filling 'the unforgiving minute with sixty seconds' worth of distance run'. He lectured for precisely three-quarters of an hour, and he never waited to answer questions. Two minutes before the end of the lecture he would quietly gather his notes together, return the watch which at one time he was in the habit of borrowing from the nearest member of his audience, and prepare to leave – lecturing all the time. Then, as he finished his last sentence, he would step off the dais and stride down the hall at top speed. If he was at all late in arriving at the lecture, he would begin it even before he entered the hall: several times the great voice came booming up the steps outside the hall door and Lewis would enter in haste, lecturing vigorously.

Summary

We begin chapter I, 'The Medieval Situation', by noting that 'Medieval man shared many ignorances with the savage, and some of his beliefs may suggest savage parallels to an anthropologist. But he did not reach these beliefs by the same route as the savage.' Medieval thought did not arise, as savage beliefs do, by a 'spontaneous response of a human group to its environment.' Nor did it arise, as it did in Egypt, by an ancient culture turning 'into something more ethical, more philosophical, even more scientific' over a period of a very long time. The peculiarity of the Middle Ages can be shown by two examples.

(1) Between 1160 and 1207 a priest called Layamon wrote a poem, the *Brut*. He did not, however, take his beliefs from the social group he lived in, but from an account of the aerial daemons by the Norman poet Wace (c. 1155) who took it from Geoffrey of Monmouth's *Historia Regum Britanniae* (before 1139). Geoffrey took it from the second-century *De Deo Socratis* of Apuleius, who was reproducing the pneumatology of Plato. If you go back far enough you come to an age 'when that mythology was coming into existence in what we suppose to be the savage fashion', but Layamon would have known nothing of this. 'He believes in these daemons because he had read about them in a book.' (2) The other example is Guillaume Deguileville's *Pèlerinage de l'Homme* of the fourteenth century, in which a character says that the frontier between their respective realms is the orbit of the Moon. It would be easy to suppose that this derived from 'savage mythopoeia, dividing the sky into a higher region peopled with higher spirits and a lower region peopled with lower', with the Moon a landmark between them. But this had little to do with either savagery or Christianity, but derived ultimately from Aristotle.

Faced with this world of 'incessant change by birth, growth, procreation, death and decay', Aristotle could discover only an 'imperfect uniformity'. The celestial bodies, so far as he could find out, were permanent. They neither came into existence nor passed away. Their movements seemed to be perfectly 'regular', and the world seemed to be divided into two regions. The lower region of change and irregularity he called Nature, and the upper world he called Sky. Above the air, in true Sky, was a different substance which he called *aether*. This *aether* encompasses the divine bodies, 'but immediately below the aethereal and divine nature comes that which is passible, mutable, perishable and subject to death.' By his introduction of the word *divine* Aristotle introduced a religious element. However, the concept of a frontier at the Moon's orbit between Sky and Nature, Aether and Air, was 'far more in response to a scientific than to a religious need'. This is the ultimate source of the passage in Deguileville.

When we speak of the Middle Ages as the age of authority we are usually thinking about the authority of the Church. But they were the age not only of her authority, but of authority. This respect for authorities differentiates the medieval period almost equally from savagery and from modern civilization. 'In a savage community you absorb your culture, in part unconsciously, from participation in the immemorial pattern of behaviour, and in part by word of mouth, from the old men of the tribe. In our society most knowledge depends, in the last resort, on observation. But the Middle Ages depended predominantly on books.'

The Romance and the Ballad are commonly thought to be characteristic Medieval products. Popular iconography, wishing to summon up the idea of the Medieval, draws a knight errant with castles, distressed damsels, and dragons in the background. This is largely owing to the fact that Ariosto, Tasso and Spenser, the lineal descendants of the medieval romancers, continued to be 'polite literature' down to the eighteenth, and even the nineteenth, century. In one sense, Romances and Ballads deserve to rank as representative of the Middle Ages.

Medieval man was not a dreamer, nor a wanderer, but an organizer, a codifier, a builder of systems. He wanted 'a place for everything and everything in the right place'. To him war was (in intention) formalized by the art of heraldry and the rules of chivalry; sexual passion (in intention) by an elaborate code of love. Every way in which a poet can write is classified in the Art of Rhetoric. Highly original philosophical speculation squeezes itself into a dialectical pattern copied from Aristotle. Studies like Law and Moral Theology, which demand the ordering of very diverse particulars especially flourish. The *Summa Theologica* of St Thomas Aquinas and Dante's *Divine Comedy* 'are as unified and ordered as the Parthenon or the *Oedipus Rex*, as crowded and varied as a London terminus on a bank holiday.' Of all modern inventions, medieval man would most have admired the card index.

Another thing worthy of note is the medieval synthesis itself – the whole organization of theology, science and history into a single, complex, harmonious mental *Model of the Universe*. The building of this Model is conditioned by the essentially bookish character of the medieval culture and their 'intense love of system'. They inherited a very hetero-geneous collection of authorities: Judaic, Pagan, Platonic, Aristotelian, Stoic, Primitive Christian, Patristic, are at once respected and made to respect each other. A Model is built which gets in everything 'without a clash'.

Chapter II, 'Reservations', deals first with reservations or clarifications concerning some of the things mentioned in the previous chapter. (1) The medieval Model of the Universe is to be seen as a backcloth to the arts; it is not the total Model. 'It takes over from the total Model only what is intelligible to a layman and only what makes some appeal to imagination and emotion. Thus our own backcloth contains plenty of Freud and little of Einstein.' (2) The total Model had a different status depending upon who was looking at it. To the great masters of science and philosophy the Model was recognized as provisional; it was a theory which 'saved appearances'. 'A scientific theory must "save" or "preserve" the appearance, the phenomena, it deals with, in the sense of getting them all in, doing justice to them.' (3) The great spiritual writers ignore the Model almost completely. 'We need to know something about the Model if we are to read Chaucer, but we can neglect it when we are reading St Bernard or *The Scale of Perfection* or the *Imitation*.' This is partly because the spiritual books were practical; they were concerned specifically with helping one's soul, not with speculations or systemizations of a general nature. Also, medieval cosmology, although firmly theistic at root and open to ideas of the supernatural, was merely 'religious', not eminently Christian.

Chapter III, 'Selected Material: The Classical Period', gives an account of some of the sources from which the Model was derived. **A. The 'Somnium Scipionis'**. This 'Dream of Scipio' is a surviving portion of the lost sixth book of Cicero's *De Republica*. Scipio Africanus Minor, one of the speakers in the dialogue, relates a remarkable dream. It is an attempt to give plausibility to a fiction by offering psychological causes. This ruse is imitated in the dream-poetry of the Middle Ages. Thus Chaucer in the Proem to the *Book of the Duchesse* reads of lovers parted by death before he dreams of them; and in the *Parlement* he reads the *Somnium Scipionis* itself and suggests this may be why he dreamed of Scipio.

The *Somnium* contains an ascent into Heaven which is the prototype of many such ascents in later literature: those in Dante, Chaucer, even Cervantes. Like much of the material which the Middle Ages inherited from antiquity, the *Somnium* is superficially close to Christianity, but actually presupposes 'a wholly Pagan ethics and metaphysics'. A good example of this is the attitude to the body. Scipio is exhorted to remember that not he, but only his body, is mortal – a sentiment with which every Christian would in some sense agree. But for Scipio the body is in 'fetters'; 'we come into it by a sort of Fall.' It is irrelevant to his nature which, in essence, is immortal and can ascend to Heaven because it came from there: 'the mind of each man is the man.' All this belongs to a circle of ideas 'wholly different from the Christian doctrines of man's creation, fall, redemption, and resurrection. The attitude to the body which it involves was to be an unfortunate legacy for medieval Christendom.' Cicero is also a source for many other aspects of the medieval Model, including the insignificance of the earth; the music of the spheres; the earth-bound ghost; the sun being the world's mind or eye; and the Moon being the boundary between eternal and perishable things.

B. Lucan. Lucan (AD 34–65) made his most important contribution to the Model when he wrote his epic on the Civil War, the *Pharsalia*. The ninth book recounts the ascent of Pompey's soul from the funeral pyre to the heavens. Pompey arrived 'where the murky air joins the star-bearing wheels', the spheres. That is, he had 'come to the great frontier between air and aether, between Aristotle's "Nature" and "Sky".' This is obviously the orbit of the Moon. 'Every detail' of the passage will meet us again 'in one author or another.' In particular, Pompey's laughter upon seeing the mockeries done to his corpse had an influence on two more famous authors: Boccaccio (when he wrote of Arcita's death in *Teseide*) and Chaucer (when he wrote of Troilus' ghost). All three ghosts laughed for the same reason – 'at the littleness of all those things that had seemed so important before they died; as we laugh, on waking, at the trifles or absurdities that loomed so large in our dreams.'

C. Statius, Claudian, and the Lady 'Natura'. Statius's *Thebaid* which appeared in AD 92 ranked in the Middle Ages with Virgil, Homer and Lucan. The vividness and importance of its personifications (*Virtus, Clementia, Pietas* and *Natura*) brought it in places very close to the fully allegorical poetry the Middle Ages delighted in. Our attention, however, is fixed on the Lady or Goddess *Natura*. The reader of Renaissance and Medieval literature will have met this goddess often. Working backwards, we met 'the veiled and numinous Nature' of Spenser, the 'genial' Nature in Chaucer's *Parlement*, and in Deguileville's *Pèlerinage* we were surprised by 'a Nature with more than a dash of the Wife of Bath in her'. And still re-ascending, we come to the Nature who dominates the *Romance of the Rose* for thousands of lines. Going back further still, we find that the ancients made very little of Nature. Why, then, did the medievals make so much of her? 'Nature may be the oldest of things, but *Natura* is the youngest of deities.' Their development of 'Lady Nature' is accounted for by the belief that Nature was not everything: 'By surrendering the dull claim to be everything, she becomes something.'

D. Apuleius, 'De Deo Socratis'. Apuleius (born c. AD 125) is the author of the *Metamorphoses* or *Golden Ass* and *De Deo Socratis*. He drew a clear distinction between 'God' and 'daemon' which was to be influential for years. Daemons are those creatures of a middle nature between gods and men – like Milton's 'Middle spirits – Betwixt the angelical and human kind.' It is through these intermediaries that mortals were to have intercourse with the gods. Apuleius tells us that these daemons inhabit the middle region between Earth and aether: that is, the air, which extends upwards as far as the orbit of the Moon. They have bodies of a finer consistency than clouds. They are rational (aerial) animals, as we are rational (terrestrial) animals, while the gods are rational (aetherial) animals.

The *De Deo Socratis* has a twofold value for medieval studies. (1) Through it Apuleius illustrates the sort of channel through which scraps of Plato trickled down to the Middle Ages (Plato wrote of daemons in the *Symposium*). (2) It introduces us to what is called 'The Principle of the Triad', the idea that two things (e.g. gods and man) cannot meet but by the agency of a third thing (e.g. daemons). The medievals endlessly act out this principle, supplying bridges, as it were, 'between reason and appetite, soul and body, king and commons'. (3) The 'Principle of Plenitude'. 'If, between aether and Earth, there is a belt of air, then, it seems to Apuleius, *ratio* herself demands that it should be inhabited.'

Chapter IV, 'Selected Materials: The Seminal Period', looks at the texts of the 'transitional' or 'seminal' period, roughly stretching from AD 205 to 533. 'This was the age which brought the characteristically medieval frame of mind into being. It also witnessed the last stand of Paganism and the final triumph of the Church.' During these centuries much that was of Pagan origin was 'built irremovably into the Model'. **A. Chalcidius**. The work of Chalcidius is an incomplete translation of Plato's *Timaeus*, and a much longer *commentarius* which 'expatiates freely on matters about which Plato had little or nothing to say.' By translating so much of the *Timaeus* and transmitting it to centuries in which little else of Plato was known, he 'determined what the name of Plato should chiefly stand for throughout the Middle Ages.' He was a Christian, and he conveyed to the medieval mind a Plato who was not a logician, nor the philosopher of love, nor the author of the *Republic*. Plato was, next to Moses, 'the great monotheistic cosmogonist, the philosopher of creation; hence, paradoxically, the philosopher of that Nature which the real Plato so often disparaged. To that extent, Chalcidius unconsciously supplied a corrective for the *contemptus mundi* inherent in neo-Platonism and early Christianity alike.'

Astronomy in Chalcidius has not yet fully settled down in its medieval form. 'Like everyone else, he declares that the Earth is infinitesimally small by cosmic standards, but the order of the planets is still open to dispute.' For him the geocentric universe is not in the least anthropocentric. If we ask why the Earth is central, the answer is that 'It is so placed in order that the celestial dance [cf. *Perelandra*] may have a centre to revolve about – in fact as an aesthetic convenience for the celestial beings.'

All daemons are for him a distinct species, and 'he applied the name *daemons* to the aetherial as well as to the aerial creatures, the former being those whom ' "the Hebrews call holy angels".' He is completely at one with Apuleius in affirming The Principle of Plenitude and that of the Triad, which has three applications in Chalcidius. (1) Aether and air, like Earth, must be populated 'lest any region be left void'. Between the immortal, celestial creature and the temporal, mortal, earthly and passible creatures there exist some 'mean' or 'intermediate beings'. (2) He finds the same triadic pattern repeated in the Ideal State and the human individual. (3) Finally, 'the common people obey. So in each man.' The summary which follows will recall to us Lewis's *Abolition of Man*. 'The rational part lives in the body's citadel ... that is, the head. In the camp or barracks ... of the chest, warrior-like, the "energy which resembles anger", that which makes a man high-spirited, has its station. Appetite, which corresponds to the common people, is located in the abdomen below them both.' The influence of Chalcidius produces its richest results in the 'twelfth-century Latin poets associated with the school of Chartres, who in their turn helped to inspire Jean de Meung and Chaucer.' Statius's and Claudian's 'Lady Natura' and the cosmogony of Chalcidius are the 'parents' of Bernardus Silvestris' *De Mundi Universitate* (the work in which Lewis discovered the term *Oyarses* which he used in *Out of the Silent Planet* and *Perelandra*).

B. Macrobius. Macrobius lived at the end of the fourth and the beginning of the fifth centuries, and he was probably a Pagan. His commentary on the *Somnius Scipionis* is a work of long-lasting influence. His ideas on dreams were of particular importance to the Middle Ages. His scheme is derived from the *Oneirocritica* of Artemidorus (first century AD), according to which there are five species of dreams, three veridical, and two which have 'no divination' in them. The veridical kinds are: (1) *Somnium*: This shows us truths veiled in an allegorical form of which Pharaoh's dream of the fat and lean kine would be a specimen. Every allegorical dream-poem in the Middle Ages records a feigned *somnium*, an example being the 'dream' in Chaucer's *Hous of Fame*. (2) *Visio*. This is a direct, literal pre-vision of the future, a type which appears as 'avisioun' in Chaucer. Lewis here mentions a book he cited in his *Dark Tower*: 'Mr Dunne's *Experiment with Time* is mainly about *visiones*.' (3) *Oraculum*. In this, one of the dreamer's parents or 'some other grave and venerable person' appears and openly declares the future or gives advice. Such dreams are Chaucer's 'oracles'. The 'useless' non-veridical kinds of dreams are: (1) *Insomnium*. This merely repeats working pre-occupations – 'the carter dremeth how his cartes goon' as Chaucer says in the *Parlement*. (2) *Visum*. This occurs when, not yet fully asleep, we see shapes rushing towards us or flitting hither and thither. Nightmares are in this class. Chaucer's 'fantom' from the *Hous of Fame* is clearly the *visum*.

C. Pseudo-Dionysius. In the Middle Ages four books, *The Celestial Hierarchies*, *The Ecclesiastical Hierarchies*, *The Divine Names* and the *Mystical Theology*, were attributed to that Dionysius who was converted by hearing St Paul's address to the Areopagus (Acts 17:34). This attribution was later disproved, and the real author was thought to have lived in Syria and to have written some time before 533. The works of pseudo-Dionysius, as he is called, are regarded as the 'main channel by which a certain kind of Theology entered the Western tradition.' We find it rooted in Plato, and its most striking representative in English is *The Cloud of Unknowing*. We are, however, more concerned with his contributions on angelology to the Model, and we confine our attention to his *Celestial Hierarchies*. Pseudo-Dionysius differs from all earlier authors in declaring the angels to be pure minds. It was his arrangement of the angelic creatures into what Spenser called their 'trinall triplicities' – into three Hierarchies containing three species each – that was finally accepted by the Church. (1) The first Hierarchy contains the three species: Seraphim, Cherubim and Thrones, the creatures closest to God; (2) The next contains the Dominations, the Powers and the Virtues. Their titles do not imply moral excellences but 'efficacies', as when we speak about the 'virtues' of a magic ring. (3) The third and lowest Hierarchy contains Princedoms (or Principalities, or Princes), Archangels and Angels. The word *angel* is a generic name for all the nine species, and a specific name for the lowest.

Pseudo-Dionysius was as certain as Plato and Apuleius that God encounters Man only through a 'mean', and he read his own philosophy into Scripture as freely as Chalcidius had read his into the *Timaeus*. 'His God does nothing directly that can be done through an intermediary; perhaps prefers the longest possible chain of intermediaries; devolution or delegation, a finely graded descent of power and goodness, is the universal principle.' In pseudo-Dionysius 'the whole universe is a sort of fugue of which the Triad (agent-mean-patient) is the "subject".' The spirit of his scheme is strongly present in the medieval Model. It is a conception of the universe utterly the reverse of the modern, and necessitates a vast re-adjustment for perceptive reading of the old poets. 'In modern, that is, in evolutionary, thought Man stands at the top of a stair whose foot is lost in obscurity; in this, he stands at the bottom of a stair whose top is invisible with light.'

D. Boethius. After Plotinus, Boethius (430–524) is the greatest author of the seminal period, and his *De Consolatione Philosophiae* was for centuries one of the most influential books written in Latin. While Boethius was a Christian and even a theologian, the 'philosophy' to which he turned for 'consolation' in the face of death 'contains few explicitly Christian elements' and its compatibility with Christian doctrine has been questioned. Apart from its contributions to the Model, its formal influence may be briefly stated. It belongs to the kind called *Satira Menippea* in which prose sections alternate with (shorter) sections in verse. From Boethius it descends to Bernardus and Alanus and even into Sannazaro's *Arcadia*. But other contributions to the Model made by the *Consolatione* are numerous.

Much of Lewis's reasoning about Providence and freedom originated from the *Consolatione*, and the chapter, 'Time and Beyond Time', in **MC** is based on Boethius's doctrine of Providence. If, as that doctrine implies, 'God sees all things that are, were, or will be ... in a single act of mind, and thus foreknows my actions, how am I free to act otherwise than He has foreseen?' We first note that the character of knowledge does not depend on the nature of the object known but on that of the 'knowing faculty'. Then, going further, eternity differs from perpetuity in that while perpetuity 'is only the attainment of an endless series of moments, each lost as soon as it is attained', eternity is 'the actual and timeless fruition of illimitable life.' God is eternal, not perpetual, and because of this: 'He never *foresees*; He simply sees. Your "future" is only an area ... of His infinite Now. He sees (not remembers) your yesterday's acts because yesterday is still "there" for Him; he sees (not foresees) your tomorrow's acts because He is already in tomorrow. As a human spectator, by watching my present act, does not at all infringe its freedom, so I am none the less free to act as I choose in the future because God, in that future (His present) watches me acting.'

Chapter V, 'The Heavens', deals with the heavens as pictured in the medieval Model. **A. The Parts of the Universe**. The fundamental concept of modern science is, or was till very recently, that of natural 'laws', and every event was described as happening in 'obedience' to them. In medieval science the fundamental concept was that of certain 'sympathies, antipathies, and strivings' inherent in matter itself. 'Everything has its right place, its home, the region that suits it, and, if not forcibly restrained, moves thither by a sort of homing instinct.'

The question is naturally raised as to whether medieval thinkers really believed that what we now call inanimate objects were sentient and purposive. If we could ask the medieval scientist, 'Why, then, do you *talk* as if they did?' he could answer with the counter-question: 'But do you intend your language about *laws* and *obedience* any more literally than I intend mine about *kindly enclyning*? Do you really believe that a falling stone is aware of a directive issued to it by some legislator and feels either a moral or a prudential obligation to conform?' We have to admit that both ways of expressing the facts are metaphorical.

Matter, for the medieval mind, had properties known as the Four *Contraries*: hot, cold, moist, dry. In combination, they form the four elements: hot and dry make fire; hot and moist, air; cold and moist, water; cold and dry, earth. Earth, the heaviest element, has gathered itself together at the centre of the sublunary world. On it lies the lighter water; above that, the still lighter air. Fire, the lightest of all, forms a sphere just below the orbit of the Moon.

The architecture of the Ptolemaic universe is well known. The central (and spherical) *Earth* is surrounded by a series of hollow and transparent globes, one above the other, and each larger than the one below. These are the 'spheres', 'heavens' or 'elements'. Fixed in each of the first seven spheres is one luminous body. Starting from *Earth*, the order is the *Moon, Mercury, Venus*, the *Sun, Mars, Jupiter* and *Saturn* – the 'seven planets'. Beyond the sphere of Saturn is the *Stellatum*, the sphere of the 'fixed' stars. Beyond that is the sphere called the *Primum Mobile*. This, since it carries no planet or stars, gives no evidence of itself to our senses; its existence has to be inferred to account for the motions of all the others. And beyond the *Primum Mobile*? 'Outside the heaven,' said Aristotle, 'there is neither place nor void nor time. Hence whatever is there is of such a kind as not to occupy space, nor does time affect it.' Adopted into Christianity, the answer is 'the very Heaven', *caelum ipsum*.

It is generally thought that medieval man knew nothing about distances between the Earth and the other planets, but this is not true. In the standard astronomical handbook used in the Middle Ages, Ptolemy's *Almagest*, the Earth, in relation to the fixed stars, has no appreciable size and must be treated as a mathematical point. The *Somnium Scipionis* pointed out that the stars are larger than the Earth, and Isidore in the sixth century knows that the Sun is larger, and the Moon smaller than the Earth. And in the very popular *South English Legendary* we are told that if a man could travel upwards at the rate of 'forty mile and yet som del mo' a day, he still would not have reached the *Stellatum* in 8000 years.

This ordered universe had two important consequences for the way men thought. (1) It provided 'an absolute up and down'. The Earth really was the centre, the lowest place; movement to it from whatever direction was downward movement. (2) Another big difference between the medieval's view of the universe and that of the modern is that to the medieval the universe 'while unimaginably large, was also unambiguously finite ... To look out on the night sky with modern eyes is like looking out over a sea that fades away into mist, or looking about one in a trackless forest – trees for ever and no horizon. To look up at the towering medieval universe is much more like looking at a great building ... Our universe is romantic, and theirs was classical.'

B. Their Operations. The medieval universe must now be set in motion. 'All power, movement, and efficacy descend from God to the *Primum Mobile* and cause it to rotate ... The rotation of the *Primum Mobile* causes that of the *Stellatum*, which causes that of the sphere of Saturn, and so on, down to the last moving sphere, that of the Moon.' Besides movement, the spheres transmitted to the Earth what were called *Influences* – the subject matter of Astrology. Astrology is not specifically medieval. The Middle Ages, having inherited it from antiquity, bequeathed it to the Renaissance.

The Church's attitude to astrology was mixed. Theologians could accept the theory that the planets had an effect on events and on psychology, and on plants and animals. But the Church objected to three offshoots of this theory: (1) The lucrative, and politically undesirable, practice of astrologically grounded predictions; (2) Astrological determinism. The doctrine of influences could be carried so far as to exclude free will; (3) Practices that implied or encouraged the worship of planets. This is easily misunderstood. Modern readers discuss whether, when Jupiter or Venus is mentioned by a medieval poet, he means the planet or the deity. 'They are planets as well as gods. Not that the Christian poet believed in the god because he believed in the planet; but all three things – the visible planet in the sky, the source of influence, and the god – generally acted as a unity upon his mind.'

Each planet exerts a different influence. **Saturn**: in the earth his influence produces lead; in man, the melancholy complexion; in history, disastrous events. **Jupiter**: he is the King, and produces in the Earth tin. 'The character he produces in man would be imperfectly expressed by the word "jovial".' The Jovial character is 'cheerful, festive, yet temperate, tranquil, magnanimous.' **Mars**: he makes iron, and 'gives men the martial temperament.' **Sun**: he produces gold and 'makes men wise and liberal'. **Venus**: her metal is copper, and in mortals she produces 'beauty and amorousness; in history, fortunate events.' **Mercury**: he produces quicksilver, and causes 'skilled eagerness' or 'bright alacrity'. **Moon**: with the Moon we cross the 'great frontier' from aether to air, from 'heaven' to 'nature', from the realm of gods (or angels) to that of daemons, from the realm of necessity to that of contingence, from the incorruptible to the corruptible. This 'great divide' needs to be fixed in our minds if we are to understand most poetry of this period. Her metal is quicksilver, and she produces 'wandering' of the wits – which is where we get the word *lunacy*.

One great difference between us and the medievals is that while we imagine that the heavenly bodies 'move in a pitch-black and dead-cold vacuity', it was not so in the medieval Model. 'As they had ... no conception of the part which the air plays in turning physical light into the circumambient colour-realm that we call Day, we must picture all the countless cubic miles within the vast concavity as illuminated ... You must conceive yourself looking up at a world lighted, warmed, and resonant with music.'

C. Their Inhabitants. God caused the *Primum Mobile* to rotate, and the answer as to how was incorporated in the medieval Model. In brief, 'The *Primum Mobile* is moved by its love for God, and, being moved, communicates motion to the rest of the universe.' It would be easy to descant on the antithesis between this Theology and that of Christianity, but this should not be regarded as a contradiction. A real universe could accommodate the 'love of God' in both senses. For instance, St John says: 'herein is love, not that we loved God, but that he loved us': but when Dante ends the *Comedy* with 'the love that moves the Sun and the other stars', he is speaking of love in the Aristotelian sense.

A modern may still want to ask why this movement should take the form of rotation. To the medieval the answer was that 'Love seeks to participate in its object, to become as like its object as it can.' The nearest approach to this divine ubiquity that the spheres can attain is the swiftest and most regular possible movement, in the most perfect form, which is circular. Resident in each sphere is 'a conscious and intellectual being' called an 'Intelligence', often referred to as the 'souls of the spheres'. Readers of Lewis's interplanetary novels will recognize that he is describing the *Oyarsa* of a planet.

Another difference between the medieval Model and the modern one is that dignity, power and speed progressively diminish as we descend from the circumference to its centre – the Earth. The Earth is 'the rim, the outside edge where being fades away on the border of nonentity.' Dante has a few lines in the *Paradiso* which stamp this on the mind for ever. There he sees God as a 'point of light'. 'Seven concentric rings of light revolve about that point, and that which is smallest and nearest to it has the swiftest movement. This is the Intelligence of the *Primum Mobile*, superior to all the rest in love and knowledge.'

Chapter VI, 'The *Longaevi*'. The *Longaevi* or 'longlivers' have been put in a separate chapter because 'their place of residence is ambiguous between air and Earth'. The name *Longaevi* comes from Martianus Capella who mentions 'dancing companies of *Longaevi* who haunt woods, glades and groves, and lakes and springs and brooks; whose names are Pans, Fauns ... Satrys, Silvans, Nymphs.' Bernardus Silvestris, without using the name *Longaevi*, speaks of similar creatures as having a 'longer life' than ours, though they are not immortal. The alternative would be to call the *Longaevi* 'Fairies', but that word is 'tarnished by pantomime and bad children's books with worse illustrations'. Instead of bringing to the subject 'some ready-made, modern concept of a Fairy and to read the old texts in the light of it', the proper method is 'to go to the texts with an open mind and learn from them what the word *fairy* meant to our ancestors.'

There are three types of *Longaevi*. (1) The first is the 'Dark Fairy', such as *Beowulf* has in mind when it ranks the elves 'along with ettins and giants as the enemies of God'. Reginald Scot in his *Discouerie of Witchcraft* (1584) gives a list of bugbears used to frighten children (a list very close to that Lewis used for similar purposes in **LWW** 14): '... spirits, witches, urchins, elves, hags, fairies, satyrs, pans, faunes, sylens, tritons, centaurs, dwarfs, giants, nymphes ... and such other bugs.' (2) There are 'the little people'. Richard Bovet in his *Pandaemonium* (1684) speaks of the fairies 'appearing like men and women of a stature generally near the smaller size of man.' It is this class, but prettified with gauzy wings, which we think of most commonly today. (3) There are the 'High Fairies', which include the *fées* of French romance, the *fays* of our own, the *fate* of the Italians. They are usually of at least fully human stature and may be male as well as female, and all are described as being hard, bright, vivid and materially splendid. The Fairy King in *Sir Orfeo* who comes with over a hundred knights and a hundred ladies on white horses is of this kind.

Chapter VII, 'Earth and Her Inhabitants'. **A. The Earth**. Unlike the celestial spheres, the Earth is not governed by an Intelligence. Being a stationary globe it was felt that she did not need one. That is, until Dante suggested that the terrestrial Intelligence was Fortune whom God ordained as 'a general minister and guide to worldly splendours; one who should from time to time transfer these deceptive benefits from one nation or stock to another in a fashion which no human wisdom can prevent.' Ordinarily Fortune has a wheel; by making it a sphere Dante 'emphasizes the new rank he has given her'. Physically considered, the Earth is a globe: 'all the authors of the high Middle Ages are agreed on this.' Again, Dante is particularly good on this. In the *Inferno* the two travellers find the giant Lucifer embedded at the centre of the earth and discover that they can climb down his shaggy sides as far as his waist, but that they have to go *up* to his feet. It is 'the first "science-fiction" effect in literature'.

The erroneous notion that the medievals were Flat-earthers has two sources. (1) The medieval maps such as the 'mappemounde' in Hereford cathedral represent the earth as a circle. This may be due either to the fact that the Cartographers had not mastered the act of projecting three dimensions on to two, or that the southern hemisphere was simply ignored as it was believed to be inaccessible. (2) The frequent references in medieval literature to the world's end – which again might be explained as references to the known world, not the world in its entirety. Indeed, a good deal of medieval cartography and geography was romantic and artistic. Authors were often more concerned to fix the site of Paradise than to provide an accurate guide for the real traveller.

B. Beasts. Compared with medieval theology, philosophy, astronomy and other disciplines, medieval zoology strikes us as childish. However, 'as there was a practical geography which had nothing to do with the *mappemounde*, so there was a practical zoology which had nothing to do with the Bestiaries.' The percentage of the population who knew a great deal about certain animals must have been far larger in medieval than in modern England, but the written zoology of the period 'is mainly a mass of cock-and-bull stories about creatures the author had never seen, and often about creatures that never existed.' This does not necessarily mean that the medievals were more easily fooled than we are. It may suggest that they were less disinclined than we to look for the *moralitas* of a given animal.

C. The Human Soul. 'Man is a rational animal, and therefore a composite being, partly akin to the angels who are rational but – on the later, scholastic view – not animal, and partly akin to the beasts which are animal but not rational. This gives us one of the senses in which he is the "little world" or microcosm.'

Rational Soul is not the only kind of soul. There is the 'Vegetable Soul', found in plants, which has the powers of nutrition, growth and propagation. There is also the 'Sensitive Soul', found in animals, which has the powers of the Vegetable Soul but has sentience in addition. Rational Soul includes Vegetable and Sensitive, and adds Reason. As Trevisa (1398), translating the thirteenth-century *De Proprietatibus Rerum* of Bartholomaeus Anglicus, puts it, there are 'thre manere soulis ... *vegetabilis* that geveth lif and no feling, *sensibilis* that geveth lif and feling and nat resoun, *racionalis* that geveth lif, feling, and resoun.' Rational Soul is sometimes called simply 'Reason', and the Sensitive Soul simply 'Sensuality'. Thus the Parson in Chaucer says 'God sholde have lordschipe over reson, and reson over sensualite, and sensualite over the body of man.'

The peculiarity of the rational soul is that it is created in each case by the immediate act of God, whereas the others come into existence by developments and transmutations within the total created order. The Book of Genesis is no doubt the source for this; but Plato had also set the creation of man apart from creation in general. 'The soul's turning to God is often treated in the poets as a returning and therefore one more instance of "kindly enclyning".' There is an instance of this in Chaucer's *Troilus*: 'Repeireth *hoom* from worldly vanitee.' However this may sound, the doctrine of pre-existence was firmly rejected in the scholastic age. 'It is not the soul's nature to leave the body; rather, the body (disnatured by the Fall) deserts the soul.'

D. Rational Soul. The Rational Soul is composed of two faculties: *Intellectus* and *Ratio*. We enjoy *intellectus* when we 'just see' a self-evident truth; we exercise *ratio* when we proceed step by step to prove a truth which is not self-evident. A cognitive life in which all truth can be simply 'seen' would be the life of an angel, an *intellectus*. But a life of unmitigated *ratio*, where nothing was 'seen', but everything had to be proved, would be impossible. The distinction between them was made by Dr Johnson who, defining *ratio*, said: 'The power by which man deduces one proposition from another, or proceeds from premises to consequences.' He gave as an example a definition from Richard Hooker: 'Reason is the director of man's will, discovering in action what is good.' But Reason meant so much more to the ancients. Aristotle made 'right reason' essential to good conduct, and St Paul, defining Natural Law§ in the Epistle to the Romans (2:14ff.), says there is a law 'written in the hearts' even of Gentiles who do not know 'the law'. Indeed, nearly all moralists before the eighteenth century regarded Reason as the 'organ of morality'. Thus, the moral conflict was between Passion and Reason, not between Passion and 'conscience', or 'duty', or 'goodness'. Moral imperatives were, therefore, uttered by Reason.

E. Sensitive and Vegetable Soul. The Sensitive Soul has ten Senses or Wits, five of which are 'outward' and five 'inward'. The 'outward' senses are what we call the Five Senses: sight, hearing, smell, taste and touch. The 'inward' five are memory, estimation, imagination, fantasy and common wit. Memory calls for no comment, but the others do. (1) Estimation covers much of what is now covered by the word *instinct*. Albertus Magnus tells us in *De Anima* that it is Estimation which enables a cow to pick out her own calf from a crowd of calves. (2) The distinction between Fantasy and Imagination is not so simple. Fantasy is the higher of the two, but Coleridge has turned the nomenclature upside down. Medieval authors would have used *invention* where we use *imagination*. 'According to Albertus, Imagination merely retains what has been perceived, and Fantasy deals with the *componendo et dividendo*, separating and uniting.'

An almost opposite fate has overtaken the word *imagination* in English, which meant not merely the retention of things perceived, but 'having in mind', or 'thinking about', or 'taking in account'. (3) Common Sense or Wit is given two functions by Albertus Magnus in *De Anima*: (a) 'It judges the operation of a sense so that when we see, we know we are seeing'; (b) it puts together the data given by the outward senses so that we can say an orange is sweet or one orange is sweeter than another. As for the Vegetable Soul, it is responsible for all the unconscious, involuntary processes in our organism: for growth, secretion, nutrition and reproduction.

F. Soul and Body. 'No Model yet devised has made a satisfactory unity between our actual experience of sensation or thought or emotion and any available account of the corporeal processes which they are held to involve.' Let us say that a chain of reasoning – that is, 'thoughts', which are 'about' or 'refer to' something other than themselves – are linked together by the logical relation of grounds and consequents. Physiologists would resolve this into a sequence of 'cerebral events'. But physical events, as such, cannot in any intelligible sense be said to be 'about' or to 'refer to' anything. They must be linked to one another not as grounds and consequents but as 'causes and effects' – a relation so irrelevant to the logical linkage that it is just as perfectly illustrated by the sequence of a maniac's thoughts as by the sequence of those of a rational man.

The chasm between the two points of view presented itself to the medieval thinker in two forms: (1) 'How can the soul, conceived as an immaterial substance, act upon matter at all? Obviously it cannot act as one body acts upon another.' (2) For Plato 'It is not possible to pass from one extreme to another but by a mean.' This would have moved the medievals to put something in between soul and body: and this *tertium quid*, this 'phantom liaison-officer', between body and soul was called *Spirit* or *spirits*. Bartholomaeus Anglicus in the *De Proprietatibus* distinguishes a triad of Natural, Vital and Animal Spirits. Their function is, as Timothy Bright says in his *Treatise of Melancholy* (1586), to be 'a true love knot to couple heaven and earth together; yea, a more divine nature than the heavens with a base clod of earth', so that the soul is 'not fettered with the bodie, as certaine Philosophers have taken it, but handfasted herewith by that golden claspe of the spirit.'

G. The Human Body. The human body gives us another sense in which man can be called a microcosm. It, like the world, is built of four contraries. In the world these combine to form the elements: fire, air, water, earth. In bodies they combine to form the 'Humours': Hot and Moist make Blood; Hot and Dry, Choler; Cold and Moist, Phlegm; Cold and Dry, Melancholy. The proportion in which the Humours are blended differs from one man to another. They constitute his *complexio* or *temperamentum*, his combination or mixture.

While the proportion of the Humours is perhaps never exactly the same in any two individuals, the 'complexions' may be grouped into four main types according to the Humour that predominates in each. One of the symptoms of a man's complexion is his *Colouring* – his 'complexion'. (1) Where *Blood* predominates we have the 'Sanguine Complexion'. (2) A '*Choleric* man' is tall and lean. (3) the *Melancholy* Complexion is described by Elyot as 'leane ... moche watch (i.e. he is a bad sleeper) ... dremes fearful ... stiff in opinions ... anger long and fretting.' (4) The *Phlegmatic* is the worst of all the Complexions. Its signs, according to Elyot, are 'fatness ... colour white ... sleepe superfluous (i.e. in excess) ... dremes of things watery or of fish ... slowness ... dulness of learning ... smallness of courage.' 'Like the planets,' Lewis warns, 'the Complexions need to be lived with imaginatively, not merely learned as concepts. They do not exactly correspond to any psychological classification we have been taught to make.' In addition to the permanent predominance of some one Humour in each individual, there is also a daily rhythmic variation which gives each of the four a temporary predominance in all of us.

H. The Human Past. To the Greeks the historical process was a meaningful flux or cyclic reiteration, and significance was to be sought 'not in the world of becoming but in that of being, not in history but in metaphysics, mathematics, and theology.' History was for them 'a story without a plot'. The Hebrews, on the other hand, saw their past 'as a revelation of the purposes of Jahweh'. And Christianity, going on from there, makes world-history in its entirety 'a single, transcendentally significant, story with a well-defined plot pivoted on Creation, Fall, Redemption and Judgement.' 'On this view,' said Lewis, 'the *differentia* of Christian historiography ought to be called what I call Historicism; the belief that by studying the past we can learn not only historical but meta-historical or transcendental truth' (see **Historicism§**).

The suggested antithesis between Pagan and Christian concepts of History is overdrawn. Virgil's *Aeneid* is an example of classical 'meta-history'. Examples of Christian 'Historicism' include Augustine's *De Civitate Dei*, Orosius's *History against the Pagans*, and Dante's *De Monarchia*. To Christians all history in the last resort must be held to be a story with a divine plot. Even so, not all Christian historiographers feel it their business to take much notice of that. To most of the medievals this 'overall plot' was festooned with a 'huge wealth of subordinate stories' which do not in the aggregate display any single trend in the world depicted. One of the things which discouraged a 'philosophy of history' was the medieval conception of Fortune. If most events happen because Fortune is turning her wheel, the ground is cut from under the feet of those who attempt 'Historicism'.

John Barbour (d. 1395) set out in his *Bruce* what he thought the true reasons for studying history: to entertain our imagination; to gratify our curiosity; and to discharge a debt we owe our ancestors. This approach differs not at all from that of authors whose matter we regard as wholly legendary – for example, the author of the fourteenth-century Troy book, the *Geste Hystoriale*, who begins very much as Barbour does. It follows that the distinction between history and fiction cannot, in its modern clarity, be applied to medieval books or to the spirit in which they were read. Stories from the past had a status in the common imagination indistinguishable – at any rate, not distinguished – from that of fact. 'It is by no means necessary to suppose that Chaucer's contemporaries believed the tale of Troy or Thebes as we believe in the Napoleonic Wars; but neither did they disbelieve as we disbelieve a novel.'

The chances are that those who read 'historical' works about Troy, Alexander, Arthur or Charlemagne believed them to be 'in the main' true. What is more certain is that they did not believe these works to be false. Everyone 'knew' that the past contained Nine Worthies: three Pagans (Hector, Alexander and Julius Caesar); three Jews (Joshua, David and Judas Maccabeus); and three Christians (Arthur, Charlemagne and Godfrey of Bouillon). Everyone 'knew' we were descended from the Trojans – as we all 'know' how King Alfred burned the cakes. 'It must be remembered throughout that the texts we should now call historical differed in outlook and narrative texture from those we should call fictions far less than a modern "history" differs from a modern novel.' Historians dealt hardly at all with the impersonal, but with individuals; their valour or villainy, their memorable sayings, their good or bad luck.

The nearest we get to a widespread 'philosophy of history' in the Middle Ages is the frequent assertion that things were once better than they are now. As we read in Wulstan's sermon: 'The world hurries on ... and speeds to its end ... thus, for men's sins it must worsen day by day.'

And yet in these chronicles or romances we do not get an impression of gloom. 'Historically as well as cosmically, medieval man stood at the foot of a stairway; looking up, he felt delight. The backward, like the upward, glance exhilarated him with a majestic spectacle, and humility was rewarded with the pleasures of admiration. And, thanks to his deficiency in the sense of period, that packed and gorgeous past was far more immediate to him than the dark and bestial past could ever be to a Lecky or a Wells ... One had one's place, however modest, in a great succession; one need be neither proud nor lonely.'

I. The Seven Liberal Arts. 'To give an educational curriculum a place in the Model of the universe may at first seem an absurdity; and it would be an absurdity if the medievals had felt about it as we feel about the "subjects" in a syllabus today.' However, for them the syllabus was regarded as immutable. The Liberal Arts had achieved a status not unlike that of nature herself. The Arts are: (1) Grammar; (2) Dialectic; (3) Rhetoric; (4) Arithmetic; (5) Music; (6) Geometry; (7) Astronomy. The first three constitute the *Trivium* or threefold way; the last four, the *Quadrivium*.

(1) Isidore defines *Grammar* as 'the skill of speech'. That is, she teaches us Latin, still then the living Esperanto of the western world, and great works were written in it. But while Grammar was thus restricted to a single tongue, it included a good deal more than literacy, such as syntax, etymology, prosody, and the explanation of allusions. (2) Having learned from Grammar how we talk, we learn from *Dialectic* 'how to talk sense, to argue, to prove and disprove'. The medieval foundation of this art was an *Isagoge* or Introduction to Aristotle written by Porphyry and translated into Latin by Boethius. 'Dialectic' in the modern Marxist sense is here a red herring – Hegelian in origin. Dialectic was really concerned with proving, and in the Middle Ages there were three kinds of proof: from Reason, from Authority, and from Experience. (3) *Rhetoric* for the ancient teachers was devoted to public speaking when that was an indispensable skill for every public man.

Chapter VIII, 'The Influence of the Model'. No one who has read the higher kinds of medieval and Renaissance poetry will have failed to notice the amount of solid instruction – of science, philosophy or history – that they carry. For instance, in the *Divine Comedy*, or Lyndsay's *Dreme* or Spenser's Mutability cantos, the theme is so chosen that it 'permits and invites' such matter. That matter may seem to us to be 'dragged in by the heels', but when, for instance, the poet of *Gawain* begins with the fall of Troy he is not padding but obeying the principle of 'a place for everything and everything in its right place'. The commonest method is by

digression. There are many such digressions in the *Roman de la Rose* –
digressions such as those on Fortune, on true nobility, on the function and
limitations of Nature, and on the immortality of gods and angels. The
simplest form of digression is that which expresses itself in 'mere
catalogue'. This may at first seem like pedantry, but it is not. Henryson
might expect, and justly, to be admired for describing the characters of the
planets so vividly in his *Trial of the Fox*, but hardly for knowing them.
These authors presented knowledge which most of their readers already
possessed. 'One gets the impression that medieval people, like Professor
Tolkien's Hobbits, enjoyed books which told them what they already
knew.'

Another explanation may be based in Rhetoric which recommended
morae – delays or padding. But this overlooks the fact that Rhetoric
explains the 'formal' and not the 'material' characteristic. That is, Rhetoric
tells you to digress, not what to put into your digressions. Besides this,
the Rhetorical explanation could hardly be expected to cover the visible
arts, where we meet the same phenomenon. They also continually re-state
what was believed about the universe. At Florence in Santa Maria del
Popolo the cupola above Chigi's tomb magnificently re-states the
Boethian doctrine of Providence and Destiny. In the Doge's palace the
planets look down from the capitals. They meet us again at Florence
strangely disguised in the Santa Maria del Fiore. And in Santa Maria
Novella the planets are paired off with the Seven Liberal Arts. In the
Salone (Palazzo della Ragione) at Padua we have the planets, their
children, the zodiacal signs, the Apostles, and the labours of men all
arranged under their appropriate months. The true explanation is that
'Poets and other artists depicted these things because their minds loved to
dwell on them.' No other age has had a Model so satisfying to the
imagination. Every fact and story became more interesting, more
pleasurable, if by being properly fitted in, 'it carried one's mind back to
the Model as a whole.'

This subordination to or humility in the face of a given significant form
may explain the most typical vice and the most typical virtue of medieval
literature. The vice is dullness (of which the *South English Legendary* or
Ormulum or part of Hoccleve are good examples). One sees how the belief
in a world of built-in significance encourages this. The writer feels
everything to be so interesting in itself that there is no need for him to
make it so. However badly a story may be re-told, the story was still
worth telling; and however badly stated the truths, they are still worth
stating.

The characteristic virtue of good medieval work is 'the absence of strain'. The best parts of Gower or of Marie de France seem so limpid and effortless that the story might be telling itself. But, in fact, art is at work, and it is 'the art of people who, no less than the bad medieval authors, have a complete confidence in the intrinsic value of their matter.' With this attitude goes the characteristically medieval type of imagination. 'It is not a transforming imagination like Wordsworth's or a penetrative imagination like Shakespeare's. It is a realizing imagination. Macaulay noted in Dante the extremely factual word-painting; the details, the comparisons, designed at whatever cost of dignity to make sure that we see exactly what he saw. Now Dante in this is typically medieval. The Middle Ages are unrivalled, till we reach quite modern times, in the sheer foreground fact, the "close-up".'

And just as the medieval writer was not ashamed imaginatively to realize what he believed 'was already there', so he was not ashamed to make use of other writers' work. 'If you had asked Layamon or Chaucer "Why do you not make up a brand-new story of your own?" I think they might have replied (in effect) "Surely we are not yet reduced to that?" ' Chaucer touches up Boccaccio; Malory touches up French prose romances; Layamon works over Wace. 'The originality which we regard as a sign of wealth might have seemed to them a confession of poverty.' Why spin something out of one's own head when the world already teems with stories which have never yet been set forth quite so well as they deserve?

Lewis begins his Epilogue with the admission: 'I have made no serious effort to hide the fact that the old Model delights me as I believe it delighted our ancestors. Few constructions of the imagination seem to me to have combined splendour, sobriety and coherence in the same degree.' It had, however, one serious defect. It was not true. On the other hand, the charge of untruthfulness can no longer have exactly the same sort of weight for us that it would have had in the nineteenth century. The meaning of the words 'know' and 'true' in this context have begun to undergo a change.

For instance, the nineteenth century held the belief that by inferences from our sense-experience we could 'know' the ultimate physical reality. They believed that the 'truth' would be a mental replica of the thing itself. Thus, mathematics were the idiom in which many of the sciences spoke. It was probably not doubted that 'there was a concrete reality *about* which the mathematics held good; distinguishable from the mathematics as a heap of apples is from the process of counting them.' That is, while it was known that it was in some respects 'not adequately represented' it was nevertheless hoped that 'ordinary imagination and conception could grasp it'. We should then, in that century, be like a man coming to know about a foreign country without visiting it. He learns about the mountains of that country from studying contour lines on a map. His knowledge is not, however, a knowledge of contour lines. Real knowledge is achieved when these lines can enable him to say 'That would be an easy ascent', or 'This is a dangerous precipice'. In going beyond the contour lines to such conclusions he is getting nearer to the reality.

It would be different if someone said to him – and he believed it – 'But it is the contour lines themselves that are the fullest reality you can get. In turning away from them to these other statements you are getting further from the reality, not nearer. All those ideas about "real" rocks and slopes and views are merely a metaphor or a parable.'

This it seems is just what has happened as regards the physical sciences in our century. 'The mathematics are now the nearest to the reality we can get. Anything imaginable, even anything that can be manipulated by ordinary (that is, non-mathematical) conceptions, far from being a further truth to which mathematics were the avenue, is a mere analogy, a concession to our weakness. Without a parable modern physics speaks not to the multitudes.' And in order to speak, even among themselves, scientists attempt to verbalize their findings. They speak of making 'models', and indeed it is from them that the word has been borrowed. But these 'models' are not, like model ships, small-scale replicas of the reality. They illustrate something by an analogy, and 'Sometimes, they do not illustrate but merely suggest, like the sayings of the mystics.' For instance, an expression such as 'the curvature of space' is strictly comparable to the old definition of God as 'a circle whose centre is everywhere and whose circumference is nowhere.'

There is, furthermore, a two-way traffic between a model of the universe and the prevailing temper of mind. 'I hope no one will think that I am recommending a return to the medieval Model,' says Lewis. 'I am only suggesting considerations that may induce us to regard all Models in the right way, respecting each and idolizing none ... No Model is a catalogue of ultimate realities, and none is a mere fantasy. Each is a serious attempt to get in all the phenomena known at a given period, and each succeeds in getting in a great many. But also, no less surely, each reflects the prevalent psychology of an age almost as much as it reflects the state of that age's knowledge. Hardly any battery of new facts could have persuaded a Greek that the universe had an attribute so repugnant to him as infinity; hardly any such battery could persuade a modern that it is hierarchical.'

Reviews

D.S. Brewer reviewing it in the *Birmingham Post* (9 June 1964) said: 'The best in the man and his books was more than generous; it was noble. It does you good to read his learned books, not because you are preached at, but because to read them is for the mind what a walk over fine, sometimes rough, country, in good weather is for the healthy body.' Helen Gardner, reviewing it in *The Listener*, 72 (16 July 1964), p. 97, said: 'Nobody else could have imposed such form on such a mass of matter, and written a book so wide in scope and implication and so curious in discovering the rare, the remote, but the exact, example. And where else in modern literary scholarship can we find so generous and enthusiastic a temper? Whether we were his pupils in the classroom or no, we are all his pupils and we shall not look upon his like again.' The reviewer in *The Times Literary Supplement* (16 July 1964), p. 632, said: 'If not a *magnum opus*, it represents Lewis the expositor at his best, and communicates the zest that he brought to the study of literature, philosophy and religion alike.' *The Church Times* (3 April 1964) said: 'An amateur medievalist is left gasping that any man who gave so much of his life to other studies could possibly have known so much about medieval literature and read so many of its Great Clerks. Over and over again he gives a list of medieval authorities on this subject or that, and says that they will all be well known to every educated man. It is very disconcerting when a lifelong student of things medieval realizes that at least some of the names on Lewis's list are entirely unknown to him. But, if the book sometimes daunts, it nearly always entrances, and, though it describes a model which has passed away into a mist, it testifies, in its reverence, for those who made it, to the greatness of the human mind.'

M.C. Bradbrook said in *New Statesman* 68 (7 August 1964), p. 188: 'The printed page transmits only part of the zest with which Lewis in his lectures demonstrated this double process, but it is invaluable to have the most famous set from the university courses preserved for posterity.' A.C. reviewing in *The Ampleforth Journal* (October 1964) said: 'We had thought to have no more from that gifted pen: it seemed as though the fruit of all that reading had passed beyond our reach ... *The Discarded Image* ... is worth having, if only for the experience of having so genial an interpreter to guide us through the realms of gold.'

KEY IDEAS

ALLEGORY: 'I am also convinced that the wit of man *cannot* devise a story in which the wit of some other man cannot find an allegory,' Lewis wrote to Father Peter Milward on 10 December 1956. 'The truth is it's one of those words which need defining in each context where one uses it.' Because Lewis had to deny so often that his Space Fiction Novels and his Chronicles of Narnia were allegories, it has become necessary to say what *he* meant by the term. Early in his life, when he was writing *The Allegory of Love*, he defined allegory as it was understood by the medieval authors he was writing about and as he continued to understand it himself:

> On the one hand you can start with an immaterial fact, such as the passions which you actually experience, and can then invent *visibilia* (visible things) to express them. If you are hesitating between an angry retort and a soft answer, you can express your state of mind by inventing a person called *Ira* (Anger) with a torch and letting her contend with another invented person called *Patientia* (Patience). This is allegory. (II).

The subject came up often after the Narnian stories were published. He was often asked if Aslan was an 'allegory'. Writing to Mrs Hook about this on 29 December 1958 (L) he said:

> By an allegory I mean a composition (whether pictorial or literary) in which immaterial realities are represented by feigned physical objects, e.g. a pictured Cupid allegorically represents erotic love (which in reality is an experience, not an object occupying a given area of space) or, in Bunyan a giant represents Despair.

John Bunyan's *Pilgrim's Progress* is one of the best-known allegories. In that work the author represents Death by a Christian lady entering a river and crossing to the other side. In **The Vision of John Bunyan**, Lewis expressed his annoyance when an artist portrayed Death as 'an old lady on her death-bed, surrounded by weeping relatives':

> This stupidity perhaps comes from the pernicious habit of reading allegory as if it were a cryptogram to be translated; as if, having grasped what an image (as we say) 'means', we threw the image away and thought of the ingredient in real life which it represents. But that method leads you continually out of the book back into the conception you started from and would have had without reading it. The right process is the exact reverse. We ought not to be thinking 'This green valley, where the shepherd boy is singing, represents humility'; we ought to be discovering, as we read, that humility is like that green valley. That way, moving always into the book, not out of it, from the concept to the image, enriches the concept. And that is what allegory is for.

See also **NARNIA** (VIII: Allegory, Supposal and Symbolism).

BULVERISM: This idea comes from the essay **'Bulverism': or, the Foundation of 20th Century Thought** in which Lewis says: 'You must show *that* a man is wrong before you start explaining *why* he is wrong. The modern method is to assume without discussion *that* he is wrong and then distract his attention from this (the only real issue) by busily explaining how he became so silly ... I have found the device so common that I have had to invent a name for it. I call it Bulverism. Some day I am going to write the biography of its imaginary inventor, Ezekiel Bulver, whose destiny was determined at the age of five when he heard his mother say to his father – who had been maintaining that two sides of a triangle were together greater than the third – "Oh you say that *because you are a man*." "At that moment," E. Bulver assures us, "there flashed across my opening mind the great truth that refutation is no necessary part of argument. Assume that your opponent is wrong, and then explain his error, and the world will be at your feet. Attempt to prove that he is wrong or (worse still) try to find out whether he is wrong or right, and the national dynamism of our age will thrust you to the wall." That is how Bulver became one of the makers of the Twentieth Century.'

CHRISTIANITY IS ABOUT 'REAL THINGS': In what was probably the first statement about his conversion, Lewis said in a letter to Arthur Greeves* of 18 October 1931 that whereas 'Pagan stories are God expressing Himself through the minds of poets ... Christianity is God expressing Himself through what we call 'real things' ... namely the actual incarnation, crucifixion and resurrection' (**TST**).

It was this belief in 'Real Things' – objective *Facts* – which made Lewis dislike intensely what he called in **MC** II, 2 'Christianity-and-water'. Christianity is God's 'statement to us of certain quite unalterable *facts* about His own nature' (**MC** II, 2). Those who turn up from time to time with 'some patent simplified religion of their own' as a substitute for Christianity are wasting time. 'We cannot compete, in simplicity, with people who are inventing religions. How could we? We are dealing with *Fact*. Of course anyone can be simple if he has no *facts* to bother about' (**MC** IV, 2). It is also pointless to talk about what the universe 'could have been' like because God is 'the rock bottom, irreducible *Fact* on which all other facts depend' (**MC** IV, 6). 'If God is the ultimate source of all concrete, individual things and events,' he argued in **M**, 'then God Himself must be concrete, and individual in the highest degree. Unless the origin of all other things were itself concrete and individual, nothing else could be so; for there is no conceivable means whereby what is abstract or general could itself produce concrete reality' (XI). Lewis had good reason to emphasize this: in **Modern Man and his Categories of Thought** he complained that 'Man is becoming as narrowly "practical" as the irrational animals. In lecturing to popular audiences I have repeatedly found it almost impossible to make them understand that I recommended Christianity because I thought its affirmations to be objectively *true*. They are simply not interested in the question of truth or falsehood. They only want to know if it will be comforting, or "inspiring", or socially useful.'

CHRONOLOGICAL SNOBBERY: This is defined in **SBJ** XIII as 'The uncritical acceptance of the intellectual climate common to our own age and the assumption that whatever has gone out of date is on that account discredited. You must find why it went out of date. Was it ever refuted (and if so by whom, where and how conclusively) or did it merely die away as fashions do? If the latter, this tells us nothing about its truth or falsehood. From seeing this, one passes to the realization that our own age is also "a period", and certainly has, like all periods, its own characteristic illusions. They are likeliest to lurk in those wide-spread assumptions which are so ingrained in the age that no one dares to attack or feels it necessary to defend them.'

In **SBJ** XIII Lewis attributed his belief in Chronological Snobbery to Owen Barfield* and in the Preface to **AOL** (dedicated to Barfield) he says, 'The friend to whom I have dedicated the book, has taught me not to patronize the past, and has trained me to see the present as itself a "period". I desire for myself no higher function than to be one of the instruments whereby his theory and practice in such matters may become more widely effective.'

CHURCH UNITY: In *The Four Loves* (IV) Lewis defines Friendship as that love which exists between those who '*see the same truth*'. The same applies, he believed, to Christian unity. There must be something for Christians to be unified *about*, and that of course is believing the same basic facts – facts such as the Incarnation, Crucifixion and Resurrection of Jesus Christ.

'It is at her centre,' he said in the Preface to **MC**, 'where her truest children dwell, that each communion is really closest to every other in spirit, if not in doctrine'. 'Hostility,' on the other hand, 'has come more from borderline people ... men not exactly obedient to any communion.' Asked whether he thought the time ripe for re-union, Lewis said in **Answers to Questions on Christianity**:

> The time is always ripe for re-union. Divisions between Christians are a sin and a scandal, and Christians ought at all times to be making contributions towards re-union, if it is only by their prayers ... In all the things which I have written and thought I have always stuck to traditional, dogmatic positions. The result is that letters of agreement reach me from what are ordinarily regarded as the most different kinds of Christians ... It seems to me that the 'extremist' elements in every church are nearest one another and the liberal and 'broad-minded' people in each body could never be united at all. The world of dogmatic Christianity is a place in which thousands of people of quite different types keep on saying the same thing, and the world of 'broad-mindedness' and watered-down 'religion' is a world where a small number of people (all of the same type) say totally different things and change their minds every few minutes. We shall never get re-union from them.

Writing to Dom Bede Griffiths* on 8 May 1939, he said: 'I am inclined to think that the immediate task is vigorous co-operation on the basis of what even now is common – combined, of course, with full admission of the differences. An *experienced* unity on some things might then prove the prelude to a confessional unity on all things' (L). Nowhere does Lewis write with such conviction and so fully about Christian unity as in his correspondence with Blessed Giovanni Calabria.* 'Common perils, common burdens,' he said on 20 September 1947, 'an almost universal hatred and contempt for the Flock of Christ can, by God's Grace, contribute much to the healing of our divisions. For those who suffer the same things from the same people for the same Person can scarcely not love each other.' Writing again on 25 November 1947 he said: 'Disputations do more to aggravate schism than to heal it: united actions, prayer, fortitude and (should God so will) united deaths for Christ – *these* will make us one' (**LDGC**).

COPY AND THE ORIGINAL, THE: Ever since his conversion Lewis had become convinced that the relation between what is usually defined as a 'copy' and an 'original' is generally the other way round. The idea appeared first in **PR** III, 9. John, the Pilgrim, is being held captive by a Giant known as 'The Spirit of the Age', when Reason, a virgin in steel armour, arrives to deliver him. Reason bets the Giant that he can't answer three riddles. He manages the first two, after which comes the third: 'By what rule do you tell a copy from the original?'

> The giant muttered and mumbled and could not answer, and Reason set spurs in her stallion and it leaped up on to the giant's mossy knees and galloped up his foreleg, till she plunged her sword into his heart. Then there was a noise and a crumbling like a landslide and the huge carcass settled down: and the Spirit of the Age became what he had seemed to be at first, a sprawling hummock of rock.

'Once rational argument is allowed,' Lewis wrote in his running headline, 'the giant is lost.' The idea came up again in **PR** IV, 2 where the Freudians assume that because the Pilgrim desires both the Island (Heaven) and 'brown girls' (lust) the first must be a 'copy' of the second. Reason, however, says to John: 'They indeed will tell you that their researches have proved that if two things are similar, the fair one is always the copy of the foul one … but in fact they assume that doctrine first and interpret their researches by it.'

Perhaps the best example of all occurs in the **LB** 15. After going through the Stable the children find themselves in a place like Narnia but which is not the same. 'That was not the real Narnia,' Lord Digory explains. 'That had a beginning and an end. It was only a shadow or a copy of the real Narnia which has always been here and always will be here: just as our own world, England and all, is only a shadow or copy of something in Aslan's real world ... It's all in Plato, all in Plato.' There are many passages in Plato that Lewis could have had in mind, but one of the most important is *Timaeus* 28c–29a:

> This is the question ... we must ask about the world. Which of the patterns had the artificer in view when he made it – the pattern of the unchangeable or of that which is created? If the world be indeed fair and the artificer good, it is manifest that he must have looked to that which is eternal, but if what cannot be said without blasphemy is true, then to the created pattern. Everyone will see that he must have looked to the eternal, for the world is the fairest of creations and he is the best of causes. And having been created in this way, the world has been framed in the likeness of that which is apprehended by reason and mind and is unchangeable, and must therefore of necessity, if this is admitted, be a copy of something.

DEMOCRACY: Lewis made his views on Democracy very clear in his essay on **Equality** of 1943 in which he says 'I am a democrat because I believe in the Fall of Man. I think most people are democrats for the opposite reason.' The proper reason, he believed, for subscribing to democracy is not because mankind is 'so wise and good' that everyone deserves a share in the government, but because 'Mankind is so fallen that no man can be trusted with unchecked power over his fellows.'

Democracy, as he often pointed out, was one 'system' out of many, a possible means to fair government, not an end in itself. He believed the success of a democracy depended largely on its conformity to Moral or Natural Law§. What is wrong cannot become right by 'majority' opinions. There is an interesting passage about this in the Introduction to EL where, writing about the emergence of civil law in the sixteenth century, he shows the relation of Democracy to Natural Law. 'For Aquinas, as for Bracton,' he said, 'political power ... is never free and never originates. Its business is to enforce something that is already there, something given in the divine reason or in the existing custom. By its fidelity in reproducing that model it is to be judged. If it tries to be original, to produce new wrongs and rights in independence of the archetype, it becomes unjust and forfeits its claim to obedience.'

The theme had been hinted at a few years before in the essay on **The Necessity of Chivalry** of 1940 in which he explained that the 'knightly character' of the medieval knight, with its combination of 'sternness' and 'meekness', was 'something that needs to be achieved, not something that can be relied upon to happen.' These high qualities are a work of *art*, not Nature. 'This knowledge is specially necessary as we grow more democratic,' he warned. The problem, as he saw it, of a 'classless society' is whether 'its *ethos* [will] be a synthesis of what was best in all the classes, or a mere "pool" with the sediment of all and the virtues of none?'

In **M** XIV he made it clear that Christianity is *not* democratic. 'Democrats by birth and education, we should prefer to think that all nations and individuals start level in the search for God ... Christianity makes no concession to this point of view. It does not tell of a human search for God at all, but of something done by God for, to, and about Man. And the way in which it is done is selective, undemocratic, to the highest degree.' Following God's 'selectiveness' in choosing Abraham from the whole of humanity, the process narrows down to 'a Jewish girl at her prayers'. While this undemocratic quality of reality permits 'on the one hand, ruthless competition, arrogance and envy: it permits on the other, modesty and ... admiration. A world in which I was *really* (and not merely by a useful legal fiction) "as good as everyone else", in which I never looked up to anyone wiser or cleverer or braver or more learned than I, would be insufferable. The very "fans" of the cinema stars and the famous footballers know better than to desire that!' See **Democratic Education§** and **Equality§**.

DEMOCRATIC EDUCATION: In **Democratic Education** (1944) Lewis said: 'Democratic education, says Aristotle, ought to mean, not the education which democrats like, but the education which will preserve democracy. Until we have realized that the two things do not necessarily go together we cannot think clearly about education.' An outline of the points he makes is as follows:

(1) 'Democratic Education' is motivated by a desire to make everyone appear equal. This explained the move in the 1940s to cease making compulsory any subject on which some boys did better than others, such as Latin and even Mathematics. Lewis feared that in time all compulsory subjects would be abolished and the curriculum made wide enough to include even the most footling subjects so that 'no boy, and no boy's parents, need feel inferior'. (2) It is improbable that 'a nation thus educated could survive', and it can only escape destruction if its rivals and enemies have the same kind of education. 'A nation of dunces can be safe only in a world of dunces.' (3) The demand for equality has two sources, one among the noblest, and the other among the basest, of human emotions. 'The noble source is the desire for fair play. But the

other source is the hatred of superiority ... There is in all men a tendency ... to resent the existence of what is stronger, subtler or better than themselves ... The kind of "democratic" education which is already looming ahead is bad because it endeavours to propitiate evil passions, to appease envy.'

(4)There are two reasons for not attempting this. First, envy is insatiable. 'The more you concede to it, the more it will demand. No attitude of humility which you can possibly adopt will propitiate a man with an inferiority complex.' Secondly, in such a system of education 'you are trying to introduce equality where equality is fatal ... It has no place in the world of the mind. Beauty is not democratic ... Virtue is not democratic ... Truth is not democratic; she demands special talents and special industry in those to whom she gives her favours. Political democracy is doomed if it tries to extend its demand for equality into these higher spheres.' (5) A 'truly democratic education' – one which will preserve democracy – must be 'ruthlessly aristocratic ... In drawing up its curriculum it should always have chiefly in view the interests of the boy who wants to know and who can know.' (6) And what about the dull boy? Is he to be sacrificed to other people's sons? Lewis replies that 'There are dozens of jobs ... in which he can be very useful and very happy. And one priceless benefit he will enjoy; he will know he's not clever ... He will be a pillar of democracy. He will allow just the right amount of rope to those clever ones ... Democracy demands that little men should not take big ones too seriously; it dies when it is full of little men who think they are big themselves.' See **Democracy§** and **Equality§**.

DISINTERESTED LOVE OF GOD: In **SBJ** XV Lewis expressed pleasure in the fact that when he converted he did not believe in a future life: 'I now number it among my greatest mercies that I was permitted for several months ... to know God and to attempt obedience without even raising that question ... There are men ... who have made immortality almost the central doctrine of their religion; but for my part I have never seen how a preoccupation with that subject at the outset could fail to corrupt the whole thing ... If you ask why we should obey God, in the last resort the answer is, "I am". To know God is to know that our obedience is due to Him ... I think it is well, even now, sometimes to say to ourselves, "God is such that if (*per impossibile*) His power could vanish and His other attributes remain, so that the supreme right were for ever robbed of the supreme might, we should still owe Him precisely the same kind and degree of allegiance as we now do."'

Still holding this to be true, in **The Weight of Glory** he turns the matter around and asks whether the promise of reward makes the Christian life a 'mercenary affair'. 'There are different kinds of reward,' he answers. 'An enjoyment of Greek poetry is certainly a proper, and not a mercenary, reward for learning Greek: but only those who have reached the stage of enjoying Greek poetry can tell from their own experience that this is so. The schoolboy beginning Greek grammar cannot look forward to his adult enjoyment of Sophocles as a lover looks forward to marriage or a general to victory. He has to begin by working for marks ... The Christian, in relation to heaven, is in much the same position as this schoolboy. Those who have attained everlasting life in the vision of God doubtless know very well that it is no mere bribe, but the very consummation of their earthly discipleship.'

This came up again on 20 May 1946 when he read a paper to the Socratic Club‡ on **Religion Without Dogma?** '[God] behaves like the rich lover in a romance who woos the maiden on his own merits, disguised as a poor man, and only when he has won her reveals that he has a throne and palace to offer ... The essence of religion, in my view, is the thirst for an end higher than natural ends; the finite self's desire for, and acquiescence in, and self-rejection in favour of, an object wholly good and wholly good for it.'

EQUALITY: In the essay on **Equality** Lewis made it clear that he believed no two people to be the same. However, because of the Fall of Man 'no man can be trusted with unchecked power over his fellows' and for this reason we need a system of government such as Democracy. *Legal fictions* such as the legal and economic equality of democracy 'are absolutely necessary remedies for the Fall'. But, he warns, to treat equality as an ideal instead of 'a medicine or a safety-gadget' breeds 'that stunted and envious sort of mind which hates all superiority'. 'Under the necessary outer covering of legal equality, the whole hierarchical dance and harmony of our deep and joyously accepted spiritual inequalities should be alive.'

'It is idle to say that men are of equal *value*,' he said in **Membership**: 'If we mean that all men are equally useful or beautiful or good or entertaining – then it is nonsense. If it means that all are of equal value as immortal souls then I think it conceals a dangerous error. The infinite value of each human soul is not a Christian doctrine. God did not die for man because of some value He perceived in him. The value of each human soul considered simply in itself, out of relation to God, is zero ... It may be that He loves all equally – He certainly loved all to the death –

and I am not certain what the expression means. If there is equality it is in His love, not in us.' 'Equality (outside mathematics),' he insisted in **Democratic Education,** 'is a purely social conception. It applies to man as a political and economic animal. It has no place in the world of the mind.'

Turning to his novels, one of the angels in **PER** 17 says of God, 'Never did He make two things the same; never did He utter one word twice … All is righteousness and there is no equality.' Perhaps the most powerful indictment of 'the factual belief that all men are equal' is found in 'Screwtape Proposes a Toast' in which Screwtape claims that the obvious advantage of such a belief is that it 'prompts a man to say *I'm as good as you*', which induces him 'to enthrone at the centre of his life a good solid, resounding lie'. See **Democracy§** and **Democratic Education§**.

FIRST AND SECOND THINGS: The theme embodied in his essay **First and Second Things** runs through everything Lewis wrote, and it is essential to the understanding of his thought. He believed that 'by valuing too highly a real but subordinate good, we … come near to losing that good itself … The woman who makes a dog the centre of her life loses, in the end, not only her human usefulness and dignity but even the proper pleasure of dog-keeping. The man who makes alcohol his chief good loses not only his job but his palate and all power of enjoying the earlier (and only pleasurable) levels of intoxication … Of course this law has been discovered before, but it will stand re-discovery. It may be stated as follows: every preference of a small good to a great, or a partial good to a total good, involves the loss of the small or partial good for which the sacrifice was made … You can't get second things by putting them first; you can get second things only by putting first things first.'

GOODNESS: Many have imagined that Lewis saw Morality as the centre of Christian life. Nothing could be further from the truth. Morality exists for the purpose of helping us to become one with Christ. 'In setting up "a good life" as our final goal,' he cautioned in **Man or Rabbit?** we have missed the very point of our existence. Morality is a mountain which we cannot climb by our own efforts; and if we could we should only perish in the ice and unbreathable air of the summit … It is *from* there that the real ascent begins. The ropes and axes are "done away" and the rest is a matter of flying.' Nowhere is the relation between Goodness and Morality put better than in this passage from **PP** IV:

The Holiness of God is something more and other than moral perfection: His claim upon us is something more and other than the claim of moral duty. I do not deny it: but this conception, like that of corporate guilt, is very easily used as an evasion of the real issue. God may be more than moral goodness: He is not less. The road to the promised land runs past Sinai. The moral law may exist to be transcended: but there is no transcending it for those who have not first admitted its claims upon them, and then tried with all their strength to meet that claim, and fairly and squarely faced the fact of their failure.

HIERARCHY: In a chapter entitled 'Hierarchy' in **PPL** Lewis provides the best definition in his writings of something he believed of great importance:

> Degrees of value are objectively present in the universe. Everything except God has some natural superior; everything except unformed matter has some natural inferior. The goodness, happiness and dignity of every being consists in obeying its natural superior and ruling its natural inferiors. When it fails in either part of this twofold task we have disease or monstrosity in the scheme of things until the peccant being is either destroyed or corrected. One or the other it will certainly be; for by stepping out of its place in the system (whether it step up like a rebellious angel or down like an uxorious husband) it has made the very nature of things its enemy. It cannot succeed.

There are many other places too in which he writes of Hierarchy, and we consider two. (1) In **PPL** XI Lewis cites the speech of Ulysses in Shakespeare's *Troilus and Cressida* (I, iii) as 'the greatest statement of the Hierarchical conception in its double reference to civil and cosmic life.' His main purpose was to illuminate the beliefs of Milton, knowing however that Ulysses's words illuminate the present time as well:

> The heavens themselves, the planets, and this centre
> Observe degree, priority, and place,
> Insisture, course, proportion, season, form,
> Office, and custom, in all line of order:
> And therefore is the glorious planet Sol
> In noble eminence enthron'd and spher'd
> Amidst the other; whose med'cinable eye

> Corrects the ill aspects of planets evil,
> And posts, like the commandment of a king,
> Sans check, to good and bad: but when the planets
> In evil mixture to disorder wander,
> What plagues, and what portents, what mutiny ...
> Take but degree away, untune that string,
> And hark! what discord follows; each thing meets
> In mere oppugnancy: the bounded waters
> Should lift their bosoms higher than the shores,
> And make a sop of all this solid globe:
> Strength should be lord of imbecility,
> And the rude son should strike his father dead:
> Force should be right; or rather, right and wrong –
> Between whose endless jar justice resides –
> Should lose their names, and so should justice too.
> Then every thing includes itself in power,
> Power into will, will into appetite;
> And appetite, a universal wolf,
> So doubly seconded with will and power,
> Must make perforce a universal prey,
> And last eat up himself (85–124).

The special importance of these lines, says Lewis, 'lies in its clear statement of the alternative to Hierarchy. If you take "Degree" away "each thing meets in mere oppugnancy", "strength" will be lord, everything will "include itself in power". In other words, the modern idea that we can choose between Hierarchy and equality is, for Shakespeare's Ulysses, mere moonshine. The real alternative is tyranny; if you will not have authority you will find yourself obeying brute force.'

(2) 'I do not believe that God created an egalitarian world,' he said in **Membership**: 'I believe the authority of parent over child, husband over wife, learned over simple to have been as much a part of the original plan as the authority of man over beast. I believe that if we had not fallen, Filmer would be right, and patriarchal monarchy would be the sole lawful government. But since we have learned sin, we have found, as Lord Acton says, that "all power corrupts, and absolute power corrupts absolutely." The only remedy has been to take away the powers and substitute a legal fiction of equality ... Authority exercised with humility and obedience accepted with delight are the very lines along which our spirits live.' See **Democracy§**, **Equality§** and **Monarchy§**.

HISTORICISM: In **Historicism** Lewis says: 'I give the name *Historicism* to the belief that men can, by the use of their natural powers, discover an inner meaning in the historical process ... I say *an inner meaning* because I am not classifying as Historicists those who find "meaning" in history in any sense whatsoever. Thus, to find causal connections between historical events is in my terminology the work of a historian not of a historicist. A historian, without becoming a Historicist, may certainly infer unknown events from known ones ... What makes all these activities proper to the historian is that in them the conclusions, like the premises, are historical. The mark of the Historicist, on the other hand, is that he tries to get from historical premises conclusions which are more than historical; conclusions metaphysical or theological or (to coin a word) altheo-logical ... It is usually theologians, philosophers and politicians who become Historicists.'

In **Modern Man and his Categories of Thought** he says 'Developmentalism, in the field of human history, becomes Historicism: the belief that the scanty and haphazard selection of facts we know about History contains an almost mystical revelation of reality, and that to grasp the *Worden* and go wherever it is going is our prime duty ... It is wholly inimical to Christianity, for it denies both creation and the Fall. Where, for Christianity, the Best creates the good and the good is corrupted by sin, for Developmentalism the very standard of good is itself in a state of flux.' For Owen Barfield's* disagreement see 'C.S.Lewis and Historicism' in **OBCSL**.

HUMANITARIAN THEORY OF PUNISHMENT, THE: This idea had appeared first in **THS** 3:iv, where 'Fairy' Hardcastle explains to Mark Studdock that 'Desert was always finite: you could do so much to the criminal and no more. Remedial treatment, on the other hand, need have no fixed limit; it could go on till it had effected a cure, and those who were carrying it out would decide when *that* was.'

Next came his full theory of it in **The Humanitarian Theory of Punishment**, first published in *20th Century: An Australian Quarterly Review*, III, No. 3 (1949), pp. 5–12. The question he handles here is not Capital Punishment as a 'morally permissible deterrent', but the 'Humanitarian Theory' of it. He argues that, according to the Humanitarian theory, 'to punish a man because he deserves it' is 'mere revenge', and the only legitimate motive for punishment is 'the desire to deter others by example or to mend the criminal.' Combined with the belief that crime is more or less pathological the whole matter becomes one of 'healing or curing' and punishment becomes 'therapeutic'. Lewis believed this doctrine, however merciful it appears, 'really means that each one of us, from the moment he breaks the law, is deprived of the rights of a human being.' This is because it 'removes from Punishment the concept of Desert' which is the 'only connecting link between punishment and justice.' When we cease to consider what a criminal 'deserves' but only what will 'cure' him, he becomes instead of a person and a subject of rights 'a mere object, a patient, a "case".'

The Humanitarian Theory removes sentences from jurists and places the criminals 'in the hands of technical experts whose special sciences do not even employ such categories as rights or justice.' Only these 'official straighteners' can say when the offender is 'cured'. Besides this, in removing a criminal from 'justice', the whole 'morality' of punishment disappears. A tyranny 'sincerely expressed for the good of its victims' may be the most oppressive. To be cured against one's will is to be 'classed with infants, imbeciles and domestic animals', but to be punished because we deserve it 'is to be treated as a human person made in God's image.' Mercy detached from Justice grows unmerciful. 'That is the important paradox. As there are plants which will flourish only in mountain soil, so it appears that Mercy will flower only when it grows in the crannies of the rock of Justice: transplanted to the marshlands of mere Humanitarianism, it becomes a man-eating weed.' As a postscript Lewis added 'One last word. You may ask why I send this to an Australian periodical. The reason is simple and perhaps worth recording: I can get no hearing for it in England.' Lewis removed the postscript when the essay was published in *The Churchman* (English) LXXIII (April–June 1959, pp. 55–60.

IMAGINATION: Lewis nowhere expounded what he called a theory of the Imagination, but he had certain clear ideas which came more and more into focus as he grew older. What follows is intended as a sketch of how he came to understand and use his imagination, with the hope that it will serve in place of a theory.

I: Fantasy and Imagination

In **SBJ** I Lewis mentions the stories he wrote as a boy about Animal-Land and Boxen, noting that 'I was living almost entirely in my imagination.' 'But imagination,' he said, 'is a vague word ... It may mean the world of reverie, daydream, wish-fulfilling fantasy ... I must insist that this was a totally different activity from the invention of Animal-Land. Animal-Land was not (in that sense) a fantasy at all. I was not one of the characters it contained. I was its creator, not a candidate for admission to it.' A sharper contrast between Fantasy and Imagination is found in **On Three Ways of Writing for Children**. *Fantasy*, he said, especially when directed on to something so close as school stories, is 'compensatory' and 'we run to it from the disappointments and humiliations of the real world: it sends us back to the real world undivinely discontented. For it is all flattery to the ego. The pleasure consists in picturing oneself the object of admiration.' *Imagination*, on the other hand, affords us a view of *reality* from many angles. For example, a fairy tale arouses in a child 'The dim sense of something beyond his reach and, far from dulling or emptying the actual world, gives it a new dimension of depth. He does not despise real woods because he has read of enchanted woods: the reading makes all real woods a little enchanted.' One very important characteristic of Imagination is that it does not leave the reader's mind 'concentrated on himself'.

A further distinction between Fantasy and Imagination is found in **Psycho-analysis and Literary Criticism**. Lewis believed that Freud posed a 'pseudo-problem' when he claimed that 'all art is traced to the fantasies – that is, the day-dreams or waking wish-fulfilments – of the artist.' There are really, he insists,

> Two activities of the imagination, one free, and the other enslaved to the wishes of its owner for whom it has to provide imaginary gratifications. Both may be the starting-point for works of art. The former or 'free' activity continues in the works it produces and passes from the status of a dream to that of art by a process which may legitimately be called 'elaboration': it is a motive power which starts the activity and is withdrawn when once the engine is running, or a scaffolding which is knocked away when the building is complete.

II: Imagination in Coleridge

By Imagination in 'the highest sense of all' (**SBJ** I) Lewis meant the Primary Imagination as defined by Coleridge in the *Biographia Literaria* (XIII):

> The primary imagination I hold to be the living power and prime Agent of all human perception, and as a repetition in the finite mind of the eternal act of creation in the infinite I AM. The secondary Imagination I consider as an echo of the former, co-existing with the conscious will, yet still as identical with the primary in the *kind* of its agency, and differing only in *degree*, and in

the *mode* of its operation. It dissolves, diffuses, dissipates, in order to re-create; or where this process is rendered impossible, yet still at all events it struggles to idealize and to unify. It is essentially *vital*, even as all objects (*as* objects) are essentially fixed and dead.

Fancy, on the contrary, has no other counters to play with but fixities and definites. The fancy is indeed no other than a mode of memory emancipated from the order of time and space; and blended with, and modified by that empirical phenomenon of the will which we express by the word *choice*. But equally with the ordinary memory it must receive all its materials ready-made from the law of association.

In brief, to Coleridge the 'Primary Imagination' is the repetition of the eternal creation of God in the finite mind of Man. The 'Secondary Imagination' is like it in kind, but less like it in degree, and is an 'echo' of the Primary Imagination in the conscious mind of Man. Fancy, on the other hand, has no power to create: it can only remember. Or, as Coleridge put it, Imagination is a '*modifying* power' while Fancy is an '*aggregating* power.'

III: Tolkien's Theory of 'sub-creation'

If there were space enough much attention would be given to that great and seminal work, *Poetic Diction: A Study in Meaning*, by Owen Barfield.* And we would include as well Owen Barfield's *What Coleridge Thought*. Let us, in any event, point out that *Poetic Diction* greatly influenced Tolkien* whose theory of 'sub-creation' was immensely important to Lewis's understanding of Imagination.[1] The theory is derived from Tolkien's essay **On Fairy Stories** and his poem 'Mythopoeia'.

According to Tolkien, you look at trees and label them 'trees' and think that ends the matter. But it was not a 'tree' until someone gave it that name. You call a star a 'star' and think it is some 'matter in a ball' moving in a mathematical course. That is only the way you *see* it. They weren't 'stars' and 'trees' until you named them that. All these things live and move at the bidding of God who is their Creator. Although Man was disgraced by the Fall and for a long time estranged from God, he is not wholly lost or changed from his original nature. He retains the image and likeness of his Maker. Man shows that he is made in the image and

---

[1] For the influence of *Poetic Diction* on Tolkien's *Mythopoeia* see Clive Tolley's 'Tolkien's "Essay on Man": A look at *Mythopoeia*' in *Inklings: Jahrbuch für Literatur und Ästhetik*, Band 10 (1992), pp. 221–35.

likeness of the Maker when, acting in a 'derivative mode', he writes stories which reflect the eternal Beauty and Wisdom. Imagination is 'the power of giving to ideal creations the inner consistency of reality.' When Man draws things from the Primary World and creates a Secondary World he is acting as a 'sub-creator'.

A Secondary World is one which the mind can enter. Because it contains this 'inner consistency of reality', what you find inside is 'true' in that it accords with the laws of that world. You therefore believe it, while you are, as it were, inside. The moment disbelief arises, the spell is broken; the magic, or rather art, has failed. You are then out in the Primary World again.

What Lewis referred to as Imagination, Tolkien called Fantasy. According to him, it has three effects: Recovery, Escape and Consolation. (1) Recovery means a regaining of 'a clear view' of the Creation. Man needs to be freed from the drab blur of triteness, familiarity and possessiveness which impair his sight. That is, he needs to see things the way they really are. The reason for this staleness and triteness is that, in acquiring them and locking these possessions away, Man has ceased to look at them. These stories open the cage, letting all those things which have been locked up fly away.

(2) Escape. Of course it will be claimed that fantastic or imaginative literature is Escape from Real Life. But who is it, asks Tolkien, that is forever thinking about Escape: *Gaolers*. 'Why should a man be scorned if, finding himself in prison, he tries to get out and go home? Or if, when he cannot do so, he thinks and talks about other topics than gaolers and prison-walls? The world outside has not become less real because the prisoner cannot see it. In using the word Escape in this way the critics ... are confusing ... the Escape of the Prisoner with the Flight of the Deserter.'

(3) Consolation. All fairy-tales and fantasy should have the 'Consolation of the Happy Ending' or *Eucatastrophe*. This is not to deny the existence of sorrow and failure: 'the possibility of these is necessary to the joy of deliverance.' Nevertheless, the Happy Ending denies 'universal final defeat' and provides 'a sudden glimpse of the underlying reality or truth.' After all, the Gospel or *Evangelium* contains 'a story of a larger kind which embraces all the essence of fairy stories.' It has entered History and the Primary World. 'The Birth of Christ is the eucatastrophe of Man's history. The Resurrection is the eucatastrophe of the story of the Incarnation. This story begins and ends in joy. It has pre-eminently the "inner consistency of reality". There is no tale ever told that men would rather find was true, and none which so many sceptical men have accepted as true on its own merits. For the Art of it has the supremely

convincing tone of Primary Art, that is, of Creation. To reject it leads either to sadness or to wrath.' We must not imagine that in God's kingdom the presence of the greatest depresses the small. The *Evangelium* has not destroyed stories, but hallowed them, especially those with the 'happy ending'. God has given Man so great a bounty that in writing Fantasy he is able to 'assist in the effoliation and multiple enrichment of creation.'

IV: The 'Baptizing' of Lewis's Imagination

The imaginative writings of Lewis's boyhood had not contained 'the sparkle and the dew-drops' of his later writings, and even those might not have contained such qualities had he not discovered George MacDonald's *Phantastes* on 4 March 1916. He was an atheist then, and describing his first reading of this book in **GMD**, he said: 'I had already been waist deep in Romanticism; and likely enough, at any moment, to flounder into its darker and more evil forms, slithering down the steep descent that leads from the love of strangeness to that of eccentricity and thence to that of perversity. Now *Phantastes* ... had about it a sort of cool, morning innocence ... What it actually did to me was to convert, even to baptize ... my imagination.'

How did the book 'baptize' his imagination? The fullest answer is found in **SBJ** XII: 'I saw the bright shadow coming out of the book into the real world and resting there, transforming all common things and yet itself unchanged. Or, more accurately, I saw the common things drawn into the bright shadow.'

V: Reason and Imagination

About the time of his conversion in 1929–31 Lewis was uncertain of the relation between Imagination and Truth, and between Imagination and Reason, and this became the subject of a poem written about that time. In 'Reason' he contrasts Reason (the 'Maid') and Imagination (Demeter or the 'mother') and the poem concludes:

> Oh who will reconcile in me both maid and mother,
> Who make in me a concord of the depth and height?
> Who make imagination's dim exploring touch
> Ever report the same as intellectual sight?
> Then could I truly say, and not deceive,
> Then wholly say, that I BELIEVE. (**P, CP**)

Unless it was written before his conversion, and copied into his notebook later, it is probable that when he wrote the poem Reason was already 'reporting the same' as Imagination. In 1931 Lewis hoped that T.S. Eliot would publish some of his essays in the *Criterion*. He had in mind his essay on **The Personal Heresy (PH)**, as well as others he hoped to write, and in his letter to Eliot of 2 June 1931 he said the completed series

> would form a frontal attack on Crocean aesthetics and state a neo-Aristotelian theory of literature ... which *inter alia* will re-affirm the romantic doctrine of imagination as a truth-bearing faculty, though not quite as the romantics understood it (**BIO** V).

VI: Myth and Imagination

Lewis was still struggling to find a clear connection between Imagination and Truth when he spent the evening of 19 September 1931 in the company of Tolkien and Hugo Dyson.* Up until then he had believed the Christian 'myth' to be as false as the Pagan myths, but Tolkien and Dyson changed that (See **Myths§**). We know from Tolkien's **On Fairy-Stories** that it was Lewis who described myth and fairy story as 'Breathing a lie through Silver', and that *Mythopoeia* was written in response to the position Lewis had held up to 19 September 1931. When Lewis wrote to Arthur Greeves on 18 October 1931 about their momentous conversation he said he was now able to accept the story of Christ as 'a true myth':

> a myth working on us in the same way as the others, but with this tremendous difference that *it really happened*: and one must be content to accept it in the same way, remembering that it is God's myth where the others are men's myths: i.e. the Pagan stories are God expressing Himself through the minds of poets, using such images as He found there, while Christianity is God expressing Himself through what we call 'real things' (**TST**).

In 1932 Lewis told the story of his conversion in the form of the allegorical *The Pilgrim's Regress* (1933). In Book VIII, chapter 8, History explains to the pilgrim John that whereas the Landlord (God) gave the Shepherds (the Jews) Rules and set their feet on a 'Road', He gave the Pagans 'pictures'. The mythology of the Pagans contained a 'divine call'. However, they (like Lewis) mistook the 'pictures' and 'desires' for what they were not, and instead of turning to Mother Kirk they became 'corrupt in their *imaginations*'. 'These pictures,' History tells John, 'this ignorance of writing – this endless desire which so easily confuses itself with other desires and, at best, remains pure only by knowing what it does *not* want – you see that it is a starting point from which *one* road leads home and a thousand roads lead into the wilderness.'

At the end of the book we learn that John has had his imagination 'baptized'. As they begin the 'regress' the Guide says: 'I should warn you of one thing – the country will look very different on the return journey' (IX, 6). As they go on, John looks in vain for the house of Mr Sensible. '"It is just as when you passed it before," said the Guide, "but your eyes are altered. You see nothing now but realities: and Mr Sensible was so near to nonentity – so shadowy even as an appearance – that he is now invisible to you."' (X, 2). This, as with *Phantastes*, is an instance of 'common things' being 'baptized' or 'altered' by being 'drawn into the bright shadow.'

VII: Imagination the 'organ of meaning'

Had Imagination finally become 'a truth-bearing faculty'? What now is the relation between Imagination and Reason? Certainly, Lewis had a clearer notion of the connection between them. His essay **Bluspels and Flalansferes**, written in the 1930s, is about a dispute as to what extent 'dead' metaphors – those whose original meaning has been forgotten – condition present meaning. He believed that 'he who would increase the meaning and decrease the meaningless verbiage in his own speech and writing, must do two things. He must become conscious of fossilized metaphors in his words; and he must freely use new metaphors, which he creates for himself. The first depends on knowledge, and therefore on leisure; the second on a certain degree of imaginative ability. The second is perhaps the more important of the two: we are never less the slaves of metaphor than when we are making metaphor, or hearing it new made.' He concludes: 'It must not be supposed that I am putting forward the imagination as the organ of truth ... For me reason is the natural organ of truth; but imagination is the organ of meaning. Imagination, producing new metaphors or revivifying old, is not the cause of truth, but its condition.'

Lewis was never able to claim as much objectivity for literature as he would have liked. Still, while he never gave up his objective approach to truth and values, he did this through being as clear and objective about his own pictures and thinking as he could. He was quick to spot why some imaginations were not 'truth-bearing', and over the years he gave a number of reasons for this. Let us look at a few. The Pagans, as he said in the **PR** had become 'corrupt in their imaginations' and this affected the pictures they used. In his 'Conclusion' to *A Preface to 'Paradise Lost'* he deplores 'stream of consciousness' literature which pretends to present '"life" in the raw':

The disorganized consciousness which it regards as specially real is in fact highly artificial. It is discovered by introspection – that is, by artificially suspending all the normal and outgoing activities of the mind and then attending to what is left. In that residuum it discovers no concentrated will, no logical thought, no morals, no stable sentiments, and (in a word) no mental hierarchy … It is like trying to see what a thing looks like when you are not looking at it … There may be a place for literature which tries to exhibit what we are doing when will and reason and attention and organized imagination are all off duty and sleep has not yet supervened. But I believe that if we regard such literature as specially realistic we are falling into illusion.

In his work on the Arthurian poems of Charles Williams* (**AT**) Lewis said in his 'Conclusions' that we demand that poems have 'Strength of Incantation', which is another instance of 'sub-creation': 'The imagined world of the poem must have a consistency and vitality which lay hold of the mind. It must not be left to *us* to keep it going. It should be difficult for us to escape from it. It should remain with us as a stubborn memory like some real place where we have once lived – a real place with its characteristic smells, sounds and colours: its unmistakable, and irreplaceable "tang".'

VIII: Myth as an 'organ of reality'

Lewis saw a clear connection between Myth and Imagination. To begin with, he would have pointed out that while Myths are works of the Imagination, it does not follow that all works of the Imagination are Myths. Most stories depend to a large degree on the actual words an author uses. In **On Stories** Lewis illustrated why this is so. In books about 'Red Indians', such as those by James Fenimore Cooper, the substitution of a pistol for a tomahawk would ruin the story. This is because we want 'not the momentary suspense but that whole world to which it belonged – the snow and the snow-shoes, beavers and canoes, war-paths and wigwams, and Hiawatha names.'

Myths, on the other hand, have no such dependence on words. 'There is … a particular kind of story which has a value in itself,' he said in **EIC** V, 'a value independent of its embodiment in any literary work. The story of Orpheus strikes and strikes deep … It is true that such a story can hardly reach us except in words. But that is logically accidental. If some perfected art of mime or silent film or serial pictures could make it clear with no words at all, it would still affect us in the same way.'

Perhaps the most remarkable claim made for Myth is found in **Myth Became Fact** where Lewis argues that:

> In the enjoyment of a great myth we come nearest to experiencing as a concrete what can otherwise be understood only as an abstraction ... [In enjoying a myth] you are not looking for an abstract "meaning" at all ... You were not knowing, but tasting; but what you were tasting turns out to be a universal principle. The moment we *state* this principle, we are admittedly back in the world of abstraction. It is only while receiving the myth as a story that you experience the principle concretely. When we translate we get abstraction – or rather, dozens of abstractions. What flows into you from the myth is not truth but reality (truth is always *about* something, but reality is that *about which* truth is), and, therefore, every myth becomes the father of innumerable truths on the abstract level.

IX: Two Commentators

We now look at the writings of two of those who have written about Lewis and the Imagination. Peter J. Schakel's *Reason and Imagination in C.S. Lewis: A Study of 'Till We Have Faces'* (1984) looks at the relation between these two things. 'This book examines,' he says in the Preface, 'the place of reason and imagination in the thought of C.S. Lewis and shows that a shift, not in basic positions or theory but certainly in emphasis and practice, occurs, not at the time of his conversion but in the late 1940s or early 1950s. Prior to that – in *Mere Christianity* and the Ransom trilogy, for example – Lewis relied heavily upon, or put his ultimate trust in, reason (the capacity for analysis, abstraction, logical deductions), with imagination (the image-making, fictionalizing, integrative power) playing a valued but limited supporting role. After that, Lewis's confidence in imaginative methods increases, and imagination becomes the more striking feature of his work from the 1950s on – in the Chronicles of Narnia, for example. My purpose is to chart the changes briefly, account for them as fully as possible, and show that in some of his later works, such as *Till We Have Faces* and *Letters to Malcolm*, reason and imagination are, at last, reconciled and unified.'

A different approach is taken by Owen Barfield* in 'Lewis, Truth, and Imagination' (**OBCSL**). He gives several reasons why he thinks Lewis was reticent to attempt anything like a theory of imagination. (1) Because he was 'in love with' imagination he 'had within him this loving impulse to protect and insulate imagination, so that it could continue to live its own pure and chaste life; to insulate it, therefore, from having anything whatever to do with *fact*.' Barfield points out that in **Is Theology Poetry?** Lewis suggested that 'there is something in belief which is hostile to perfect imaginative enjoyment.'

(2) If imagination is taken as a 'way of *thinking*, and therefore of acquiring knowledge', then 'the kind of thinking it is bears a strong superficial resemblance to that blur of confused impressions into which ... Lewis found the intellectual world as a whole degenerating under the influence of subjectivism and relativism – a sort of mishmash, in which nothing is definitely anything, because everything is also everything else ... when any question was at issue bearing on truth or knowledge, he preferred to leave out imagination altogether.'

(3) It is characteristic of images that 'they interpenetrate one another' but when there is interpenetration of one determinate meaning with another determinate meaning we get equivocation. 'Lewis's just hatred of his sworn foe, mishmash, led him beyond mere reticence on the subject of imagination and into a strong repugnance to the idea of interpenetration of any sort, whether material or psychic or spiritual. Compare the imagery of Dante's *Paradiso* with the imagery Lewis employs for his dream of heaven in *The Great Divorce*. The beings in Dante's heaven are constantly presented in terms of light, of lights mirroring each other, entering each other, interpenetrating each other, indwelling each other, after the manner of luminous beams. In the heaven of *The Great Divorce* what is remorselessly emphasized is the impenetrable *solidity* of everything and everybody. There is indeed a realm where the opposite obtains, where *nothing* is solid, and whose inhabitants have the capacity of ultimately interpenetrating, or absorbing, or slithering into, one another. But for Lewis, and I think also for his friend Charles Williams, the name of this particular part of the spiritual world was hell.'

Barfield concludes that it was in his religious writings, even more than in his work on English literature, that Reason and Imagination 'came nearest to joining hands'. This is best illustrated by Lewis's sermon, **Transposition**. 'In it,' says Mr Barfield, 'he begins by directing attention to one particular instance where the problem of meaning, or the relation between apparent meaninglessness and actual meaning, arises in an acute form; namely, the phenomenon of glossolalia, or "speaking in tongues". Hysteria, or the Holy Spirit bearing witness with our spirit? Mishmash, or valid, though nonlogical, communication?' 'His argument,' says Mr Barfield,

is that 'what is happening in the lower medium can be understood only if we know the higher medium.' Confronted with a picture in two dimensions, only a mind which had some experience or knowledge of the real world of three dimensions could discern that what the picture represents is not a copy, but a kind of *transposition*, of such a real world. He gives other examples ... For instance, what [some] would call 'a man without imagination' he calls 'the observer who knows only the lower medium', and he adds that the world of such a man must necessarily be 'all fact and no meaning'. It took me some time to realize that, whatever else it is as well, 'Transposition' can be seen as a theory of imagination ... I am not sure whether there is anything like it anywhere else in Lewis's writing, but that little sermon 'Transposition' amounts in my view to a theory of imagination, in which imagination is not mentioned.

To this theory we should add a point made by Owen Barfield in 'Some Reflections on *The Great Divorce*' (**OBCSL**). 'In *The Great Divorce*,' he said, 'mythopoeic Lewis, with a touch of violence that is itself perhaps more characteristic of atomic Lewis, employs not only material shapes but *materiality itself* to symbolize immateriality. All the description concentrates on heaven as a *solid* place. Heaven itself almost *is* solidity, and its inhabitants are regularly referred to as "the solid People" by contrast with the wraithlike visitants from hell ... In other words, mythopoeic Lewis, the builder, filches from atomic Lewis the concrete-reality principle, which he had always kept so fastidiously at arm's length, and inserts it as the keystone of his supporting arch!'

INNER RING: In the essay of this title Lewis says 'I believe that in all men's lives at certain periods, and in many men's lives at all periods between infancy and extreme old age, one of the most dominant elements is the desire to be inside the local Ring and the terror of being left outside.' One form of this desire is snobbery, but Lewis's interest is in another kind. A man with an 'itch' for this inner ring wants 'the sacred little attic or studio, the heads bent together, the fog of tobacco smoke, and the delicious knowledge that we – we four or five all huddled beside this stove – are the people who *know*.' Not all 'rings' are in themselves evil, and most of those between friends are good. The real 'inner ringer' is different. To him the desire to be on the 'inside' is one of the 'permanent mainsprings' of life. He values being on the 'inside' mainly because others are 'outside', and he is willing to become a great scoundrel rather than find himself being thrust back into the 'cold outer world'.

Mark Studdock in **THS** is the 'inner ringer' *par excellence*. When Lord Feverstone has a private word with him about College matters 'the giddy sensation of being suddenly whirled up from one plane of secrecy to another ... prevented him from speaking' (2:i). At Belbury, while having to work with the insignificant Cosser, 'it came over Mark what a terrible bore this little man was, and in the same moment he felt utterly sick of the N.I.C.E. But he reminded himself that one could not expect to be in the interesting set at once' (4:vi). When Stone falls out of favour with the Inner Ring at Belbury Mark is afraid to speak to him. 'He knew by experience how dangerous it is to be friends with a sinking man or even to be seen with him: you cannot keep him afloat and he may pull you under' (5:ii). After the N.I.C.E. has him write some dishonest articles for the newspapers, 'The idea of the immense dynamo which had been placed for the moment at his disposal, thrilled through his whole being ... The child inside him whispered how splendid and how triumphantly grown up it was to [have] ... all the inner ring of the N.I.C.E. depending on him, and nobody ever again having the least right to consider him a nonentity or cipher' (6:iv). Much later, when he is disgraced and forced to attend to the tramp who is thought to be Merlin, Mark finds an 'inner ring' that is not corrupting: 'Here, where there was no room for vanity and no more power or security than that of "children playing in a giant's kitchen", he had unaware become a member of a "circle", as secret and as strongly fenced against outsiders as any that he had dreamed of' (14:iv).

ITCH FOR THE HYPOTHETICAL, THE: Lewis was a master of 'supposals' which brought the imagination into play, such as inventing Narnia, but which did not contradict the real. On the other hand, he regarded the attempt to avoid the truth by way of the hypothetical extremely unhealthy. A good example is found in the chapter on 'Divine Omnipotence' in PP II. In a discussion about the words 'With God all things are possible' (Matthew 19:26), he says 'If you choose to say "God can give a creature free-will and at the same time withhold free-will from it," you have not succeeded in saying *anything* about God: meaningless combinations of words do not suddenly acquire meaning simply because we prefix to them the two other words "God can" ... nonsense remains nonsense even when we talk it about God.' In *Perelandra* we find the Itch for Repetition and the Itch for the Hypothetical combined. The Un-man taunts Ransom for shrinking 'back from the wave that is coming towards us' because he would like 'to bring back the wave that is past' (9) while urging the Lady to consider what would happen *if* she disobeyed Maleldil. 'The ideas of the Great Deed, of the Great Risk, of a kind of martyrdom, were presented to her every day' (10).

An example of a different sort is found in the chapter on 'The Fall of Man' in **PPL** where the right time for asking the great 'if' is not raised at the right time. Lewis is discussing Milton's *Paradise Lost* and he regrets that Adam, following his wife's fall, does not scold or even chastize Eve and intercede with God on her behalf. 'We see the results of our actions,' he says, 'but we do not know what would have happened if we had abstained. For all Adam knew, God might have had other cards in His hand; but Adam never raised the question, and now nobody will ever know. Rejected goods are invisible.'

The most delightful example of this itch is found in the chapter 'The Bell and the Hammer' in **MN** where Digory is made wildly curious by the verse on the bell:

> *Make your choice, adventurous Stranger;*
> *Strike the bell and bide the danger,*
> *Or wonder, till it drives you mad,*
> *What would have followed if you had.*

In **PC** 10 the children fail to follow Aslan. Lucy asks Aslan what '*would* have happened' if they had done as they should have. 'Nobody is ever told that,' he says, 'but anyone can find out what *will* happen.' And in **HHB** 11 when Shasta asks to understand the action of Aslan in Aravis's life, the Lion says: 'I tell no one any story but his own.'

ITCH FOR REPETITION, THE: The best example of this itch is found in **PER** 4. Ransom, having found one of the bubble fruit sufficient for his needs, is tempted to plunge 'through the whole lot of them and to feel, all at once, that magical refreshment multiplied tenfold.' Then he thinks: 'This itch to have things over again, as if life were a film that could be unrolled twice or even made to work backwards ... was it possibly the root of all evil? No: of course the love of money was called that. But money itself – perhaps one valued it chiefly as a defence against chance, a security for being able to have things over again, a means of arresting the unrolling of the film.'

In **LTM** V Lewis regrets that we often 'sulkily, reject the good that God offers us because, at that moment, we expected some other good ... we are always harking back to some occasion which seemed to us to reach perfection, setting that up as a norm, and depreciating all other occasions by comparison ... It would be rash to say that there is any prayer which God *never* grants. But the strongest candidate is the prayer we might express in the single word *encore*. And how should the Infinite repeat

Himself? All space and time are too little for Him to utter Himself in them *once.'*

JOY: In **SBJ** I Lewis said the 'central story of my life is about nothing else,' and he went on to define Joy: 'It is an unsatisfied desire which is itself more desirable than any other satisfaction. I call it Joy, which is here a technical term and must be sharply distinguished both from Happiness and from Pleasure. Joy (in my sense) has indeed one characteristic, and one only, in common with them; the fact that anyone who has experienced it will want it again ... It might almost equally well be called a particular kind of unhappiness or grief. But then it is a kind we want.' The idea – or one very close to it – first appeared in his poem 'Joy' (1923). After his conversion it became the dominant theme in his semi-autobiographical **PR** (1933). But, apart from **SBJ**, the clearest exposition is to be found in the Preface of the new and revised edition of **PR** (1943). Central to an understanding of Joy is the sermon, **The Weight of Glory**.

LAW OF INATTENTION, THE: This law enjoins us to appreciate the Quiddity§ of things and to look away from the Self. Not named as such by Lewis, this principle is fundamental to his thought and so frequently adumbrated as to be nearly ubiquitous in his writing. At the level of practical guidance (and for the sake of illustration) Lewis reminds us that we are often *least* reverential when at worship, or *least* in love on our wedding day, respectively *because*, aware as we are of the emotions that ought to accompany these occasions, we attempt to manufacture them in ourselves. The proper technique, he says, is to forget the Self entirely and, instead, to pay attention to God (the object of our reverence) or to our beloved (the object of our love). Ultimately based upon Lewis's distinction (from **Meditation in a Toolshed**) between 'looking at' and 'looking along' (which itself derives from Samuel Alexander's *Space, Time and Deity,* a book of overwhelming importance to Lewis), it is centrally expressed in **SBJ** XV, immediately following Lewis's discussion of Alexander's book and his declaration of the distinction as 'an indispensable tool of thought': 'The surest way of spoiling a pleasure [is] to start examining your satisfaction ... [It follows] that all introspection is in one respect misleading. In introspection we try to look "inside ourselves" and see what is going on. But nearly everything that was going on a moment before is stopped by the very act of our turning to look at it.'

This epistemological insight Lewis applies to many activities, from prayer to literary experience; and it is the premise of his attack upon emotion as a suitable basis on which to accept as true any given proposition, religious or otherwise. 'To see things as the poet sees them,' he said in **PH** I, 'I must share his consciousness and not attend to it; I must look where he looks and not turn round to face him; I must make of him not a spectacle but a pair of spectacles: in fine, as Professor Alexander would say, I must *enjoy* him and not *contemplate* him.' 'The disorganized consciousness which ['stream of consciousness' critics] regard as specially real is in fact highly artificial. It is discovered by introspection – that is, by artificially suspending all the normal and outgoing activities of the mind and then attending to what is left. In that residuum it discovers no concentrated will, no logical thought, no morals, no stable sentiments, and (in a word) no mental hierarchy. Of course not; for we have deliberately stopped all these things in order to introspect. The poet who finds by introspection that the soul is mere chaos is like a policeman who, having himself stopped all the traffic in a certain street, should then solemnly write down in his notebook "The stillness in this street is highly suspicious" ... The very nature of such unfocused consciousness is that it is not attended to. Inattention makes it what it is' (**PPL** XIX). In paying excessive attention to our own emotions we thus miss out on the world and, ultimately, on God Himself, who 'walks everywhere' but is 'everywhere *incognito*' (**LTM** XIV).

LOVE AND KINDNESS – the difference between: In **PP** III Lewis points out that 'By the goodness of God we mean nowadays almost exclusively His lovingness ... And by Love ... most of us mean kindness – the desire to see others than the self happy; not happy in this way or in that, but just happy ... When kindness ... is separated from the other elements of Love, it involves a certain fundamental indifference to its object, and even something like contempt of it ... It is for people whom we care nothing about that we demand happiness on any terms: with our friends, our lovers, our children, we are exacting and would rather see them suffer much than be happy in contemptible and estranging modes.'

We are certainly urged to be more 'exacting' in **The Weight of Glory** where Lewis points out that as there are no *'ordinary* people', only 'possible gods and goddesses', 'Our charity must be a real and costly love, with deep feeling for the sins in spite of which we love the sinner – no mere tolerance, or indulgence which parodies love.' But perhaps the most astringent example of the necessity of putting Love before Kindness is found in **GD** XIII where Lewis complains to George MacDonald that some people say that 'the final loss of one soul gives the lie to all the joy of those who are saved.' MacDonald answers that while this 'sounds very merciful' what lurks behind it is 'The demand of the loveless and the self-imprisoned that they should be allowed to blackmail the universe: that till they consent to be happy (on their own terms) no one else shall taste joy: that theirs should be the final power; that Hell should be able to *veto* Heaven.'

MERE CHRISTIANITY: Lewis borrowed the phrase from Richard Baxter, who used it in *Church-History of the Government of Bishops* (1680). 'What History is Credible, and what not.' Lewis used it first in his Introduction to Sister Penelope's* translation of *The Incarnation of the Word of God* (1944). In the Introduction, reprinted as **On the Reading of Old Books**, he spoke of 'a standard of plain, central Christianity ('mere Christianity' as Baxter called it),' and he went on to say:

> If any man is tempted to think ... that 'Christianity' is a word of so many meanings that it means nothing at all, he can learn beyond all doubt, by stepping out of his own century, that this is not so. Measured against the ages 'mere Christianity' turns out to be no insipid interdenominational transparency, but something positive, self-consistent, and inexhaustible ... We are all rightly distressed, and ashamed also at the divisions of Christendom ... They are bad, but such people do not know what it looks like from without. Seen from there, what is left intact, despite all the divisions, still appears (as it truly is) an immensely formidable unity.

We find the phrase next used in the Preface to *Mere Christianity* where it is defined as 'the belief that has been common to nearly all Christians at all times.' The fullest understanding of the term is to be had from reading the book.

MONARCHY: In **Equality** Lewis complained that 'When equality is treated not as a medicine or a safety-gadget but as an ideal we begin to breed that stunted and envious sort of mind which hates all superiority. That mind is the special disease of democracy ... The man who cannot conceive a joyful and loyal obedience on the one hand, nor an unembarrassed and noble acceptance of that obedience on the other, the man who has never wanted to kneel or to bow, is a prosaic barbarian.' He goes on to say that the answer to this in Britain is the Monarchy:

> We Britons should rejoice that we have contrived to reach much legal democracy ... without losing our ceremonial Monarchy. For there, right in the midst of our lives, is that which satisfies the craving for inequality, and acts as a permanent reminder that

medicine is not food. Hence, a man's reaction to Monarchy is a kind of test. Monarchy can easily be 'debunked'; but watch the faces, mark well the accents, of the debunkers. These are the men whose tap-root in Eden has been cut: whom no rumour of the polyphony, the dance, can reach – men to whom pebbles laid in a row are more beautiful than an arch. Yet even if they desire mere equality they cannot reach it. Where men are forbidden to honour a king they honour millionaires, athletes, or film-stars instead: even famous prostitutes or gangsters. For spiritual nature, like bodily nature, will be served; deny it food and it will gobble poison.

A year later, drawing on *Pride and Prejudice*, he raised the question in **Myth Became Fact** as to whether Monarchy is rational. '"Would not conversation be much more rational than dancing?" said Jane Austen's Miss Bingley. "Much more rational," replied Mr Bingley, "but much less like a ball."

In the same way, it would be much more rational to abolish the English monarchy. But how if, by doing so, you leave out the one element in our State which matters most? How if the monarchy is the channel through which all the *vital* elements of citizenship – loyalty, the consecration of secular life, the hierarchical principle, splendour, ceremony, continuity – still trickle down to irrigate the dustbowl of modern economic Statecraft?

At this time Lewis was at work on **THS** in which his central character, Jane Studdock, an extreme democrat averse to obedience in marriage, begins to practise a 'joyful and loyal obedience' towards God and her husband. This came as a result of meeting Ransom who, though not a king, she recognizes as her superior: 'For the first time in all those years she tasted the word *King* itself with all linked associations of battle, marriage, priesthood, mercy and power', and 'her world was unmade' (7:i). The books in which Lewis most rejoiced in Monarchy and Inequality are, of course, the Chronicles of Narnia.

The Narnian Monarchy is never allowed absolute rule, but owes obedience to Aslan who is 'the King of the wood and the son of the great Emperor-Beyond-the-Sea' (**LWW** 8), and 'The High King above all kings' (**HHB** 11). In establishing the Monarchy in the **MN** 11, Aslan says 'As Adam's race has done the harm, Adam's race shall help to heal it.' In administering what might be called the Coronation oath to King Frank I, Aslan says:

You shall rule and name all these creatures, and do justice among
them, and protect them from their enemies when enemies arise ...
Can you use a spade and a plough and raise food out of the earth?
... Can you rule these creatures kindly and fairly, remembering that
they are not slaves like the dumb beasts of the world you were born
in? ... And would you bring up your children and grandchildren to
do the same? ... And you wouldn't have favourites either among
your own children or among the other creatures or let any hold
another under or use it hardly? ... And if enemies came against the
land ... and there was war, would you be the first in the charge and
the last in the retreat?

Defending the monarchical impulse caused by the Narnian stories, Lewis
said in a letter to Patricia Hillis of Austin, Texas, on 10 March 1959:
'American children, as I know from the letters they write me, are just as
"Aslan-olatrous" as English ones. The world of fairy-tale, as the world of
Christianity, makes the heart and imagination royalist in a sense which
mere politics hardly [touches]. What my stories do is to liberate – to free
from inhibitions – a spontaneous impulse to serve and adore, to have a
"dearest dread", which the modern world starves, or diverts to film-stars,
crooners, and athletes.'

When Mrs Mary Willis Shelburne asked him about the Coronation of
Elizabeth II, Lewis made a serious point about monarchy in his reply of 10
July 1953. 'Over here,' he said,

people did *not* get that fairy-tale feeling about the coronation. What
impressed most who saw it was the fact that the Queen herself
appeared to be quite overwhelmed by the sacramental side of it.
Hence, in the spectators, a feeling of (one hardly knows how to
describe it) – awe – pity – pathos – mystery. The pressing of that
huge, heavy crown on that small, young head becomes a sort of
symbol of the situation of *humanity* itself: humanity called by God
to be His vice-regent and high priest on earth, yet feeling so
inadequate. As if He said, 'In my inexorable love I shall lay upon
the dust that you are glories and dangers and responsibilities
beyond your understanding.' Do you see what I mean? One has
missed the whole point unless one feels that we have all been
crowned and that coronation is somehow, if splendid, a tragic
splendour (**LAL**). (see **Equality**§.)

MYTH:

I: Myth as Falsehood

In **SBJ** IV Lewis said one of the reasons he ceased to believe in Christianity when he was a schoolboy was because the editors of Classical texts 'took it for granted from the outset that these religious ideas were sheer illusion. No one ever attempted to show in what sense Christianity fulfilled Paganism or Paganism prefigured Christianity.' As a result, when he wrote to Arthur Greeves* on 12 October 1916 he said he had reached the conclusion that 'All religions, that is all mythologies to give them their proper name, are merely man's own invention – Christ as much as Loki' **(TST)**.

II: Christianity a 'True Myth'

This view of myth as falsehood remained mainly intact until 1931. Following a conversation with J.R.R. Tolkien* and Hugo Dyson* about Christian and Pagan Myth on 19 September 1931 Lewis wrote to Arthur Greeves on 1 October to say he had 'just passed on from believing in God to definitely believing in Christ – in Christianity ... Dyson and Tolkien had a good deal to do with it' **(TST)**. Then, in a letter of 18 October he explained that

> what Dyson and Tolkien showed me was this: that if I met the idea of sacrifice in a Pagan story I didn't mind it at all: again, that if I met the idea of a god sacrificing himself to himself ... I liked it very much and was mysteriously moved by it: again, that the idea of a dying and reviving god (Balder, Adonis, Bacchus) similarly moved me provided I met it anywhere *except* in the gospels. The reason was that in Pagan stories I was prepared to feel the myth as profound and suggestive of meanings beyond my grasp even though I could not say in cold prose 'what it meant'. Now the story of Christ is simply a true myth: a myth working on us in the same way as the others, but with this tremendous difference that *it really happened*: and one must be content to accept it in the same way, remembering that it is God's myth where the others are men's myths: i.e. the Pagan stories are God expressing Himself through the minds of poets, using such images as He found there, while Christianity is God expressing Himself through what we call 'real things'. Therefore it is *true*, not in the sense of being a "description" of God (that no finite mind could take in) but in the sense of being the way in which God chooses to (or can) appear to our faculties.

The "doctrines" we get *out of* the true myth are of course *less* true: they are translations into our *concepts* and *ideas* of that which God has already expressed in a language more adequate, namely the actual incarnation, crucifixion, and resurrection (**TST**).

It was not long after this that Lewis wrote *The Pilgrim's Regress* (1933). In this allegorical account of his conversion History explains to the pilgrim John that whereas the Landlord (God) gave the Shepherds (the Jews) Rules and set their feet on a 'Road,' He gave the Pagans 'pictures'. The mythology of the Pagans contained a 'divine call'. But they (like Lewis with his early misunderstanding about 'Joy') mistook the 'pictures' and 'desires' for what they were not, and instead of turning to Mother Kirk they became 'corrupt in their imaginations' (IX: 8). Later on John meets Mother Kirk who says:

> Child, if you will, it *is* mythology. It is but truth, not fact: an image, not the very real. But then it is My mythology. The words of Wisdom are also myth and metaphor: but since they do not know themselves for what they are, in them the hidden myth is master, where it should be servant: and it is but of man's inventing. But this is My inventing, this is the veil under which I have chosen to appear even from the first until now. For this end I made your senses and for this end your imagination, that you might see My face and live. What would you have? Have you not heard among the Pagans the story of Semele? Or was there any age in any land when men did not know that corn and wine were the blood and body of a dying and yet living God? (IX: 5).

This had become clearer to Lewis by the time he gave his talks on **What Christians Believe** over the BBC in January–February 1942. In the one called **The Shocking Alternative**, (**MC** II: 3) he said God took three actions about the Fall, one of which was to send the human race 'what I call good dreams: I mean those queer stories scattered all through the heathen religions about a god who dies and comes to life again and, by his death, has somehow given new life to men.'

III: Myth as Fact

Myth Became Fact (1944) contains Lewis's fullest statement about Myth. He cites the Incarnation as the supreme example of Myth becoming fact. 'Human intellect,' he said, 'is incurably abstract ... Yet the only realities we experience are concrete – this pain, this pleasure, this dog, this man.

While we are loving the man, bearing the pain, enjoying the pleasure, we are not intellectually apprehending Pleasure, Pain or Personality. When we begin to do so, on the other hand, the concrete realities sink to the level of mere instances or examples ... This is our dilemma – either to taste and not to know or to know and not to taste – or, more strictly, to lack one kind of knowledge because we are in an experience or to lack another kind because we are outside it.' Of this tragic dilemma, he says,

> myth is the partial solution. In the enjoyment of a great myth we come nearest to experiencing as a concrete what can otherwise be understood only as an abstraction. At this moment, for example, I am trying to understand something very abstract indeed – the fading, vanishing of tasted reality as we try to grasp it with the discursive reason ... If I remind you, instead, of Orpheus and Eurydice, how he was suffered to lead her by the hand but, when he turned round to look at her, she disappeared, what was merely a principle becomes imaginable. You may reply that you never till this moment attached that 'meaning' to that myth. Of course not. You are not looking for an abstract 'meaning' at all ... You were not knowing, but tasting; but what you were tasting turns out to be a universal principle. The moment we *state* this principle, we are admittedly back in the world of abstraction. It is only while receiving the myth as a story that you experience the principle concretely. When we translate we get abstraction – or rather, dozens of abstractions. What flows into you from the myth is not truth but reality (truth is always *about* something, but reality is that *about which* truth is), and, therefore, every myth becomes the father of innumerable truths on the abstract level. Myth is the mountain whence all the different streams arise which become truths down here in the valley ... Or, if you prefer, myth is the isthmus which connects the peninsular world of thought with that vast continent we really belong to. It is not, like truth, abstract; nor is it, like direct experience, bound to the particular.

> Now as myth transcends thought, Incarnation transcends myth. The heart of Christianity is a myth which is also a fact. The old myth of the Dying God, *without ceasing to be myth*, comes down from the heaven of legend and imagination to the earth of history. It *happens* – at a particular date, in a particular place, followed by definable historical consequences. We pass from a Balder or an Osiris, dying nobody knows when or where, to a historical Person crucified (it is all in order) *under Pontius Pilate*.

In 1944 Lewis read a paper to the Socratic Club‡ entitled **Is Theology Poetry?** in which he expanded on the relation between the 'divine call' found in Pagan myths and the 'condensation of the myth as it becomes fact and also quite real':

> The Pagan stories are all about someone dying and rising, either every year, or else nobody knows where and nobody knows when. The Christian story is about a historical personage, whose execution can be dated pretty accurately ... It is not the difference between falsehood and truth. It is the difference between a real event on the one hand and dim dreams or premonitions of that same event on the other. It is like watching something come gradually into focus: first it hangs in the clouds of myth and ritual, vast and vague, then it condenses, grows hard and in a sense small, as a historical event in first century Palestine ... The essential meaning of all things came down from the 'heaven' of myth to the 'earth' of history. In so doing, it partly emptied itself of its glory, as Christ emptied Himself of His glory to be Man ... This is the humiliation of myth into fact, of God into Man: what is everywhere and always, imageless and ineffable, only to be glimpsed in dream and symbol and the acted poetry of ritual, becomes small, solid – no bigger than a man who can lie asleep in a rowing boat on the Lake of Galilee.

He did not mean that all Pagan myths were equally a 'divine hinting' of Christian truth. In **Religion Without Dogma?**, read to the Socratic Club in 1946, he said, 'I believe that in the huge mass of mythology which has come down to us a good many different sources are mixed – true history, allegory, ritual, the human delight in story-telling, etc. But among these sources I include the supernatural, both diabolical and divine.'

He was to mention the myth of the 'Dying and Reviving God' again in **M** (1947), where in chapter XV he says in footnote 1: 'My present view ... would be that just as, on the factual side, a long preparation culminates in God's becoming incarnate as Man, so, on the documentary side, the truth first appears in *mythical* form and then by a long process of condensing or focusing finally becomes incarnate as History. This involves the belief that Myth in general is not merely misunderstood history ... nor diabolical illusion ... nor priestly lying ... but, at its best, a real though unfocused gleam of divine truth falling on human imagination.'

IV: General Characteristics of Myth

Hitherto Lewis had been writing about the Myth of God incarnate, but in the Preface to his **GMD** (1946) he considers some general characteristics of myth:

> Myth does not essentially exist in *words* at all. We all agree that the story of Balder is a great myth, a thing of inexhaustible value. But of whose version – whose *words* – are we thinking when we say this? ...
>
> If the story is anywhere embodied in words, that is almost an accident. What really delights and nourishes me is a particular pattern of events, which would equally delight and nourish if it had reached me by some medium which involved no words at all – say a mime, or a film ...
>
> In poetry the words are the body, and the 'theme' or 'content' is the soul. But in myth the imagined events are the body and something inexpressible is the soul: the words, or mime, or film, or pictorial series are not even clothes – they are not much more than a telephone.

Much of this was later incorporated into the chapter **On Myth** in **EIC** in which he goes into greater detail. He cites the following as characteristics of Myth: (1) It is 'extra-literary'. (2) 'The pleasure of myth depends hardly at all on such usual narrative attractions as suspense or surprise.' (3) 'Human sympathy is at a minimum. We do not project ourselves at all strongly into the characters. They are like shapes moving in another world. We feel indeed that the pattern of their movements has a profound relevance to our own life.' (4) 'Myth is always, in one sense of that word, "fantastic".' (5) 'The experience may be sad or joyful but it is always grave.' (6) 'The experience is not only grave but awe-inspiring ... It is as if something of great moment had been communicated to us. The recurrent efforts of the mind to grasp – we mean, chiefly, to conceptualize – this something, are seen in the persistent tendency of humanity to provide myths with allegorical explanation. And after all allegories have been tried, the myth itself continues to feel more important than they.' See **Imagination§, Myth§** and **Pagan Christs§**.

NATURAL LAW: The classical definition of this is found in St Thomas Aquinas: 'The natural law is nothing other than the light of understanding placed in us by God; through it we know what we must do and what we must avoid. God has given this light or law at the creation' (*Collationes in decem praeceptis* 1). But long before that Cicero said (51 BC) in *De Republica*

11:33: 'There is in fact a true law – namely, right reason – which is in accordance with nature, applies to all men and is unchangeable and eternal.' The chief New Testament text on which Natural Law is based is Romans 2:14–15 where St Paul affirms that 'When Gentiles who have not the law do by nature what the law requires, they are a law to themselves, even though they do not have the law. They show that what the law requires is written on their hearts, while their conscience also bears witness.' Lewis in **AOM** (I) defines it as 'the doctrine of objective value, the belief that certain attitudes are really true, and others really false, to the kind of thing the universe is and the kind of things we are.'

I: Right and Wrong

Lewis was to devote an important part of his writings to explaining and defending Natural Law, although it should be pointed out that he did not always call it 'Natural Law' but used a variety of terms for the sake of freshness. His first series of BBC talks, **Right and Wrong as a Clue to the Meaning of the Universe** (**MC** Book I) is entirely about Natural Law. In the first talk he said: 'This Law or Rule about Right and Wrong used to be called the Law of Nature. Nowadays, when we talk of the "laws of nature" we usually mean things like gravitation, or heredity, or the laws of chemistry. But when the older thinkers called the Law of Right and Wrong "the Law of Nature", they really meant the Law of *Human* Nature. The idea was that, just as all bodies are governed by the law of gravitation and organisms by biological laws, so the creature called man also had *his* law – with this great difference, that a body could not choose whether it obeyed the law of gravitation or not, but a man could choose either to obey the Law of Human Nature or to disobey it.' He ended with these two points:

> First ... human beings, all over the earth, have this curious idea that they ought to behave in a certain way, and cannot really get rid of it. Secondly ... they do not in fact behave in that way. They know the Law of Nature; they break it. These two facts are the foundation of all clear thinking about ourselves and the universe we live in.

II: On Ethics

About the same time that he gave his **Right and Wrong** talks, Lewis wrote an essay **On Ethics** much of which later went into *The Abolition of Man*. 'It is often asserted in modern England,' he began, 'that the world must return to Christian ethics in order to preserve civilization, or even in order to save the human species from destruction.' From there he goes on to refute two propositions: (1) Regarding the proposition 'That Christian

Ethics is one among several alternative bodies of injunctions ... clearly distinct from one another,' he said

> A Christian who understands his own religion laughs when unbelievers expect to trouble him by the assertion that Jesus uttered no command which had not been anticipated by the Rabbis – few, indeed, which cannot be paralleled in classical, ancient Egyptian, Ninevite, Babylonian or Chinese texts. We have long recognized that truth with rejoicing. Our faith is not pinned on a crank.

(2) To the proposition that we are able to stand 'outside all these systems in a sort of ethical vacuum, ready to enter whichever of them is most convincingly recommended to us', he replied:

> A man with no ethical allegiance can have no ethical motive for adopting one. If he had, it would prove that he was not really in the vacuum at all.

He goes on to argue that some, in an attempt to evade this difficulty, and to preserve the idea that they are able to exist in a moral vacuum, insist that 'the preservation of our species is not a moral imperative but an end prescribed by Instinct.' To this he replied: (a) *Instinct* is often 'used for what ought to be called appetite: thus we speak of the sexual instinct. *Instinct* in this sense means an impulse which appears in consciousness as desire, and whose fulfilment is marked by pleasure':

> That we have no instinct (in this sense) to preserve our species, seems to me self-evident. Desire is directed to the concrete – this woman, this plate of soup, this glass of beer: but the preservation of the species is a high abstraction which does not even enter the minds of unreflective people, and affects even cultured minds most at those times when they are least instinctive.

(b) To the argument that *Instinct* means 'a natural, unreflective, spontaneous impulse to ... preserve our offspring', he said: 'I do not find that I have this impulse, and I do not see evidence that other men have it':

> The truth seems to me to be that we have such an impulse to preserve our children and grandchildren, an impulse which progressively weakens as we carry our minds further and further into the abyss of future generations, and which ... soon dies out altogether.

Supposing, however, that we are 'outside all ethical systems', and with an instinct for the 'preservation of our species'. Why, he asks, should *this* instinct be preferred to all one's other instincts? It is often not even the strongest instinct we have. He believed that the attempt to argue on behalf of Instinct conceals a 'surreptitious re-introduction of the ethical':

> Those who expect us to adopt a moral code as a means to the preservation of the species have themselves already a moral code and tacitly assume that we have one too. Their starting point is a purely moral maxim *that humanity ought to be preserved*. The introduction of instinct is futile. If you do not arrange our instincts in a hierarchy of comparative dignity, it is idle to tell us to obey instinct, for the instincts are at war. If you do, then you are arranging them in obedience to a moral principle, passing an ethical judgement upon them.
>
> If instinct is your only standard, no instinct is to be preferred to another: for each of them will claim to be gratified at the expense of all the rest. Those who urge us to choose a moral code are already moralists. We may throw away the preposterous picture of a wholly unethical man confronted with a series of alternative codes and making his free choice between them. Nothing of the kind occurs. When a man is wholly unethical he does not choose between ethical codes. And those who say they are choosing between ethical codes are already assuming a code.

Where then do we get the maxim *that humanity ought to be preserved*? We find it in all the major religions, and 'from my point of view,' said Lewis, 'there is no particular mystery about this maxim. It is what I have been taught, explicitly and implicitly, by my nurse, my parents, my religion, by sages or poets from every culture of which I have any knowledge.' 'It is no more possible,' he said,

> to invent a new ethics than to place a new sun in the sky. Some precept from traditional morality always has to be assumed. We never start from a *tabula rasa*: if we did, we should end, ethically speaking, with a *tabula rasa*. New Moralities can only be contractions or expansions of something already given.

Lewis believed that in modern thought there had been a very serious exaggeration of the ethical differences between different cultures. This is enshrined in the word *ideologies*, which suggests that 'the whole moral and philosophical outlook of a people can be explained without remainder in terms of their method of production, their economic organization, and their geographical position.' Are they *really* very different? 'I would suggest,' said Lewis,

> that the appearance is somewhat illusory. It seems to me to result from a concentration on those very elements in each culture which are most variable (sexual practice and religious ritual) and also from a concentration on the savage. I have even found a tendency in some thinkers to treat the savage as the normal or archetypal man. But surely he is the exceptional man. It may indeed be true that we were all savages once, as it is certainly true that we were all babies once. But we do not treat as normal man the imbecile who remains in adult life what we all were (intellectually) in the cradle ...
>
> And if we turn to civilized man, I claim that we shall find far fewer differences of ethical injunction than is now popularly believed. In triumphant monotony the same indispensable platitudes will meet us in culture after culture. The idea that any of the new moralities now offered us would be simply one more addition to a variety already almost infinite, is not in accordance with the facts.

Finally, he insists that there are no 'ethical alternatives' that one may choose instead of traditional morality, or Natural Law. 'Those who urge us to adopt new morality,' he said

> are only offering us the mutilated or expurgated text of a book which we already possess in the original manuscript. They all wish us to depend on them instead of on that original, and then to deprive us of our full humanity. Their activity is in the long run always directed against our freedom.

III: The Abolition of Man

The most substantial contribution Lewis made to the subject comes in that powerful work *The Abolition of Man*. However, as it is covered elsewhere in this volume it is enough to mention a passage in which, using the Chinese word *Tao* for Natural Law, Lewis insisted that:

> This thing which I have called for convenience the *Tao*, and which others may call Natural Law ... is not one among a series of possible systems of value. It is the sole source of all value judgements. If it is

rejected, all value is rejected. If any value is retained, it is retained. The effort to refute it and raise a new system of value in its place is self-contradictory. There never has been, and never will be, a radically new judgement of value in the history of the world. What purport to be new systems or (as they now call them) 'ideologies', all consist of fragments from the *Tao* itself, arbitrarily wrenched from their context in the whole and then swollen to madness in their isolation, yet still owing to the *Tao* and to it alone such validity as they possess ... The human mind has no more power of inventing a new value than of imagining a new primary colour, or, indeed, of creating a new sun and new sky for it to move in (II).

IV: The Poison of Subjectivism

He returned to the subject in his essay **The Poison of Subjectivism**. By 'subjectivity' he meant the abandonment of objective *truth* and *reality* for whatever 'practical results' or 'ideologies' we happen to like. 'Until modern times,' he said, 'no thinker of the first rank ever doubted that our judgements of value were rational judgements or that what they discovered was objective. It was taken for granted that in temptation passion was opposed, not to some sentiment, but to reason. Thus Plato thought, thus Aristotle, thus Hooker, Butler and Doctor Johnson. The modern view is very different. It does not believe that value judgements are really judgements at all. They are sentiments, or complexes, or attitudes, produced in a community by the pressure of its environment and its traditions, and differing from one community to another. To say that a thing is good is merely to express our feelings about it; and our feeling about it is the feeling we have been socially conditioned to have.' 'On the contrary,' he warns,

> except on the supposition of a changeless standard, progress is impossible. If good is a fixed point, it is at least possible that we should get nearer and nearer to it; but if the terminus is as mobile as the train, how can the train progress towards it? Our ideas of the good may change, but they cannot change either for the better or the worse if there is no absolute and immutable good to which they can approximate or from which they can recede. We can go on getting a sum more and more nearly right only if the one perfect right answer is 'stagnant'.

Lewis suggests two propositions that should be 'written into our minds with indelible ink': (1) 'The human mind has no more power of inventing a new value than of planting a new sun in the sky or a new primary colour in the spectrum.' (2) 'Every attempt to do so consists in arbitrarily selecting some one maxim of traditional morality, isolating it from the rest, and erecting it into an *unum necessarium*'.

The second proposition needs illuminating because it is especially offended against by the modern reformer who, isolating some one precept from all the rest, insists that he *is* obeying Natural Law. Lewis explains how this works:

> By taking the second precept alone you construct a Futurist Ethic in which the claims of 'posterity' are the sole criterion. Ordinary morality tells us to keep promises and also to feed the hungry. By taking the second precept alone you get a Communist Ethic in which 'production', and distribution of the products to the people, are the sole criteria. Ordinary morality tells us, *ceteris paribus* (other things being equal or unchanged), to love our kindred and fellow citizens more than strangers. By isolating this precept you can get either an Aristocratic Ethic with the claims of our class as sole criterion, or a Racialist Ethic where no claims but those of blood are acknowledged. These monomaniac systems are then used as a ground from which to attack traditional morality; but absurdly, since it is from traditional morality alone that they derive such semblance or validity as they possess … The trunk to whose root the reformer would lay the axe is the only support of the particular branch he wishes to retain.

Lewis provides a brilliant illustration in *Out of the Silent Planet* (20) of what happens when one maxim of traditional morality is isolated from all the rest and erected into an *unum necessarium*. The Oyarsa of Malacandra is speaking to Dr Weston:

> I see now how the lord of the silent world has bent you. There are laws that all *hnau* know, of pity and straight dealing and shame and the like, and one of these is the love of kindred. He has taught you to break all of them except this one, which is not one of the greatest laws; this one he has bent till it becomes folly and has set it up, thus bent, to be a little, blind Oyarsa in your brain. And now you can do nothing but obey it, though if we ask you why it is a law you can give no other reason for it than for all the other and greater laws which it drives you to disobey.

V: The Euthyphro Dilemma

This is a term used by philosophers which refers to a dilemma posed in Plato's *Euthyphro*. In this dialogue between Socrates and Euthyphro the former makes a distinction fundamental in reasoning: that the good is not good because the gods approve it, but the gods approve it because it is good.

The dilemma came up a number of times in Lewis's writings. (1) In *The Problem of Pain* VI he argued that 'Paradisal man always chose to follow God's will. In following it he also gratified his own desire, both because all the actions demanded of him were, in fact, agreeable to his blameless inclination, and also because the service of God was itself his keenest pleasure ... But we inherit a whole system of desires which do not necessarily contradict God's will but which, after centuries of usurped autonomy, steadfastly ignore it. If the thing we like doing is, in fact, the thing God wants us to do, yet that is not our reason for doing it; it remains a mere happy coincidence.' He goes on to state the Euthyphro Dilemma:

> It has sometimes been asked whether God commands certain things because they are right, or whether certain things are right because God commands them. With Hooker, and against Dr Johnson, I emphatically embrace the first alternative. The second might lead to the abominable conclusion ... that charity is good only because God arbitrarily commanded it – that He might equally well have commanded us to hate Him and one another and that hatred would then have been right.

(2) It came up again in *Reflections on the Psalms* VI where, discussing the Psalmists, he states the dilemma: 'There were in the eighteenth century terrible theologians who held that "God did not command certain things because they are right, but certain things are right because God commanded them".' It would, he said

> be better and less irreligious to believe in no God and to have no ethics than to have such an ethics and such a theology as this. The Jews of course never discuss this in abstract and philosophical terms. But at once, and completely, they assume the right view ... They know that the Lord (not merely obedience to the Lord) is 'righteous' and commands 'righteousness' because He loves it ... He enjoins what is good because it is good, because He is good. Hence His laws have *emeth* 'truth', intrinsic validity, rock-bottom reality, being rooted in His own nature.

(3) In between writing these two passages, Lewis discussed the dilemma at some length and more philosophically in **The Poison of Subjectivism**. 'If we grant that our practical reason,' he said, 'is really reason and that its fundamental imperatives are as absolute and categorical as they claim to be, then unconditional allegiance to them is the duty of man. So is absolute allegiance to God.' He found both sides of the dilemma 'intolerable' and he explained why:

> We must remind ourselves that Christian theology does not believe God to be a person. It believes Him to be such that in Him a trinity of persons is consistent with a unity of Deity ... It is ... possible that the duality which seems to force itself upon us when we think, first, of our Father in Heaven, and, secondly, of the self-evident imperatives of the moral law, is not a mere error but a real ... perception of things that would necessarily be two in any mode of being which enters our experience, but which are not so divided in the absolute being of the superpersonal God. When we attempt to think of a person and a law, we are compelled to think of this person either as obeying the law or as making it. And when we think of Him as making it we are compelled to think of Him either as making it in conformity to some yet more ultimate pattern of goodness ... or else as making it arbitrarily ... But ... God neither *obeys* nor *creates* the moral law. The good is uncreated; it never could have been otherwise; it has in it no shadow of contingency; it lies, as Plato said, on the other side of existence. It is the *Rita* of the Hindus by which the gods themselves are divine, the *Tao* of the Chinese from which all realities proceed. But we, favoured beyond the wisest pagans, know what lies beyond existence, what admits no contingency, what lends divinity to all else, what is the ground of all existence, is not simply a law but also a begetting love, a love begotten, and the love which, being between these two, is also immanent in all those who are caught up to share the unity of their self-caused life. God is not merely good, but goodness; goodness is not merely divine, but God.

VI: Subjectivity and the Western Mind

Since he wrote these works Subjectivity has become the hallmark of the Western mind. Those who would like to investigate the foundations of Natural Law more deeply will find it discussed in detail in what is the basis for all studies in Natural Law – St Thomas Aquinas's *Summa*

Theologica Part I–II, Questions 91–100. In Article 6 of Question 94, he raised the question 'Whether the Law of Nature Can Be Abolished from the Heart of Man?' In the article, surely of immense relevance today, he says:

> There belong to the natural law, first, certain most general precepts, that are known to all; and secondly, certain secondary and more detailed precepts, which are, as it were, conclusions following closely from first principles. As to these general principles, the natural law, in the abstract, can nowise be blotted out from men's hearts. But it is blotted out in the case of a particular action, in so far as reason is hindered from applying the general principle in a particular point of practice, on account of concupiscence or some other passion. But as to the other, i.e., the secondary precepts, the natural law can be blotted out from the human heart, either by evil persuasions, just as in speculative matters errors occur in respect of necessary conclusions; or by vicious customs and corrupt habits, as among some men, theft, and even unnatural vices, as the Apostle states (Romans 1), were not esteemed sinful.

The *Summa Theologica* is a work Lewis used constantly. It is long, but not difficult to understand. The beginner could hardly do better than read the abridgement in English edited by Peter Kreeft. It contains the famous section on Natural Law, and the translation is the well-known one made in 1920 by the Fathers of the English Dominican Province. It is called *A Summa of the 'Summa': The Essential Philosophical Passages of St Thomas Aquinas' 'Summa Theologica', Edited and Explained for Beginners* (San Francisco: Ignatius Press, 1990).

Increasingly theologians and lawyers see the close connection between Natural Law and Democracy. The most recent defence of Natural Law is Pope John Paul II's *Veritatis Splendor* (1993) in which, speaking of the relation between objective moral norms and 'genuine democracy', he says:

> There can be no freedom apart from or in opposition to the truth … Only by obedience to universal moral norms does man find full confirmation of his personal uniqueness and the possibility of authentic moral growth … These norms in fact represent the unshakeable foundation and solid guarantee of a just and peaceful human coexistence, and hence of genuine democracy, which can come into being and develop only on the basis of the equality of all its members, who possess common rights and duties. *When it is a matter*

of the moral norms prohibiting intrinsic evil, there are no privileges or exceptions for anyone. It makes no difference whether one is the master of the world or the 'poorest of the poor' on the face of the earth.

Before the demands of morality we are all absolutely equal (96).

Besides the works mentioned above, the reader will want to see Peter Kreeft, *C.S. Lewis for the Third Millennium* (San Francisco: Ignatius Press, 1994) which contains an essay on Lewis and Thomas Aquinas entitled 'Can the Natural Law Ever Be Abolished from the Heart of Man?' Other recent and important works on the subject are Janine Marie Idziak's *Divine Command Morality: Historical and Contemporary Readings* (New York: Edwin Mellen Press, 1979); John Finnis, *Natural Law and Natural Rights* (Oxford: Oxford University Press, 1980); Germain Grisez, *The Way of the Lord Jesus: Vol. I: Christian Moral Principles* (Chicago: Franciscan Herald Press, 1983); and Cardinal Joseph Ratzinger's Fisher Lecture at Cambridge University on 25 January 1988. It is entitled 'Consumer Materialism and Christian Hope' and is primarily about *The Abolition of Man*. The lecture is published in *Briefing 88*, vol. 18, No 3 (5 February 1988), pp. 43–50.

ORIGINALITY: It may be that Lewis's disdain of any attempt at originality is one of the most original things about him. His sympathies were not against Originality as such, but the attempt to *be* 'original'. Soon after his conversion to Christianity he came to the realization, as he said in **Christianity and Literature**, that '"Originality" in the New Testament is quite plainly the prerogative of God alone ... The duty and happiness of every other being is placed in being derivative ... in becoming clean mirrors filled with the image of a face that is not ours.' And because Supernature made Nature, he said in **Bulverism**, 'we can create nothing new, but can only rearrange our material provided through sense data.'

Lewis adopted a very unfashionable view in arguing that there is nothing 'eternal and inviolable' about Personality as such. 'True personality lies ahead,' he said in **Membership**, in which he warned against the 'un-Christian worship of the human individual simply as such ... the pestilent notion (one sees it in literary criticism) that each of us starts with a treasure called "personality" locked up inside him, and that to expand and express this, to guard it from interference, to be "original", is the main end of life. This is Pelagian, or worse, and it defeats even itself. No man who values originality will ever be original. But try to tell the truth as you see it, try to do any bit of work as well as it can be done for the work's sake, and what men call originality will come unsought.' 'The pother about "originality",' he wrote to the poet Martyn Skinner on 23 April 1942, 'all comes from the people who have nothing to say: if they had they'd be original without noticing it' (**L**).

Lewis was, naturally, particularly interested in the relation between originality and literature, and even before he became a Christian, a phrase of Dr Johnson's became dear to him. Writing to his brother on 2 August 1928 he noted the truth of Dr Johnson's remark that '"People more frequently require to be reminded than instructed".' (**L**). It was clear to Nevill Coghill,* that Lewis never made the slightest attempt to be original, and he once asked Lewis how it was that he was invited to write for so many popular magazines. 'What I do,' replied Lewis, 'is to recall as well as I can, what my mother used to say on the subject, eke it out with a few similar thoughts of my own, and so produce what would have been strict orthodoxy in about 1900.'[2]

His thoughts about originality never changed. 'We ... never in the ultimate sense, *make*,' he said in his last book. 'We only build. We always have materials to build from. All we can know about the act of creation must be derived from what we can gather about the relation of the creatures to their Creator' (**LM** XIV). See **Stock Responses**§.

PAGAN CHRISTS: Lewis came across the notion of Christ as one of many 'Dying and Reviving Gods' in J.G. Frazer's *Golden Bough* which was being published when he was with W. T. Kirkpatrick* in 1914–17. The same thing was suggested to him when he was a schoolboy by those editors of the classics who never 'attempted to show in what sense Christianity fulfilled Paganism or Paganism prefigured Christianity' (**SBJ** IV). Partly as a result of this he became an atheist, and on 12 October 1916 he insisted to Arthur Greeves* that: 'All religion, that is, all mythologies to give them their proper name, are merely man's own invention – Christ as much as Loki' (**TST**).

The proper relationship between Paganism and Christianity was to elude him until the time of his conversion. 'Pagan stories are God expressing Himself through the minds of poets,' he wrote excitedly to Arthur Greeves on 18 October 1931, 'while Christianity is God expressing Himself through what we call "real things"' (**TST**). This did not, however, mean that the Pagan myths were simply 'lies'. Seeing the true relation between Paganism and Christianity, he argued in **Myth Became Fact** that 'We must not be nervous about "parallels" and "Pagan Christs". They *ought* to be there – it would be a stumbling block if they weren't.'

[2] Nevill Coghill, 'The Approach to English', **LCSL**.

He went on to argue in **Religion Without Dogma?** that the use you make of these Pagan Christs will depend on whether you are a Naturalist or a Christian:

> To me, who first approached Christianity from a delighted interest in, and reverence for, the best pagan imagination, who loved Balder before Christ and Plato before St Augustine, the anthropological argument against Christianity has never been formidable. On the contrary, I could not believe Christianity if I were forced to say that there were a thousand religions in the world of which 999 were pure nonsense and the thousandth (fortunately) true. My conversion, very largely, depended on recognizing Christianity as the completion, the actualization, the entelechy, of something that had never been wholly absent from the mind of man. And I still think that the agnostic argument from similarities between Christianity and paganism works only if you know the answer. If you start by knowing on other grounds that Christianity is false, then the pagan stories may be another nail in its coffin: just as if you started by knowing that there were no such things as crocodiles then the various stories about dragons might help to confirm your disbelief.

We meet the theme again in **Is Theology Poetry?** 'The difference,' he said, 'between the Pagan Christs (Balder, Osiris, etc.) and the Christ Himself is much what we should expect to find ... It is not the difference between falsehood and truth. It is the difference between a real event on the one hand and dim dreams or premonitions of that same event on the other' (See **Myth§**).

PERSONAL HERESY: E.M.W. Tillyard complained in his *Milton* (1930) that such matters as style 'have concerned the critics far more than what the poem is really about, the true state of Milton's mind when he wrote it.' Lewis dubbed such criticism the 'Personal Heresy'. In an essay **The Personal Heresy in Criticism**, which became the first chapter of a joint work between him and Tillyard, *The Personal Heresy: A Controversy* (1939), he argued that the 'concealed major premise' in Dr Tillyard's book 'is plainly the proposition that all poetry is about the poet's state of mind.'

'I maintain,' Lewis said, 'that when we read poetry as poetry should be read, we have before us no representation which claims to be the poet, and frequently no representation of a *man*, a *character*, or a *personality* at all.' Indeed, in so far as we can 'know' a poet, it is 'by sharing his consciousness, not by studying it':

> I look with his eyes, not at him. He, for the moment, will be precisely what I do not see; for you can see any eyes rather than the pair you see with, and if you want to examine your own glasses you must take them off your own nose. The poet is not a man who asks me to look at *him*; he is a man who says 'look at that' and points; the more I follow the pointing of his finger the less I can possibly see of *him*.

QUIDDITY: There are few things more characteristic of Lewis than his 'zest for rubbing one's nose in the mere quiddity' of things (SBJ XIII), his 'love of everything which has its own strong flavour' (SBJ XV). He gave much of the credit for this to his undergraduate friend, A.K. Hamilton Jenkin,* of whom he said in SBJ XIII:

> I learned from him that we should attempt a total surrender to whatever atmosphere was offering itself at the moment; in a squalid town to seek out those very places where its squalor rose to grimness and almost grandeur, on a dismal day to find the most dismal and dripping wood, on a windy day to seek the windiest ridge. There was no Betjemannic irony about it; only a quiddity of each thing, to rejoice in its being (so magnificently) what it was.

There are numerous examples of Lewis's growing delight in 'the quiddity of things' in AMR. He records that on 7 November 1922 he and Jenkin stole into a private wood where: 'We were as pleased as two children revelling in the beauty, the secrecy, and the thrill of trespassing. Jenkin's undisguised delight in the more elementary pleasures of a ramble always bucks me.'

REASON: Reason is the capacity for logical, rational and analytical thought, and there are few things Lewis respected as much or mentioned so often in his writings.

I: Early treatment of Reason
In his poem **Reason** written about the time of his conversion, Lewis associates Reason with the goddess Athena:

> Set on the soul's acropolis the reason stands
> A virgin, arm'd, commercing with celestial light,
> And he who sins against her has defiled his own
> Virginity: no cleansing makes his garment white;
> So clear is reason.

Reason's next appearance is in *The Pilgrim's Regress,* an allegorical account of Lewis's conversion. In **PR** III:9 John, the Pilgrim, is imprisoned by the Spirit of the Age until he is set free by the 'rational argument' of Reason – 'a sun-bright virgin clad in complete steel, with a sword naked in her hand.' He learns that she never decides anything without evidence. When he says that he cannot remain in doubt about a certain question, she replies:

> In Eschropolis, indeed, it is impossible, for the people who live there have to give an opinion once a week or once a day, or else Mr Mammon would soon cut off their food. But out here in the country you can walk all day and all the next day with an unanswered question in your head: you need never speak until you have made up your mind (IV:3).

John tells Reason that when he tried to argue with the Spirit of the Age he was told that he was 'rationalizing' his own desires, the Spirit of the Age implying that his own doctrines were true. Reason's 'cure' for this was an argument repeated often in Lewis's later works:

> You must ask them whether any reasoning is valid or not. If they say no, then their own doctrines, being reached by reasoning, fall to the ground. If they say yes, then they will have to examine your arguments and refute them on their merits: for if some reasoning is valid, for all they know, your bit of reasoning may be one of the valid bits (IV:4).

Reason leads John as far as Mother Kirk and leaves him. Later, when on the point of believing in Christianity, he struggles to remain free. Reason appears and will not allow it (IX:2). John returns to the Church of Christ, and when he and his companion set out on the rest of their journey Reason 'rode with the company, talking to them at will and not visiting them any longer by sudden starts, nor vanishing suddenly' (IX:5).

II: How Reason Works

Miracles is one of Lewis's most philosophical works, and it contains his clearest statements about Reason. A particularly fine definition of Reason is found in chapter III in which he says, 'It is clear that everything we know, beyond our own immediate sensations, is inferred from those sensations. I do not mean that we begin as children, by regarding our sensations as "evidence" and thence arguing consciously to the existence of space, matter, and other people. I mean that if we are old enough to understand the question, our confidence in the existence of anything else ... is challenged, our argument in defence of it will have to take the form of inferences from our immediate sensations. Put in its most general form the inference would run:

'Since I am presented with colours, sounds, shapes, pleasures and pains which I cannot perfectly predict or control, and since the more I investigate them the more regular their behaviour appears, therefore there must exist something other than myself and it must be systematic.' Inside this very general inference, all sorts of special trains of inference lead us to more detailed conclusions. We infer Evolution from fossils: we infer the existence of our own brains from what we find inside the skulls of other creatures like ourselves in the dissecting room.

All possible knowledge, then, depends on the validity of reasoning. If the feeling of certainty which we express by words like *must be* and *therefore* and *since* is a real perception of how things outside our own minds really 'must' be, well and good. But if this certainty is merely a feeling *in* our own minds and not a genuine insight into realities beyond them – if it merely represents the way our minds happen to work – then we can have no knowledge. Unless human reasoning is valid no science can be true.

It follows that no account of the universe can be true unless that account leaves it possible for our thinking to be a real insight. A theory which explained everything else in the whole universe but which made it impossible to believe that our thinking was valid, would be utterly out of court. For our theory would itself have been reached by thinking, and if thinking is not valid that theory would, of course, be itself demolished. It would have destroyed its own credentials. It would be an argument which proved that no argument was sound – a proof that there are no such things as proofs – which is nonsense.

Thus a strict materialism refutes itself for the reason given long ago by Professor Haldane: 'If my mental processes are determined wholly by the motions of atoms in my brain, I have no reason to suppose that my beliefs are true ... and hence I have no reason for supposing my brain to be composed of atoms.'

Another example of 'self-contradiction' in materialism is found in **Answers to Questions on Christianity**: 'If *their* thoughts – i.e., of Materialism and Astronomy – are merely accidental by-products, why should we believe them to be true? I see no reason for believing that one accident should be able to give me a correct account of all the other accidents. It's like expecting that the accidental shape taken by the splash when you upset a milk-jug should give you a correct account of how the jug was made and why it was upset.'

III: Reason a part of Supernature

In **M** IV Lewis argues that there is no 'interlocking' of Reason and Nature. The 'frontier' between them is not one between 'mind' and 'matter' or between 'soul' and 'body', but between Reason and 'the whole mass of irrational events whether physical or psychological.' In daily life we use our Reason to alter the course of Nature as when we use mathematics to build bridges, and by Reason we alter the course of psychological nature when we apply arguments to alter our own emotions. Nature, on the other hand, is powerless to produce Rational thought:

Every object you see before you at this moment – the walls, ceiling and furniture, the book, your own washed hands and cut finger-nails, bears witness to the colonization of Nature by Reason: for none of this matter would have been in these states if Nature had had her way ... If, on the other hand, a toothache or an anxiety is at this very moment preventing you from attending, then Nature is indeed interfering with your consciousness: but not to produce some new variety of reasoning, only (so far as in her lies) to suspend Reason altogether.

There is, thus, an 'Unsymmetrical Relation' between Reason and Nature. A symmetrical relation is this: if A is the brother of B, then B is the brother of A. An Unsymmetrical Relation is this: if A is the father of B, B is *not* the father of A. Reason is not related to Nature as Nature is related to Reason. Whereas Nature is a creation produced by God, 'eternal, self-existent Reason' is part of Supernature.

Of course Rational Thinking is conditioned in its exercise by a natural object such as the brain. For instance, 'It is temporarily impaired by alcohol, or a blow on the head', and 'It wanes as the brain decays and vanishes when the brain ceases to function' (**M** VI). Nevertheless,

> The rational and moral element in each human mind is a point of force from the Supernatural working its way into Nature, exploiting at each turn those conditions which Nature offers, repulsed where the conditions are hopeless and impeded when they are unfavourable. A man's Rational thinking is *just so much* of his share in eternal Reason as the state of the brain allows to become operative ... The voice of the Announcer is just so much of a human voice as the receiving set lets through. Of course it varies with the state of the receiving set, and deteriorates as the set wears out, and vanishes altogether if I throw a brick at it. It is conditioned by the apparatus but not originated by it (**M** IV).

Lewis insisted in **De Futilitate** that 'We must give up talking about "*human* reason". In so far as thought is merely human, merely a characteristic of one particular biological species, it does not explain our knowledge. Where thought is strictly rational it must be, in some odd sense, not ours, but cosmic or super-cosmic. It must be something not shut up inside our heads but already "out there" – in the universe or behind the universe: either as objective as material Nature or more objective still ... Total reason – cosmic or super-cosmic Reason – *corrects* human imperfections of Reason. Now correction is not the same as mere contradiction. When your false reasoning is corrected you "see the mistakes": the true reasoning thus takes up into itself whatever was already rational in your original thought. You are not moved into a totally new world; you are given *more* and *purer* of what you already had in a small quantity and badly mixed with foreign elements.'

V: Moral Judgements are Made by Reason

One of the major theses of Lewis's writings is that, besides reasoning about matters of fact, it is by Reason that men make moral judgements, as when they say 'I *ought* to do this,' or 'I *ought not* to do that', 'This is *good*', or 'This is *evil*'. All moral principles he believed to be rationally perceived. The point is argued over and over again in his writings, but principally in Book I of **MC** - **Right and Wrong as a Clue to the Meaning of the Universe,** *The Abolition of Man*, **The Poison of Subjectivism, De Futilitate,** and **M** V.

'We "just see", he says in **M** V, 'that there is no reason why my neighbour's happiness should be sacrificed to my own, as we "just see" that things that are equal to the same thing are equal to one another. If we cannot prove either axiom, that is not because they are irrational but because they are self-evident and all proofs depend on them. Their intrinsic reasonableness shines by its own light. It is because all morality is based on such self-evident principles that we say to a man, when we would recall him to right conduct, "Be Reasonable".'

There is a difficulty,' Lewis warned in **MC** II:3, 'about arguing with God. He is the source from which all your reasoning power comes: you could not be right and He wrong any more than a stream can rise higher than its own source. When you are arguing against Him you are arguing against the very power that makes you able to argue at all.'

V: The Enemies of Reason

Mere *feelings* are a powerful enemy against Reason. In his important little essay, **Religion: Reality or Substitute?** Lewis insisted that all our knowledge depends on Authority, Reason and Experience, and that *feelings* are sometimes the enemy of all three. 'Though Reason is divine,' he said, 'human reasoners are not. When once passion takes part in the game, the human reason, unassisted by Grace, has about as much chance of retaining its hold on truths already gained as a snowflake has of retaining its consistency in the mouth of a blast furnace. The sort of arguments against Christianity which our reason can be persuaded to accept at the moment of yielding to temptation are often preposterous. Reason may win truth; without Faith she will retain them just so long as Satan pleases. There is nothing we cannot be made to believe or disbelieve. If we wish to be rational, not now and then, but constantly, we must pray for the gift of faith, for the power to go on believing not in the teeth of reason but in the teeth of lust and terror and jealousy and boredom and indifference to that which reason, authority or experience, or all three, have once delivered to us for truth.'

Another enemy of Reason is *subjectivity* about Reason itself, and nowhere did Lewis write more cogently about the problem than in **The Poison of Subjectivism.** He pointed out there that:

After studying his environment man has begun to study himself. Up to that point, he had assumed his own reason and through it seen all other things. Now, his own reason has become the object: it is as if we took out our eyes to look at them. Thus studied, his own reason appears to him as the epiphenomenon which accompanies chemical or electrical events in a cortex which is itself the by-product of a blind evolutionary process. His own logic, hitherto the king whom events in all possible worlds must obey, becomes merely subjective. There is no reason for supposing that it yields truth.

A weapon Lewis employed constantly against this 'anti-Naturalism' was the unanswerable argument that you cannot *prove* that there is no such thing as proof, or hold it to be *true* that there is no such thing as truth. Or to use the argument already quoted from Professor Haldane: 'If my mental processes are determined wholly by the motions of atoms in my brain, I have no reason to suppose that my beliefs are true ... and hence I have no reason for supposing my brain to be composed of atoms.' See **Natural Law§**.

RENAISSANCE, THE: *The Oxford Companion to English Literature* defines the 'Renaissance' as: 'The great flowering of art, architecture, politics, and the study of literature, usually seen as the end of the Middle Ages and the beginning of the modern world, which came about under the influence of Greek and Roman models. It began in Italy in the late 14th century, culminated in the High Renaissance in the early 16th century ... and spread to the rest of Europe in the 15th century and afterwards. Its emphasis was humanist: that is, on regarding the human figure and reason without a necessary relating of it to the superhuman.'

Those who have read Nevill Coghill's* 'The Approach to English' in **LCSL** will recall him saying that Lewis often threw out 'powerful assertions that challenged discussion', one of which was about the Renaissance. One day, said Coghill:

I saw him coming slowly towards me, his round, rubicund face beaming with pleasure to itself. When he came within speaking distance, I said 'Hullo, Jack! You look very pleased with yourself; what is it?'

'I believe,' he answered, with a modest smile of triumph, 'I *believe* I have proved that the Renaissance never happened in England. *Alternatively*' – he held up his hand to prevent my astonished exclamations – 'that if it did, *it had no importance!*'

Lewis had been throwing out hints about the Renaissance almost since he began lecturing in the University. In *The Allegory of Love* (VI, v) he speaks of that 'complex of heterogeneous events ... known as the Renaissance' as 'not a landmark of primary importance.' However, most of what he believed about what was and was not a 'Renaissance' is found in *English Literature in the Sixteenth Century*. In the Introduction he said that 'It is ... true that many movements of thought which affected our literature would have been impossible without the recovery of Greek. But if there is any closer connection than that between the *renascentia* and the late sixteenth-century efflorescence of English literature, I must confess that it has escaped me.' He goes on to provide a valuable explanation of what he means by 'the Renaissance':

The word has sometimes been used merely to mean the 'revival of learning', the recovery of Greek, and the 'classicizing' of Latin. If it still bore that clear and useful sense, I should of course have employed it. Unfortunately it has, for many years, been widening its meaning, till now 'the Renaissance' can hardly be defined except as 'an imaginary entity responsible for everything the speaker likes in the fifteenth and sixteenth centuries.' If it were merely a chronological label, like 'pre-Dynastic' or 'Caroline', it might be harmless. But words, said Bacon, shoot back upon the understandings of the mightiest. Where we have a noun we tend to imagine a thing. The word *Renaissance* helps to impose a factitious unity on all the untidy and heterogeneous events which were going on in those centuries as in any others. Thus the 'imaginary entity' creeps in. *Renaissance* becomes the name for some character or quality supposed to be immanent in all the events, and collects very serious emotional overtones in the process. Then, as every attempt to define this mysterious character or quality turns out to cover all sorts of things that were there before the chosen period, a curious procedure is adopted. Instead of admitting that our definition has broken down, we adopt the desperate expedient of saying that 'the Renaissance' must have begun earlier than we had thought. Thus Chaucer, Dante, and presently St Francis of Assisi, become 'Renaissance' men. A word of such wide and fluctuating meaning is of no value.

REPELLENT DOCTRINES: In **The Weight of Glory** Lewis argued that 'If our religion is something objective, then we must never avert our eyes from those elements in it which seem puzzling or repellent; for it will be precisely the puzzling or the repellent which conceals what we do not yet know and need to know ... Having followed up what seemed puzzling and repellent in the sacred books, I find, to my great surprise, looking back, that the connection is perfectly clear.'

That is the first formulation of a rule Lewis followed in writing Christian apologetics. Nearly all the most difficult ideas and doctrines he writes about, such as Pain and Miracles, were 'repellent' to him when he was an atheist. It was by thinking them through to 'the absolute ruddy end' that he arrived at his orthodox position. In both *Surprised by Joy* and the earlier *Pilgrim's Regress* he explains how repellent the connection between 'Joy' and Heaven would have been at one time, and how by a 'lived dialectic' the connection was revealed. As he said in the Preface to the 1943 edition of *The Pilgrim's Regress*: 'It appeared to me ... that if a man diligently followed this desire, pursuing the false objects until their falsity appeared and then resolutely abandoning them, he must come out at last into the clear knowledge that the human soul was made to enjoy some object that is never fully given ... in our present mode of subjective and spatio-temporal experience ... The dialectic of Desire, faithfully followed, would retrieve all mistakes, head you off from all false paths, and force you not to propound, but to live through, a sort of ontological proof.'

The discussing of 'repellent doctrines' was a weekly feature of the Oxford University Socratic Club‡ during Lewis's presidency. In his article **The Founding of the Oxford Socratic Club** he said: 'Socrates had exhorted men to "follow the argument wherever it led them": the Club came into existence to apply his principle to one particular subject matter – the *pros* and *cons* of the Christian Religion.' It was in 1945, when addressing the clergy of Wales on **Christian Apologetics**, that Lewis provided the most complete formulation of this key idea: 'The doctrines which one finds easy are the doctrines which give Christian sanction to truths you already knew. The new truth which you do not know and which you need, must, in the very nature of things, be hidden precisely in the doctrines you least like and least understand. It is just the same here as in science ... Science progresses because scientists, instead of running away from such troublesome phenomena or hushing them up, are constantly seeking them out. In the same way, there will be progress in Christian knowledge only as long as we accept the challenge of the difficult or repellent doctrines. A "liberal" Christianity which considers itself free to alter the faith whenever the Faith looks perplexing or repellent *must* be completely stagnant. Progress is made only into a *resisting* material.'

SCIENCE and SCIENTISM: In considering this subject we would do well to recall a passage from Chad Walsh's *C.S. Lewis: Apostle to the Skeptics* (1949). Walsh said that when he asked Lewis whether he was 'against science', 'He answered – with unusual warmth – that he was not. "Science is neither an enemy nor a friend," he said. "Science is not a *person*!"' (16). Lewis is, nevertheless, often criticized for traducing science and scientists. This is not true.

What he attacked, particularly in his science fiction, is 'Scientism'§ which he defined as 'A certain outlook on the world which is casually connected with the popularization of the sciences, though it is much less common among real scientists than among their readers' (**A Reply to Professor Haldane**). In this **Reply** he pointed out that the only real scientist in his science fiction is William Hengist, a chemist, who leaves the National Institute of Co-ordinated Experiments after finding out what its purpose is. 'I came here,' he tells Mark, 'because I thought it had something to do with science. Now that I find it's something more like a political conspiracy, I shall go home' (**THS** 3:iv). Lewis's own viewpoint was voiced by Ransom who says that the sciences are 'good and innocent in themselves' although 'scientism' is creeping into them (9:v).

Screwtape was a believer in 'scientism'. 'Above all,' he says, 'do not attempt to use science (I mean, the real sciences) as a defence against Christianity. They will positively encourage him to think about realities he can't touch and see. There have been sad cases among the modern physicists. If he must dabble in science, keep him on economics and sociology' (**SL** I).

Lewis said in the Preface to **THS** that his book was a '"tall story" about devilry' which contains 'a serious "point" which I have tried to make in my *Abolition of Man*.' The 'point' was how the jettisoning of the *Tao* or **Natural Law**§ can lead to the 'abolition of Man' by Nature.

What Man gains by eugenics and scientific education is 'the power to make its descendants what it pleases' because 'all men who live after it are the patients of that power.' Thus, 'Man's conquest of Nature, if the dreams of some scientific planners are realized, means the rule of a few hundreds of men over billions upon billions of men.' In the end Man, subject to his 'Conditioners', who are themselves subject to Nature, would be ruled by their impulses. Their motives will, as a result, derive from such things as heredity, digestion, the weather and the association of ideas. By reducing things to *mere Nature* Man is able to conquer Nature. However, this wresting of powers *from* Nature is also the surrendering of things *to* Nature, and the final stage of surrender is reached when we reduce our own species – Man himself – to the level of a mere 'natural object'.

'Nothing I can say,' Lewis goes on, 'will prevent some people from describing this … as an attack on science. I deny the charge … I even suggest that from Science herself the cure might come.' Magic and applied science are united by the fact that both are separated from the 'wisdom' of earliest ages:

> For the wise men of old the cardinal problem had been how to conform the soul to reality, and the solution had been knowledge, self-discipline and virtue. For magic and applied science alike the problem is how to subdue reality to the wishes of men.

What Lewis called a 'regenerate science' would explain things without explaining them away. 'When it spoke of the parts it would remember the whole. While studying the *IT* it would not lose what Martin Buber calls the *Thou*-situation. The analogy between the *Tao* of Man and the instinct of an animal species would mean for it new light cast on the unknown thing, Instinct, by the inly known reality of conscience and not a reduction of conscience to the category of Instinct.'

Returning to **THS** we find there one who was born co-operating with Nature. This is Merlin, brought back from the fifth century to help with the destruction of this modern Tower of Babel. He is 'the last vestige of an old order in which matter and spirit were, from our modern point of view, confused. For him every operation on Nature is a kind of personal contact, like coaxing a child or stroking one's horse. After him came the modern man to whom Nature is something dead – a machine to be worked, and taken to bits if it won't work the way he pleases' (see Dr John Laurent's 'C.S. Lewis and Animal Rights', *Journal of Myth, Fantasy and Romanticism*, The Journal of the Mythopoeic Literature Society of Australia, vol. 2, No 1 (April 1993), pp. 14–24.

SEEING THROUGH: Lewis often drew attention to those who claim to 'see through' an experience they have never had. The first example of this is found in the pilgrim John's talk with Angular in **PR** (VI:3). After Angular brushes aside John's talk about the Island for which he is searching, John says, 'I know this by experience as I know a dozen things about it of which you betray your ignorance as often as you speak … How is it possible that you can advise me in this matter? Would you recommend a eunuch as confessor to a man whose difficulties lay in the realm of chastity? Would a man born blind be my best guide against the lust of the eye?'

The sternest of all the warnings Lewis issued is found in **AOM** III in which he protested: 'You cannot go on "seeing through" things for ever. The whole point of seeing through something is to see something through it. It is good that the window should be transparent, because the street or garden beyond it is opaque. How if you saw through the garden too? It is no use trying to "see through" first principles. If you see through everything, then everything is transparent. But a wholly transparent world is an invisible world. To "see through" all things is the same as not to see.'.

STOCK RESPONSES: These are the correct symbols, the organized and willed responses, the conventional reactions we assume when writing or talking about important matters. To say that Virtue is lovely is a Stock Response. Lewis borrowed the idea from the literary critic, I. A. Richards (1893–1979), and rehabilitated it for his own use. In his *Practical Criticism: A Study of Literary Judgement* (1929) Richards described Stock Responses as one of the 'chief difficulties of criticism'. These 'critical traps', he says in the 'Introductory' chapter:

> have their opportunity whenever a poem seems to, or does, involve, views and emotions already fully prepared in the reader's mind, so that what happens appears to be more of the reader's doing than the poet's. The button is pressed, and then the author's work is done, for immediately the record starts playing in quasi- (or total) independence of the poem which is supposed to be its origin or instrument.

Dr Richards argued that Stock Responses are 'disadvantageous and even dangerous, because they may get in the way of, and prevent, a response more appropriate to the situation.'

Lewis wrote at length about Stock Responses in **PPL** VIII where he deplores the exchange of 'direct free play of experience' for willed Stock Responses such as finding love sweet, death bitter, and virtue lovely. 'In my opinion,' he said, 'such deliberate organization is one of the first necessities of human life, and one of the main functions of art is to assist it. All that we describe as constancy in love or friendship, as loyalty in political life, or, in general, as perseverance – all solid virtue and stable pleasure – depends on organizing chosen attitudes and maintaining them against the eternal flux.'

He assigned as causes for this: (1) 'The decay of Logic, resulting in an untroubled assumption that the particular is real and the universal is not.' (2) 'A Romantic Primitivism ... which prefers the merely natural to the elaborated, the un-willed to the willed.' (3) 'A confusion ... between the organization of a response and the pretence of a response.' (4) 'A belief ... that a certain elementary rectitude of human response is "given" by nature herself, and may be taken for granted, so that poets, secure of this basis are free to devote themselves to the more advanced work of teaching us ever finer and finer discrimination. I believe this to be a dangerous delusion. Children like dabbling in dirt; they have to be *taught* the stock response to it. Normal sexuality, far from being a *datum*, is achieved by a long and delicate process of suggestion and adjustment which proves too difficult for some individuals and, at times, for whole societies' (**PPL** VIII).

Lewis goes on to say that 'The Stock response to pain has become uncertain; I have heard Mr Eliot's comparison of evening to a patient on an operating table praised, nay gloated over, not as a striking picture of sensibility in decay, but because it was so "pleasantly unpleasant" ... That elementary rectitude of human response, at which we are so ready to fling the unkind epithets of "stock", "crude", "bourgeois" and "conventional", so far from being "given" is a delicate balance of trained habits, laboriously acquired and easily lost, on the maintenance of which depend both our virtues and our pleasures and even, perhaps, the survival of our species. For though the human heart is not unchanging ... the laws of causation are. When poisons become fashionable they do not cease to kill' (**PPL** VIII).

T. S. Eliot's poems, such as 'The Love Song of J. Alfred Prufrock', were for Lewis the supreme instance of the destruction of the right Stock Response. Just how seriously he viewed the harm such poems might cause is made clear by a letter to Katharine Farrer* who sent him a copy of her novel, *The Cretan Counterfeit* (1954). He was struck by her expression, 'the faint oval of the moon dodged in and out of the clouds like the white face of an idiot lost in a wood' (IX). 'Dear Lady,' he said on 3 February 1954, 'this is simply Eliotic: for (a) It illustrates what we've all seen by what most of us have *not* seen (b) It denigrates, in the leering modern mode, the high creatures of God. If I were your *directeur* you'd learn Psalm 136 by heart. Not safe, either, to be rude to goddesses ... Artemis still owes Aphrodite a come-back for the Hippolytus affair and we should hate you to be the target.'

When Mrs Farrer objected, he wrote again on 9 February saying: 'I'm afraid you came in for the backwash of my feeling about a widespread tendency in modern literature which strikes me as horrid: I mean, the readiness to admit extreme uses of the pathetic fallacy in contexts where there is nothing to justify them and always of a kind that belittles or "sordidizes" ("sordifies") nature. Eliot's evening "like a patient etherized upon a table" is the *locus classicus*. I don't believe one person in a million, under any emotional stress, would see evening like that. And even if they did, I believe that anything but the most sparing admission of such images is a very dangerous game. To invite them, to recur willingly to them, to come to regard them as normal, surely poisons us?'

It was probably this exchange with Mrs Farrer that caused Lewis, later that same year, to defend Stock Responses in his poem, 'A Confession':

> I'm like that odd man Wordsworth knew, to whom
> A primrose was a yellow primrose, one whose doom
> Keeps him forever in the list of dunces,
> Compelled to live on stock responses,
> Making the poor best that I can
> Of dull things ... peacocks, honey, the Great Wall, Aldebaran,
> Silver weirs, new-cut grass, wave on the beach, hard gem,
> The shapes of horse and woman, Athens, Troy, Jerusalem.

THRILLS, A DISTRUST OF: Lewis's distrust of thrills and raptures developed early in his life, and probably began with his youthful tendency to mistake the feelings accompanying 'Joy'§ for what Joy pointed to – Heaven. By the time he came to write the story of his conversion in the allegorical **PR** he had a well developed notion of what purpose thrills and raptures fill. In **PR** VIII:10 John tells History that his desire for the Island '*is* a thrill – a physical sensation.' 'You must fear thrills,' replies History. 'It is only a foretaste of that which the real Desirable will be when you have found it ... Do you not know how it is with love? First comes delight: then pain: then fruit. And then there is joy of the fruit, but that is different again from the first delight. And mortal lovers must not try to remain at the first step: for lasting passion is the dream of a harlot and from it we wake in despair. You must not try to keep the raptures: they have done their work.'

The transitory nature of all emotions is something Lewis believed young couples need to be warned against. In **MC** III:6 he said: 'No feeling can be relied on to last in its full intensity, or even to last at all. Knowledge can last, principles can last, habits can last; but feelings come and go ... It is just the people who are ready to submit to the loss of the thrill and settle down to the sober interest, who are then most likely to meet new thrills in some quite different direction ... Let the thrill go – let it die away – go on through that period of death into the quieter interest and happiness that follows – and you will find you are living in a world of new thrills all the time.'

This caution appears frequently in his letters. When a former pupil was on the point of marrying he wrote on 18 April 1940: 'The modern tradition is that the proper reason for marrying is the state described as "being in love". Now I have nothing to say against "being in love": but the idea that this is or ought to be the exclusive reason or that it can ever be by itself an *adequate* basis seems to be simply moonshine ... Many ages, many cultures, and many individuals don't experience it ... It often unites most unsuitable people ... Is it not usually transitory? Doesn't the modern emphasis on "love" lead people either into divorce or into misery, because when that emotion dies down they conclude that their marriage is a "failure," though in fact they have just reached the point at which *real* marriage begins. Fourthly, it would be undesirable, even if it were possible, for people to be "in love" all their lives. What a world it would be if most of the people we met were perpetually in this trance!' (L). To another friend he said: 'Feelings come and go, but they especially *go!*'

WHO'S WHO

Aldwinckle, Elia Estelle 'Stella' (1907–90): founder of the Oxford University Socratic Club.‡ She was born in Johannesburg on 16 December 1907, the second of four children of English parents. When she was three-and-a-half the family moved to South America, where her father, an architect, hoped to find work. In 1915 the family returned to England and Stella was sent to Westcliff School in Weston-super-Mare. Sometime later the family returned to South Africa, where Stella rejoined them at Brits, in the Magaliesberg Mountains. At the age of twenty-one, alone by the banks of the Crocodile River, she decided that she should give her life to helping people find God.

To prepare herself mentally, she returned to England. After learning Greek and the other subjects she needed to pass the entrance examination to Oxford, she gained a place at St Anne's College, Oxford, in 1932, and read Theology, taking a BA in 1936 and an MA in 1941. On leaving Oxford she taught Divinity in Yorkshire for three years, and then at St Christopher's College in Blackheath.

Gradually she realized that her calling was pastoral, and she returned to Oxford in 1941 and joined the Oxford Pastorate. This was a team of workers attached to St Aldate's Church whose work was principally that of spiritual counselling of the University's undergraduates. She had found exactly the work that suited her and she was a Chaplain to Women Students 1941–66. Almost immediately after joining the Pastorate, she was sent to Somerville College, one of the women's colleges, to act as an adviser to the students there. She enjoyed controversy and was stung into action when one of them complained that no one seemed ready to discuss the questions agnostics raise about God.

In Michaelmas Term 1941 she put up a notice exhorting 'all atheists, agnostics, and those who are disillusioned about religion or think they are' to meet in the Junior Common Room. Together they decided that the

University needed an 'open forum for the discussion of the intellectual difficulties connected with religion and with Christianity in particular.' The society had to have a senior member from the University, and Miss Aldwinckle felt that C.S. Lewis was exactly the right person. Lewis agreed to help and the Oxford University Socratic Club was founded shortly after Christmas 1941, with Stella Aldwinckle as its Chairman, and Lewis as its President. Over the years it became one of the best-known and best-attended university societies in Oxford. It declined steeply when Lewis went to Cambridge in 1955, but by the time it ended in 1972 Stella had more than accomplished what she had set out to do.

Stella Aldwinckle was also a knowledgeable horsewoman, and in 1958 she founded the Oxford University Horsemanship Club, using this too as a pastoral contact. After retiring from the Oxford Pastorate in 1966 she devoted herself full-time to a philosophical treatise on some of the theoretical ontological problems that had always interested her. She was given much help and encouragement by the theologian Austin Farrer.* The subject of her thesis gradually evolved into a poem *Christ's Shadow in Plato's Cave: A Meditation on the Substance of Love* (Oxford: The Amate Press, 1990), published the year of her death. Perhaps her most enduring monuments are the five volumes of the *Socratic Digest* she edited 1942–52. See **Socratic Club‡** and Walter Hooper's account of the Socratic Club, 'Oxford's Bonny Fighter' in **ABT**.

Anscombe, Gertrude Elizabeth Margaret FBA (1919–   ), member of the Socratic Club,‡ was Professor of Philosophy, Cambridge University, 1970–86 and is a translator and co-editor of posthumous works of Ludwig Wittgenstein. She was born 18 March 1919, the daughter of **Allen Wells Anscombe** and **Gertrude Elizabeth (Thomas) Anscombe**. She says that 'As a result of my teenage conversion to the Catholic Church – itself the fruit of reading done from 12 to 15 – I read a work called *Natural Theology*.' Thus began her lifelong interest in Philosophy. A year after taking a First in Greats from St Hugh's College, Oxford, in 1941, she moved to Cambridge where, as a research student at Newnham College, she met Wittgenstein and became his pupil. In 1946 she was appointed to a Research Fellowship at Somerville College, Oxford, and she was a Fellow of Somerville College 1964–70.

Professor Anscombe is married to the philosopher **Peter Geach**, and they have seven children. Her books include *An Introduction to Wittgenstein's Tractatus* (1959) and (with Peter Geach) *Three Philosophers* (1961). Those interested in her theological beliefs should see Vol. III of her Collected Philosophical Papers, *Ethics, Religion and Politics*, which contains her celebrated essay on 'Contraception and Chastity'. See *Intention and Intentionality: Essays in Honour of G.E.M. Anscombe* (with photograph), ed. Cora Diamond and Jenny Teichman (1979), p. xi.

To many, Professor Anscombe is known only for her debate with Lewis at the Socratic Club, and over the years the substance of that debate has become greatly misunderstood. There has grown up the belief that she defeated Lewis's case for Christianity. Such was not her purpose, and nothing could be further from the truth. Professor Anscombe is a devout Roman Catholic and her paper is really about 'Causation'. In 1947 Lewis had published *Miracles*, in chapter III of which, on 'The Self-Contradiction of the Naturalist', he contended that 'A theory which explained everything else in the whole universe but which made it impossible to believe that our thinking was valid, would be utterly out of court ... We may in fact state it as a rule that *no thought is valid if it can be fully explained as the result of irrational causes.*' On 2 February 1948 Professor Anscombe gave a paper to the Socratic entitled 'A Reply to Mr C.S. Lewis's Argument That "Naturalism" Is Self-Refuting' which was afterwards published in the *Socratic Digest*, No 4 [1948], along with Lewis's **Reply**.

Her argument, about the nature of causation, is complex and difficult for anyone not a philosopher to understand. The crucial points of it are: (1) that a distinction must be made between 'irrational causes' and 'non-rational causes'; (2) it must be made clear what is meant by 'valid' reasoning; (3) the Naturalist can be allowed to explain a chain of reasoning as a result of 'non-rational' causes – with the meanings of the words *valid, invalid, rational* and *irrational* left intact; (4) it is necessary to distinguish between the 'ground' and the 'cause' of a conclusion.

Lewis believed that Professor Anscombe had misunderstood his argument. However, he accepted that he was unclear about a certain point in his paper and he revised chapter III of *Miracles*, giving it the new title 'The Cardinal Difficulty of Naturalism', for the edition Collins (London) published as a Fontana Book in 1960. The revised chapter III appeared in the Macmillan (New York) edition in 1978. Professor Anscombe's original article is reprinted in Vol. II of her Collected Philosophical Papers, *Metaphysics and the Philosophy of Mind* (1981). In the Introduction she says that the revised chapter III

does correspond more to the actual depth and difficulty of the questions being discussed ... The fact that Lewis rewrote that chapter, and rewrote it so that it now has these qualities, shows his honesty and seriousness. The meeting of the Socratic Club at which I read my paper has been described by several of his friends as a horrible and shocking experience which upset him very much. Neither Dr Havard* (who had Lewis and me to dinner a few weeks later) nor Professor Jack Bennett* remembered any such feelings on Lewis's part ... My own recollection is that it was an occasion of sober discussion of certain quite definite criticisms, which Lewis's rethinking and rewriting showed he thought were accurate. I am inclined to construe the odd accounts of the matter by some of his friends – who seem not to have been interested in the actual arguments or the subject matter – as an interesting example of the phenomenon called 'projection'.

Baker, Leo Kingsley (1898–1986), Oxford friend. He was born in London on 14 August 1898, the son of **Laura Jane Baker** and **James Leopold Hawes**. He was educated at St George's School, Harpenden, 1909–17, where he was a School Prefect, the Captain of Rugby and the Captain of Cricket. After matriculating at Wadham College, Oxford, in June 1917 he enlisted in the Royal Flying Corps. He was commissioned a Second Lieutenant in November 1917, and a First Lieutenant in April 1918. In May 1918 he went to France as a pilot with the 80th Squadron of the Royal Air Force. After being severely wounded in August 1918, he was awarded the Distinguished Flying Cross.

Leo Baker returned to Oxford in 1919 and read Modern History. He and Lewis, who shared a love of poetry, met during 1919. They worked together on an anthology of poetry, but it was never published. It was Leo Baker who introduced Owen Barfield,* also of Wadham, to Lewis in 1919. He was a frequent visitor at Lewis's and Mrs Janie Moore's* home, and there are many references to him in **AMR**.

After taking his BA, he was from 1922–25 an actor with the Old Vic Company under Lilian Bayliss. His experience included parts in thirty Shakespeare plays, some Old Comedy, and two years of stage management. In 1925 he married **Eileen Brookes** and they had three daughters, **Susan Mary** (b. 1930), **Elizabeth Margaret** (b. 1933), and **Rachel Mary Rosalind** (b. 1939). He had to give up the theatre owing to troubles resulting from his war wounds, and he and his wife set up a handloom weaving business in Chipping Campden, known as the Kingsley Weavers. This was dissolved on the outbreak of the war in 1939. Meanwhile, in 1933 he became a priest with the Christian Community, and when the war broke out he took the family out of London to Gloucester, where he taught at a Rudolf Steiner School. He left the school in 1942 to become Drama Adviser for Gloucestershire, and in 1946 he became National Drama Adviser for the Carnegie United Kingdom Trust.

On his retirement at 65 he became head of acting for the Rose Bruford College of Speech and Drama in Sidcup, having been the Chairman of the Governors when it was founded. His final retirement was at the age of 72. His wife suffered a severe stroke in 1976, and for five and a half years he devotedly visited her in hospital every day. She was paralysed and unable to speak. Leo Baker died on 5 September 1986 at the age of 88, his intellectual faculties as bright as ever. Lewis's letters to him are in the Bodleian Library.‡

Barfield, Owen (1898–1997): an Inkling and 'the wisest and best of my unofficial teachers', as Lewis said in the dedication to *The Allegory of Love*. He was born in North London on 9 November 1898, the son of **Arthur Edward Barfield** and **Elizabeth (Shoults) Barfield**. His father was a solicitor and his mother an ardent suffragette. Owen Barfield was educated at Highgate School, where he became friends with Cecil Harwood.* During the First War he served as a Wireless Officer in the Signal Service of the Royal Engineers – now the Royal Corps of Signals. The wireless (or radio) was at that time in its infancy, and still using the Morse code. In 1919 he went up to Wadham College, Oxford, on a Classical Scholarship. It was during his first term there that he met Lewis, and they became friends from that point onwards. 'Barfield towers above us all', Lewis wrote in his diary of 9 July 1922. This diary (**AMR**) covering the years 1922–27, contains much about their early meetings and conversations. Lewis's finest tribute to Barfield is found in **SBJ** XIII:

> There is a sense in which Arthur [Greeves]* and Barfield are the types of every man's First Friend and Second Friend. The First is the *alter ego*, the man who first reveals to you that you are not alone in the world by turning out (beyond hope) to share all your most secret delights. There is nothing to be overcome in making him your friend; he and you join like raindrops on a window. But the Second Friend is the man who disagrees with you about everything. He is not so much the *alter ego* as the anti-self. Of course he shares your interests; otherwise he would not become your friend at all. But he has approached them all at a different angle. He has read all the right books but has got the wrong thing out of every one. It is as if he spoke your language but mispronounced it. How can he be so nearly right and yet, invariably, just not right? He is as fascinating (and infuriating) as a woman. When you set out to correct his heresies, you find he forsooth has decided to correct yours! And then you go at it, hammer and tongs, far into the night,

night after night, or walking through fine country that neither gives a glance to, each learning the weight of the other's punches, and often more like mutually respectful enemies than friends. Actually (though it never seems so at the time) you modify one another's thought; out of this perpetual dogfight a community of mind and a deep affection emerge. But I think he changed me a good deal more than I him. Much of the thought which he afterward put into *Poetic Diction* had already become mine before that important little book appeared. It would be strange if it had not. He was of course not so learned then as he has since become; but the genius was already there.

When he wrote to his son, Christopher Tolkien,* on 24 November 1944 about a meeting of the Inklings, J.R.R. Tolkien* said: 'O.B. is the only man who can tackle C.S.L. making him define everything and interrupting his most dogmatic pronouncements with subtle *distinguo's*' (**LJRRT**). After taking a BA in 1921, Barfield began a B.Litt. thesis on 'Poetic Diction'. This work, published in 1928, was to have a profound influence on Lewis and Tolkien. It is about the relation between word and meaning, and it contains many of the author's leading philosophic ideas. Barfield's first book was a fairy tale, *The Silver Trumpet* (1925), and after this he published *History in English Words* (1926), which is not merely about the changes in the meanings of words over time but what he called 'evolution of consciousness'.

Barfield became a follower of Rudolf Steiner in 1923, and was involved with the Anthroposophical Society all his life. While writing his thesis on 'Poetic Diction' his beliefs about it had led him to the Romantic poets and their doctrines of imagination, and then to the conclusion that Romanticism had never fulfilled itself, never been philosophically 'justified'. However, on reading Steiner he found that Steiner had understood all this before him. In the Introduction to *Romanticism Comes of Age* (1944), which contains Barfield's debt to Steiner, he wrote: 'Anthroposophy included and transcended not only my own poor stammering theory of poetry as knowledge, but the whole Romantic philosophy. It was nothing less than Romanticism grown up.' Lewis rejected Steiner out of hand, and there resulted his 'Great War'‡ with Barfield in letters and other documents.

As an undergraduate Barfield had been interested in folk dancing, and on 11 April 1923 he married **Matilda ('Maud') Douie**, a professional dancer and producer who had worked with Gordon Craig. They lived in Long Crendon after their marriage, and Lewis often visited them there.

Barfield was baptized in the Church of England in 1949. 'Welcome, welcome, welcome,' Lewis wrote on 23 June 1949. 'No, of course it won't mean the end of the Great War.' The Barfields had three children, **Alexander** (b. 30 January 1928), **Lucy** (b. 2 November 1935) who is Lewis's godchild and to whom he dedicated *The Lion, the Witch and the Wardrobe*, and **Geoffrey** (b. 6 June 1940) to whom Lewis dedicated *The Voyage of the 'Dawn Treader'*.

While Barfield's chief loves were to remain literature and philosophy, his father needed him in his law practice, and in 1929 he joined the London firm of Barfield and Barfield. He received a BCL from Oxford in 1930, and spent the next twenty-eight years as a solicitor in London. In the 1940s Lewis asked him to set up a charitable trust into which he could direct most of his royalties, which trust was administered by Barfield. Those who would know more about the 'Agapargyry' (love + money), as they called the trust, should see Barfield's *This Ever Diverse Pair* (1950). (See **Agape Fund‡**). In this charming *jeu d'esprit* 'Burgeon' is the idealistic alter ego or 'sleeping partner' of the practical-minded solicitor named 'Burden'. They represent the tension between the demands of the legal profession and the need to live in the larger world of thought and letters. Chapter VI is about a client named 'Ramsden' who is based on Lewis, and it deals in a humorous way with the charitable trust Barfield set up for his friend. This chapter of the book is reprinted in a work containing nearly everything Barfield has written about Lewis, *Owen Barfield on C.S. Lewis*, ed. G.B. Tennyson (1990).

A revolution in his life came about when he was sixty. Following his retirement in 1959 he found time to write many of his best books. They include his own favourite – *Saving the Appearances* (1957) – as well as *Worlds Apart* (1963), *Unancestral Voice* (1965), *Speaker's Meaning* (1967), *What Coleridge Thought* (1971), *The Rediscovery of Meaning, and Other Essays* (1977), and *History, Guilt and Habit* (1979). For the first two decades of this second part of his life he was a visiting scholar in many American colleges and universities. There was always a welcome for his American friends at his home 'Orchard View' in Dartford, Kent. His wife died there on 13 February 1980. He moved to Forest Row, Sussex, in 1986 and died there on 14 December 1997.

Barfield was a Fellow of the Royal Society of Literature. *Evolution of Consciousness: Studies in Polarity*, ed. Shirley Sugerman (1976) is a volume of essays offered him. An excellent review of his life is found in the Introduction to *A Barfield Sampler: Poetry and Fiction by Owen Barfield* (1993) by the editors, Jeanne Clayton Hunter and Thomas Kranidas. Of the many studies of his writings he thought the best was Gareth Knight's *The Magical World of the Inklings: J.R.R. Tolkien, C.S. Lewis, Charles Williams,*

Owen Barfield (1990). Photos in **IHW** and **TJB**. See **Anthroposophy**.‡

Baynes, Pauline Diana (1922–   ) is the illustrator of the Chronicles of Narnia. She was born in Brighton on 9 September 1922, the daughter of **Frederick William Wilberforce Baynes** and **Jessie Harriet Maude (Cunningham) Baynes**. Her father was a Commissioner in the Indian Civil Service, and she spent her first five years in India. She was educated at several private schools, after which she followed her older sister, **Angela**, to Farnham School of Art (1937). She was a student in the Slade 1939–40, when it was evacuated to Oxford. During the Second War Farnham Castle was the Camouflage Development Training Centre of the Royal Engineers, and she and her sister worked there as assistant model-makers 1940–42. While there she did her first illustrations, which accompanied some of the tales in the *Perry Colour Books*. From there she went to Bath to draw charts for the Admiralty Hydrographic Department 1942–45. After this she taught art at Beaufort School in Camberley 1946–47.

Miss Baynes's professional work began when she happened to draw a picture in the margin of a letter she wrote to a friend. He showed it to Frank Whittaker of *Country Life*, and this led to a commission to illustrate three books by Victoria Stevenson: *Clover Magic* (1944), *The Magic Footstool* (1946) and *The Magic Broom* (1950). Before she finished the third of these commissions she had illustrated a book of her own, *Victoria and the Golden Bird* (1948).

Her long association with Lewis and J.R.R. Tolkien* began with Tolkien's strong dislike of some illustrations his publishers had chosen for *Farmer Giles of Ham*. He complained to Allen & Unwin about the ugly 'fashionableness' of the drawings, and in his letter of 5 August 1948 said they were 'wholly out of keeping with the style or manner of the text' (**LJRRT**). Pauline Baynes had left a portfolio with Allen & Unwin, and when the publishers showed Tolkien some comical ink-and-watercolour cartoons she had drawn after medieval manuscript decorations, he felt her work exactly suited his book. He was delighted with the ones she drew for him. 'They are more than illustrations,' he wrote to Allen & Unwin on 16 March 1949, 'they are a collateral theme. I showed them to my friends whose polite comment was that they reduced my text to a commentary on the drawings' (**LJRRT**).

Not long afterwards Lewis asked her to illustrate *The Lion, the Witch and the Wardrobe*. He may have been one of those who had seen the illustrations to *Farmer Giles*, but Miss Baynes has said: 'C.S. Lewis told me that he had actually gone into a bookshop and asked the assistant there if she could recommend someone who could draw children and animals. I don't know whether he was just being kind to me and making me feel that I was more important than I was or whether he'd simply heard about me from his friend Tolkien' (**PWD** 6). She and Lewis met for the first time on 31 December 1949 at a luncheon party Lewis gave in Magdalen College.‡ Lewis was so impressed by her traditional style of drawing that he wanted her to illustrate all the Narnian stories. At a meeting on 1 January 1951 they discussed a map of Narnia for the end pages of *Prince Caspian*. On 5 January Lewis sent her a little map he had made (now in the Bodleian‡) and a few suggestions: 'My idea was that the map should be more like a medieval map than an Ordnance Survey – mountains and castles drawn – perhaps winds blowing at the corners – and a few heraldic-looking ships, whales and dolphins in a sea.' When we compare these simple instructions with the map in the end pages of *Prince Caspian* and the grand poster-sized map of Narnia which came out in 1968, we realize how much our picture of Lewis's imaginary world owes to the skill and imagination of this lady.

As time went on, Lewis found her work improving and her range widening. 'It is delightful to find,' he said on 21 January 1954 after seeing the drawings for *The Horse and His Boy*, 'that you do each book a little bit better than the last … Both the drawings of Lasaraleen in her litter were a rich feast of line and of fantastic-satiric imagination … Shasta among the tombs (in the new technique, which is lovely) was exactly what I wanted. The pictures of Rabadash hanging on the hook and just turning into an ass were the best comedy you've done yet. The Tiscoc was superb: far beyond anything you were doing five years ago … The crowds are beautiful, realistic yet also lovely wavy compositions: but your crowds always were. How did you do Tashbaan? We only got its full wealth by using a magnifying glass! The result is exactly right' (**L**). When *The Last Battle* won the Carnegie Medal for the best children's book of 1956 she wrote to congratulate him. He replied on 4 May 1957: 'Is it not rather "our" Medal?'

The Narnian tales had just come to an end when Pauline Baynes was helping Tolkien again. He wanted illustrations, he told her on 6 December 1961, that are 'bright and clear visions of things that one might really see' (**LJRRT**). This resulted in more of her charming mock-medieval drawings for *The Adventures of Tom Bombadil* (1962). A few years later she illustrated Tolkien's *Smith of Wootton Major* (1967). In the same year that she won the Kate Greenaway Medal for her illustrations to Grant Uden's *Dictionary of Chivalry* (1968) the Tolkiens moved to Bournemouth. It was there that Tolkien and his wife came to know Pauline's husband.

Pauline Baynes met **Fritz Otto Gasch** in early 1961 and they married on 25 March 1961. Gasch, who was born in Auerswalde, Saxony, Germany, was taken prisoner while serving in the Afrika Corps and brought to England, via the USA, as a prisoner of war. 'We only knew each other a few months before we decided to get married,' she said. 'Meeting Fritz was the best thing that ever happened to me; he was a splendid man and a wonderful husband who was completely tolerant of his wife's obsession to draw!' Following the marriage they settled in the village of Dockenfield, near Farnham, where Fritz was a garden contractor. He died in 1988.

Miss Baynes has illustrated over a hundred books, some of the best known of which are Amabel Williams-Ellis's *The Arabian Nights* (1957) and *Fairy Tales from the British Isles* (1960), Hans Christian Andersen's *Andersen's Fairy Tales* (1963), Richard Barber's *Companion to World Mythology* (1979), and Beatrix Potter's *Country Tales* (1987). She has also written and illustrated a number of books, among which are *The Song of the Three Holy Children* (1986), *How Dog Began* (1986), *Good King Wenceslaus* (1987), *Noah and the Ark* (1988) and *In the Beginning* (1991). She is the editor and illustrator of *Thanks Be to God: Prayers from around the World* (1990).

Her recent work includes illustrations to Brian Sibley's *Land of Narnia* (HarperCollins, London, 1990); a special edition of *The Lion, the Witch and the Wardrobe* which contains, besides the original illustrations, her map of Narnia and 17 full-page additional illustrations in colour (HarperCollins, London, 1991); and *A Book of Narnians: The Lion, the Witch and the Others*. The latter is a picture book of the Narnian characters, with text by James Riordan, and illustrated by Pauline Baynes (HarperCollins, London, 1994). The original poster-map of Narnia and some of the Narnian illustrations are in the Wade Center‡ at Wheaton; her map of Tolkien's Middle Earth and some of the Narnian illustrations are in the Bodleian.‡ For more about her Narnian illustrations see **NARNIA**. Further information about Pauline Baynes can be found in *Contemporary Authors* (USA), *Illustrators of Children's Books* (1978) and *Something about the Author*, vol. 19 (1980) and vol. 59 (1990). Photos in **IHW** and **TJB**.

Bennett, Jack Arthur Walter, FBA (1911–81), Inkling and colleague at Magdalen College,‡ was born in Auckland, New Zealand on 28 February 1911. He was the son of **Ernest Bennett** and his wife **Alexandra (Corrall) Bennett**, both natives of Leicester. His father emigrated to New Zealand in 1907 and his mother in 1909. Jack Bennett was educated at Mount Albert Grammar School and then Auckland University College, where he sat under a teacher who turned his mind to Middle English.

After taking an MA in Auckland University College, he left for Merton College, Oxford, where he matriculated in 1933. His tutorials with

Edmund Blunden led to a lifetime friendship, and he attended the lectures of C.L. Wrenn,* J.R.R. Tolkien* and C.T. Onions. After taking a First Class degree in English in 1935, he was supervised by Kenneth Sisam in the writing of a doctoral thesis on 'Old English and Old Norse studies in England from the time of Francis Junius till the end of the eighteenth century', for which he was awarded the D.Phil. in 1938. He was elected to a junior research fellowship at The Queen's College, Oxford, in 1938.

Bennett was in New Zealand at the outbreak of the Second World War, and was in New York on his way back to England when the British Information Services there asked for his help. In the end he spent five years in the US, first as Head of the Research Department, and later as a Director. He returned to the Queen's College in September 1945 and began teaching on the English faculty. In 1947 he was elected to a fellowship at Magdalen College, where he was able to take over the teaching of Anglo-Saxon for Lewis. At the same time he helped C.T. Onions edit *Medium Aevum*, of which he was sole editor 1956–80. In 1957 his *Parlement of Foules* was published, and in 1958 the first volume of the Clarendon Medieval and Tudor Series appeared under his General Editorship.

In 1964 Bennett succeeded Lewis as Professor of Medieval and Renaissance English in Cambridge, becoming at the same time a Fellow of Magdalene College.‡ He devoted his inaugural lecture in November 1964 to Lewis. It is entitled *The Humane Medievalist* (1965), and amongst the warm tributes he pays his predecessor he offers the following appreciation of Lewis's literary gifts:

> The whole man was in all his judgements and activities, and a discriminating zest for life, for 'common life', informs every page he wrote. 'Grete clerke' as he was, he was never wilfully esoteric: quotations and allusions rose unbidden to the surface of his full and fertile mind, but whether they are to Tristram Shandy or James Thurber they elucidate not decorate. His works are all of a piece: a book in one genre will correct, illumine or amplify what is latent in another. Hence the opening chapters of the *Allegory* must now be read in the light of the closing pages of *The Four Loves* – where he retracts his view that passionate love was largely a literary phenomenon; whilst those same pages lead us straight to the first theme of *The Discarded Image* – namely the appearance of pagan, or neoplatonic elements in the formative writers of the medieval Christian tradition. The Merlin who in a very literal sense underlies the action of *That Hideous Strength* is the Merlin who was to figure

in his selections from Layamon's *Brut*. And in *Till We Have Faces* the expositor of allegory himself writes an allegory so haunting and so suggestive that it makes Fulgentius's allegorical interpretation of his tale of Cupid and Psyche seem strained and Boccaccio's gloss on it merely mechanical (pp. 26–7).

Bennett was quite unlike Lewis. Describing some of their differences, John Stevens said in the *Magdalene College Magazine and Record*, New Series, No. 25 (1980–81), p. 6:

> As J.A.W.B. became more distant from the actual needs, and ignorances, of present-day undergraduates, so his formal lecturing … became for most undergraduates a medium of impenetrable difficulty. In this he was markedly different from his Magdalen predecessor, C.S. Lewis, the first holder of the Cambridge Chair. Lewis was amongst other things a popularizer of genius and a lecturer who enjoyed finding how he could engage the minds of his audience … It was in fact as a sole performer that J.A.W.B. was at his best; and in such single performances as his lectures on Carlyle's *Past and Present*, 'From Casaubon to Mr Casaubon', the T.S. Eliot papers, and Gibbon he showed his virtuoso powers of scholarship, his elegance of expression, his mastery of sustained and subtle argument in a way that those who were privileged to hear him will never forget.

J.A.W. Bennett was a great medievalist. Over the years he published numerous editions of medieval texts, and these include *The Knight's Tale* (1954) and *Devotional Pieces in Verse and Prose* (1955). He wrote three works on Chaucer, *The Parlement of Foules: An Interpretation* (1957), *Chaucer's Book of Fame* (1968) and *Chaucer at Oxford and at Cambridge* (1974). He persuaded Lewis to contribute an essay on 'The English Prose "Morte"' to his *Essays on Malory* (1963). He contributed an essay, 'Gower's "Honest Love"', to *Patterns of Love and Courtesy: Essays in Memory of C.S. Lewis* (1966), and he wrote a biography of Lewis for the **DNB**.

J.A.W. Bennett's marriage in 1937 to **Edith Bannister** was annulled in 1949. In 1951 he married **Gwyneth Mary Nicholas**, and they had two sons, **Edmund** and **Anselm**. He and his wife were devout Catholics, and one of the unfashionable causes to which Bennett devoted much energy and scholarship was the preservation of the old liturgy. His unofficial translation of the *Order of Mass* was published by the Association for the Latin Liturgy in 1974. He retired in 1978. Gwyneth Bennett died in 1980, and it was while he was at the airport in Los Angeles, on his way to New Zealand, that Jack Bennett died suddenly on 29 January 1981. There is a short biography of him and a list of his published writings by P.L. Heyworth in *Medieval Studies for J.A.W. Bennett*, ed. P.L. Heyworth (1981). See also Emrys Jones's biography in **DNB**, and Norman Davis's 'J.A.W. Bennett (1911–81)' in *Medium Aevum*, L, No. 1 (1981), pp. 1–2. There is a photo in **IHW**, and one of Bennett and his wife in the *Magdalene College Magazine and Record*, New Series, No. 25 (1980–81).

Betjeman, (Sir) John (1906–84): The Poet Laureate was Lewis's pupil in Magdalen College.‡ He was born in London on 28 August 1906, the son of **Ernest Betjemann** and **Mabel Bessie Dawson Betjemann**. He was educated at Highgate Junior School 1915–17, after which he went to the Dragon School in Oxford where he remained until 1920. It was while cycling around Oxford that the other great interest of his life began to flower – churches. He arrived at Marlborough College in 1920 and was there until he went up to Magdalen College in the Michaelmas Term of 1925.

Lewis was Betjeman's tutor in English language and literature. While it was reasonable to suppose they would be compatible because of their mutual love of poetry and literature, they were not. Lewis's first mention of Betjeman in his diary (**AMR**) was on 28 April 1926: 'Another very dark, clouded day – less apocalyptic, but more depressing. Pupils in the morning. Yorke for language. Then Betjeman and Valentin to stumble through the *Voyage of Ohthere*.'

He would not work and in the end Betjeman failed the University's Divinity examination. After being 'rusticated' for a term, he chose not to take his final examination and he left Oxford without a degree. He blamed Lewis for this, and from that point on Lewis appeared as a figure of fun in a number of his poems. In *Ghastly Good Taste* (1933) Betjeman said: 'Finally, the author is indebted to Mr C.S. Lewis … whose jolly personality and encouragement to the author in his youth have remained an unfading memory for the author's declining years.' In *Continual Dew* (1937) he again expressed indebtedness to Lewis 'for the footnote on p. 256'. (There was no p. 256.) In 'A Hike on the Downs', in *Continual Dew*, he has this verse:

> Objectively, our Common Room
> Is like a small Athenian State –
> Except for Lewis; he's all right
> But do you think he's *quite* first-rate?

And, finally, in 'May-Day Song for North Oxford' (*New Bats in Old Belfries*, 1945), Betjeman wrote:

> Oh! well-bound Wells and Bridges!
> Oh! earnest ethical search
> For the wide high-table λογος
> of St C.S. Lewis's Church.

Betjeman's *Letters: Volume One: 1926 to 1951*, edited by his daughter Candida Lycett Green (1994) contains a long letter to Lewis on 13 December 1939 in which the author spells out his case against him. However, by the time he wrote to Martyn Skinner on 23 February 1960 he was willing to take part of the blame: 'Lewis was my undoing at Magdalen as well as my own temperament' (*Letters: Volume Two: 1951 to 1989* (1995)).

On 29 July 1933 Betjeman married **Penelope Chetwode**, the daughter of Field Marshal Sir Philip Walhouse Chetwode. They had two children, **Paul** (b. 1937) and **Candida** (now **Candida Lycett Green**) (b. 1942). Besides working as film critic to the *Evening Standard* 1934–35, Betjeman wrote many articles and reviews and contributed a number of poems to various journals. His first two collections of poems were *Mount Zion* (1931) and *Continual Dew* (1937). In his article about Betjeman in **DNB**, Kingsley Amis speaks of his poems as showing 'a poet already fully formed, with the impeccable ear, delight in skill, and assured mastery of a wide range of tones and themes that so distinguished all his subsequent work in verse ... In a remarkable variety of metres and manners the poems make an equally clear-cut impression on the reader, never drifting into obscurity and never once tainted with the modernism then fashionable. Here too he gave glimpses of the world of gas-lit Victorian churches and railway stations, of grim provincial cities and leafy suburbs that he was to make his own, not forgetting the grimmer contemporary developments, shopping arcades, and bogus Tudor bars, that he saw effacing it and strove to resist.' Many of these concerns are reflected in the collection *Ghastly Good Taste* (1933). Betjeman's career flourished with *Old Lights for New Chancels* (1940), *New Bats in Old Belfries* (1945) and *A Few Late Chrysanthemums* (1954).

In World War II he volunteered for the RAF, but after being rejected he joined the Ministry of Information. He was the UK press attaché in Dublin (1941–43), and he afterwards worked in the Publications Department in the Admiralty. Between 1944 and 1951 he was a regular book reviewer for the *Daily Herald*. But no account of his life would be complete without mentioning his 'Church of England thoughts'. After years of 'sermon tasting', he became a member of the Church of England and a communicant in 1937. It is an understatement to say Betjeman cared passionately for the Anglican Church. He had a deep and abiding love of the Faith itself, quite apart from his love for its buildings and liturgy. In 1946–78 he served on the Oxford Diocesan Advisory Committee, and for much of that time on the London Diocesan Advisory Committee.

In later years Betjeman and Lewis were reconciled, but they never became close friends. In a letter to Betjeman of 28 May 1938 Lewis said, 'Why do you never drop in and see me?' Betjeman became warmer towards Lewis as time went on, and when Owen Barfield* said to him in the 1950s, 'I hear you don't like Lewis,' Betjeman replied, 'Oh, I do *now*!'

His very popular *Collected Poems* came out in 1958, and in 1960 he won the Queen's Gold Medal for Poetry. He was elected a Companion of Literature by the Royal Society of Literature in 1968, and in 1969 he was knighted. In 1972 he was chosen as Poet Laureate. In the 1970s Betjeman began suffering from Parkinson's disease. Lady Betjeman died in 1985, and he died at Trebetherick, Cornwall, on 19 May 1984.

Bide, The Rev. Peter William (1912–   ): friend who performed Lewis's marriage. He was born in Uxbridge, Middlesex on 18 November 1912, the elder son of **Jesse** and **Katherine Bide**. He left Cranbrook School in Kent at 17 and, after a brief spell in Germany, he joined the staff of British Dyestuffs Corporation, Manchester, a subsidiary of Imperial Chemical Industries (ICI), as a dyehouse assistant. In 1935 his parents sold their business and gave him and his brother £500 each. He gave up his position with ICI, got a job in Germany, now under Hitler, teaching a hotel proprietor English while he learned elementary Latin.

In the Michaelmas Term of 1936 he went up to Oxford to read English Language and Literature at St Catherine's Society. 'Almost the first thing,' he said, 'that happened when I came up was being told to go and attend the lectures of someone called Lewis of whom I'd never heard.' Bide took his BA in 1939, and recalls this period as three moderately successful and blissful years with a 'good Second' at the end of it.

In 1940 Bide was gazetted a Second Lieutenant in the Royal Marines. He became engaged shortly afterwards to **Margaret Garrett** and they were married the following year on his return from the disastrous Dacca expedition. They had four children: **Carol**, b. 4 February 1944; **Stephen**, b. 2 December 1946; **Penelope**, b. 25 August 1949; and **Mark**, b. 15 January 1954.

In 1943 Bide, promoted Captain, became Brigade Intelligence Officer and posted himself to the School of Military Intelligence at Cambridge, responsible for training the Normandy Expeditionary Force in German Infantry weapons and tactics. In one way and another he remained in Intelligence for the rest of the war, leaving with the rank of Major. He was offered and accepted a peace-time appointment with Foreign Office Intelligence. During these war years Bide had kept up with Lewis, visiting him when he passed through Oxford.

In 1948 he was recommended for ordination and trained at Wells Theological College. He was ordained Deacon in 1949 by the Bishop of Chichester, George Bell, to the title of St Helen's, Hangleton, a tiny Sussex downlands church. Ordained priest the following year he was later the first Vicar of Hangleton since the Middle Ages.

In the spring of 1954 there was a terrible polio epidemic in the area. These were the days before the Salk vaccine. 'I remember,' he says, 'the stream of ambulances up to the "fever hospital" where I was Chaplain. Some died between the ambulance and the ward. I was told that the Gallagher boy was seriously ill. This was a Roman Catholic family, one of the first to move into the Council Estate which was busily extending my parish. I went round to see them and found the whole family and relations crammed into the tiny sitting room, Mother twisting a soaked hanky between her fingers. "Michael's in the hospital," she said, "and they say he's dying." "The doctors haven't got the gift of life and death," I said, "that belongs to God. What you have to do is to relax your fear and stress, as far as you are able, and rest on the Mercy of God. I will go and see him." When I got to the hospital it was obvious that the child was very seriously ill. If any child was dying it was Michael. It wasn't polio, as I had expected, but cerebral meningitis. Sister was sitting in the ward with him. I went on my knees by the bedside and uttered a very simple and naïve prayer: "Look down, O Lord, on this Thy child, and if it be Thy gracious Will, let him recover. For the sake of Jesus Christ our Lord. Amen." I didn't touch him. I got up and said to Sister, "Now I hope he'll be all right." She looked at me as though I were mad – not unnaturally.

'This was Lent and in the neighbouring Parish of St Nicholas, Portslade, I had been giving a series of addresses on Faith. The previous week I had been talking on the Healing of Jairus's daughter. It makes a very good story for discussing Faith and what is involved in the profession of Faith. And I said to the congregation, "Now, here is Michael Gallagher. I'm sure since last week you have in your prayers and thoughts concerned yourself with the nature of Faith. If you will rest on everything you have learned in this church, all the many blessings that have come to you through Sacrament, and Worship, and put Michael's welfare at the heart of this, then he will get better." I heard myself say those terrible and presumptuous words. I was putting all these people's Faith at risk and drawing a blank cheque on the Holy Spirit which is not, in my judgement, a good thing to do. Afterwards I went straight up to the hospital. The Night Sister was sitting in the Ward. "How is he?" I said. "Well, it's an extraordinary thing," she said, "but he's rather better." Two days later the Chief Physician of Brighton's Children's Hospital rang up to ask the result of the autopsy and was told he was sitting up and having his breakfast!

'Now I found this theologically extremely puzzling. I had other patients in the hospital with whom I had prayed and laid hands on some of them, and they had died. Of course I was glad for Michael and his family. But why had he been selected in, apparently, so arbitrary a fashion? The next time I saw Jack Lewis I discussed this with him. I do not remember that there was much clarification of the problem – how could there be? But this is the basis on which he asked me to go up later on.'

Two years later – 23 April 1956 – Lewis married Joy Gresham* in a civil ceremony with the purpose of giving her British nationality. By the spring of 1957 she was in the Wingfield-Morris Hospital (now the Nuffield Orthopaedic Centre) with cancer. She was believed to be dying and both she and Lewis wanted the Sacrament of Marriage before that happened.

This did not seem unduly complicated to Lewis who took the position of the Catholic Church regarding matrimony. That is to say, because Joy's husband had been married before, her marriage to Gresham was invalid. The Anglican Church, however, regards all marriages as valid, even if some are irregular. Thus, when Lewis appealed to the Bishop of Oxford (Harry Carpenter) for permission to marry he was refused. 'Lewis had been married in a Register Office,' said Bide, 'and the peculiar position of the Anglican Church as the Established Church of these Islands meant that it recognized such marriages as valid. You cannot be married twice to the same person. The fact is that *official* Anglicanism in England does not recognize the sacramental nature of the Marriage Service (see Article XXV of the 39 Articles). They order these things differently abroad where customarily a civil marriage precedes the marriage in church.'

In these circumstances Lewis wrote to Bide and asked him to come up and stay the night and lay hands on Joy. Here is his account of what followed:

When Joy was diagnosed as having a sarcoma Jack wrote to me and asked me to come up and lay hands on her. I hesitated. The Michael case had mercifully made little or no noise but I had been aware of how easy it would have been for me to assume the role of 'a priest with a gift of healing' so I made no attempt to exploit the gift, if gift it was. I have stuck to that ever since. But Jack was a special case. Not only did I owe a considerable intellectual debt but the ordinary demands of friendship would have made it churlish to say no. So I went. And that was the beginning. He had sent for me to lay hands on Joy.

Shortly after my arrival at The Kilns he said to me, 'Peter, I know this isn't fair, but do you think you could marry us? I asked the Bishop; I've asked my parish priest; I've asked all my friends on the Faculty; and they've said no. Joy is dying and she wants the Sacrament before she dies.' He then outlined the problem which I have set out above which clearly baffled him. I had myself for some time found the Church's attitude to remarriage in church after divorce difficult. The Church rested everything on the previous marriage vows. It was stated by moral philosophers that it was impossible to countenance the renewal of vows which had so flagrantly been broken. But the Church itself was guilty of an obvious inconsistency. If, after the marriage, consummation for one reason or another failed, then the Church accepted the State's decree of nullity. But if non-consummation did not come under 'for better or worse' what did? But unease is not repudiation. I had no jurisdiction in the Diocese of Oxford or in its many parishes. The example of my fellow priests showed that I should be guilty of a grave breach of Church law. A minor public school instils an exaggerated respect for authority, and confrontation has never been one of my strongest points. I asked Jack to leave me alone for a while and I considered the matter. In the end there seemed only one Court of Appeal. I asked myself what He would have done and that somehow finished the argument.

The following morning I married them in the hospital ward with the Ward Sister and Warnie Lewis* as witnesses. I laid hands on Joy and she lived for another three years.[1]

---

[1] Lewis referred to this in **The Efficacy of Prayer**. 'I have stood by the bedside of a woman,' he said, 'whose thigh-bone was eaten through with cancer and who had thriving colonies of the disease in many other bones as well. It took three people to move her in bed. The doctors predicted a few months of life: the nurses (who often know better), a few weeks. A good man laid his hands on her and prayed. A year later the patient was walking (uphill, too, through rough woodland) and the man who took the last X-ray photos was saying, "These bones are solid as rock. It's miraculous."'

Then the pigeons began to come home. I went straight to see the Bishop of Oxford and tell him what I had done. He tore me off a strip – quite properly – and then said, 'I will not give you a penance. You are to go straight home and tell your own Bishop what you have done.' I loved George Bell and the idea of going and telling him something of which I knew he would not approve was very difficult. Bishop Carpenter knew what he was about!

When I got home I rang up Mary Balmer, George's secretary, and asked for an appointment. 'Oh Mr Bide, he had been trying to get in touch with you. Come in tomorrow morning at 10 a.m.' Oh dear, I thought, bad news travels fast. But when I got to Chichester he had no idea why I wanted to see him. I told him the story, sitting across the desk from the Bishop, and under the steady gaze of those piercing blue eyes. When I had finished he paused and then said 'Peter, what *did* you think you were doing? They were married already.' I tried to explain that the sacramental aspect of Christian marriage meant a great deal to a dying woman and that she felt that the marriage service would give her some final sense of acceptance. But he remained baffled. 'Anyway, you won't do it again will you Peter?' I was able to give him that assurance. 'Now,' he said, and went on to offer me Goring-by-Sea, one of the plums of his Diocese!

Alas, Peter Bide was not to enjoy Goring for long. His own wife also developed cancer. That same year Bide was appointed the Anglican Assistant General Secretary of the British Council of Churches responsible for local councils of churches throughout the British Isles, including both Ulster and Eire. He also became the full-time secretary of the Faith and Order Committee.

Margaret Bide died in early September 1960. With four motherless children he could not cope with his job which called for constant travel. He married again in 1961, **Penelope Voelcker**, who was the secretary to his boss, Kenneth Slack. They had two further children: **Katharina**, b. 11 April 1962, and **Nicola**, b. 8 January 1967. In 1968, after serving four years each in two further parishes, he received the wholly unexpected request to apply for the Chaplaincy of Lady Margaret Hall, the oldest of Oxford's women's colleges. There he spent thirteen years as chaplain and tutor in theology. When he retired in 1980 he spent a further two years at the invitation of the Dean of Christ Church as Precentor of Oxford Cathedral. He now lives in Boxgrove, West Sussex.

Bles, Geoffrey (1886–1957) was born in Alderly Edge, Cheshire, on 5 September 1886, the son of **Joseph Bles**. He was educated at Charterhouse, and in 1905 he matriculated at Merton College, Oxford, where he read Greats. After taking his BA in 1909, he joined the Indian Civil Service in 1910, and was with the 17th Cavalry in the Indian Army for a while during the First World War. In 1920 he married **Evelyn Constance Halse**.

In 1923 he created his own publishing firm in London. Among his early successes was the publication of a translation of Vicki Baum's novel *Grand Hotel* (1930). This same year he began publishing religious books, and introduced Nicolas Berdyaev and Jacques Maritain to Britain. He was as well the publisher of J.B. Phillips. Working with him was another London publisher, Ashley Sampson, of The Centenary Press, whom Bles bought out in about 1930. Sampson remained with the Centenary Press and worked for Bles, and it was he who first spotted C.S. Lewis. He had been so impressed by *The Pilgrim's Regress* that he asked Lewis to contribute *The Problem of Pain* to his 'Christian Challenge Series'. Thus it was that Geoffrey Bles Ltd became the major publisher of Lewis's religious books. Bles also had a scholar's love for Latin and Greek, and this made for a very lively correspondence with Lewis. He retired in 1954 and his controlling shares in the business were purchased by William Collins,* Sons & Co. Ltd. He left behind two colleagues on the Board of the company, J.G. Lockhart and Jocelyn Gibb* who became the Managing Director. He died on 3 April 1957.

Calabria, Blessed Giovanni (1873–1954), who corresponded with Lewis for some years, was described by Pope John Paul II as 'a champion of the charity of the Gospel'. Giovanni Calabria was born into a very poor family in Verona on 8 October 1873, the son of **Luigi** and **Angela Foschio**. He attended the State Secondary School. From the first he had an urge to give away whatever he had and this led him to the priesthood. He was ordained on 11 August 1901 and served as a curate at St Stephen's, Verona. Besides visiting the hospitals, the prisons, and the homes of the poor, Don Giovanni set out to rescue some of the many orphans from the streets.

He became parish priest of St Benedict's al Monte in 1907, and on 26 November conceived the idea for his great 'work', the San Zeno Orphanage, the Casa Buoni Fanciulli (Home of Good Children), in Verona. On 6 November 1908 he settled with his many orphans in a quarter of Verona known as San Zeno in Monte. To help with his work Don Giovanni established a Congregation of priests and laity to be called 'The Poor Servants of Divine Providence'. By the time the Order was approved by his Bishop in 1932 the Congregation numbered some hundred and fifty priests and laymen, attached to about twenty houses in the Provinces of Verona, Vicenza, Ferrara, Milan, Rome and other parts of Italy. Those students who enter the Congregation are housed, fed and given an elementary education, after which they are free to enter any seminary or religious missionary institute they please. At the same time, the poor children – who now number over 2500 in the various houses – are looked after and prepared for life. In the same year (1947) that Don Giovanni's Congregation of The Poor Servants of Divine Providence won the approval of Pope Pius XII he began a correspondence with C.S. Lewis.

Don Giovanni had been passionately interested in Christian unity for a long time and after reading *Le Lettere di Berlicche* – an Italian translation of *The Screwtape Letters* – he decided to write to the author. As he could neither read nor write English, he chose the only language he believed they shared – Latin. In his letter of 1 September 1947, he said that he had 'begun to propagate the holding of an "octave of prayers for the unity of the Church"' and that Lewis seemed 'to be able to contribute much in the Lord, with your great influence not only in your own most noble country but even in other lands ... Poor as I am, I promise to pray strenuously that God and our Lord Jesus Christ will see fit to illuminate and strengthen you that you may be able to perform something of greater moment in the Lord's vineyard.' Lewis replied on 6 September – in Latin of course – that he had tried 'to leave completely aside the subtler questions about which the Roman Church and Protestants disagree ... and in my own books to expound, rather, those things which still, by God's grace, after so many sins and errors, are shared by us.' This was the beginning of a correspondence which meant much to both of them and which continued for the rest of Don Giovanni's life.

During this time Don Giovanni was kept very busy with the Congregation and the Casa Buoni Fanciulli. Father Domenico Mondrone SJ says in his short biography, 'God's Care-Taker' in *The Month* (October 1956), that Don Giovanni's 'administrative wisdom' was certainly not of this world. Rather, it was contained in the words of Our Lord: 'Be not solicitous for your life', 'Behold the birds of the air', 'Seek ye first the Kingdom of God.' It is not surprising that when a wealthy Roman benefactor offered him a million lire to open a house in Primavalle, Don Giovanni replied, 'Thank you, but there is no need for it. If God wants this work to be done, it will be done. But I beg you to take back this cheque.' In his last letter to Lewis, of 3 September 1953, he said, 'I wish that for your love of me, you would see fit to write what you think about the moral state of our times ... I would like you to indicate saving remedies, so far as they seem opportune to you, for reparation and the removal of evil, for the renewal of courage, for advancing the unity of hearts in charity ... Divine Providence binds us together with the sweet bonds of love, even if we have never known each other personally. But in love and mutual prayer we know each other well.'

Don Giovanni died on 4 December 1954 and was beatified by Pope John Paul II in Verona on 17 April 1988. Lewis corresponded with another priest of the Order, Don Luigi Pedrollo, until his death. The correspondence between Lewis, Blessed Giovanni and Don Luigi Pedrollo was translated by Martin Moynihan and published with the original Latin letters as *Letters: C.S. Lewis–Don Giovanni Calabria, A Study in Friendship* (1989). There is also a very scholarly Italian edition of the correspondence, with some additional letters between Lewis, Blessed Giovanni, Don Luigi Pedrollo, and one from Warren Lewis* to Don Luigi Pedrollo. *Una Gioia Insolita: Lettere tra un prete cattolico e un laico anglicano*, as it is called, is edited with an introduction and notes by Luciano Squizzato, and the Latin text of the letters is given as well as the translation into Italian by Patrizia Morelli (Milan: Editoriale Jaca Book SpA, 1995). *Una Gioia Insolita* contains biographies of Lewis, Don Calabria and Don Luigi Pedrollo, as well as an exhaustive list of works by and about Blessed Giovanni Calabria.

Father Mondrone's 'God's Care-Taker' is an abridgement of a longer work, 'Una Gemma del Clero Italiano, Don Giovanni Calabria,' in *La Civiltà Cattolica*, I (1955), pp. 37–52. Father Mondrone has also published 'Don Giovanni Calabria e i Fratelli Separati', in *La Civiltà Cattolica*, IV (1964), pp. 344–53. The official biography of Giovanni Calabria is Ottorino Foffano's *Il Servo di Dio Don Giovanni Calabria* (Verona: 1959). Another work of importance, and which contains a discussion about the correspondence with Lewis, is Eugenio dal Corso's thesis *Il Servo di Dio, Don Giovanni Calabria e i Fratelli Separati* ('The Servant of God, Don Giovanni Calabria, and the Separated Brethren') (Rome: Pontificia Universita Lateranense, 1974).

Capron, Robert ('Oldy' or 'Oldie') (1851–1911), Headmaster of Wynyard School,‡ which Lewis called 'Belsen' in **SBJ** II. Capron was born in Brampton, Devon, on 29 October 1851, and received a BA and a BSc from the University of London in 1873 and 1875 respectively. From 1873 to 1878 he was a teacher at Bowdon College in Altrincham, Cheshire. Ordained an Anglican clergyman in 1878, he was Curate of Wordsley, Staffordshire, and in 1881 he moved to what is now 99 Langley Road, Watford, where he founded Wynyard School.

In 1882 he married **Ellen Barnes** (1849–1909); they had three daughters, **Norah, Dorothy** and **Eva**, and one son, **John Wynyard** (1883–1959). The school was successful for a while, and at its height it could accommodate thirty boarders and as many day-boys. Robert Capron was in his day remarkably successful in teaching of the Classics, and he was proud of the fact that some of his boys gained scholarships to Charterhouse, Malvern, Uppingham and Rugby. His son won scholarships to Eton and King's College, Cambridge.

In 1896 a boy from Watford, Ernest Benskin, enrolled at Wynyard. In 1963 he published an account of his years as an India Forest Adviser, *Jungle Castaway*. However, it is in an unpublished autobiography that he explained what brought Capron to the brink of ruin. He was there when Capron, who had already shown evidence of cruelty, went into such a rage that he battered a pupil named 'Punch' Hickmott so unmercifully that the boy's parents took legal proceedings against him in the High Court. From this point onwards the school began to decline.

Albert Lewis* knew nothing about all this when he enrolled Warren at Wynyard. 'It is difficult to understand how this came about,' wrote Warren Lewis, 'having in view the careful and exhaustive enquiries which had culminated in the narrowing of the choice to three or four schools, of which Wynyard was not one' (**LP** III:33). In any event, Warren arrived there with his mother on 11 May 1905. In his reminiscences of his years there (**LP** III:33–41) Warren describes Capron:

> A fine forehead surmounted a pair of piercing eyes of the shade of brown which is nearly black. He wore a short grey beard and moustaches, and his hair, which was plentiful, was of the same colour; his complexion was ruddy, healthy, and weather beaten. The face was marred by the nose, which was small, had the appearance of being varnished, and from which the lobe of the right nostril had at some time been removed. He was, I imagine, above middle height, and was a well built and extremely powerful man physically; I have seen him lift a boy of twelve or so from the floor by the back of his collar, and, holding him at arms length as one might a dog, proceed to refresh the unfortunate youth's memory by applying his cane to his calves.

By the time C.S. Lewis entered Wynyard on 18 September 1908, Capron had been examined by a brain specialist who found him mad. The school had dwindled to eight boarders and about as many day-boys. Capron's only assistants at this time were his daughters and John Wynyard Capron who was ordained in 1909. It was not long before Jack was as appalled by Capron's cruelty as Warren, and he wrote of this in **SBJ** II.

When a blast of Capron's temper fell upon Warren on 19 September 1908 both boys wrote to their father. Warren said: 'I have stood this sort of thing for three years and I cannot stand it any longer. Please let us leave at once.' Jack said: 'Please may we not leave on Saturday? We simply *cannot* wait in this hole till the end of term.' Mr Lewis had lost his wife Flora Lewis* the month before, and trying to be helpful he replied on 20 September 1908: 'All schools – whether for boys or the larger school of life for men – press hardly and sorely at times. Otherwise they would not be schools. But I am sure you will face the good and the bad like a brave Christian boy, for dear, dear Mammy's sake' (**LP** III:140). They did not have to hold on as long as they expected. Mrs Capron died on 1 March 1909, and Warren left to go to Malvern in July 1909. Reduced to a handful of pupils, the school began to sink. Capron wrote to Albert Lewis on 27 April 1910 to say he was 'giving up school work'. The school closed in July 1910, Capron having been inducted into the living at Radwell on 13 June 1910. There he began flogging the choirboys and, when they tried to stop it, the churchwardens as well. He was put under restraint, certified insane, and resigned his living in June 1911. He died of pneumonia in Camberwell House Asylum, Peckham, Kent, on 18 November 1911. His body lies with that of his wife in Watford Cemetery.

Cecil, David (Lord Edward Christian David Gascoyne) (1902–86), Inkling and colleague. Lord David Cecil was born at Hatfield House on 9 April 1902, the youngest son of the fourth Marquess of Salisbury. He was educated at Eton and Christ Church, Oxford, where he took a First Class degree in History in 1924. Believing that his tastes were probably more academic than political, he accepted a Fellowship at Wadham College in 1924, and taught Modern History and then English Literature until 1931.

The first mention we have of Lord David in Lewis's writings comes in **AMR** where on 15 June 1926 he records a conversation about Gertrude Stein, whom Lewis found a great sham. At a meeting in her honour, he said, 'Cecil of Wadham rose to ask her what she meant by the same things being "absolutely identical and absolutely different" to which Stein ... replied "Well, you and the man next you are abs-o-lute-ly identical the way you both jump up to ask questions, but abs-o-lute-ly different in character.'

One of his fellow dons at Wadham at this time was Maurice Bowra, the Tutor in Classics, who said of him in his *Memories* (1966):

> He ... liked gay, good-natured argument and was unusually adept at it, having at his command a sharp intelligence which punctured most forms of nonsense. He was extremely quick at taking a point and making the most of it, and had an eager curiosity about all kinds of human behaviour. Though he had strong convictions on religion and politics, he never forced them on you, and was much too tolerant to make you feel that your own opinions were absurd (p. 117).

On 13 October 1932 Lord David married **Rachel**, the daughter of Sir Desmond MacCarthy, and they went to live at their home in Rockbourne, Hampshire, with the purpose of pursuing literary work. 'A happier marriage than his to Rachel one could hardly have imagined.'[2] They had two sons, **Jonathan** (b. 1939) and **Hugh** (b. 1941), and one daughter, **Laura** (b. 1947). In 1938 Lord David returned to Oxford as a Fellow of English at New College, and he moved with his family to 7 Linton Road in Summertown. He had strong convictions based on his deeply-held Christian beliefs, and in this he never changed. His love for Anglo-Catholicism caused him to go sometimes into the centre of Oxford for High Mass at St Mary Magdalen. Professionally, he was, like Lewis, one of the most popular lecturers in the English School. L.P. Hartley, one of his closest friends, said that at this time

> Few of his contemporary undergraduates would have guessed that this frail, slight figure, with its loping, plunging gait, almost a sprite, a leprechaun, was not an apparition sent to be a moment's ornament, but had in him the stamina to become one of the University's best-known and best-loved teachers.[3]

Another friend who remembered his lecturing said (*The Times*, 1 January 1986):

> Cecil was an excellent teacher. He had a gift of going straight to the heart of a subject and was quick to expose what he thought shoddy

[2] Patricia Hambledon in *David Cecil: A Portrait by his Friends*, Collected and Introduced by Hannah Cranborne (1991), p. 37.
[3] 'Lord David Cecil,' in *Essays and Poems Presented to Lord David Cecil*, ed. W.W. Robson (1970).

or silly, although he did so with such wit and humour that it was difficult to feel offence. Unlike some talkers he was an exceptionally stimulating listener. This was one of the sources of his success as a teacher and of the pleasure his company gave. In his lectures he drew large audiences, and if his personal mannerisms were unusually marked in them, and he was not always perfectly audible, his hearers were delighted by his lack of pomposity and by the contrast between his ethereal, even rather frail, appearance and the vigour and robust good sense of many of his comments. He displayed the two qualities he demanded of a critic, commonsense and uncommon sensibility.

Cecil was actually a man of letters rather than an academic. He was not drawn towards traditional scholarship, editing, or large-scale literary history, and he was uninterested in critical theory ... His own interest was in works of art as the expression of individual imaginations, shaped but not limited by historical circumstances. This led him to biography and to the critical essay on a single author or on a single author's *oeuvre*.

Lord David's first book, *The Stricken Deer* (1929), is a deeply sympathetic life of William Cowper. After this he wrote biographies of some of his favourite writers: *Sir Walter Scott* (1933) and *Jane Austen* (1935). His *Early Victorian Novelists* (1934) is a set of essays based on his Oxford lectures in which he set out to defend writers then under a cloud of critical disapproval and neglect. Not unnaturally as the grandson of the long-serving Victorian Prime Minister, Lord Salisbury (1830–1903), he chose another Prime Minister to write about. This resulted in a two-volume biography of Lord Melbourne, *The Young Melbourne* (1939) and *Lord Melbourne* (1954). This more than anything he wrote showed his inborn grasp of the realities of politics. 'He did not have to write,' L.P. Hartley said in his memoir, 'he did not have to rely on writing or teaching for his living,' but

he chose to partly because his impulse to write was stronger than his impulse to resist writing and also because the *noblesse oblige* feeling of his family, diverted in his case from politics to literature, forbade him to bury the talent that he had and that *au fond* he enjoyed using, whatever pain it cost him.

Lewis was delighted to welcome Lord David back to Oxford, and it was natural that he became a member of the Inklings. He had so many friends that it is not surprising that he was unable to attend many of their meetings. Not all the Inklings were as enthusiastic about Tolkien's *Lord of the Rings* as Lewis, but Lord David was one who heard it read in the Inklings meetings and loved it. Warnie Lewis was able to capture some of Lord David's contributions to the meetings in **BF**.

In 1948 his success as a writer and a lecturer made him an obvious choice for the newly founded Goldsmith's Chair of English Literature, and he was able to remain at New College as the chair is attached to that college. In 1949 he was made a Companion of Honour, a very early age to receive so high a distinction and a sign of the repute in which he was held. His remarkable output of writing continued, and during this period he published *Two Quiet Lives* (1948), a study of Thomas Gray and Dorothy Osborne, *Poets and Story-Tellers* (1949), and his delightful biography of Max Beerbohm, *Max* (1964). His wife Rachel published a novel entitled *Theresa's Choice* (1958).

Lewis sometimes dined with the Cecils at their home in Linton Road. In 1953 Lord David revealed that his eleven-year-old son, Hugh, wanted Lewis to read the history of his imaginary world. When Lewis had dinner with the Cecils at 7 Linton Road on 27 January 1953 he borrowed Hugh's history, and was so pleased with it that he lent the boy one of the earliest manuscripts of his imaginary world, the *History of Animal-Land*. Hugh Cecil copied down as much of Lewis's history as he could before the manuscript had to be returned, which was fortunate because the original manuscript was lost and only Hugh's copy of the *History* has survived.

Following his retirement in 1969, Lord David and his wife settled at Cranborne, where he remained as busy as ever. He appeared frequently on TV programmes about the Arts as well as on Brains Trusts. He also used this time as an opportunity to turn to pictorial biography. Out of this period came *Visionary and Dreamer: Two Poetic Painters – Samuel Palmer and Edward Burne-Jones* (1969), *A Portrait of Charles Lamb* (1983), and a further study of Jane Austen entitled *A Portrait of Jane Austen* (1978). In *The Cecils of Hatfield House* (1973) he provided an affectionate history of his own family, who had given service to the Crown since the age of Elizabeth I. Lord David's wife died in 1982, and he died on 1 January 1986. See Julian Fane, *Best Friends: Memories of Rachel and David Cecil, Cynthia Asquith, L.P. Hartley and some others* (1990), and *David Cecil: A Portrait by his Friends*, Collected and Introduced by Hannah Cranborne (1991).

Coghill, Nevill Henry Kendal Aylmer (1899–1980), Inkling. This scion of the Anglo-Irish Protestant gentry was born on 19 April 1899 at Castle Townshend, Skibbereen, County Cork. He was the son of **Sir Egerton**

Bushe Coghill, fifth baronet, a noted amateur landscape painter, and **Elizabeth Hildegarde Augusta Somerville** – sister of the writer Edith Anna Oenone Somerville. He was educated at Bilton Grange and Haileybury College, after which he was commissioned a Second Lieutenant in the trench mortar division of the Royal Artillery, and served as a gunner on the Salonika front in 1918. He went up to Exeter College, Oxford, in 1919 and read History and then English. He gained a First in English in 1923.

Coghill and Lewis began reading English together, and the first mention of Coghill occurs in Lewis's diary (**AMR**) of 2 February 1923 after they had attended George Gordon's 'Discussion Class': 'He seems an enthusiastic sensible man, without nonsense, and a gentleman, much more attractive than the majority.' It was the practice of the Discussion Class to keep the minutes of the meetings in verse. After Lewis read a paper on Spenser on 9 February 1923 Coghill wrote the minutes in some of the same Chaucerian verse for which he was to become so famous. Describing Lewis's paper on Spenser, he said:

> Sir Lewis was ther; a good philosópher
> He hade a noblé paper for to offer.
> Well couthe he speken in the Greeké tongue;
> And yet, his countenance was swythé yong.

Lewis was an unbeliever when he met Coghill, and in **SBJ** XIV he explained the 'disturbing factors in Coghill' which threatened his atheism:

> I soon had the shock of discovering that he – clearly the most intelligent and best-informed man in that class – was a Christian and a thoroughgoing supernaturalist. There were other traits that I liked but found ... oddly archaic; chivalry, honour, courtesy, 'freedom', and 'gentilesse'. One could imagine him fighting a duel. He spoke much 'ribaldry' but never 'villeinye'.

After teaching for a while in the Royal Naval College at Dartmouth, Coghill was elected a research fellow at Exeter in 1924. He became an official fellow and librarian in 1925. In 1927 he married **Elspeth Nora Harley** and they had a daughter, **Carol**. The marriage was dissolved in 1933. Over the years he developed his very considerable talents as a dramatic producer. After his production of *Samson Agonistes* in Exeter College in 1930, he went on to produce many plays for the OUDS (Oxford

University Dramatic Society). When he was casting *Measure for Measure* in 1944 he chose a young man from his own college to play the part of Angelo. He was destined for great fame. Although baptized Richard Jenkins, he later took the name Richard Burton. He and Coghill became and remained good friends. A detailed account of Coghill's contributions to OUDS, with a photo of Coghill rehearsing *Dr Faustus* with Richard Burton, is found in Humphrey Carpenter's *O.U.D.S.: A Centenary History of the Oxford University Dramatic Society* (1985).

John Wain,* who acted in Coghill's OUDS production of *The Taming of the Shrew* in 1945, left a delightful portrait of Nevill Coghill in *Dear Shadows* (1986):

> He was a big man, with a tallness that would not be remarkable now that so many people are tall, but also built on generous lines, broad-shouldered and deep-chested. His head was large, and brown hair, greying in middle life, curled and clustered on it as wiry as heather. He smiled easily, revealing somewhat battered teeth, and indeed his whole face had a slightly rough, knocked-about quality, like a chipped statue. I had one friend who used to say that he looked like one of the emperors' heads outside the Sheldonian ... But if his head was statue-like, it was a noble statue, generous in expression and bearing. His voice was deep and strong, his speech soft and gentle; and this contrast was carried through everything. He was totally courteous, a gentleman by instinct as well as by tradition ... In fact, he was more endowed with grace of manner and of mind than anyone I ever met (p. 13).

In 1957 Coghill was elected the Merton Professor of English Literature. He was a scholar of Middle English literature and his translation into contemporary English of Chaucer's *The Canterbury Tales* (1951) has enjoyed a wide audience. Lewis thought highly of it and he was pleased that Coghill had succeeded in making Chaucer understandable to many who would have never otherwise been able to read him. Coghill's translation of Langland's *Piers Plowman* was published as *Visions from Piers Plowman* in 1949, and his translation of Chaucer's *Troilus and Criseyde* in 1971.

Lewis and Coghill saw one another often, and Coghill attended a good many meetings of the Inklings. He was one of the best known and best loved men in Oxford. After running into him at a concert on 11 November 1947, Warnie Lewis* said in his diary: 'How I envy that man his apparently effortless ease in always speaking *en honnête homme*! To me tonight he said "I always like to see you at a concert because then I know it's going to be a good one"' (**BF**). Coghill liked both the Lewis brothers. He spoke of C.S. Lewis's 'habitual generosity of mind' in his essay, 'Love and "Foul Delight": Some Contrasted Attitudes', found in *Patterns of Love and Courtesy: Essays in Memory of C.S. Lewis* (1966). In his 'Approach to English' (**LCSL**) he evaluates his gifts.

In 1966, the year of his retirement, Coghill directed his former pupil Richard Burton and Elizabeth Taylor in *Dr Faustus* at the Oxford Playhouse. The following year the film, with almost the same cast, was shot in Rome, with Coghill and Burton co-directing. In 1968 he mounted a very successful musical version of *The Canterbury Tales* which ran for five years at the Phoenix Theatre in London. In the late 1960s Coghill went to live with his brother Sir Jocelyn Coghill at Aylburton, Gloucester. He died in Cheltenham on 6 November 1980. See *To Nevill Coghill from Friends*, Collected by John Lawlor and W.H. Auden (1966), and John Carey's biography in the **DNB**. Photo in **IHW**.

Collins, Sir William ('Billy') (1900–76): publisher of Lewis's books, was born in Glasgow on 23 May 1900, the son of **William Alexander Collins** and **Grace (Brander) Collins**. His family had for four consecutive generations headed the firm of William Collins, Sons & Co, Ltd. They were the leading Scottish publishers of books, stationery, Bibles, classics and diaries. He was educated at Harrow, and Magdalen College,‡ Oxford, where he read Modern History but distinguished himself most as a sportsman. Shortly after taking his BA in 1922 he joined the family firm. In 1924 he married **Priscilla Marian Lloyd**, the daughter of **Samuel Janson Lloyd** and **Margaret Ellen (Philips) Lloyd** of Pipewell Hall, Kettering. **Priscilla** or **Pierre**, as her friends called her, was born in Brigstock, Northampton on 9 October 1901. Collins and his wife had two sons and two daughters.

During the years before World War II he and his cousin Hope gradually took over most of the business from his father and his uncle, Sir Godfrey Collins. In time Billy Collins was drawn to London where his list relied heavily on Bibles, the classics and cheap books for children. However, over the 1940s and 1950s he attracted many successful authors to his firm – Thomas Armstrong, Nigel Balchin, Marguerite Steen, Norman Collins and Howard Spring amongst others. Collins was helped enormously by several people on his staff, most notably Ronald Politzer, perhaps the greatest book promoter of his generation, and his own wife Pierre.

Pierre was the inspiration behind the move into religious publishing, and it was she who was the pre-eminent builder of the Fontana religious list. A serious illness in the 1940s led to a religious crisis and she emerged a devout Catholic. By acquiring the firm of Geoffrey Bles in 1953 the Collinses were able to publish inexpensive paperback editions of both C.S. Lewis and J.B. Phillips. Of their many fine accomplishments one of the most notable was the launching of Fontana paperbacks into a market hitherto dominated by Penguin and Pan. This launch got off to a wonderful start with the works of Agatha Christie and Hammond Innes. Collins was appointed CBE in 1966 and knighted in 1970. He died at his home in Kent on 21 September 1976.

Lady Collins continued working with the firm after her husband died and loved going to the Frankfurt Book Fair. When she finally gave up work – when she was well over eighty – she remained cheerful and interested, and her Catholic faith brought her great comfort. She died at her flat in St James Place on 23 April 1990. In an obituary entitled 'Lady Fontana' (*The Tablet*, 5 May 1990) the author said:

> Her Fontana mind was always on C.S. Lewis and J.B. Phillips and it was not long before she had obtained the paperback rights on both these successful authors from Geoffrey Bles. When Bles ran into difficulties, she found an ally in its director Jocelyn Gibb* (said to be the last of the gentlemen publishers), employed him and took over the profitable titles for Fontana … When her husband died in 1976, her enthusiasm for publishing seemed to diminish, and it was through the purchase of her shares that Rupert Murdoch eventually acquired the family firm. But she made her mark and that tall, slim, vibrant figure is not forgotten. She was indeed a great publisher.

See R.A. Denniston's article on Sir William Collins in **DNB**, and his obituary, 'Lady Collins', in *The Bookseller* (4 May 1990), p. 1438.

Dunbar of Hempriggs, Dame Maureen Daisy Helen, Baronetess (1906–97), lifelong friend. She was born in Delgany, County Wicklow, Ireland, on 19 August 1906, the daughter of **Courtenay Edward Moore** and **Jane King Askins Moore**,* and the sister of **Edward Francis Courtenay 'Paddy' Moore**.* Following her parents' separation, Maureen moved with her mother and Paddy to Bristol in 1908. In June 1917 she and her mother took rooms in Wellington Square, Oxford, so that they could be near Paddy while he was training with the Officers' Training Corps in Keble College. She met Lewis soon after his arrival there on 7 June. He became a favourite with her family, and paid several visits to their home in Bristol during the next few months. It was on one of these visits, shortly before Lewis and her brother left for France, that she heard them promise that if one of them survived the war he would look after Lewis's father and Paddy's mother. Paddy was killed in action in France in March 1918 and awarded the Military Cross. After the war she and her mother returned to Oxford to be near Lewis.

Maureen was educated at Headington School, Lewis giving her tutorials in Latin and Greek for the School Certificate. Lewis's diary, *All My Road Before Me*, contains much about their joint life, and the various places they lived. Mrs Moore did much to encourage Maureen's interest in music. She had taken lessons in Bristol, and these were continued in Oxford. After leaving Headington School she went to the Royal College of Music, where she obtained her Licentiate of the Royal Academy of Music in 1928. She taught music at Monmouth School for Girls 1930–33; Oxford High School 1935–40; and at Malvern College 1957–68. On 27 August 1940 she married **Leonard Blake** (b. 7 October 1907), who had been Director of Music at Worksop College since 1935, and who in 1945 became Director of Music at Malvern College. They had two children, **Richard Francis Blake**, Lewis's godson, born on 8 January 1945; and **Eleanor Margaret Blake** born on 16 November 1949.

From Malvern she did what she could to look after her mother. After Mrs Moore became old and frail it was often difficult for Lewis both to teach and look after her. Maureen and her family would spend what time they could at The Kilns,‡ making it possible for Jack and Warnie to have a holiday in their home. She helped look after Joy Lewis's boys in 1957 when Joy was in hospital by having them to stay during the school holidays in Malvern.

On 4 February 1963 a distant relative, Sir George Cospatrick Duff-Sutherland-Dunbar, died. He was unmarried and Maureen Blake discovered that she was next in line, through her father's side of the family, to a baronetcy and an estate in Caithness, Scotland. She became the 8th Baronet. She had not seen Lewis since this happened when, in July 1963, she visited him in hospital. He had not recognized others that day, and she said: 'Jack, it is Maureen.' 'No,' he replied, 'it's Lady Dunbar of Hempriggs.' 'Oh, Jack,' she said, 'how could you remember that?' 'On the contrary,' he replied, 'how could I forget a fairy-tale?'

In August 1965 Maureen was proved to be the successor to the baronetcy by The Lord Lyon, chief of Heralds in Edinburgh. The Hempriggs Baronetcy, a 'Nova Scotia' one, was created in 1706 'to heirs whomsoever, whether male or female'. On 6 August 1965 *The Times* carried an article headlined on page 10, **Woman Wins Claim to Title – Baronetess of Scotland Recognized**.

'The court, in a judgement issued today,' it said, 'granted a petition brought by Mrs Maureen Daisy Helen Moore or Blake, of The Lees, Malvern, Worcestershire, and recognized her as Dame Maureen Daisy Helen Dunbar of Hempriggs, Baronetess.' The article goes on to say:

> Sir Thomas Innes of Learney, the Lord Lyon King of Arms, ruled that there was no reason why a woman could not inherit a baronetcy. The court held that the petitioner has the right to the arms of Dunbar of Hempriggs ... and that she is Baronetess of Hempriggs ...
>
> One of the principal legal points argued before the Lyon Court was whether a female could succeed to a baronetcy. In his judgement the Lord Lyon said: 'I cannot myself see any reason why a woman cannot inherit a baronetcy, just as she would any other hereditary dignity, and accordingly I find the petitioner heir of line, next of blood and representer of the line of Dunbar of Hempriggs' ...
>
> The title of baronet is usually limited to heirs male of the original holder, but the Dunbar baronetcy of Nova Scotia, which was created in 1706, is one of the few with remainder 'to heirs whomsoever'. Other Nova Scotia baronetcies have in the past been transmitted through females.
>
> Two baronetesses were created in the seventeenth century. In 1635 a widow was made a baronetess of Scotland, with a grant of land in Nova Scotia. In 1686 another widow, Mrs Debora Speelman, whose husband's patent of baronetcy was not sealed before his death, was made a baronetess of England for life.

Lady Dunbar and her family began spending a month each summer at Ackergill Tower, near Wick, Caithness – in the very far north of Scotland. This inheritance did not bring Maureen wealth, rather it brought added responsibilities. Still, it furnished her and her husband with a great deal of interest, and they managed to go up North every summer. When they retired from teaching at Malvern, they moved to a small village in Gloucestershire. Her husband died on 1 August 1989. Lady Dunbar died on 15 February 1997, her son becoming the 9th Baronet, Sir Richard Dunbar of Hempriggs, Bart. For more information see *They Stand Together* and George Sayer's *Jack*. Photos in **IHW**, **TJB** and *Jack*.

Dundas-Grant, James Harold ('D.G.') (1896–1985), Inkling. He was born in London on 13 April 1896, the son of a Scotsman, **Sir James Dundas-Grant**, an ear and throat specialist, and his wife, **Helen Frith**. He was educated at a preparatory school run by Mr Browne in Eastbourne, then at Eton College 1910–12. At the beginning of the War he entered the Navy and volunteered for the Air Branch. He became a Major and served in the Home Waters, Italy and France. An attack of poison gas took him back home and into hospital. After the war he became a Lloyd's underwriter, and a member of the Royal Naval Volunteer Reserve. He was recalled at the beginning of the Second War. In October 1944 he began his last appointment as commander of the Oxford University Naval Division, and it was after taking up residence in Magdalen College‡ that he met Lewis.

They were soon friends. Most of the Inklings were specialists in some academic field, and this inevitably led to Dundas-Grant being asked which one he worked in. 'I dinna work in any *field*!' he would exclaim. He was a humble man, and in his article, 'From an "Outsider",' in **ABT** he describes his gradual assimilation into both the Thursday evening and Tuesday morning meetings of the Inklings. He said that sometimes when Lewis received a large ham from his friends abroad ...

> He would approach me with a conspiratorial glint in his eye. 'D.G.,' he said, using the nickname he had given me, 'I've got a rather nice ham in my room. Would you care to come up tonight and have some?' It was thus I came to meet his great friend Tolkien:* tall, sweptback grey hair, restless. He read to us parts of his manuscript for *Lord of the Rings*, asking for criticism. Colin Hardie* was there and sometimes our doctor friend Havard,* known as Humphrey. His brother,* too, was usually in attendance. It was at these sessions that I found out how much one learned just sitting and listening ...
>
> Then one day Jack said to Humphrey: 'Don't you think that D.G. should join us at The Bird and Baby‡ on Tuesday?' ... Thus began my real acquaintance with Jack – perhaps I should say that acquaintance turned to friendship.

D.G. was a devout Catholic, and his love of music led him to run several choirs, one at Greyfriars in Oxford and another at the USAF Base at Brize Norton. Following his retirement from Magdalen he and his wife, **Katherine Galloway Dundas-Grant**, leased a house in Iffley Road, Oxford, and took charge of eight Catholic undergraduates. They were allowed to turn their garage into a chapel. In later life they moved to

Woking in Surrey. He died on 29 October 1985. There are references to him in **BF**. He is on the far left of the photo of the Inklings sitting on the terrace at the Trout Inn,‡ Godstow, c. 1947 published in **INK** and **TJB**.

Dyson, Henry Victor Dyson, 'Hugo' (1896–1975), an Inkling, was born on 7 April 1896 in Hove. He was educated at Brighton College, and the Royal Military College at Sandhurst. He was a First Lieutenant in the Queen's Own Royal West Kent Regiment, and during 1915–18 he served in France and Belgium. He was seriously wounded at Passchendaele. He came up to Exeter College, Oxford, in October 1919 and read English, taking a BA in 1921. After this he wrote a thesis on John Ford and took a B.Litt. in 1924, and his MA in 1925. 'Hugo' Dyson was Lecturer and Tutor in English at Reading University 1924–45, during which time he was an Oxford Extension Lecturer and an Oxford examiner for St Andrews and Durham. In 1925 he married **Margaret Mary Bosworth Robinson** of Wantage.

Dyson was introduced to Lewis in 1930 through their mutual friend Nevill Coghill.* Lewis described their second meeting in a letter to Arthur Greeves* of 29–30 July 1930. Dyson and Coghill had dined with Lewis in Magdalen College on 29 July and remained until 3 o'clock in the morning: 'Having met him once I liked him so well that I determined to get to know him better. My feeling was apparently reciprocated and I think we sat up so late with the feeling that heaven knew when we might meet again and the new friendship had to be freed past its youth and into maturity in a single evening. Although my head aches this morning I do not regret it. Such things come rarely and are worth a higher price than this. He is a man who really loves truth: a philosopher and a religious man: who makes his critical and literary activities depend on the former – none of your damned dilettanti' (**TST**).

When Lewis next wrote to Greeves about Dyson concerned an even more important evening at Magdalen – 19 September 1931 – this time with J.R.R. Tolkien.* This time their 'memorable talk' went on until 4 in the morning, and when Lewis wrote to Greeves on 1 October he said: 'I have just passed on from believing in God to definitely believing in Christ – in Christianity ... Dyson and Tolkien had a good deal to do with it' (**TST**). Lewis did not greatly like to have a friend spring a wife on him, but writing to Warnie on 22 November 1931 about a weekend with the Dysons, he said: 'Rare luck to stay with a friend whose wife is so nice that one *almost* (I can't say quite) *almost* regrets the change when he takes us up to his study for serious smoking and for the real midnight talking' (**L**).

There were to be more of such meetings when Dyson became a Fellow and Tutor of Merton College in 1945 and moved to Oxford. Warnie Lewis* had met him in 1933, and his diary provides an excellent description of Dyson's wit and vivacious spirits. He is, Warnie wrote on 18 February 1933: 'a man who gives the impression of being made of quick silver: he pours himself into a room on a cataract of words and gestures, and you are caught up in the stream – but after the first plunge, it is exhilarating' (**BF**). There is much evidence of this 'cataract of words' in the book he wrote with John Butt, *Augustans and Romantics 1689–1830* (1940). Jack wrote to Warnie on 3 March 1940 about reading the book in proof. 'It is, as one would expect,' he said, 'almost too bright, but some of the sparks are admirable.'

Dyson shared Warnie's disappointment in Jack having chosen Mrs Janie Moore* as his companion. On 8 August 1946 Warnie dined with Hugo Dyson in Merton, and that night he wrote in his diary: 'He was in high spirits when I met him, and his spirits rose steadily for the rest of the evening. I was more than ever struck with his amazing knowledge of Shakespeare; I don't suppose there is a man in Oxford – with the possible exception of [C.T.] Onions – who can quote so happily, e.g. tonight, apropos of J[ack]: 'O cursed spite that gave thee to the Moor': poor [Jack's] whole catastrophe epitomized in nine words!'

His works include *Pope* (1933), '"The Old Cumberland Beggar" and the Wordsworthian Unities' in *Essays on the Eighteenth Century Presented to David Nichol Smith* (1945), and *The Emergence of Shakespeare's Tragedy* (1950). Patrick Garland, the producer, had been one of his pupils, and at his instigation Dyson gave several television talks on Shakespeare for the BBC, as well as introducing Garland's television series *Famous Gossips*. In 1965 he made an appearance in John Schlesinger's film *Darling*, which starred Julie Christie and Dirk Bogarde. He died 6 June 1975. See letters of 22 September and 1 and 18 October 1931 in **TST** for his part in Lewis's conversion, and Humphrey Carpenter's *The Inklings*. Photo in **IHW**.

Eliot, Thomas Stearns (1888–1965), poet, playwright, critic, editor and publisher. He was born in St Louis, Missouri, on 26 September 1888, the son of **Henry Ware Eliot** and his wife **Charlotte Chauncy Stearns**. He took his BA from Harvard in 1909. It was while he was still an undergraduate at Harvard that Eliot contributed some poems to the *Harvard Advocate*. He hoped to become a professor of Philosophy, and entered the Harvard Graduate School where he took an MA in 1910. While writing a doctoral dissertation on the philosophy of F.H. Bradley for Harvard he spent the year 1914–15 at Merton College, Oxford, on a travelling fellowship. During this time he met Ezra Pound, and it was largely through his influence that he made several momentous decisions.

He gave up philosophy for poetry; he decided to settle in England; and he married **Vivien Haigh-Wood**. Pound helped Eliot to publish some of his poems, one of the first of which was 'The Love Song of J. Alfred Prufrock' in 1915. Eliot then took up school teaching, and during 1915–16 he had John Betjeman* as one of his pupils at Highgate Junior School in London. In 1917 he began working in Lloyds Bank in London, where he remained until 1925. It was while at Lloyds that he secured a position as both poet and critic. His first volume of verse, *Prufrock and other Observations* (1917) was followed by *Poems* in 1919. In 1922 Eliot founded a quarterly review called *The Criterion*, in the first issue of which he published 'The Waste Land', a poem which, more than any other, established him as the voice of a disillusioned generation.

In 1925 Eliot left Lloyds to become a director of the publishing firm Faber & Gwyer (later Faber & Faber). In 1927 he became a British subject and was baptized into the Church of England. Not long afterwards he characterized himself as 'classical in literature, royalist in politics, and Anglo-Catholic in religion'. His High Anglicanism is chartered in a number of poems and culminates in the *Four Quartets* (1935–42). Eliot became a very active churchman and lay apologist, and in 1939 he published *The Idea of a Christian Society*. He did much in the 1930s to revive poetic drama; the best known of his own dramas is *Murder in the Cathedral* (1935) which is about the martyrdom of Thomas à Becket. His many works of criticism include *The Sacred Wood: Essays on Poetry and Criticism* (1920), *Selected Essays* (1932) and *Notes Towards the Definition of Culture* (1948). The ill health of Eliot's wife, mental and physical, led to their separation. She died in 1947. In 1948 Eliot received the Nobel Prize for Literature and the Order of Merit. In 1957 he married **Valerie Fletcher**, with whom he lived very happily for the rest of his life. He died on 4 January 1965, and his ashes were buried in St Michael's Church in East Coker.

From the time Lewis began reading Eliot's poetry in the 1920s he disliked it and feared its effect on modern poetry. When he became a Christian, he allegorized Eliot in *The Pilgrim's Regress* (VI:3). More than anything else, as he made clear in *A Preface to 'Paradise Lost'*, he disliked Eliot's poetry because he used, in his opinion, the wrong Stock Responses§. 'I hope the fact that I find myself often contradicting you in print,' he wrote to Eliot on 22 February 1943, 'gives no offence; it is a kind of tribute to you – whenever I fall foul of some wide-spread contemporary view about literature I always seem to find that you have expressed it most clearly. One aims at the officers first in meeting an attack!'

Real friendship had to wait until 1959 when Lewis and Eliot became members of the Archbishops' 'Commission to Revise the Psalter'. Now, at last, they were engaged in a common task and saw one another frequently. Lewis could easily have been speaking of Eliot and himself when he said in *The Four Loves* IV: 'Friendship arises out of mere Companionship when two or more of the companions discover that they have in common some insight or interest or even taste which the others do not share and which, till that moment, each believed to be his own unique treasure (or burden).' 'My dear Eliot,' Lewis began all his letters after that. He had come to love Eliot as a result of their companionship over a shared interest (see **LIFE XXXI**).

Farrer, Austin Marsden (1904–68), philosopher and theologian. He was born in London on 1 October 1904, the son of the Rev. **Augustus John Daniel Farrer**, a Baptist minister who was for many years Secretary and Librarian of New College, London, and his wife **Evangeline (Archer) Farrer**. From St Paul's School, Austin Farrer went up to Balliol College, Oxford, as a Classical Scholar in 1923. He read Classical Honour Moderations,‡ *Literae Humaniores*,‡ and Theology, and took First Class degrees in each. He was confirmed in the Church of England in 1924, and after being ordained a priest in 1929 he served his title at All Saints', Dewsbury. He was 'catholic' in doctrine and 'high church' in style.

In 1931 Farrer returned to Oxford as Chaplain and Tutor of St Edmund Hall, where he remained until 1935. He was Fellow and Chaplain of Trinity College from 1935 until 1960, and Warden of Keble College from 1960 until 1968. He had great influence as a biblical scholar and theologian. He described his intellectual goal as 'to understand how the first cause works through the secondary causes by using and not over-riding the activity proper to their created nature', and 'to discern what kind of natural philosophy is most congenial to Christian belief'. These themes are prominent in his *Finite and Infinite* (1943) and *Freedom of the Will* (1958). In 1948 he delivered the Bampton Lectures (*The Glass of Vision: The Making of St John's Apocalypse*) in which he maintained that religious truth can only be communicated to human intelligences through images. He had a strong poetic streak, and some biblical scholars have found his works too imaginative. His other works on the New Testament include *St Matthew and St Mark* (1954) and *The Revelation of St John the Divine* (1964).

He was both a brilliant scholar and a humble priest. When the Socratic Club‡ was founded in 1941 he gave it his full support, and during the early years he gave a paper nearly every term. It was through the Socratic that he and Lewis became friends. His essay on 'The Christian Apologist' in **LCSL** is an excellent assessment of Lewis as an apologist. He admired Lewis's gifts as one, and regretted that he could not write in the same vein.

He first met **Katharine Dorothy Newton** in 1932 when he was visiting his parents in Rickmansworth. They were married in Ashwell Church on 15 April 1937, and had one child, **Caroline**. He and his wife, Katharine Farrer* – or K as she always signed letters to friends – were extremely successful with students, and they often entertained in the Gate House of Trinity College. Those who admired Farrer's scholarship were often very surprised to find, not only how warm he could be, but that he considered himself first and foremost a priest. His Chapel Services were well-attended, and he had a great influence on the ordinands who came under his influence. He loved the Rosary and used it regularly. Out of term he often celebrated the Eucharist at Pusey House or St Mary Magdalen.

Some of his college sermons were published as *The Crown of the Year* (1952) and *Said or Sung* (1960). In his Preface to the American edition of *Said or Sung* – entitled *A Faith of Our Own* (1960) – Lewis said: 'He writes everywhere as one who both has authority and is under authority ... Because he writes with authority, he has no need to shout. The truth and importance of what he says are already vouched for. It is assumed that we acknowledge both. He is there to expound, to explain, to remind: to draw again any lines in the bright diagram that have been smudged ... To talk to us thus Dr Farrer makes himself almost nothing, almost nobody. To be sure, in the event, his personality stands out from the pages as clearly as that of any author; but this is one of heaven's jokes – nothing makes a man so noticeable as vanishing.'

When he was elected Warden of Keble in 1960 many imagined that he would be too unpractical and too shy. Such presumption was quickly dispelled. The ease with which he took on the work surprised everyone. He was a firm and decisive Warden, as well as being an immensely kind pastor. Students found him wise, unsentimental and very easy to talk with. His wife, 'K', was delighted with the new position and referred to herself as the 'wardress'. His relaxations included working in his rose garden and upholstery. His lithe figure was once seen inspecting the roof of the college. Here, as in Trinity, he and his wife extended a warm welcome to visitors. No one could forget the pleasure of being with them. Their sophisticated conversation over 4.15 tea (Mrs Farrer always served Lapsang Souchong) was immensely civilizing. They delighted in one another, and nothing seemed to please Austin Farrer so much as hearing someone praise his wife's books. They had known Lewis since the 1940s, and they were some of the first of his friends to welcome Joy Gresham.*

Austin Farrer was a witness to Lewis's register office marriage on 23 April 1956, and he presided at Joy's funeral in 1960. It was his wish to retire some day to a country parish. In this he was forestalled by dying suddenly and unexpectedly on 29 December 1968. His papers and letters are in the Bodleian Library,‡ and there is a portrait in the hall of Keble College. 'In His Image', an address read at a Memorial Service to C.S. Lewis, is published in **ABT**. A biography by Philip Curtis is entitled *A Hawk among Sparrows* (1985).

Farrer, Katharine Dorothy (1911–72), friend, and wife of Austin Farrer.* She was born at Chippenham, Wiltshire, on 27 September 1911, the daughter of the Rev. **Frederick Henry Joseph Newton** and **Edith Grace (Sanders) Newton**. She was brought up in two successive parsonages in Hertfordshire, first in Rickmansworth, where her father was Vicar from 1921 to 1933, and then in Ashwell, Baldock. She was educated at St Helen's School, Northwood. In 1929 she matriculated at St Anne's College, Oxford, where she read Classical Honour Moderations‡ and Greats.‡ While an undergraduate she published her first stories under a pen-name in *The Cherwell*. After taking a BA in 1933, she took a course in Education and then taught at Gerrard's Cross.

In 1932 she met **Austin Farrer**, Chaplain of Trinity College, Oxford, who was in Rickmansworth visiting his father. They saw one another frequently after this, but he refused to propose until she had taken her degree. They were married in Ashwell Church on 15 April 1937. Their daughter, **Caroline**, was born on 5 April 1939. Katharine had given up writing, but when their daughter went away to school she began again. Her first book was a translation of Gabriel Marcel's *Etre et Avoir*, which was published as *Being and Having* in 1949. This was followed by three detective novels, *The Missing Link* (1952), *Cretan Counterfeit* (1954) and *Gownsman's Gallows* (1957). What she called her only 'straight' novel was *At Odds with Morning* (1960). 'K', as she signed herself when writing to friends, had the fragile beauty of fine porcelain. She was a fey, elegant and cultivated hostess. After she and her husband had been to tea at The Kilns,‡ Lewis said, 'It was like entertaining elves.' She also knew J.R.R. Tolkien,* Charles Williams* and Dorothy L. Sayers* (whom she met through the Detection Club). Many authors sought her help and encouragement, and Lewis and Tolkien discussed *Till We Have Faces* and *The Lord of the Rings* with her as they were being written. 'How pleased … Mrs Farrer will be,' Lewis wrote to Tolkien on 13 November 1952, on learning that *The Lord of the Rings* had found a publisher.

She was one of the first of Lewis's friends to be introduced to Joy Gresham,* and this proved a wise choice. On the evening of 18 October 1956 she suddenly knew something was wrong with Joy. 'I *must* ring her!' she said to her husband. At the very moment that she was dialling the number, Joy tripped over the telephone wire. The bone in her leg snapped as she fell to the floor, and, lying there, she heard Katharine talking to her. The Farrers were able to get Joy into the hospital where the doctors discovered that her bone had been eaten through by cancer. After Joy died, Lewis wrote to the Farrers on 22 July 1960 saying, 'She loved you both very much. And getting to know you both better is one of the many permanent gains I have got from my short married life.' Lewis dedicated *Reflections on the Psalms* to them. Warnie records in his diary of 13 July 1960 that, on her deathbed, Joy left her fur coat to Katharine. She wore the musquash coat until her death in 1971, and her daughter Caroline wore it until 1992.

During their time at Keble College, Katharine accompanied Austin when he lectured in the United States. When they visited Louisiana in 1966, their hosts found it necessary to drive through a very large swamp to get them to Baton Rouge. They did not know Katharine Farrer wrote detective novels, and as the car passed through the swamp they were shocked to hear her say 'What a lovely place to hide a body!' Mrs Farrer was the victim of acute insomnia, and this was a great trouble to her. After her husband's death she moved to 71 Lonsdale Road, Oxford. She died there on 25 March 1972 and she is buried with her husband in the churchyard of St Cross.‡ See Philip Curtis, *A Hawk among Sparrows: A Biography of Austin Farrer* (1985).

Fox, Adam (1883–1977), Inkling and colleague at Magdalen College.‡ He was born at Kensington on 15 July 1883, the son of **William Henry Fox** and **Ellen (Frost) Fox**. In 1897 he went to Winchester College as a scholar, and in 1902 he matriculated at University College,‡ Oxford. Fox took his BA in 1906, after which he joined the staff of Lancing College where he was to remain until 1918. Meanwhile he was ordained by the Bishop of Chichester in 1911. In 1918 he succeeded Selwyn as Warden of Radley College.

Fox carried out a very successful reorganization of the school, which had been necessary as the result of war conditions. However, it greatly affected his constitution, which was never robust, and he gave way under the strain of work. Following medical advice, in 1924 he accepted an invitation to go to South Africa as a temporary assistant master at the Diocesan College, Rondebosch. His health was restored, and he afterwards spoke of his years there as among the happiest of his life.

In 1929 he returned to Oxford as Fellow and Dean of Divinity at Magdalen College, where he was to remain until 1942. One of the duties of the Dean is to conduct 'Dean's Prayers' in the Chapel at 8 o'clock every morning, after which he would join his colleagues for breakfast in the Common Room. Two of the colleagues he came to know over breakfast, and whom he liked very much, were Paul Benecke and J.A. Smith. His essay, 'At the Breakfast Table' (**ABT**) is about the fourth member of this group, Lewis.

While he had a very modest notion of his abilities as a poet, Fox had been awarded the Sacred Poem Prize at Oxford in 1929, and in 1937 he published a long narrative poem entitled *Old King Cole*, a poem Lewis liked very much. In Oxford the Professorship of Poetry falls vacant every five years, and the election of a new professor by the Masters of Arts of Oxford University is an occasion when feelings run high. In 1937 Sir Edmund Chambers was proposed as the next Professor of Poetry. 'He would not have been my choice,' said Fox ...

> and when at breakfast one morning I read that Chambers was proposed, I said without any thought of being taken literally, 'This is simply shocking; they might as well make me Professor of Poetry.' Whereupon, Lewis said instantly, 'Well, we will.' And they did.

Lewis was to make himself very unpopular with a good many people who thought he acted irresponsibly when he and J.R.R. Tolkien* campaigned for Fox against the other candidates, Sir Edmund Chambers and Lord David Cecil.* Fox was elected and writing to Sir Stanley Unwin on 4 June 1938, Tolkien revealed 'Fox is a member of our literary club of *practising poets* – before whom the *Hobbit*, and other works ... have been read' (**LJRRT**). Lewis certainly did not think he and Tolkien acted irresponsibly. His reasons for admiring Fox are found in an unsigned article, imitating Doctor Johnson's *Lives of the English Poets*, entitled 'From Johnson's *Life of Fox*'. It was published in *The Oxford Magazine* (9 June 1938), p. 737, and he says there:

> The poetry of *Fox*, which is now to be considered, is more simple and unadorned than that of any other writer; nor need it excite the wonder of posterity if the regularity of nature and the sobriety of reason were not sufficient to save his compositions from disgust in an age when taste was formed on the incoherent excursions of *Eliot* and the petulant obscurity of *Pound*. But since the modes of error

are agitated by continual change while truth remains always the same, his poetry now shines with undiminished lustre when the false wit of the *Fantasticks* is neglected by the polite, condemned by the judicious, and read by the learned with frigid indifference ...

If his poetry never disgusts us by the vacuity of affectation or the tremor of disproportionate splendour, it sometimes chills us with imbecility and avoids excellences as well as faults. Yet he has left no poem which does not please as a whole. He always performs more than he promises. The reader who at first expected only amusement finds himself insensibly transported, and wonders at last by what stealth a composition which seems to owe so little to art has afforded him so much pleasure and so much instruction.

The Inklings were delighted to have Fox as a member. When Jack wrote to Warnie on 3 February 1940, he said: 'The Inklings is now really very well provided, with Fox as chaplain, you as army, Barfield as lawyer, Havard as doctor – almost all the estates!' (L). On 3 March 1940 he wrote again to say that at another meeting: 'Fox read us his latest "Paradisal" on Blenheim Park in winter. The only line I can quote (which seems to me very good) is "Beeches have figures; oaks, anatomies." It was in the *Troilus* stanza and full of his own "cool, mellow flavour" as the tobacconists say. He has really in some respect a considerable similarity to Miss Sackville West' (L).

In 1942 Fox was appointed to a canonry at Westminster Abbey, and he transferred to the Abbey much of the devotion he had given Magdalen. He had very considerable gifts as a preacher, and had been Select Preacher both at Oxford and Cambridge. In 1947 he was awarded an honorary DD by St Andrews. Included in his many books of this period are *Plato for Pleasure* (1945), *English Hymns and Hymn Writers* (1947), *Meet the Greek Testament* (1952) and *Dean Inge* (1960). Adam Fox retired in 1963, and after his death on 17 January 1977 his ashes were buried in Poets' Corner, Westminster Abbey. See Lord Redcliffe-Maud's obituary in *University College Record* (1977) and the one in *The Times* (19 January 1977), p. 16.

Gibb, Jocelyn Easton ('Jock') CBE (1907–79), Managing Director of Geoffrey Bles Ltd. The Gibb family from William (1736–91) down to **Sir Alexander Gibb** (1872–1958), Jock's father, were all engineers involved in a vast range of famous engineering projects: bridges, railways, harbours, to name a few. In 1922 Jock's father founded the firm of Sir Alexander Gibb & Partners, Consulting Engineers, whose work is famous on every continent.

In 1900 **Alexander Gibb** married **Norah Isobel Monteith**, and Jock was born on 18 May 1907 at Goytree House, near Abergavenny, when his father was working on Newport Dock. He went to preparatory school at Scaitcliffe, Englefield Green, Surrey, and to Rugby 1921–24. Due to ill health he transferred to Switzerland and to Chillon College at Montreux-Territet, Canton de Vaud. Here he edited the college magazine, perhaps the earliest sign of literary leanings. He entered Pembroke College, Cambridge, in October 1926, but took a year out. He read the ordinary degree subjects: Engineering, English and History, and left Cambridge with his BA in June 1930. He became an MA in 1950.

Jock's father, though presumably disappointed at this turn, generously determined to equip him for this new career, and because Leipzig was then considered to be in the forefront of colour printing and methods of reproduction, he went to acquire some German. This was followed by an apprenticeship in Hutchinson under the late Sir Robert Lusty. His first step into publishing proper came when he was made production manager in Methuen & Co, London, in the mid-1930s. It was there that he met his wife, **Evelyn Elizabeth Balfour Milne** who was secretary to the Publicity Manageress. They married on 21 April 1937 and their son, **Robert**, was born on 31 March 1939.

Gibb had become a Territorial in the Royal Wiltshire Yeomanry, and he left Methuen when he was called up just before the outbreak of war. He went with that regiment to Palestine. Due to ill health he was returned to service in England. His twin daughters, **Alison** and **Jean**, were born on 22 December 1942. At the end of the war he was released as a Lieutenant-Colonel and returned to civilian life to explore the possibilities of publishing books on his own account.

Eventually he entered Geoffrey Bles as production manager. When Bles* retired in 1954 he became Managing Director. It was here that he came in contact with C.S. Lewis. The firm was publishing the Narnian stories, and he was the ideal one to take over the books from Bles. From 1954 until Lewis's death in 1963 he was a kind and discerning man who was not only interested in what Lewis had to say, but did much to encourage him. He visited Lewis in Oxford and Cambridge, and their correspondence is that of close friends.

Geoffrey Bles had been bought by William Collins & Sons as far back as 1954, and although Collins began publishing the paperbacks of Lewis's works in 1955, the imprint of 'Geoffrey Bles Ltd' remained on the hardcover books until Gibb's retirement in 1974. Between 1957–72 Gibb edited the house magazine of Geoffrey Bles, *Fifty-Two* (after the address of the firm: 52 Doughty Street, London WC1). When Lewis died Gibb edited and published *Light on C.S. Lewis* (1965), which contains some of the earliest and best of the reminiscences by his friends. Gibb also contributed the article on Lewis to the fifteenth edition of *The Encyclopedia Britannica* (1974). Another writer to whom he gave much attention was J.B. Phillips. Perhaps his masterpiece of publishing, and one of those for which he was justly proud, was *Phoenix at Coventry: The Building of a Cathedral* (1962) by Basil Spence.

During the many years that he was giving his attention so generously to Lewis and his other authors and concerns, he was farming a hundred acres at home in Sussex, as well as a small farm where the Gibb family originated in West Lothian, and he was tenant farmer of a hill farm in Wester Ross. In addition, he was Chairman of the Land Settlement Association 1958–77, an association of horticultural small-holding co-operatives in England, and for this he received his CBE. This last 'gentleman publisher', as he is often called, died at his home, Mousehall, Tidebrook, in Sussex on 4 April 1979. Photo in **IHW**.

Green, Roger Lancelyn (1918–87), friend and author, was born 2 November 1918 at Norwich. He was the son of **Gilbert Arthur Lancelyn Green** and **Helena Mary Phyllis (Sealy) Green**, and for most of his life he lived at Poulton Hall, Poulton-Lancelyn, Wirral, Cheshire, an estate which his ancestors had held for almost nine hundred years. He was educated at Dane Court, Pyrford, Surrey, and Liverpool College, and privately for a number of years due to ill health. He matriculated at Merton College, Oxford, in 1937, where he took an Honours Degree in English Language and Literature. He had been attending Lewis's 'Prolegomena' lectures on Medieval and Renaissance Literature for some time before they met in November 1939. Lewis invited him to port and coffee – thus beginning a friendship that would last for twenty-five years. His BA was followed by a B.Litt. – his thesis on 'Andrew Lang and the Fairy Tale' was supervised by J.R.R. Tolkien.*

On leaving Oxford he pursued a number of brief careers. He was a teacher, an antiquarian bookseller, and an actor. Humphrey Carpenter's *O.U.D.S.: A Centenary History of the Oxford University Dramatic Society* (1985) contains a photo of him taking the part of Biondello in the OUDS's Diamond Jubilee production of *The Taming of the Shrew* given in Wadham College in June 1945.

Between 1945 and 1950 he was Deputy Librarian of Merton College, and the William Noble Research Fellow at Liverpool University 1950–52. It was, however, while playing one of the pirates in a production of *Peter Pan* in 1942–43 that he became fascinated by the story of the boy who did not want to grow up. This led him to write his highly acclaimed history of its production, *Fifty Years of Peter Pan* (1954). Many other biographies followed, amongst which were those of Andrew Lang, Lewis Carroll, A.E.W. Mason, Mrs Molesworth, Rudyard Kipling and C.S. Lewis. He edited the *Diaries* of Lewis Carroll in 1953, and his *Works* in 1965.

In 1948 he married **June Burdett**, and after returning to Poulton Hall in 1950, devoted himself to writing. It is unfortunate that his success as a compiler and reteller of tales has tended to overshadow his own stories for children. They include: *The Wonderful Stranger* (1950), *The Luck of the Lynns* (1952), *The Secret of Rusticoker* (1953), *The Theft of the Golden Cat* (1955), *The Land of the Lord High Tiger* (1958), *Mystery at Mycenae* (1957) and *The Luck of Troy* (1961). Many know of Lewis's immense debt to Roger Lancelyn Green for his advice and criticism while the Chronicles of Narnia were being written (see **NARNIA**). But it was sometimes Lewis who was talking or writing to Roger Lancelyn Green about *his* books. Lewis thought his retelling of tales unparalleled. His favourite was *King Arthur and his Knights of the Round Table* (1953) which is based on Malory and many other Arthurian sources as well. 'The non-Malory parts are just as good as the Malory parts,' Lewis said in a letter of 10 July 1953. 'You have managed the events, such as the begetting of Galahad, which present difficulties in a children's book, with wonderful skill. The style is exactly right.' Other retellings which have become classics are *The Adventures of Robin Hood* (1956), *The Saga of Asgard* – later renamed *Myths of the Norsemen* (1960), *Heroes of Greece and Troy* (1960). Other favourites of Lewis's were Green's study of children's writers, *Tellers of Tales* (1946) and a book dedicated to Lewis – *Into Other Worlds: Space-Flight in Fiction, from Lucian to Lewis* (1957).

The same remarkable gift which made Roger Lancelyn Green's books so well-written and congenial made him a faithful and easy friend. He was a very good listener, and this flowering of his many literary talents coincided with Lewis's writing of the Narnian Chronicles. He proved to be an invaluable critic and encouragement to Lewis. He was a friend of Tolkien's as well, and over the years he was present at many of the Tuesday morning Inklings meetings. Lewis visited Roger and June Lancelyn Green several times at Poulton Hall, where he met their three children, **Scirard** (b. 1949), **Priscilla** (b. 1951) and **Richard** (b. 1953). Roger Lancelyn Green was for many years Editor of *The Kipling Journal*, and an enthusiastic member of the Sherlock Holmes Society of London. After his son Richard acquired a taste for the Sherlock Holmes stories, Roger helped him erect in the attic of Poulton Hall a replica of Holmes' study at 221B Baker Street. Since that time his son has gone on to publish a bibliography of the writings of Conan Doyle and to edit some of his uncollected writings.

Amongst the many honours heaped upon him, those he valued particularly highly were the dedication to him of Lewis's last book – *The Discarded Image* (1964) – and an Honorary D.Litt. from the University of Liverpool in 1981. In 1963 he published the Bodley Head monograph on *C.S. Lewis* which he dedicated to 'Jack and Joy in memory of "a pub-crawl through the golden isles of Greece".' In 1974 he co-authored *C.S. Lewis: A Biography*, which contains the diary he kept during that marvellous holiday, or 'pub-crawl', when he and his wife toured Greece with Lewis and Joy in April 1960. He died at Poulton Hall on 8 October 1987. For information about his family and home see his *Poulton-Lancelyn: The Story of an Ancestral Home* (1948). There is a photo in **IHW**.

Greeves, Joseph Arthur (1895–1966), boyhood friend, was born in Belfast on 27 August 1895, the youngest of five children born to **Joseph Malcomson Greeves** and **Mary Margretta Gribbon** of Brooklyn, New York. Their home, 'Bernagh', was directly across the road from 'Little Lea',‡ where Lewis's family lived. Arthur's father was the Director of J. & T.M. Greeves, Ltd, flax spinners. The family had traditionally been members of the Society of Friends, but had converted to the Plymouth Brethren in 1830. The only formal education Arthur had was at Campbell College,‡ Belfast, between 1906 and 1912. He enrolled at the Slade School of Fine Art in London in 1921, and left with a Certificate in 1923. For years he had tried to get to know Jack and Warnie Lewis, but without success. Then, said Lewis in **SBJ** VIII:

> It was shortly before the beginning of my last term at [Malvern] that I received a message saying that Arthur was in bed, convalescent, and would welcome a visit. I can't remember what led me to accept this invitation, but for some reason I did.
>
> I found Arthur sitting up in bed. On the table beside him lay a copy of *Myths of the Norsemen*.
>
> 'Do *you* like that?' said I.
>
> 'Do *you* like that?' said he.

Next moment the book was in our hands, our heads were bent close together, we were pointing, quoting, talking – soon almost shouting – discovering in a torrent of questions that we liked not only the same thing, but the same parts of it and in the same way; that both knew the stab of Joy and that, for both, the arrow was shot from the North. Many thousands of people have had the experience of finding the first friend, and it is none the less a wonder; as great a wonder (*pace* the novelists) as first love, or even greater. I had been so far from thinking such a friend possible that I had never even longed for one; no more than I longed to be King of England.

They were to be friends for half a century. They began corresponding in June 1914, and for a number of years they wrote to one another weekly. There seems to be almost nothing that Jack did not discuss in his letters with him. After Lewis's father died in 1929 Jack became a frequent visitor to 'Bernagh'. It was in this house, during the summer of 1932, that Lewis wrote *The Pilgrim's Regress*. Unfortunately, Lewis did not preserve many of Arthur's letters, but Arthur saved nearly all of Lewis's and they were published as *They Stand Together* in 1979. When compiling the **Lewis Papers‡** from 1933–35 Warnie Lewis wrote a portrait of Arthur (Vol. IV, pp. 181–2) in which he said:

> His circumstances have been such that he has never been compelled to face the issues of life, to know it as it is, to gauge the degree of toleration which the community owes to the individual and the individual to the community. I do not here refer to the fact that he has never had to earn his living, but mean that with a child's liking for being liked he has the child's distress at the obtuseness of the grown ups who cannot see that if only everyone would always do as he wants them to do, the world would be a very delightful place to live in.

Jack felt obliged to supplement this portrait with something from his own pen (**LP** X: 218–20), and he said of his friend:

> Arthur was the youngest son of a doting mother and a harsh father, two evils whereof each increased the other. The mother soothed him the more, to compensate for the father's harshness, and the father became harsher to counteract the ill effects of the mother's indulgence. Both thus conspired to aggravate a tendency ... towards self-pity ... It can easily be imagined how such a child grew up: but who could have foretold that he would be neither a liar nor a tale bearer, neither a coward nor a misanthrope?
> He was the frankest of men. Many of the most ludicrous episodes which could be told against him, turn on his failure to acquire that 'visor to the human race' which such a training usually

teaches a man to wear. He was the most faithful of friends, and carried the innumerable secrets of my own furtive and ignoble adolescence locked in a silence which is not commonly thought effeminate. Under illness or inconvenience he was impatient – a loud and violent, but not a lengthy grumbler: but danger left him unmoved ...

During the earlier years of our acquaintance he was (as always) a Christian, and I was an atheist. But though (God forgive me) I bombarded him with all the thin artillery of a seventeen-year-old rationalist, I never made any impression on his faith – a faith both vague and confused, and in some ways too indulgent to our common weaknesses, but inexpugnable. He remains victor in that debate. It is I who have come round. The thing is symbolical of much in our joint history. He was not a clever boy, he was even a dull boy; I was a scholar. He had no 'ideas'. I bubbled over with them. It might seem that I had much to give him, and that he had nothing to give me. But this is not the truth. I could give concepts, logic, facts, arguments, but he had feelings to offer, feelings which most mysteriously – for he was always very inarticulate – he taught me to share. Hence, in our commerce, I dealt in superficies, but he in solids. I learned charity from him and failed, for all my efforts, to teach him arrogance in return.

Being unable to work because of his bad heart, Greeves managed on an income from the family business. He nevertheless won some recognition as a landscape painter, and was exhibited in 1936. He was a member of the Royal Hibernian Academy. Much of his time was spent painting in and around his beloved County Down, where he spent the whole of his life.

After his mother's death in 1949 he moved to Crawfordsburn, County Down, where Lewis often stayed. It was here that Arthur entertained Jack and Joy during the summers of 1958 and 1959. The last time Jack and Arthur were together was a weekend spent at The Kilns‡ in June 1961. Jack was making plans to visit Arthur in Ireland during the summer of 1963, but a heart attack prevented this. 'It looks as if you and I shall never meet again in this life,' he wrote on 11 September 1963, 'Oh, Arthur, never to see you again!' (**TST**).

In later life Arthur began searching for a religious position that suited him. In the forties he became associated with the Unitarians. In later life he joined the Baha'i Faith, and when he was an older man, he became, as his ancestors had before him, a member of the Society of Friends. This seems to have brought him some of the peace he was looking for. There is a good deal about him in **SBJ, AMR** and the Introduction to **TST**. There are photos of him in the **LP**, as well as in **TJB** and **AMR**.

Gresham, David Lindsay (1944–   ), stepson of C.S. Lewis. He was born in New York City on 27 March 1944, the elder son of the novelist, **William Lindsay Gresham** (1909–62), and **Helen Joy Davidman** (1915–60)*. His brother **Douglas Howard Gresham*** was born in 1945. Following the publication of his father's *Nightmare Alley* in 1946, the family moved to Ossining, New York, and then to Staatsburg, in Dutchess County, New York, where they lived in Endekill Road. Marital problems began to develop. His mother had long been interested in England and its literature, and this as well as a desire to meet C.S. Lewis, caused her to go to England in August 1952. She and Lewis met and they became friends.

In November 1953 Joy Gresham left her husband and returned to England with David and Douglas. From the beginning David never liked his new home, and he missed New York. He found the regional accents of the English hard to understand, and the accents of the educated unattractive.

The first place at which they lived in England was the Avoca House Hotel, 43 Belsize Park, Hampstead, London, but after a short while they moved into a flat in an annex of the hotel in 14 Belsize Park. David first met Lewis on 17 December 1953 when he, his mother and brother spent four days at The Kilns.‡ Writing to Bill Gresham on 22 December, Joy said the boys 'were a big success with the Lewises' and that, after the Lewis brothers had taught him to play chess, David 'astonished them by learning instantly and doing very well' (**AGCI** chapter 4, p. 104). It was during this visit that Lewis promised to dedicate *The Horse and His Boy* to David and his brother. In January 1954 the brothers were enrolled at Dane Court, a preparatory school at Pyrford, near Woking in Surrey. 'I would describe it as athletic and snobbish,' said David, 'and although I would have hated it anyway (after being taken away from the USA), it was made much worse by the rampant anti-Americanism then prevalent in Britain.'

In 1954 his parents were divorced. Then, in August 1955 his mother moved them to 10 Old High Street, Headington, a pleasant house with a large garden. As they now lived about a mile from The Kilns, his mother persuaded Lewis to tutor David in Latin. When his mother was unable to have her visa renewed, she and Lewis married in a register office on 23 April 1956. This act gave Joy the right to British citizenship, and the 'patrial' status entitled David and Douglas to claim British citizenship.

When, in October 1956, his mother was found to have cancer David and his brother went to live with Lewis at The Kilns. On 21 March 1957 his mother and Lewis were married by a Church of England priest in the Wingfield-Morris Hospital, Oxford. There was a remission of the cancer, and Joy joined her sons at The Kilns. Lewis had written to Sister Penelope* on 6 March 1957 saying: 'I don't doubt that Joy and I (and David and Douglas, the two boys) will have your prayers. Douglas is an absolute charmer (11½). David, at first sight less engaging, is at any rate a comically appropriate stepson for me (13), being almost exactly what I was – bookworm, pedant, and a bit of a prig' (L).

In September 1957 David left Dane Court and became a day-boy at Magdalen College School, Oxford. Following his mother's death on 13 July 1960, his love for Judaism, which he had been interested in since he was eleven, came into its own. He believes the 'real reason' behind this love to be 'divine grace', because the main concern of Judaism is one's 'coming to God'. David was also spurred on by his Anglophobia and the need for an identity.

While at Magdalen College School he began to have private lessons in Hebrew from Ronald May, who was working as a proof-reader for the Oxford University Press, and who later became a teacher at the Oxford Centre for Post-Graduate Hebrew Studies. While studying for the Hebrew O-level examination, he began a study of Yiddish on his own. He was fortunate in making the acquaintance of Professor Chone Shmeruk of the Hebrew University of Jerusalem, one of the world's leading Yiddish scholars, who was in Oxford doing research on medieval Yiddish manuscripts. He kindly gave David lessons in this language during the winter of 1961–62.

Encouraged by Rabbi M.Y. Young, a master at Carmel College, a Jewish secondary school in Wallingford, on 10 April 1962 David visited a yeshiva (a Jewish parochial school) at Gateshead in the north of England. One of the rabbis there advised him to go to a Jewish school in London to finish his A-level examinations before going to a yeshiva. On 15 April he went to London, and after a few months became a student at the North West London Talmudical College in Finchley Road, where he was to remain for a year.

After the year in London, he returned to the United States where he studied until the beginning of 1966, mostly in the Mesivta Rabbi Chaim Berlin, of which Rabbi Isaac Hutner was the Rosh Yeshiva. Later that same year he settled briefly in London, and then he moved to Cambridge. He had decided to go to university, and he needed to pass the A-level examination. After a period of private study he passed in German, Logic and Biblical Hebrew. In 1967 he went to Israel, where he studied for about nine months at the Hebron Yeshiva in Jerusalem, and then for a year at the Hebrew University where he started to learn Arabic. He returned to England in 1969, and that autumn entered Cambridge University where he was a member of Magdalene College,‡ of which his step-father had been a Fellow. There he read Oriental Studies (Arabic, Turkish, Hebrew), graduating in 1972.

In 1974 David Gresham went to live in Spain, where he remained until 1977, when he went to live in Paris. During these years he devoted himself to the study of Hebrew, Latin and modern languages. In 1980 he moved to Montreux in Switzerland, where he studied at the Montreux Yeshiva. This yeshiva was transferred to Jerusalem in 1984, and in 1985 David moved to Ireland, where he now lives.

Since 1983 he had been in the habit of spending three or four months a year in India. On 1 November 1992 he married Miss **Padmavati Hariharan** at the Magen Aboth Synagogue in Alibag, Maharashtra. Their son, **Joseph Isaac**, was born on 17 May 1994. David Gresham has said: 'My main occupation is the study of the Hebrew Bible and the Talmud and their commentaries, and languages and literature, and I take an interest in furthering Jewish education.' For further information see Douglas Gresham, *Lenten Lands* (1988) and Lyle Dorsett, *And God Came In* (1983).

Gresham, Douglas Howard (1945–   ), stepson of C.S. Lewis. He was born on 10 November 1945 in the city of New York, the second son of the novelist, **William Lindsay Gresham** (1909–62), and **Helen Joy Davidman** (1915–60)*. His brother **David Lindsay Gresham*** was born in 1944. After the publication of his father's *Nightmare Alley* in 1946, the family moved to Ossining, New York, and thence to Staatsburg. It was not long afterwards, however, that marital problems began, and in 1952 his mother went to England in the hope of meeting C.S. Lewis. While there she became friends with Lewis and spent Christmas with the Lewis brothers in Oxford. After breaking with William Gresham, his mother returned to England in November 1953 with her sons. Their first home was 14 Belsize Park, London.

Douglas has given a vivid account of their first visit with Lewis during December 1953 in his autobiography *Lenten Lands: My Childhood with Joy Davidman and C.S. Lewis* (1988). He expected the creator of Narnia to be wearing 'silver chain mail and be girt about with a jewel-encrusted sword-belt', but what he really found was 'a slightly stooped, round-shouldered, balding gentleman' (7). His surprise was hardly greater than Lewis's.

Writing about the visit to Ruth Pitter* on 21 December 1953, he said: 'I never knew what we celibates are shielded from. I will never laugh at parents again. Not that the boys weren't a delight: but a delight like surf-bathing which leaves one breathless and aching. The energy, the *tempo*, is what kills. I have now perceived (what I always suspected from memories of my own childhood) that the way to a child's heart is quite simple: treat them with seriousness and ordinary civility – they ask no more. What they can't stand (quite rightly) is the common adult assumption that everything they say should be twisted into a kind of jocularity.'

In January 1954 Douglas went to Dane Court School in Pyrford, Surrey. His parents were divorced that same year, on 5 August. The next year the family moved to 10 Old High Street, Headington, Oxford, where they were to see more of Lewis. For reasons which remain unexplained, Joy Gresham was unable to have her visa renewed, and in 1956 she and Lewis were married in a civil ceremony. This act gave Joy British citizenship, and the 'patrial' status entitled Douglas and his brother to claim British citizenship. Not long afterwards his mother was discovered to have cancer, and she appeared to be dying. Lewis took the two boys into his household at The Kilns, while their mother was in hospital. On 21 March 1957 she and Lewis were married by a Church of England clergyman in the Wingfield-Morris Hospital, Oxford. Shortly thereafter she went into remission and soon joined the family at The Kilns. 'Douglas is an absolute charmer,' Lewis said to Sister Penelope* on 6 March 1957. Later that year his mother's cancer was diagnosed as 'arrested', and there followed several happy years for all of them. Douglas left Dane Court School in September 1957. However, by the time he went off to Lapley Grange School at Machynlleth, Montgomeryshire, in 1960, his mother was ill again. Lapley Grange, however, suited him admirably, and while there he became Head Prefect. In the summer of 1960 he and his brother were brought home to be with their mother before her death on 13 July. When he wrote to Arthur Greeves on 30 August 1960 about his wife's death, Lewis said: 'Douglas – the younger boy – is, as always, an absolute brick, and a very bright spot in my life' (TST).

In September 1960 Douglas Gresham was enrolled in Magdalen College School, Oxford, where he remained until December 1962. From there he went to a small private school, Applegarth, Mark Way, Godalming, Surrey. Here, too, he was to know much grief. His father, whom he had last seen in the summer of 1960, died by his own hand in September 1962. On 22 November 1963 he learned, first, that President Kennedy had been killed in Dallas, Texas, and then that Lewis had died of heart failure.

From Applegarth he went to 'Chargot', the farm of Sir Edward Malet in Somerset, to gain agricultural experience. During his six months there, he met and fell in love with Sir Edward Malet's niece, **Meredith ('Merrie') Conan-Davies**, a nurse at St Thomas's Hospital, London. After further training at Glympton Park Estate, a large intensive mixed farm a few miles from Woodstock in Oxfordshire, and a year at an agricultural college, Douglas and Merrie were married in Westminster Cathedral on 20 February 1967. For some time he had thought of farming in Australia, and shortly after the wedding, he and Merrie sailed for Tasmania. Over the many and eventual years they spent in Australia, he was a farmer, a radio and television broadcaster, a restaurateur and many other things besides. It was there that their children were born: **James** in 1968; **Timothy** in 1969, **Dominick** in 1971, and **Lucinda** in 1976. In 1990 they adopted **Melody**, then five years old, from Korea.

Since 1973 Douglas Gresham has worked untiringly with all aspects of the Estate of C.S. Lewis, and in 1993 the family moved to Ireland so that he could give it more of his attention. He has many other interests as well. He and his wife, both of whom are committed Christians, have made their home in County Carlow available as the European centre of the Institute for Pregnancy Loss and Child Abuse Research and Recovery. They also run Rathvinden Ministries, a multi-faceted house ministry in Ireland. *Lenten Lands* is not only about his life with his mother and stepfather. It contains much information about W.H. Lewis,* the best portrait we have of Fred Paxford,* and many photos. See also Lyle Dorsett's biography of Joy Davidman, *And God Came In*.

Griffiths, Dom Bede OSB (1906–93): pupil and friend. He was born **Alan Richard Griffiths** on 17 December 1906 in Walton-on-Thames, the son of **Walter Griffiths** and his wife **Harriet Lilian Frampton-Day**. He was brought up there and in New Milton, Hampshire. His family, who were members of the Church of England, moved to the Isle of Wight when he was fourteen. He was educated at Christ's Hospital in Horsham, and then at Magdalen College,‡ Oxford, his matriculation in 1925 coinciding exactly with Lewis's appointment as Fellow of English.

After reading Classical Honour Moderations, Alan decided not to proceed to Greats, but to read English Literature instead. As he later recorded in his autobiography, *The Golden String* (1954), he was not a Christian at the time, and he had lost faith in intellect and reason. Before he left Oxford he and his friends, Martyn Skinner and Hugh l'Anson Fausset, began spending their vacations in the Cotswolds getting close to the rhythm of nature and the country people. It was there that he first read the Bible, and as the real content of it penetrated into his mind he felt forced to take religion seriously. He was preparing himself for ministry in the Church of England when a reading of John Henry Newman's *Essay on the Development of Christian Doctrine* changed his concept of Christianity and the Church. He said in *The Golden String* (7):

> I believed that the Church which Christ had founded was a historical reality, that it had had a continuous history from the time of the Apostles to the present day. I had thought that this continuity might be found in the Church of England, but now the overwhelming weight of evidence for the continuity of the Roman Church was presented to my mind.

Griffiths and Lewis became Christians in 1931. On Christmas Eve 1931 Griffiths was received into the Catholic Church. A few months later he decided to try his vocation as a monk at Prinknash, the Benedictine priory at Winchcombe, and on 20 December 1932 he was clothed as a novice. It was at this point that he changed his name to **Bede** after St Bede 'The Venerable' (c. 673–735), after which he was known as **Dom Bede Griffiths**. He made his solemn vows on 21 December 1936.

From the time he became a Catholic, Dom Bede began trying to argue the merits of their respective positions with Lewis. Lewis was determined that he would only speak of those which *unified* Christians. 'The result,' said Dom Bede in 'The Adventure of Faith' (**ABT**), was that we agreed not to discuss our differences any more, and this was perfectly satisfactory to Lewis; for me it was a great embarrassment. It meant that I could never really touch on much that meant more to me than anything else, and there was always a certain reserve therefore afterward in our friendship.' Despite this, Lewis's side of their correspondence during this period contains some of his finest theological observations.

After making his solemn vows, Dom Bede began a study of Thomas Aquinas's *Summa Theologica*, and this led to a great deal of correspondence with Lewis on philosophy and the part it can play in the salvation of souls. When Lewis thought Dom Bede might be relying on it too much, he reminded him in a letter of 8 January 1937 that 'we have no abiding city even in philosophy: all passes, except the Word.' Not long after Dom Bede was ordained a priest on 9 March 1940, Lewis asked for his help with the radio scripts he was preparing for the BBC.

On 29 April 1947 Dom Bede went to the priory at Farnborough as Prior, and in 1951 he was sent to the new Scottish priory at Pluscarden as novice master. Several years before the move to Scotland, Dom Bede, partly through the influence of Christopher Dawson, had taken up the study of oriental thought. 'I realized,' he said in *The Golden String* (10), 'that a Christian civilization could no longer be of a merely European character. Not only was the Church now extended throughout the world, but we were becoming more and more aware of the importance of Asia and Africa both as political and as cultural powers.' He goes on in that same chapter to explain this new way of thought that was to make such a drastic change in his life:

> For centuries now Christianity has developed in a westerly direction, taking on an ever more western character of thought and expression. If it is ever to penetrate deeply into the East it will have to find a correspondingly eastern form, in which the genius of the peoples of the East will be able to find expression. For Christianity will never realize its full stature as a genuine Catholicism, that is, as the universal religion of mankind, until it has incorporated into itself all that is valid and true in all the different religious traditions.

Dom Bede argued with such force on behalf of Hinduism that on 27 September 1949 Lewis said:

> I ... feel that the kind of union (with God) which they are seeking is precisely the opposite to that which He really intends for us ... To what end was creation except to separate us in order that we may be reunited to Him in that unity of love which is utterly different from mere numerical unity and indeed presupposes that lover and beloved be distinct? Thus the whole Indian aim seems to me to be *backward* towards a sort of unity which God deliberately rejected and not onward to the true one.

And in a letter dated 'April 15' and which was probably written in 1949, Lewis went even further:

> I now believe that refined, philosophical eastern Pantheism is *far further* from the true Faith than the semi-barbarous pagan religions ... The man who rushed with the Maenads on the mountains to tear and eat the beast which also was the god ... is far nearer the truth than Hinduism. I am inclined to think that Paganism is the primitive revealed truth corrupted by devils and that Hinduism is neither of divine nor diabolical origin but profoundly and *hopelessly* natural.

After this, Dom Bede kept fairly quiet about the East when writing to Lewis. In 1954 he learned that he was being sent to India to assist in the formation of a Benedictine monastery there. He arrived in India in 1955. It was not a success, but two years later, assisted by an Indian priest and a Cistercian monk, he founded Kurisumala Ashram, a Benedictine monastery of the Syrian rite in Kerala. A few years later Dom Bede outlined in *Christian Ashram* (1966), or *Christian in India* (1967) as it is called in the United States, his ideas about how Indian Catholicism and the future universal Church might develop.

In 1968 Dom Bede went to Saccidananda Ashram, Shantivanam, in Tamil Nadu. This ashram was a pioneer attempt in India to found a Christian community following the customs of a Hindu ashram and adapting itself to Hindu ways of life and thought. Under Dom Bede's leadership this Ashram became one of the world's great centres of interfaith spirituality. The monks lived in individual thatched huts, met three times a day for informal prayers, which included texts not only from the Bible and the Christian tradition, but from the *Vedas* (the Hindu sacred texts), the *Koran*, and the *Granth Sahib* of the Sikhs.

Over the years Dom Bede won a great deal of recognition through his books, which include *Vedanta and Christian Faith* (1973), *Return to the Centre* (1976), *The Marriage of East and West* (1982), *The Cosmic Revelation* (1983), and *A New Vision of Reality* (1989) in which he challenged the assumptions of modern society. He envisaged the breakdown of modern civilization, based on exploitation of scientific knowledge without regard for people or the world as a whole. By this time Dom Bede was regarded as a guru, and the young in particular travelled from England, the United States, Australia and other places to visit him. In his saffron robe, with a white beard, this exceptionally gentle man became much loved and respected. Many local villagers would turn up at his ashram for blessing and counsel. When they touched his feet in traditional reverence he would turn to his Western visitors and explain: 'Of course it is not me they are worshipping you know, but God in me.'

He was not without critics. Many in the Catholic Church have felt as Lewis did, that he was selling the Christian Faith short by his attempt at syncretism. Before his death on 13 May 1993, Dom Bede had been working on an anthology of world scriptures, showing how all religions begin and finally meet in the experience of nonduality. This work, *Universal Wisdom: A Journey through the Sacred Wisdom*, was published in 1994. See Kathryn Spink, *A Sense of the Sacred: A Biography of Bede Griffiths* (1988), which contains many photographs. Shirley Du Boulay's biography *Dom Bede Griffiths* will be published by Rider Publishers of London in 1998.

Hardie, Colin (1906–   ), Inkling and colleague at Magdalen College.‡ He is one of the sons of **William Ross Hardie** (1862–1916), the distinguished classical scholar, and his wife **Isabella Wall Stevenson**. His brother, **William Francis Ross Hardie**, who was President of Corpus Christi College, Oxford, 1950–69 is mentioned frequently in Lewis's diary (**AMR**).

Colin Hardie was born in Edinburgh on 16 February 1906. From the Edinburgh Academy he went to Balliol College, Oxford, where he took a First Class degree in Classical Moderations in 1926, and a First Class degree in *Literae Humaniores* in 1928. After winning the Gaisford Prize for Greek Prose in 1927 he was a Junior Research Fellow of Balliol 1928–29, and a Fellow and Classical Tutor of Balliol 1930–33. In 1933 he became Director of the British School at Rome.

In 1936 he returned to Oxford as Fellow and Classical Tutor at Magdalen College. It was there that he met Lewis. In his account of their friendship, 'A Colleague's Note on C.S. Lewis' in the *Inklings-Jahrbuch* (1985), he said that on his arrival in Magdalen he was 'A little like his Mark Studdock in *That Hideous Strength*' and 'inclined at that time towards the "Progressive Element".' Before the war, however, they found a common interest in Dante, both being members of the Oxford Dante Society (founded in 1876 and limited to a group of twelve who meet once a term). 'It was only after the war,' he said, 'that he became closer to Lewis. 'By this time my beliefs were very different from those of until 1941 or so. I felt that what was good enough for the not very orthodox Dante would do for me.'

In 1940 he married **Christian Viola Mary Lucas**. They have two sons, **Nicholas** (to whom *The Silver Chair* is dedicated) and **Anthony**. The family lived in 63 High Street, directly across from Magdalen, and it was during the War that Colin Hardie became a regular member of the Thursday evening Inklings meetings and the Tuesday morning gatherings in the Bird and Baby. Writing about the post-war meetings in his 'Colleague's Note', he said: 'This entry into C.S.L.'s circle was when his many admirers in the USA sent choice foods to him in still beleaguered and … rationed Britain. These included what we had not seen for six years, fine hams, which it became my congenial task to carve for the party.' His carving ability was exercised on one of the most memorable of the Inklings's 'ham feasts' – 11 March 1948 – when eight of them sat down to a ham sent by Dr Warfield M. Firor of Baltimore. There is a photograph of their letter of appreciation to Dr Firor in Humphrey Carpenter's *The Inklings*. When he wrote about the dinner in his diary, Warnie Lewis said 'Colin covered himself with glory in the ungrateful role of carver' (**BF**).

His edition of the *Vitae Vergilianae Antiquae* was published by the Clarendon Press in 1954. Other works on Virgil include *The 'Georgics': A Transitional Poem* (1971). Following his election to the Oxford Dante Society in 1938 he was its secretary for thirty years. During this time he edited the Society's *Centenary Essay on Dante* (1965), which includes his 'The symbol of the Gryphon in *Purgatorio* xxix.108 and following Cantos.' His other works on Dante include 'Dante and the Tradition of Courtly Love' in *Patterns of Love and Courtesy*, ed. John Lawlor (1966) and an edition of Edward Moore's *Studies in Dante* (1968–69).

Hardie was Public Orator of the University of Oxford from 1967 until 1973. This meant composing a good many speeches in Latin, because the Public Orator presents those who are to be admitted to honorary degrees. One of the last he made was on 3 June 1972 when J.R.R. Tolkien* was awarded the Doctorate of Letters. The address contained several references to Tolkien's stories of Middle-earth, and he concluded with the hope 'that in such green leaf, as the Road goes ever on, he will produce from his store Silmarillion and scholarship.' The original Latin text of the speech is found in the *Oxford University Gazette*, No 3511, vol. CII (8 June 1972) p. 1079.

Since Hardie and his wife retired to Sussex in 1973 he has been busy with a number of projects. He has been Honorary Professor of Ancient Literature at the Royal Academy of Arts since 1971. On the occasion of the founding of the *Inklings-Gesellschaft* in Aachen in 1983, he composed some Latin Elegiacs as a Greeting. They were published with a 'Paraphrase and Commentary' in the *Inklings-Jahrbuch* of 1983. His wife Christian Hardie was also a friend of Lewis's, and his letters to her are found in her article, 'Three Letters from C.S. Lewis,' in *The Chesterton Review*, C.S. Lewis Special Issue, (Vol. XVII, No 3, August 1991 and Vol. XVII, No 4, November 1991), pp. 392–8. There is a photo of Colin Hardie with James Dundas-Grant,* R.E. Havard,* and Lewis at The Trout‡ in **INK** and **TJB**. The photo in **INK** of Colin Hardie and J.R.R. Tolkien was made on 3 June 1972 after the degree ceremony.

Harwood, Alfred Cecil (1898–1975), lifelong friend. He was born on 5 January 1898 in Highbury, London, where his father, the Rev. **William Hardy Harwood** was a Congregational minister. He was educated at Highgate School, London, and it was there that he met Owen Barfield* in 1910. In 1916 both young men won Classical Scholarships to Oxford, Barfield to Wadham College, and Harwood to Christ Church. Immediately upon leaving school Harwood joined the Royal Warwickshires and served with the infantry as a Second Lieutenant. He saw some active service in France. At one point he was asked to take his platoon to a village held by the Germans, but, to his relief, they had already left. A case of appendicitis, which caused him to be invalided out of France, probably saved him from dying in the trenches. He went up to Oxford in Hilary Term 1919, and Barfield followed him there shortly afterwards. Harwood met Lewis through Barfield, and thus began a lifelong friendship.

After taking his BA in 1921 Harwood and Barfield returned to Oxford for post-graduate studies. They lived for a time in 'Bee Cottage' in Beckley, where Lewis was a frequent visitor. Their great mutual interest was poetry, and Lewis valued Harwood's criticism highly. Harwood read Lewis's *Dymer* as it was being written, and in his diary of 24 May 1922 Lewis recorded that Cecil Harwood '"danced with joy" over it' and 'advised me to drop everything else and go on with it' (**AMR**). Many of the poems Harwood wrote during these years, and which Lewis found 'original, quaint and catchy' are found in *The Voice of Cecil Harwood*, ed. Owen Barfield (1979). Another of their shared interests was the Walking Tour,‡ and such was his enthusiasm for these that Lewis dubbed him the 'Lord of the Walks'.

After leaving Oxford he had a temporary job with the British Empire Exhibition in London, after which he went into publishing. Writing about this period in his life in the Anthroposophical Society's *Supplement to Members' News Sheet* (February 1976), Barfield said: 'He was at that time making a rather half-hearted attempt to turn himself into what used to be called a "young man about town", and even the Bloomsbury set were not wholly outside his orbit. I don't think the experiment could ever have succeeded. But there was another reason why it did not last long.'

The other 'reason' is related to something that happened a few years earlier. During his second year in Oxford, Harwood followed Owen Barfield into the English Folk Dance Society. In the summer of 1922 they joined an amateur concert party touring some Cornish towns and villages. A friend of the organizers, **The Honourable Daphne Olivier**, was invited, and this was Harwood's first meeting with the woman he was to marry. Daphne Olivier was the daughter of Sydney Haldane Olivier (Lord Olivier), Governor of Jamaica from 1907 to 1913. She read the Medieval and Modern Languages Tripos at Newnham College, Cambridge, and after taking her BA in 1913, became a teacher. In 1922 she attended a conference on 'Spiritual Values in Education and Social Life' held at Manchester College, Oxford, 15–29 August, and it was at this conference that she first heard Rudolf Steiner lecture. She became a convinced and devoted follower. The next summer she attended an

Educational Conference at Ilkley in Wharfedale, Yorkshire, 4–18 August 1923, when Steiner lectured on 'Education and the Spiritual Life of Today'. Immediately afterwards (18 August–1 September) she went to the first International Summer School promoted by the Anthroposophical Society at Penmaenmawr in Wales. There Steiner gave a special course of lectures entitled 'Spiritual and Physical Evolution of the World and Humanity, past, present, and future, from the point of view of Anthroposophy'. It was during the conference at Ilkley that a group of teachers, including Daphne Olivier, expressed their desire to found a co-educational day school in England on the basis of Dr Steiner's educational principles and along the lines of the Waldorf School in Germany. Steiner approved the formation of a Founders' Committee, whose job it was to find a way of bringing about such a school. The Committee purchased a house in London big enough to accommodate 200 children, and Steiner accepted four teachers who were able to begin work: Helen Fox, Dorothy Martin, Effie G. Wilson and Daphne Harwood.

Meanwhile, the Anthroposophical Society of Great Britain was having regular meetings and lectures in London. Writing about this period in the Anthroposophical Society's *Supplement to Members' News Sheet* (February 1976), Owen Barfield said it was through Daphne Olivier that he and Harwood 'heard of anthroposophy and began, rather sceptically, attending together some weekly lecture-readings which George Adams (then George Kaufmann) was conducting at 46 Gloucester Place. This went on for some time and, if my memory is correct, Cecil's detachment lasted a little longer than my own, and it was I who first raised between us the question whether it was not about time we joined the Society. I believe I did actually join a few weeks or months before he did.'

Harwood visited Lewis shortly after this. In his diary of 7 July 1923 Lewis said: 'Harwood ... told me of his new philosopher, Rudolf Steiner, who has "made the burden roll from his back" ... I was very much disappointed to hear that both Harwood and Barfield were impressed by him' (**AMR**). But more was to come. Harwood accompanied Miss Olivier to the second International Summer School held at Torquay from 9–23 August 1924 where Rudolf Steiner gave a course of lectures on 'True and False Paths of Spiritual Investigation'. During this conference Steiner met with the four women who wanted to found a Steiner school in London, and recommended that they would do well to have some male assistance. Pointing to Harwood, he said, 'What about him?' This, said Barfield in the *Members' News Sheet*, 'changed everything ... I recall very vividly a telephone conversation after his return, in which he briefly informed me that Rudolf Steiner was a simply astounding man, and that he himself had decided to become a teacher in a School that was still to be founded. He did not say so, but it was clear, even through the microphone, that he had become a dedicated man.'

Harwood was committed to Anthroposophy for the rest of his life, and he was to have a very large part to play in its dissemination in this country. 'The New School', as it was called, was founded in January 1925 at 40 Leigham Court Road, Streatham, London, with Harwood and Miss Olivier as two of its original five teachers. On 14 August 1925 Harwood and Daphne married, and moved into a house in 51 Angles Road. Very little was known about Steiner in the country as a whole, and Harwood, who had a talent for lecturing, did much during the early years to spread the knowledge of Anthroposophy throughout the English-speaking world. His first public lecture for the Anthroposophical Society was given in the Court House, Oxford Street, London, on 8 November 1925 when he talked on 'Rudolf Steiner's Gift to Education'. Shortly afterwards he was elected to the Executive Council of the Anthroposophical Society in Great Britain, and in 1937 he became Chairman, a post he held until 1974. Some ten years after its founding, at a ceremony which included building a meteorite into the wall, the Streatham school was renamed Michael Hall School.

The Harwoods' first child John (who had Lewis as his tutor at Magdalen College‡) was born 31 May 1926. They were to have four more children: Lois was born 26 January 1929; Laurence, born on 12 June 1933, was Lewis's godson; Mark was born 4 October 1934; and Sylvia was born 16 May 1937. Lewis saw Cecil and Daphne often during these years. In his essay 'About Anthroposophy' (ABT) Harwood said that when accepting their invitation to stay with them in Argyle Street, Lewis reminded them (28 October 1926) that he did not agree with some of the tenets of Anthroposophy. In other letters to Cecil and Daphne Harwood, quoted extensively in the article on Anthroposophy, Lewis gave his objections. Thanks, however, to good will on all sides, their differences seem not to have hurt the friendship. Lewis was often a visitor to their house, and in 1947 he dedicated Miracles to them. One of the highlights of Lewis's life was the annual walking tour with Harwood and Barfield. The best known of his tributes to Harwood is found in SBJ XIII:

> Closely linked with Barfield of Wadham was his friend (and soon mine) A.C. Harwood of The House, later a pillar of Michael Hall, the Steinerite school at Kidbrooke. He was different from either of us; a wholly imperturbable man. Though poor (like most of us) and wholly without 'prospects', he wore the expression of a

nineteenth-century gentleman with something in the Funds. On a walking tour when the last light of a wet evening had just revealed some ghastly error in map-reading (probably his own) and the best hope was 'Five miles to Mudham (if we could find it) and we *might* get beds there', he still wore that expression. In the heat of argument he wore it still. You would think that he, if anyone, would have been told to 'take that look off his face'. But I don't believe he ever was. It was no mask and came from no stupidity. He has been tried since by all the usual sorrows and anxieties. He is the sole Horatio known to me in this age of Hamlets; no 'stop for Fortune's finger'.

When war broke out in 1939, the school was evacuated to Minehead in Somerset, where it remained throughout the war. Harwood moved there with his family, and there, too, Lewis visited them. Harwood served in the Home Guard during the war. Then in 1945 he discovered the Kidbrooke Park property in Forest Row, Sussex, and the whole Michael Hall school moved to this new location, where it remains. Cecil had a great sorrow in July 1950 when Daphne Harwood died. He, nevertheless, continued his teaching, lecturing and writing. On 1 November 1954 he married **Marguerite Lundgren**, the founder of the London School of Eurythmy. This system of dance is explained in *Eurythmy and the Impulse to Dance, with Sketches for Eurythmy figures by Rudolf Steiner* (1974) which she wrote with Cecil Harwood and Marjorie Raffé. After his retirement Harwood remained in Forest Row. Even during his last years, when he was afflicted with diabetes, he did not lose that remarkable imperturbability Lewis admired so much. He died on 22 December 1975. Many of his poems, stories and essays are collected in *The Voice of Cecil Harwood*. His other works include *The Way of a Child, an Introduction to the Work of Rudolf Steiner for Children* (1940), *The Recovery of Man in Childhood* (1958), and *Shakespeare's Prophetic Mind* (1964). His essay, 'About Anthroposophy' and the 'Toast to his [Lewis's] Memory' are found in **ABT**. See Owen Barfield's 'Cecil Harwood' in *The Anthroposophical Quarterly*, 21 (Summer 1976). Photos in **TJB** and *The Voice of Cecil Harwood*.

Havard, Robert Emlyn ('Humphrey') (1901–85), Inkling, member of the Socratic Club,‡ and Lewis's doctor. He was born on 15 March 1901 in Faldingworth, Lincolnshire, where he spent his boyhood. His father was the Rev. **John Emlyn Havard**, Vicar of Faldingworth and Buslingthorpe in Lincolnshire 1908–30. Robert Havard was educated at Wolverly School in Kidderminster, and he came up to Keble College in 1919 where he read Chemistry. He took a First Class degree in 1921.

Not long afterwards he was received into the Catholic Church by Ronald Knox, Catholic Chaplain to the University. This was a very serious step, and as Keble College had a ban against Catholics he had to give up membership there until the ban was lifted in the 1940s. However, he was given a place in Queen's College, Oxford, and he received his BM and B.Chem. from there in 1927. After this he was a Research Student at Guy's Hospital and in London Hospital, returning to Oxford as an Assistant House Surgeon at the Radcliffe Infirmary, and Demonstrator in the Biochemistry Department of Oxford University. He then taught in the Biochemistry Department of Leeds University.

While in Leeds, he married **Grace Mary Middleton** on 29 December 1931. She had taken a BA from St Anne's College, Oxford, in 1929. They had five children: **John Edward Havard** (b. 13 October 1932); **Mark Emlyn Havard** (b. 9 June 1935); **Mary Penrose Clare Havard**, to whom Lewis dedicated *Prince Caspian* (b. 28 December 1936); **Peter Laurence Havard** (b. 5 February 1939); and **David Thomas Havard** (b. 29 December 1942).

Havard returned to Oxford in 1934 to take over a medical practice with surgeries in Headington and St Giles. That same year he was given a Schorstein Research Fellowship by Queen's College, and he was awarded the Oxford Doctorate of Medicine. He met Lewis sometime after this when making a call at The Kilns.‡ In his essay 'Philia: Jack at Ease' (**ABT**) he said: 'On my first visit we spent some five minutes discussing his influenza, which was straightforward, and then half an hour or more in a discussion of ethics and philosophy. Lewis was something of a Berkleyan and had returned to Christianity via Idealism … whereas I, as a scientist of sorts, had been attracted to the realism of St Thomas Aquinas. Our differences laid the foundation of a friendship that lasted, with some ups and downs, until his death nearly thirty years later.'

In the same essay he described the delightful occasion at the end of August 1939 when Jack and Warnie Lewis,* Hugo Dyson* and he (as navigator) spent a few days sailing up the Thames on Warnie's cabin cruiser, the *Bosphorus*. They were at Godstow when they learned that Hitler had invaded Poland. They hurried back to Oxford, and he said that Lewis 'tried to lift the gloom by saying, "Well, at any rate, we now have less chance of dying of cancer".'

While waiting to know when he might be called up, Havard continued with his practice and became a regular member of the Inklings. Lewis was reading aloud *The Problem of Pain* at the time, and he asked Havard to contribute an Appendix on 'the observed effects of pain … from clinical experience.' Havard was very helpful in getting the Socratic Club‡ started, and at its first meeting on 26 January 1942 he read a paper entitled

'Won't Mankind Outgrow Christianity in the Face of the Advance of Science and of Modern Ideologies?'

It was, incidentally, through the Inklings that he acquired various nicknames. The best known of them, 'Humphrey', was given him by Hugo Dyson. Lewis named the doctor in *Perelandra* 'Humphrey' as a tribute to him. In 1943 he was called up, and served in the Navy as a medical officer. While at sea he grew a beard so ruddy in hue that Lewis labelled him 'The Red Admiral'. On another occasion Warnie was annoyed with him for not turning up with his car and dubbed him 'The Useless Quack' or 'U.Q.' 'The Useless Quack has returned to Oxford!' J.R.R. Tolkien* wrote to Christopher Tolkien on 1 March 1944 (**LJRRT**).

Although a busy husband, father and doctor, he was nevertheless one of the most faithful of the Inklings, rarely ever failing to show up for a meeting. He was one of the few who could drive a car, and most of their expeditions to country pubs would have been impossible without him. There are numerous references to him in Warnie Lewis's diary, one of the most charming of which concerns an Inklings meeting in September 1949. Warnie had not been there, but in his diary of 5 October he wrote: 'The best Inkling story of my absence is of Humphrey's instructing young Mark [Havard] in the elements of Christianity. "God" said Humphrey "has no body." "Do you mean, Daddy, that His legs join straight on to His head?"' (**BF**).

Grace Havard died on 10 September 1950, leaving him deeply saddened and with immense responsibilities. He nevertheless continued to attend Inkling gatherings. After his retirement in 1968 he was awarded the Papal Knighthood of St Sylvester. He and his wife were Benedictine Oblates (Tertiaries) of Ampleforth, and following his retirement he went to live in a home for elderly and handicapped men run by an unofficial group of lay Dominicans at Weston Manor on the Isle of Wight. He died there 17 July 1985, and he is buried at St Philip's Priory, Begbroke, near Oxford. There are two photographs of him in **TJB** (as well as an interview). In one he appears with James Dundas-Grant,* Colin Hardie,* Lewis* and Peter Havard; the other shows him in the Eagle and Child pub‡ in 1978.

Head, the Rev. Ronald Edwin (1919–91), was Lewis's parish priest. He was born on 5 November 1919 at 35 Quinton Street, London, the son of **Alfred Head** and **Beatrice Maud (Forward) Head**. He received his BD from King's College London in 1949 and he went on to take a B.Litt. from Exeter College, Oxford, in 1959. His thesis was published as *Royal Supremacy and the Trials of Bishops 1558–1725* (1962). He was ordained an Anglican priest in 1950 and was a curate of St Peter's, Vauxhall, 1949–52.

He became the curate of the Church of the Holy Trinity, Headington Quarry, Oxford in 1952, and was Vicar from 1956 until his retirement in 1990. Father Head was a man of many parts, a priest, a scholar, a musician. He stood firmly within the Catholic tradition of the Church of England, and abided by its twin pillars of Scripture and Tradition. He never departed from the Book of Common Prayer of 1662. He was horrified by many of the recent pronouncements from the Anglican hierarchy, but equally dismayed by those of the Second Vatican Council. Warnie Lewis* was churchwarden of Holy Trinity when Father Head arrived there, and when he came across Lewis, and before he knew who he was, he said 'you must be the churchwarden's brother.'

He was devoted to the Lewis brothers, and he was delighted when C.S. Lewis came to the Vicarage to consult his copy of the celebrated Latin commentaries on the Scriptures by Cornelius à Lapide (1567–1637). *Letters to Malcolm* owes much to Father Head. In later years he explained why he would not read books *about* Lewis. 'I've never done so,' he said, 'because one of the great dangers of this thing is if you do your own recollections become totally clouded, because they take in other people's thoughts about the thing and you then imagine that you've had them yourself, which makes memory quite useless.' Thus it was that his memories were always fresh.

It might have been supposed that he would have been too old-fashioned to welcome Mrs Joy Lewis* into his parish, but he liked her immensely and was deeply impressed by her courage in the face of death. He showed a similar courage when he was dying. He is buried beside his parents, a few yards from the grave of the Lewis brothers. See 'A Personal Recollection of Father Head' by W.A. Day in *Headington Quarry Parish Magazine* (February 1991). A cassette is available from Holy Trinity Church (The PCC Holy Trinity, The Vicarage, Quarry Road, Oxford OX3 8NU) entitled 'Reminiscences of C.S. Lewis by the Revd Canon R.E. Head.' Photo in **IHW**.

Jenkin, Alfred Kenneth Hamilton (1900–80), friend from undergraduate days. He was born on 29 October 1900 at 378 Green Lane, Redruth, Cornwall, the son of **Alfred Hamilton Jenkin** and **Amy Louisa (Keep) Jenkin**. His family had lived in Redruth since the eighteenth century. Jenkin matriculated at University College,‡ Oxford, in 1919. There he read English. This was an unhappy year for him, for while out on a bicycle ride with his father, the latter suffered a heart attack, and Kenneth had to leave him dying at the roadside while he sought help. He nevertheless took his BA in 1922, after which he stayed on to write a thesis on Richard Carew for a Bachelor of Letters.

Jenkin and Lewis became friends at University College in 1919. Both were members of the Martlets Society,‡ and Lewis's diary (**AMR**) is filled with details of their walks, their bicycle rides, and their talk. Jenkin was a frequent visitor at the house Lewis shared with Mrs Janie Moore*, and in his diary of 25 June 1922, Lewis observed that he and Mrs Moore 'were amused to notice again how in his conversation all roads lead to Cornwall.'

There was no keeping Jenkin from his native county, and while they met infrequently after he left Oxford, Lewis was always indebted to him for teaching him to enjoy 'the very quiddity of each thing'. (See **Quiddity**§). Lewis wrote to him on 4 November 1925 to complain that he had no one with whom to share the pleasure of crossing Magdalen deer park in the moonlight. 'I do it for the love of it,' he said,

> when I might just as well go in past the porter's lodge. And if there is no moon ... perhaps instead there will be thick darkness and drumming rain and the hoofs of the deer (invisible) scampering away – and ahead the long lighted line of the cloisters in New Buildings. I wish there was anyone here childish enough (or *permanent* enough, not the slave of his particular and outward age) to share it with me ... I go to Barfield* for sheer wisdom and a sort of richness of spirit. I go to you for some smaller and yet more intimate connection with the feel of things, for a certain gusto and complete *rightness* of palate: to Harwood* for 'humours' and the appreciation of them.

Lewis wrote about their friendship in **SBJ** XIII, where he said:

> The first lifelong friend I made at Oxford was A.K. Hamilton Jenkin, since known for his books on Cornwall. He continued (what Arthur [Greeves]* had begun) my education as a seeing, listening, smelling, receptive creature. Arthur had had his preference for the Homely. But Jenkin seemed to be able to enjoy everything; even ugliness. I learned from him that we should attempt a total surrender to whatever atmosphere was offering itself at the moment; in a squalid town to seek out those very places where its squalor rose to grimness and almost grandeur, on a dismal day to find the most dismal and dripping wood, on a windy

day to seek the windiest ridge. There was no Betjemannic irony about it; only a serious, yet gleeful, determination to rub one's nose in the very quiddity of each thing, to rejoice in its being (so magnificently) what it was.

In Cornwall, Jenkin lived in St Ives, where he worked as a journalist and broadcaster. His first major work was *The Cornish Miner: An account of his life above and underground from early times* (1927), the standard work on the subject and one which established him as a historian. This was followed in the next decade by *Cornish Seafarers* (1932), *Cornwall and the Cornish* (1933), *Cornish Homes and Customs* (1934), and *The Story of Cornwall* (1934). In the 1960s he brought out his vast 16-part series on *Mines and Miners of Cornwall* (1961–78), running to nearly a thousand pages and embodying the results of some sixteen years' research involving visits to some 2000 Cornish mines.

In 1926 Jenkin married **Luned Jacobs**, the daughter of the novelist W.W. Jacobs. They had two daughters, **Jennifer Hamilton Heseltine** (b. June 1929) and **Honor Bronwen Goldsmid** (b. June 1930). The marriage was dissolved about 1934. During the War Jenkin met **Elizabeth Lenton** (née **Le Sueur**) at Mullion Cove Hotel, where she was Managing Director. They married in 1948, and together managed the Poldu Hotel, Mullion, whilst Kenneth also continued his research into *News from Cornwall* (1951). When Elizabeth fell ill in 1954, he took her to live in the family home in Redruth, Trewirgie House, where his family had been since 1770. One of the early occupants of this house had been his great-great grandfather, William Jenkin, who became in later life steward to the Lanhydrock family estates. Elizabeth died in 1977.

Jenkin assisted in the formation of Old Cornwall societies, and he was elected President of the Federation of Old Cornwall Societies 1959–60. In 1962 he became the Federation's first Life Vice-President, which honour he held for the rest of his life. At the Gorsedd of Cornwall in 1978 he was presented with a medal, most appropriately struck in tin, which commemorated the fact that he was one of only two living Bards who were initiated by Henry Jenner at the first Gorsedd in 1928. He took the bardic name of Lef Stenoryon – 'Voice of the Tinners'. That same year he was awarded a D.Litt. by Exeter University. Jenkin was largely responsible for setting up the Cornwall County Record Office in Truro, one of the finest in the country. A.K. Hamilton Jenkin died on 20 August 1980. He left his printed books and pamphlets to the Redruth public library and his historical notes, documents, photos, maps and MSS to the County Record Office in Truro. His letters from Lewis are in the Bodleian Library.‡

Kirkpatrick, William Thompson 'The Great Knock' (1848–1921), was Headmaster of Lurgan College, County Armagh, Northern Ireland, 1876–99. Albert Lewis* had been his pupil at Lurgan 1877–79, and W.H. Lewis* and C.S. Lewis were tutored by him. Chapter IX of **SBJ** is devoted to this extraordinary man, and he is the model for MacPhee in *The Dark Tower* and *That Hideous Strength*. He was born in Boardmills, Co. Down, 10 January 1848, the son of **James** and **Sarah Kirkpatrick**. He was brought up in the Presbyterian Church and matriculated at the Royal Belfast Academical Institution, a liberal Presbyterian boys' school, in 1862. From there he went to Queen's College, Belfast (now Queen's University) where he graduated in July 1868 with First Class Honours in English, History and Metaphysics. He wrote the English Prize essay under the nom-de-plume 'Tamberlaine'. That same year he was awarded a Double Gold Medal by the Royal University of Ireland. He took an MA from Queen's College in 1870.

In 1868 Kirkpatrick entered the teaching profession as Assistant Master in the English Department of the Royal Belfast Academical Institution where he remained for eight years. That same year he also entered the Assembly's College (the Presbyterian seminary in Belfast) and spent the normal three years in theological studies for ordination in the Irish Presbyterian Church. He took classes in Christian Ethics, Oriental Languages, Biblical Criticism, Ecclesiastical History and Rhetoric. Mr Kirkpatrick became a licentiate – i.e. he had fulfilled the Church's academic and other demands for ordinands – but he was never ordained, and appears in the records of the General Assembly as a licentiate under the care of the Belfast Presbytery for ten years, 1871–80.

It was, however, as a teacher that he excelled. The large and extravagant personality which Lewis wrote about in **SBJ** struck one of his pupils there as forcefully as it did Lewis years later. Robert M. Jones, writing in *Royal Belfast Academical Institution. Centenary Volume (1810–1910)* (Belfast: 1913) by John H. Robb, said: 'No boy and no man could be in his company for even a very short time without being impressed by the fact that he was in the presence of a man of unusual mental power and grasp, of an overmastering influence on the mind, and of an intellectual honesty and vigour before which pretence and make-believe were dissipated like smoke before a strong wind. None who knew him could be surprised that it was he who subsequently made Lurgan College for many years one of the most remarkable and successful schools in Ireland. He became an almost incomparable teacher, and under him the boys swept on to victory over their work and to mastery of their subjects and of themselves. His pistol never missed fire; but he gave you the impression that, if it did, as Goldsmith said of Johnson, you would be knocked down by the butt-end.'

From there he went on to become Headmaster of Lurgan College, Co. Armagh, 1876–99. The school had been founded in 1873 on the endowment of Samuel Watts, a prominent local businessman, with extensive interests in brewing and tobacco. At his death in 1850 he left almost £10,000 to endow an 'English, Classical and Agricultural School for boys' in Lurgan. The will was remarkable in that it laid down that no clergyman, or person in Holy Orders, could have any part in the teaching or the management of the school. It further prohibited the teaching of any religious instruction during the hours normally laid down for school lessons. These provisions have always been seen as controversial. It is suggested, however, that it was Watt's intention to establish a school for older boys that would be on the same foundation as those National Schools envisaged by the Government in the 1830s, and which combined secular and separate religious instruction. Mr Kirkpatrick had applied for the position as Headmaster of Lurgan College in 1873, but the position was given to Edward Vaughan Boulger. When Boulger left Lurgan in December 1875, Mr Kirkpatrick succeeded him. The second time he applied he took pains to prove that he was not 'in Holy Orders'. Whatever Mr Kirkpatrick's beliefs were at this time, he was insistent that religious instruction was given to boarders, and he attended the local Presbyterian church every Sunday with the Presbyterian boarders. He had brought with him to Lurgan his sister, **Anna Mussen Kirkpatrick** (b. 8 December 1845), who helped with the management of them.

Mr Kirkpatrick's years at Lurgan College were exceptionally successful. There were sixteen pupils when he arrived in 1876, and when Albert Lewis was there he would have witnessed a considerable expansion because in only four years Mr Kirkpatrick had built it up to over sixty. By the late 1880s Lurgan College was one of the top schools in Ireland. Mr Kirkpatrick may have felt he needed a helpmeet by this time because on 15 July 1881 he married **Louisa Ashmore Smyth** of 81 Pembroke Road, Dublin, in St Bartholomew's Church, Dublin. Louisa was the daughter of George Smyth, a stockbroker. Two days earlier, on 13 July, Anna Kirkpatrick had married a former assistant at Lurgan, Alexander Stewart Mitchell, in St Anne's Church, Belfast. W.T. Kirkpatrick's only child, **George Louis**, was born on 23 May 1882 and educated at Charterhouse 1896–99.

Lewis was tutored by Mr Kirkpatrick in 1914–17, and describing him in **SBJ** (IX) he said: 'He had been a Presbyterian and was now an Atheist ... I hasten to add that he was a "Rationalist" of the old, high and dry nineteenth-century type. For Atheism has come down in the world since those days, and mixed itself with politics and learned to dabble in dirt.' As a licentiate of the Presbyterian Church, who preached on a number of occasions, Mr Kirkpatrick almost certainly entertained the ambition of becoming a minister. What led to his loss of faith? The Royal Belfast Academical Institution was a haven of liberalism when he was there. This was a time when liberalism was far from popular, and the dogmatism of the majority of his co-religionists may have caused him to become frustrated.

Mr Kirkpatrick had timed his retirement for 1899 so that while Louis was articled to the electrical engineers Browett, Lindley & Co., Engine Makers of Patricroft, Manchester, he and his wife could live nearby in 'Sharston House', Northenden. Later, while Louis was in Berlin gaining experience with electric tramways, the Kirkpatricks moved to Great Bookham in Surrey where they were to spend the rest of their lives. It was there that he had Warren Lewis as a pupil in 1913, and CSL 1914–17. He sent glowing opinions of them to their father, who acted as his solicitor. He died 22 March 1921.

Mrs Kirkpatrick lived until 1933. Louis, who was married but had no children, was General Manager of Bruce Peebles & Co. (Engineers) in Edinburgh from 1932 until his death in 1943. Many of W.T. Kirkpatrick's letters survive in the **LP**. The only known photograph of him, taken by W.H. Lewis, is found in **TJB** and **BIO** (2nd Ed.). There is a drawing of him by C.S. Lewis in **IHW**. On his years at Lurgan College, see 'A History of Lurgan College, Part II - Consolidation 1876–1899' by J.I. Wilson in *Ulula (Lurgan College School Magazine)* (1977), pp. 67–74.

Ladborough, Richard William (1908–72), friend and colleague at Cambridge. He was born in London on 12 September 1908, the son of **W.F. Ladborough**. He was educated at Malvern College‡ 1922–27, and he went up to Magdalene College,‡ Cambridge, in 1927, where he read French and Latin for the Modern and Medieval Languages Tripos, taking his BA in 1930. He remained in residence as a research student and gained his D.Phil. in 1935 with a thesis on Maucroix.

For the next two years he worked at the British Museum on the Book Catalogue. In 1936 he was appointed Lecturer in French at the then University College of Southampton. He remained there for nine years, serving as Vice-Warden of Connaught Hall during the war years. In 1954 he returned to Cambridge as University Lecturer in French. He was elected Fellow and Director of Studies at his old college, Magdalene, where he also served as Dean and Pepys Librarian. He organized the first complete catalogue of the Pepys Library. He excelled as a teacher, but he is equally admired for his many years of loyalty to Magdalene.

Ladborough gave Lewis a very warm welcome when he became a Fellow of Magdalene in 1955, and as they both lived in College they saw one another often. His essay, 'In Cambridge' (**ABT**), is the fullest account yet written of Lewis's years in Cambridge. 'It was Lewis,' Ladborough says in the essay, 'who first broke the ice. I remember how grateful I felt when I, perhaps among others, received a little note from him in his crabbed handwriting: "Dear Dick, May I call you that? Yours, Jack."' While he was astonished that Lewis visited the Pepys Library only once, he seemed happy to forgive him because, as he said in his essay, Lewis 'read the whole of Pepys Diary with insight and, of course, with intelligence, and made one of the best speeches on Pepys I have ever heard.'

In a memorial essay (with an excellent photograph) found in the *Magdalene College Magazine and Record*, N.S., No 16 (1971–72), R.F.B. said:

> Dick was in one sense the last of his generation. Casual acquaintances soon realized that his habits of thought as well as the ceremonious courtliness of his manner belonged to the past rather than to the present, but his friends knew that lately the outlook had aged far faster than the man, and they always excepted his scholarship when they thought of him as old-fashioned – for he followed modern work on his subject with close attention however much he might repudiate some of its conclusions. Too young to be deeply marked by the First World War, he was set in his ways before the Second cast its darkest shadows; in many respects he was a man of the Thirties, but of the Thirties at their most carefree. For in spite of the sad paradox that he was often worried and preoccupied in recent years, his was a fundamentally gay and happy nature ...
>
> One of the most striking things about Dick was an exuberant sense of fun, which he communicated to old and young alike. Laughter was never far away, and a cheerful grin always lighted up his face when one called at his rooms or met him in the street. His stories were endless and always amusing. Many, told quite unselfconsciously out of sheer delight in the joke, were against himself. He was a master of the art of the gaffe, and must have dropped more bricks on his own toes than a dozen other men (pp. 3–4).

His published writings include: 'Translations from the Ancient in Seventeenth-century France', *Journal of the Warburg Institute*, II, 2 (1938) pp. 85–104; 'François Maucroix's friendship with La Fontaine', *Modern Language Review*, xxiv, 2 (1939) pp. 223–9; 'The Sixteenth Century ... An annotated and classified list', *The Year's Work in Modern Language Studies*, ix (1939) pp. 48–56; Jean de Routou's *Le Véritable Saint Genest*, Edited R.W. Ladborough (Cambridge: 1954); and 'Pepys and Pascal', *French Studies* x, 2 (1956) pp. 133–9.

Richard Ladborough was an Anglo-Catholic and showed his love for the Faith by his support for the College Chapel and Little St Mary's in Cambridge. When he died on 30 April 1972 a Memorial Service was held for him in Little St Mary's on 30 May at which the Archbishop of Canterbury (Michael Ramsay) said in an address found in the 1971–1972 issue of the *Magdalene College Magazine and Record*:

> There are Christians who talk a lot about their faith and what it means to them. There are Christians who press their creed upon their work and upon their neighbours. Not so Dick. His piety was of the Tractarian kind, hidden and reserved. It was a part of him, and quietly people came to know it. His Christianity resembled St Paul's words: 'Your life is hid with Christ in God.' Next to his loving loyalty to the Chapel of St Mary Magdalene and its altar he found that the worship here in Little St Mary's meant much to him. Hidden with Christ in God his life was one which faced trials with serenity, cared for others both young and old, and could never be solemn, least of all solemn about itself (p. 5).

Lean, Edward Tangye CBE (1911–74), founder of 'The Inklings' literary group in University College,‡ Oxford. He was born on 23 February 1911, the second son of **Francis William la Bount Lean** and **Helena Anne Tangye**. He was educated at Leighton Park, and matriculated at University College in 1929. He read Modern Languages the first year, and then changed to Philosophy, Politics and Economics. He took a Second in PPE in 1933. During his three years at Univ. he founded a society of dons and undergraduates who met in his rooms to read unpublished manuscripts aloud, after which there would be comments and criticism. Lewis and Tolkien* were both members, and in a letter to William Luther White of 11 September 1967, Tolkien said:

> Tangye-Lean ... was more aware than most undergraduates of the impermanence of their clubs and fashions, and had an ambition to

found a club that would prove more lasting. Anyway, he asked some 'dons' to become members. C.S.L. was an obvious choice, and he was probably at that time Tangye-Lean's tutor ... In the event both C.S.L. and I became members. The club met in T.-L.s rooms in University College; its procedure was that at each meeting members should read aloud unpublished compositions. These were supposed to be open to immediate criticism ... Tangye-Lean proved quite right. The club soon died ... but C.S.L. and I at least survived. Its name was then transferred (by C.S.L.) to the un-determined and unelected circle of friends who gathered about C.S.L., and met in his rooms in Magdalen. Although our habit was to read aloud compositions of various kinds (and lengths!), this association and its habit would in fact have come into being at that time, whether the original short-lived club had ever existed or not (LJRRT).

It is unlikely that Lean had Lewis as his tutor, but besides the 'Inklings' group, they met as fellow members of the Martlets Society‡ in University College. Lean became a member of this society in 1930, and was President 1931–32. On occasion he read some of his own stories to the Martlets, and he published many other things in the student magazine, *Isis*. It is recorded in the Martlets minute books that at their 333rd meeting on 2 March 1932:

The President, Mr E. Tangye Lean, having written practically the whole of the *Isis* during the early part of 1931, became a sub-editor in October, and Editor the following June. His first novel *Of Unsound Mind* was published by Cobden Sanderson in February 1932, and an essay *Spirit of Death* by the White Owl Press in June 1932; we gather that a second novel will appear soon.

The title of the second novel Lean published as an undergraduate is *Storm in Oxford* (1933). He was the editor of *Isis* 1932–33. After leaving Oxford he was a writer and editor for the *News Chronicle* 1934–36. He began working for the German Service of the BBC in 1942, one of the most talented of their wartime broadcasters. His *Voices in the Darkness* (1943) is a vivid account of the task of the BBC's wartime broadcasts. His *Study in Toynbee* was published in 1947. As time went on he found the opportunity to write becoming submerged in the growing responsibilities of administration.

He retired at the age of 56 and returned to his first love. His work on *The Napoleonists* (1970) is a controversial study of the motives of certain eminent British men and women who favoured Napoleon's cause. He married **Doreen Myra Sharp** and had two sons and a daughter. He died on 28 October 1974. He was the brother of David Lean, the film director.

Lewis, Albert James (1863–1929), father of W.H. Lewis* and CSL, was born on 23 August 1863 in Cork. He was one of six children of **Richard Lewis** (1832–1908) and his wife **Martha Gee Lewis** (1831–1903) who had emigrated to Cork from Hawarden, Flintshire, in Wales. In 1868 the family moved to Belfast when Richard became a partner in 'MacIlwaine and Lewis: Boiler Makers, Engineers, and Iron Ship Builders'.

Albert attended the District Model National School, after which he spent 1877–79 at Lurgan College, in Lurgan, County Armagh. These were some of the happiest years of his life, owing in large part to the encouragement he received from the headmaster, W. T. Kirkpatrick.* Mr Kirkpatrick did much to foster Albert's literary bent, and the writing of poetry and the life-long keeping of literary chapbooks began at Lurgan. They were to remain life-long friends. On 9 August 1880 Albert was articled to the law firm of Maclean, Boyle, and Maclean in Dublin. Although his first love was always to be the Law, two others were to flourish during his time in Dublin: the liturgy of the Church of Ireland and English Literature. Writing to his father on 6 May 1883 about a high church service he attended there he said: 'Anything which renders to a certain extent the intangible tangible is certainly not useless and not a sin' **(LP** II: 91). He was elected a member of the Belmont Literary Society in 1881.

After qualifying as a solicitor on 10 June 1885, he set up a practice of his own at 83 Royal Avenue, Belfast. Mr Kirkpatrick had already engaged him as his solicitor the previous year, being much impressed by Albert's rhetorical abilities. 'Woe to the poor jury man who wants to have any mind of his own,' he said. 'He will find himself borne down by a resistless Niagara' **(LP** II: 98). In time Albert became Sessional Solicitor of the Belfast City Council and the Belfast and County Down Railway Company. He was Solicitor as well to the National Society for the Prevention of Cruelty to Children.

Albert emerged as a political speaker of considerable importance for the Conservative Party, the newspapers containing numerous references to his ability. One who did not thaw to him quite as fast as the others was the daughter of his parish priest, **Florence Augusta 'Flora' Hamilton.*** The Lewis family had long been parishioners of St Mark's, Dundela, and so would have known the Rev. Thomas Hamilton and his family since their arrival there in 1874. Albert first took serious notice of Flora in 1885, and found her friendly but cool. When he proposed to her in September 1886 she had already rejected his brother William, and she told Albert that she 'had nothing but friendship to give' (**LP** II:152). Albert turned to corresponding about literary subjects, a wise move since both liked writing stories. The publication of Flora's 'The Princess Rosetta' in *The Household Journal* of 1889 delighted him, and it led to further literary discussions through the post. Eventually, Albert got what he wanted. He and Flora became engaged in 1893 and were married in St Mark's on 29 August 1894.

Thus began a short but exceptionally happy married life for both. **Warren Hamilton Lewis*** was born in Dundela Villas‡ in 1895, and **Clive Staples Lewis** in 1898. With increased prosperity, Albert had a new house built for his family, and in 1905 the family moved into 'Little Lea'.‡ In February 1908 Flora was found to have cancer. Following an operation which seemed to leave her better, Albert's father died. Flora was ill again by June 1908, and she died with Albert beside her on 23 August. He was devastated by the loss and he never recovered. He treasured all his wife's last sayings, and the family preserved the sheet from the Shakespearean daily calendar which stood on Flora's mantlepiece on the day of her death. The quotation read:

> Men must endure
> Their going hence, even as their coming hither:
> Ripeness is all (*King Lear* V:ii).

His attempts to be a better father left Warnie and Jack feeling smothered by his love, and over the years each quarrelled with him. The fact remains, however, that he did the best he could, and more than most fathers attempt. He had always worked too hard, but Flora had been able to protect him from excess. With Flora gone, he practically lived in his law office. When he was persuaded to relax it was usually with Flora's brother, Augustus ('Gussie'), perhaps his best friend. 'He was never happier' said CSL, 'than when closeted for an hour or so with one or two of my uncles exchanging 'wheezes' (as anecdotes were oddly called in our family)' (**SBJ** I). When he wrote to his sons he nearly always included the latest 'wheeze', while they sent him the ones they picked up. When the boys were home from school he liked taking them to the music hall. Albert was not a wealthy man, but he nevertheless provided for all CSL's undergraduate years at Oxford and until he had a job of his own. His interest in his parish church never flagged, and he served as a churchwarden for a number of years. Still, his greatest natural consolation came from his work as a solicitor. He continued at his practice until his death on 25 September 1929.

There is a short biography (and photograph) of him in the 'Contemporary Biographies' section of Robert M. Young's *Belfast and the Province of Ulster in the 20th Century* (Brighton, 1909) p. 520. His correspondence with his sons and Mr Kirkpatrick is found in the **LP**. Over the years Lewis and Warren preserved one hundred of their father's dicta which they copied into a notebook entitled 'Pudaita Pie' after Albert's 'low' Irish pronunciation of 'potato'. Many of the sayings later went into **SBJ**. The manuscript of 'Pudaita Pie' is in Wheaton College. See also **SBJ**, Warren's 'Memoir' in **L**, and **AMR**. Photos in **L** (1st ed. 1966), **IHW, I, TJB** and **BIO** (2nd ed.), A photograph of the portrait of Albert painted by A.R. Baker in 1917 is found in Walter Hooper's 'The Lewis That Stayed Behind', in the *Magdalen College Record* (1995).

Lewis, Florence Augusta 'Flora' (1862–1908), the mother of W.H. Lewis* and CSL, was one of two daughters and two sons born to the Rev. **Thomas Robert Hamilton** and **Mary Warren Hamilton**. At the time of her birth on 18 May 1862 in Queenstown, County Cork, her father was a Chaplain with the Royal Navy. During 1870–74 the family lived in Rome, where Thomas Hamilton was Chaplain of Holy Trinity Church. There survives from this period the earliest document in Flora's hand. It is an account of a miracle she witnessed in one of the Catholic churches of Rome when she was 12 years old, and which WHL thought evidence of an eminent degree of her 'matter of factness'. Describing the body of a young female saint in a glass case beneath the altar, Flora said, 'the beautiful waxen figure with its flowers and candles had a great fastenation [sic] for me, so I went back by myself to look at it again ... I was gazing fixedly at her when she slowly lifted her eyelids and looked at me; I was terribly frightened and felt myself getting cold – I had hardly time to look at or admire her large blue eyes when she again closed them.' Later, her mother 'laughed and said it was nonsense', thus causing Flora to conclude that 'it was all done by cords' (**LP** I:312).

From Rome the Hamiltons moved to Belfast where Flora's father was Rector of St Mark's, Dundela, 1874–1900. Flora attended 'Ladies' Classes' at the Methodist College Belfast, in the sessions 1881–82, 1883–84 and 1884–85, at the same time as she was going to Queen's University, Belfast (then the Royal University of Ireland). She performed brilliantly at Queen's. She took a first degree in 1880, and in her second examinations in 1881 she passed with First Class Honours in Geometry and Algebra. In 1885 she passed the second university examination with First Class Honours in Logic and Second Class Honours in Mathematics, and took a BA in 1886.

Flora would have known **Albert Lewis's*** family since the Hamiltons arrived in Belfast, but it was not until almost a decade had passed that they suddenly seemed to need one another's opinion on a good many things. 'Where was the best place to stay in Dublin?' asked Albert. 'Will you come in to tea after church? We want to get some information from you,' said Flora. Albert obviously thought it best to save really serious matters until after he had qualified as a solicitor in 1885. However, when he proposed to her in 1886 she had already turned down his brother, William, and he seems to have understood this as increasing his own chance. However, in her reply of 21 September 1886 Flora said, 'I always thought you knew that I had nothing but friendship to give you' (**LP** II: 152). In this she was not being conventional: she really did like Albert's friendship, and, indeed, seemed to value all friendships highly.

CSL has described his mother as 'a voracious reader of good novels' (**SBJ** I), and this love of literature which she and Albert shared certainly made Albert a more interesting suitor than his brother. A particular opportunity came to hand in 1889 when Flora had a story, 'The Princess Rosetta', published in *The Household Journal* of London. Albert said at once that he hoped that 'to the collegiate honours' Strandtown had already gained through Flora, 'will be added the higher distinction of producing a great novelist.' Flora presented him with the manuscript of the 'Princess Rosetta', and Albert assured her that not even the Bodleian Library or the British Museum could persuade him to part with it. It is a pity that it was not given to one of these libraries for no copies of *The Household Journal* containing Flora's story, nor any of the other stories she wrote, can be traced. Flora and Albert were to exchange many letters after this, but only Flora's have survived.

In comparing the Lewises and the Hamiltons, CSL said his father's people were 'sentimental, passionate, and rhetorical', while the Hamiltons were 'cooler', their minds 'critical and ironic' (**SBJ** I). The thirty letters Flora wrote to Albert before they were married, and the forty-eight she wrote afterwards (preserved in **LP**) provide evidence of this. They supply as well a clue as to where Lewis got his own clarity of thought. 'I am not quite sure that I would like it if you *only* talk to me on "sensible subjects",' Flora wrote to Albert on 5 July 1893. 'Why should it bore me to hear about your love for me? You know it does not. I like you to love me, and if your love bored me, your society would, still more, so there would be no use in your talking to me on any subject at all ... Gussie [her brother] is right about our not being a demonstrative family. I don't think we are, but do you know I really think it is better than being too demonstrative; men soon get tired of that sort of thing' (**LP** II: 251–2).

Up until they became engaged in June 1893, Flora, a well-brought up lady, addressed Albert as 'Dear Mr Lewis'. Now, writing to him on 26 June 1893 she calls him 'My dear Allie', and asks:

> I wonder do I love you? I am not quite sure. I know that at least I am very fond of you, and that I should never think of loving anyone else. I said 'yes' the other day, partly because I knew that if I said 'no', we should have had to have given up seeing each other altogether … The thing that makes me most doubtful about the whole thing is the fear lest you be disappointed in me. You see, you really care too much about me to know what I am like. I am afraid you think I am far better and far nicer than I really am, and that when you find out that I am just about the same as other people, you will not be satisfied with me …
>
> In spite of all this, I think and hope that we shall be happier together than apart, and even if I don't succeed in making you perfectly happy in the future as your wife, I should at least have made you unhappy in the present by refusing, so let us hope that I have done what is best for you (**LP** II: 248–9).

They were married in St Mark's on 29 August 1894, and following a honeymoon in North Wales, they moved into the Dundela Villas,‡ Dundela, Belfast. They were immensely devoted to one another. **Warren Hamilton Lewis*** was born in 1895 and named after the two sides of Flora's family; **Clive Staples Lewis** was born in 1898. Warren has said in his 'Memoir' how much his father 'loathed' holidays away from home. The responsibility of taking the boys on holiday thus fell on Flora, and 'Warnie' and 'Jack' were never to forget what a large stock of their happiness came from these holidays. No matter how short the distance from home, Flora wrote almost daily to Albert. In the holiday to Castlerock in 1901 she learned that he was fussing over life insurance. 'I wish I could make you feel more satisfied about things of this sort,' she wrote, 'but I am afraid it is your nature to take a gloomy view of life' (**LP** II: 316).

In 1905 the family moved into 'Little Lea'‡ on the outskirts of Belfast, which Albert had specially built for Flora. Warnie went to Wynyard School‡ in England soon afterwards, while Jack's education began at home, with Flora teaching him French and Latin, and Annie Harper, his governess, teaching him everything else. Flora's last holiday with the boys was in Berneval in the summer of 1907. In the little diary Jack wrote the following Christmas – 'My life During the Exmas Holadys of 1907' – we glimpse the contentment of the happy Lewis family. He said his father was 'very sensible' and 'nice when not in a temper' while his mother is 'like most middle-aged ladys, stout, brown hair, spectaciles, kniting her chief industry.' As Christmas draws near we learn how Warnie comes home from school, of the various Lewis and Hamilton relations who drop in, how 'Mamy stoned raisins for the Xmas pudding', of how Jack and Warnie take to 'rushing about the house' and of the play which Jack is writing to perform for the family on Christmas Day. The document ends with the words 'The old year out and the new year in' (**LP** III: 88–92).

Not far into the new year Flora fell ill. On 7 February 1908 she was operated on at home. The doctor found cancer. Flora rallied for a while, but by June 1908 the trouble had returned, the nurses were back, and Flora was confined to bed. There her faithful husband attended her with touching devotion, rarely leaving her bedside. She died on 23 August 1908, deeply lamented by Albert, Warnie and Jack. There is a good deal about her in **LP**, **SBJ** and in Warren's 'Memoir'. Photos in **L, IHW, TI, TJB**.

Lewis, Joy Davidman Gresham (1915–60), Lewis's wife. (For a detailed treatment of her life see **LIFE XXII–XXIII**). She was born in New York City on 18 April 1915, of Jewish parents from Europe. Her father, **Joseph Isaac Davidman** was born in Poland in 1887 and arrived in New York in 1893; her mother, **Jeannette (Spivack) Davidman**, came from the Ukraine.

At the age of eight she read Wells' *Outline of History*, and declared herself an atheist. She was educated in New York public schools, and she received a BA from Hunter College in 1934, and an MA from Columbia University in 1935. After teaching English in New York high schools she devoted herself to writing. Her first book of verse, *Letter to a Comrade*, won the Yale Series of Younger Poets Award for 1938. The Depression of the 1930s affected her so deeply that in 1938 she joined the Communist Party and became a journalist and critic on the Party's magazine, *New Masses*. After an unsuccessful six months as a junior screen writer for Metro-Goldwyn-Mayer in Hollywood during 1939 she returned to New York. Her first novel, *Anya*, was published in 1940, and her second, *Weeping Bay*, in 1950. She edited an anthology, *War Poems of the United Nations*, published in 1944.

In 1942 she married the writer, **William Lindsay Gresham**, and they had two sons, **David*** (b. 1944) and **Douglas*** (b. 1945). In 1946 they moved to Pleasant Plains, New York, and in 1948 they became Christians. Each told the story of his conversion in *These Found the Way: Thirteen Converts to Protestant Christianity*, ed. David Wesley Soper (1951).

In 1950 Joy began corresponding with Lewis, and they met for the first time when she spent several months in England in 1952. While there she completed another book, *Smoke on the Mountain: An Interpretation of the Ten Commandments* (1953). She went home to find that her husband had taken a mistress. In November 1953 she returned to England with her sons, and took rooms in Belsize Park, London.

Joy and her husband were divorced on 5 August 1954, and in August 1955 she moved with her sons to 10 Old High Street, Headington. For reasons which remain unknown, Joy was unable to have her visa renewed, and rather than see her return unwillingly to the United States, Lewis married her in a register office on 23 April 1956. This act gave her the right to British citizenship, and the 'patrial' status entitled David and Douglas to claim British citizenship.

Although she was only 41, Joy began suffering from pains in her right leg. On 18 October 1956 she was discovered to have cancer in her leg and other parts of her body. The doctors believed her to be dying, and on 21 March 1957 she and Lewis were married by the Rev. Peter Bide.* In April 1957 she joined her sons and Lewis at The Kilns.‡ By the autumn of 1957 she had improved greatly and was almost without pain. Lewis, however, began experiencing a great deal of pain, and it was his belief that he was allowed to carry this burden for his wife. The improvement continued, and in July 1958 they had a honeymoon in Ireland.

During a routine examination on 13 October 1959 X-rays revealed that cancerous spots were returning to many of her bones. She and Lewis had planned to accompany Roger Lancelyn Green* and his wife to Greece in 1960, and despite much pain she fulfilled this life-long ambition when the four of them had a holiday there, 3–14 April. She grew progressively worse after this, but her courage never flagged. She died on 13 July 1960. See Douglas Gresham's *Lenten Lands: My Childhood with Joy Davidman and C.S. Lewis* (1988), and Lyle Dorsett's *And God Came In: The Extraordinary Story of Joy Davidman, Her Life and Marriage to C.S. Lewis* (1983) – renamed *Joy and C.S. Lewis* (1994). Both contain photographs.

Lewis, Warren Hamilton ('Warnie') (1895–1973), brother of CSL. He was born in Dundela Villas,‡ Belfast, on 16 June 1895, the son of **Albert James Lewis*** and **Florence Hamilton Lewis***. The family was still in Dundela Villas when his brother **Clive Staples ('Jack')**, was born in 1898. They became and remained for the rest of their lives the best of friends. Shortly after the family moved to Little Lea‡ in 1905 he was sent to Wynyard School‡ in Watford, Hertfordshire, where he passed four miserable years. His recollections of the school and Robert Capron,* the headmaster, are found in **LP** III: 33–42.

He entered Malvern College‡ in September 1909, and here he was content. Although he described Shakespeare as 'dreary rubbish' (**LP** III:299) he won praise as a writer of essays. In a little article he wrote for the College *Beacon* (1954) he said:

> Work was never a problem for S[chool] H[ouse], for the House had discovered the value of specialization long before my day. In a house over fifty strong, we argued, there must be many who can do some one thing better than the average; so why have fifty men wasting their time trying to do half a dozen things? Let the Grecian do Greek, the Latinist Latin, and so forth, all *pro bono publico*. This suited me down to the ground; the only thing that I was interested in was writing English essays, and as time went on and my clientèle expanded, I was able to make this almost a whole time job; for of course, the bulk of my other work was traded off against the essays.

He was made a Prefect in May 1913 when he also began considering a career in the Royal Army Service Corps (RASC). After leaving Malvern in July 1913 he was prepared for the Sandhurst entrance examination by Albert Lewis's old headmaster, W.T. Kirkpatrick,* then living in Surrey. Reflecting later on his time with Mr Kirkpatrick, he said, 'When I went to Bookham I had what would now be called "an inferiority complex", partly the result of Wynyard, partly of my own idleness, and partly of the *laissez faire* methods of Malvern. A few weeks of Kirk's generous but sparing praise of my efforts, and of his pungent criticisms of the Malvern masters, restored my long-lost self confidence: I saw that whilst I was not brilliant or even clever, I had in the past been unsuccessful because I was lazy, and not lazy because I was unsuccessful' (**LP** IV: 62).

Mr Kirkpatrick wrote to Albert Lewis on 20 September 1913 saying: 'He is one of the nicest, best tempered, personally amiable boys I have ever met. To live in the house with him is a pleasure, and no one could sit working along with him so long as I have done without developing an affection for him. Not naturally of the strenuous type I should say, but he is conscientious and ready to do what he can with any work you impose on him' (**LP** IV: 69). In 1914 Warnie won a Price Cadetship to Sandhurst after placing twenty-first out of 201 successful candidates.

Due to wartime need his officer's training was accelerated to nine months instead of two years, and in November 1914 he was sent to France with the 4th Company 7th Divisional Train, British Expeditionary Force, as an officer with the Royal Army Service Corps. During the First World War he served in France, and it was during this time that he came across the book that led to his flowering as a historian. 'One day in 1919 in St Omer,' he said, 'I saw in a shop window an abridgement of St Simon's *Memoirs*, bought it as a change from French novels, and became a life-addict to the period.' After the Armistice, in 1919 he was reassigned to service in England. In March 1921 he left to serve in Sierra Leone, West Africa, where he remained until April 1922. It was while visiting Jack in Oxford that he first met Mrs Janie Moore* on 5 August 1922. On 11 April 1927 he sailed for China where he was in command of the supply depot at Shanghai for much of the time he was there. He learned of his father's death in October 1929.

On 4 March 1930, when standing before the Great Buddha of Kamakura, Warnie became convinced of the truth of Christianity. He wrote in his diary of 13 May 1931: 'I started to say my prayers again after having discontinued doing so for more years than I care to remember: this was no sudden impulse but the result of a conviction of the truth of Christianity which has been growing on me for a considerable time ... I intend to go to Communion once again ... The wheel has now made the full revolution – indifference, scepticism, atheism, agnosticism, and back again to Christianity' (**BF**). He returned home in April 1930 and was assigned to Bulford. During Christmas 1931 at The Kilns‡ he began the mammoth task of editing the **Lewis Papers**.‡ In October 1931 he left for his second tour of duty in China, and was in Shanghai when the Japanese attacked on 29 January 1932.

After he returned home in December 1932 he retired from the RASC, and went to live at The Kilns‡ with his brother. During 1933–35 he completed his editing of the **Lewis Papers**, eleven volumes of family papers. On 4 September 1939 he was recalled to active service and sent to Le Havre. After his evacuation in May 1940 he was transferred to Reserve of Officers and sent to Oxford, where he served as a private soldier with the 6th Oxford City Home Guard Battalion.

In 1943 he began acting as his brother's secretary, and over the years he was to type many letters for him. He was also a very active member of the Inklings,‡ and his diary, *Brothers and Friends* (1982) is a prime source of information about the group. He wrote so well that his readers can only share his regret that he did not keep a fuller record. 'Oh if only I could have known in time that he was to die first,' he said of his brother on 8 April 1966, 'how I would have Boswellized him!' (**BF**). Warnie was greatly loved by the other Inklings, and writing about their meetings John Wain* said in *Sprightly Running* (V):

There was no fixed etiquette, but the rudimentary honours would be done partly by Lewis and partly by his brother, W.H. Lewis, a man who stays in my memory as the most courteous I have ever met – not with mere politeness, but with a genial, self-forgetful considerateness that was as instinctive to him as breathing.

J.R.R. Tolkien* is another who thought highly of him, and he praised Warnie's first book, *The Splendid Century: Some Aspects of French Life in the Reign of Louis XIV* (1953) when it was read aloud to the Inklings. Warnie's hobby of seventeenth and eighteenth century France ('the best escapist resort in the world') bore much fruit over the next ten years. *The Splendid Century* was followed by *The Sunset of the Splendid Century: The Life and Times of Louis Auguste de Bourbon, Duc de Maine, 1670–1736* (1955), *Assault on Olympus: The Rise of the House of Gramont between 1604 and 1678* (1958), *Louis XIV: An Informal Portrait* (1959), *The Scandalous Regent: A Life of Philippe, Duc D'Orleans, 1674–1723* (1961), and *Levantine Adventurer: The Travels and Missions of the Chevalier d'Arvieux, 1653–1697* (1962). He also published an edition of the *Memoirs of the Duc de Saint-Simon* (1964). One of his admirers was the historian J.H. Plumb who said 'W.H. Lewis knows Versailles better than any man living.' He was astonished to learn that he had never been there. Like his brother, he preferred his enjoyment of places to come *through books*. When invited to visit Versailles he said 'Oh no! That would ruin it!'

He had a problem with drink that went back many years, but which became serious in the 1940s. During a holiday in Ireland in June of 1947 he collapsed and was hospitalized in Our Lady of Lourdes Hospital, Drogheda, run by the Medical Missionaries of Mary (see **BF** 30 June 1947). Over the years he struggled hard to overcome the problem. Although the reasons for his alcoholism were numerous and complex, one of them was his shyness. In their youth Warnie was gregarious and Jack was to some extent a recluse. As time went on they seemed to exchange positions. While Jack's fame as a Christian apologist drove him to mingle with all sorts of people, most of whom he came to like, Warnie withdrew more and more into the company of books and fewer friends. Alcohol gave him back, albeit temporarily, the gregariousness that was draining away. Austin and Katharine Farrer* were primarily Jack's friends, but when it became necessary for him to spend his weekdays in Cambridge, Mrs Farrer wondered if Warnie might sometimes like to lunch with them. In his reply of 2 April 1955 Jack provided an insight into his brother's temperament:

He's as evasive as Mr Badger. His *first* thought on receiving any invitation is not whether he should accept but how he can most plausibly and politely refuse. This includes invitations from people he likes best as well as from the greatest bores.

Warnie was devastated by his brother's death. Fearing that he would not be able to keep up The Kilns, he bought a small semi-detached house in nearby 51 Ringwood Road and moved into it in May 1964. He was unhappy there, and in April 1967 he returned to The Kilns. For the first few years he retreated more and more to Ireland where he enjoyed the company of an old friend, Major Frank Henry. Eventually Our Lady of Lourdes Hospital was unable to accommodate him, and this forced him to remain in Oxford. It was, however, during these lonely years that he edited the *Letters of C.S. Lewis* (1966), to which he attached a touching 'Memoir'.

He was subject to fits of anxiety, and on 2 January 1972 he damaged his heart through drink. The following summer he was on holiday in Drogheda, began drinking and became ill. The Medical Missionaries of Mary took him in and nursed him for the next nine months. He left the hospital at the beginning of April 1973, and died at The Kilns on 9 April. He is buried in the same grave as his brother at Holy Trinity Church,‡ Headington Quarry. Selections from his diary are published as *Brothers and Friends*, ed. Clyde Kilby and Marjorie Lamp Mead (1982), and there are numerous letters and reminiscences by him in **LP**. Photos in **L** (1st ed.), **IHW, TJB, AMR.**

McCallum, Ronald Buchanan 'Mac' (1898–1973), Inkling. He was born 28 August 1898 at Paisley, Renfrewshire, the son of **Andrew Fisher McCallum** and his wife **Catherine Buchanan (Gibson) McCallum**. After being educated at Paisley Grammar School and Trinity College, Glenalmond, he served for two years with the Labour Corps of the British Expeditionary Force in France 1917–19.

In 1919 he matriculated at Worcester College, Oxford, where he read Modern History. He obtained First Class Honours in 1922. Following a year at Princeton and a year at Glasgow University as a history lecturer, he was elected Fellow and Tutor of History at Pembroke College, Oxford, in 1925. One colleague, who had been there since 1912, was the distinguished philosopher and historian, R.G. Collingwood. Another who arrived the same year as McCallum was J.R.R. Tolkien,* the Professor of Anglo-Saxon and a Fellow of Pembroke. McCallum was the ideal of an Oxford don. One of those who began history tutorials with him in 1927 was Frank Ziegler who, in the *Pembroke College Record* (1973), described McCallum's use of that great Oxford institution, the vacation Reading Party:

> At our cottage a huge teapot would dominate our substantial breakfasts, while other meals retain even now a lasting savour of Cotswold lamb. We would read from about 9 till 12, and from 5 till 7.30, and I recall that my tutor's own reading, Spengler's *Decline of the West*, somewhat worried him even in those early days of western decline. In the afternoon, with Collingwood's *Roman Britain* as a guide, we would go for long walks seeking out the disused stretches of the Fosse Way. On one of them my tutor asked me: 'If you came to a cross-roads and found the signpost lying in a ditch, how would you use it to find your way?' I was happy to have passed that little examination when he added: 'It stumped one of our generals during the war in France' (pp. 26–7).

McCallum took great interest in *The Oxford Magazine*. He edited it, then wrote for it, he believed in it, he was perhaps its greatest friend. He was twice the Editor, the first time in 1932, and again in 1972 when, on the revival of the magazine, he accepted the responsibility of re-floating it. Many of his colleagues will know that he sometimes wrote under the pseudonym 'Vernon Fork'.

Born and brought up in a radical constituency, it is not surprising that McCallum's first book was a *Life of Asquith* (1936). Nor is it surprising that, as a tutor of undergraduates in British and foreign history, his next should be *England and France, 1939–1943* (1944). In his most controversial, *Public Opinion and the Last Peace* (1944), he analysed British attitudes to the treaty of Versailles. This was followed by (with Alison Readman) *The British General Election of 1945* (1947). His other works include an edition of J.S. Mill's *On Liberty and Considerations on Representative Government* (1946) and *The Liberal Party from Earl Grey to Asquith* (1963). Amongst the many things he will be remembered for is coining the word 'psephology', defined by the *Oxford English Dictionary* as 'study of trends in elections and votings ... [f. Gk. *psēphos* pebble, vote + -o- + -logy].'

It is not known when he began attending meetings of the Inklings, but Warnie Lewis's diary first mentions him in 1948. He was introduced to the group by Tolkien. Writing about a meeting on 4 February 1949, Warnie said: 'An enjoyable Inklings in the evening. Present, J, McCallum, Colin [Hardie],* Hugo [Dyson]* and myself ... The talk drifted, by channels which I have forgotten, to torture, Tertullian ... the contractual theory in medieval kingship, odd surnames and place names. McCallum very good on kingship; he much improves as time goes on, and if one gets the impression in listening to him that you are having a tutorial, well I suppose a history don cannot very well talk history in any other way' (**BF**). He was unable to attend many of the Thursday evening sessions, but he was often present at the Tuesday meetings in the Eagle and Child.‡

After holding a number of positions in the College, McCallum was elected Master of Pembroke in 1955. Describing his mastership, Z.A. Pelczyniski said in his **DNB** biography:

> The twelve years of McCallum's mastership saw a marked transformation of Pembroke. The number of tutorial fellows increased and began to include natural scientists. The quality of undergraduates and their academic performance improved. A new quadrangle was created in 1962 by converting and incorporating a row of historic houses between Pembroke Street and Beef Lane. McCallum was an ideal master for this expansionary period in the college's history. He combined traditional beliefs in the virtues of Oxford education with the recognition of a need to bring the college into the post-1944 Butler Education Act era. His sense of fairness and toleration of views with which he disagreed were valuable qualities in a governing body that became increasingly large and diverse.

McCallum married **Ischtar Gertrude Bradley** in 1932, and they had two daughters. She died in 1944, and in 1950 he married **Evelyn Margaret Veale**, and they had two sons and a daughter. McCallum resigned his mastership in 1967 in order to become principal of St Catharine's, Cumberland Lodge, Windsor Great Park, a position he held until 1971. In 1967 he was awarded an honorary LLD by Dundee University in recognition of his advice on the university's constitution and development. Worcester College made him an honorary fellow in 1961, and he became an honorary fellow of Pembroke in 1968. After Lewis died McCallum was one of the Inklings who attempted to keep the Monday morning meetings going. But when it was clear that the group could not survive without Lewis, he pronounced its epitaph: 'When the Sun goes out there is no more light in the solar system.' He died on 18 May 1973. A portrait of him by John Ward hangs in Pembroke College hall. See Godfrey Bond's 'R.B. McCallum' in *Pembroke College Record* (1973), pp. 13–18; *The Times* (21 May 1973); and the first R.B. McCallum memorial lecture, by J.W. Fulbright, 24 October 1975.

McNeill, Jane Agnes 'Janie' (1889–1959), life-long friend from Belfast to whom C.S. Lewis dedicated *That Hideous Strength* and W.H. Lewis* dedicated *The Sunset of the Splendid Century*. She was born at 3 West Elmwood, Belfast, on 23 November 1889, the daughter of **James Adams McNeill** and **Margaret (Cunningham) McNeill**. 'Flora' Lewis* had been taught by Mr McNeill when he was Mathematics Master at Methodist College, Belfast. From 1890 until his death in 1907 he was the Headmaster of Campbell College.‡ Janie McNeill remained attached to Campbell College all her life. She had very little formal education, but she was given some private tuition by Lewis Alden ('Octie'), Senior English Master at Campbell 1898–1930. She then went to Victoria College, Belfast, from 1902 until 1907, and was thereafter a loyal and devoted alumna.

After her father's death, Jane continued to live with her mother in their big Victorian house, 'Lisnadene', at 191 Belmont Road, Strandtown. She was a member of Belmont Presbyterian Church, and for a good many years taught Sunday School to the girls of Victoria College. She edited the College magazine, *The Victorian*, from 1931 to 1941 and again from 1952 to 1959. Janie McNeill was widely read, and her interest in literature was stimulated by her attendance at the 'Drawing room Circle', a literary club founded in 1926 by Mary Bell Morwood, which flourished until the later 1970s. Jane read a number of papers at their meetings. The obituary in the Campbell School magazine, *The Campbellian* (July 1959) said of her: 'An authority on early ballads and early Scottish poetry, she loved to discuss Henryson, Dunbar and Alexander Scott. Her knowledge of French medieval literature was profound, but dearest to her heart was the lore of Mysticism and the early Mystics. All her love of literature stemmed from a profound knowledge of the Bible.'

In his letters to Arthur Greeves,* *They Stand Together*, as well as in his diary, *All My Road Before Me*, Lewis was sometimes caustic about Janie or 'Chanie' or 'Tchainie', as he sometimes called her in imitation of her mother's pronunciation. However, over time he came to love and admire her. 'Damn Tchainie's impudence for thinking I am to be a critic,' he said to Greeves on 14 February 1920 about a most prophetic remark (**TST**). It was while visiting his father in January 1923 that Lewis suddenly caught a glimpse of how frustrating it must have been for Janie never to venture far from home. 'I had some real and serious conversation with Janie,' he wrote in his diary on 9 January. 'She talked about her longing to get away from Strandtown and the impossibility of doing so, as she could neither leave nor transplant her mother. Her idea of going to Oxford or Cambridge had been knocked on the head years ago by her father's death' (**ABR**).

One of Janie's closest friends from her days at Victoria College was the medieval scholar and translator, Helen Waddell (1889–1965), who wrote *The Wandering Scholars* (1927), *Medieval Latin Lyrics* (1929), and *Peter Abelard* (1933). Writing to her friend George Pritchard Taylor in about 1920, Helen Waddell provided a touching sketch of Jane:

> Do you remember the girl I used to coach, the daughter of the old headmaster of Campbell? Jane is very fat; outsiders think her a very nice ordinary good-natured girl, jollier perhaps than most – 'but isn't it a pity she's so fat? She'd be quite nice-looking if only ...'
>
> By dint of much knowing, I've begun to fathom Jane: a curious, very appreciative, very sensitive mind, not ill stocked, and an extraordinary *mélange* of out-of-the-way stuffs in it: and almost the biggest heart I know. She is one of the few people who only want to give.[4]

In 1924 Miss Waddell took Janie and Mrs McNeill on a motoring tour around Touraine. In a letter to her sister, Margaret, from Hotel de l'Univers in Tours, she said:

> Jane is triumphant because in heat so fierce that I was sleeping with only a sheet she packed woollen knickers and a burberry ... We went to High Mass in the Cathedral today, and Mrs McNeill knelt and bowed to the altar like a good Papist. I do love her, more every day. When I talk to her about the Middle Ages, she listens as if I were the Ancient Mariner. I was describing Chartres, where so many of my great bishops lived, and since then it's always: 'Now tell me more about Ivo.' Also, what so few people realize, she said one day: 'Helen, it's good company you keep in your work. I'd like to have the Fathers all round me like that.' Jane is really behaving awfully well. I heard a good deal of her own excellence as a traveller, till in self-defence I produced a rhyme which gets added to every day:

> JANE or *The Perfect Traveller*
> She likes to travel in the train
> She never smells an open drain.
> On boats she talks to stewardesses,
> And gives advice in their distresses.

[4] D. Felicitas Corrigan, *Helen Waddell: A Biography* (1986). p. 168.

> She is not sick in any swell,
> But only in each new hotel.
> And even in Paris summer heat
> She wears goloshes on her feet.[5]

Lewis had been a guest in their home on numerous occasions and when Mrs McNeill died in 1947 he was deeply saddened. 'As for Mrs McNeill,' he wrote to Arthur on 5 January 1947, 'well, what could you and I *say* about it even if we were together? It's just a flood of queer, absurd, adorable memories, isn't it? – something that you and I could both respond to, and in exactly the same way as long as we remained ourselves.' Lewis remembered the McNeills in his autobiography where he said 'I think we Strandtown and Belmont people had among us as much kindness, wit, beauty, and taste as any circle of the same size that I have ever known' (**SBJ** X).

Another of Jane's friends, Mary Rogers, recorded in 'Jane McNeill and C.S. Lewis' (**CSL**, vol. 10, No 10 August 1979), that Janie felt Lewis neglected his academic work for apologetics. Following the publication of *Miracles* in 1947, Mrs Rogers says 'She expressed herself to me forcefully: "He's done enough now. He ought to stop it, and write more works like *The Allegory of Love*." She was also very critical about his self-commitment to Mrs Moore* (from 1921–51). She was never very explicit about this, so it was not until later that I understood an outburst like: "A promise is a promise, I suppose, but he goes too far! He's ruining his chances of having his own home and family' ... Janie's reaction to *That Hideous Strength* was very strong: "I hate it! I wish he'd dedicated any book other than this to me!"'

As time went on Jane became increasingly crippled and could only walk with the aid of two sticks. Still, she would not give up and she almost never missed a school concert or prizegiving at Victoria College. She was editing the centenary edition of *The Victorian* when she died suddenly at her home on 24 March 1959. Lewis's obituary of her was published in *The Campbellian* (July 1959):

Molliter Ossa Cubent[6]

Of Miss McNeill the charitable lady, the teacher, the member of committees, I saw nothing. My knowledge is of Janie McNeill; even of Chanie, as we sometimes called her, for she had the habit,

---

[5] Monica Blackett, *The Mark of the Maker: A Portrait of Helen Waddell* (1973), pp. 62–3.

[6] 'Soft may her bones lie.' Ovid, *Tristia*, III, iii, 76.

common in some Scottish dialects, of 'unvoicing' the consonant 'J'. Obviously there is a great deal I never knew. Someone writes to me describing her as a mystic. I would never have guessed it. What I remember is something as boisterous, often as discomposing but always as fresh and tonic, as a high wind. Janie was the delight and terror of a little Strandtown and Belmont circle, now almost extinct. I remember wild walks on the (still unspoiled) Holywood hills, preposterous jokes shouted through the gale across half a field, extravagantly merry (yet also Lucullan) lunches and suppers at Lisnadene, devastating raillery, the salty tang of an immensely vivid personality. She was a religious woman, a true, sometimes a grim, daughter of the Kirk; no less certainly, the broadest-spoken maiden lady in the Six Counties. She was a born satirist. Every kind of sham and self-righteousness was her butt. She deflated the unco-gude with a single ironic phrase, then a moment's silence, then the great gust of her laughter. She laughed with her whole body. When I consider how all this was maintained through years of increasing loneliness, pain, disability, and inevitable frustration I am inclined to say she had a soul as brave and uncomplaining as any I ever knew. Few have come nearer to obeying Dunbar's magnificent recipe (she knew her Dunbar):

> Man, please thy Maker and be merry
> And give not for this world a cherry.

Most of the papers given by the 'Drawing room Circle' are now in the Public Records Office in Belfast. There is an obituary of Jane McNeill in *The Victorian*, No 44 (June 1959) pp. 36–7. A small snapshot of Jane taken about 1923 by Warren Lewis is found at the Wade Centre.‡ It faces p. 315 in the **LP** VII. Keith Haines's *Neither Rogues nor Fools: A History of Campbell College and Campbellians* (1993) contains a good deal about James McNeill, and there is a photograph of him on p. 11.

Mathew, Father Anthony Gervase OP (1905–76), Inkling. He was given the name **Anthony** when he was born in Chelsea on 14 March 1905, the second son of **Francis James Mathew**, barrister-at-law and novelist, and his wife **Agnes Elizabeth Anna Woodroffe**. His elder brother was **David James Mathew** (1902–75), Archbishop of Apamea in Bithynia.

After being educated privately by his father, Anthony went up to Balliol College, Oxford, in 1925 where he read Modern History. He joined the Catholic Order of Dominicans in 1928 and took the name **Gervase**.

From this time onwards Blackfriars, in St Giles, Oxford, was home for the rest of his life. He was ordained in 1934, the same year that he and his brother published *The Reformation and the Contemplative Life*. Father Mathew was an eccentric, lovable man and an immensely loyal friend. One who knew him well said that if for some reason you were sent to prison, he would be the first to visit you. What seemed his air of 'drifting vagueness' was an illusion because he had great clarity of mind.

His enthusiasm for Byzantine art was fired by a visit to Ravenna at the age of 16, and in 1928 he visited Istanbul, Mistra and Cyprus. He lectured in the Modern History, Theology and English Faculties of the University of Oxford, and in 1947 was appointed University Lecturer in Byzantine Studies, which post he held until 1971, and for which he never drew a salary. He was one of the main creators of Byzantine studies at Oxford, and his lectures on topics such as 'Church and State in the Byzantine Empire' and 'The Ravenna Mosaics' attracted enthusiastic followers. He took part in archaeological surveys in Africa and the Middle East. In 1963 he and Roland Oliver edited the first volume of a *History of East Africa*.

Gervase Mathew began attending the Inklings meetings about 1939 although Warnie first mentions his attendance on 28 March 1946 (**BF**). On 13 July of that year he described how he went with his brother to hear Father Mathew lecture on Byzantine civilization in the garden of St Hugh's College:

> Gervase was excellent, and had got a capital collection of slides for his discourse. Byzantine painting grows on one; at first their portraits seem primitive, then they 'focus' with extraordinary rapidity ... The most interesting thing Gervase said was that Charles [Williams],* to whom the results of modern Byzantine research were unknown, had managed to give a much truer account of Byzantium in *Taliessin* than that given by Gibbon, his sole authority (**BF**).

On 1 June 1951 Warnie wrote an interesting account of lunch at Blackfriars with Father Mathew. Jack and Nevill Coghill* were also there, and Warnie seems not to have appreciated the fact that he was in a *Dominican* house. 'Shades of Grandfather Hamilton,' he said, 'that I should find myself a guest in a Benedictine monastery! ... Lunch over ... Gervase showed us over the house. The architect who built it knew his business. Peace, light, simplicity were the dominating tones; the beauty of austerity everywhere, nothing of that tinselly effect which RC interiors are so apt to have ... Gervase also took us to what he called "my chapel", a really lovely little building built in an arch not I should think bigger than Hertford's "Bridge of sighs". Here, he told me, Charles [Williams], not long before his death, had Gervase say a Mass for all those whom he loved, and acted as server at it' (BF).

In his joint biography of Gervase and David Mathew in the DNB, Fergus Kerr said:

> The two brothers, always in clerical dress though otherwise distressingly dishevelled and unkempt, were often to be seen in the streets of Oxford, sometimes arm in arm, as they made their way somewhat ponderously to a small French restaurant for a special celebration (at which the sweet trolley was always their great delight), or pottering over to Blackwell's to leaf through the latest book by one of their many friends. The enigmatic silences, the sudden hilarity which ended with the disconcerting abruptness with which it began, and the oracular manner, which the brothers shared, alarmed many people; but many others found in their love for one another, and in the absolute simplicity of their religion, a touchstone of fidelity.

Father Gervase's books include *Byzantine Painting* (1950), *Bede Jarrett, of the Order of Preachers*, with Kenneth Wykeham George (1952), *Byzantine Aesthetics* (1963) and *The Court of Richard II* (1968). He wrote many essays, amongst which are 'Byzantium to Oxford', in *For Hilaire Belloc: Essays in Honour of his 72nd Birthday*, ed. D. Woodruff (1942), 'Marriage and *Amour Courtois* in Late-Fourteenth-Century England' in ECW, 'Ideals of Friendship', in *Patterns of Love and Courtesy: Essays in Memory of C.S. Lewis*, ed. John Lawlor (1966), and 'Orator' in ABT. For many years Gervase Mathew suffered from emphysema, and he survived his brother by only four months, dying on 4 April 1976. Photo in IHW.

Moore, Edward Francis Courtenay 'Paddy' (1898–1918), room-mate and friend from Officers' Training Corps, Oxford, 1917. He was born at 8 Windsor Terrace, Kingstown, County Dublin, Ireland on 17 November 1898, the son of **Courtenay Edward Moore** and **Janie King (Askins) Moore**.* When his parents separated, he moved with his mother and sister, **Maureen** (see **Dunbar of Hempriggs, Lady***), to Bristol where his mother's brother, Dr Robert Askins, was a government medical officer. Paddy became a pupil at Clifton College in May 1908. He lived in the 'South Town' boarding house, and was at Clifton until April 1917.

He joined the Officers' Training Corps on 8 June 1917, and he and Lewis found themselves room-mates in Keble College, Oxford. They became friends, and he introduced Lewis to his mother and sister who were living close by in Wellington Square. In a letter to his father of 10 June 1917 Lewis described some of those he had come to know in the OTC. 'Moore of Clifton, my room companion,' he said, 'is a little too childish for real companionship, but I will forgive him much for his appreciation of Newbolt' (**L**). Writing the same day to Arthur Greeves,* he said: 'My room-mate Moore (of Clifton) is quite a good fellow ... though a little too childish and virtuous for "common nature's daily food"' (**TST**).

As time went by the young men became closer, and when Lewis wrote to his father on 18 June he said, 'Moore, my room-mate, comes from Clifton and is a very decent sort of man.' 'His mother, an Irish lady,' he said mentioning her for the first time, 'is staying up here and I have met her once or twice' (**LP** V: 224). On 27 August 1917 he told his father about a week of manoeuvres in Warwick. 'The following week,' he said, 'I spent with Moore at the digs of his mother who, as I mentioned, is staying at Oxford. I like her very much and thoroughly enjoyed myself' (**L**). Of all Paddy's friends, Lewis seemed the one he was closest to. Lewis invited Paddy to see his room in University College‡ (Staircase XII, Room 5). Paddy took a photograph through Jack's college window (found in **LP** VII:49). Two photographs of this period, probably taken with Paddy's camera, and reproduced in *All My Road Before Me* (as well as **TJB, DL, BIO**), show Lewis and Paddy with other OTC cadets on bivouac, and punting on the Cherwell. When all is said, those months of preparing for France were very happy.

On 26 September 1917 they were commissioned Second Lieutenants and given a month's leave. They had hoped to be in the same regiment, but Paddy was assigned to the Rifle Brigade, and Jack to the Somerset Light Infantry. Instead of going directly to Belfast, Lewis went to the Moores' home at 56 Ravenswood Road, Redlands, Bristol, where he spent the first three weeks of his leave. That period in Bristol was to be momentous for all of them. Besides his love of the poetry of Sir Henry Newbolt – like himself, an Old Cliftonian – Paddy loved Clifton College, and on Sunday 30 September he took Lewis to see it. They made a solemn promise to one another. Such a large percentage of officers were being killed at the front – most Oxford colleges lost a quarter of their members in the war – that it was natural for Jack and Paddy to want to make some provision against this. Maureen afterwards recalled hearing Lewis and her brother promise that if one survived the war he would look after Paddy's mother and Lewis's father. Mrs Moore knew of the promise as well, and writing to Albert Lewis on 1 October 1918, she said: 'My poor son asked him to look after me if he did not come back' (**LP** VI: 44–45).

Jack Lewis turned up at home on 12 October 1917, and it was while there that news arrived that he was to join his regiment at Crownhill in Devon on 19 October. Paddy had, meanwhile, been placed in the 5th Battalion of the Rifle Brigade and he crossed to France in October. Jack was still in Devon when he wrote to his father on 5 November 1917 saying: 'I have really been very lucky in getting here ... Paddy Moore, in the Rifle Brigade, seems to have got in with a most terrible lot of outsiders, so after all our separation was a blessing in disguise. He also seems to be much harder worked than I.'

Paddy took part in resisting the great German attack which began 21 March 1918. William W. Seymour's *History of the Rifle Brigade in the War of 1914–1918*, vol. II (1936) gives a full account of the 2nd Battalion of the Rifle Brigade during the battle in which Paddy played an heroic part.

Lewis was wounded in the Battle of Arras on 15 April 1918 and was in the hospital at Etaples when Mrs Moore was informed by the War Office that Paddy was missing. When he wrote to Albert Lewis on 14 May, Jack said: 'My friend Mrs Moore is in great trouble – Paddy has been missing for over a month and is almost certainly dead. Of all my own particular set at Keble he has been the first to go, and it is pathetic to remember that he at least was always certain that he would come through' (**L**). An account of Paddy's part in what happened appeared in Clifton College's school magazine, *The Cliftonian*, CCXCV (May 1918), p. 225. It contains a letter from the Adjutant of Paddy's battalion to Mrs Moore in which he said:

> Your very gallant son was reported missing on the 24th [March]. He was last seen on the morning of that day with a few men defending a position on a river bank against infinitely superior numbers of the enemy. All the other officers and most of the men of his company have become casualties, and I fear it is impossible to obtain more definite information. He did really fine work on the previous night in beating off a party of Germans who had succeeded in rushing a bridgehead in our lines. We all feel his loss very deeply, and I cannot express too strongly our sympathy with you.

In September 1918 it was confirmed that Paddy had died at Pargny. That Christmas was a sad one for Mrs Moore and Maureen, but they could nevertheless take pride when on 2 December 1918 Paddy was awarded the Military Cross for 'conspicuous gallantry and initiative'. In the *List of*

Officers and Other Ranks of The Rifle Brigade Awarded Decorations, or Mentioned in Despatches, for Services During the Great War, compiled by T.R. Eastwood and H.G. Parkyn (1936), the citation (pp. 64–5) reads:

> Moore, 2nd Lieut. E.F.C. (2nd Bn) M.C. 2.12.18. For conspicuous gallantry and initiative. When a party of the enemy succeeded in rushing a bridgehead in the dark, their officer, whose company was in support, immediately led forward, under heavy machine-gun fire, a small party to get in touch with the enemy. He did so, and having killed two or three of them returned with information which led to the destruction of them all and the recapture of the bridge. He rendered excellent service.

Paddy Moore's name is one of the 600 inscribed on the Memorial Gateway of Clifton College, and boys are urged to offer gratitude to these brave men as they pass through. It would have pleased Paddy to see over their names the following lines by Sir Henry Newbolt:

> From the great Marshal to the last recruit,
>   These, Clifton, were thy Self, thy Spirit in Deed,
> Thy flower of Chivalry, thy fallen fruit,
>   And thine immortal seed.

Moore, Janie King 'Minto' (1872–1951), friend and companion of many years. She was born in Pomeroy, County Tyrone, Northern Ireland, on 28 March 1872, the eldest of three daughters and two sons of the Rev. **William James Askins** (1842–95) and **Jane King Askins** (1846–90), daughter of the Ven. Francis King. The family moved to Dunany, County Louth, Ireland, in 1872 where Mr Askins was Vicar of Dunany and Dunleer from 1872 to 1895. It was at Dunany that Janie grew up. Her brothers and sisters were: **Edith 'Edie' Askins** (1873–1936), **John Hawkins Askins** (1877–1923), **William James Askins** (1879–1955), **Robert Askins** (1880–1935) and **Sarah Askins**. After the death of her mother in 1890 Janie, as the eldest child, had the task of bringing up the younger children. Her parents are buried at Dunleer.

On 1 August 1897 she married **Courtenay Edward Moore** (b. 26 June 1870). He too was from a clerical family, his father being Canon Courtenay Moore (1840–1922), Rector of Michaelstown in County Cork. Courtenay Edward Moore had taken a BA from Trinity College Dublin in 1893 and at the time of their marriage was a Civil Engineer in Dublin. They had two children, **Edward Francis Courtenay 'Paddy'*** (b. 17

November 1898) and **Maureen*** (b. 19 August 1906). It turned out to be an unhappy marriage, and Janie left her husband and moved to Bristol with the children in 1907. Her brother, Robert, was a doctor there, and Paddy became a pupil at Clifton College. Mrs Moore and her husband were never divorced.

In the spring of 1917 Paddy joined the Officers' Training Corps, and in June 1917 was sent to Keble College, Oxford. Mrs Moore moved there with Maureen, and took rooms in Wellington Square. It was probably during the second week of June 1917 that she and Lewis met for the first time. 'I like her immensely,' Lewis wrote to his father on 27 August (**L**). Very quickly, Lewis came to prefer the company of the Moores to that of his father. After Lewis and Paddy were given a month's leave before embarking overseas, Lewis spent three weeks of it with the Moores at their home at 56 Ravenswood Road, Redlands, Bristol, and only a week in Belfast with his father. It was during this visit to Bristol that Paddy and Lewis promised that if one or other were spared, the survivor would look after Paddy's mother and Lewis's father.

The young men did not see one another again. In October Paddy was sent to France with the Rifle Brigade, and Lewis followed him over in November with the Somerset Light Infantry. Lewis was wounded on 15 April 1918 and was in the hospital when Paddy took part in resisting the great German attack around Pargny which began on 21 March. He fought gallantly and was reported missing on 24 March. His death was confirmed in April, and in December 1918 he was awarded the Military Cross.

After receiving a letter of sympathy from Albert Lewis,* Mrs Moore wrote to him on 1 October 1918 saying:

> I just lived all my life for my son, and it is hard to go on now. I had built such hopes on my only son, and they are buried with so many others in that wretched Somme ... Jack has been so good to me. My poor son asked him to look after me if he did not come back (**LP** VI:44–45).

Before going to France, Lewis had told Arthur Greeves* of his feelings for Mrs Moore, and he later said to him in a letter of 2 February 1918 that 'there is room for other things besides love in a man's life' (**TST**). After Lewis came back from the war, and returned to Oxford in January 1919, Mrs Moore took a place there to be near him. From this time onwards they were to share a house for the rest of her life. Lewis's diary, *All My Road Before Me*, covering the years 1922–27, provides more information about their day-to-day life at this time than any other document. Clearly, Lewis was very happy in the home she made for him. Besides this, she sacrificed much to ensure that her daughter had a good education. After years of near-poverty and living in rented accommodation, she was joyous when in 1930 they bought The Kilns‡.

A particularly sad aspect of this long affair was the deceit Lewis practised on his father. He received money from him under the pretence that he needed it for college expenses. Years later Lewis said to Rhona Bodle on 24 March 1954: 'I treated my own father abominably and no sin in my whole life now seems to be so serious.' Whatever Lewis's feelings for Mrs Moore were at the beginning, over time she became a mother to him and in most letters from about 1940 onwards he speaks of her as his 'Mother'.

Mrs Moore was still to some extent a mother to her brothers and sisters, and she did much to help them. John, William and Robert Askins had all gone to Trinity College, Dublin. John and Robert became doctors, and when John became fatally ill in 1923 Mrs Moore nursed him in her home up until his death. William Askins became a clergyman in the Church of Ireland and was Dean of Kilmore Cathedral from 1931 to 1955.

On 27 October 1929 Mrs Moore wrote to Warnie saying: 'I hope you will spend your leaves with us [here] or wherever we are. We hope some day to get a larger house, [where] things would be more comfortable for you, so please do think of our home as your home, and be assured always of a very hearty welcome' (LP X: 197). When Warnie returned from the Far East in December 1932, he found that Mrs Moore and Jack had added two extra rooms to The Kilns for him.

Mrs Moore was an atheist most of her later life, and it annoyed her greatly when Lewis was converted to Christianity. 'She nags J about having become a believer,' Warnie recorded in his diary (BF) on 21 December 1933. Mrs Moore blamed God for her son's death, and Owen Barfield remembered her chiding Jack and Warnie for going to those 'blood feasts' in their parish church every Sunday morning. In her declining years Mrs Moore became, like so many others, senile and grumbling. Often she was in much pain, and in April 1950 she went into a nursing home in Oxford where Lewis visited her every day. She died on 12 January 1951 and is buried in the churchyard of Holy Trinity Church‡ in Headington Quarry. Mr Moore, with whom she was never reconciled, died in Dublin on 9 June 1951.

Opinions about Mrs Moore vary drastically. Warnie gives a very unflattering and, one suspects, an unlikely picture of her in his **Memoir** and the pages of his diary. Many of those who knew her regret that his account has been the dominant one and counted for so much. Owen Barfield* knew her over many years and liked her, and in the Foreword to **AMR** he said: 'One of the things that make me welcome its appearance in print is, that it will do much to rectify the false picture that has been painted of her as a kind of baneful stepmother and inexorable taskmistress ... If she imposed some burdens on him, she saved him from others by taking them on herself even against his protestations. Moreover she was deeply concerned to further his career.' 'Her main virtue was kindness,' George Sayer* said in *Jack* 6, 'especially to those in any sort of need. Her main fault, that of being too autocratic and controlling, was the almost inevitable result of having to take charge, at an early age, of a large house and family.' For information and photos see **L, IHW, TJB, DL, BIO, AMR** and *Jack*.

Moynihan, Martin John, CMG, MC, (1916–) member of the British Diplomatic Service, was a pupil of Lewis's and the translator of *Letters: C.S. Lewis – Don Giovanni Calabria* (1988). He was born in Birkenhead on 17 February 1916, the son of **William John Moynihan** and **Phoebe (Alexander) Moynihan**. He was educated at Birkenhead School and then at Magdalen College,‡ Oxford. He read Modern Greats under T.D. Weldon 1934–37, and English under Lewis and C.L. Wrenn* in 1938. In Lewis's 'Beer and Beowulf'‡ evenings he heard him defend Idealism against the tide of scepticism (Russell) and Logical Positivism. He has written of these tutorials in 'C.S. Lewis and T.D. Weldon' (*Seven*, 5, 1984).

After Oxford he joined the India Office and was with the Indian Army (Corps of Guides) during the Second World War, serving with the Punjab Frontier Force in the North West Frontier and Burma. He afterwards published *South of Fort Hertz: A Tale in Rhyme* (1956) about the Burma campaigns. Lewis took pleasure in its use of place names in verse. In 1946 he married **Monica Hopwood** and joined the Commonwealth and later Diplomatic Service, becoming H.M. Consul General, Philadelphia, Ambassador in Liberia and High Commissioner in Lesotho.

He last saw Lewis when he and Monica attended the memorable Inaugural Lecture (**De Descriptione Temporum**) at Cambridge on 29 November 1954, and talked with him afterwards. On Lewis's death he subscribed to a plaque to his memory in Magdalen College Chapel (which Lewis daily attended during term time). In 1985 his attention was drawn by Barbara Reynolds to the Latin correspondence between Lewis and Don Giovanni Calabria* of Verona. He was asked to translate it, and after giving us a foretaste of the letters in *The Latin Letters of C.S. Lewis* (1987), he published a translation of the complete *Letters: C.S. Lewis – Don*

Giovanni Calabria in 1988, during which year he was invited to Don Giovanni's beatification in Verona.

In his retirement he has administered the Kennedy Scholarships. At the same time, he has continued to contribute essays and talks. He has given several papers to the Oxford University C.S. Lewis Society.‡ In 1983 he attended the Inaugural Session of the Inklings-Gesellschaft‡ in Aachen, transmitting the Latin elegiacs composed for the occasion by Colin Hardie* and giving a paper on 'C.S. Lewis and the Arthurian Tradition'. The Elegiacs with Mr Moynihan's translation and his paper on the Arthurian Tradition were published in the *Inklings-Jahrbuch* (1983). He chaired an international summer school on Lewis at Hawarden in North Wales in 1984, and his account of 'The Inklings' in *Litterature*, No 8 (University of Genoa, 1985) is a valuable addition to the history of that group. He has an essay on 'Charles Williams and the Occult' in the *Inklings–Jahrbuch* (1987). Currently he is considering the similarity between the theme of the *Letters* of Lewis and Don Giovanni Calabria (No 27 of 1953) and of *The Abolition of Man* – namely, that moral relativity is the main problem of our times – and Cardinal Ratzinger's Fisher Lecture, Cambridge, 1988, and the Pope's recent encyclical, *Veritatis Splendor*. His latest publication was 'C.S. Lewis and G.K. Chesterton' in *The Chesterton Review* (vol. XVII, Nos 3 and 4, August/November 1991). Photo in **TJB**.

Paxford, Frederick William Calcutt 'Fred' (1898–1979), gardener and general handyman at The Kilns.‡ He was born in the village of Fifield, Oxfordshire, on 5 August 1898, the son of **Alice Sophia Paxford**, a domestic servant. Mrs Janie Moore* and Lewis hired him shortly after they moved into The Kilns in 1930, and he remained there until Lewis's death. Over the years he became as much a part of their lives as the house itself, and he was much loved. There was a great deal of work for all when the property was acquired, and during the early years Paxford cleared much of the nine acres. He organized a garden and an orchard, and he helped Mrs Moore with her chickens. He was not married, and lived in a small bungalow at The Kilns.

No man was less of a busybody. Even so, he had distinct ideas about nearly everything, and when you asked a question you had to accept the consequences. He spoke in a long, drill-like manner that some found irritating. It did not bother Mrs Moore, who was dedicated to him and sought his advice about almost everything. It was partly because she depended on him so much that many of the references to him in Warren Lewis's*' diary are extremely negative. Warren was often driven to fury by Mrs Moore's talk, and as a result of her frequent references to Paxford, he bore much of the blame.

Much that Warnie found annoying his brother found amusing. It would have been difficult to find a man who *said* such gloomy things, but who was himself so free from anxiety. Douglas Gresham* recalled what his conversation was like (**LL**, chapter 11, p. 98):

> 'Good morning, Fred,' I might say. 'Ah, looks loike rain afore lunch though, if'n it doan't snow ... or 'ail that is,' might well be his reply.

Paxford did the shopping for the household, and while he could hardly be said to be anxious in the sense condemned by Our Lord ('Take no thought for your life ... '), he often seemed worried about what was in the larder of The Kilns when the end of the world came. One of those who worked in The Kilns for a short time has said:

> I was often worried as to whether there would be enough sugar in the house. This indispensable item, of which Lewis was so fond, comes in both two- and one-pound bags. It was typical of Paxford to buy only half a pound at a time if he could find someone to take the other half. As Lewis entertained a number of distinguished visitors, and as most used sugar in their tea, I was in constant fear of there not being enough. I talked this over with Paxford, who invariably said, 'Well, you never know when the end of the world will come and we don't want to be left with sugar on our hands. What'll we do with it then, eh?' (**PWD** 6).

It was this inwardly optimistic, outwardly pessimistic, view of things that caused Lewis to use him as the model for one of his most delightful Narnian creatures, Puddleglum the Marshwiggle. Although not a church-goer, Paxford loved hymns and he could be heard singing such favourites as 'Abide with me' in such a loud voice that sometimes the neighbours complained. Douglas Gresham remembered that:

> One would hear the first line of a song perhaps, or part thereof, and then a very long silence, broken only by the snick-clack of his hedging shears or whatever, as he continued this song in his head, and then suddenly he would roar out a few words of wherever he had reached in the song. 'Oh Molly, this London's a wonderful ... ' long pause, snick-clack! ... snick-clack! 'And boi noight they ... ' snick-clack! ... 'pertaters er bairley er wheat' snick-clack! snick-clack! (Sotto voce) 'Bugger it!' Then bellowing again, 'Fer gold all the day in the street, doo doo doo doo!' (**LL** chapter 11, pp. 97–8).

Paxford was a dedicated bachelor, and when asked if he might marry, he invariably came out with the verse:

> A little puff of powder,
> A little touch of paint,
> Makes a woman look
> Just like what she *ain't*!

As for the rest, he was perfectly content with his radio, his Sunday paper, the occasional pint, and a seemingly endless supply of roll-your-own cigarettes. After Lewis's death, he retired to the little village of Churchill, a few miles from where he was born. There, in his cottage, No 5 The Square, he had a small garden all for himself. Writing about a visit there in 1973, Douglas Gresham said,

> Someone had told him that I was coming and, living though he was in abject poverty, he'd laid in a bottle of gin and a supply of pre-rolled fags. He poured me a huge tumblerful of gin and watched over me to make sure I drank it as we talked and smoked together for an hour or so and then, with his arm across my shoulders, we walked unsteadily out to inspect his patch of gyaarden. It was neat and weedless. He had 'caulis, taters, roobub, purple sproutin' (broccoli) and a variety of other plants. I left him, finally, waving from his cottage door (**LL**, chapter 11, p. 100).

Fred Paxford died in his cottage at Churchill on 10 August 1979. His own story of life at The Kilns is told in 'Observations of his Gardener', *The Canadian C.S. Lewis Journal*, No 55 (Summer 1986), pp. 8–13. Photos in **IHW, TJB**.

Penelope CSMV, Sister (1890–1977), friend. Sister Penelope was born **Ruth Penelope Lawson** in Clent, Worcestershire, on 20 March 1890. She was the daughter of the Rev. **Frederick Robert Lawson**, Vicar of Clent 1878–1908. In September 1899 she went to the Worcester High School, now the Alice Ottley School, where she developed a devotion to the Blessed Virgin and a love of Greek and Latin. In her 'spiritual autobiography', *Meditation of a Caterpillar* (1962), she described two 'fundamental things' in Miss Ottley's teaching which affected her decision to enter a religious order:

> The first was that it was my duty as a Christian to examine my conscience before Communion, and to confess to God specifically

what I found amiss ... The other thing she taught me personally and unknown to herself, on the evening of 15 March 1904 ... I knew with overwhelming certainty that she was living in a world of most intense reality, to which I was, as yet, a total stranger. I was outside it utterly, but *it existed* (pp. 27–8).

In 1912 she entered the Convent of the Community of St Mary the Virgin at Wantage, and from this time on was **Sister Penelope CSMV**. The Community, founded in 1848 by the Rev. W.J. Butler, was one of the first of the Anglican religious Orders founded since the Reformation. Wantage was only a short distance from Oxford, and Sister Penelope was able to study theology under B.J. Kidd, the Warden of Keble College, and the distinguished medievalist R.W. Hunt. She wrote well and easily, and over the years she published twenty-five works of theology, and translated seventeen volumes of the Church Fathers. It was not the practice at that time for nuns to write under their own names, and most of her books were written as by 'A Religious of CSMV'.

One of her first books was *The Wood for The Trees: An Outline of Christianity* (1935), which contains her defence of the Church of England as a 'real *via media*, retaining all the essentials of Catholicity and with singular freedom for development' (XXII:vi).

On 5 August 1939 she wrote to tell Lewis that *Out of the Silent Planet* 'has given and still gives me a joy and delight quite impossible to put into words.' She went on to say:

It provokes thought in just the directions where I have always wanted to think; and wherever it is most delightfully suggestive one senses the most profound scriptural basis ... There are bits – Augray's views about the different sorts of bodies, the relations of the unfallen creatures with Oyarsa, their social order, their peaceful awareness of the spiritual world – which are more lovely and more satisfying than anything I have met before.

Thus began a friendship and a fruitful correspondence which lasted for the rest of Lewis's life. He spoke of Sister Penelope as his 'elder sister' in the Faith, and she more than anyone helped him to appreciate the Catholic side of Anglicanism. When she sent him a photograph of the Turin Shroud, he acknowledged it in a letter of 9 October 1941, saying: 'Thank you very much for the photo of the Shroud. It raises a whole question on which I shall have to straighten out my thoughts one of these days.' He wrote again a month later (9 November) saying: 'It has grown upon me wonderfully ... The great value is to make one realize that He really was a man, and once even a dead man. There is so much difference between a doctrine and a realization.' He kept the photograph on the wall of his bedroom for the rest of his life.

In 1942 the Mother Superior of CSMV invited him to talk to the Junior Sisters, and he and Sister Penelope met when he stayed in the Community's guest house 20–22 April 1942. Lewis later dedicated *Perelandra* 'To some Ladies at Wantage' by which he meant the nuns of the Community of St Mary the Virgin. It amused Sister Penelope that the Portuguese edition translated this 'To some wanton ladies'. She had a delightful sense of humour and enjoyed telling the story of how, when she was a girl, she heard a missionary preach on the evils of alcohol. 'Bring up your son to hate the bottle,' he said, 'and when he is a grown man he will never depart from it!'

On 9 October 1941 Lewis sent her the manuscript of *The Screwtape Letters.* 'I enclose,' he said, 'the MS of *Screwtape.* If it is not a trouble I should like you to keep it safe until the book is printed (in case the one the publisher has got blitzed) – after that it can be made into spills or used to stuff dolls or anything' (L). When, years later, she asked if he wanted the MS back he replied on 18 June 1956: 'If you can persuade any "sucker" (as the Americans say) to buy the MS of *Screwtape*, pray do, and use the money for any pious or charitable object you like.' In her annotations to his letters she said:

> I wrote to him again begging him to let me send it back ... He would not have it, and would only have destroyed it if I had insisted ... Very reluctantly, when we were hard put to it for funds for doing up St Michael's chapel, did I venture to ask him if I might dispose of it ... It is now in the Berg Collection in the New York Public Library.

Lewis contributed an Introduction (reprinted as **On the Reading of Old Books**) to the most famous of her translations, Athanasius's *The Incarnation of the Word of God* (1944). Such was her vitality that she began translating St Hugh of Victor when she was eighty. Sister Penelope died in her beloved Convent on 15 May 1977.

Pitter, Ruth CBE, (1898–1992) friend, was born in Ilford, Essex, on 7 November 1897, the daughter of **George Pitter**, an Elementary Schoolmaster. She was educated at Downshall Elementary School and the Coburn School for Girls in Bow. After serving in the War Office 1916–18, she became a painter for the Walberswick Peasant Pottery Company in Suffolk. In 1930 she and a fellow worker, Kathleen O'Hara, set up a partnership producing gift items in Chelsea. They became lifelong friends and shared a house. During the War they abandoned their business and went to work in a factory in south London. The work drove Ruth nearly to despair, and while listening to Lewis's *Mere Christianity* radio broadcasts she was converted and joined the Church of England. In 1952 she and Kathleen O'Hara moved to Long Crendon in Buckinghamshire where she continued her painting.

Her first poems were published in *New Age* when she was only 13. Her first volume of poems, *First Poems*, was published in 1920, and she went on to write and publish many more during her long life. They include *A Mad Lady's Garland* (1935), *A Trophy of Arms*, for which she won the Hawthornden Prize in 1936, *Pitter on Cats* (1947), and *Poems 1926–66* (1968).

In 1946 she wrote to Lewis, thanking him for his books and asking if they could meet. He was an admirer of her poems, and in his reply of 13 July 1946 he said, 'What you should be "trepidant" about in calling on a middle-aged don I can't imagine ... Would Wednesday July 17 suit?' They became friends and, while Ruth Pitter's letters have not survived, those from Lewis are some of his finest and contain many valuable comments about poetry. Over the years they visited one another often. Lewis could not drive but George Sayer* took him to her house at Long Crendon a number of times between 1953 and 1955. 'It was obvious,' Sayer said in *Jack* 19:

> that he liked her very much. He felt at ease in her presence – and he did not feel relaxed with many people. In fact, he seemed to be on intimate terms with her. The conversation was a mixture of the literary and the domestic. They discussed Eddison's romances and the poems of R.S. Thomas and Andrew Young. Each suggested amusing and improbable books for the other to write ... After one visit in 1955, he remarked that, if he were not a confirmed bachelor, Ruth Pitter would be the woman he would like to marry.

Ruth Pitter was certainly not 'trepidant' during Lewis's visit on 12 June 1954. She wrote a short piece about it:

Ruth Pitter defeats C.S. Lewis in Argument
On 12 June 1954, David and Rachel Cecil came to lunch, bringing the two Lewises, 'Warnie' and CS. I asked CS if I might catechize him a bit about the delectable *Lion, Witch and Wardrobe*, in which I

thought I had detected a weakness. Permission courteously given;

RP The Witch makes it always winter and never summer?

CS (In his fine reverberating voice) She does.

RP Does she allow any foreign trade?

CS She does not.

RP Am I allowed to postulate a *deus ex machina*, perhaps on the lines of Santa Claus with the tea-tray? (This is where CS lost the contest. If he had allowed the deus-ex-m., for which Santa gives good precedent, he would have saved himself.)

CS You are not.

RP Then how could the Beavers have put on the splendid lunch?

CS They caught the fish through holes in the ice.

RP Quite so, but the dripping to fry them? The potatoes – a plant that perishes at a touch of the frost – the oranges and sugar and suet and flour for the lovely surprise Marmalade Roll – the malt and hops for Mr Beaver's beer – the milk for the children?

CS (with great presence of mind) I must refer you to a further study of the text.

Warnie Nonsense, Jack; you're stumped and you know it.[7]

The only time Ruth Pitter met Joy Gresham* was at a luncheon Lewis gave at the Eastgate Hotel in Oxford on 1 February 1954. On 28 January 1957 Lewis wrote to her about Joy's illness: 'Alas, all is not well. The disease is cancer ... She may get through *this* time ... I am sure she would love a letter from you though, for the mechanical reason, she will not be able to scrawl more than ten words in answer.' In her annotation to this letter Ruth Pitter said:

[7] If he had not thought it ungenerous to do so, Lewis might have saved his bacon. Years before he pointed out in an essay **On Stories** that 'The logic of a fairy-tale is as strict as that of a realistic novel, though different.' He goes on to consider the animals in Kenneth Grahame's *Wind in the Willows*. 'They are like children in so far as they have no responsibilities, no struggle for existence, no domestic cares. Meals turn up; one does not even ask who cooked them. In Mr Badger's kitchen 'plates on the dresser grinned at pots on the shelf'. Who kept them clean? Where were they bought? How were they delivered to the Wild Wood? ... In that way the life of all the characters is that of children for whom everything is provided and who take everything for granted. But in other ways it is the life of adults. They go where they like and do what they please, they arrange their own lives. To that extent the book is a specimen of the most scandalous escapism.'

I had of course seen the announcement of his marriage and (so tragically soon after) the news of his wife's illness. Not being near enough to help practically (supposing this would have been acceptable) I thought it best not to bother him, except for an occasional brief message requiring no answer.

I had been taught in youth that a woman's friendship with a married man must be by grace and favour of his wife, and as Joy recovered and lived on so amazingly, I did from time to time write to her: but there was never any reply, so I decided to be thankful for this correspondence and friendship with so rare a creature as Lewis, and to leave it at that.

Owen Barfield* took Lewis to see Miss Pitter on 12 July 1961. Their last visit was on 15 August 1962 when Ruth Pitter went to see him at The Kilns.‡ Her *Collected Poems* were published in 1969. She was made a Commander of the British Empire in 1979, a Companion of Literature in 1974, and she was the first woman to receive the Queen's Gold Medal for Poetry (1955). Ruth Pitter died on 29 February 1992. See *Ruth Pitter: Homage to a Poet*, Edited by Arthur Russell with an introduction by David Cecil* (1969).

Sayer, George Sydney Benedict (1914–), pupil, friend, and sometimes Inkling,‡ was born in Bradfield, Berkshire, on 1 June 1914, the son of **Sydney Sayer** and his wife **Hilda Julia Frances (Payne) Sayer**. His father was an irrigation engineer whose business was mainly in Egypt. He was educated at what he described as a 'brutal Eastbourne preparatory school', and Trinity College, Glenalmond, a 'dull, unacademic school, that nevertheless taught him to love the Scottish countryside.' He went up to Magdalen College‡ in 1933, and read English with Lewis. The flavour of his tutorials is brilliantly captured in the Preface to his biography *Jack: C.S. Lewis and His Times* (1988; 2nd ed. 1994). During his third year in Oxford he realized that Lewis was a Christian, and in his own search for truth he was led to the Catholic Church. He took his BA in 1938 and his MA in 1947. Over time his friendship with Lewis led him to become friends with Warnie Lewis,* Mrs Janie Moore* and Maureen Moore* as well.

After leaving Oxford he tried his hand at writing, but when the war broke out he joined the Army and served in Military Intelligence. In 1940 he married **Moira Casey** (1913–77), a barrister's daughter. Still finding little success as a writer he turned to teaching, and in 1949 he became the Senior English Master at Lewis's old school, Malvern College,‡ where he remained until his retirement in 1974.

Lewis and his brother were often visitors to Sayer's house, 'Hamewith', in Malvern. In his essay 'Jack on Holiday' (**ABT**) Sayer recounts some of Lewis's visits there, as well as their walks in the Malvern Hills. 'The most unselfish man I have ever gone about with,' Lewis said of him in a letter to Ruth Pitter* of 5 March 1955 (**L**). Some of Sayer's other reminiscences of Lewis's visits to 'Hamewith' are found in 'A Guest in the House' (*In Search of C.S. Lewis*, ed. Stephen Schofield, 1983). When the Lewis brothers were in Malvern during August 1947 Warnie wrote in his diary (19 August) about a drive in Sayer's car: 'Sayer has the supreme car driving virtue that he is always ready to *stop*; and stop we frequently did to drink in the beauty and peace of it all' (**BF**).

George Sayer was invited to the luncheon Lewis gave Joy Gresham* and her friend Phyllis Williams at Magdalen College in September 1952, shortly after Joy first arrived in England. Lewis sought Sayer's advice when he thought of marrying Joy, but he did not take it. Chapter 19 of *Jack* contains a good deal about the marriage. After C.S. Lewis's death he was a consoling friend to Warnie. In his diary of 7 March 1967 Warnie mentions a holiday with the Sayers: 'Hamewith is a house in which one always feels at home, and by the time I went to bed I felt as if I had been established there for weeks' (**BF**).

Following the death of **Moira** in 1977 after a long illness, in 1983 Sayer married **Margaret Cronin** (1932–   ). They still live in Malvern and enjoy family life with three children and four grandchildren. He has an essay on 'C.S. Lewis and George MacDonald' in the *Inklings-Jahrbuch*‡ (1988). Sayer has reviewed a number of books by and about Lewis for *Blackfriars* and other periodicals, and sometimes lectures on Lewis, J.R.R. Tolkien* and Charles Williams*. The recordings he made in 1952 of Tolkien reading from *The Hobbit* and *The Lord of the Rings* were issued by Caedmon Records in 1975. He is writing a Memoir of Warnie Lewis. See **BF** and **LJRRT**.

Sayers, Dorothy Leigh (1893–1957), friend, translator of Dante, theologian, and author of the Lord Peter Wimsey detective novels. She was born in Oxford on 13 June 1893, the daughter of the Rev. **Henry Sayers** and **Helen Mary (Leigh) Sayers**. Her father was at the time Headmaster of the Choir School of Christ Church. The family moved to Bluntisham-cum-Earith in Huntingdonshire in 1897, and it was there that Dorothy L. Sayers spent her girlhood. She went to Somerville College, Oxford, in 1912 and took a First in Modern Languages. In 1926 she married **Oswold Arthur Fleming**, a reporter and writer.

Her first job was as an advertiser's copywriter with S.H. Benson Ltd, 1921–31. She came to fame through the introduction of her detective nobleman, Lord Peter Wimsey, in *Whose Body?* (1923). This was followed by other Wimsey novels including *Clouds of Witness* (1926), *Strong Poison* (1930), *The Nine Tailors* (1934) and *Gaudy Night* (1935). But it was her theological writings which attracted Lewis, his favourites being *The Mind of the Maker* (1941), the radio drama, *The Man Born to be King* (1943), and *The Other Six Deadly Sins* (1943). Writing to her about the last of these on 18 March 1943, he said: 'It is one of the very few things which I find, within its limits, perfect.'

In 1943 she was offered the Lambeth Degree of Doctor of Divinity, but chose not to accept it. Her son, **John Anthony Fleming** (b. 3 January 1924; d. 26 November 1984) followed his mother to Oxford. He won a scholarship to Balliol College (Lord Peter Wimsey's college) in 1941 and took a First Class degree in Modern Greats.

Dorothy L. Sayers was delighted with Lewis's *Screwtape Letters*, and in 1942 she asked him to contribute to her *Bridgeheads* series of theological books. Thus began a long correspondence, with occasional meetings, about shared interests. Lewis relished her letters, and on 10 December 1945 said: 'Although you have so little time to write letters you are one of the great English letter writers. (Awful vision for you – "It is often forgotten that Miss Sayers was known in her own day as an Author. We who have been familiar from childhood with the Letters can hardly realize! ... "' (**L**).

Her interest in Dante began in 1943 when she read Charles Williams's* *Figure of Beatrice*. She and Williams became friends, and one result was her translations of Dante's *Inferno* (1949) and *Purgatorio* (1955). The *Paradiso* (1962), unfinished at her death, was completed by Barbara Reynolds whose story of these translations is told in Barbara Reynolds' *The Passionate Intellect* (1989). The suggestion that Miss Sayers was a member of the Inklings‡ was contradicted by Lewis in a letter, 'Wain's Oxford', in *Encounter*, XX, 1 (January 1963): 'Dorothy Sayers, so far as I know, was not even acquainted with any of us except Charles Williams and me. We two had got to know her at different times and in different ways. In my case, the initiative came from her. She was the first person of importance who ever wrote me a fan-letter. I liked her, originally, because she liked me; later for the extraordinary zest and edge of her conversation – as I like a high wind ... Needless to say, she never met our own club, and probably never knew of its existence.'

After her death on 17 December 1957 Lewis composed a **Panegyric for Dorothy L. Sayers** which was read at a memorial service on 15 January 1958. The two major biographies are James Brabazon's *Dorothy L. Sayers: The Life of a Courageous Woman* (1981) and Barbara Reynolds' superb

Dorothy L. Sayers: Her Life and Soul (1993), both of which contain many excellent photographs. Nearly the whole of her correspondence with Lewis is intact, and there are copies of both sides of it in the Bodleian‡ and the Wade Center.‡

Stevens, Courtenay Edward 'Tom Brown' (1905–76), Inkling‡ and colleague at Magdalen College.‡ Stevens, a distinguished ancient historian, was born in London on 14 April 1905, the son of **Courtenay Stevens** and his wife **Melior Frances Barker**. He was educated at Winchester College, and matriculated at New College, Oxford, in 1924 where he read *Literae Humaniores*‡ under the formidable philosopher tutor H.W.B. Joseph and the historian R.G. Collingwood. After taking a First Class degree in 1928, he wrote a B.Litt. thesis (1930) published in 1933 as *Sidonius Apollinaris and His Age*. In 1929 he became a Robinson Exhibitioner at Oriel College, after which he won a University Senior Scholarship. During the time he was a Craven Fellow (1931–33) he studied Celtic land tenure in Belfast, teaching himself Irish in the course of his work. In 1933 Stevens was elected a Fellow of Magdalen by Special Election.

'Tom Brown Stevens', as he was known to one and all, had known Jack and Warnie Lewis* since he arrived at Magdalen. In 1940 he left for service in the Foreign Office. During the War he worked on 'black propaganda', as an intelligence officer with Radio Atlantic, the service beamed at U-boat crews. An obituary in *The Times* (2 September 1976), p. 14, recalls that:

> His sharp intelligence and imagination, devious cleverness and inventiveness, here found ideal employment. And he left his mark deep in a whole generation of Europeans, for it was at his inspired suggestion that the four opening notes of Beethoven's Fifth Symphony (the 'V' in Morse Code) were adopted as the most famous broadcasting theme of the war.

Stevens returned to Magdalen in 1946 as an Official Fellow and Tutor in Ancient History. He had not been back long when Lewis made a bet with him. We find it in the college 'Betting Book', written in Lewis's hand: 'Lewis bet Stevens that the word ΕΡΩΣ does not occur in the *Odyssey* (a bottle of port) 14 May '46.' There follows in Stevens's hand: 'Paid by Mr Stevens.' Warnie Lewis recorded in his diary that at the Inklings meeting on 23 October 1947 his brother 'suggested that Stevens should be invited to become an Inkling, and all those present were in favour. I should like to see him join us' (**BF**). Stevens made his debut as an Inkling on 27 November, and recalling the event, Warnie Lewis wrote:

A very pleasant meeting: Tollers, J, self, Stevens and Humphrey [Havard].* We talked of Bishop [Ernest William] Barnes, of the extraordinary difficulty of interesting the uneducated indifferent in religion: savage and primitive man and the common confusion between them: how far pagan mythology was a substitute for theology: bravery and panache. Stevens said that Vauban's fortresses killed the old style panache: and told me a very interesting thing, viz., that our stand in the actual forts built by Vauban at Calais enabled the bulk of the BEF [British Expeditionary Force] to escape through Dunkirk in 1940 (**BF**).

It is a pity that Stevens was away from Oxford during some of the Inklings' best years. While they met for other occasions, such as ham-suppers, the regular Thursday evening meetings ended in October 1949. To this day it is a mystery as to how Stevens had any time left from his professional work for recreation. The author of his obituary in *The Times* (2 September 1976) said that, after Stevens became Vice President of Magdalen in 1950, his 'fantastic career' as a tutor began:

His most unlikely partnership with the late J.L. Austin furnished Magdalen with the most powerful tutorial combination in Oxford Greats. At its peak, in 1950, it secured five of the eight Firsts awarded. But Magdalen could not contain his energies, nor yet New College, for whom he also taught Roman History. Pupils both male and female were harvested from all quarters, and taught at all hours and in all surroundings: in one stupendous week he taught 72 hours, and totals over 50 were commonplace. His enthusiasm and devotion never faltered or flagged: each pupil felt himself the centre of his attention, all were swept away on the tidal wave of his ebullience, originality and vinous hospitality.

For him each tutorial hour remained an adventure and a challenge: there were examiners (those natural enemies) to be outwitted and cut down to size, established theories to be toppled, whole sweeps of history to be rewritten. For those who could stand the pace – and fill in the gaps – it was wonderfully exhilarating. His public lectures too were hilariously popular and vastly informative. Of course his published work suffered, yet it was considerable and wide-ranging, sometimes even magisterial, though sometimes marred (especially in political history) by over-ingeniousness and a delight in cleverness for its own sake – like Stanley Matthews, his footwork was a joy to behold, but he did not often score goals ...

He was a great Oxford character; boisterous, noisily sociable, infuriatingly knowledgeable in the oddest corners of other men's specialities, untidy, disconcerting and unpredictable. A visit from him could set any Oxford common room on its ears. A man of great warmth and humanity, he won many friends – and, from his pupils, much love.

Apart from his two books, *Sidonius Apollinaris and His Age* (1933) and *The Building of Hadrian's Wall* (1966), it was generally assumed that Stevens did not have time to publish many things. When, however, his pupils and colleagues produced a collection of essays to mark his seventieth birthday, *The Ancient Historian and his Materials: Essays in honour of C.E. Stevens*, ed. Barbara Levick (1975), a bibliography of his books and numerous articles and reviews surprised everyone. He was married three times: (1) In 1938 to **Leila Evelyn Porter** by whom he had a son; (2) in 1949 to **Norma Gibbs**; and (3) in 1962 to **Mrs Olive Sergeant**. Stevens retired in 1972, and died 1 September 1976. There is a photograph in *The Ancient Historian*.

Tolkien, Christopher Reuel (1924–), Inkling. He is the third son of **John Ronald Reuel Tolkien*** and **Edith Mary (Bratt) Tolkien**. He was born in Leeds on 21 November 1924, where his father was Professor of Anglo-Saxon. The family moved to Oxford in 1926 when his father became Professor of Anglo-Saxon in the University of Oxford. Christopher was educated at the Dragon School in Oxford and the Oratory School at Woodcote in Berkshire. As a boy he was a frequent listener to his father's stories of Middle Earth, and in the 1930s he and Lewis read *The Hobbit* as a serial.

In 1942 he matriculated at Trinity College, Oxford, but left in July 1944 when he joined the RAF, who sent him to South Africa to train as a pilot. The letters his father wrote to him at this time, many of which are found in **LJRRT**, are a valuable source of information about the Inklings and the progress of *The Lord of the Rings* and *The Silmarillion*. During much of 1944 his father sent him the chapters which make up Book IV of *The Lord of the Rings*. 'Christopher was my real primary audience,' Tolkien wrote to Stanley Unwin on 18 March 1945:

who has read, vetted and typed all of the new Hobbit, or The Ring, that has been completed. He was dragged off in the middle of making maps. I have squandered almost the only time I have had to spare for writing in continuing our interrupted conversations by epistles: he occupied the multiple position of audience, critic, son, student in my department, and my tutorial pupil! **(LJRRT)**

At the end of the War, Christopher returned to Trinity College, where he read English. He took his BA in 1949. During this time he continued to assist his father with *The Lord of the Rings*, and drew the maps for the book. The Lewis brothers were delighted to have him back, and he was quickly absorbed into the Inklings. In his diary Warnie Lewis* mentions his attendance at a number of meetings.

After taking his degree in 1949 Christopher Tolkien was a University Lecturer in Anglo-Saxon, Middle English and Old Norse at several Oxford colleges. He was at the same time working on a B.Litt. thesis, a translation of the Icelandic *Saga of King Heidrek the Wise* which was published in 1960. During this time he and Nevill Coghill* edited *The Pardoner's Tale* (1958) and *The Nun's Priest's Tale* (1959). After lecturing in Oxford for a number of years New College elected him to a fellowship in 1965.

He married (1) **Faith Faulconbridge** on 2 April 1951, and they had one son, **Simon (Mario Reuel Tolkien)** born on 12 January 1959. Faith Tolkien is a sculptor; her portrait head of J.R.R. Tolkien is in the English Faculty Library at Oxford, and her head of Lewis is in Magdalen College. After their marriage was dissolved in 1967, Christopher Tolkien married (2) **Baillie Klass** on 18 September 1967. They have two children, **Adam (Reuel Tolkien)**, born on 3 March 1969, and **Rachel (Clare Reuel Tolkien)**, born on 13 February 1971. Baillie Tolkien is the editor of J.R.R. Tolkien's *The Father Christmas Letters* (1976).

When Tolkien died in 1973 he left behind a massive number of 'Middle Earth' manuscripts and other papers. In 1975 Christopher Tolkien resigned his Fellowship at New College and soon afterwards moved to France, where he has devoted his time to the gigantic task of editing his father's papers. His impeccable editions include *Sir Gawain and the Green Knight, Pearl, and Sir Orfeo* (1975), *Pictures by J.R.R. Tolkien* (1979), *The Monsters and the Critics and Other Essays* (1983), and *Tree and Leaf, including the poem 'Mythopoeia'* (1988).

His most impressive accomplishment, one for which he was uniquely qualified, has been the editing of the 'Middle Earth' manuscripts. This began with *The Silmarillion* (1977), the *Unfinished Tales of Númenor and Middle-earth* (1980), and those volumes which make up the vast History of Middle-Earth: (1) *The Book of Lost Tales, Part One* (1983); (2) *The Book of Lost Tales, Part Two* (1984); *The Lays of Beleriand* (1985); (4) *The Shaping of Middle-Earth: The Quenta, The Ambarkanta and the Annals* (1986); (5) *The Lost Road and Other Writings* (1987); (6) *The Return of the Shadow: The History of The Lord of the Rings, Part One* (1988); (7) *The Treason of Isengard: The History of The Lord of the Rings, Part Two* (1989); (8) *The War of the Ring: The History of The Lord of the Rings, Part Three* (1990); (9) *Sauron Defeated: The End of the Third Age (The History of the Lord of the Rings, Part Four)* (1992); (10) *Morgoth's Ring: The Later Silmarillion, Part I, The Legends of Aman* (1993); (11) *The War of the Jewels: The Later Silmarillion, Part Two, The Legends of Beleriand* (1994); (12) *The Peoples of Middle-Earth* (1996). For more information see Humphrey Carpenter's *J.R.R. Tolkien: A Biography* (1977), *The Letters of J.R.R. Tolkien*, ed. Humphrey Carpenter (1981) and *The Tolkien Family Album* (1992) by John and Priscilla Tolkien.

Tolkien, John Ronald Reuel CBE (1892–1973), Inkling and close friend. He was born in Bloemfontein, South Africa, to English parents, on 3 January 1892. His father, **Arthur Reuel Tolkien,** who had married **Mabel Suffield** in 1891, was the manager of the Bank of Africa in Bloemfontein. His brother **Hilary Arthur Reuel Tolkien** was born on 17 February 1894. Because the intense heat was harming Ronald, Mrs Tolkien returned to England with the boys in 1895 and settled at 5 Gracewell, Sarehole, near Birmingham. Before they could rejoin him in South Africa, Arthur Tolkien died in 1896.

In 1900 Mabel Tolkien, despite strong opposition from her family, became a Roman Catholic and began to instruct her sons in the Catholic religion. That same year Ronald was sent to King Edward's School, Birmingham, where his love of languages was already in flower. In order that her sons could receive a Catholic education, in 1902 the family moved to 26 Oliver Road, Edgbaston, so that Ronald and Hilary could be educated by the priests of Birmingham Oratory at St Philip's School. One of the Oratorian priests who was to become a lifelong friend was Father Francis Xavier Morgan. However, after winning a Scholarship, Ronald returned to King Edward's School in 1903.

After a long illness, Mrs Tolkien died on 14 November 1904. Her many sacrifices to raise her children as Catholics were not lost on Ronald, who later wrote: 'My own mother was a martyr indeed, and it is not to everybody that God grants so easy a way to his great gifts as he did to Hilary and myself, giving us a mother who killed herself with labour and trouble to ensure us keeping the faith.' The boys went to live with their aunt, Beatrice Suffield, in Birmingham.

Tolkien came up to Exeter College, Oxford, in 1911 and read Honour Moderations. For his special subject he chose Comparative Philology and was taught by Joseph Wright. He then read English Language and

Literature, taking a First in 1915. It was during these undergraduate years that he developed his interest in painting and drawing. Tolkien was a Lieutenant with the Lancashire Fusiliers 1915–18, and took part in the Battle of the Somme. While convalescing from an illness he began writing *The Silmarillion*, the myths and legends of what later became known as 'the First Age of the World'.

Meanwhile, he married **Edith Mary Bratt** on 22 March 1916. They were to have four children: **John** (b. 16 November 1917), **Michael** (b. 22 October 1920), **Christopher*** (b. 21 November 1924), and **Priscilla** (b. 18 June 1929). After demobilization from the army in November 1918 he moved to Oxford, where he worked for a while on the Oxford Dictionary. He became a Reader in English Language at the University of Leeds in 1920, and Professor of English Language there in 1924. Then, in 1925 he returned to Oxford as the Rawlinson and Bosworth Professor of Anglo-Saxon. You have only to glance at the list of lectures he gave to see what a demanding job this was. Tolkien was elected Merton Professor of English Language and Literature in 1945, becoming at the same time a Fellow of Merton College.

Although they may have seen one another before this, it would appear that he and Lewis first met at a faculty meeting on 11 May 1926: 'He is a smooth, pale, fluent little chap,' wrote Lewis in his diary that day. 'Thinks the language is the real thing in the school' (**AMR**). The next year Tolkien enrolled Lewis in his Kolbítar‡ or Coalbiters, a society he founded in the Michaelmas Term of 1926 for the purpose of reading the Icelandic sagas and myths in the original Old Icelandic or Old Norse. Writing to Arthur Greeves* on 3 December 1929, Lewis said, 'One week I was up till 2.30 on Monday (talking to the Anglo-Saxon professor Tolkien who came back with me to College from a society and sat discoursing of the gods and giants and Asgard for three hours)' (**TST**). After this they were meeting regularly, usually on Monday mornings, and this could be taken as the beginnings of The Inklings.‡

Lewis was converted to Christianity in 1931, and in a letter to Dom Bede Griffiths* of 21 December 1941, he spoke of Hugo Dyson* and Tolkien as 'the immediate human carriers' of his conversion. The part these men played in this is explained in detail in the letter to Arthur Greeves of 18 October 1931 (**TST**). Further light is shed on Lewis's conversion and Tolkien's understanding of Myth§ by Tolkien's poem, 'Mythopoeia', which is found in *Tree and Leaf*, ed. Christopher Tolkien, (2nd edition: 1988).

The two men had other things in common as well. Tolkien was a born philologist, and he and Lewis did much to improve the 'language' side of the English syllabus. Tolkien's lectures at Oxford on *Beowulf* and particularly his British Academy lecture of 1936, 'Beowulf: the Monsters and the Critics', revolutionized studies of this poem. Another work which was to have immense importance for Lewis was Tolkien's essay 'On Fairy Stories'.

Although *The Silmarillion* was in draft form during the 1920s, Tolkien turned from it to *The Hobbit* (1937), which he began in about 1930 to amuse his children. The next work to emerge from the huge mythological world of *The Silmarillion* was *The Lord of the Rings* which he began in 1937. Much of what the Inklings called 'the new Hobbit' was read aloud to them while it was being written. When, after many frustrating delays, this most famous of all Tolkien's works was published it appeared in three volumes. The first volume, *The Fellowship of the Ring* came out in 1954, and the other two volumes, *The Two Towers* and *The Return of the King* in 1955. Few works of literature had ever meant so much to Lewis. 'But for the encouragement of CSL,' Tolkien wrote to Clyde S. Kilby on 18 December 1965, 'I do not think that I should ever have completed or offered for publication *The Lord of the Rings*' (**LJRRT**).

Despite that encouragement, Tolkien's friendship with Lewis had begun to cool before the publication of *The Lord of the Rings*, and this was one of the reasons the Thursday evening Inklings meetings came to an end in 1949. The Tuesday morning meetings continued, and Tolkien and Lewis still saw one another fairly often, but it was never the same. There are several reasons which, while they certainly do not exhaust this very complicated matter, help explain Tolkien's feelings. Lewis had clearly overestimated what Charles Williams* would mean to the other members of the Inklings, especially Tolkien, when he invited him to become a member. 'We were separated first by the sudden apparition of Charles Williams, and then by his marriage,' Tolkien wrote to Michael Tolkien in a letter dated November or December 1963 (**LJRRT**). 'CSL was my closest friend from about 1927 to 1940,' Tolkien told Christopher Bretherton on 16 July 1964, 'and remained very dear to me ... But in fact we saw less and less of one another after he came under the dominant influence of Charles Williams, and still less after his very strange marriage' (**LJRRT**).

Tolkien retired in 1959. Since 1953 he and his wife had been living at 76 Sandfield Road in Headington. Mrs Tolkien was by now quite lame from arthritis, and increasingly Tolkien withdrew from the active life of the University to spend more time with her. This was not easy. While the publication of *The Lord of the Rings* brought fame and wealth, it also brought visitors and an enormous number of fan letters. Still, he continued work on *The Silmarillion*, and his publications over the next few years included *The Adventures of Tom Bombadil and other verses from The Red Book* (1962), *Tree and Leaf* (1964), and *Smith of Wootton Major* (1967).

Tolkien saw Lewis occasionally after Lewis went to Cambridge, and in 1962–63 Tolkien visited him twice at The Kilns. When Lewis died suddenly in November 1963 no one could have been more generous with praise. In a letter of 26 November 1963, to his daughter, Priscilla, he compared the death of Lewis to 'an axe-blow near the roots'. 'Very sad that we should have been so separated in the last years; but our time of close communion endured in memory for both of us. I had a Mass said this morning, and was there, and served' (**LJRRT**). To his son Michael he wrote in November or December 1963: 'We owed each a great debt to the other, and that tie, with the deep affection that it begot, remains. He was a great man of whom the cold-blooded official obituaries only scraped the surface' (**LJRRT**).

In 1965 Tolkien's publishers learned that an American publisher planned to issue an unauthorized paperback edition of *The Lord of the Rings*. To remedy the situation Tolkien had to make a number of textual changes in his book so that it could be reprinted as the 'authorized' paperback. This was exhausting work but in the end he revised both *The Hobbit* and *The Lord of the Rings*. The new editions were published in 1966. That same year Tolkien and his wife celebrated their golden wedding anniversary.

For some years they had been taking holidays at the Miramar Hotel in Bournemouth. In 1968 they moved into a bungalow at 19 Lakeside Road, which was only a short taxi-ride to the Catholic church and the Miramar. They were thus able to divide their time between their home and the hotel. Both of them liked the Miramar very much, and it was where their children stayed when they visited. With a secretary to deal with the fan-mail, Tolkien returned to *The Silmarillion*. It existed in many versions, and one of his problems was harmonizing it with *The Lord of the Rings*.

Mrs Tolkien died on 29 November 1971. This was a terrible shock to Tolkien. Following her burial in Oxford, Merton College invited him to become a resident honorary Fellow, and they gave him a set of rooms in 21 Merton Street. He had his children around him, and he was able to take whatever meals he liked in the College. On 28 March 1972 he went to Buckingham Palace to be presented with a CBE by the Queen. Amongst the many honorary degrees conferred on him, perhaps the one that meant most was the honorary Doctorate of Letters from his own University on 4 June 1972. On 28 August 1973 he went to Bournemouth to stay with some friends. While there he was taken ill with a bleeding ulcer, and moved to a private hospital. The reports of his condition were at first optimistic, but he developed a chest infection and died in the company of two of his children, John and Priscilla, on 2 September 1973.

In 1917 Tolkien wrote the story 'Of Beren and Lúthien', the chief part of *The Silmarillion*. It describes the love of the mortal man Beren for the immortal elven-maid Lúthien. In a letter to his son, Christopher, of 11 July 1972, Tolkien asked that the name 'Lúthien' be added to that of 'Edith Mary Tolkien' on her gravestone. The Wolvercote Cemetery in Oxford has a small area reserved for Catholics. Above a single grave in this part of the cemetery is a stone of Cornish granite on which is inscribed: *Edith Mary Tolkien, Lúthien, 1889–1971. John Ronald Reuel Tolkien, Beren, 1892–1973.* For information and photos see Humphrey Carpenter's *J.R.R. Tolkien: A Biography* (1977), and *The Inklings* (1978); *The Letters of J.R.R. Tolkien*, ed. Humphrey Carpenter (1981); the numerous Forewords by Christopher Tolkien to editions of his father's works; and *The Tolkien Family Album* (1992) by John and Priscilla Tolkien.

Tynan, Kenneth Peacock (1927–80), pupil and theatre critic. He was born in Birmingham on 2 April 1927, the son of **Sir Peter Peacock**, and **Letitia Rose Tynan**. From King Edward's School in Birmingham, he won a demyship to Magdalen College,‡ Oxford, in 1945. He found that Lewis was to be his tutor. At the time Oxford was filled with ex-soldiers in army greatcoats and uniforms with the insignia torn off. There was as well such a lack of fuel that during the 3-month freeze-up of 1946–47 there was very little fuel for fires, perhaps a bucket of coal or so a week. Into this grey world there stepped the gaunt figure of Kenneth Tynan in a purple suit in fine doeskin, with perhaps an opera cloak.

It might be thought that, after suffering the relatively mild eccentricities of John Betjeman* in the 1920s, Lewis would find Tynan too much. Such was not the case. Lewis had mellowed, and he came to like Tynan very much. This affection was certainly reciprocated by Tynan. 'C.S. Lewis, my tutor, is terribly sound and sunny,' he wrote to Julian Holland on 30 October 1945 (*Letters of Kenneth Tynan*, ed. Kathleen Tynan (1994), p. 95). He had not been in Oxford long before he discovered that his tutor was to be found at the Socratic Club‡ every Monday evening in term, and on at least one occasion Tynan went along to hear him. The programme for the evening of 28 January 1946 was a debate between Shaw Desmond and Lewis on 'Religion in the Post-War World'. Desmond, after advocating a wild mishmash of beliefs, deplored the teaching of dogma. Lewis replied that to teach religion in schools without dogma would lead to exactly the kind of religion the speaker recommended. Writing about it to Holland on 4 February 1946, Tynan said he had heard 'a very witty unrehearsed debate between Shaw Desmond and C.S. Lewis. (Desmond: You speak plainly, Mr Lewis, but your wisdom is cheaply got. C.S.L.: I am prepared to admit, sir, that *my* part in this argument has been to propound the penny-wise and the penny-plain)' (*Letters*, p. 106).

Lewis expected Tynan to take a First, and Tynan certainly did work hard. But he was at the same time finding his feet as an actor and a theatre critic. His first review appeared in February 1946. He was as well the Editor of *The Cherwell* 1946–47, the President of the Experimental Theatre Club in 1947, and Secretary of the Oxford Union Society in 1948. Thus it was that in Hilary Term of 1948 Tynan asked Lewis's permission to postpone his final examination until November. He had a bad bronchial condition and had been in and out of hospitals for several months. As well, the girl to whom he was engaged dropped him for someone else. Finally, Tynan, in a state of despair, said: 'Not only do I want to postpone the examinations, I really don't see any reason for living.' In his interview with Stephen Schofield published in the latter's *In Search of C.S. Lewis* (1983) Tynan recalled Lewis's reply:

'Tynan, am I right in thinking that you once told me that during the war, when you were about twelve years old, living in Birmingham, there was an air raid on the town?'

I answered, 'Yes.' (We were heavily bombed in Birmingham.)

Lewis reminded me of something else. 'Didn't you tell me that one plane dropped a landmine by parachute and that it nearly blew up your house, missing it only by inches?'

'Yes,' I admitted.

'Now if the wind had blown that bomb a few inches nearer your house, you would be dead. So ever since then – and that was seven years ago – all the time you have lived has been a bonus. It is a gift. It is a fantastic present you have been given. And now you are talking about giving up this incredible gift and you could have been dead for eight years. You have had eight years of life that you had no reason to expect. How can you be so ungrateful?'

'Suddenly,' said Tynan, 'I saw my little problems in perspective.' He took his examination in November 1948 and received a Second. Lewis wrote to him, explaining that the 'authorities of the castle' had found the language papers inadequate. 'All this,' he said, 'I imagine, is much what you expected – i.e. that you had the troops on the dash but in the excitement of the battle did not manoeuvre as well as we hoped. Don't let it become a trauma! It signifies comparatively little' (Kathleen Tynan, *The Life of Kenneth Tynan* (1988), p. 78). He did not let it become a trauma. After leaving Oxford he soon made his mark as an actor, director, critic and man of the theatre. His first book, *He That Plays the King* (1950) was a brilliant survey of the current theatre as he saw it. In 1951 he became drama critic of *The Spectator*. After this he was drama critic for the *Evening Standard* 1952–53; the *Daily Sketch* 1953–54; the *Observer* 1954–63; and the *New Yorker* 1958–60. Much of the work done at this time is found in *Persona Grata* (1953). Another book which appeared in 1953 was *Alec Guinness*.

It was while Tynan was still with *The Spectator* that he married the novelist-playwright **Elaine Dundy**. They had a daughter **Tracy Peacock Tynan**, born 12 May 1952. Tynan and his wife were divorced in 1964. In 1967 he married the novelist and screenwriter **Kathleen Halton** (b. 25 January 1937). They had a daughter, **Roxana Nell Tynan**, b. 14 September 1967, and a son, **Matthew Blake Tynan**, b. 9 June 1971.

His best years as a drama critic coincided with what has been called the New Drama in England, exemplified by such playwrights as John Osborne. Over time Tynan became identified with the drama of social protest and a theatre of social responsibility. His books, *Curtains* (1961) and *Tynan Right and Left* (1967) give a good idea of his thoughts on the aims and ends of the theatre during these years. He also attempted to prove himself as a creator, spending the years 1955–57 as a script editor for Ealing Films. In 1963 he gave up drama criticism to become Literary Manager of the National Theatre under Sir Laurence Olivier. Of this period in Tynan's life, the author of his obituary in *The Times* (29 July 1980, p. 14) said:

> He was seldom from the centre of the theatrical scene though seemingly confused by the multiplicity of his own talents and unsure how they might be used to best advantage. And always the reproach that he might in some obscure way be failing to live up to his early promise.

One effect of this unsureness was that Tynan increasingly turned to the works of Lewis. Not the literary studies, as one might imagine, but the theological writings. In his Journal of 4 April 1971 he wrote: 'Living a mile from Stonehenge, near the heart of Old Albion, and the places of Arthur, I again come across the books of C.S. Lewis – on sale in Salisbury Cathedral. I read *That Hideous Strength* and once more the old tug reasserts itself – a tug of genuine war with my recent self. How thrilling he makes goodness seem – how tangible and radiant! But what problems he raises! ... the film Andy Braunsberg wants me to write and – greatest, most consummate of temptations – to *direct* has an erotic and anally sadistic theme. To do this work may well be a wicked act. Am I being tempted with sin, or tested with the chance of committing myself to responsible work?' (*Life*, p. 308). A re-reading of *The Problem of Pain* caused him to note in his Journal on 3 May 1975: 'As ever, I respond to his powerful suggestion that feelings of guilt and shame are not conditioned by the world in which we live but are real apprehensions of the standards obtaining in an eternal world' (*Life*, p. 347).

For years Tynan had been having trouble with his lungs, and in 1976 he and his family moved to Los Angeles. There he began writing a series of profiles for the *New Yorker* which were subsequently published as *Show People* (1980). In 1979 he wrote to his agent about a projected auto-biography, but he was too ill to get far. He died on 26 July 1980. Tynan had hoped that his body could lie as close as possible to Lewis's. When his ashes were buried in the churchyard of St Cross, Oxford, on 17 September 1980, his daughter Roxana read over his grave a passage from Lewis's **The Weight of Glory** which was probably the most important lesson Lewis ever taught him:

> The books or the music in which we thought the beauty was located will betray us if we trust to them; it was not *in* them, it only came *through* them, and what came through them was longing. These things – the beauty, the memory of our own past – are good images of what we really desire; but if they are mistaken for the thing itself, they turn into dumb idols, breaking the hearts of their worshippers. For they are not the thing itself; they are only the scent of a flower we have not found, the echo of a tune we have not heard, news from a country we have never yet visited.

Wain, John CBE (1925–94), Inkling. He was a novelist, a poet and a critic. John was born in Stoke-on-Trent on 14 March 1925, the son of **Arnold Wain** and **Anne Wain**. After leaving Newcastle-under-Lyme High School he matriculated at St John's College, Oxford, in 1943, where he read English. Because of the situation created by the war, he was sent to Magdalen‡ for tuition with Lewis. His *Sprightly Running: Part of an Autobiography* (1962) includes an account of tutorials, meetings of the Inklings‡ and the Socratic Club.‡

Lewis did not allow Wain's account of the Inklings to go without correction. In chapter V of *Sprightly Running* he had described them as 'A circle of instigators, almost of incendiaries, meeting to urge one another on in the task of redirecting the whole current of contemporary art and life' (V). Replying in *Encounter*, XX (January 1963), p. 81, Lewis said: 'The whole picture of myself as one forming a cabinet, or cell, or coven, is erroneous. Mr Wain has mistaken the purely personal relationships for alliances. He was surprised that these friends were "so different from one another". But were they more different from one another than he is from all of them? Aren't we always surprised at our friend's other friendships? As at all his tastes? One may even discover (not without horror) that one's friend prefers bottled beer to beer, or processed cheese to cheese. We have to face it.'

While an undergraduate, Wain founded a magazine entitled *Mandrake*, which contains some of his early verses. He did some acting as well, and in 1945 played opposite Richard Burton in the OUDS production of *Measure for Measure*. After taking a brilliant First Class degree in 1947 he held for a brief while a research fellowship at St John's. Then, in 1947, he left Oxford to become a Lecturer in English Literature at the University of Reading, where he remained until 1955. While there he wrote his first novel, *Hurry on Down* (1953), which because of its affinities with such books as Kingsley Amis's *Lucky Jim* and John Braine's *Room at the Top*, stamped him as one of the Angry Young Men of the 1950s. In 1947 he married **Marianne Urmston**, and they were divorced in 1956.

In 1955 he resigned from Reading to become a freelance author and critic. Some time later he moved to Wolvercote, Oxford, where he spent the rest of his life. He remained in close touch with Lewis, and over the years was present at many of the Tuesday morning meetings of the Inklings in the Eagle and Child pub.‡ Over the following years his novels and stories included *The Contenders* (1958), *A Travelling Woman* (1959), *Nuncle and Other Stories* (1960), *The Smaller Sky* (1967) and *A Winter in the Hills* (1970). His best poetry is found in *Mixed Feeling* (1951) and *Weep Before God* (1961).

Instead of becoming the Angry Young Man some hoped for, he espoused traditional values and had much in common with his own literary heroes, Dr Johnson, Arnold Bennett and George Orwell. His *Samuel Johnson: A Biography* (1974) has been called 'a model of lucid and sympathetic exposition'. John Wain was also a prolific literary journalist and radio and television broadcaster. He was much occupied during his last years on his Oxford trilogy of novels, *Where Rivers Meet* (1988), *Comedies* (1990) and *Hungry Generations* (1994). His other partly-autobiographical work is *Dear Shadows: portraits from memory* (1986). A complete list of his writings is found in David Gerard's *John Wain: A Bibliography* (1987).

In 1971 he was made the Fellow in Creative Arts at Brasenose College, Oxford, and in 1973 he was elected to the Chair of Poetry in Oxford

University. He was appointed CBE in 1984. In 1960 he married **Eirian James**, and they had three sons: **William Brunswick** (b. 18 October 1960), **Ianto Samuel** (b. 22 December 1962), and **Tobias Hamnett** (b. 26 May 1966). During a long illness, which led to her death in 1988, he nursed his wife with touching devotion. In 1989 he married **Patricia Adams**.

John Wain died on 24 May 1994. 'Contrasting as we were, Lewis and I had one thing in common,' he said in *Sprightly Running* (V), 'we both loved innocent conviviality. A tobacco-clouded room, the unhampered talk and laughter of men who trusted each other, and a jug of beer on the table – that was all that Lewis needed to make him happy, and I was the same.' Those who came across this kind and congenial man in the Eagle and Child, or any other pub, would have soon understood why Lewis loved him so much.

Walsh, Chad (1914–91), friend. He was a distinguished poet and teacher, and the author of many books ranging from literary criticism, Christian apologetics and children's books. Born in South Boston, Virginia, on 10 May 1914, he took a BA in French from the University of Virginia in 1938, and a D.Phil. in English Literature from the University of Michigan in 1943. He was a Research Analyst with the US War Department, 1943–45. He joined the English Department of Beloit College, Wisconsin, in 1945, eventually becoming Professor of English, Writer in Residence and Poet in Residence. He was Chairman of the department 1962–70. Chad Walsh was ordained in the Episcopal Church in 1948, and served as an assistant at St Paul's Episcopal Church, Beloit, 1948–77.

In 1938 he married **Eva Tuttle** and they had four daughters, **Damaris, Madeline, Sarah-Lindsay** and **Alison**. He discovered Lewis through reading *Perelandra* in 1945, a book which affected him deeply. Writing about it in 'Impact on America' (**LCSL**), he said 'It was as though an intellectual abstraction or speculation had become flesh and dwelt in its solid bodily glory among us.' He wrote to Lewis on 30 November 1945, and the following year he published 'C.S. Lewis, Apostle to the Skeptics' in *The Atlantic Monthly* (September 1946). At this time very little was known about Lewis, and Eva urged him to expand his *Atlantic* article into a book. He met Lewis several times during the summer of 1948, and the following year Macmillan of New York published his *C.S. Lewis: Apostle to the Skeptics*. It was the first book about Lewis, and it remains one of the best.

One of those who wrote to thank him for *Apostle to the Skeptics* was Joy Davidman Gresham.* After establishing a friendship by mail, Joy and her husband, William Lindsay Gresham, visited the Walshes at their summer place in Vermont in 1951 and 1952. The friendship deepened and when Chad, Eva, Damaris and Madeline travelled to England in the summer of

1955, they went to Oxford for a visit with Lewis and Joy, who was staying with Lewis at the time. Following Lewis's marriage to Joy, the exchange of letters continued. Lewis dedicated *The Four Loves* to the friend who had been partly responsible for bringing them together. Chad had a final visit with Lewis in 1961. He died on 17 January 1991.

Walsh's critical writings about Lewis include 'The Re-education of the Fearful Pilgrim' in *The Longing for a Form*, ed. Peter J. Schakel (1977) and *The Literary Legacy of C.S. Lewis* (1979). His biographical writings include 'The Man and the Mystery' in *Shadows of Imagination*, ed. Mark R. Hillegas (1969) and the Afterword to the Bantam edition (1976) of *A Grief Observed*. He is the editor of *The Visionary Christian: 131 Readings from C.S. Lewis* (1981). Some of his many volumes of poems are *The Psalm of Christ*, *The End of Nature*, *The Unknown Dance* and *Hang Me Up My Begging Bowl*. Of his many books on religion Lewis's favourite was *Behold the Glory*. His letters to and from Lewis are in the Wade Center‡ at Wheaton College, with copies in the Bodleian. Other collections of his writings are found in the Newberry Library in Chicago and in the Roanoke College Library, Salem, Virginia.

Williams, Charles Walter Stansby (1886–1945), Inkling. He was born in London on 20 September 1886, the son of **Richard Walter Stansby Williams** and **Mary (Wall) Williams**. He was educated at St Albans School and the University of London. He joined the Oxford University Press in 1908, and never left it. On 12 April 1917 he married another devoted Anglican and Londoner, **Florence 'Michal' Conway**. Their only child, **Michael Stansby Williams**, was born in 1922.

A few years before he married, while reading the proofs of a translation of Dante's *Divine Comedy*, he was enraptured by one of his most remarkable ideas, the 'Beatrician experience'. This is a recovery of that vision which would have been common to each of us if Man had not fallen. In his first book, *The Silver Stair* (1912), he explains how earthly love can be a staircase to God. The fullest explanation of the experience is found in 'The Theology of Romantic Love' from *He Came Down from Heaven* (1938). In Lewis's opinion, the works in which Romantic Love found the most perfect expression are *Taliessin Through Logres* (1938) and *The Region of the Summer Stars* (1944).

Lewis's discovery of Williams came through one of Williams's seven 'supernatural thrillers', *The Place of the Lion* (1931). 'I have just read what I think a really great book,' Lewis wrote to Arthur Greeves* on 26 February 1936. On 11 March Lewis expressed his thanks to Williams for the book, and was answered by return of post. 'If you had delayed writing another 24 hours,' Williams said on 12 March, 'our letters would have crossed. It has never before happened to me to be admiring an author of a book while he at the same time was admiring me ... To be exact, I finished on Saturday looking – too hastily – at proofs of your *Allegorical Love Poem* ... I regard your book as practically the only one that I have ever come across, since Dante, that shows the slightest understanding of what this very peculiar identity of love and religion means.'

The men met shortly afterwards in London, and Lewis was even more impressed by Williams himself. 'After this,' Lewis said in the Preface to **ECW**:

> our friendship rapidly grew inward to the bone. Until 1939 that friendship had to subsist on occasional meetings, though, even thus, he had already become as dear to all my Oxford friends as he was to me. There were many meetings both in my rooms at Magdalen and in Williams's tiny office at Amen House ...
>
> But in 1939 the Oxford University Press, and he with it, was evacuated to Oxford. From that time until his death we met one another about twice a week, sometimes more ... The removal to Oxford also produced other changes. The English Faculty was depleted by war, and Williams was soon making an Oxford reputation both as a lecturer and a private tutor ...
>
> In appearance he was tall, slim, and straight as a boy, though grey-haired. His face we thought ugly: I am not sure that the word 'monkey' has not been murmured in this context. But the moment he spoke it became, as was also said, like the face of an angel – not a feminine angel in the debased tradition of some religious art, but a masculine angel, a spirit burning with intelligence and charity ... There was something of recklessness, something even of *panache*, in his gait ... He always carried his head in the air. When he lectured, wearing his gown, his presence was one of the stateliest I have ever seen.

Writing to Warnie Lewis* on 19 November 1939 about a lecture Williams gave in one of the women's colleges on 16 November, Lewis said: 'On Tuesday evening, I went to the J.C.R. of St Hugh's to hear Williams read a paper – or rather not "read" but "spout" – i.e. deliver without a single note a perfectly coherent and impassioned meditation, variegated with quotations in his incantatory manner. A most wonderful performance and impressed his audience, specially the young women, very much. And it really is remarkable how that ugly, almost simian, face, becomes transfigured.' On 29 January 1940 Williams gave his famous lecture on

Milton's *Comus* in Divinity School. This was followed by other lectures in English Literature. During his years at Oxford he wrote *The Figure of Beatrice* (1943) and this fired a friendship with Dorothy L. Sayers,* and influenced her translation of Dante.

The War in Europe ended on 9 May 1945, but as Williams prepared to return to London he died suddenly on 15 May. He is buried in the churchyard of St Cross,‡ Oxford. His many works include (NOVELS: *War in Heaven* (1930), *Many Dimensions* (1931), *The Place of the Lion* (1931), *The Greater Trumps* (1932), *Shadows of Ecstasy* (1933), *Descent into Hell* (1937), *All Hallows' Eve* (1945); OTHER: *Bacon* (1933), *Judgement at Chelmsford* (1939), *The Descent of the Dove* (1939). See especially *Arthurian Torso* for Lewis's commentary on Williams's Arthurian poems. For information and photos see Alice Mary Hadfield, *Charles Williams: An Exploration of His Life and Work*, **L, BF, BIO, IHW, INK**.

Wrenn, Charles Lesley (1895–1969), Inkling, and Rawlinson and Bosworth Professor of Anglo-Saxon in Oxford University 1946–63. He was born on 30 December 1895 at Westcliffe-on-Sea, the son of **H.W. Wrenn**. He was educated privately, and then became an undergraduate at Queen's College, Oxford. After taking his BA he was a Lecturer in English at Durham University 1917–20, Principal and Professor of English at Pachaiyappa's College, Madras, 1920–21; Fellow of Madras University 1920; Head of Department of English, University of Dacca, 1921–27.

Wrenn returned to England in 1928 when he was made a Lecturer in English at Leeds University, where he was to remain until 1930. In that year he became a Lecturer in English Language in Oxford, where he was able to help J.R.R. Tolkien* with the teaching of Anglo-Saxon. Wrenn had married **Agnes Wright** in 1919, and they were to have one daughter. Tolkien's wife, Edith, had not found many friends among her husband's acquaintances, but in Agnes Wrenn she discovered a very good one. In 1939 Charles Wrenn was appointed Professor of English Language and Literature at the University of London, and there he was to remain until 1946.

His name appears only a few times in accounts of Inkling meetings. On 5 November 1939 Jack Lewis wrote to his brother about one in which Wrenn had been prominent:

> I had a pleasant evening on Thursday with [Charles] Williams,* Tolkien and Wrenn, during which Wrenn *almost* seriously expressed a strong wish to burn Williams, or at least maintained that conversation with Williams enabled him to understand how inquisitors had felt it right to burn people ...

The occasion was a discussion of the most distressing text in the Bible ('narrow is the way and few they be that find it') and whether one really could believe in a universe where the majority were damned and also in the goodness of God. Wrenn, of course, took the view that it mattered precisely nothing whether it conformed to your ideas of goodness or not, and it was at that stage that the combustible possibilities of Williams revealed themselves to him in an attractive light. The general sense of the meeting was in favour of a view on the lines taken in *Pastor Pastorum* – that Our Lord's replies are never straight answers and never gratify curiosity, and that whatever this one meant its purpose was certainly not statistical (**L**).

On 21 July 1946 Tolkien wrote to Sir Stanley Unwin to say: 'I have removed to Merton, as the Merton Professor of English Language and Literature: Professor Wrenn, from King's College, London, is coming to take Anglo-Saxon off my shoulders' (**LJRRT**). Wrenn was to hold the post Tolkien had managed so magnificently, that of Rawlinson and Bosworth Professor of Anglo-Saxon, until his retirement in 1963. He was a devoted and enthusiastic teacher, and as a professor gave much personal help and instruction. He was a very conscientious Chairman of the Council of the London University School of Slavonic and East European Studies, 1945–49. Writing about this side of his life, the author of his obituary in *The Times* (4 June 1969) said:

> He refused to allow political opinions to interfere with the cultural co-operation between Britain and Russia, and he visited the Soviet Union in 1952. In 1956 he took a sabbatical year in the US. His zeal for co-operation on the cultural plane with Russia at one time brought him under suspicion of being near-communist in sympathy but to those who knew him nothing could have been more ridiculous.
>
> Many of the universities of Great Britain and Ireland enjoyed his services, and his influence in making appointments in universities was considerable. But he looked also beyond these islands and his greatest single contribution to international academic co-operation was the founding of the International Conference of University Professors of English. He organized the successful first conference at Magdalen College, Oxford, in 1950 (p. 12).

Wrenn's works include an edition of *Beowulf: A Revision of Clark Hall's translation* (1940), *The Poetry of Caedmon* (1947), *An Old English Grammar* (with R. Quirk) (1955) and *A Study of Old English Literature* (1967).

WHAT'S WHAT

Addison's Walk: This walk lies within the grounds of Magdalen College‡ and runs from alongside New Buildings northwards between Long Meadow and the Fellows' Garden until it reaches *Mesopotamia*.‡ It was originally named Water Walks for the river banks that it follows but was renamed after Joseph Addison (1672–1719), a fellow of Magdalen, best known for his contributions to the *Spectator* and his interest in landscape gardening. Lewis walked here nearly every day.

Agape Fund (or 'Agapony', or 'Agapargyry' = love + money): In the 1940s Lewis asked Owen Barfield* to set up a charitable trust into which he could direct most of his royalties. The trust was administered by Barfield, who dispensed the money as Lewis directed, but all gifts were made anonymously. Owen Barfield devoted a chapter to this fund in his book *This Ever Diverse Pair*, which chapter is reprinted in **OBCSL**.

Anglicanism: 'Anglicanism' is the system of doctrine, practice and services based on the Church of England's *Book of Common Prayer*‡ upheld by those churches throughout the world which are in communion with the See of Canterbury. Anglicanism's three sources of authority are Scripture, Tradition and Reason. It claims to have preserved the Apostolic Succession whereby the ministry of the Christian Church is held to be derived from the Apostles by a continuous succession of Bishops. Until 250 years after the Reformation the Anglican Communion consisted solely of the Churches of England (the only part still retaining State Establishment), Ireland and Wales, and the Episcopal Church in Scotland. The Episcopal Church in the United States came into existence in 1787.

Very little is known about Christianity in Britain before Pope Gregory the Great despatched St Augustine of Canterbury (d. 604) to England in 597 to refound the English Church. After Christianity had been formally adopted by Ethelbert, King of Kent, Augustine was consecrated Archbishop of Canterbury. With the Norman Conquest in 1066 the English Church entered more fully into the mainstream of European religion.

Although the causes of the English Reformation lay very deep, the occasion of it was the famous divorce of Henry VIII from Catherine of Aragon which caused him to break with Rome by the Act of Supremacy. The original formulation of Anglican principles, however, did not take place until the reign of Elizabeth I (1533–1603) who became Queen in 1558. It was under her that Anglicanism as a doctrinal system came into existence, a church claiming to be both Catholic and Reformed.

Throughout its four-hundred-year history, the Church of England has accommodated a wide variety of opinion within its fold: at times the 'high' church, with its doctrines inclining more towards those of Rome, has prevailed. At others, the 'low', more Protestant, view has been to the fore. There is also a third strand, called the 'liberal', increasingly strong in the twentieth century but with its roots much further back, which promotes dialogue with what may be called the spirit of the age.

Lewis was baptized in the Church of Ireland in 1899. He gave up going to church when an undergraduate at Oxford, and picked it up again after his conversion in 1931. See **Book of Common Prayer**.‡

Anthroposophy: It means literally 'the wisdom of mankind'. It is a religious system evolved by Rudolf Steiner (1861–1925) who studied natural science at Vienna University and for a number of years was engaged on the works of Goethe. In 1902 he became the leader of a German section of the Theosophical Society, but rejected its predominantly Eastern associations. In 1913 he founded the Anthroposophical Society as an independent association, his aim being to develop the faculty of spirit cognition inherent in ordinary people and to put them in touch with the spiritual world from which materialism had caused them to be estranged.

Anthroposophy teaches a highly elaborated doctrine of the origin of the world, the original nobility of the human spirit, the various epochs of mankind, a doctrine of immortality, reincarnation, and 'Karma', but it places man in union with God in the centre. It was condemned by the Catholic Church in 1919. Steiner's works include *Philosophy of Spiritual Activity*, *Occult Science* and *Knowledge of Higher Worlds*.

Lewis strongly disapproved of Anthroposophy, and it was a cause of disagreement with his friends Owen Barfield* and Cecil Harwood* who became Anthroposophists in 1923. Some of Lewis's objections were made when he was an atheist, and others when he was a Christian, so he was not always arguing from the same position. The best work on his objections is Cecil Harwood's 'About Anthroposophy' in **ABT**. See also Lionel Adey's *C.S. Lewis's 'Great War' with Owen Barfield* (1978).

Beer and Beowulf Evenings: *Beowulf* is an eighth-century poem in Old English which tells of how the young Geatish hero, Beowulf, fights and kills the monster Grendel, and afterwards Grendel's mother. Fifty years later, when king of the Geats, Beowulf fights a dragon which has attacked his people, and in the combat Beowulf and the dragon are mortally wounded.

Beowulf is one of the finest poems in the English language, but because Old English is very difficult it is a required subject for those reading English at Oxford. Lewis had good reason for making it as interesting as possible. A glance at those passages of his diary which deal with the bad teaching he had as an undergraduate and you can almost smell the ink burning the pages. The culprit was H.C.K. Wyld ('the Cad!'), Merton Professor of English Language and Literature between 1920 and 1945. Besides Wyld's inept lecturing, Lewis had to depend on his books when he began teaching Old English to his pupils.

He was hammering away at Wyld's *Historical Study of the Mother Tongue* when, on 17 January 1927, he found a way of making the sound-laws of Old English clearer. 'I worked from breakfast to lunch on language,' he wrote, 'mainly constructing a Mnemonic for "O.E. to M.E. [Old English to Middle English] (Vowels)." I am beginning to enjoy this stuff and have certainly got further this time than in any of my innumerable previous attempts to calm that chaos. What a brute Wyld is – no order, no power of exposition, no care for the reader. It is satisfaction to see that no amount of learning can save a fool' (**AMR**). He was still working on this system for improving the memory when he said to Owen Barfield* on 7 June 1928 (**L**): 'I am writing a great new poem – also a Mnemonic rime on English sound changes in octosyllabic verse

> (Thus Æ to Ĕ they soon were fetchin',
> Cf. such forms as ÞÆC and ÞECCEAN.)

There thus came about Lewis's famous 'Beer and Beowulf' evenings. At these sessions he introduced his pupils to the mnemonic devices he had invented, chanted *Beowulf* aloud, and passed around the beer-jug.

Bird and Baby: *See* **Eagle and Child‡**

Bodleian Library: This is one of the oldest libraries in the world, and one of the most beautiful buildings in Oxford. It is the library of the University of Oxford, and it contains one of the two largest collections of Lewis's manuscripts there are, the other being in the Wade Center‡ of Wheaton College. The original University Library of the fourteenth century was housed in a room above the church of St Mary the Virgin. In time the books outgrew the room, and in about 1489 they were placed, with the library of Duke Humfrey of Gloucester, in a room built above the Divinity School. For various reasons Duke Humfrey's Library was empty of books and furniture by 1556. It was refounded in 1598 by Sir Thomas Bodley, after whom the Bodleian takes its name, and it opened officially to the public in 1602. The other parts of the Bodleian which adjoin Duke Humfrey's Library were added later in the century. Since the 17th Century the Bodleian has been a copyright library, entitled to a free copy of every book published in Britain. This, combined with its numerous benefactions over the centuries, means that the Bodleian now contains 5.6 million books on 90.9 miles of shelving.

It was in the Bodleian that Lewis did most of his reading and research. He had been working there on *The Allegory of Love* when he wrote to his father on 31 March 1928 saying:

> If only you could smoke, and if only there were upholstered chairs, the Bodleian would be one of the most delightful places in the world. I sit in 'Duke Humphrey's Library', the oldest part, a fifteenth-century building with a very beautiful painted wooden ceiling above me and a little mullioned window at my left hand, through which I look down on the garden of Exeter where, these mornings, I see the sudden squalls of wind and rain driving the first blossoms off the fruit trees and snowing the lawn with them ... By a merciful provision, however many books you may send for, they will all be left on your chosen table at night for you to resume work next morning: so that one gradually accumulates a pile as comfortably as in one's own room. There is not, as in modern libraries, a forbidding framed notice to shriek 'Silence': on the contrary, a more moderate request 'Talk little and tread lightly'. There is indeed always a faint murmur going on of semi-whispered conversations in neighbouring boxes. It disturbs no one. I rather like to hear the hum of the hive (**L**).

The Bodleian began its collection of the manuscripts of C.S. Lewis in 1967 when Sister Penelope* donated her fifty-six letters from Lewis. As Lewis had worked in the Bodleian most of his life, Walter Hooper believed that it was the right place for his papers, and beginning in 1968 he undertook the collecting of Lewis manuscripts on their behalf. The Bodleian's 'Lewis Collection' contains over 2,300 letters, but not all are originals. There is a reciprocal photocopying agreement between the Bodleian and the Wade Center, so that each library possesses photocopies of the letters in the other's collection. Amongst the Bodleian's collection of original letters are those to Pauline Baynes,* Geoffrey Bles,* Arthur C. Clarke, Nevill Coghill,* E.R. Eddison, Jocelyn Gibb,* Roger Lancelyn Green,* Cecil Harwood,* Richard Ladborough,* Ruth Pitter,* Kathleen Raine, Sheldon Vanauken, Lawrence Whistler and numerous others.

The Bodleian has the entire manuscripts of some of Lewis's books, including *Arthurian Torso, A Grief Observed, The Dark Tower, Letters to Malcolm* and *Studies in Words.* The collection also includes fragments of such works as *Surprised by Joy* and *That Hideous Strength*, various Narnian fragments including Lewis's own map of Narnia, and the originals of a great many of his essays and shorter works. There are also many related manuscripts and letters, including a microfilm of the **Lewis Papers‡** and some hundreds of Lewis's books in translation. See **Translations of Lewis's writings.‡**

Book of Common Prayer, The (BCP): There are numerous references to this, and quotations from it, in the writings of Lewis. It is the official service book of the Church of England, and variations of it are used in all churches of the Anglican Communion (see **Anglicanism‡**). It contains the daily offices of Morning and Evening Prayer, the Psalter, the forms of administration of the Sacraments (such as Holy Communion or the Eucharist) and other rites. Following the break with Rome in 1533, Thomas Cranmer and others sought to simplify the Latin service of the medieval Church and to produce a convenient book in English. The first BCP was published in 1549. There were to be a good many revisions until the BCP of 1662, which remained relatively unchanged until the Church of England issued the Alternative Service Book in 1980. The 1662 BCP, which Lewis grew up with, was always used in his parish church in Headington Quarry. He used the Coverdale translation of the Psalter (as found in the BCP) in **ROP**. Lewis wrote glowingly about the BCP in **EL** where he says:

> There are of course many good, and different, ways both of writing prose and praying. Its temper may seem cold to those reared in other traditions but no one will deny that it is strong. It offers little

and concedes little to merely natural feelings: even religious feelings it will not heighten till it has first sobered them; but at its greatest it shines with a white light hardly surpassed outside the pages of the New Testament itself (Book II, Part 1).

See **Anglicanism‡**.

Booklist: In response to *The Christian Century's* question 'What books did most to shape your vocational attitude and your philosophy of life?', Lewis sent the following list: '*Phantastes*, by George MacDonald; *The Everlasting Man*, by G.K. Chesterton; *The Aeneid*, by Virgil; *The Temple*, by George Herbert; *The Prelude*, by William Wordsworth; *The Idea of the Holy*, by Rudolf Otto; *The Consolation of Philosophy*, by Boethius; *Life of Samuel Johnson*, by James Boswell; *Descent into Hell*, by Charles Williams; *Theism and Humanism*, by Arthur James Balfour.' The list appeared in *The Christian Century* (6 June 1962), and is reprinted in *The Canadian C.S. Lewis Journal*,‡ No 58 (Spring 1987), p. 27.

Books of C.S. Lewis: *See* **Library of C.S. Lewis.‡**

C.S. Lewis Foundation: One of its officers writes: 'Founded in 1986, this US non-profit education foundation, with offices in Redlands, California, is committed to promoting the open expression of Christian thought and artistry particularly within mainstream university academic and cultural forums. In support of its primary mission, the Foundation seeks to encourage the public's awareness of, and interest in, the life and work of C.S. Lewis, who is viewed as an exemplary twentieth-century Christian scholar. It also seeks to facilitate international networking among Christian scholars and artists of all communions; is actively engaged in seeking alternative approaches to higher education that promise greater opportunity for constructive interaction between Christians and non-Christians; and, finally, seeks generally to advance the cause of academic freedom for all scholars of faith.

'Consistent with its strategic objectives, the Foundation has been active since 1986 in conducting Round Tables for Christian faculty working within largely secular colleges and universities; it conducts the triennial C.S. Lewis Summer Institute at Oxford and Cambridge; it has acquired and is in the process of restoring "The Kilns", C.S. Lewis's long-time residence in Oxford, for future use as a Christian study centre, museum and residence for visiting Christian faculty and artists (projected opening date: 1998); and hopes ultimately to found a proto-type "Mere

Christian" college in the United States, to be named after C.S. Lewis. The college, which is envisioned as a modified Great Books college with a school of visual and performing arts, would be distinctive in its dual commitment both to Christian orthodoxy and to meaningful interaction with non-Christians within the framework of a larger secular university environment somewhat in the tradition of Oxford and Cambridge (projected opening date: 1999–2001).' For more information concerning the work of the Foundation, please contact Dr J. Stanley Mattson, President, P.O. Box 8008, Redlands, California 92375, U.S.A. Tel. 909-793-0949; Fax 909-335-3501.

Campbell College, Belfast: After Wynyard School‡ collapsed in the summer of 1910, Lewis was a boarder here between September and December 1910. This school for boys, only a mile from Little Lea,‡ was named after Henry James Campbell (1813–89), who left a large estate to be used for the founding of a school 'for the purpose of giving therein a superior liberal Protestant education'. The school was founded in 1890 with 213 boys on the register. Writing about it in **SBJ** III, Lewis said:

> From my point of view the great drawback was that one had, so to speak, no home. Only a few very senior boys had studies. The rest of us, except when seated at table for meals or in a huge 'preparation room' for evening 'Prep', belonged nowhere. In out-of-school hours one spent one's time either evading or conforming to all those inexplicable movements which a crowd exhibits as it thins here and thickens there ... One was always 'moving on' or 'hanging about' ... It was very like living permanently in a large railway station.

He goes on to say in **SBJ** III, 'Much the most important thing that happened to me at Campbell was that I there read *Sohrab and Rustum* in form under an excellent master whom we called Octie.' 'Octie' was Lewis Alden (d. 1941), an Exhibitioner of Wadham College, Oxford, who was Senior English Master at Campbell from 1898 until 1930. Lewis Alden is not to be confused with a close friend of the Lewis family, James Adams McNeill (1853–1907), who was the first Headmaster of Campbell. His daughter, Jane McNeill,* is the friend to whom Lewis dedicated *That Hideous Strength*. See Keith Haines, *Neither Rogues nor Fools: A History of Campbell College and Campbellians* (1993).

Canadian C.S. Lewis Journal, The: The first 83 numbers of this quarterly journal, which ran from 1979 to 1993, were edited by Stephen Schofield. He was a Canadian journalist who emigrated to England, living first in Godalming and then in Yorkshire. This charming man was always on the lookout for 'scoops' and his journal is rich in unpublished Lewis letters, interviews with friends of Lewis, and lively letters to the Editor. Some of the best of Schofield's interviews from the *Journal* were published in *In Search of C.S. Lewis*, ed. S. Schofield (1983). Beginning with No 84 (Autumn 1993) the *Journal*, now edited by Roger Stronstad, can be obtained by writing to *The Canadian C.S. Lewis Journal*, c/o Western Pentecostal Bible College, P.O. Box 1700, Abbotsford, B.C., Canada V2S 7E7. Copies in the Bodleian Library‡ and the Wade Center.‡

Cherbourg School: This is the school called 'Chartres' in **SBJ** IV. Jack Lewis joined this preparatory school in Malvern, Worcestershire, in January 1911 after leaving Campbell College.‡ It was made up of about twenty boys between the ages of 8 and 12. The school opened in 1907 under the headmastership of Arthur Clement Allen (1868–1957). Allen was educated at Repton and New College, Oxford, where he read Classics. After taking a BA in 1891, he was a teacher at Silloth School from 1902 until 1907.

With Warnie Lewis* nearby in Malvern College,‡ Jack got on quite well here. Certainly his schoolwork prospered, and he won a scholarship to Malvern College. It was here that he came across Richard Wagner, as a result of which, as he said in **SBJ** V, 'Pure "Northernness" engulfed me.' It was also at Cherbourg, as he says in **SBJ** IV, that he 'ceased to be a Christian', partly owing to the Matron, Miss Cowie, who was 'floundering in the mazes of Theosophy, Rosicrucianism, Spiritualism; the whole Anglo-American Occultist tradition.' Another influence mentioned in that chapter was the master to whom he gave the nickname 'Pogo' – P.G.K. Harris. Arthur C. Allen was Headmaster until 1917 when he became Joint Headmaster. He moved Cherbourg School to Wood Norton, Evesham, in 1925, and the school closed when he retired in 1931.

Classical Honour Moderations: *See* **Literae Humaniores.**

'Clerk', 'N.W.' : *See* **Pseudonyms.**‡

Coalbiters: *See* **Kolbítar.**‡

Colleges: When Lewis was at Magdalen College‡ twenty-four men's colleges and five women's colleges made up the University of Oxford. (Now thirty-six colleges make up the University, and all admit men and women with the exception of St Hilda's, which admits only women). The colleges are completely autonomous, owning the buildings they occupy. Each is self-contained, with rooms for fellows and students, chapel, library, dining hall, etc. All these colleges together form the **University of Oxford.‡**

Cowley Fathers: This is a name used of the Anglican religious community, the Society of St John the Evangelist. It was founded in Oxford in 1866 by the Rev. Richard Meux Benson, at that time Vicar of Cowley. In 1868 the Fathers moved into the Mission House in Marston Street, Cowley, beside the Church of St John the Evangelist. Writing to Sister Penelope* on 24 October 1940, Lewis said, 'I am going to make my first confession next week.' This was the beginning of Lewis's regular confessions to one of the Cowley priests, Father Walter Adams SSJE. The merits of 'Fr A.' are mentioned in a letter to Mary Neylan of 30 April 1941: 'If I have ever met a holy man, he is one' (*The Chesterton Review*, XVII, Aug. and Nov. 1991, p. 409). And it was of Father Adams that Lewis spoke when he wrote to Don Giovanni Calabria* on 14 April 1952 saying, 'My aged confessor and most loving father in Christ has just died. While he was celebrating at the altar, suddenly, after a sharp but (thanks be to God) very brief attack of pain, he expired; and his last words were, "I come, Lord Jesus." He was a man of ripe spiritual wisdom – noble minded but of an almost childlike simplicity and innocence: *buono fanciullo*, if I may put it so' (**LDGC**). In 1980 the mother house of the Cowley Fathers moved to St Edward's House in Westminster.

CSL: The Bulletin of the New York C.S. Lewis Society: *See* **New York C.S. Lewis Society.‡**

Dedicatees (those to whom Lewis dedicated his books): (1) The first impression of the poem *Dymer* (1926) was not dedicated to anyone; the 2nd impression with a Preface of 1950 was dedicated to the late **Marjorie Milne.** Owen Barfield* introduced Miss Milne to Lewis in the 1940s. She was a devout Anglo-Catholic who felt Lewis should occupy the place of a figurehead in a new religious movement. Her adulation was such that, when he wrote to Owen Barfield on 22 December 1947, Lewis said: 'Never communicate any troubles of mine again to M. Milne. Through no will of my own I occupy already a larger place in her thoughts than I could wish, and the degree of her sympathy is such as to make her miserable and to embarrass me.'

Warnie Lewis* mentions her in his diary of 19 September 1950: 'J had by appointment that indefatigable talker Marjorie M, at 5 p.m. She had come to "consult" him, but supplied at least 90 per cent of the conversation. This is the woman of whom Owen Barfield remarked in his dry way: "She's a good creature when all's said and done: especially when all's said and done"' (**BF**). Her essay 'Dymer: Myth or Poem?' is found in *The Month*, VIII (September 1952), pp. 170–73.

(2) *The Pilgrim's Regress* (1933) is dedicated to Lewis's boyhood friend **Arthur Greeves*** (1895–1966) in whose home it was written. (3) The dedication to *The Allegory of Love* (1936) runs: 'To Owen Barfield/ Wisest and Best/ of my/ Unofficial Teachers.' They met in 1919 and **Owen Barfield*** was one of Lewis's closest friends. (4) *Out of the Silent Planet* (1938) is dedicated 'To my Brother/ W.H.L./ a lifelong critic of the/ space-and-time story.' **Warren Hamilton Lewis*** was a member of the Inklings‡ and heard the story read aloud as it was being written. (5) *Rehabilitations and Other Essays* (1939) is dedicated 'To/ Hugo Dyson'. Dyson* was Lecturer and Tutor in English at Reading University 1921–45, and a Fellow of Merton College 1945–1963.

(6) *The Problem of Pain* (1940) is dedicated 'To/ The Inklings'. **The Inklings‡** are the group of friends who met in Lewis's rooms in Magdalen College and read and discussed the works they were writing. (7) *The Screwtape Letters* (1942) is dedicated 'To/ J.R.R. Tolkien.' **J.R.R. Tolkien**,* an Inkling and the author of *The Lord of the Rings*, was Rawlinson and Bosworth Professor of Anglo-Saxon at Oxford 1925–45, and then Merton Professor of English Language and Literature.

(8) The dedication of *A Preface to 'Paradise Lost'* (1942) 'To Charles Williams' is in the form of a letter in which Lewis says that to think of **Charles Williams's*** lectures from which this book developed 'is to think of those other lectures at Oxford in which you partly anticipated, partly confirmed, and most of all clarified and matured, what I had long been thinking about Milton.' (9) *Perelandra* is dedicated 'To/ Some Ladies/ at/ Wantage'. Those ladies were **Sister Penelope CSMV*** and the other nuns of The Community of St Mary the Virgin in Wantage, Berkshire. (10) *That Hideous Strength* (1945) is dedicated 'To/ J. McNeill'. This was Lewis's old friend from Belfast, **Jane McNeill.***

(11) *The Great Divorce* (1945) is dedicated 'To/ Barbara Wall/ Best and most long-suffering of scribes'. (For whatever reason the American edition does not contain the dedication.) Mrs **Barbara Wall** is the sister of Christian Hardie, who is the wife of Colin Hardie.* During the War Lewis

was looking for someone who would type his books, and Colin Hardie introduced him to his sister-in-law, Barbara Wall, who was living in Oxford. She typed *That Hideous Strength*, *The Great Divorce* and *Miracles*. Barbara Wall, born Barbara Lucas on 9 October 1911, is the daughter of Perceval and Madeline (Meynell) Lucas. In 1935 she married the writer Bernard Wall, and they have two daughters. She has written a number of theological books under the name Barbara Wall, and these include *And Was Crucified* (1939), *Great Saints and Saintly Figures* (1963), and (with Bernard Wall) *Thaw at the Vatican* (1964). Her novels, all of which are published under her maiden name, include *Stars Were Born* (1934), *The Trembling of the Sea* (1936), *Anna Collett* (1946), *More Ado About Nothing* (1969) and *Widows and Widowers* (1979).

(12) *George MacDonald: An Anthology* (1946) is dedicated 'To/ Mary Neylan'. Mrs Neylan (1908–   ) was a pupil and friend of C.S. Lewis. In 'My Friendship with C.S. Lewis', *The Chesterton Review*, C.S. Lewis Special Issue (Vol. XVII, No 3, August 1991 and Vol. XVII, No 4, November 1991), pp. 405–11, she wrote:

> I first met C.S. Lewis in 1931 when I was his pupil at Oxford. He had been encouraged to accept me by his friend, Hugo Dyson,* who had previously been my tutor at Reading University. I found Lewis's tutorials intensely interesting. He was then working on the Prolegomena to the *Allegory of Love*, and his discussions on moral and literary questions surprised and fascinated me, so that when *The Pilgrim's Regress* appeared in the window of Blackwell's bookshop in Oxford during 1933, I immediately purchased it. It was a book which chimed in with my own experience and eventually influenced me to become a convert to Christianity.

Mrs Neylan was the recipient of those letters addressed 'To a Former Pupil' and 'To a Lady' scattered throughout Lewis's *Letters*.

(13) *Miracles* (1947) is dedicated 'To/ Cecil and Daphne Harwood'. Lewis provided us with a portrait of **Cecil Harwood*** in **SBJ** XIII. (14) *Arthurian Torso: Containing the Posthumous Fragment of 'The Figure of Arthur' by Charles Williams and A Commentary on the Arthurian Poems of Charles Williams by C.S. Lewis* (1948) is dedicated 'To/ Michal Williams/ without whose permission this book could not/ have been made'. **Michal Williams** was the wife of Charles Williams,* and while part of the book belonged to her anyway, Lewis arranged for her to receive all the royalties from it.

(15) The best-known of all the dedications, found in *The Lion, the Witch and the Wardrobe*, is that to his god-daughter Lucy Barfield, the adopted daughter of Owen Barfield.* Mr Barfield says of **Lucy Barfield** (b. 2 November 1935):

> The question whether Lucy Pevensie was 'named after' Lucy Barfield is one I never put to Lewis. I should have thought the opening words of the Dedication were a sufficiently appropriate answer.
>
> Whether he had her personally in mind in portraying Lucy Pevensie is another matter, and I think the answer must be No; because, although he had very willingly consented to be her Godfather, they saw very little of each other in the latter years of his life. This was due to residential and occupational circumstances and was a matter of great regret to me.
>
> Lucy Barfield was a very lively and happy child – apt for instance to be seen turning somersault-wheels in the garden immediately after a meal. From an early age she showed marked musical taste and ability. After a short-lived ambition to become a ballet dancer, she eventually qualified as a professional teacher of music and was employed for a year or two as such by a well-known Kentish school for girls. But the cruel onset of multiple sclerosis soon obliged her to abandon all idea of living a normal life and she has remained for decades a (now almost) totally disabled patient in a wheel chair.

(16) *Prince Caspian* (1951) is dedicated 'To/ Mary Clare Havard'. **Mary Clare Havard** is the daughter of Dr R.E. 'Humphrey' Havard.* She was born 28 December 1936, and took her BA from St Anne's College, Oxford, in 1958. She is now married to Patrick Sheahan, and they live in London. She wrote on 21 November 1994:

> I was born at the end of 1936, and met Lewis quite often as I was growing up, mainly because we children were occasionally invited to join the Inklings at the 'Bird and Baby' (it was some time before I learnt that it had another name) or at Studley Priory where my father and Jack and friends sometimes went for Sunday lunch. Although rather in awe of Jack because of what seemed to me his immeasurable breadth of learning, I enjoyed these outings, and found his conversation fascinating. He had the gift of talking to children as though their opinions were as valuable and interesting

as those of anybody else, which was all the more refreshing as it was very unusual in those days. He asked me to read the typescript of *The Lion, the Witch and the Wardrobe* and tell him what I thought of it, so I wrote a solemn criticism for him, saying what I liked about it – and what I didn't. One thing I did not like was the presence of a lamppost when the children first arrived in Narnia; I don't suppose I knew the word anachronistic, but that's what I thought it was. I was rather pleased when he explained how the lamppost arrived in Narnia in one of the later books. He dedicated *Prince Caspian* to me as a thank you for doing that. I also wrote a poem and sent it to him, which he sent back to me with his kindly comments.

When I went to university, and later worked in London, I really only heard news of him via my father. I later married and had four children – all of them brought up on the Narnia books of course.

(17) *The Voyage of the 'Dawn Treader'* (1952) is dedicated 'to Geoffrey Corbett'. '**Jeffrey**', as he now spells his name, is the foster son of Owen* and Maud Barfield. He was born in London on 6 June 1940 near the beginning of the War. His mother being unable to provide for him, the Barfields agreed to foster him for a while. When it came time to give him up Mrs Barfield could not bear this, and she turned to Lewis for help. He took over Jeffrey's school fees, thus making it possible for the Barfields to keep him. They lived in Long Crendon, Buckinghamshire, until 1947 when they moved to Uckfield in Sussex. There Jeffrey went to Warren House School at Crowborough, and he remembers meeting Lewis there in 1949. After the family moved to 28 Menelik Road, Hampstead in 1951 he became a pupil at St Mary Town and Country.

Eventually, in 1957, they moved to Hartley, Kent, where the family had two acres of uncultivated land. Jeffrey had by this time become interested in horticulture and, after a year's study (1960), he qualified with a Kent Horticultural Certificate and a certificate from the Royal Horticultural Society. He worked in landscaping until 1976, after which he turned to metal fabrication welding.

'Soon after he came to us,' Owen Barfield writes, 'he was baptized in the Church of England and was brought up accordingly. In 1962 or thereabouts, following on a close relation he had developed with some neighbours, he became deeply attached to a congregation with an evangelical or pentecostal emphasis and his work and his association with them became his principal interest in life. He has preached in a number of evangelical churches and has received letters addressed to

"Pastor Barfield". Upon his attaining his majority I suggested his changing his name. He was at first opposed to it but by 1962 he had changed his mind and the switch to Barfield was duly effected.' In 1969 the Barfields moved to 'Orchard View' in Dartford, Kent, and from 1976 until 1988 Jeffrey owned and operated his own business. During all these years during which Jeffrey lived with his parents, he was indispensable to them. Mrs Barfield died in 1980, and in 1986 Owen Barfield moved to Forest Row. Jeffrey now lives in Gravesend, Kent. The name **Geoffrey Barfield** has now replaced his original name in copies of *The Voyage of the 'Dawn Treader'*.

(18) *The Silver Chair* (1953) is dedicated 'To/ Nicholas Hardie'. He was born on 12 November 1945, and is the eldest son of Colin Hardie.* He was educated at Magdalen College School and Balliol College. After receiving his BA in 1970 he did an MBA from Lancaster University. In 1971 he married Jane Howe.

(19) *The Horse and His Boy* (1954) is dedicated 'to **David and Douglas Gresham**'. David Gresham* and Douglas Gresham* are the sons of William Lindsay Gresham and Joy Gresham.* (20) *The Magician's Nephew* (1955) is dedicated 'To/ The Kilmer Family'. In 1950 Mr and Mrs Kilmer of Washington, D.C. put their friend Mary Willis Shelburne, also of Washington, D.C., in touch with Lewis. Out of this grew a correspondence that has been published as *Letters to an American Lady*. Running side by side with this correspondence was one with the Kilmer family, which began in 1954 when Mrs Shelburne sent Lewis a bundle of letters and pictures 'from the eight children of Mr and Mrs Kilmer'. Many of Lewis's letters to these children are found in *Letters to Children*. Replying to them on 24 January 1954 Lewis began:

> Dear Hugh, Anne, Noelie (There is a name I never heard before; what language is it, and does it rhyme with *oily* or *mealy* or *Kelly* or *early* or *truly*?), Nicholas, Martin, Rosamund, Matthew, and Miriam ...
>
> You *are* a fine big family! I should think your mother sometimes feels like the Old-Woman-who-lived-in-a-Shoe (you know that rhyme?). I'm so glad you like the books. The next one, *The Horse and His Boy*, will be out quite soon. There are to be seven altogether.

(21) *Surprised by Joy* (1955) is dedicated 'To/ Dom Bede Griffiths, OSB'. **Dom Bede Griffiths OSB*** was Lewis's pupil at Magdalen College.‡ (22) *Till We Have Faces: A Myth Retold* (1956) is dedicated 'To/ Joy Davidman'.* This is Lewis's wife.

(23) *Reflections on the Psalms* (1958) is dedicated 'To/ Austin and Katharine/ Farrer'. **Austin Farrer*** was a distinguished philosopher, theologian and biblical scholar. His wife, **Katharine Farrer*** was a novelist. (24) *The Four Loves* (1960) is dedicated 'To/ Chad Walsh'. **Chad Walsh*** did much to make Lewis known in America.

(25) *Studies in Words* (1960) is dedicated 'To/ Stanley and/ Joan Bennett'. Lewis had known them from the 1930s, and during his years in Cambridge he was a frequent visitor at their home. **Stanley Bennett** (1889–1972) trained as a teacher in Chelsea, and was an elementary schoolmaster 1909–15. During the War he served with the 22nd London Regiment in France. A severe wound led to the amputation of his right foot, and on leaving the army in 1918 he entered Emmanuel College, Cambridge, where he read the English tripos. He was elected a Fellow of Emmanuel in 1933, and he served for twenty-five years as Librarian to the College. His many scholarly works include *Life on the English Manor* (1937), the first part of Vol. II of the *Oxford History of English Literature* (1947), *English Books and Readers 1475–1557* (1952) and *Six Medieval Men and Women* (1955). **Joan Bennett** (1896–1986) was born in London, the daughter of Arthur Frankau and his wife Julia, who enjoyed great popularity in her day as the novelist Frank Danby. Gilbert Frankau, the novelist, was Joan's brother. In 1920 she married Stanley Bennett, and they had one son and three daughters. Joan Bennett was a Fellow of Girton College, Cambridge, and a Lecturer in English at Cambridge University 1936–64. Her contributions to the study of seventeenth-century literature and of George Eliot are highly respected. Her works include *Sir Thomas Browne* (1962) and *Five Metaphysical Poets* (1965). See *The Times* (22 July 1986), p. 14.

(26) *The Discarded Image: An Introduction to Medieval and Renaissance Literature* (1964) is dedicated 'To/ Roger Lancelyn Green'. **Roger Lancelyn Green*** heard these lectures given in the English School at Oxford.

Documentary Film of C.S. Lewis: A three-part documentary film of Lewis's life, *Through Joy and Beyond*, was made by Lord & King Associates of West Chicago, Illinois, in 1978. The film is directed by Bob O'Donnell, with Peter Ustinov as the voice of C.S. Lewis. The script was written by Walter Hooper and Anthony Marchington, and the film is narrated by Walter Hooper. *Through Joy and Beyond* was filmed in Magdalen College and other places in Oxford, as well as in Lewis's boyhood home in Belfast. The documentary is in three one-hour parts; the first two parts cover Lewis's life, while Part III, entitled 'Jack

Remembered', consists of interviews with Owen Barfield,* Pauline Baynes,* R.E. Havard,* Martin Moynihan,* and John and Priscilla Tolkien. It received its premiere in twenty cities in the United States during the spring of 1979.

Since Lord & King Associates was dissolved, the only part of *Through Joy and Beyond* which is available is a condensed one-hour version of Parts I and II from Bridgestone Management Group, 2091 Las Palmas Drive, Carlsbad, California 92009. Enquiries about the entire film may be addressed to: Bob O'Donnell, 28 W. 120 Robin Lane, West Chicago, Illinois 60185. *Through Joy and Beyond: A Pictorial Biography of C.S. Lewis*, by Walter Hooper (New York: Macmillan, 1982) is based on the documentary.

Don(s): In English universities a 'don' is a head, a fellow or a tutor of a college. The word derives from the Latin *dominus* (lord, or person of distinction).

Dundela Villas (Belfast): C.S. Lewis and his brother Warnie Lewis* were born in one of this now extinct pair of semi-detached houses which used to adjoin a coach house in an area of Belfast known as Dundela. The villas were probably built in the middle of the nineteenth century by Thomas Keown (1860–1935), a Belfast banker who later became an insurance agent.

In 1883 Thomas Keown married Albert Lewis's* elder sister, Sarah Jane 'Jeannie' Lewis, and their first home was Dundela Villas. By the time, however, that Albert Lewis and Flora Hamilton were married in 1894, the Keowns had moved with their family to Duncairn Gardens, and Thomas Keown rented one of the Villas to Albert. Here Albert and Flora Lewis spent the first nine years of their marriage, and here CSL and WHL were born, before the family moved to 'Little Lea'‡ in 1905. After the death of Thomas Keown in 1935, his son Harry sold his half of Dundela Villas. After changing hands a number of times they became derelict and were demolished in 1952. Their place is now covered by Dundela Flats, the address of which is 47 Dundela Avenue, Belfast. Photos in **L** (1st Ed.) and **TJB**.

Eagle and Child (or **'Bird and Babe'** or **'Bird and Baby'**): This is the pub at 49 St Giles, Oxford, where the Inklings‡ met for many years. Although the building is much older, it has been an inn since 1650, when it was named after the family of the Earl of Derby, whose crest was a coronet with an eagle and child. During the early part of the 17th century it and the adjoining house served as a payhouse for the Royalist army in the Civil War. A few years later it was much frequented by the diarist Anthony Wood. During the years 1939–62 it was the regular meeting place of the Inklings. The pub was licensed to Charles Blagrove who permitted the Inklings to meet in the little family parlour ('The Rabbit Room') at the back of the pub, every Tuesday morning.

In this little back room, with its own coal fire, Lewis, Tolkien,* Hugo Dyson,* Charles Williams,* Warren Lewis,* Colin Hardie,* Owen Barfield,* 'Humphrey' Havard* and others sat over a pint or two of bitter or cider from about 11.30 a.m. to 1.00. Here they read the proofs of *The Lion, the Witch and the Wardrobe*, and here they discussed Tolkien's *Lord of the Rings* as it was being written. In 1962 the Inklings transferred their meetings across St Giles to the Lamb and Flag pub.‡ A major renovation took place in 1984 when the pub was extended. However, the Rabbit Room is much as it was and contains a plaque to the Inklings as well as other memorials. There are references to it in **BF** and **LJRRT**.

English Language and Literature: This is the school or course that Lewis read in 1922–23. It involves the literary and the linguistic. Candidates are required to show knowledge of the English language at all periods. The philological study is divided into three periods: Old English, Middle English and Modern English Philology. There is also a paper called Modern English which covers an historical knowledge of English from c. 1400 to the present time, especially of grammar, idiom and vocabulary. The literary part begins with such Old English texts as *Beowulf* and follows on with Middle English texts up to Chaucer. English literature from 1400 to 1900 is set without prescribed authors. Shakespeare and contemporary English dramatists form a subject by itself. There is also a general paper of critical questions about English Literature. This is one of the Final Honour Schools that normally takes three years to read.

Films: *See* **Shadowlands**,‡ **Television Films of the Chronicles of Narnia**‡ and **Documentary Film of C.S. Lewis**.‡

Great War, The: 'Barfield's conversion to Anthroposophy‡ marked the beginning of what I can only describe as the Great War between him and me,' wrote Lewis. It was never, thank God, a quarrel, though it could have become one in a moment if he had used to me anything like the violence I allowed myself to him. But it was an almost incessant disputation, sometimes by letter and sometimes face to face, which lasted for years. And this Great War was one of the turning points of my life' (**SBJ** XIII).

For a full and excellent account of this see Lionel Adey's *C.S. Lewis's 'Great War' with Owen Barfield*, English Literary Studies No 14 (University of Victoria: 1978). The 'Great War' manuscripts consist of letters written 1925–27, as well as several treatises: (1) *Clivi Hamiltonis Summae Metaphysices contra Anthroposophos* (November 1928) – better known as 'the *Summa*' – by Lewis who was using his pseudonym 'Clive Hamilton'; *Replicit* and *Autem* (1929) by Barfield; *Replies to Objections* and *Note on the Law of Contradiction* (1929) by Lewis; *De Bono et Malo* (1930?) by Lewis; *De Toto et Parte* (1930?) by Barfield; and the unfinished *Commentarium in De Toto et Parte* by Lewis (1931?). See **Anthroposophy**.‡

'Greats': see **Literae Humaniores** and **Schools**.‡

Guardian, The: This was a weekly Anglican religious newspaper founded in 1846 by R.W. Church (1815–90) and others to uphold High Church Tractarian principles – after the *Tracts for the Times* published by the Oxford Movement clergymen, John Henry Newman, E.B. Pusey, John Keble and others 1833–41 – and to show their relevance to the best secular thought. R.W. Church was a defender of the Tractarians and it was his intention to make *The Guardian* an offspring of the Tractarian Movement. Lewis was a subscriber, and it was in the pages of *The Guardian* that *The Screwtape Letters* and *The Great Divorce* first appeared. See **BIBLIOGRAPHY**. It was when *The Guardian* began serializing *Screwtape* in thirty-one instalments, one a week, 2 May–28 November 1941, that Lewis began donating two-thirds of his income to charities. The paper ceased publication in 1951.

Hamilton, Clive: *See* **Pseudonyms**.‡

Holy Trinity Church, Headington Quarry: This was Lewis's parish church, about a mile from **The Kilns**.‡ It was designed by George Gilbert Scott in fifteenth-century style, and it is built of Headington stone. The foundation stone was laid in 1848, and the building was consecrated in 1849. The east-window glass, depicting Christ in Glory, was designed by Ninian Comper and was installed in 1951 as a memorial to those in the parish who fell in the Second World War. In the north aisle there is a brass plate marking where Lewis and his brother always sat. A few feet away is the Narnian Window, decorated with scenes from the Narnian stories and etched on glass by Sally Scott. The Window, dedicated on 2 July 1991, was placed there at the bequest of George and Kathleen Howe in memory of their son and daughter

William and Gillian who died in childhood. Lewis and his brother are buried in the churchyard in a single grave. Mrs Janie King Moore* is buried nearby in the same grave as Alice Hamilton Moore (no relation). Photos of interior and exterior of church, the Lewis brothers' grave and the Rev. R.E. Head* in **IHW**; photo of grave in **TJB**.

Inklings, The: This was an informal group of friends which included Lewis, Warren Lewis,* Owen Barfield,* J.R.R. Tolkien* and others who met weekly from about 1930 to 1949 in Lewis's rooms in Magdalen College to talk, drink and read aloud whatever any of them were writing. There would then be discussion and criticism of the work. Some of the books read aloud by members as they were being written were Lewis's *Screwtape Letters*, Warren Lewis's *The Splendid Century*, J.R.R. Tolkien's *Lord of the Rings*, and Charles Williams's* *All Hallows' Eve*. The same group also met every Tuesday morning in The Eagle and Child‡ or some other Oxford pub from about 1930 up until Lewis's death. When Lewis's former pupil Dom Bede Griffiths* asked who the Inklings were, Lewis replied on 21 December 1941: 'We meet on Friday evenings in my rooms, theoretically to talk about literature, but in fact nearly always to talk about something better. What I owe to them all is incalculable.' (For more details, see the **LIFE** in this volume.)

Most first-hand information about the Inklings is found in Lewis's *Letters, The Letters of J.R.R. Tolkien*, Warren Lewis's *Brothers and Friends*, John Wain's *Sprightly Running*, and Colin Hardie's 'A Colleague's Note on C.S. Lewis' in the *Inklings-Jahrbuch* (1985), and Owen Barfield's 'The Inklings Remembered' in *The World and I* (April 1990).

Humphrey Carpenter's *The Inklings: C.S. Lewis, J.R.R. Tolkien, Charles Williams and their friends* (1978) is the most exhaustive history of the group. An excellent short account is Martin Moynihan's 'The Inklings', in *Litterature* (University of Genoa), No 8 (1985). Also to be recommended is G.B. Tennyson's 'Owen Barfield: First and Last Inkling', in *The World and I* (April 1990). In another piece on The Inklings by G.B. Tennyson entitled 'On Location, Without Tears', in the *California Political Review*, Vol. 5, No 1 (Winter 1994), the author said the Inklings,

in addition to being friends of C.S. Lewis – perhaps *because* of being friends of C.S. Lewis – were something like a literary movement or at least a reasonably coherent literary school that shared not only Lewis's friendship but in their own ways Lewis's dedication to Christianity. This view holds that the writings of the Inklings constitute a congruous body of literature imbued with an imaginative Christian sensibility especially strong in the area of fantasy and fairy-tales ... The Inklings stand for something real and important that speaks to the issues of literature and belief and their relation to the modern world.

Inklings-Gesellschaft (Germany): This society is specially devoted to the study and discussion of the works of C.S. Lewis, J.R.R. Tolkien,* Charles Williams,* Dorothy L. Sayers,* G.K. Chesterton and George MacDonald. It was founded in March 1983 in Aachen by Dr Gisbert Kranz, and it has about 340 members, primarily professors, undergraduates and writers, from all over the world. It publishes an annual, *Inklings-Jahrbuch*, of up to 384 pages in English and in German (with English summaries), and three times a year it publishes a newsletter, *Inklings-Rundbrief*. For members there is *Die Inklings-Bibliothek*, a special collection of 1,400 books, 2,400 articles in periodicals, and 270 holographs by Chesterton, Tolkien, Lewis, Barfield and their friends. Some 300 titles may be lent out, while the rest is a reference library used by scholars doing research on C.S. Lewis or one of the other authors.

The *Inklings-Gesellschaft* has organized, in more than 30 cities, exhibitions with conferences and International Symposia: in 1983 on C.S. Lewis, in 1986 on Charles Williams, in 1992 on Tolkien, and in 1993 on Dorothy L. Sayers. The President is Raimund B. Kern, MA; the Vice-President is Irene Oberdörfer (1993). For information write to: Inklings, c/o Frau Irene Oberdörfer, Wilhelm-Tell-Strasse 3, D-40219 Düsseldorf, Germany. Send books for review to: Dr Gisbert Kranz, Rote-Haag-Weg I 31, D-52076 Aachen, Germany; send papers for inclusion in *Inklings-Jahrbuch* to Herren Christian Rendel, MA, Gartenstrasse 6, D-37213 Witzenhausen, Germany.

Japan C.S. Lewis Society, The: Interest in the writings of C.S. Lewis has built up steadily in Japan over the years. This owes much to Lewis's pupil, Father Peter Milward SJ, who joined the teaching staff of Sophia University, Tokyo, in 1962. Besides reviews of some of Lewis's books, he contributed an article on 'C.S. Lewis on Allegory' to *Eigo Seinen (The Rising Generation)* of April 1958. In 1966 a translation of the Narnian stories by Teiji Seta was published by Iwanami Shoten. This was followed by translations of his scholarly writings, such as Mr Yasuo Tamaizumi's translation of *The Allegory of Love* (1972) and Professor Kazumi Yamagata's translation of *An Experiment in Criticism* (1968). It is worthy of note that in 1985 Father Milward's pupil, Sister Setsuo Nakao ACJ was awarded the degree of Ph.D. from the Sophia Faculty of Literature for her thesis on 'The Theme of Salvation in the Fiction of C.S. Lewis'. Sister Setsuko is now President of Seisen Women's College, Tokyo. For more on these early years see Father Milward's 'G.K. Chesterton and C.S. Lewis in Japan', *Inklings-Jahrbuch*, 6 (1988), pp. 165–74.

The Japan C.S. Lewis Society was founded on 2 November 1985 by Professor Kazumi Yamagata (Tsukuba University), with the collaboration of Father Peter Milward SJ. At this inaugural meeting at the Sacred Heart University in Tokyo, Father Milward gave a lecture on 'Memories of C.S. Lewis'. It has since been published as 'A Jesuit Remembers Lewis' in *The Chesterton Review*, vol. XVII, Nos 3 and 4 (August, November 1991), pp. 385–8. The Society holds workshops two or three times a year, and its membership in 1995 was 77. Besides their annual *Japan C.S. Lewis Newsletter* (Vols 1–8) in Japanese, they have published *C.S. Lewis no Sekai (The World of C.S. Lewis)*, ed. Kazumi Yamagata (1983); second, revised and enlarged edition, 1988, and *A Readers' Guide to the Chronicles of Narnia* (in Japanese, with co-operation of several members) (1988); revised and enlarged edition forthcoming. The Secretary of The Japan C.S. Lewis Society is Professor Kazuo Takeno, Faculty of Humanities, Keisen Women's College, 8-10-1 Minamino, Tama-shi, Tokyo 206, Japan. Many Japanese translations of Lewis's writings are found in the Bodleian Library.‡

Kilns, The: This was Lewis's home in Oxford. The original house was built in 1922, probably for those who operated the brick kilns adjoining it. Lewis and his brother Warnie first saw it on 6 July 1930. Warnie wrote in his diary: 'We did not go inside the house, but the eight-acre garden is such stuff as dreams are made of. I never imagined that for us any such garden would ever come within the sphere of discussion. The house ... stands at the entrance to its own grounds at the northern foot of Shotover at the end of a narrow lane, which in turn opens off a very bad and little used road, giving as great privacy as can reasonably be looked for near a large town: to the left of the house are the two brick kilns from which it takes its name – in front, a lawn and hard tennis court – then a large bathing pool, beautifully wooded, and with a delightful circular brick seat overlooking it: after that a steep wilderness broken with ravines and nooks of all kinds runs up to a little cliff topped by a thistly meadow: and then the property ends in a thick belt of fir trees, almost a wood: the view from the cliff over the dim blue distance of the plain is simply glorious ... we want to build on two more rooms' (**BF** 7 July 1930; **BF** also contains photos of The Kilns from Shotover Hill as it looked in 1930).

The Kilns was bought for £3,300, Mrs Janie Moore* being the nominal owner, but with a settlement whereby it would be the Lewis brothers' home for the rest of their lives, after which it would pass to Mrs Moore's daughter. They moved into The Kilns on 11 October 1931, and for all it seemed a dream come true. 'Oh!' said Lewis writing to Arthur Greeves,* 'I never hoped for the like' (TST 29 October 1930).

In October 1931 Warren left for a second tour of duty in China. When he returned in December 1932 the family had built two additional rooms to the ground floor of The Kilns. They extend from the back of the left side of the house (if you are facing it), and consist of a study and a bedroom for Warnie. After Lewis's death the brick kilns, sheds and Fred Paxford's* bungalow were demolished, and in 1968 a number of houses were built in the grounds of the house, thus destroying the rustic beauty it once had. In 1969 the 7½ acres of woodlands, and the pond, north of the house were acquired by the Berkshire, Buckinghamshire and Oxfordshire Naturalists' Trust and made into the 'Henry Stephen/C.S. Lewis Nature Reserve'. The Kilns was acquired by the **C.S. Lewis Foundation** of Redlands, California, in 1984. The Director of the Foundation, Dr Stanley Mattson, began a restoration of the house in 1993.

Kolbítar (or Coalbiters, a term which means 'men who lounge so close to the fire in winter that they bite the coal'): This society was founded in Oxford University by J.R.R. Tolkien* in the Michaelmas Term of 1926, for the purposes of reading the Icelandic sagas and myths in the original Old Icelandic or Old Norse. Tolkien felt that Old Icelandic deserved a prominent place among early and medieval studies, and when he became the Professor of Anglo-Saxon at Oxford in 1925 he introduced a class in 'Old Icelandic Texts'. At the same time he founded the Kolbítar. The original members, all of whom were dons,‡ included R.M. Dawkins (Professor of Byzantine and Modern Greek), C.T. Onions (of the Oxford Dictionary), G.E.K. Braunholz (Professor of Comparative Philology) and John Frazer (Professor of Celtic). These men were able to read Old Icelandic, but they were soon joined by a few dons who could not. These last included John Bryson (Fellow of English in Balliol College), Nevill Coghill* (Fellow of English in Exeter College) and Lewis, who became a member in 1927. Tolkien knew the language well, and after translating perhaps a dozen pages, those with a working knowledge of Old Icelandic would translate a page or two, followed by the beginners who would attempt to translate a paragraph or so.

Lewis was such a beginner, and in his diary of 8 February 1927 he said: 'Spent the morning partly on the *Edda* ... Hammered my way through a couple of pages in about an hour, but I am making some headway. It is an exciting experience, when I remember my first passion for things Norse under the initiation of Longfellow (Tegner's *Drapa* and *Saga of K. Olaf*) at about the age of 9: and its return much stronger when I was about 13, when the high priests were M. Arnold, Wagner's music, and the Arthur Rackham *Ring*. It seemed impossible then that I should ever come to read these things in the original. The old authentic thrill came back to me once or twice this morning: the mere names of god and giant catching my eye as I turned the pages of Zoega's dictionary was enough' (**AMR**).

Lamb and Flag: This pub is located at 12 St Giles, Oxford, and is directly across the road from **The Eagle and Child**.‡ Its name is taken from the badge of St John's College, who bought the property from Godstow Abbey and opened it as an inn around 1695. In 1962, when the inner parlour of the 'Eagle and Child' was opened to the public and joined on to the main bar, the Inklings migrated to the front room of the 'Lamb and Flag' where they had more privacy. The pub has been much modernized since Lewis died.

Lamp-Post, The: This is the quarterly publication of the Southern California C.S. Lewis Society which was founded by Paul F. Ford in 1974. The journal began publication in January 1977 and contains articles, book reviews, news and letters. The editor since 1992 has been James Prothero. For information write to: *The Lamp-Post*, The Southern California C.S. Lewis Society, P.O. Box 533, Pasadena, CA 91102, USA. Society meetings are on the third Wednesday of each month except July, August and December, at 7.30 p.m. in the Faculty Common Room at Fuller Theological Seminary in Pasadena. The members meet for a week every summer at St Andrew's Abbey in Valyermo, CA.

Lenten Lands: My Childhood with Joy Davidman and C.S. Lewis, by Lewis's step-son, Douglas Gresham,* was published by Macmillan Publishing Company, New York, and Collins Publishers, London, in 1988. It is of a significance with *Brothers and Friends: The Diaries of Major Warren Hamilton Lewis*, being a first-hand account of life with Joy Davidman* and Lewis. It is remarkable that the author could endure such concentrated suffering – his mother, his father, and Lewis died within three years of one another – and yet remain sunny in disposition, and blessed with an uncanny memory for what was best and most intimate about Lewis and the other inhabitants of The Kilns.‡ The very tone of these valuable reminiscences explains why Lewis said to a friend on 30 August 1960:

'Douglas ... is, as always, an absolute brick, and a very bright spot in my life' (L).

Lewis Papers, The: These are eleven bound volumes of typescript compiled by W.H. Lewis* 1933–35. The volumes are actually titled 'Memoirs of the Lewis Family: 1850–1930' and they contain the diaries, letters and other family mementoes of the Lewis family up to 1930. They provide a detailed account of the early history of Albert,* Warnie and Jack Lewis. The original is in the Marion E. Wade Center,‡ and they are on microfilm in the Bodleian Library‡ and the Southern Historical Collection‡ in Chapel Hill, North Carolina.

Library of C.S. Lewis: From the time he bought The Kilns‡ in 1930 and up until he retired from Magdalene College‡ in August 1963, Lewis's library was spread between his home and his college rooms. Even then he never had enough shelf space, and now and then he sold books he could do without. Following his retirement from Cambridge he found it necessary to sell a good many of his books because The Kilns was not large enough to hold them. Amongst those he parted with were St Thomas Aquinas' *Summa Theologica* and bound sets of *Medium Aevum* and *Essays in Criticism*. Lewis gave his Temple Edition of Shakespeare to Magdalene College.

At his death he left his library of about 3000 volumes to his brother, W.H. Lewis,* but with the request that his Trustees, Owen Barfield* and Cecil Harwood* be allowed 'to take such of the said books as they wish unless he wants them for his own use, and in making this request I have chiefly in mind my Greek and Latin and medieval and philosophical books.' After Warren Lewis had decided which books he would keep, he invited several other friends, notably George Sayer* and J.A.W. Bennett,* to choose a memento from the library. J.A.W. Bennett wrote in *The Humane Medievalist* (1965), 'Given the choice of a book from Lewis's library, and foiled in my search for his *Bernardus Silvestris*, I lighted on his annotated copy of ... Newman's *History of my religious opinions*' [*Apologia Pro Vita Sua*, Oxford ed., 1913].

The rest of the books were sold to B.H. Blackwell Booksellers. Walter Hooper bought about 200 of them, and the remaining 2710 volumes were sold to Wroxton College, Banbury, a few miles from Oxford. (Wroxton College is a branch of Fairleigh Dickinson University of Rutherford, New Jersey.) Walter Hooper gave 176 of the volumes he bought to the Southern Historical Collection‡ of the University of North Carolina at Chapel Hill and a number of others to the Bodleian Library.‡

During the time the remainder of the library was at Wroxton College, they were catalogued by Margaret Anne Rogers for her thesis 'C.S. Lewis: A Living Library' (Fairleigh Dickinson University). Unfortunately, there was a security problem at Wroxton College and a number of the books were stolen. They eventually decided to sell the library and it was bought for the Wade Center‡ of Wheaton College. By the time Lewis's Library reached the Wade Center, where it is now housed, it consisted of 2,363 volumes.

Literae Humaniores ('Greats'): This is the study of the Classics, Philosophy and Ancient History. It is the first and the most celebrated of the arts courses at Oxford, and it differs from most of the other schools in being a four-year course. Midway in their second year students take their First Public Examination in what is called **Classical Honour Moderations** or '**Mods**'. This is an examination in Latin and Greek, and it includes (i) unseen translation from Latin and Greek into English; (ii) 'prose composition', which is rendering passages of English prose into Latin or Greek – not just any Latin or Greek, but the authentic style of the great classical authors; (iii) the works of Homer and Virgil, and a number of the great classical writers, poets, orators and historians. Some of the works of these authors have to be studied textually with great care; and (iv) there are special subjects, such as Deductive Logic, Greek Literary Criticism, etc., one of which may be chosen at the option of the candidate. Classical Honour Moderations is meant as the completion of the classical studies which the student began at school, and it is meant to prepare him for the Final Honour School.

Final Honour School, which is what is usually called 'Greats', is the second part of *Literae Humaniores*. It is a combined school of history and philosophy. The student is required to study the Greek or Latin historians and philosophers in the original. It involves a very deep enquiry into the nature of Greek and Roman civilization through the minds of its greatest writers. The historical studies involve about three centuries of Greek history and a longer period of Roman history. The latest date to which a candidate may go is the death of the Emperor Trajan in AD 117. The philosophy is based on Plato and Aristotle, and especially Plato's *Republic* and Aristotle's *Ethics*. To this is added the study of modern philosophy from Descartes onwards, which is examined in a paper on Logic and Moral Philosophy. The purpose of this school is to develop 'accurate thought and speech and a keen and critical intellect'.

Lewis began reading Classical Honour Moderations in April 1917, but stopped to serve in the Army. He began again in January 1919, and took

Schools (= examinations) in March 1920. He began reading the Final Honour School or Greats in April 1920 and he took Schools in June 1922. See **Schools**.‡

Little Lea (Belfast): This was the Lewis family home from 1905–30. It is located at 76 Circular Road, Strandtown, Belfast. Albert Lewis had it built, and the family spent their first night there on 21 April 1905. Jack and Warnie loved it. 'The New House,' Lewis wrote, 'is almost a major character in my story. I am a product of long corridors, empty sunlit rooms, upstairs indoor silences, attics explored in solitude, distant noises of gurgling cisterns and pipes, and the noise of wind under the tiles ... I soon staked out a claim to one of the attics and made it "my study"' (**SBJ** I).

In the first of Lewis's surviving notebooks there is a floor plan he drew of the house in 1906, and this shows the location of the principal rooms. He did not mark it in the plan, but his 'study', which came to be called 'the little end room', is the one to the right of the 'servants' room' with Jack's and Warnie's bedroom just below. Warnie was in China when Albert Lewis died on 25 September 1929, but after his return he and Jack made one final visit there. On 23 April 1930 Jack and Warnie packed their Boxen toys into a box and buried it in the garden of Little Lea. They spent their last night there on 24 April (see **BF** 23–24 April 1930). In 1978 the house was bought by Denis Rogers, who has done much to restore it. On the outside of the house is a plaque commemorating C.S. Lewis. For further information see **SBJ**, **Memoir**, and **BF**. Photos in **LP**, **IHW**, **B** (2nd ed.), **TJB** (photos inside and outside), **BF**, **J** and **AMR**.

Magdalen College (Oxford): Lewis was a Fellow of this college 1925–54. It is the College of St Mary Magdalen, but the college retains its 15th-century pronunciation, 'Maudele'n'. It was founded by William of Waynflete in 1458 and work on the building began in 1474 under Magdalen's first President, William Tybard. By 1480–1 the Chapel, Hall, Founder's Tower and much of the Cloisters had been erected under the second President, Richard Mayew. His abiding monument is the Great Tower which was commenced in 1492 and completed in 1505. In 1491 William Grocyn, Divinity Reader at Magdalen, gave the first lectures in Greek in Oxford. One of the college Fellows promoted to the episcopate was Thomas Wolsey (?1475–1530), Lord Chancellor under Henry VIII and founder of Christ Church. Unfortunately, Magdalen fared much worse than University College‡ during the Reformation, which purged the Chapel of its medieval furnishings and vestments. What Lewis used to see in Chapel, and the visitor still sees today, is the interior as it was restored in 1828–35. The altarpiece, Christ carrying the Cross, is attributed to Valdés Leal. There is a brass commemorating Lewis in the ante-chapel.

Lewis became a Fellow of Magdalen in 1925 and lived in Rooms 3 on Staircase 3 of 'New Buildings', the construction of which began in 1733. These rooms – which are not open to the public – look north into a deer park, and south to the Great Tower. 'My external surroundings are beautiful beyond expectation and beyond hope,' he wrote to his father* on 21 October 1925 (L). During the times visitors are permitted, they may enjoy the completely unspoiled Addison's Walk,‡ which runs alongside the Cherwell and New Buildings. The College owns a bronze bust of Lewis sculpted by Faith Tolkien.

Magdalene College (Cambridge): Lewis became a Fellow of this College upon his becoming the Professor of Medieval and Renaissance English at Cambridge in 1954. It was founded by the Benedictine Order. In 1428 Abbot Lytlington of Crowland Abbey near Peterborough was licensed to acquire the site north of the River Cam so that a hostel could be established in Cambridge for student monks of the Benedictine Order. It became known as Monk's Hostel. Between 1470 and 1472 Henry Stafford, second Duke of Buckingham, collaborated with John de Wisbech, Abbot of Crowland, in planning the First Court and building the Chapel. After this individual Benedictine abbeys were each allowed to build a staircase for their student monks, and these were constructed between 1472 and 1483. As a result of the Duke's patronage the name of the institution was changed from Monk's Hostel to Buckingham College.

The next most important development was in 1519 when Edward Stafford, third Duke of Buckingham, built the Hall. This was followed by Henry VIII's Dissolution of the Monasteries in 1536 and 1539, but although Crowland Abbey was destroyed the College somehow managed to remain open. Following the Reformation some of the Benedictine abbeys involved in the College came into the possession of Thomas, Lord Audley. Audley had, as Lord Chancellor, presided over the trials of Sir Thomas More and Anne Boleyn, and he helped Henry VIII to get rid of two more wives, as well as Thomas Cromwell. He refounded Buckingham College as the College of St Mary Magdalene in 1542. From that time the name of the College was pronounced 'maudele'n' (just as the one in Oxford is). When Audley died in 1544 the College was inadequately endowed and struggling with extreme poverty.

The College afterwards went through many years of mismanagement which caused the rest of the College to be built very slowly. The Pepys

Building, the principal ornament of the College, took fifty years to build and was not finished until after 1700. It is named after the great diarist Samuel Pepys who gave his library to the College. The fortunes of the College improved greatly under one of its most famous Masters, A.C. Benson. He was a Fellow there from 1904 and the Master from 1915 to 1925. Many more improvements were made between 1950 and 1970. First Court, the oldest part of the College which you walk into from the street, was built from about 1470 to about 1585.

The beautiful rooms Lewis occupied in the 'North range' of First Court are on the second floor of Staircase 3. These rooms are not open to the public, but one can usually visit the little fifteenth-century Chapel where Lewis attended services and where he preached **A Slip of the Tongue** at Evensong on 29 January 1956. Directly across the street from the main gate of the College is 'The Pickerel Inn' where Lewis often stopped for a pint. The best overall picture of Lewis in Cambridge is the essay 'In Cambridge' (**ABT**) by Richard Ladborough.*

Malvern College (Malvern, Worcestershire): This is one of the finest public schools in England, and it stands only a short distance from Cherbourg House.‡ Lewis came here directly from Cherbourg House in 1912, and in **SBJ** VI and VII, where he describes his time here, he gives it the name 'Wyvern'. The College was founded in 1863, and next to the medieval Priory, the buildings of Malvern College are the most striking architectural feature of the area. They were built in the beautiful Malvern Hills and they command a grand view of the Severn Valley. Most of the buildings date from 1863, although the Chapel was built in 1897 to the designs of Sir Arthur Blomfield, and is very handsome. Then, in July 1936 the college decided to increase the accommodation for modern scientific teaching and the science laboratories date from that time. On the occasion of the college's centenary George Sayer* edited *Age Frater: A Portrait of a School* (1965) which contains many photographs.

Warren Lewis had come direct from Wynyard House‡ and was here from 1909 to 1913. He loved the college very much and wore a Malvern tie most of his life. Jack Lewis arrived here from Cherbourg in September 1913 and left in July 1914. The headmaster at the time was Sydney Rhodes James. In **SBJ** VI and VII Lewis is scathing about what he disliked about Malvern. On the positive side he lists the 'Grundy', the college library, and the English master whom he called 'Smewgy' but whose name was Harry Wakelyn Smith (1861–1918). From Malvern Lewis went for private tuition to W.T. Kirkpatrick.* For information about Malvern at the time the Lewis brothers were there, see Sydney Rhodes James, *Seventy Years:*

Random Reminiscences and Reflections (1926), and George Sayer,* *Jack* (1988, 2nd ed. 1994).

Martlets, The: This is a literary society founded in University College‡ in 1892. Lewis became a member in January 1919, and writing to his father on 4 February he said: 'I have had "greatness thrust upon me". There is a literary club in College called the Martlets, limited to twelve undergraduate members ... I have been elected Secretary ... And so if I am forgotten of all else, at least a specimen of my handwriting will be preserved' (**L**). He became a very active member after this, becoming President of the Martlets in October 1919. Some of his most interesting literary ideas (William Morris, narrative poetry, Spenser, the Personal Heresy) were worked out in the papers he read to this society.

The many well-known figures who have read papers to the Martlets include Maurice Bowra, Nevill Coghill,* R.G. Collingwood, Ronald Knox, Edward Tangye Lean,* Sir Michael Sadleir and Charles Williams.* The minute books of the Martlets are in the Bodleian Library.‡ Lewis's pupil, Peter Bayley, has an essay on 'The Martlets' in the *University College Record* (1949–50). Walter Hooper's essay on 'To the Martlets', in *C.S. Lewis: Speaker and Teacher*, ed. Carolyn Keefe (1971), contains extracts from the minute books about Lewis's talks to the society.

'Mesopotamia': The name, from Greek, means 'between the rivers', and originally referred to the district between the Rivers Euphrates and Tigris, now part of Iraq. In Oxford it refers to a narrow strip of land between the River Cherwell on one side and a branch of the Cherwell on the other. There is a path of about three-quarters of a mile running along the bank of the river, beautifully shaded by trees. In the summer long, narrow boats called Punts are used on the Cherwell. Lewis loved punting and swimming in the Cherwell and he writes about it in **TST** and **AMR**. See **Parson's Pleasure**.‡

Mythopoeic Society: This society describes itself as an 'international literary and educational organization devoted to the study, discussion, and enjoyment of the works of J.R.R. Tolkien,* C.S. Lewis and Charles Williams*. It believes these writers can be more completely understood and appreciated by studying the realm of myth; the genres of fantasy; and the literary, philosophical, and spiritual traditions which underlie their works, and from which they have drawn and enriched.'

It was founded in 1967 by Glen H. GoodKnight, and from its first meeting in Southern California it has grown to be an international organization. Its first annual Mythopoeic Conference was held in 1971. In 1972 the Tolkien Society of America merged with it. The Society publishes a monthly newsletter, *Mythprint*, and since 1969 it has published a quarterly journal called *Mythlore: A Journal of J.R.R. Tolkien, C.S. Lewis, Charles Williams and the Genres of Myth and Fantasy Studies*. For information write to: *Mythlore* (or *Mythprint*), P.O. Box 6707, Altadena, California 91003, USA. Copies of both periodicals are found in the Bodleian,‡ the Wade Center‡ and a number of other libraries.

Narnian Stories on Television: *See* **Television Films of The Chronicles of Narnia.**‡

'Nat Whilk' and **'N.W.':** *See* Pseudonyms.‡

New York C.S. Lewis Society: This was the first formal group devoted to Lewis's writings, and the largest. The Society has members throughout the English-speaking world, most of them living far from New York. The earliest members were those who responded to a letter from Henry Noel that appeared in the *National Review* (23 September 1969). From this beginning a Society was founded by him, and its first meeting was on 1 November 1969. The group has been meeting in Manhattan on the second Friday of each month (except August) since then. The Society has been publishing a monthly bulletin, *CSL*, since November 1969, and over the years its editors have been: Henry Noel 1969–74; Eugene McGovern 1974–81; Jerry L. Daniel 1981–91; James Como 1991– . For much of its history, the Society owed most to Hope Kirkpatrick.

A number of authors well-known for their works on Lewis have spoken at the Society's meetings, and several of the essays in *C.S. Lewis at the Breakfast Table*, ed. James T. Como (1979) were first published in **CSL**. The Society focuses closely on Lewis's writings, giving little attention to other writers; his Christian works receive the most attention, but the Society is not a religious group. Meetings are presently held at 7.45 p.m. on the second Friday of the month (excluding August) at The Church of the Ascension, 12 West 11th Street, Manhattan, New York. For information write to: Clara Sarrocco, 84-23 77th Avenue, Glendale, New York 11385, USA. Copies of **CSL** are in the Bodleian‡ and Wade Center.‡

Oxford University C.S. Lewis Society: This society was founded on 8 January 1982 by Gregory Wolfe of Mansfield College. Gregory Wolfe was elected President, Suzanne Pierce was elected Treasurer, and Jeffrey Steenson of Christ Church became the first Secretary. All Oxford clubs must be supported by a Senior Member of the University, and during the first year the Senior Member of the Society was the Precentor of Christ Church Cathedral, the Rev. Peter Bide.* In his 'Notes towards the Definition of a C.S. Lewis Society', Wolfe said:

> Lewis, of course, would smile at the thought of a university society bearing his name – he might even worry that such a society would commit the 'personal heresy' and concentrate on him. But the purpose of the CSL Society we have in mind is broader: the name 'C.S. Lewis' is an important indication of what the society will be like, for like Dr Johnson, Lewis was a focus of an intellectual world. The Society would thus be interested not in Lewis as a man so much as the world Lewis inhabited and the intellectual and spiritual colleagues and fellow travellers he knew or admired. These latter include Tolkien, Williams, Sayers, MacDonald, Chesterton, Eliot, Barfield, and others.

The first public meeting was held in Christ Church on 3 February 1982 at 8.15 p.m. On that occasion there was a reading of Lewis's then unpublished essay on **Modern Man and his Categories of Thought**, now found in Lewis's *Present Concerns* (1986). In 1983 the Society moved to Pusey House in St Giles, where there are meetings in the Frederic Hood Room every Tuesday during Term at 8.15 p.m.

The Society attempts to have talks on several of the authors mentioned above nearly every term. Following the meetings, the speaker is taken to the 'Eagle and Child' pub‡ for refreshments. The Society preserves audiotapes of the talks given at the meetings. To honour the twentieth anniversary of Lewis's death it published a hundred copies of an unpublished *jeu d'esprit* between Owen Barfield* and Lewis entitled *A Cretaceous Perambulator (The Re-examination of)* (1983). In 1990 the Society reprinted a hundred copies of another lark, *Mark vs. Tristram: Correspondence between C.S. Lewis and Owen Barfield*, first published at Harvard in 1967, but this time with illustrations by Pauline Baynes.* Copies in the Bodleian‡ and the Wade Center.‡

Parson's Pleasure: A bathing place for men on the River Cherwell much enjoyed by Lewis, but now turned into a park. It lay north of Magdalen College, where two branches of the Cherwell come together to form the area known as 'Mesopotamia'‡ after the ancient country between the Tigris and the Euphrates. It was known as 'Patten's Pleasure' in the 17th century, and as 'Loggerhead' in the 19th century, and it seems to have acquired the name Parson's Pleasure no earlier than this century. It was always used for men bathing and sunbathing in the nude, and it was customary for ladies to disembark from their punts before reaching Parson's Pleasure and walk around to a series of metal rollers where they could pick them up again.

'Some kind friend lent me a bicycle and thus we set out,' Lewis wrote to Arthur Greeves* on 13 May 1917. 'It was a perfectly lovely morning with a deep blue sky, all the towers and pinnacles gleaming in the sun and bells ringing everywhere. We passed down through quieter streets among colleges and gardens to the river, and after about quarter of an hour's ride along the bank came to the bathing places. Here, without the tiresome convention of bathing things, we enjoyed a swim' (**TST**). There are references to Parson's Pleasure in **AMR**. See the drawing on p. 44 of **TJB**. See **Punting.‡**

Pseudonyms: Lewis used a variety of pseudonyms over the years. (1) The first was **Clive Hamilton**, under which name he published his first book, *Spirits in Bondage*, in 1919. This is a combination of his own first name – Clive – and his mother's family name. 'Clive Hamilton' was also used for the poem, 'Death in Battle', taken from *Spirits in Bondage* and published in *Reveille*, No 3 (February 1919), and for the poem, 'Joy', published in *The Beacon*, III, No 31 (May 1924). It was last used for his long narrative poem *Dymer* (1926).

(2) A pseudonym first used in 1936 for a poem, 'The Shortest Way Home' in *The Oxford Magazine* (19 May 1934) was **Nat Whilk** or **N.W.** This is Anglo-Saxon for 'I know not whom'. He used the name, or the initials, for all the poems he published in *Punch*. In *Perelandra* (I, fn.1) he cites a non-existent work by 'Nativilcius', which is Latin for Nat Whilk.

(3) The third pseudonym was **N.W. Clerk** which he used for *A Grief Observed* (1961). Although the grief in the title is his grief for his own wife, Lewis wanted the book to have a wide application, and for this reason he decided to publish under a pseudonym. He first took the name 'Dimidius' (= Half), and he had his agents, Curtis Brown Ltd, send the book to Faber and Faber, where it was read by T.S. Eliot* and his wife. In a letter to Spencer Curtis Brown of 20 October 1960 Eliot said he could guess who the author was, and that if he really wanted anonymity a 'plausible English pseudonym would hold off enquirers better than Dimidius'. Lewis had used the initials 'N.W.' before, and, as he said to a friend, 'because I am by medieval standards a "clerk", they came together as 'N.W. Clerk'.

Punting: A punt is a long, narrow boat native to the River Thames. It is square-ended and handled with a long pole with which you propel the craft. Punting on the River Cherwell is very popular in Oxford. There is a photo of Lewis and Paddy Moore* in a punt on p. 49 of **TJB**, and the photo on p. 59 shows some students punting near Magdalen Bridge.

Recordings of C.S. Lewis: (A) **BBC Recordings:** (1) All but three of the broadcasts that Lewis made over the BBC during 1941–44, and which were later published as *Mere Christianity*, were delivered live. The three recorded on disc were from the last series entitled *Beyond Personality*. However, the only one of these three talks which has survived is the one entitled **The New Man**. It was recorded on 21 March 1944 and is 14'12" long. It was to appear, with various additions and changes, as the last chapter of *Mere Christianity*. (2) Lewis made a recording on 27 February 1948 of the Preface to *The Great Divorce*. It was broadcast on 9 May 1948 and is 1'57" long. (3) A talk on 'Charles Williams' was recorded on 11 February 1949 and broadcast that same day. It is 18'12" long. A text of this talk appears in *Of This and Other Worlds* (=**OS**). (4) 'The Great Divide' is an adaptation made by Lewis of the Inaugural lecture he gave at Cambridge on 29 November 1954 and entitled *De Descriptione Temporum* (**SLE**). It was recorded on 1 April 1955 and broadcast on 6 April. It is 37'10" in length. (5) A talk on John Bunyan's *Pilgrim's Progress* was recorded on 16 October 1962 and broadcast on 11 November 1962. It is 26' long. A text of this talk appears in **SLE**.

(B) **The Episcopal Radio-TV Foundation, Inc. Recordings:** In 1957 the Episcopal Radio-TV Foundation of Atlanta, Georgia, asked Lewis to make some recordings to be played over the air in the United States. Lewis agreed, choosing 'The Four Loves' – Affection, Friendship, Eros and Agape – as his subject. The Foundation's Executive Director, Caroline Rakestraw, met Lewis in London and the recordings were made there on 19–20 August 1958. They were played over a number of radio stations in the United States, and in 1970 the Foundation put them on four cassettes entitled *Four Talks on Love* – later changed to *The Four Loves*. There is an hour's playing time on each cassette. They are available from the Foundation. Lewis used the radio scripts as a basis for his book, *The Four Loves*.

In 1982 the Foundation issued a number of other cassettes: (1) A nine-cassette album of Michael York reading *Mere Christianity*. Included in this album was a cassette containing Lewis's BBC talk on **The New Man**. (2) Three cassettes entitled 'C.S. Lewis: Comments and Critiques' which contain all the other BBC broadcasts listed under the **BBC** above. One cassette contains the Preface to *The Great Divorce* and the talk on 'Charles Williams', a second contains 'The Great Divide'; and a third contains the talk on John Bunyan's *Pilgrim's Progress*. The album of Michael York's reading of *Mere Christianity* is no longer available, but *The Four Loves* and the three cassettes of 'C.S. Lewis: Comments and Critiques' are available from The Episcopal Radio-TV Foundation, Inc., 3379 Peachtree Road, N.E., Atlanta, Georgia 30326, USA. Telephone (404) 233-5419; Fax (404) 233-3597.

Recordings of the 'Chronicles of Narnia': I: Radio Dramatizations: (1) **Lance Sieveking's Dramatization.** The first performance over radio was a dramatization of *The Lion, the Witch and the Wardrobe* by Lance Sieveking. This was the only dramatization approved by Lewis, who first met Sieveking on 5 September 1957 to discuss the idea. The play was broadcast over the BBC Home Service's 'Children's Hour' in six 40-minute parts on successive Friday evenings at 5.15 to 5.55 from 18 September to 23 October 1959. The play was produced by David Davis, and the part of Peter was played by Glyn Dearman; Susan by Carol Marsh; Edmund by Jean England; Lucy by Ann Totten; Mr Tumnus by Preston Lockwood; the White Witch by Jill Balcon, and Aslan by Deryck Guyler.

(2) **Brian Sibley Dramatizations.** The following dramatizations by Brian Sibley were produced by Geoffrey Taylor-Marshall, directed by John Taylor, and produced on cassettes by the BBC Radio Collection. (a and b) In 1988 the BBC broadcast *The Magician's Nephew* and *The Lion, the Witch and the Wardrobe* over Radio 4's For School programme. The stories were run together, one after the other, between 14 January and 24 March, 10.20-10.45 a.m. Each story was produced on a double audio cassette in 1992. (c) *The Horse and His Boy* was broadcast in four half-hour weekly parts over BBC Radio 4 from 6.30 p.m. on 4 to 25 September 1994, and produced on a double cassette in 1994. (d) *Prince Caspian* was broadcast in four half-hour weekly parts over BBC Radio 4 from 7.00 p.m. on 18 June to 9 July 1995, and produced on a double cassette in 1995. (e) *The Voyage of the 'Dawn Treader'* was broadcast in four half-hour weekly parts over BBC Radio 4 from 25 September to 15 October 1995 and produced on a double cassette in 1995. (f) *The Silver Chair* was broadcast in four half-hour weekly parts over BBC Radio 4 from 15 September to 6 October 1996 and produced on a double cassette in 1996. (g) *The Last Battle* was broadcast in four half-hour weekly parts over BBC Radio 4 from 7.00 p.m. on 2 to 23 March 1997 and produced on a double cassette in 1997.

Single Voice Recordings: (1) Between 1978 and 1981 Caedmon of New York brought out gramophone records of the Chronicles of Narnia. The stories are abridged to about an hour each. *The Magician's Nephew* and *Prince Caspian* are read by Claire Bloom; *The Lion, the Witch and the Wardrobe* and *The Silver Chair* by Ian Richardson; *The Horse and His Boy* and *The Voyage of the 'Dawn Treader'* by Anthony Quayle; and *The Last Battle* by Michael York. These recordings were issued on cassette by Caedmon of New York and HarperCollins of London. In the US Caedmon has now been taken over by HarperAudio. *The Chronicles of Narnia* (boxed set of all seven titles), *Selections from The Chronicles of Narnia* (boxed set of the four titles read by Ian Richardson) and *The Lion, the Witch and the Wardrobe* were issued by HarperAudio in the autumn of 1995.

(2) In 1980 Academy Studios, London, released gramophone records of the seven stories, all of which are read by Sir Michael Hordern. They were abridged by Harvey Usill, with music by Marisa Robles. The stories run to a little over two hours each. These recordings are available on cassettes from HarperCollins of London.

St Cross, Church of, Holywell: Many of Lewis's friends and acquaintances lie in the cemetery adjacent to this ancient church in St Cross Road, Oxford. The earliest parts of the church date from the late 11th or early 12th century, but most of what is seen was added during the 14th-16th centuries. Charles Williams* went to services here during his years in Oxford, and Dorothy L. Sayers* chose it for the 'marriage' of Lord Peter Wimsey and Harriet Vane in *Busman's Honeymoon*. The cemetery contains the graves of many notable people, among whom are: Stella Aldwinckle;* Sir Maurice Bowra (1898–1971), Warden of Wadham College; H.V.D. 'Hugo' Dyson;* Austin Farrer;* Katharine Farrer;* Kenneth Grahame (1859–1932), author of *The Wind in the Willows*; Lord Redcliffe-Maud (1906–82), Master of University College and Founder of UNESCO; Kenneth Tynan;* Charles Williams.

St Mark's Church, Dundela, Belfast: This was the church in which Lewis was baptized (29 January 1899), confirmed (6 December 1914) and brought up. When his grandfather, the Rev. Thomas Robert Hamilton (1826–1905), arrived in Belfast in 1874 as the first Rector of St Mark's, services were being held in a coachhouse nearby. The foundation stone of the church, which was designed by William Butterfield, was laid on 13 October 1876, and the tower and nave were consecrated on 22 August 1878. Thirteen years later the Ewart family built the chancel and transepts.

The Lewis family's associations with the churches go back to its beginnings when Albert Lewis* became its first Sunday School Superintendent. It was here that he met and married the Rector's daughter, Florence Lewis* on 29 August 1894. The Lewis family gave the Communion silver, which bears their name, and the brass Lectern is also connected with them. In 1935 the Lewis brothers gave the stained glass window (second from the back on the right-hand side) in memory of their parents. It was designed by Michael Healey.

Schools: Lewis uses this word a great deal, particularly in **AMR**. It means three things: (1) **A course of study;** (2) **An examination in a particular study;** and (3) **Examination Schools** or **'Schools'** which is the 19th-century building in the High Street, Oxford, where lectures are given and in which students sit the examinations. As an example, Lewis began reading the school (= subject or course of study) of English Language and Literature in October 1922 and he took schools (= an examination) in Schools (= Examination School in High Street) in June 1923.

Academic study in Oxford University is organized under eighteen Faculties, or courses of study, for the BA degree. Students in the Arts are usually examined at the end of their third year of residence as a student. There is, however, a First Public Examination which is usually taken at the end of the second term of residence, and which is sometimes called 'Smalls' (**TST** 6 June 1920). If a student passes this examination there follows a stretch of about two years of terms during which he prepares for the final ordeal of the Second Public Examination in the form of the Final Honour School. The Faculties which Lewis read, or studied, were *Literae Humaniores* (or 'Greats')‡ and *English Language and Literature*.‡ See **Terms.**‡

Seven: An Anglo-American Literary Review: In 1980 Dr Barbara Reynolds, Dr Clyde S. Kilby and Dr Beatrice Batson founded this annual review for the discussion and assessment of the seven writers, Owen Barfield,* George MacDonald, G.K. Chesterton, C.S. Lewis, J.R.R. Tolkien,* Charles Williams,* and Dorothy L. Sayers.* It is published by the Marion E. Wade Center‡ at Wheaton College and is intended for both the general and the specialized reader. Nine issues were published between 1980 and 1988, and they contain some of the best essays ever written on these writers. After an interval of five years, publication was resumed in 1993. For information write to: The Marion E. Wade Center, Wheaton College, Wheaton, Illinois 60187-5593, USA. Tel. (708) 752-5908; FAX: (708) 752-5855.

Shadowlands: This drama by William Nicholson is about Lewis and his marriage to Joy Davidman.* There have been three slightly different versions of it. (1) It had its original performance over the BBC on 22 December 1985. This TV version was directed by Norman Stone and produced by David Thompson. The part of Lewis was played by Joss Ackland, and that of Joy Davidman by Claire Bloom.

(2) It opened as a stage play at the Theatre Royal, Plymouth, on 5 October 1989, and was first presented in London at The Queen's Theatre, Shaftesbury Avenue, on 23 October, by Brian Eastman and Armada Productions in association with The Theatre Royal, Plymouth. It was directed by Elijah Moshinsky. The two leading parts were played by Nigel Hawthorne and Jane Lapotaire. The script of William Nicholson's play, *Shadowlands: A Play*, was published by Samuel French, London, in 1989. A revised version was published in 1992.

(3) The story was made into a film by Richard Attenborough with Brian Eastman. It was also directed by Richard Attenborough. In this version Anthony Hopkins played Lewis, and Debra Winger played Joy Davidman. It had its world première in the Mann National Theater in Westwood, Los Angeles, California, on 5 December 1993, and went on national release in the United States on 7 January 1994. The English première, in the presence of HRH The Prince of Wales, was at the Odeon, West End, Leicester Square, London, on 3 March 1994. The Oxford première was in the MGM Cinema in Magdalen Street on 9 March 1994.

(4) A radio version, adapted by William Nicholson from his stage play, was broadcast over BBC Radio 4 on 4 October 1997, 2.30 to 4.00 p.m. It was directed by Elijah Moshinsky, with Michael Williams playing Lewis and Zoë Wanamaker as Joy.

Criticism (of the film by Richard Attenborough): (1) Lewis's step-son, Douglas Gresham,* says:

> When William Nicholson set out to write the first *Shadowlands* script, he was neither attempting nor intending to write an historically accurate biographical documentary. Nor was he trying to examine or portray the Christian behaviour or faith of C.S. Lewis. He was, rather, exploring and expounding one of the most remarkable love stories of modern times, the two protagonists of which were two of the most remarkable people of modern times. In the execution of this aim and in the transitions from Television to Stage to Film, the script has necessarily been 'fictionalized'. Those who go to the film *Shadowlands* seeking a factual history or a Christian apologetic are missing the point. *Shadowlands* is a love story designed to entertain. The basis of it is true; those people did exist, and the essential phenomena of the film did happen. Where Bill has fictionalized is in the dialogue, the scenery, and the

inessential details which fill out the bare bones of the true story. The emotional values and transitions of the film are absolutely accurate, and that is what is important. *Shadowlands* is a very good film, it makes one laugh, it makes one cry, it is visually beautiful, and in the end the film leaves one with a sense of hope and joy.

To those who wish to criticize *Shadowlands* for not being the film that they wished to see, I would have two suggestions. The first is to apply the same critical philosophies to Jack's *Till We Have Faces*. You will find that it has suddenly become a very bad book. It does not accurately follow the 'true' myth of Cupid and Psyche, and it does not accurately expound the pantheism of ancient Greece. My second suggestion to those who wish to see a very different film about C.S. Lewis, is that they should make one. However, if I were a sculptor, I would be very wary of trying to better Michaelangelo Buonarotti's Pietà.

(2) Other views of the film have been expressed in *Seven*,‡ Vol. 11 (1994) by Marjorie Lamp Mead, Peter Schakel, George Sayer,* James Como, Lyle W. Dorsett, Douglas Gresham, Walter Hooper, Martin Moynihan,* and Claude Rawson in a section entitled '*Shadowlands* Observed'. In his piece on 'The De-Christianization of a Christian Love Story' George Sayer complained that:

> The film keeps to the bare bones of the story, but de-Christianizes it. Thus, the remission [of cancer] is attributed just to chemo-therapy: prayer is not mentioned. This is a most serious distortion, because for Lewis, prayer of one sort or another was about the most important activity of his life. It tempts the viewer to think that, although Lewis wrote books on prayer, he did not practise what he preached. Again, the purpose of depicting him at the end of the film as the great apologist with his faith weakened, perhaps shattered, is no doubt to present him as a truly tragic character, but the accusation is not true …
>
> In the leading role, Anthony Hopkins was never recognizable as Lewis. Lewis had wit, a glorious sense of humour (he regarded this as one of God's greatest gifts to man) and a rather boyish sense of fun, qualities that made him a joy to meet and a wonderful companion. Hopkins … was usually solemn and, frankly, rather dull – something that Lewis never was. He seemed to be an unhappy character suffering from an obscure sense of guilt. Lewis had none of this. He had repented of his sins, been of course

forgiven, and was therefore quite free of any feeling of guilt. He was also usually cheerful ...

The film gave no idea of the qualities of enthusiasm and zest for literature (for life, too) that made [Lewis], with the help of his rich and resonant voice with its slight Northern Irish brogue, very much the most exciting and popular lecturer in his subject. Nor did it provide even a glimpse of the imaginative depths from which his imaginative writing and profound spiritual insights came.

James Como in 'Shadowlands: "Even Though ... ?"' said:

I remain happy to have this film; happy that it is not, though it easily could have been, very much worse, and happier than if it had not been made in the first place. Happy, even though ... Rocky Balboa is more religious than C.S. Lewis. He prayed more often and more submissively. He sought out blessings when at risk. *He* went to church to petition Jesus to save *his* stricken wife ...

Even on its own soap-operatic terms the film could have been 'thicker' – and far, far less condescending than it was. And why, then, was it not? ... Nicholson told me that ... Lewis was incapable of making *any* commitments, until he met Joy. Attenborough and Nicholson were not going to allow the intrusion of anything that would, according to Nicholson, 'dilute the intensified love story.' Note: Not the *actual* love story but the *intensified* love story ...

How might it – indeed, how should it – have been a different film, and therefore a better story? ... Get rid of the Whistler sub-plot. Not only does he seem to have dropped in from another film, but if Lewis is going to be someone *else's* foil better that he be lessoned (if he be lessoned at all) by a Tolkien or the like. Next, depict the actual seven years that Lewis and Joy had, not an absurd two. Joy could then change, as she must have, Douglas be a much more affecting adolescent when his mother dies, instead of a sentimentalized juvenile, and Jack could evidence his *multi-faceted* intensity, including his humour, rather than some perpetual waiting-room resignation.

After all, George Sayer, in the second edition of his biography of Lewis, allows that Lewis might have married Ruth Pitter, in whose company he 'seemed unusually quiet and peaceful', after Joy died, had only his health been better ... And last, excise the nonsensically reiterated 'pain-megaphone' line: Not only did Lewis both know and say better, but he positively refuted the very 'dilemma' posited in the film. At least then he might be worthy of going a few rounds with Rocky.

Societies and Journals (Lewis): There are numerous C.S. Lewis Societies and Journals throughout the world, in England, Canada, Germany, Ireland, Japan, the United States, and other countries. However, it has been impossible to gain information about all of them, for some are coming into being as others disappear. For this reason, our information is restricted to the following: **C.S. Lewis Foundation, Canadian C.S. Lewis Journal, Inklings-Gesellschaft, Japan C.S. Lewis Society, The Lamp-Post, Mythopoeic Society, New York C.S. Lewis Society, Oxford University C.S. Lewis Society, Seven.**

Society of St John the Evangelist: *See* **Cowley Fathers.**‡

Socratic Club, The Oxford University: Socrates had exhorted men to 'follow the argument wherever it led them'. This club was founded by Elia Estelle 'Stella' Aldwinckle* in December 1941 'to apply his principle to one particular subject-matter – the *pros* and *cons* of the Christian Religion.' C.S. Lewis was the Club's first President, and in the Preface he wrote for the first issue of the *Socratic Digest* (1942–43), reprinted as **The Founding of the Oxford Socratic Club**, he said: 'In any fairly large and talkative community such as a university there is always the danger that those who think alike should gravitate together into coteries where they will henceforth encounter opposition only in the emasculated form of rumour that the outsiders say thus and thus. The absent are easily refuted, complacent dogmatism thrives, and differences of opinion are embittered by group hostility. Each group hears not the best, but the worst, that the other groups can say. In the Socratic all this was changed. Here a man could get the case for Christianity without all the paraphernalia of pietism and the case against it without the irrelevant *sansculottisme* of our common anti-God weeklies. At the very least we helped to civilize one another.'

The Socratic met every week during term. It was their practice to have two speakers at every meeting, one to read a paper and another to reply, after which there was a general discussion. During Lewis's presidency it was one of the best-attended societies in Oxford. After Lewis went to Cambridge in 1955 there was a sharp decline in interest, and the Socratic came to an end in 1972. The Club published five *Socratic Digests*, copies of which are in the Bodleian.‡ An account of the Socratic with a list of speakers up to 1954 is found in Walter Hooper's 'Oxford's Bonny Fighter' in **ABT**. See Austin Farrer's 'The Christian Apologist' in **LCSL** and John Wain* on Lewis's 'knock-down-and-drag-out performances' in *Sprightly Running* (3).

Southern California C.S. Lewis Society: *See* **Lamp-Post, The.‡**

Southern Historical Collection: Wilson Library, The University of North Carolina. This Collection is the largest and oldest component of the Manuscripts Department of the University of North Carolina. Included in it are the papers of Walter Hooper, a native of North Carolina. The 6000 items which make up the papers concern Walter Hooper's role as the Literary Advisor to the Estate of C.S. Lewis. The collection includes 9 letters from C.S. Lewis (copies in the Bodleian Library‡ and the Wade Center‡), 71 letters from W.H. Lewis,* as well as letters from Roger Lancelyn Green,* R.E. Havard,* Sister Penelope,* Chad Walsh* and others. The library has 176 volumes from Lewis's library and a microfilm of the **Lewis Papers.‡** The Curator says: 'Since the Manuscripts Department continues to receive additional material from Walter Hooper, the papers are restricted until all additions have been received and processing is complete. Interested researchers should write to the Manuscripts Department for further details.' The Manuscripts Department, CB#3926, Wilson Library, The University of North Carolina at Chapel Hill, Chapel Hill, North Carolina, 27514-8890, USA.

Stage Plays of the Chronicles of Narnia: There have been numerous adaptations of several of the Narnian stories for the stage, the most popular being *The Lion, the Witch and the Wardrobe*. Those produced by Aldersgate Productions Ltd, The Westminster Theatre, and Vanessa Ford Productions, of London, with the approval of the Estate of C.S. Lewis, have been very successful.

(1) *The Lion, the Witch and the Wardrobe* was adapted for the stage by Glyn Robbins, and directed by Richard Williams. It was a joint production of Aldersgate, Westminster, and Vanessa Ford Productions. The play had its première in the Westminster Theatre, London, on 19 November 1984, after which it toured the country until 15 January 1985. In the cast were: The Professor/Aslan played by Barry Woolgar; Lucy by Veronica Smart; Edmund by Ian Puleston-Davies; Susan by Elizabeth Anson; Peter by Nicholas Farr; and the White Witch by Susannah Morley. (2) It opened again at the Westminster Theatre, London, on 18 November 1985, and from then until 20 January 1986 it toured 25 regional theatres, with 108 performances. (3) There was a third tour nationwide between 24 November 1986 and 19 January 1987; (4) a fourth between 16 January and 2 February 1989, followed by a fifth and a sixth tour with two of the other plays (see below).

(2) *The Voyage of the 'Dawn Treader'* was adapted by Glyn Robbins, directed by Richard Williams, and produced by Aldersgate Productions Ltd. It was first performed at the Theatre Royal, Bath, on 9 September 1986. It subsequently went on tour and then to Sadler's Wells Theatre, London on 23 December 1987, after which it toured the country until 6 February 1988. It went on tour again with *The Lion, the Witch and the Wardrobe* between 26 December 1988 and 4 February 1989. In the cast were: Miraz/Aslan played by Yannis Lazarides; Bern by Andrew Jolly; Octesian/Drinian by Tim Killick; Restimar by Robin Watson; Revilian by Alan Corser; Mavramorn by Sharon Lloyd; Argoz by Michael Bennett; Edmund by Paul Ryan; Eustace by Kieron Smith; Lucy by Tacye Lynette; Caspian by Nicholas Farr; Rynelf by Robin Watson; and Reepicheep by Franny O'Loughlin.

(3) *The Magician's Nephew* was adapted by Glyn Robbins, directed by Richard Williams, and produced by Vanessa Ford Productions in association with Aldersgate Productions. It had its première at the Ashcroft Theatre, Croydon, on 20 September 1988, and subsequently went on tour, then to the Westminster Theatre, London, on 20 November, after which it toured the country until 24 December 1988. In the cast were: Aslan played by Robert Neil Kingham; Digory by Kieron Smith; Polly by Antonia Loyd; Uncle Andrew by John Hester; Jadis by Elizabeth Elvin; and Aunt Letitia by Judith Carpenter. It had another Westminster première and nationwide tour with *The Lion, the Witch and the Wardrobe* between 16 January 1989 and 2 February 1990.

(4) *The Horse and His Boy* was adapted by Glyn Robbins, directed by Richard Williams, and produced by Vanessa Ford Productions at the Charter Theatre, Preston, on 25 September 1990, and subsequently went on tour and to the Lyric Theatre, Hammersmith. In the cast were: Shasta played by Kieron Smith; Arsheesh/Aslan by Mark Faith; Rabadash by Tim Charrington; Bree by Robert Neil Kingham; Aravis by Felicity Duncan; Hwin by Stephen Omer; Edmund by Nicholas Fard; Lasaraleen by Benedikte Faulkner; Susan by Vanessa Heywood; Corin by Brian Back; and King Lune by Rob Swinton. These tours, managed by Vanessa Ford Productions and Glyn Robbins, went on for more than five years, and the plays were seen by more than one and a half million people.

The texts of these plays, all written by Glyn Robbins, were published by Samuel French Ltd of London: *The Lion, the Witch and the Wardrobe* (1987), *The Magician's Nephew* (1990), *The Voyage of the 'Dawn Treader'* (1992).

In addition to the Glyn Robbins versions there are: *The Lion, the Witch and the Wardrobe*, music, book and lyrics by Irita Kutchmy (1985), published by Josef Weinberger Ltd, 12–14 Mortimer Street, London W1N

7RD. In the United States: *The Lion, the Witch and the Wardrobe* dramatized by Joseph Robinette; *Narnia* based on *The Lion, the Witch and the Wardrobe*, book by Jules Tasca, lyrics by Ted Drachman, music by Thomas Tierney; *The Magician's Nephew* dramatized by Aurand Harris. All published by The Dramatic Publishing Company, 311 Washington Street, Woodstock, Illinois 60098, USA.

Television Films of the Chronicles of Narnia: (1) The first of these stories to be televised was *The Lion, the Witch and the Wardrobe*. It was an ABC Television Network Production shown on ITV (UK) in 1967. This live-action drama in black and white consisted of nine twenty-minute episodes broadcast between 9 July and 3 September 1967, produced by Pamela Lonsdale, and adapted by Trevor Preston. The part of Aslan was played by Bernard Kay; the Professor by Jack Woolgar; Peter by Paul Woller; Susan by Zuleika Robson; Edward by Edward McMurray; and Lucy by Elizabeth Crowther.

After seeing the first episode of this production W.H. Lewis* wrote in his diary of 9 July 1967: 'On Television last night I saw the opening instalment of J's *Lion, Witch and Wardrobe* by which I was agreeably surprised. Lucy is good, and looks the part, and Tumnus comes off ... It's very promising and I think J would have been pleased with it – no hint so far of what he feared, a touch of Disneyland ... The scenery was first rate, and there really was something of magic about the transition from the wardrobe to the dim-lit snow-covered Narnia. How I wish J was here to talk it over with me!' (**BF**).

(2) An animated film by Steve and Bill Melendez of *The Lion, the Witch and the Wardrobe*, consisting of two one-hour parts, was made jointly by the Episcopal Radio-TV Foundation of Atlanta, Georgia, and the Children's Television Workshop, New York. It was broadcast over CBS-TV on 1 and 2 April 1976, one part each evening. On 1 and 2 April 1979 the film was broadcast over CBS television. This same year (1979) the Episcopal Radio-TV Foundation issued a special edition of Macmillan Publishing Company's 'Collier Edition' of *The Lion, the Witch and the Wardrobe* containing a Study Guide by the Rt Rev. Harold Barrett Robinson and the Rev. Patricia Cadwallader. This same version of the film, but with a different sound-track, was broadcast in Britain by ATV on Easter Sunday, 6 April 1980. It was improved by having professional actors do the voices. Aslan was played by Stephen Thorne; the White Witch by Sheila Hancock; Mr Beaver by Arthur Lowe; Mrs Beaver by June Whitfield; the Professor by Leo McKern.

(3) The third version of *The Lion, the Witch and the Wardrobe* was produced by BBC Television. It consisted of 6 half-hour episodes broadcast between 13 November and 18 December 1988 from 5.45 to 6.15 p.m. The story was dramatized by Alan Seymour, and combined live action and animation. It was produced by Paul Stone, and directed by Marilyn Fox, with music by Geoffrey Burgon. The White Witch was played by Barbara Kellerman; Peter by Richard Dempsey; Edmund by Jonathan R. Scott; Susan by Sophie Cook; Lucy by Sophie Wilcox; and Aslan by Ailsa Berk and William Todd-Jones.

(4) *Prince Caspian* was broadcast over the BBC in 2 episodes on 19 and 26 November 1989 between 5.45 and 6.15 p.m. It was produced by Paul Stone and directed by Alex Kirby. The Pevensie children were played by the same actors as were in *The Lion, the Witch and the Wardrobe*. Prince Caspian (the boy) was played by Jean-Marc Perret; Reepicheep by Warwick Davis; King Miraz by Robert Lang; and Trumpkin by Big Mick.

(5) *The Voyage of the 'Dawn Treader'* followed directly from *Prince Caspian*. It was broadcast over the BBC in 4 episodes between 26 November and 24 December 1989, again from 5.45 to 6.15 p.m. It was produced by Norman Stone and directed by Alex Kirby. The Pevensie children were the same as in the other BBC productions. Aslan was played by Ailsa Berk, William Todd-Jones and Tim Rose; Aslan's voice came from Ronald Pickup; King Caspian was Samuel West; and Captain Drinian was John Hallam.

(6) *The Silver Chair* was broadcast in 6 episodes between 18 November and 23 December 1990, from 5.45 to 6.15 p.m. It was produced by Paul Stone and directed by Alex Kirby. The part of Eustace was played by David Thwaites; Jill Pole by Camilla Power; Puddleglum by Tom Baker; Prince Rilian by Richard Henders; the Green Lady by Barbara Kellerman; the Black Knight by Richard Henders; the Giant King by Stephen Reynolds; the Giant Queen by Lesley Nicol; and Glimfeather by Warwick Davis.

These BBC productions have been issued by the BBC on three video cassettes: *The Lion, the Witch and the Wardrobe* in October 1989; *Prince Caspian* and *The Voyage of the 'Dawn Treader'* in November 1990, and *The Silver Chair* in October 1991. The cassettes were re-released in April 1995. All except *The Voyage of the 'Dawn Treader'* were distributed on video cassette in the United States by Public Media Incorporated (PMI) of Chicago in 1991.

Terms: There are three terms each in the Oxford University year: Michaelmas, Hilary and Trinity. (1) Michaelmas Term, which is the first of the academic year, begins on and includes 1 October and ends on 17

December; (2) Hilary Term begins on and includes 7 January and ends on and includes 25 March or the Saturday before Palm Sunday; (3) Trinity Term begins on and includes 20 April or the Wednesday after Easter, whichever is the later, and ends on and includes 6 July.

Translations of Lewis's Writings: There are many hundreds of translations of Lewis's books, and the list grows longer all the time. *The Chronicles of Narnia* are some of the most popular and they have been translated into Afrikaans, Chinese, Czech, Danish, Dutch, Finnish, French, German, Greek, Hebrew, Hungarian, Icelandic, Italian, Japanese, Norwegian, Polish, Portuguese, Russian, Slovene, Spanish, Swedish, Welsh and a number of other languages. (*The Lion, the Witch and the Wardrobe* is even translated into Hawaiian.) The science fiction trilogy (*Out of the Silent Planet, Perelandra* and *That Hideous Strength*) are almost as popular and they have been translated into Chinese, Czech, Dutch, Finnish, French, German, Hungarian, Icelandic, Italian, Japanese, Portuguese, Slovene, Spanish and Swedish.

Lewis said little about the translations of his books except on one occasion. In May 1960 his publisher, Jocelyn Gibb* of Geoffrey Bles, wrote to him about someone who wanted to translate *Miracles* into Japanese with certain expurgations. Replying to Gibb about this on 9 May, Lewis said:

> I am afraid I can't agree to a Japanese version of *Miracles* with those expurgations. Small though they are, their aim clearly is that I should be disguised as a fundamentalist and a non-smoker. I should be trying to attract a particular public under false pretences. I have hitherto been acceptable to a good many different 'denominations' without such camouflage, and I won't resort to it now. The Baptist translator, may if he pleases, add notes of his own, warning readers that the book is at these points, in his opinion, pernicious. But he must not remove them.

There is probably no library that contains copies of all the translations that have been made, but the Bodleian Library‡ in Oxford and the British Library in London contain most of them. The Wade Center‡ also has a collection. There is a great deal of detailed information about translations of Lewis's books up to 1980 in the 33 volumes of the *Index Translationum: International Bibliography of Translations* (UNESCO) which, unhappily, ceased publication in 1985. The published volumes of the *British Library General Catalogue of Printed Books to 1975* lists all their books up to 1975. It has been followed by a *British Library General Catalogue of Printed Books 1976–1989* on microfiche. The *Index Translationum* and the *British Library General Catalogues* are available in most university libraries. The Bodleian's large collection of translations are listed in its various library catalogues.

Trout, The: This is one of the loveliest places in Oxford. It is on Godstow Road and faces the Thames. At present a pub and a restaurant, it was originally a fisherman's house in the 16th century. By 1625 it was serving as an inn. The two-storey building was largely rebuilt in 1737, and the interior is very cosy with its flagstone floor, beamed ceiling and log fires. Collections of old clocks, prints, pewter tankards and a stuffed pike line the walls. In 1988 the stable to the left of the inn was opened up to provide more room. The Inklings‡ came here often in the summertime when they could have their drinks outdoors beside the river, and watch the peacocks wander about the garden. There is a photo of The Trout in **IHW** and **TJB**, and a photo of J. Dundas-Grant,* Colin Hardie,* R.E. Havard* and Lewis at The Trout in **TJB**.

Tutorials: This is the system of teaching favoured at Oxford and Cambridge. Once a week a student goes to each of his tutors for an hour. During the tutorial he reads an essay on a subject assigned by the tutor and afterwards they discuss it or some other academic matters, perhaps over a glass of sherry. A tutor will occasionally take two pupils at a time, as we find Lewis did when he took John Betjeman* and D.R. Valentin together (see **AMR**). Occasionally, especially in some of the smaller colleges, it is necessary for a student to go to a tutor in another college for tuition or supervision. In **AMR** we find Lewis, when an undergraduate, going to St Hugh's College for tutorials in Anglo-Saxon, and we find him giving tutorials in Lady Margaret Hall after he became a fellow of Magdalen.‡

University College: It is in the High Street, Oxford, and was Lewis's college as an undergraduate and Tutor in Philosophy. He was elected to a Scholarship in December 1916, and matriculated on 28 April 1917. At the same time that he was reading Honour Moderations (see **Literae Humaniores‡**) he was in the Officers' Training Corps, and after he joined the Army on 7 June 1917 he moved to Keble College. Following his training there he went to France. He returned to University College in January 1919 and took his BA in 1922. He also taught Philosophy there in 1924. He lived in Room 5 on Staircase XII. For College photos of Lewis see **TJB**.

'Univ.', as it is called, is the first collegiate foundation in Oxford, and indeed in Great Britain. However, there is an amiable dispute about seniority between University, Merton and Balliol colleges. Balliol College had the first site, Merton the first statutes, but University the first benefactor. This was William of Durham who in 1249 bequeathed 310 marks to the University for the buying of property. The first of the properties was bought in 1280. Other properties on the south side of High Street were added until they were amalgamated. No buildings earlier than 1634 survive. The front quad, which is entered from High Street, was built 1634–1677. In about 1380 the Fellows asserted that Univ. had been founded by King Alfred. This spurious claim was upheld, and even today King Alfred is still prayed for on college feast days.

During the 16th century Univ. was fortunate in being spared divisions during the period of religious vacillations by Henry VIII. This was to happen again in the 17th century when the Catholic master, Obadiah Walker, set up a Mass-chapel in rooms in the quadrangle, a statue of James II on the tower, and a printing press for Catholic books. One of Lewis's favourite poets, Percy Bysshe Shelley, was expelled from Univ. in 1811 for circulating a pamphlet, *The Necessity of Atheism*, which he wrote with Thomas Jefferson Hogg. Visitors to the college may see the Shelley memorial which Lewis refers to in **TST** 28 April 1917. Beneath a dome the naked figure of Shelley after drowning lies on a slab of Connemara marble supported by winged lions in bronze.

University of Oxford: The University is a self-governing corporation, subject only to Parliament and the courts of law. It consists wholly of members of the colleges. The relation between the University and the colleges of Oxford is this: while the functions of the colleges are teaching and research, the University does those things which demand uniformity of treatment or need to be done on a large scale. For instance, it sees that all members of the University have the same examinations, and it confers degrees. The University also provides those things which it would be foolish or too expensive for colleges to provide individually, such as scientific laboratories, public lectures, and the Bodleian Library.‡ For more information on the various parts of the University and Oxford generally see *The Encyclopaedia of Oxford*, ed. Christopher Hibbert and Edward Hibbert (1988).

Wade Center, Marion E., Wheaton College, Wheaton, Illinois: The Center, founded in 1965, contains a collection of the writings and papers of 'The Seven': Owen Barfield,* G.K. Chesterton, C.S. Lewis, George

MacDonald, J.R.R. Tolkien,* Dorothy L. Sayers,* and Charles Williams.* This collection of 'The Seven' contains more than 20,000 letters, 12,000 books (first editions and critical works) and 1000 manuscripts. The C.S. Lewis holdings include over 2,300 letters, some of the original Boxen stories, the **Lewis Papers,**‡ the diaries of W.H. Lewis,* 2,363 books from Lewis's own library, and family photographs. The Marion E. Wade Center and the Bodleian Library‡ exchange photocopies of many of their Lewis holdings, so that the greater part of their material is accessible in both places.

No account of this fine collection would be complete without recognition of its founder, the late Clyde S. Kilby (1902–86) who has been called 'the godfather of Lewis interest in America'. Dr Kilby came to Wheaton in 1935 as an Assistant Professor in the English Department, and was Chairman of the Department from 1951 to 1966. Deploring the poor quality of evangelical writing, he said in the Wheaton College *Alumni Magazine* of 1961: 'I am afraid that the problem of Christian writing is not so much that of making it Christian as making it structurally and intellectually sound ... As long as we suppose writing to be an after-dinner exercise in sentimentality, we shall continue to produce trash.' His admiration for Lewis's books led him to write his excellent *The Christian World of C.S. Lewis* (1964). In 1965 he conceived the idea of collecting the writings of the seven authors. Some of the first letters given to Wheaton were those from Lewis to Mary Willis Shelburne, and they were edited by Dr Kilby as *Letters to an American Lady* (1967).

In 1974 the Lewis Collection was renamed in honour of Marion E. Wade, founder of The ServiceMaster Company, L.P. During Dr Kilby's years as Curator of the Marion E. Wade Center he worked tirelessly to collect the writings of 'the Seven' and to promote them throughout the United States. His other works include *A Mind Awake: An Anthology of C.S. Lewis* (1968); (with Douglas Gilbert) *C.S. Lewis: Images of His World* (1973); and *Tolkien and The Silmarillion* (1976). In 1987 Martha Kilby gave her husband's papers to the Wade Center. For information write to: The Marion E. Wade Center, Wheaton College, Wheaton, Illinois 60187-5593, USA. Tel. (708) 752-5908; Fax: (708) 752-5855.

Walking Tours: 'My happiest hours are spent with three or four old friends in old clothes tramping together and putting up in small pubs,' Lewis wrote in a little portrait on the dust jacket of the original American edition of *Perelandra*. Lewis had always liked walking, and his diary of the 1920s (**AMR**) is filled with details about many solitary walks. 'Walking Tours,' however, involved going with several friends to a pre-arranged place by train or car and then walking for several days. They were *not camping*: it was essential that they spend the nights in village pubs or small hotels where they could get supper, drinks and beds for the night. It was the walking tours that Lewis was recalling in the chapter on 'Friendship' in the FL IV where he speaks of those 'golden sessions'

> when four or five of us after a hard day's walking have come to our inn; when our slippers are on, our feet spread out towards the blaze and our drinks at our elbows; when the whole world, and something beyond the world, opens itself to our minds as we talk; and no one has any claim on or any responsibility for another, but all are freemen and equals as if we had first met an hour ago, while at the same time an Affection mellowed by the years enfolds us. Life – natural life – has no better gift to give. Who could have deserved it?

Lewis and his walking companions described themselves as 'cretaceous perambulators', because, in choosing a place to walk, it was necessary that the soil be chalky, and thus dry, and the grass be short. The Walking Tours originated with Cecil Harwood* and Owen Barfield.* They had been walking for some time before Lewis joined them. In an undated letter of either 1925 or 1926 to Harwood, Lewis explained that neither he nor Barfield were in a league with him: 'You, happy man, are the common theme of walking whereon he and I are but alternative variations.'

In a letter to Warren Lewis* of 26 April 1927 we get a description of a walk taken over the Berkshire Downs by Lewis, Harwood, Barfield, and Walter 'Wof' Field from 19–25 April. On this occasion the walkers met at Goring and set off from there. 'We were,' Lewis wrote to Warnie, 'on the broad grass track of the Icknield Way, the grass very short and fine and perfectly dry, as it is nearly all the year round in these chalk hills.' As this letter is found in *Letters* the reader can follow the whole length of this walking tour. Most of the planning for the walks was done by Harwood, and in a delightfully funny letter to Harwood of 24 April 1931 Lewis informs him that he is 'Lord of the Walks'.

On another occasion in April 1936 Harwood and Barfield spent several days walking in Hampshire. Lewis had been unable to go with them, and their 'revenge' consisted in making him take an examination before he could be re-admitted into the 'College of Cretaceous Perambulators'. Lewis surprised them with some very amusing answers to their questions. The questions and answers were published in a limited edition by the Oxford University C.S. Lewis Society‡ in 1983 under the title *A*

Cretaceous Perambulator (The Re-examination of), copies of which are in the Bodleian Library‡ and the Wade Center.‡ In 1931 Lewis introduced his brother, Warnie, to walking tours, and in his diary (**BF**) Warnie writes about the eight tours they took between 1931 and 1939.

Wynyard School ('Belsen'): This boys' preparatory school, hated by both Lewis brothers, is called 'Belsen' in **SBJ** II. It was founded in 1881 by the Rev. Robert Capron* and stood on the site of 99 Langley Road, Watford, Hertfordshire, until it was pulled down in 1992. It was the first school Warren Lewis* and CSL attended. Warren was a student there 1905–09, and in his recollections, found in the **LP** III: 33–41, he provided the following description:

> Wynyard was one of a pair of semi-detached houses, each standing in about two acres of ground, enclosed by an oak paling, and containing some pine trees. The house itself was of that hideous yellow brick not uncommon in Hertfordshire. A flight of stone steps led up to the centrally situated hall door, flanked on either side by bow windows on the ground and second storey, over which a gabled storey of attics was surmounted by a flat roof enclosed with an ornamental iron railing; in front of the house, a drive of the yellowish gravel characteristic of the county, swept in a curve across a lawn and disappeared round the house to the left. On this side the house was rendered irregular by a low two-storeyed addition which comprised the school buildings. The ground floor room, half the depth of the house, and some four feet below the level of its ground floor, was entered from the dining room by a little staircase descending from a small raised platform. This room, the one and only school room, and the only room in the house to which the boys had unrestricted access, contained a table, two benches, two master's desks, and four or five rows of other desks under the frosted windows at either end of the room; a map of the world, two oil lamps hanging over the table, a bookshelf loaded with slates, a blackboard, and a cane hanging from the pale green iron mantelpiece opposite the dining room door, completed its appointments. A door at the back of the room gave access to a porch containing a wash basin; a further door opened into the playground. Above the school room, a very low roofed dormitory completed the boys' indoor accommodation.

In **SBJ** II Lewis said: 'The school, as I first knew it, consisted of some eight or nine boarders and about as many day-boys ... I was one of the last survivors, and left the ship only when she went down under us.' Robert Capron had been declared mad as far back as 1906, and shortly after the school closed permanently in 1910 he was certified insane. He died in Camberwell House Asylum, Peckham, Kent, in 1911. There is a photo of the school in **TJB**. See Walter Hooper, 'C.S. Lewis in Hertfordshire's "Belsen" ' in *Hertfordshire Countryside*, vol. 37, September and October 1982.

A BIBLIOGRAPHY
OF THE WRITINGS
OF C.S. LEWIS

This bibliography includes only writings *by* C.S. Lewis. For writings *about* him see Joe R. Christopher and Joan K. Ostling, *C.S. Lewis: An Annotated Checklist of Writings about him and his Works*, Kent, Ohio: Kent State University Press, [1974]. This includes critical works up to June 1972. It was followed by Susan Lowenberg, *C.S. Lewis: A Reference Guide 1972–1988*, New York: G.K. Hall & Co, 1993.

A: Books

1. **SPIRITS IN BONDAGE**/*A Cycle of Lyrics*. London: William Heinemann, hardback 20 March 1919 (under the pseudonym of Clive Hamilton).

   U.S. A new edition edited with a Preface by Walter Hooper. New York: Harcourt Brace Jovanovich, paperback 6 January 1984. *Spirits in Bondage* is included in *Collected Poems* (A70).

2. **DYMER**. London: J.M. Dent, hardback 20 September 1926 (under the pseudonym Clive Hamilton); reprinted with a new Preface, as by C.S. Lewis, hardback 19 October 1950.

   U.S. New York: E.P. Dutton, hardback 1926; Macmillan, hardback 19 October 1950. *Dymer* is included in *Narrative Poems* (A51).

3. **THE/ PILGRIM'S/ REGRESS**/*An Allegorical Apology/ for/ Christianity, Reason and Romanticism*. London: J.M. Dent, hardback 25 May 1933. This was followed by a second edition published by Sheed & Ward of London in October 1935. Lewis was worried about obscurity in the book, and this edition from Sheed & Ward differs from the first in having a short 'Argument' at the beginning of each of the ten books. A 'New and Revised Edition' was published by Geoffrey Bles of London in 1943.

Besides a valuable Preface in which Lewis explains what he meant by 'Romanticism', he makes his story clearer still with the occasional footnote and running headlines on every page explaining exactly what the story is about. These running headlines take the place of the 'Arguments' in the Sheed & Ward edition.

When the book was published as a Fount Paperback by Collins of London in 1977 it was found necessary to change the pagination. Because of this, the running headlines were gathered into short sections which precede each chapter.

U.S. The Sheed & Ward edition of 1935 was published by Sheed & Ward Inc. of New York in 1935. It was printed in England, and there is no difference between it and the one published in London. Sheed & Ward of New York published the New and Revised Edition in 1944.

4. **THE/ ALLEGORY/ OF LOVE/** *A Study in/Medieval Tradition.* Oxford: Clarendon Press, hardback 21 May 1936; reprinted with corrections, London: Oxford University Press, 1938. Oxford Paperback 10 November 1977.

    U.S. New York: Oxford University Press, Galaxy Book paperback 18 February 1960.

5. **OUT OF THE SILENT/ PLANET.** London: John Lane The Bodley Head, hardback 23 September 1938. Paperback published by Pan Books of London 16 June 1952. **THE COSMIC TRILOGY:** *Out of the Silent Planet, Perelandra, That Hideous Strength* published in hardback and paperback by The Bodley Head 22 September 1990.

    U.S. New York: Macmillan Company in hardback 28 September 1943. This was followed by a paperback from Avon Book Division of New York in 1949; Macmillan Paperbacks Edition 1965.

6. **REHABILITATIONS/** *And Other Essays.* London: Oxford University Press 23 March 1939. (Contents: Preface, 'Shelley, Dryden, and Mr Eliot', 'William Morris', 'The Idea of an "English School"', 'Our English Syllabus', 'High and Low Brows', 'The Alliterative Metre', 'Bluspels and Flalansferes: A Semantic Nightmare', 'Variation in Shakespeare and Others', 'Christianity and Literature'.)

7. (With E.M.W. Tillyard) **THE/ PERSONAL/ HERESY/** *A Controversy.* London: Oxford University Press, hardback 27 April 1939; Oxford Paperback 17 June 1965.

8. **THE PROBLEM OF PAIN**. London: The Centenary Press, hardback 18 October 1940; Fount Paperbacks 4 February 1957.

U.S. New York: Macmillan, hardback 26 October 1943; Macmillan Paperback 1962.

The French edition of this book, *Le Problème de la Souffrance*, Traduit de l'anglais par Marguerite Faguer, Préface de Maurice Nédoncelle, Paris: Desclée de Brouwer, 1950, contains a footnote (chapter ix, p. 163) and Preface written specially for it by Lewis.

9. **THE/ SCREWTAPE LETTERS**. London: Geoffrey Bles, hardback 9 February 1942. (The *Letters* were first published in *The Guardian*.‡ See D24–55.) Published as a Fontana Paperback by Collins 14 February 1955.

U.S. New York: Macmillan, hardback 16 February 1943. The back cover of this edition featured a drawing of Screwtape by Lewis. Macmillan Paperback 1976.

Reprinted with a new Screwtape letter as **THE SCREWTAPE LETTERS/ AND/ SCREWTAPE PROPOSES A TOAST**, with a new and additional Preface (dated 18 May 1960), London: Geoffrey Bles, hardback 27 February 1961.

U.S. New York: Macmillan, hardback 1962; Revised Macmillan Paperback Edition 1982.

THE/ SCREWTAPE/ LETTERS/ WITH/ SCREWTAPE/ PROPOSES A TOAST. *Revised Edition*. New York: Macmillan, a 'Revised Macmillan Paperback Edition' 1982. (This edition contains a hitherto unpublished piece by C.S. Lewis that serves as a Preface to 'Screwtape Proposes a Toast.')

10. **A PREFACE TO/ 'PARADISE LOST'/** *Being the Ballard Matthews Lectures/ Delivered at University College, North Wales, 1941/ Revised and Enlarged*. London: Oxford University Press, hardback 8 October 1942; Oxford Paperback 15 September 1960.

11. **BROADCAST TALKS/** *Reprinted with some alterations from two series/ of Broadcast Talks ('Right and Wrong: A Clue to/ the Meaning of the Universe' and 'What Christians/ Believe') given in 1941 and 1942*. London: Geoffrey Bles: The Centenary Press, hardback 13 July 1942.

U.S. New York: Macmillan, published as a hardback under the title **THE CASE/ FOR CHRISTIANITY**, 7 September 1943.

12. **CHRISTIAN BEHAVIOUR/** *A Further series of Broadcast Talks.* (The original eight talks Lewis gave over the BBC with four additional chapters on 'The Cardinal Virtues', 'Christian Marriage', 'Charity' and 'Hope'.) London: Geoffrey Bles: The Centenary Press, hardback 19 April 1943.

   U.S. New York: Macmillan, hardback 18 January 1944.

13. **PERELANDRA/** *A Novel.* London: John Lane The Bodley Head, hardback 20 April 1943. The first paperback published under the title *Voyage to Venus* by Pan Books of London 14 August 1953.

   U.S. New York: Macmillan, hardback 11 April 1944. The first paperback was published by Avon Publications of New York in [1944]. Avon reprinted it [c. 1950] as *Perelandra: World of the New Temptation.* Macmillan Paperbacks Edition 1965.

14. **THE ABOLITION OF MAN/** *or/ Reflections on Education with Special/ Reference to the Teaching of English/ in the Upper Forms of School.* Riddell Memorial Lectures, Fifteenth Series. London: Oxford University Press, paperback 6 January 1943. A new edition with some alterations was published by Geoffrey Bles: The Centenary Press, 12 August 1946. Fount Paperbacks 1978.

   U.S. New York: Macmillan, hardback 8 April 1947; Macmillan Paperback Edition 1965.

15. **BEYOND PERSONALITY/** *The Christian Idea of God.* London: Geoffrey Bles: The Centenary Press, hardback 9 October 1944. (The talks originally appeared in *The Listener* 11 February–6 April 1944. Lewis added four new chapters before its publication by Bles.)

   U.S. New York: Macmillan, hardback 20 March 1945.

16. **THAT/ HIDEOUS/ STRENGTH/** *a modern fairy-tale for grown-ups.* London: John Lane The Bodley Head, hardback 16 August 1945. John Lane included it in **THE COSMIC TRILOGY:** *Out of the Silent Planet, Perelandra, That Hideous Strength,* hardback and paperback on 22 February 1990.

   U.S. New York: Macmillan, hardback 21 May 1946. (This edition differs in a number of ways from the one published by Bodley Head. See Note on pp. 240–2.) Macmillan Paperback 1965.

   THE/ TORTURED/ PLANET/ (That Hideous Strength) is an Abridged Edition specially prepared by Lewis from the Bodley Head Edition for publication in paperback by Avon Books of New York [c. 1946]. The Abridged Edition was published by Pan Books of London in

1955 as **THAT HIDEOUS/ STRENGTH**. In 1983 Pan Books published a paperback of the Macmillan Edition of the work.

17. **THE/ GREAT DIVORCE/** *A Dream*. London: Geoffrey Bles: The Centenary Press, hardback 14 January 1946. (It was mistakenly dated November 1945.) The book was originally published in parts in *The Guardian‡* (see D87–113). Fontana Paperbacks 1972.

    U.S. New York: Published as **THE/ GREAT DIVORCE**, Macmillan, hardback 26 February 1946; Macmillan Paperback 1976.

18. **MIRACLES/** *A Preliminary Study*. London: Geoffrey Bles: The Centenary Press, hardback 12 May 1947. First published as a Fontana Book with a revision of chapter III 9 May 1960.

    U.S. New York: Macmillan, hardback 16 September 1947; Macmillan Paperback with revised chapter III, 1978. An abridgement in paperback with a specially written preface by the author, New York: The Association Press, a Reflection Book, 1958.

19. **ARTHURIAN TORSO/** *Containing the posthumous fragment of/ The Figure of Arthur/ by/ Charles Williams/ and/ A Commentary on The Arthurian Poems of/ Charles Williams/ by/ C.S. Lewis*. London: Oxford University Press, hardback 21 October 1948.

    U.S. *Taliessin Through Logres/ The Region/ of the Summer Stars/ by Charles Williams/ and Arthurian Torso/ by Charles Williams/ and C.S. Lewis*. Introduction by Mary McDermott Shideler, Grand Rapids, Michigan: Eerdmans paperback 1974.

20. **TRANSPOSITION/** *And Other Addresses*. London: Geoffrey Bles, 1949. (Contents: Preface, 'Transposition', 'The Weight of Glory', 'Membership', 'Learning in War-Time', 'The Inner Ring'.)

    U.S. New York: Macmillan, published as a hardback under the title **THE/ WEIGHT OF/ GLORY** *And Other/ Addresses*, 13 September 1949.

    THE WEIGHT/ OF GLORY/ *And Other Addresses*. Revised and Expanded Edition. Edited, with an Introduction, by Walter Hooper. New York: Macmillan, Macmillan Paperbacks Edition, 1980. (Contents: Introduction, 'The Weight of Glory', 'Learning in War-Time', 'Why I Am Not a Pacifist', 'Transposition' (expanded version), 'Is Theology Poetry?', 'The Inner Ring', 'Membership', 'On Forgiveness', 'A Slip of the Tongue'.)

21. **THE LION, THE WITCH/ AND/ THE WARDROBE/** *A Story for Children*. Illustrations by Pauline Baynes. London: Geoffrey Bles, hardback 16 October 1950; Puffin Book by Penguin Books 29 October 1959; Lion paperback by HarperCollins November 1992.

U.S. New York: Macmillan, hardback 7 November 1950; Collier Books paperback 1970. First HarperCollins edition in hardback, trade paperback and HarperTrophy paperback May 1994. (See **NARNIA**, Publication Record, pp. 451–6).

22. **PRINCE CASPIAN/** *The Return to Narnia*. Illustrations by Pauline Baynes. London: Geoffrey Bles, hardback 15 October 1951; Puffin Book by Penguin Books 19 April 1962; Lion paperback by HarperCollins November 1992.

New York: Macmillan, hardback 16 October 1951; Collier Books paperback 1970. First HarperCollins edition in hardback, trade paperback and HarperTrophy paperback May 1994. (See **NARNIA**, Publication Record, pp. 451–6.)

23. **MERE CHRISTIANITY/** *A revised and amplified edition, with a / new introduction, of the three books, 'Broadcast Talks', 'Christian Behaviour' and 'Beyond Personality'*. London: Geoffrey Bles, hardback 7 July 1952; Fontana Paperbacks 14 February 1955.

U.S. As **MERE CHRISTIANITY/** *A revised and enlarged edition,/ with a new introduction, of the/ three books 'The Case for Christ-/ ianity', 'Christian Behaviour' and/ 'Beyond Personality'* by Macmillan of New York, 11 November 1952; Macmillan Paperback 1960.

MERE/ CHRISTIANITY/ *An Anniversary Edition of/ The Three Books/ 'The Case for Christianity', 'Christian Behaviour'/ and/ 'Beyond Personality'*. Edited with an Introduction by Walter Hooper. New York: Macmillan, 1981. This edition contains the original broadcasts of those talks entitled 'Some Objections' and 'Sexual Morality', as well as part of a programme called 'The Anvil' in which Lewis took part. (An edition of this book, without the Introduction and appendices, was published by Collins of London, 1988.)

24. **THE VOYAGE OF THE/ 'DAWN TREADER'.** Illustrations by Pauline Baynes. London: Geoffrey Bles, hardback 15 September 1952; Puffin Book by Penguin Books 25 March 1965; Lion paperback by HarperCollins November 1992.

U.S. New York: Macmillan, hardback 30 September 1952; Collier Books paperback 1970. First HarperCollins edition in hardback, trade paperback and HarperTrophy paperback May 1994. (See **NARNIA**, Publication record, pp. 451–6.)

25. **THE SILVER CHAIR**. Illustrations by Pauline Baynes. London: Geoffrey Bles, hardback 7 September 1953; Puffin Book by Penguin Books 24 June 1965; Lion paperback by HarperCollins November 1992.

U.S. New York: Macmillan, hardback 6 October 1953; Collier Books paperback 1970. First HarperCollins edition in hardback, trade paperback and HarperTrophy paperback May 1994. (See **NARNIA**, Publication Record, pp. 452–6.)

26. **THE HORSE AND HIS BOY**. Illustrations by Pauline Baynes. London: Geoffrey Bles, hardback 6 September 1954; Puffin Book by Penguin Books 30 September 1965; Lion paperback by HarperCollins November 1992.

U.S. New York: Macmillan, hardback 5 October 1954; Collier Books paperback 1970. First HarperCollins edition in hardback, trade paperback and HarperTrophy paperback May 1994. (See **NARNIA**, Publication Record, pp. 452–6.).

27. **ENGLISH LITERATURE/ IN THE/ SIXTEENTH CENTURY/ EXCLUDING DRAMA**. The Completion of 'The Clark Lectures', Trinity College, Cambridge, 1944. (*The Oxford History of English Literature*, Vol. III). Oxford: Clarendon Press, hardback 16 September 1954; Oxford Paperback 29 March 1973. Reprinted as **POETRY AND PROSE/ IN THE/ SIX-TEENTH CENTURY**. Oxford: Clarendon Press, hardback 29 March 1990.

U.S. New York: Oxford University Press, hardback 16 September 1954.

28. **THE/ MAGICIAN'S NEPHEW**. Illustrations by Pauline Baynes. London: The Bodley Head, hardback 2 May 1955; Puffin Book by Penguin Books 27 June 1963; Lion paperback by HarperCollins November 1992.

U.S. New York: Macmillan, hardback 4 October 1954; Collier Books paperback 1970. First HarperCollins edition in hardback, trade paperback and HarperTrophy paperback May 1994. (See **NARNIA**, Publication Record, pp. 452–6.).

29. **SURPRISED BY JOY**/ *The Shape of My Early Life*. London: Geoffrey Bles, hardback 19 September 1955; Fontana paperback 4 May 1959; Fount Paperbacks 1977.

U.S. New York: Harcourt, Brace & World, hardback 1 February 1956; Harvest/HBJ Book (paperback) 9 July 1970.

30. **THE LAST BATTLE/** *A Story for Children*. Illustrations by Pauline Baynes. London: The Bodley Head, hardback 19 March 1956; Puffin Book by Penguin Books 30 January 1964; Lion paperback by HarperCollins November 1992.

    U.S. As **THE/ LAST BATTLE**, New York: Macmillan, hardback 4 September 1956; Collier Books paperback 1970. First HarperCollins edition in hardback, trade paperback and HarperTrophy paperback May 1994. (See **NARNIA**, Publication Record, pp. 452–6.).

31. **TILL WE HAVE FACES/** *A Myth Retold*. London: Geoffrey Bles, hardback 10 September 1956; Fount Paperbacks 1978.

    U.S. New York: Harcourt, Brace & World, hardback 9 January 1957. It contains a 'Note' by Lewis about Apuleius's version of the myth of Cupid and Psyche. Harvest Book paperback 9 July 1980.

32. **REFLECTIONS ON THE PSALMS**. London: Geoffrey Bles, hardback 8 September 1958; Fontana Paperbacks 2 January 1961.

    U.S. New York: Harcourt, Brace & World, hardback 5 November 1958. Harvest Book paperback 7 October 1964.

33. **THE FOUR LOVES**. London: Geoffrey Bles, hardback 28 March 1960; Fontana Paperbacks 7 January 1963.

    U.S. New York: Harcourt, Brace & World, hardback 27 July 1960. Harvest Book paperback 29 September 1971.

34. **STUDIES IN/ WORDS**. Cambridge: Cambridge University Press, 9 September 1960. (Contents: Preface, 'Introduction', 'Nature', 'Sad', 'Wit', 'Free', 'Sense', 'Simple', 'Conscience and Conscious', 'At the Fringe of Language', Index.) The Second Edition includes three new and additional chapters on 'World', 'Life', and 'I Dare Say', hardback and paperback 6 July 1967.

35. **THE WORLD'S LAST NIGHT/** *And Other Essays*. New York: Harcourt, Brace & World, hardback 10 February 1960. (Contents: 'The Efficacy of Prayer', 'On Obstinacy in Belief', 'Lilies that Fester', 'Screwtape Proposes a Toast', 'Good Work and Good Works', 'Religion and Rocketry', 'The World's Last Night'.) Harvest Book paperback 24 October 1973.

36. **A GRIEF OBSERVED**. London: Faber and Faber, hardback 29 September 1961 (under the pseudonym N.W. Clerk); reprinted as by C.S. Lewis in 1964; Faber Paper Covered Editions 7 April 1966.

U.S. Greenwich, Connecticut: Seabury Press, hardback 14 February 1963 (under the pseudonym N.W. Clerk). Reprinted as by C.S. Lewis 1964. It was published with an Afterword by Chad Walsh* as a paperback by Bantam Books of New York, March 1976. Published by HarperCollins, San Francisco with a Foreword by Douglas Gresham* 1995.

37. **AN/ EXPERIMENT IN CRITICISM**. Cambridge: Cambridge University Press, hardback 13 October 1961; paperback 18 November 1965.

38. **THEY ASKED FOR A PAPER/** *Papers and Addresses*. London: Geoffrey Bles, hardback 26 February 1962. (Contents: Acknowledgements, *'De Descriptione Temporum'*, 'The Literary Impact of the Authorized Version', 'Hamlet: The Prince or the Poem?', 'Kipling's World', 'Sir Walter Scott', 'Lilies that Fester', 'Psycho-analysis and Literary Criticism', 'The Inner Ring', 'Is Theology Poetry?', 'Transposition' (an expanded version of the one in A20), 'On Obstinacy in Belief', 'The Weight of Glory'.)

39. **U.S. BEYOND/ THE BRIGHT BLUR**. New York: Harcourt, Brace & World, hardback 25 December 1963. (On the flyleaf: *'Beyond the Bright Blur* is taken from *Letters to Malcolm: Chiefly on Prayer* (chapters 15, 16, 17) by C.S. Lewis, which will be published in the year 1964. This limited edition is published as a New Year's greeting to friends of the author and his publisher.')

40. **LETTERS TO MALCOLM/ CHIEFLY ON PRAYER**. London: Geoffrey Bles, hardback 27 January 1964; Fontana Paperbacks, 10 January 1966.

U.S. New York: Harcourt, Brace & World, hardback 12 February 1964. Harvest Book paperback 21 March 1973.

41. **THE/ DISCARDED IMAGE/** *An Introduction to/ Medieval and Renaissance/ Literature*. Cambridge: Cambridge University Press, hardback 7 May 1964; paperback 11 January 1968.

42. **POEMS**. Edited by Walter Hooper. London: Geoffrey Bles, hardback 26 October 1964. *Poems* is included in *Collected Poems* (A70).

U.S. New York: Harcourt, Brace & World, hardback 24 March 1965; Harvest/HBJ paperback 5 December 1977.

43. **SCREWTAPE/ PROPOSES A/ TOAST/** *and other pieces*. Preface and Acknowledgements by J.[ocelyn] E.[aston] G.[ibb]. London: Collins, Fontana Paperbacks 4 January 1965. (Contents: 'Screwtape Proposes a Toast', 'On Obstinacy in Belief', 'Good Work and Good Works', 'The Inner Ring', 'Is Theology Poetry?', 'Transposition', 'The Weight of Glory', 'A Slip of the Tongue'.)

44. **STUDIES IN MEDIEVAL/ AND RENAISSANCE/ LITERATURE.** Edited by Walter Hooper. Cambridge: Cambridge University Press, hardback 9 June 1966. (Contents: Preface by Walter Hooper, *'De Audiendis Poetis'*, 'The Genesis of a Medieval Book', 'Imagination and Thought in the Middle Ages', 'Dante's Similes', 'Imagery in the Last Eleven Cantos of Dante's *Comedy'*, 'Dante's Statius', 'The *Morte Darthur'*, 'Tasso', 'Edmund Spenser: 1552–99', 'On Reading *The Faerie Queene'*, 'Neoplatonism in the Poetry of Spenser', 'Spenser's Cruel Cupid', 'Genius and Genius', 'A Note on *Comus'*, Additional Editorial Notes, Index.)

45. **LETTERS OF/ C.S. LEWIS.** Edited, with a Memoir, by W.H. Lewis. London: Geoffrey Bles, hardback 18 April 1966. London: Collins, Revised and enlarged Edition. Edited by Walter Hooper, Fount Paperbacks, 17 November 1988.
    U.S. New York: Harcourt, Brace & World, hardback 16 November 1966; Harvest Book paperback 12 March 1975. San Diego: Harcourt Brace & Company, Revised and Enlarged Edition, Harvest Original paperback 15 April 1994 (mistakenly dated 1993).

46. **OF OTHER WORLDS/** *Essays and Stories*. Edited by Walter Hooper. London: Geoffrey Bles, hardback 5 September 1966. (Contents: Preface, ESSAYS: 'On Stories', 'On Three Ways of Writing for Children', 'Sometimes Fairy Stories May Say Best What's to be Said', 'On Juvenile Tastes', 'It All Began with a Picture ...', 'On Criticism', 'On Science Fiction', 'A Reply to Professor Haldane', 'Unreal Estates'; STORIES: 'The Shoddy Lands', 'Ministering Angels', 'Forms of Things Unknown', *After Ten Years* (fragment of a novel), *Notes on After Ten Years* by Roger Lancelyn Green and Alastair Fowler.) These pieces appear with others in *Of This and Other Worlds* (A59).
    U.S. New York: Harcourt, Brace & World, hardback 22 February 1967; Harvest Book paperback 15 October 1975.

47. **CHRISTIAN REFLECTIONS**. Edited by Walter Hooper. London: Geoffrey Bles, hardback 23 January 1967; Fount Paperbacks 1981. (Contents: Preface, 'Christianity and Literature', 'Christianity and Culture', 'Religion: Reality or Substitute?', 'On Ethics', *De Futilitate*', 'The Poison of Subjectivism', 'The Funeral of a Great Myth', 'On Church Music', 'Historicism', 'The Psalms', 'The Language of Religion', 'Petitionary Prayer: A Problem Without an Answer', 'Modern Theology and Biblical Criticism' [= 'Fern-seed and Elephants'], 'The Seeing Eye'.)

U.S. Grand Rapids, Michigan; Eerdmans, hardback 1967.

48. **SPENSER'S/ IMAGES OF LIFE**. Edited by Alastair Fowler. Cambridge: Cambridge University Press, hardback 2 November 1967.

49. **U.S. LETTERS TO/ AN AMERICAN LADY** (Mary Willis Shelburne). Edited by Clyde S. Kilby. Grand Rapids, Michigan: Eerdmans, hardback 1967.

U.K. London: Hodder and Stoughton, hardback June 1969; Hodder and Stoughton paperback 1971.

50. **A MIND AWAKE/** *An Anthology of C.S. Lewis*. Edited by Clyde S. Kilby. London: Geoffrey Bles, hardback 4 March 1968.

U.S. New York: Harcourt, Brace & World, hardback 3 December 1969; Harvest/HBJ paperback 9 September 1980.

51. **NARRATIVE POEMS**. Edited by Walter Hooper. London: Geoffrey Bles, hardback 27 October 1969. (Contents: Preface, *Dymer*, *Launcelot*, *The Nameless Isle*, *The Queen of Drum*, Notes). London: HarperCollins, Fount Paperbacks 30 May 1994.

U.S. New York: Harcourt Brace Jovanovich, hardback 23 February 1972; Harvest/HBJ paperback 6 February 1978.

52. **SELECTED/ LITERARY/ ESSAYS**. Edited by Walter Hooper. Cambridge: Cambridge University Press, hardback 4 December 1969. (Contents: Preface, *'De Descriptione Temporum'*, 'The Alliterative Metre', 'What Chaucer Really Did to *Il Filostrato*', 'The Fifteenth-Century Heroic Line', 'Hero and Leander', 'Variation in Shakespeare and Others', 'Hamlet: The Prince or the Poem?', 'Donne and Love Poetry in the Seventeenth Century', 'The Literary Impact of the Authorized Version', 'The Vision of John Bunyan', 'Addison', 'Four-Letter Words', 'A Note on Jane Austen', 'Shelley, Dryden, and Mr Eliot', 'Sir Walter Scott', 'William Morris', 'Kipling's World', 'Bluspels and Flalansferes: A Semantic

Nightmare', 'High and Low Brows', 'Metre', 'Psycho-analysis and Literary Criticism', 'The Anthropological Approach', Index.)

53. **U.S. GOD IN THE DOCK/** *Essays on Theology and Ethics*. Edited by Walter Hooper. Grand Rapids, Michigan: Eerdmans, hardback 30 November 1970. (Contents: Preface, 'Evil and God', 'Miracles', 'Dogma and the Universe', 'Answers to Questions on Christianity', 'Myth Became Fact', '"Horrid Red Things"', 'Religion and Science', 'The Laws of Nature', 'The Grand Miracle', 'Christian Apologetics', 'Work and Prayer', 'Man or Rabbit?', 'On the Transmission of Christianity', '"Miserable Offenders"', 'The Founding of the Oxford Socratic Club', 'Religion without Dogma?', 'Some Thoughts', 'The Trouble with "X" ...', 'What Are We to Make of Jesus Christ?', 'The Pains of Animals', 'Is Theism Important?', 'Rejoinder to Dr Pittenger', 'Must Our Image of God Go?', 'Dangers of National Repentance', 'Two Ways with the Self', 'Meditation on the Third Commandment', 'On the Reading of Old Books', 'Two Lectures', 'Meditation in a Toolshed', 'Scraps', 'The Decline of Religion', 'Vivisection', 'Modern Translations of the Bible', 'Priestesses in the Church?', 'God in the Dock', 'Behind the Scenes', 'Revival or Decay?', 'Before We Can Communicate', 'Cross-Examination', '"Bulverism", or The Foundation of 20th-Century Thought', 'First and Second Things', 'The Sermon and the Lunch', 'The Humanitarian Theory of Punishment', 'Xmas and Christmas: A Lost Chapter from Herodotus', 'What Christmas Means to Me', 'Delinquents in the Snow', 'Is Progress Possible?: Willing Slaves of the Welfare State', 'We Have No "Right to Happiness"': LETTERS: 'The Conditions for a Just War', 'The Conflict in Anglican Theology', 'Miracles', 'Mr C.S. Lewis on Christianity', 'A Village Experience', 'Correspondence with an Anglican Who Dislikes Hymns', 'The Church's Liturgy, Invocation and Invocation of Saints', 'The Holy Name', 'Mere Christians', 'Canonization', 'Pittenger-Lewis and Version Vernacular', 'Capital Punishment and Death Penalty', Index.)

    U.K. As **UNDECEPTIONS**/ *Essays on Theology and Ethics*. London: Geoffrey Bles, hardback 1971.

54. **FERN-SEED/ AND ELEPHANTS**: *and Other Essays on Christianity*. Edited by Walter Hooper. London: Collins, Fontana Paperbacks 29 September 1975. (Contents: Preface, 'Membership', 'Learning in War Time', 'On Forgiveness', 'Historicism', 'The World's Last Night', 'Religion and Rocketry', 'The Efficacy of Prayer', 'Fern-Seed and Elephants' (= 'Modern Theology and Biblical Criticism').)

55. **THE DARK TOWER/** *And Other Stories.* Edited by Walter Hooper. London: Collins, hardback 28 February 1977; Fount Paperbacks 28 July 1983. (Contents: Preface, *The Dark Tower*, Note on *The Dark Tower*, 'The Man Born Blind', 'The Shoddy Lands', 'Ministering Angels', 'Forms of Things Unknown', *After Ten Years*, Notes on *After Ten Years* by Roger Lancelyn Green and Alastair Fowler.)

U.S. New York: Harcourt Brace Jovanovich, hardback and Harvest/ HBJ paperback 18 April 1977.

56. **U.S. THE JOYFUL CHRISTIAN/** *127 Readings from C.S. Lewis.* Edited with a Foreword by Henry William Griffin. New York: Macmillan hardback 1977; Macmillan Paperbacks Edition 1984.

57. **GOD IN THE/ DOCK/** *Essays on Theology.* Edited by Walter Hooper. London: Collins, Fontana Paperbacks 29 March 1979. (Contents: Preface, 'Miracles', 'Dogma and the Universe', 'Myth Became Fact', 'Religion and Science', 'The Laws of Nature', 'The Grand Miracle', 'Man or Rabbit?', 'The Trouble with "X" ...', 'What are We to Make of Jesus Christ?', 'Must Our Image of God Go?' 'Priestesses in the Church?', 'God in the Dock', 'We Have No "Right to Happiness"'.)

58. **THEY STAND/ TOGETHER/** *The Letters of/ C.S. Lewis to Arthur Greeves/ (1914–63).* Edited by Walter Hooper. London: Collins, hardback 19 April 1979. (Contents: Introduction, Editor's Note, 296 letters from C.S. Lewis to Arthur Greeves, 2 letters from W.H. Lewis to Arthur Greeves, 1 letter from Joy Davidman to Arthur Greeves, and 4 letters from Arthur Greeves to C.S. Lewis, Index.)

U.S. New York: Macmillan: 1979; Macmillan Collier Books Edition paperback retitled *The Letters of/ C.S. Lewis to Arthur Greeves/ (1914–63)*, 1986.

59. **OF THIS/ AND/ OTHER WORLDS.** Edited by Walter Hooper. London: Collins, hardback 6 September 1982; Fount Paperbacks 1984. (Contents: Preface, 'On Stories', 'The Novels of Charles Williams', 'A Tribute to E.R. Eddison', 'On Three Ways of Writing for Children', 'Sometimes Fairy Stories May Say Best What's to be Said', 'On Juvenile Tastes', 'It All Began with a Picture ...', 'On Science Fiction', 'A Reply to Professor Haldane', 'The Hobbit', 'Tolkien's *The Lord of the Rings*', 'A Panegyric for Dorothy L. Sayers', 'The Mythopoeic Gift of Rider Haggard', 'George Orwell', 'The Death of Words', 'The Parthenon and the Optative', 'Period Criticism', 'Different

Tastes in Literature', 'On Criticism', 'Unreal Estates'.) This book contains all the essays that were in *Of Other Worlds* (A46).

U.S. As *On Stories: and Other Essays on Literature*, New York: Harcourt, Brace, Jovanovich, hardback and paperback 24 June 1982.

60. **THE BUSINESS/ OF HEAVEN**/ *Daily Readings from/ C.S. Lewis*. Edited by Walter Hooper. London: Collins, Fount Paperbacks 15 March 1984. (Contents: Preface, 365 Readings for the Year, Movable Fasts and Feasts.)

U.S. New York: Harcourt, Brace, Jovanovich, a Harvest/HBJ paperback 5 July 1984.

61. **BOXEN/** *The Imaginary World of/ the Young/ C.S. Lewis*. Edited by Walter Hooper. London: Collins, hardback 28 May 1985, paperback 10 October 1985. (Contents: Introduction, ANIMAL-LAND STORIES: 'The King's Ring', 'Manx Against Manx', 'The Relief of Murry', 'History of Mouse-land from Stone-Age to Bublish I', 'History of Animal-Land', 'The Chess Monograph', 'The Geography of Animal-Land'; BOXEN STORIES: 'Boxen: or Scenes from Boxonian City Life', 'The Locked Door and Than-Kyu', 'The Sailor'; ENCYCLOPEDIA BOXONIANA.)

U.S. San Diego, California: Harcourt, Brace, Jovanovich, hardback 17 October 1985, Harvest/HBJ paperback 26 November 1986.

62. **U.S. LETTERS TO/ CHILDREN**. Edited by Lyle W. Dorsett and Marjorie Lamp Mead, with a Foreword by Douglas H. Gresham. New York: Macmillan, hardback 11 April 1985, paperback April 1988.

U.K. London: Collins, hardback 31 October 1985 and Fount Paperbacks 13 October 1986.

63. **FIRST AND/ SECOND THINGS**: *Essays on Theology and Ethics*. Edited by Walter Hooper. London: Collins, Fount Paperbacks 11 July 1985. (Contents: Preface, 'Bulverism', 'First and Second Things', 'On the Reading of Old Books', '"Horrid Red Things"', 'Work and Prayer', 'Two Lectures', 'Meditation in a Toolshed', 'The Sermon and the Lunch', 'On the Transmission of Christianity', 'The Decline of Religion', 'Vivisection', 'Modern Translations of the Bible', 'Some Thoughts', 'The Humanitarian Theory of Punishment', 'Xmas and Christmas', 'Revival or Decay?', 'Before We Can Communicate'.)

64. **PRESENT CONCERNS**. Edited by Walter Hooper. London: Collins, Fount Paperbacks 10 July 1986. (Contents: Introduction, 'The Necessity of

Chivalry', 'Equality', 'Three Kinds of Men', 'My First School', 'Is English Doomed?', 'Democratic Education', 'A Dream', 'Blimpophobia', 'Private Bates', 'Hedonics', 'After Priggery – What?', 'Modern Man and his Categories of Thought', 'Talking about Bicycles', 'On Living in an Atomic Age', 'The Empty Universe', 'Prudery and Philology', 'Interim Report', 'Is History Bunk?', 'Sex in Literature'.)

U.S. San Diego, California: Harcourt, Brace, Jovanovich, hardback and Harvest/HBJ paperback 25 March 1987.

65. **TIMELESS AT HEART/** *Essays on Theology*. Edited by Walter Hooper. London: Collins, Fount Paperbacks 16 July 1987. (Contents: Preface, 'Christian Apologetics', 'Answers to Questions on Christianity', 'Why I Am Not a Pacifist', 'The Pains of Animals', 'The Founding of the Oxford Socratic Club', 'Religion Without Dogma?', 'Is Theism Important?', 'Rejoinder to Dr Pittenger', 'Willing Slaves of the Welfare State', Letters.)

66. **LETTERS/ C.S. LEWIS/ DON GIOVANNI CALABRIA/** *A study in friendship*. Translated and edited by Martin Moynihan. London: Collins, hardback January 1989.

U.S. Ann Arbor, Michigan: Servant Books, paperback 1 November 1988. (This is a correspondence in Latin between C.S. Lewis and Don Giovanni Calabria,* Founder of the Casa Buoni Fanciulli in Verona. The book contains 28 letters from Lewis, and 7 from Don Giovanni in the original Latin with an English translation.)

67. **CHRISTIAN/ REUNION:** *And Other Essays*. Edited by Walter Hooper. London: Collins, Fount Paperbacks 15 August 1990. (Contents: Introduction, 'Christian Reunion', 'Lilies that Fester', 'Evil and God', 'Dangers of National Repentance', 'Two Ways with the Self', 'Meditation on the Third Commandment', 'Scraps', 'Miserable Offenders', 'Cross-Examination', 'Behind the Scenes', 'What Christmas Means to Me', 'Delinquents in the Snow'.)

68. **ALL MY ROAD/ BEFORE ME/** *The Diary of C.S. Lewis 1922–27*. Edited by Walter Hooper. London: HarperCollins, hardback 18 April 1991; Fount Paperbacks 18 March 1993.

U.S. San Diego, California: Harcourt, Brace, Jovanovich, hardback 24 July 1991; Harvest/HBJ paperback 13 November 1992.

69. **DAILY READINGS WITH/ C.S. LEWIS**. Edited by Walter Hooper. London: HarperCollins, Fount Paperbacks 18 June 1992. Reissued by

HarperCollins as a Fount Paperback on 10 July 1995 under the title **C.S. LEWIS: READINGS FOR REFLECTION AND MEDITATION.**

70. **THE COLLECTED POEMS OF C.S. LEWIS.** Edited by Walter Hooper. London: HarperCollins, Fount Paperbacks 30 May 1994. (Contents: *Poems*; *Spirits in Bondage*; and A Miscellany of Additional Poems which consists of 17 previously unpublished poems.)

B: Short Stories

1. 'The Shoddy Lands', *The Magazine of Fantasy and Science Fiction*, X (February 1956) pp. 68–74. Repr. **OOW, DT**.

2. 'Ministering Angels', *The Magazine of Fantasy and Science Fiction*, XIII (January 1958) pp. 5–14. Repr. **OOW, DT**.

3. 'Forms of Things Unknown', *Fifty-Two: A Journal of Books & Authors* [from Geoffrey Bles], No 18 (August 1966) pp. 3–9. (An abridgement of the story that appears in *Of Other Worlds* and *The Dark Tower*.) Repr. **OOW, DT**.

4. 'The Man Born Blind', *Church Times*, No 5947 (4 February 1977) pp. 4–5. Repr. **OOW, DT**.

C: Books Edited or with Prefaces by C.S. Lewis

1. St Athanasius, *The Incarnation of the Word of God: Being the Treatise of St Athanasius' 'De Incarnatione Verbi Dei'* with an Introduction by C.S. Lewis. (Translated and edited by A Religious of CSMV [Sister Penelope CSMV = R.P. Lawson].) Lewis's Introduction is reprinted as 'On the Reading of Old Books' in **GID = U, FST**.

2. *George MacDonald: An Anthology*. Edited by C.S. Lewis. London: Geoffrey Bles, 18 March 1946 [Macmillan, 1947].

3. B.G. Sandhurst, *How Heathen is Britain?* with a Preface by C.S. Lewis. London: Collins, 1946. Lewis's Preface is reprinted as 'On the Transmission of Christianity' in **GID = U** and **FST**.

4. Eric Bentley, *The Cult of the Superman: A Study of the Idea of Heroism in Carlyle and Nietzsche, with Notes on Other Hero-Worshippers of Modern Times*, with an Appreciation by C.S. Lewis. London: Geoffrey Bles, 1947.

5. J.B. Phillips, *Letters to Young Churches: A Translation of the New Testament Epistles*, with an Introduction by C.S. Lewis. London: Geoffrey Bles, 1947. Lewis's Introduction is reprinted as 'Modern Translations of the Bible' in **GID = U, FST**.

6. C.S. Lewis (editor), *Essays Presented to Charles Williams*. London: Oxford University Press, 1947. (With a Preface and an essay, 'On Stories', by C.S. Lewis.)

7. D.E. Harding, *The Hierarchy of Heaven and Earth: A New Diagram of Man in the Universe*, with a Preface by C.S. Lewis. London: Faber & Faber, 1952. Lewis's Preface is reprinted as 'The Empty Universe' in **PRCON**.

8. Joy Davidman, *Smoke on the Mountain: An Interpretation of the Ten Commandments in Terms of Today*, with a Foreword by C.S. Lewis. London: Hodder & Stoughton, 1955.

9. Austin Farrer, *A Faith of Our Own*, with a Preface by C.S. Lewis. Cleveland, Ohio: World Publishing Co., 1960.

10. Layamon, *Selection from Layamon's 'Brut'*. Edited by G.L. Brook, with an Introduction by C.S. Lewis. Oxford: Clarendon Press, 1963.

11. *The Play and its Critic: Essays for Eric Bentley*. Edited by Michael Bertin, with an Appreciation by C.S. Lewis. Lanham, Maryland: University Press of America, 1986. The Appreciation consists of two letters of recommendation which Lewis wrote about his pupil, Eric Bentley, in 1938 and 1940.

D: Essays, Pamphlets and Miscellaneous Pieces

1. 'The Expedition to Holly Bush Hill', *Cherbourg School Magazine* (November 1912). Reproduced in **LP** III:310–11.[1]

2. 'Are Athletes Better than Scholars?', *Cherbourg School Magazine*, No 2 (1913). Reproduced in **LP** III:318–19.

---

[1] It has been impossible to discover any copies of the *Cherbourg School Magazine*, once published by the long-defunct Cherbourg School in Malvern, Worcestershire. Lewis's contributions are, however, reproduced in the unpublished 'Lewis Papers: Memoirs of the Lewis Family 1850–1930' (**LP**). The original of the **LP** is in Wheaton College, and there is a microfilm in the Bodleian Library.

3. 'The Expedition to Holly Bush Hill', *Cherbourg School Magazine* (July 1913). This is a different expedition from the one in D1. Reproduced in **LP** IV:51.

4. 'A Note on *Comus*', *The Review of English Studies*, VIII (April 1932), pp. 170–6. Repr. **SMRL**.

5. 'What Chaucer Really Did to *Il Filostrato*', *Essays and Studies by Members of the English Association*, XVII (1932), pp. 56–75. Repr. **SLE**.

6. 'The Personal Heresy in Criticism', *Essays and Studies by Members of the English Association*, XIX (1934) pp. 7–28; Repr. **PH**; cf. E.M.W. Tillyard, 'The Personal Heresy in Criticism: A Rejoinder', ibid., XX (1935) pp. 7–20. Repr. **PH**.

7. 'A Metrical Suggestion', *Lysistrata*, II (May 1935), pp. 13–24. Repr. as 'The Alliterative Metre' in **R** and **SLE**.

8. 'Genius and Genius', *The Review of English Studies*, XII (April 1936), pp. 189–94. Repr. **SMRL**.

9. 'Open Letter to Dr Tillyard', *Essays and Studies by Members of the English Association*, XXI (1936), pp. 153–68. Repr. **PH**.

10. 'Donne and Love Poetry in the Seventeenth Century', *Seventeenth-Century Studies Presented to Sir Herbert Grierson*. Oxford: Clarendon Press, 1938, pp. 64–84. Repr. **SLE**.

11. 'From Johnson's *Life of Fox*', *The Oxford Magazine*, LVI (9 June 1938), pp. 737–78 (Unsigned).

12. 'The Fifteenth-Century Heroic Line', *Essays and Studies by Members of the English Association*, XXIV (1939), pp. 28–41. Repr. **SLE**.

13. 'None Other Gods: Culture in War Time', a sermon before the Church of St Mary the Virgin, Oxford. Mimeographed by the Church of St Mary the Virgin, 22 October 1939. Reprinted in pamphlet form as *The Christian in Danger*, London: Student Christian Movement, 1939; Repr. as 'Learning in War Time' in **T (WG)** and **FE**.

14. 'Christianity and Culture', *Theology*, XL (March 1940), pp. 166–79. Repr. as Part I of 'Christianity and Culture' in **CR**. cf. S.L. Bethell and E.F. Carritt, 'Christianity and Culture: Replies to Mr Lewis', ibid. XL (May 1940), pp. 356–66.

15. C.S. Lewis, 'Christianity and Culture' (a letter), ibid. XL (June 1940), pp. 475–7. Repr. as Part II of 'Christianity and Culture' in **CR**. cf. George Every, 'In Defence of Criticism', ibid. XLI (Sept. 1940), pp. 159–65.

16. 'Dangers of National Repentance', *The Guardian* (15 March 1940), p. 127. Repr. **GID, CRR**.

17. 'Two Ways with the Self', *The Guardian* (3 May 1940), p. 215. Repr. **GID, CRR**.

18. 'Notes on the Way', *Time and Tide*, XXI (17 August 1940), p. 841. Reprinted as 'Importance of an Ideal', *Living Age*, CCCLIX (October 1940), pp. 109–11. Repr. as 'The Necessity of Chivalry' in **PRCON**.

19. 'Peace Proposals for Brother Every and Mr Bethell', *Theology*, XLI (December 1940), pp. 339–48. Repr. as Part III of 'Christianity and Culture' in **CR**.

20. 'Meditation on the Third Commandment', *The Guardian* (10 January 1941), p. 18. Repr. **GID, CRR**.

21. 'Evil and God', *The Spectator*, CLXVI (7 February 1941), p. 141. Repr. **GID = U, CRR**.

22. 'Edmund Spenser', *Fifteen Poets*. London: Oxford University Press, 1941, pp. 40–3. Repr. as 'On Reading *The Faerie Queene*' in **SMRL**.

23. 'Notes on the Way', *Time and Tide* XXII (29 March 1941), p. 261. Repr. and expanded as '"Bulverism", or, The Foundation of 20th Century Thought', in *The Socratic Digest*, No 2 (June 1944), pp. 16–20. Expanded version repr. **GID = U, FST**.

24. 'The Screwtape Letters – I', *The Guardian* (2 May 1941), pp. 211–12. Repr. **SL**.

25. 'The Screwtape Letters – II', *The Guardian* (9 May 1941), pp. 223–4. Repr. **SL**.

26. 'The Screwtape Letters – III', *The Guardian* (16 May 1941), pp. 235–6. Repr. **SL**.

27. 'The Screwtape Letters – IV', *The Guardian* (23 May 1941), pp. 246, 249. Repr. **SL**.

28. 'The Screwtape Letters – V', *The Guardian* (30 May 1941), pp. 259–60. Repr. **SL**.

29. 'The Screwtape Letters – VI', *The Guardian* (6 June 1941), pp. 270, 273. Repr. **SL**.

30. 'The Screwtape Letters – VII', *The Guardian* (13 June 1941), p. 282. Repr. **SL**.

31. 'The Screwtape Letters – VIII', *The Guardian* (20 June 1941), pp. 291–2. Repr. **SL**.

32. 'The Screwtape Letters – IX', *The Guardian* (27 June 1941), pp. 307–8. Repr. **SL**.

33. 'The Screwtape Letters – X', *The Guardian* (4 July 1941), pp. 319–20. Repr. **SL**.

34. 'The Screwtape Letters – XI', *The Guardian* (11 July 1941), pp. 331–2. Repr. **SL**.

35. 'The Screwtape Letters – XII', *The Guardian* (18 July 1941), pp. 343–4. Repr. **SL**.

36. 'The Screwtape Letters – XIII', *The Guardian* (25 July 1941), pp. 355–6. Repr. **SL**.

37. 'The Screwtape Letters – XIV', *The Guardian* (1 August 1941), pp. 367–8. Repr. **SL**.

38. 'The Screwtape Letters – XV', *The Guardian* (8 August 1941), pp. 378, 382. Repr. **SL**.

39. 'The Screwtape Letters – XVI', *The Guardian* (15 August 1941), pp. 391–2. Repr. **SL**.

40. 'The Screwtape Letters – XVII', *The Guardian* (22 August 1941), p. 402. Repr. **SL**.

41. 'The Screwtape Letters – XVIII', *The Guardian* (29 August 1941), pp. 417–18. Repr. **SL**.

42. 'The Screwtape Letters – XIX', *The Guardian* (5 September 1941), p. 426. Repr. **SL**.

43. 'The Screwtape Letters – XX', *The Guardian* (12 September 1941), pp. 443–4. Repr. **SL**.

44. 'The Screwtape Letters – XXI', *The Guardian* (19 September 1941), pp. 451–2. Repr. **SL**.

45. 'The Screwtape Letters – XXII', *The Guardian* (26 September 1941), p. 465. Repr. **SL**.

46. 'Religion: Reality or Substitute?', *World Dominion*, XIX (September–October 1941), pp. 277–81. Repr. **CR**.

47. 'The Screwtape Letters – XXIII: The Historical Jesus', *The Guardian* (3 October 1941), pp. 475–6. Repr. **SL**.

48. 'The Screwtape Letters – XXIV: Spiritual Pride', *The Guardian* (10 October 1941), p. 490. Repr. **SL**.

49. 'The Screwtape Letters – XXV: The Enemy Loves Platitudes', *The Guardian* (17 October 1941), pp. 498, 502. Repr. **SL**.

50. 'The Screwtape Letters – XXVI: The Generous Conflict Illusion', *The Guardian* (24 October 1941), p. 514. Repr. **SL**.

51. 'The Screwtape Letters – XXVII: The Historical Point of View', *The Guardian* (31 October 1941), p. 526. Repr. **SL**.

52. 'The Screwtape Letters – XXVIII', *The Guardian* (7 November 1941), p. 531. Repr. **SL**.

53. 'The Screwtape Letters – XXIX: Cowardice', *The Guardian* (14 November 1941), p. 550. Repr. **SL**.

54. 'The Screwtape Letters – XXX', *The Guardian* (21 November 1941), p. 558. Repr. **SL**.

55. 'The Screwtape Letters – XXXI', *The Guardian* (28 November 1941), p. 570. Repr. **SL**.

56. 'The Weight of Glory', *Theology*, XLIII (November 1941), pp. 263–74. Repr. as a pamphlet, London, SPCK, 1942. Repr. **T (WG), TAFP, SPT**.

57. 'Psycho-analysis and Literary Criticism', *Essays and Studies by Members of the English Association*, XXVII (1942), pp. 7–21. Repr. **TAFP, SLE**.

58. 'Hamlet: The Prince or the Poem?', Annual Shakespeare Lecture, 1942, *The Proceedings of the British Academy*, XXVIII, London: Oxford University Press, 1942. Repr. **TAFP, SLE**.

59. 'Notes on the Way', *Time and Tide*, XXIII (27 June 1942), pp. 519–20. Repr. as 'First and Second Things' in **GID = U. FST**.

60. 'Miracles', *The Guardian* (2 October 1942), p. 316.

61. 'Miracles', *Saint Jude's Gazette*, No 73 (October 1942), pp. 4–7. (Published by St Jude on the Hill Church, Golders Green, London.) This version of 'Miracles', which is an expansion of the one printed in *The Guardian* (above), is repr. in **GID = U, gid**.

62. 'This Was a Very Frank Talk – Which We Think Everyone Should Read', *Daily Mirror* (13 October 1942), pp. 6–7. This broadcast on 'Sexual Morality' was published illegally before its appearance in **CB** and **MC**.

63. Preface to *The Socratic Digest*, No 1 (1942–43), pp. 3–5. Repr. as 'The Founding of the Oxford Socratic Club' in **GID=U, TAH**.

64. 'Dogma and the Universe', *The Guardian* (19 March 1943), p. 96. Repr. **GID = U, gid**.

65. 'Three Kinds of Men', *The Sunday Times*, No 6258 (21 March 1943), p. 2. Repr. **PRCON**.

66. 'Dogma and Science', *The Guardian* (26 March 1943), pp. 104, 107. This article, which concludes 'Dogma and the Universe' (above), is repr. as 'Dogma and the Universe' in **GID = U, gid**.

67. 'The Poison of Subjectivism', *Religion in Life*, XII (Summer 1943), pp. 356–65. Repr. **CR**.

68. 'Equality', *The Spectator*, CLXXI (27 August 1943), p. 192. Repr. **PRCON**.

69. 'Notes on the Way', *Time and Tide*, XXIV (4 September 1943), p. 717. Repr. as 'My First School' in **PRCON**.

70. 'Is English Doomed?', *The Spectator*, CLXXII (11 February 1944), p. 121. Repr. **PRCON**.

71. 'The Map and the Ocean', *The Listener*, XXXI (24 February 1944), p. 216. Repr. **BP, MC**.

72. 'God in Three Persons', *The Listener*, XXXI (2 March 1944), p. 224. Repr. **BP, MC**.

73. 'The Whole Purpose of the Christian', *The Listener*, XXXI (9 March 1944), p. 272. Repr. **BP, MC**.

74. 'Notes on the Way', *Time and Tide*, XXV (11 March 1944), p. 213. Repr. as 'The Parthenon and the Optative' in **OTOW = OS**.

75. 'The Obstinate Tin Soldiers', *The Listener*, XXXI (16 March 1944), p. 300. Repr. **BP, MC**.

76. 'Let us Pretend', *The Listener*, XXXI (23 March 1944), p. 328. Repr. **BP, MC**.

77. 'Is Christianity Hard or Easy?', *The Listener*, XXXI (30 March 1944), p. 356. Repr. **BP, MC**.

78. 'The New Man', *The Listener*, XXXI (6 April 1944), p. 384. Repr. **BP, MC**.

79. 'What France Means to You', (par Raymond Mortimer, Gilbert Murray, J.H.F. McEwen, C.S. Lewis, Harold Nicholson, David Eccles, et

Michael Roberts) *La France Libre*, VII, 42 (15 Avril 1944), pp. 403–4. In this periodical, published by Hamish Hamilton Ltd in London, each of the contributors wrote in French. Lewis's essay is reprinted with a translation in *The Canadian C.S. Lewis Journal*,‡ No 87 (Spring 1995), pp. 6–10.

80. *Answers to Questions on Christianity.* Electric and Musical Industries Christian Fellowship, Hayes, Middlesex [1944], 24 pp. (From the Preface: 'A "One Man Brains Trust" held on 18 April 1944, at the Head Office of Electric and Musical Industries, Ltd' H.W. Bowen, Question master.) Repr. **GID = U, TAH**.

81. 'Notes on the Way', *Time and Tide*, XXV (29 April 1944), pp. 369–70. Repr. as 'Democratic Education' in **PRCON**.

82. 'A Dream', *The Spectator*, CLXXIII (28 July 1944), p. 77. Repr. in **PRCON**.

83. 'Blimpophobia', *Time and Tide*, XXV (9 September 1944), p. 785. Repr. **PRCON**.

84. 'The Death of Words', *The Spectator*, CLXXIII (22 September 1944), p. 261. Repr. **OTOW = OS**.

85. 'Myth Became Fact', *World Dominion*, XXII (September–October 1944), pp. 267–70. Repr. **GID = U, gid**.

86. '"Horrid Red Things"', *Church of England Newspaper*, LI (6 October 1944), pp. 1–2. Repr. **GID = U, FST**.

87. 'Who Goes Home? or The Grand Divorce I', *The Guardian* (10 November 1944), pp. 399–400. ('I seemed to be standing ... as far as the eye could reach.') Repr. **GD**.[2]

88. 'Who Goes Home? or The Grand Divorce II', *The Guardian* (17 November 1944), pp. 411, 413. ('I was not left very long ... But he didn't seem able to stop it.') Repr. **GD**.

---

[2] *Who Goes Home? or The Great Divorce* was published in twenty-three consecutive parts in the pages of *The Guardian* before it was published as a book under the title *The Great Divorce*. To show how these parts compare with the segments of the book, the beginning and end of each part is shown.

89. 'Who Goes Home? or The Grand Divorce III', *The Guardian* (24 November 1944), pp. 421–2. ('From the vibrations I gathered that the bus ... And still the light grew.') Repr. **GD**.

90. 'Who Goes Home? or The Grand Divorce IV', *The Guardian* (1 December 1944), pp. 431–2. ('A cliff had loomed up ahead ... The rest of us huddled closer to one another.') Repr. **GD**.

91. 'Who Goes Home? or The Grand Divorce V', *The Guardian* (8 December 1944), pp. 442, 445. ('As the solid people came nearer ... it picked its way over the sharp grasses, it made off.') Repr. **GD**.

92. 'Who Goes Home? or The Grand Divorce VI', *The Guardian* (15 December 1944), pp. 453–4. ('For a moment there was silence ... "I'm not sure that I've got the exact point you are trying to make," said the Ghost.') Repr. **GD**.

93. 'Who Goes Home? or The Grand Divorce VII', *The Guardian* (22 December 1944), pp. 463–5. ('"I am not trying to make any point," ... walking very fast indeed I made very little progress.') Repr. **GD**.

94. 'Who Goes Home? or The Grand Divorce VIII', *The Guardian* (29 December 1944), pp. 472–4. ('The cool smooth skin of the bright water ... even greater caution till I lost sight of it.') Repr. **GD**.

95. 'Private Bates', *The Spectator*, CLXXIII (29 December 1944), p. 596. Repr. **PRCON**.

96. 'Religion and Science', *The Coventry Evening Telegraph* (3 January 1945), p. 4. Repr. **GID = U, gid**.

97. 'Who Goes Home? or The Grand Divorce IX', *The Guardian* (5 January 1945), pp. 4, 8. ('Although I watched the misfortunes of the Ghost ... A few minutes later he moved off.') Repr. **GD**.

98. 'Who Goes Home? or The Grand Divorce X', *The Guardian* (12 January 1945), pp. 15, 18. ('I sat still on a stone by the river's side ... So I never saw the end of that interview.') Repr. **GD**.

99. 'Who Goes Home? or The Grand Divorce XI', *The Guardian* (19 January 1945), pp. 25–6. ('"Where are ye going?," said a voice with a strong Scotch accent ... And how *can* they choose it?"') Repr. **GD**.

100. 'Who Goes Home? or The Grand Divorce XII', *The Guardian* (26 January 1945), pp. 34, 37. ('"Milton was right," said my Teacher ... still accompanied by the bright patience at her side, moved out of hearing.') Repr. **GD**.

101. 'Who Goes Home? or The Grand Divorce XIII', *The Guardian* (2 February 1945), pp. 45, 48. ('"What troubles ye, son?" ... Those that hate goodness are sometimes nearer than those that know nothing at all about it and think they have it already.') Repr. **GD**.

102. 'Who Goes Home? or The Grand Divorce XIV', *The Guardian* (9 February 1945), p. 52. ('"Whist, now!," said my Teacher ... And without listening to the Spirit's reply, the spectre vanished.') Repr. **GD**.

103. 'Who Goes Home? or The Grand Divorce XV', *The Guardian* (16 February 1945), pp. 63–4. ('This conversation also we overheard ... A sour, dry smell lingered in the air for a moment and then there was no Ghost to be seen.') Repr. **GD**.

104. 'Who was Right – Dream Lecturer or Real Lecturer?', *The Coventry Evening Telegraph* (21 February 1945), p. 4. Repr. as 'Two Lectures' in **GID** = **U, FST**.

105. 'Who Goes Home? or The Grand Divorce XVI', *The Guardian* (23 February 1945), pp. 73, 77. ('One of the most painful meetings we witnessed ... "We will go a bit further," said my Teacher, laying his hand on my arm.') Repr. **GD**.

106. 'Who Goes Home? or The Grand Divorce XVII', *The Guardian* (2 March 1945), p. 84. ('"Why did you bring me away, Sir?," ... "I cannot kill it against your will. It is impossible. Have I your permission?"') Repr. **GD**.

107. 'Who Goes Home? or The Grand Divorce XVIII', *The Guardian* (9 March 1945), pp. 95–6. ('The Angel's hands were almost closed on the Lizard ... "Is there *another* river, Sir" I asked.') Repr. **GD**.

108. 'Who Goes Home? or The Grand Divorce XIX', *The Guardian* (16 March 1945), p. 104. ('The reason why I asked if there were another river ... He was like a seedy actor of the old school.') Repr. **GD**.

109. 'Who Goes Home? or The Grand Divorce XX', *The Guardian* (23 March 1945), p. 114. ('"Darling! At last!" said the Lady ... It just won't work.') Repr. **GD**.

110. 'Who Goes Home? or The Grand Divorce XXI', *The Guardian* (29 March 1945), p. 124. ('I do not know that I ever saw another more terrible ... bending with its light feet the grasses I could not bend.') Repr. **GD**.

111. 'The Laws of Nature', *The Coventry Evening Telegraph* (4 April 1945), p. 4. Repr. **GID = U, gid**.

112. 'Who Goes Home? or The Grand Divorce XXII', *The Guardian* (6 April 1945), p. 132. ('Presently the lady got up ... your terrestrial Pacific itself is only a molecule.') Repr. **GD**.

113. 'Who Goes Home? or The Grand Divorce XXIII', *The Guardian* (13 April 1945), p. 141. ('"I see," said I at last ... the clock striking three, and the siren howling overhead.') Repr. **GD**.

114. Recollection of George Gordon's 'Discussion Class' in M.[ary] C. G.[ordon], *The Life of George S. Gordon* 1881–1942. London: Oxford University Press, 1945, p. 77.

115. 'The Grand Miracle', *The Guardian* (27 April 1945), pp. 161, 165. Repr. **GID = U, gid**.

116. 'Charles Walter Stansby Williams (1886–1945)', *The Oxford Magazine*, LXIII (24 May 1945), p. 265 (obituary).

117. 'Work and Prayer', *The Coventry Evening Telegraph* (28 May 1945), p. 4. Repr. **GID = U, FST**.

118. 'Membership', *Sobornost*, No 31, New Series (June 1945), pp. 4–9. Repr. **T = WG, FE**.

119. 'Hedonics', *Time and Tide*, XXVI (16 June 1945), pp. 494–5. Repr. **PRCON**.

120. 'Oliver Elton (1861–1945)', *The Oxford Magazine*, LXIII (21 June 1945), pp. 318–19 (obituary).

121. 'Meditation in a Toolshed', *The Coventry Evening Telegraph* (17 July 1945), p. 4. Repr. **GID = U, FST**.

122. 'Addison', *Essays on the Eighteenth Century Presented to David Nichol Smith*. Oxford: Clarendon Press, 1945, pp. 1–14. Repr. **SLE**.

123. 'The Sermon and the Lunch', *Church of England Newspaper*, No 2692 (21 September 1945), pp. 1–2. Repr. **GID = U, FST**.

124. 'Scraps', *St James' Magazine* (December 1945), pp. [4–5]. (Published by St James' Church, Birkdale, Southport.) Repr. **GID = U, CRR**.

125. 'After Priggery – What?', *The Spectator*, CLXXV (7 December 1945), p. 536. Repr. **PRCON**.

126. 'Is Theology Poetry?', *The Socratic Digest*, No 3 (1945), pp. 25–35. Repr. **TAFP, SPT**.

127. *Man or Rabbit?* Student Christian Movement in Schools [1946?], 4 pp. Repr. **GID = U, gid**.

128. Sermon in *Five Sermons by Laymen*. St Matthew's Church, Northampton (April – May 1946), pp. 1–6. Repr. with slight alterations as '*Miserable Offenders*': *An Interpretation of Prayer Book Language*, Advent Paper No 12. Boston: Church of the Advent [n.d.] 12 pp. Also repr. **GID = U, CRR**.

129. 'Notes on the Way', *Time and Tide*, XXVII (25 May 1946), p. 486. Repr. as first part of 'Different Tastes in Literature' in **OTOW = OS**.

130. 'Notes on the Way', *Time and Tide*, XXVII (1 June 1946), pp. 510–11. Repr. as second part of 'Different Tastes in Literature' in **OTOW = OS**.

131. 'Talking about Bicycles', *Resistance* (October 1946), pp. 10–13. Repr. **PRCON**.

132. 'Notes on the Way', *Time and Tide*, XXVII (9 November 1946), pp. 1070–71. Repr. as 'Period Criticism' in **OTOW = OS**.

133. 'The Decline of Religion', *The Cherwell*, XXVI (29 November 1946), pp. 8–10. Repr. **GID = U, FST**.

134. 'A Christian Reply to Professor Price', *Phoenix Quarterly*, I, No 1 (Autumn 1946), pp. 31–44; cf. H.H. Price, 'The Grounds of Modern Agnosticism', ibid., pp. 10–30. (Despite the fact that 'Religion Without Dogma?' was published later, 'A Christian Reply to Professor Price' is a revision of 'Religion Without Dogma?')

135. 'On Stories', *Essays Presented to Charles Williams*. London: Oxford University Press, 1947, pp. 90–105. Repr. **OTOW=OS**.

136. *Vivisection*, with a portrait of Lewis, and a Foreword by George R. Farnum. Boston: New England Anti-Vivisection Society, [1947], 11 pp. (Repr., with portrait, and a Foreword by R. Fielding-Ould. London, National Anti-Vivisection Society, [1948] 11 pp.) Repr. **GID = U, FST**.

137. 'Kipling's World', *Literature and Life: Addresses to the English Association*, I. London: Harrap and Co., 1948, pp. 57–73. Repr. **TAFP, SLE**.

138. 'Some Thoughts', *The First Decade: Ten Years' Work of the Medical Missionaries of Mary*. Dublin: At the Sign of the Three Candles, [1948], pp. 91–4. Repr. **GID = U, FST**.

139. 'Religion Without Dogma?', *The Socratic Digest*, No 4 [1948], pp. 82–94; cf. H.H. Price, 'Reply', ibid., pp. 94–102. Repr. **GID = U, TAH**.

140. 'Reply – Note', *The Socratic Digest*, No 4 [1948], pp. 15–16; G.E.M. Anscombe, 'A Reply to Mr C.S. Lewis's Argument that "Naturalism" is Self-refuting', ibid., pp. 7–15. The argument Miss Anscombe was criticizing is found in the original third chapter of Lewis's *Miracles* (1947). Lewis's 'Reply – Note' repr. **GID = U, TAH**.

141. 'The Trouble with "X" ...', *Bristol Diocesan Gazette*, XXVII (August 1948), pp. 3–6. Repr. **GID = U, gid**.

142. 'Notes on the Way', *Time and Tide*, XXIX (14 August 1948), pp. 830–1. Repr. as 'Priestesses in the Church?' in **GID = U, gid**.

143. 'Difficulties in Presenting the Faith to Modern Unbelievers', (English text with French translation) *Lumen Vitae*, III (September 1948), pp. 421–26. Repr. as 'God in the Dock' in **GID = U, gid**.

144. 'Note' on Programme of Owen Barfield's play *Orpheus*, produced by the Sheffield Educational Settlement at The Little Theatre, Shipton Street, Sheffield, on 25 September [1948], p. 8. This 'Note' is reprinted on the cover of Owen Barfield, *Orpheus: A Poetic Drama*, ed. John C. Ulrich, Jr. (West Stockbridge, Massachusetts: The Lindisfarne Press, 1983.)

145. "On Living in an Atomic Age", *Informed Reading*, VI [1948], pp. 78–84. Repr. **PRCON**.

146. 'On Church Music', *English Church Music*, XIX (April 1949), pp. 19–22. Repr. **CR**.

147. 'The Humanitarian Theory of Punishment', *20th Century: An Australian Quarterly Review*, III. No 3 (1949), pp. 5–12; cf. Norval Morris and Donald Buckle, 'A Reply to C.S. Lewis', ibid. VI, No 2 (1952), pp. 20–6. Both articles were reprinted in *Res Judicate*, VI (June 1953), pp. 224–30, 231–7. Lewis's article repr. with 'On Punishment: A Reply' in **GID = U, FST**.

148. (With C.E.M. Joad) 'The Pains of Animals: A Problem in Theology', *The Month*, CLXXXIX (February 1950), pp. 95–104. Repr. **GID = U, TAH**.

149. *The Literary Impact of the Authorized Version*, The Ethel M. Wood Lecture delivered before the University of London on 20 March 1950. London: The Athlone Press, 1950, 26 pp. Repr. **TAFP, SLE**.

150. 'What are we to make of Jesus Christ?', *Asking Them Questions* (Third Series). Edited by Ronald Selby Wright. London: Oxford University Press, 1950, pp. 48–53. Repr. **GID = U, gid**.

151. 'Historicism', *The Month*, IV (October 1950), pp. 230–43. Repr. **CR, FE**.

152. 'Christian Hope – Its Meaning for Today', *Religion in Life*, XXI (Winter 1951–52), pp. 20–32. Repr. as 'The World's Last Night' in **WLN, FE**.

153. *Hero and Leander*, Wharton Lecture on English Poetry, British Academy, 1952. *The Proceedings of the British Academy*, XXXVIII. London: Oxford University Press, [1952], 15 pp. Repr. **SLE**.

154. 'Is Theism Important? A Reply', *The Socratic [Digest]*, No 5 (1952), pp. 48–51; cf. H.H. Price, 'Is Theism Important?', ibid., pp. 39–47. Repr. as 'Is Theism Important?' in **GID = U, TAH**.

155. 'On Three Ways of Writing for Children', *Library Association. Proceedings, Papers and Summaries of Discussions at the Bournemouth Conference on 29 April to 2 May 1952*. London: Library Association (1952), pp. 22–8. Repr. **OOW, OTOW = OS**.

156. 'Edmund Spenser, 1552–99', *Major British Writers*, Vol. I. Edited by G.B. Harrison. New York: Harcourt, Brace & Co., 1954, pp. 91–103. Repr. **SMRL**.

157. 'On Punishment: A Reply', *Res Judicatae*, VI (August 1954), pp. 519–23; cf. J.J.C. Smart, 'Comment: The Humanitarian Theory of Punishment', ibid. VI (February 1954), pp. 368–71. Repr. with 'The Humanitarian Theory of Punishment', in **GID = U, FST**.

158. Reminiscence of P.V.M. Benecke in Margaret Deneke, *Paul Victor Mendelssohn Benecke 1868–1944*. Oxford: Privately printed by A.T. Broome and Son [1954], pp. 9, 31–34.

159. 'A Note on Jane Austen', *Essays in Criticism*, IV (October 1954), pp. 43–4. Repr. **SLE**.

160. 'Xmas and Christmas: A Lost Chapter from Herodotus', *Time and Tide*, XXXV (4 December 1954), p. 1607. Repr. **GID = U, FST**.

161. 'George Orwell', *Time and Tide*, XXXVI (8 January 1955), pp. 43–4. Repr. **OTOW = OS**.

162. 'Prudery and Philology', *The Spectator*, CXCIV (21 January 1955), pp. 43–4. Repr. **PRCON**.

163. *De Descriptione Temporum*, An Inaugural Lecture by the Professor of Medieval and Renaissance English Literature in the University of Cambridge. Cambridge: Cambridge University Press, 1955, 22 pp. Repr. **SLE**.

164. 'Lilies that Fester', *Twentieth Century*, CLVII (April 1955), pp. 330–41. Repr. **WLN, TAFP, CRR**.

165. 'On Obstinacy in Belief', *The Sewanee Review*, LXIII (Autumn 1955), pp. 525–38. Repr. **WLN, TAFP, SPT**.

166. [A Toast to] 'The Memory of Sir Walter Scott', *The Edinburgh Sir Walter Scott Club Forty-ninth Annual Report,* 1956, Edinburgh, 1956, pp. 13–25. Repr. **TAFP, SLE**.

167. 'Critical Forum: *De Descriptione Temporum*', *Essays in Criticism*, VI, (April 1956), p. 247.

168. 'Interim Report', *The Cambridge Review* (21 April 1956), pp. 468–71. Repr. **PRCON**.

169. 'Sometimes Fairy Stories May Say Best What's to Be Said', *The New York Times Book Review, Children's Book Section* (18 November 1956), p. 3. Repr. **OOW, OTOW = OS**.

170. 'Behind the Scenes', *Time and Tide*, XXXVII (1 December 1956), pp. 1450–51. Repr. **GID = U, CRR**.

171. 'Is History Bunk?' *The Cambridge Review*, LXXVIII (1 June 1957), pp. 647, 649. Repr. **PRCON**.

172. 'Dante's Statius', *Medium Aevum*, XXV, No 3 (1957), pp. 133–9. Repr. **SMRL**.

173. 'What Christmas Means to Me', *Twentieth Century*, CLXII (December 1957), pp. 517–18. Repr. **GID = U, CRR**.

174. 'Delinquents in the Snow', *Time and Tide*, XXXVIII (7 December 1957), pp. 1521–2. Repr. **GID = U, CRR**.

175. 'Will We Lose God in Outer Space?', *Christian Herald*, LXXXI (April 1958), pp. 19, 74–6. Repr. as a pamphlet *Shall We Lose God in Outer Space?*. London: SPCK, 1959, 11 pp, and repr. as 'Religion and Rocketry' in **WLN, FE**.

176. 'Revival or Decay?', *Punch*, CCXXXV (9 July 1958), pp. 36–8. Repr. **GID = U, FST**.

177. 'Willing Slaves of the Welfare State', (No 2 of the series 'Is Progress Possible?'), *The Observer* (20 July 1958), p. 6; cf. C.P. Snow, 'Is Progress Possible? – I: Man in Society', ibid. (13 July 1958), p. 12. Repr. **GID = U, TAH**.

178. 'The Psalms as Poetry', *Fifty-Two: A Journal of Books and Authors* [from Geoffrey Bles], No 3 (Autumn 1958), pp. 9–12. (Part of the Introductory chapter to *Reflections on the Psalms*.)

179. 'Rejoinder to Dr Pittenger', *The Christian Century*, LXXV (26 November 1958), pp. 1359–61; cf. W. Norman Pittenger, 'Apologist Versus Apologist: A Critique of C.S. Lewis as "defender of the faith",' ibid., LXXV (1 October 1958), pp. 1104–7. Lewis's article repr. **GID = U, TAH**.

180. 'On Juvenile Tastes', *Church Times, Children's Supplement* (28 November 1958), p. i. Repr. **OOW, OTOW = OS**.

181. 'The Efficacy of Prayer', *The Atlantic Monthly*, CCIII (January 1959), pp. 59–61. Repr. **WLN, FE**.

182. '*Molliter Ossa Cubent*', *The Cambellian* (the School Magazine of Campbell College, Belfast), XIV, No 9 (July 1959), pp. 692–3. (An obituary of Jane Agnes McNeill.*) Repr. **TST**.

183. *A Series of Ten Radio Talks on Love*, Atlanta, Georgia: The Episcopal Radio-TV Foundation, 1959. (These ten individual pamphlets are the radio scripts Lewis recorded on to tape in 1958, which tapes were issued in 1970 on four cassettes called *Four Talks on Love*. The scripts served as a basis for Lewis's book, *The Four Loves*.)

184. 'Affection – Friendship – Eros – Charity', *Fifty-Two: A Journal of Books and Authors* [from Geoffrey Bles], No 4 (Autumn 1959), p. 20. (An extract from the Introduction to *The Four Loves*.)

185. 'Screwtape Proposes a Toast', *The Saturday Evening Post*, CCXXXII (19 December 1959), pp. 36, 88–9. Repr. **SL&SPT, WLN, SPT**.

186. 'Good Work and Good Works', *Good Work*, XXIII (Christmas 1959), pp. 3–10. Repr. **WLN, SPT**.

187. 'Metre', *A Review of English Literature*, I (January 1960), pp. 45–50. Repr. **SLE**.

188. 'Undergraduate Criticism', *Broadsheet* (Cambridge University), VIII, No 17 (9 March 1960).

189. 'It All Began with a Picture ...', *Radio Times, Junior Radio Times*, CXLVIII (15 July 1960) [2]. Repr. **OOW, OTOW = OS**.

190. 'Haggard Rides Again', *Time and Tide*, XLI (3 September 1960), pp. 1044–5. Repr. as 'The Mythopoeic Gift of Rider Haggard' in **OTOW = OS**.

191. 'Four-letter Words', *The Critical Quarterly*, III (Summer 1961), pp. 118–22. Repr. **SLE**.

192. 'Before We Can Communicate', *Breakthrough*, No 8 (October 1961), p. 2. Repr. **GID = U, FST**.

193. 'The Anthropological Approach', *English and Medieval Studies Presented to J.R.R. Tolkien on the Occasion of his Seventieth Birthday*. Edited by Norman Davis and C.L. Wrenn. London: Allen and Unwin, 1962, pp. 219–30. Repr. **SLE**.

194. 'Sex in Literature', *The Sunday Telegraph*, No 87 (30 September 1962), p. 8. Repr. **PRCON**.

195. 'The Vision of John Bunyan', *The Listener*, LXVIII (13 December 1962), pp. 1006–8. Repr. **SLE**.

196. 'Going into Europe: A Symposium', *Encounter*, XIX (December 1962), p. 57.

197. 'Thoughts of a Cambridge Don', *The Lion* (the magazine of St Mark's, Dundela, Belfast) (January 1963) [11–21]; Repr. in an enlarged form as 'A Slip of the Tongue' in **SPT, WG (Rev)**.

198. 'The English Prose "Morte"', *Essays on Malory*. Edited by J.A.W. Bennett. Oxford: Clarendon Press, 1963, pp. 7–28.

199. 'Onward, Christian Spacemen', *Show*, III (February 1963), pp. 57, 117. Repr. as 'The Seeing Eye' in **CR**.

200. 'Must Our Image of God Go?', *The Observer* (24 March 1963), p. 14; cf. J.A.T. Robinson, 'Our Image of God Must Go', ibid. (17 March 1963), p. 21. Lewis's article repr. in *The Honest to God Debate: Some Reactions to the Book 'Honest to God' with a new chapter by its author, J.A.T. Robinson, Bishop of Woolwich*. Edited by David L. Edwards, London: SCM Press, 1963, p. 91, and in **GID = U, gid**.

201. 'I Was Decided Upon', *Decision*, II (September 1963), p. 3. (Answers to questions when interviewed by Sherwood E. Wirt of the Billy Graham Evangelistic Association on 7 May 1963). Repr. with 'Heaven, Earth and Outer Space' as 'Cross-Examination' in **GID = U, CRR**.

202. 'Heaven, Earth and Outer Space', *Decision*, II (October 1963), p. 4. (Answers to questions when interviewed by Sherwood E. Wirt of the Billy Graham Evangelistic Association on 7 May 1963). This essay and 'I Was Decided Upon' are parts of a single interview, and are repr. as 'Cross-Examination' in **GID = U, CRR**.

203. A Note on the meaning of Civilization in the *Chronicles of Narnia* found in Roger Lancelyn Green, *C.S. Lewis* (A Bodley Head Monograph). London: The Bodley Head, 1963, p. 51.

204. 'We Have No "Right to Happiness"', *The Saturday Evening Post*, CCXXXVI (21–28 December 1963), pp. 10, 12. Repr. **GID = U, gid**.

205. 'Heaven? – It's a Venture', *Fifty-Two: A Journal of Books and Authors* [from Geoffrey Bles], No 13 (Spring 1964), pp. 3–5. (An extract from chapter 22 of *Letters to Malcolm*.)

206. '"The establishment must die and rot ..."', C.S. Lewis Discusses Science Fiction with Kingsley Amis, *SF Horizons*, No 1 (Spring 1964), pp. 5–12. (An informal conversation between Lewis, Kingsley Amis, and Brian Aldiss recorded on tape in Lewis's rooms in Magdalene College, Cambridge, on 4 December 1962. Repr. as 'Unreal Estates' in *Encounter*, XXIV (March 1965) and **OOW, OTOW = OS**.

207. 'Dante's Similes', *Nottingham Mediaeval Studies* (Dante Centenary Number), IX (1965), pp. 32–41. Repr. **SMRL**.

208. *Mark vs. Tristram: Correspondence between C.S. Lewis and Owen Barfield.* Edited by Walter Hooper. Cambridge, Massachusetts: The Lowell House

Printers. A hand-printed edition limited to 126 copies. November 1967, 11 pp; another edition, Oxford: Oxford University C.S. Lewis Society, 1990, 18 pp. This new edition, limited to 100 copies, contains illustrations specially drawn for it by Pauline Baynes.

209. Boxen Manuscripts quoted in Walter Hooper's Preface to Lewis's *Of Other Worlds: Essays and Stories*. Edited by Walter Hooper. London: Geoffrey Bles, 1966; New York: Harcourt, Brace & World, 1967, pp. vii, viii. Repr. **BOX**.

210. Wynyard School Diary (November 1909) in Walter Hooper, 'C.S. Lewis', *The Franciscan*, Vol. IX, No 4 (September 1967), p. 163.

211. Oxford Diary: [14 February 1923] quoted in Walter Hooper's Preface to C.S. Lewis, *Selected Literary Essays*. Edited by Walter Hooper. Cambridge: Cambridge University Press, 1969, p. xii. Repr. **AMR**.

212. Oxford Diary: (2 April 1922) on p. x; (23 November 1922) on p. xi; (9 September 1923) on p. xi; (16 and 21 January 1927) on pp. xii–xiii: quoted in Walter Hooper's Preface to C.S. Lewis, *Narrative Poems*. Edited by Walter Hooper. London: Geoffrey Bles, 1969; New York: Harcourt, Brace & World, 1972, pp. x–xiii. Repr. **AMR**.

213. Definition of Myth, in Walter Hooper, 'Past Watchful Dragons: The Fairy Tales of C.S. Lewis', *Imagination and the Spirit*. Edited by Charles A. Huttar. Grand Rapids: Eerdmans, 1971, p. 286. Repr. **PWD**.

214. Boxen Manuscripts: ('The Locked Door') in Walter Hooper, 'Past Watchful Dragons: The Fairy Tales of C.S. Lewis', *Imagination and the Spirit*. Edited by Charles A. Huttar. Grand Rapids: Eerdmans, 1971, pp. 279–80. Repr. **PWD**.

215. Narnian Manuscripts. (1) 'Outline of Narnian history so far as it is known', on pp. 298–301; Repr. **PWD**. (2) Outline of *The Voyage of the 'Dawn Treader'* (holograph and printed) on pp. 302, 303; (3) Galley proofs of *The Silver Chair* on p. 304; (4) Portion of 'The Lefay Fragment' (an early version of *The Magician's Nephew*) on pp. 304–7; (5) 'Eustace's Diary' on p. 309; (6) Original Map of Narnia (holograph) on p. 310; drawing of Monopods (holograph) on p. 313; in Walter Hooper, 'Past Watchful Dragons: The Fairy Tales of C.S. Lewis', *Imagination and the Spirit*. Edited by Charles A. Huttar. Grand Rapids: Eerdmans, 1971. Repr. **PWD**.

216. Fragment of a story beginning 'It was in autumn', quoted in Walter Hooper, 'Past Watchful Dragons: The Fairy Tales of C.S. Lewis', *Imagination and the Spirit*. Edited by Charles A. Huttar. Grand Rapids: Eerdmans, 1971, p. 291.

217. Martlet Society Minutes of 12 March and 14 June 1919, in Walter Hooper, 'To the Martlets', in *C.S. Lewis: Speaker and Teacher*. Edited by Carolyn Keefe. Grand Rapids, Michigan: Zondervan, 1971, pp. 43, 44.

218. Oxford Diary of 9 February 1923, about Martlet Society meeting, quoted in Walter Hooper, 'To the Martlets', in *C.S. Lewis: Speaker and Teacher*. Edited by Carolyn Keefe. Grand Rapids, Michigan: Zondervan, 1971, pp. 47–50. Repr. **AMR**.

219. Passage from lecture on 'Innate Ideas' (1924) quoted in Walter Hooper, 'To the Martlets', in *C.S. Lewis: Speaker and Teacher*. Edited by Carolyn Keefe. Grand Rapids, Michigan: Zondervan, 1971, p. 52.

220. Passage from fragment of 'Ulster Novel' (c. 1927) quoted in Walter Hooper's Preface to Kathryn Ann Lindskoog, *The Lion of Judah in Never-Never Land*. Grand Rapids, Michigan: Eerdmans, 1973, p. 9. The 'Ulster Novel' is found in the *Lewis Papers* vol. IX, pp. 291–300.

221. Earliest known Manuscript (c. 1939) of *The Lion, the Witch and the Wardrobe* quoted in Walter Hooper's Preface to Kathryn Ann Lindskoog, *The Lion of Judah in Never-Never Land*. Grand Rapids, Michigan: Eerdmans, 1973, p. 12. (This manuscript is written on the back of the first page of the manuscript of *The Dark Tower*, found in the Bodleian Library.) Repr. **BIO** X.

222. Holograph of 'To Mars and back', the fragment of a story written by Lewis when a child, in Douglas Gilbert and Clyde S. Kilby, *C.S. Lewis: Images of His World*. Grand Rapids: Eerdmans, 1973, p. 104.

223. Little Lea Diary ('My Life During the Exmas Holadys of 1907') quoted in Roger Lancelyn Green and Walter Hooper, *C.S. Lewis: A Biography*. London: Collins; New York: Harcourt Brace Jovanovich, 1974, p. 24.

224. Wynyard School Diary: (November 1909) quoted in Roger Lancelyn Green and Walter Hooper, *C.S. Lewis: A Biography*. London: Collins; New York: Harcourt Brace Jovanovich, 1974.

225. Oxford Diary: (24 May 1922) on pp. 69–70; [11 June 1922] on p. 71; [9–23 September 1922] on p. 71; [13, 15, 17 October 1922] on p. 72; (18 October 1922) on p. 72; [7 November 1922] on p. 72; [15 November 1922] on p. 72; [18 January 1923] on p. 73; (26 January; 2 February 1923) on p. 73; (11 February 1923) on pp. 73–4; (1 June 1923) on p. 75; (10 July 1923) on p. 75; [13–25 July 1923] on p. 76; [17–25 March 1924] on p. 76; (8 September 1923) on p. 77; [13 September 1923] on p. 77; (29 February 1924) on pp. 78–9; [21–24 June 1924] on p. 80; [3, 4 July 1924] on p. 80; (10 February 1925) on pp. 81–2; [5 February 1927] on p. 86; [5 May 1926] on p. 87; [10 May 1926] on p. 88; (11 May 1926) on p. 88; [10 June 1926] on pp. 88–9; [6 July 1926] on p. 89; (18 January 1927) on p. 90; (8 February 1927) on pp. 90–1; [1 March 1927] on p. 91; (24 January 1927) on pp. 90–1; (12 September 1923) on p. 175; (27 April 1923) on p. 250; (9 September 1923) on p. 261; (23 November 1922) on p. 161; quoted in Roger Lancelyn Green and Walter Hooper, *C.S. Lewis: A Biography*. London: Collins; New York: Harcourt Brace Jovanovich, 1974. Repr. **AMR**.

226. Pen portraits of Arthur Greeves's family on p. 40; of Arthur Greeves on p. 98; from **The Lewis Papers**,‡ quoted in Roger Lancelyn Green and Walter Hooper, *C.S. Lewis: A Biography*. London: Collins; New York: Harcourt Brace Jovanovich, 1974.

227. Early Prose Autobiography (the story of 'Joy') quoted in Roger Lancelyn Green and Walter Hooper, *C.S. Lewis: A Biography*. London: Collins; New York: Harcourt Brace Jovanovich, 1974, p. 113.

228. Passages from *The Dark Tower* quoted in Roger Lancelyn Green and Walter Hooper, *C.S. Lewis: A Biography*. London: Collins; New York: Harcourt Brace Jovanovich, 1974, pp. 166–8. Repr. **DT**.

229. Excerpts from unpublished *Clivi Hamiltonis Summae Metaphysices contra Anthroposophos*, quoted in Lionel Adey, 'The Barfield-Lewis "Great War"', *CSL: The Bulletin of the New York C.S. Lewis Society*, VI, No 10 (August 1975), pp. 10–13.

230. Testimonial for Frank Goodridge (c. 1952) quoted in *CSL: The Bulletin of the New York C.S. Lewis Society*, Whole No 75 (January 1976), p. 13.

231. 'Great War' Documents. Excerpts from *Clivi Hamiltonis Summae Metaphysices contra Anthroposophos Libri II*, quoted in Lionel Adey, "Enjoyment, Contemplation, and Hierarchy in *Hamlet*", *Evolution of*

Consciousness: Studies in Polarity. Edited by Shirley Sugerman. Middletown, Connecticut: Wesleyan University Press, 1976, p. 151.

232. Annotations to Shakespeare, quoted in Lionel Adey, 'C.S. Lewis's Annotations to His Shakespeare Volumes', *CSL: The Bulletin of the New York C.S. Lewis Society*. Vol. 8, No 7 (May 1977), pp. 1–8.

233. Little Lea Diary: ('My Life During the Exmas Holadys of 1907'), quoted in Humphrey Carpenter, *The Inklings: C.S. Lewis, J.R.R. Tolkien, Charles Williams, and their friends.* London: Allen & Unwin, 1978, pp. 3, 4.

234. Wynyard School Diary: (November 1909) quoted in Humphrey Carpenter, *The Inklings: C.S. Lewis, J.R.R. Tolkien, Charles Williams, and their friends.* London: Allen & Unwin, 1978.

235. Oxford Diary: [13 September 1923] on p. 11; [4 July 1923; 27 November 1922] on p. 12; [15–25 July 1923] on p. 13; [16 October; 2 November 1922] on p. 14; [21 February 1923] on p. 15; [19 January 1927] on p. 20; [15 June 1926] on p. 21; [11 May 1926] on p. 22; [8 February 1927] on p. 28; [5 January 1924] on p. 39; [26 May 1926] on p. 40; [13 June 1926] on p. 40; [18 January 1927] on p. 40; [9 July 1922] on p. 164; [Autumn 1923 – visit to Owen Barfield] on p. 164; quoted in Humphrey Carpenter, *The Inklings: C.S. Lewis, J.R.R. Tolkien, Charles Williams, and their friends.* London: Allen & Unwin, 1978. Repr. **AMR**.

236. Pen Portraits of Michael Denne Parker on p. 18; T.D. Weldon on p. 18; quoted in Humphrey Carpenter, *The Inklings: C.S. Lewis, J.R.R. Tolkien, Charles Williams, and their friends.* London: Allen & Unwin, 1978. Repr. in the 'Magdalen College Appendix' of **AMR**.

237. 'Commentary on the Lay of Leithian' (for J.R.R. Tolkien) quoted in Humphrey Carpenter, *The Inklings: C.S. Lewis, J.R.R. Tolkien, Charles Williams, and their friends.* London: Allen & Unwin, 1978, pp. 30–31.

238. Oxford Diary: (7 July 1923); quoted in Lionel Adey, *C.S. Lewis's 'Great War' with Owen Barfield.* Victoria, B.C.: University of Victoria, 1978, p. 13. Repr. **AMR**.

239. Boxen Manuscripts ('Boxen: or Scenes from Boxonian City Life') quoted in Chad Walsh, *The Literary Legacy of C.S. Lewis.* New York: Harcourt Brace Jovanovich, 1979, pp. 123–5. Repr. **BOX**.

240. 'The Quest of Bleheris', quoted in Chad Walsh, *The Literary Legacy of C.S. Lewis*. New York: Harcourt Brace Jovanovich, 1979, pp. 126–7, 128.

241. Boxen Manuscripts. (1) 'The Lefay Fragment' on pp. 48–65; (2) 'Eustace's Dairy' on pp. 68–71; in Walter Hooper, *Past Watchful Dragons: The Narnian Chronicles of C.S. Lewis*. New York: Macmillan, 1979; London: Collins, 1980.

242. Oxford Diary: (4 and 5 August 1922) on pp. 22–3; (9–23 September 1922) on p. 292; (11 July 1923) on pp. 294–5; (18 July 1922) on p. 310; quoted in C.S. Lewis, *They Stand Together: The Letters of C.S. Lewis to Arthur Greeves (1914–1963)*. Edited by Walter Hooper, 1979. Repr. **AMR**.

243. Pen portraits of Arthur Greeves's parents on pp. 16–18; of Arthur Greeves, on pp. 24–6; quoted from **LP**,‡ in *They Stand Together*, 1979.

244. Minutes of the Martlets Society for 26 February 1919 (University College, Oxford) quoted in *They Stand Together*, p. 250, Note 6.

245. Testimonial for Norman Bradshaw (4 December 1938) in *The Canadian C.S. Lewis Journal*, No 11 (November 1979), p. 2. (Reprinted in Stephen Schofield, *In Search of C.S. Lewis*, pp. 17–18.)

246. Quotations from the original Spenser lecture notes used in Cambridge, quoted in Margaret Hannay, *C.S. Lewis*. New York: Frederick Ungar, 1981, pp. 158–63. (Dr Hannay was quoting from the holograph pages in *Spenser's Images of Life*.)

247. Parts of original BBC Broadcasts (1942) not included in the published versions quoted in Walter Hooper's Introduction to C.S. Lewis, *Mere Christianity*. Anniversary Edition. Edited by Walter Hooper. New York: Macmillan, 1981, pp. xiv–xv, xvii–xviii, xx–xxi.

248. 'Answers to Listeners' Questions', holograph of the typescript Lewis read over the BBC on 3 September 1941, in Appendix A of *Mere Christianity*, Anniversary Edition. This was rewritten to form chapter II ['Some Objections'] in *Broadcast Talks*.

249. 'The Anvil', BBC broadcast in which Lewis took part, 22 July 1943. Included as 'Appendix C' in *Mere Christianity*. Anniversary Edition, pp. 207–11.

250. Wynyard School Diary: (November 1909) quoted in Walter Hooper, *Through Joy and Beyond: A Pictorial Biography of C.S. Lewis*. New York: Macmillan, 1982, p. 19.

251. Wynyard School Diary (November 1909) quoted in Walter Hooper, 'C.S. Lewis in Hertfordshire (2): Wynyard School's Tormenter', *Hertfordshire Countryside*, Vol. 37 (October 1982), p. 35.

252. *A Cretaceous Perambulator (The Re-examination of)*, by Owen Barfield and C.S. Lewis. Edited by Walter Hooper. Oxford: The Oxford University C.S. Lewis Society, 1983. This 18-page pamphlet is in a limited edition of 100 copies.

253. Passage from essay on 'Christian Reunion' in Walter Hooper's Foreword to John Randolph Willis, *Pleasures Forevermore: The Theology of C.S. Lewis*. Chicago: Loyola University Press, 1983, p. xv. Repr. **CR**.

254. 'Great War' Documents. *Summae Metaphysices contra Anthroposophos* quoted in Stephen Thorson, 'Knowing and Being in C.S. Lewis's "Great War" with Owen Barfield', *CSL: The Bulletin of the New York C.S. Lewis Society*. Vol. 169 (November 1983), pp. 1–8.

255. Oxford Diary: (25 December 1922) quoted in Kathryn Lindskoog, 'C.S. Lewis on Christmas', *Christianity Today* (16 December 1983), pp. 24–5. Repr. **AMR**.

256. 'Great War' Documents. Annotations to *Summae Metaphysices contra Anthroposophos* quoted in Lionel Adey, 'A Response to Dr Thorson', and in Stephen Thorson, 'A Reply', *CSL: The Bulletin of the New York C.S. Lewis Society*, Vol. 173 (March 1984) pp. 6–11.

257. Oxford Diary: (4 July 1922; 12 September 1923; 22 February 1924; 3 June 1926) on p. 44; quoted in Peter J. Schakel, *Reason and Imagination in C.S. Lewis: A Study of 'Till We Have Faces'*. Grand Rapids: Eerdmans, 1984. Repr. **AMR**.

258. 'Commentary on the Lay of Leithian' in J.R.R. Tolkien, *The Lays of Beleriand*. Edited by Christopher Tolkien. London: George Allen & Unwin, 1985, pp. 315–29.

259. 'Eric Bentley: An Appreciation' in *The Play and its Critic: Essays for Eric Bentley*. Edited by Michael Bertin. Lanham, Maryland: University Press of America, 1986, pp. 4–7. The 'Appreciation' consists of two letters of recommendation which Lewis wrote about his pupil, Eric Bentley, in 1938 and 1940.

260. 'The Emancipation of Women', a portion of the essay 'Modern Man and His Categories of Thought' published in full in *Present Concerns*. The essay was written for the World Council of Churches Assembly, Commission II materials on 'God's Design and Man's Witness', October 1946, and this portion was published in *CSL: The Bulletin of the New York C.S. Lewis Society*, Vol. 17, No 4 (February 1986), pp. 4–5.

261. Oxford Diary: (November–December 1923) on p. 15; (29 May 1923) on p. 21; (12 September 1923) on p. 21; (1 May 1926) on p. 27; [28 April 1926] on pp. 29–30; (12 May 1926) on p. 30; (24 January 1927) on p. 37; [5 February 1927] on p. 38; (10 February 1927) on p. 38; quoted in William Griffin, *Clive Staples Lewis: A Dramatic Life*. San Francisco, Harper & Row, 1986; Tring: Lion, 1988. Repr. **AMR**.

262. 'The Moral Good – Its Place Among the Values', (The fourteen lectures Lewis gave in the University of Oxford 1924–25). The section called the 'Critique of Locke' is quoted in James Patrick, *The Magdalen Metaphysicals: Idealism and Orthodoxy at Oxford 1901–45*. Macon, Georgia: Mercer University Press, 1987, pp. 116–17.

263. Pen portraits of P.V.M. Benecke on p. 111; of T.D. Weldon on p. 132; quoted in George Sayer, *Jack: C.S. Lewis and His Times*. London: Macmillan, 1988, p. 111. Repr. in the 'Magdalen College Appendix' of **AMR**.

264. 'The Quest of Bleheris' (prose romance written in 1916) quoted in George Sayer, *Jack: C.S. Lewis and His Times*. London: Macmillan, 1988, pp. 59–60.

265. Little Lea Diary: ('My Life During the Exmas Holadys of 1907') on p. 20; (23 February 1908) on p. 21; Oxford Diary: [3 April; 25 April; 6 April; 3 June 1922] on p. 93; [14 July; 19 August; 3 August 1922] on p. 95; [8 August 1922] on p. 96; (29 February 1924) on p. 102; [13–25 July 1923] on p. 102; [19 May 1924] on p. 103; [23 May; 24 May 1924] on p. 104; (5 June 1924) on p. 105; [12 June; 21–24 June 1924] on p. 105; (6 February 1925) on

p. 105; (10 February 1925) on p. 106; (29 July 1924) on p. 106; [1–3 August 1924] on p. 107; [17 August 1925] on pp. 107–8; [5 February 1927] on p. 118; [1 February 1927] on p. 120; [24 January 1927] on p. 120; (18 January 1927) on p. 131; quoted in George Sayer, *Jack: C.S. Lewis and His Times*. London: Macmillan, 1988. (The entries from the Oxford Diary are reprinted in **AMR**.)

266. Boxen Manuscripts quoted in A.N. Wilson, *C.S. Lewis: A Biography*. London: Collins; New York: W.W. Norton, 1990, pp. 17, 34. Repr. **BOX**.

267. Essay on Richard Wagner (1911) quoted in A.N. Wilson, *C.S. Lewis: A Biography*. London: Collins; New York: W.W. Norton, 1990, pp. 30, 32.

268. Little Lea Diary: ('My Life During the Exmas Holadys of 1907') on p. 17; Oxford Diary: [25 May 1923] on p. 69; [24 June 1922] on p. 74; [20 June 1923] on p. 76; [1 June 1923] on p. 80; [4 February 1923] on p. 81; [21 February, 23 February, 12 March 1923] on p. 82; [18 June 1923, 21 June 1922] on p. 84; [5 January 1924] on p. 86; [18 June 1922], [13–25 July 1923] on p. 88; [29 August 1925] on pp. 93–4; [27 May 1926] on p. 98; [24 January 1927] on p. 99; [13–25 July 1923] on p. 101; [11 May 1926] on p. 105; quoted in A.N. Wilson, *C.S. Lewis: A Biography*. London: Collins; New York: W.W. Norton, 1990. (All but the first two entries repr. **AMR**.)

E: Single Short Poems

(Lewis wrote most of his poems under the pseudonym **Nat Whilk** (Anglo-Saxon for 'I know not whom') or **N.W.** Even though many were revised and given new titles by the author, most of the following appear in both *Poems* and *Collected Poems*.)

1. '*Quam Bene Saturno*', *Cherbourg School Magazine* (July 1913). Repr. **LP** IV: 51–2.

2. 'Death in Battle', *Reveille*, No 3 (February 1919), p. 508. Repr. **SIB, CP**.

3. 'Joy', *The Beacon*, III, No 31 (May 1924), pp. 444–5 (under pseudonym Clive Hamilton). Repr. **CP**.

4. (With Owen Barfield) 'Abecedarium Philosophicum', *The Oxford Magazine*, LII (30 November 1933), p. 298.

5. 'The Shortest Way Home', *The Oxford Magazine*, LII (10 May 1934), p. 665 (Nat Whilk). Revised and retitled 'Man is a Lumpe Where All Beasts Kneaded Be' in **P** and **CP**.

6. 'Scholar's Melancholy', *The Oxford Magazine*, LII (24 May 1934), p. 734 (Nat Whilk). Repr. **P, CP**.

7. 'The Planets', *Lysistrata*, II (May 1935), pp. 21–4. (A portion of the poem is quoted in Lewis's essay 'A Metrical Suggestion'.) Repr. **P, CP**.

8. 'Sonnet', *The Oxford Magazine*, LIV (14 May 1936), p. 575 (Nat Whilk). Repr. **P, CP**.

9. 'Coronation March', *The Oxford Magazine*, LV (6 May 1937), p. 565 (Nat Whilk). Repr. **P, CP**.

10. 'After Kirby's *Kalevala*' (a translation), *The Oxford Magazine*, LV (13 May 1937), p. 505 (Nat Whilk). Repr. **P, CP**.

11. 'The Future of Forestry', *The Oxford Magazine*, LVI (10 February 1938), p. 383 (Nat Whilk). Repr. **P, CP**.

12. '*Chanson D'Aventure*', *The Oxford Magazine*, LVI (19 May 1938), p. 638 (Nat Whilk). Revised and retitled 'What the Bird Said Early in the Year' in **P** and **CP**.

13. 'Experiment', *The Spectator*, CLXI (9 December 1938), p. 998. The poem is also found in *Augury: An Oxford Miscellany of Verse and Prose*. Edited by A.M. Hardie and K.C. Douglas. Oxford: Basil Blackwell, 1940, p. 28. It is there called 'Metrical Experiment', and it is a slightly different version of the poem that appeared earlier in *The Spectator* or which was revised yet again and appears as 'Pattern' in **P** and **CP**.

14. 'To Mr Roy Campbell', *The Cherwell*, LVI (6 May 1939), p. 35 (Nat Whilk). Revised and retitled 'The Author of *Flowering Rifle*' in **P** and **CP**.

15. 'Hermione in the House of Paulina', *Augury: An Oxford Miscellany of Verse and Prose*. Edited by Alec M. Hardie and Keith C. Douglas. Oxford: Basil Blackwell, 1940, p. 28. Revised and repr. **P, CP**.

16. 'Essence', *Fear No More: A Book of Poems for the Present Time by Living English Poets*. Cambridge: Cambridge University Press, 1940, p. 4. Repr. in **CP** but not **P**.

NOTE: All the poems in *Fear No More* are published anonymously. There are, however, six copies containing an additional leaf giving the names of the authors of the poems, and one of these is in the Bodleian Library, Oxford.

17. 'Break, Sun, my Crusted Earth', *Fear No More: A Book of Poems for the Present Time by Living English Poets*. Cambridge: Cambridge University Press, 1940, p. 72. This is a revised version of the last three stanzas of 'A Pageant Played in Vain'.

18. 'The World is Round', *Fear No More: A Book of Poems for the Present Time by Living English Poets*. Cambridge: Cambridge University Press, 1940, p. 85. This is a revised version of 'Poem for Psychoanalysts and/or Theologians'.

19. 'Arise my Body', *Fear No More: A Book of Poems for the Present Time by Living English Poets*. Cambridge: Cambridge University Press, 1940, p. 89. This is a revised version of 'After Prayers, Lie Cold'.

20. 'Epitaph', *Time and Tide*, XXIII (6 June 1942), p. 460. Retitled 'Epigrams and Epitaphs, No 11.' Repr. **P, CP**.

21. 'To G.M.', *The Spectator*, CLXIX (9 October 1942), p. 335. Revised and retitled 'To a Friend'. Repr. **P, CP**.

22. 'Awake, My Lute!', *The Atlantic Monthly*, CLXXII (November 1943), pp. 113, 115. Repr. in **CP** but not **P**.

23. 'The Salamander', *The Spectator*, CLXXIV (8 June 1945), p. 521; see erratum: 'Poet and Printer', ibid. (15 June 1945), p. 550. Repr. **P, CP**.

24. 'From the Latin of Milton's *De Idea Platonica Quemadmodum Aristoteles Intellexit*' (a translation), *English*, V, No 30 (1945), p. 195.

25. 'On the Death of Charles Williams', *Britain Today*, No 112 (August 1945), p. 14. Revised and retitled 'To Charles Williams' in **P** and **CP**.

26. 'Under Sentence', *The Spectator*, CLXXV (7 September 1945), p. 219. Revised and retitled 'The Condemned' in **P** and **CP**.

27. 'On the Atomic Bomb (Metrical Experiment)', *The Spectator*, CLXXV (28 December 1945), p. 619. Repr. **P** and **CP**.

28. 'On Receiving Bad News', *Time and Tide*, XXVI (29 December 1945), p. 1093. Retitled 'Epigrams and Epitaphs, No 12' in **P** and **CP**.

29. 'The Birth of Language', *Punch*, CCX (9 January 1946), p. 32 (N.W.). Revised and repr. **P** and **CP**.

30. 'On Being Human', *Punch*, CCX (8 May 1946), p. 402 (N.W.). Revised and repr. in **P** and **CP**.

31. 'Solomon', *Punch*, CCXI (14 August 1946), p. 136 (N.W.). Revised and repr. **P** and **CP**.

32. 'The True Nature of Gnomes', *Punch*, CCXI (16 October 1946), p. 310 (N.W.). Repr. **P** and **CP**.

33. 'The Meteorite', *Time and Tide*, XXVII (7 December 1946), p. 1183. Repr. **P, CP**.

34. 'Pan's Purge', *Punch*, CCXII (15 January 1947), p. 71 (N.W.). Repr. **P, CP**.

35. 'The Romantics', *The New English Weekly*, XXX (16 January 1947), p. 130. Revised and retitled 'The Prudent Jailer' in **P** and **CP**.

36. 'Dangerous Oversight', *Punch*, CCXII (21 May 1947), p. 434 (N.W.). Revised and retitled 'Young King Cole' in **P** and **CP**.

37. 'Two Kinds of Memory', *Time and Tide*, XXVIII (7 August 1947), p. 859. Revised and repr. in **P** and **CP**.

38. '*Le Roi S'Amuse*', *Punch*, CCXIII (1 October 1947), p. 324 (N.W.). Revised and repr. in **P** and **CP**.

39. 'Donkeys' Delight', *Punch*, CCXIII (5 November 1947), p. 442 (N.W.). Revised and repr. in **P** and **CP**.

40. 'The End of the Wine', *Punch*, CCXIII (3 December 1947), p. 538 (N.W.). Revised and retitled 'The Last of the Wine' in **P** and **CP**.

41. '*Vitrea Circe*', *Punch*, CCXIV (23 June 1948), p. 543 (N.W.). Revised and repr. in **P** and **CP**.

42. 'Epitaph', *The Spectator*, CLXXXI (30 July 1948), p. 142. Revised and retitled 'Epigrams and Epitaphs, No 14' in **P** and **CP**.

43. 'The Sailing of the Ark', *Punch*, CCXV (11 August 1948), p. 124 (N.W.). Revised and retitled 'The Late Passenger' in **P** and **CP**.

44. 'The Landing', *Punch*, CCXV (15 September 1948), p. 237 (N.W.). Revised and repr. in **P** and **CP**.

45. 'The Turn of the Tide', *Punch* (Almanac), CCXV (1 November 1948), p. 237 (N.W.). Revised and repr. in **P** and **CP**.

46. 'The Prodigality of Firdausi', *Punch*, CCXV (1 December 1948), p. 510 (N.W.). Revised and repr. in **P** and **CP**.

47. 'Epitaph in a Village Churchyard', *Time and Tide*, XXX (19 March 1949), p. 272. Retitled 'Epigrams and Epitaphs, No 16' in **P** and **CP**.

48. 'On a Picture by Chirico', *The Spectator*, CLXXXII (6 May 1949), p. 607. Revised and repr. in **P** and **CP**.

49. 'Adam at Night', *Punch*, CCXVI (11 May 1949), p. 510 (N.W.). Revised and retitled 'The Adam at Night' in **P** and **CP**.

50. 'Arrangement of Pindar', *Mandrake*, I, No 6 (1949), pp. 43–5. Revised and retitled 'Pindar Sang' in **P** and **CP**.

51. 'Epitaph', *The Month*, II (July 1949), p. 8. Retitled 'Epigrams and Epitaphs, No 17' in **P** and **CP**.

52. 'Conversation Piece: The Magician and the Dryad', *Punch*, CCXVII (20 July 1949), p. 71 (N.W.). Revised and retitled 'The Magician and the Dryad' in **P** and **CP**.

53. 'The Day with a White Mark', *Punch*, CCXVII (17 August 1949), p. 170 (N.W.). Revised and repr. in **P** and **CP**.

54. 'A Footnote to Pre-History', *Punch*, CCXVII (14 September 1949), p. 304 (N.W.). Revised and retitled 'The Adam Unparadised' in **P** and **CP**.

55. 'As One Oldster to Another', *Punch*, CCXVIII (15 March 1950), pp. 294–5 (N.W.). Revised and repr. in **P** and **CP**.

56. 'A Cliché Came Out of its Cage', *Nine: A Magazine of Poetry and Criticism*, II (May 1950), p. 114. Revised and repr. in **P** and **CP**.

57. 'Ballade of Dead Gentlemen', *Punch*, CCXX (23 March 1951), p. 386 (N.W.). Repr. **P**, **CP**.

58. 'The Country of the Blind', *Punch*, CCXXI (12 September 1951), p. 303 (N.W.). Repr. **P**, **CP**.

59. 'Pilgrim's Problem', *The Month*, VII (May 1952), p. 275. Repr. **P**, **CP**.

60. 'Vowels and Sirens', *The Times Literary Supplement*, Special Autumn Issue (29 August 1952), p. xiv. Revised and repr. **P** and **CP**.

61. 'Impenitence', *Punch*, CCXXV (15 July 1953), p. 91 (N.W.). Repr. **P**, **CP**.

62. 'March for Drum, Trumpet, and Twenty-one Giants', *Punch*, CCXXV (4 November 1953), p. 553. Revised and repr. in **P** and **CP**.

63. 'To Mr Kingsley Amis on His Late Verses', *Essays in Criticism*, IV (April 1954), p. 190; cf. Kingsley Amis, 'Beowulf', ibid. (January 1954), p. 85.

64. 'Odora Canum Vis (A defence of certain modern biographers and critics)', *The Month*, XI (May 1954), p. 272. Revised and repr. in **P** and **CP**.

65. 'Cradle-Song Based on a Theme from Nicolas of Cusa', *The Times Literary Supplement* (11 June 1954), p. 375. Revised and retitled 'Science-Fiction Cradlesong' in **P** and **CP**.

66. 'Spartan Nactus', *Punch*, CCXXVII (1 December 1954), p. 685 (N.W.). Revised and retitled 'A Confession' in **P** and **CP**.

67. 'On Another Theme from Nicolas of Cusa', *The Times Literary Supplement* (21 January 1955), p. 43. Revised and retitled 'On a Theme from Nicolas of Cusa' in **P** and **CP**.

68. 'Legion', *The Month*, XIII (April 1955), p. 210. Revised and repr. in **P** and **CP**.

69. 'After Aristotle', *The Oxford Magazine*, LXXIV (23 February 1956), p. 296 (N.W.). Repr. **P** and **CP**.

70. 'Epanorthosis (for the end of Goethe's *Faust*)', *The Cambridge Review*, LXXVII (26 May 1956), p. 610 (N.W.). Revised and retitled 'Epigrams and Epitaphs, No 15' in **P** and **CP**.

71. 'Evolutionary Hymn', *The Cambridge Review*, LXXIX (30 November 1957), p. 227 (N.W.). Repr. **P** and **CP**.

72. 'An Expostulation (against too many writers of science fiction)', *The Magazine of Fantasy and Science Fiction*, XVI (June 1959), p. 47. Repr. **P, CP**.

73. 'Re-Adjustment', *Fifty-Two: A Journal of Books and Authors* [from Geoffrey Bles], No 14 (Autumn 1964), p. 4. Repr. **P, CP**.

74. 'The Old Grey Mare', Quoted in Roger Lancelyn Green, 'C.S. Lewis', *Puffin Post*, IV, No 1 (1970), pp. 14–15.

75. 'Leaving For Ever the Home of One's Youth', *Occasional Poets: An Anthology*. Edited by Richard Adams. Harmondsworth, Middlesex: Penguin Books, 1986, p. 101. Repr. **CP**.

76. 'Finchley Avenue', *Occasional Poets: An Anthology*. Edited by Richard Adams. Harmondsworth, Middlesex: Penguin Books, 1986, pp. 102–4. Repr. **CP**.

77. 'West Germanic to Primitive Old English' (fifteen lines of a mnemonic poem) quoted in Walter Hooper's Preface to C.S. Lewis, *Selected Literary Essays*. Edited by Walter Hooper. Cambridge: Cambridge University Press, 1969, p. xv.

78. 'Loki Bound' (seven lines of a poem written in 1914) quoted in Walter Hooper's Preface to C.S. Lewis, *Narrative Poems*. Edited by Walter

Hooper. London: Geoffrey Bles, 1969; New York: Harcourt, Brace & World, 1972, p. xiii.

79. Epitaph for his Wife (a holograph) in Douglas Gilbert and Clyde S. Kilby, *C.S. Lewis: Images of His World*. Grand Rapids: Eerdmans, 1973, p. 65. (Lewis had written two versions of this epitaph, one of which is found in *Poems*. Joy Davidman chose one for her own epitaph, and Lewis revised it extensively in 1963 before it was cut into the stone seen in this photograph.) The poem is repr. in **CP**.

80. Verses in imitation of Ovid's *Pars estis pauci* quoted in Roger Lancelyn Green and Walter Hooper, *C.S. Lewis: A Biography*. London: Collins; New York: Harcourt Brace Jovanovich, 1974, p. 38.

81. A stanza of the 'Ballade of a Winter's Morning', quoted in Roger Lancelyn Green and Walter Hooper, *C.S. Lewis: A Biography*. London: Collins; New York: Harcourt Brace Jovanovich, 1974, p. 44.

82. 'I think, if it be truth, as some have taught', in Roger Lancelyn Green and Walter Hooper, *C.S. Lewis: A Biography*. London: Collins; New York: Harcourt Brace Jovanovich, 1974, p. 49.

83. 'You rest upon me all my days', with preface to the manuscript 'Half Hours with Hamilton' quoted in Roger Lancelyn Green and Walter Hooper, *C.S. Lewis: A Biography*. London: Collins; New York: Harcourt Brace Jovanovich, 1974, p. 112. This is an earlier version of the poem published in *The Pilgrim's Regress* (Book 8, Chapter vi) and it is reprinted as 'Caught' in **P** and **CP**.

84. Narrative Verse Autobiography (the story of 'Joy'; the only surviving lines) in Roger Lancelyn Green and Walter Hooper, *C.S. Lewis: A Biography*. London: Collins; New York: Harcourt Brace Jovanovich, 1974, p. 127.

85. 'Perelandra' (a fragment of verse which appears to be the idea for *Perelandra*) quoted in Roger Lancelyn Green and Walter Hooper, *C.S. Lewis: A Biography*. London: Collins; New York: Harcourt Brace Jovanovich, 1974, p. 171 n. 1.

86. 'Prayer for a Brother', (written when his brother was away during World War II) in Roger Lancelyn Green and Walter Hooper, *C.S. Lewis: A Biography*, 1974, p. 183.

87. 'Cupid and Psyche' (lines from a fragmentary poem written in 1923 and later retold in *Till We Have Faces*) quoted in Roger Lancelyn Green and Walter Hooper, *C.S. Lewis: A Biography*, 1974, pp. 250, 262.

88. 'Two at the table ...' (in the metre of *Beowulf* about J.R.R. Tolkien and E.V. Gordon examining in the English School) quoted in Humphrey Carpenter, *The Inklings: C.S. Lewis, J.R.R. Tolkien, Charles Williams, and their friends*. London: Allen & Unwin, 1978, p. 55.

89. 'Poem for Arthur Greeves' (1913) in C.S. Lewis, *They Stand Together: The Letters of C.S. Lewis to Arthur Greeves* (1914–63). Edited by Walter Hooper. London: Collins; New York: Macmillan, 1979, p. [5].

90. 'Song' (an earlier version of the one in *Spirits in Bondage*) quoted in the letter of 23 May 1918; in *They Stand Together*, 1979, pp. 215–16.

91. 'Nimue' (the only surviving lines of a poem later destroyed) quoted in the letter of 18 September 1919; in C.S. Lewis, *They Stand Together*, 1979, p. 261.

92. 'Lilith' (an earlier version of the poem which was first published in *The Pilgrim's Regress* (1933) and later revised for the edition of 1943) quoted in the letter of 29 April 1930; in *They Stand Together*, 1979, pp. 353–4. (Lewis gave it no title.)

93. 'Poem for Jill Flewett' written in the front of a copy of *The Screwtape Letters*; in Jill (Flewett) Freud's 'Lewis teaches the Retarded', *The Canadian C.S. Lewis Journal*, No 16 (April 1980), p. 5. (Reprinted in Stephen Schofield, *In Search of C.S. Lewis*, South Plainfield, N.J.: Bridge, 1983, p. 59.)

94. 'Two Kinds of Memory.' This holograph poem is found in Eugene McGovern, 'C.S. Lewis', *Dictionary of Literary Biography*. Vol. 15 of British Novelists 1930–59. Detroit: Gale Publishers, 1983, p. 304. There are substantial differences between this version and the one in **P** and **CP**.

95. 'Loki Bound' (nine lines, different from those in the Preface to *Narrative Poems*, written in 1914) quoted in Walter Hooper's Preface to a reprint of C.S. Lewis, *Spirits in Bondage: A Cycle of Lyrics*. New York: Harcourt Brace Jovanovich, 1984, p. xvi.

96. 'Posturing' (An early version – 1929 – of the poem which was first published in *The Pilgrim's Regress*) in Lewis's 'Commentary on the Lay of Leithian' found in J.R.R. Tolkien, *The Lays of Beleriand*. Edited by Christopher Tolkien. London: George Allen & Unwin, 1985, pp. 321–2.

97. An earlier version ('They tell me, Lord ...') of 'Prayer' included in **P**, is found in C.S. Lewis, *Letters to Malcolm: Chiefly on Prayer* – A40. A slightly different version, found in a letter to Dom Bede Griffiths of *c*. June 1931, is reproduced in William Griffin, *Clive Staples Lewis: A Dramatic Life*. San Francisco: Harper & Row, 1986, pp. 149–50. This biography is published in England by Lion in Tring, Hertfordshire, under the title *C.S. Lewis: The Authentic Voice*, 1988. The pagination is different in the English version and the poem is found on p. 152.

98. An earlier version of 'Pattern' in *Poems* entitled 'Some Believe'. This earlier version appears to be a revision of the poem entitled 'Experiment' – E13. It is reproduced in William Griffin, *Clive Staples Lewis: A Dramatic Life*. San Francisco: Harper & Row, 1986, pp. 258–9. Published in England by Lion in Tring, Hertfordshire, under the title *C.S. Lewis: The Authentic Voice*, 1988. Because the pagination is different, the poem is found on pp. 248–9.

99. 'Epigram ("Call *him* a Fascist?")', included in a letter to Ruth Pitter of 6 June 1947, reproduced in William Griffin, *Clive Staples Lewis: A Dramatic Life*. San Francisco: Harper & Row, 1986, p. 270. Published in England by Lion in Tring, Hertfordshire, under the title *C.S. Lewis: The Authentic Voice*, 1988. Because the pagination is different, the poem is found on p. 258.

100. 'The Hills of Down' (1915) first of two stanzas quoted in A.N. Wilson, *C.S. Lewis: A Biography*. London: Collins; New York: W.W. Norton, 1990, p. 48. Repr. **CP**.

101. Fragment (describing W.T. Kirkpatrick) of Autobiographical Poem quoted in A.N. Wilson, *C.S. Lewis: A Biography*. London: Collins; New York: W.W. Norton, 1990. p. 251.

F: Book Reviews
1. Evelyn Waugh, *Rossetti: His Life and Works. The Oxford Magazine*, XLVII (25 October 1928), pp. 66, 69 (Unsigned).

2. Hugh Kingsmill, *Matthew Arnold*. The Oxford Magazine, XLVII (15 November 1928), p. 177.

3. W.P. Ker, *Form and Style in Poetry*. Edited by R.W. Chambers. The Oxford Magazine, XLVII (6 December 1928), pp. 283–4.

4. H.W. Garrod, *Collins*. The Oxford Magazine, XLVIII (16 May 1929), p. 633.

5. Ruth Mohl, *The Three Estates in Medieval and Renaissance Literature*. Medium Aevum, III (February 1934), pp. 68–70.

6. E.K. Chambers, *Sir Thomas Wyatt and Some Collected Studies*. Medium Aevum, III (October 1934), pp. 237–40.

7. T.R. Henn, *Longinus and English Criticism*. The Oxford Magazine, LIII (6 December 1934), p. 264.

8. Dorothy M. Hoare, *The Works of Morris and of Yeats in Relation to Early Saga Literature*. 'The Sagas and Modern Life: Morris, Mr Yeats and the Originals', *The Times Literary Supplement* (29 May 1937), p. 409 (Unsigned).

9. J.R.R. Tolkien, *The Hobbit: or There and Back Again*. 'A World for Children', *The Times Literary Supplement* (2 October 1937), p. 714 (Unsigned). Repr. as 'The Hobbit' in **OTOW = OS**.

10. J.R.R. Tolkien, *The Hobbit: or There and Back Again*. 'Professor Tolkien's Hobbit', *The Times* (8 October 1937), p. 20 (Unsigned).

11. Charles Williams, *Taliessin Through Logres*. 'A Sacred Poem', *Theology*, XXXVIII (April 1939), pp. 268–76.

12. A.C. Bouquet (Editor), *A Lectionary of Christian Prose from the Second Century to the Twentieth Century*. Theology, XXXIX (December 1939), pp. 467–8.

13. D. de Rougemont, *Passion and Society* (Translated by M. Belgion); Claude Chavasse, *The Bride of Christ*. Theology, XL (June 1940), pp. 459–61.

14. Lord David Cecil (Editor), *The Oxford Book of Christian Verse*. The Review of English Studies, XVII (January 1941), pp. 95–102.

15. Helen M. Barrett, *Boethius: Some Aspects of His Times and Work. Medium Aevum*, X (February 1941), pp. 29–34.

16. Logan Pearsall Smith, *Milton and His Modern Critics. The Cambridge Review* (21 February 1941), p. 280.

17. Dorothy L. Sayers, *The Mind of the Maker. Theology*, XLIII (October 1941), pp. 248–9.

18. Andreas Capellanus, *The Art of Courtly Love* (with introduction, translation, and notes by John Jay Parry). *The Review of English Studies*, XIX (January 1943), pp. 77–9.

19. J.W.H. Atkins, *English Literary Criticism: The Medieval Phase. The Oxford Magazine*, LXII (10 February 1944), p. 158.

20. Owen Barfield, *Romanticism Comes of Age*. '"Who gaf me Drink?"', *The Spectator*, CLXXIV (9 March 1945), p. 224.

21. Charles Williams, *Taliessin Through Logres. The Oxford Magazine*, IXIV (14 March 1946), pp. 248–50.

22. Douglas Bush, *'Paradise Lost' in Our Time: Some Comments. The Oxford Magazine*, LXV (13 February 1947), pp. 215–17.

23. Sir Thomas Malory, *The Works of Sir Thomas Malory* (Edited by E. Vinaver). 'The Morte Darthur', *The Times Literary Supplement* (7 June 1947), pp. 273–4 (Unsigned). Repr. **SMRL**.

24. G.A.L. Burgeon (= Owen Barfield), *This Ever Diverse Pair*. 'Life Partners', *Time and Tide*, XXXI (25 March 1950), p. 286.

25. Howard Rollin Patch, *The Other World, According to Descriptions in Medieval Literature. Medium Aevum*, XX (1951), pp. 93–4.

26. Alan M.F. Gunn, *The Mirror of Love: A Reinterpretation of 'The Romance of the Rose'. Medium Aevum*, XXII, No 1 (1953), pp. 27–31.

27. J.R.R. Tolkien, *The Fellowship of the Ring* (being the First Part of *The Lord of the Rings*). 'The Gods Return to Earth', *Time and Tide*, XXXV (14

August 1954), pp. 1082–3. Repr. with G28 as 'Tolkien's *The Lord of the Rings*' in **OTOW = OS**.

28. J.R.R. Tolkien, *The Two Towers* (being the Second Part of *The Lord of the Rings*); *The Return of the King* (being the Third Part of *The Lord of the Rings*). 'The Dethronement of Power', *Time and Tide*, XXXVI (22 October 1955), pp. 1373–4. Repr. with G27 as 'Tolkien's *The Lord of the Rings*' in **OTOW = OS**.

29. W. Schwarz, *Principles and Problems of Biblical Translation. Medium Aevum*, XXVI, No 2 (1957), pp. 115–17.

30. R.S. Loomis (Editor), *Arthurian Literature in the Middle Ages: A Collaborative Study*, 'Arthuriana', *The Cambridge Review*, LXXXI (13 February 1960), pp. 355, 357.

31. M. Pauline Parker, *The Allegory of the 'Faerie Queen'*. *The Cambridge Review*, LXXXI (11 June 1960), pp. 643, 645.

32. John Vyvyan, *Shakespeare and the Rose of Love. The Listener*, LXIV (7 July 1960), p. 30.

33. Robert Ellrodt, *Neoplatonism in the Poetry of Spenser. Etudes Anglaises*, XIV (April–June 1961), pp. 107–16. Repr. as 'Neoplatonism in the Poetry of Spenser' in **SMRL**.

34. George Steiner, *The Death of Tragedy*. 'Tragic Ends', *Encounter*, XVIII (February 1962), pp. 97–101.

35. David Loth, *The Erotic in Literature*. 'Eros on the Loose', *The Observer* (Weekend Review), No 8905 (4 March 1962), p. 30.

36. Sir John Hawkins, *The Life of Samuel Johnson* (Edited by B.H. Davis). 'Boswell's Bugbear', *Sunday Telegraph*, No 61 (1 April 1962), p. 8.

37. Homer, *The Odyssey* (Translated by Robert Fitzgerald). 'Odysseus Sails Again', *Sunday Telegraph*, No 84 (9 September 1962), p. 6.

38. John Jones, *On Aristotle and Greek Tragedy*. 'Ajax and Others', *Sunday Telegraph*, No 98 (16 December 1962), p. 6.

39. Harold Bloom, *The Visionary Company: A Reading of English Romantic Poetry*. 'Poetry and Exegesis', *Encounter*, XX (June 1963), pp. 74–6.

40. Dorothy L. Sayers, *The Poetry of Search and the Poetry of Statement*. 'Rhyme and Reason', *Sunday Telegraph*, No 148 (1 December 1963), p. 18.

G: Published Letters

1. 'The Kingis Quair', *The Times Literary Supplement* (18 April 1929), p. 315.

2. 'Spenser's Irish Experiences and *The Faerie Queene*', *The Review of English Studies*, VII (January 1931), pp. 83–5.

3. 'The Genuine Text', *The Times Literary Supplement* (2 May 1935), p. 288; cf. J. Dover Wilson, ibid. (16 May 1935), p. 313.

4. 'The Genuine Text', *The Times Literary Supplement* (23 May 1935), p. 331; cf. J. Dover Wilson, ibid. (30 May 1935), p. 348; J. Dover Wilson, ibid. (13 June 1935), p. 380.

5. 'On Cross-Channel Ships', *The Times* (18 November 1938), p. 12.

6. 'The Conditions for a Just War', *Theology*, XXXVIII (May 1939), pp. 373–4. Repr. **GID = U, TAH**.

7. 'Christianity and Culture', *Theology*, XL (June 1940), pp. 475–7. Repr. **CR**.

8. 'The Conflict in Anglican Theology', *Theology*, XLI (November 1940), p. 304. Repr. **GID = U, TAH**.

9. Open Letter, *The Christian News-Letter*, No 119 (4 February 1942), p. 4.

10. 'Miracles', *The Guardian* (16 October 1942), p. 331. Repr. **GID = U, TAH**.

11. Letter to Publisher on dust cover of C.S. Lewis, *Perelandra*. New York: Macmillan, 1944.

12. 'Mr C.S. Lewis on Christianity', *The Listener*, XXXI (9 March 1944), p. 273; cf. W.R. Childe, ibid. (2 March 1944), p. 245; W.R. Childe, ibid. (16 March 1944), p. 301. Repr. **GID = U, TAH**.

13. 'Basic Fears', *The Times Literary Supplement* (2 December 1944), p. 583; cf. S.H. Hooke, ibid. (27 January 1945), p. 43.

14. 'Basic Fears', *The Times Literary Supplement* (3 February 1945), p. 55; cf. S.H. Hooke, ibid. (10 February 1945), p. 67.

15. 'Above the Smoke and Stir', *The Times Literary Supplement* (14 July 1945), p. 331; cf. B.A. Wright, ibid. (4 August 1945), p. 367.

16. 'Above the Smoke and Stir', *The Times Literary Supplement* (29 September 1945), p. 463; cf. B.A. Wright, ibid. (27 October 1945), p. 511.

17. 'A Village Experience', *The Guardian* (31 August 1945), p. 335. Repr. **GID = U, TAH.**

18. 'Socratic Wisdom', *The Oxford Magazine*, LXIV (13 June 1946), p. 359.

19. 'Poetic Licence', *The Sunday Times* (11 August 1946), p. 6.

20. Letter to Publisher on dust cover of *Essays Presented to Charles Williams* (Edited by C.S. Lewis). London: Oxford University Press, 1947.

21. 'A Difference of Outlook', *The Guardian* (27 June 1947), p. 283; cf. A Correspondent, 'Adult Colleges', ibid. (30 May 1947), pp. 235, 240.

22. 'Public Schools', *Church Times*, CXXX (3 October 1947), p. 583.

23. 'The New Miltonians', *The Times Literary Supplement* (29 November 1947), p. 615.

24. (With Erik Routley) 'Correspondence with an Anglican who Dislikes Hymns', *The Presbyter*, VI, No 2 (1948), pp. 15–20. (The two letters from Lewis, dated 16 July and 21 September 1946, are printed over the initials 'A.B.'). Repr. **GID = U, TAH.**

25. 'Charles Williams', *The Oxford Magazine*, LXVI (29 April 1948), p. 380.

26. 'Othello', *The Times Literary Supplement* (19 June 1948), p. 345.

27. 'The Church's Liturgy', *Church Times*, CXXXII (20 May 1949), p. 319; cf. E.L. Mascall, *'Quadringentesimo Anno'*, ibid. (6 May 1949), p. 282; W.D.F.

Hughes, 'The Church's Liturgy', ibid. (24 June 1949), p. 409. Repr. **GID = U, TAH.**

28. 'The Church's Liturgy', *Church Times*, CXXXII (1 July 1949), p. 427; cf. Edward Every, 'Doctrine and Liturgy', ibid. (8 July 1949), pp. 445–6. Repr. **GID = U, TAH.**

29, 'Invocation', *Church Times*, CXXXII (15 July 1949), pp. 463–4; cf. Edward Every, 'Invocation of Saints', ibid. (22 July 1949), pp. 481–2. Repr. **GID = U, TAH.**

30. 'Invocation of Saints', *Church Times*, CXXXII (5 August 1949), p. 513. Repr. **GID = U, TAH.**

31. 'Text Corruptions', *The Times Literary Supplement* (3 March 1950), p. 137; J. Dover Wilson, ibid. (10 March 1950), p. 153.

32. Letter on '*Robinson Crusoe* as a Myth', *Essays in Criticism*, I (July 1951), p. 313; cf. Ian Watt, '*Robinson Crusoe* as a Myth', ibid. (April 1951), pp. 95–119; Ian Watt, ibid. (July 1951), p. 313.

33. 'The Holy Name', *Church Times*, CXXXIV (10 August 1951), p. 541; cf. Leslie E.T. Bradbury, ibid. (3 August 1951), p. 525. Repr. **GID = U, TAH.**

34. 'Mere Christians', *Church Times*, CXXXV (8 February 1952), p. 95; cf. R.D. Daunton-Fear, 'Evangelical Churchmanship', ibid. (1 February 1952), p. 77. Repr. **GID = U, TAH.**

35. 'The Sheepheard's Slumber', *The Times Literary Supplement* (9 May 1952), p. 313.

36. Letter to Dorothy L. Sayers quoted in Miss Sayers's 'Ignorance and Dissatisfaction', *Latin Teaching*, XXVIII, No 3 (October 1952), p. 91. (The article is reprinted as 'The Teaching of Latin' in Dorothy L. Sayers's *The Poetry of Search and the Poetry of Statement*. London: Victor Gollancz, 1963).

37. 'Canonization', *Church Times*, CXXXV (24 October 1952), p. 763; cf. Eric Pitt, ibid. (17 October 1952), p. 743. Repr. **GID = U, TAH.**

38. Letter to the Publisher on dust cover of A Religious of CSMV [R.P. Lawson], *The Coming of the Lord: A Study in the Creed*. London: A.R. Mowbray, 1953.

39. Letter to the Publisher on dust cover of J.R.R. Tolkien, *The Fellowship of the Ring*. London: George Allen & Unwin, 1954.

40. Letter to Joy Davidman of 22 December 1953 quoted on cover of paperback of A.C. Clarke, *Childhood's End*. London: Sidgwick and Jackson, 1954.

41. Letter to the Milton Society of America, *A Milton Evening in Honor of Douglas Bush and C.S. Lewis*. Modern Language Association (28 December 1954), pp. 14–15. Repr. **L**.

42. Letter to Don Luigi Pedrollo of 16 December 1954 in *L'Amico die Buoni Fanciulli*, No 1 (Verona, 1955), p. 75. Repr. **LDGC**.

43. (With Dorothy L. Sayers) 'Charles Williams', *The Times* (14 May 1955), p. 9.

44. 'Portrait of W.B. Yeats', *The Listener*, LIV (15 September 1955), p. 427.

45. Letter to the Publisher on the dust cover (a portion of one letter on the inside front flap and a portion of another on the back flap) of C.S. Lewis, *Till We Have Faces: A Myth Retold*. London: Geoffrey Bles, 1956.
   The letter or 'Note' from the back flap was printed in full in the Time Special Edition of *Till We Have Faces* published in paperback in New York by Time Inc., 1966, pp. 273–5. Both the letter and the 'Note' are printed in the Fount Paperback edition of *Till We Have Faces* (1978).

46. Letter to J.B. Phillips (3 August 1944) quoted in *Fifty-Two: A Journal of Books and Authors* [from Geoffrey Bles], No 1 (Autumn 1957), p. 9.

47. Letter to the Publisher on dust cover of E.R. Eddison, *The Mezentian Gate*. London: Printed at the Curwen Press, 1958. Repr. as 'A Tribute to E.R. Eddison' in **OTOW = OS**.

48. (With others) 'Mgr R.A. Knox', *Church Times*, CXLI (6 June 1958), p. 12.

49. 'Books for Children', *The Times Literary Supplement* (28 November 1958), p. 689; cf. 'The Light Fantastic', ibid., *Children's Book Section* (21 November 1958), p. x.

50. 'Version Vernacular', *The Christian Century*, LXXV (31 December 1958), p. 1515. Repr. **GID = U, TAH.**

51. Letter to the Publisher on dust cover of Mervyn Peake, *Titus Alone*. London: Eyre and Spottiswoode, 1959.

52. 'Spelling Reform', *The Times Educational Supplement* (1 January 1960), p. 13.

53. Letter to the Publisher on dust cover of David Bolt, *Adam*. London: J.M. Dent, 1960.

54. Letter to Charles Moorman in Charles Moorman, *Arthurian Triptych: Mystic Materials in Charles Williams, C.S. Lewis and T.S. Eliot*. Berkeley and Los Angeles: University of California Press (1960), p. 161.

55. Letter to Mahmoud Manzalaoui quoted in M. Manzalaoui's 'Lydgate and English Prosody', *Cairo Studies in English* (1960), p. 94.

56. Letter to the Editor, *Delta: The Cambridge Literary Magazine*, No 23 (February 1961), pp. 4–7; cf. The Editors, 'Professor C.S. Lewis and the English Faculty', ibid., No 22 (October 1960), pp. 6–17; C.S. Lewis, 'Undergraduate Criticism', *Broadsheet* (Cambridge), VIII, No 17 (9 March 1960) [i].

57. Letters to 'A Member of the Church of the Covenant', quoted in the pamphlet, *Encounter with Light*. Lynchburg, Virginia: Church of the Covenant [June 1961], pp. 11–16, 20. (The three letters from C.S. Lewis were written [14 December 1950; 23 December 1950; 17 April 1951] respectively.) Reprinted, as by Sheldon Vanauken, by Wheaton College, Wheaton, Illinois [1976].

58. 'Capital Punishment', *Church Times*, CXLIV (1 December 1961), p. 7; cf. Claude Davis, ibid. (8 December 1961), p. 14. Repr. **GID = U, TAH.**

59. 'Death Penalty', *Church Times*, CXLIV (15 December 1961), p. 12; cf. Claude Davis, ibid. (8 December 1961), p. 14. Repr. **GID = U, TAH.**

60. 'And Less Greek', *Church Times*, CXLV (20 July 1962), p. 12.

61. Letter to the Editor, *English*, XIV (Summer 1962), p. 75.

62. 'Wain's Oxford', *Encounter*, XX (January 1963), p. 81.

63. Letter to Roger Lancelyn Green [28 December 1938] quoted in Roger Lancelyn Green, *C.S. Lewis*. London: The Bodley Head, 1963, p. 26.

64. Letter to Edward Meskys (3 October 1963) in *Niekas*, No 7 (December 1963), no p.n.

65. Letter quoted in Rose Macaulay, *Letters to a Sister* (Edited by Constance Babington Smith). London: Collins, 1964, p. 261 n. (Quotations from a letter C.S. Lewis wrote to Dorothea Conybeare, who had asked him to explain the title of his book *Till We Have Faces*.)

66. Letter to the Publisher on flyleaf of Austin Farrer, *Saving Belief: A Discussion of Essentials*. London: Hodder & Stoughton, 1964.

67. Letters to Clyde S. Kilby (of 10 February 1957, 7 May 1959 and 11 January 1961) and Thomas Howard quoted in Clyde S. Kilby, *The Christian World of C.S. Lewis*. Grand Rapids, Michigan: Eerdmans (1964), pp. 58, 136, 153–4, 189–90.

68. Letter to John Warwick Montgomery (of 29 August 1963) in J.W. Montgomery, *History and Christianity*. Donner's Grove, Illinois: Inter-Varsity Press (1964), pp. 6–7.

69. 'Conception of *The Screwtape Letters*', *Fifty-Two: A Journal of Books and Authors* [from Geoffrey Bles], No 14 (Autumn 1964), p. 3. (A letter C.S. Lewis wrote to his brother on 21 July 1940 which divulges the original idea for *The Screwtape Letters*.) Repr. L.

70. Letters to Owen Barfield ('Great War Letter' c. 1927, beginning 'After writing lectures all morning') on p. xviii; to Charles A. Huttar (30 March 1962) on p. xix; and to John Lawlor (1954) on p. 77, quoted in *Light on C.S. Lewis*. Edited by Jocelyn Gibb. London: Geoffrey Bles, 1965; New York: Harcourt, Brace & World, 1966.

71. 'Two letters from C.S. Lewis', *Fifty-Two: A Journal of Books and Authors* [from Geoffrey Bles], No 17 (Spring 1966), pp. 18–19. (Letters to his father about the writing of *The Allegory of Love* on 20 July 1928 and his visit to Cambridge in 1920.) Repr. **L**.

72. A letter to James E. Higgins of 2 December 1962 in J.E. Higgins, 'A Letter from C.S. Lewis', *The Horn Book Magazine*, XLII (October 1966), pp. 533–4.

73. Letter to William Borst (*c*. 1954) of Harcourt, Brace & World, quoted in Walter Hooper's Preface to C.S. Lewis, *Studies in Medieval and Renaissance Literature*. Edited by Walter Hooper. Cambridge: Cambridge University Press, 1966, pp. viii–ix.

74. Letter to Dom Bede Griffiths [*c*. 1934] quoted in Walter Hooper's Preface to C.S. Lewis, *Christian Reflections*. Edited by Walter Hooper. London: Geoffrey Bles, 1967; Grand Rapids, Eerdmans, 1967, p. vii.

75. Letter to Walter Hooper [of 30 November 1954] in 'Prof. Burton's Class', *The Greensboro Daily News*, North Carolina (8 October 1967), p. 4. Repr. **BOH** (15 July).

76. Letters to Peter Milward SJ, of 22 September, 17 December 1955; 9 May, 22 September, 10 December 1956; 24 September, 25 December 1959; 7 March 1960 quoted in Peter Milward, 'C.S. Lewis on Allegory', *Bigo Seinen: The Rising Generation*, Tokyo, CXIV, No 4 (April 1968), pp. 227–31.

77. Letter to a little girl [Ruth Broady] (26 October 1963) quoted in C.S. Lewis, *A Mind Awake*. Edited by Clyde S. Kilby. London: Geoffrey Bles, 1968; New York, Harcourt, Brace & World, 1969, p. 123.

78. Letter to his father (14 August 1925) quoted in Walter Hooper's Preface to C.S. Lewis, *Selected Literary Essays*. Edited by Walter Hooper. Cambridge: Cambridge University Press, 1969, p. xiii. Repr. **L**.

79. Letters to Arthur Greeves (2 December 1918; 14 July, 18 September 1919) quoted in Walter Hooper's Preface to C.S. Lewis, *Narrative Poems*. Edited by Walter Hooper. London: Geoffrey Bles, 1969, pp. ix–x. Repr. **TST**.

80. Letter to John Warwick Montgomery (29 August 1963), printed in Appendix B, John Warwick Montgomery, *Where Is History Going?* Grand Rapids: Zondervan, 1969, p. 222.

81. Letter to the Publisher on dust cover of Francis Warner, *Poetry of Francis Warner*. Philadelphia: Pilgrim Press, 1970.

82. Letters to Anthony Boucher (of 5 February 1953) and Susan Salzberg (of 5 February 1960) in *CSL: The Bulletin of the New York C.S. Lewis Society*, II, No 10 (August 1971), p. 3.

83. Letters to J.S.A. Ensor (of 13 March, 31 March and 28 April 1944), Owen Barfield (of 1943) and the Rt. Rev. Henry I. Louttit (of 5 January 1958) quoted in *C.S. Lewis: Speaker and Teacher*. Edited by Carolyn Keefe. Grand Rapids, Michigan: Zondervan Publishing Co. (1971), pp. 17–18, 102–3, 123, 132.

84. Letters to [Arthur Greeves] (13 and 30 August 1930); quoted in Glenn Sadler, 'Fantastic Imagination in George MacDonald' (pp. 218, 225, 226); letters to Arthur Greeves (of 12 October 1916) and Pauline Baynes (of 21 January 1954) quoted in Walter Hooper, 'Past Watchful Dragons' (pp. 282, 312), *Imagination and the Spirit: Essays in Literature and the Christian Faith presented to Clyde S. Kilby*. Edited by Charles Huttar. Grand Rapids: Eerdmans, 1971.

85. 'Letters of C.S. Lewis to E. Vinaver' (Edited by Richard C. West), *Orchrist* (Special C.S. Lewis Issue), No 6 (Winter 1971–1972), pp. 3–5. (Contained are five letters to Professor Eugène Vinaver and one to Mrs Vinaver.)

86. Letter to Anne and Martin Kilmer [7 August 1957] quoted in Margaret Hannay, 'C.S. Lewis Collection at Wheaton College', *Mythlore*, Vol. 2, No 4 (Winter 1972), p. 20.

87. Letter to Nina Howell Starr (of 1 November 1960) in Nathan C. Starr, 'C.S. Lewis: A Personal Memoir', *Unicorn*, II, No 2 (Spring 1972), p. 11.

88. Letter to an American Girl [Hila Newman: 23 June 1953] on p. 16; and letter to Kathryn Ann Lindskoog [of 29 October 1957] quoted on back cover of Kathryn Ann Lindskoog, *The Lion of Judah in Never-Never Land*. Grand Rapids, Michigan: Eerdmans (1973).

89. Letters to Arthur Greeves [18 October 1916] on p. 17; [29 May 1918] on p. 18; (10 January 1932) on pp. 20–1; (13 May 1917) on p. 24; [2 June 1919] on p. 34; [24 December 1930] on p. 58; (26 June 1931) on p. 70; [4 May 1915] on p. 74; [1 June 1930] on p. 75; [3 August 1930] on p. 76; [30 March 1915] on p. 93; [29 April 1930] on pp. 119, 136; (23 April 1935) on p. 138; [5 January 1930] on p. 139; (24 July 1917) on p. 145; [29 November 1916] on p. 158; (15 June 1930) on p. 162; [17 August 1933] on p. 168–71; (1 October 1934) on p. 173; (19 January 1931) on p. 178; holograph letter to Owen Barfield (no date) on p. 45; holograph letter to Michal Williams (22 November 1947) on p. 189; and a holograph inscription to his father on the end leaf of a copy of *Spirits in Bondage* (29 March 1919) on p. 188; quoted in Douglas Gilbert and Clyde S. Kilby, *C.S. Lewis: Images of His World*. Grand Rapids: Eerdmans, 1973.

90. Letters to Alfred Cecil Harwood (of 28 October 1926) and Daphne Harwood (of 28 March 1933 and March 1942) quoted in A.C. Harwood, 'C.S. Lewis and Anthroposophy', *Anthroposophical Quarterly*, XVIII, No 4 (Winter 1973), pp. 40–2. Article repr. **ABT**.

91. Letters to Arthur Greeves and Owen Barfield quoted in Lionel Adey, 'The Light of Holiness: some comments on Morris by C.S. Lewis', *The Journal of the William Morris Society*, III, No 1 (Spring 1974), pp. 11, 12, 13, 14, 15, 16. Letters to Arthur Greeves repr. **TST**.

92. Letters to Mervyn Peake (20 June 1959; 2 October 1958) quoted in Maeve Gilmore and Shelagh Johnson, *Mervyn Peake: Writings and Drawings*. London: Academy Editions; New York: St Martin's Press, 1974, pp. 46, 83.

93. Letters to Corbin Scott Carnell (of 13 October and 10 December 1958) quoted in Corbin Scott Carnell, *Bright Shadows of Reality: C.S. Lewis and the Feeling Intellect*. Grand Rapids, Michigan: Eerdmans (1974), pp. 69, 71, 79.

94. Letter to John Warwick Montgomery (of 21 January 1960) in *Myth, Allegory and Gospel: An Interpretation of J.R.R. Tolkien, C.S. Lewis, G.K. Chesterton, Charles Williams* (edited by John Warwick Montgomery). Minneapolis: Bethany Fellowship (1974), pp. 145–7.

95. Letters to Arthur Greeves [of 8 June 1915, 12 October 1915, 22 April 1923, 25 March 1933, 1 June 1930, 26 December 1945, 24 July 1915, December 1935, 5 November 1933, 26 December 1934, 4 May 1915, 17 July

1918, 29 December 1935, 17 June 1918, 17 August 1933, 5 September 1931, 1 February 1931] quoted in Clyde S. Kilby and Linda J. Evans, 'C.S. Lewis and Music', *Christian Scholar's Review*, IV, No 1 (1974), pp. 1, 11, 12, 13, 14, 15. Repr. **TST**.

96. Letters to his father [19 September 1908] on pp. 27-8; (January 1911) on p. 29; [? September 1913] on p. 34; [28 September 1913] on pp. 34-5; (18 March 1913) on p. 35; [22 June 1914] on pp. 37-8; [7 December 1916] on p. 46; [28 January 1917] on p. 47; [8 February 1917] on p. 47; [10 June 1917] on p. 51; (27 August 1917) on p. 52; [10 September 1917] on p. 52; (15, 16 November; 13 December 1917) on p. 53; (17 April 1918) on p. 55; (14 May 1918) on p. 55; [20? June 1918] on p. 57; (8 December 1918) on p. 59; (27 January 1919) on p. 60; [4 February 1919] on p. 61; [5 March 1919] on p. 62; (25 May 1919) on p. 64; (4 April 1920) on p. 65; (18 May 1922) on p. 68; (1 July 1923) on p. 75; [22 November 1923] on p.78; [Note to end of 1923 diary] on p. 78; [15 October 1924] on pp. 80-1; [11 February 1925] on p. 82; [April 1925] on p. 82; [14 August 1925] on p. 83; (21 October 1925) on pp. 84-5; (4 December 1925) on p. 86; (25 January 1926) on pp. 86-7; (5 June 1926) on p. 88; [29 July 1927] on p. 93; (10 July 1928) on p. 96; [9 July 1929] on p. 96; (10 July 1928) on p. 148; (30 March 1927) on p. 181; quoted in Roger Lancelyn Green and Walter Hooper, *C.S. Lewis: A Biography*. London: Collins; New York: Harcourt Brace Jovanovich, 1974.

97. Letters to Mrs Edward A. Allen (26 November 1955) on p. 286;
　　to Delmar Banner (6 June 1954) on p. 281;
　　to Owen Barfield (6 May 1932) on p. 127; (29 October 1932) on p. 128;
　　to Pauline Baynes (21 January 1954) on p. 246;
　　to Geoffrey Bles (20 March 1953) on pp. 245-6; (11 March 1953) on p. 248;
　　to Charles A. Brady (23 October 1944) on p. 164;
　　to R.W. Chapman (18 September 1935) on pp. 132-3;
　　to Claude Chavasse (25 February 1934) on p. 130;
　　to Arthur C. Clarke (7 December 1943) on p. 173; [14 February 1953] on pp. 177-8;
　　to E. R. Eddison (16 November, 19 December, 29 December 1942) on p. 213;
　　to T.S. Eliot (19 April 1931) on pp. 125-6; (2 June 1931) on p. 126; (18 May 1962) on p. 296;
　　to Vera Gebbert (15 July 1960) on pp. 276-7;
　　to Jocelyn Gibb (28 June 1963) on p. 233; (16, 29 February 1956) on p. 261; (9 May 1960) on p. 275;

to Roger Lancelyn Green [16 September 1945] on p. 70; (28 December 1938) on p. 163; (17 November 1957) on pp. 163–4; [25 March 1962] on p. 240; [4 April 1950] on p. 244; (6 March 1951) on p. 244; (26 September 1952) on p. 245; (22 February 1954) on p. 248; (1 May 1952) on p. 255; (29 March 1952) on p. 258; (5 February 1957) on p. 268; (8 May 1957) on p. 268; (10 December 1957) on p. 268; ([16] July 1953) on pp. 282–3; (29 August 1958) on p. 294; ([6] September 1961) on p. 295; ([28 January] 1963) on p. 297; (11 August 1963) on p. 303; (1 November 1963) on p. 306;

to Joy Davidman Gresham (22 December 1953) on p. 178;

to Cyril Hartmann (25 July and n.d. 1919) on p. 65;

to A.K. Hamilton Jenkin (21 March 1930) on p. 106;

to Walter Hooper ([2] July 1962) on p. 298;

to William L. Kinter (30 July 1954; 14 February 1951; 27 November 1951; 28 March 1953; 30 July 1954) on p. 179;

to Richard Ladborough (28 October 1963) on p. 306;

to W.H. Lewis [3 September 1927] on p. 93; [12 December 1927] on pp. 94, 95; [1] April 1928) on p. 95; (25 August; 29 September 1929) on p. 97; [12 January 1930] on p. 99; [22 November 1931] on p. 124; (3 December 1939) on p. 186; (21 July 1940) on p. 191; (2, 18 September 1939) on p. 238;

to Sister Penelope (9 November 1941) on p. 170; (11 May 1942) on p. 170; [6 September 1944] on pp. 177; (28 May 1945) on pp. 179–80, 224, 226; (24 October 1940) on pp. 198, 221–2; (4 November 1940) on p. 198; (9 October 1941) on p. 199; (15 May 1941) on p. 205; (30 December 1950) on pp. 229–30; (5 June 1951) on p. 257; (30 July 1960) on p. 281; ([15 February] 1954) on p. 297; ([17] September 1963) on p. 304;

to the Marquess of Salisbury (9 March 1947) on p. 228;

to the Editor of *The Saturday Evening Post* (17 October 1963) on pp. 304–5;

to Alec Vidler (23 March 1939) on p. 137;

to Chad Walsh (21 October 1959) on p. 270; (23 May 1960) on pp. 275–6;

to Mrs Watt (28 August 1958) on p. 269;

to James W. Welch (10 February 1941) on p. 202;

to Laurence Whistler (9 January 1947) on p. 153; [April 1947] on pp. 153–4;

to Basil Willey (26 October 1956) on p. 289; (22 October 1963) on p. 306; quoted in Roger Lancelyn Green and Walter Hooper, *C.S. Lewis: A Biography*. London: Collins; New York: Harcourt Brace Jovanovich, 1974.

98. Letters to Arthur Greeves [26 September 1914] on p. 42; [6 October 1914] on p. 43; [26 January 1915] on p. 44; [7 March 1916] on p. 44; [27 September 1916] on p. 45; [15 February; 28 February 1917] on p. 48; (12

October 1916) on pp. 48–9; [6 March 1917] on p. 50; [28 April 1917] on pp. 50–1; [13 May 1917] on p. 51; [10 June 1917] on pp. 51–2; [8 July 1917] on p. 52; (28 October 1917) on p. 53; (29 May 1918) on p. 55; (12 September 1918) on p. 58; [6? October 1918] on p. 58; (2 November 1918) on p. 58; (2 December 1918) on p. 59; [26 January 1919] on p. 61; [5 May 1919] on pp. 63–4; [June 1921] on pp. 65–6; [22 April 1923] on p. 77; ([3] December 1929) on p. 88; [26 June 1927] on p. 93; [5 November 1929] on p. 97; [22, 26 December 1929] on p. 98; (9 January 1930) on p. 104; (5, 26 January 1930) on p. 105; (30 January 1930) on pp. 105–6; (7 June 1930) on pp. 106–7; (30 June 1930) on pp. 107–8; (8 July 1930) on p. 108; (15 June 1930) on p. 109; (29 July 1930) on pp. 109–10; (18 August 1930) on p. 110; (22 June 1930) on p. 111; (28 August 1930) on p. 111; (10 January 1931) on p. 113; (17 January 1931) on p. 114; (1 June 1930) on p. 114; (5 September 1931) on p. 115; (1 October 1931) on p. 116; (11 October 1931) on pp. 117–8; (1 October 1931) on pp. 119–20; (6 December 1931) on p. 121; (25 March 1933) on p. 128; [17 December 1932] on p. 129; (4 December 1932) on p. 129; (4 February 1933) on p. 131; (17 August 1933) on p. 131; (26 February 1936) on pp. 133–4; (23 December 1941) on pp. 170, 203, 206; quoted in Roger Lancelyn Green and Walter Hooper, *C.S. Lewis: A Biography*. London: Collins; New York: Harcourt Brace Jovanovich, 1974. Repr. **TST**.

99. Letter to Lucy Matthews [of 11 September 1958] quoted in *Amon Hen: The Bulletin of the Tolkien Society of Great Britain*, No 14 (February 1975), p. 2.

100. Letters to Arthur Greeves (6 March 1917) and to his father (4 December 1915), quoted in Roger Lancelyn Green, 'C.S. Lewis and Andrew Lang', *Notes and Queries*, N.S., XXII (May 1975), pp. 208–9. (Repr. *CSL: The Bulletin of the New York C.S. Lewis Society*, VI, No 9 (July 1975), p. 11.)

101. Letters to R.W. Ladborough quoted in R.W. Ladborough, 'C.S. Lewis in Cambridge', *CSL: The Bulletin of the New York C.S. Lewis Society*, VI, No 9 (July 1975), pp. 8, 10. Repr. **ABT**.

102. Letter to A.C. Harwood (of 7 May 1934) quoted in A.C. Harwood, 'A Toast to the Memory of C.S. Lewis proposed at Magdalen College, 4 July 1975', *CSL: The Bulletin of the New York C.S. Lewis Society*, VI, No 11 (September 1975), p. 2. Repr. **ABT**.

103. Letter to Chad Walsh (*c.* 1949) quoted in Chad Walsh's Afterword to C.S. Lewis, *A Grief Observed*. New York: Bantam, 1976, p. 110.

104. Letters to Kathryn Stillwell (Lindskoog) (24 April 1956, 29 October 1957) in Kathryn Lindskoog, 'C.S. Lewis: Reactions from Women', *Mythlore*, Vol. 3, No 4 (June 1976), p. 19. The same letters (24 April 1956, 29 October 1957) in *Voyage to Narnia Response Book*. Lifestyle Series for Young Adults. Elgin, Illinois: David C. Cook, 1978, pp. 6–7. Holograph letter (29 October 1957) in the *Canadian C.S. Lewis Journal*, No 48 (Autumn 1984), pp. 14–15. Part of the letter of 29 October 1957 appears on the back cover of G88: Kathryn Lindskoog, *The Lion of Judah in Never-Never Land*.

105. Letter to Francis Anderson (23 September 1963) on p. 76; to Charles Brady (29 October 1944) on p. 48; to Arthur Greeves [30 January 1930, 4 February 1933], (3 December 1929, 22 September 1931, 22 June 1930, 26 February 1936, 11 January 1944) on pp. 47, 48, 69, 70, 72, 73; to Thomas Howard (28 October 1958) on p. 48; to W.H. Lewis (10 September 1939) on p. 70; to Sister Penelope (24 August 1939) on p. 75; quoted in Clyde S. Kilby, *Tolkien and the Silmarillion*. Wheaton: Harold Shaw, 1976.

106. Letters to J.R.R. Tolkien [of 7 December 1929, 27 October 1949, 13 November 1952, 7 December 1953] quoted in Humphrey Carpenter, *J.R.R. Tolkien: A Biography*. London: Allen & Unwin (1977), pp. 145, 204, 215 and 219 respectively.

107. Letters to Owen Barfield (undated) on p. 216; to Gracia Fay Bouman (of 19 July 1960) on p. 3; to Arthur Greeves (of 4 February 1933, 22 September 1931, 8 November 1931 [1 July 1930], 1 June 1930, 18 October 1931, 1 October 1931, 12 September 1933 [18 October 1916]) on pp. 137, 138, 141, 142–3, 155, 221, 273; to Dom Bede Griffiths (of 8 January 1936, 1934) on pp. 143, 221; to Mr Lennox (of 25 May 1959) on pp. 40–1; to Ruth Pitter (of 16 April 1952) on p. xv, quoted in *The Longing for a Form: Essays on the Fiction of C.S. Lewis* (Edited by Peter J. Schakel). Kent, Ohio: Kent State University Press, 1977.

108. Letters to Sheldon Vanauken. The following letters are given in full: (14 December 1950) on pp. 88–90; (23 December 1950) on pp. 91–3; (17 April 1951) on pp. 101–2; (1951) on p. 104; (5 January 1951) on pp. 105–6; (8 January 1951) on p. 106; (24 March 1952) on p. 110; (1952) on p. 123; (22 April 1953) on pp. 134–5; (14 May 1954) on pp. 146–8; (23 November 1954) on pp. 167–8; (10 February 1955) on pp. 183–4; (20 February 1955) on pp. 186–7; (6 April 1955) on pp. 188–9; (27 August 1956) on p. 191; (5 June 1955) on pp. 205–6; (8 May 1955) on pp. 209–10; (7 March 1957) on p. 225; (27 November 1957) on pp. 227–8, 232. The following letters are

excerpted: (26 April 1958) on p. 228; (15 December 1958) on p. 228; (16 April 1960) on p. 228; (July-August 1960) on p. 229; (23 September 1960) on p. 229; (30 June 1962) on p. 229; in Sheldon Vanauken, *A Severe Mercy: C.S. Lewis and a pagan love invaded by Christ, told by one of the lovers.* London: Hodder & Stoughton; San Francisco: Harper & Row, 1977.

109. Letter to Bernard Acworth [of 5 March 1960] quoted in Malcolm Bowden, *Ape-men – Fact or Fallacy?* London: Sovereign Publications (1977), p. 35.

110. Letters to Arthur Greeves (15 February 1917) on p. 7; [4 October 1916] on p. 8; (15 February 1917) on p. 8; (26 January 1919) on p. 10; (15 October 1918) on p. 12; (3 December 1929) on p. 28; (30 January 1930) on p. 32; (22 September 1931) on p. 33; (29 April 1930) on p. 35; [25 May 1940] on p. 38; (29 July 1930) on p. 42; (22 September 1931) on pp. 43–4, 45; (18 October 1931) on pp. 44, 46; (1 October 1931) on p. 45; (8 November 1931) on p. 47; (25 March 1933) on p. 53; (4 February 1933) on p. 57; (26 February 1936) on p. 99; (30 January 1944) on p. 101; (27 December 1940) on p. 131; (30 January 1944) on pp. 179, 185; (25 December 1941) on p. 189; (5 January 1947) on p. 207; (11 October 1952) on p. 233; (11 September 1963) on p. 249; quoted in Humphrey Carpenter, *The Inklings: C.S. Lewis, J.R.R. Tolkien, Charles Williams, and their friends.* London: Allen & Unwin, 1978. Repr. **TST**.

111. Letters to his father [18 March 1914] on pp. 5, 6; [10 July 1928] on p. 17; [3 November 1928] on p. 18.
  to W.H. Lewis [12 January 1930] in p. 14; [26 April 1927; 15 April 1928] on p. 34; (25 December 1931; (24 October 1931) on p. 55; (4 May 1940) on p. 115; (18 November 1939; 28 January 1940) on p. 118; (11 February 1940) on p. 119; (18 September 1939) on p. 174;
  to Edward A. Allen (5 December 1955) on p. 231;
  to Mrs Edward A. Allen (17 January 1955) on p. 231;
  to Leo Baker (September 1920) on p. 39; (? 1921) on p. 158;
  to Owen Barfield ('Great War Letter' [27 May 1928] beginning 'After an unconscionable delay') on p. 18; (Letter [1928] beginning 'You might like to know') on p. 42; (18 May 1945) on p. 203; (28 June 1936) on p. 219; (16 December 1947) on p. 224;
  to Derek Brewer (16 November 1959) on p. 156;
  to Arthur C. Clarke (26 January 1954) on p. 158;
  to Edward T. Dell (29 April 1963) on p. 175; (25 October 1949) on p. 189;
  to E.R. Eddison (16 November 1942) on p. 190;

to George Every (4 February 1941) on p. 64;

to Katharine Farrer (9 February 1954) on p. 158; (4 December 1953) on p. 160;

to W.O. Field (10 May 1943) on p. 35;

to Mrs Vera Gebbert (23 December 1953) on p. 237;

to Joy Davidman Gresham (22 December 1953) on p. 219;

to Dom Bede Griffiths (25 May 1942) on p. 116; (10 May 1945) on p. 199; (22 April 1954) on p. 218;

to A.K. Hamilton Jenkin (4 November 1925) on p. 22; (21 March 1930) on p. 41;

to Mrs Heck (29 December 1958) on p. 223;

to Mr Hutter (30 March 1962) on p. 186;

to William L. Kinter (29 September 1951) on p. 66;

to Father Peter Milward SJ (25 December 1959) on p. 247;

to Sister Penelope (30 December 1950) on p. 233;

to Ruth Pitter (29 September 1945) on p. 47;

to Kathleen Raine (5 December 1958) on p. 246;

to J.R.R. Tolkien (7 December 1929) on p. 30; (21 October 1949) on p. 226; (20 November 1962) on p. 249;

to Basil Willey (22 October 1963) on p. 246;

to Michal Williams (22 May 1945) on p. 203;

quoted in Humphrey Carpenter, *The Inklings: C.S. Lewis, J.R.R. Tolkien, Charles Williams, and their friends*. London: Allen & Unwin, 1978.

112. 'Great War' Letter to Owen Barfield: (Beginning 'I hope to return your sister's plays ...') on p. 37; quoted in Humphrey Carpenter, *The Inklings: C.S. Lewis, J.R.R. Tolkien, Charles Williams, and their friends*. London: Allen & Unwin, 1978.

113. Letters to Arthur Greeves [9 January 1930] on p. 11; [18 October 1916] on p. 15; (21 December 1929) on p. 18; ([24] December 1929) on p. 18; [24 July 1915; 12 October 1916; 18 October 1916] on p. 126; to Owen Barfield (24 January 1926) on p. 14; (28 February 1936) on p. 15; quoted in Lionel Adey, *C.S. Lewis's 'Great War' with Owen Barfield*. Victoria, B.C.: University of Victoria, 1978.

114. Letters to Lucy Matthews (14 September 1957, 11 September 1958), quoted in *Eglerio! In Praise of Tolkien*. Edited by Anne Etkin. Greencastle, Pennsylvania: Quest Communications (1978), pp. 42–4. The second of these is G99 in this section of the Bibliography.

115. Letters to Walter Hooper (11 October 1963) on p. 31; to his father (4 and 14 May 1918, 29 June 1919, 16 February 1921) on pp. 213, 258, 299; to his brother (9 June 1919) on pp. 257–8; and to Leo Baker (September 1920, 23 December 1920) on pp. 284–5; quoted in C.S. Lewis, *They Stand Together: The Letters of C.S. Lewis to Arthur Greeves (1914–63)*. Edited by Walter Hooper. London: Collins; New York: Macmillan, 1979.

116. Letters to Corbin Scott Carnell (5 April 1953) and to Clyde S. Kilby (7 May 1959) in Michael Christensen, *C. S. Lewis on Scripture*. Waco, Texas: Word Books (1979), pp. 97–9.

117. Letter to Rosamund Rieu (28 September 1942) in *The Canadian C.S. Lewis Journal*, No 4 (April 1979), p. 9. Repr. in *In Search of C.S. Lewis*.

118. Letter to Patricia Mary Mackey (8 June 1960) in Walter Hooper, *Past Watchful Dragons: The Narnian Chronicles of C.S. Lewis*. New York: Macmillan (1979); London: Collins (1980), pp. 109–10.

119. Letter to William L. Kinter (30 July 1954) quoted in Peter J. Schakel, *Reading with the Heart: The Way into Narnia*. Grand Rapids: Eerdmans (1979), p. 9.

120. Letters to W.H. Lewis (17 April 1932) on p. 26; to Lucy Matthews (11 September 1958) on p. 76; to Arthur Greeves (c. 1916; 15 September 1930; 20 December 1943) on pp. 136, 156–7; quoted in Kathryn Lindskoog, *The Gift of Dreams: A Christian View*. New York: Harper & Row, 1979.

121. Letter to Mrs William L. Krieg (6 May 1955) – see also G99 – quoted in Martha C. Sammons, *A Guide Through Narnia*. Wheaton: Harold Shaw, 1979, pp. 76–7.

122. Letter to Harvey Karlsen (30 October 1961) on pp. 73, 76; to Dom Bede Griffiths (19[13] November 1950) on p. 100; (8 January 1936) on p. 114; (July 1936) on pp. 157, 161; (23 May 1936) on pp. 157–8; to William L. Kinter (23 December 1952) on p. 105; to Sister Penelope (9 July [August] 1939) on p. 154; to Susan Salzberg (5 February 1960) on p. 158; quoted in Leanne Payne, *Real Presence: The Holy Spirit in the Works of C.S. Lewis*. Westchester, Illinois: Cornerstone Books, 1979.

123. Letters to Stephen Schofield (23 August 1956 and 26 February 1959) in *The Canadian C.S. Lewis Journal*, III (March 1979) p. 13. Repr. in Stephen Schofield, *In Search of C.S. Lewis*.

124. Letter to Gracia Fay Ellwood (19 July 1960) in Gracia Fay Ellwood's 'Of Creation and Love', *Mythlore*, Vol. 6, No 4 (Fall 1979), p. 19.

125. Letter to W.H. Lewis (28 January 1940) quoted in Walter Hooper's Introduction to C.S. Lewis, *The Weight of Glory and Other Addresses.* Revised and Expanded Edition. Edited by Walter Hooper. New York: Macmillan (1980) xvi.

126. Letters to Laurence Krieg and his mother, Mrs William L. Krieg (6 May 1955, 21 April 1957, 23 December 1957) and to Mrs Hook (29 December 1958), quoted in Paul F. Ford, *A Companion to Narnia.* San Francisco: Harper & Row, 1980, pp. xxii–xxiii. The entire Lewis-Krieg correspondence was printed in Jeanette Anderson Bakke's 'The Lion and the Lamb and the Children', an unpublished Ph.D. dissertation (University of Minnesota, 1975), pp. 110–11, 342–8, along with a commentary by Laurence Krieg. Lewis's letters to Mrs William L. Krieg (6 May 1955) and to Laurence Krieg (24 October 1955, 27 April 1956, 21 April 1957, 23 December 1957) are found in C.S. Lewis, *Letters to Children.* Edited by Lyle W. Dorsett and Marjorie Lamp Mead. New York: Macmillan; London: Collins (1985) pp. 52–3, 57–8, 61–2, 68–9, 76.

127. Letters to Spencer Curtis Brown (1963) on p. 53; to H. Lyman Stebbins (9 May 1945) on pp. 95–7; quoted in Christopher Derrick, *C.S. Lewis and the Church of Rome.* San Francisco: Ignatius, 1981.

128. Letters to J.W. Welch (10 February 1941, 24 November 1945) on pp. xi, xxxiv; to Eric Fenn (17 May and 14 November 1941; 4 January, 23 February, 28 June and 30 November 1942; 16 June, 1 July, 27 and 31 December 1943; 5 January, 10 February, and 25 March 1944) on pp. xiii, xvi, xvii, xxi, xxii, xxiv, xxvi–xxviii, xxx, xxxi, xxxv; to J.R. Williams (30 September 1941) on p. xvi to R.S. Lee (6 and 23 October 1944) on pp. xxxiii, xxxiv; to Rhona Bodle (11 April 1950) on p. xxxvi; quoted in Walter Hooper's Introduction to C.S. Lewis, *Mere Christianity.* Anniversary Edition. New York: Macmillan, 1981.

129. Letters to Rhona Bodle (11 April 1950) on pp. 1, 10; (28 April 1955) on p. 100; to Sister Madaleva (3 October 1963) on p. 11; to Ruth Pitter (17 July 1951) on p. 11; to Miss Jacob (3 July 1941) on p. 16; (13 August 1941) on p. 38; to Dom Bede Griffiths (8 January 1936) on p. 17; (27 June 1949) on p. 81; (c. 1933) on p. 81; (27 September 1948) on p. 84; (27? June 1937) on pp. 87–8; (20 December 1946) on p. 103; to Sister Penelope (30 December 1950)

on p. 34; to Mr Canfield (28 February 1955) on pp. 57–8; to Keith Masson (6 March 1956) on pp. 97–8; quoted in Richard L. Purtill, *C.S. Lewis's Case for the Christian Faith*. San Francisco: Harper & Row, 1981.

130. Letters to Leo Baker [April 1920; September 1920] on p. 11; [July 1921] on p. 12;

to Owen Barfield (2 September 1937) on p. 26;

to Harry Blamires (14 March 1954) on pp. 37, 123–4;

to Rhona Bodle (24 March 1954) on p. 35;

to Charles A. Brady (16 November 1956) on p. 36;

to Arthur C. Clarke (20 January 1956) on p. 38;

to E. R. Eddison (16 November 1942) on pp. 31, 107, 220 [note 13]; [29? December 1942] on pp. 213 [note 64], 105; (29 April 1943) on pp. 78, 105;

to Allen C. Emery, Jr (18 August 1953) on pp. 36, 131;

to Katharine Farrer (4 December 1953) on p. 37; (2 April 1955) on p. 187; (10 June 1952) on p. 188; (9 July 1955) on p. 188;

to Warfield M. Firor (27 June 1953) on p. 37; (15 October 1949) on p. 41;

to Joy Davidman Gresham (22 December 1953) on p. 38;

to Dom Bede Griffiths (8 January 1936) on pp. 26–7; (20 December 1946) on pp. 32–3, 124; (25 March 1948) on p. 172;

to George Rostrevor Hamilton (29 April 1943) on p. 213 [note 71];

to A.K. Hamilton Jenkin (4 November 1925) on pp. 13–14; (27 July [1928]) on pp. 15–16; (11 January 1939) on p. 28; (30 May 1949) on p. 35; (27 May 1925) on p. 107;

to Carl Henry (28 September 1955) on p. 131;

to Miss Jacob (13 August 1941) on p. 29;

to Martin Kilmer (28 April 1958) on p. 214 [note 95];

to William L. Kinter (28 March 1953) on p. 35; (30 July 1954) on pp. 36, 108;

to Joan Lancaster (20 April 1959) on pp. 39, 189; (31 August 1958) on p. 40; (15 April 1954; 7 May 1954) on p. 179;

to Keith Masson (3 June 1956) on p. 41;

to Vera Mathews (31 October 1949) on p. 220 [note 15];

to Father Peter Milward (4 July 1955) on p. 214 [note 95]; (4 July 1955) on pp. 77, 109;

to Sister Penelope (4 November 1940) on pp. 28, 92; (22 August 1942) on p. 29; (25 March 1943) on pp. 30, 106; (31 August 1948) on p. 35; (24 October 1940) on p. 92; (9 November 1941) on p. 92; (24 September 1943) on p. 106;

to Ruth Pitter (4 January 1947) on p. 33; (24 July 1946) on p. 34; (10 August 1946) on p. 34; (21 December 1953) on p. 38; (20 Aug 1962) on p. 41;

to Kathleen Raine (4 October 1956) on p. 194;

to Susan Salzberg (5 February 1960) on p. 36;

to Mrs Sandeman (10 December 1952) on p. 41;

to Martyn Skinner (31 December 1959) on p. 220 [note 32]; quoted in Donald E. Glover, *C.S. Lewis: The Art of Enchantment*. Athens, Ohio: Ohio University Press, 1981.

131. Letters to Dorothy L. Sayers (23 October and 14 December 1945; 23 and 29 July, and 8 August 1946; 11 November 1949) quoted in James Brabazon, *Dorothy L. Sayers: the Life of a Courageous Woman*. London: Gollancz; New York, Scribners (1981), pp. 235–6, 251–2.

132. Letters to W.H. Lewis (8 April 1932) on p. 18; to Ruth Pitter (29 December 1951) on p. 22; to Mr Welbore (18 September 1936) on p. 228; to Sister Penelope CSMV (10 January 1952) on p. 180 of Margaret Patterson Hannay, *C.S. Lewis*. New York: Frederick Ungar, 1981.

133. Letter to Cecil Roth (*c.* 1960) quoted in Irene Roth, *Cecil Roth: Historian Without Tears. A Memoir*. New York: Sepher-Herman Press (1982), p. 153.

134. Letters to Ruth Pitter (4 January 1947) and Roger Lancelyn Green (28 December 1938) quoted in Walter Hooper's Preface to C.S. Lewis, *Of This and Other Worlds*. London: Collins, 1982, pp. 17, 18; as *On Stories and Other Essays on Literature*. New York: Harcourt Brace Jovanovich (1982), pp. xvi, xvii.

135. Letter to Sarah Neylan (3 April 1949) quoted in George Sayer, 'Reviews', *Seven: An Anglo-American Literary Review*, Vol. 3 (1982), p. 132.

136. Letters to Owen Barfield [3? February 1930] on p. 78; to Sister Penelope (30 July 1954) on p. 129; to Dorothy L. Sayers (24 December 1956) on p. 141; (25 June 1957) on pp. 143–5; to Kathleen Raine (25 October 1961) on p. 151; quoted in Walter Hooper, *Through Joy and Beyond: a Pictorial Biography of C. S. Lewis*. New York: Macmillan (1982).

137. Letters to Dom Bede Griffiths (*c.* 1931) on p. 97; to Sister Madeleva (7 June 1934) on p. 98; to Charles Williams (20 July 1940) on p. 99; to Theodora Bosanquet (27 August 1942) on p. 99; to E. R. Eddison (16 November 1942) on p. 99; to T.S. Eliot (22 February 1943) on p. 101; and to Alastair Fowler (7 January 1961) on p. 102; quoted in Fred D. Crawford,

Mixing Memory and Desire. University Park: Pennsylvania State University, 1982.

138. Letters to his father ([19 September] and 29 September 1908) quoted in Walter Hooper, 'C.S. Lewis in Hertfordshire's "Belsen" (1)', *Hertfordshire Countryside*, Vol. 37 (September 1982), p. 18.

139. Letter to his father (1 March 1909) quoted in Walter Hooper, 'C.S. Lewis in Hertfordshire (2): Wynyard School's Tormentor', *Hertfordshire Countryside*, Vol. 37 (October 1982), p. 35.

140. Letters to Clyde S. Kilby (20 November 1962) and to Owen Barfield (September 1929 and 28 July 1927) quoted in Peter J. Schakel, 'Seeing and Knowing: The Epistemology of C. S. Lewis's *Till We Have Faces*', *Seven: An Anglo-American Literary Review*, Vol. 4 (1983), pp. 85, 87, 89, 91.

141. Letters to Owen Barfield (16 December 1947, and no date) quoted in John C. Ulreich Jr's Afterword to Owen Barfield, *Orpheus: A Poetic Drama*. Edited by John C. Ulrich, Jr, West Stockbridge, MA: Lindisfarne (1983) p. 118.

142. Letters to Vera Mathews Gebbert (23 December 1953) on pp. 105–6; to Dom Bede Griffiths (1 August 1957) on p. 128; to William Lindsay Gresham (6 April 1957, two letters on same date) on pp. 134–5; to Sister Penelope CSMV (12 February 1958) on p. 137; quoted in Lyle W. Dorsett, *And God Came In* (a biography of Joy Davidman). New York: Macmillan; London: Collins, 1983.

143. Letter to Nicholas Fridsma (15 February 1946) in *CSL: The Bulletin of the New York C. S. Lewis Society*, XV, No 169 (November 1983), p. 10.

144. Letters to his brother (25 December 1931, 24 December 1939) quoted in Kathryn Lindskoog, 'C.S. Lewis on Christmas', *Christianity Today* (16 December 1983), pp. 25–6.

145. Letter to Stephen Schofield (10 October 1956) in Stephen Schofield, *In Search of C.S. Lewis*. New Jersey: Bridge, 1983, p. 195.

146. Letters to Ruth Pitter (4 January 1947), a different portion from G95, on p. 138; and to Stephen Schofield (23 August, 10 October 1956, 26 February 1959, 31 January 1960, and *c.* 26 July 1960) on pp. 193–7 quoted

in Stephen Schofield, *In Search of C. S. Lewis*. South Plainfield, New Jersey: Bridge, 1983.

147. Letters to his father (14 October 1914) on pp. xvii, xx; (3 November 1914) on p. xxi; (8 November 1914) on p. xviii; (17 May 1917) on p. xxvii; (13 December 1917) on p. xxx; (3 September 1918) on p. xxxiv; (9 September 1918) on p. xxxiv; (18 September 1918) on p. xxxv; (19 September 1918) on p. xiii; (10 November 1918) on pp. xxxv–vi; quoted in Walter Hooper's Preface to a reprint of C.S. Lewis, *Spirits in Bondage: A Cycle of Lyrics*. New York: Harcourt Brace Jovanovich, 1984.

148. Letter to Richard Selig (7 June 1954) in John Kirkpatrick, 'A Lewis Pupil, Richard Selig 1929–57', *CSL: The Bulletin of the New York C.S. Lewis Society*, Vol. XV, No 180 (October 1984), p. 5.

149. Letters to Dabney (Adams) Hart (1 June 1956), to Mr Crow, her faculty advisor (28 May 1956) on pp. 5–6; and to M.L. Charlesworth (9 April 1940) on p. 81; quoted in Dabney Hart, *Through the Open Door: A New Look at C.S. Lewis*. University, Alabama: University of Alabama Press, 1984.

150. Letters to J.B. Phillips (3 August 1943) on pp. 100, 107; (1956) on p. 172; quoted in J.B. Phillips, *The Price of Success*. London: Collins; Wheaton: Harold Shaw, 1984.

151. Letters to Dom Bede Griffiths (5 October 1938) on p. 129; quoted in Peter J. Schakel, *Reason and Imagination in C.S. Lewis: A Study of 'Till We Have Faces'*. Grand Rapids: Eerdmans, 1984.

152. Letters to Don Giovanni Calabria* (20 September 1947) on p. 7; (3 January 1961; 26 December 1951; 13 September 1951 on p. 8; [14 April 1952]) on p. 10; ([19 November 1949] 25 November 1947; 20 September 1947; 10 August 1953; [14 April 1952]; 17 March 1953) on p. 11; ([3 October 1947]; 27 March 1948; 14 January 1949) on p. 12; ([5 January 1953]; [15 September 1953]; 27 March 1948) on p. 14; ([14 April 1952]; 26 December 1951) on p. 15; ([26 December 1951]; 14 April 1952; [27 March 1948]) on p. 16; (28 March 1959) on p. 17; ([5 December 1954]) on p. 18; (4 January 1959) on p. 19; letters to Don Luigi Pedrollo [16 December 1954] on p. 9; (16 April 1960; 8 April 1961) on p. 18; 'The Latin Letters, 1947–61, of C.S. Lewis to Don Giovanni Calabria of Verona (1873–1954) and to Members of his Congregation', by Martin Moynihan in *Seven: An Anglo-American*

Literary Review, Vol. 6 (1985) pp. 7–22. (This essay was published as a booklet under the title *The Latin Letters of C.S. Lewis to Don Giovanni Calabria of Verona and to Members of His Congregation, 1947 to 1961* by Bookmakers Guild, Inc. of Longmont, Colorado, and the Marion E. Wade Center, Wheaton College, Wheaton, Illinois, 1985.) Letters repr. **LDGC**.

153. Letter to Cynthia Donnelly (14 August 1954) in *CSL: The Bulletin of the New York C.S. Lewis Society*, XVII, No 185 (March 1985), p. 7.

154. Letters to W. H. Lewis [November 1906 and *c.* September 1906] in the Introduction to C.S. Lewis, *Letters to Children*. Edited by Lyle W. Dorsett and Marjorie Lamp Mead. New York: Macmillan; London: Collins (1985), pp. 13–14.

155. Letters to W. H. Lewis (*c.* September 1906 and *c.* June 1907 and [5 October 1927]) quoted in Walter Hooper's Introduction to C.S. Lewis, *Boxen: The Imaginary World of the Young C.S. Lewis*. Edited by Walter Hooper. London: Collins; New York: Harcourt Brace Jovanovich (1985), pp. 10, 19.

156. Letter to J.R.R. Tolkien (7 December 1929) quoted in J.R.R. Tolkien, *The Lays of Beleriand*. Edited by Christopher Tolkien. London: George Allen & Unwin; Boston: Houghton-Mifflin (1985), pp. 150–1.

157. Letter to Peter Philip (3 March 1955) quoted in *The Canadian C.S. Lewis Journal*, No 49 (Winter 1985), p. 15.

158. Letter to John Beversluis (3 June 1963) in John Beversluis, *C.S. Lewis and the Search for Rational Religion*. Grand Rapids: Eerdmans (1985), pp. 156–57.

159. Letter to Joyce Pearce (20 July 1943) in *The Canadian C.S. Lewis Journal*, No 51 (Summer 1985), pp. 1, 3.

160. Letter of 30 August 1958 quoted in Katherine Gardiner, 'C.S. Lewis as a Reader of Edmund Spenser', *CSL: The Bulletin of the New York C.S. Lewis Society*, Vol. 16, No 191 (September 1985), p. 7.

161. Letter to Owen Barfield (28 June 1936) quoted in M.L. Mead's Afterword to Owen Barfield, *The Silver Trumpet*. Edited by Marjorie Lamp Mead. Longmont, Colorado: Bookmakers Guild (1986), p. 121.

162. Letters to Sister Penelope (25 March 1943); to Dom Bede Griffiths (26 May 1943); and to Arthur C. Clarke (20 January 1954) in Kath Filmer, 'The Polemic Image: The Role of Metaphor and Symbol in the Fiction of C.S. Lewis' in *Seven: An Anglo-American Literary Review*, Vol. 7 (1986), pp. 67, 73.

163. Letters to his father (27 August 1917) on p. 7; to [his father] (19 March 1921) on p. 25; (10 July 1928) on p. 51; [November 1928] on pp. 51–2; (9 July, 5 August 1929) on p. 54; (31 March 1928) on p. 181;

to W.H.Lewis (1 July 1921) on p. 4; (13 March 1921) on p. 11; (1 March, 10 May 1921) on p. 20; (25 August 1929) on p. 54; (19 May 1929) on pp. 54–5; (29 August 1929) on pp. 55, 56; (29 September 1929) on pp. 55–6; (27 September 1929) on p. 57; (11 February 1940) on p. 176;

to Father Frederick J. Adelmann SJ (21 September 1960) on p. 421;

to Edward A. Allen (10 March 1948) on p. 282; (6 December 1948) on p. 292; (8 January 1951) on p. 317; (10 December 1962) on pp. 434–5;

to Delmar Banner (6 June 1954) on p. 354;

to Owen Barfield [March–April 1926] on p. 33; (27 May 1928) on p. 48; (9 September 1929) on p. 55; (6, 12 May 1932) on p. 85; (12 September 1938) on p. 156; (23 July 1939) on p. 161; [1943] on p. 218; (19 December 1945) on p. 251; (25, 28 May 1945) on p. 255; (1 November 1948) on p. 290; (23 June 1949) on p. 300; (22 August 1949) on p. 301; (8 November 1954) on p. 357;

to Pauline Baynes (2 October 1954) on p. 356; (4 May 1957) on p. 387;

to Nell Berners-Price (9 May 1952) on p. 330;

to John Betjeman (28 May 1938) on p. 151;

to Harry Blamires (12 October 1945) on p. 250; (12 December 1955) on pp. 372–3;

to Rhona Bodle (31 December 1947) on p. 279; (10 February, 3 March 1948) on p. 281; (24 June 1948) on p. 284; (24 October 1948) on p. 290;

to Charles A. Brady (29 October 1944) on p. 238; (27 October 1956) on pp. 380-81;

to Joseph M. Canfield (28 February 1955) on p. 364;

to Corbin Scott Carnell (31 October 1958) on p. 400;

to H. C. Chang (22 June 1956) on p. 378;

to Arthur C. Clarke (14, 16 February 1953) on p. 339; (20 January 1954) on p. 348;

to Nevill Coghill (4 February 1926) on p. 27;

to Harold Dawson (6 February 1958) on pp. 392–3;

to Edward T. Dell, Jr (25 October 1949) on p. 303; (22 April 1963) on p. 536;

to Bonamy Dobrée (7 November 1963) on p. 446;

to Brian D. Doud (5 June 1960) on p. 415;

to Jane Douglass (3 May 1960) on p. 414;

to E.R. Eddison (29 April 1943) on p. 218;

to T.S. Eliot (19 April 1931) on p. 76; (23 February 1944) on p. 228; (14 June 1959) on p. 406;

to Allan C. Emery (18 April 1959) on p. 403;

to John S.A. Enson (31 March 1944) on pp. 229–30;

to I.O. Evans (22 December 1954) on p. 361;

to Austin and Katharine Farrer (22 July 1960) on p. 420;

to Warfield M. Firor (13 September, 1 October 1947) on pp. 276–7; [29 March 1948] on p. 283; (10 July, 25 September 1948) on p. 288; (5 January 1949) on pp. 292–3; (22 March 1949) on p. 296; (15 October, 5 December 1949) on p. 304; (12 March 1950) on p. 306; (14 April 1950) on p. 307; (26 July 1950) on pp. 310, 311; (6 December 1950) on p. 314; [23 April 1951] on p. 321; (20 December 1951) on p. 326; (27 June 1953) on p. 342;

to B. Ginder (18 August 1960) on p. 420;

to Joy Davidman Gresham (30 December 1953) on p. 437;

to William Lindsay Gresham (30 December 1956) on p. 383; (6 April and 6 April 1957) on p. 386, 387; (15 July 1960) on p. 418;

to Dom Bede Griffiths (26 December 1934) on p. 114; (8 January 1936) on p. 125; [20 February 1936] on p. 128; (24 April 1936) on p. 130; (14 September 1936) on p. 131; (29 April 1938) on p. 150; (5 October 1938) on p. 156; (16 April 1940) on p. 171; (26 May 1943) on p. 219; (10 May 1945) on p. 245; (20 December 1946) on p. 266; (13 November 1950) on p. 313; (17 May 1952) on p. 331; (1 November 1954) on p. 356; (1 August 1957) on p. 388; (30 April 1959) on p. 403; (20 December 1961) on p. 428;

to George Rostrevor Hamilton (11 March 1947) on p. 267; (14 August 1949) on p. 300;

to [A.K.Hamilton Jenkin] (4 November 1925) on pp. 20-1, 22;

to Carl Henry (28 September 1955) on p. 370;

to Patricia Hillis (10 March 1959) on p. 403;

to Mrs W.W. Johnson (14 November 1956) on p. 380;

to Mrs Frank Jones (7 December 1950) on p. 314; (16 November 1963) on p. 447;

to Bishop Girault M. Jones (1 May 1958) on p. 394;

to Harvey Karlsen (13 October 1961) on p. 427;

to William L. Kinter (28 March 1953) on p. 340;

to Richard W. Ladborough (9 October 1961) on p. 427; (28 October 1963) on p. 446;

to Joan Lancaster (26 December 1955) on p. 373; (11 July 1963) on p. 439;

to Sister Madeleva (6 June 1934) on p. 109; [18 April 1951] on p. 321;

to Keith Masson (11 April 1956) on p. 375;

to Vera Mathews (Gebbert) (24 November 1947) on p. 278; (10, 19 March 1948) on p. 282; (7 March 1949) on p. 294; (1 October 1949) on p. 302; (9 November 1949) on p. 303; (30 November 1949) on p. 304; (8 November 1950) on p. 312; (20 November 1950) on p. 313; (27 March 1951) on pp. 320–1; (18 October 1951) on p. 325; (17 February 1952) on p. 327; (23 May 1952) on p. 331; (14 October 1952) on p. 333; (28 October 1952) on p. 334; (9 December 1952, 23 March 1953) on p. 340; (20 June 1953) on p. 341; (7 November 1953) on p. 345; (23 December 1953) on p. 347; (18 January 1954) on p. 348; (26 October 1954) on p. 356; (15 June 1955) on p. 366; (19 December 1955) on p. 373; (9 May 1956) on p. 376; (10 December 1956) on pp. 382–3; (31 December 1956) on p. 383; (12 November 1957) on p. 391; (16 December 1957) on p. 391; (30 May 1958) on p. 395; (17 January 1960) on p. 411; (29 January 1962) on pp. 428–9;

to Father Peter Milward (23 May 1951) on pp. 322–3; (17 December 1955) on p. 373; (15 December 1959) on p. 411; (7 March 1960) on p. 412;

to John Warwick Montgomery (21 January 1960) on p. 412;

to Marg-Riette Montgomery (10 June 1952) on p. 332;

to National Association of Evangelicals (3 March 1949) on p. 294;

to J.B. Phillips (3 August 1943) on pp. 221–2;

to Joan B. Pile (5 June 1952) on p. 332;

to Sister Penelope (9 August 1939) on p. 162; (24 October 1940) on pp. 180, 181; (4 November 1940) on pp. 181–2; (22 August 1942) on p. 204; (15 May 1942) on p. 206; (22 December 1942) on p. 211; (10 April 1943) on p. 218; (5 October 1943) on p. 224; (3 January 1945) on p. 241; (28 May 1945) on p. 246; (21 October 1946) on p. 261; to [Sister Penelope] (21 November 1947) on p. 278; (31 January 1949) on p. 293; (30 December 1950) on p. 316; (15 February 1954) on p. 349; (18 June 1956) on pp. 377–8; (23 June 1962) on p. 429;

to Ruth Pitter (17 July 1946) on p. 257; (19 July 1946) on p. 258; (24 July 1946) on pp. 258–9; (28 August 1946) on p. 260; (4 January 1947) on p. 266; (9 August 1947) on p. 274; (31 August 1948) on p. 288; [22 September 1949] on p. 302; (6 January 1951) on p. 316; (17 March 1951) on p. 320; (26 March 1951) on p. 321; (12 September 1951) on p. 324; (29 December 1951) on p. 326; (8 January 1952) on p. 327; (2 January 1953) on p. 337; (1 October 1953) on pp. 343–4; (21 December 1953) on p. 347; (19 March 1955) on p. 365; (5 August 1955) on pp. 368–9; (31 January 1956) on p. 374; (9 July 1956) on p. 378; (28 January 1957) on p. 384; (15 April 1957) on p. 387;

to Kathleen Raine (11 April 1956) on p. 375; (21 October 1961) on p. 427; (7 November 1963) on p. 446;

to T. Wilkinson Riddle (16 July 1946) on p. 258;

to Royal Society of Literature (19 March 1949) on p. 283;

to Mrs Roderick Watson (22 December 1952) on p. 336;

to Stephen Schofield (31 January 1960) on p. 412;

to Kathryn Stillwell (29 October 1957) on pp. 390–1;

to Mrs Stone (17 June 1960) on p. 415;

to Mary Willis Shelburne (17 October 1963) on p. 445;

to Basil Willey (26 October 1956) on p. 380; (22 October 1963) on p. 446;

to Michal Williams (Mrs Charles Williams) (22 May 1945) on p. 246;

to Sir Henry Willink (3 December 1959) on p. 411; (25 October 1963) on p. 446;

quoted in William Griffin, *Clive Staples Lewis: A Dramatic Life*. San Francisco: Harper & Row, 1986; Tring: Lion, under the title *C.S. Lewis: The Authentic Voice*, 1988. (The pagination in the English edition of this biography is different from that in the American edition. The page numbers of the American edition are those given above.)

164. Letter to Janet Wise (5 October 1955) in *The Canadian C.S. Lewis Journal*, No 53 (Winter 1986), pp. 1–2.

165. Letters to his father (30 November 1913) on p. 40; (29 September 1913) on p. 42; [? November 1914] on p. 48; (8 February 1917) on p. 63; [3 May 1917] on p. 67; [10? June 1917] on p. 69; [27 August 1917] on p. 70; [24 September 1917] on p. 70; [13 December 1917] on p. 72; (4 March 1918) on p. 73; [14 May 1918] on p. 73; [30 May 1918] on p. 74; [29 June 1918] on pp. 74–5; (18 November [October] 1918) on p. 77; [3 September [November] 1918) on p. 77; [17? November 1918] on p. 78; [8 December 1918] on p. 78; [4 February 1919] on p. 80; [5 March 1919] on p. 85; [4 April 1920] on p. 90; [25 July 1920] on p. 90; [19 January 1921] on p. 91; (9 July 1921) on p. 92; [11 May 1924] on p. 103; (15 October 1924) on p. 105; (28 August 1924) on p. 105; [3 November 1928] on pp. 119–20;

to W.H. Lewis [8 January 1917] on p. 62; [1 July 1921] on p. 92; (19 November 1939) on pp. 112–13; (29 September 1929) on p. 133; (2 September 1939) on p. 162;

to Delmar Banner (1 November 1963) on p. 250;

to Dom Bede Griffiths [1932] on p. 144;

to George Sayer (15 August 1951) on p. 206; (15 August 1958) on p. 228; (November 1959) on p. 230;

to Chad Walsh (21 October 1959) on p. 230; (23 May 1960) on pp. 230–1;

quoted in George Sayer, *Jack: C.S. Lewis and His Times*. London: Macmillan; San Francisco: Harper & Row, 1988.

166. Letters to Dorothy L. Sayers (30 June 1945) on pp. 47–8; (6 July 1945) on p. 48; (29 December 1946) on p. 48; (18 December 1945) on p. 49; (24 December 1945) on p. 51; (11 November 1949) on pp. 114, 115; (15 November 1949) on p. 114; to Owen Barfield (16 December 1947) on p. 242; quoted in Barbara Reynolds, *The Passionate Intellect: Dorothy L. Sayers's Encounter with Dante.* Kent, Ohio: Kent State University Press, 1989.

167. Letters to Richard Ladborough (3 June 1959) on p. 36; to Jocelyn Gibb (9 May 1960) on p. 42; to Walter Hooper (2 July 1962) on p. 43; quoted in Walter Hooper's 'C.S. Lewis and C.S. Lewises', in *The Riddle of Joy: G.K. Chesterton and C.S. Lewis.* Edited by Michael H. Macdonald and Andrew A. Tadie. Grand Rapids, Michigan: Eerdmans, 1989.

168. Letters to W.H. Lewis ([18] May 1907) pp. 18–19; (9 June 1919) on p. 57; [10 July 1920] on p. 68; [10 May 1921] on p. 73; (25 March 1931) on pp. 131–2; (22 November 1931) on p. 136;

to his father [29 June 1914] on p. 35; [10 September 1917] on p. 53; [29 June 1919] on p. 67; [11 April 1920] on p. 68; [1 May 1920] on p. 68; [19 March 1921] on p. 71;

to Nevill Coghill (3 February 1926) on p. 101;

to Rhona Bodle (25[24] March 1954) on p. 114;

to Sister Penelope [24 October 1940] on p. 175;

to Mrs Flewett (1944 and 4 January 1945) on p. 203; (5 April 1955) on p. 253;

to Mrs Frank Jones (16 November 1963) on pp. 215, 297;

to Nan Dunbar [7 March 1956 and 20 April 1956] on pp. 254–5;

to J.R.R. Tolkien [1962] on p. 294;

quoted in A.N. Wilson, *C.S. Lewis: A Biography.* London: Collins; New York: W.W. Norton, 1990.

169. Letters to Sister Madeleva (19 March 1963) on p. 33 in Richard L. Purtill, 'Did C.S. Lewis Lose His Faith?' in *A Christian for All Christians: Essays in Honour of C.S. Lewis.* Edited by Andrew Walker and James Patrick. London: Hodder & Stoughton, 1990.

170. Letters to Delmar Banner (7 June 1944, 30 November 1942) in *The Canadian C.S. Lewis Journal*, No 72 (Autumn 1990), pp. 5–6.

171. Letters to Ruth Pitter (10 August 1946) on pp. 87, 92; (24 July 1946) on p. 95; to Laurence Whistler (30 October 1961) on p. 88; to Leo Baker

(September 1920) on p. 92; to Roger Longacre (19 June 1952) on p. 95; to Katharine Farrer (9 February 1954) on p. 96; to Rhona Bodle (24 June 1949) on p. 106; quoted in Charles A. Huttar, 'A Lifelong Love Affair with Language: C.S. Lewis's Poetry', to Paul Piehler (22 October 1963) on p. 215; quoted in Paul Piehler, 'Myth or Allegory? Archetype and Transcendence in the Fiction of C.S. Lewis', found in *Word and Story in C.S. Lewis*. Edited by Peter J. Schakel and Charles A. Huttar. Columbia, Missouri: University of Missouri Press, 1991.

172. Holograph letter to Roger Poole (19 October 1961) in *The Canadian C.S. Lewis Journal*, No 75 (Summer 1991), p. 1.

173. Letter to Barbara Reynolds (19 March 1959) in her 'Memories of C.S. Lewis in Cambridge' on pp. 383–4; to Thomas Howard [1958?] in his 'C.S. Lewis and Purgatory: An Anecdote' on p. 390; to Christian Hardie (22 and 27 March 1951, Palm Sunday [6 April] 1952) in her 'Three Letters from C.S. Lewis' on pp. 394–9; to Mary Neylan (21 March 1939, 26 April, 30 April, 9 May, 2 October 1941) in her 'My Friendship with C.S. Lewis' on pp. 407–11; to D.E. Harding (1951) on p. 486 in *The Chesterton Review*, Vol. XVII, No 3 and No 4 (August and November 1991).

174. Letters of 14 March and 30 October 1941 to Sir Emrys Evans (Principal of the University of North Wales) in *The Canadian C.S. Lewis Journal*, No 81 (Winter 1993), pp. 1, 3.

175. Letter to Dorothy L. Sayers (13 July 1948) in Barbara Reynolds, *Dorothy L. Sayers: Her Life and Soul*. London: Hodder & Stoughton (1993), p. 358.

ACKNOWLEDGEMENTS

The author and publisher gratefully acknowledge permission to reproduce extracts from copyright material in this book. All works are by C.S. Lewis unless other indicated, and are copyright © C.S. Lewis Pte Ltd. (W) denotes that world permission has been obtained from the source given.

In the United Kingdom:

The Bodley Head: *Out of the Silent Planet; Perelandra; That Hideous Strength* (all W).

Cambridge University Press: *The Discarded Image; An Experiment in Criticism* (both W).

Curtis Brown, London: *Arthurian Torso* (W), *Essays Presented to Charles Williams* (W); *God in the Dock: Essays on Theology and Ethics* (USA); *The Personal Heresy* (W); *Letters to Don Giovanni Calabria* (W); *Selected Literary Essays* (W).

Faber & Faber Ltd: *A Grief Observed*.

HarperCollins: *The Abolition of Man* (W); *All My Road Before Me; Boxen; Christian Reflections; Christian Reunion* (W); *Collected Poems; The Dark Tower; Fern-Seed and Elephants* (W); *First and Second Things* (W); *The Four Loves; God in the Dock: Essays on Theology; The Great Divorce* (W); *The Horse and His Boy* (W); *The Last Battle* (W); *Letters of C.S. Lewis; Letters to Children; Letters to Malcolm; The Lion, the Witch and the Wardrobe* (W); *The Magician's Nephew* (W); *Mere Christianity* (W); *Miracles* (W); *Narrative Poems; Of This and Other Worlds; Poems* (UK); *The Pilgrim's Regress* (W); *Present Concerns; Prince Caspian* (W); *The Problem of Pain* (W); *Reflections on the Psalms; The Screwtape Letters* (W); *Screwtape Proposes a Toast; The Silver Chair* (W); *Surprised by Joy; They Stand Together; Till We Have Faces; Timeless at Heart*

(W); *The Voyage of the 'Dawn Treader'* (W).

Oxford University Press: *English Literature in the Sixteenth Century; A Preface to 'Paradise Lost'* (both W).

Unwin Hyman Ltd: *The Letters of J.R.R. Tolkien* (edited by Humphrey Carpenter) (W).

Watson, Little Ltd: *Jack: C.S.Lewis and His Times by George Sayer* (W).

In the United States:

Harcourt Brace: *All My Road Before Me; Boxen; The Dark Tower; The Four Loves; Letters of C.S. Lewis; Letters to Malcolm; Narrative Poems; On Stories; Poems; Reflections on the Psalms; Screwtape Proposes a Toast; Spirits in Bondage; Surprised by Joy; Till We Have Faces.*

HarperCollins: *A Grief Observed.*

Willam B. Eerdmans Publishing Company: *Christian Reflections; Letters to an American Lady* (W).

Macmillan Publishing Company, Inc: *They Stand Together; Letters to Children;* the Preface to *The Screwtape Letters and Screwtape Proposes a Toast;* the expanded version of 'Transposition'.

Marion E. Wade Center: *Brothers and Friends: The Diaries of Major Warren Hamilton Lewis* (W).

INDEX